SCHOOL OF GOVERNMENT
North Carolina Benchmarking Project

Final Report on City Services for Fiscal Year 2016–2017

PERFORMANCE AND COST DATA

MARCH 2018

COSPONSORED BY:

THE CITIES OF APEX, ASHEVILLE, CHAPEL HILL, CHARLOTTE, CONCORD, GOLDSBORO, GREENSBORO, GREENVILLE, HICKORY, HIGH POINT, RALEIGH, SALISBURY, WILSON, AND WINSTON-SALEM

SCHOOL OF GOVERNMENT

NORTH CAROLINA LOCAL GOVERNMENT BUDGET ASSOCIATION

The School of Government at the University of North Carolina at Chapel Hill works to improve the lives of North Carolinians by engaging in practical scholarship that helps public officials and citizens understand and improve state and local government. Established in 1931 as the Institute of Government, the School provides educational, advisory, and research services for state and local governments. The School of Government is also home to a nationally ranked Master of Public Administration program, the North Carolina Judicial College, and specialized centers focused on community and economic development, information technology, and environmental finance.

As the largest university-based local government training, advisory, and research organization in the United States, the School of Government offers up to 200 courses, webinars, and specialized conferences for more than 12,000 public officials each year. In addition, faculty members annually publish approximately 50 books, manuals, reports, articles, bulletins, and other print and online content related to state and local government. The School also produces the *Daily Bulletin Online* each day the General Assembly is in session, reporting on activities for members of the legislature and others who need to follow the course of legislation.

Operating support for the School of Government's programs and activities comes from many sources, including state appropriations, local government membership dues, private contributions, publication sales, course fees, and service contracts.

Visit sog.unc.edu or call 919.966.5381 for more information on the School's courses, publications, programs, and services.

CB# 3330 Knapp Building,
The University of North Carolina at Chapel Hill,
Chapel Hill, NC 27599-3330

Preparation and printing of this report were made possible
by funding from the participating cities.

Printed in the United States of America

22 21 20 19 18 1 2 3 4 5

ISBN 978-1-56011-925-8

CONTENTS

UNC | SCHOOL OF GOVERNMENT
North Carolina Benchmarking Project

PREFACE

North Carolina municipalities are continually looking for ways to improve the efficiency and effectiveness of service delivery. As part of this effort, a group of municipalities joined together with the School of Government and the North Carolina Local Government Budget Association to create an ongoing project to compare performance and cost data for selected governmental services. This joint undertaking is known as the North Carolina Local Government Performance Measurement Project or, more commonly, as the North Carolina Benchmarking Project. This report presents performance and cost data for the fiscal year ending June 30, 2017, for the fourteen North Carolina municipalities participating in the benchmarking project —Apex, Asheville, Chapel Hill, Charlotte, Concord, Goldsboro, Greensboro, Greenville, Hickory, High Point, Raleigh, Salisbury, Wilson, and Winston-Salem. Twenty-two previous reports have been published regarding municipal services.

The benchmarking project is a collaborative effort. Officials from the participating local governments have made vital contributions to the success of the project, including budget and finance staff, program and service staff, and city and town managers. Special thanks are owed to the members of the steering committee, who provide the necessary leadership demanded by such a project: Suzanne Parmentier, Accounting and Budget Manager, and Amanda Grogan, Budget and Management Analyst of Apex; Tony McDowell, Budget and Financial Reporting Manager, and Lauren Brune, Budget Analyst of Asheville; David Finley, Budget and Management Analyst of Chapel Hill; Justin Amos, Budget Analyst, and Rachel Wood, Strategy Manager of Charlotte; Robin Barham, Budget and Performance Manager, and Lesley Reder, Management Analyst, of Concord; Kaye Scott, Finance Director of Goldsboro; Jon Decker, Budget Analyst of Greensboro; Shelley Leach, Financial Analyst of Greenville; Cameron McHargue, Budget Analyst of Hickory; Roslyn McNeil, Budget Analyst, and Laura Altizer, Senior Budget Analyst, of High Point; Monica Chaparro, Strategic Planning and Performance Manager, and Amber Smith, Assistant Budget Director, of Raleigh; Anna Bumgarner, Purchasing Manager of Salisbury; Lanette Pridgen, Financial Analyst of Wilson; and Scott Tesh, Director of the Office of Performance and Accountability, and Heather Curry, Budget and Evaluation Analyst of Winston-Salem.

The benchmarking project receives contributions from other individuals who strongly support benchmarking and performance measurement. William C. Rivenbark and David N. Ammons, faculty members with the School of Government, serve as project advisors. Special thanks go to Michael R. Smith, dean of the School of Government, and Thomas H. Thornburg, senior associate dean of the School of Government, for their leadership and support of the benchmarking project. The author wishes to acknowledge other School of Government staff who have contributed many hours to the benchmarking project, including Jennifer Henderson and Dan Soileau in Strategic Communications.

Dale J. Roenigk
April 2018

UNC | SCHOOL OF GOVERNMENT
North Carolina Benchmarking Project

Performance and Cost Data

INTRODUCTION

UNC | SCHOOL OF GOVERNMENT
North Carolina Benchmarking Project

INTRODUCTION

Can local governments measure their performance and cost in a meaningful way? Can performance measures in one local government be legitimately compared to the performance of another? In the fall of 1995, fourteen large municipalities and counties in North Carolina agreed to participate in a collaborative project to answer these and other questions relating to benchmarking. Seven of the jurisdictions were municipalities, forming Phase I of what is now known as the North Carolina Local Government Performance Measurement Project or, more commonly, the North Carolina Benchmarking Project. The other seven jurisdictions were counties, constituting Phase II of the benchmarking project. A third phase of the benchmarking project began in January 1997, consisting of fourteen municipal and county, small- and medium-size North Carolina jurisdictions. These phases represented the pilot stage of the benchmarking project.

Since that beginning, the benchmarking project has proceeded with an ongoing agreement to collect, clean, and report comparative performance and cost data from the participating municipalities. Listed below are the fourteen municipalities that are included in this report:

- Apex
- Asheville
- Chapel Hill
- Charlotte
- Concord
- Goldsboro
- Greensboro
- Greenville
- Hickory
- High Point
- Raleigh
- Salisbury
- Wilson
- Winston-Salem

This project was the result of a joint undertaking of the participating municipalities, the School of Government, and the North Carolina Local Government Budget Association. The North Carolina League of Municipalities and the Local Government Commission also contributed to the development of this project. The goals of the benchmarking project are as follows:

1. To develop/expand the use of performance measurement in local government
2. To produce reliable performance and cost data for comparison
3. To facilitate the use of performance and cost data for service improvement

SERVICES

This report presents performance and cost data and accompanying explanatory information for the following service areas:

- Residential Refuse Collection
- Household Recycling
- Yard Waste/Leaf Collection
- Police Services
- Emergency Communications
- Asphalt Maintenance and Repair
- Fire Services
- Building Inspections
- Fleet Maintenance
- Central Human Resources
- Water Services
- Wastewater Services
- Core Parks and Recreation

The participating units did not agree to continue the benchmarking project to endure the challenges of data collection and "data cleaning" simply to produce a report. They continue with the belief that performance measurement and benchmarking are catalysts to service improvement. No jurisdiction can be the best in every service that it provides, highlighting the notion that even outstanding performers can learn from the practices of others. Performance measurement and benchmarking are about tracking performance and cost data and making changes based on both internal and external comparisons over time.

This report is the twenty-second publication representing municipal services. The previous twenty-one reports are listed below along with their publication dates:

- *Performance and Cost Data: Phase I City Services* (October 1997)
- *Performance and Cost Data: Phase III City Services* (March 1999)
- *Final Report on City Services for Fiscal Year 1997–98* (March 1999)
- *Final Report on City Services for Fiscal Year 1998–99* (February 2000)
- *Final Report on City Services for Fiscal Year 1999–2000* (February 2001)
- *Final Report on City Services for Fiscal Year 2000–2001* (February 2002)
- *Final Report on City Services for Fiscal Year 2001–2002* (February 2003)
- *Final Report on City Services for Fiscal Year 2002–2003* (February 2004)
- *Final Report on City Services for Fiscal Year 2003–2004* (February 2005)
- *Final Report on City Services for Fiscal Year 2004–2005* (February 2006)
- *Final Report on City Services for Fiscal Year 2005–2006* (February 2007)
- *Final Report on City Services for Fiscal Year 2006–2007* (February 2008)
- *Final Report on City Services for Fiscal Year 2007–2008* (February 2009)
- *Final Report on City Services for Fiscal Year 2008–2009* (February 2010)
- *Final Report on City Services for Fiscal Year 2009–2010* (February 2011)
- *Final Report on City Services for Fiscal Year 2010–2011* (February 2012)
- *Final Report on City Services for Fiscal Year 2011–2012* (February 2013)

- *Final Report on City Services for Fiscal Year 2012–2013* (February 2014)
- *Final Report on City Services for Fiscal Year 2013–2014* (February 2015)
- *Final Report on City Services for Fiscal Year 2014–2015* (February 2016)
- *Final Report on City Services for Fiscal Year 2014–2015* (May 2016)
- *Final Report on City Services for Fiscal Year 2015–2016* (May 2017)

REPORTING FORMAT

This is primarily a data report. It incorporates graphs, summary tables, and explanatory information to present the performance and cost results for each service area under study. The results of each service area by municipality are displayed with a standard, two-page format. The following information is contained in this report:

1. **Explanatory Information.** This segment of the report describes how the service is provided and identifies conditions or dimensions that affect performance and cost data of service delivery.
2. **Municipal Profile.** This includes a limited number of characteristics of each municipality, such as population density and median family income, which may affect service performance and cost. Some of the general characteristics, such as population, appear in the municipal profiles for all of the service areas. Others, such as weather and tax base served, appear only in selected profiles.
3. **Service Profile.** This area provides input and output data and identifies important dimensions of service delivery.
4. **Full Cost Profile.** A cost accounting model is used to calculate full or total cost of providing each service area under study. Although the cost data were collected in detail, using a collection instrument with more than seventy specific line items, the reporting format aggregates the detailed cost data into three general categories for the purpose of presentation: personal services for the direct expenses of salaries, wages, and related fringe benefits; operating costs that include direct operating expenses and indirect cost allocations; and capital costs that represent depreciation for equipment and facilities.
5. **Resource Measures.** These measures gauge the amount of resources or inputs municipalities allocate for the provision of a given service.
6. **Performance Measures.** Three types of performance measures are used and reported—workload, efficiency, and effectiveness. A municipality's performance is compared to the performance average, noting that the average is based on services with numerous variations and should be viewed with caution. The measures used in this report do not assess total service performance. They gauge certain service dimensions and should be approached with an understanding of the service being provided.

SUMMARY OF OVERALL RESULTS

What the project has achieved

1. The project's methodology, consisting of service profiles, performance measures, cost accounting, and explanation of results, works extremely well for data consistency and comparability. The project's accounting model is especially effective in producing reliable and materially accurate cost data.
2. The performance data have been used in numerous jurisdictions for service improvement, especially in the areas of residential refuse collection, household recycling, police services, and fleet services.
3. The project's success is directly correlated with consensus about service definitions and measurement formulas, involving numerous local government officials from the participating units.

What we have learned

1. Local governments can produce accurate, reliable, and comparable performance and cost data, which can then be used for service improvement.
2. Specific service definitions are vital to performance measurement, including explanatory information.
3. Data availability and quality are very important to performance measurement.
4. Performance measurement and cost accounting are time consuming. However, performance measures provide valuable feedback when the goal is to deliver quality services at reasonable cost.

READING THE REPORT

This report presents the performance and cost data for the fourteen North Carolina municipalities participating in the benchmarking project for the fiscal year ending June 30, 2017. It also presents multiyear data for participants based on the number of fiscal years that each municipality has participated in the benchmarking project. The following table provides the five fiscal years of performance measures (by final report) contained within the present report and the corresponding municipalities by fiscal year of participation.

Final Report	Jurisdictions
Final Report on City Services for Fiscal Year 2012–2013	Apex, Asheville, Burlington, Cary, Charlotte, Concord, Durham, Greensboro, Greenville, Hickory, High Point, Salisbury, Wilmington, Wilson, and Winston-Salem
Final Report on City Services for Fiscal Year 2013–2014	Apex, Asheville, Burlington, Cary, Charlotte, Concord, Greensboro, Greenville, Hickory, High Point, Salisbury, Wilson, and Winston-Salem
Final Report on City Services for Fiscal Year 2014–2015	Apex, Asheville, Burlington, Cary, Chapel Hill, Concord, Greensboro, Greenville, Hickory, High Point, Salisbury, Wilson, and Winston-Salem
Final Report on City Services for Fiscal Year 2015–2016	Apex, Asheville, Burlington, Cary, Chapel Hill, Charlotte, Concord, Greensboro, Greenville, Hickory, High Point, Raleigh, Salisbury, Wilson, and Winston-Salem

Final Report on City Services for Fiscal Year 2016–2017	Apex, Asheville, Chapel Hill, Charlotte, Concord, Goldsboro, Greensboro, Greenville, Hickory, High Point, Raleigh, Salisbury, Wilson, and Winston-Salem

The municipal profile, full cost profile, service profile, and explanatory information for each municipality are based solely on performance and cost data for the fiscal year ending June 30, 2017. Readers should be extremely careful when interpreting the performance and cost data for municipalities with multiyear data. Municipal profiles, full cost profiles, service profiles, and explanatory information that support performance measures for the fiscal years ending June 30, 2013, through June 30, 2016, are located in prior year performance and cost data reports and can be obtained from the School of Government.

The benchmarking project considers new service areas and service changes on an annual basis under the guidance of the steering committee. Asphalt Maintenance and Repair represented a new service area for the fiscal year ending June 30, 2000. This service was previously reported as Street Pavement Maintenance. Police Services represented a new service area for the fiscal year ending June 30, 2001. This service was presented as Police Patrol and Police Investigations in prior reports. Fleet Maintenance represented a new service area for the fiscal year ending June 30, 2002. Central Human Resources represented a new service area for the fiscal year ending June 30, 2004. Water Services represented a new service area added in the fiscal year ending June 30, 2007. Wastewater Services was added in the fiscal year ending June 30, 2012. Finally, Core Parks and Recreation was added in the fiscal year ending June 30, 2013.

Municipalities do not participate in every service area for a variety of reasons. Certain ones do not participate in Emergency Communications and Building Inspections because those services are often county functions. In some cases, a municipality may not participate due to organizational structures or other issues. The following table provides the jurisdictions participating in each service area contained in this report.

Service Area	Jurisdictions
Residential Refuse Collection	Apex, Asheville, Chapel Hill, Charlotte, Concord, Goldsboro, Greensboro, Greenville, Hickory, High Point, Raleigh, Salisbury, Wilson, and Winston-Salem
Household Recycling	Apex, Asheville, Charlotte, Concord, Goldsboro, Greensboro, Greenville, Hickory, High Point, Raleigh, Salisbury, Wilson, and Winston-Salem
Yard Waste/Leaf Collection	Apex, Asheville, Chapel Hill, Charlotte, Concord, Goldsboro, Greensboro, Greenville, Hickory, High Point, Raleigh, Salisbury, Wilson, and Winston-Salem
Police Services	Apex, Asheville, Chapel Hill, Concord, Goldsboro, Greensboro, Greenville, Hickory, High Point, Raleigh, Salisbury, Wilson, and Winston-Salem
Emergency Communications	Apex, Asheville, Concord, Greensboro, Greenville, Hickory, High Point, Raleigh, and Winston-Salem

Service Area	Jurisdictions
Asphalt Maintenance and Repair	Apex, Asheville, Chapel Hill, Charlotte, Concord, Goldsboro, Greensboro, Greenville, Hickory, High Point, Raleigh, Salisbury, Wilson, and Winston-Salem
Fire Services	Apex, Asheville, Chapel Hill, Charlotte, Concord, Goldsboro, Greensboro, Greenville, Hickory, High Point, Raleigh, Salisbury, Wilson, and Winston-Salem
Building Inspections	Apex, Asheville, Chapel Hill, Goldsboro, Greensboro, Greenville, High Point, Raleigh, Wilson, and Winston-Salem
Fleet Maintenance	Apex, Asheville, Chapel Hill, Charlotte, Concord, Goldsboro, Greensboro, Greenville, Hickory, High Point, Raleigh, Salisbury, Wilson, and Winston-Salem
Central Human Resources	Apex, Asheville, Chapel Hill, Charlotte, Concord, Goldsboro, Greensboro, Greenville, Hickory, High Point, Raleigh, Salisbury, Wilson, and Winston-Salem
Water Services	Apex, Asheville, Charlotte, Concord, Goldsboro, Greensboro, Hickory, High Point, Raleigh, Salisbury, Wilson, and Winston-Salem
Wastewater Services	Apex, Charlotte, Concord, Goldsboro, Greensboro, Hickory, High Point, Raleigh, Salisbury, Wilson, and Winston-Salem
Core Parks and Recreation	Apex, Asheville, Chapel Hill, Concord, Goldsboro, Greensboro, Greenville, Hickory, High Point, Raleigh, Salisbury, Wilson, and Winston-Salem

It also should be noted that not all municipalities submit performance and cost data for each performance measure contained within the respective service area. Therefore, data are missing for selected performance measures regardless of service participation.

Performance and Cost Data

RESIDENTIAL REFUSE COLLECTION

UNC | SCHOOL OF GOVERNMENT
North Carolina Benchmarking Project

PERFORMANCE MEASURES FOR RESIDENTIAL REFUSE COLLECTION

SERVICE DEFINITION

This is regularly scheduled collection of household refuse or "garbage" from residential premises and other locations, including small businesses, using containers small enough that residents and/or workers can move or lift them manually. The service excludes collection of waste from dumpsters; regular or special collection of yard waste and leaves; collection of recyclable materials, white goods, or other bulky items; and any special or non-routine service provided to residences. Transportation of refuse to a landfill or a transfer station is included, but the disposal of refuse and tipping costs are excluded.

NOTES ON PERFORMANCE MEASURES

1. Tons of (Residential) Refuse Collected per 1,000 Population and per 1,000 (Residential) Collection Points

"Tons of refuse collected" is widely used as a measure of workload for this service. A collection point or pickup point is a single locale (active address) from which residential refuse is collected. It can be a single-family residence, a condominium, an apartment, or a small business that uses containers that residents or sanitation workers can move or lift. Pickup points directly generate collection work, so this measure provides a good assessment of workload. "Tons of refuse collected per 1,000 population" and "per 1,000 collection points" also serve as measures of need for this service. Because of citizen expectations and public health requirements, sanitation crews or contractors must pick up all or virtually all household refuse that residents put out for collection.

2. Cost per Ton of Residential Refuse Collected and Cost per Residential Collection Point

These are the project's principal measures of efficiency for this service. Because of differences in the number of people per household and the percentage of the municipal population served by curbside collection, comparisons for these two efficiency measures can vary.

3. Full-Time Equivalent (FTE) Positions

The number of full-time equivalent (FTE) positions for residential refuse collection is the number of employees directly involved in providing the service as approved in the annual operating budget during the fiscal year. This number includes both full-time and part-time workers and both permanent and temporary workers. One FTE equates to 2,080 hours of work per year. Any combination of employees providing 2,080 hours of work annually equals one FTE. Cost data reflect all such workers. The measure "tons collected per collection FTE," however, includes only those workers who actually collect refuse and not supervisory or support personnel.

4. Number of Complaints and Number of Valid Complaints

All of the participating units take calls about residential refuse collection, and nearly all maintain records of one kind or another about such calls. However, the municipalities follow very different procedures in processing and recording these calls and in determining which ones are complaints and which are not. For these reasons, the project is able to present limited comparative data about complaints or valid complaints for residential refuse collection or other solid waste services. Nonetheless, the project recommends that the participating municipalities devise common criteria for identifying complaints and procedures for processing and recording calls.

Residential Refuse Collection

Summary of Key Dimensions of Service

City or Town	Normal Collection Location	Collection Points	Tons Collected	Weekly Routes	Percentage Contracted Service	Crew Size (most commonly used)	City FTE Collection Positions	Main Equipment		Landfill/Transfer	
								Packers	Automated	Trips per Day	Distance
Apex	Curbside	15,357	12,735	5	100%	Contracted	NA	NA	NA	NA	NA
Asheville	Curbside	30,280	22,187	37	0%	1 & 3 person	14	1	7	2	6 miles
Chapel Hill	Curbside	12,075	6,686	28	0%	1 & 3 person	12.71	7	0	1	18 miles
Charlotte	Curbside	216,922	189,383	320	0%	1 & 2 person	79	7	57	1.24	21 miles
Concord	Curbside	31,211	24,453	25	100%	Contracted	0.5	NA	NA	1	8 miles
Goldsboro	Curbside	14,372	11,253	16	1%	1 & 3 person	6	1	3	6	11 miles
Greensboro	Curbside	89,214	57,615	68	0%	1 & 2 person	27	3	23	1.8	8 miles
Greenville	Curbside and backyard	39,362	28,813	28	0%	1 & 3 person	11	2	5	2	5 miles
Hickory	Curbside	12,200	7,292	15	0%	1 & 2 person	3.75	0.25	3.25	2	5 miles
High Point	Curbside	49,918	38,320	44	0%	1 & 3 person	22.5	0.5	9	2	10 miles
Raleigh	Curbside	126,075	94,252	120	0%	1 & 3 person	68	10	22	2	10 miles
Salisbury	Curbside	11,095	9,223	15	0%	1 & 2 person	5	2	3	1	10 miles
Wilson	Curbside	20,017	23,080	27	0%	1 & 3 person	11	2	5	2	10 miles
Winston-Salem	Curbside	81,589	57,707	104	0%	1 & 3 person	82	12	12	1	10 miles

NOTES

All of the municipalities currently collect residential refuse once per week.
All of the municipalities have special provisions for collecting from the back or side yards of individuals with disabilities or mobility restrictions.

EXPLANATORY FACTORS

These are factors that the project found affected residential refuse collection performance and cost in one or more of the municipalities:

Backyard or curbside collection
Routing
Climate
Topographic conditions
Population density
Size of crews
Type of equipment used (automated)
Privatization
Participation in recycling program
Economies of scale
Distance to landfill/transfer station
Fee policies (volume-based or other)

Fiscal Year 2016–17

Explanatory Information

Service Level and Delivery

Apex contracts with Waste Industries for refuse collection, disposal, and recycling. Only the refuse collection is reflected on this page.

Residents pay $7.97 per month for collection. Refuse is collected once a week curbside, although backyard collection is provided for disabled customers at no additional charge. Residents receiving service are provided with one ninety-six-gallon container. The service also includes a small number of businesses in the downtown area who use the standard carts but receive service twice a week.

The contractor collects five days a week from different routes. Trash is trucked to the landfill.

The contractor collected 12,735 tons of residential refuse during FY 2016–17, at a cost of $87 per ton. The cost per ton does not include the disposal cost at the landfill.

Conditions Affecting Service, Performance, and Costs

Municipal Profile

Population (OSBM 2016)	46,688
Land Area (Square Miles)	20.61
Persons per Square Mile	2,265
Median Family Income U.S. Census 2010	$97,201

Service Profile

FTE Positions—Collection	Contractor
FTE Positions—Other	Contractor
Type of Equipment	Contractor
Size of Crews (most commonly used)	Contractor
Weekly Routes	5
Average Distance to Disposal Site	NA
Average Daily Trips to Disposal Site	NA
Percentage of Service Contracted	100%
Collection Frequency	1 x week
General Collection Location	Curbside
Residential Customers (number represents collection points)	15,357
Tons Collected	12,735
Monthly Service Fee	$7.97

Full Cost Profile

Cost Breakdown by Percentage	
Personal Services	0.0%
Operating Costs	100.0%
Capital Costs	0.0%
TOTAL	100.0%
Cost Breakdown in Dollars	
Personal Services	$0
Operating Costs	$1,103,508
Capital Costs	$0
TOTAL	$1,103,508

Key: Apex ▒ Benchmarking Average — Fiscal Years 2013 through 2017

Resource Measures

Residential Refuse Collection Costs per Capita

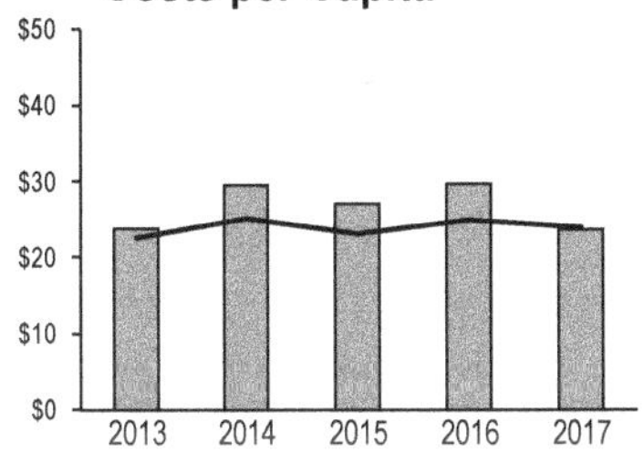

	2013	2014	2015	2016	2017
Apex	$23.83	$29.57	$27.10	$29.73	$23.64
Average	$22.61	$25.23	$23.10	$24.98	$23.97

Residential Refuse FTEs per 10,000 Population

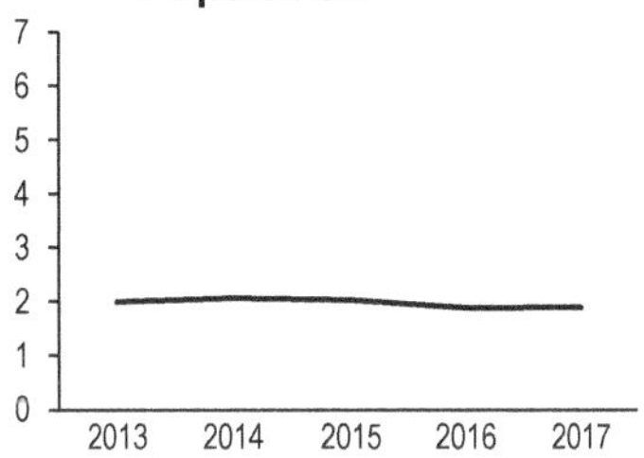

	2013	2014	2015	2016	2017
Apex					
Average	1.98	2.05	2.02	1.87	1.88

Workload Measures

Residential Refuse Tons per 1,000 Population

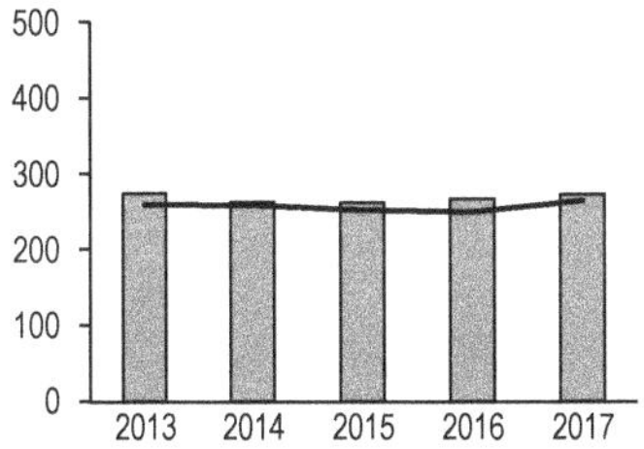

	2013	2014	2015	2016	2017
Apex	274	262	262	267	273
Average	259	258	251	249	264

Residential Refuse Tons per 1,000 Collection Points

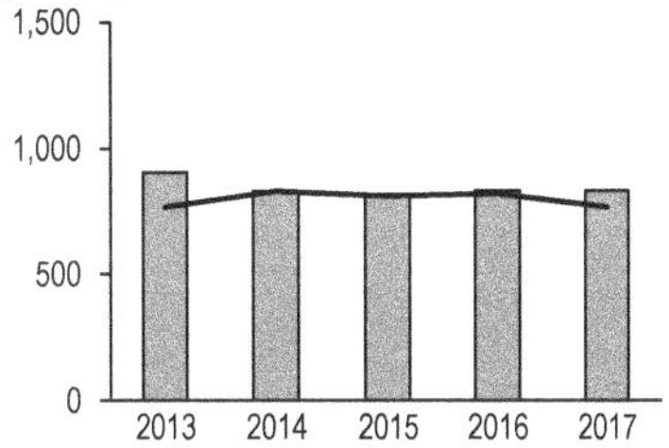

	2013	2014	2015	2016	2017
Apex	905	827	816	829	829
Average	767	831	811	819	767

Efficiency Measures

Residential Refuse Collection Cost per Ton Collected

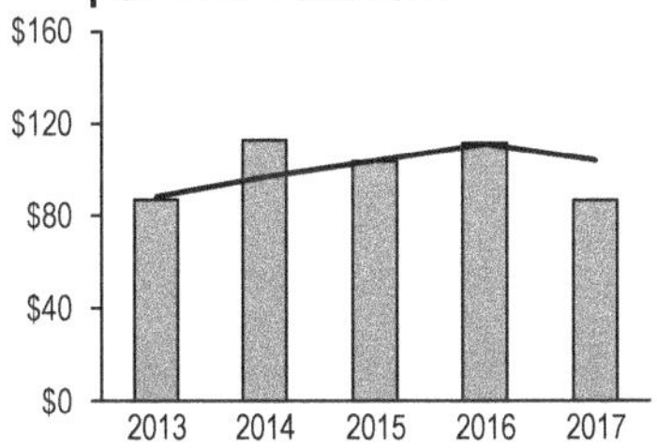

	2013	2014	2015	2016	2017
Apex	$87	$113	$104	$112	$87
Average	$88	$97	$104	$111	$104

Residential Refuse Collection Cost per Collection Point

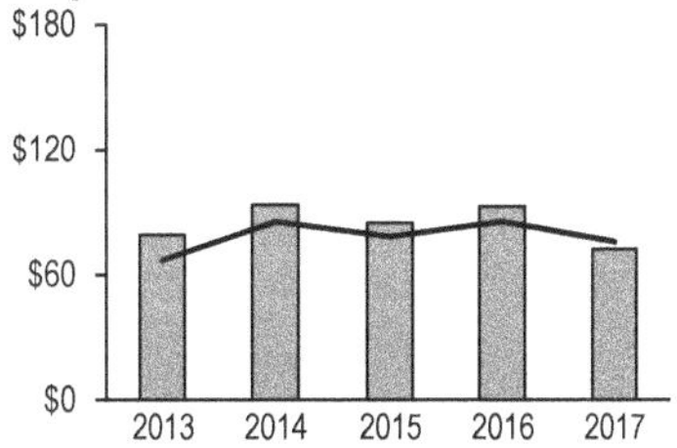

	2013	2014	2015	2016	2017
Apex	$79	$93	$85	$92	$72
Average	$67	$85	$78	$85	$75

Refuse Tons Collected per Municipal Collection FTE

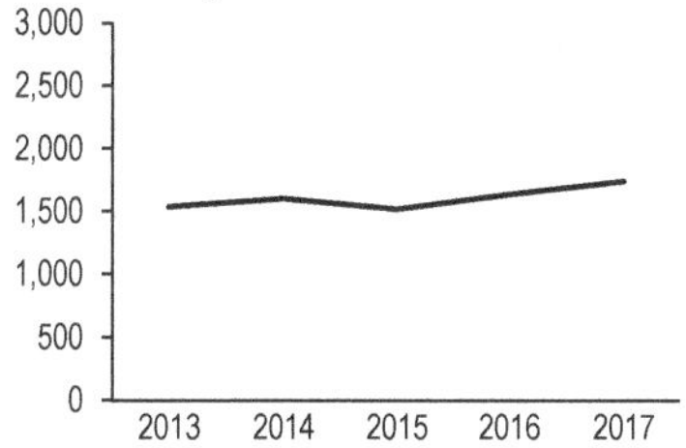

	2013	2014	2015	2016	2017
Apex					
Average	1,531	1,598	1,514	1,632	1,735

Effectiveness Measures

Complaints per 1,000 Collection Points

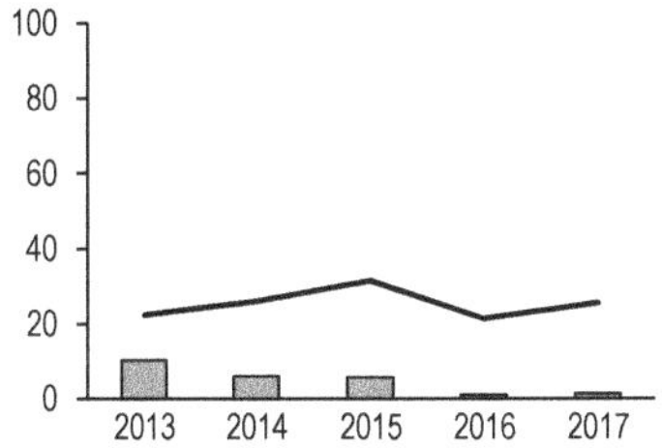

	2013	2014	2015	2016	2017
Apex	10.4	6.2	5.8	1.0	1.3
Average	22.5	26.1	31.5	21.4	25.6

Valid Complaints per 1,000 Collection Points

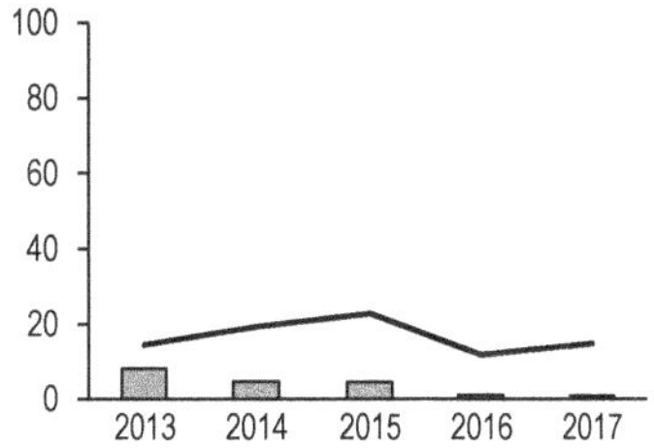

	2013	2014	2015	2016	2017
Apex	8.3	4.6	4.4	1.0	0.8
Average	14.6	19.4	22.8	11.9	14.8

Fiscal Year 2016–17

Explanatory Information

Service Level and Delivery
Asheville collects residential refuse once a week at curbside, although backyard collection is provided for disabled customers at no charge and for other customers for a fee.

The city uses seven automated trucks, each with one driver, from Monday to Thursday working ten-hour days. Two rear packers with two- and three-person crews are used from Monday to Thursday for the collection of bulky items, clean-ups, and streets not accessible by automated trucks.

There are thirty-three main collection routes served by the automated trucks. The average number of trips to the transfer station is two per day per route. Nearly all trash goes to the transfer station before going to the landfill. The average distance to the transfer station is six miles. Two rear packers serve seven collection routes.

The city collected 22,187 tons of residential refuse during FY 2016–17, at a cost of $67 per ton. The cost per ton does not include the disposal cost of $43 per ton at the transfer station. The transfer station is the primary disposal point for Asheville's trucks.

Residents receiving automated service are provided with one container. The majority of the containers are ninety-five-gallon capacity. Some residents use containers of sixty-five-gallon or thirty-five-gallon capacity. Residents may rent more containers if desired for $14 per month. Residents receiving rear-loading service provide their own containers. They are able to use up to six containers or bags. There is a $14 per month waste fee regardless of container size.

Conditions Affecting Service, Performance, and Costs
Asheville is highly automated in the area of residential refuse collection.

Municipal Profile

Population (OSBM 2016)	91,929
Land Area (Square Miles)	45.52
Persons per Square Mile	2,019
Median Family Income U.S. Census 2010	$53,350

Service Profile

FTE Positions—Collection	14.0
FTE Positions—Other	4.0
Type of Equipment	7 automated packers 1 packer
Size of Crews (most commonly used)	1 & 3 person
Weekly Routes	37
Average Distance to Disposal Site	6 miles
Average Daily Trips to Disposal Site	2
Percentage of Service Contracted	0%
Collection Frequency	1 x week
General Collection Location	Curbside
Residential Customers (number represents collection points)	30,280
Tons Collected	22,187
Monthly Service Fee	$14.00

Full Cost Profile

Cost Breakdown by Percentage	
Personal Services	43.0%
Operating Costs	41.0%
Capital Costs	16.0%
TOTAL	100.0%
Cost Breakdown in Dollars	
Personal Services	$642,971
Operating Costs	$612,640
Capital Costs	$238,895
TOTAL	$1,494,506

Asheville

Residential Refuse Collection

Key: Asheville ▒ Benchmarking Average — Fiscal Years 2013 through 2017

Resource Measures

Residential Refuse Collection Costs per Capita

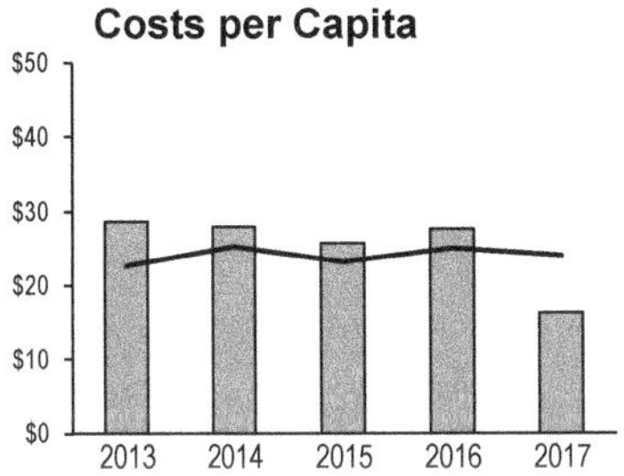

	2013	2014	2015	2016	2017
Asheville	$28.57	$27.89	$25.64	$27.57	$16.26
Average	$22.61	$25.23	$23.10	$24.98	$23.97

Residential Refuse FTEs per 10,000 Population

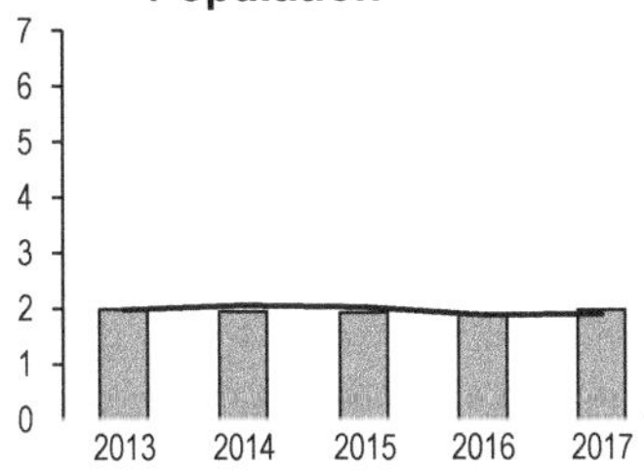

	2013	2014	2015	2016	2017
Asheville	1.9719976	1.93	1.90	1.87	1.96
Average	1.98	2.05	2.02	1.87	1.88

Workload Measures

Residential Refuse Tons per 1,000 Population

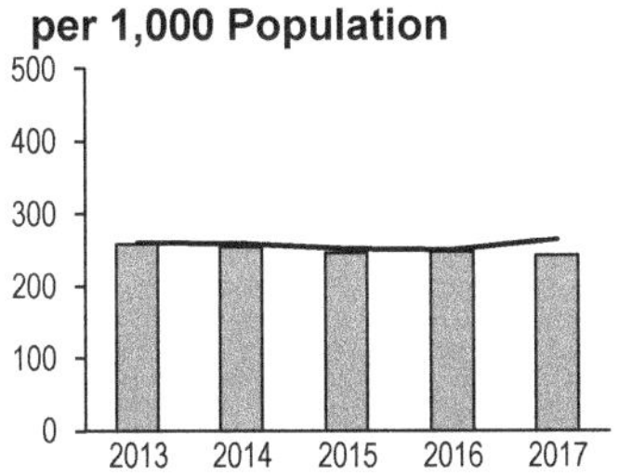

	2013	2014	2015	2016	2017
Asheville	257.33	253	245	247	241
Average	259	258	251	249	264

Residential Refuse Tons per 1,000 Collection Points

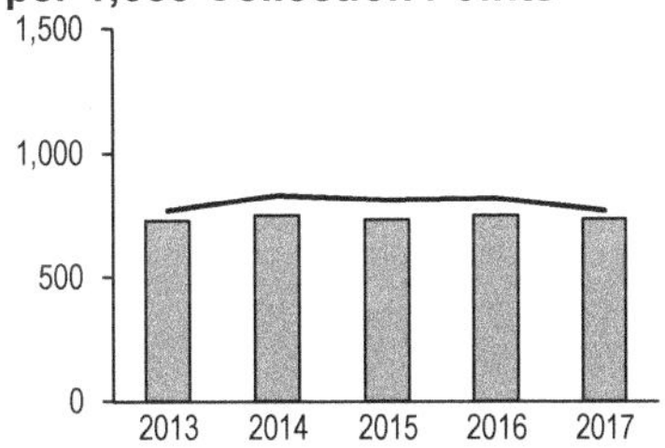

	2013	2014	2015	2016	2017
Asheville	725	747	731	745	733
Average	767	831	811	819	767

Efficiency Measures

Residential Refuse Collection Cost per Ton Collected

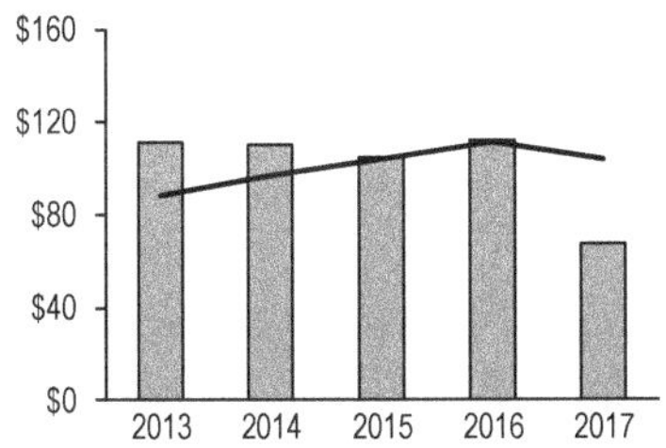

	2013	2014	2015	2016	2017
Asheville	$111	$110	$105	$112	$67
Average	$88	$97	$104	$111	$104

Residential Refuse Collection Cost per Collection Point

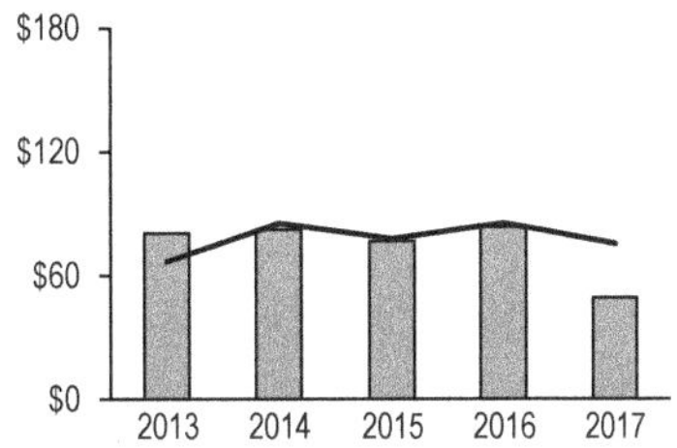

	2013	2014	2015	2016	2017
Asheville	$81	$82	$76	$83	$49
Average	$67	$85	$78	$85	$75

Refuse Tons Collected per Municipal Collection FTE

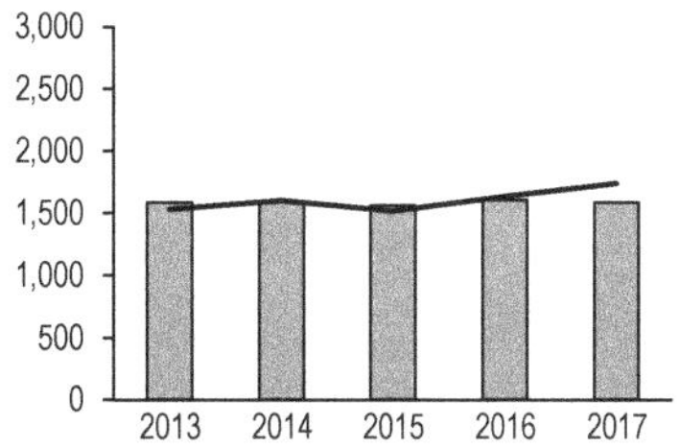

	2013	2014	2015	2016	2017
Asheville	1,585	1,591	1,561	1,601	1,585
Average	1,531	1,598	1,514	1,632	1,735

Effectiveness Measures

Complaints per 1,000 Collection Points

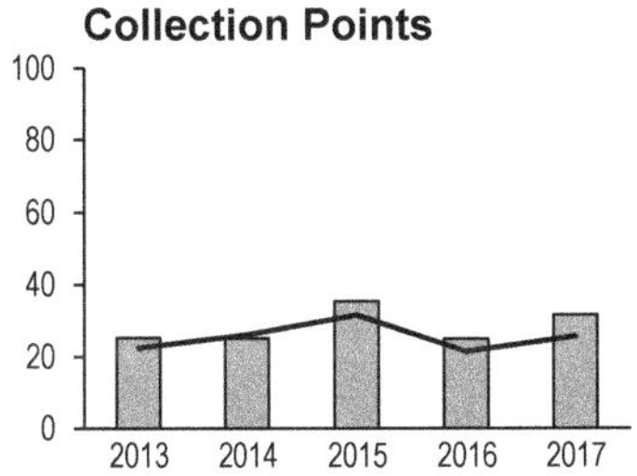

	2013	2014	2015	2016	2017
Asheville	25.3	25.2	35.3	25.0	31.6
Average	22.5	26.1	31.5	21.4	25.6

Valid Complaints per 1,000 Collection Points

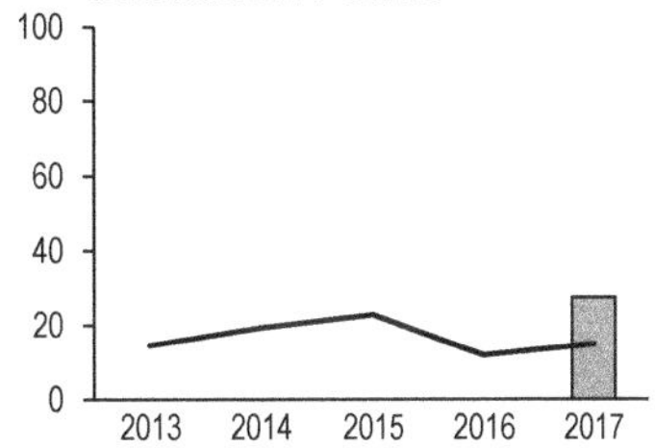

	2013	2014	2015	2016	2017
Asheville					27.4
Average	14.6	19.4	22.8	11.9	14.8

Chapel Hill — Residential Refuse

Fiscal Year 2016–17

Explanatory Information

Service Level and Delivery

Chapel Hill residential refuse collection is performed by the Solid Waste Services Division under the Public Works Department. The Town provides weekly household waste collection Mondays and Tuesdays with no fees charged.

Residential refuse is collected by seven 3-person crews using rear packers two days per week. The packer crews are staffed with three persons, one driver and two collectors. The trucks average one trip to the transfer station with the distance averaging 18 miles one way. A lift gate truck is also used to collect bulky items and electronics for a fee five days per week running two routes per day. Two pickup trucks are also used to collect medical exemptions, pedestrian trash cans, and streets not accessible to rear packers with one truck running seven days per week and the other running two days per week.

The town collected 6,686 tons of residential refuse during the fiscal year at a cost of $322 per ton or $178 per collection point. The cost does not include the disposal cost of $44 per ton at the transfer station for the tipping fee. Residents receive one roll-out cart at no charge. Residents can also purchase their own trash cans, but these must be 32 gallons or smaller and weigh less than 60 pounds when full.

Conditions Affecting Service, Performance, and Costs

The Town of Chapel Hill began participation in the benchmarking project in July 2015, with FY 2014–15 being the first reporting year.

The out-of-town transfer station is the primary disposal location for Chapel Hill. Orange County had the highest waste reduction rate (64 percent) in North Carolina in FY 2014–15. The town provides special exemptions for backyard collections for 475 collection points, which represents 3.93 percent of the total collection points.

Municipal Profile

Population (OSBM 2016)	59,852
Land Area (Square Miles)	21.21
Persons per Square Mile	2,822
Median Family Income U.S. Census 2010	$61,405

Service Profile

FTE Positions—Collection	12.7
FTE Positions—Other	1.1
Type of Equipment	7 packers 1 Lift-Gate Truck and 2 Pickups
Size of Crews (most commonly used)	1 & 3 person
Weekly Routes	28
Average Distance to Disposal Site	18 miles
Average Daily Route Trips to Disposal Site	1
Percentage of Service Contracted	0%
Collection Frequency	1 x week
General Collection Location	Curbside
Residential Customers (number represents collection points)	12,075
Tons Collected	6,686
Monthly Service Fee	No

Full Cost Profile

Cost Breakdown by Percentage	
Personal Services	38.1%
Operating Costs	47.7%
Capital Costs	14.2%
TOTAL	100.0%

Cost Breakdown in Dollars	
Personal Services	$820,603
Operating Costs	$1,025,194
Capital Costs	$305,317
TOTAL	$2,151,114

Key: Chapel Hill ▒ Benchmarking Average — Fiscal Years 2013 through 2017

Resource Measures

Residential Refuse Collection Costs per Capita

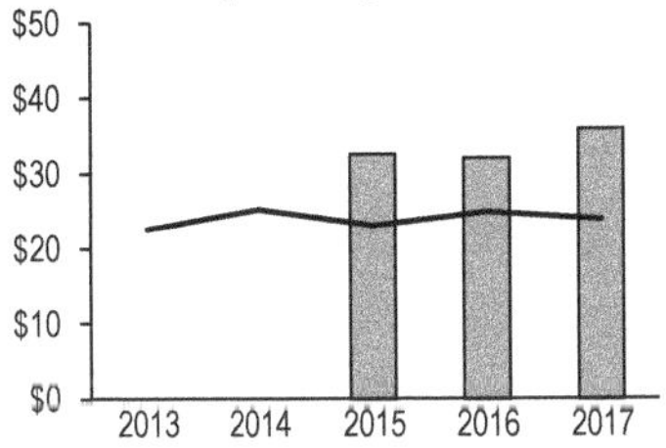

	2013	2014	2015	2016	2017
Chapel Hill			$32.63	$32.09	$35.94
Average	$22.61	$25.23	$23.10	$24.98	$23.97

Residential Refuse FTEs per 10,000 Population

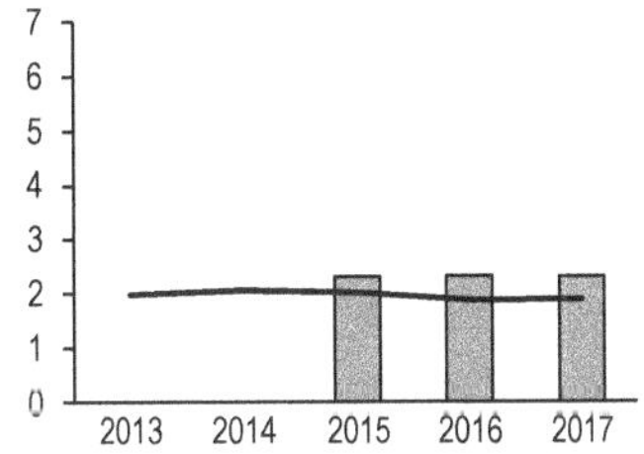

	2013	2014	2015	2016	2017
Chapel Hill			2.31	2.32	2.31
Average	1.98	2.05	2.02	1.87	1.88

Workload Measures

Residential Refuse Tons per 1,000 Population

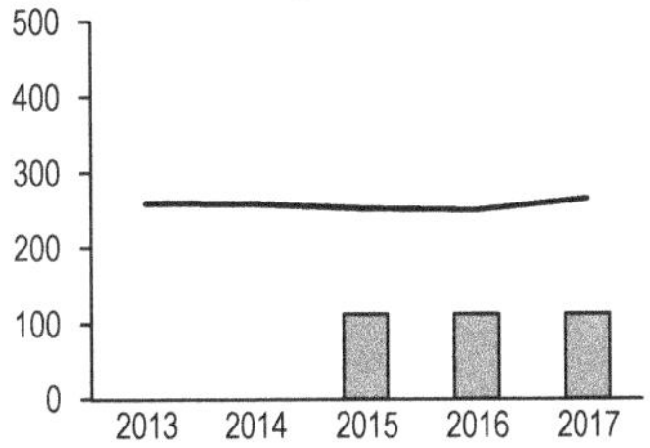

	2013	2014	2015	2016	2017
Chapel Hill			111	112	112
Average	259	258	251	249	264

Residential Refuse Tons per 1,000 Collection Points

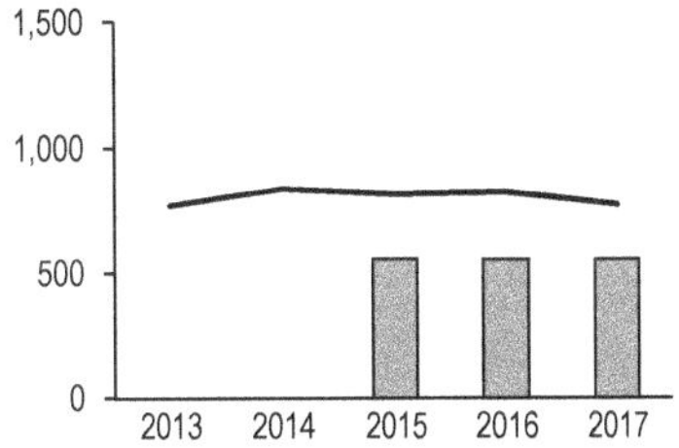

	2013	2014	2015	2016	2017
Chapel Hill			556	553	554
Average	767	831	811	819	767

Efficiency Measures

Residential Refuse Collection Cost per Ton Collected

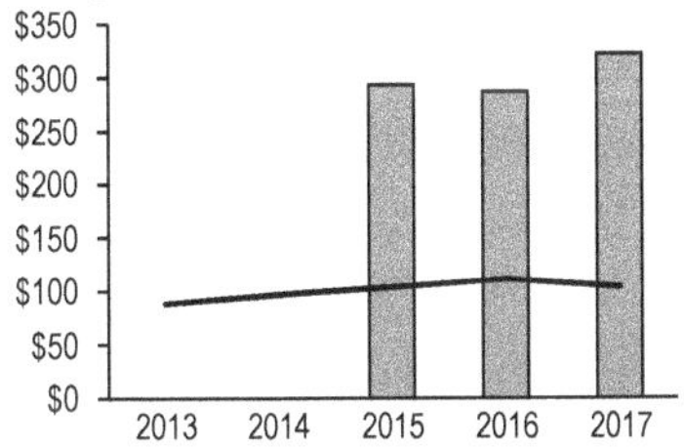

	2013	2014	2015	2016	2017
Chapel Hill			$293	$287	$322
Average	$88	$97	$104	$111	$104

Residential Refuse Collection Cost per Collection Point

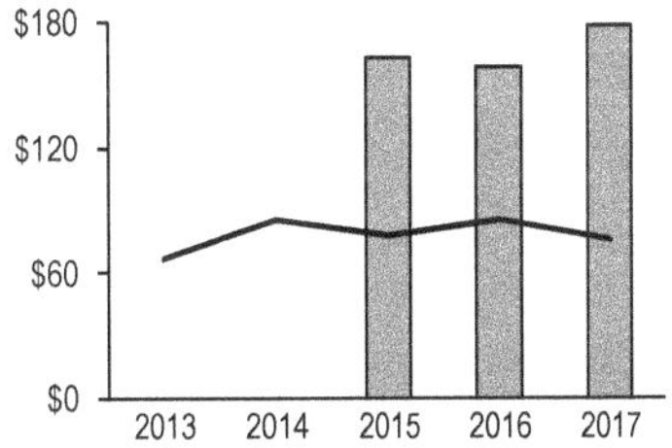

	2013	2014	2015	2016	2017
Chapel Hill			$163	$159	$178
Average	$67	$85	$78	$85	$75

Refuse Tons Collected per Municipal Collection FTE

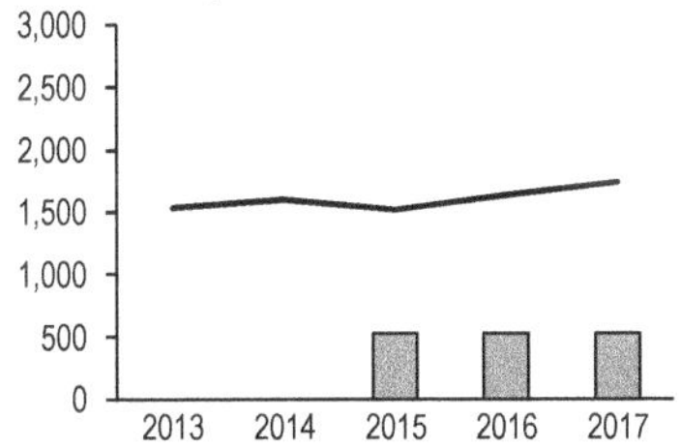

	2013	2014	2015	2016	2017
Chapel Hill			523	525	526
Average	1,531	1,598	1,514	1,632	1,735

Effectiveness Measures

Complaints per 1,000 Collection Points

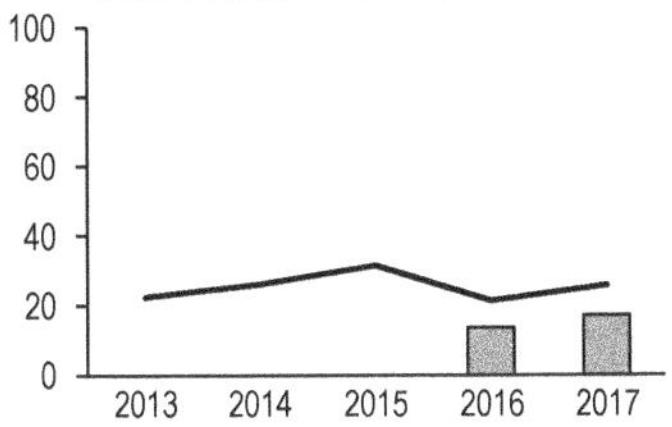

	2013	2014	2015	2016	2017
Chapel Hill				13.5	17.1
Average	22.5	26.1	31.5	21.4	25.6

Valid Complaints per 1,000 Collection Points

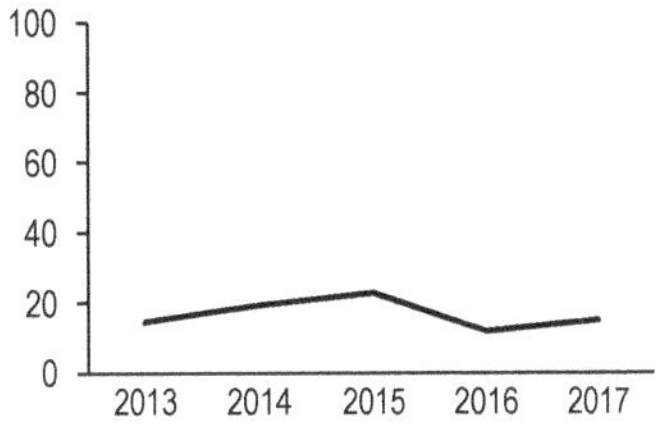

	2013	2014	2015	2016	2017
Chapel Hill					
Average	14.6	19.4	22.8	11.9	14.8

Fiscal Year 2016–17

Explanatory Information

Service Level and Delivery

Charlotte collects residential refuse once a week at curbside. Backyard service is available only to those persons with valid medical reasons and physician certification. The city charges an annual fee of $33 for refuse services which is paid on the property tax bill; the fee applies to both collection and disposal costs and is meant to be just a portion of cost recovery for services.

City crews are composed primarily of one driver, each operating an automated packer. There were fifty-seven of these crews for FY 2016–17. In addition, three crews, each composed of one driver and one laborer, collected refuse using semi-automated packers. These crews are used primarily for backyard service for those citizens with disabilities and some multi-family complexes with less than thirty units. Small business garbage is collected by four crews, each composed of one driver and one laborer, using rear loaders. Costs include reserve crews that were used as needed throughout the year.

The city serviced 320 daily collection routes once each week during FY 2016–17, with an average of 1.24 trips to the landfill per day per route at an average one-way distance of twenty-one miles. Each single-family residence is provided one ninety-six-gallon rollout container. An additional receptacle may be purchased for a nominal one-time fee. Charlotte collected 189,383 tons of residential refuse during the fiscal year, at a cost of $90 per ton. The cost per ton does not include the disposal cost of $30.50, representing the landfill tipping fee.

Conditions Affecting Service, Performance, and Costs

Charlotte did not participate in the Benchmarking Project during FY 2014–15. No data are available for that year.

Charlotte is highly automated in the area of residential refuse collection. It considers all complaints to be valid complaints.

Charlotte's Solid Waste Services division has been focused on improving customer service since FY 2013–14, explaining the drop in complaints.

Municipal Profile

Population (OSBM 2016)	830,258
Land Area (Square Miles)	305.48
Persons per Square Mile	2,718
Median Family Income U.S. Census 2010	$61,405

Service Profile

FTE Positions—Collection	79.0
FTE Positions—Other	7.0
Type of Equipment	57 automated packers 7 packers
Size of Crews (most commonly used)	1 & 2 person
Weekly Routes	320
Average Distance to Disposal Site	21 miles
Average Daily Trips to Disposal Site	1.24
Percentage of Service Contracted	0%
Collection Frequency	1 x week
General Collection Location	Curbside
Residential Customers (number represents collection points)	216,922
Tons Collected	189,383
Annual Service Fee	$33 per year

Full Cost Profile

Cost Breakdown by Percentage	
Personal Services	32.6%
Operating Costs	47.5%
Capital Costs	20.0%
TOTAL	100.0%
Cost Breakdown in Dollars	
Personal Services	$5,567,000
Operating Costs	$8,115,723
Capital Costs	$3,415,997
TOTAL	$17,098,720

Charlotte

Residential Refuse Collection

Key: Charlotte ▒ Benchmarking Average — Fiscal Years 2013 through 2017

Resource Measures

Residential Refuse Collection Costs per Capita

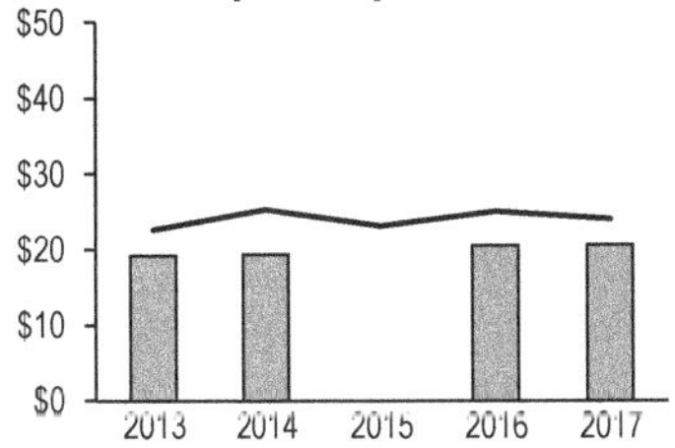

	2013	2014	2015	2016	2017
Charlotte	$19.16	$19.31		$20.50	$20.59
Average	$22.61	$25.23	$23.10	$24.98	$23.97

Residential Refuse FTEs per 10,000 Population

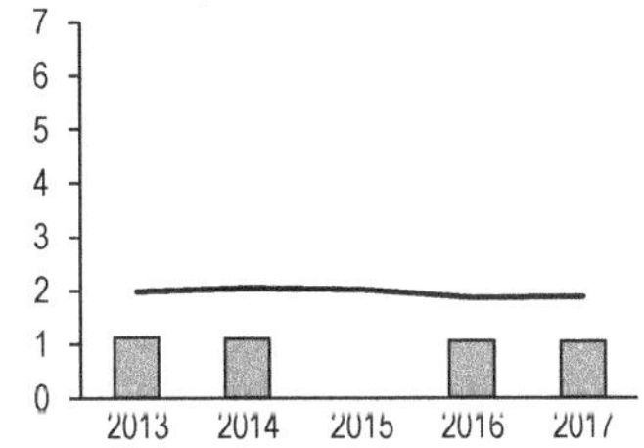

	2013	2014	2015	2016	2017
Charlotte	1.12	1.10		1.05	1.04
Average	1.98	2.05	2.02	1.87	1.88

Workload Measures

Residential Refuse Tons per 1,000 Population

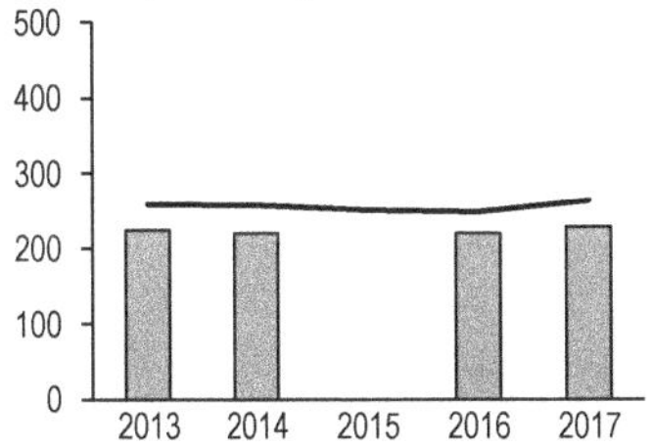

	2013	2014	2015	2016	2017
Charlotte	224	220		220	228
Average	259	258	251	249	264

Residential Refuse Tons per 1,000 Collection Points

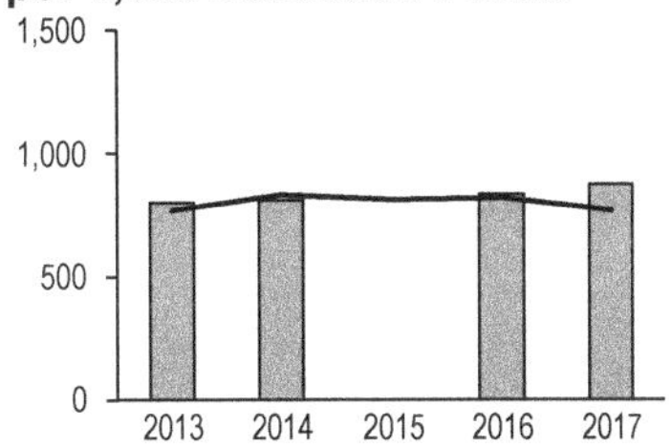

	2013	2014	2015	2016	2017
Charlotte	800	809		834	873
Average	767	831	811	819	767

Efficiency Measures

Residential Refuse Collection Cost per Ton Collected

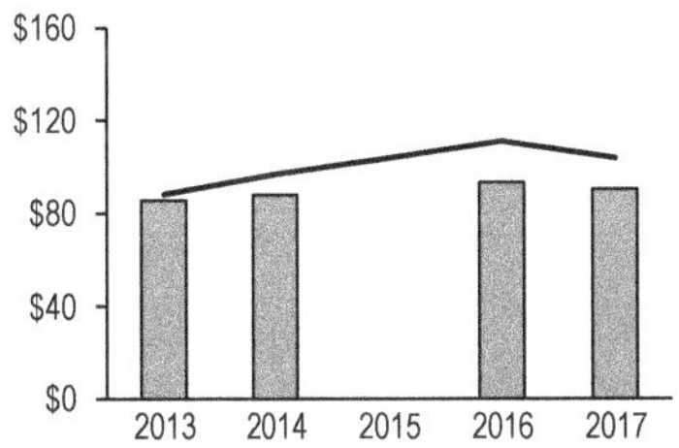

	2013	2014	2015	2016	2017
Charlotte	$86	$88		$93	$90
Average	$88	$97	$104	$111	$104

Residential Refuse Collection Cost per Collection Point

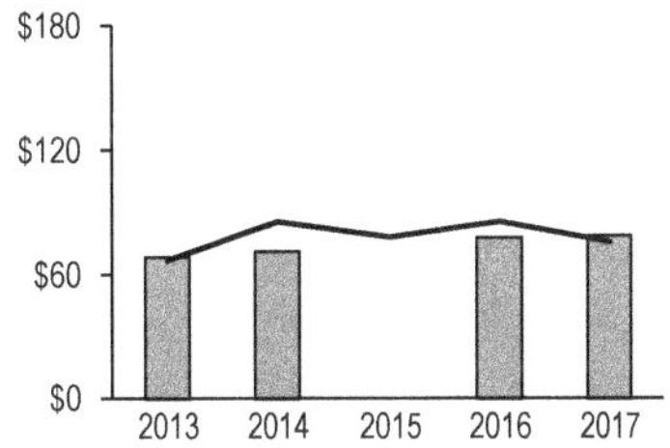

	2013	2014	2015	2016	2017
Charlotte	$69	$71		$78	$79
Average	$67	$85	$78	$85	$75

Refuse Tons Collected per Municipal Collection FTE

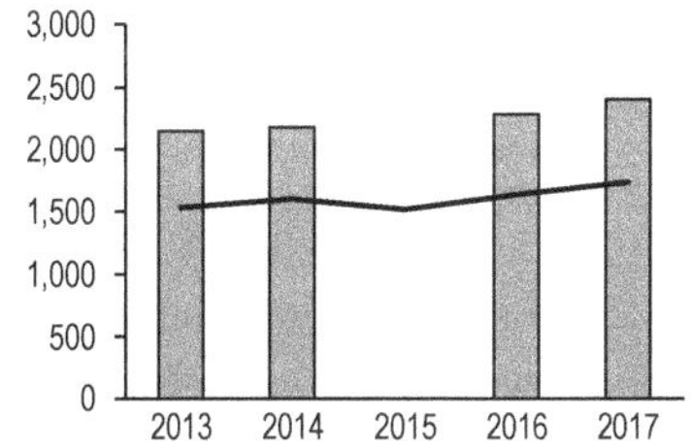

	2013	2014	2015	2016	2017
Charlotte	2,140	2,168		2,276	2,397
Average	1,531	1,598	1,514	1,632	1,735

Effectiveness Measures

Complaints per 1,000 Collection Points

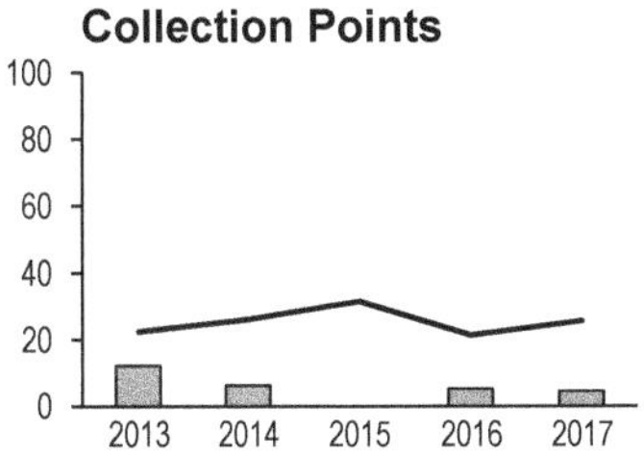

	2013	2014	2015	2016	2017
Charlotte	12.4	6.5		5.3	4.7
Average	22.5	26.1	31.5	21.4	25.6

Valid Complaints per 1,000 Collection Points

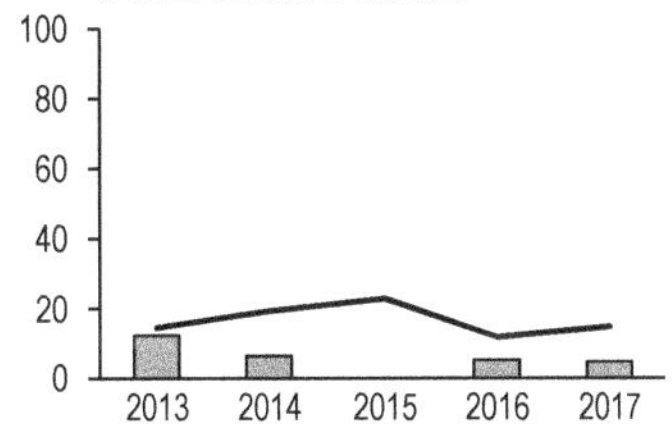

	2013	2014	2015	2016	2017
Charlotte	12.4	6.5		5.3	4.7
Average	14.6	19.4	22.8	11.9	14.8

Fiscal Year 2016–17

Explanatory Information

Service Level and Delivery
Residential refuse collection service is provided once a week at curbside to Concord residents. Backyard service is available for the elderly and disabled. The city has provided residential refuse collection service under contract for many years, but it changed the contractor used in FY 2010–11. The cost of the contract for the year was approximately $1.70 million.

The contractor primarily used five automated packers, each with one person. Residents used one ninety-five-gallon cart, with extra carts available for larger families or unusual circumstances.

The contractor serviced twenty-five collection routes each week, with an average distance per route per day to the landfill of eight miles. The packers made an average of one trip to the landfill per day per route. The contractor collected 24,453 tons of residential refuse during the fiscal year, at a cost of $85 per ton.

Conditions Affecting Service, Performance, and Costs
Concord is one of only two jurisdictions participating in the benchmarking project that contracts 100 percent of its residential refuse collection service. Therefore, "tons collected per collection FTE" is not used for Concord as a performance measure, as this reflects only municipal workers.

Concord's "total tons collected" includes bulk trash, which is collected along with residential refuse and cannot be separated for reporting purposes.

Concord defines valid complaints to mean any missed collection or request for service as determined by the city to result from contractor negligence or omission.

Concord discontinued its old system, which required citizens to schedule the collection of bulky items. Too many collections were not called in, resulting in bulky items being left curbside for days and generating complaints. The drop in complaints in FY 2013–14 was the result of a new system where the city scouts out items to be picked up and citizens are not required to call in. Pickup is improved and additional costs for the scouting have been offset by savings from avoided costs through improved collection efficiencies.

Municipal Profile

Population (OSBM 2016)	88,815
Land Area (Square Miles)	62.61
Persons per Square Mile	1,419
Median Family Income U.S. Census 2010	$63,643

Service Profile

FTE Positions—Collection	0.5 City
FTE Positions—Other	1.64 City
Type of Equipment	5 automated packers
Size of Crews (most commonly used)	Contractor
Weekly Routes	25
Average Distance to Disposal Site	8 miles
Average Daily Trips to Disposal Site	1
Percentage of Service Contracted	100%
Collection Frequency	1 x week
General Collection Location	Curbside
Residential Customers (number represents collection points)	31,211
Tons Collected	24,453
Monthly Service Fee	No

Full Cost Profile

Cost Breakdown by Percentage	
Personal Services	7.1%
Operating Costs	92.7%
Capital Costs	0.2%
TOTAL	100.0%
Cost Breakdown in Dollars	
Personal Services	$148,225
Operating Costs	$1,931,592
Capital Costs	$4,020
TOTAL	$2,083,836

Key: Concord ▒ Benchmarking Average — Fiscal Years 2013 through 2017

Resource Measures

Residential Refuse Collection Costs per Capita

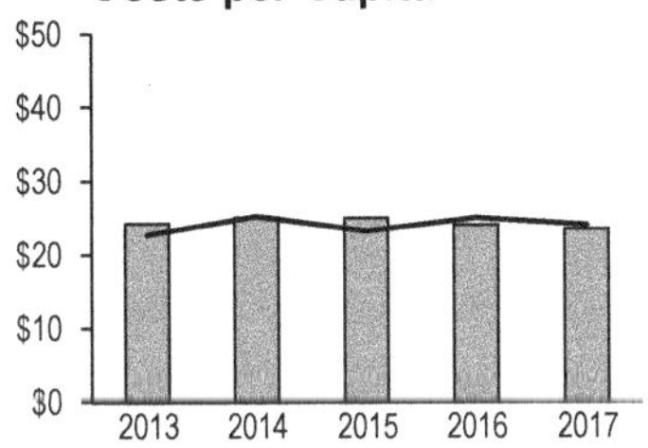

	2013	2014	2015	2016	2017
Concord	$24.27	$25.16	$25.01	$24.04	$23.46
Average	$22.61	$25.23	$23.10	$24.98	$23.97

Residential Refuse FTEs per 10,000 Population

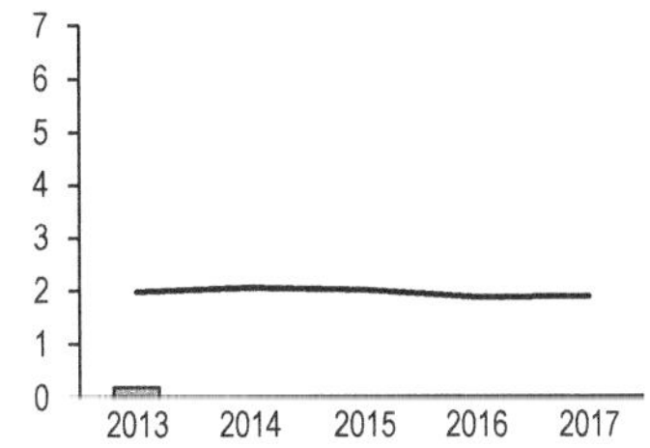

	2013	2014	2015	2016	2017
Concord	0.20				
Average	1.98	2.05	2.02	1.87	1.88

Workload Measures

Residential Refuse Tons per 1,000 Population

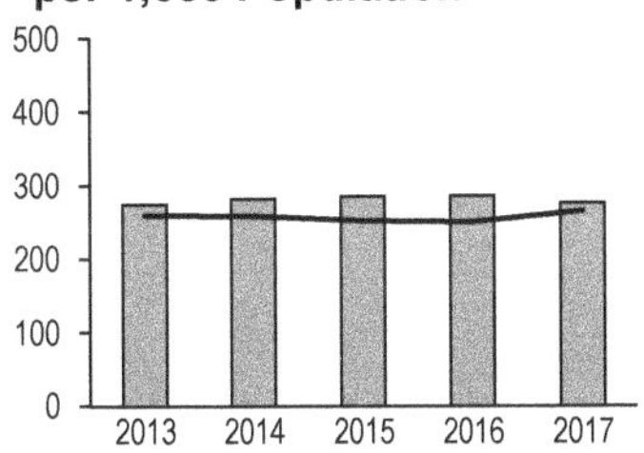

	2013	2014	2015	2016	2017
Concord	274	281	285	286	275
Average	259	258	251	249	264

Residential Refuse Tons per 1,000 Collection Points

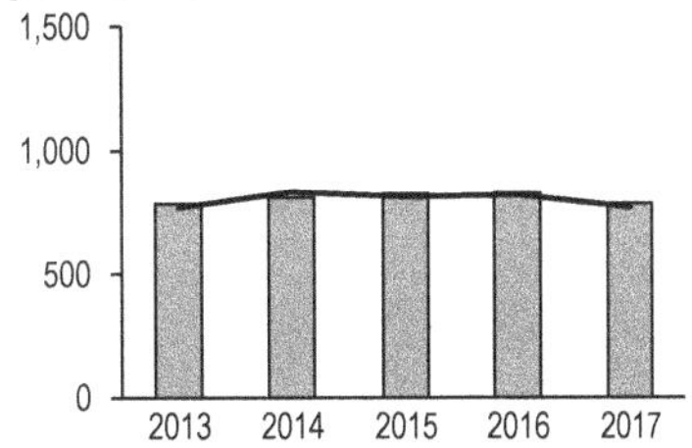

	2013	2014	2015	2016	2017
Concord	782	808	823	825	783
Average	767	831	811	819	767

Efficiency Measures

Residential Refuse Collection Cost per Ton Collected

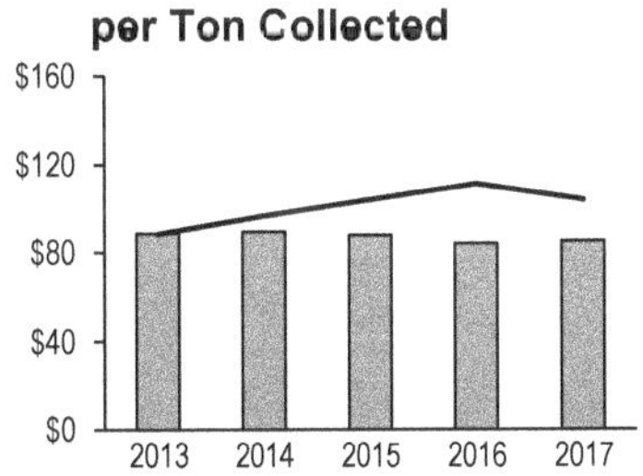

	2013	2014	2015	2016	2017
Concord	$89	$89	$88	$84	$85
Average	$88	$97	$104	$111	$104

Residential Refuse Collection Cost per Collection Point

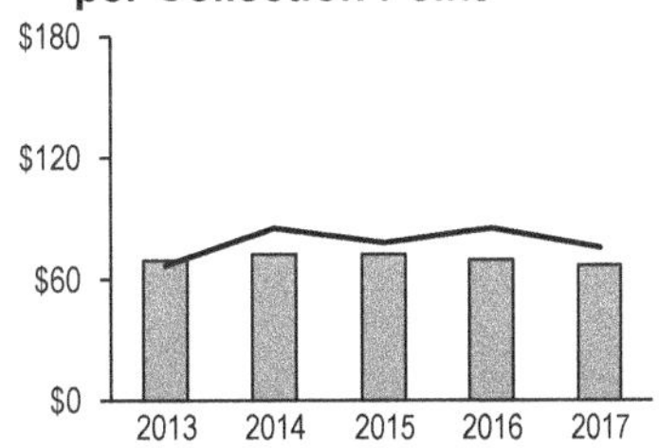

	2013	2014	2015	2016	2017
Concord	$69	$72	$72	$69	$67
Average	$67	$85	$78	$85	$75

Refuse Tons Collected per Municipal Collection FTE

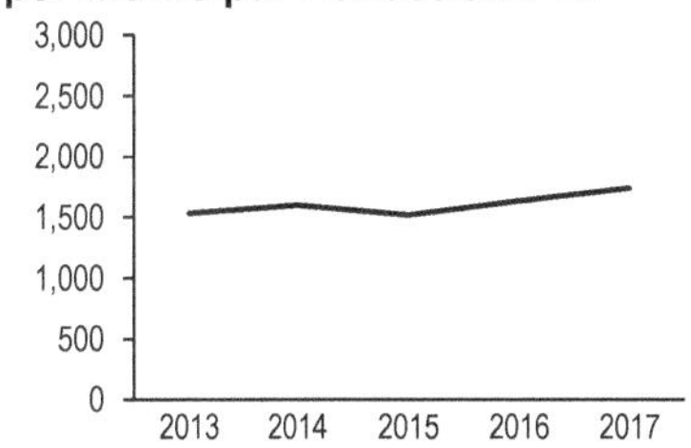

	2013	2014	2015	2016	2017
Concord					0
Average	1,531	1,598	1,514	1,632	1,735

Effectiveness Measures

Complaints per 1,000 Collection Points

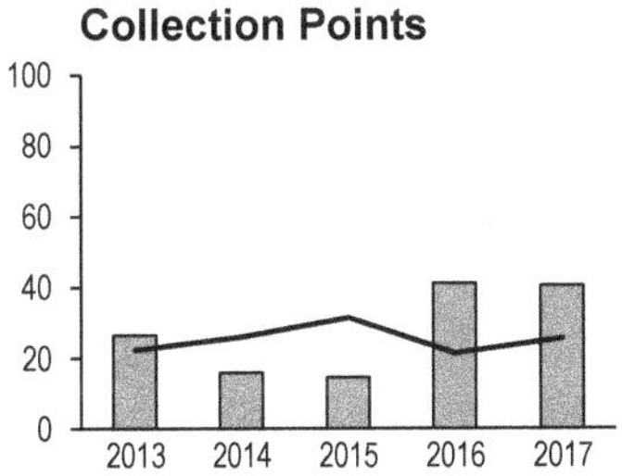

	2013	2014	2015	2016	2017
Concord	26.7	16.0	14.7	41.2	40.5
Average	22.5	26.1	31.5	21.4	25.6

Valid Complaints per 1,000 Collection Points

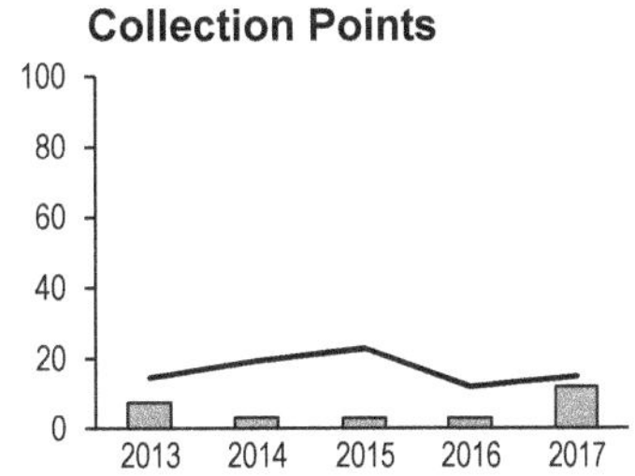

	2013	2014	2015	2016	2017
Concord	7.5	3.2	3.0	3.1	12.0
Average	14.6	19.4	22.8	11.9	14.8

Goldsboro — Residential Refuse

Fiscal Year 2016–17

Explanatory Information

Service Level and Delivery
Goldsboro provides residential refuse collection once a week at curbside for residents. Collection is done by the Solid Waste Division of the Public Works Department. Backyard collection is available for the disabled. Currently the city charges a monthly fee of $22 which includes refuse, recycling, and leaf and limb pickup.

There are three automated trucks with a single driver and one crew with a driver and two collectors using a rear loader. Collection trucks run four days per week. Crews drive eleven miles to a transfer station.

The city collected 11,253 tons of residential refuse during the fiscal year from 14,372 collection points. The collection costs do not include a disposal cost at the transfer station of $31.50 per ton.

Conditions Affecting Service, Performance, and Costs
The city of Goldsboro joined the Benchmarking Project in July 2017 with the first year of data showing for FY 2016–17.

Goldsboro contracts refuse collection for one small neighborhood where a hill and tight roads make it infeasible to use city trucks.

Municipal Profile

Population (OSBM 2016)	34,793
Land Area (Square Miles)	29.35
Persons per Square Mile	1,186
Median Family Income U.S. Census 2010	$33,879

Service Profile

FTE Positions—Collection	6.0
FTE Positions—Other	1.3
Type of Equipment	3 automated packers 1 packer
Size of Crews (most commonly used)	1 & 3 person
Weekly Routes	16
Average Distance to Disposal Site	11 miles
Average Daily Trips to Disposal Site	6
Percentage of Service Contracted	0.7%
Collection Frequency	1 x week
General Collection Location	Curbside
Residential Customers (number represents collection points)	14,372
Tons Collected	11,253
Monthly Service Fee	$22

Full Cost Profile

Cost Breakdown by Percentage	
Personal Services	50.3%
Operating Costs	33.3%
Capital Costs	16.4%
TOTAL	100.0%
Cost Breakdown in Dollars	
Personal Services	$375,447
Operating Costs	$248,671
Capital Costs	$122,000
TOTAL	$746,118

Key: Goldsboro ▒ Benchmarking Average — Fiscal Years 2013 through 2017

Resource Measures

Residential Refuse Collection Costs per Capita

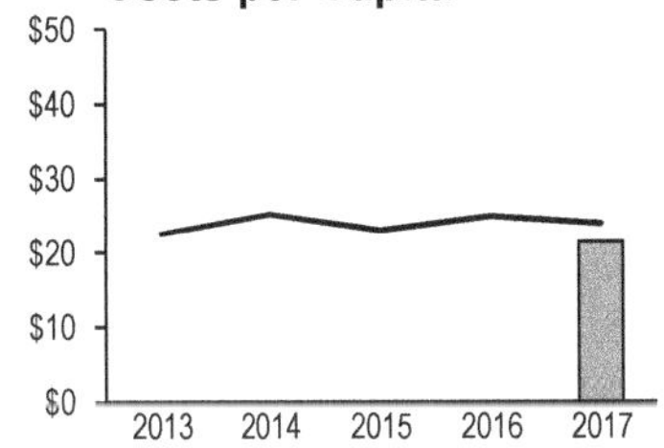

	2013	2014	2015	2016	2017
Goldsboro					$21.44
Average	$22.61	$25.23	$23.10	$24.98	$23.97

Residential Refuse FTEs per 10,000 Population

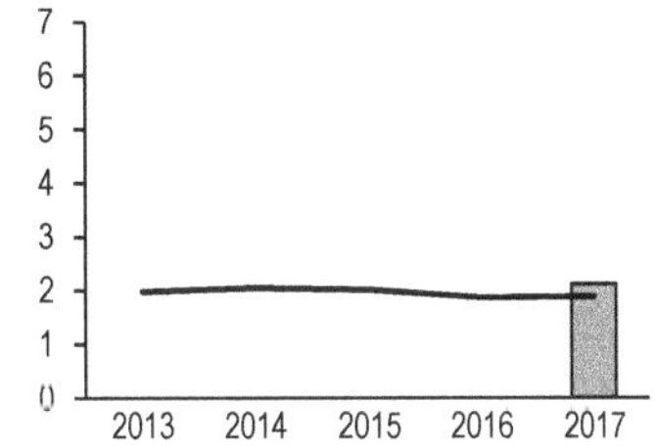

	2013	2014	2015	2016	2017
Goldsboro					2.11
Average	1.98	2.05	2.02	1.87	1.88

Workload Measures

Residential Refuse Tons per 1,000 Population

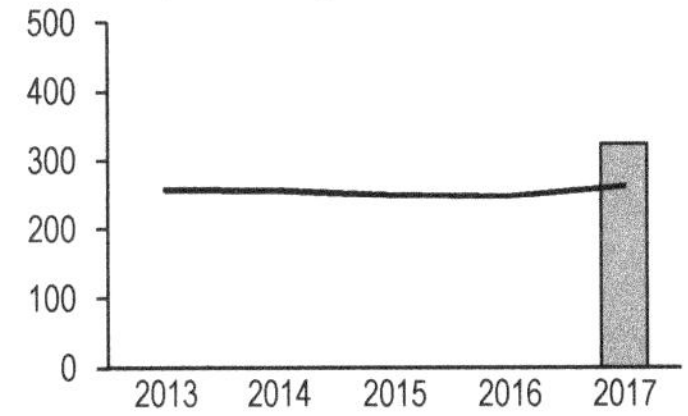

	2013	2014	2015	2016	2017
Goldsboro					323
Average	259	258	251	249	264

Residential Refuse Tons per 1,000 Collection Points

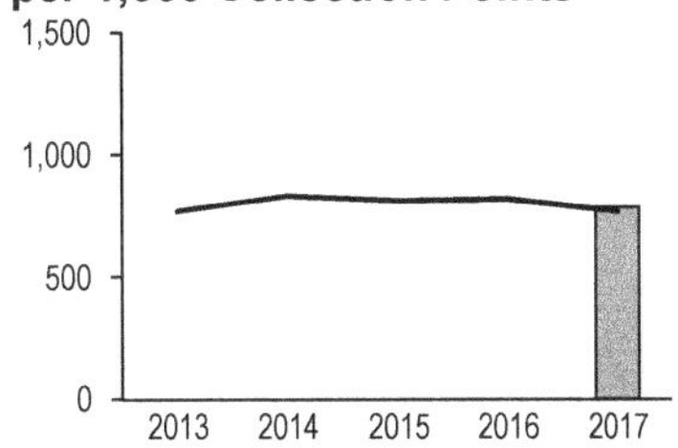

	2013	2014	2015	2016	2017
Goldsboro					783
Average	767	831	811	819	767

Efficiency Measures

Residential Refuse Collection Cost per Ton Collected

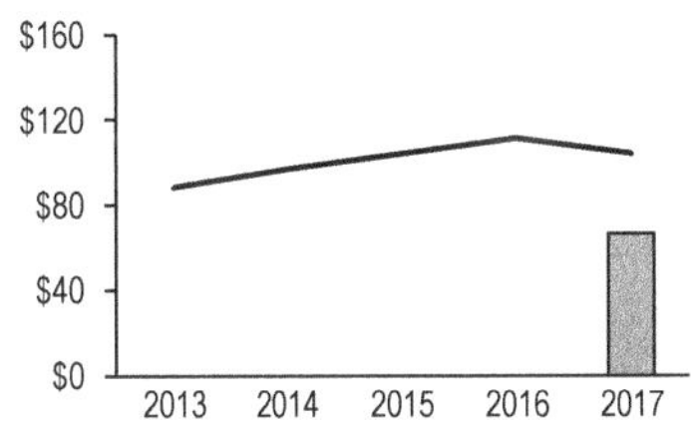

	2013	2014	2015	2016	2017
Goldsboro					$66
Average	$88	$97	$104	$111	$104

Residential Refuse Collection Cost per Collection Point

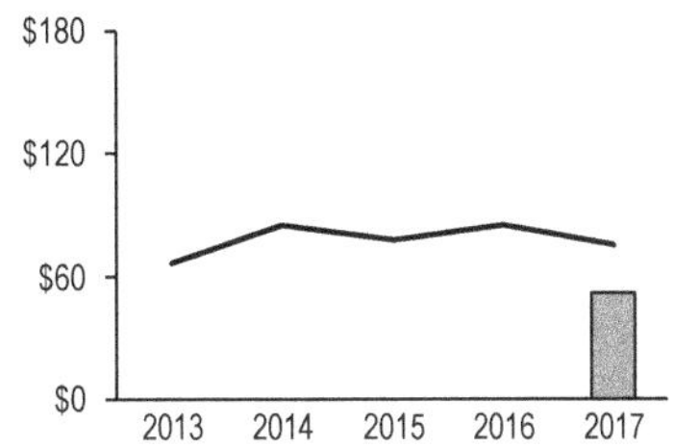

	2013	2014	2015	2016	2017
Goldsboro					$52
Average	$67	$85	$78	$85	$75

Refuse Tons Collected per Municipal Collection FTE

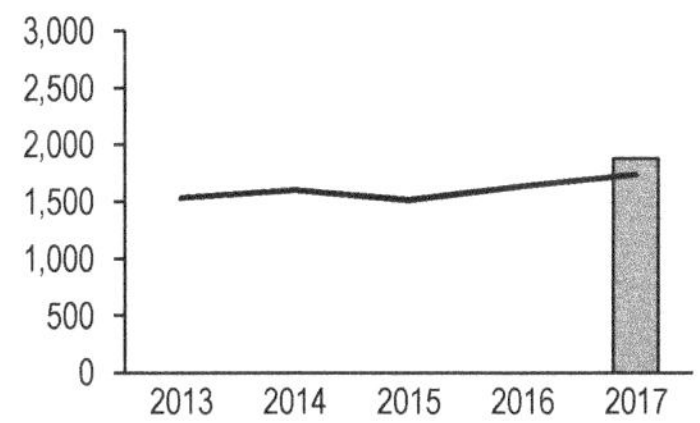

	2013	2014	2015	2016	2017
Goldsboro					1,874
Average	1,531	1,598	1,514	1,632	1,735

Effectiveness Measures

Complaints per 1,000 Collection Points

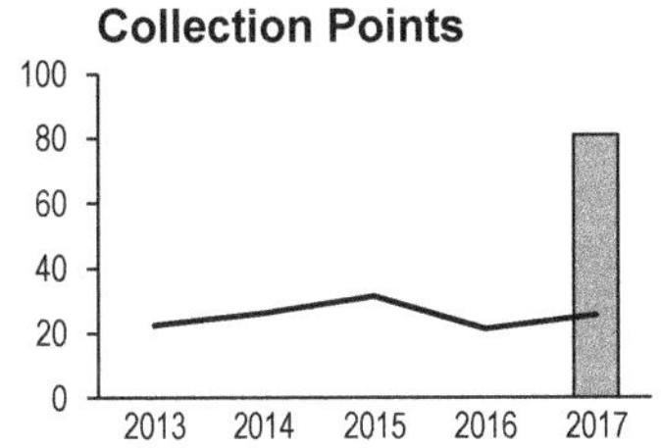

	2013	2014	2015	2016	2017
Goldsboro					81.0
Average	22.5	26.1	31.5	21.4	25.6

Valid Complaints per 1,000 Collection Points

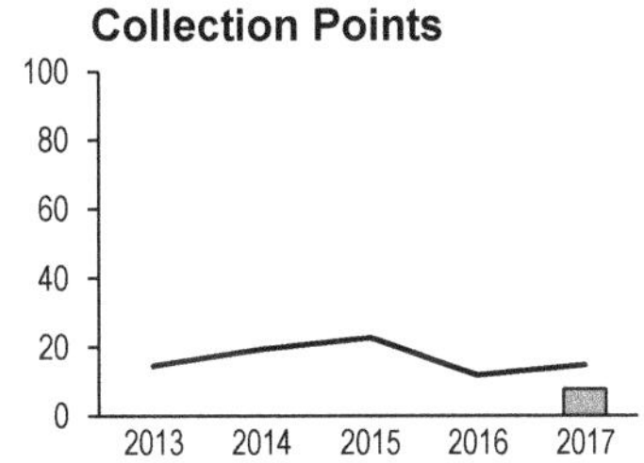

	2013	2014	2015	2016	2017
Goldsboro					7.7
Average	14.6	19.4	22.8	11.9	14.8

Fiscal Year 2016–17

Explanatory Information

Service Level and Delivery
Greensboro provides once-a-week collection of residential refuse at curbside. Each resident is provided up to two ninety-gallon carts. Currently there is no fee for residential collection of refuse.

There were twenty-one city crews for FY 2016–17. Eighteen crews each have one driver operating an automated packer. Three crews use rear loaders.

The city used sixty-eight collection routes during the fiscal year, with each packer making an average of 1.8 trips per day to a municipal solid waste transfer station and the travel distance averaging eight miles.

The city collected 57,615 tons of residential refuse during FY 2016–17, at a cost of $64 per ton.

Greensboro defines automated packers as one-armed automated-loading packers that are operated by one person. Rear loaders are rear-loading packer trucks.

Conditions Affecting Service, Performance, and Costs
Greensboro is highly automated in the area of residential refuse collection.

Municipal Profile

Population (OSBM 2016)	284,343
Land Area (Square Miles)	128.72
Persons per Square Mile	2,209
Median Family Income U.S. Census 2010	$52,752

Service Profile

FTE Positions—Collection	27.0
FTE Positions—Other	4.0
Type of Equipment	23 automated packers 3 packers
Size of Crews (most commonly used)	1 & 2 person
Weekly Routes	68
Average Distance to Disposal Site	8 miles
Average Daily Trips to Disposal Site	1.8
Percentage of Service Contracted	0%
Collection Frequency	1 x week
General Collection Location	Curbside
Residential Customers (number represents collection points)	89,214
Tons Collected	57,615
Monthly Service Fee	No

Full Cost Profile

Cost Breakdown by Percentage	
Personal Services	33.8%
Operating Costs	66.2%
Capital Costs	0.0%
TOTAL	100.0%
Cost Breakdown in Dollars	
Personal Services	$1,252,777
Operating Costs	$2,454,922
Capital Costs	$0
TOTAL	$3,707,699

Greensboro — Residential Refuse Collection

Key: Greensboro ▒ Benchmarking Average — Fiscal Years 2013 through 2017

Resource Measures

Residential Refuse Collection Costs per Capita

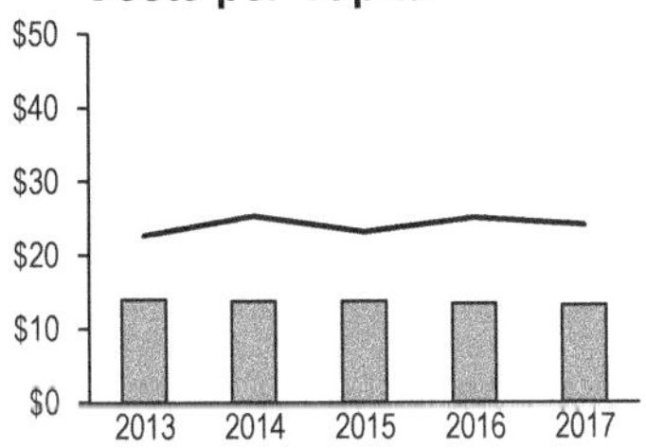

	2013	2014	2015	2016	2017
Greensboro	$13.89	$13.62	$13.66	$13.27	$13.04
Average	$22.61	$25.23	$23.10	$24.98	$23.97

Residential Refuse FTEs per 10,000 Population

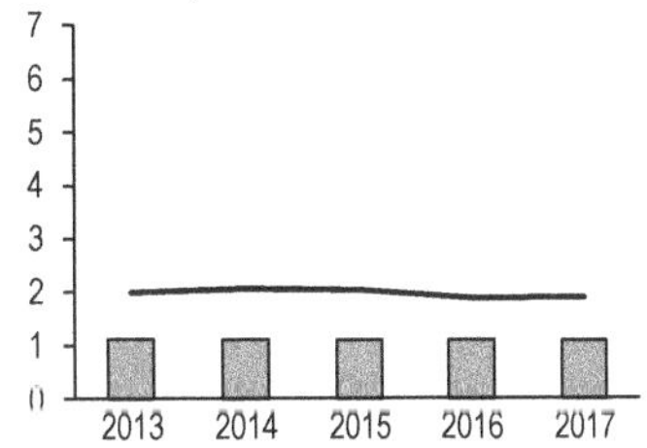

	2013	2014	2015	2016	2017
Greensboro	1.13	1.11	1.10	1.10	1.09
Average	1.98	2.05	2.02	1.87	1.88

Workload Measures

Residential Refuse Tons per 1,000 Population

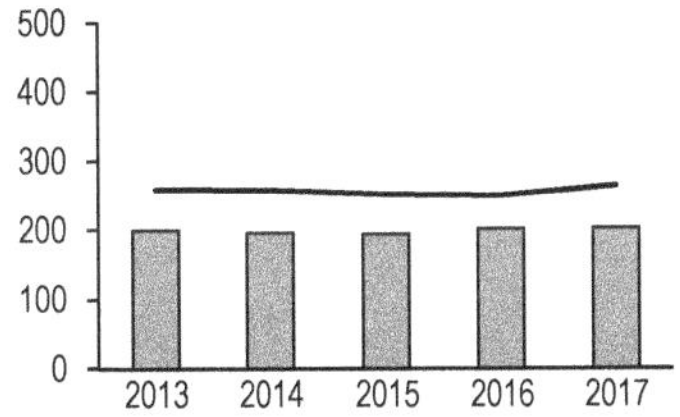

	2013	2014	2015	2016	2017
Greensboro	199	196	195	202	203
Average	259	258	251	249	264

Residential Refuse Tons per 1,000 Collection Points

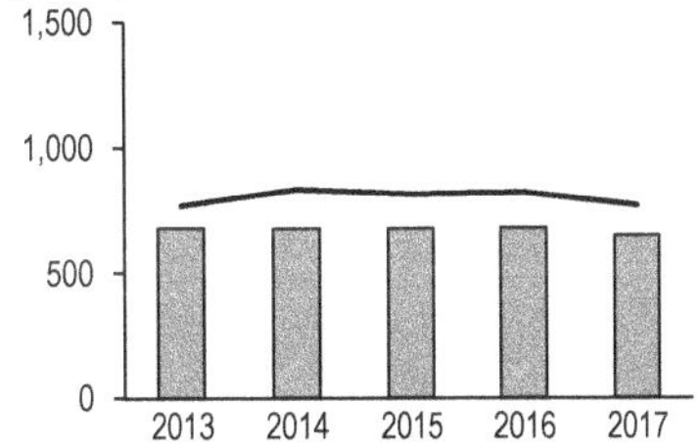

	2013	2014	2015	2016	2017
Greensboro	677	675	674	678	646
Average	767	831	811	819	767

Efficiency Measures

Residential Refuse Collection Cost per Ton Collected

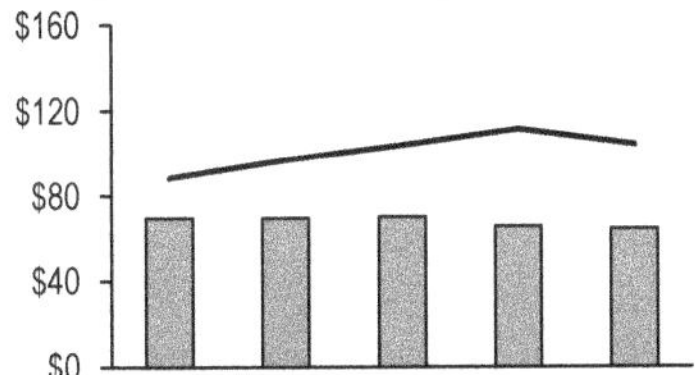

	2013	2014	2015	2016	2017
Greensboro	$70	$69	$70	$66	$64
Average	$88	$97	$104	$111	$104

Residential Refuse Collection Cost per Collection Point

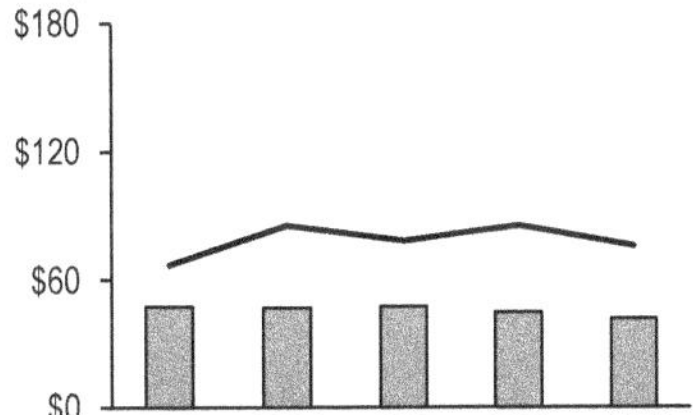

	2013	2014	2015	2016	2017
Greensboro	$47	$47	$47	$45	$42
Average	$67	$85	$78	$85	$75

Refuse Tons Collected per Municipal Collection FTE

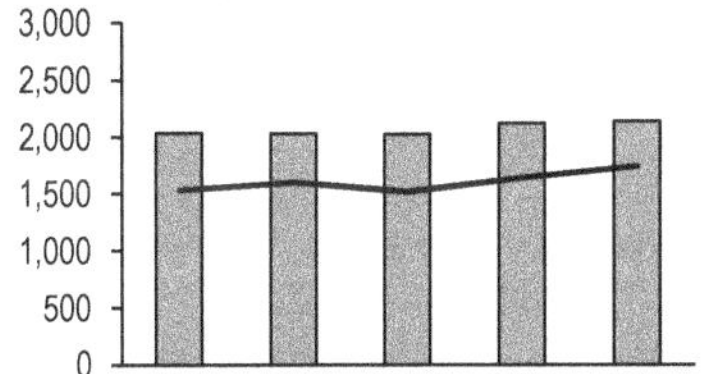

	2013	2014	2015	2016	2017
Greensboro	2,032	2,027	2,025	2,116	2,134
Average	1,531	1,598	1,514	1,632	1,735

Effectiveness Measures

Complaints per 1,000 Collection Points

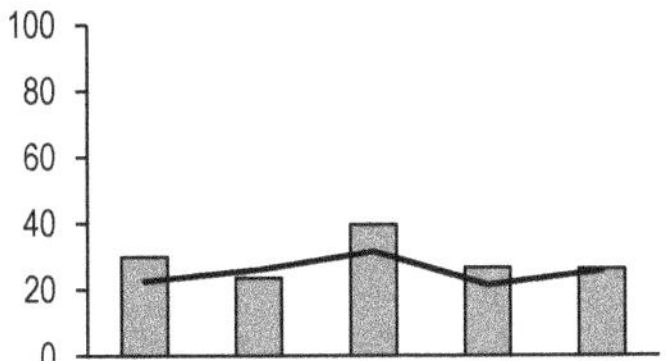

	2013	2014	2015	2016	2017
Greensboro	30.0	23.6	39.6	26.6	26.2
Average	22.5	26.1	31.5	21.4	25.6

Valid Complaints per 1,000 Collection Points

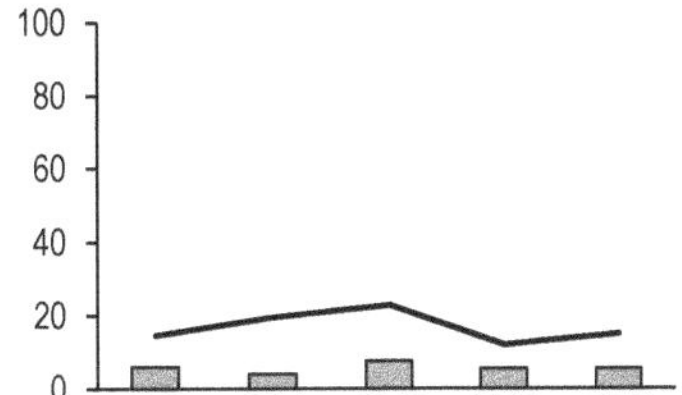

	2013	2014	2015	2016	2017
Greensboro	6.0	4.1	7.6	5.4	5.5
Average	14.6	19.4	22.8	11.9	14.8

Fiscal Year 2016–17

Explanatory Information

Service Level and Delivery

Greenville collects refuse from residential premises once a week at both curbside and backyard. Residents can choose which level of service to receive at different costs. Curbside collection is priced at $15.75 per month while backyard collection is notably higher. Most residents have chosen curbside. Curbside recycling of white goods and electronic is included in the residential refuse fee.

The city uses five one-person crews operating automated trucks and two trucks with a crew of three persons using rear-loading vehicles. The crews run collection routes four days a week.

Twenty-eight collection routes were used during FY 2016–17, with an average of two trips to the transfer station per day per route. The average distance to the transfer station per route was five-and-a-half miles.

Greenville collected 28,813 tons of residential refuse during FY 2016–17, at a cost of $71 per ton. The cost per ton does not include the disposal cost of $31.66, representing the tipping fee at the transfer station.

Conditions Affecting Service, Performance, and Costs

Greenville was the only municipality participating in this benchmarking project that continues to collect residential refuse from the backyard for many customers as a service offering rather than just for customers needing special assistance. This is a relatively labor-intensive process and represents a high level of service.

The apparent drop in the data in the graphs that look at tons collected is due to reporting improvements. In earlier years, Greenville could not easily separate out refuse collected from multi-family units. Improvements in what the county landfill is able to track and report back to the city mean that the most recent year includes just single-family units.

Greenville made substantial changes during FY 2013–14, including new trucks and new carts. Additionally, early retirement incentives were given to some employees to reduce staff size, which raised costs on a one-time basis.

Municipal Profile

Population (OSBM 2016)	87,989
Land Area (Square Miles)	35.41
Persons per Square Mile	2,485
Median Family Income U.S. Census 2010	$50,395

Service Profile

FTE Positions—Collection	11.0
FTE Positions—Other	1.4
Type of Equipment	5 automated packers 2 packers
Size of Crews (most commonly used)	1 & 3 person
Weekly Routes	28
Average Distance to Disposal Site	5 miles
Average Daily Trips to Disposal Site	2
Percentage of Service Contracted	0%
Collection Frequency	1 x week
General Collection Location	Curbside and backyard
Residential Customers (number represents collection points)	39,362
Tons Collected	28,813
Monthly Service Fee	$15.75 Curbside

Full Cost Profile

Cost Breakdown by Percentage	
Personal Services	38.3%
Operating Costs	45.5%
Capital Costs	16.2%
TOTAL	100.0%

Cost Breakdown in Dollars	
Personal Services	$784,984
Operating Costs	$932,996
Capital Costs	$330,916
TOTAL	$2,048,896

Greenville — Residential Refuse Collection

Key: Greenville ▒ Benchmarking Average — Fiscal Years 2013 through 2017

Resource Measures

Residential Refuse Collection Costs per Capita

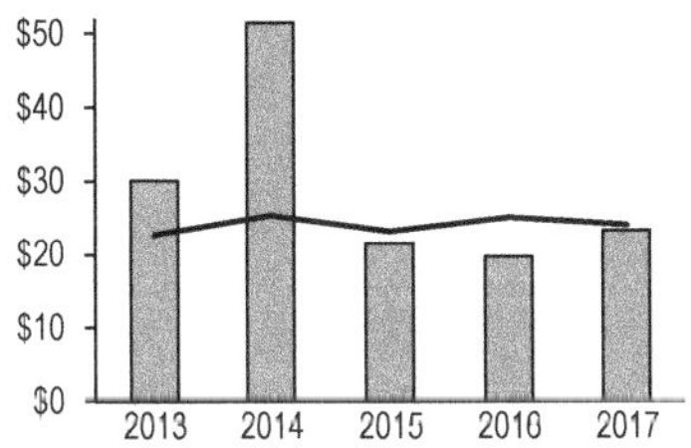

	2013	2014	2015	2016	2017
Greenville	$30.14	$51.48	$21.54	$19.73	$23.29
Average	$22.61	$25.23	$23.10	$24.98	$23.97

Residential Refuse FTEs per 10,000 Population

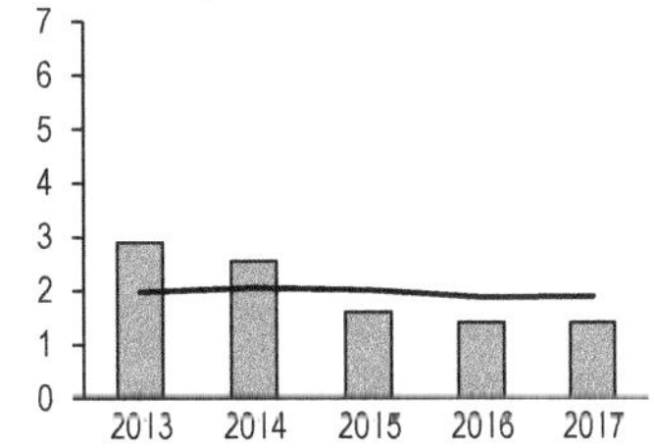

	2013	2014	2015	2016	2017
Greenville	2.90	2.54	1.60	1.41	1.41
Average	1.98	2.05	2.02	1.87	1.88

Workload Measures

Residential Refuse Tons per 1,000 Population

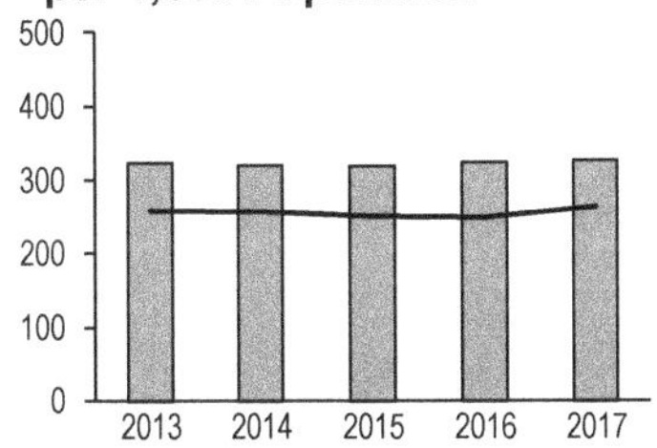

	2013	2014	2015	2016	2017
Greenville	324	320	320	325	327
Average	259	258	251	249	264

Residential Refuse Tons per 1,000 Collection Points

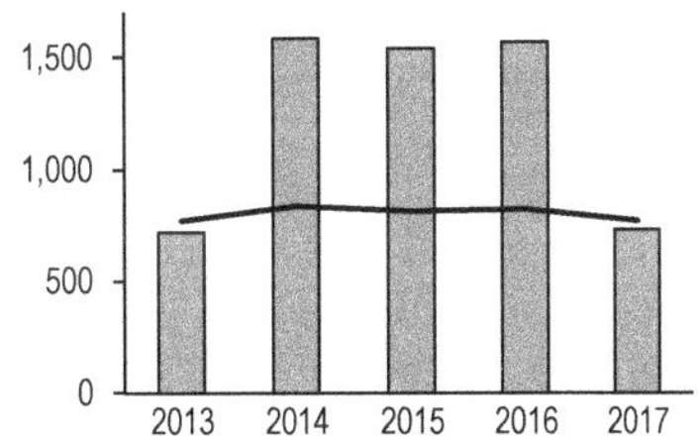

	2013	2014	2015	2016	2017
Greenville	719	1,587	1,543	1,569	732
Average	767	831	811	819	767

Efficiency Measures

Residential Refuse Collection Cost per Ton Collected

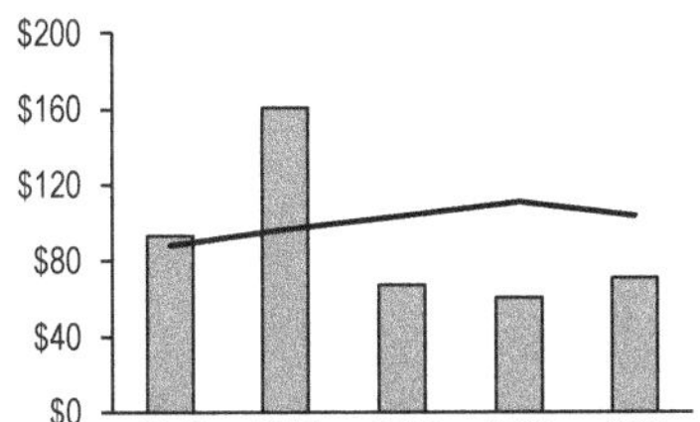

	2013	2014	2015	2016	2017
Greenville	$93	$161	$67	$61	$71
Average	$88	$97	$104	$111	$104

Residential Refuse Collection Cost per Collection Point

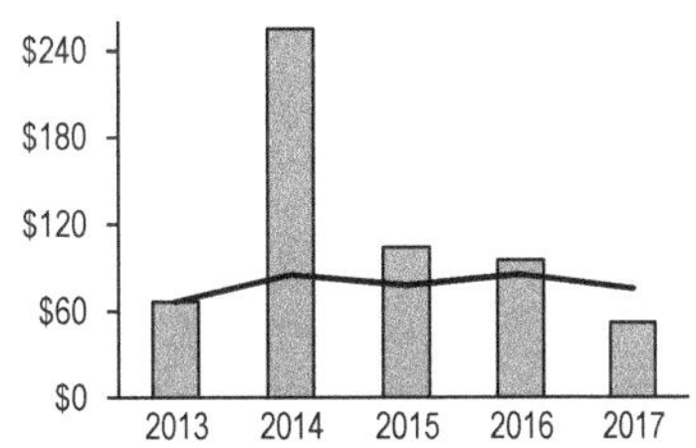

	2013	2014	2015	2016	2017
Greenville	$67	$255	$104	$95	$52
Average	$67	$85	$78	$85	$75

Refuse Tons Collected per Municipal Collection FTE

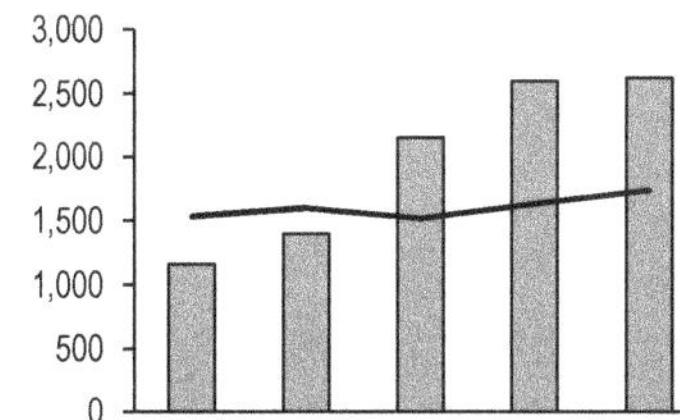

	2013	2014	2015	2016	2017
Greenville	1,162	1,398	2,150	2,596	2,619
Average	1,531	1,598	1,514	1,632	1,735

Effectiveness Measures

Complaints per 1,000 Collection Points

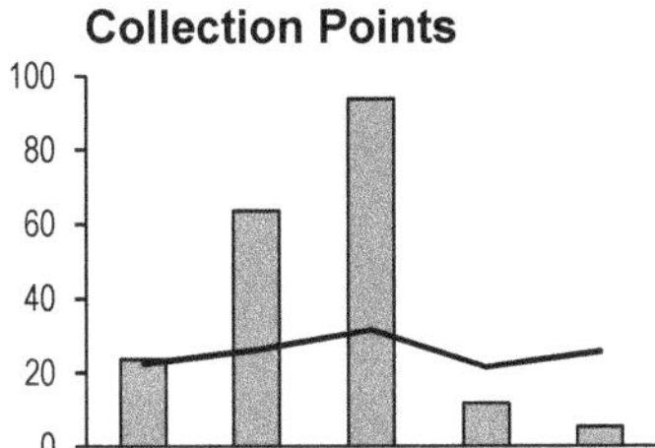

	2013	2014	2015	2016	2017
Greenville	23.6	63.5	93.7	11.8	5.3
Average	22.5	26.1	31.5	21.4	25.6

Valid Complaints per 1,000 Collection Points

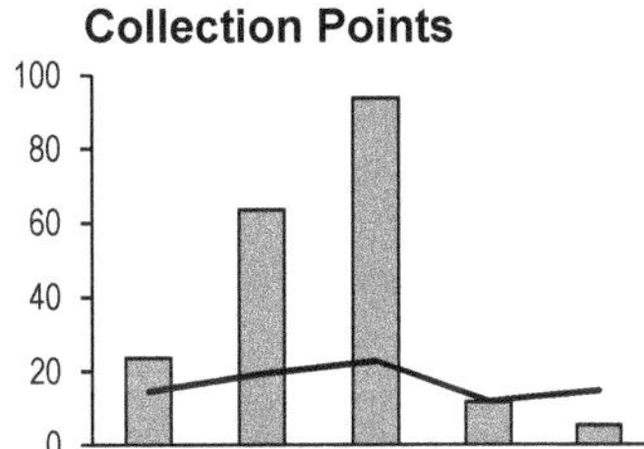

	2013	2014	2015	2016	2017
Greenville	23.6	63.5	93.7	11.8	5.3
Average	14.6	19.4	22.8	11.9	14.8

Fiscal Year 2016–17

Explanatory Information

Service Level and Delivery

Hickory collects refuse from residential premises once a week at curbside, although backyard collection is provided for elderly and disabled citizens. A monthly solid waste fee of $19.50 per cart was charged for residential refuse collection service during FY 2016–17. Each residence uses a cart provided by the city for residential refuse collection. Each cart has a capacity of ninety-six gallons and is provided at no charge. Upon request, a second cart is provided to the customer for an additional solid waste fee.

The city used four one-person crews operating automated packers, with three of these trucks running full-time and one one-fourth of the time. A regular packer truck with one driver and one crew member works about half-time collecting on one-way streets and dead ends.

Fifteen collection routes were used during FY 2016–17, with an average of two trips to the transfer station per day per route. The average distance to the transfer station per route was five miles.

Hickory collected 7,292 tons of residential refuse during FY 2016–17, at a cost of $76 per ton. The cost per ton does not include the disposal cost of $33, representing the tipping fee at the Catawba County landfill.

Hickory defines automated packers as trucks with mechanical arms.

Conditions Affecting Service, Performance, and Costs

Hickory is highly automated in the area of residential refuse collection.

Municipal Profile

Population (OSBM 2016)	40,453
Land Area (Square Miles)	29.90
Persons per Square Mile	1,353
Median Family Income U.S. Census 2010	$54,093

Service Profile

FTE Positions—Collection	3.75
FTE Positions—Other	0.82
Type of Equipment	4 automated packers 1 packer
Size of Crews (most commonly used)	1 & 2 person
Weekly Routes	15
Average Distance to Disposal Site	5 miles
Average Daily Trips to Disposal Site	2
Percentage of Service Contracted	0%
Collection Frequency	1 x week
General Collection Location	Curbside
Residential Customers (number represents collection points)	12,200
Tons Collected	7,292
Monthly Service Fee	$19.50 per cart

Full Cost Profile

Cost Breakdown by Percentage	
Personal Services	44.6%
Operating Costs	38.6%
Capital Costs	16.8%
TOTAL	100.0%
Cost Breakdown in Dollars	
Personal Services	$247,072
Operating Costs	$213,618
Capital Costs	$92,845
TOTAL	$553,535

Hickory **Residential Refuse Collection**

Key: Hickory ▒ Benchmarking Average — Fiscal Years 2013 through 2017

Resource Measures

Residential Refuse Collection Costs per Capita

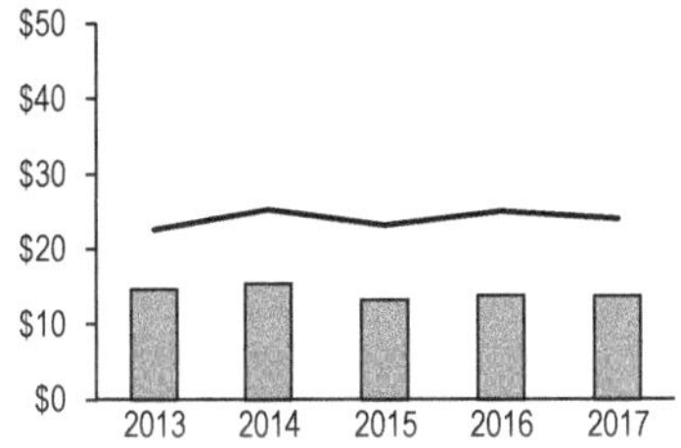

	2013	2014	2015	2016	2017
Hickory	$14.66	$15.38	$13.23	$13.80	$13.68
Average	$22.61	$25.23	$23.10	$24.98	$23.97

Residential Refuse FTEs per 10,000 Population

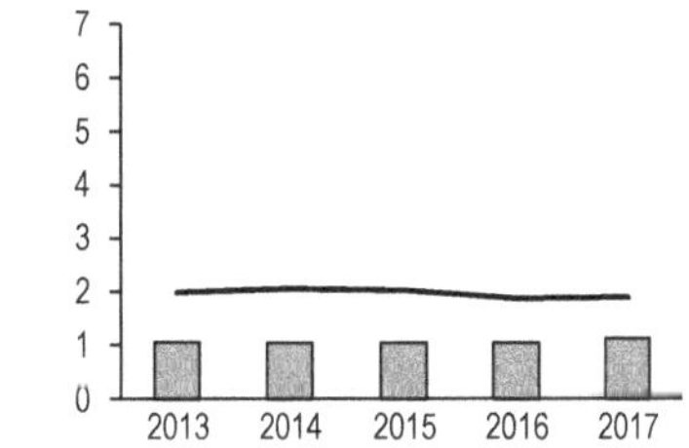

	2013	2014	2015	2016	2017
Hickory	1.06	1.05	1.05	1.05	1.13
Average	1.98	2.05	2.02	1.87	1.88

Workload Measures

Residential Refuse Tons per 1,000 Population

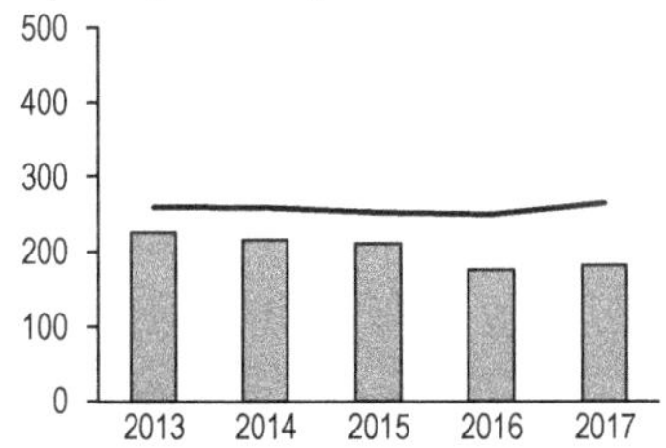

	2013	2014	2015	2016	2017
Hickory	224	215	210	175	180
Average	259	258	251	249	264

Residential Refuse Tons per 1,000 Collection Points

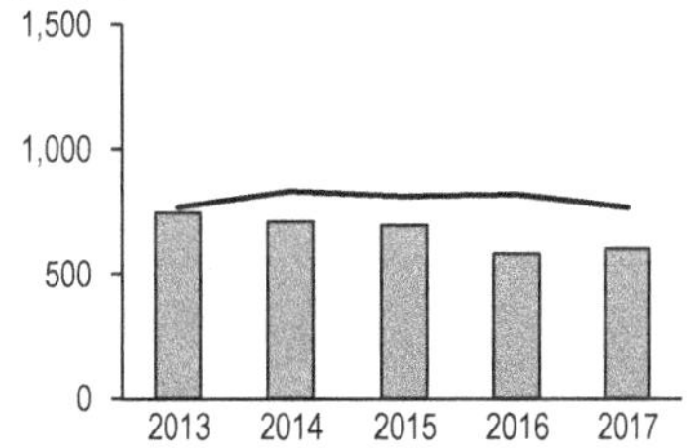

	2013	2014	2015	2016	2017
Hickory	742	708	694	579	598
Average	767	831	811	819	767

Efficiency Measures

Residential Refuse Collection Cost per Ton Collected

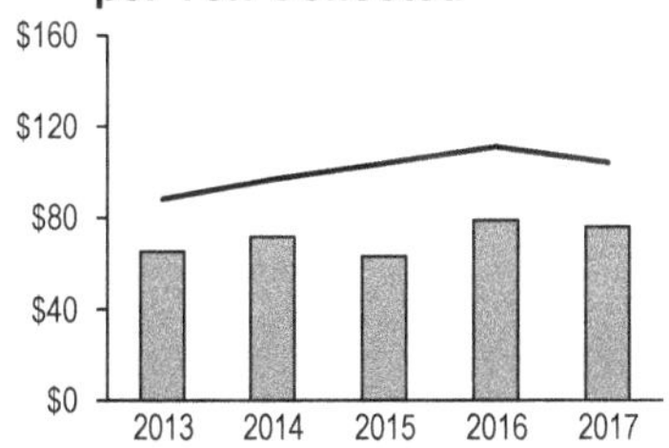

	2013	2014	2015	2016	2017
Hickory	$65	$72	$63	$79	$76
Average	$88	$97	$104	$111	$104

Residential Refuse Collection Cost per Collection Point

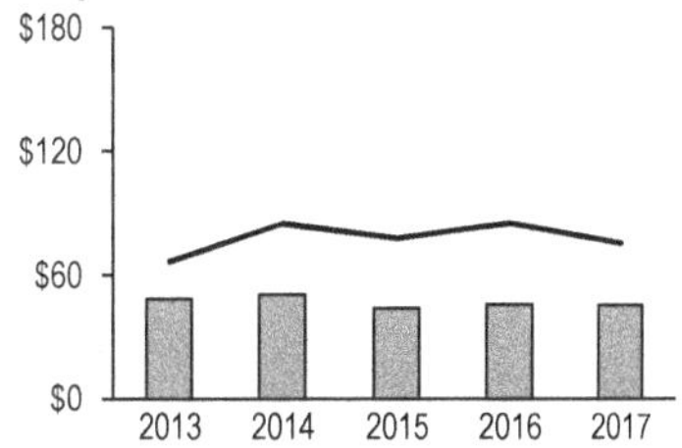

	2013	2014	2015	2016	2017
Hickory	$49	$51	$44	$46	$45
Average	$67	$85	$78	$85	$75

Refuse Tons Collected per Municipal Collection FTE

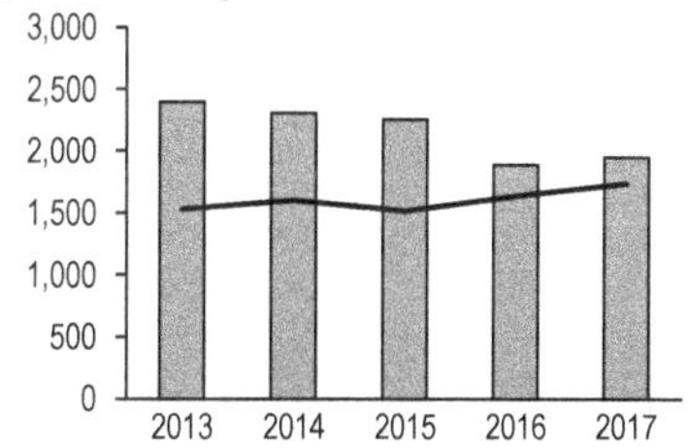

	2013	2014	2015	2016	2017
Hickory	2,395	2,305	2,259	1,883	1,945
Average	1,531	1,598	1,514	1,632	1,735

Effectiveness Measures

Complaints per 1,000 Collection Points

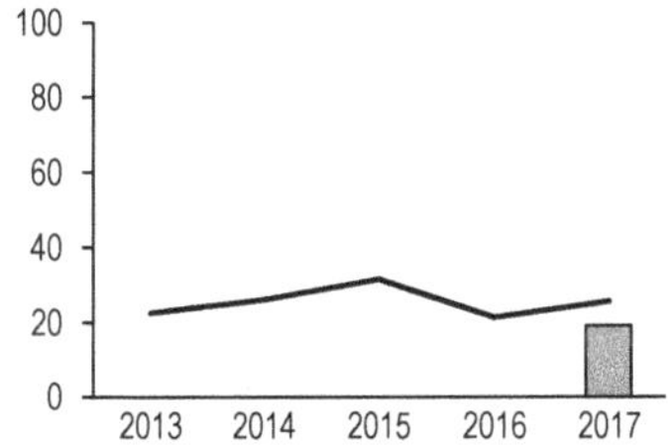

	2013	2014	2015	2016	2017
Hickory					19.2
Average	22.5	26.1	31.5	21.4	25.6

Valid Complaints per 1,000 Collection Points

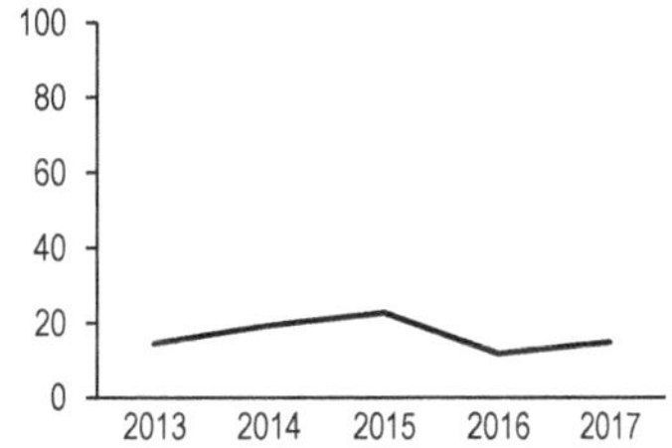

	2013	2014	2015	2016	2017
Hickory					
Average	14.6	19.4	22.8	11.9	14.8

Fiscal Year 2016–17

Explanatory Information

Service Level and Delivery

High Point collects residential refuse once a week at curbside, although backyard collection is provided for residents with verified medical disabilities. High Point also has a contract for the collection of refuse from dumpsters at multi-family units, but these costs and tons are not included in this reporting. There is a $14 per month fee for residential refuse collection.

The city primarily collects residential refuse with nine automated trucks, each with one person. There are forty-four collection routes. The average number of trips to the landfill is two per day per route. The average distance to the landfill is ten miles.

The city collected 38,320 tons of residential refuse during FY 2016–17, at a cost of $70 per ton. The cost per ton does not include the disposal cost of $31, representing the landfill tipping fee.

Residents may use up to two roll-out carts constructed so that they can be emptied by the lifting devices mounted on city trucks. The cart size is ninety-six gallons.

Conditions Affecting Service, Performance, and Costs

High Point is now fully automated in its pickups, other than those involving special needs.

Municipal Profile

Population (OSBM 2016)	110,244
Land Area (Square Miles)	55.14
Persons per Square Mile	1,999
Median Family Income U.S. Census 2010	$49,720

Service Profile

FTE Positions—Collection	22.5
FTE Positions—Other	2.0
Type of Equipment	9 automated packers 3 special
Size of Crews (most commonly used)	1 & 3 person
Weekly Routes	44
Average Distance to Disposal Site	10 miles
Average Daily Trips to Disposal Site	2
Percentage of Service Contracted	0%
Collection Frequency	1 x week
General Collection Location	Curbside
Residential Customers (number represents collection points)	49,918
Tons Collected	38,320
Monthly Service Fee	$14.00

Full Cost Profile

Cost Breakdown by Percentage	
Personal Services	47.1%
Operating Costs	31.2%
Capital Costs	21.7%
TOTAL	100.0%
Cost Breakdown in Dollars	
Personal Services	$1,270,937
Operating Costs	$841,742
Capital Costs	$584,667
TOTAL	$2,697,346

Key: High Point ▒ Benchmarking Average — Fiscal Years 2013 through 2017

Resource Measures

Residential Refuse Collection Costs per Capita

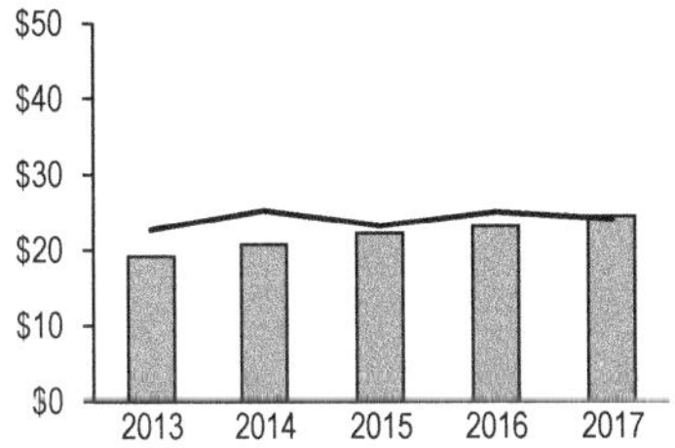

	2013	2014	2015	2016	2017
High Point	$19.20	$20.76	$22.24	$23.13	$24.47
Average	$22.61	$25.23	$23.10	$24.98	$23.97

Residential Refuse FTEs per 10,000 Population

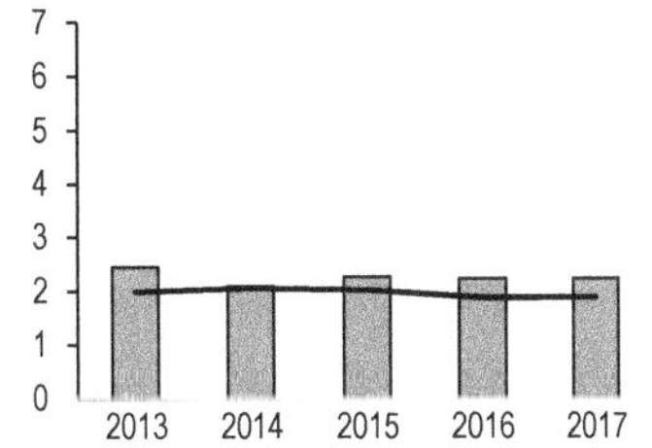

	2013	2014	2015	2016	2017
High Point	2.44	2.09	2.26	2.23	2.22
Average	1.98	2.05	2.02	1.87	1.88

Workload Measures

Residential Refuse Tons per 1,000 Population

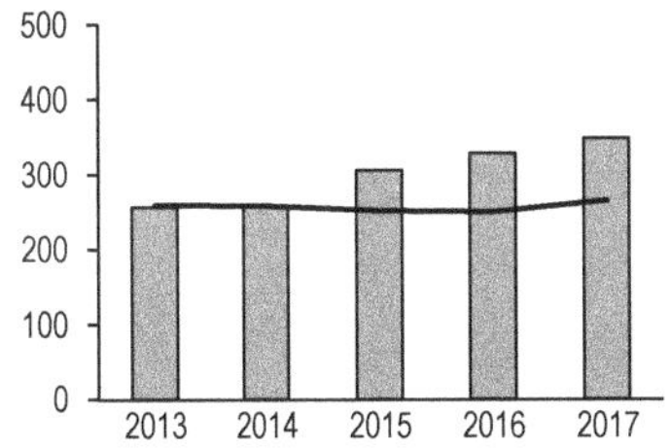

	2013	2014	2015	2016	2017
High Point	256	257	306	327	348
Average	259	258	251	249	264

Residential Refuse Tons per 1,000 Collection Points

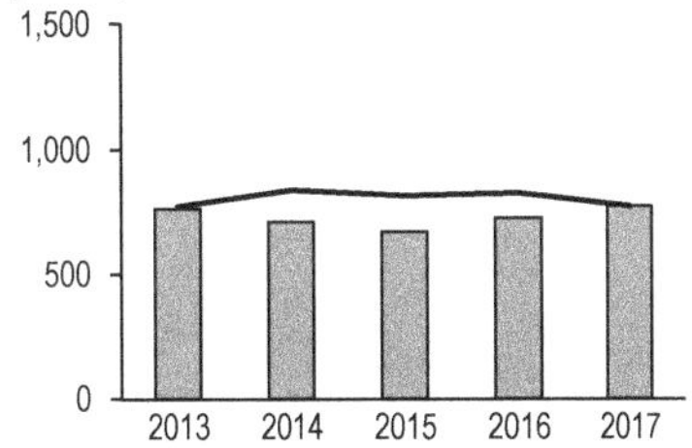

	2013	2014	2015	2016	2017
High Point	758	706	665	720	768
Average	767	831	811	819	767

Efficiency Measures

Residential Refuse Collection Cost per Ton Collected

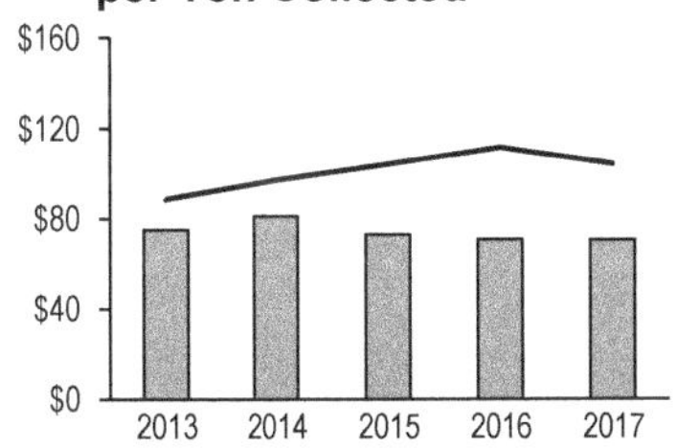

	2013	2014	2015	2016	2017
High Point	$75	$81	$73	$71	$70
Average	$88	$97	$104	$111	$104

Residential Refuse Collection Cost per Collection Point

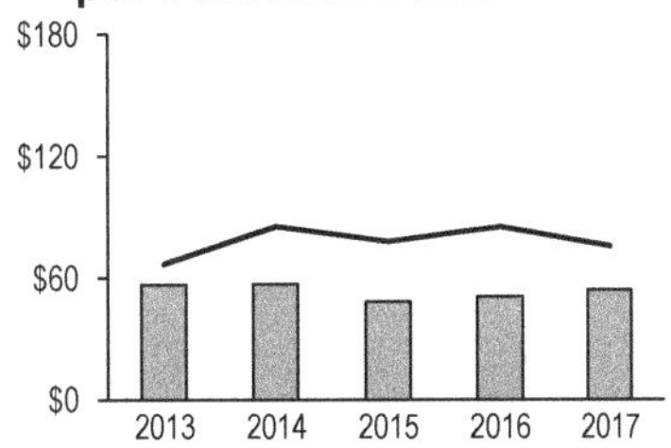

	2013	2014	2015	2016	2017
High Point	$57	$57	$48	$51	$54
Average	$67	$85	$78	$85	$75

Refuse Tons Collected per Municipal Collection FTE

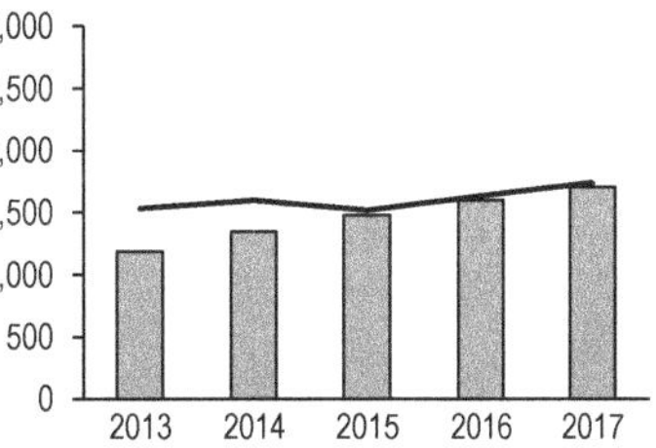

	2013	2014	2015	2016	2017
High Point	1,184	1,347	1,475	1,597	1,703
Average	1,531	1,598	1,514	1,632	1,735

Effectiveness Measures

Complaints per 1,000 Collection Points

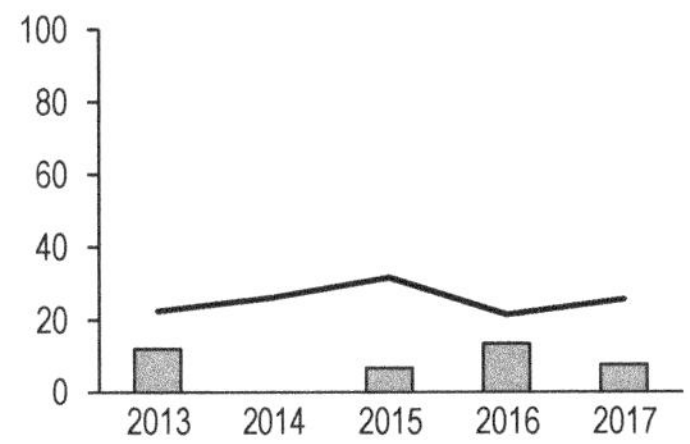

	2013	2014	2015	2016	2017
High Point	12.0		6.8	13.5	7.7
Average	22.5	26.1	31.5	21.4	25.6

Valid Complaints per 1,000 Collection Points

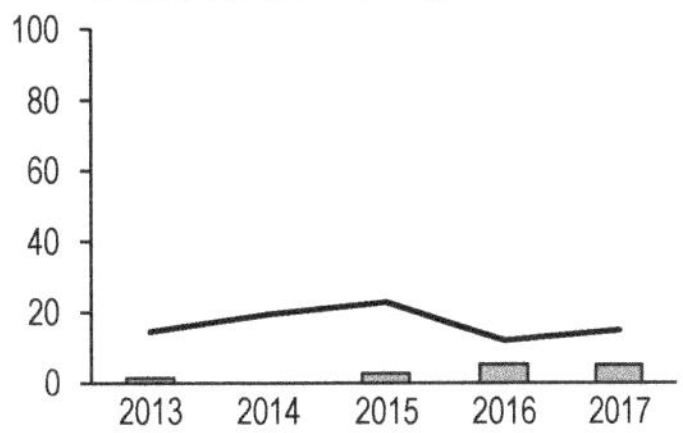

	2013	2014	2015	2016	2017
High Point	1.5		2.7	5.3	5.1
Average	14.6	19.4	22.8	11.9	14.8

Raleigh

Residential Refuse

Fiscal Year 2016–17

Explanatory Information

Service Level and Delivery

Raleigh provides residential refuse collection service once per week at curbside. Backyard collection service is provided for customers who have been certified by a physician as being unable to move a cart to the curb and who have no able-bodied resident to provide assistance. The city charges a monthly fee of $12.95 for refuse collection.

The city employed twenty automated trucks with a single driver and ten crews of three on semi-automated trucks for primary collection. A total of 120 collection routes were used per week with a average truck making two trips per day to the disposal site covering a distance of ten miles.

Each customer has up to two ninety-five-gallon roll-out carts provided and paid for by the city. The city collected 94,252 tons of residential refuse during FY 2016–17, at a cost per ton of $169 or $126 per collection point. Not included in the cost per ton was a $30 landfill tipping fee.

Conditions Affecting Service, Performance, and Costs

Raleigh rejoined the Benchmarking Project in July 2016 with the first year of data showing for FY 2015–16.

Municipal Profile

Population (OSBM 2016)	448,706
Land Area (Square Miles)	145.57
Persons per Square Mile	3,083
Median Family Income U.S. Census 2010	$68,678

Service Profile

FTE Positions—Collection	68.0
FTE Positions—Other	6.0
Type of Equipment	22 automated packers 10 packersl
Size of Crews (most commonly used)	1 & 3 person
Weekly Routes	120
Average Distance to Disposal Site	10 miles
Average Daily Trips to Disposal Site	2
Percentage of Service Contracted	0%
Collection Frequency	1 x week
General Collection Location	Curbside
Residential Customers (number represents collection points)	126,075
Tons Collected	94,252
Monthly Service Fee	$12.95

Full Cost Profile

Cost Breakdown by Percentage	
Personal Services	22.1%
Operating Costs	59.3%
Capital Costs	18.7%
TOTAL	100.0%
Cost Breakdown in Dollars	
Personal Services	$3,518,226
Operating Costs	$9,453,026
Capital Costs	$2,976,492
TOTAL	$15,947,744

Resource Measures

Residential Refuse Collection Costs per Capita

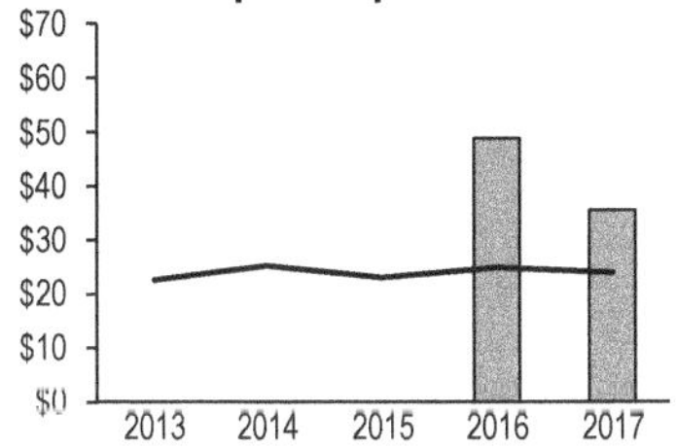

	2013	2014	2015	2016	2017
Raleigh				$48.80	$35.54
Average	$22.61	$25.23	$23.10	$24.98	$23.97

Residential Refuse FTEs per 10,000 Population

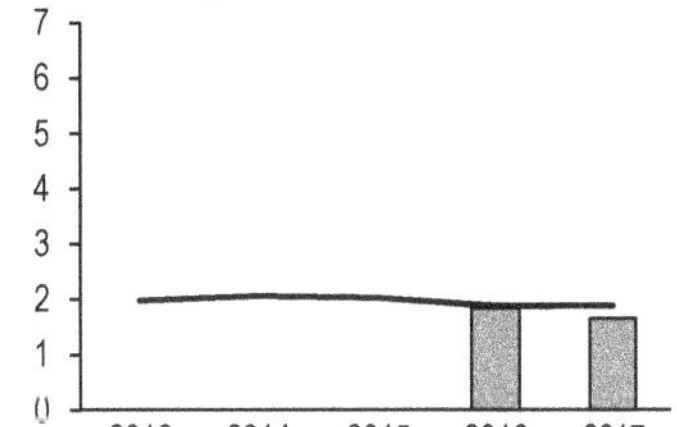

	2013	2014	2015	2016	2017
Raleigh				1.84	1.65
Average	1.98	2.05	2.02	1.87	1.88

Workload Measures

Residential Refuse Tons per 1,000 Population

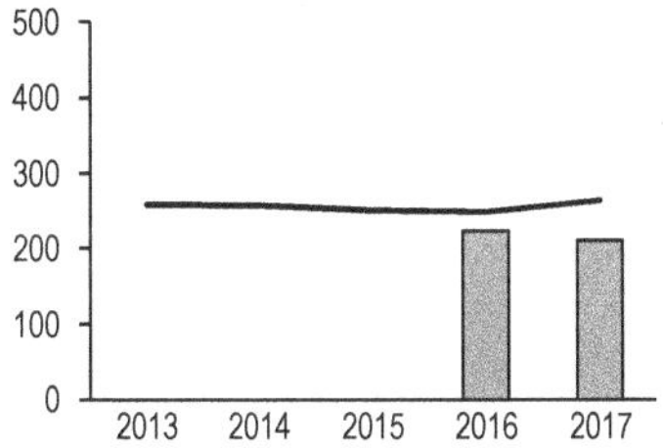

	2013	2014	2015	2016	2017
Raleigh				222	210
Average	259	258	251	249	264

Residential Refuse Tons per 1,000 Collection Points

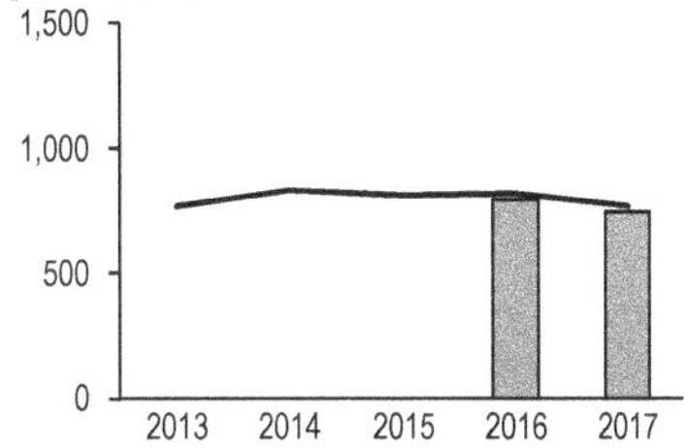

	2013	2014	2015	2016	2017
Raleigh				797	748
Average	767	831	811	819	767

Efficiency Measures

Residential Refuse Collection Cost per Ton Collected

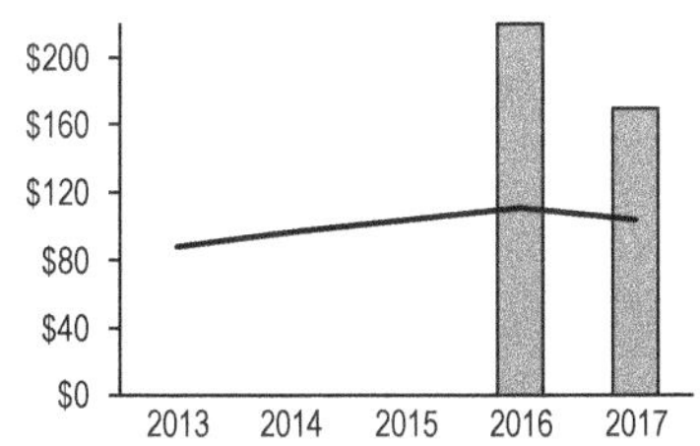

	2013	2014	2015	2016	2017
Raleigh				$219	$169
Average	$88	$97	$104	$111	$104

Residential Refuse Collection Cost per Collection Point

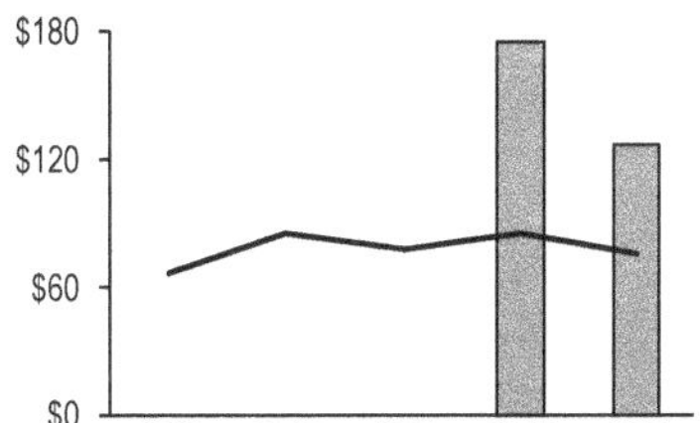

	2013	2014	2015	2016	2017
Raleigh				$175	$126
Average	$67	$85	$78	$85	$75

Refuse Tons Collected per Municipal Collection FTE

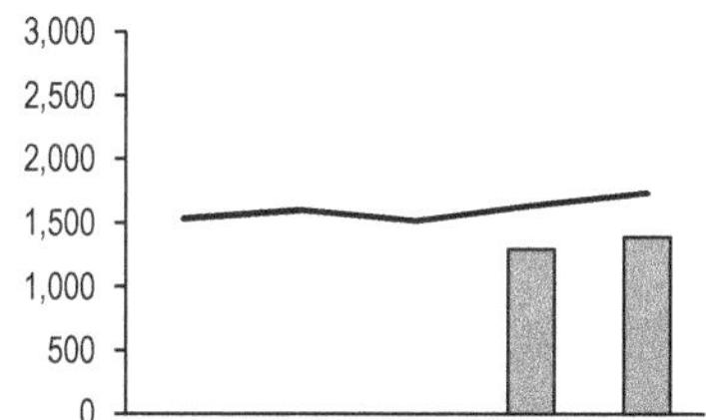

	2013	2014	2015	2016	2017
Raleigh				1,290	1,386
Average	1,531	1,598	1,514	1,632	1,735

Effectiveness Measures

Complaints per 1,000 Collection Points

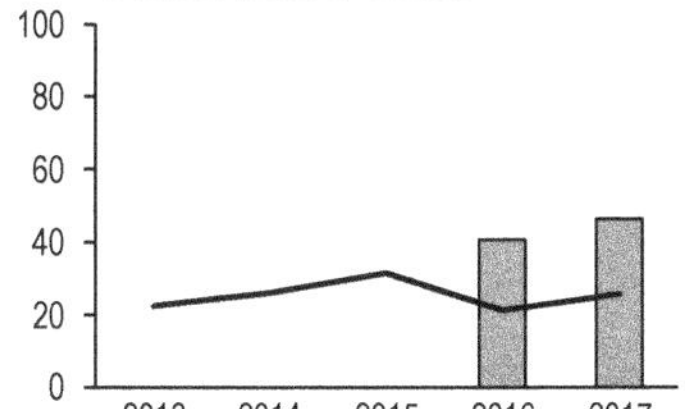

	2013	2014	2015	2016	2017
Raleigh				40.6	46.3
Average	22.5	26.1	31.5	21.4	25.6

Valid Complaints per 1,000 Collection Points

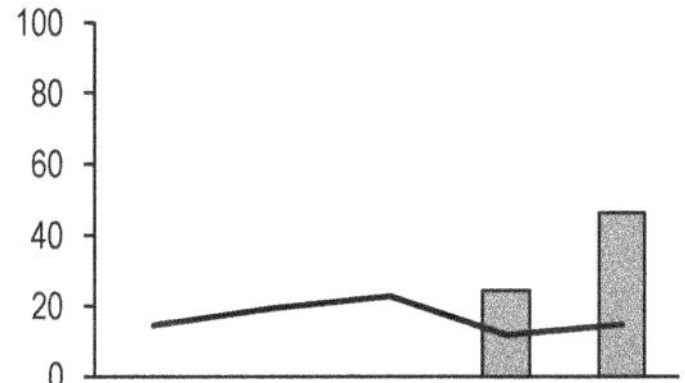

	2013	2014	2015	2016	2017
Raleigh				24.4	46.3
Average	14.6	19.4	22.8	11.9	14.8

Fiscal Year 2016–17

Explanatory Information

Service Level and Delivery

Salisbury provides residential refuse collection service once per week at curbside. Backyard collection service is provided for disabled customers only. The city charges a monthly fee of $15.12 for all solid waste collection.

The city used one-person crews in FY 2016–17, typically in four trucks. Fifteen collection routes were serviced, with an average of one ten-mile trip per route per day to the landfill.

Each resident has one ninety-six-gallon roll-out cart provided and paid for by the city. A second cart may be obtained. The city collected 9,223 tons of residential refuse during FY 2016–17, at a cost per ton of $103. Not included in the cost per ton was a $36 landfill tipping fee.

Salisbury defines its semi-automated packers as low-entry compactors that can be driven from either side of the truck, with the refuse being dumped in the rear of the truck from roll-out carts. The city is relying mostly on one-arm collection trucks.

Conditions Affecting Service, Performance, and Costs

Salisbury's total tons collected includes bulk trash, which is collected along with residential refuse and cannot be separated for reporting purposes.

Municipal Profile

Population (OSBM 2016)	34,459
Land Area (Square Miles)	22.28
Persons per Square Mile	1,547
Median Family Income U.S. Census 2010	$40,192

Service Profile

FTE Positions—Collection	5.0
FTE Positions—Other	1.0
Type of Equipment	3 automated packers 2 packers
Size of Crews (most commonly used)	1 & 2 person
Weekly Routes	15
Average Distance to Disposal Site	10 miles
Average Daily Trips to Disposal Site	1
Percentage of Service Contracted	0%
Collection Frequency	1 x week
General Collection Location	Curbside
Residential Customers (number represents collection points)	11,095
Tons Collected	9,223
Monthly Service Fee	$15.12

Full Cost Profile

Cost Breakdown by Percentage	
Personal Services	39.6%
Operating Costs	29.9%
Capital Costs	30.5%
TOTAL	100.0%
Cost Breakdown in Dollars	
Personal Services	$377,850
Operating Costs	$285,657
Capital Costs	$290,793
TOTAL	$954,299

Key: Salisbury ▒ Benchmarking Average — Fiscal Years 2013 through 2017

Resource Measures

Residential Refuse Collection Costs per Capita

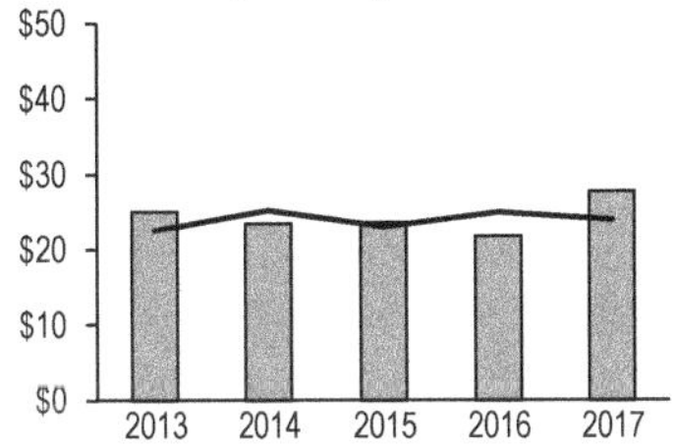

	2013	2014	2015	2016	2017
Salisbury	$25.05	$23.51	$23.66	$21.77	$27.69
Average	$22.61	$25.23	$23.10	$24.98	$23.97

Residential Refuse FTEs per 10,000 Population

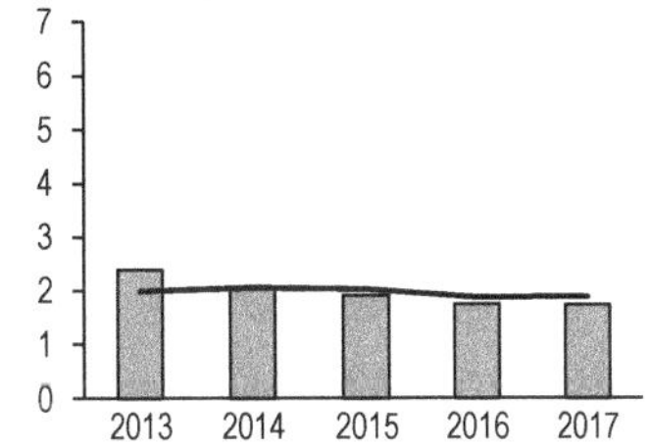

	2013	2014	2015	2016	2017
Salisbury	2.39	2.08	1.91	1.75	1.74
Average	1.98	2.05	2.02	1.87	1.88

Workload Measures

Residential Refuse Tons per 1,000 Population

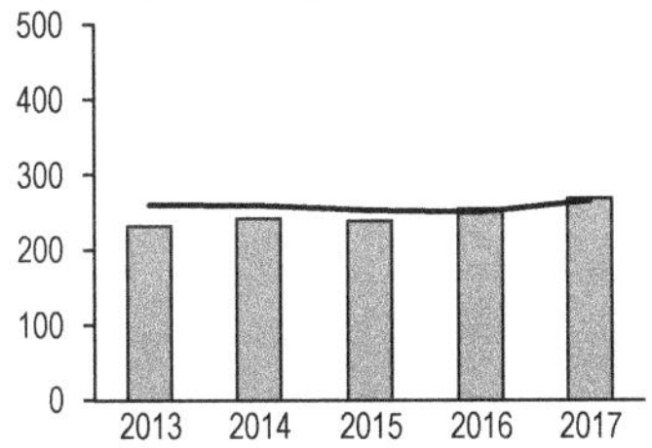

	2013	2014	2015	2016	2017
Salisbury	231	241	238	254	268
Average	259	258	251	249	264

Residential Refuse Tons per 1,000 Collection Points

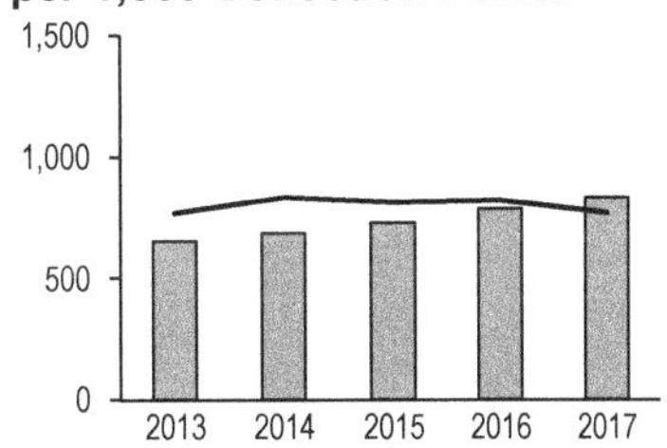

	2013	2014	2015	2016	2017
Salisbury	651	684	727	784	831
Average	767	831	811	819	767

Efficiency Measures

Residential Refuse Collection Cost per Ton Collected

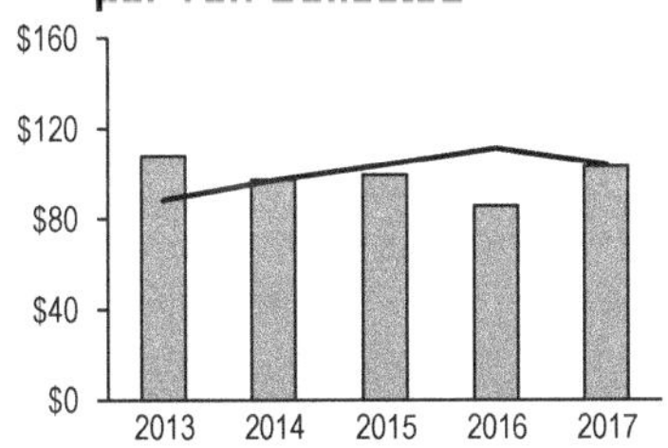

	2013	2014	2015	2016	2017
Salisbury	$108	$98	$100	$86	$103
Average	$88	$97	$104	$111	$104

Residential Refuse Collection Cost per Collection Point

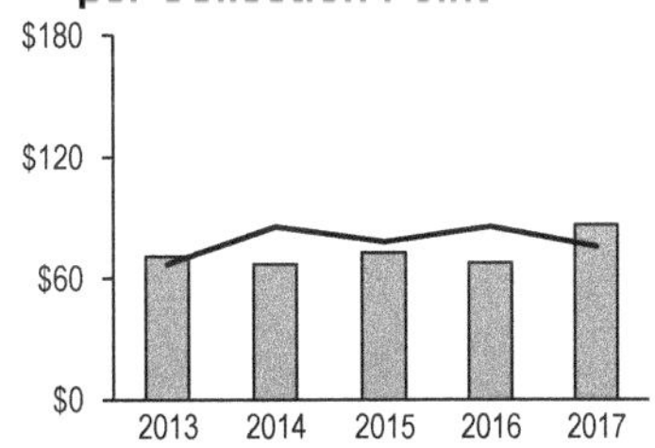

	2013	2014	2015	2016	2017
Salisbury	$71	$67	$72	$67	$86
Average	$67	$85	$78	$85	$75

Refuse Tons Collected per Municipal Collection FTE

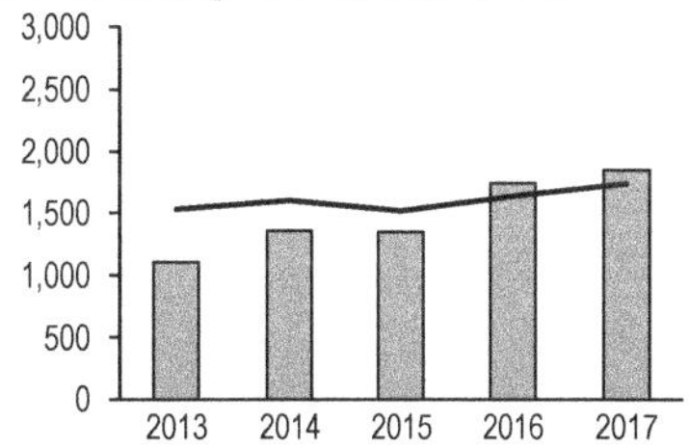

	2013	2014	2015	2016	2017
Salisbury	1,105	1,355	1,345	1,739	1,845
Average	1,531	1,598	1,514	1,632	1,735

Effectiveness Measures

Complaints per 1,000 Collection Points

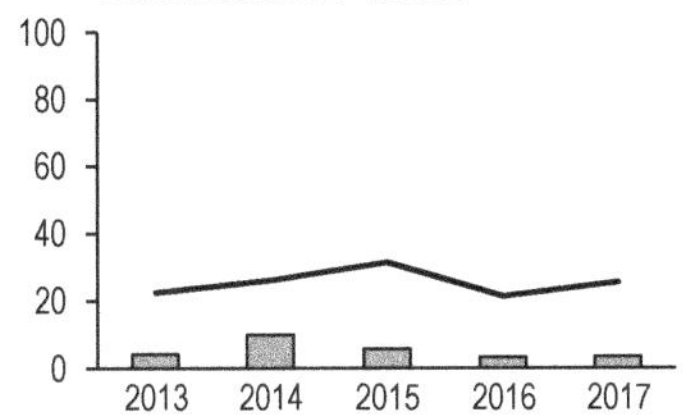

	2013	2014	2015	2016	2017
Salisbury	4.2	9.9	5.8	3.2	3.6
Average	22.5	26.1	31.5	21.4	25.6

Valid Complaints per 1,000 Collection Points

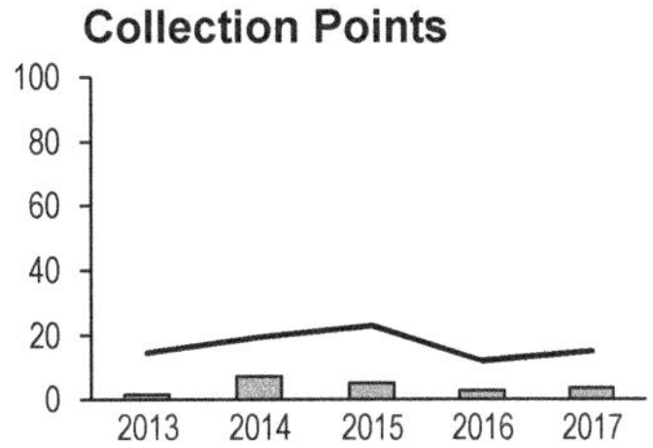

	2013	2014	2015	2016	2017
Salisbury	1.7	7.2	5.0	2.8	3.5
Average	14.6	19.4	22.8	11.9	14.8

Fiscal Year 2016–17

Explanatory Information

Service Level and Delivery
Residential refuse collection service is provided once a week at curbside to Wilson residents. Senior citizens and disabled persons may apply for and receive backyard pickup. There is currently a monthly $20.00 fee per household for residential refuse collection service.

During FY 2016–17, the city used five one-person crews working from automated packers. The city also used two three-person crews, each composed of one driver and two collectors working from semi-automated rear loaders. Residents are required to use ninety-six-gallon roll-out containers.

The city serviced seventeen collection routes each week during FY 2016–17. The packers made an average of two trips to the disposal facility per day per route, with the distance to the transfer station being ten miles.

Wilson collected 23,080 tons of residential refuse during the fiscal year, at a cost of $65 per ton. The cost per ton does not include the disposal cost of $39.32, representing the tipping fee at the transfer station.

Wilson defines automated packers as fully automated trucks requiring one driver. Packers are rear-loading, semi-automated trucks requiring one driver and two collectors.

Conditions Affecting Service, Performance, and Costs
The city of Wilson considers all complaints to be valid complaints.

Municipal Profile

Population (OSBM 2016)	49,406
Land Area (Square Miles)	30.60
Persons per Square Mile	1,615
Median Family Income U.S. Census 2010	$43,442

Service Profile

FTE Positions—Collection	11.0
FTE Positions—Other	1.0
Type of Equipment	5 automated packers 2 packers
Size of Crews (most commonly used)	1 & 3 person
Weekly Routes	27
Average Distance to Disposal Site	10 miles
Average Daily Trips to Disposal Site	2
Percentage of Service Contracted	0%
Collection Frequency	1 x week
General Collection Location	Curbside
Residential Customers (number represents collection points)	20,017
Tons Collected	23,080
Monthly Service Fee	$20.00

Full Cost Profile

Cost Breakdown by Percentage	
Personal Services	40.2%
Operating Costs	37.3%
Capital Costs	22.5%
TOTAL	100.0%
Cost Breakdown in Dollars	
Personal Services	$520,895
Operating Costs	$483,917
Capital Costs	$291,006
TOTAL	$1,295,818

Wilson — Residential Refuse Collection

Key: Wilson ▒ Benchmarking Average — Fiscal Years 2013 through 2017

Resource Measures

Residential Refuse Collection Costs per Capita

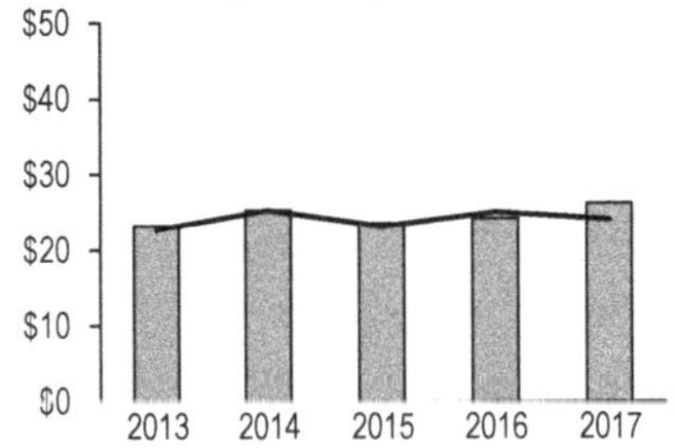

	2013	2014	2015	2016	2017
Wilson	$23.21	$25.33	$23.58	$24.19	$26.23
Average	$22.61	$25.23	$23.10	$24.98	$23.97

Residential Refuse FTEs per 10,000 Population

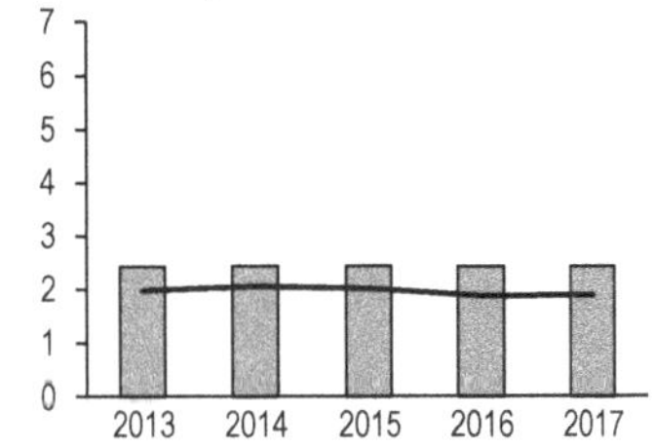

	2013	2014	2015	2016	2017
Wilson	2.43	2.44	2.44	2.43	2.43
Average	1.98	2.05	2.02	1.87	1.88

Workload Measures

Residential Refuse Tons per 1,000 Population

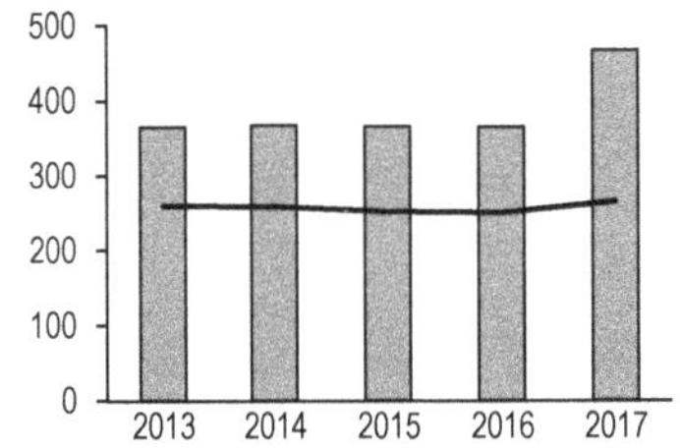

	2013	2014	2015	2016	2017
Wilson	364	367	366	365	467
Average	259	258	251	249	264

Residential Refuse Tons per 1,000 Collection Points

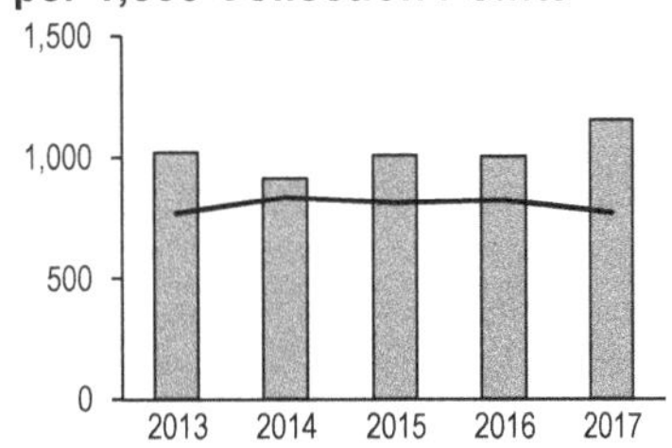

	2013	2014	2015	2016	2017
Wilson	1,020	911	1,008	1,001	1,153
Average	767	831	811	819	767

Efficiency Measures

Residential Refuse Collection Cost per Ton Collected

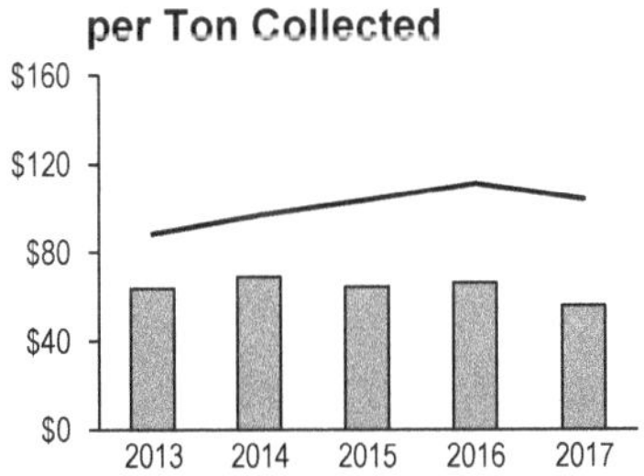

	2013	2014	2015	2016	2017
Wilson	$64	$69	$64	$66	$56
Average	$88	$97	$104	$111	$104

Residential Refuse Collection Cost per Collection Point

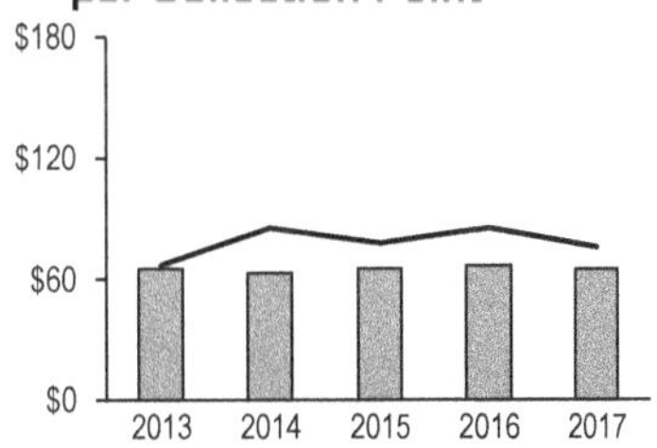

	2013	2014	2015	2016	2017
Wilson	$65	$63	$65	$66	$65
Average	$67	$85	$78	$85	$75

Refuse Tons Collected per Municipal Collection FTE

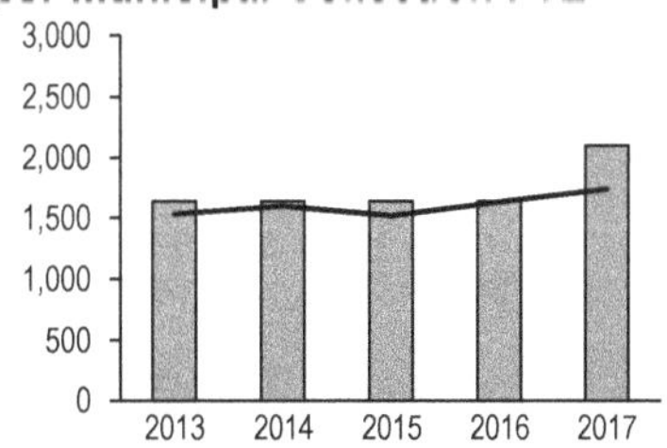

	2013	2014	2015	2016	2017
Wilson	1,636	1,636	1,636	1,636	2,098
Average	1,531	1,598	1,514	1,632	1,735

Effectiveness Measures

Complaints per 1,000 Collection Points

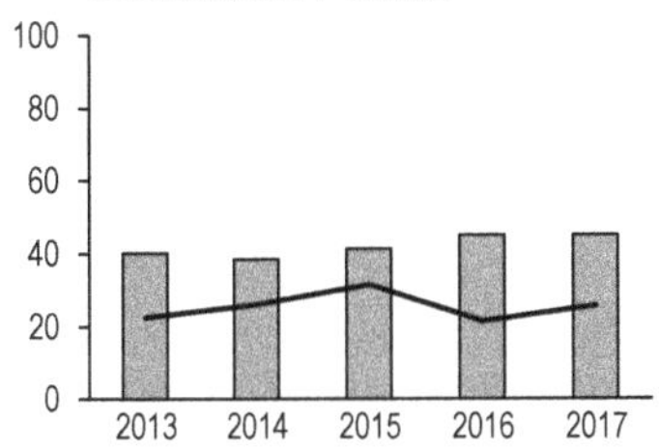

	2013	2014	2015	2016	2017
Wilson	40.1	38.4	41.4	45.1	45.1
Average	22.5	26.1	31.5	21.4	25.6

Valid Complaints per 1,000 Collection Points

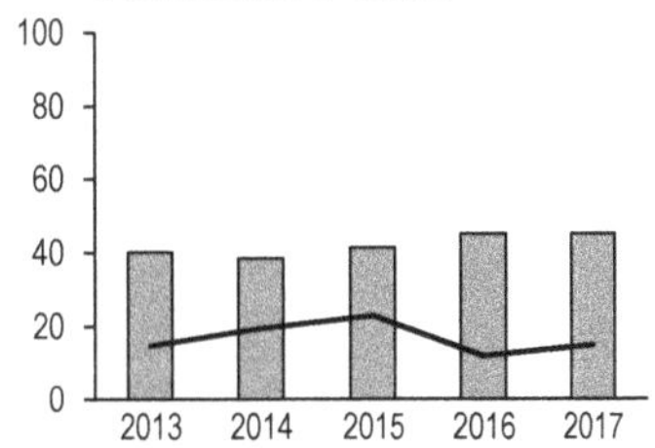

	2013	2014	2015	2016	2017
Wilson	40.1	38.4	41.4	45.1	45.1
Average	14.6	19.4	22.8	11.9	14.8

Fiscal Year 2016–17

Explanatory Information

Service Level and Delivery

Winston-Salem collects residential refuse once a week from backyards and at curbside. The city implemented a voluntary curbside collection program in March 2005. In October 2010, the city began the transition to mandatory curbside collection. The transition to a curbside only collection system was complete during FY 2011–2012.

The city uses sixteen three-person crews, each composed of a driver and two collectors equipped with rear-loading packers, to collect most of the residential refuse. In addition, there are ten automated trucks with one person each, one special collections truck with one person, and one central business district crew with one driver and one collector.

Residents may use three thirty-two-gallon containers or one ninety-six-gallon roll-out cart. There was no fee for the residential refuse service during FY 2016–17.

The city collected 57,707 tons of residential refuse during FY 2016–17 from 81,589 collection points. The cost per ton was $126, which does not include the tipping fee of $36 per ton. The city serviced 104 collection routes during the fiscal year, with an average of one trip per route per day to the landfill. The average distance to the landfill was ten miles.

Winston-Salem primarily uses rear-loading packers, which are trucks that load from the back. Two lifters are on the back of each truck. The crews hook their carts onto these lifters and dump the refuse into the back of the truck. The compactor blade also is located in the back of the truck.

Conditions Affecting Service, Performance, and Costs

Municipal Profile

Population (OSBM 2016)	240,603
Land Area (Square Miles)	132.55
Persons per Square Mile	1,815
Median Family Income U.S. Census 2010	$51,491

Service Profile

FTE Positions—Collection	82.0
FTE Positions—Other	3.0
Type of Equipment	12 automated packers 12 packers
Size of Crews (most commonly used)	1 & 3 person
Weekly Routes	104
Average Distance to Disposal Site	10 miles
Average Daily Trips to Disposal Site	1
Percentage of Service Contracted	0%
Collection Frequency	1 x week
General Collection Location	Curbside
Residential Customers (number represents collection points)	81,589
Tons Collected	57,707
Monthly Service Fee	No

Full Cost Profile

Cost Breakdown by Percentage	
Personal Services	49.9%
Operating Costs	31.0%
Capital Costs	19.2%
TOTAL	100.0%
Cost Breakdown in Dollars	
Personal Services	$3,637,904
Operating Costs	$2,260,664
Capital Costs	$1,398,329
TOTAL	$7,296,897

Key: Winston-Salem ▩ Benchmarking Average — Fiscal Years 2013 through 2017

Resource Measures

Residential Refuse Collection Costs per Capita

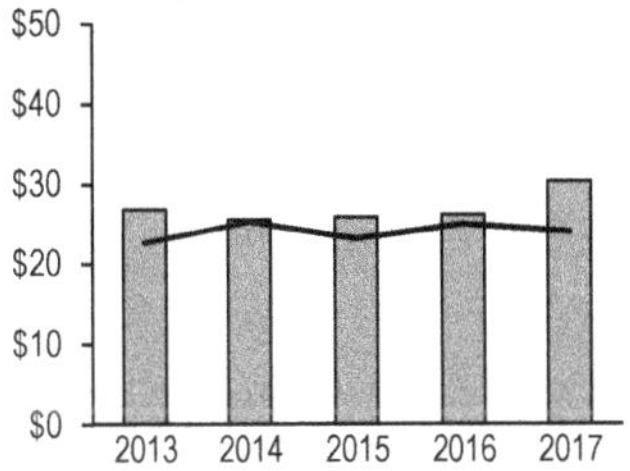

	2013	2014	2015	2016	2017
Winston-Salem	$26.77	$25.48	$25.85	$26.13	$30.33
Average	$22.61	$25.23	$23.10	$24.98	$23.97

Residential Refuse FTEs per 10,000 Population

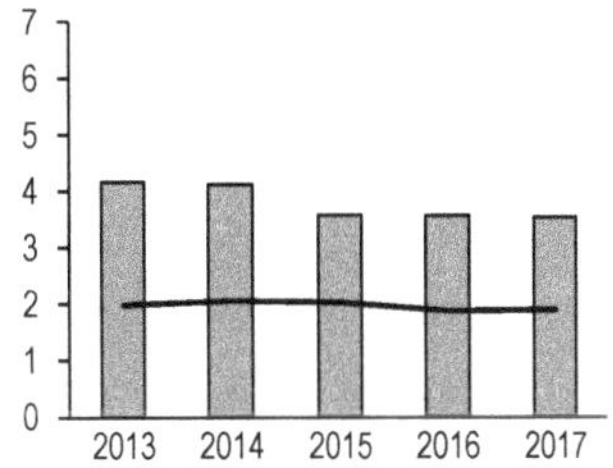

	2013	2014	2015	2016	2017
Winston-Salem	4.17	4.12	3.57	3.56	3.53
Average	1.98	2.05	2.02	1.87	1.88

Workload Measures

Residential Refuse Tons per 1,000 Population

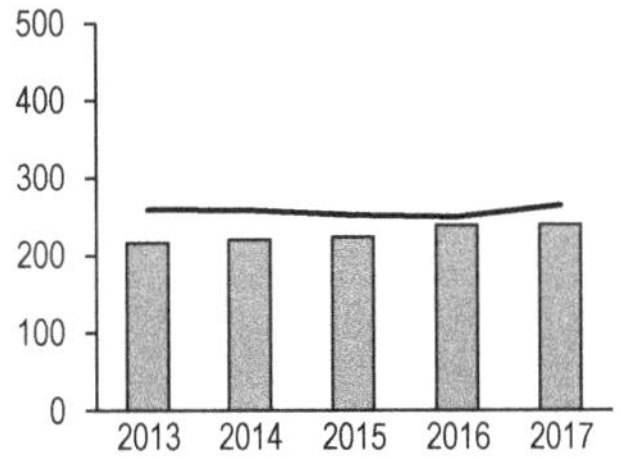

	2013	2014	2015	2016	2017
Winston-Salem	216	221	224	239	240
Average	259	258	251	249	264

Residential Refuse Tons per 1,000 Collection Points

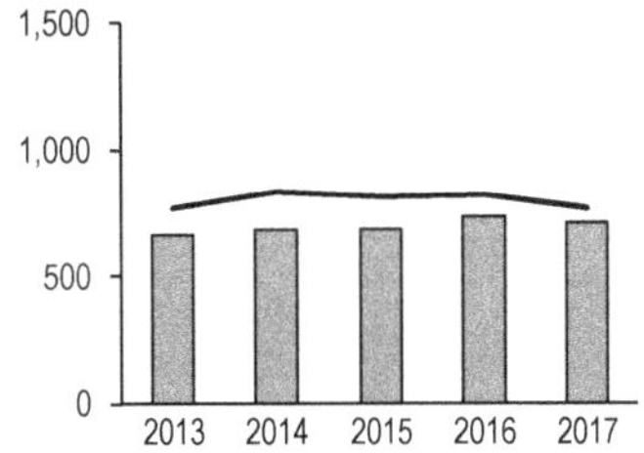

	2013	2014	2015	2016	2017
Winston-Salem	661	682	683	732	707
Average	767	831	811	819	767

Efficiency Measures

Residential Refuse Collection Cost per Ton Collected

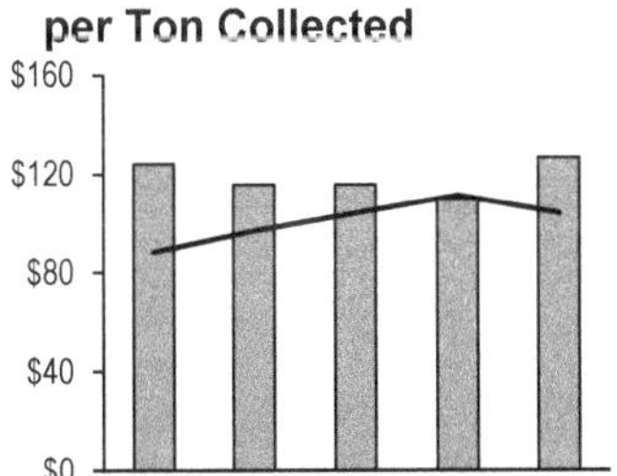

	2013	2014	2015	2016	2017
Winston-Salem	$124	$115	$116	$109	$126
Average	$88	$97	$104	$111	$104

Residential Refuse Collection Cost per Collection Point

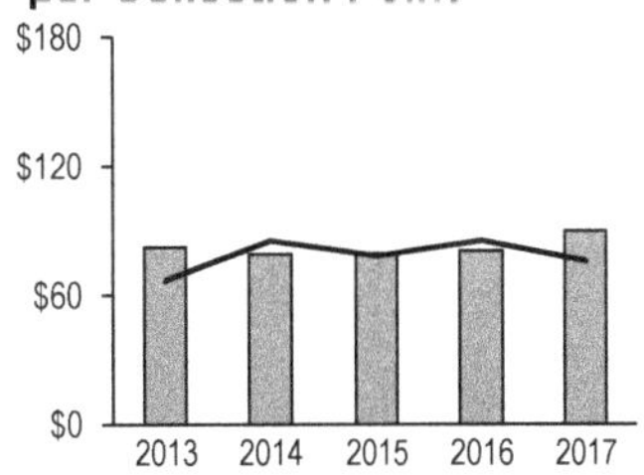

	2013	2014	2015	2016	2017
Winston-Salem	$82	$79	$79	$80	$89
Average	$67	$85	$78	$85	$75

Refuse Tons Collected per Municipal Collection FTE

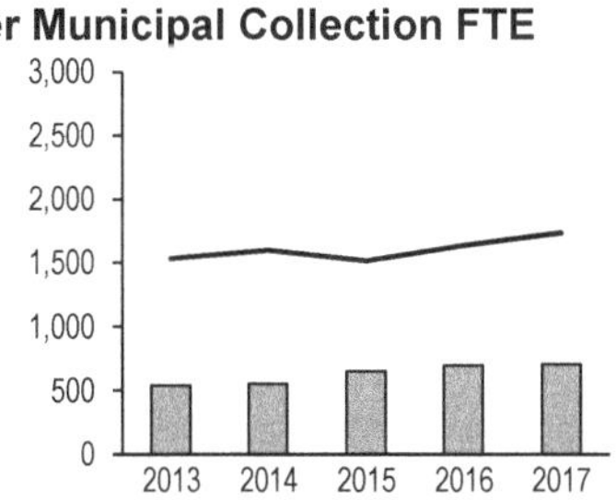

	2013	2014	2015	2016	2017
Winston-Salem	535	553	649	696	704
Average	1,531	1,598	1,514	1,632	1,735

Effectiveness Measures

Complaints per 1,000 Collection Points

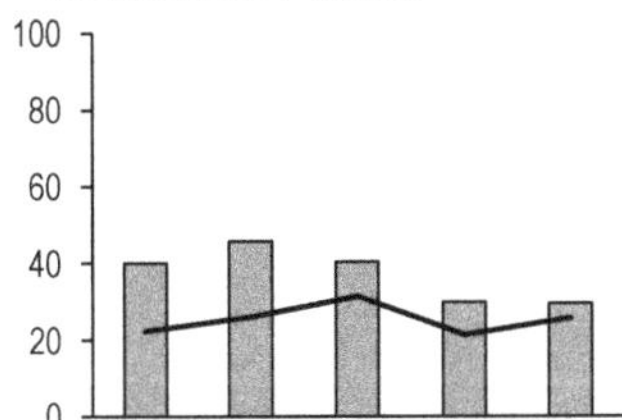

	2013	2014	2015	2016	2017
Winston-Salem	40.0	45.7	40.3	29.9	29.5
Average	22.5	26.1	31.5	21.4	25.6

Valid Complaints per 1,000 Collection Points

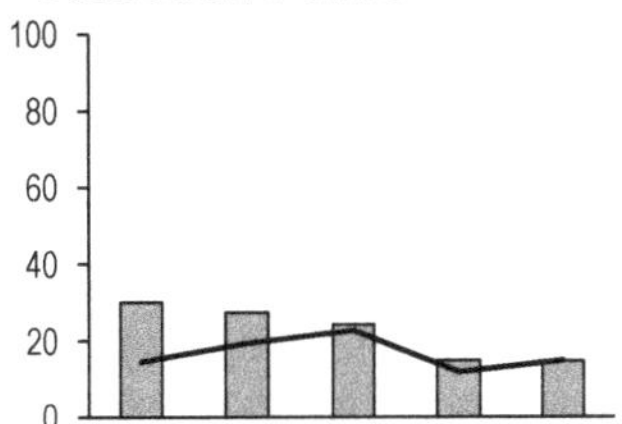

	2013	2014	2015	2016	2017
Winston-Salem	30.0	27.4	24.2	15.0	14.7
Average	14.6	19.4	22.8	11.9	14.8

UNC | SCHOOL OF GOVERNMENT
North Carolina Benchmarking Project

Performance and Cost Data

HOUSEHOLD RECYCLING

PERFORMANCE MEASURES FOR HOUSEHOLD RECYCLING

SERVICE DEFINITION

This includes both curbside collection and processing of household recyclable materials from residences and certain other locations and the drop-off of such materials by citizens at recycling stations or centers. The recyclable materials collected are mainly aluminum and steel cans, plastics, glass bottles, newspapers, magazines, and cardboard. The curbside portion of this service involves regularly scheduled collection that utilizes containers small enough that residents and/or workers can move or lift them. Excluded are collection of yard waste, leaves, and commercial recycling.

NOTES ON PERFORMANCE MEASURES

1. Workload and Efficiency Measures

The same sorts of workload and efficiency measures are used for household recycling as for residential refuse collection. The project's workload measures for household recycling are tons of recyclable materials collected per 1,000 population and per 1,000 collection points, and the efficiency measures for this service are cost per ton of recyclable materials collected, cost per collection point, and tons of household recyclable materials collected per full-time equivalent (FTE) position directly involved in household recycling. FTEs for recycling are calculated in the same way as they are for residential refuse collection. Only those FTE positions that actually collect recyclables are used for the measure "tons collected per FTE."

2. Tons of Solid Waste Landfilled per 1,000 Population

"Tons solid waste landfilled per 1,000 population" is used as a workload measure. Although not all residential refuse is recyclable, much more of it is likely to be recycled in the future as recycling technology improves and markets for recyclable materials grow. Thus, tons of solid waste landfilled per 1,000 population serves as a useful indicator of the need for household recycling.

3. Community Set-Out Rate in Household Recycling

The project uses this as a measure of household recycling effectiveness. Residents in municipalities with curbside recycling choose whether to participate in the program and decide the extent of their participation. As the portion of households participating in household recycling grows, the more effective recycling is likely to be in reducing the volume of residential refuse. This measure combines the set-out rate for those participating and the participation rate to estimate the percentage of potential households that are actually recycling.

4. Tons of Household Recyclable Materials Collected as a Percentage of the Sum of Tons of Residential Refuse Collected Plus Tons of Household Recyclable Materials Collected

This measure assesses the magnitude of household recycling in relation to residential refuse collected for disposal. A household recycling program is effective to the extent it diverts residential refuse from the disposal stream.

Household Recycling

Summary of Key Dimensions of Service

City or Town	Drop-Off Sites		Collection Frequency	Recyclables Sorted at Curb?	Collection Points	Community Set-Out Rate	Tons Collected	Percentage of Waste Stream Diverted from Landfill	Percentage Service Contracted	Municipal FTE Collection Positions
	City Owned	Other								
Apex	0	0	1 x week	No	15,607	91%	3,951	24%	100%	NA
Asheville	0	1	1 x 2 weeks	No	29,343	97%	8,748	28%	100%	NA
Charlotte	0	11	1 x 2 weeks	No	215,602	37%	45,859	19%	100%	NA
Concord	0	1	1 x 2 weeks	No	31,211	74%	6,002	20%	100%	1.1
Goldsboro	0	0	1 x 2 weeks	No	14,372	na	1,085	9%	1%	4.0
Greensboro	20	0	1 x 2 weeks	No	89,214	63%	17,217	23%	0%	15
Greenville	224	0	1 x week	No	19,294	NA	4,394	13%	0%	11
Hickory	2	0	1 x 2 weeks	No	12,200	65%	2,622	26%	92%	0.5
High Point	16	0	1 x 2 weeks	No	42,418	75%	12,262	24%	0%	6
Raleigh	2	2	1 x 2 weeks	No	185,746	68%	28,412	23%	0%	37
Salisbury	0	0	1 x 2 weeks	No	11,095	58%	1,581	15%	100%	NA
Wilson	0	0	1 x week	No	20,017	53%	1,705	7%	0%	7
Winston-Salem	11	0	1 x 2 weeks	No	76,452	57%	14,911	21%	100%	NA

NOTES

Community Set-Out Rate is a combination of the participation rate and the participant's set-out rate.

EXPLANATORY FACTORS

These are factors that the project found affected household recycling collection performance and cost in one or more of the municipalities:

Types of items eligible for recycling
Landfill tipping fees for solid waste
Commitment of city officials to recycling
Number of drop-off centers
Community education
Market prices for recyclable materials
Demographic makeup of community

Fiscal Year 2016–17

Explanatory Information

Service Level and Delivery

Apex contracts with Waste Industries for refuse collection, disposal, and recycling. Only the recycling collection is reflected on this page. The town offers curbside recycling to all residents. Residents pay a $3.31 fee per container per month. Most residents have a sixty-four-gallon cart though some have eighteen-gallon containers.

The following materials are collected:

- plastics
- paperboard
- chipboard
- paper tubes
- corrugated cardboard
- aluminum
- tin and steel cans
- glass
- newspaper
- magazines and catalogs
- phone books.

Residents living within Apex are encouraged to participate in the curbside recycling program. The program serves 15,607 residences.

Conditions Affecting Service, Performance, and Costs

Municipal Profile

Population (OSBM 2016)	46,688
Land Area (Square Miles)	20.61
Persons per Square Mile	2,265
Median Family Income U.S. Census 2010	$97,201

Service Profile

FTE Positions—Collection	Contractor
FTE Positions—Other	Contractor
Number of City Drop-Off Centers	0
Other Drop-Off Centers	0
Percentage of Service Contracted	100%
Collection Frequency	1 x week
General Collection Location	Curbside
Recyclables Sorted at Curb	No
Collection Points	15,607
Tons of Recyclables Collected	
Curbside	3,951
City Drop-Off Centers	0
Total Tons Collected	3,951
Monthly Service Fee	$3.31
Revenue from Sale of Recyclables	$0
Sale Revenue as Percentage of Cost	NA

Full Cost Profile

Cost Breakdown by Percentage	
Personal Services	0.0%
Operating Costs	100.0%
Capital Costs	0.0%
TOTAL	100.0%
Cost Breakdown in Dollars	
Personal Services	$0
Operating Costs	$614,978
Capital Costs	$0
TOTAL	$614,978

Key: Apex ▒ Benchmarking Average — Fiscal Years 2013 through 2017

Resource Measures

Recycling Services Cost per Capita

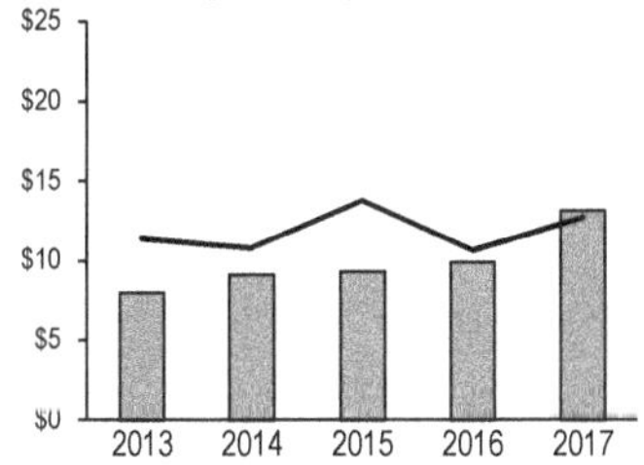

	2013	2014	2015	2016	2017
Apex	$8.00	$9.12	$9.34	$9.92	$13.17
Average	$11.39	$10.81	$13.79	$10.66	$12.74

Recycling Services FTEs per 10,000 Population

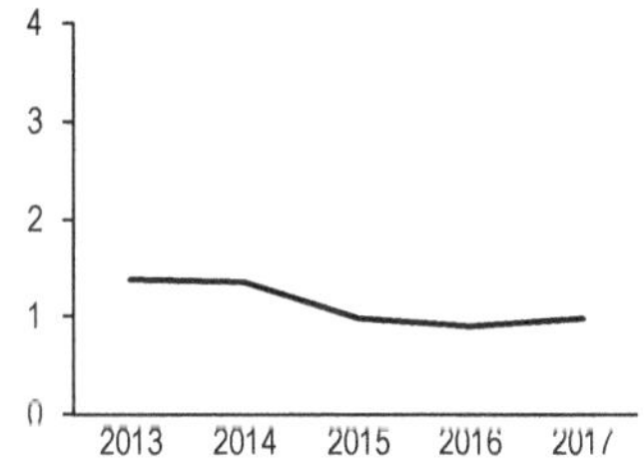

	2013	2014	2015	2016	2017
Apex					
Average	1.37	1.35	0.98	0.89	0.98

Workload Measures

Tons Recyclables Collected per 1,000 Population

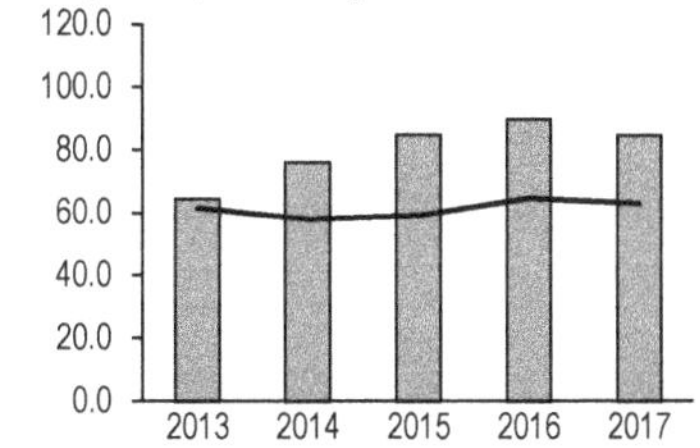

	2013	2014	2015	2016	2017
Apex	64.5	76.1	84.8	89.7	84.6
Average	61.4	57.7	58.9	64.4	62.8

Tons Recyclables Collected per 1,000 Collection Points

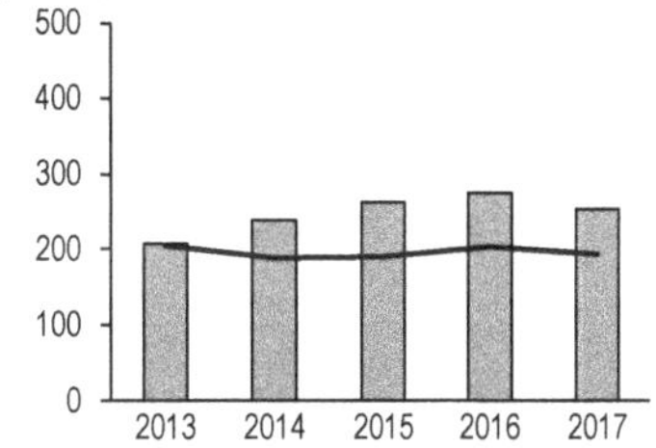

	2013	2014	2015	2016	2017
Apex	207	238	262	275	253
Average	205	188	190	203	193

Tons Solid Waste Landfilled per 1,000 Population

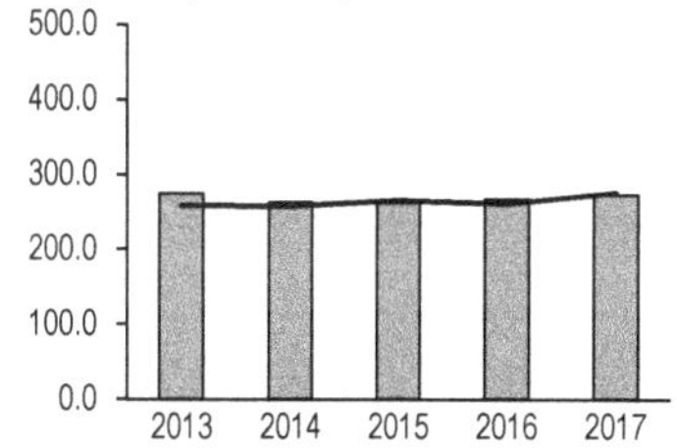

	2013	2014	2015	2016	2017
Apex	274.0	262.2	261.8	266.6	272.8
Average	258.5	257.6	264.9	260.6	275.7

Efficiency Measures

Recycling Services Cost per Ton Collected

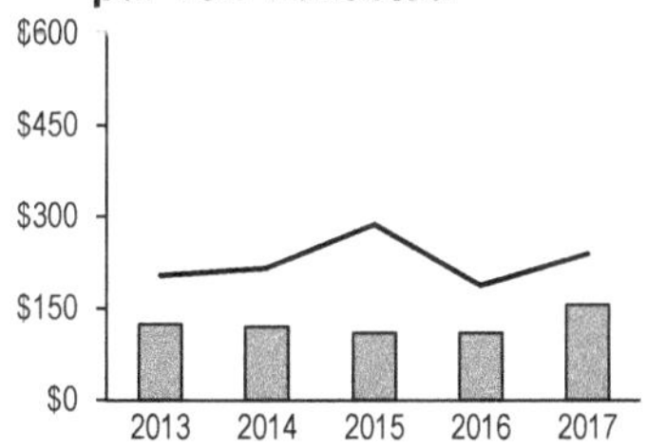

	2013	2014	2015	2016	2017
Apex	$124	$120	$110	$111	$156
Average	$204	$215	$286	$187	$239

Recycling Services Cost per Collection Point

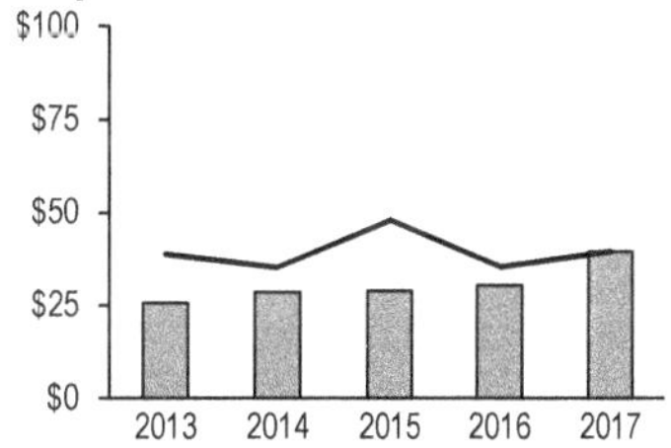

	2013	2014	2015	2016	2017
Apex	$25.63	$28.52	$28.88	$30.38	$39.40
Average	$38.72	$35.13	$47.74	$35.39	$39.44

Tons Collected Curbside per Municipal FTE

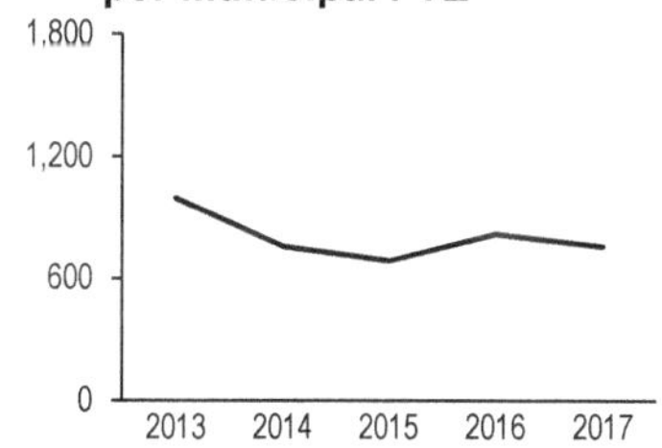

	2013	2014	2015	2016	2017
Apex					
Average	994	758	684	816	757

Effectiveness Measures

Community Set-Out Rate

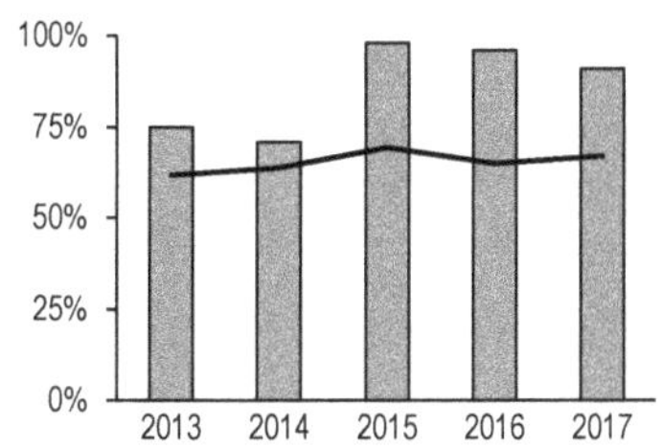

	2013	2014	2015	2016	2017
Apex	75.0%	71.0%	98.0%	96.0%	91.0%
Average	61.9%	63.8%	69.4%	65.1%	67.1%

Tons Recycled as Percentage of Tons Refuse and Recyclables Collected

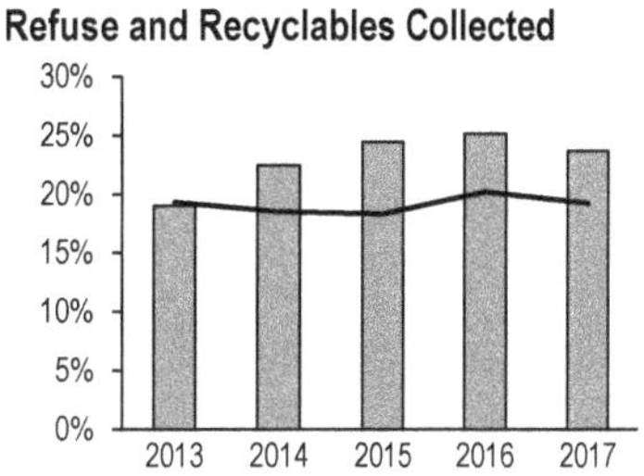

	2013	2014	2015	2016	2017
Apex	19.1%	22.5%	24.5%	25.2%	23.7%
Average	19.4%	18.5%	18.4%	20.2%	19.3%

Asheville — Household Recycling

Fiscal Year 2016–17

Explanatory Information

Service Level and Delivery

The city offers curbside recycling service to all residential customers. The service was provided by contract during FY 2016–17 by Curbside Management Incorporated. The contracted service also includes daily collection of approximately 250 on-street recycling cans located in the city.

Asheville charged a $14 monthly fee for all solid waste services. Recyclables are collected using a two-bin system. The following materials are collected:

- mixed paper
- newspaper
- corrugated cardboard
- clear, green, and brown glass bottles
- all plastic bottles
- aluminum and steel cans
- telephone books (seasonal)
- aerosol cans.

Residents living within the city of Asheville are encouraged to participate in the curbside recycling program. The program serves 29,343 residences, with each residence receiving a ninety-five-gallon or in some cases a sixty-five-gallon cart. Recycling is collected every other week on the regular trash day. A curbside recycling truck comes to each neighborhood on a predetermined schedule and separates the recyclables at the curb.

There is one drop-off center within Asheville. This center is set up for people who do not have curbside recycling pickup at their homes or businesses. Anyone can use this center to drop off their recycling during transfer station operating times.

Conditions Affecting Service, Performance, and Costs

Municipal Profile

Population (OSBM 2016)	91,929
Land Area (Square Miles)	45.52
Persons per Square Mile	2,019
Median Family Income U.S. Census 2010	$53,350

Service Profile

FTE Positions—Collection	Contractor
FTE Positions—Other	Contractor
Number of City Drop-Off Centers	0
Other Drop-Off Centers	1
Percentage of Service Contracted	100.0%
Collection Frequency	Every 2 weeks
General Collection Location	Curbside
Recyclables Sorted at Curb	No
Collection Points	29,343
Tons of Recyclables Collected	
Curbside	8,748
City Drop-Off Centers	0
Total Tons Collected	8,748
Monthly Service Fee	$0.00
Revenue from Sale of Recyclables	$0
Sale Revenue as Percentage of Cost	NA

Full Cost Profile

Cost Breakdown by Percentage	
Personal Services	0.0%
Operating Costs	100.0%
Capital Costs	0.0%
TOTAL	100.0%
Cost Breakdown in Dollars	
Personal Services	$0
Operating Costs	$1,228,766
Capital Costs	$0
TOTAL	$1,228,766

Key: Asheville ▒ Benchmarking Average — Fiscal Years 2013 through 2017

Resource Measures

Recycling Services Cost per Capita

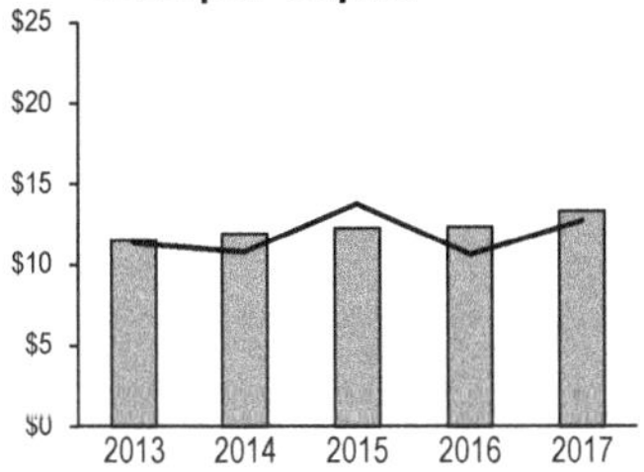

	2013	2014	2015	2016	2017
Asheville	$11.54	$11.97	$12.32	$12.41	$13.37
Average	$11.39	$10.81	$13.79	$10.66	$12.74

Recycling Services FTEs per 10,000 Population

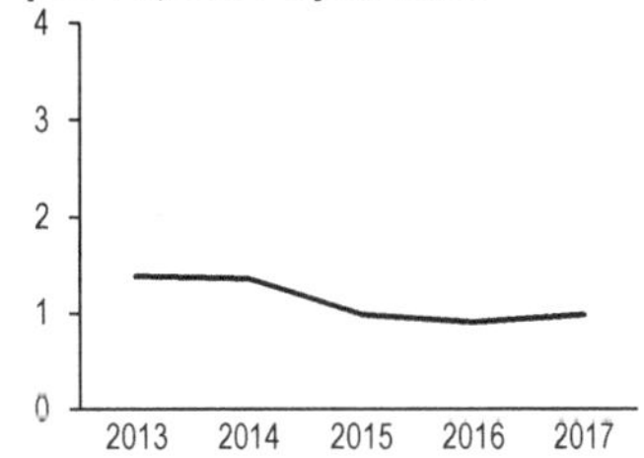

	2013	2014	2015	2016	2017
Asheville					
Average	1.37	1.35	0.98	0.89	0.98

Workload Measures

Tons Recyclables Collected per 1,000 Population

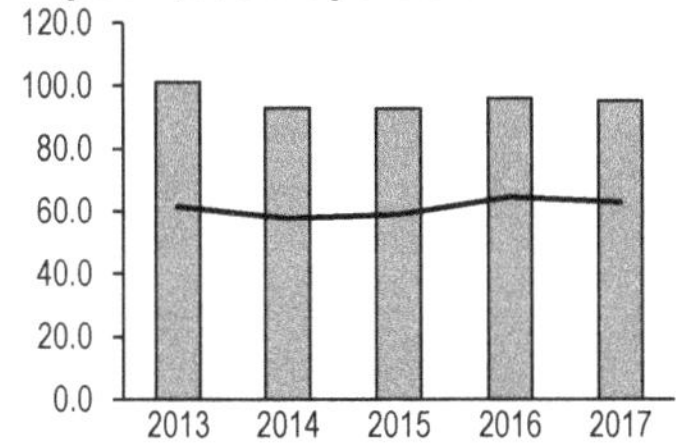

	2013	2014	2015	2016	2017
Asheville	101.0	92.8	92.7	96.0	95.2
Average	61.4	57.7	58.9	64.4	62.8

Tons Recyclables Collected per 1,000 Collection Points

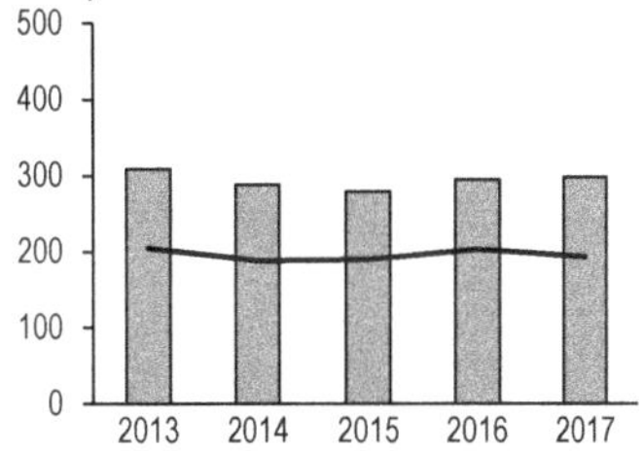

	2013	2014	2015	2016	2017
Asheville	309	288	279	294	298
Average	205	188	190	203	193

Tons Solid Waste Landfilled per 1,000 Population

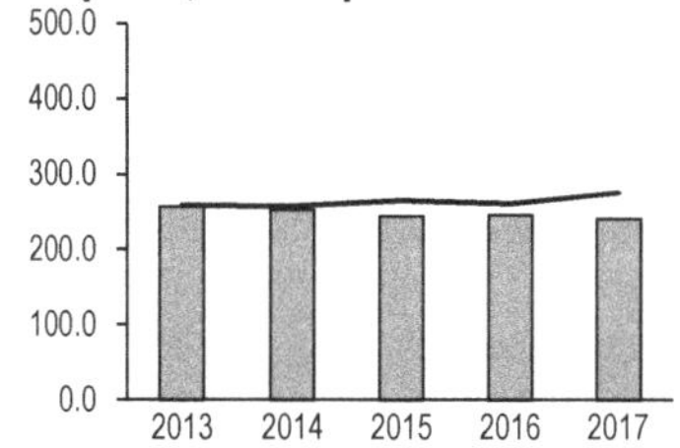

	2013	2014	2015	2016	2017
Asheville	257.3	253.1	244.9	246.5	241.3
Average	258.5	257.6	264.9	260.6	275.7

Efficiency Measures

Recycling Services Cost per Ton Collected

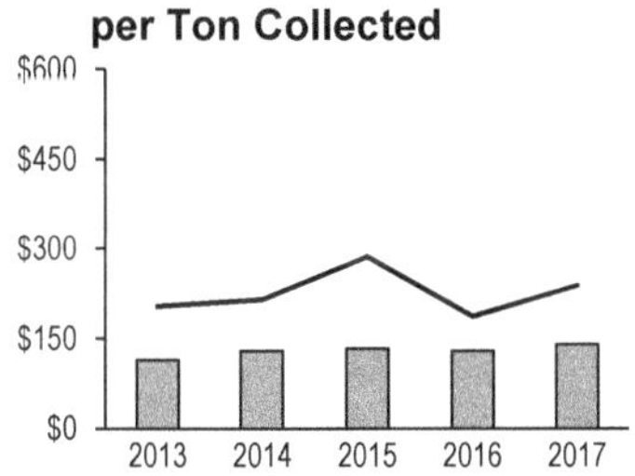

	2013	2014	2015	2016	2017
Asheville	$114	$129	$133	$129	$140
Average	$204	$215	$286	$187	$239

Recycling Services Cost per Collection Point

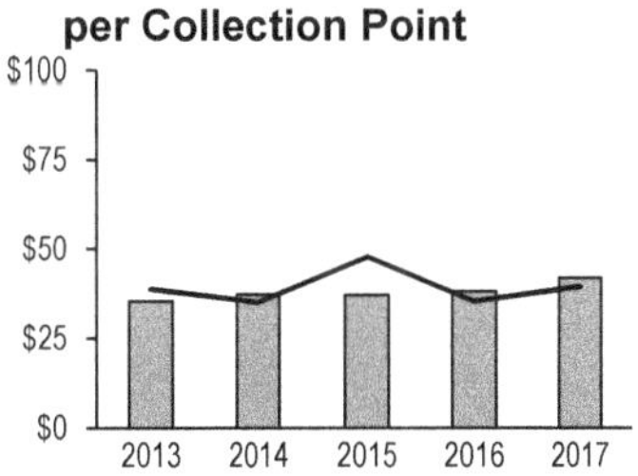

	2013	2014	2015	2016	2017
Asheville	$35.27	$37.20	$37.07	$38.04	$41.88
Average	$38.72	$35.13	$47.74	$35.39	$39.44

Tons Collected Curbside per Municipal FTE

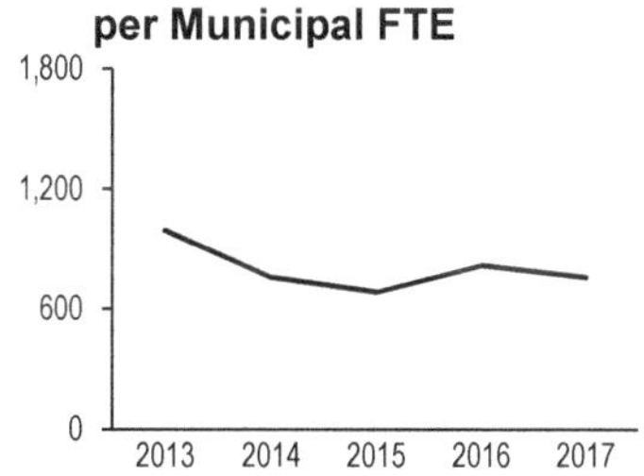

	2013	2014	2015	2016	2017
Asheville					
Average	994	758	684	816	757

Effectiveness Measures

Community Set-Out Rate

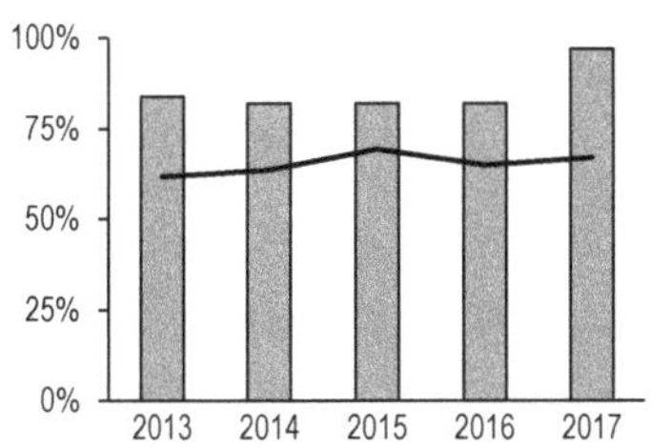

	2013	2014	2015	2016	2017
Asheville	84.0%	82.0%	82.0%	82.0%	97.0%
Average	61.9%	63.8%	69.4%	65.1%	67.1%

Tons Recycled as Percentage of Tons Refuse and Recyclables Collected

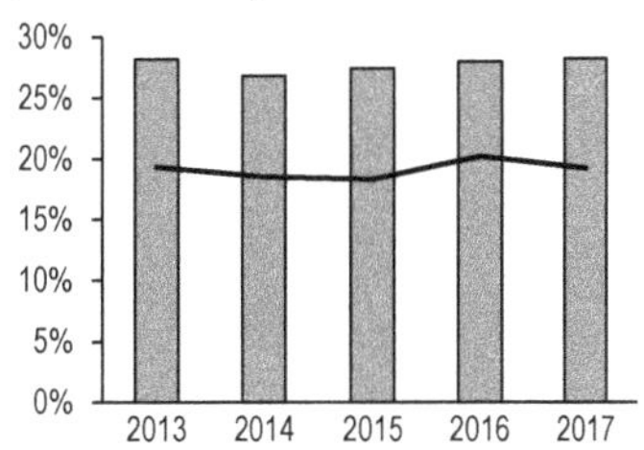

	2013	2014	2015	2016	2017
Asheville	28.2%	26.8%	27.4%	28.0%	28.3%
Average	19.4%	18.5%	18.4%	20.2%	19.3%

Fiscal Year 2016–17

Explanatory Information

Service Level and Delivery

Charlotte provides curbside recycling collection to single-family residential customers once every two weeks. Recycling collection is entirely provided by a contractor. Materials collected in the recycling program include the following:

- glass
- plastic
- aluminum
- newspaper
- magazines
- catalogs
- phone books
- cardboard
- milk cartons
- aerosol cans
- juice boxes.

The majority of users have ninety-five or ninety-six-gallon roll-out containers. The city receives a modest amount from sale of recyclables, which totaled $210,062 for the year.

The county operates several recycling drop-off centers that are available for use by citizens of Charlotte and Mecklenburg County. Tonnage from the drop-off centers is not included in this report.

Conditions Affecting Service, Performance, and Costs

Charlotte did not participate in the Benchmarking Project during FY 2014–15. No data are available for that year.

The set-out rate is calculated daily, as the trucks are outfitted with Radio Frequency Identification (RFID) readers and the recycling carts have RFID chips installed.

During FY 2013–14, the recycling contractor implemented substantial route changes, leading to confusion and a rise in complaints.

Municipal Profile

Population (OSBM 2016)	830,258
Land Area (Square Miles)	305.48
Persons per Square Mile	2,718
Median Family Income U.S. Census 2010	$61,405

Service Profile

FTE Positions—Collection	Contractor
FTE Positions—Other	Contractor
Number of City Drop-Off Centers	0
Other Drop-Off Centers	11
Percentage of Service Contracted	100%
Collection Frequency	Every 2 weeks
General Collection Location	Curbside
Recyclables Sorted at Curb	No
Collection Points	215,602
Tons of Recyclables Collected	
Curbside	45,859
City Drop-Off Centers	0
Total Tons Collected	45,859
Monthly Service Fee	0
Revenue from Sale of Recyclables	$210,062
Sale Revenue as Percentage of Cost	3.2%

Full Cost Profile

Cost Breakdown by Percentage	
Personal Services	0.0%
Operating Costs	99.5%
Capital Costs	0.5%
TOTAL	100.0%
Cost Breakdown in Dollars	
Personal Services	$0
Operating Costs	$6,499,655
Capital Costs	$29,501
TOTAL	$6,529,156

Charlotte — Household Recycling

Key: Charlotte ▒ Benchmarking Average — Fiscal Years 2013 through 2017

Resource Measures

Recycling Services Cost per Capita

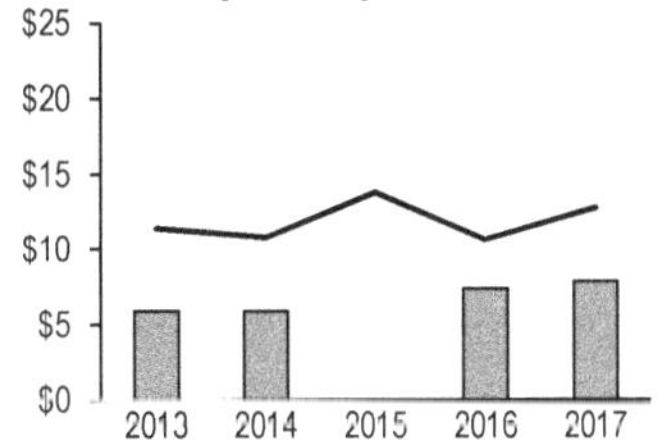

	2013	2014	2015	2016	2017
Charlotte	$5.90	$5.90		$7.39	$7.86
Average	$11.39	$10.81	$13.79	$10.66	$12.74

Recycling Services FTEs per 10,000 Population

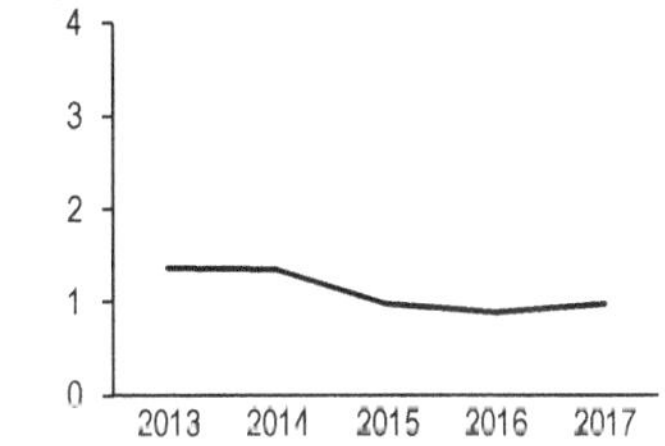

	2013	2014	2015	2016	2017
Charlotte					
Average	1.37	1.35	0.98	0.89	0.98

Workload Measures

Tons Recyclables Collected per 1,000 Population

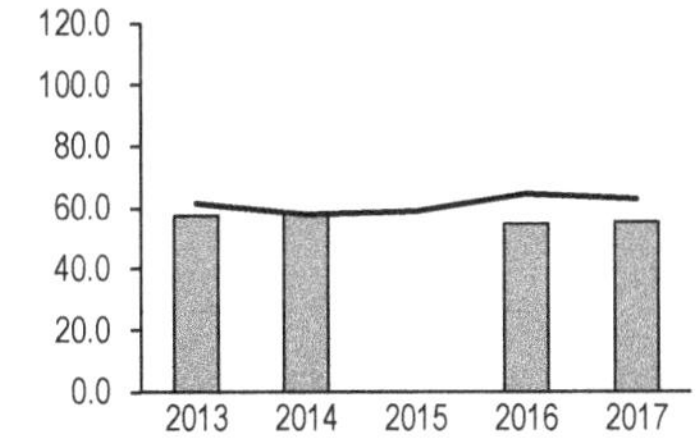

	2013	2014	2015	2016	2017
Charlotte	57.4	58.1		54.7	55.2
Average	61.4	57.7	58.9	64.4	62.8

Tons Recyclables Collected per 1,000 Collection Points

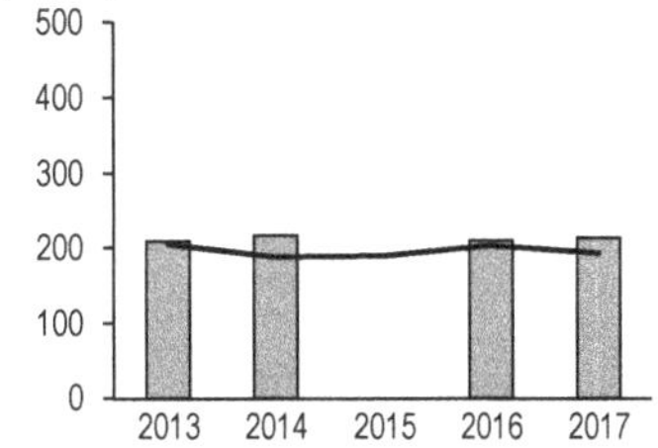

	2013	2014	2015	2016	2017
Charlotte	208	216		209	213
Average	205	188	190	203	193

Tons Solid Waste Landfilled per 1,000 Population

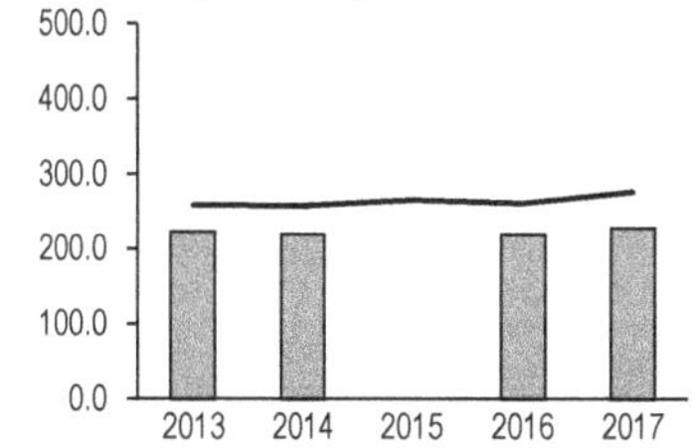

	2013	2014	2015	2016	2017
Charlotte	223.6	219.8		219.7	228.1
Average	258.5	257.6	264.9	260.6	275.7

Efficiency Measures

Recycling Services Cost per Ton Collected

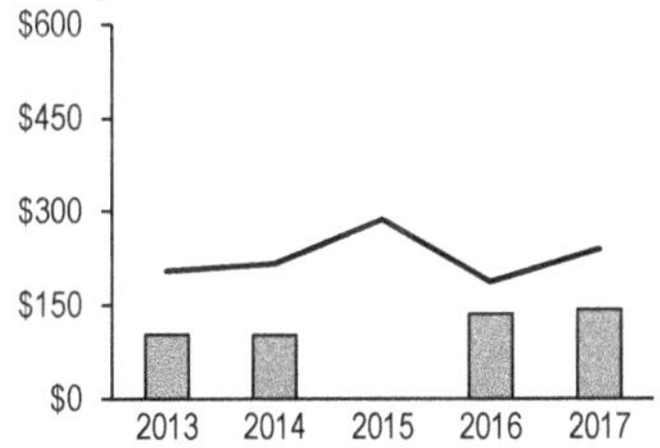

	2013	2014	2015	2016	2017
Charlotte	$103	$101		$135	$142
Average	$204	$215	$286	$187	$239

Recycling Services Cost per Collection Point

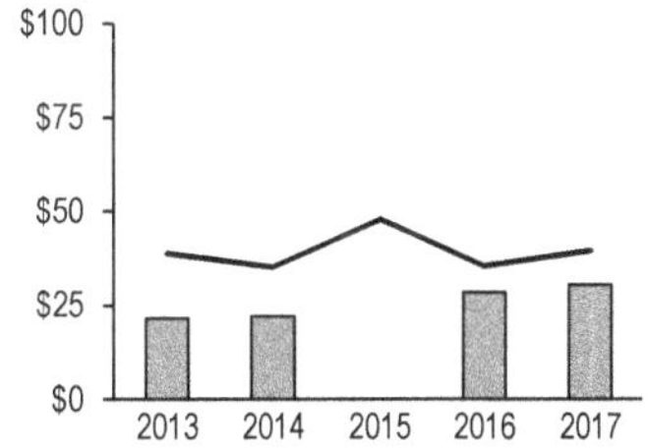

	2013	2014	2015	2016	2017
Charlotte	$21.43	$21.93		$28.29	$30.28
Average	$38.72	$35.13	$47.74	$35.39	$39.44

Tons Collected Curbside per Municipal FTE

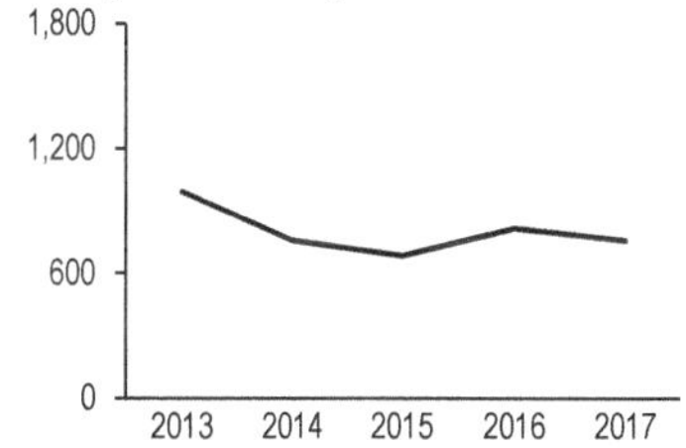

	2013	2014	2015	2016	2017
Charlotte					
Average	994	758	684	816	757

Effectiveness Measures

Community Set-Out Rate

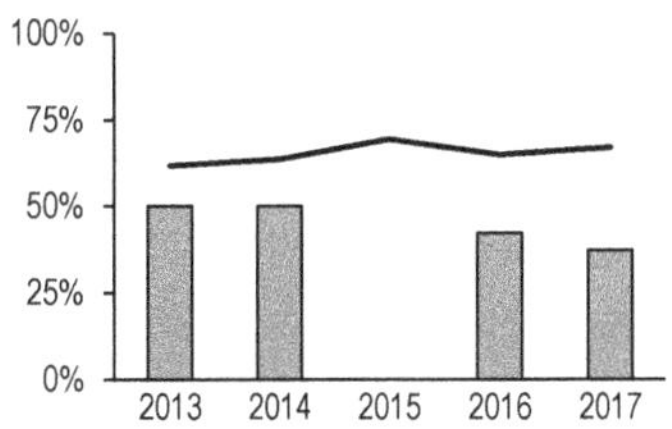

	2013	2014	2015	2016	2017
Charlotte	50.0%	50.0%		42.2%	37.2%
Average	61.9%	63.8%	69.4%	65.1%	67.1%

Tons Recycled as Percentage of Tons Refuse and Recyclables Collected

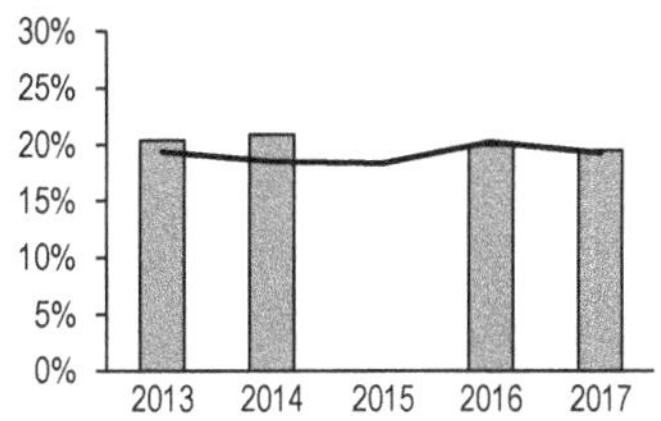

	2013	2014	2015	2016	2017
Charlotte	20.4%	20.9%		19.9%	19.5%
Average	19.4%	18.5%	18.4%	20.2%	19.3%

Fiscal Year 2016–17

Explanatory Information

Service Level and Delivery
Concord provides biweekly curbside collection of recyclable materials from households. The city uses a contractor to provide recycling collection. Residents place materials into a ninety-five-gallon cart. The recyclable materials collected include:

- glass
- newspaper
- magazines
- mixed paper and mail
- No. 1 and No. 2 plastics
- metal and aluminum food and beverage containers.

Concord uses a contract collector for regular residential curbside recycling. The materials are collected on a commingled basis biweekly from each participating resident and delivered to a materials recovery facility (MRF) in Charlotte for separation and marketing.

The city received $167,820 from the sale of recyclables during the year offsetting some of the costs.

Conditions Affecting Service, Performance, and Costs
The set-out rate is calculated twice a year.

Municipal Profile

Population (OSBM 2016)	88,815
Land Area (Square Miles)	62.61
Persons per Square Mile	1,419
Median Family Income U.S. Census 2010	$63,643

Service Profile

FTE Positions—Collection	1.1
FTE Positions—Other	1.44
Number of City Drop-Off Centers	0
Other Drop-Off Centers	1
Percentage of Service Contracted	100%
Collection Frequency	Every 2 weeks
General Collection Location	Curbside
Recyclables Sorted at Curb	No
Collection Points	31,211
Tons of Recyclables Collected	
Curbside	6,002
City Drop-Off Centers	0
Total Tons Collected	6,002
Monthly Service Fee	0
Revenue from Sale of Recyclables	$167,820
Sale Revenue as Percentage of Cost	14.8%

Full Cost Profile

Cost Breakdown by Percentage	
Personal Services	14.3%
Operating Costs	83.9%
Capital Costs	1.9%
TOTAL	100.0%
Cost Breakdown in Dollars	
Personal Services	$161,852
Operating Costs	$951,630
Capital Costs	$21,415
TOTAL	$1,134,897

Key: Concord ▒ Benchmarking Average — Fiscal Years 2013 through 2017

Resource Measures

Recycling Services Cost per Capita

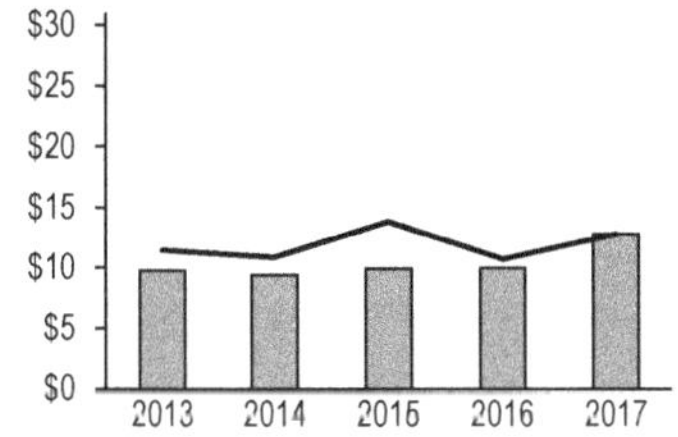

	2013	2014	2015	2016	2017
Concord	$9.76	$9.41	$9.91	$9.96	$12.78
Average	$11.39	$10.81	$13.79	$10.66	$12.74

Recycling Services FTEs per 10,000 Population

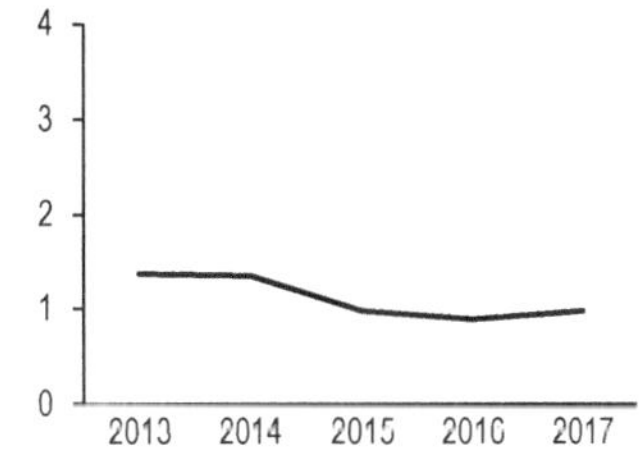

	2013	2014	2015	2016	2017
Concord					
Average	1.37	1.35	0.98	0.89	0.98

Workload Measures

Tons Recyclables Collected per 1,000 Population

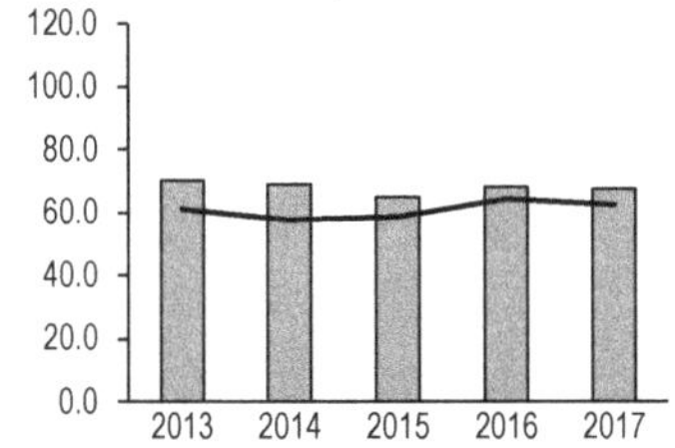

	2013	2014	2015	2016	2017
Concord	70.4	69.0	65.0	68.2	67.6
Average	61.4	57.7	58.9	64.4	62.8

Tons Recyclables Collected per 1,000 Collection Points

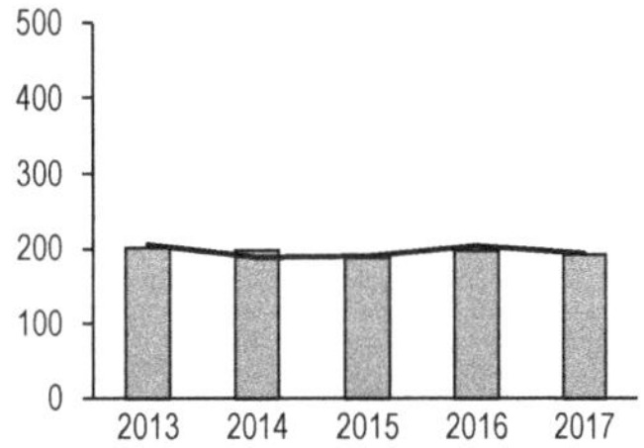

	2013	2014	2015	2016	2017
Concord	201	198	188	197	192
Average	205	188	190	203	193

Tons Solid Waste Landfilled per 1,000 Population

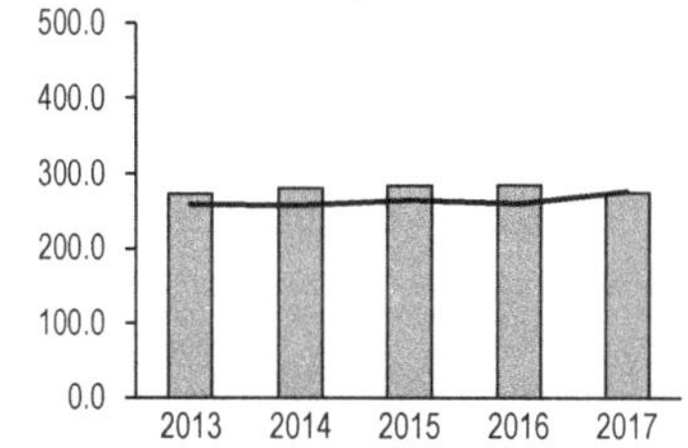

	2013	2014	2015	2016	2017
Concord	273.7	281.4	284.6	285.6	275.3
Average	258.5	257.6	264.9	260.6	275.7

Efficiency Measures

Recycling Services Cost per Ton Collected

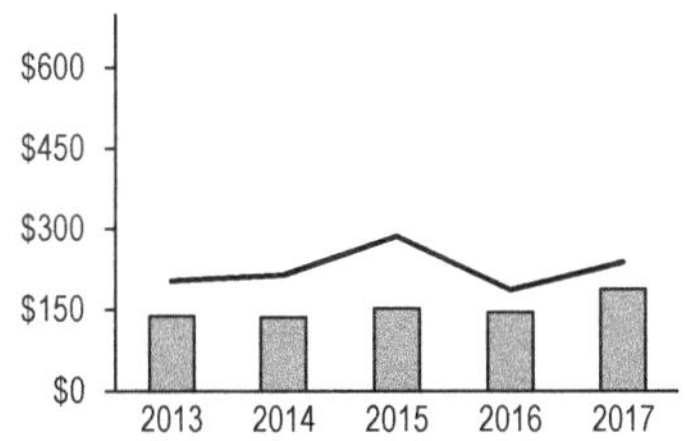

	2013	2014	2015	2016	2017
Concord	$139	$136	$152	$146	$189
Average	$204	$215	$286	$187	$239

Recycling Services Cost per Collection Point

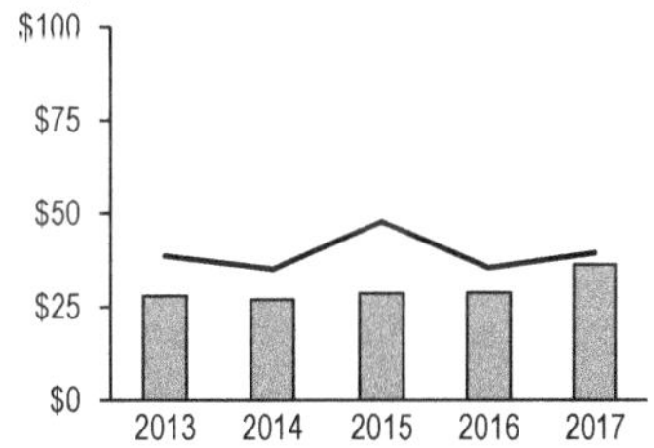

	2013	2014	2015	2016	2017
Concord	$27.88	$27.03	$28.65	$28.77	$36.36
Average	$38.72	$35.13	$47.74	$35.39	$39.44

Tons Collected Curbside per Municipal FTE

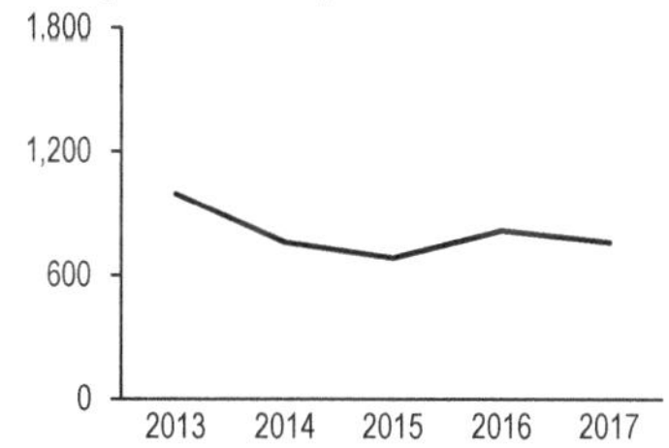

	2013	2014	2015	2016	2017
Concord					
Average	994	758	684	816	757

Effectiveness Measures

Community Set-Out Rate

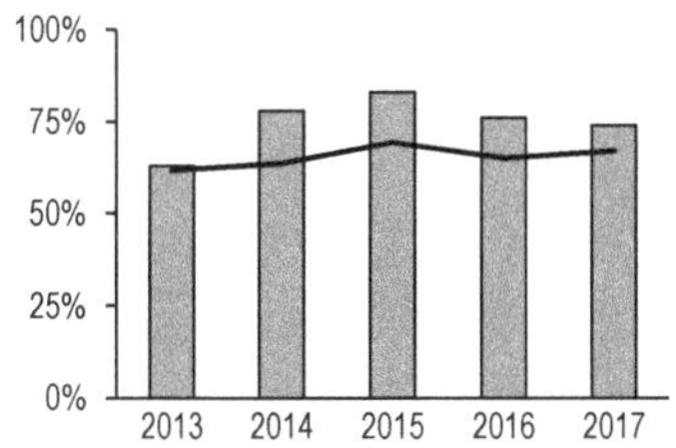

	2013	2014	2015	2016	2017
Concord	63.0%	78.0%	83.0%	76.0%	74.0%
Average	61.9%	63.8%	69.4%	65.1%	67.1%

Tons Recycled as Percentage of Tons Refuse and Recyclables Collected

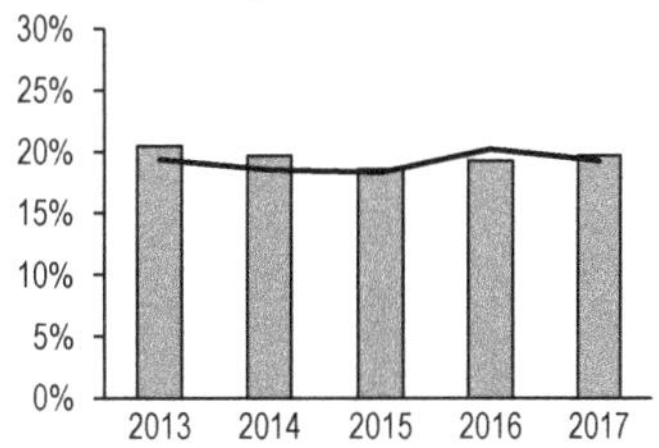

	2013	2014	2015	2016	2017
Concord	20.4%	19.7%	18.6%	19.3%	19.7%
Average	19.4%	18.5%	18.4%	20.2%	19.3%

Goldsboro

Household Recycling

Fiscal Year 2016–17

Explanatory Information

Service Level and Delivery

Goldsboro operates a reycling system with curbside collection for residents. Recycling is picked up the the Solid Waste Division of the Public Works Department. Collection is done every two weeks. Residents pay a fee which covers all solid waste services including recycling. Residents use a ninety-five-gallon container provided by the city.

Goldsboro's recycling is not sorted curbside. Materials collected by the household recycling program include:

- No. 1 and No. 2 plastics
- newspaper
- magazines
- telephone books
- cardboard
- aluminum and steel cans
- glass jars and bottles
- plastic soda bottles and milk jugs
- office paper.

Conditions Affecting Service, Performance, and Costs

The city of Goldsboro joined the Benchmarking Project in July 2017 with the first year of data showing for FY 2016–17.

Goldsboro contracts recyling collection for one small neighborhood where a hill and tight roads make it infeasible to use city trucks.

.

Municipal Profile

Population (OSBM 2016)	34,793
Land Area (Square Miles)	29.35
Persons per Square Mile	1,186
Median Family Income U.S. Census 2010	$33,879

Service Profile

FTE Positions—Collection	4.0
FTE Positions—Other	1.3
Number of City Drop-Off Centers	0
Other Drop-Off Centers	0
Percentage of Service Contracted	0.7%
Collection Frequency	Every 2 weeks
General Collection Location	Curbside
Recyclables Sorted at Curb	No
Collection Points	14,372
Tons of Recyclables Collected	
Curbside	1,085
City Drop-Off Centers	0
Total Tons Collected	1,085
Monthly Service Fee	0
Revenue from Sale of Recyclables	$0
Sale Revenue as Percentage of Cost	NA

Full Cost Profile

Cost Breakdown by Percentage	
Personal Services	51.7%
Operating Costs	48.3%
Capital Costs	0.0%
TOTAL	100.0%
Cost Breakdown in Dollars	
Personal Services	$316,048
Operating Costs	$295,828
Capital Costs	$0
TOTAL	$611,876

Goldsboro

Household Recycling

Key: Goldsboro ▒ Benchmarking Average — Fiscal Years 2013 through 2017

Resource Measures

Recycling Services Cost per Capita

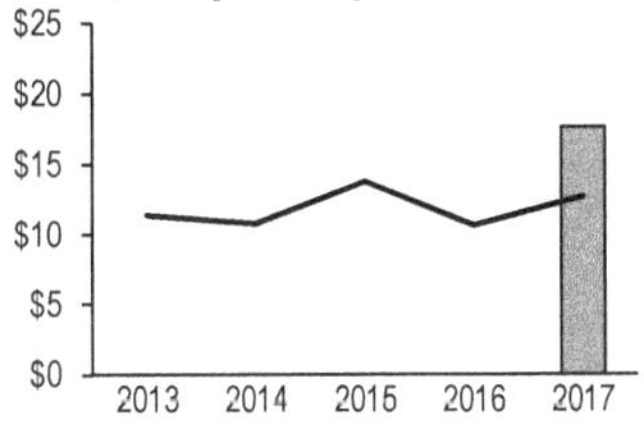

	2013	2014	2015	2016	2017
Goldsboro					$17.59
Average	$11.39	$10.81	$13.79	$10.66	$12.74

Recycling Services FTEs per 10,000 Population

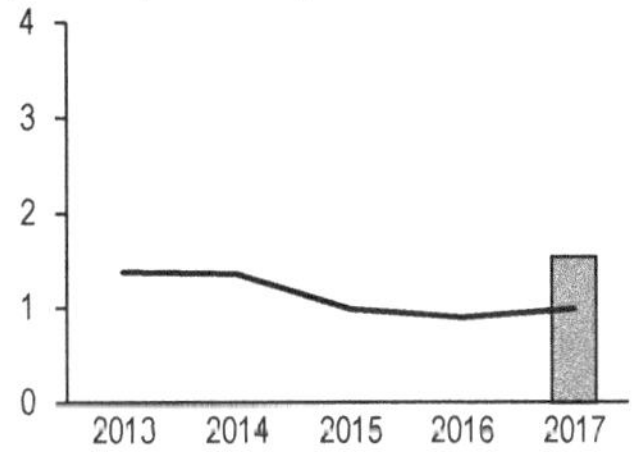

	2013	2014	2015	2016	2017
Goldsboro					1.53
Average	1.37	1.35	0.98	0.89	0.98

Workload Measures

Tons Recyclables Collected per 1,000 Population

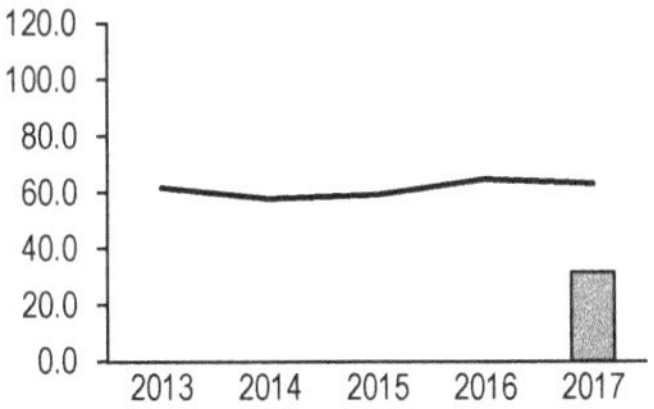

	2013	2014	2015	2016	2017
Goldsboro					31.2
Average	61.4	57.7	58.9	64.4	62.8

Tons Recyclables Collected per 1,000 Collection Points

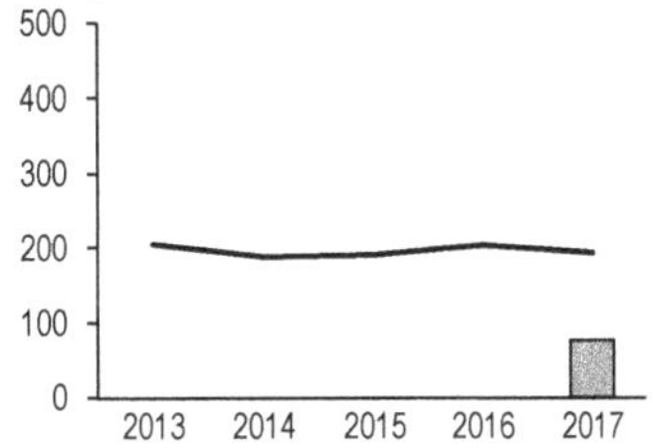

	2013	2014	2015	2016	2017
Goldsboro					75
Average	205	188	190	203	193

Tons Solid Waste Landfilled per 1,000 Population

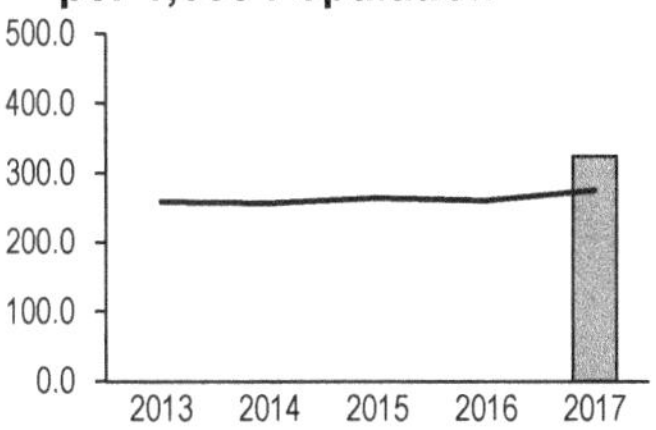

	2013	2014	2015	2016	2017
Goldsboro					323.4
Average	258.5	257.6	264.9	260.6	275.7

Efficiency Measures

Recycling Services Cost per Ton Collected

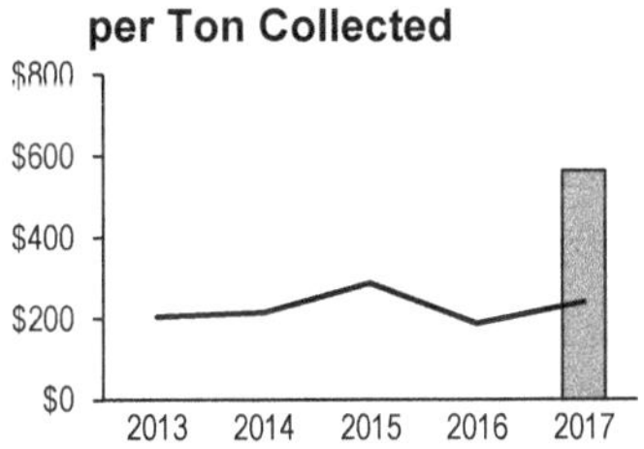

	2013	2014	2015	2016	2017
Goldsboro					$564
Average	$204	$215	$286	$187	$239

Recycling Services Cost per Collection Point

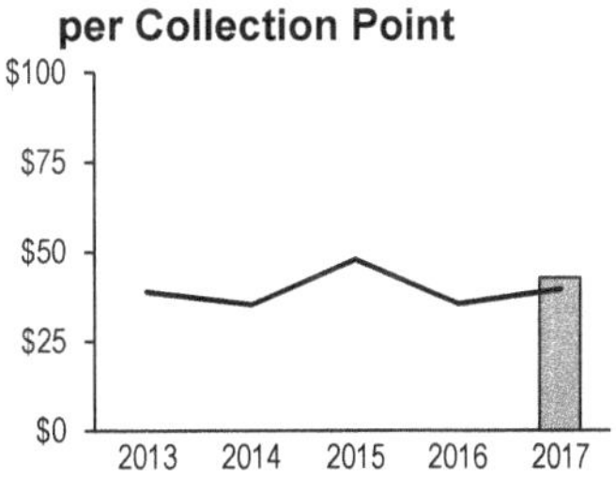

	2013	2014	2015	2016	2017
Goldsboro					$42.57
Average	$38.72	$35.13	$47.74	$35.39	$39.44

Tons Collected Curbside per Municipal FTE

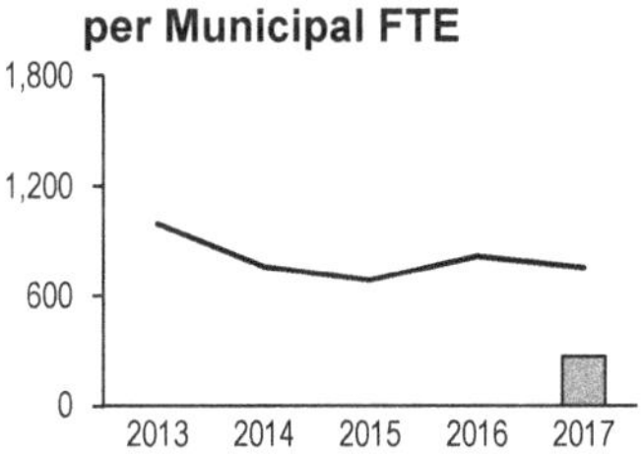

	2013	2014	2015	2016	2017
Goldsboro					271
Average	994	758	684	816	757

Effectiveness Measures

Community Set-Out Rate

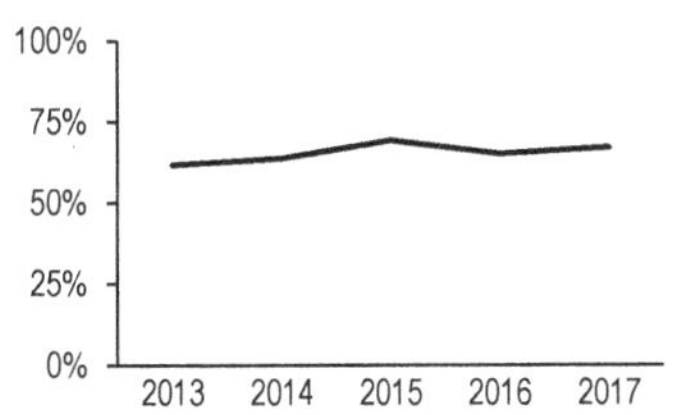

	2013	2014	2015	2016	2017
Goldsboro					
Average	61.9%	63.8%	69.4%	65.1%	67.1%

Tons Recycled as Percentage of Tons Refuse and Recyclables Collected

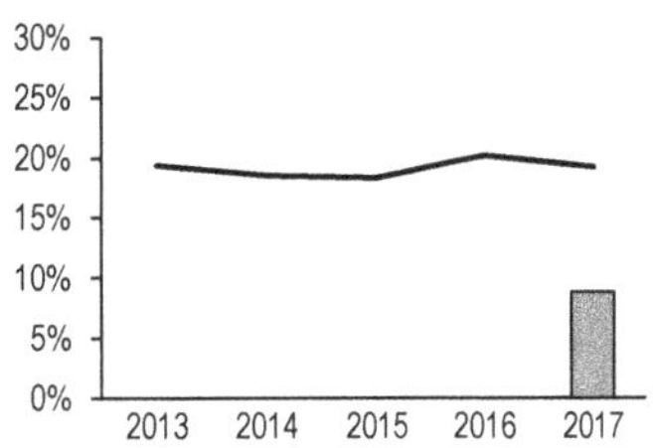

	2013	2014	2015	2016	2017
Goldsboro					8.8%
Average	19.4%	18.5%	18.4%	20.2%	19.3%

Fiscal Year 2016–17

Explanatory Information

Service Level and Delivery
Greensboro operates a voluntary commingled collection process for its recycling customers. Recycling services are provided to the community by means of single ninety-six or sixty-four-gallon automated containers and by green translucent bags. Partnerships also are maintained with fire departments, the county school system, the extension office, and the parks department for providing drop-off sites. There are twenty city-owned drop-off sites, but these collected tons are not reported in Greensboro's data.

Recycling pickup is done ever other week. Recycling materials are not sorted curbside. Instead, they are set out in one container, picked up by an automated-collection crew, and taken to an off-site contractor that sorts and recycles the materials. Greensboro provides the collection pickup and delivery to the contractor's location, while the contractor provides for recovery of materials and disposal of the residuals it is unable to recycle.

Materials collected by Greensboro's household recycling program include:

- No. 1 and No. 2 plastics
- newspaper
- magazines
- telephone books
- cardboard
- aluminum and steel cans
- chipboard (cereal boxes)
- glass jars and bottles
- plastic soda bottles and milk jugs
- office paper
- empty aerosol cans.

Greensboro contracts with a private firm for separation, packaging, and sale of recyclable materials. City payments to the contractor for FY 2016–17 are included in total cost. The contractor pays the city 50 percent of the net proceeds it receives from the sale of recyclable items. The estimated revenues for sale of recyclables for residential recycling for FY 2016–17 was $364,266, partially offsetting program costs. Greensboro gets additional revenues from the sale of recyclables from non-residential sources, but these are not counted here.

Conditions Affecting Service, Performance, and Costs
Greensboro is highly automated in gathering materials from its recycling program.

The set-out rate was based on a manual count done on a bi-weekly basis.

Municipal Profile

Population (OSBM 2016)	284,343
Land Area (Square Miles)	128.72
Persons per Square Mile	2,209
Median Family Income U.S. Census 2010	$52,752

Service Profile

FTE Positions—Collection	15.0
FTE Positions—Other	4.0
Number of City Drop-Off Centers	20
Other Drop-Off Centers	0
Percentage of Service Contracted	0%
Collection Frequency	Every 2 weeks
General Collection Location	Curbside
Recyclables Sorted at Curb	No
Collection Points	89,214
Tons of Recyclables Collected	
Curbside	17,217
City Drop-Off Centers	0
Total Tons Collected	17,217
Monthly Service Fee	0
Revenue from Sale of Recyclables	$364,266
Sale Revenue as Percentage of Cost	13.4%

Full Cost Profile

Cost Breakdown by Percentage	
Personal Services	34.7%
Operating Costs	65.3%
Capital Costs	0.0%
TOTAL	100.0%
Cost Breakdown in Dollars	
Personal Services	$943,766
Operating Costs	$1,779,129
Capital Costs	$0
TOTAL	$2,722,895

Key: Greensboro ▒ Benchmarking Average — Fiscal Years 2013 through 2017

Resource Measures

Recycling Services Cost per Capita

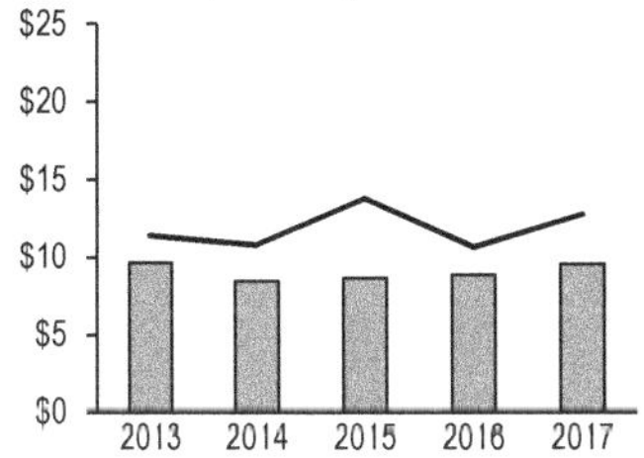

	2013	2014	2015	2016	2017
Greensboro	$9.64	$8.45	$8.66	$8.86	$9.58
Average	$11.39	$10.81	$13.79	$10.66	$12.74

Recycling Services FTEs per 10,000 Population

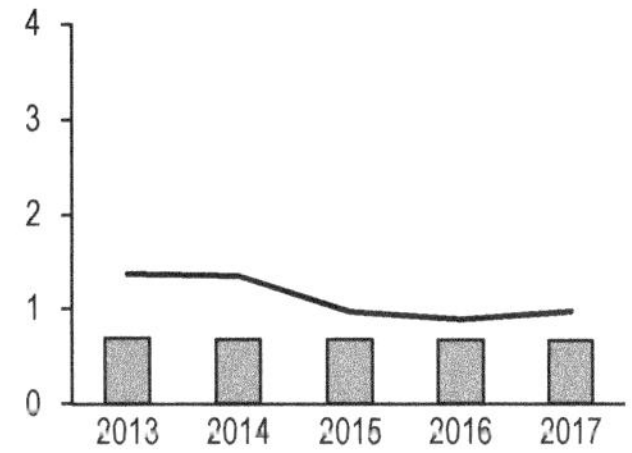

	2013	2014	2015	2016	2017
Greensboro	0.69	0.68	0.68	0.67	0.67
Average	1.37	1.35	0.98	0.89	0.98

Workload Measures

Tons Recyclables Collected per 1,000 Population

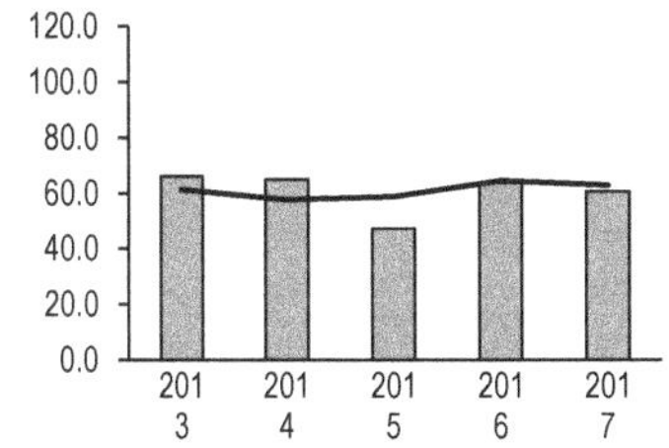

	2013	2014	2015	2016	2017
Greensboro	66.0	64.9	47.1	63.8	60.5
Average	61.4	57.7	58.9	64.4	62.8

Tons Recyclables Collected per 1,000 Collection Points

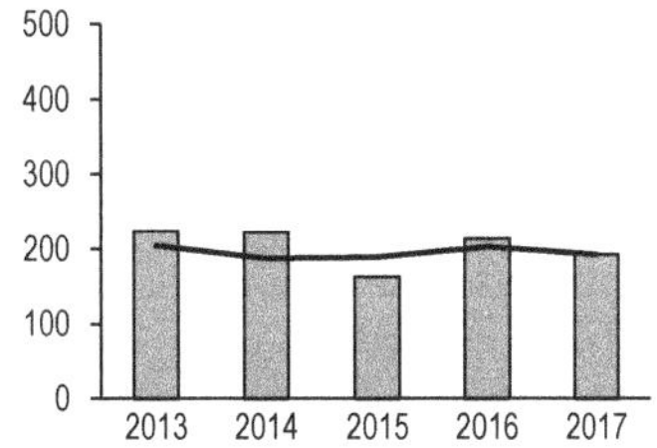

	2013	2014	2015	2016	2017
Greensboro	224	223	163	214	193
Average	205	188	190	203	193

Tons Solid Waste Landfilled per 1,000 Population

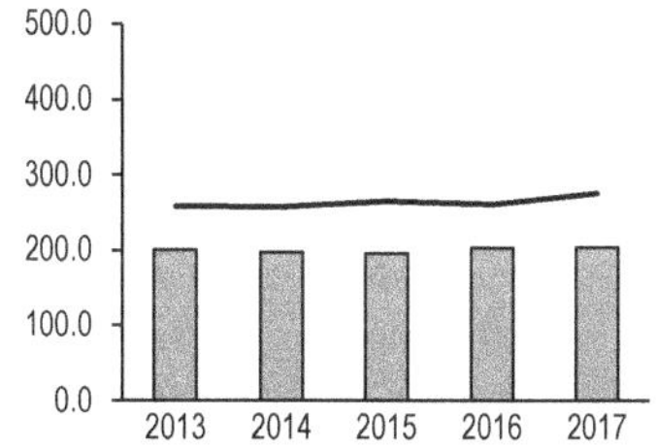

	2013	2014	2015	2016	2017
Greensboro	199.5	196.4	194.7	202.0	202.6
Average	258.5	257.6	264.9	260.6	275.7

Efficiency Measures

Recycling Services Cost per Ton Collected

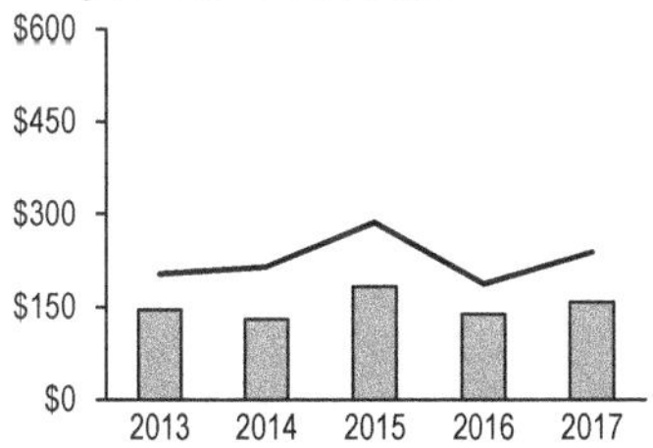

	2013	2014	2015	2016	2017
Greensboro	$146	$130	$184	$139	$158
Average	$204	$215	$286	$187	$239

Recycling Services Cost per Collection Point

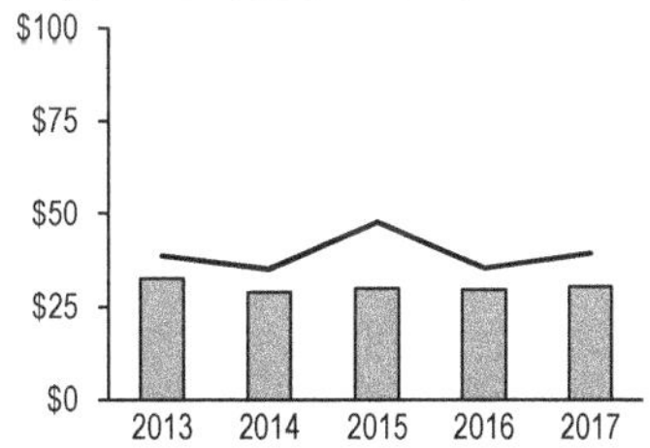

	2013	2014	2015	2016	2017
Greensboro	$32.69	$29.04	$29.98	$29.74	$30.52
Average	$38.72	$35.13	$47.74	$35.39	$39.44

Tons Collected Curbside per Municipal FTE

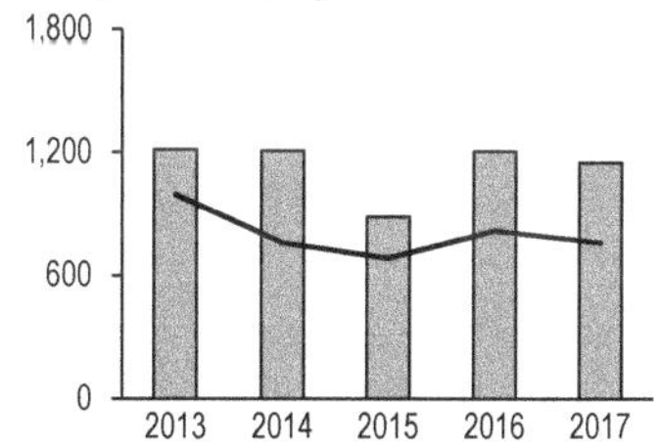

	2013	2014	2015	2016	2017
Greensboro	1,211	1,205	882	1,204	1,148
Average	994	758	684	816	757

Effectiveness Measures

Community Set-Out Rate

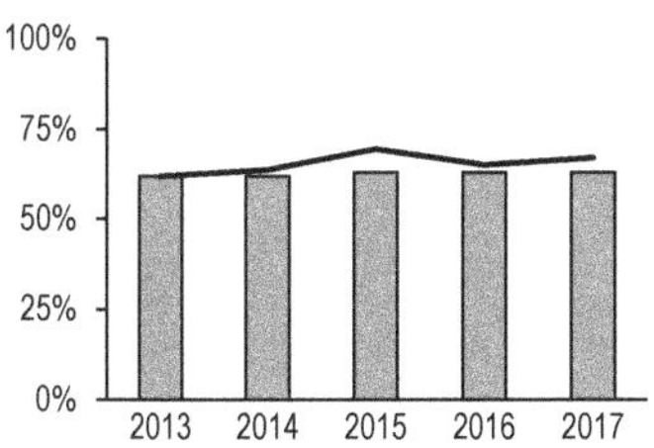

	2013	2014	2015	2016	2017
Greensboro	62.0%	62.0%	63.0%	63.0%	63.0%
Average	61.9%	63.8%	69.4%	65.1%	67.1%

Tons Recycled as Percentage of Tons Refuse and Recyclables Collected

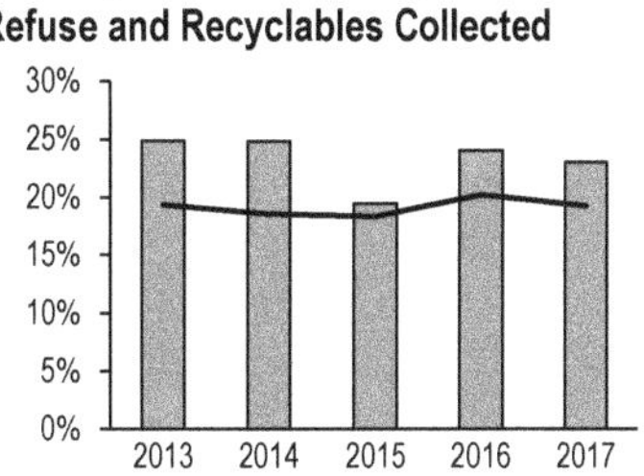

	2013	2014	2015	2016	2017
Greensboro	24.9%	24.8%	19.5%	24.0%	23.0%
Average	19.4%	18.5%	18.4%	20.2%	19.3%

Fiscal Year 2016–17

Explanatory Information

Service Level and Delivery
Greenville offers once-a-week curbside or backyard collection of recyclable materials to its residents through a city-run program. Residents can choose to have backyard collection for a fee. The recycling fee is included in the solid waste fee for residential refuse collection. The recycling materials include:

- newspaper and magazines
- cardboard
- aluminum and steel cans
- No. 1 and No. 2 plastics
- glass of all colors
- white goods.

Greenville's household recycling program also uses three city-owned drop-off recycling centers and over 200 other sites connected to multi-family complexes. Tonnage and cost for these other drop-off sites are not included in the performance and cost data.

Conditions Affecting Service, Performance, and Costs
Greenville does not track the number of households that set out recyclables on a weekly basis.

The apparent drop in the graphs for collected tonnage in FY 2013–14 reports only items which were taken to the local material recovery facility. The drop appears to reflect more accurate reporting, excluding items such as concrete, tree limbs, and other material rather than actual service change in recyclables.

Greenville introduced new recycling carts in FY 2013–14, which generated service complaints during the transition period.

Municipal Profile

Population (OSBM 2016)	87,989
Land Area (Square Miles)	35.41
Persons per Square Mile	2,485
Median Family Income U.S. Census 2010	$50,395

Service Profile

FTE Positions—Collection	11.0
FTE Positions—Other	1.2
Number of City Drop-Off Centers	224
Other Drop-Off Centers	0
Percentage of Service Contracted	0%
Collection Frequency	1 x week
General Collection Location	Curbside
Recyclables Sorted at Curb	No
Collection Points	19,294
Tons of Recyclables Collected	
Curbside	4,394
City Drop-Off Centers	0
Total Tons Collected	4,394
Monthly Service Fee	0
Revenue from Sale of Recyclables	$0
Sale Revenue as Percentage of Cost	NA

Full Cost Profile

Cost Breakdown by Percentage	
Personal Services	37.8%
Operating Costs	46.1%
Capital Costs	16.1%
TOTAL	100.0%
Cost Breakdown in Dollars	
Personal Services	$763,054
Operating Costs	$929,610
Capital Costs	$325,614
TOTAL	$2,018,278

Greenville — Household Recycling

Key: Greenville ▩ Benchmarking Average — Fiscal Years 2013 through 2017

Resource Measures

Recycling Services Cost per Capita

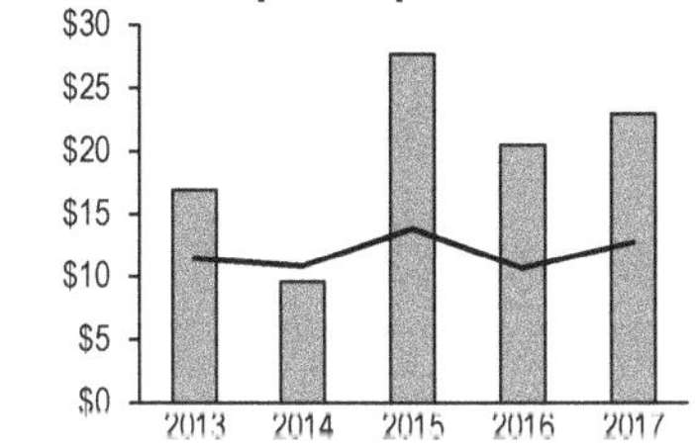

	2013	2014	2015	2016	2017
Greenville	$16.92	$9.61	$27.67	$20.49	$22.94
Average	$11.39	$10.81	$13.79	$10.66	$12.74

Recycling Services FTEs per 10,000 Population

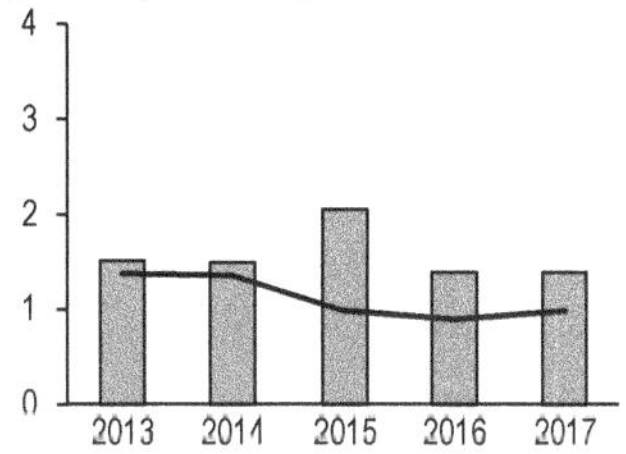

	2013	2014	2015	2016	2017
Greenville	1.51	1.49	2.06	1.39	1.39
Average	1.37	1.35	0.98	0.89	0.98

Workload Measures

Tons Recyclables Collected per 1,000 Population

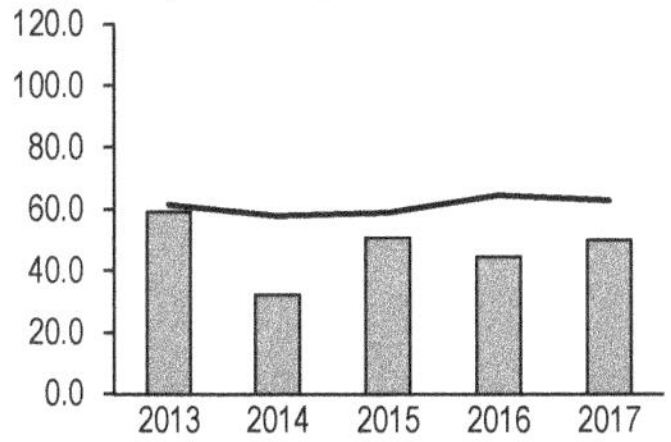

	2013	2014	2015	2016	2017
Greenville	59.2	32.3	50.8	44.6	49.9
Average	61.4	57.7	58.9	64.4	62.8

Tons Recyclables Collected per 1,000 Collection Points

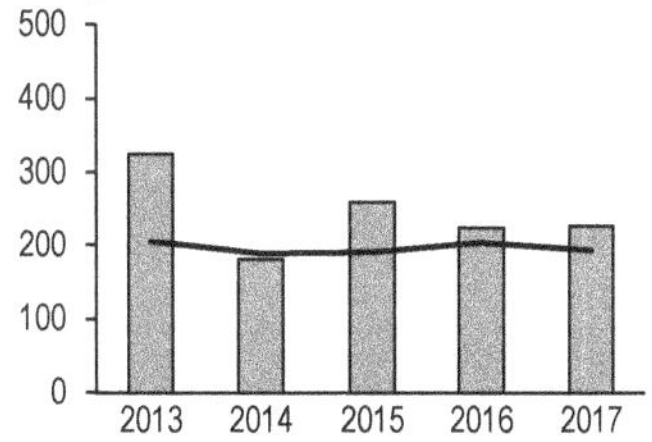

	2013	2014	2015	2016	2017
Greenville	325	181	259	225	228
Average	205	188	190	203	193

Tons Solid Waste Landfilled per 1,000 Population

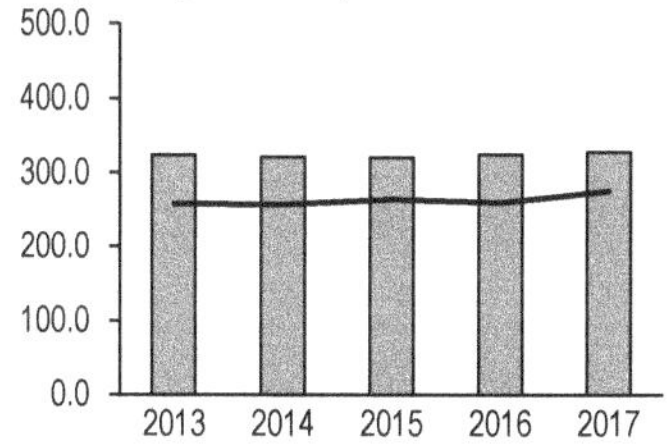

	2013	2014	2015	2016	2017
Greenville	323.7	320.4	319.7	324.7	327.5
Average	258.5	257.6	264.9	260.6	275.7

Efficiency Measures

Recycling Services Cost per Ton Collected

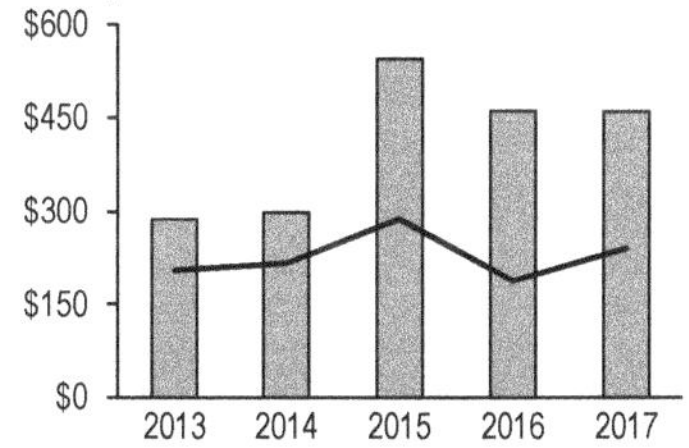

	2013	2014	2015	2016	2017
Greenville	$286	$297	$544	$460	$459
Average	$204	$215	$286	$187	$239

Recycling Services Cost per Collection Point

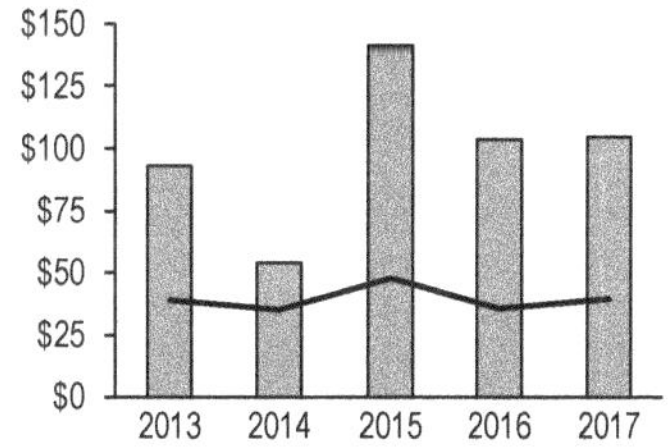

	2013	2014	2015	2016	2017
Greenville	$92.80	$53.89	$141.1	$103.5	$104.6
Average	$38.72	$35.13	$47.74	$35.39	$39.44

Tons Collected Curbside per Municipal FTE

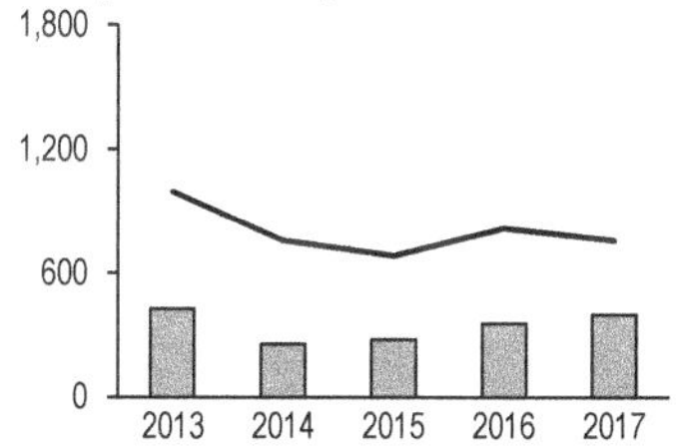

	2013	2014	2015	2016	2017
Greenville	425	256	278	356	399
Average	994	758	684	816	757

Effectiveness Measures

Community Set-Out Rate

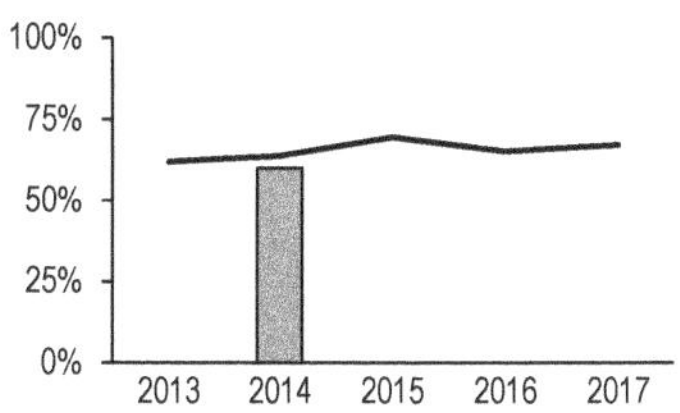

	2013	2014	2015	2016	2017
Greenville		60.0%			
Average	61.9%	63.8%	69.4%	65.1%	67.1%

Tons Recycled as Percentage of Tons Refuse and Recyclables Collected

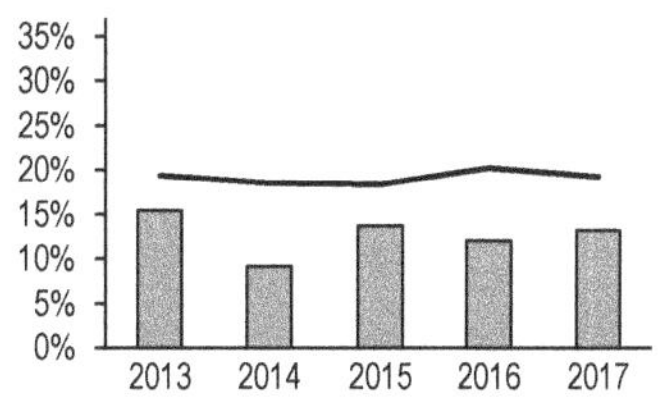

	2013	2014	2015	2016	2017
Greenville	15.5%	9.2%	13.7%	12.1%	13.2%
Average	19.4%	18.5%	18.4%	20.2%	19.3%

Fiscal Year 2016–17

Explanatory Information

Service Level and Delivery
Hickory offers curbside collection every other week of recyclable materials to its residents through a contractual agreement. The recycling materials collected include:

- newspaper and magazines
- aluminum and steel cans
- No. 1 and No. 2 plastics
- glass—all colors
- phone books and junk mail.

Hickory's household recycling program also uses two drop-off recycling centers. One is staffed, and the other is not. These centers collect antifreeze and oil in addition to the same household materials that are collected at the curb. Tonnage and costs for this service are included in the performance and cost data.

A separate commercial recycling program that services businesses and multi-family units is operated by the city. The program utilizes city workers and equipment to collect cardboard and paper in addition to the curbside materials. The performance and cost data do not include the commercial program.

The city charges residents a monthly fee for recycling, which is included in the monthly solid waste fee. In FY 2016–17 the city collected $67,127 in revenue from the sale of recyclables partially offsetting program costs.

Conditions Affecting Service, Performance, and Costs
The set-out rate is calculated on a monthly basis by the contractor. While not tracked, missed recycling pickups are minimal and average less than one per month.

Municipal Profile

Population (OSBM 2016)	40,453
Land Area (Square Miles)	29.90
Persons per Square Mile	1,353
Median Family Income U.S. Census 2010	$54,093

Service Profile

FTE Positions—Collection	0.5 City
FTE Positions—Other	0.27 City
Number of City Drop-Off Centers	2
Other Drop-Off Centers	0
Percentage of Service Contracted	92%
Collection Frequency	Every 2 weeks
General Collection Location	Curbside
Recyclables Sorted at Curb	No
Collection Points	12,200
Tons of Recyclables Collected	
Curbside	2,409
City Drop-Off Centers	213
Total Tons Collected	2,622
Monthly Service Fee	0
Revenue from Sale of Recyclables	$67,127
Sale Revenue as Percentage of Cost	18.5%

Full Cost Profile

Cost Breakdown by Percentage	
Personal Services	9.7%
Operating Costs	88.5%
Capital Costs	1.8%
TOTAL	100.0%
Cost Breakdown in Dollars	
Personal Services	$35,121
Operating Costs	$320,698
Capital Costs	$6,572
TOTAL	$362,391

Hickory

Household Recycling

Key: Hickory ▒ Benchmarking Average — Fiscal Years 2013 through 2017

Resource Measures

Recycling Services Cost per Capita

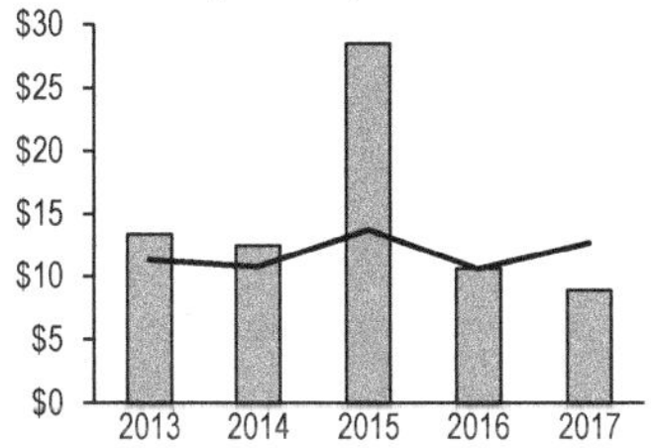

	2013	2014	2015	2016	2017
Hickory	$13.43	$12.53	$28.56	$10.68	$8.96
Average	$11.39	$10.81	$13.79	$10.66	$12.74

Recycling Services FTEs per 10,000 Population

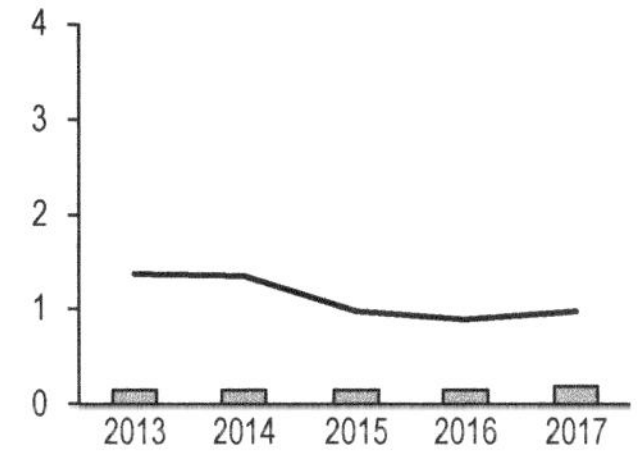

	2013	2014	2015	2016	2017
Hickory	0.15	0.15	0.15	0.15	0.19
Average	1.37	1.35	0.98	0.89	0.98

Workload Measures

Tons Recyclables Collected per 1,000 Population

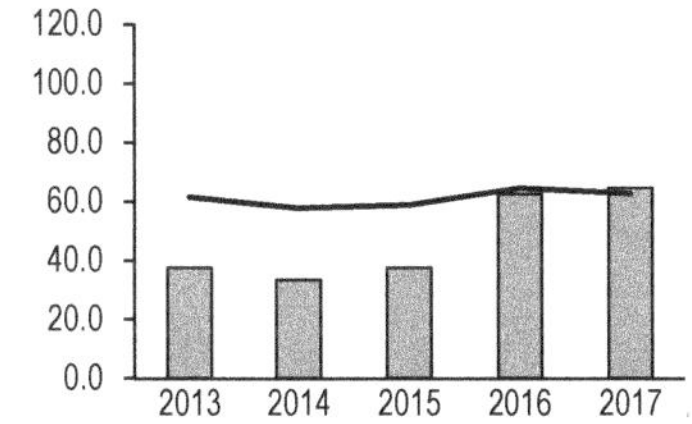

	2013	2014	2015	2016	2017
Hickory	37.4	33.2	37.4	62.5	64.8
Average	61.4	57.7	58.9	64.4	62.8

Tons Recyclables Collected per 1,000 Collection Points

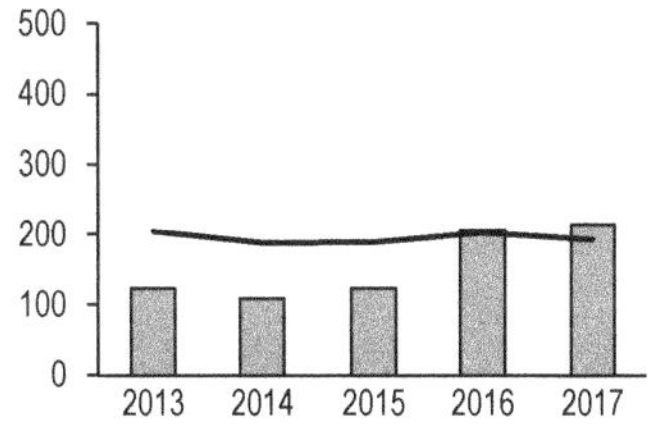

	2013	2014	2015	2016	2017
Hickory	124	110	124	207	215
Average	205	188	190	203	193

Tons Solid Waste Landfilled per 1,000 Population

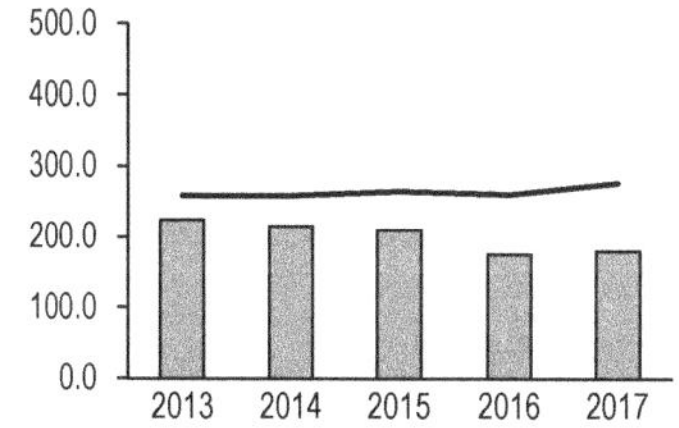

	2013	2014	2015	2016	2017
Hickory	224.3	214.9	210.0	175.0	180.3
Average	258.5	257.6	264.9	260.6	275.7

Efficiency Measures

Recycling Services Cost per Ton Collected

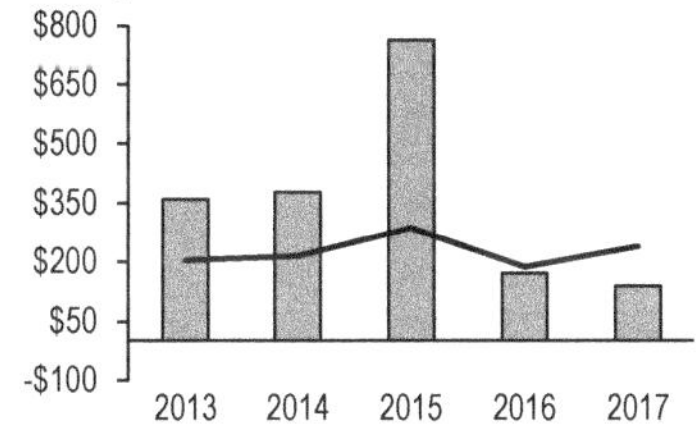

	2013	2014	2015	2016	2017
Hickory	$359	$377	$763	$171	$138
Average	$204	$215	$286	$187	$239

Recycling Services Cost per Collection Point

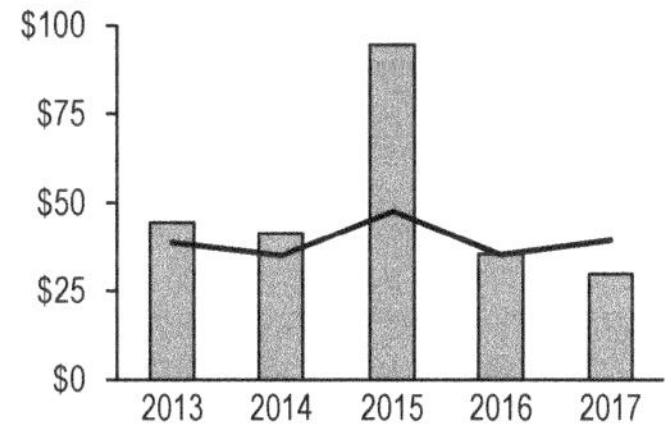

	2013	2014	2015	2016	2017
Hickory	$44.44	$41.32	$94.41	$35.34	$29.70
Average	$38.72	$35.13	$47.74	$35.39	$39.44

Tons Collected Curbside per Municipal FTE

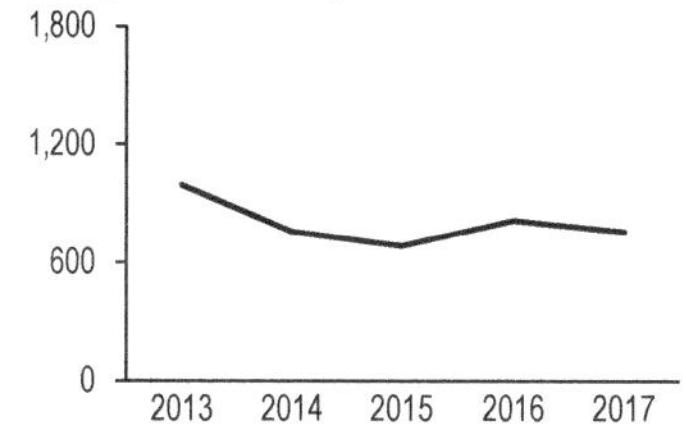

	2013	2014	2015	2016	2017
Hickory					
Average	994	758	684	816	757

Effectiveness Measures

Community Set-Out Rate

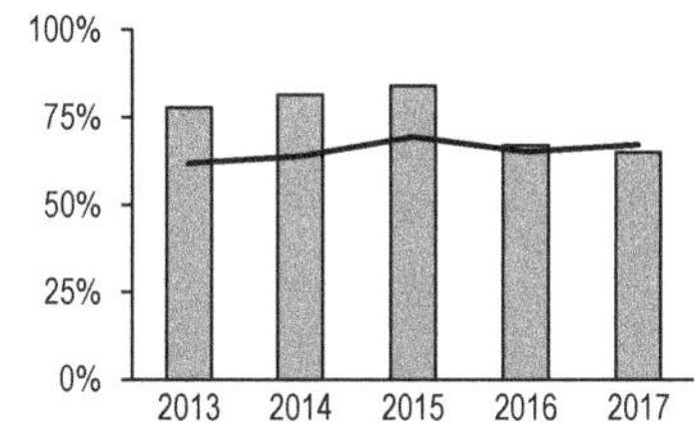

	2013	2014	2015	2016	2017
Hickory	77.8%	81.4%	84.0%	67.0%	65.0%
Average	61.9%	63.8%	69.4%	65.1%	67.1%

Tons Recycled as Percentage of Tons Refuse and Recyclables Collected

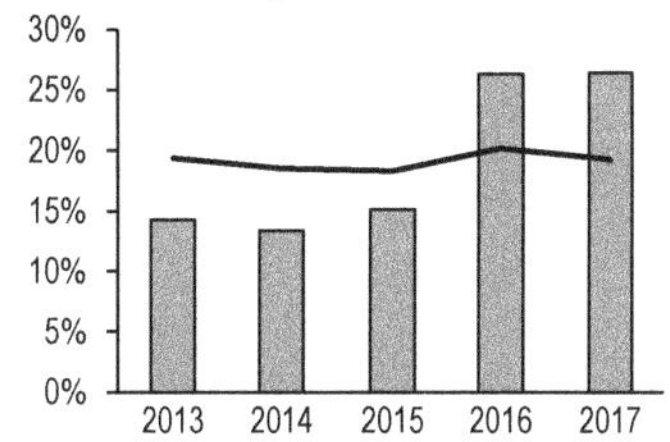

	2013	2014	2015	2016	2017
Hickory	14.3%	13.4%	15.1%	26.3%	26.4%
Average	19.4%	18.5%	18.4%	20.2%	19.3%

Fiscal Year 2016–17

Explanatory Information

Service Level and Delivery
High Point offers curbside collection every other week. Large ninety-six-gallon containers are provided to customers. Additional carts may be purchased. The recycling program is a city function.

Recyclables are collected using four recycling crews that work in the Environmental Services Division. The pickup trucks are automated with one driver. A truck for special circumstances, such as downtown collection, uses a crew with a driver and one laborer. There are sixteen drop-off sites throughout the city and a number of multi-family sites at which the city collects. Materials collected include:

- plastic
- glass
- metal and aluminum cans
- magazines
- newspaper
- phone books
- cardboard
- mixed paper.

The city also operates and owns a material recovery facility (MRF). There is a buy-back center at the MRF to service individuals selling recyclables.

Conditions Affecting Service, Performance, and Costs
The city used a random sample to determine the set-out rate.

High Point has been working on improving efficiency and processing of recyclables for resale. Sales of recyclable materials were $469,148 for the year, partially offsetting program costs.

In addition to the tons of recyclables collected by the city, a further 1,056 tons of cardboard was collected by private haulers during the Furniture Market held in High Point. These tons are not included in the reported totals and the costs are solely born by the private entities involved. The city allows private haulers to bring this cardboard to the MRF to keep it off the streets during the Furniture Market.

High Point is fully automated in its pickups, other than those involving special requests.

Municipal Profile

Population (OSBM 2016)	110,244
Land Area (Square Miles)	55.14
Persons per Square Mile	1,999
Median Family Income U.S. Census 2010	$49,720

Service Profile

FTE Positions—Collection	6.0
FTE Positions—Other	1.5
Number of City Drop-Off Centers	16
Other Drop-Off Centers	0
Percentage of Service Contracted	0%
Collection Frequency	Every 2 weeks
General Collection Location	Curbside
Recyclables Sorted at Curb	No
Collection Points	42,418
Tons of Recyclables Collected	
Curbside	10,424
City Drop-Off Centers	782
Total Tons Collected	11,206
Monthly Service Fee	$14.00
Revenue from Sale of Recyclables	$469,148
Sale Revenue as Percentage of Cost	45.1%

Full Cost Profile

Cost Breakdown by Percentage	
Personal Services	37.4%
Operating Costs	34.4%
Capital Costs	28.1%
TOTAL	100.0%
Cost Breakdown in Dollars	
Personal Services	$389,062
Operating Costs	$357,975
Capital Costs	$292,334
TOTAL	$1,039,371

High Point

Household Recycling

Key: High Point ▒ Benchmarking Average — Fiscal Years 2013 through 2017

Resource Measures

Recycling Services Cost per Capita

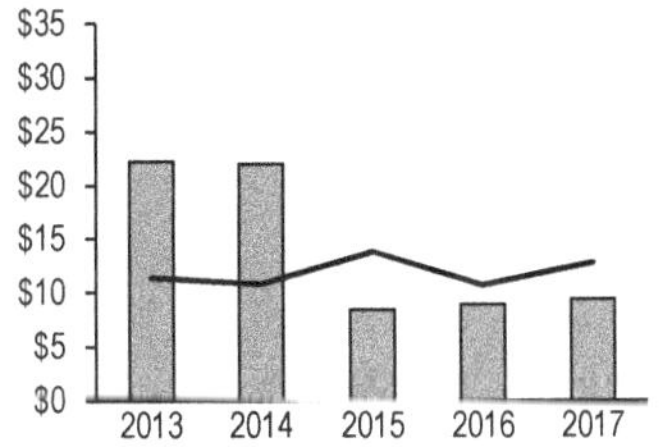

	2013	2014	2015	2016	2017
High Point	$22.29	$22.04	$8.46	$8.94	$9.43
Average	$11.39	$10.81	$13.79	$10.66	$12.74

Recycling Services FTEs per 10,000 Population

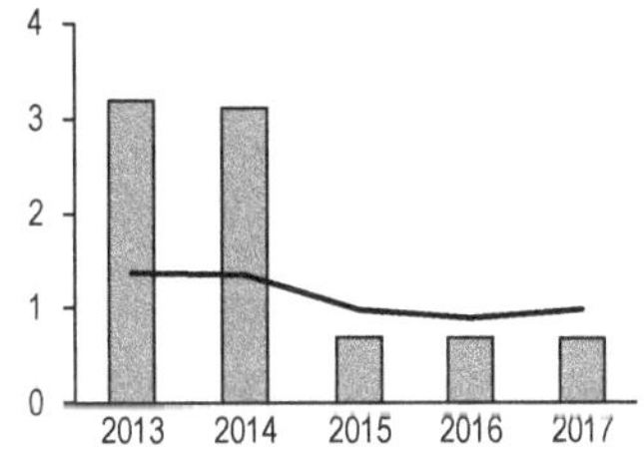

	2013	2014	2015	2016	2017
High Point	3.20	3.11	0.69	0.68	0.68
Average	1.37	1.35	0.98	0.89	0.98

Workload Measures

Tons Recyclables Collected per 1,000 Population

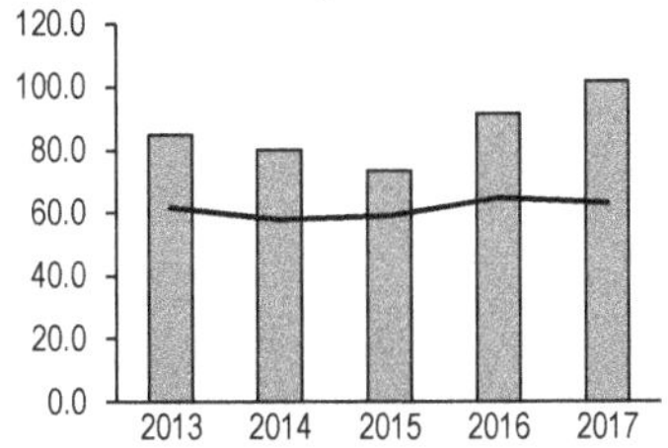

	2013	2014	2015	2016	2017
High Point	84.8	80.0	73.3	91.4	101.6
Average	61.4	57.7	58.9	64.4	62.8

Tons Recyclables Collected per 1,000 Collection Points

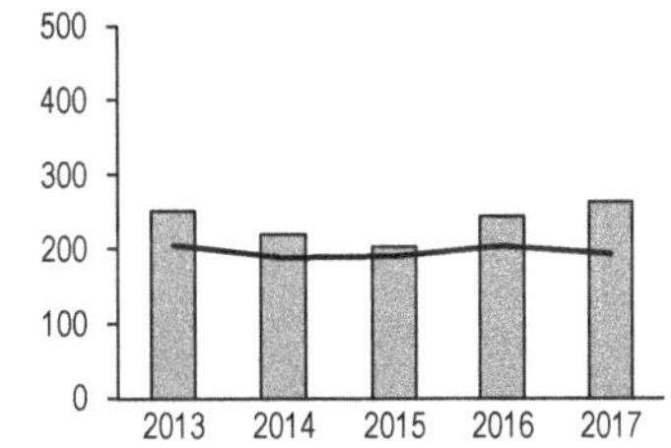

	2013	2014	2015	2016	2017
High Point	251	220	203	243	264
Average	205	188	190	203	193

Tons Solid Waste Landfilled per 1,000 Population

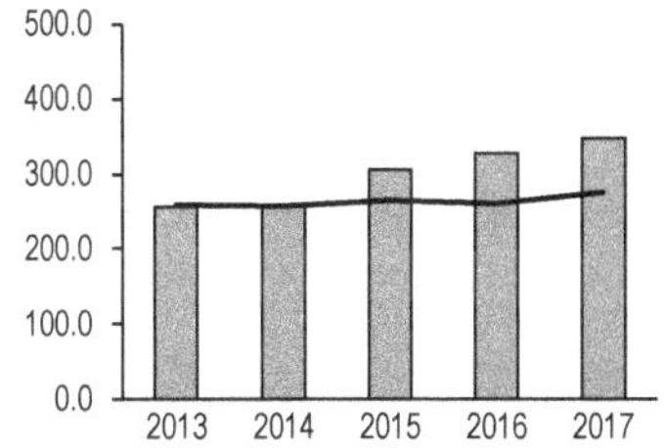

	2013	2014	2015	2016	2017
High Point	256.0	256.5	305.7	327.4	347.6
Average	258.5	257.6	264.9	260.6	275.7

Efficiency Measures

Recycling Services Cost per Ton Collected

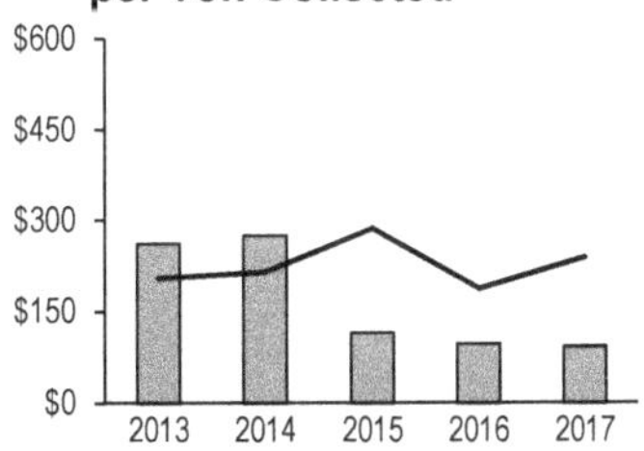

	2013	2014	2015	2016	2017
High Point	$263	$275	$115	$98	$93
Average	$204	$215	$286	$187	$239

Recycling Services Cost per Collection Point

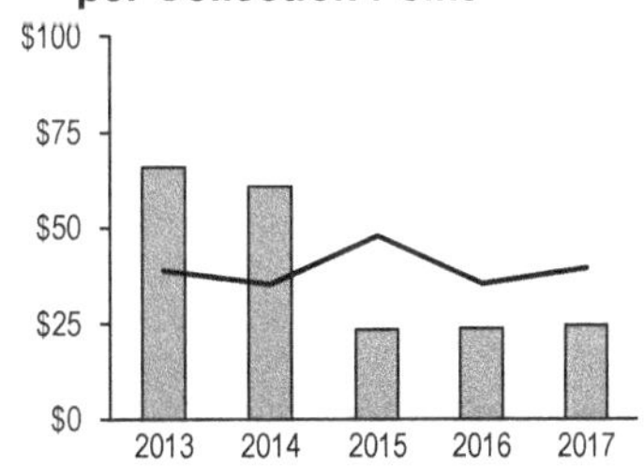

	2013	2014	2015	2016	2017
High Point	$65.99	$60.67	$23.40	$23.80	$24.50
Average	$38.72	$35.13	$47.74	$35.39	$39.44

Tons Collected Curbside per Municipal FTE

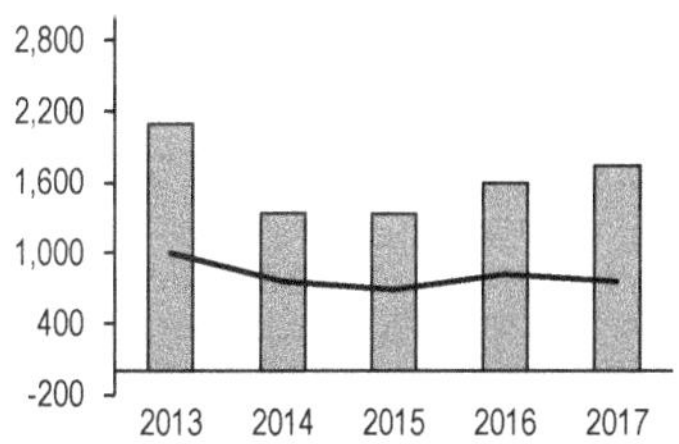

	2013	2014	2015	2016	2017
High Point	2,093	1,329	1,326	1,592	1,737
Average	994	758	684	816	757

Effectiveness Measures

Community Set-Out Rate

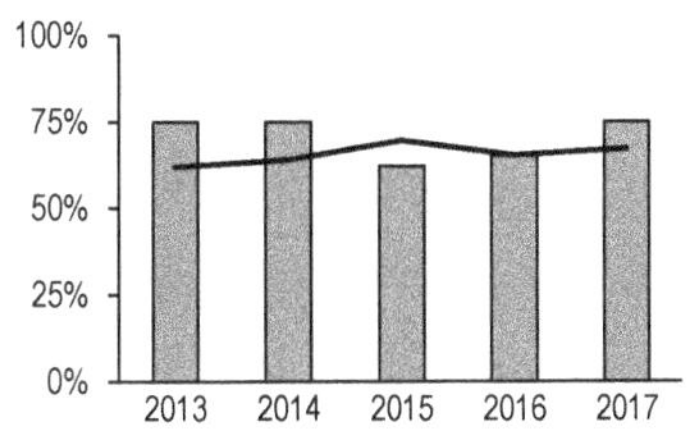

	2013	2014	2015	2016	2017
High Point	75.0%	75.0%	62.0%	65.0%	75.0%
Average	61.9%	63.8%	69.4%	65.1%	67.1%

Tons Recycled as Percentage of Tons Refuse and Recyclables Collected

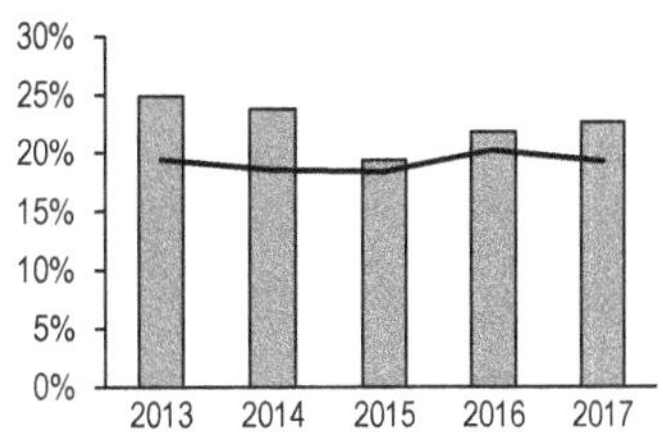

	2013	2014	2015	2016	2017
High Point	24.9%	23.8%	19.3%	21.8%	22.6%
Average	19.4%	18.5%	18.4%	20.2%	19.3%

Fiscal Year 2016–17

Explanatory Information

Service Level and Delivery
Raleigh provides curbside collection of recyclables every other week. Four drop-off centers for use by all residents and small businesses are also available. Customers are allowed two ninety-five-gallon carts. A few townhome locations use smaller eighteen-gallon bins due to the difficulty of moving carts to a pickup location.

Recyclables collected include:

- plastic
- glass
- metal and aluminum cans
- magazines
- newspaper
- phone books
- cardboard
- mixed paper.

The city received revenue from resale of recyclables of $332,354 during the fiscal year offsetting some program costs.

Conditions Affecting Service, Performance, and Costs
Raleigh rejoined the Benchmarking Project in July 2016 with the first year of data showing for FY 2015–16.

Municipal Profile

Population (OSBM 2016)	448,706
Land Area (Square Miles)	145.57
Persons per Square Mile	3,083
Median Family Income U.S. Census 2010	$68,678

Service Profile

FTE Positions—Collection	37.0
FTE Positions—Other	2.0
Number of City Drop-Off Centers	2
Other Drop-Off Centers	2
Percentage of Service Contracted	0%
Collection Frequency	Every 2 weeks
General Collection Location	Curbside
Recyclables Sorted at Curb	No
Collection Points	185,746
Tons of Recyclables Collected	
Curbside	27,557
City Drop-Off Centers	855
Total Tons Collected	28,412
Monthly Service Fee	$2.60
Revenue from Sale of Recyclables	$332,354
Sale Revenue as Percentage of Cost	4.3%

Full Cost Profile

Cost Breakdown by Percentage	
Personal Services	27.1%
Operating Costs	40.0%
Capital Costs	32.9%
TOTAL	100.0%
Cost Breakdown in Dollars	
Personal Services	$2,117,128
Operating Costs	$3,118,117
Capital Costs	$2,569,755
TOTAL	$7,805,000

Raleigh

Household Recycling

Key: Raleigh ▒ Benchmarking Average — Fiscal Years 2013 through 2017

Resource Measures

Recycling Services Cost per Capita

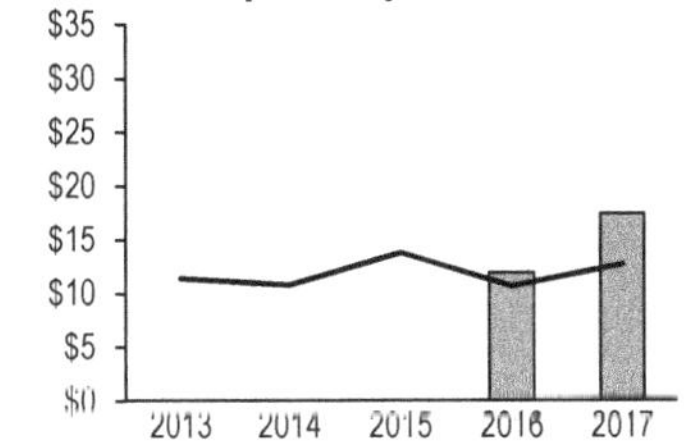

	2013	2014	2015	2016	2017
Raleigh				$11.90	$17.39
Average	$11.39	$10.81	$13.79	$10.66	$12.74

Recycling Services FTEs per 10,000 Population

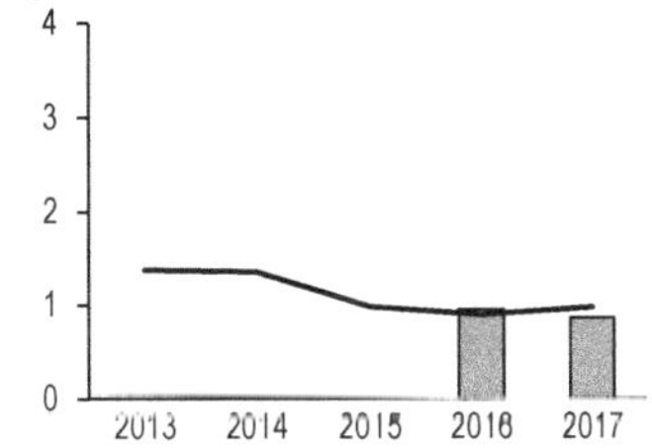

	2013	2014	2015	2016	2017
Raleigh				0.95	0.87
Average	1.37	1.35	0.98	0.89	0.98

Workload Measures

Tons Recyclables Collected per 1,000 Population

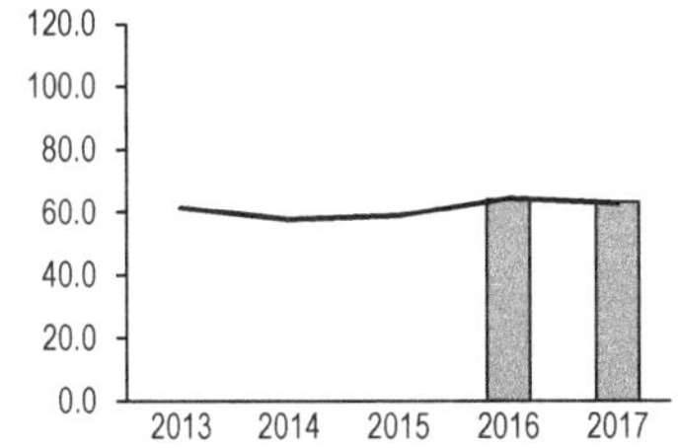

	2013	2014	2015	2016	2017
Raleigh				64.1	63.3
Average	61.4	57.7	58.9	64.4	62.8

Tons Recyclables Collected per 1,000 Collection Points

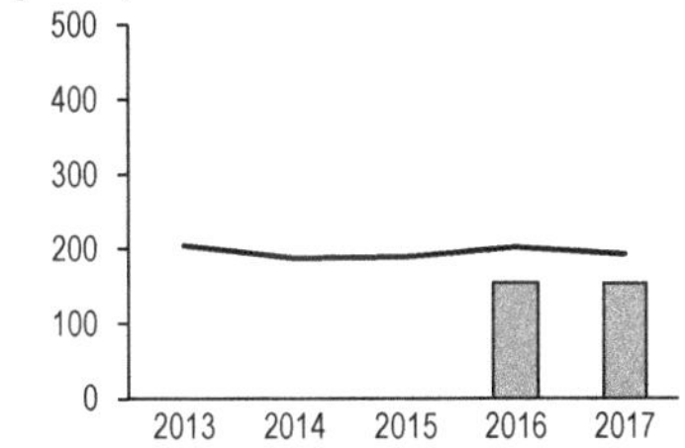

	2013	2014	2015	2016	2017
Raleigh				154	153
Average	205	188	190	203	193

Tons Solid Waste Landfilled per 1,000 Population

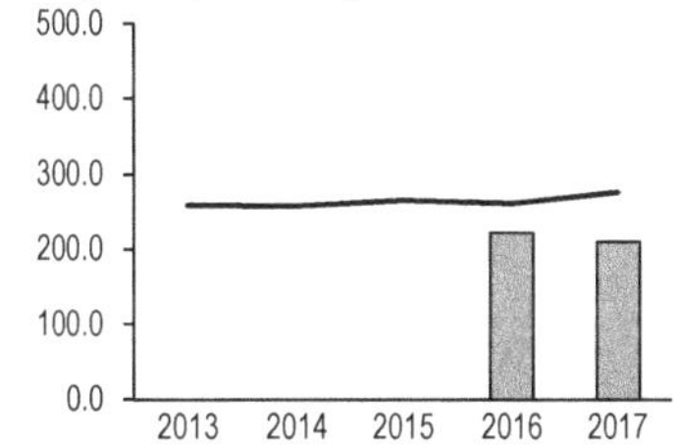

	2013	2014	2015	2016	2017
Raleigh				222.4	210.1
Average	258.5	257.6	264.9	260.6	275.7

Efficiency Measures

Recycling Services Cost per Ton Collected

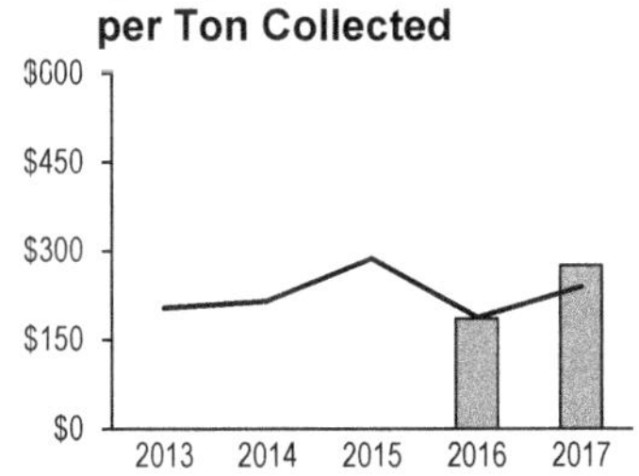

	2013	2014	2015	2016	2017
Raleigh				$186	$275
Average	$204	$215	$286	$187	$239

Recycling Services Cost per Collection Point

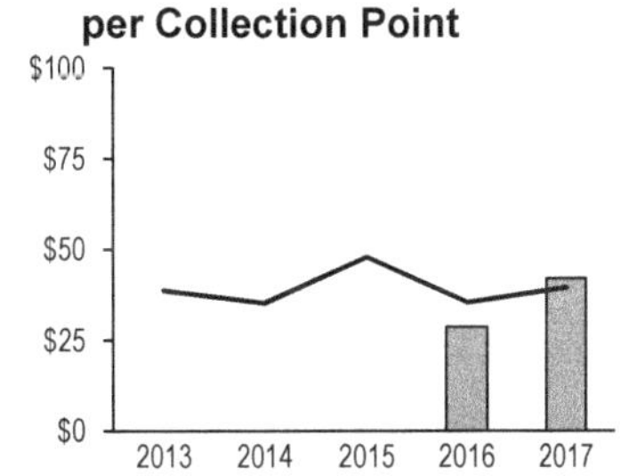

	2013	2014	2015	2016	2017
Raleigh				$28.65	$42.02
Average	$38.72	$35.13	$47.74	$35.39	$39.44

Tons Collected Curbside per Municipal FTE

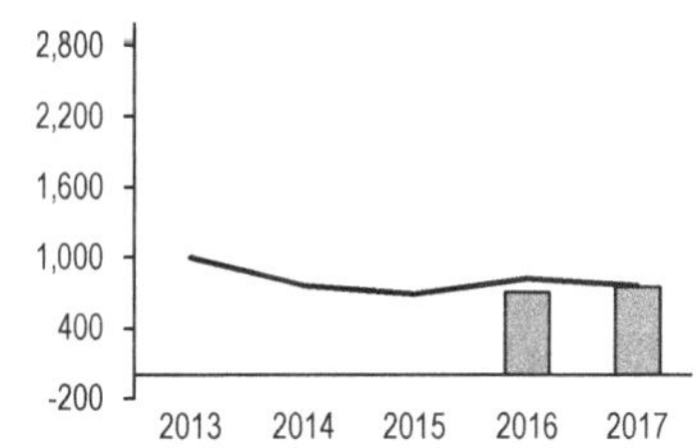

	2013	2014	2015	2016	2017
Raleigh				702	745
Average	994	758	684	816	757

Effectiveness Measures

Community Set-Out Rate

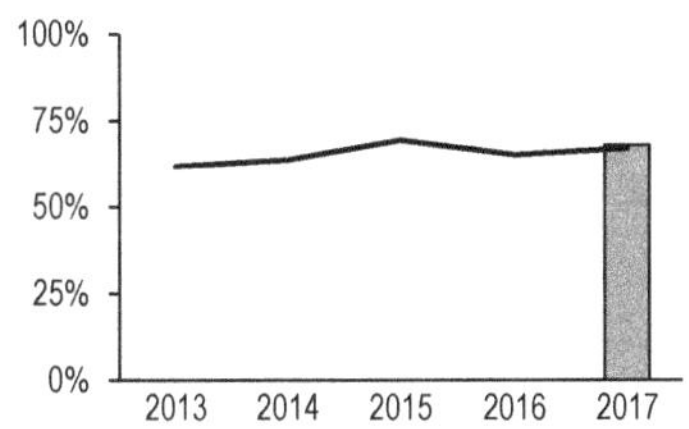

	2013	2014	2015	2016	2017
Raleigh					68.0%
Average	61.9%	63.8%	69.4%	65.1%	67.1%

Tons Recycled as Percentage of Tons Refuse and Recyclables Collected

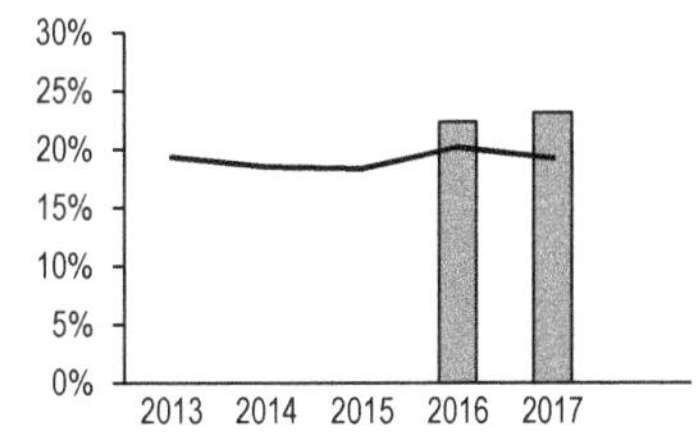

	2013	2014	2015	2016	2017
Raleigh				22.4%	23.2%
Average	19.4%	18.5%	18.4%	20.2%	19.3%

Fiscal Year 2016–17

Explanatory Information

Service Level and Delivery

Salisbury provides every other week curbside collection of recyclable materials from households. The city charged a monthly recycling fee of $4.03 in FY 2016–17. Through the city contractor residents are provided with a ninety-six-gallon recycling roll-out container. The city contracts 100 percent of its recycling program. Recyclables are collected by the contractor and taken to the recycling site.
The recyclable materials collected include:

- glass (all colors)
- newspaper
- magazines and catalogs
- mixed paper and mail
- telephone books
- cardboard—broken down and cereal boxes
- all plastics
- aluminum cans
- steel cans.

Conditions Affecting Service, Performance, and Costs

The set-out rate was reported monthly by the contractor. The city reserves the right to conduct unannounced follow-up inspections of the collection process.

Municipal Profile

Population (OSBM 2016)	34,459
Land Area (Square Miles)	22.28
Persons per Square Mile	1,547
Median Family Income U.S. Census 2010	$40,192

Service Profile

FTE Positions—Collection	Contractor
FTE Positions—Other	Contractor
Number of City Drop-Off Centers	0
Other Drop-Off Centers	0
Percentage of Service Contracted	100%
Collection Frequency	Every 2 weeks
General Collection Location	Curbside
Recyclables Sorted at Curb	No
Collection Points	11,095
Tons of Recyclables Collected	
Curbside	1,581
City Drop-Off Centers	0
Total Tons Collected	1,581
Monthly Service Fee	$0.00
Revenue from Sale of Recyclables	$0
Sale Revenue as Percentage of Cost	NA

Full Cost Profile

Cost Breakdown by Percentage	
Personal Services	0.0%
Operating Costs	100.0%
Capital Costs	0.0%
TOTAL	100.0%
Cost Breakdown in Dollars	
Personal Services	$0
Operating Costs	$319,466
Capital Costs	$0
TOTAL	$319,466

Key: Salisbury ▒ Benchmarking Average — Fiscal Years 2013 through 2017

Resource Measures

Recycling Services Cost per Capita

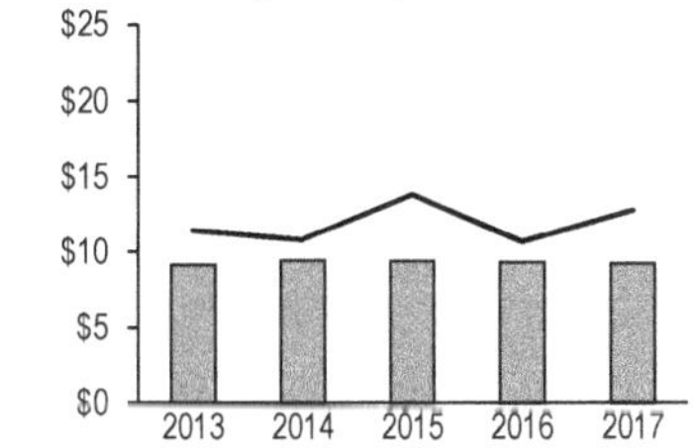

	2013	2014	2015	2016	2017
Salisbury	$9.18	$9.45	$9.42	$9.32	$9.27
Average	$11.39	$10.81	$13.79	$10.66	$12.74

Recycling Services FTEs per 10,000 Population

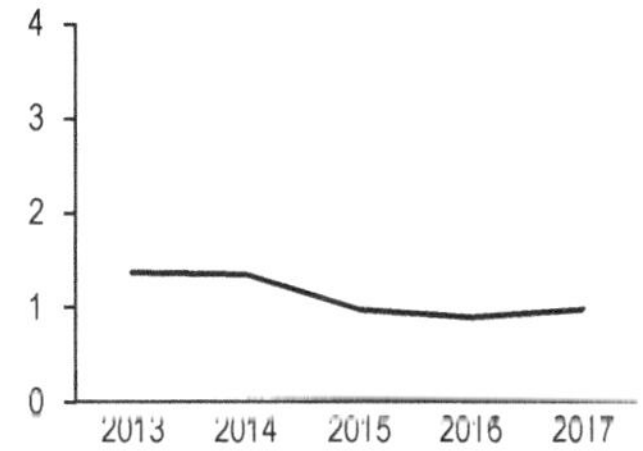

	2013	2014	2015	2016	2017
Salisbury					
Average	1.37	1.35	0.98	0.89	0.98

Workload Measures

Tons Recyclables Collected per 1,000 Population

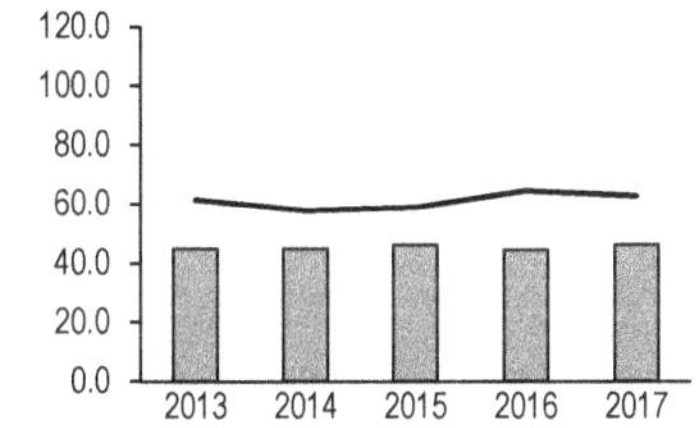

	2013	2014	2015	2016	2017
Salisbury	44.8	44.7	45.9	44.3	45.9
Average	61.4	57.7	58.9	64.4	62.8

Tons Recyclables Collected per 1,000 Collection Points

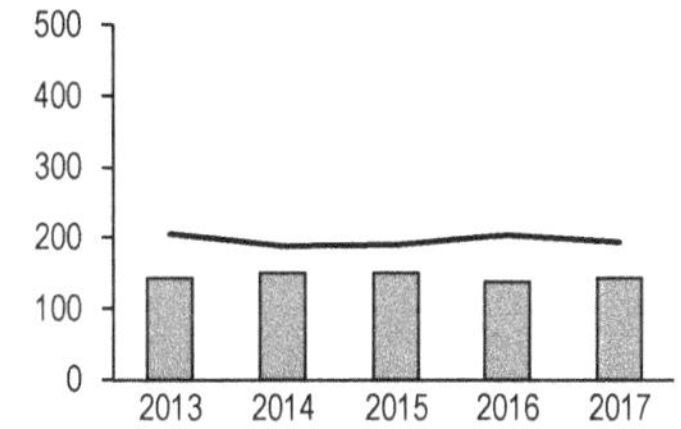

	2013	2014	2015	2016	2017
Salisbury	143	150	149	137	143
Average	205	188	190	203	193

Tons Solid Waste Landfilled per 1,000 Population

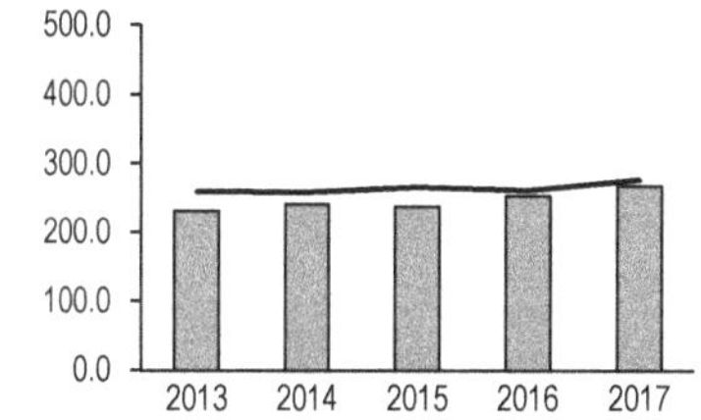

	2013	2014	2015	2016	2017
Salisbury	231.3	241.1	237.7	253.6	267.7
Average	258.5	257.6	264.9	260.6	275.7

Efficiency Measures

Recycling Services Cost per Ton Collected

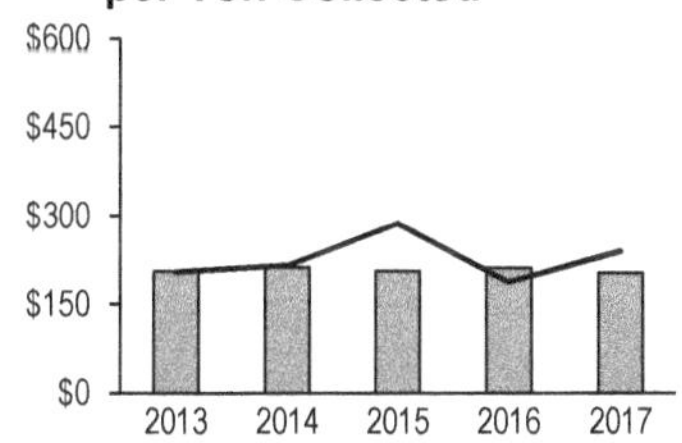

	2013	2014	2015	2016	2017
Salisbury	$205	$212	$205	$210	$202
Average	$204	$215	$286	$187	$239

Recycling Services Cost per Collection Point

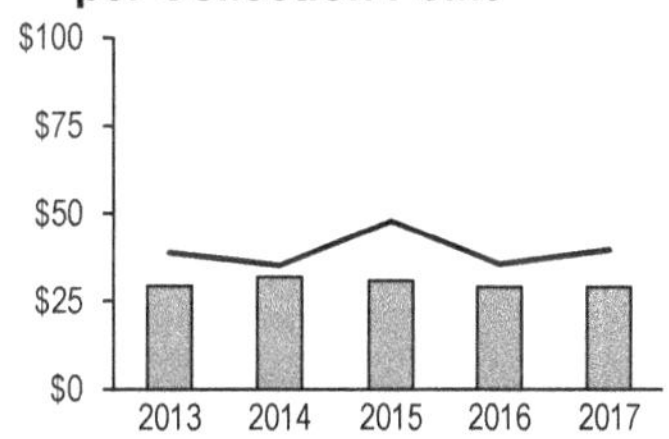

	2013	2014	2015	2016	2017
Salisbury	$29.25	$31.69	$30.66	$28.79	$28.79
Average	$38.72	$35.13	$47.74	$35.39	$39.44

Tons Collected Curbside per Municipal FTE

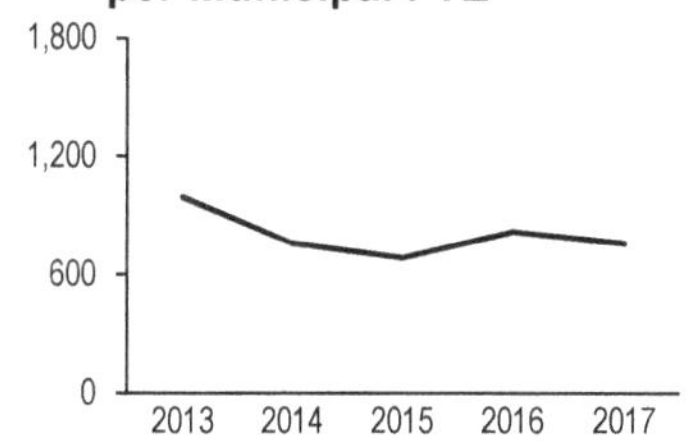

	2013	2014	2015	2016	2017
Salisbury					
Average	994	758	684	816	757

Effectiveness Measures

Community Set-Out Rate

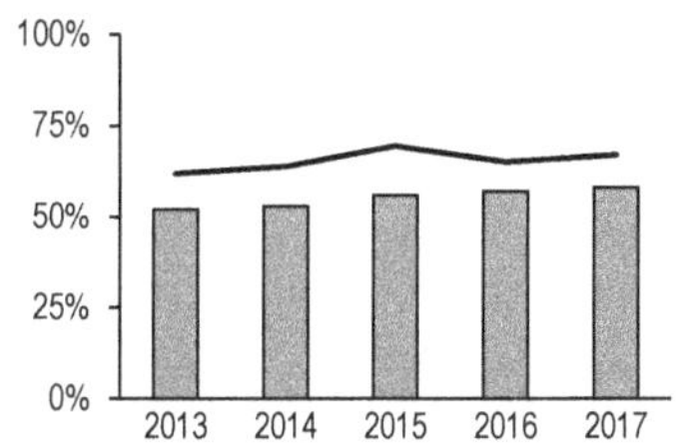

	2013	2014	2015	2016	2017
Salisbury	52.0%	53.0%	56.0%	57.0%	58.0%
Average	61.9%	63.8%	69.4%	65.1%	67.1%

Tons Recycled as Percentage of Tons Refuse and Recyclables Collected

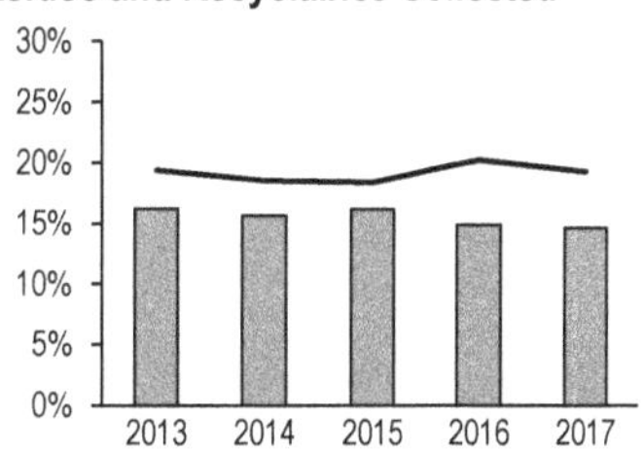

	2013	2014	2015	2016	2017
Salisbury	16.2%	15.6%	16.2%	14.9%	14.6%
Average	19.4%	18.5%	18.4%	20.2%	19.3%

Fiscal Year 2016–17

Explanatory Information

Service Level and Delivery

Wilson's household recycling program provides curbside pickup of materials once each week to residents on the same day as residential refuse collection but by different crews. Wilson began a pilot program in July 2015 shifting to collection done once every two weeks. This pilot phase initially covered about 2,800 homes and each received a ninety-six-gallon roll out cart. The transition is continuing for almost half the homes and is expected to be done in the next fiscal year for all households. The recycling program is part of the Division of Environmental Services.

The following materials are collected:

- aluminum and steel cans
- No. 1 and No. 2 plastic containers
- newsprint
- clear, green, and brown glass
- waste oil on a call-in basis.

Wilson used two three-person crews during the year, consisting of one driver and two collectors each.

Conditions Affecting Service, Performance, and Costs

The set-out rate was calculated on a monthly basis by drivers on the recycling trucks using counters.

The initial pilot phase for recycling begun in July 2015 helped lower overall costs notably.

Municipal Profile

Population (OSBM 2016)	49,406
Land Area (Square Miles)	30.60
Persons per Square Mile	1,615
Median Family Income U.S. Census 2010	$43,442

Service Profile

FTE Positions—Collection	7.0
FTE Positions—Other	0.5
Number of City Drop-Off Centers	0
Other Drop-Off Centers	0
Percentage of Service Contracted	0%
Collection Frequency	
for 96-gallon carts	Every 2 weeks
for 18-gallon cart	Every week
General Collection Location	Curbside
Recyclables Sorted at Curb	No
Collection Points	20,017
Tons of Recyclables Collected	
Curbside	1,705
City Drop-Off Centers	0
Total Tons Collected	1,705
Monthly Service Fee	$20.00
Revenue from Sale of Recyclables	$0
Sale Revenue as Percentage of Cost	NA

Full Cost Profile

Cost Breakdown by Percentage	
Personal Services	27.9%
Operating Costs	59.7%
Capital Costs	12.4%
TOTAL	100.0%
Cost Breakdown in Dollars	
Personal Services	$228,465
Operating Costs	$488,142
Capital Costs	$101,394
TOTAL	$818,001

Key: Wilson ▒ Benchmarking Average — Fiscal Years 2013 through 2017

Resource Measures

Recycling Services Cost per Capita

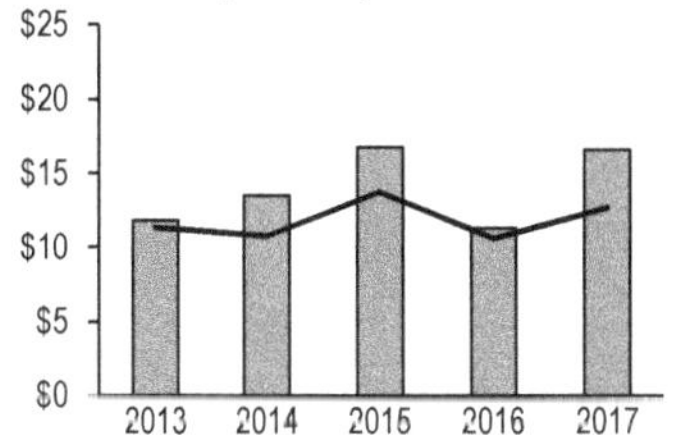

	2013	2014	2015	2016	2017
Wilson	$11.80	$13.49	$16.74	$11.31	$16.56
Average	$11.39	$10.81	$13.79	$10.66	$12.74

Recycling Services FTEs per 10,000 Population

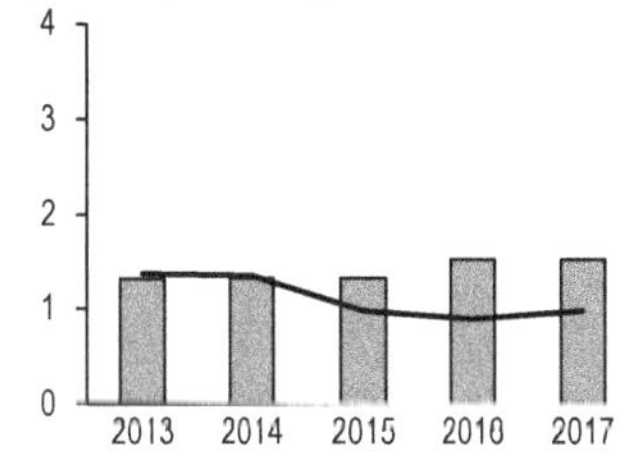

	2013	2014	2015	2016	2017
Wilson	1.31	1.32	1.32	1.52	1.52
Average	1.37	1.35	0.98	0.89	0.98

Workload Measures

Tons Recyclables Collected per 1,000 Population

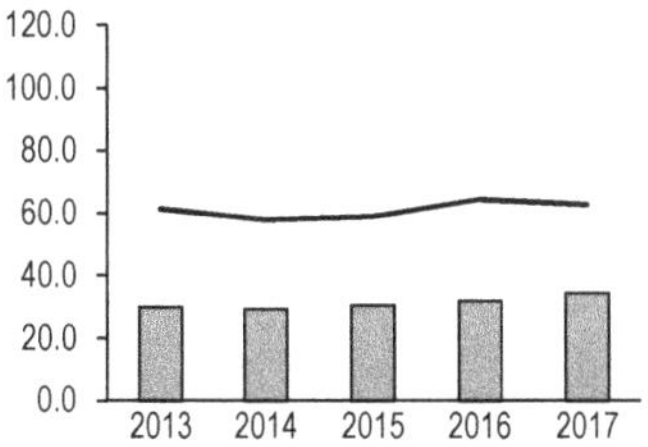

	2013	2014	2015	2016	2017
Wilson	30.0	29.3	30.7	32.1	34.5
Average	61.4	57.7	58.9	64.4	62.8

Tons Recyclables Collected per 1,000 Collection Points

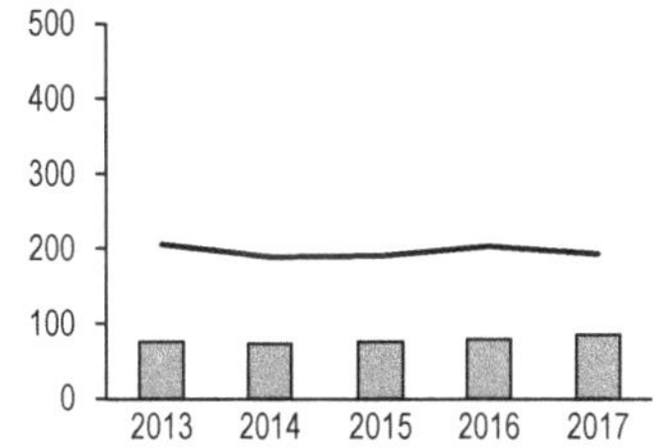

	2013	2014	2015	2016	2017
Wilson	76	73	76	79	85
Average	205	188	190	203	193

Tons Solid Waste Landfilled per 1,000 Population

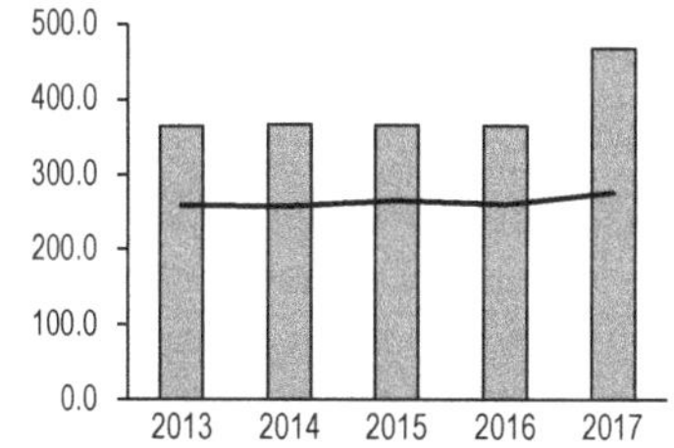

	2013	2014	2015	2016	2017
Wilson	364.1	366.6	365.7	364.7	467.1
Average	258.5	257.6	264.9	260.6	275.7

Efficiency Measures

Recycling Services Cost per Ton Collected

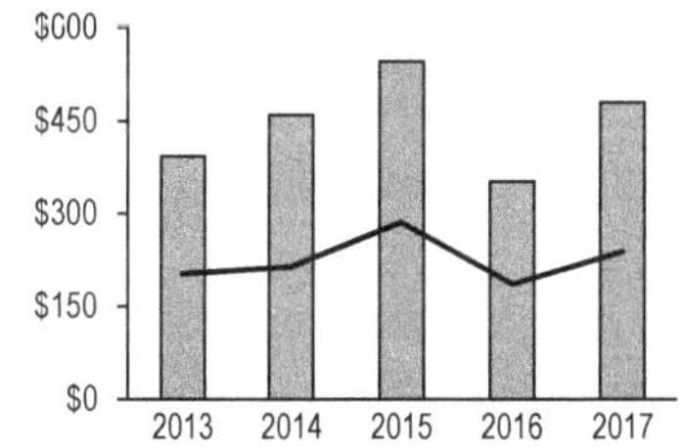

	2013	2014	2015	2016	2017
Wilson	$393	$460	$546	$352	$480
Average	$204	$215	$286	$187	$239

Recycling Services Cost per Collection Point

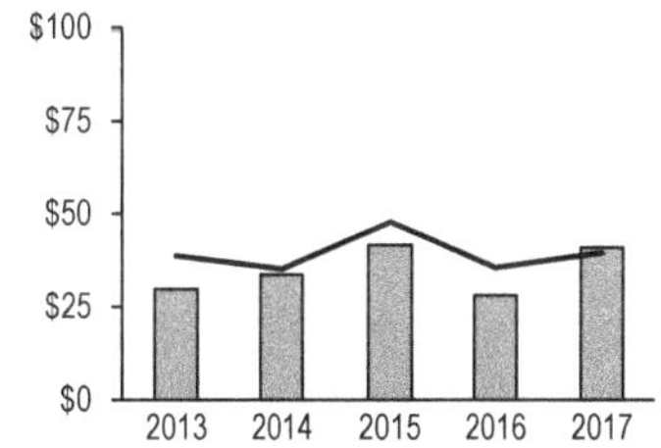

	2013	2014	2015	2016	2017
Wilson	$29.69	$33.55	$41.51	$27.96	$40.87
Average	$38.72	$35.13	$47.74	$35.39	$39.44

Tons Collected Curbside per Municipal FTE

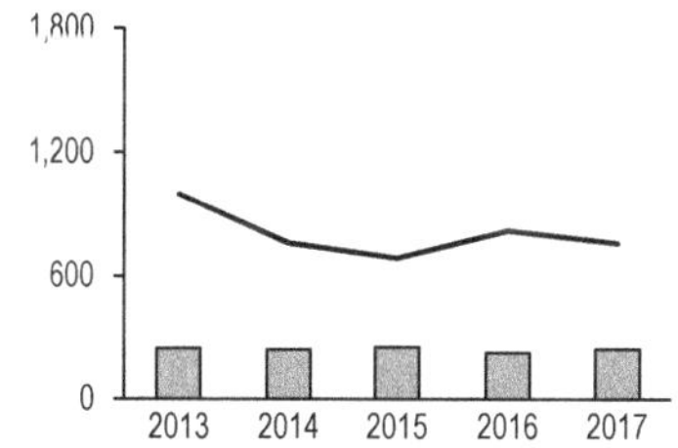

	2013	2014	2015	2016	2017
Wilson	248	240	252	227	244
Average	994	758	684	816	757

Effectiveness Measures

Community Set-Out Rate

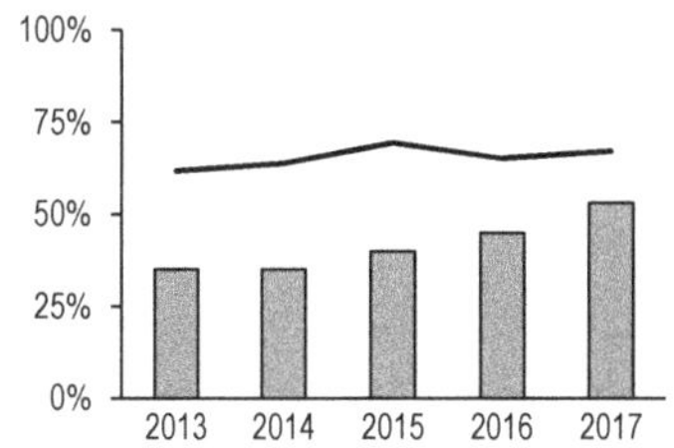

	2013	2014	2015	2016	2017
Wilson	35.0%	35.0%	40.0%	45.0%	53.0%
Average	61.9%	63.8%	69.4%	65.1%	67.1%

Tons Recycled as Percentage of Tons Refuse and Recyclables Collected

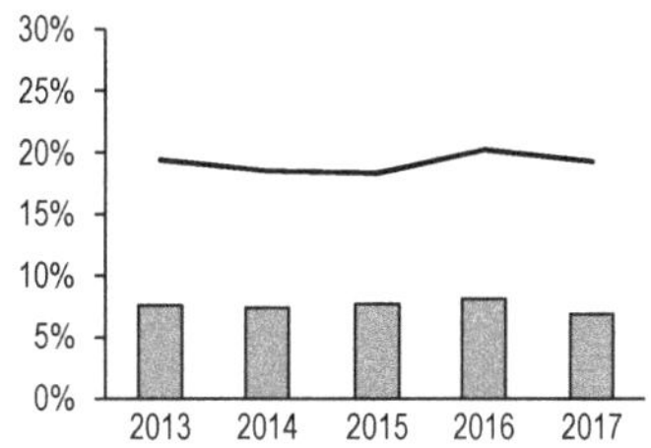

	2013	2014	2015	2016	2017
Wilson	7.6%	7.4%	7.7%	8.1%	6.9%
Average	19.4%	18.5%	18.4%	20.2%	19.3%

Fiscal Year 2016–17

Explanatory Information

Service Level and Delivery

Winston-Salem provides biweekly curbside household recycling service to its single-family residences using ninety-six-gallon carts. The city provides nine drop-off sites for cardboard at its fire stations plus two full-service drop-off sites. Items collected in the city's curbside household recycling program include:

- aluminum and steel cans
- all plastic bottles
- green, amber, and clear glass
- newspaper
- magazines, telephone books, and junk mail
- chipboard
- corrugated cardboard (no bundling requirement)
- office paper
- aerosol cans.

The city contracts for 100 percent of its curbside household recycling program. The city does not charge a recycling fee. Revenue to the city for the sale of recyclables was $166,640 during the year, partially offsetting program costs.

Conditions Affecting Service, Performance, and Costs

In April 2012, the city implemented a single-stream recycling program in which residents place all recyclables into a city-issued ninety-six-gallon cart that is rolled to the curb for collection. The service was also changed to a biweekly collection. The city anticipates signficant cost savings and increased participation from a single-stream program.

Municipal Profile

Population (OSBM 2016)	240,603
Land Area (Square Miles)	132.55
Persons per Square Mile	1,815
Median Family Income	$51,491
U.S. Census 2010	

Service Profile

FTE Positions—Collection	Contractor
FTE Positions—Other	2.0
Number of City Drop-Off Centers	11
Other Drop-Off Centers	0
Percentage of Service Contracted	100%
Collection Frequency	Every 2 weeks
General Collection Location	Curbside
Recyclables Sorted at Curb	No
Collection Points	76,452
Tons of Recyclables Collected	
Curbside	14,609
City Drop-Off Centers	302
Total Tons Collected	14,911
Monthly Service Fee	0
Revenue from Sale of Recyclables	$166,640
Sale Revenue as Percentage of Cost	10.3%

Full Cost Profile

Cost Breakdown by Percentage	
Personal Services	4.9%
Operating Costs	95.1%
Capital Costs	0.0%
TOTAL	100.0%
Cost Breakdown in Dollars	
Personal Services	$80,333
Operating Costs	$1,543,626
Capital Costs	$0
TOTAL	$1,623,959

Key: Winston-Salem ▒ Benchmarking Average — Fiscal Years 2013 through 2017

Resource Measures

Recycling Services Cost per Capita

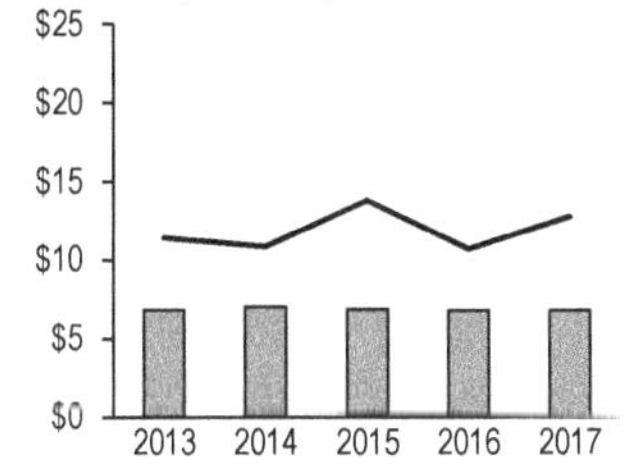

	2013	2014	2015	2016	2017
Winston-Salem	$6.80	$6.98	$6.84	$6.73	$6.75
Average	$11.39	$10.81	$13.79	$10.66	$12.74

Recycling Services FTEs per 10,000 Population

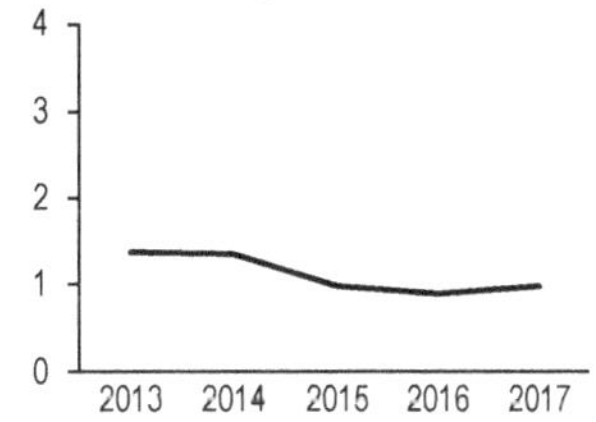

	2013	2014	2015	2016	2017
Winston-Salem					
Average	1.37	1.35	0.98	0.89	0.98

Workload Measures

Tons Recyclables Collected per 1,000 Population

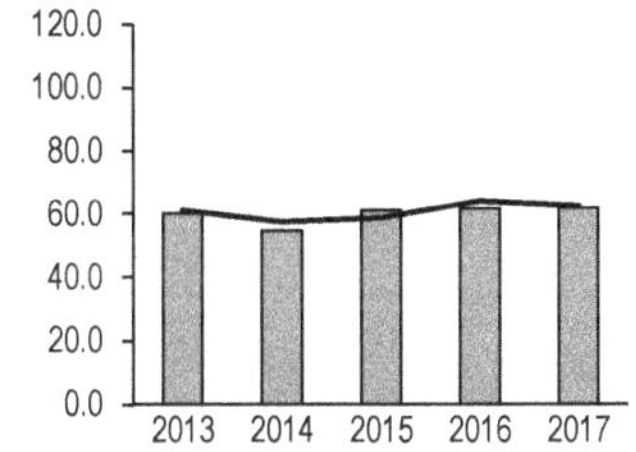

	2013	2014	2015	2016	2017
Winston-Salem	60.1	54.7	61.2	61.7	62.0
Average	61.4	57.7	58.9	64.4	62.8

Tons Recyclables Collected per 1,000 Collection Points

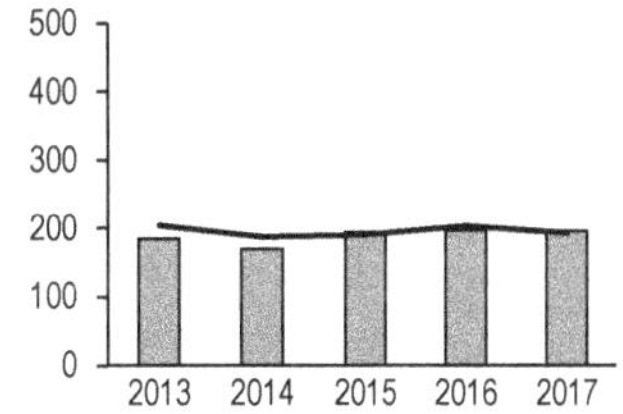

	2013	2014	2015	2016	2017
Winston-Salem	184	169	194	196	195
Average	205	188	190	203	193

Tons Solid Waste Landfilled per 1,000 Population

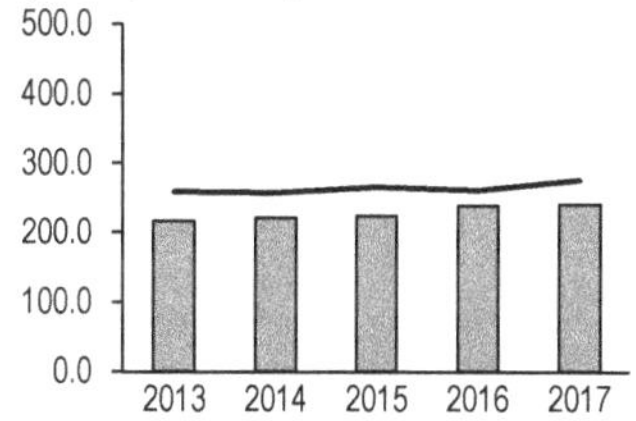

	2013	2014	2015	2016	2017
Winston-Salem	216.1	220.8	223.7	238.9	239.8
Average	258.5	257.6	264.9	260.6	275.7

Efficiency Measures

Recycling Services Cost per Ton Collected

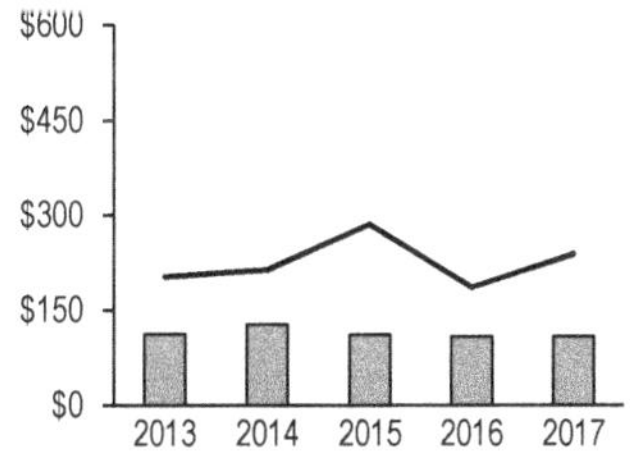

	2013	2014	2015	2016	2017
Winston-Salem	$113	$128	$112	$109	$109
Average	$204	$215	$286	$187	$239

Recycling Services Cost per Collection Point

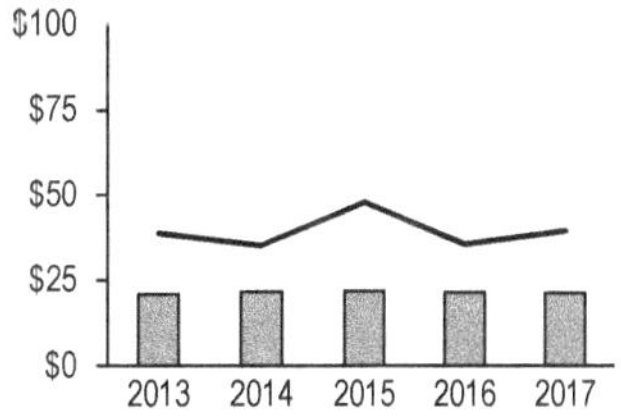

	2013	2014	2015	2016	2017
Winston-Salem	$20.85	$21.62	$21.69	$21.44	$21.24
Average	$38.72	$35.13	$47.74	$35.39	$39.44

Tons Collected Curbside per Municipal FTE

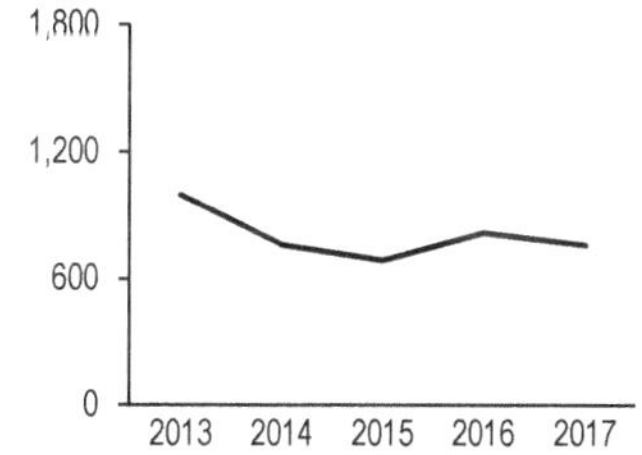

	2013	2014	2015	2016	2017
Winston-Salem					
Average	994	758	684	816	757

Effectiveness Measures

Community Set-Out Rate

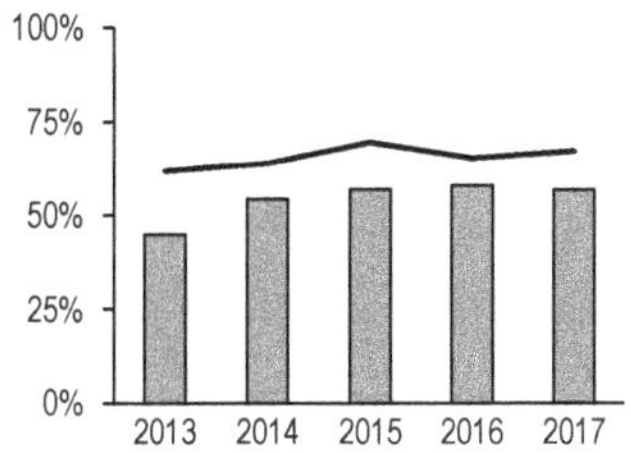

	2013	2014	2015	2016	2017
Winston-Salem	44.9%	54.2%	56.8%	57.9%	56.7%
Average	61.9%	63.8%	69.4%	65.1%	67.1%

Tons Recycled as Percentage of Tons Refuse and Recyclables Collected

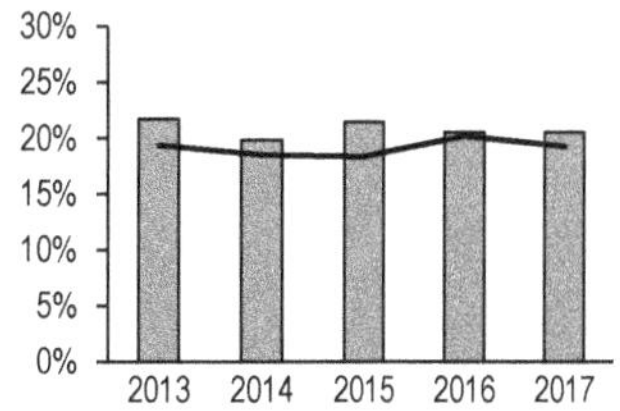

	2013	2014	2015	2016	2017
Winston-Salem	21.8%	19.8%	21.5%	20.5%	20.5%
Average	19.4%	18.5%	18.4%	20.2%	19.3%

UNC | SCHOOL OF GOVERNMENT
North Carolina Benchmarking Project

Performance and Cost Data

YARD WASTE / LEAF COLLECTION

PERFORMANCE MEASURES FOR YARD WASTE/LEAF COLLECTION

SERVICE DEFINITION

Yard waste and leaf collection includes regularly scheduled or special collection of these items. Such collection may occur from the curb, backyard, or another locale. Yard waste and leaves may be bagged, placed in containers, or loose. The service definition excludes the collection of white goods and other bulky items. Although some municipalities collect yard waste and leaves with household refuse or other trash, they separate the items at some point in the collection process because yard waste and leaves cannot be placed in landfills.

NOTES ON PERFORMANCE MEASURES

1. Tons Collected per 1,000 Population and per 1,000 Collection Points

These are the same performance measures that are used for residential refuse collection, except that tonnage is for yard waste, leaves, and miscellaneous trash rather than residential refuse. "Collection points" refers to the number of residential premises served by regularly scheduled collection of yard waste, leaves, and miscellaneous trash.

2. Cost per Ton Collected

Cost is measured using the project's full cost accounting model, calculating direct, indirect, and capital costs. Tons are as defined above.

3. Tons Collected per Collection FTE

The number of full-time equivalent (FTE) positions refers to the number of employees or laborers who were directly involved in collection of yard waste, leaves, and miscellaneous trash during the fiscal year. This number includes temporary, permanent, full-time, and part-time workers. Such workers can be sanitation, street, or other municipal employees. One FTE equals 2,080 hours of work per year. Any combination of employees providing 2,080 hours of work per year is one FTE.

4. Complaints (and Valid Complaints) per 10,000 Collection Points

Complaints are those tracked by each jurisdiction, using its own criteria and procedures. Collection points are as defined above. The municipalities follow very different procedures in processing and recording these calls and in determining which ones are complaints and which are not. For these reasons, the project is able to present limited comparative data about complaints or valid complaints. Nonetheless, the project recommends that the participating municipalities devise common criteria for identifying complaints and procedures for processing and recording calls.

Yard Waste/Leaf Collection

Summary of Key Dimensions of Service

City or Town	Yard Waste Collection		Seasonal Loose Leaf Collection	Collection Points	Tons Collected		Collection FTE Positions
	Location	Frequency			Yard Waste	Seasonal Leaves	
Apex	Curbside	1 x week	NA	14,662	6,531	NA	11.9
Asheville	Curbside	2 x month	NA	30,280	6,204	NA	14.9
Chapel Hill	Curbside	1 x week	5-6 sweeps	12,075	2,578	5,104	16.6
Charlotte	Curbside	1 x week	NA	215,602	55,535	NA	74.0
Concord	Curbside	1 x week	3 sweeps	31,211	6,829	1,946	24.6
Goldsboro	Curbside	1 x 2 weeks	1 x 2 weeks	14,372	6,936	3,360	17.0
Greensboro	Curbside	1 x week	2 sweeps	89,214	12,800	10,565	45.9
Greenville	Curbside	1 x week	1 x week	19,294	5,725	910	21.6
Hickory	Curbside	1 x week	2 sweeps	12,200	6,302	3,870	10.4
High Point	Curbside	1 x week	2 sweeps	42,418	4,243	2,803	16.9
Raleigh	Curbside	1 x week	2 sweeps	126,075	17,946	12,352	64.0
Salisbury	Curbside	1 x week	1 x 3 weeks	10,961	1,743	2,541	8.8
Wilson	Curbside	1 x week	1 x 3 weeks	20,017	9,211	1,204	15.5
Winston-Salem	Curbside	Yard Waste Cart 1 x week Brush every 10 days	3 sweeps	81,589	20,974	11,025	75.9

NOTES

Municipalities with no reported seasonal leaf collection collect leaves as part of their yard waste collection programs.

EXPLANATORY FACTORS

These are factors that the project found affected yard waste and leaf collection performance and cost in one or more of the municipalities:

Whether or not a fee is charged for collection
Residential/commercial/industrial nature of the community
Policies regarding sizes and types of items collected
Extent of seasonal leaf collection service
Landfill policies and tipping fees

Fiscal Year 2016–17

Explanatory Information

Service Level and Delivery
The Town of Apex collects yard waste curbside once per week for all city residents. The town collects vegetative matter from residential landscaping. The town does not operate a seasonal leaf collection, but leaves are collected year-round as part of the weekly service. Land clearing debris is not collected. The town charges $6.85 per month for collection of yard waste.

There are three grass/vacuum trucks, two two-person limb-chipping crews, and one grapple-truck operator for larger items. These crews cover the town every week using a five-day-a-week schedule.

Conditions Affecting Service, Performance, and Costs
Apex made a major purchase of new leaf and grappler trucks for leaf collection in FY 2013–14, which pushed up capital costs but helped with productivity.

Municipal Profile

Population (OSBM 2016)	46,688
Land Area (Square Miles)	20.61
Persons per Square Mile	2,265
Median Family Income U.S. Census 2010	$97,201

Service Profile

FTE Positions—Collection	11.0
FTE Positions—Other	0.9
Collection Frequency	
Yard Waste	1 x week
Collection Points	14,662
Tons Collected	
Yard Waste	6,531
Seasonal Leaves	with yard waste
Total Tons Collected	6,531
Monthly Service Fee	$6.85

Full Cost Profile

Cost Breakdown by Percentage	
Personal Services	50.8%
Operating Costs	30.2%
Capital Costs	19.1%
TOTAL	100.0%
Cost Breakdown in Dollars	
Personal Services	$706,740
Operating Costs	$420,103
Capital Costs	$265,233
TOTAL	$1,392,076

Apex

Yard Waste/Leaf Collection

Key: Apex ▒ Benchmarking Average — Fiscal Years 2013 through 2017

Resource Measures

Yard Waste and Leaf Collection Costs per Capita

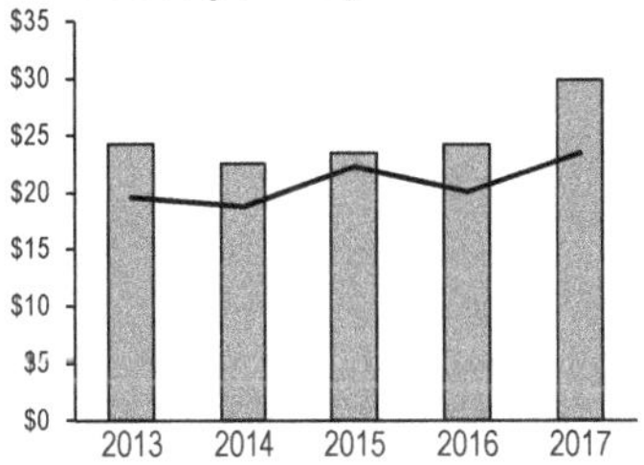

	2013	2014	2015	2016	2017
Apex	$24.23	$22.53	$23.42	$24.19	$29.82
Average	$19.59	$18.82	$22.33	$20.10	$23.48

Yard Waste and Leaf Collection FTEs per 10,000 Population

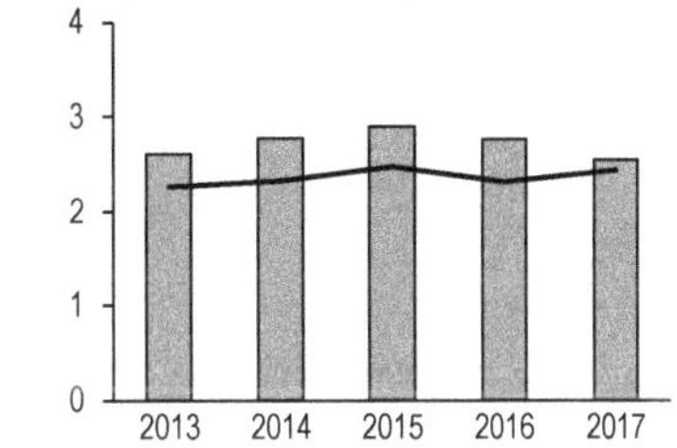

	2013	2014	2015	2016	2017
Apex	2.6	2.8	2.9	2.8	2.5
Average	2.3	2.3	2.5	2.3	2.4

Workload Measures

Yard Waste and Leaf Tons Collected per 1,000 Population

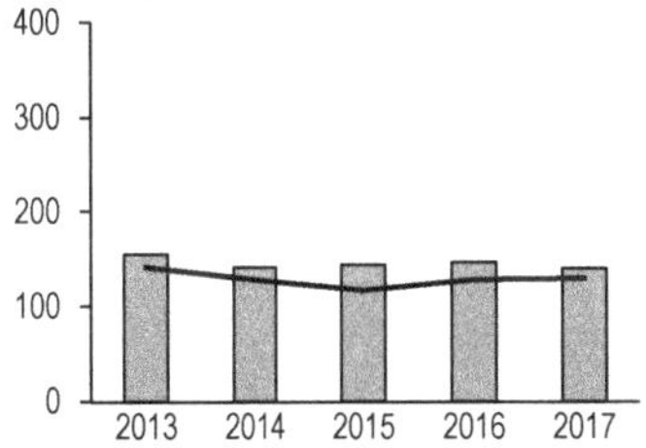

	2013	2014	2015	2016	2017
Apex	155	141	144	146	140
Average	141	128	117	128	129

Yard Waste and Leaf Tons Collected per 1,000 Collection Points

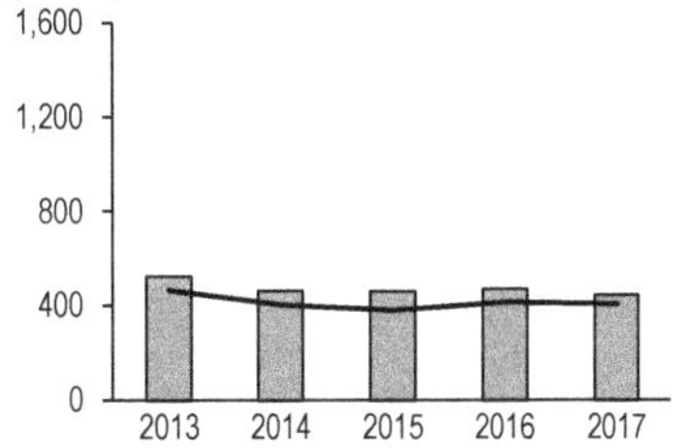

	2013	2014	2015	2016	2017
Apex	526	463	462	471	445
Average	468	404	384	416	406

Efficiency Measures

Yard Waste and Leaf Collection Cost per Collection Point

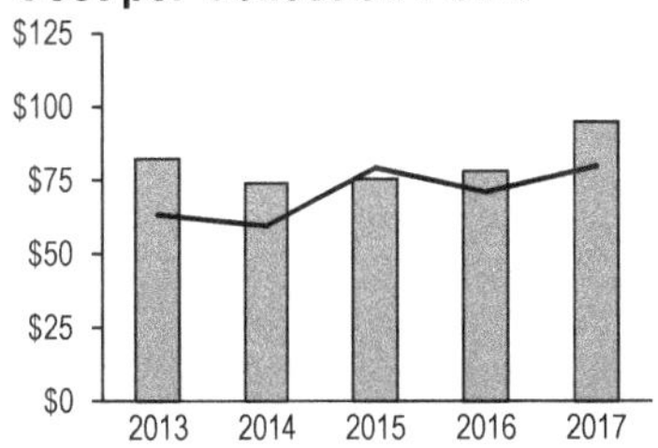

	2013	2014	2015	2016	2017
Apex	$82	$74	$75	$78	$95
Average	$63	$59	$79	$71	$79

Yard Waste and Leaf Collection Cost per Ton Collected

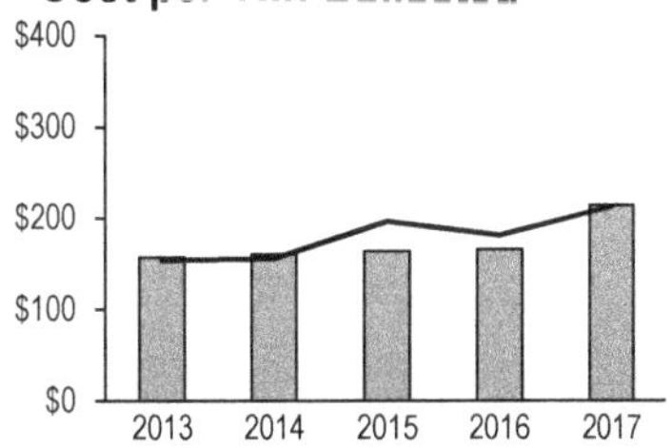

	2013	2014	2015	2016	2017
Apex	$156	$160	$163	$165	$213
Average	$153	$155	$196	$180	$212

Yard Waste and Leaf Tons Collected per Collection FTE

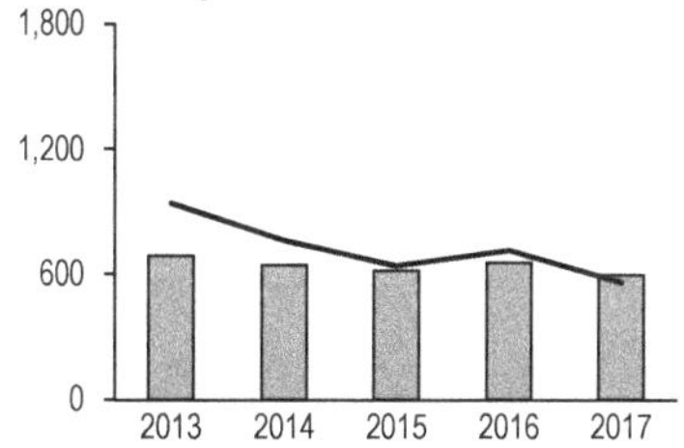

	2013	2014	2015	2016	2017
Apex	685	642	613	654	594
Average	937	760	637	711	558

Effectiveness Measures

Collection Complaints per 10,000 Collection Points

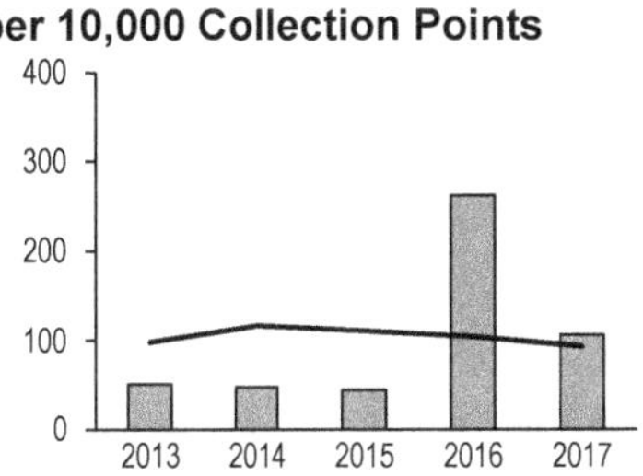

	2013	2014	2015	2016	2017
Apex	51	48	45	262	106
Average	98	117	111	105	93

Valid Complaints per 10,000 Collection Points

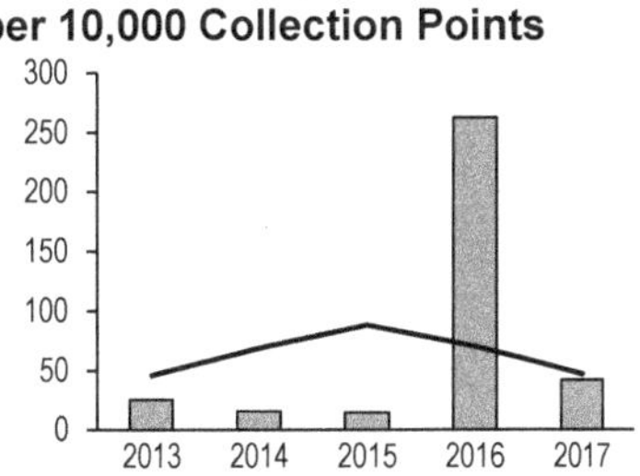

	2013	2014	2015	2016	2017
Apex	26	16	15	262	42
Average	46	69	88	70	47

Asheville — Yard Waste/Leaf Collection

Fiscal Year 2016–17

Explanatory Information

Service Level and Delivery

Asheville collects yard waste curbside twice per month for all city residents. The city collects yard trimmings no longer than 4 feet and no wider than 6 inches. Grass clippings and materials cut by contractors are not collected.

There are three one-person crews on knucklebooms, scheduled for approximately three-and-one-half days per week. Three three-person crews operating rear packers collect yard waste four days per week.

The city does not charge a fee for yard waste collection. A $5 fee is charged for white goods, and a $10 fee is charged for dead animals.

Asheville does not have a separate leaf collection program. Instead, leaves are collected as part of the normal twice-a-month yard waste collection.

The city transfers yard waste to a contractor's site for grinding. The city does not recieve any of the grindings. The disposal costs for this are not included in the collection costs reported here.

Conditions Affecting Service, Performance, and Costs

Municipal Profile

Population (OSBM 2016)	91,929
Land Area (Square Miles)	45.52
Persons per Square Mile	2,019
Median Family Income U.S. Census 2010	$53,350

Service Profile

FTE Positions—Collection	14.0
FTE Positions—Other	0.9
Collection Frequency	
Yard Waste	2 x month
Collection Points	30,280
Tons Collected	
Yard Waste	6,204
Seasonal Leaves	with yard waste
Total Tons Collected	6,530
Monthly Service Fee	No

Full Cost Profile

Cost Breakdown by Percentage	
Personal Services	43.0%
Operating Costs	41.0%
Capital Costs	16.0%
TOTAL	100.0%
Cost Breakdown in Dollars	
Personal Services	$642,971
Operating Costs	$612,640
Capital Costs	$238,895
TOTAL	$1,494,506

Asheville

Yard Waste/Leaf Collection

Key: Asheville ▒ Benchmarking Average — Fiscal Years 2013 through 2017

Resource Measures

Yard Waste and Leaf Collection Costs per Capita

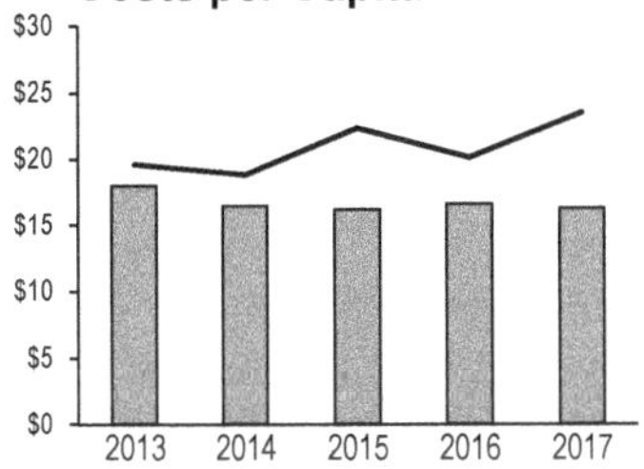

	2013	2014	2015	2016	2017
Asheville	$17.99	$16.46	$16.18	$16.61	$16.26
Average	$19.59	$18.82	$22.33	$20.10	$23.48

Yard Waste and Leaf Collection FTEs per 10,000 Population

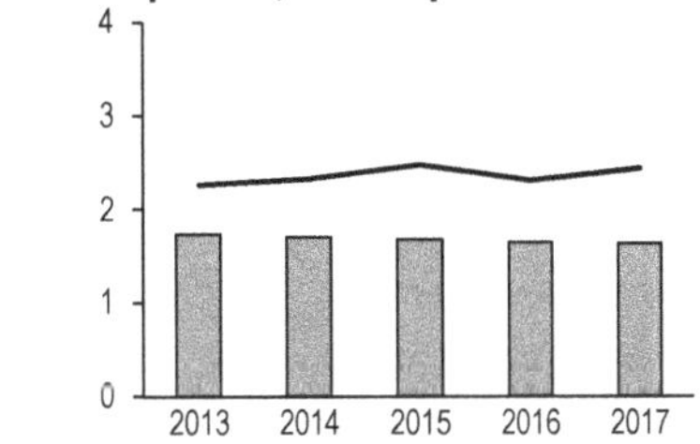

	2013	2014	2015	2016	2017
Asheville	1.7	1.7	1.7	1.6	1.6
Average	2.3	2.3	2.5	2.3	2.4

Workload Measures

Yard Waste and Leaf Tons Collected per 1,000 Population

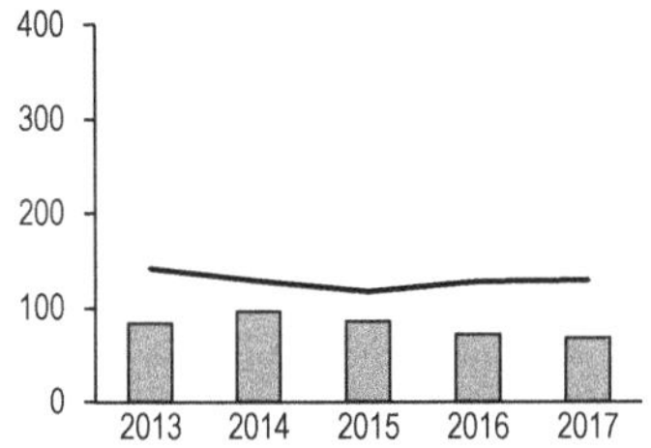

	2013	2014	2015	2016	2017
Asheville	83	96	85	72	67
Average	141	128	117	128	129

Yard Waste and Leaf Tons Collected per 1,000 Collection Points

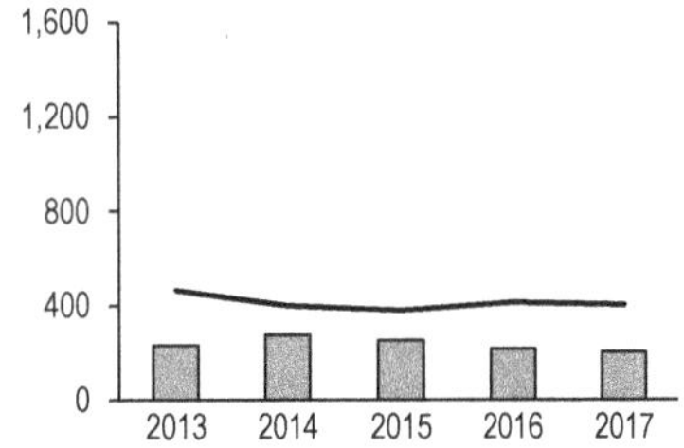

	2013	2014	2015	2016	2017
Asheville	234	277	255	217	205
Average	468	404	384	416	406

Efficiency Measures

Yard Waste and Leaf Collection Cost per Collection Point

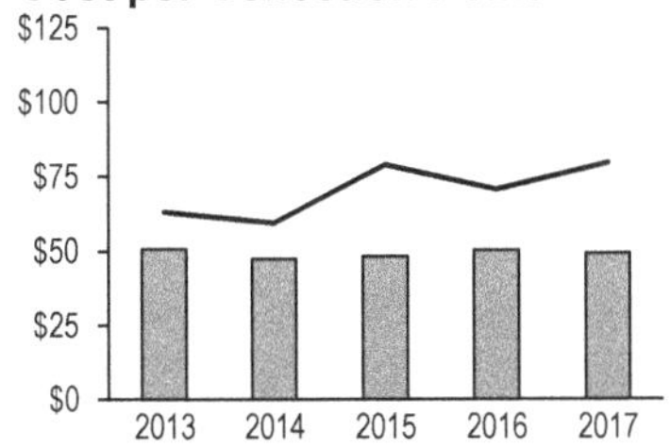

	2013	2014	2015	2016	2017
Asheville	$51	$47	$48	$50	$49
Average	$63	$59	$79	$71	$79

Yard Waste and Leaf Collection Cost per Ton Collected

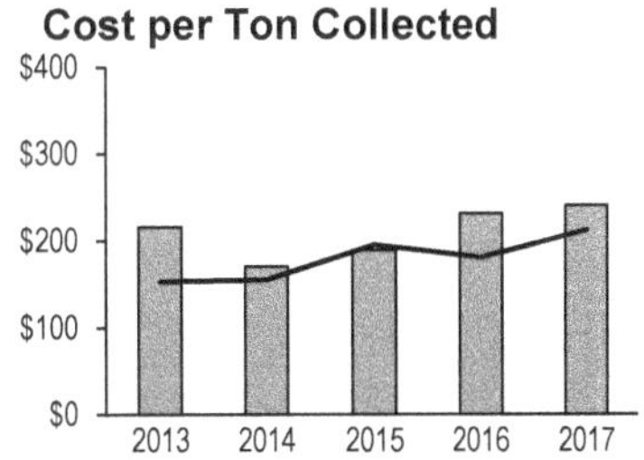

	2013	2014	2015	2016	2017
Asheville	$216	$171	$189	$231	$241
Average	$153	$155	$196	$180	$212

Yard Waste and Leaf Tons Collected per Collection FTE

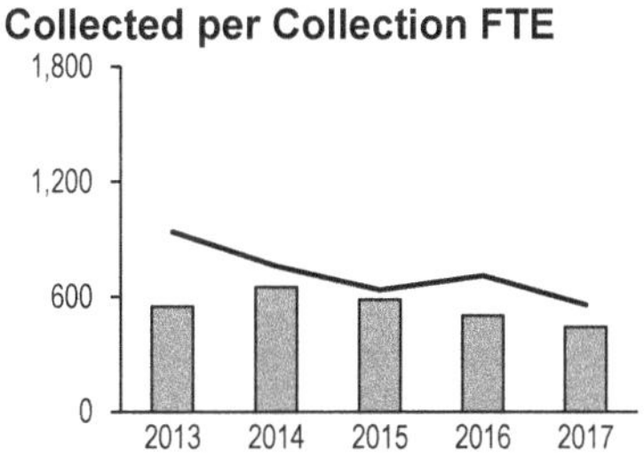

	2013	2014	2015	2016	2017
Asheville	552	652	586	502	443
Average	937	760	637	711	558

Effectiveness Measures

Collection Complaints per 10,000 Collection Points

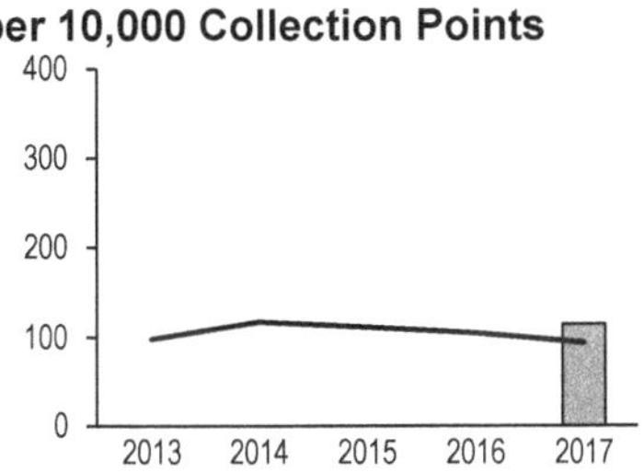

	2013	2014	2015	2016	2017
Asheville					114
Average	98	117	111	105	93

Valid Complaints per 10,000 Collection Points

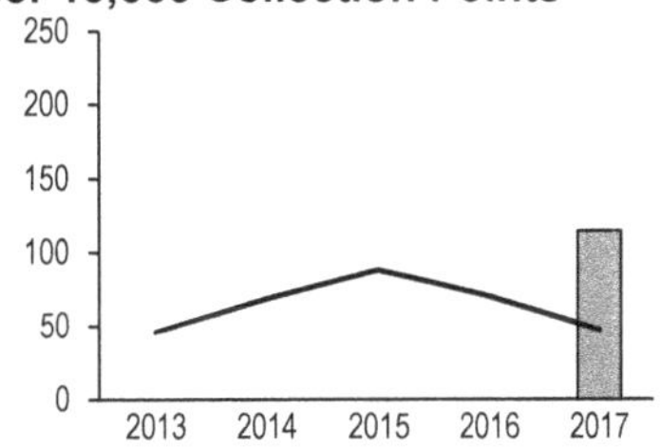

	2013	2014	2015	2016	2017
Asheville					114
Average	46	69	88	70	47

Fiscal Year 2016–17

Explanatory Information

Service Level and Delivery

Yard waste collection is managed by the Solid Waste Services Division of the Public Works Department. Yard waste includes organic materials including leaves, stems, grass, limbs, and other residential organic matter. The town does not collect large logs or stumps, or debris from lot clearing.

Yard waste is collected once per week curbside with no monthly fee. Yard waste is collected by seven three-person crews using rear packers two days per week. The Town collects small yard waste materials placed in roll carts, other rigid containers, or paper yard waste bags for collection. The Town collects large yard waste materials in loose piles. Yard waste piles larger than three cubic yards are collected for a fee. The Town does not collect yard waste in plastic bags.

Residents can rent a 10-cubic-yard roll-off container or schedule a paid knuckle boom collection for large projects. These larger loads are collected by a one-person crew using a knuckle boom truck and a hook-lift truck 5 days per week. Residents pay a fee of $35 per day or $60 per week to rent a roll-off container for collection. The fee for a knuckle boom collection is $125.

Seasonal leaf collection is managed by the Streets and Construction Services Division of the Public Works Department. Seasonal leaf collection is run with five or six cycles in a season from mid-October to early March. Only loose leaves and pine straw free of limbs or other debris are collected curbside. Leaf crews consist of a driver, a raker, and a machine operator. Crews may make use of seasonal labor, and three to six crews are used depending on the volume of leaves at the curb for collection. During peak leaf fall, crews also pull the curb line in conjunction with street sweepers from the Stormwater Program of the Public Works Department.

Conditions Affecting Service, Performance, and Costs

The Town of Chapel Hill began participation in the benchmarking project in July 2015, with FY 2014–15 being the first reporting year.

Complaints only include leaf collection. In FY 2014–15 complaints were not tracked for yard waste.

Municipal Profile

Population (OSBM 2016)	59,852
Land Area (Square Miles)	21.21
Persons per Square Mile	2,822
Median Family Income U.S. Census 2010	$61,405

Service Profile

FTE Positions—Collection	15.1
FTE Positions—Other	1.5
Collection Frequency	
Yard Waste	1 x week
Seasonal Leaf Collection	5-6 sweeps
Collection Points	12,075
Tons Collected	
Yard Waste	2,578
Seasonal Leaves	5,104
Total Tons Collected	7,682
Monthly Service Fee	Resdients may purchase cart for $50 but not required

Full Cost Profile

Cost Breakdown by Percentage	
Personal Services	41.1%
Operating Costs	39.7%
Capital Costs	19.2%
TOTAL	100.0%
Cost Breakdown in Dollars	
Personal Services	$988,935
Operating Costs	$953,921
Capital Costs	$462,122
TOTAL	$2,404,979

Chapel Hill — Yard Waste/Leaf Collection

Key: Chapel Hill ▒ Benchmarking Average — Fiscal Years 2013 through 2017

Resource Measures

Yard Waste and Leaf Collection Costs per Capita

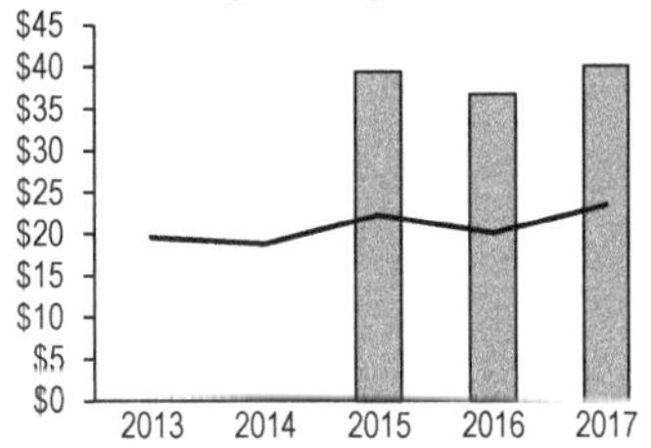

	2013	2014	2015	2016	2017
Chapel Hill			$39.50	$36.77	$40.18
Average	$19.59	$18.82	$22.33	$20.10	$23.48

Yard Waste and Leaf Collection FTEs per 10,000 Population

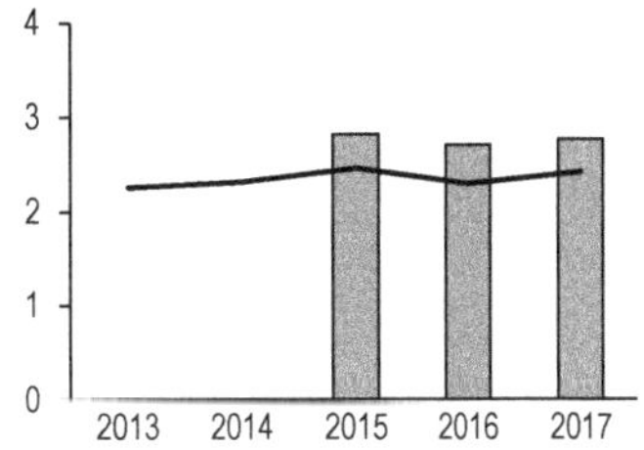

	2013	2014	2015	2016	2017
Chapel Hill			2.8	2.7	2.8
Average	2.3	2.3	2.5	2.3	2.4

Workload Measures

Yard Waste and Leaf Tons Collected per 1,000 Population

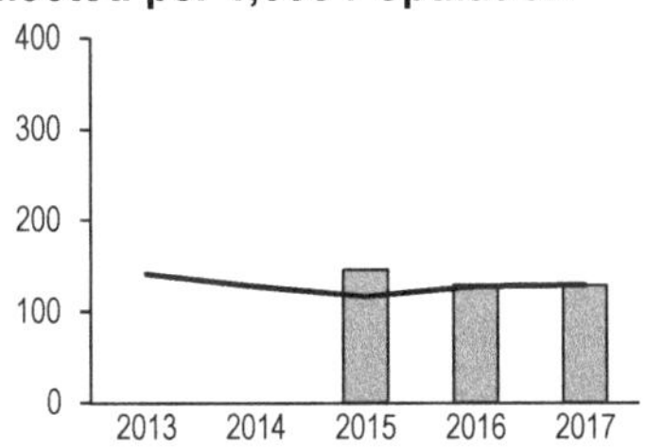

	2013	2014	2015	2016	2017
Chapel Hill			146	129	128
Average	141	128	117	128	129

Yard Waste and Leaf Tons Collected per 1,000 Collection Points

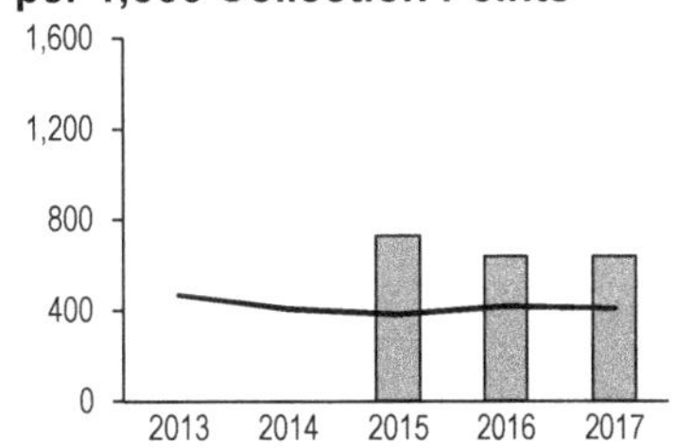

	2013	2014	2015	2016	2017
Chapel Hill			727	636	636
Average	468	404	384	416	406

Efficiency Measures

Yard Waste and Leaf Collection Cost per Collection Point

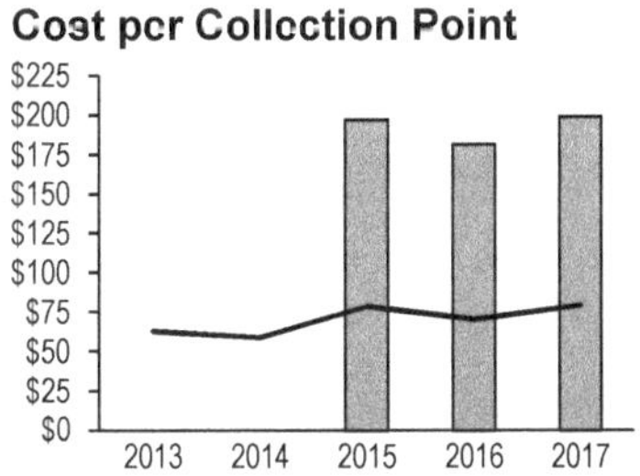

	2013	2014	2015	2016	2017
Chapel Hill			$197	$182	$199
Average	$63	$59	$79	$71	$79

Yard Waste and Leaf Collection Cost per Ton Collected

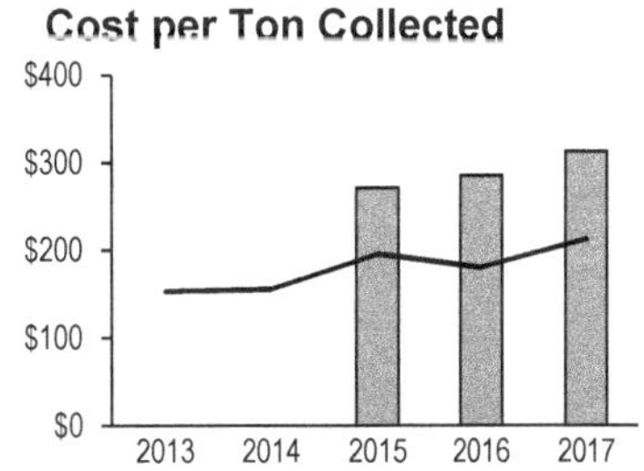

	2013	2014	2015	2016	2017
Chapel Hill			$271	$286	$313
Average	$153	$155	$196	$180	$212

Yard Waste and Leaf Tons Collected per Collection FTE

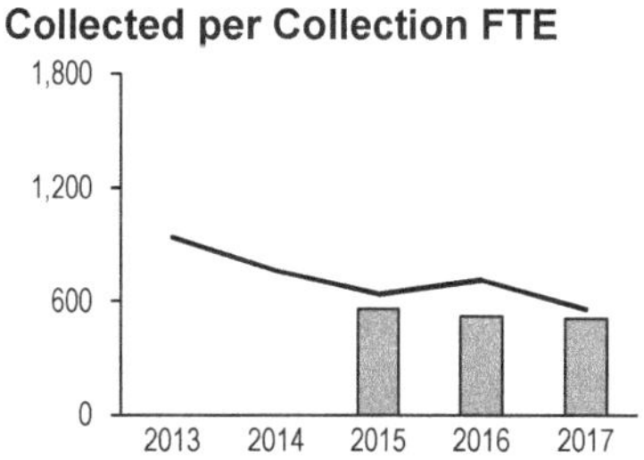

	2013	2014	2015	2016	2017
Chapel Hill			558	519	509
Average	937	760	637	711	558

Effectiveness Measures

Collection Complaints per 10,000 Collection Points

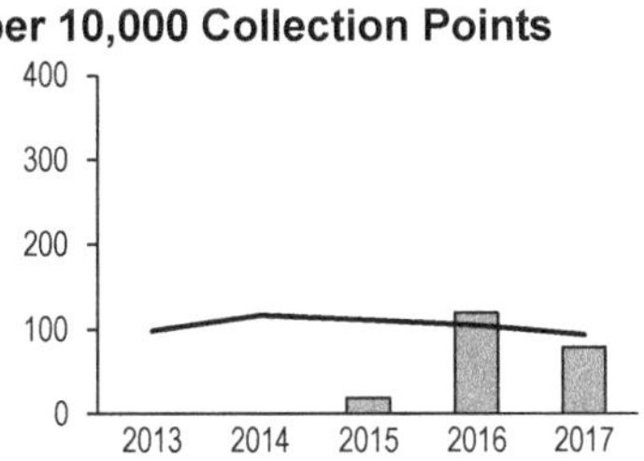

	2013	2014	2015	2016	2017
Chapel Hill			19	119	79
Average	98	117	111	105	93

Valid Complaints per 10,000 Collection Points

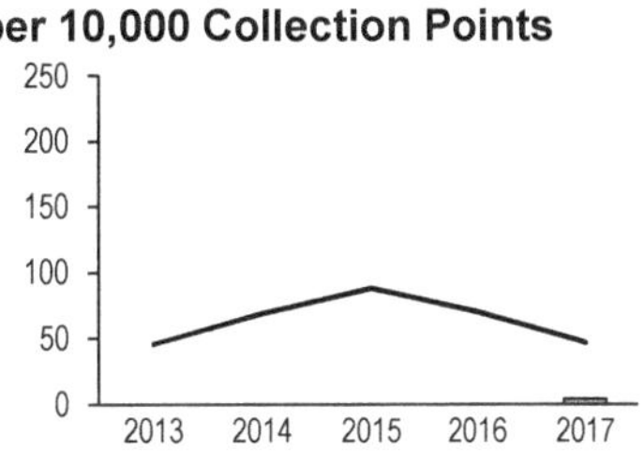

	2013	2014	2015	2016	2017
Chapel Hill					4
Average	46	69	88	70	47

Fiscal Year 2016–17

Explanatory Information

Service Level and Delivery
Charlotte collects yard waste once per week curbside. The city performs all yard waste collection.

Yard waste includes leaves, stems, grass, limbs, and other residential organic matter. Limbs should be separated into piles small enough for one individual to handle. Leaves and grass clippings must be placed in untied plastic bags or in uncovered trash cans. Yard waste placed at the curb by a commercial landscaping service will not be collected by the city. The city of Charlotte used thirty-four two-person crews working from rear loaders to service the entire city. Additional trucks and staff are allocated as a yard waste reserve.

Leaves are collected in bags and are debagged at the curb as part of the regular yard waste service. A special seasonal leaf collection is not done by the city of Charlotte.

Conditions Affecting Service, Performance, and Costs
Charlotte did not participate in the Benchmarking Project during FY 2014–15. No data are available for that year.

Charlotte's Solid Waste Services division focussed on improving customer service in FY 2013–14, explaining the drop in complaints.

Municipal Profile

Population (OSBM 2016)	830,258
Land Area (Square Miles)	305.48
Persons per Square Mile	2,718
Median Family Income U.S. Census 2010	$61,405

Service Profile

FTE Positions—Collection	74.00
FTE Positions—Other	0.00
Collection Frequency	
Yard Waste	1 x week
Collection Points	215,602
Tons Collected	
Yard Waste	55,535
Seasonal Leaves	with yard waste
Total Tons Collected	55,535
Monthly Service Fee	No

Full Cost Profile

Cost Breakdown by Percentage	
Personal Services	40.6%
Operating Costs	45.1%
Capital Costs	14.3%
TOTAL	100.0%
Cost Breakdown in Dollars	
Personal Services	$4,244,088
Operating Costs	$4,706,423
Capital Costs	$1,494,335
TOTAL	$10,444,847

Key: Charlotte ▒ Benchmarking Average — Fiscal Years 2013 through 2017

Resource Measures

Yard Waste and Leaf Collection Costs per Capita

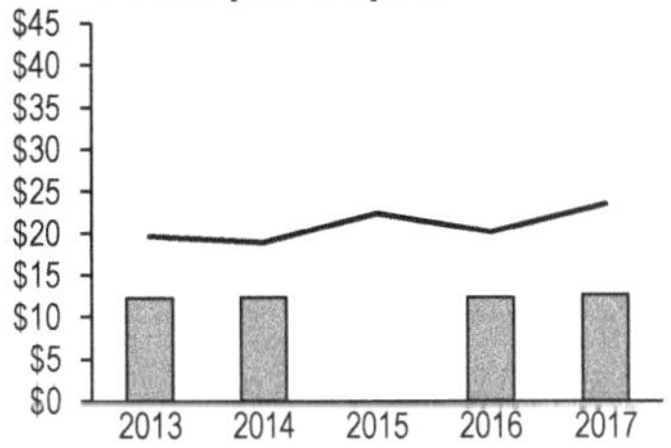

	2013	2014	2015	2016	2017
Charlotte	$12.20	$12.29		$12.25	$12.58
Average	$19.59	$18.82	$22.33	$20.10	$23.48

Yard Waste and Leaf Collection FTEs per 10,000 Population

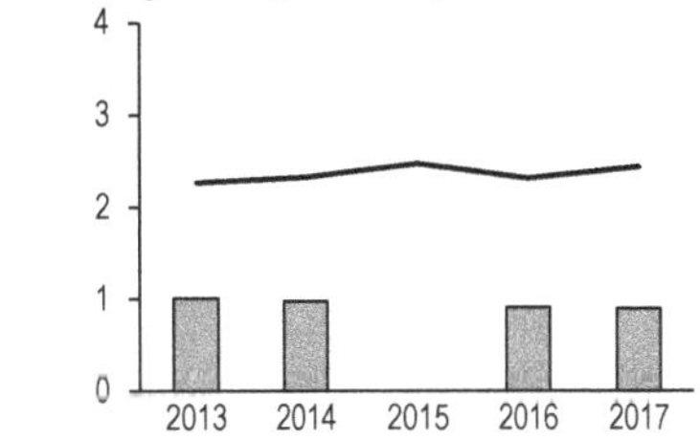

	2013	2014	2015	2016	2017
Charlotte	1.0	1.0		0.9	0.9
Average	2.3	2.3	2.5	2.3	2.4

Workload Measures

Yard Waste and Leaf Tons Collected per 1,000 Population

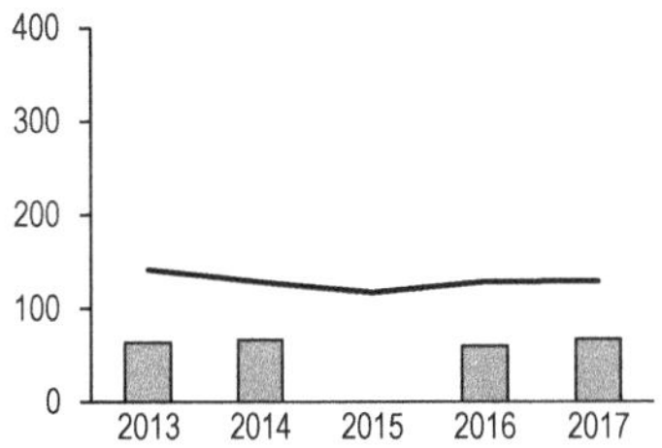

	2013	2014	2015	2016	2017
Charlotte	64	66		60	67
Average	141	128	117	128	129

Yard Waste and Leaf Tons Collected per 1,000 Collection Points

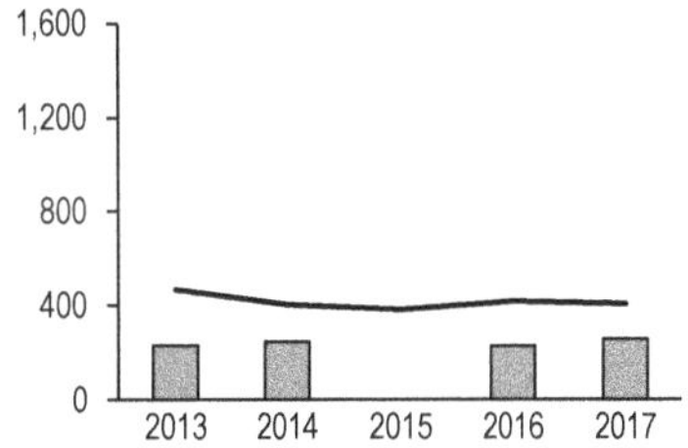

	2013	2014	2015	2016	2017
Charlotte	231	247		228	258
Average	468	404	384	416	406

Efficiency Measures

Yard Waste and Leaf Collection Cost per Collection Point

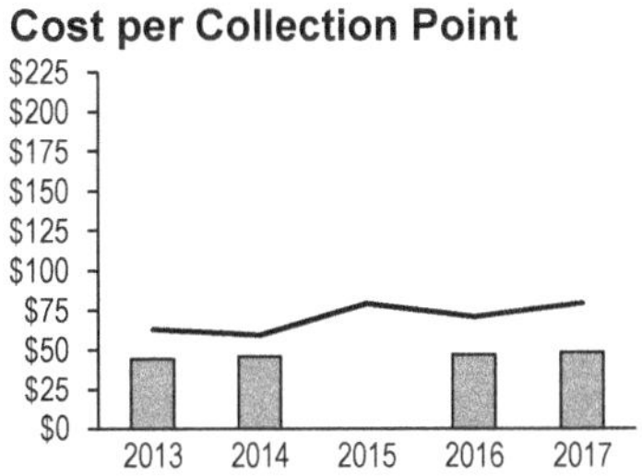

	2013	2014	2015	2016	2017
Charlotte	$44	$46		$47	$48
Average	$63	$59	$79	$71	$79

Yard Waste and Leaf Collection Cost per Ton Collected

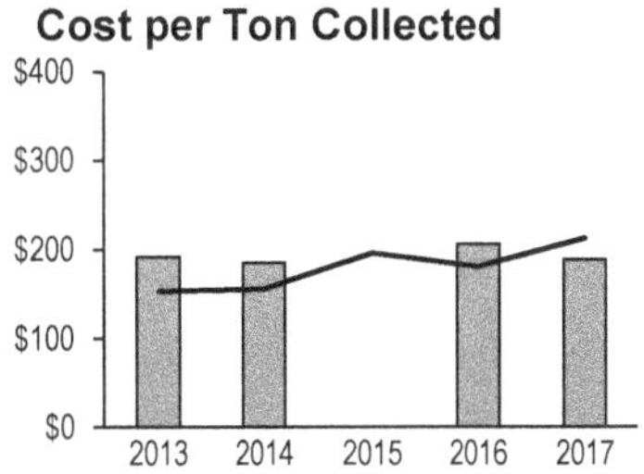

	2013	2014	2015	2016	2017
Charlotte	$192	$185		$206	$188
Average	$153	$155	$196	$180	$212

Yard Waste and Leaf Tons Collected per Collection FTE

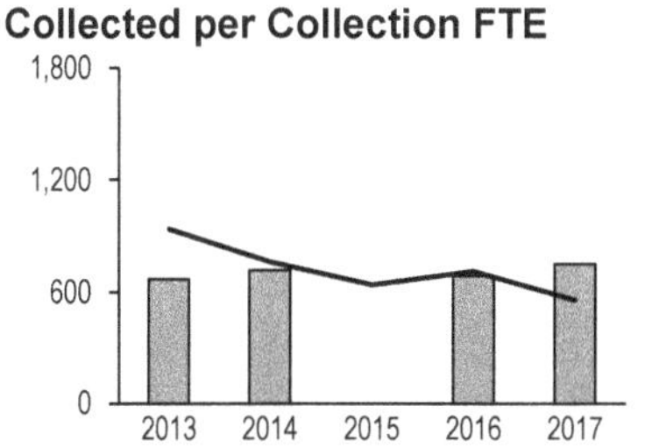

	2013	2014	2015	2016	2017
Charlotte	667	717		687	750
Average	937	760	637	711	558

Effectiveness Measures

Collection Complaints per 10,000 Collection Points

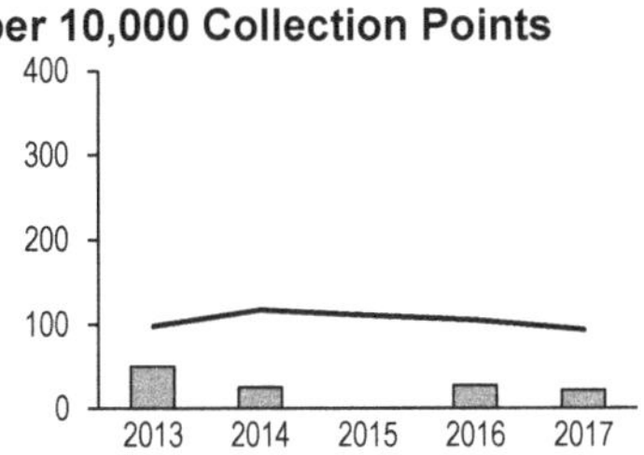

	2013	2014	2015	2016	2017
Charlotte	50	25		27	21
Average	98	117	111	105	93

Valid Complaints per 10,000 Collection Points

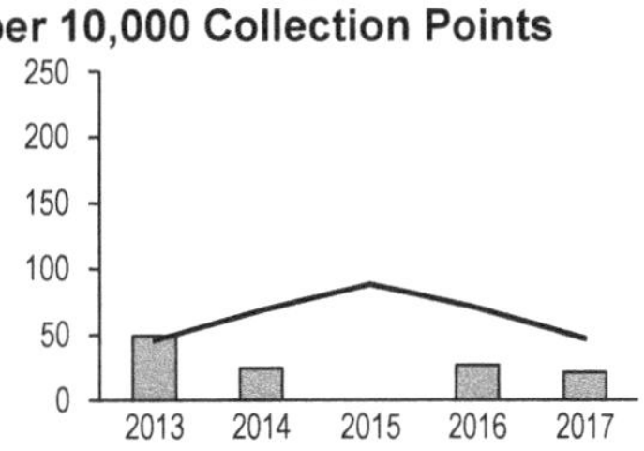

	2013	2014	2015	2016	2017
Charlotte	50	25		27	21
Average	46	69	88	70	47

Concord

Yard Waste/Leaf Collection

Fiscal Year 2016–17

Explanatory Information

Service Level and Delivery

Concord collects all yard waste once per week. Yard waste includes limbs, logs, grass clippings, shrubbery clippings, and leaves.

Concord uses three two-person crews with garbage trucks and a one-person crew with a dump truck to collect yard waste. Four two-person crews also are used to collect limbs and brush with knuckleboom trucks on a weekly basis.

Concord's seasonal loose leaf collection runs from mid-October through mid-February. Each street is serviced following a publicized schedule a minimum of three times for loose leaf collection during this period. Residents who bag their leaves receive weekly collection along with the normal yard waste collection program.

Conditions Affecting Service, Performance, and Costs

Municipal Profile

Population (OSBM 2016)	88,815
Land Area (Square Miles)	62.61
Persons per Square Mile	1,419
Median Family Income	$63,643
U.S. Census 2010	

Service Profile

FTE Positions—Collection	22.50
FTE Positions—Other	2.07
Collection Frequency	
Yard Waste	1 x week
Seasonal Leaf Collection	3 sweeps
Collection Points	31,211
Tons Collected	
Yard Waste	6,829
Seasonal Leaves	1,946
Total Tons Collected	8,775
Monthly Service Fee	No

Full Cost Profile

Cost Breakdown by Percentage	
Personal Services	50.0%
Operating Costs	30.5%
Capital Costs	19.5%
TOTAL	100.0%
Cost Breakdown in Dollars	
Personal Services	$1,188,183
Operating Costs	$723,650
Capital Costs	$462,239
TOTAL	$2,374,071

Key: Concord ▒ Benchmarking Average — Fiscal Years 2013 through 2017

Resource Measures

Yard Waste and Leaf Collection Costs per Capita

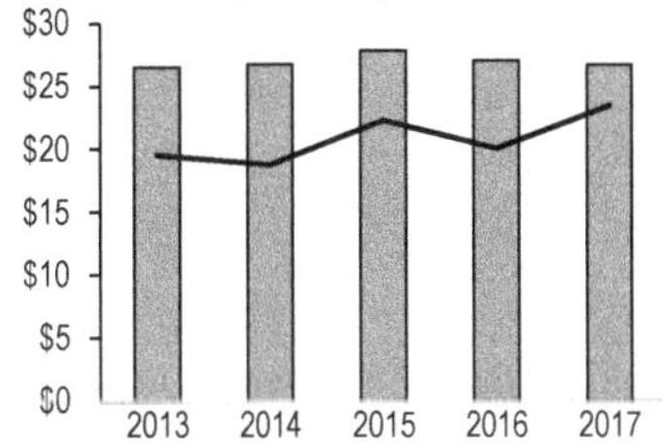

	2013	2014	2015	2016	2017
Concord	$26.55	$26.81	$27.90	$27.10	$26.73
Average	$19.59	$18.82	$22.33	$20.10	$23.48

Yard Waste and Leaf Collection FTEs per 10,000 Population

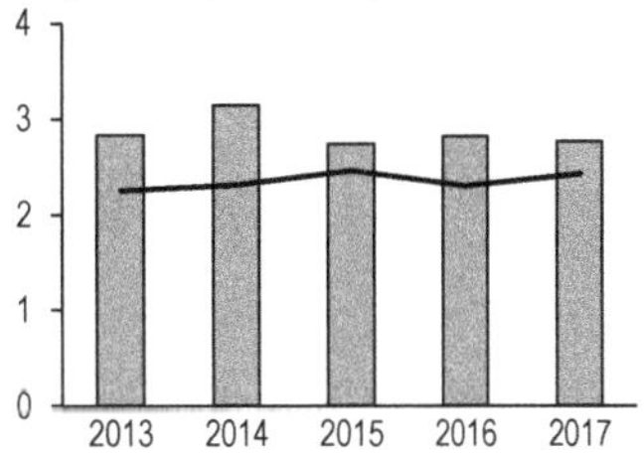

	2013	2014	2015	2016	2017
Concord	2.8	3.1	2.7	2.8	2.8
Average	2.3	2.3	2.5	2.3	2.4

Workload Measures

Yard Waste and Leaf Tons Collected per 1,000 Population

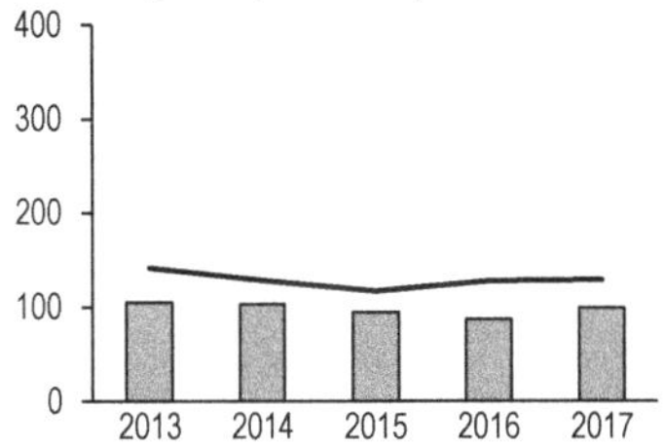

	2013	2014	2015	2016	2017
Concord	105	103	95	87	99
Average	141	128	117	128	129

Yard Waste and Leaf Tons Collected per 1,000 Collection Points

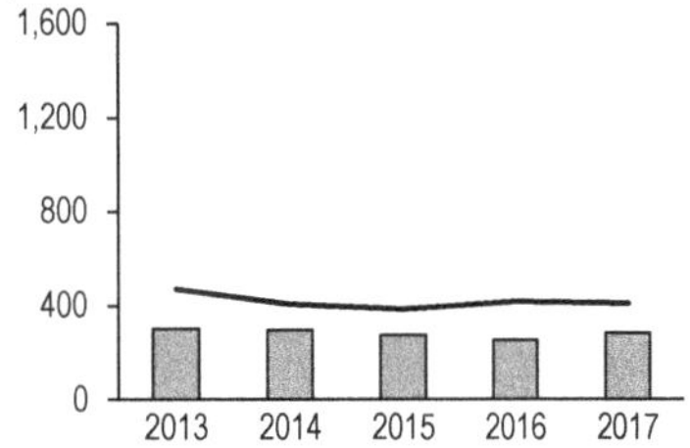

	2013	2014	2015	2016	2017
Concord	300	296	274	251	281
Average	468	404	384	416	406

Efficiency Measures

Yard Waste and Leaf Collection Cost per Collection Point

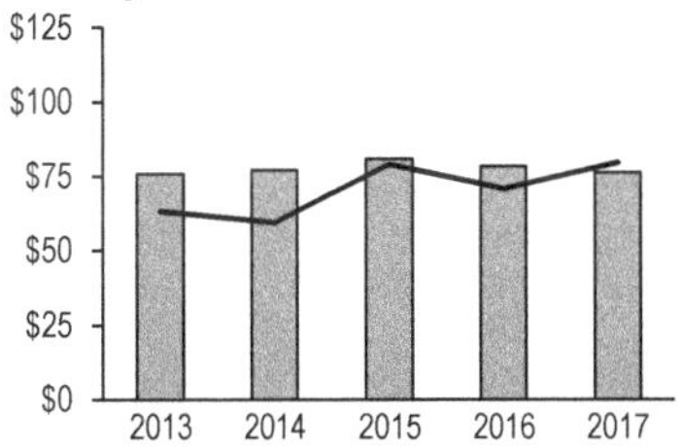

	2013	2014	2015	2016	2017
Concord	$76	$77	$81	$78	$76
Average	$63	$59	$79	$71	$79

Yard Waste and Leaf Collection Cost per Ton Collected

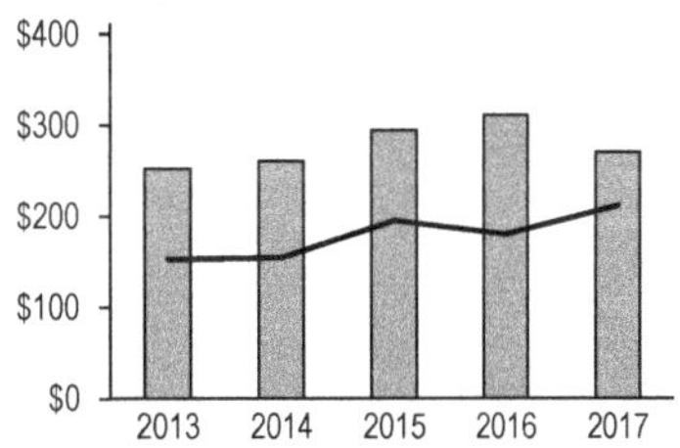

	2013	2014	2015	2016	2017
Concord	$252	$260	$295	$311	$271
Average	$153	$155	$196	$180	$212

Yard Waste and Leaf Tons Collected per Collection FTE

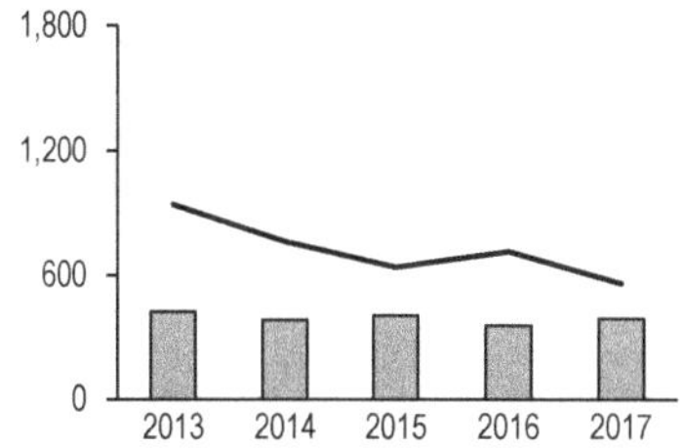

	2013	2014	2015	2016	2017
Concord	422	382	403	358	390
Average	937	760	637	711	558

Effectiveness Measures

Collection Complaints per 10,000 Collection Points

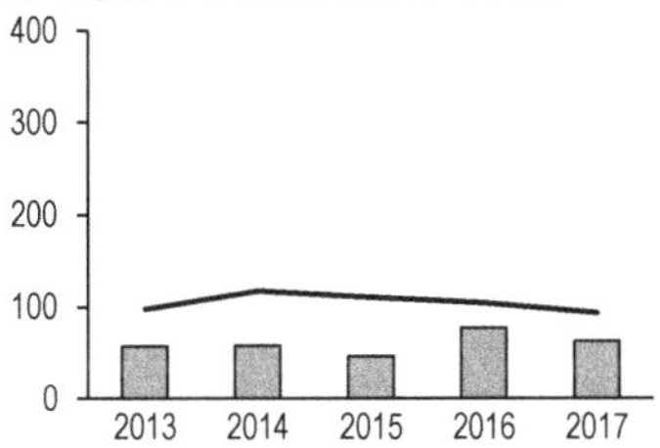

	2013	2014	2015	2016	2017
Concord	57	58	47	78	63
Average	98	117	111	105	93

Valid Complaints per 10,000 Collection Points

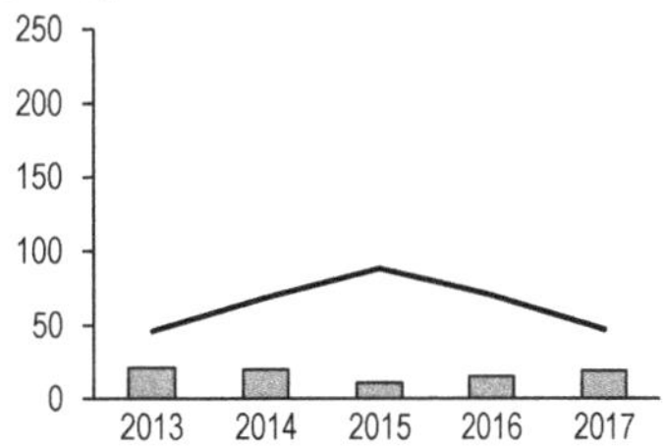

	2013	2014	2015	2016	2017
Concord	22	20	12	16	20
Average	46	69	88	70	47

Fiscal Year 2016–17

Explanatory Information

Service Level and Delivery

Goldsboro provides yard waste and seasonal leaf collection through the Solid Waste Divison of the Public Works Department. Yard waste includes grass clippings, vines, garden and hedge trimmings, shrubbery, and other vegetative debris. Yard waste must be placed at the curbside in loose piles.

Yard waste is collected by four two-person crews consisting of one driver and one collector. Yard waste is collected every two weeks rotating through diffferent sections of the city.

Seasonal leaf collection is done during the months of October through February. Collection is done every two weeks. Five crews are used for seasonal leaf collection consisting of one driver and two collectors per crew. One of the seasonal collectors is a temporary employee while the driver and the other collector are permanent employees. Leaves must be placed loose or in a leaf cage at the curb.

Conditions Affecting Service, Performance, and Costs

The city of Goldsboro joined the Benchmarking Project in July 2017 with the first year of data showing for FY 2016–17.

Municipal Profile

Population (OSBM 2016)	34,793
Land Area (Square Miles)	29.35
Persons per Square Mile	1,186
Median Family Income U.S. Census 2010	$33,879

Service Profile

FTE Positions—Collection	15.00
FTE Positions—Other	2.00
Collection Frequency	
Yard Waste	1 x 2 weeks
Seasonal Leaf Collection	1 x 2 weeks
Collection Points	14,372
Tons Collected	
Yard Waste	6,936
Seasonal Leaves	3,360
Total Tons Collected	10,296
Monthly Service Fee	No

Full Cost Profile

Cost Breakdown by Percentage	
Personal Services	59.7%
Operating Costs	40.3%
Capital Costs	0.0%
TOTAL	100.0%
Cost Breakdown in Dollars	
Personal Services	$867,116
Operating Costs	$584,491
Capital Costs	$0
TOTAL	$1,451,607

Key: Goldsboro ▒ Benchmarking Average — Fiscal Years 2013 through 2017

Resource Measures

Yard Waste and Leaf Collection Costs per Capita

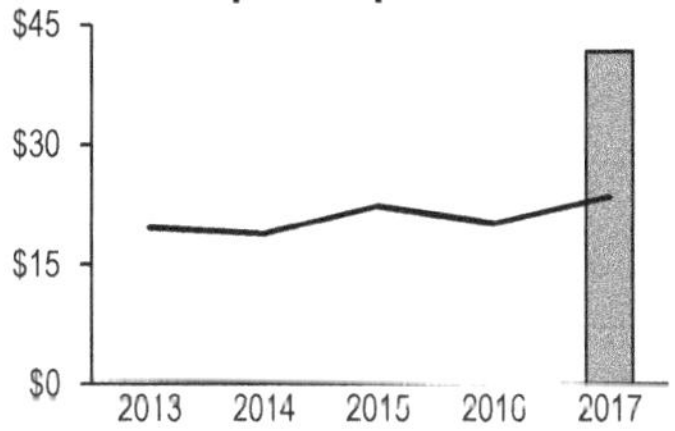

	2013	2014	2015	2016	2017
Goldsboro					$41.72
Average	$19.59	$18.82	$22.33	$20.10	$23.48

Yard Waste and Leaf Collection FTEs per 10,000 Population

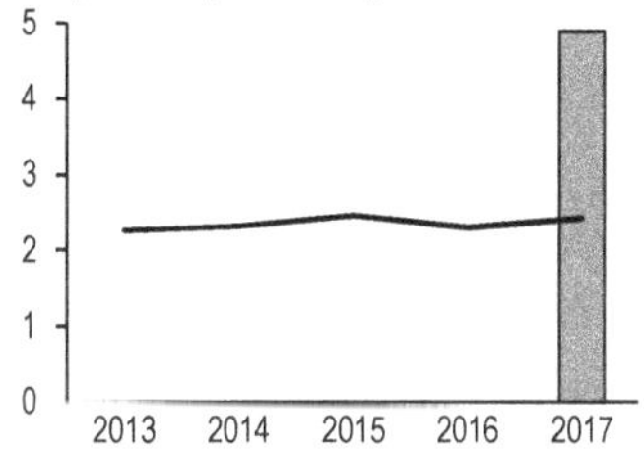

	2013	2014	2015	2016	2017
Goldsboro					4.9
Average	2.3	2.3	2.5	2.3	2.4

Workload Measures

Yard Waste and Leaf Tons Collected per 1,000 Population

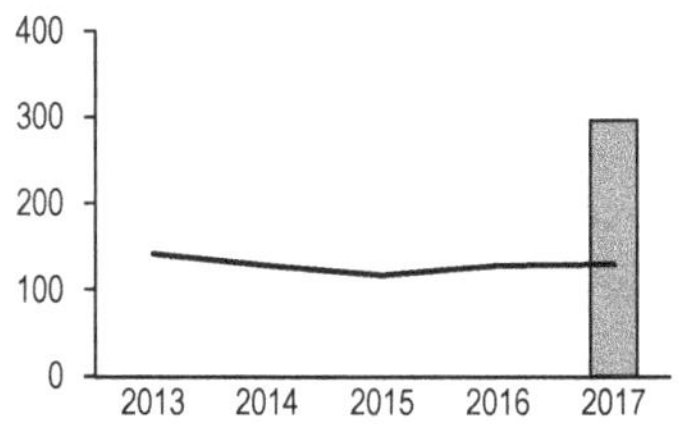

	2013	2014	2015	2016	2017
Goldsboro					296
Average	141	128	117	128	129

Yard Waste and Leaf Tons Collected per 1,000 Collection Points

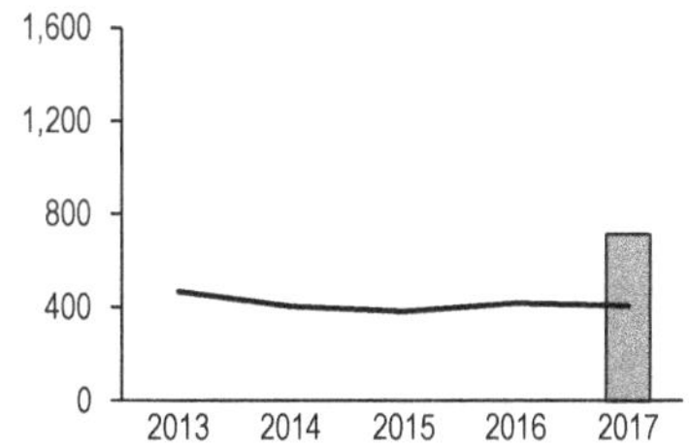

	2013	2014	2015	2016	2017
Goldsboro					716
Average	468	404	384	416	406

Efficiency Measures

Yard Waste and Leaf Collection Cost per Collection Point

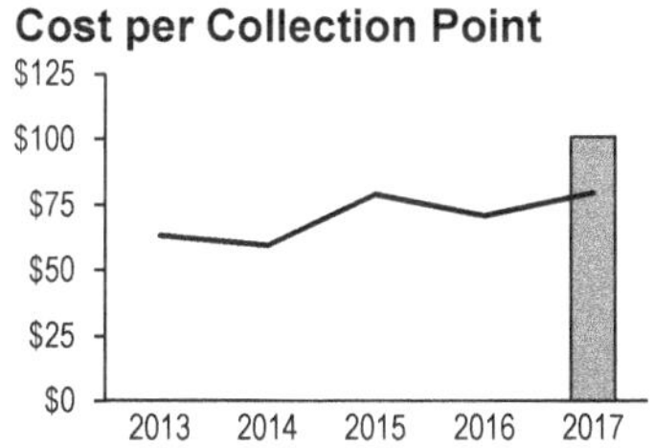

	2013	2014	2015	2016	2017
Goldsboro					$101
Average	$63	$59	$79	$71	$79

Yard Waste and Leaf Collection Cost per Ton Collected

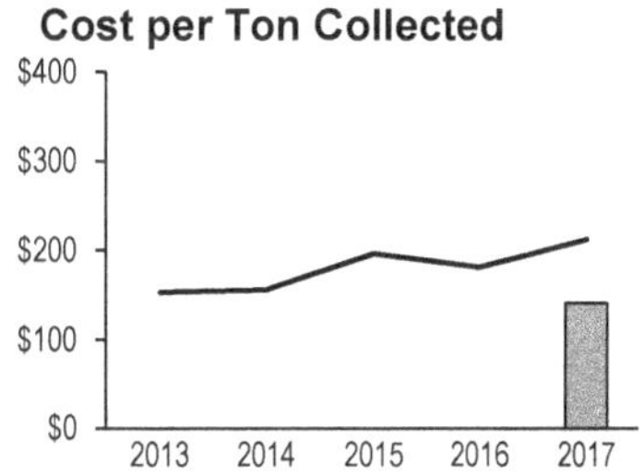

	2013	2014	2015	2016	2017
Goldsboro					$141
Average	$153	$155	$196	$180	$212

Yard Waste and Leaf Tons Collected per Collection FTE

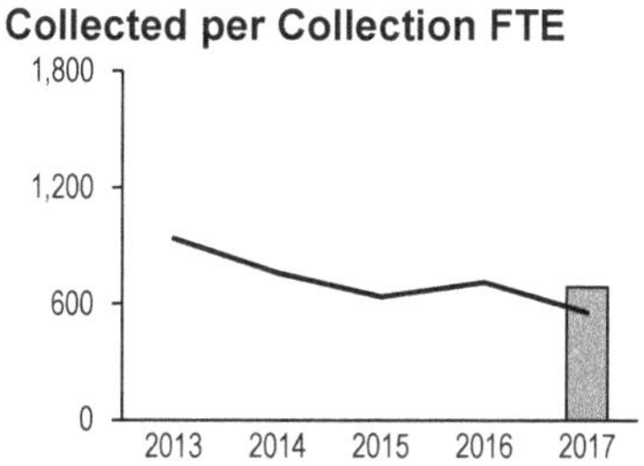

	2013	2014	2015	2016	2017
Goldsboro					686
Average	937	760	637	711	558

Effectiveness Measures

Collection Complaints per 10,000 Collection Points

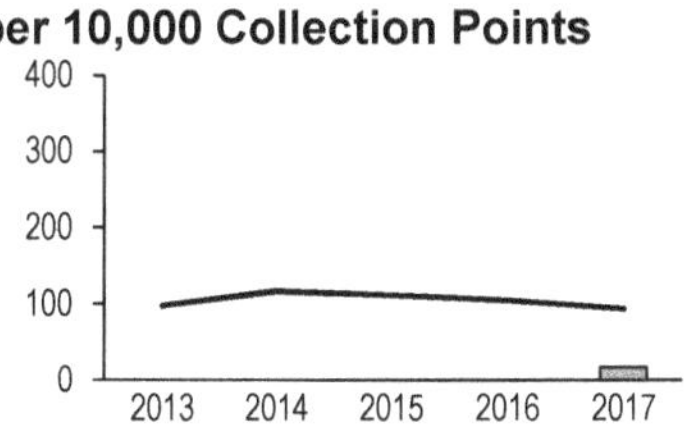

	2013	2014	2015	2016	2017
Goldsboro					17
Average	98	117	111	105	93

Valid Complaints per 10,000 Collection Points

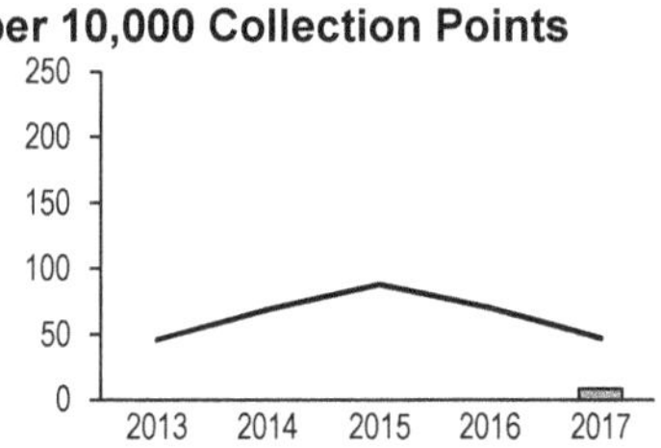

	2013	2014	2015	2016	2017
Goldsboro					8
Average	46	69	88	70	47

Fiscal Year 2016–17

Explanatory Information

Service Level and Delivery

Greensboro collects yard waste once per week curbside, either in clear plastic bags, thirty-five-gallon containers, or tied in bundles not to exceed 50 pounds or 5 feet in length. Yard waste includes grass, weeds, leaves, tree trimmings, plants, shrubbery trimmings, and other materials generated in yard maintenance. Yard waste does include some bagged leaves during the fall, and this waste is not broken out separately into leaf collection.

The city provides yard waste service to all single-family residences inside the city limits. Yard waste crews include nine two-person crews that rotate between driver and collector. The crews work four days per week, ten hours per day.

Seasonal leaf collection (October through January) is provided by Greensboro's Field Operations Division. Leaves are picked up a minimum of two times from November until mid-January by vacuuming the leaves from the curb.

Conditions Affecting Service, Performance, and Costs

Municipal Profile

Population (OSBM 2016)	284,343
Land Area (Square Miles)	128.72
Persons per Square Mile	2,209
Median Family Income U.S. Census 2010	$52,752

Service Profile

FTE Positions—Collection	44.79
FTE Positions—Other	1.15
Collection Frequency	
Yard Waste	1 x week
Seasonal Leaf Collection	2 sweeps
Collection Points	89,214
Tons Collected	
Yard Waste	12,800
Seasonal Leaves	10,565
Total Tons Collected	23,365
Monthly Service Fee	No

Full Cost Profile

Cost Breakdown by Percentage	
Personal Services	32.5%
Operating Costs	67.5%
Capital Costs	0.0%
TOTAL	100.0%
Cost Breakdown in Dollars	
Personal Services	$1,008,923
Operating Costs	$2,096,549
Capital Costs	$0
TOTAL	$3,105,472

Key: Greensboro ▒ Benchmarking Average — Fiscal Years 2013 through 2017

Resource Measures

Yard Waste and Leaf Collection Costs per Capita

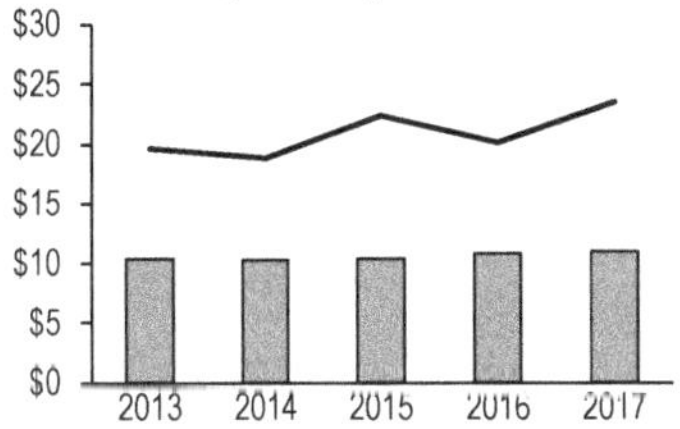

	2013	2014	2015	2016	2017
Greensboro	$10.32	$10.24	$10.36	$10.74	$10.92
Average	$19.59	$18.82	$22.33	$20.10	$23.48

Yard Waste and Leaf Collection FTEs per 10,000 Population

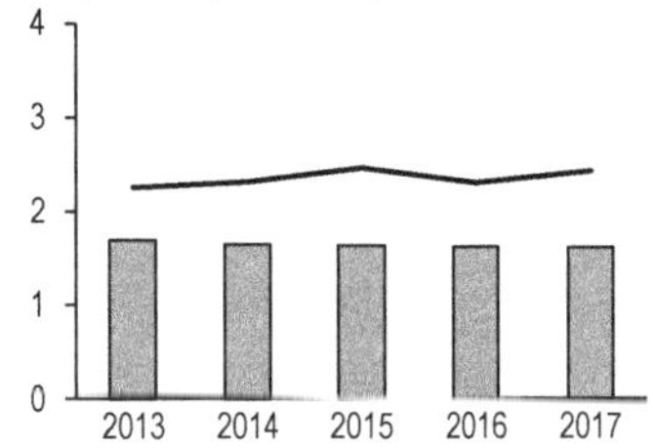

	2013	2014	2015	2016	2017
Greensboro	1.7	1.6	1.6	1.6	1.6
Average	2.3	2.3	2.5	2.3	2.4

Workload Measures

Yard Waste and Leaf Tons Collected per 1,000 Population

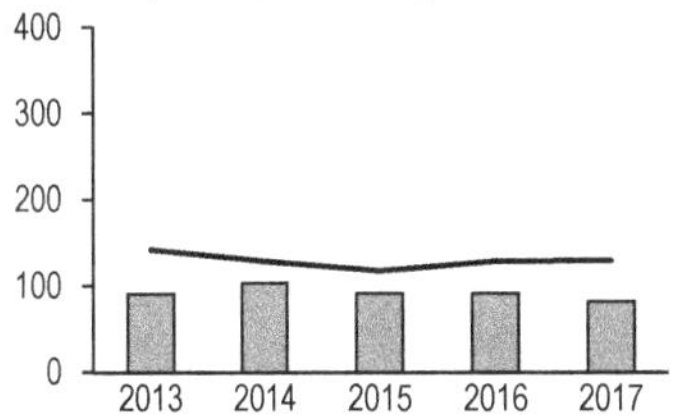

	2013	2014	2015	2016	2017
Greensboro	91	103	92	92	82
Average	141	128	117	128	129

Yard Waste and Leaf Tons Collected per 1,000 Collection Points

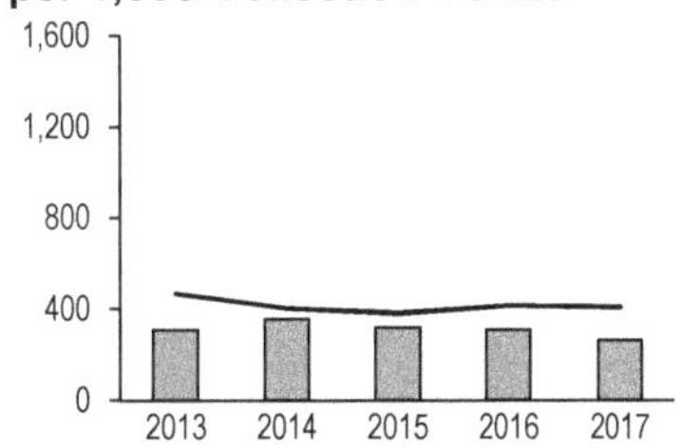

	2013	2014	2015	2016	2017
Greensboro	308	355	318	308	262
Average	468	404	384	416	406

Efficiency Measures

Yard Waste and Leaf Collection Cost per Collection Point

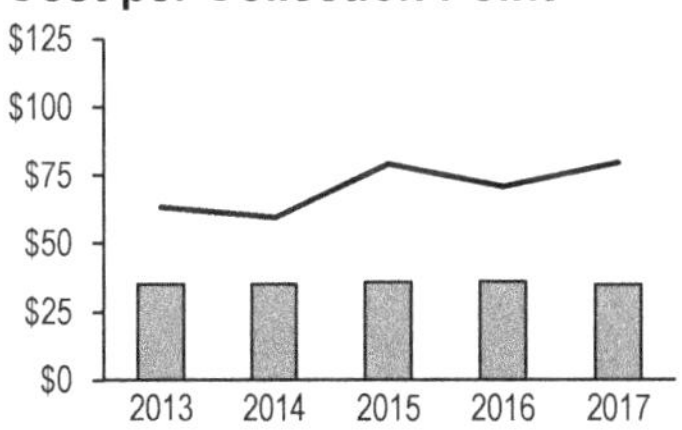

	2013	2014	2015	2016	2017
Greensboro	$35	$35	$36	$36	$35
Average	$63	$59	$79	$71	$79

Yard Waste and Leaf Collection Cost per Ton Collected

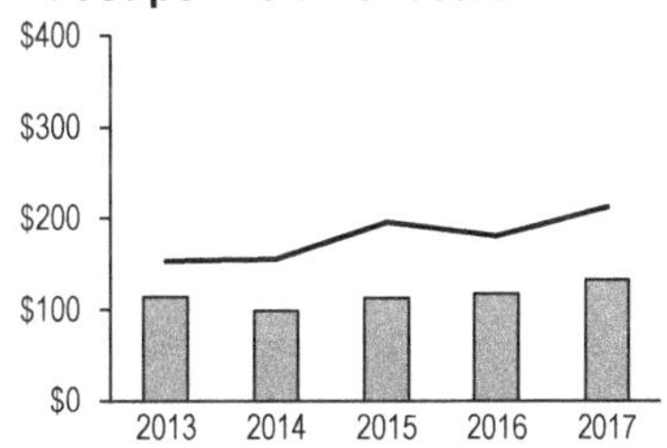

	2013	2014	2015	2016	2017
Greensboro	$114	$99	$113	$117	$133
Average	$153	$155	$196	$180	$212

Yard Waste and Leaf Tons Collected per Collection FTE

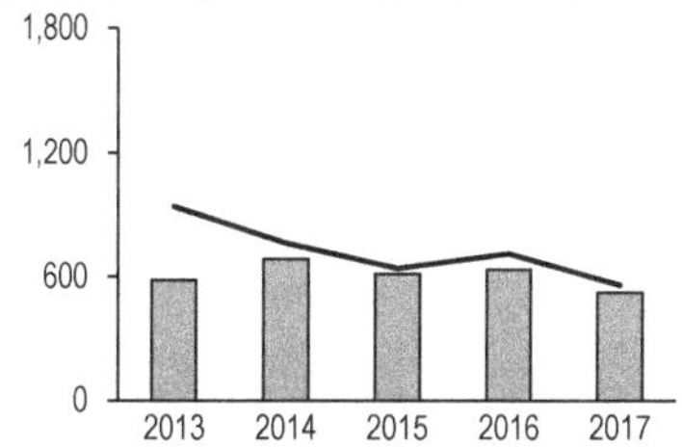

	2013	2014	2015	2016	2017
Greensboro	582	683	611	632	522
Average	937	760	637	711	558

Effectiveness Measures

Collection Complaints per 10,000 Collection Points

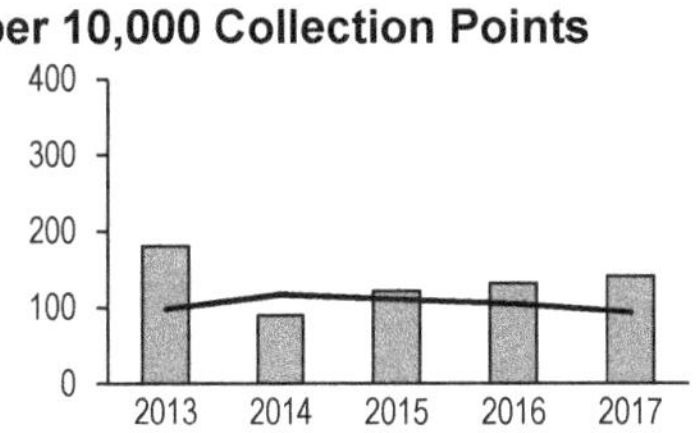

	2013	2014	2015	2016	2017
Greensboro	180	90	122	132	141
Average	98	117	111	105	93

Valid Complaints per 10,000 Collection Points

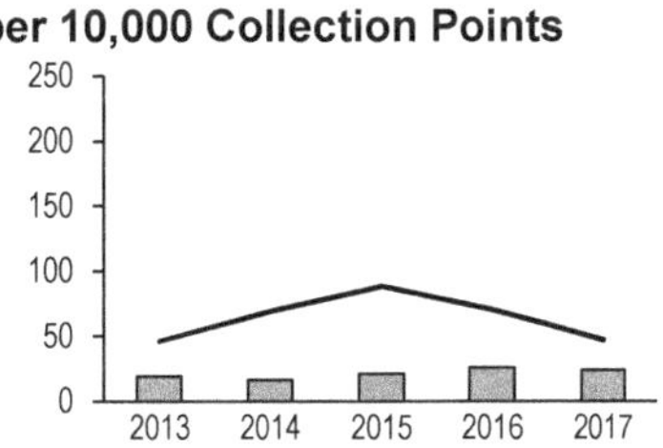

	2013	2014	2015	2016	2017
Greensboro	19	16	21	26	24
Average	46	69	88	70	47

Fiscal Year 2016–17

Explanatory Information

Service Level and Delivery

Greenville collects yard waste once per week curbside. Yard waste includes tree limbs up to 6 feet in length or 4 inches in diameter, bushes, grass clippings, and other vegetative matter. The city does not charge a separate fee for yard waste, leaves, or bulky items. It is part of the solid waste fee.

Greenville uses two-person crews to collect yard waste. Crews are made up of a driver and a collection worker. Each crew has an assigned route for each day.

The city's seasonal leaf collection service runs from November to February. Leaves are collected weekly from the backs of curbs. The city uses five crews, each having a driver and two collection workers. The leaf collection crews are all seasonal employees.

Conditions Affecting Service, Performance, and Costs

Greenville experienced equipment breakdowns and personnel changes during FY 2013–14, which led to a high level of complaints.

Municipal Profile

Population (OSBM 2016)	87,989
Land Area (Square Miles)	35.41
Persons per Square Mile	2,485
Median Family Income	$50,395
U.S. Census 2010	

Service Profile

FTE Positions—Collection	20.3
FTE Positions—Other	1.3
Collection Frequency	
Yard Waste	1 x week
Seasonal Leaf Collection	1 x week
Collection Points	19,294
Tons Collected	
Yard Waste	5,725
Seasonal Leaves	910
Total Tons Collected	6,635
Monthly Service Fee	No

Full Cost Profile

Cost Breakdown by Percentage	
Personal Services	40.4%
Operating Costs	42.4%
Capital Costs	17.2%
TOTAL	100.0%
Cost Breakdown in Dollars	
Personal Services	$1,351,061
Operating Costs	$1,415,495
Capital Costs	$575,174
TOTAL	$3,341,730

Key: Greenville ▒ Benchmarking Average — Fiscal Years 2013 through 2017

Resource Measures

Yard Waste and Leaf Collection Costs per Capita

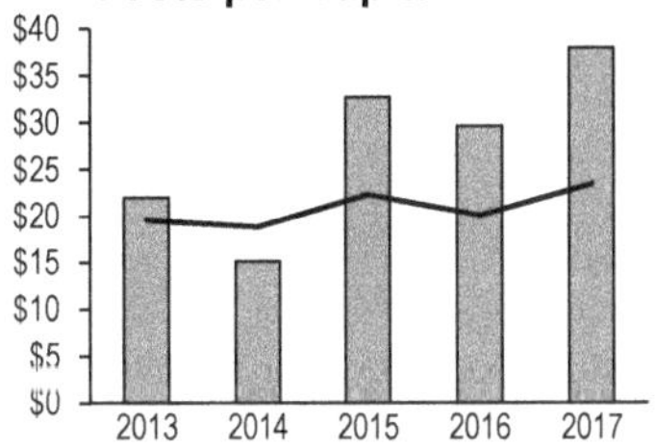

	2013	2014	2015	2016	2017
Greenville	$21.94	$15.10	$32.73	$29.59	$37.98
Average	$19.59	$18.82	$22.33	$20.10	$23.48

Yard Waste and Leaf Collection FTEs per 10,000 Population

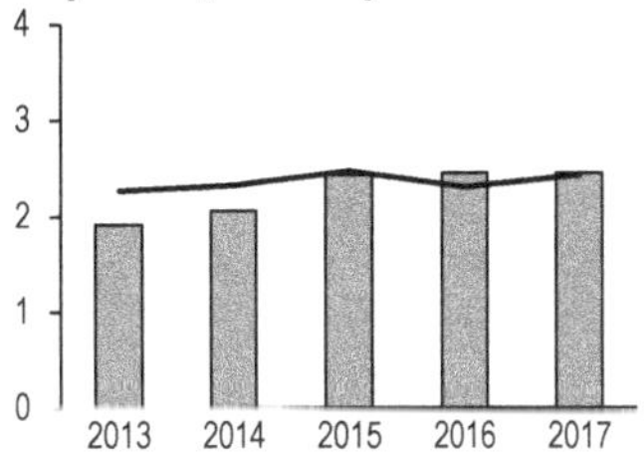

	2013	2014	2015	2016	2017
Greenville	1.9	2.1	2.4	2.5	2.5
Average	2.3	2.3	2.5	2.3	2.4

Workload Measures

Yard Waste and Leaf Tons Collected per 1,000 Population

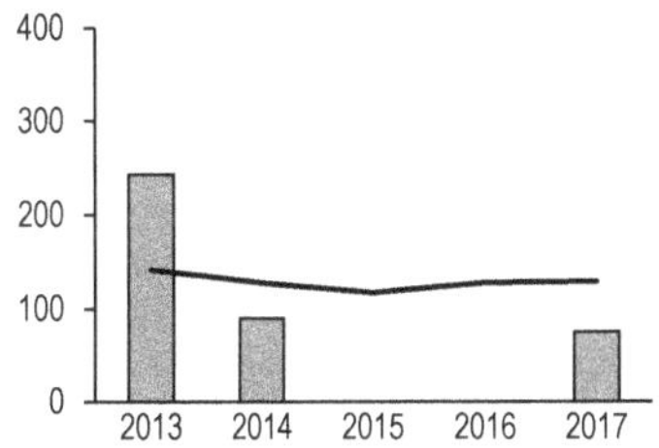

	2013	2014	2015	2016	2017
Greenville	244	90			75
Average	141	128	117	128	129

Yard Waste and Leaf Tons Collected per 1,000 Collection Points

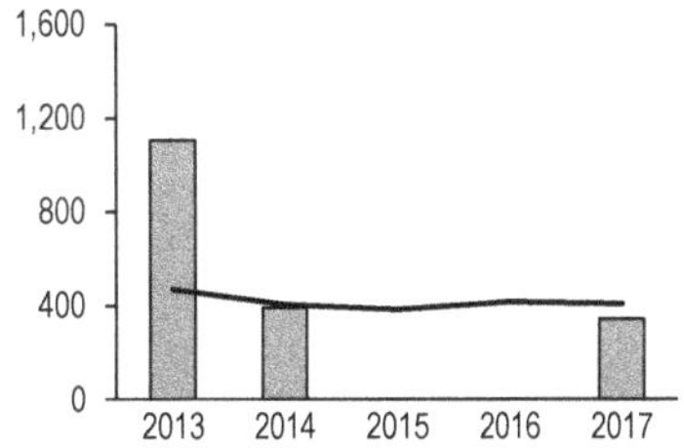

	2013	2014	2015	2016	2017
Greenville	1,105	392			344
Average	468	404	384	416	406

Efficiency Measures

Yard Waste and Leaf Collection Cost per Collection Point

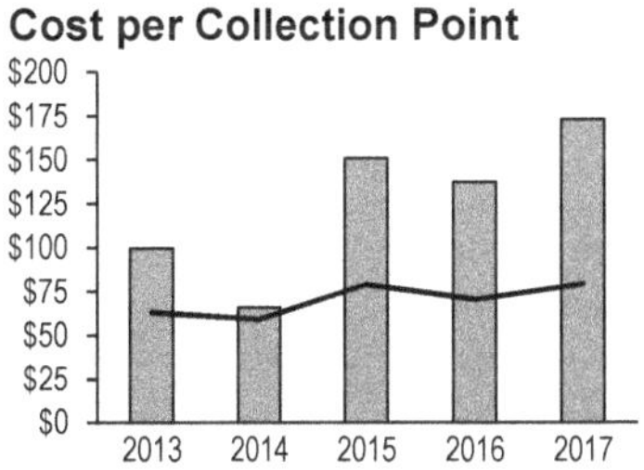

	2013	2014	2015	2016	2017
Greenville	$99	$66	$151	$137	$173
Average	$63	$59	$79	$71	$79

Yard Waste and Leaf Collection Cost per Ton Collected

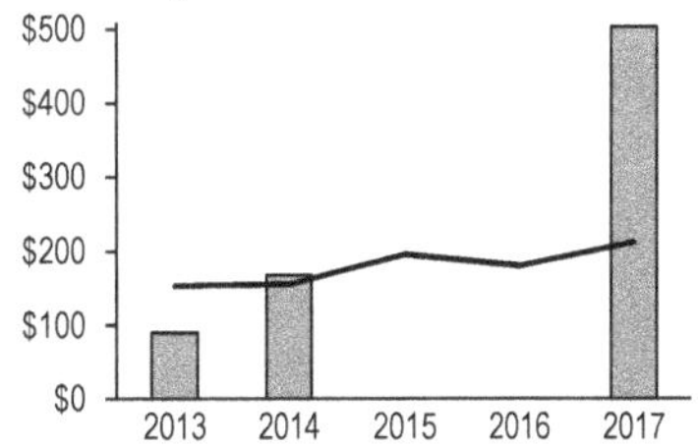

	2013	2014	2015	2016	2017
Greenville	$90	$168			$504
Average	$153	$155	$196	$180	$212

Yard Waste and Leaf Tons Collected per Collection FTE

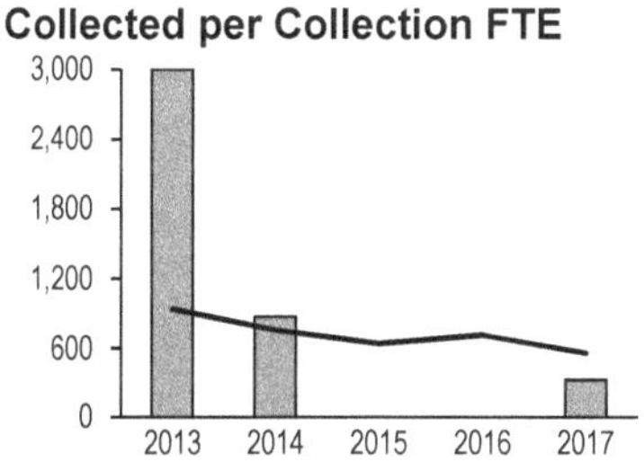

	2013	2014	2015	2016	2017
Greenville	3,000	872			327
Average	937	760	637	711	558

Effectiveness Measures

Collection Complaints per 10,000 Collection Points

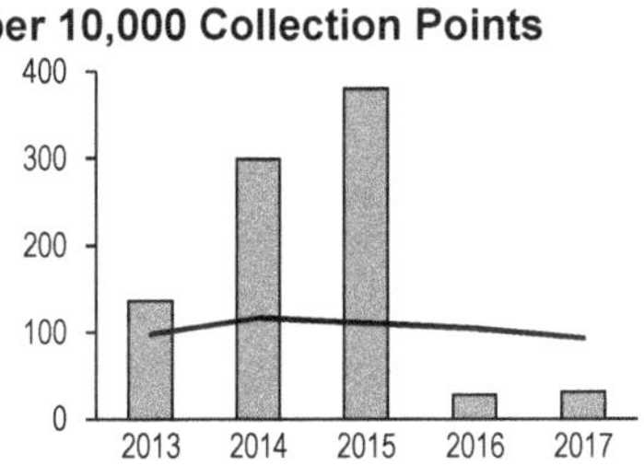

	2013	2014	2015	2016	2017
Greenville	136	299	380	27	31
Average	98	117	111	105	93

Valid Complaints per 10,000 Collection Points

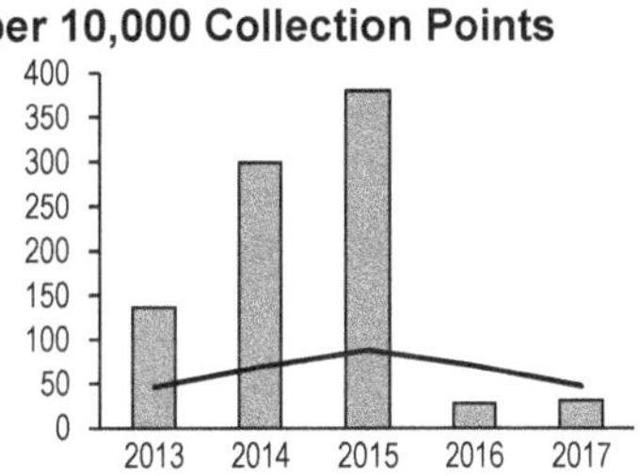

	2013	2014	2015	2016	2017
Greenville	136	299	380	27	31
Average	46	69	88	70	47

Fiscal Year 2016–17

Explanatory Information

Service Level and Delivery

Hickory collects yard waste once per week curbside. Yard waste includes tree limbs less than 6 feet in length and 6 inches in diameter, shrubs, grass clippings, leaves, and other vegetative matter. The city does not charge a separate fee for yard waste, leaves, or bulky items. It is part of the solid waste fee. Residents use either clear plastic bags or open containers.

Hickory is divided into five sections for the yard waste program. Three routes are serviced each day within each section, using three rear loaders with crews comprised of one driver and one laborer each. Large piles are collected with a knuckleboom loader with one driver on a scheduled basis working about half-time.

All yard waste is collected and stockpiled at the city yard waste facility. Debris is ground into mulch or compost and sold back to citizens or used for city projects.

The city's seasonal leaf collection service runs from November to January. There are two sweeps down each city street during this time. City crews use leaf vacuums to collect leaves in box trucks. Hickory uses temporary contract workers to help with leaf collection. These seasonal employees are counted in the total employee count, but only for the one-fourth of the year they work.

Conditions Affecting Service, Performance, and Costs

Hickory's yard waste collection is set up to provide regular service but also takes requests for service when collection is needed. These calls for service cannot be separated out from actual complaints, so complaint data cannot be reported for this service area.

Municipal Profile

Population (OSBM 2016)	40,453
Land Area (Square Miles)	29.90
Persons per Square Mile	1,353
Median Family Income U.S. Census 2010	$54,093

Service Profile

FTE Positions—Collection	9.75
FTE Positions—Other	0.7
Collection Frequency	
Yard Waste	1 x week
Seasonal Leaf Collection	2 sweeps
Collection Points	12,200
Tons Collected	
Yard Waste	6,302
Seasonal Leaves	3,870
Total Tons Collected	10,172
Monthly Service Fee	No

Full Cost Profile

Cost Breakdown by Percentage	
Personal Services	38.1%
Operating Costs	47.6%
Capital Costs	14.3%
TOTAL	100.0%
Cost Breakdown in Dollars	
Personal Services	$278,612
Operating Costs	$347,836
Capital Costs	$104,698
TOTAL	$731,146

Key: Hickory ▒ Benchmarking Average — Fiscal Years 2013 through 2017

Resource Measures

Yard Waste and Leaf Collection Costs per Capita

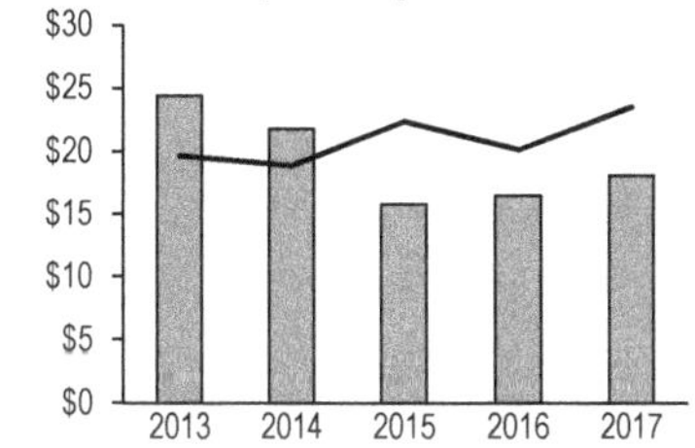

	2013	2014	2015	2016	2017
Hickory	$24.38	$21.78	$15.80	$16.47	$18.07
Average	$19.59	$18.82	$22.33	$20.10	$23.48

Yard Waste and Leaf Collection FTEs per 10,000 Population

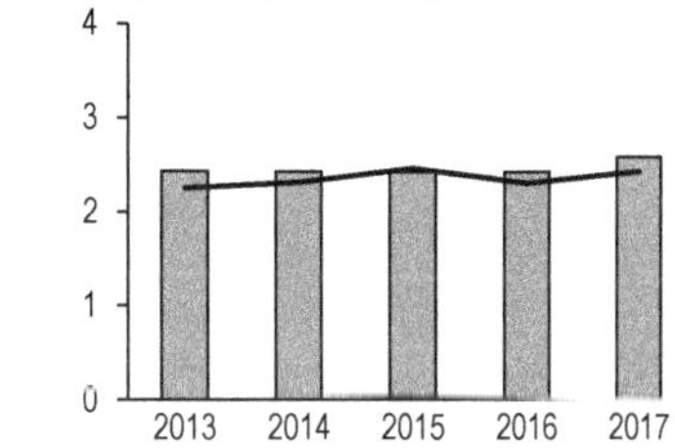

	2013	2014	2015	2016	2017
Hickory	2.4	2.4	2.4	2.4	2.6
Average	2.3	2.3	2.5	2.3	2.4

Workload Measures

Yard Waste and Leaf Tons Collected per 1,000 Population

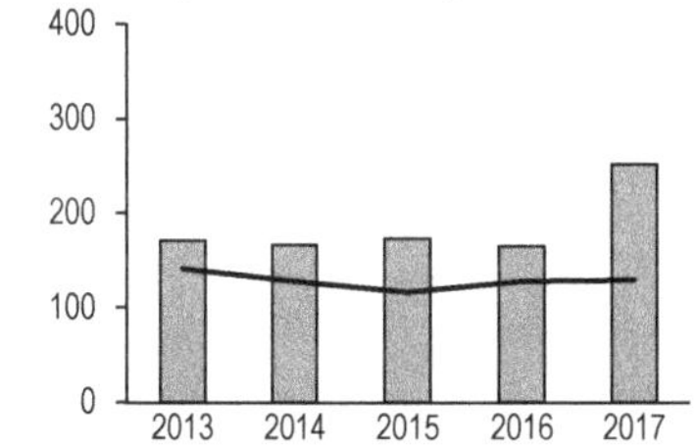

	2013	2014	2015	2016	2017
Hickory	171	166	173	164	251
Average	141	128	117	128	129

Yard Waste and Leaf Tons Collected per 1,000 Collection Points

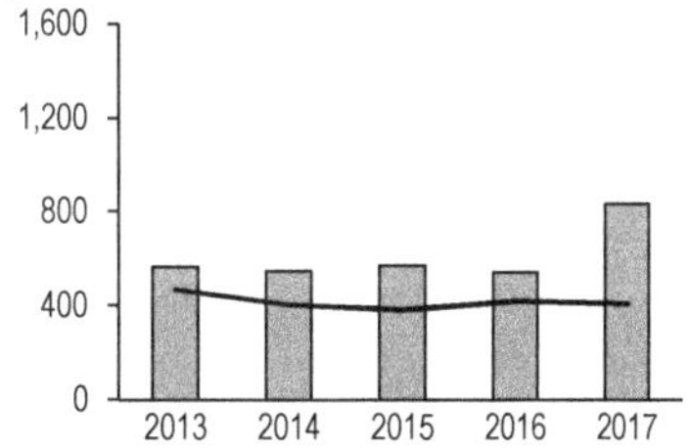

	2013	2014	2015	2016	2017
Hickory	565	546	571	543	834
Average	468	404	384	416	406

Efficiency Measures

Yard Waste and Leaf Collection Cost per Collection Point

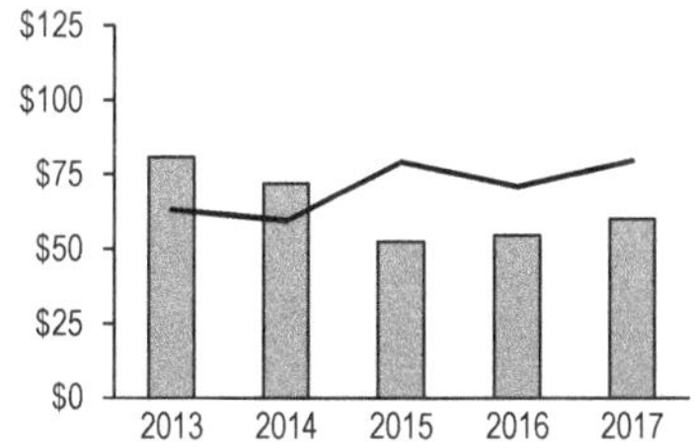

	2013	2014	2015	2016	2017
Hickory	$81	$72	$52	$54	$60
Average	$63	$59	$79	$71	$79

Yard Waste and Leaf Collection Cost per Ton Collected

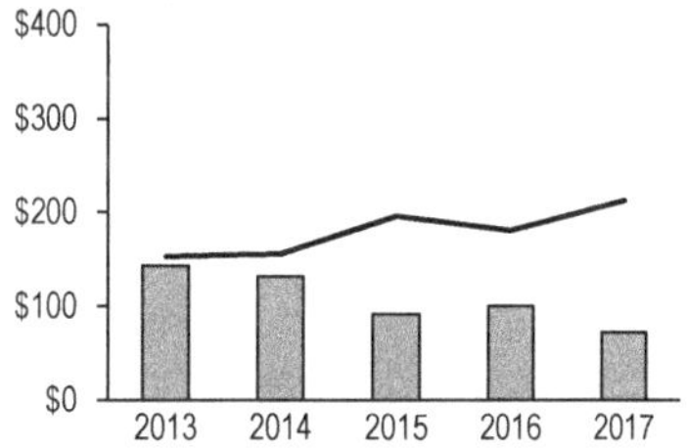

	2013	2014	2015	2016	2017
Hickory	$143	$131	$92	$100	$72
Average	$153	$155	$196	$180	$212

Yard Waste and Leaf Tons Collected per Collection FTE

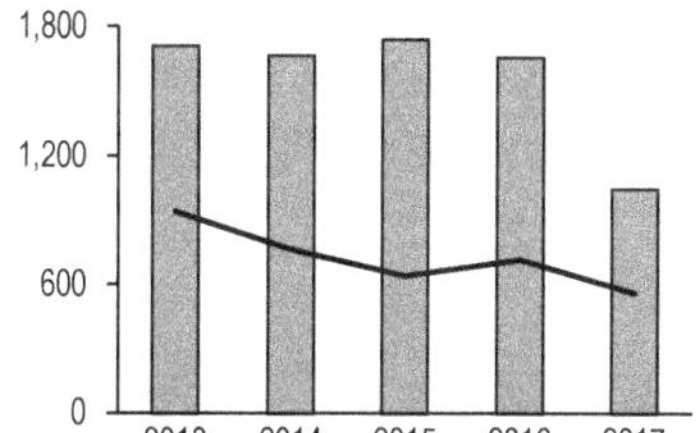

	2013	2014	2015	2016	2017
Hickory	1,709	1,667	1,741	1,657	1,043
Average	937	760	637	711	558

Effectiveness Measures

Collection Complaints per 10,000 Collection Points

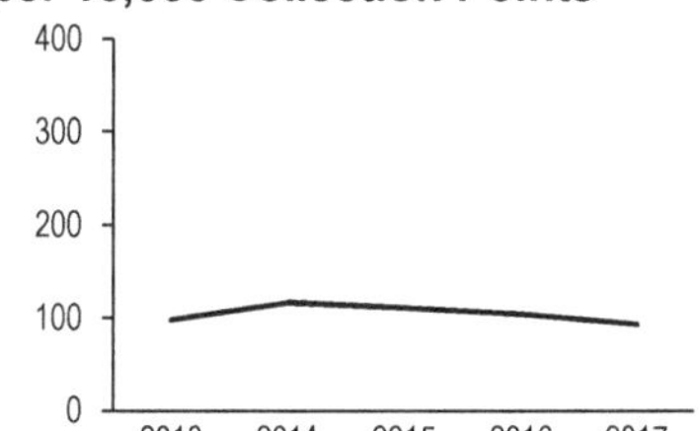

	2013	2014	2015	2016	2017
Hickory					
Average	98	117	111	105	93

Valid Complaints per 10,000 Collection Points

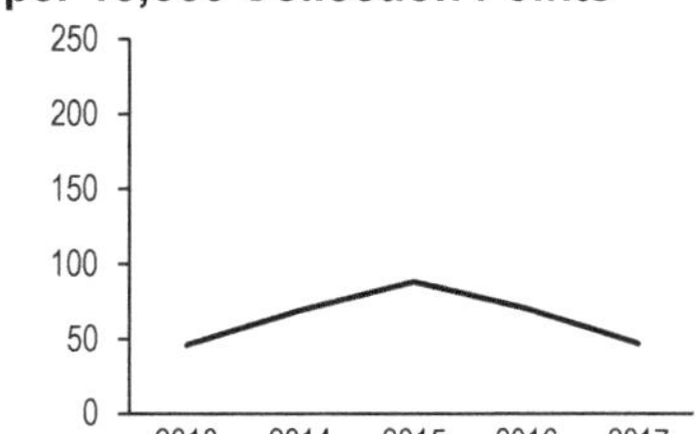

	2013	2014	2015	2016	2017
Hickory					
Average	46	69	88	70	47

Fiscal Year 2016–17

Explanatory Information

Service Level and Delivery

Collectible yard waste in High Point's program consists solely of vegetative matter resulting from landscaping and lawn maintenance, including grass clippings, leaves, brush, tree branches, flowers, and other organic materials.

Yard waste is collected once each week curbside using three-person crews. Each crew is composed of one driver and two collectors. The work schedule is from Monday through Thursday. There is no separate fee charged for yard waste collection.

The city provides two citywide cycles of loose leaf collection beginning mid-November and continuing through mid-January. There are seven crews of one person each operating a truck mounted leaf vacumm with in-cab controls. There are usually two additional crews consisting of five permanent employees using a self-contained leaf vacumm pulled behind a small dump truck. This operation requires employees to manually rake leaves and operate teh suction hose. The addition of more of the single operator leaf collection units has allowed the city to reduce the number of employees needed for loose leaf collection. Bagged leaves are collected once per week with the regular yard waste.

Conditions Affecting Service, Performance, and Costs

Municipal Profile

Population (OSBM 2016)	110,244
Land Area (Square Miles)	55.14
Persons per Square Mile	1,999
Median Family Income	$49,720
U.S. Census 2010	

Service Profile

FTE Positions—Collection	16.1
FTE Positions—Other	0.8
Collection Frequency	
Yard Waste	1 x week
Seasonal Leaf Collection	2 sweeps
Collection Points	42,418
Tons Collected	
Yard Waste	4,243
Seasonal Leaves	2,803
Total Tons Collected	7,046
Monthly Service Fee	No

Full Cost Profile

Cost Breakdown by Percentage	
Personal Services	49.6%
Operating Costs	31.2%
Capital Costs	19.2%
TOTAL	100.0%
Cost Breakdown in Dollars	
Personal Services	$860,657
Operating Costs	$542,222
Capital Costs	$333,525
TOTAL	$1,736,404

Key: High Point ▒ Benchmarking Average — Fiscal Years 2013 through 2017

Resource Measures

Yard Waste and Leaf Collection Costs per Capita

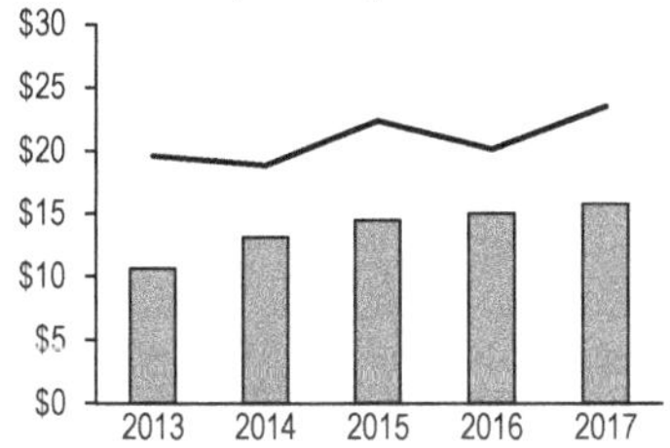

	2013	2014	2015	2016	2017
High Point	$10.61	$13.08	$14.41	$14.97	$15.75
Average	$19.59	$18.82	$22.33	$20.10	$23.48

Yard Waste and Leaf Collection FTEs per 10,000 Population

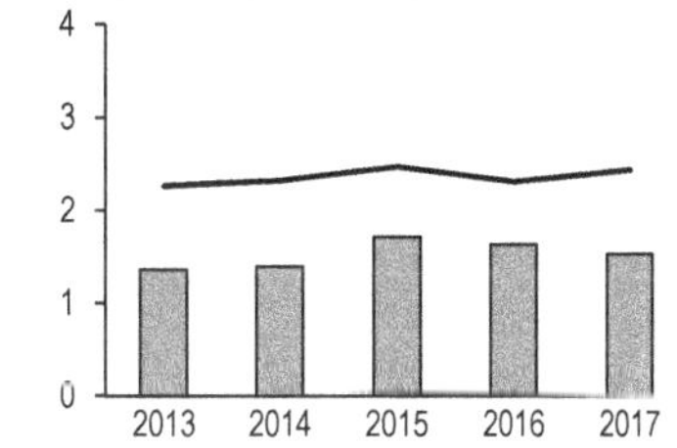

	2013	2014	2015	2016	2017
High Point	1.4	1.4	1.7	1.6	1.5
Average	2.3	2.3	2.5	2.3	2.4

Workload Measures

Yard Waste and Leaf Tons Collected per 1,000 Population

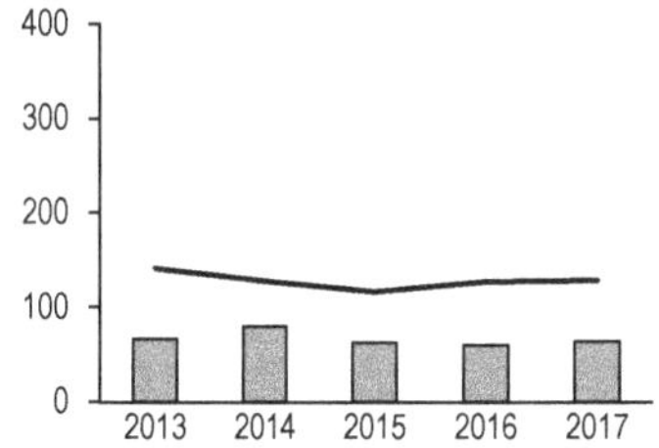

	2013	2014	2015	2016	2017
High Point	67	80	63	60	64
Average	141	128	117	128	129

Yard Waste and Leaf Tons Collected per 1,000 Collection Points

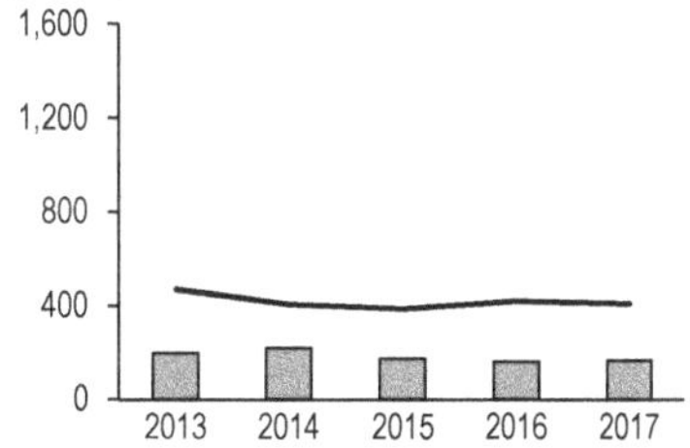

	2013	2014	2015	2016	2017
High Point	197	219	173	159	166
Average	468	404	384	416	406

Efficiency Measures

Yard Waste and Leaf Collection Cost per Collection Point

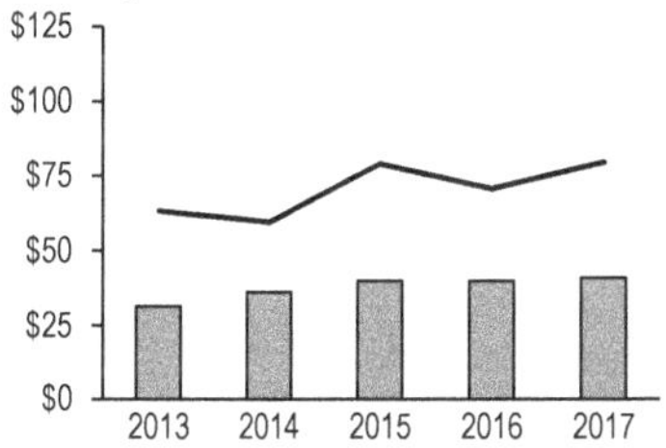

	2013	2014	2015	2016	2017
High Point	$31	$36	$40	$40	$41
Average	$63	$59	$79	$71	$79

Yard Waste and Leaf Collection Cost per Ton Collected

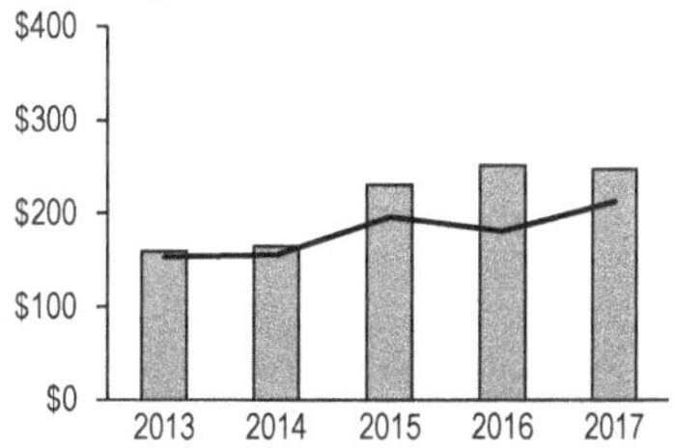

	2013	2014	2015	2016	2017
High Point	$159	$164	$230	$251	$246
Average	$153	$155	$196	$180	$212

Yard Waste and Leaf Tons Collected per Collection FTE

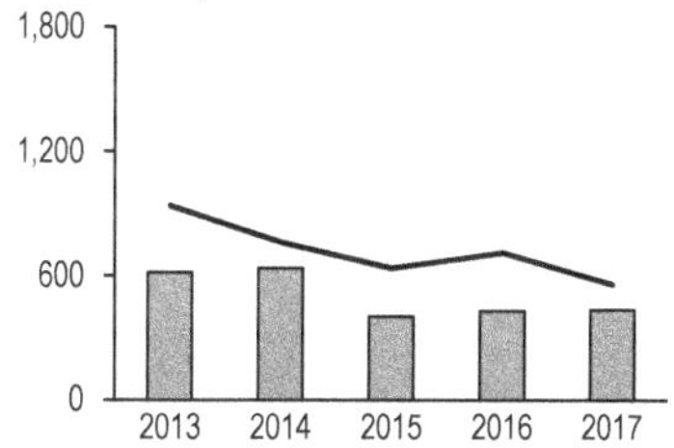

	2013	2014	2015	2016	2017
High Point	616	634	405	430	438
Average	937	760	637	711	558

Effectiveness Measures

Collection Complaints per 10,000 Collection Points

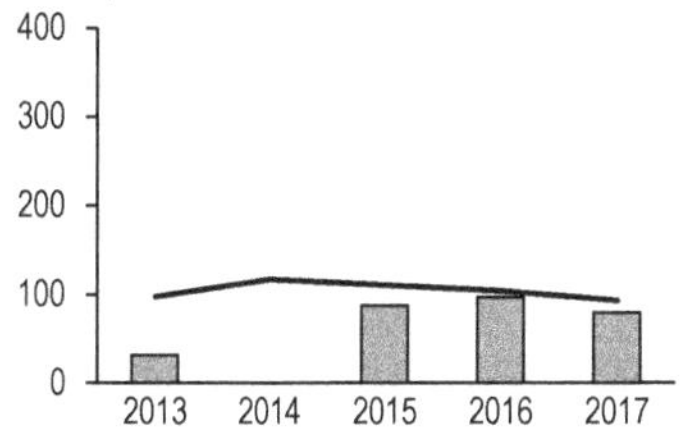

	2013	2014	2015	2016	2017
High Point	32		88	97	80
Average	98	117	111	105	93

Valid Complaints per 10,000 Collection Points

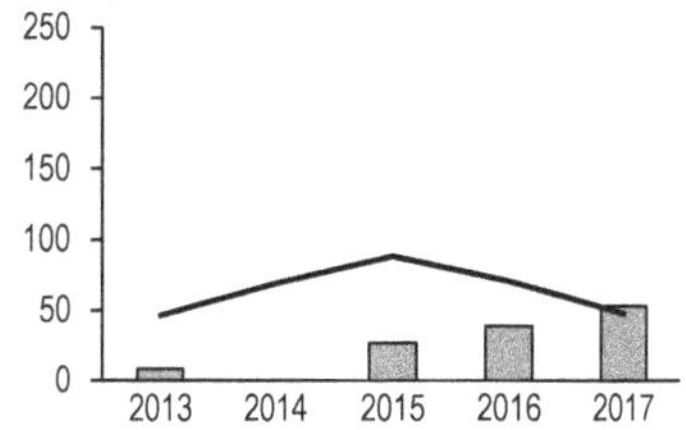

	2013	2014	2015	2016	2017
High Point	9		27	39	53
Average	46	69	88	70	47

Raleigh

Yard Waste/Leaf Collection

Fiscal Year 2016–17

Explanatory Information

Service Level and Delivery

Yard waste is picked up weekly at the curb in Raleigh. Yard waste must be bagged or containerized with a limit of fifteen bags. Bags must be clear or biodegradeable.

The city uses twelve three-person crews to collect yard waste on the same day as trash collection. Temporary crews may be added during leaf season as yard waste volume picks up.

Loose leaves are collected curbside during leaf season, which runs from November to February. Two sweeps of the City are completed during leaf season. The first sweep is usually completed by Christmas and the second sweep is usually completed by the end of February. Loose leaves must be placed at the street and must be free of debris to be collected.

A total of 45 employees made up of supervisors, support staff, and temporary employees are utilized during leaf season. This staff makes up seven crews of one to two for automated trucks and eleven crews of three for pull behind leaf trucks. This makes eighteen total crews.

Conditions Affecting Service, Performance, and Costs

Raleigh rejoined the Benchmarking Project in July 2016 with the first year of data showing for FY 2015–16.

Municipal Profile

Population (OSBM 2016)	448,706
Land Area (Square Miles)	145.57
Persons per Square Mile	3,083
Median Family Income U.S. Census 2010	$68,678

Service Profile

FTE Positions—Collection	64.0
FTE Positions—Other	7.0
Collection Frequency	
Yard Waste	1 x week
Seasonal Leaf Collection	2 sweeps
Collection Points	126,075
Tons Collected	
Yard Waste	17,946
Seasonal Leaves	12,352
Total Tons Collected	30,298
Monthly Service Fee	No

Full Cost Profile

Cost Breakdown by Percentage	
Personal Services	32.3%
Operating Costs	42.4%
Capital Costs	25.4%
TOTAL	100.0%
Cost Breakdown in Dollars	
Personal Services	$2,098,158
Operating Costs	$2,756,005
Capital Costs	$1,648,446
TOTAL	$6,502,609

Raleigh — Yard Waste/Leaf Collection

Key: Raleigh ▒ Benchmarking Average — Fiscal Years 2013 through 2017

Resource Measures

Yard Waste and Leaf Collection Costs per Capita

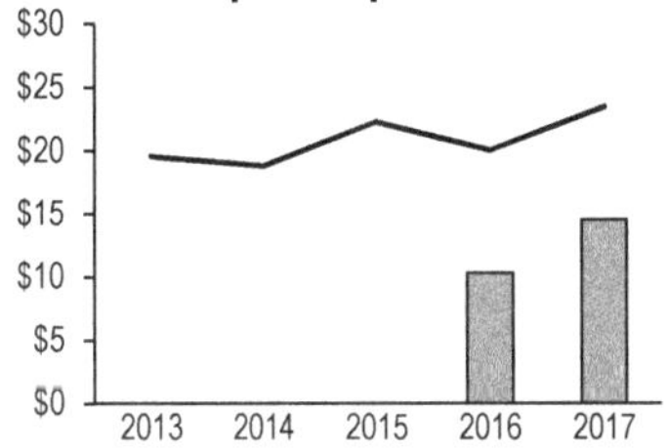

	2013	2014	2015	2016	2017
Raleigh				$10.31	$14.49
Average	$19.59	$18.82	$22.33	$20.10	$23.48

Yard Waste and Leaf Collection FTEs per 10,000 Population

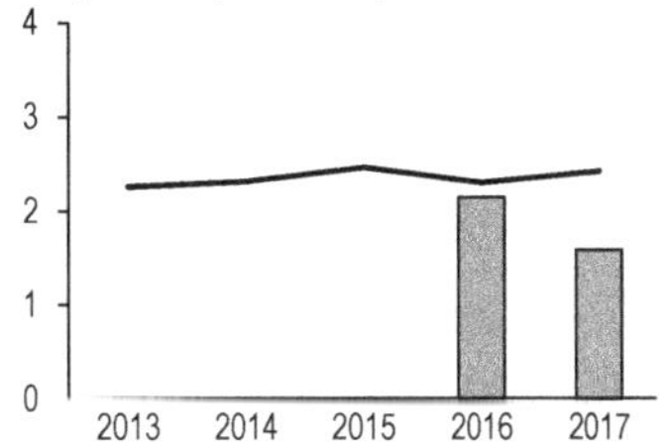

	2013	2014	2015	2016	2017
Raleigh				2.2	1.6
Average	2.3	2.3	2.5	2.3	2.4

Workload Measures

Yard Waste and Leaf Tons Collected per 1,000 Population

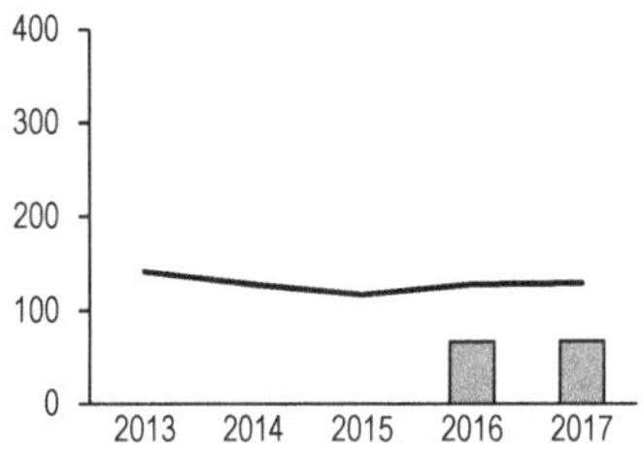

	2013	2014	2015	2016	2017
Raleigh				67	68
Average	141	128	117	128	129

Yard Waste and Leaf Tons Collected per 1,000 Collection Points

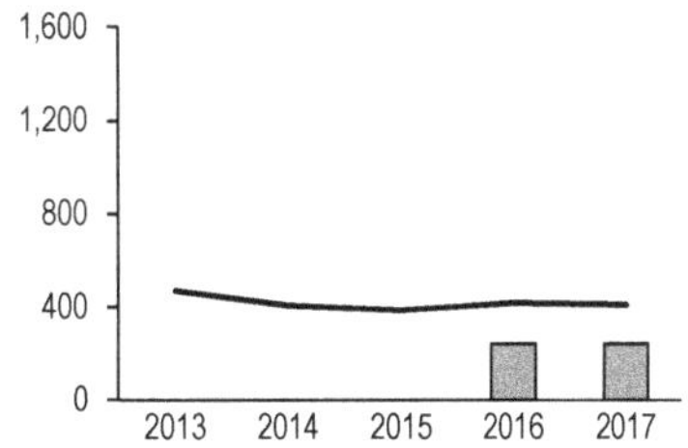

	2013	2014	2015	2016	2017
Raleigh				239	240
Average	468	404	384	416	406

Efficiency Measures

Yard Waste and Leaf Collection Cost per Collection Point

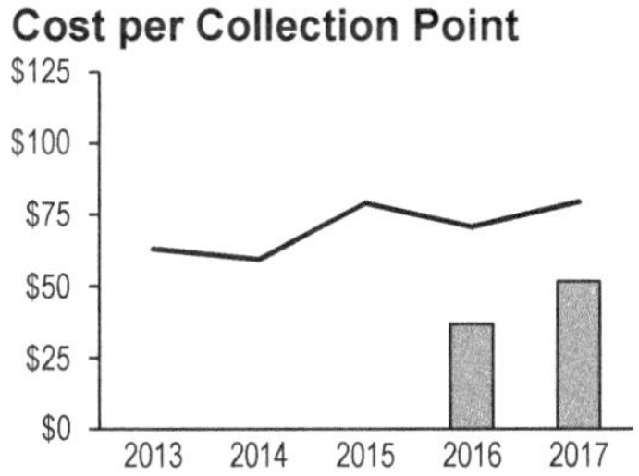

	2013	2014	2015	2016	2017
Raleigh				$37	$52
Average	$63	$59	$79	$71	$79

Yard Waste and Leaf Collection Cost per Ton Collected

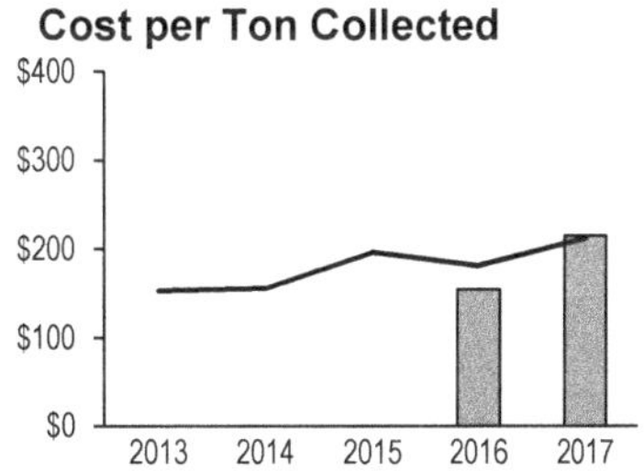

	2013	2014	2015	2016	2017
Raleigh				$154	$215
Average	$153	$155	$196	$180	$212

Yard Waste and Leaf Tons Collected per Collection FTE

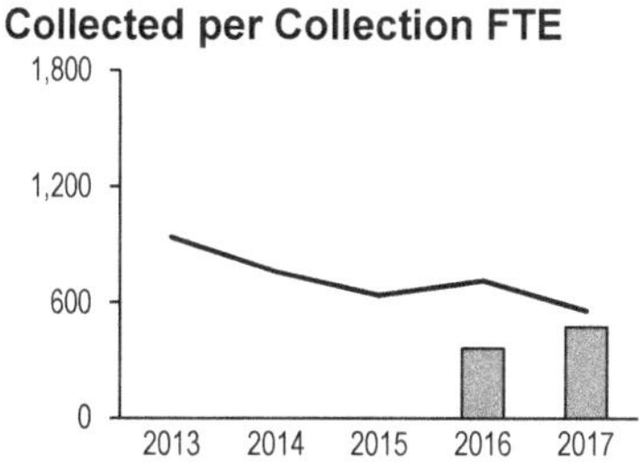

	2013	2014	2015	2016	2017
Raleigh				364	473
Average	937	760	637	711	558

Effectiveness Measures

Collection Complaints per 10,000 Collection Points

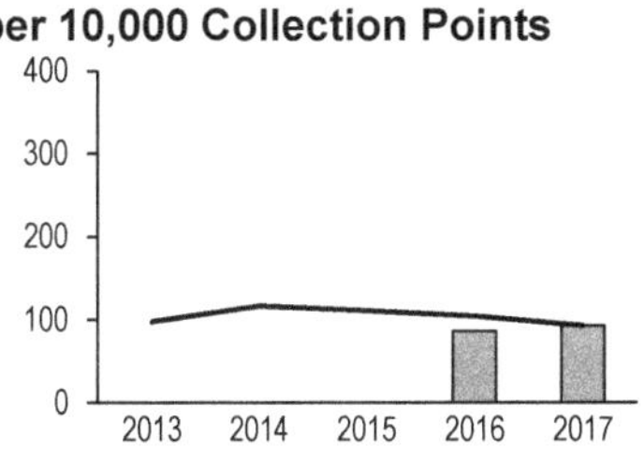

	2013	2014	2015	2016	2017
Raleigh				86	93
Average	98	117	111	105	93

Valid Complaints per 10,000 Collection Points

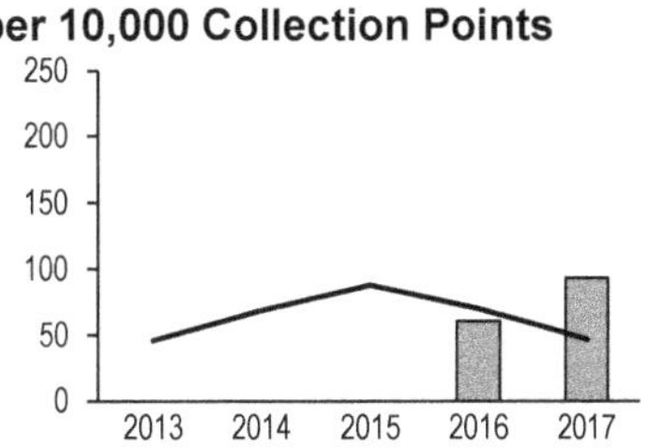

	2013	2014	2015	2016	2017
Raleigh				60	93
Average	46	69	88	70	47

Salisbury — Yard Waste/Leaf Collection

Fiscal Year 2016–17

Explanatory Information

Service Level and Delivery

Yard waste is picked up weekly at the curb in Salisbury. Yard waste includes limbs, shrubs, bagged grass clippings, and bagged leaves. It is collected the same day as trash and recycling materials for city residents.

The city uses two or three two-person crews, each consisting of a driver and laborer, on packer trucks for yard waste collection. One to two additional two-member crews operating two knuckleboom trucks collect large brush piles and limbs. One supervisor patrols the routes throughout the day, coordinating pickups and responding to citizen requests.

Loose leaves are collected curbside during leaf season, which runs from mid-October through March. Loose leaves are collected every third week during leaf season. Bagged leaves are collected as part of the weekly yard waste program.

One to seven crews, each composed of an operator, a street maintenance worker, and a seasonal worker, are used for the annual leaf collection program. This service includes costs to manage a treatment and process site where material is ground up and a composting site. Three positions operate these sites and are included in the positions.

Conditions Affecting Service, Performance, and Costs

The startup of the Salisbury composting site caused some of the data on tons of material collected to be lost during the transition. The tonnage numbers reported for FY2014–15 are lower than the actual numbers but an adjustment was not possible.

Yard waste tonnage in the fiscal year was lower than in previous years. This is due to improved accuracy in reporting by better matching volume and estimated weight in the yard waste stream.

Municipal Profile

Population (OSBM 2016)	34,459
Land Area (Square Miles)	22.28
Persons per Square Mile	1,547
Median Family Income	$40,192
U.S. Census 2010	

Service Profile

FTE Positions—Collection	8.0
FTE Positions—Other	0.75
Collection Frequency	
Yard Waste	1 x week
Seasonal Leaf Collection	1 x 3 weeks
Collection Points	10,961
Tons Collected	
Yard Waste	1,743
Seasonal Leaves	2,541
Total Tons Collected	4,283
Monthly Service Fee	No

Full Cost Profile

Cost Breakdown by Percentage	
Personal Services	55.8%
Operating Costs	23.9%
Capital Costs	20.3%
TOTAL	100.0%
Cost Breakdown in Dollars	
Personal Services	$357,631
Operating Costs	$153,009
Capital Costs	$130,157
TOTAL	$640,797

Key: Salisbury ▒ Benchmarking Average — Fiscal Years 2013 through 2017

Resource Measures

Yard Waste and Leaf Collection Costs per Capita

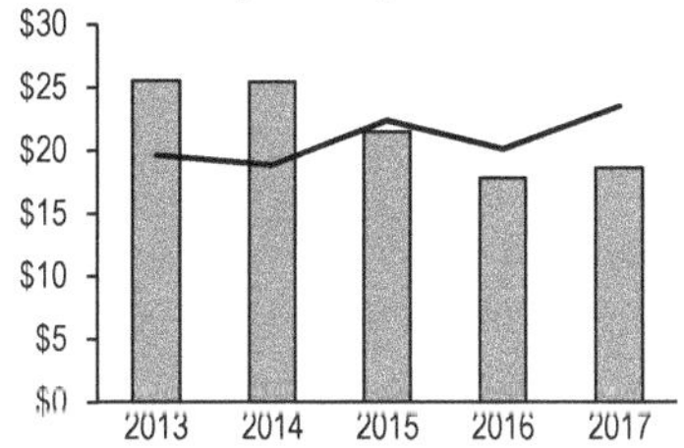

	2013	2014	2015	2016	2017
Salisbury	$25.52	$25.40	$21.46	$17.78	$18.60
Average	$19.59	$18.82	$22.33	$20.10	$23.48

Yard Waste and Leaf Collection FTEs per 10,000 Population

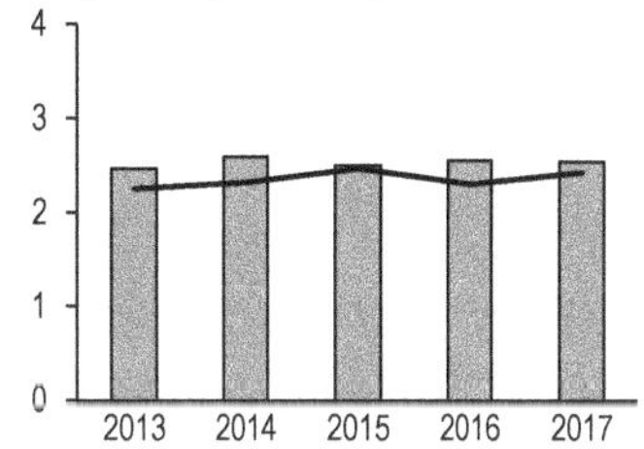

	2013	2014	2015	2016	2017
Salisbury	2.5	2.6	2.5	2.6	2.5
Average	2.3	2.3	2.5	2.3	2.4

Workload Measures

Yard Waste and Leaf Tons Collected per 1,000 Population

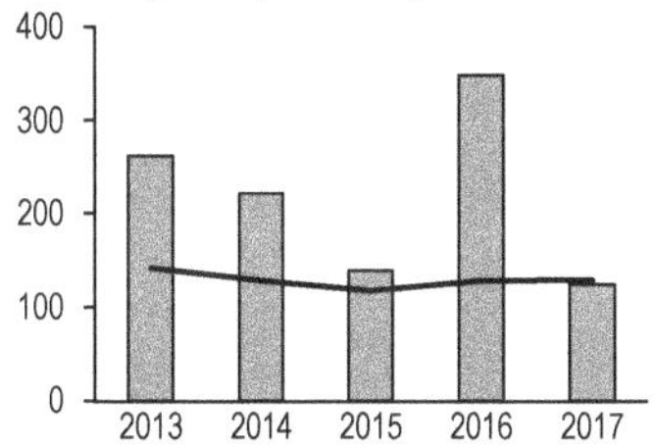

	2013	2014	2015	2016	2017
Salisbury	262	221	138	348	124
Average	141	128	117	128	129

Yard Waste and Leaf Tons Collected per 1,000 Collection Points

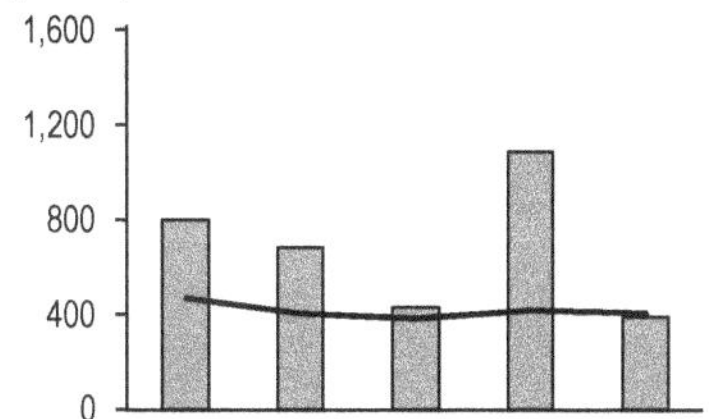

	2013	2014	2015	2016	2017
Salisbury	798	681	429	1,088	391
Average	468	404	384	416	406

Efficiency Measures

Yard Waste and Leaf Collection Cost per Collection Point

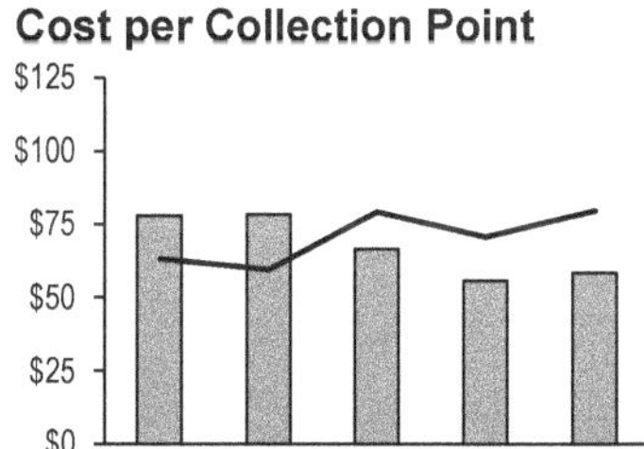

	2013	2014	2015	2016	2017
Salisbury	$78	$78	$66	$56	$58
Average	$63	$59	$79	$71	$79

Yard Waste and Leaf Collection Cost per Ton Collected

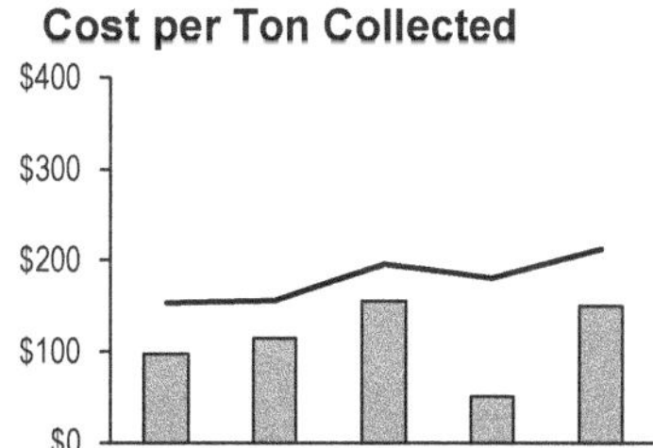

	2013	2014	2015	2016	2017
Salisbury	$98	$115	$155	$51	$150
Average	$153	$155	$196	$180	$212

Yard Waste and Leaf Tons Collected per Collection FTE

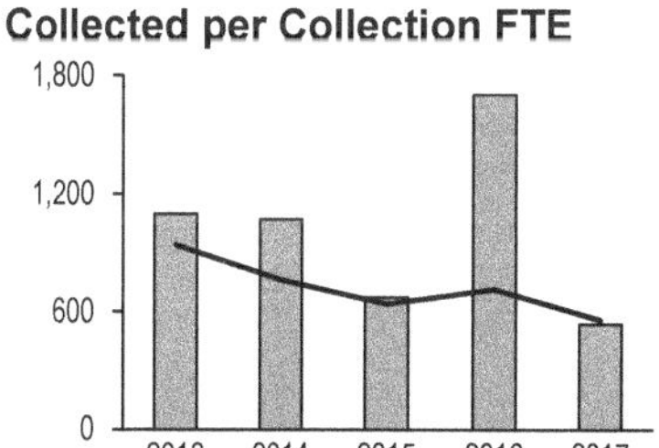

	2013	2014	2015	2016	2017
Salisbury	1,094	1,066	672	1,704	535
Average	937	760	637	711	558

Effectiveness Measures

Collection Complaints per 10,000 Collection Points

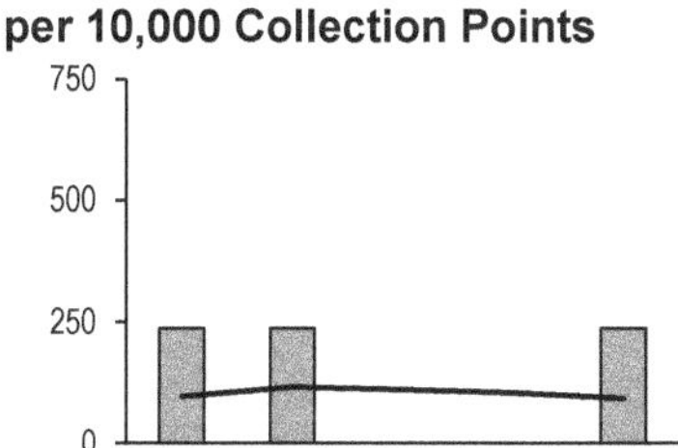

	2013	2014	2015	2016	2017
Salisbury	237	237			237
Average	98	117	111	105	93

Valid Complaints per 10,000 Collection Points

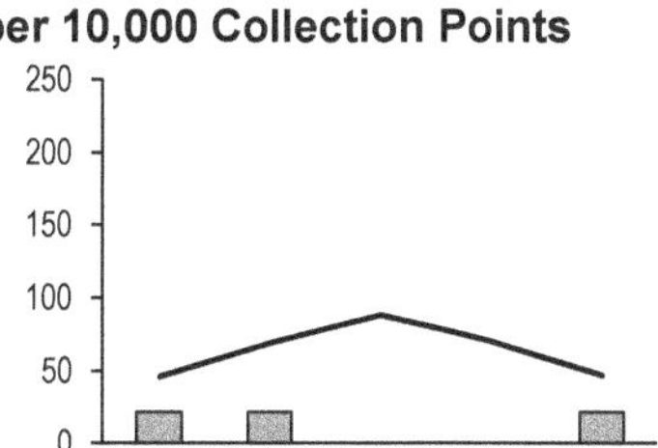

	2013	2014	2015	2016	2017
Salisbury	22	22			22
Average	46	69	88	70	47

Fiscal Year 2016–17

Explanatory Information

Service Level and Delivery

Yard waste is containerized in bags, sheets, roll-out containers, or other container types for collection by rear-loader packers. Yard waste is collected once per week by compost crews on the same day as residential refuse collection.

The city uses two three-person crews on Tuesdays and Fridays and three or four three-person crews on Mondays and Thursdays to collect yard waste. Each crew is composed of one driver and two workers. These crews rotate collection between residential refuse and yard waste. A one-person crew uses a knuckleboom truck to collect large limbs daily.

The city's leaf season is from mid-October to mid-January. Leaves are collected loose at the curb on a one-to-three-week cycle. The city uses leaf vacuum machines and compacting leaf trucks to collect loose leaves.

Six to eight three-person crews are used to collect loose leaves. The drivers are permanent employees. Collectors are seasonal employees.

Conditions Affecting Service, Performance, and Costs

Municipal Profile

Population (OSBM 2016)	49,406
Land Area (Square Miles)	30.60
Persons per Square Mile	1,615
Median Family Income U.S. Census 2010	$43,442

Service Profile

FTE Positions—Collection	15.5
FTE Positions—Other	0.0
Collection Frequency	
Yard Waste	1 x week
Seasonal Leaf Collection	1 x 3 weeks
Collection Points	20,017
Tons Collected	
Yard Waste	9,211
Seasonal Leaves	1,204
Total Tons Collected	10,415
Monthly Service Fee	Included in solid waste fee

Full Cost Profile

Cost Breakdown by Percentage	
Personal Services	46.9%
Operating Costs	28.8%
Capital Costs	24.2%
TOTAL	100.0%
Cost Breakdown in Dollars	
Personal Services	$476,956
Operating Costs	$293,098
Capital Costs	$246,090
TOTAL	$1,016,143

Wilson

Yard Waste/Leaf Collection

Key: Wilson ▪ Benchmarking Average — Fiscal Years 2013 through 2017

Resource Measures

Yard Waste and Leaf Collection Costs per Capita

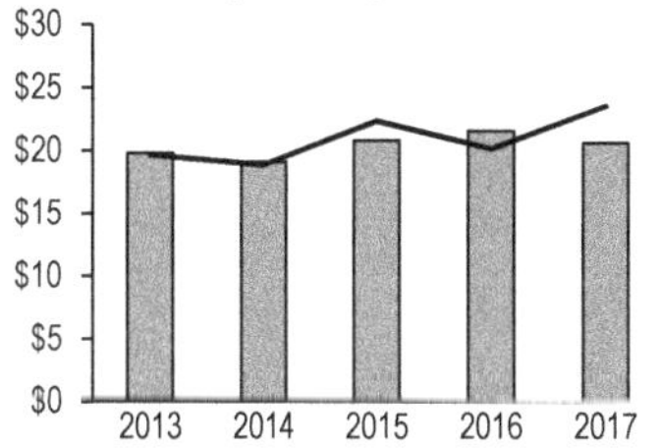

	2013	2014	2015	2016	2017
Wilson	$19.76	$19.07	$20.76	$21.50	$20.57
Average	$19.59	$18.82	$22.33	$20.10	$23.48

Yard Waste and Leaf Collection FTEs per 10,000 Population

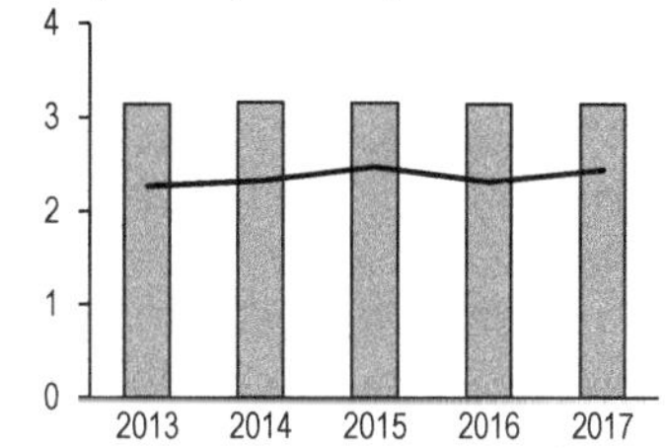

	2013	2014	2015	2016	2017
Wilson	3.1	3.2	3.1	3.1	3.1
Average	2.3	2.3	2.5	2.3	2.4

Workload Measures

Yard Waste and Leaf Tons Collected per 1,000 Population

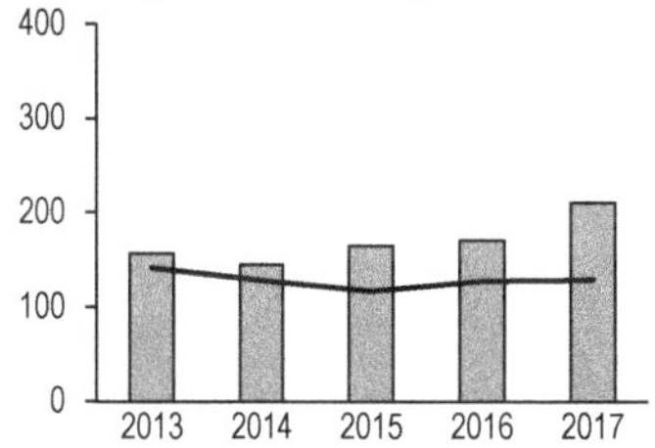

	2013	2014	2015	2016	2017
Wilson	157	145	165	171	211
Average	141	128	117	128	129

Yard Waste and Leaf Tons Collected per 1,000 Collection Points

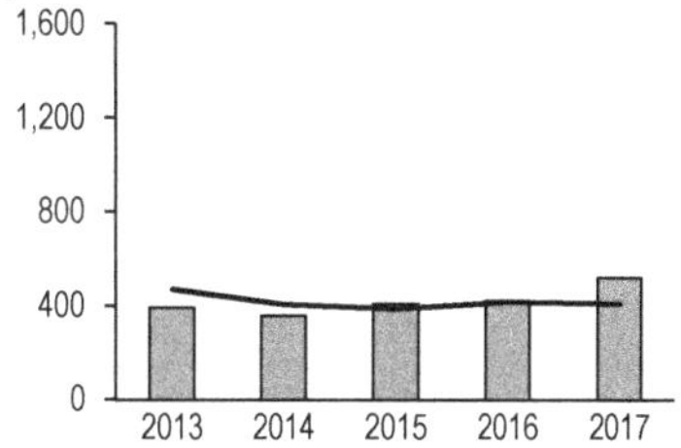

	2013	2014	2015	2016	2017
Wilson	394	360	408	422	520
Average	468	404	384	416	406

Efficiency Measures

Yard Waste and Leaf Collection Cost per Collection Point

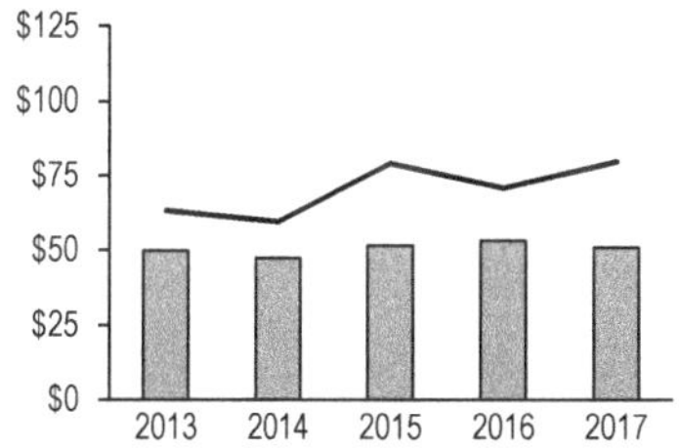

	2013	2014	2015	2016	2017
Wilson	$50	$47	$51	$53	$51
Average	$63	$59	$79	$71	$79

Yard Waste and Leaf Collection Cost per Ton Collected

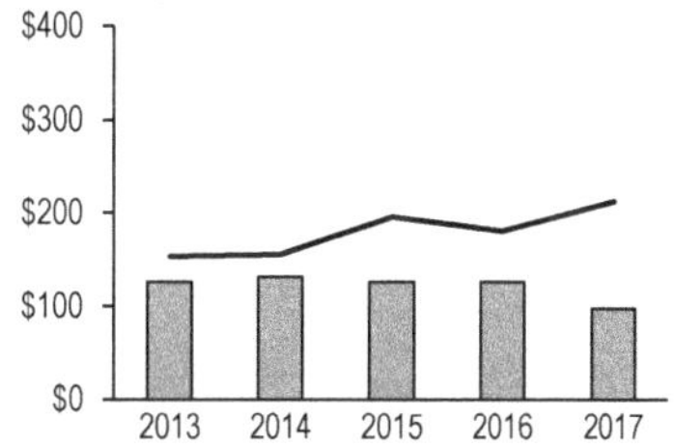

	2013	2014	2015	2016	2017
Wilson	$126	$132	$126	$126	$98
Average	$153	$155	$196	$180	$212

Yard Waste and Leaf Tons Collected per Collection FTE

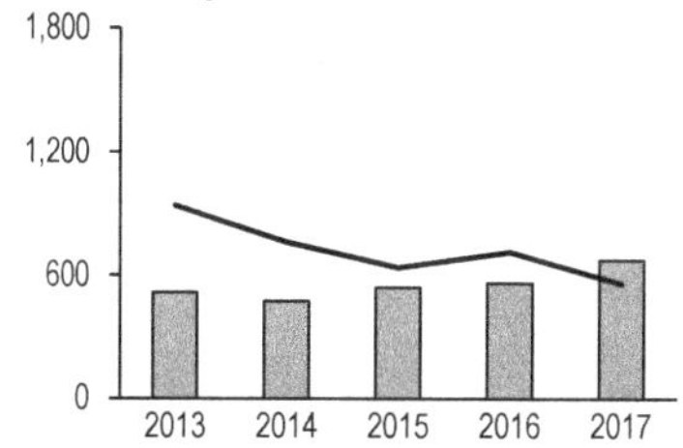

	2013	2014	2015	2016	2017
Wilson	516	474	540	562	672
Average	937	760	637	711	558

Effectiveness Measures

Collection Complaints per 10,000 Collection Points

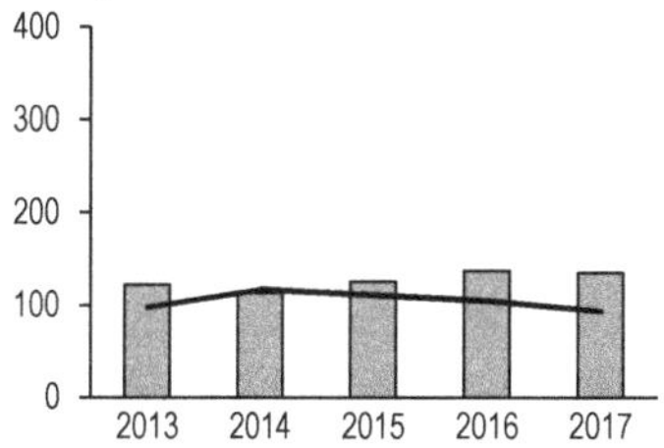

	2013	2014	2015	2016	2017
Wilson	122	113	126	137	135
Average	98	117	111	105	93

Valid Complaints per 10,000 Collection Points

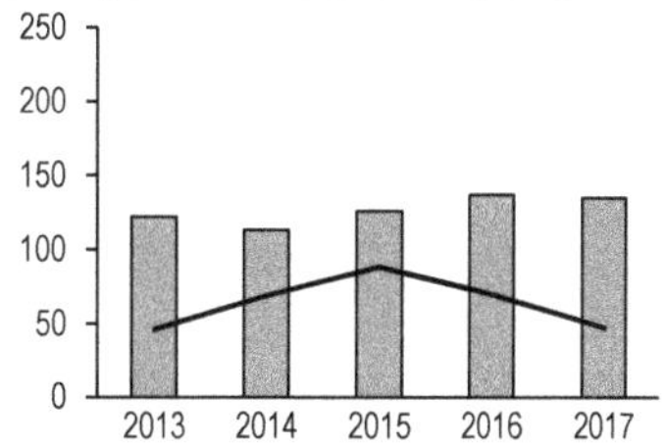

	2013	2014	2015	2016	2017
Wilson	122	113	126	137	135
Average	46	69	88	70	47

Winston-Salem — Yard Waste/Leaf Collection

Fiscal Year 2016–17

Explanatory Information

Service Level and Delivery

The city operates a curbside collection program for brush, leaves, and bulky items. Brush is collected throughout the year, while leaves and bulky items are collected on a seasonal basis. Brush is defined as small tree limbs, branches, and shrubbery clippings. Tree and shrubbery limbs cannot be larger than 6 inches in diameter or 6 feet in length. A city ordinance requires that brush be collected once every ten working days except during leaf season. There are no separate fees for the curbside collection program. The brush collection program gathered 14,146 tons across the city.

The yard waste cart program provides weekly collection of containerized yard waste placed in ninety-six-gallon carts. The city uses six one-person crews using automated packers and one two-person crew using a rear-loading packer to service these carts. Collection is provided Monday through Thursday. Carts are delivered on Friday. Residents who participate in the yard waste cart program pay an annual $60 fee. Residents also pay for the ninety-six-gallon carts at a cost of $60 if the cart is picked up or $65 if the cart is delivered. A household can have up to three carts. The yard cart program serviced 13,843 customers in the fiscal year picking up 6,828 tons.

The city's seasonal leaf collection program picks up leaves that are deposited at the curb between November 1 and January 15. Loose leaves are vacuumed two to three times during this time period. Containerized leaves are collected throughout the year as part of the yard waste program. The city uses thirty-two crews for seasonal leaf collection, with a combination of equipment operators, maintenance workers, and both permanent and seasonal workers.

Conditions Affecting Service, Performance, and Costs

The performance measure "cost per collection point" is based on a total 81,589 collection points.

Municipal Profile

Population (OSBM 2016)	240,603
Land Area (Square Miles)	132.55
Persons per Square Mile	1,815
Median Family Income U.S. Census 2010	$51,491

Service Profile

FTE Positions—Collection	74.5
FTE Positions—Other	1.4
Collection Frequency	
Yard Waste	1 x week
Seasonal Leaf Collection	1 x 3 weeks
Brush	1 x 10 days
Collection Points	81,589
Tons Collected	
Yard Waste	20,974
Seasonal Leaves	11,025
Total Tons Collected	31,999
Monthly Service Fee	$60 per year for cart

Full Cost Profile

Cost Breakdown by Percentage	
Personal Services	50.1%
Operating Costs	27.4%
Capital Costs	22.6%
TOTAL	100.0%
Cost Breakdown in Dollars	
Personal Services	$3,019,356
Operating Costs	$1,648,995
Capital Costs	$1,360,740
TOTAL	$6,029,091

Winston-Salem — Yard Waste/Leaf Collection

Key: Winston-Salem ▒ Benchmarking Average — Fiscal Years 2013 through 2017

Resource Measures

Yard Waste and Leaf Collection Costs per Capita

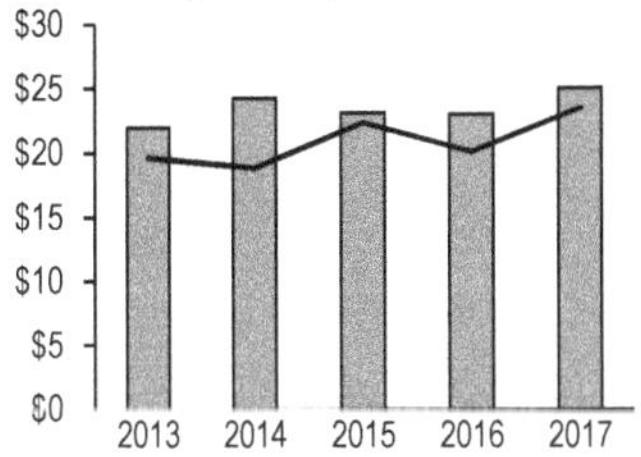

	2013	2014	2015	2016	2017
Winston-Salem	$21.99	$24.26	$23.11	$23.03	$25.06
Average	$19.59	$18.82	$22.33	$20.10	$23.48

Yard Waste and Leaf Collection FTEs per 10,000 Population

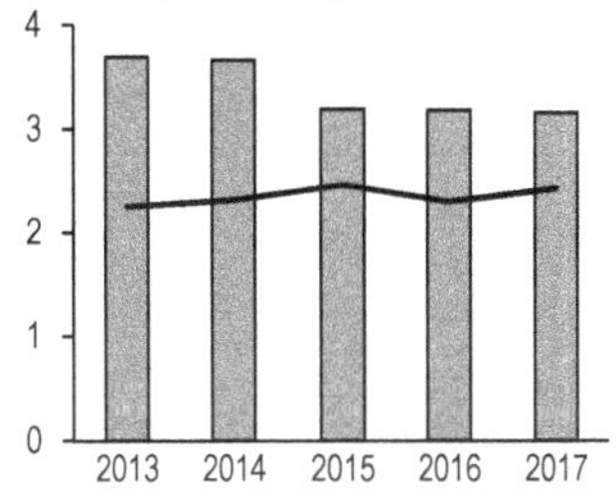

	2013	2014	2015	2016	2017
Winston-Salem	3.7	3.7	3.2	3.2	3.2
Average	2.3	2.3	2.5	2.3	2.4

Workload Measures

Yard Waste and Leaf Tons Collected per 1,000 Population

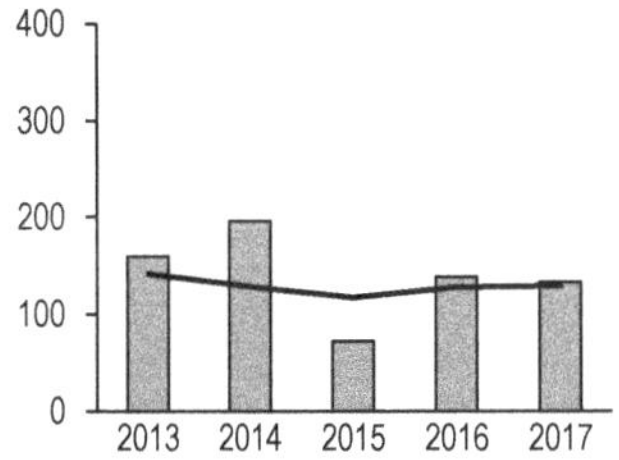

	2013	2014	2015	2016	2017
Winston-Salem	159	196	72	138	133
Average	141	128	117	128	129

Yard Waste and Leaf Tons Collected per 1,000 Collection Points

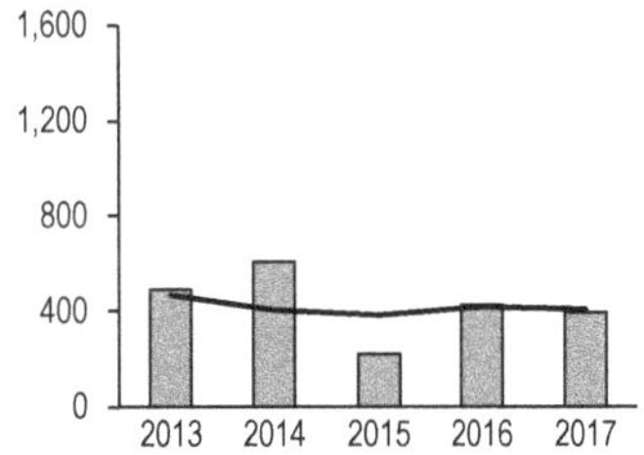

	2013	2014	2015	2016	2017
Winston-Salem	489	607	219	424	392
Average	468	404	384	416	406

Efficiency Measures

Yard Waste and Leaf Collection Cost per Collection Point

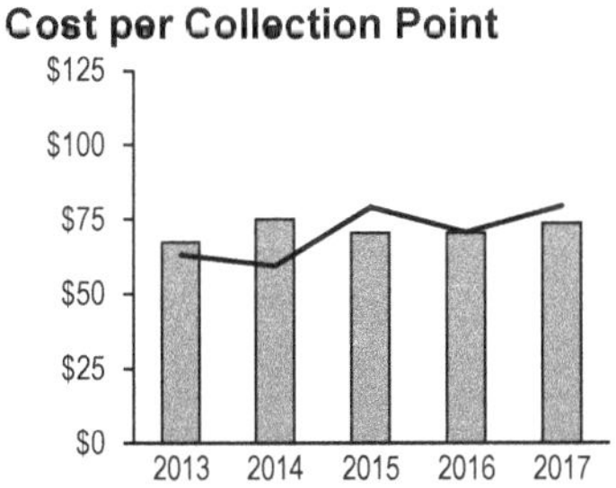

	2013	2014	2015	2016	2017
Winston-Salem	$67	$75	$71	$71	$74
Average	$63	$59	$79	$71	$79

Yard Waste and Leaf Collection Cost per Ton Collected

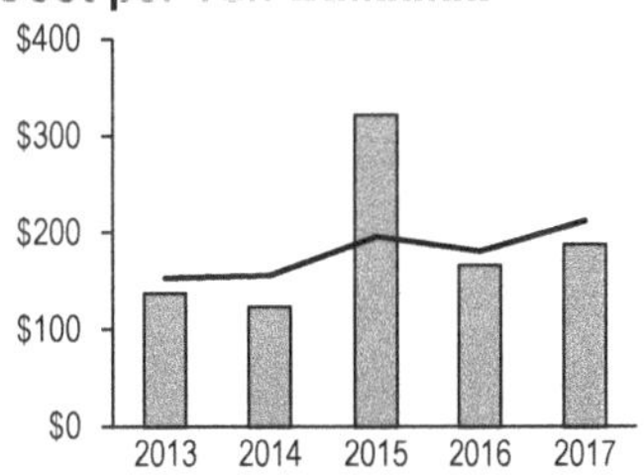

	2013	2014	2015	2016	2017
Winston-Salem	$138	$124	$323	$167	$188
Average	$153	$155	$196	$180	$212

Yard Waste and Leaf Tons Collected per Collection FTE

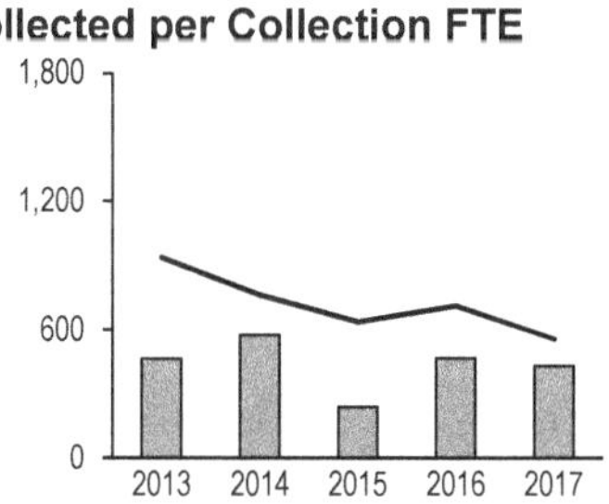

	2013	2014	2015	2016	2017
Winston-Salem	464	575	241	466	430
Average	937	760	637	711	558

Effectiveness Measures

Collection Complaints per 10,000 Collection Points

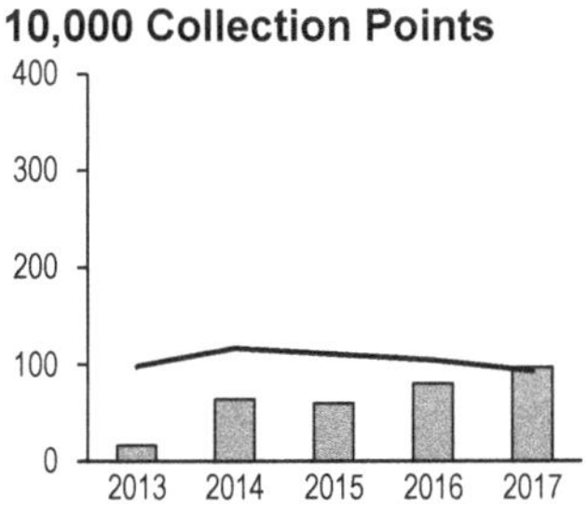

	2013	2014	2015	2016	2017
Winston-Salem	16	64	60	80	97
Average	98	117	111	105	93

Valid Complaints per 10,000 Collection Points

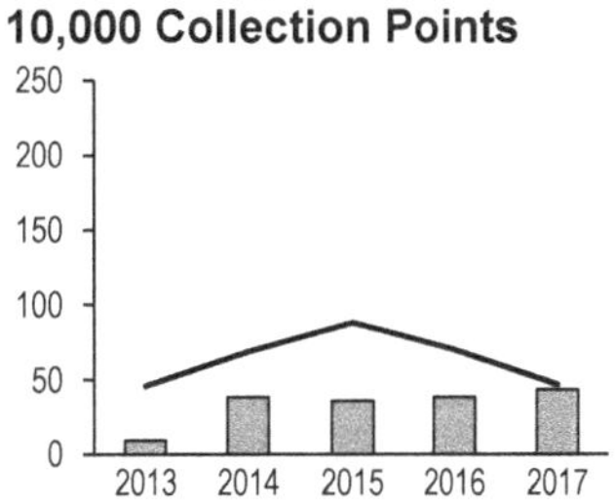

	2013	2014	2015	2016	2017
Winston-Salem	9	39	36	39	44
Average	46	69	88	70	47

UNC | SCHOOL OF GOVERNMENT
North Carolina Benchmarking Project

Performance and Cost Data

POLICE SERVICES

PERFORMANCE MEASURES FOR POLICE SERVICES

SERVICE DEFINITION

Police Services consist of all police activities performed by sworn and non-sworn personnel. This includes, but is not limited to, activities performed by patrol, traffic, investigations, special units, support staff, supervisors, and police administration. This definition captures all functions of the police department except for emergency communications.

NOTES ON PERFORMANCE MEASURES

1. Dispatched Calls

These are calls resulting in the dispatch of an officer. Most dispatches result from calls coming into the emergency communications center or the police department, but some are self-initiated by officers on duty. Multiple calls resulting in the dispatch of several officers are counted as one.

2. Uniform Crime Reporting (UCR) Part I Crimes

Uniform Crime Reporting (UCR) Part I crimes include crimes against persons (criminal homicide, forcible rape, robbery, and aggravated assault) and crimes against property (burglary, larceny, motor vehicle theft, and arson).

3. Incident-Based Reporting (IBR) Part I Crimes

Incident-Based Reporting (IBR) Part I crimes include crimes against persons (criminal homicide, forcible rape, robbery, and aggravated assault) and crimes against property (burglary, larceny, motor vehicle theft, and arson). The difference between the UCR method and the IBR method for reporting crimes is that IBR counts crime and arrest activities at the incident level, as opposed to counting only the most serious crime with multiple offenses.

4. Full-Time Equivalent (FTE) Positions: Sworn Officers

The number of full-time equivalent (FTE) positions is the number of budgeted positions for sworn officers during the fiscal year.

5. Response Time to High Priority Calls

Each police department defines high priority calls somewhat differently. The definitions generally refer to crimes in progress or situations where there are risks of injury or threats to life or property. Response time commences with the dispatch of an officer and ends with the arrival of the officer at the scene of the incident. The officer may be dispatched while on patrol or from the police station.

Police Services

Summary of Key Dimensions of Service

City or Town	Police Department Accredited?	Number of Sworn Officers	Average Length of Service for Sworn Officers (Years)	Number of Patrol Vehicles	Reporting Format	Part I Crimes			Part II Crimes	Dispatched Calls	Number of Traffic Accidents
						Against Persons	Against Property	Total			
Apex	Yes	77	14.4	80	IBR	43	694	737	1,566	41,917	1,184
Asheville	Yes	222	8.2	208	IBR	488	4,327	4,815	5,222	118,790	8,292
Chapel Hill	No	119	12.5	80	UCR	96	1,621	1,717	3,395	35,266	2,143
Concord	No	184	9.6	187	IBR	111	2,105	2,216	1,963	125,323	3,983
Goldsboro	No	110	10.1	97	UCR	356	1,964	2,320	2,283	55,237	2,234
Greensboro	Yes	673	10.9	223	IBR	1,540	10,021	11,561	15,674	224,955	11,030
Greenville	Yes	194	13.0	163	UCR	604	3,776	4,380	4,323	85,416	4,811
Hickory	No	116	9.1	155	IBR	175	2,000	2,175	3,375	88,167	3,555
High Point	No	247	10.9	246	UCR	654	4,179	4,833	4,624	118,511	5,109
Raleigh	Yes	800	na	803	NIBRS	1,637	11,699	13,336	NA	362,289	27,621
Salisbury	Yes	81	11.9	94	IBR	239	1,709	1,948	2,035	37,459	1,965
Wilson	Yes	121	10.1	128	UCR	262	1,879	2,141	2,887	99,227	2,596
Winston-Salem	Yes	570	12.3	473	IBR	2,339	12,873	15,212	34,454	225,958	10,573

EXPLANATORY FACTORS

These are factors that the project found affected police services performance and cost in one or more of the municipalities:

Demographic makeup of the community
Community policing policies
Population density and land area
Downtown area characteristics
Use of incident-based reporting
Presence of unique problems in particular areas, such as drugs or gangs
Emphasis on quick response to all calls
Vehicle take-home policy
Beat structure
Use of special units

Fiscal Year 2016–17

Explanatory Information

Service Level and Delivery

The Town of Apex Police Department provides an array of police services, including patrol, investigations, a special response unit, and school resource officers at the high school and middle schools located in the town.

The city had 76.5 sworn officer positions authorized for the year, with an average length of service of over fourteen years. Police services occupies a headquarters located in downtown Apex, newly built in 2010, which houses all divisions in the department. There is also an unmanned substation attached to one of the town fire stations.

Officers in Apex in the partrol division work twelve-hour modified DuPont schedules. Each patrol squad is also assigned a flex officer. The traffic unit works a modified DuPont schedule based on crash statistics. The investigations division works Monday through Friday from 8 a.m. to 5 p.m., with one investigator working from 2 p.m. to 11 p.m. The investigator working the late shift is also the on-call investigator, and this position rotates every week.

Patrol and investigation units are assigned individual vehicles. Command staff also have individually assigned vehicles, which are the only take-home vehicles in the fleet.

The police department was successful in clearing a total of 246 Part I cases in FY 2016–17.

The definition of a high priority call in Apex is any call when the immediate arrival and presence of the police may prevent death or injury or alleviate the threat of death or injury.

Conditions Affecting Service, Performance, and Costs

Municipal Profile

Population (OSBM 2016)	46,688
Land Area (Square Miles)	20.61
Persons per Square Mile	2,265
Median Family Income U.S. Census 2010	$97,201

Service Profile

FTE Positions—Sworn	76.5
FTE Positions—Other	6.8
Marked and Unmarked Patrol Vehicles	80
Part I Crimes Reported	
Homicide	0
Rape	7
Robbery	11
Assault	25
Burglary	104
Larceny	564
Auto Theft	22
Arson	4
TOTAL	737
Part II Crimes Reported	1,566
Part I Crimes Cleared	
Persons	33
Property	213
TOTAL	246
Reporting Format	IBR
Number of Calls Dispatched	41,917
Number of Traffic Accidents	1,184
Property Damage for Accidents	$4,893,343

Full Cost Profile

Cost Breakdown by Percentage	
Personal Services	66.3%
Operating Costs	22.4%
Capital Costs	11.3%
TOTAL	100.0%
Cost Breakdown in Dollars	
Personal Services	$7,082,874
Operating Costs	$2,394,556
Capital Costs	$1,202,260
TOTAL	$10,679,690

Apex

Police Services

Key: Apex ▒ Benchmarking Average — Fiscal Years 2013 through 2017

Resource Measures

Police Services Costs per Capita

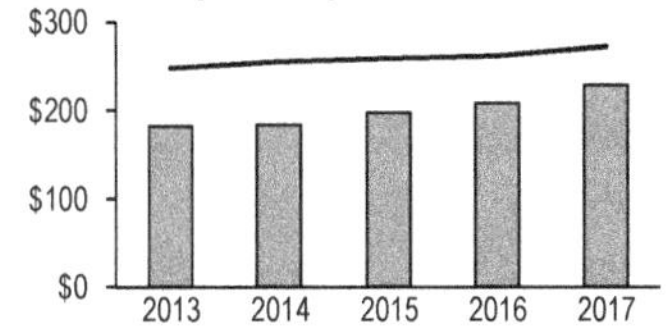

	2013	2014	2015	2016	2017
Apex	$182	$184	$197	$209	$229
Average	$249	$256	$260	$263	$273

Total Police Services Personnel per 10,000 Population

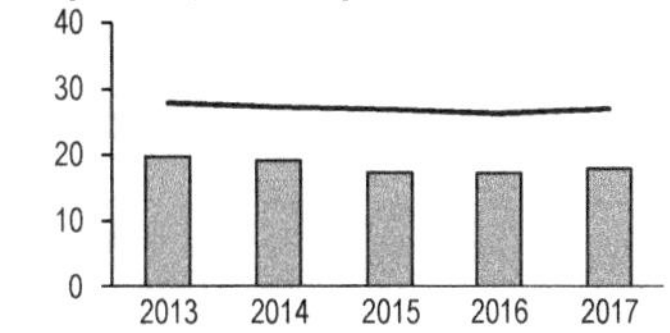

	2013	2014	2015	2016	2017
Apex	19.6	19.1	17.3	17.2	17.8
Average	27.9	27.3	26.9	26.2	26.9

Sworn Police Officers per 10,000 Population

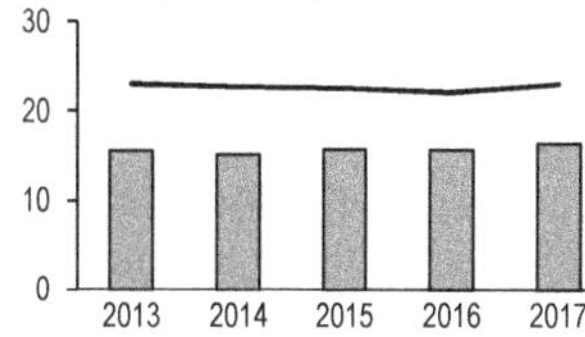

	2013	2014	2015	2016	2017
Apex	15.6	15.1	15.7	15.6	16.4
Average	23.1	22.8	22.6	22.1	23.0

Workload Measures

Calls Dispatched per 1,000 Population

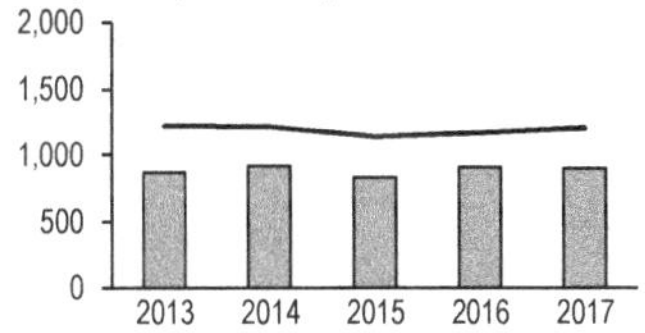

	2013	2014	2015	2016	2017
Apex	866	915	830	905	898
Average	1,220	1,213	1,134	1,166	1,203

Part I Crimes per 1,000 Population

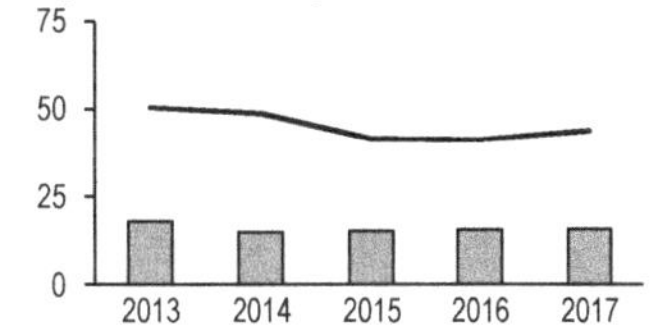

	2013	2014	2015	2016	2017
Apex	17.9	14.8	15.2	15.5	15.8
Average	50.5	48.8	41.4	41.1	43.8

Efficiency Measures

Police Services Cost per Call Dispatched

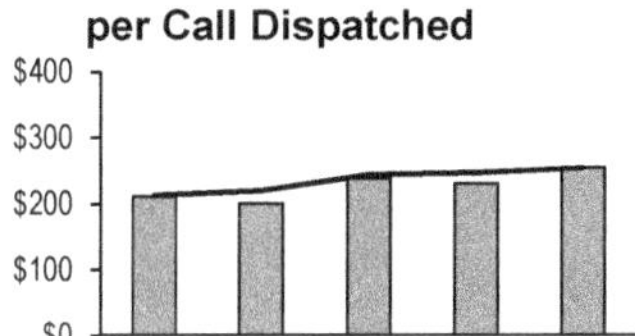

	2013	2014	2015	2016	2017
Apex	$211	$201	$238	$230	$255
Average	$213	$219	$243	$247	$254

Calls Dispatched per Sworn Officer

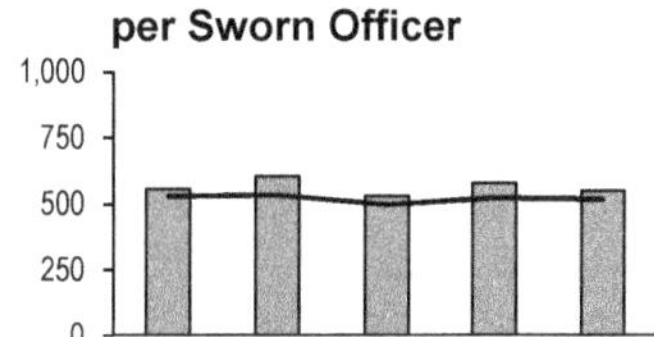

	2013	2014	2015	2016	2017
Apex	555	604	529	578	548
Average	528	532	496	521	516

Police Services Cost per Part I Case Cleared

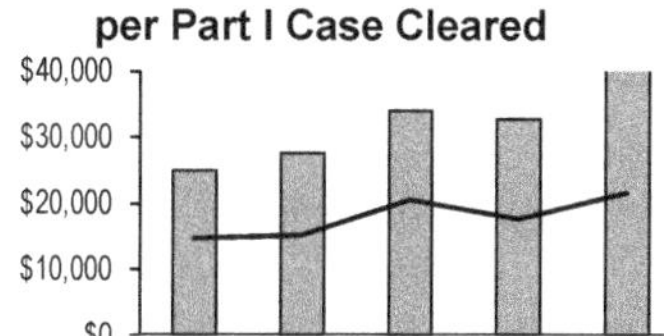

	2013	2014	2015	2016	2017
Apex	$25,093	$27,720	$34,131	$32,860	$43,413
Average	$14,685	$15,183	$20,524	$17,593	$21,594

Part I Cases Cleared per Sworn Officer

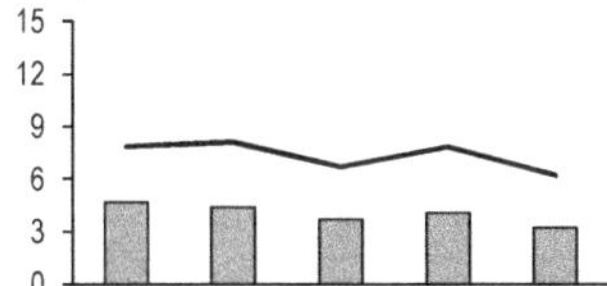

	2013	2014	2015	2016	2017
Apex	4.7	4.4	3.7	4.1	3.2
Average	7.9	8.1	6.7	7.8	6.2

Effectiveness Measures

Percentage of Part I Cases Cleared of Those Reported

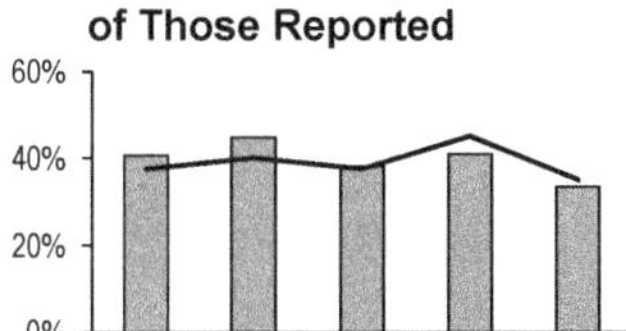

	2013	2014	2015	2016	2017
Apex	40.7%	44.7%	38.1%	40.9%	33.4%
Average	37.5%	40.0%	37.6%	45.0%	35.0%

Response Time to High Priority Calls in Minutes

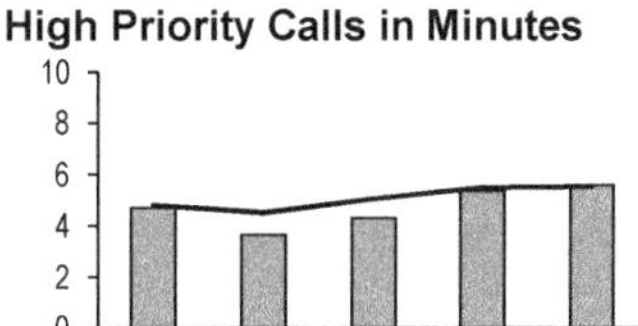

	2013	2014	2015	2016	2017
Apex	4.7	3.7	4.3	5.4	5.6
Average	4.8	4.5	5.0	5.5	5.5

Fiscal Year 2016–17

Explanatory Information

Service Level and Delivery

The Asheville Police Department provides an array of police services, including patrol, investigations, a telephone response unit, a canine unit, a special response unit, animal control, a drug enforcement unit, a hostage negotiation team, a hazardous device team, and several other special programs.

The city had 222 sworn officer positions authorized for the year, with an average length of service of about 8.2 years. Police services occupies five facilities: the main downtown facility shared by the fire department and four substations.

Officers in Asheville work a varied DuPont schedule based on a fourteen-day period, working six twelve-hour days and one eight-hour day. The schedule requires two or three days on followed by two days off in alternating sequences over the two-week period. A power squad is assigned to work the evening shift during the peak time of calls. Detectives work four ten-hour days, with half the detectives off Mondays and the other half off on Fridays. Detective supervisors work five eight-hour days.

Specialty units such as traffic, SWAT, and detectives have assigned take-home cars. Additionally, sergeants and higher-ranked officers also have assigned vehicles. Patrol cars have multiple users.

The police department was successful in clearing a total of 1,617 Part I cases in FY 2016–17. The definition of a high priority call in Asheville is any call dealing with a crime in progress or a situation where there is immediate danger to a person.

Conditions Affecting Service, Performance, and Costs

Significant efforts have been made, starting in FY 2006–07, to reduce drug crime in Asheville. The number of Part I crimes has declined, which is believed to be due in part to the focus on reducing drug crime.

The average response time to high priority calls reflects the response time of the first arriving unit. Self-initiated calls are not included in the response time. Due to a better classification of high priority calls at the Asheville communications unit, police have been able to lower their response time to high priority calls.

Municipal Profile

Population (OSBM 2016)	91,929
Land Area (Square Miles)	45.52
Persons per Square Mile	2,019
Median Family Income U.S. Census 2010	$53,350

Service Profile

FTE Positions—Sworn	222.0
FTE Positions—Other	62.0
Marked and Unmarked Patrol Vehicles	208
Part I Crimes Reported	
Homicide	6
Rape	40
Robbery	175
Assault	267
Burglary	735
Larceny	3,269
Auto Theft	313
Arson	10
TOTAL	4,815
Part II Crimes Reported	5,222
Part I Crimes Cleared	
Persons	307
Property	1,310
TOTAL	1,617
Reporting Format	IBR
Number of Calls Dispatched	118,790
Number of Traffic Accidents	8,292
Property Damage for Accidents	$24,842,599

Full Cost Profile

Cost Breakdown by Percentage	
Personal Services	65.7%
Operating Costs	24.8%
Capital Costs	9.4%
TOTAL	100.0%
Cost Breakdown in Dollars	
Personal Services	$18,868,964
Operating Costs	$7,131,122
Capital Costs	$2,699,604
TOTAL	$28,699,690

Key: Asheville ▒ Benchmarking Average — Fiscal Years 2013 through 2017

Resource Measures

Police Services Costs per Capita

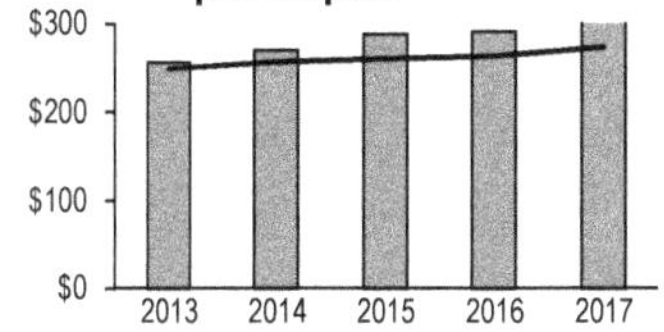

	2013	2014	2015	2016	2017
Asheville	$256	$270	$288	$291	$312
Average	$249	$256	$260	$263	$273

Total Police Services Personnel per 10,000 Population

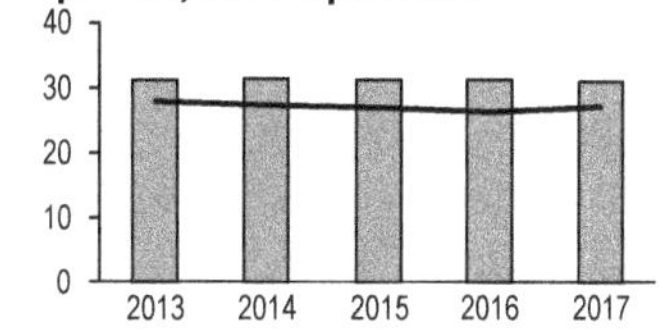

	2013	2014	2015	2016	2017
Asheville	31.2	31.4	31.1	31.2	30.9
Average	27.9	27.3	26.9	26.2	26.9

Sworn Police Officers per 10,000 Population

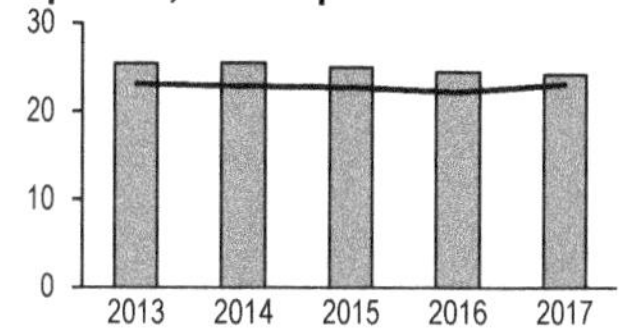

	2013	2014	2015	2016	2017
Asheville	25.4	25.5	25.0	24.4	24.1
Average	23.1	22.8	22.6	22.1	23.0

Workload Measures

Calls Dispatched per 1,000 Population

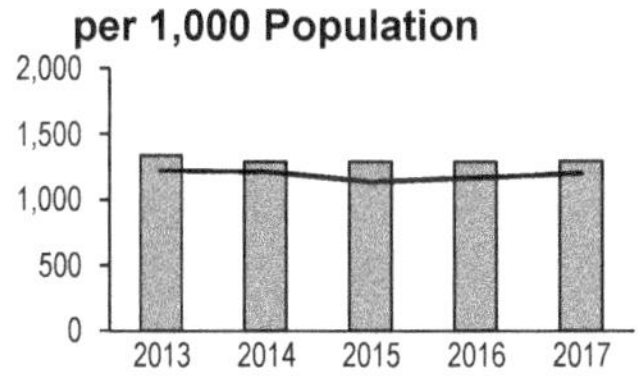

	2013	2014	2015	2016	2017
Asheville	1,338	1,289	1,288	1,287	1,292
Average	1,220	1,213	1,134	1,166	1,203

Part I Crimes per 1,000 Population

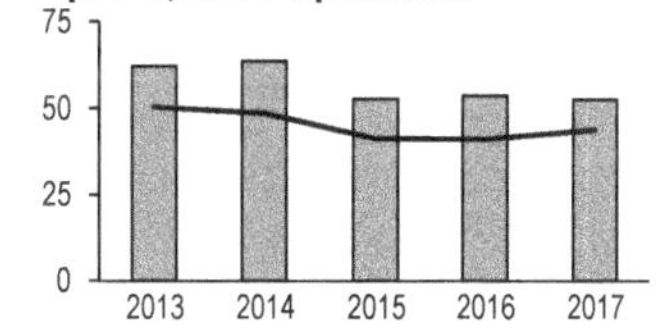

	2013	2014	2015	2016	2017
Asheville	62.1	63.6	52.7	53.4	52.4
Average	50.5	48.8	41.4	41.1	43.8

Efficiency Measures

Police Services Cost per Call Dispatched

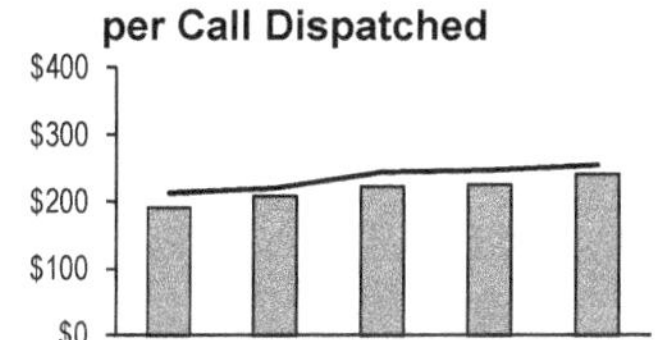

	2013	2014	2015	2016	2017
Asheville	$191	$209	$224	$226	$242
Average	$213	$219	$243	$247	$254

Calls Dispatched per Sworn Officer

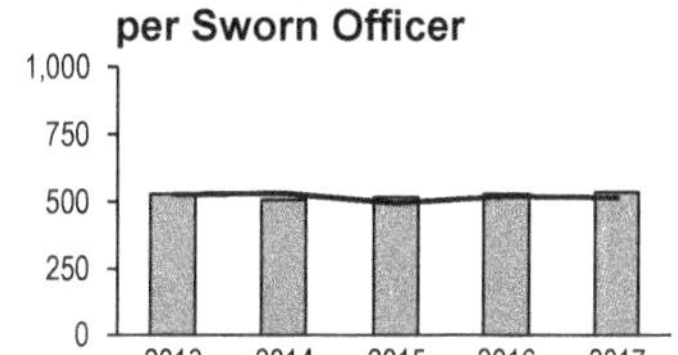

	2013	2014	2015	2016	2017
Asheville	527	506	515	527	535
Average	528	532	496	521	516

Police Services Cost per Part I Case Cleared

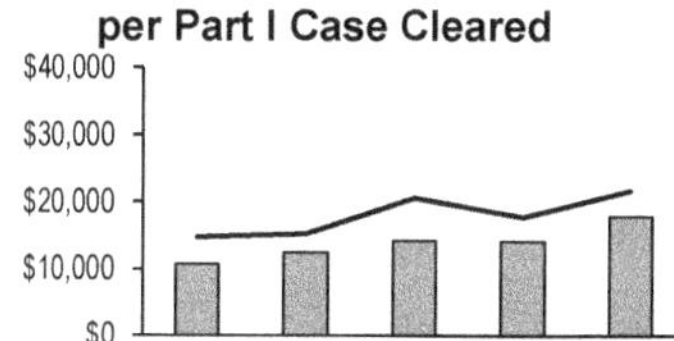

	2013	2014	2015	2016	2017
Asheville	$10,684	$12,350	$14,133	$14,038	$17,749
Average	$14,685	$15,183	$20,524	$17,593	$21,594

Part I Cases Cleared per Sworn Officer

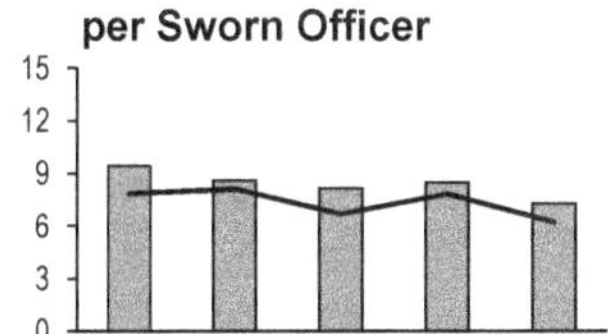

	2013	2014	2015	2016	2017
Asheville	9.4	8.6	8.2	8.5	7.3
Average	7.9	8.1	6.7	7.8	6.2

Effectiveness Measures

Percentage of Part I Cases Cleared of Those Reported

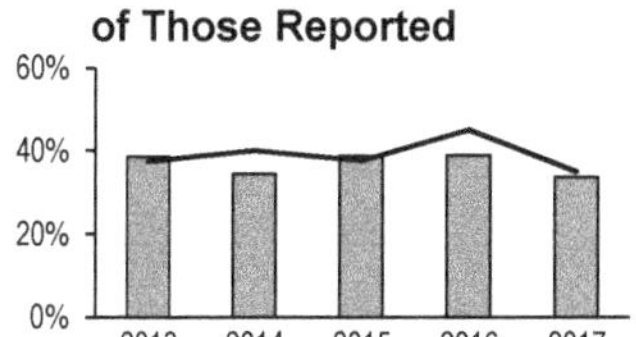

	2013	2014	2015	2016	2017
Asheville	38.6%	34.4%	38.7%	38.8%	33.6%
Average	37.5%	40.0%	37.6%	45.0%	35.0%

Response Time to High Priority Calls in Minutes

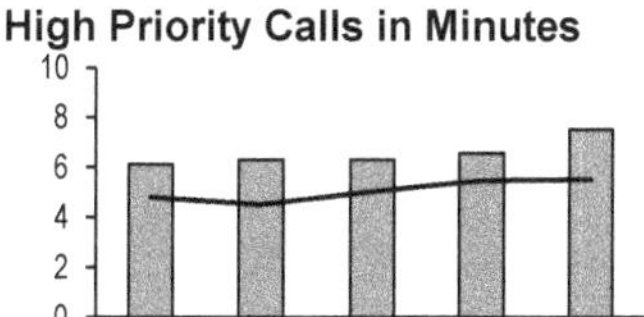

	2013	2014	2015	2016	2017
Asheville	6.1	6.3	6.3	6.6	7.5
Average	4.8	4.5	5.0	5.5	5.5

Fiscal Year 2016–17

Explanatory Information

Service Level and Delivery

The Town of Chapel Hill Police Department provides an array of police services, including patrol, investigations, a special response unit, bicycle patrol, drug enforcement, limited laboratory work, and a canine unit.

The town had 119 sworn officer positions authorized for the fiscal year, with an average length of service of 12.47 years. Police headquarters is located in a separate building. The department also operates four substations. Three of the substations function as offices for community services, and the fourth is located downtown and functions as a space for report processing but is not regularly staffed.

In order to provide continuous service to the citizens of Chapel Hill, officers work twelve hour shifts and are assigned to either day (6 a.m. to 6 p.m.) or night (6 p.m. to 6 a.m.) shifts. Each shift selects a number of officers to report 1-2 hours early to cover calls that occur leading up to shift change.

Vehicles are allocated to divisions in the department and are assigned by unit level supervisors. Individual assignments are made for certain positions, but the only officers allowed to take home vehicles are K9 units and administrative oficers and on-call investigators.

The town defines a high priority call as one that requires immediate police attention to protect persons or render emergency aid.

The police department was successful in clearing a total of 424 Part I cases in FY 2016–17.

Conditions Affecting Service, Performance, and Costs

The Town of Chapel Hill began participation in the benchmarking project in July 2015, with FY 2014–15 being the first reporting year.

Reported cases cleared was up in FY 2015–16 by 68 percent for Part I crimes over the prior year. This was due to an improvement in data tracking.

The average response time to high priority calls reflects the response time of the first arriving unit. Self-initiated calls with a response time of zero are included in the average response time to high priority calls.

Municipal Profile

Population (OSBM 2016)	59,852
Land Area (Square Miles)	21.21
Persons per Square Mile	2,822
Median Family Income U.S. Census 2010	$61,405

Service Profile

FTE Positions—Sworn	119.0
FTE Positions—Other	15.0
Marked and Unmarked Patrol Vehicles	80
Part I Crimes Reported	
Homicide	2
Rape	17
Robbery	31
Assault	46
Burglary	283
Larceny	1,255
Auto Theft	75
Arson	8
TOTAL	1,717
Part II Crimes Reported	3,395
Part I Crimes Cleared	
Persons	65
Property	359
TOTAL	424
Reporting Format	UCR
Number of Calls Dispatched	35,266
Number of Traffic Accidents	2,143
Property Damage for Accidents	$5,580,407

Full Cost Profile

Cost Breakdown by Percentage	
Personal Services	67.0%
Operating Costs	25.0%
Capital Costs	8.1%
TOTAL	100.0%
Cost Breakdown in Dollars	
Personal Services	$9,875,613
Operating Costs	$3,683,355
Capital Costs	$1,188,439
TOTAL	$14,747,408

Chapel Hill — Police Services

Key: Chapel Hill ▒ Benchmarking Average — Fiscal Years 2013 through 2017

Resource Measures

Police Services Costs per Capita

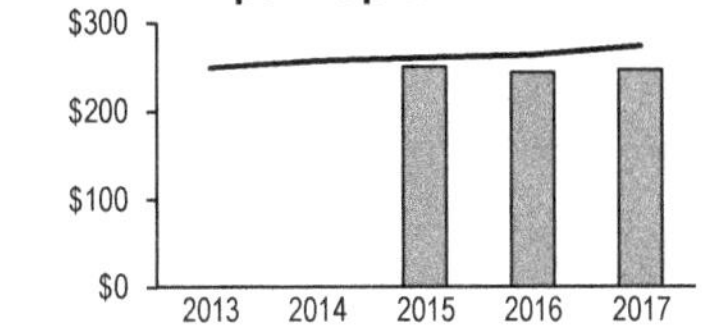

	2013	2014	2015	2016	2017
Chapel Hill			$250	$243	$246
Average	$249	$256	$260	$263	$273

Total Police Services Personnel per 10,000 Population

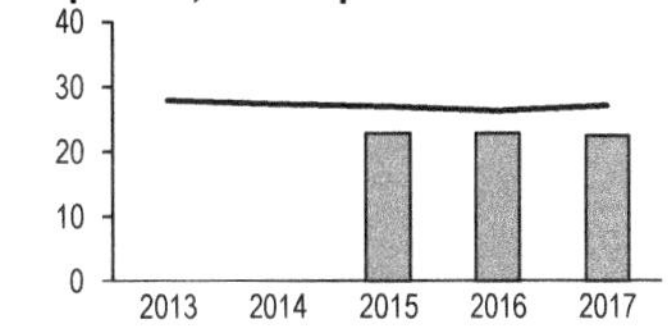

	2013	2014	2015	2016	2017
Chapel Hill			22.8	22.8	22.4
Average	27.9	27.3	26.9	26.2	26.9

Sworn Police Officers per 10,000 Population

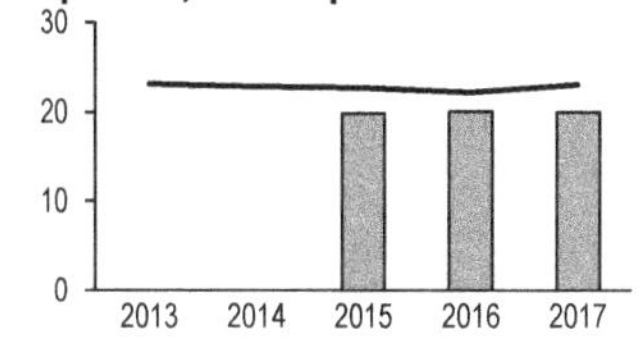

	2013	2014	2015	2016	2017
Chapel Hill			19.7	20.0	19.9
Average	23.1	22.8	22.6	22.1	23.0

Workload Measures

Calls Dispatched per 1,000 Population

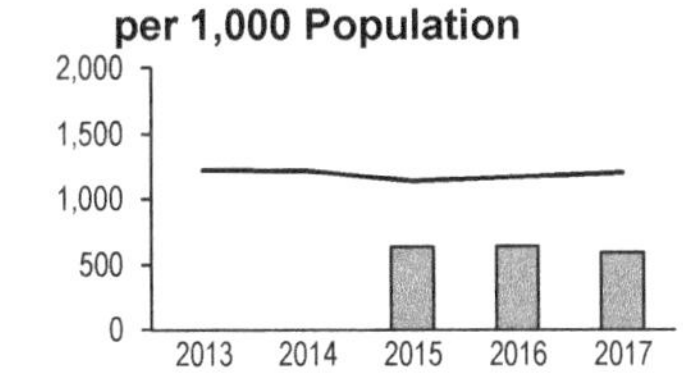

	2013	2014	2015	2016	2017
Chapel Hill			633	638	589
Average	1,220	1,213	1,134	1,166	1,203

Part I Crimes per 1,000 Population

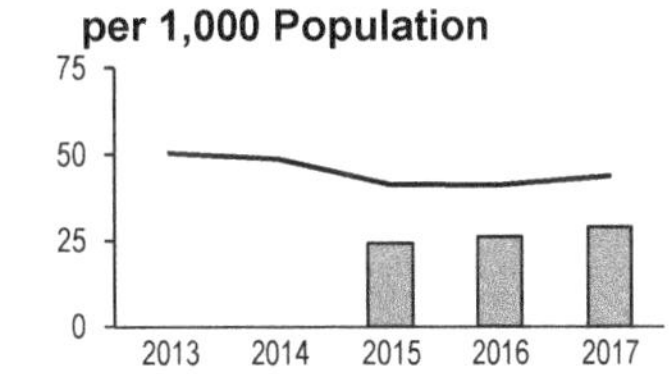

	2013	2014	2015	2016	2017
Chapel Hill			24.1	26.0	28.7
Average	50.5	48.8	41.4	41.1	43.8

Efficiency Measures

Police Services Cost per Call Dispatched

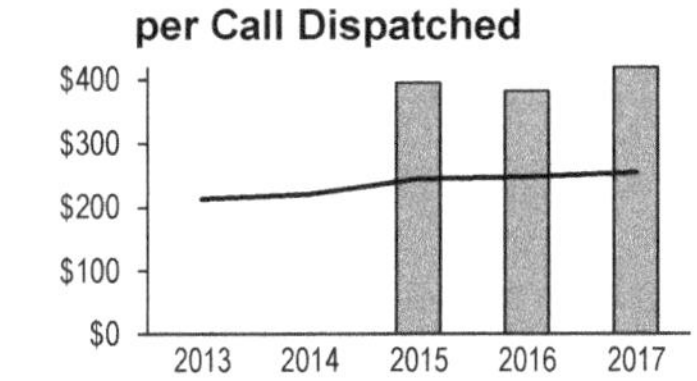

	2013	2014	2015	2016	2017
Chapel Hill			$395	$381	$418
Average	$213	$219	$243	$247	$254

Calls Dispatched per Sworn Officer

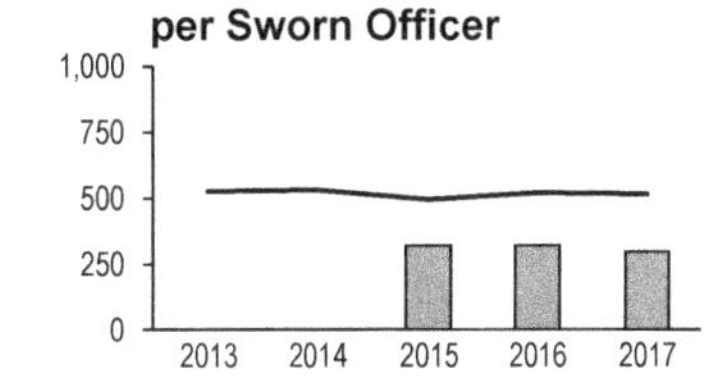

	2013	2014	2015	2016	2017
Chapel Hill			320	319	296
Average	528	532	496	521	516

Police Services Cost per Part I Case Cleared

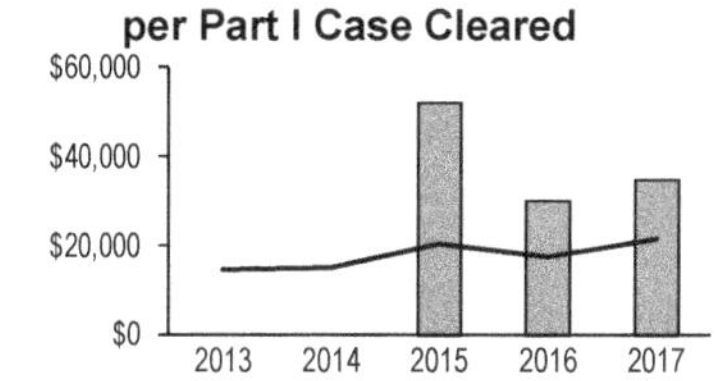

	2013	2014	2015	2016	2017
Chapel Hill			$52,020	$30,063	$34,782
Average	$14,685	$15,183	$20,524	$17,593	$21,594

Part I Cases Cleared per Sworn Officer

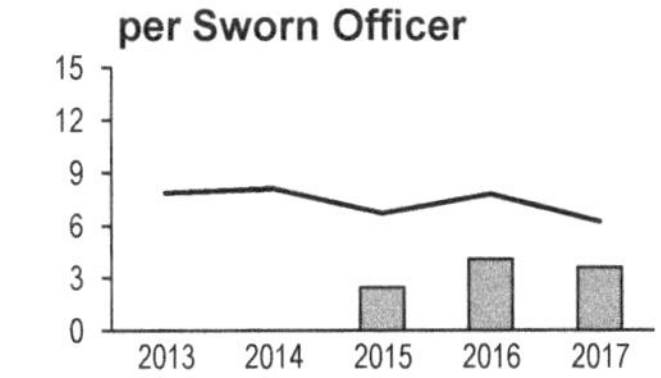

	2013	2014	2015	2016	2017
Chapel Hill			2.4	4.1	3.6
Average	7.9	8.1	6.7	7.8	6.2

Effectiveness Measures

Percentage of Part I Cases Cleared of Those Reported

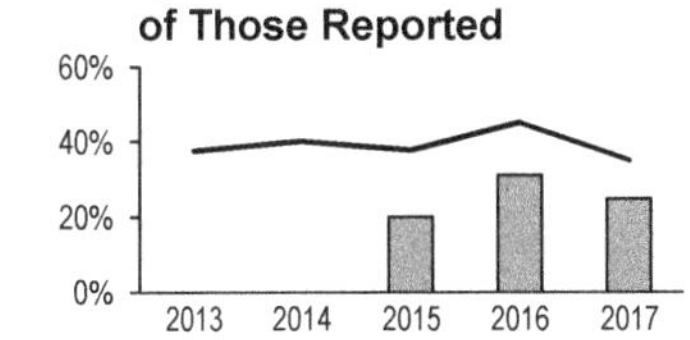

	2013	2014	2015	2016	2017
Chapel Hill			19.9%	31.1%	24.7%
Average	37.5%	40.0%	37.6%	45.0%	35.0%

Response Time to High Priority Calls in Minutes

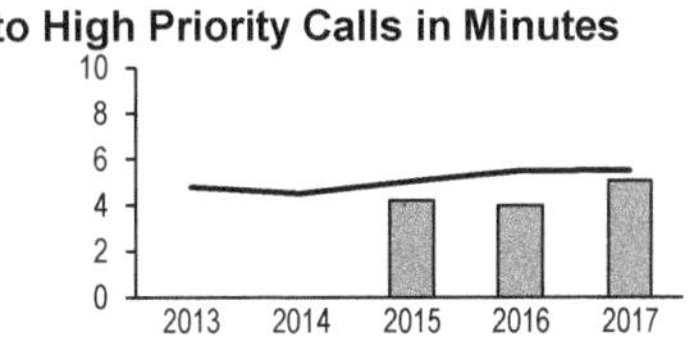

	2013	2014	2015	2016	2017
Chapel Hill			4.2	4.0	5.1
Average	4.8	4.5	5.0	5.5	5.5

Fiscal Year 2016–17

Explanatory Information

Service Level and Delivery

Concord's police department provides an array of police services, including patrol, investigations, a traffic unit, a telephone response unit, a canine unit, a special response unit, a bicycle patrol unit, a drug enforcement unit, a limited forensic laboratory, and other programs such as school resource officers.

The city had 184 sworn officer positions authorized for the fiscal year, with an average length of service of 9.6 years. The police headquarters is in a new separate building located downtown. Four substations are used, two in fire stations and two in shopping malls.

Uniformed patrol officers work twelve-hour rotating shifts. Investigators work five eight-hour days on first and second shifts. District Commanders have the authority to change individual schedules to meet peak demands.

The city defines high priority emergency calls as those involving an assault in progress, personal injury, breaking and entering, or robbery in progress.

Concord uses a one-on-one car plan. Officers may take their vehicles home if they live in the city or within one mile of the city limits.

The police department was successful in clearing a total of 1,805 Part I cases in FY 2016–17.

Conditions Affecting Service, Performance, and Costs

The average response time to high priority calls reflects the response time of the first arriving unit. Self-initiated calls are not included.

Concord's high clearance rate has been driven by a focus on clearing larceny cases by arrest or by exhausting leads as quickly as possible. Since larcenies are the largest category of Part I crimes, this effort has substantially improved the overall clearance rate.

Municipal Profile

Population (OSBM 2016)	88,815
Land Area (Square Miles)	62.61
Persons per Square Mile	1,419
Median Family Income U.S. Census 2010	$63,643

Service Profile

FTE Positions—Sworn	184.00
FTE Positions—Other	20.0
Marked and Unmarked Patrol Vehicles	187
Part I Crimes Reported	
Homicide	2
Rape	12
Robbery	45
Assault	52
Burglary	335
Larceny	1,675
Auto Theft	88
Arson	7
TOTAL	2,216
Part II Crimes Reported	1,963
Part I Crimes Cleared	
Persons	114
Property	1,691
TOTAL	1,805
Reporting Format	IBR
Number of Calls Dispatched	125,323
Number of Traffic Accidents	3,983
Property Damage for Accidents	$14,487,436

Full Cost Profile

Cost Breakdown by Percentage	
Personal Services	64.8%
Operating Costs	25.8%
Capital Costs	9.4%
TOTAL	100.0%
Cost Breakdown in Dollars	
Personal Services	$13,731,623
Operating Costs	$5,459,880
Capital Costs	$1,999,211
TOTAL	$21,190,714

Key: Concord ▒ Benchmarking Average — Fiscal Years 2013 through 2017

Resource Measures

Police Services Costs per Capita

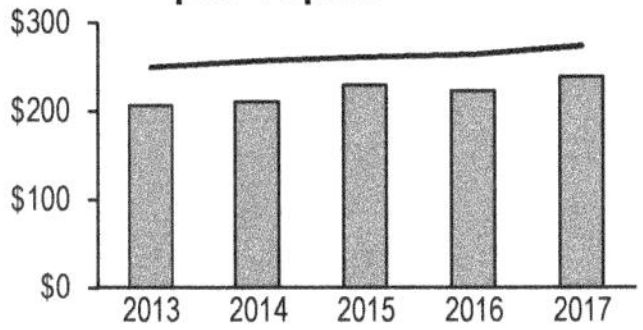

	2013	2014	2015	2016	2017
Concord	$205	$210	$229	$223	$239
Average	$249	$256	$260	$263	$273

Total Police Services Personnel per 10,000 Population

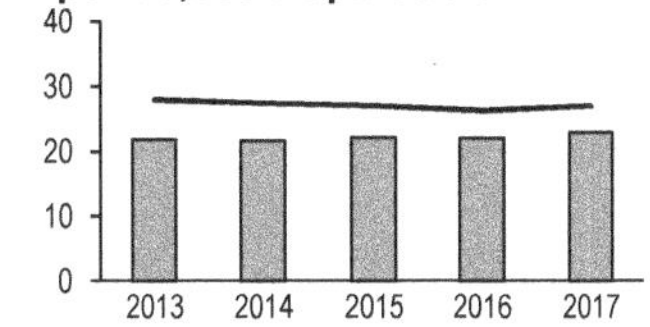

	2013	2014	2015	2016	2017
Concord	21.9	21.6	22.2	22.1	23.0
Average	27.9	27.3	26.9	26.2	26.9

Sworn Police Officers per 10,000 Population

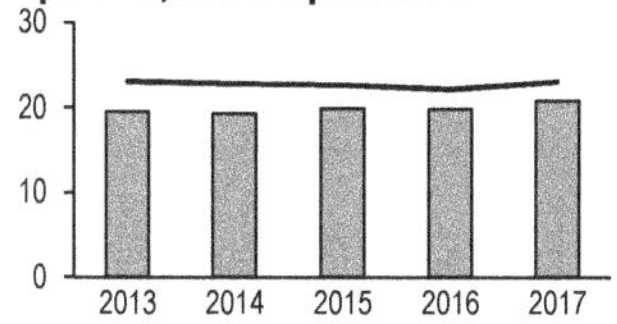

	2013	2014	2015	2016	2017
Concord	19.4	19.2	19.8	19.8	20.7
Average	23.1	22.8	22.6	22.1	23.0

Workload Measures

Calls Dispatched per 1,000 Population

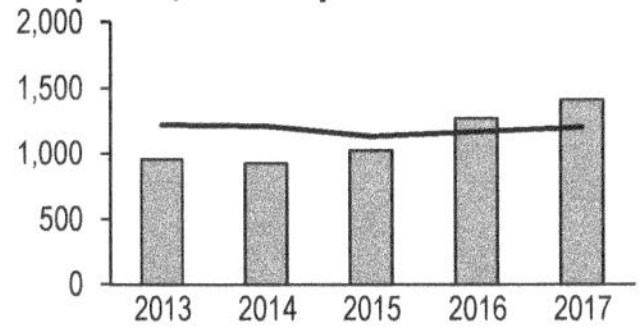

	2013	2014	2015	2016	2017
Concord	952	923	1,024	1,271	1,411
Average	1,220	1,213	1,134	1,166	1,203

Part I Crimes per 1,000 Population

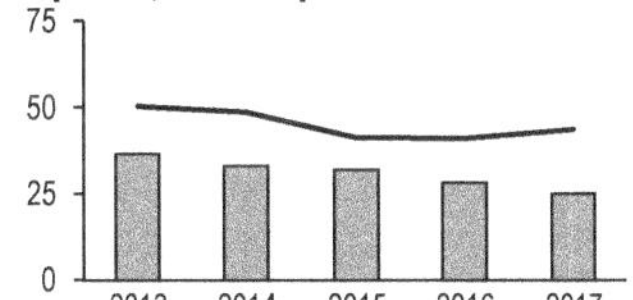

	2013	2014	2015	2016	2017
Concord	36.7	33.0	31.8	28.3	25.0
Average	50.5	48.8	41.4	41.1	43.8

Efficiency Measures

Police Services Cost per Call Dispatched

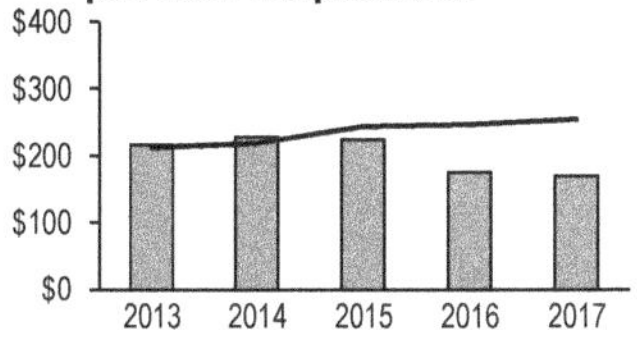

	2013	2014	2015	2016	2017
Concord	$216	$227	$223	$175	$169
Average	$213	$219	$243	$247	$254

Calls Dispatched per Sworn Officer

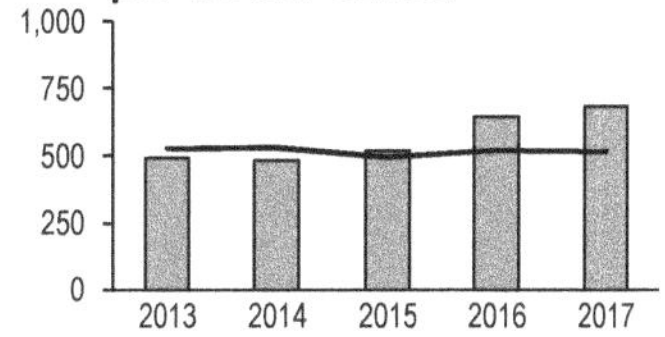

	2013	2014	2015	2016	2017
Concord	490	480	517	643	681
Average	528	532	496	521	516

Police Services Cost per Part I Case Cleared

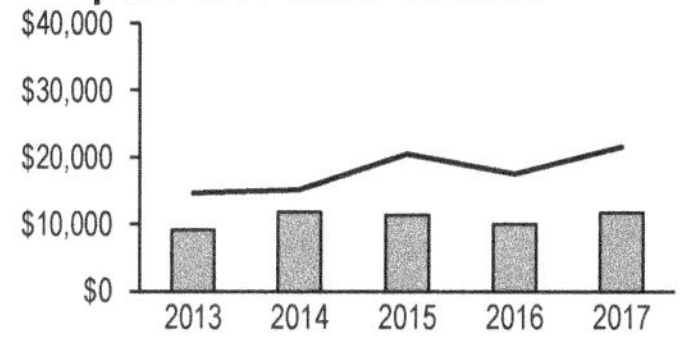

	2013	2014	2015	2016	2017
Concord	$9,161	$11,882	$11,381	$9,999	$11,740
Average	$14,685	$15,183	$20,524	$17,593	$21,594

Part I Cases Cleared per Sworn Officer

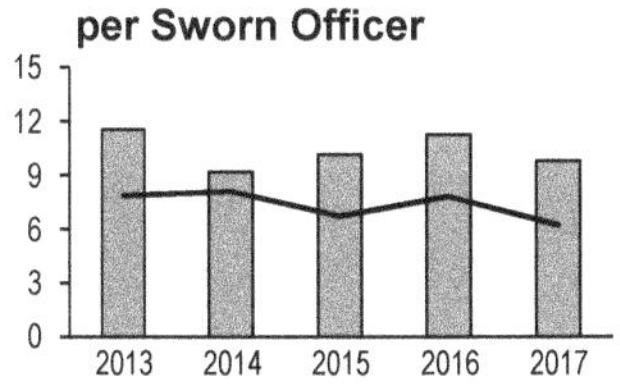

	2013	2014	2015	2016	2017
Concord	11.5	9.2	10.1	11.3	9.8
Average	7.9	8.1	6.7	7.8	6.2

Effectiveness Measures

Percentage of Part I Cases Cleared of Those Reported

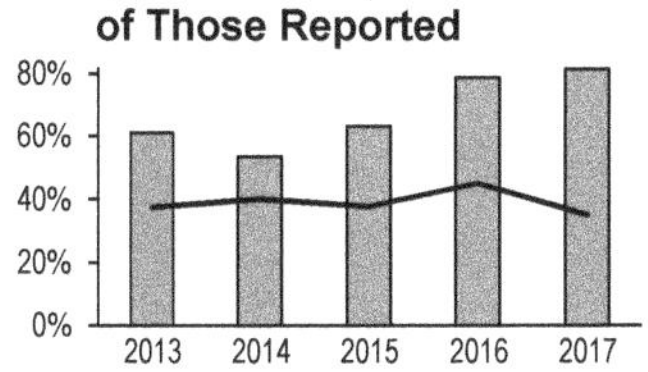

	2013	2014	2015	2016	2017
Concord	61.2%	53.5%	63.1%	78.7%	81.5%
Average	37.5%	40.0%	37.6%	45.0%	35.0%

Response Time to High Priority Calls in Minutes

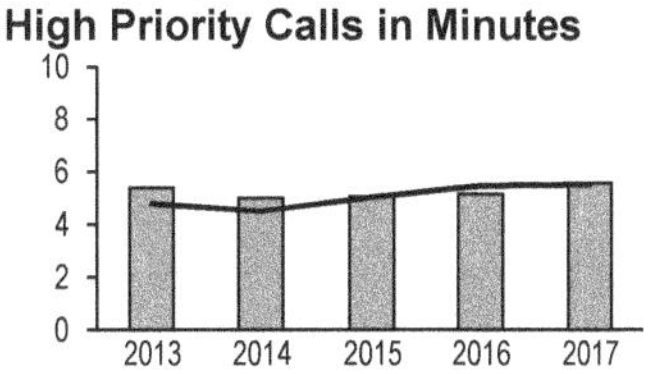

	2013	2014	2015	2016	2017
Concord	5.4	5.0	5.1	5.2	5.6
Average	4.8	4.5	5.0	5.5	5.5

Goldsboro — Police Services

Fiscal Year 2016–17

Explanatory Information

Service Level and Delivery

Goldsboro provides comprehensive police services, including patrol, investigations, a canine unit, a bicycle patrol unit, a drug enforcement unit, animal control, and a limited service forensics unit. The bicycle unit is made up of officers assigned to the housing unit and selective enforcement unit and is not a stand-alone unit.

The city had 110 sworn officers authorized for the fiscal year with an average length of service of just over ten years. The police department is housed in a complex that is shared with the fire department, with each department having its own entrance but sharing a gym and locker rooms.

Uniformed officers work a total of 2,052 hours per year while investigators work a total of 2,080 hours. Schedules can be adjusted at any time according to call demand, special events, or special incidents. Officers are assigned a vehicle once they are out of field training. They can drive a vehicle home if they live within Wayne County.

Goldsboro currently does not have a specific definition for "high priority calls." The police department is currently implementing a new system which will be able to track call types and times more efficiently in the future. Call times for the current fiscal year for high priority calls were not available.

Conditions Affecting Service, Performance, and Costs

The city of Goldsboro joined the Benchmarking Project in July 2017, with the first year of data showing for FY 2016–17.

Municipal Profile

Population (OSBM 2016)	34,793
Land Area (Square Miles)	29.35
Persons per Square Mile	1,186
Median Family Income	$33,879
U.S. Census 2010	

Service Profile

FTE Positions—Sworn	110.0
FTE Positions—Other	11.0
Marked and Unmarked Patrol Vehicles	97
Part I Crimes Reported	
Homicide	12
Rape	2
Robbery	75
Assault	267
Burglary	401
Larceny	1,473
Auto Theft	88
Arson	2
TOTAL	2,320
Part II Crimes Reported	2,283
Part I Crimes Cleared	
Persons	125
Property	477
TOTAL	602
Reporting Format	UCR
Number of Calls Dispatched	55,237
Number of Traffic Accidents	2,234
Property Damage for Accidents	NA

Full Cost Profile

Cost Breakdown by Percentage	
Personal Services	73.0%
Operating Costs	23.8%
Capital Costs	3.1%
TOTAL	100.0%
Cost Breakdown in Dollars	
Personal Services	$6,916,980
Operating Costs	$2,258,336
Capital Costs	$297,195
TOTAL	$9,472,511

Key: Goldsboro ▒ Benchmarking Average — Fiscal Years 2013 through 2017

Resource Measures

Police Services Costs per Capita

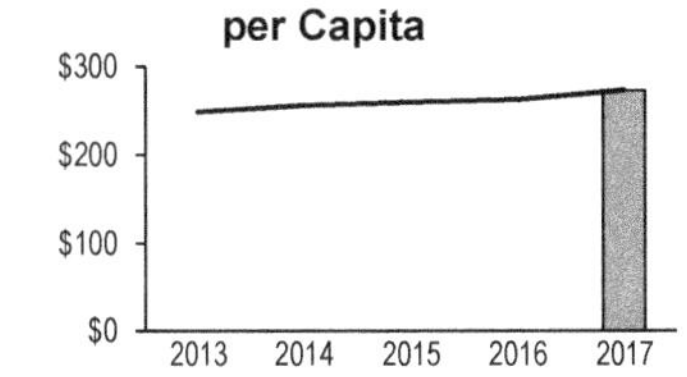

	2013	2014	2015	2016	2017
Goldsboro					$272
Average	$249	$256	$260	$263	$273

Total Police Services Personnel per 10,000 Population

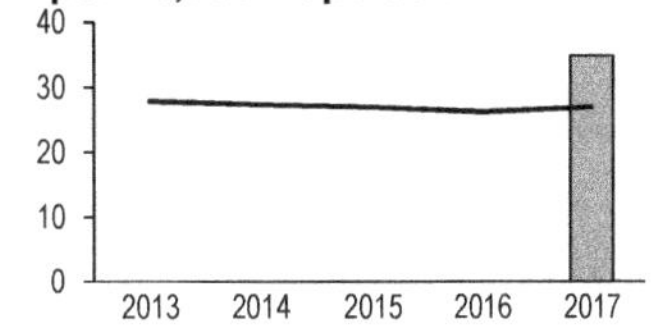

	2013	2014	2015	2016	2017
Goldsboro					34.8
Average	27.9	27.3	26.9	26.2	26.9

Sworn Police Officers per 10,000 Population

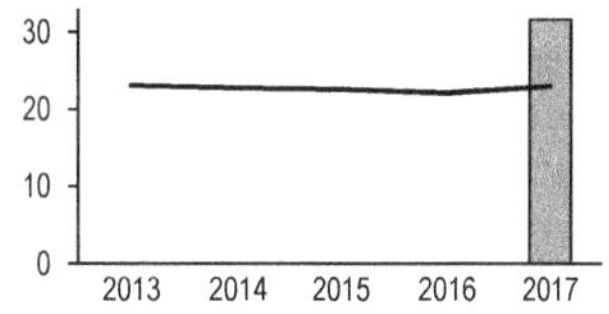

	2013	2014	2015	2016	2017
Goldsboro					31.6
Average	23.1	22.8	22.6	22.1	23.0

Workload Measures

Calls Dispatched per 1,000 Population

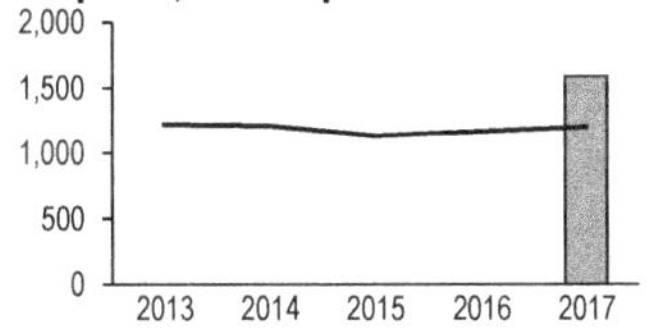

	2013	2014	2015	2016	2017
Goldsboro					1,588
Average	1,220	1,213	1,134	1,166	1,203

Part I Crimes per 1,000 Population

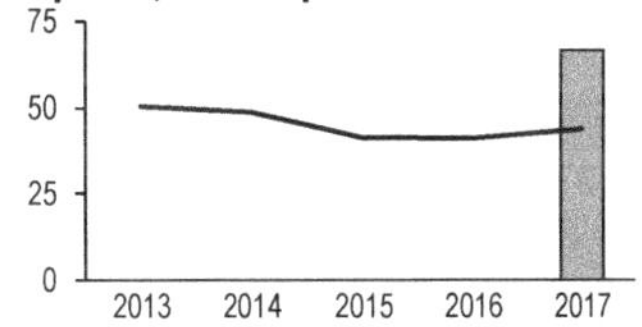

	2013	2014	2015	2016	2017
Goldsboro					66.7
Average	50.5	48.8	41.4	41.1	43.8

Efficiency Measures

Police Services Cost per Call Dispatched

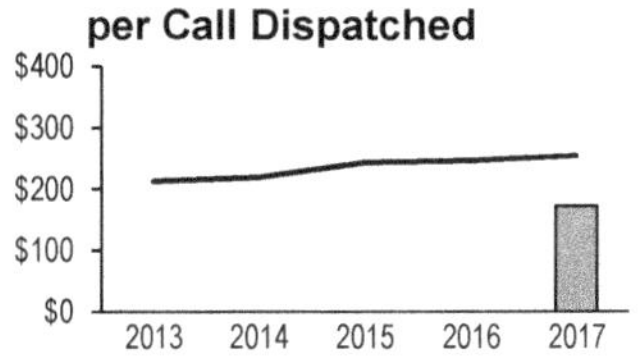

	2013	2014	2015	2016	2017
Goldsboro					$171
Average	$213	$219	$243	$247	$254

Calls Dispatched per Sworn Officer

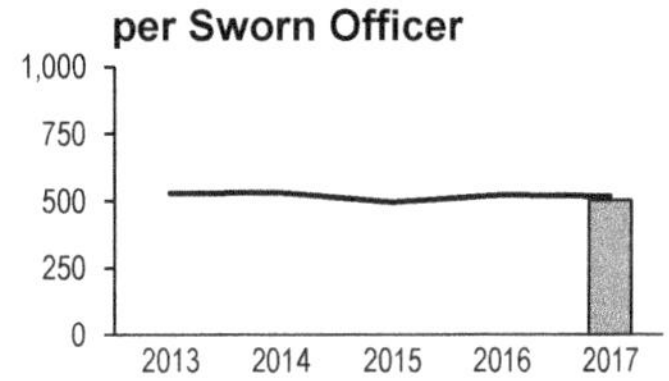

	2013	2014	2015	2016	2017
Goldsboro					502
Average	528	532	496	521	516

Police Services Cost per Part I Case Cleared

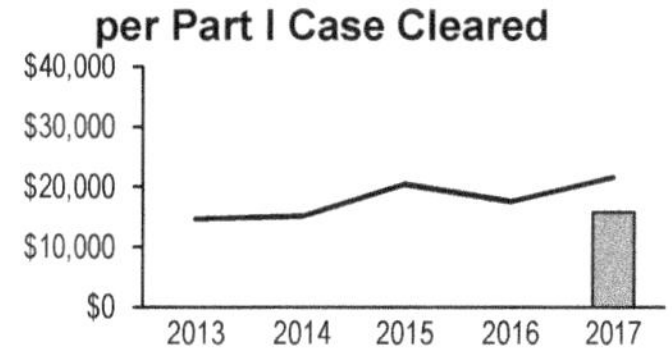

	2013	2014	2015	2016	2017
Goldsboro					$15,735
Average	$14,686	$16,183	$20,621	$17,593	$21,594

Part I Cases Cleared per Sworn Officer

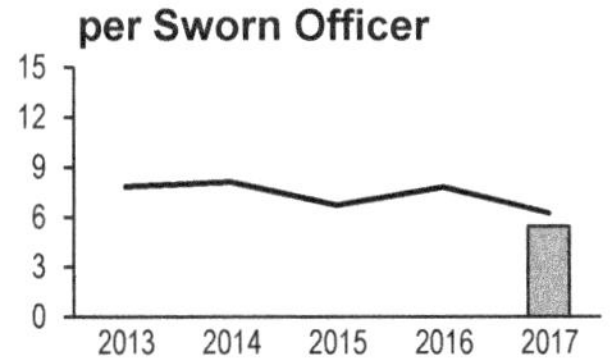

	2013	2014	2015	2016	2017
Goldsboro					5.5
Average	7.9	8.1	6.7	7.8	6.2

Effectiveness Measures

Percentage of Part I Cases Cleared of Those Reported

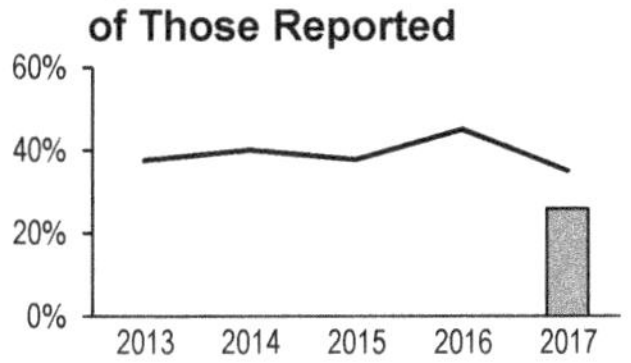

	2013	2014	2015	2016	2017
Goldsboro					25.9%
Average	37.5%	40.0%	37.6%	45.0%	35.0%

Response Time to High Priority Calls in Minutes

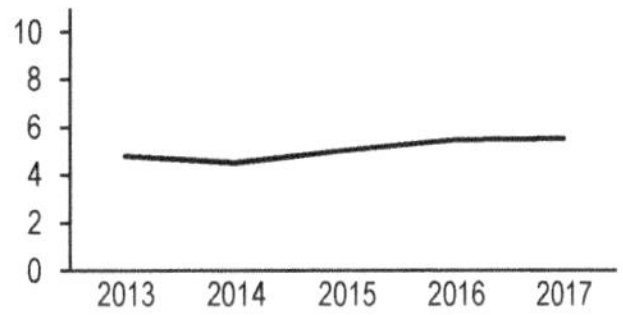

	2013	2014	2015	2016	2017
Goldsboro					
Average	4.8	4.5	5.0	5.5	5.5

Fiscal Year 2016–17

Explanatory Information

Service Level and Delivery

Greensboro provides comprehensive police services, including patrol, investigations, a traffic unit, a telephone response unit, a forensics laboratory, a canine unit, a motorcycle unit, a special response unit, a bicycle patrol unit, a drug enforcement unit, and a student outreach and recruiting program.

The city had 673 sworn officer positions authorized for the fiscal year, with an average length of service of nearly eleven years. The police department is housed in a downtown facility with other city departments. The city also has three substations that serve as remote line-up facilities.

Patrol officers work a four-days-on and four-days-off fixed schedule. There are four shifts each day, with each patrol officer shift lasting eleven hours. Investigators and administrative personnel work Monday through Friday from 8 a.m. to 5 p.m. Schedules can be adjusted at any time according to call demand, special events, or special incidents.

Line patrol officers do not take vehicles home. Patrol supervisors, division commanders, and some investigators take vehicles home, depending on their assignments.

Greensboro defines a high priority emergency call as one where there is a potential for imminent serious injury or death. The police department was successful in clearing a total of 3,421 Part I cases in FY 2016–17.

Conditions Affecting Service, Performance, and Costs

The average response time to high priority calls reflects the response time of the first arriving unit. Self-initiated calls with a response time of zero are included in the average response time to high priority calls with the exception of traffic stops and report-only calls.

Municipal Profile

Population (OSBM 2016)	284,343
Land Area (Square Miles)	128.72
Persons per Square Mile	2,209
Median Family Income U.S. Census 2010	$52,752

Service Profile

FTE Positions—Sworn	673.0
FTE Positions—Other	112.0
Marked and Unmarked Patrol Vehicles	223
Part I Crimes Reported	
Homicide	47
Rape	83
Robbery	637
Assault	773
Burglary	2,266
Larceny	6,924
Auto Theft	714
Arson	117
TOTAL	11,561
Part II Crimes Reported	15,674
Part I Crimes Cleared	
Persons	658
Property	2,763
TOTAL	3,421
Reporting Format	UCR
Number of Calls Dispatched	224,955
Number of Traffic Accidents	11,030
Property Damage for Accidents	$45,341,325

Full Cost Profile

Cost Breakdown by Percentage	
Personal Services	76.8%
Operating Costs	23.2%
Capital Costs	0.0%
TOTAL	100.0%
Cost Breakdown in Dollars	
Personal Services	$60,239,868
Operating Costs	$18,243,335
Capital Costs	$0
TOTAL	$78,483,203

Resource Measures

Police Services Costs per Capita

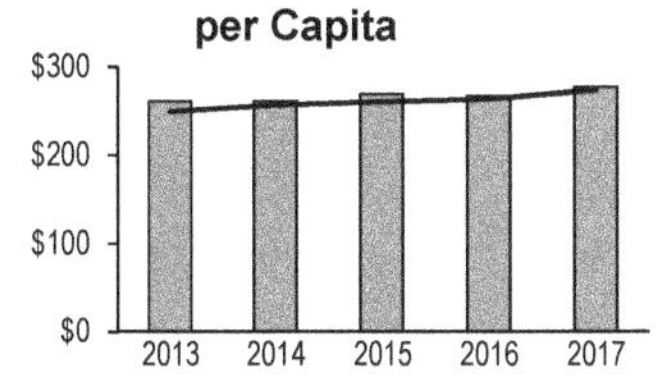

	2013	2014	2015	2016	2017
Greensboro	$260	$260	$268	$266	$276
Average	$249	$256	$260	$263	$273

Total Police Services Personnel per 10,000 Population

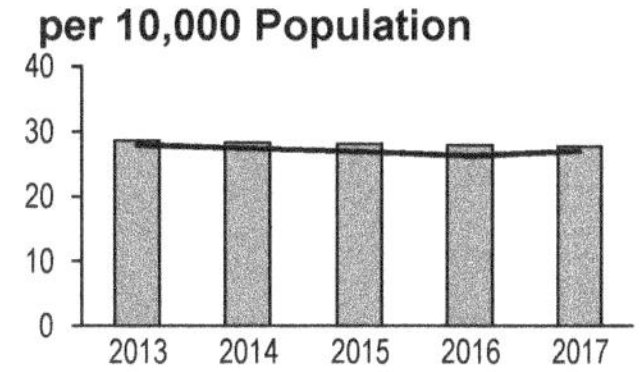

	2013	2014	2015	2016	2017
Greensboro	28.5	28.2	28.0	27.8	27.6
Average	27.9	27.3	26.9	26.2	26.9

Sworn Police Officers per 10,000 Population

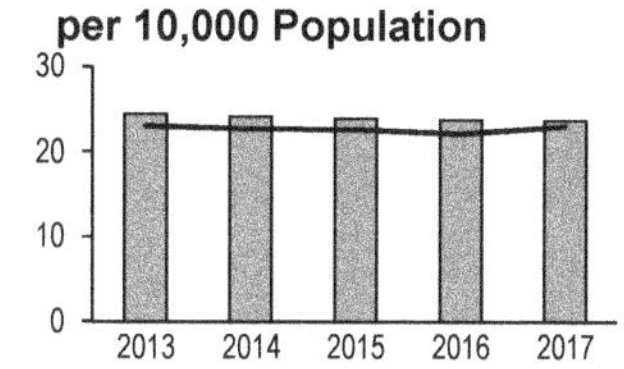

	2013	2014	2015	2016	2017
Greensboro	24.5	24.2	24.0	23.8	23.7
Average	23.1	22.8	22.6	22.1	23.0

Workload Measures

Calls Dispatched per 1,000 Population

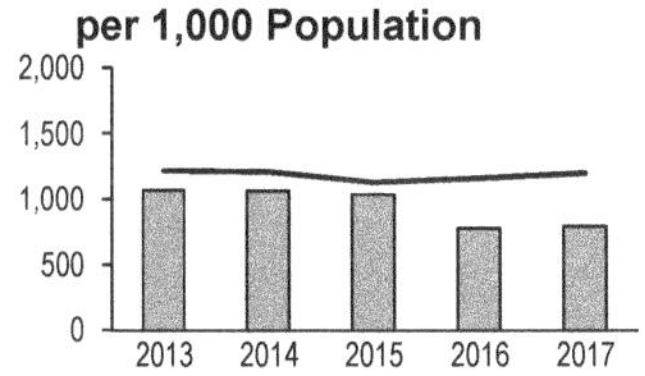

	2013	2014	2015	2016	2017
Greensboro	1,073	1,064	1,036	779	791
Average	1,220	1,213	1,134	1,166	1,203

Part I Crimes per 1,000 Population

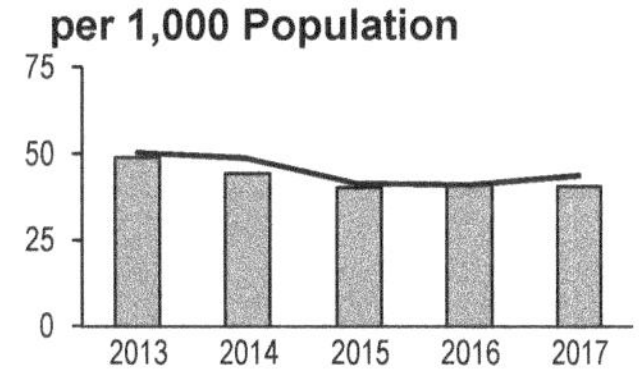

	2013	2014	2015	2016	2017
Greensboro	49.0	44.4	40.3	41.0	40.7
Average	50.5	48.8	41.4	41.1	43.8

Efficiency Measures

Police Services Cost per Call Dispatched

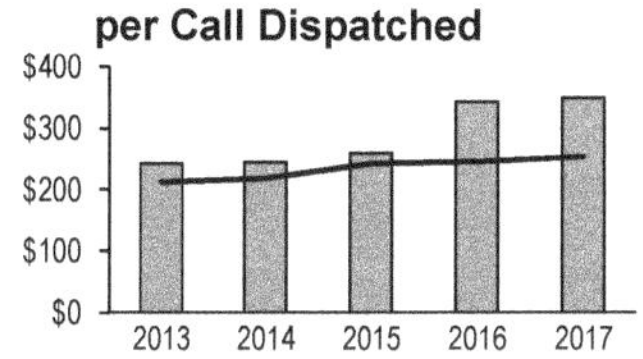

	2013	2014	2015	2016	2017
Greensboro	$242	$245	$259	$342	$349
Average	$213	$219	$243	$247	$254

Calls Dispatched per Sworn Officer

	2013	2014	2015	2016	2017
Greensboro	439	441	432	327	334
Average	528	532	496	521	516

Police Services Cost per Part I Case Cleared

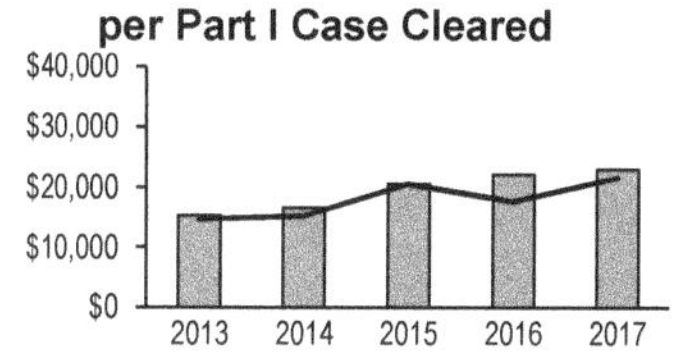

	2013	2014	2015	2016	2017
Greensboro	$15,323	$16,548	$20,484	$22,107	$22,942
Average	$14,085	$15,183	$20,524	$17,593	$21,594

Part I Cases Cleared per Sworn Officer

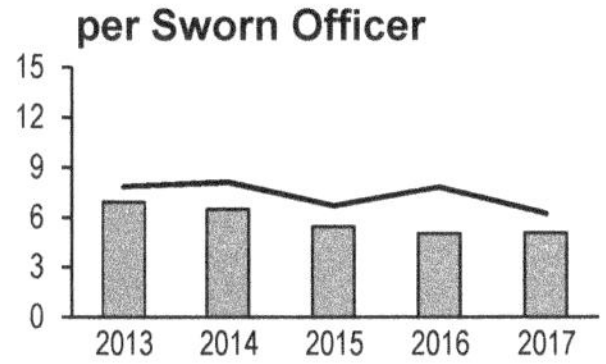

	2013	2014	2015	2016	2017
Greensboro	6.9	6.5	5.5	5.1	5.1
Average	7.9	8.1	6.7	7.8	6.2

Effectiveness Measures

Percentage of Part I Cases Cleared of Those Reported

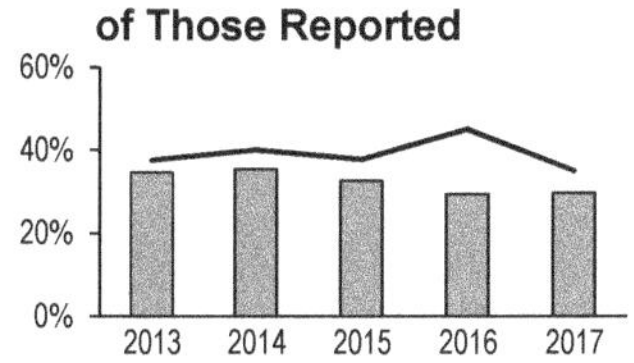

	2013	2014	2015	2016	2017
Greensboro	34.7%	35.4%	32.5%	29.4%	29.6%
Average	37.5%	40.0%	37.6%	45.0%	35.0%

Response Time to High Priority Calls in Minutes

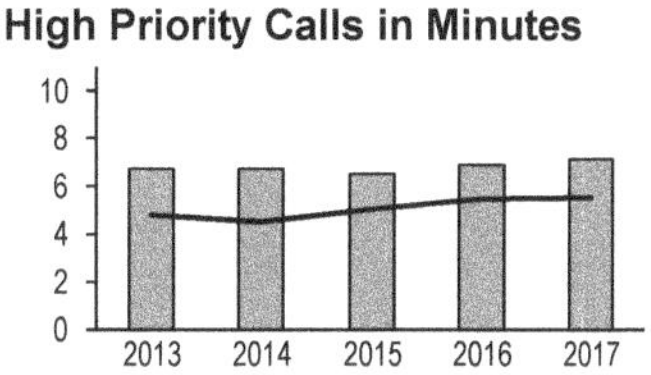

	2013	2014	2015	2016	2017
Greensboro	6.7	6.7	6.5	6.9	7.1
Average	4.8	4.5	5.0	5.5	5.5

Fiscal Year 2016–17

Explanatory Information

Service Level and Delivery

Greenville provides a full array of police services, including patrol, investigations, a canine unit, a special response unit, bicycle patrol, and drug enforcement.

The city had 194 sworn officer positions authorized for the fiscal year, with an average length of service of thirteen years. The police department occupies space in the city government building.

Patrol officers work a rotating schedule of two on/two off/three on/two off/two on/three off. There are four shifts each day for patrol officers, with the shifts lasting eleven hours. Investigators and administrative personnel work Monday through Friday, with eight-hour shifts. Schedules are subject to change based on call demand, special events, or unusual events.

Some patrol officers have take-home vehicles. There are seven or eight take-home cars per shift. They are assigned by seniority and whether or not the officer lives in the city limits. Officers on a shift who do not have a take-home car are assigned a pool car to drive each day. All investigators and administative personnel (with one exception) have take-home cars.

Greenville defines high priority emergency calls as those situations that present a potential for imminent serious injury or death. These calls are dispatched to the first available patrol unit, which may require a citywide dispatch.

The police department was successful in clearing a total of 1,132 Part I cases in FY 2016–17.

Conditions Affecting Service, Performance, and Costs

The average response time to high priority calls reflects the response time of the first arriving unit. Self-initiated calls are not included in the response times.

Municipal Profile

Population (OSBM 2016)	87,989
Land Area (Square Miles)	35.41
Persons per Square Mile	2,485
Median Family Income U.S. Census 2010	$50,395

Service Profile

FTE Positions—Sworn	194.0
FTE Positions—Other	49.0
Marked and Unmarked Patrol Vehicles	163
Part I Crimes Reported	
Homicide	7
Rape	13
Robbery	138
Assault	446
Burglary	1,159
Larceny	2,509
Auto Theft	99
Arson	9
TOTAL	4,380
Part II Crimes Reported	4,323
Part I Crimes Cleared	
Persons	190
Property	942
TOTAL	1,132
Reporting Format	UCR
Number of Calls Dispatched	85,416
Number of Traffic Accidents	4,811
Property Damage for Accidents	NA

Full Cost Profile

Cost Breakdown by Percentage	
Personal Services	63.3%
Operating Costs	27.1%
Capital Costs	9.5%
TOTAL	100.0%
Cost Breakdown in Dollars	
Personal Services	$16,698,054
Operating Costs	$7,150,675
Capital Costs	$2,511,032
TOTAL	$26,359,761

Key: Greenville ▒ Benchmarking Average — Fiscal Years 2013 through 2017

Resource Measures

Police Services Costs per Capita

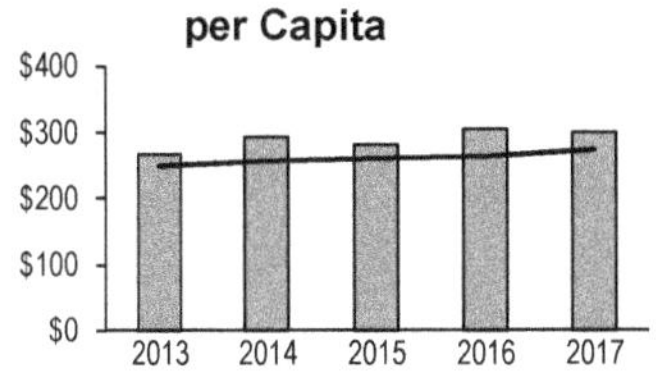

	2013	2014	2015	2016	2017
Greenville	$267	$293	$281	$305	$300
Average	$249	$256	$260	$263	$273

Total Police Services Personnel per 10,000 Population

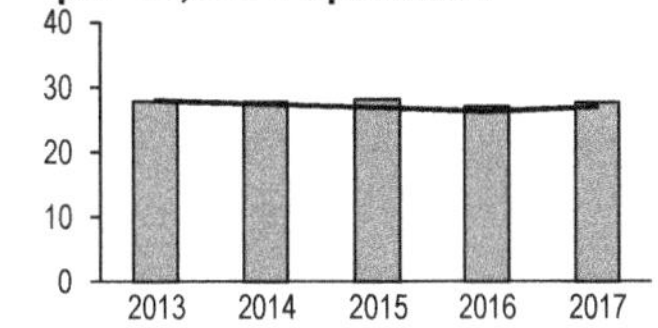

	2013	2014	2015	2016	2017
Greenville	27.9	27.7	28.1	27.1	27.6
Average	27.9	27.3	26.9	26.2	26.9

Sworn Police Officers per 10,000 Population

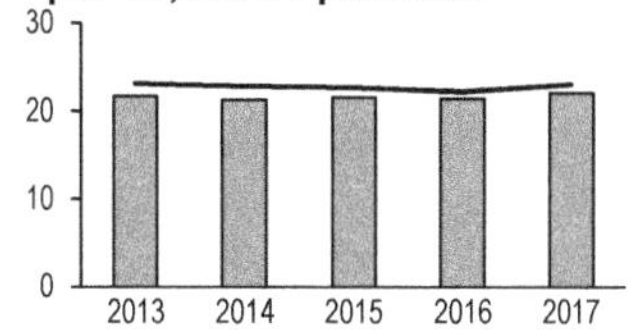

	2013	2014	2015	2016	2017
Greenville	21.7	21.2	21.5	21.4	22.0
Average	23.1	22.8	22.6	22.1	23.0

Workload Measures

Calls Dispatched per 1,000 Population

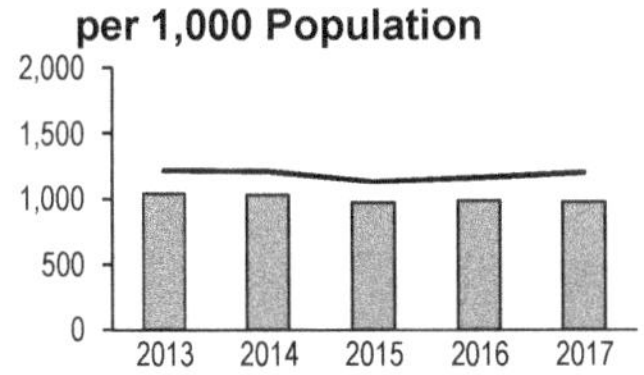

	2013	2014	2015	2016	2017
Greenville	1,031	1,023	964	981	971
Average	1,220	1,213	1,134	1,166	1,203

Part I Crimes per 1,000 Population

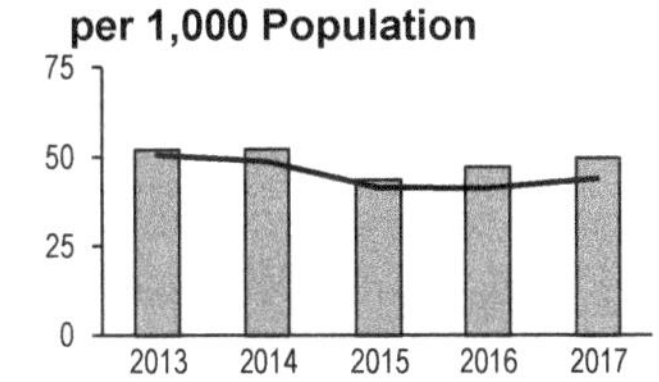

	2013	2014	2015	2016	2017
Greenville	52.2	52.3	43.6	47.3	49.8
Average	50.5	48.8	41.4	41.1	43.8

Efficiency Measures

Police Services Cost per Call Dispatched

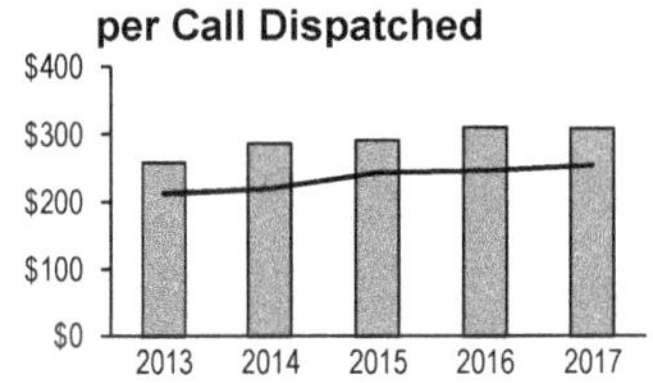

	2013	2014	2015	2016	2017
Greenville	$259	$287	$292	$311	$309
Average	$213	$219	$243	$247	$254

Calls Dispatched per Sworn Officer

	2013	2014	2015	2016	2017
Greenville	475	482	448	459	440
Average	528	532	496	521	516

Police Services Cost per Part I Case Cleared

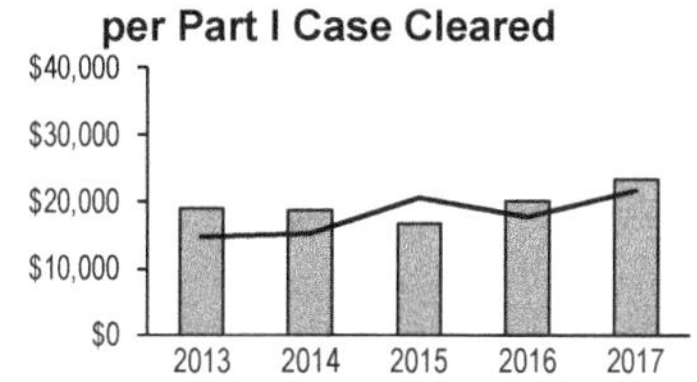

	2013	2014	2015	2016	2017
Greenville	$18,963	$18,646	$16,689	$19,992	$23,286
Average	$14,685	$15,183	$20,524	$17,593	$21,594

Part I Cases Cleared per Sworn Officer

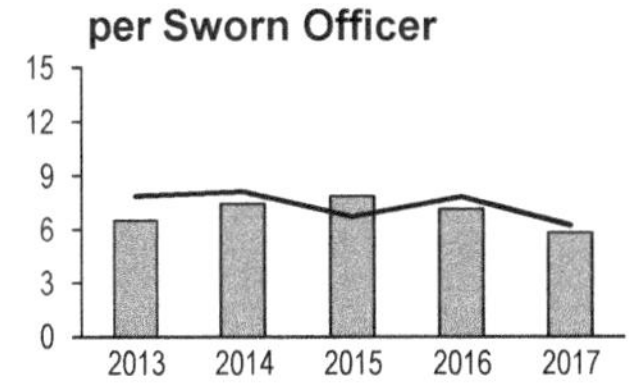

	2013	2014	2015	2016	2017
Greenville	6.5	7.4	7.8	7.1	5.8
Average	7.9	8.1	6.7	7.8	6.2

Effectiveness Measures

Percentage of Part I Cases Cleared of Those Reported

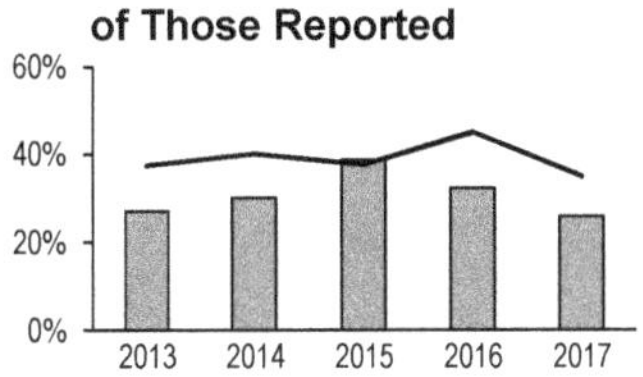

	2013	2014	2015	2016	2017
Greenville	27.0%	30.1%	38.7%	32.2%	25.8%
Average	37.5%	40.0%	37.6%	45.0%	35.0%

Response Time to High Priority Calls in Minutes

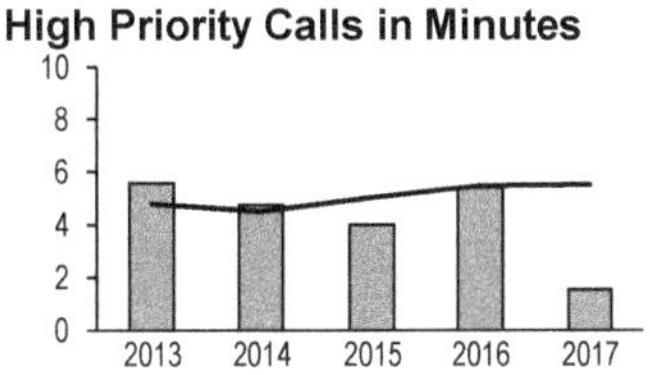

	2013	2014	2015	2016	2017
Greenville	5.6	4.8	4.0	5.4	1.5
Average	4.8	4.5	5.0	5.5	5.5

Fiscal Year 2016–17

Explanatory Information

Service Level and Delivery
Hickory provides a full array of police services, including patrol, investigations, a traffic unit, a small laboratory facility, a canine unit, a special response unit, bicycle patrol, a jail/holding facility, animal control, drug enforcement, and a DARE program.

The city had 116 sworn officer positions authorized for the fiscal year, with an average length of service of 9.1 years. The police department occupies its own three-story facility, completed in January 1996. Each of the five community police areas has an office located in its respective community. These offices are not staffed. They are used for interviews, to obtain information, to store supplies, and to make phone calls.

Patrol officers work a fourteen-day, 80.5-hour cycle. During this period, officers work seven 11.5-hour days. Each of the five districts is commanded by a lieutenant who establishes schedules based on need.

Investigators work Monday through Friday, either from 8:30 a.m. to 5:00 p.m. or 3:30 p.m. to 12:00 a.m. for the second-shift on-call investigators.

Hickory uses the one-officer, one-car plan. Officers take vehicles home if they live in or within one mile of the city. Officers who are members of specialized units needed for emergency response, such as special operations, K-9, or criminial investigations, may also take their vehicles home.

Hickory defines high priority emergency calls as those situations that present an in-progress threat to life or serious property loss. Officers are authorized to utilize blue lights and sirens during responses and may exceed posted speed limits by up to 20 miles per hour.

The police department was successful in clearing a total of 774 Part I cases in FY 2016–17.

Conditions Affecting Service, Performance, and Costs
The average response time to high priority calls reflects the response time of the first arriving unit. Self-initiated calls with a response time of zero are included in the average response time to high priority calls.

Municipal Profile

Population (OSBM 2016)	40,453
Land Area (Square Miles)	29.90
Persons per Square Mile	1,353
Median Family Income	$54,093
U.S. Census 2010	

Service Profile

FTE Positions—Sworn	116.0
FTE Positions—Other	36.0
Marked and Unmarked Patrol Vehicles	155
Part I Crimes Reported	
Homicide	4
Rape	16
Robbery	65
Assault	90
Burglary	333
Larceny	1,513
Auto Theft	144
Arson	10
TOTAL	2,175
Part II Crimes Reported	3,375
Part I Crimes Cleared	
Persons	84
Property	690
TOTAL	774
Reporting Format	IBR
Number of Calls Dispatched	88,167
Number of Traffic Accidents	3,555
Property Damage for Accidents	$9,593,910

Full Cost Profile

Cost Breakdown by Percentage	
Personal Services	67.4%
Operating Costs	24.8%
Capital Costs	7.8%
TOTAL	100.0%
Cost Breakdown in Dollars	
Personal Services	$8,001,077
Operating Costs	$2,942,725
Capital Costs	$927,767
TOTAL	$11,871,570

Key: Hickory ▒ Benchmarking Average — Fiscal Years 2013 through 2017

Resource Measures

Police Services Costs per Capita

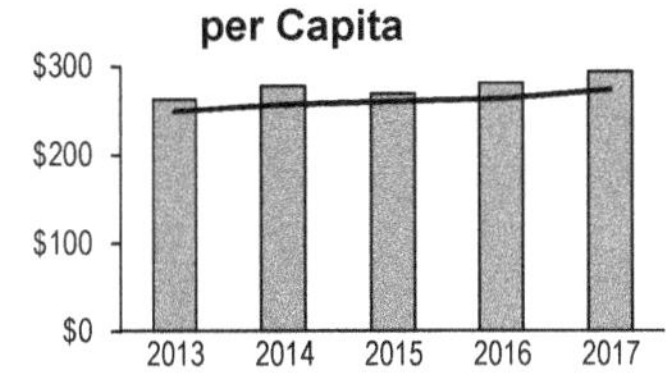

	2013	2014	2015	2016	2017
Hickory	$262	$277	$269	$281	$293
Average	$249	$256	$260	$263	$273

Total Police Services Personnel per 10,000 Population

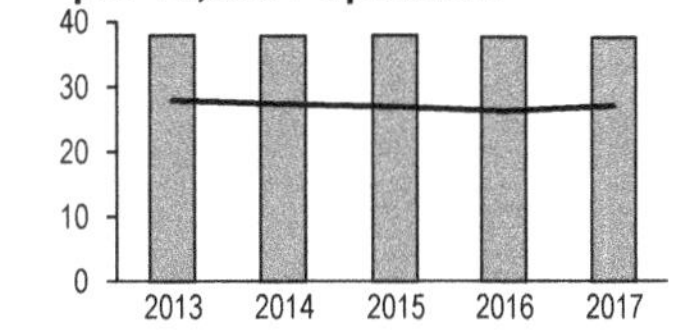

	2013	2014	2015	2016	2017
Hickory	38.0	37.8	37.9	37.7	37.6
Average	27.9	27.3	26.9	26.2	26.9

Sworn Police Officers per 10,000 Population

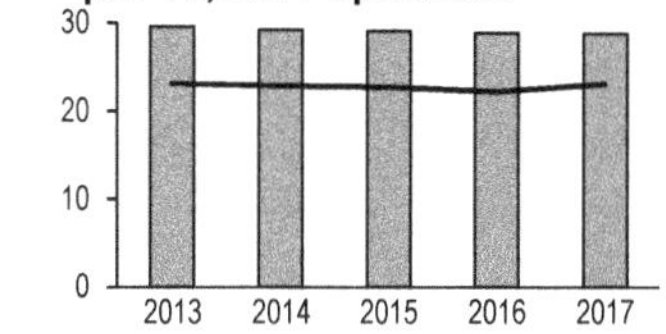

	2013	2014	2015	2016	2017
Hickory	29.5	29.1	29.0	28.7	28.7
Average	23.1	22.8	22.6	22.1	23.0

Workload Measures

Calls Dispatched per 1,000 Population

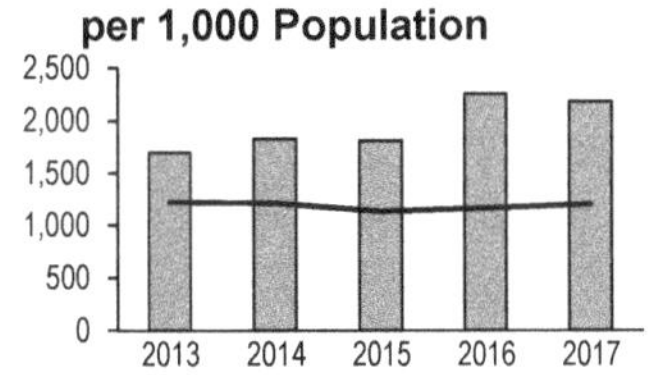

	2013	2014	2015	2016	2017
Hickory	1,697	1,825	1,805	2,253	2,179
Average	1,220	1,213	1,134	1,166	1,203

Part I Crimes per 1,000 Population

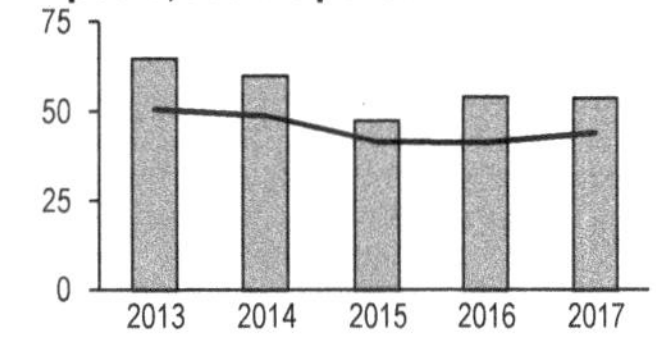

	2013	2014	2015	2016	2017
Hickory	64.9	60.0	47.5	54.2	53.8
Average	50.5	48.8	41.4	41.1	43.8

Efficiency Measures

Police Services Cost per Call Dispatched

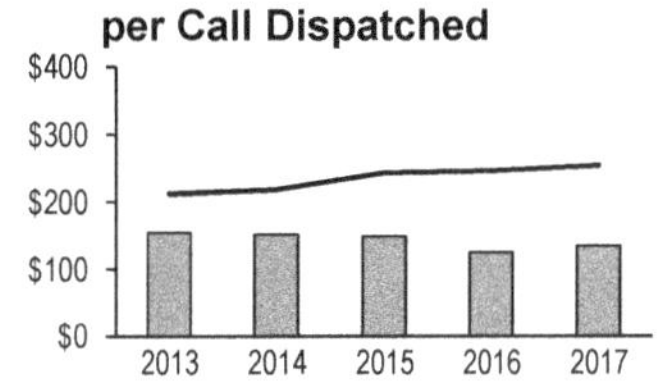

	2013	2014	2015	2016	2017
Hickory	$155	$152	$149	$125	$135
Average	$213	$219	$243	$247	$254

Calls Dispatched per Sworn Officer

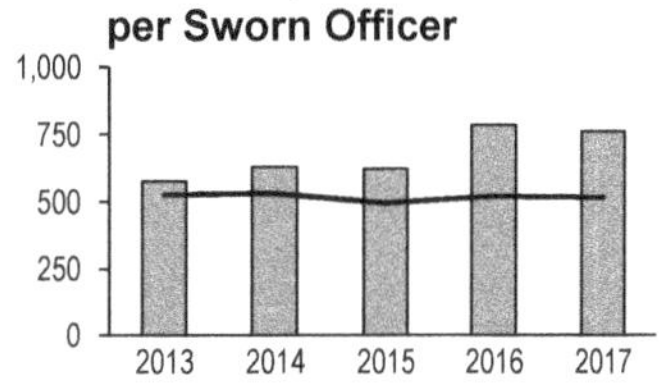

	2013	2014	2015	2016	2017
Hickory	576	627	622	784	760
Average	528	532	496	521	516

Police Services Cost per Part I Case Cleared

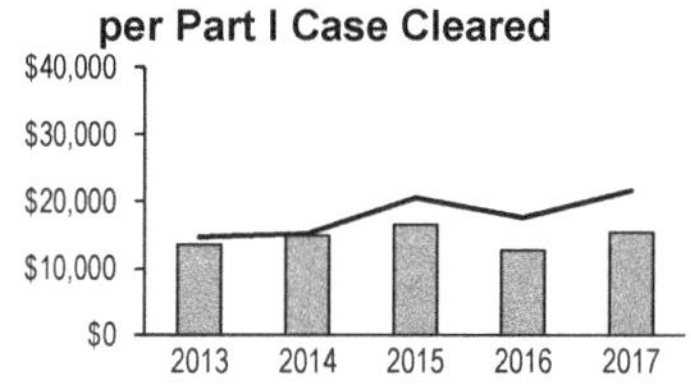

	2013	2014	2015	2016	2017
Hickory	$13,517	$14,836	$16,472	$12,697	$15,338
Average	$14,685	$15,183	$20,524	$17,593	$21,594

Part I Cases Cleared per Sworn Officer

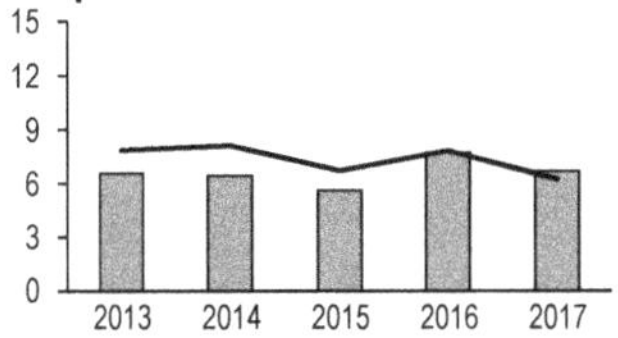

	2013	2014	2015	2016	2017
Hickory	6.6	6.4	5.6	7.7	6.7
Average	7.9	8.1	6.7	7.8	6.2

Effectiveness Measures

Percentage of Part I Cases Cleared of Those Reported

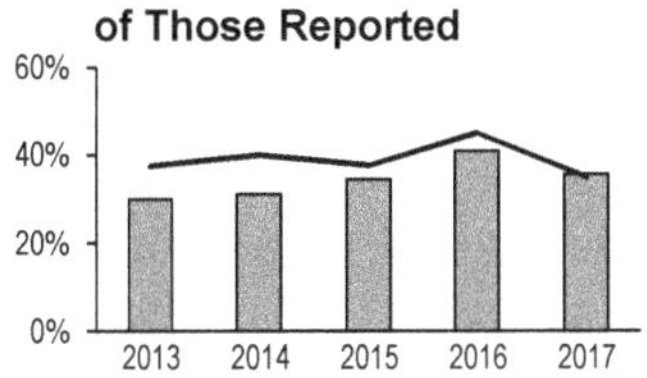

	2013	2014	2015	2016	2017
Hickory	29.9%	31.1%	34.4%	40.9%	35.6%
Average	37.5%	40.0%	37.6%	45.0%	35.0%

Response Time to High Priority Calls in Minutes

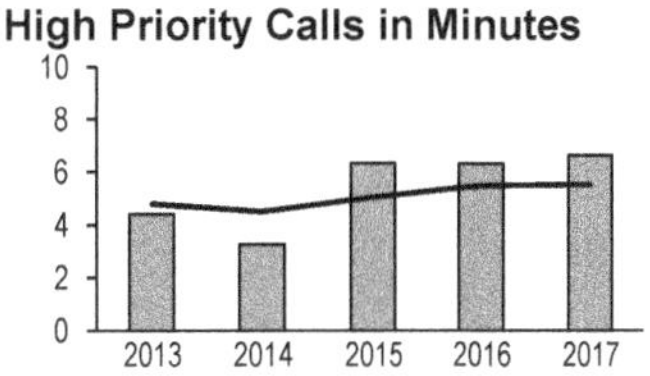

	2013	2014	2015	2016	2017
Hickory	4.4	3.3	6.3	6.3	6.6
Average	4.8	4.5	5.0	5.5	5.5

Fiscal Year 2016–17

Explanatory Information

Service Level and Delivery

High Point's police department provides an array of police services, including patrol, investigations, traffic, a telephone response unit, a forensics laboratory, a canine unit, a motorcycle unit, a special response unit, a bicycle patrol unit, an animal control function, a drug enforcement unit, and other programs such as school resource officers.

The city had 247 sworn officer positions authorized for the fiscal year, with an average length of service of 10.9 years. The police department is located in a separate building from city hall.

Patrol officers work a 10.5-hour shift on either the first, second, or third shift. Officers are assigned to separate teams and alternate four days on and four days off. In order to provide coverage for peak hours, the second and third shifts overlap by 5.5 hours. This applies to both daytime and night coverage.

Detectives work a twenty-eight-day cycle of five days on and two days off. The first shift is from 8 a.m. to 5 p.m., and the second shift is from 4 p.m. to 12 a.m. Each week, three detectives rotate to cover the second shift.

Each officer is assigned a vehicle. Officers living within the city limits take vehicles home. If the officer lives outside of the city limits, the vehicle must be parked at an approved location within the city.

The city defines high priority emergency calls as those where the threat of physical injury or the level of danger created by a suspect or condition requires such a quick response.

The police department was successful in clearing a total of 2,930 Part I cases in FY 2016–17.

Conditions Affecting Service, Performance, and Costs

The average response time to high priority calls reflects the response time of the first arriving unit. Self-initiated calls with a response time of zero are not included in the average response time to high priority calls.

High Point conducted a large audit of open cases in FY 2013–14 and then again in FY 2015–16. A large number of open cases were discovered which had not been cleared going back over a decade before the implementation of the current case management software system. An effort was made to go back through these older open cases. Many were found to have been resolved but not recorded in prior years, and some others were cleared as inactive. As a result of this auditing work, the number of cleared cases for High Point jumped noticeably for the fiscal year. These are likely to be special jumps and not long-term patterns.

Municipal Profile

Population (OSBM 2016)	110,244
Land Area (Square Miles)	55.14
Persons per Square Mile	1,999
Median Family Income U.S. Census 2010	$49,720

Service Profile

FTE Positions—Sworn	247.0
FTE Positions—Other	41.0
Marked and Unmarked Patrol Vehicles	246
Part I Crimes Reported	
Homicide	15
Rape	38
Robbery	239
Assault	362
Burglary	854
Larceny	3,059
Auto Theft	257
Arson	9
TOTAL	4,833
Part II Crimes Reported	4,624
Part I Crimes Cleared	
Persons	578
Property	2,352
TOTAL	2,930
Reporting Format	UCR
Number of Calls Dispatched	118,511
Number of Traffic Accidents	5,109
Property Damage for Accidents	$18,979,497

Full Cost Profile

Cost Breakdown by Percentage	
Personal Services	73.8%
Operating Costs	22.5%
Capital Costs	3.8%
TOTAL	100.0%
Cost Breakdown in Dollars	
Personal Services	$22,376,499
Operating Costs	$6,812,000
Capital Costs	$1,144,498
TOTAL	$30,332,997

High Point — Police Services

Key: High Point ▒ Benchmarking Average — Fiscal Years 2013 through 2017

Resource Measures

Police Services Costs per Capita

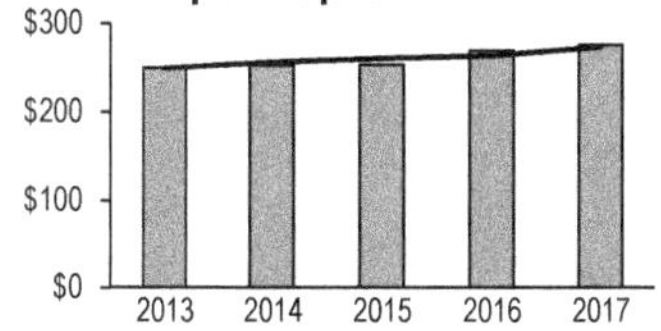

	2013	2014	2015	2016	2017
High Point	$249	$252	$253	$268	$275
Average	$249	$256	$260	$263	$273

Total Police Services Personnel per 10,000 Population

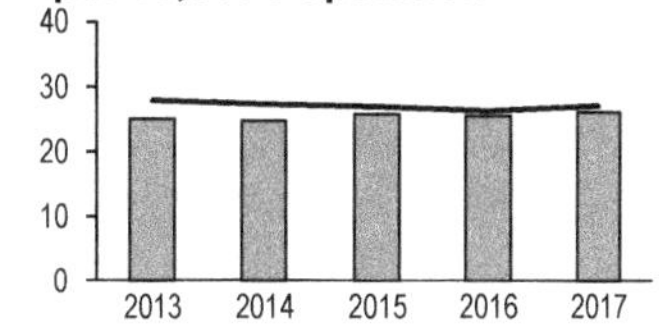

	2013	2014	2015	2016	2017
High Point	25.1	24.8	25.8	25.5	26.1
Average	27.9	27.3	26.9	26.2	26.9

Sworn Police Officers per 10,000 Population

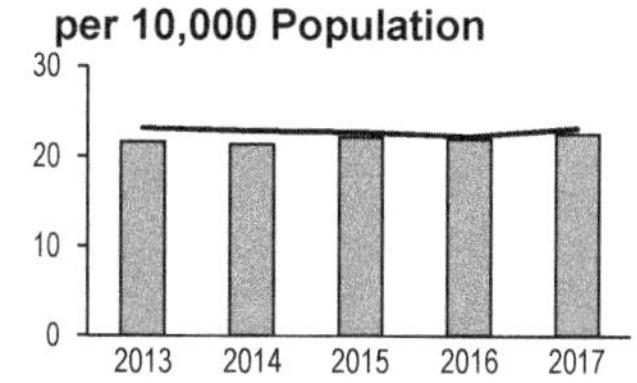

	2013	2014	2015	2016	2017
High Point	21.5	21.3	22.0	21.8	22.4
Average	23.1	22.8	22.6	22.1	23.0

Workload Measures

Calls Dispatched per 1,000 Population

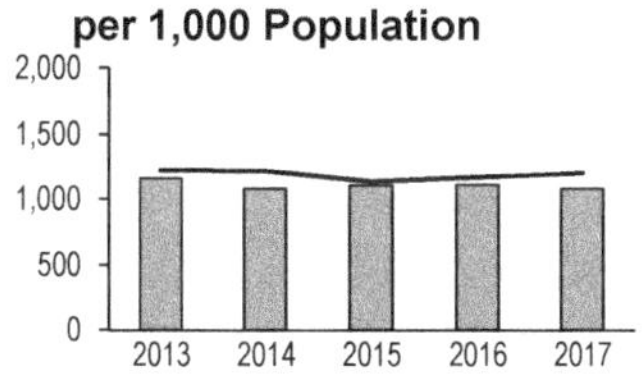

	2013	2014	2015	2016	2017
High Point	1,150	1,075	1,099	1,101	1,075
Average	1,220	1,213	1,134	1,166	1,203

Part I Crimes per 1,000 Population

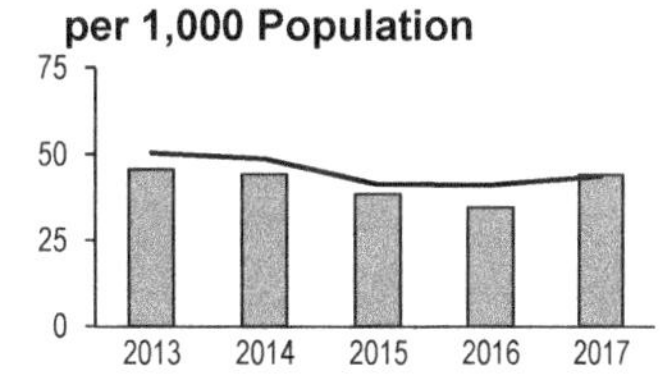

	2013	2014	2015	2016	2017
High Point	45.7	44.1	38.2	34.4	43.8
Average	50.5	48.8	41.4	41.1	43.8

Efficiency Measures

Police Services Cost per Call Dispatched

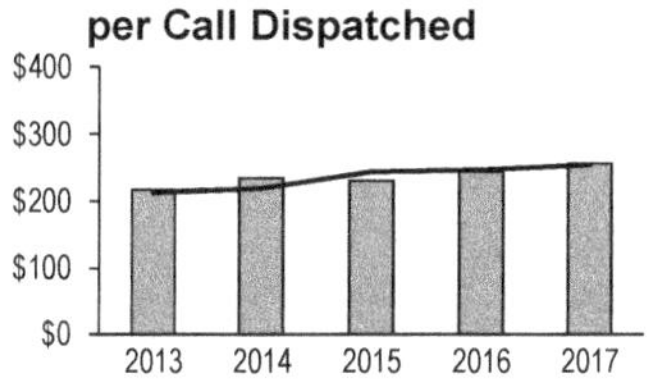

	2013	2014	2015	2016	2017
High Point	$217	$234	$230	$244	$256
Average	$213	$219	$243	$247	$254

Calls Dispatched per Sworn Officer

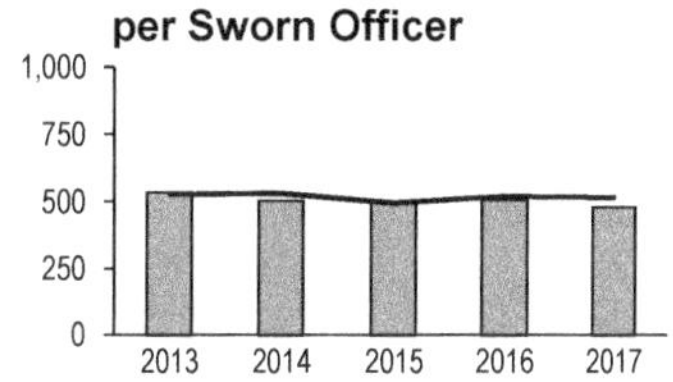

	2013	2014	2015	2016	2017
High Point	535	505	499	506	480
Average	528	532	496	521	516

Police Services Cost per Part I Case Cleared

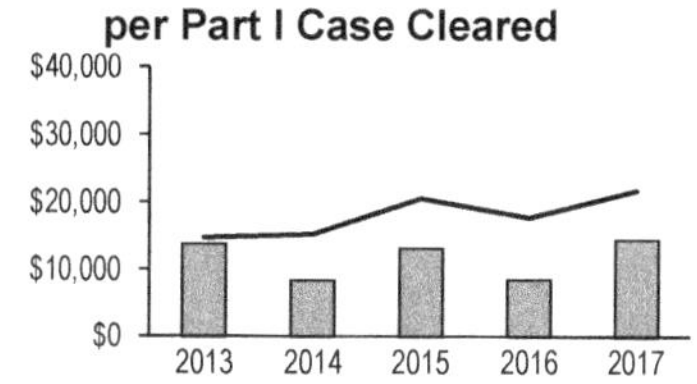

	2013	2014	2015	2016	2017
High Point	$13,798	$8,357	$13,172	$8,538	$14,431
Average	$14,685	$15,183	$20,524	$17,593	$21,594

Part I Cases Cleared per Sworn Officer

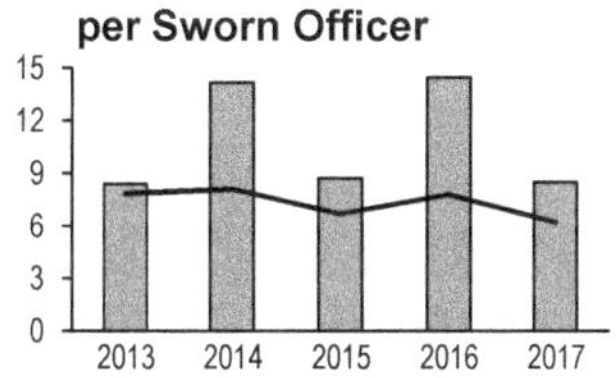

	2013	2014	2015	2016	2017
High Point	8.4	14.2	8.7	14.4	8.5
Average	7.9	8.1	6.7	7.8	6.2

Effectiveness Measures

Percentage of Part I Cases Cleared of Those Reported

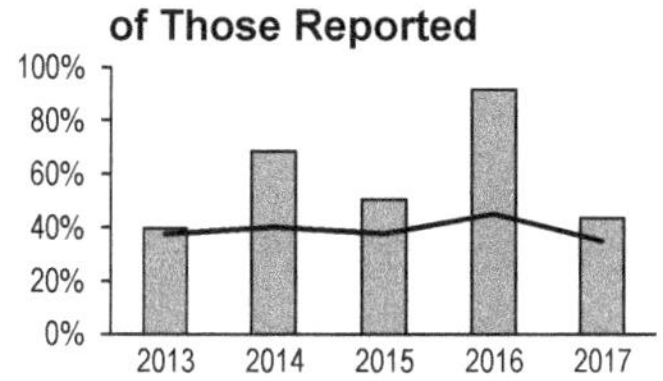

	2013	2014	2015	2016	2017
High Point	39.5%	68.2%	50.3%	91.5%	43.5%
Average	37.5%	40.0%	37.6%	45.0%	35.0%

Response Time to High Priority Calls in Minutes

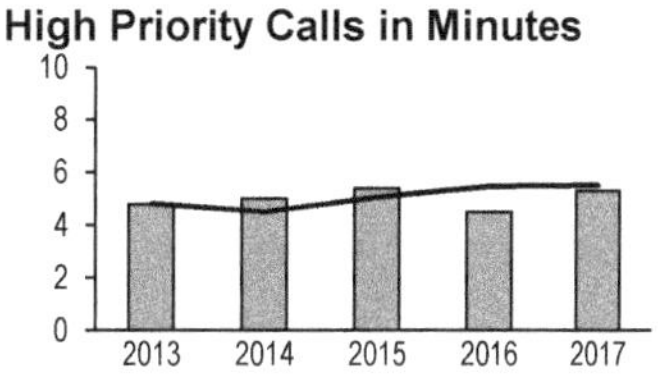

	2013	2014	2015	2016	2017
High Point	4.8	5.0	5.4	4.5	5.3
Average	4.8	4.5	5.0	5.5	5.5

Fiscal Year 2016–17

Explanatory Information

Service Level and Delivery
Raleigh's police department provides an array of police services, including patrol, investigations, canine unit, special response unit, mounted equine unit, motorcycle unit, drug enforcement units, and other programs.

The city had 800 sworn officer positions authorized for the fiscal year. The police department has ten substations around the city.

Patrol officers work a twelve-hour schedule rotating between days and nights every twenty-eight days. Detectives work an 8.4 hour schedule each weekday rotating between a day shift and an evening shift. Most detectives are in a pool that shares responsibilities to cover weekend duty and midnight shifts.

Field Operations Division has a take-home vehicle program for officers with two years of service and living inside the city limits with a safe driving record. Detectives and Special Operation Divisions have take-home vehicles for units on call or call-back status.

The police department was successful in clearing a total of 3,609 Part I cases in FY 2016–17.

The city defines high priority emergency calls as those involving crimes that are in progress or calls that are life-threatening or potentially life-threatening.

Conditions Affecting Service, Performance, and Costs
Raleigh rejoined the Benchmarking Project in July 2016 with the first year of data showing for FY 2015–16.

The average response time to high priority calls reflects the response time of each arriving unit. Self-initiated calls are not included in the average response time to high priority calls.

Municipal Profile

Population (OSBM 2016)	448,706
Land Area (Square Miles)	145.57
Persons per Square Mile	3,083
Median Family Income U.S. Census 2010	$68,678

Service Profile

FTE Positions—Sworn	800.0
FTE Positions—Other	103.0
Marked and Unmarked Patrol Vehicles	803
Part I Crimes Reported	
Homicide	30
Rape	151
Robbery	640
Assault	816
Burglary	2,265
Larceny	8,442
Auto Theft	937
Arson	55
TOTAL	13,336
Part II Crimes Reported	NA
Part I Crimes Cleared	
Persons	789
Property	2,820
TOTAL	3,609
Reporting Format	NIBRS
Number of Calls Dispatched	362,289
Number of Traffic Accidents	27,621
Property Damage for Accidents	$3,288,314

Full Cost Profile

Cost Breakdown by Percentage	
Personal Services	74.3%
Operating Costs	13.8%
Capital Costs	11.8%
TOTAL	100.0%
Cost Breakdown in Dollars	
Personal Services	$76,747,870
Operating Costs	$14,256,381
Capital Costs	$12,226,890
TOTAL	$103,231,141

Key: Raleigh ▒ Benchmarking Average — Fiscal Years 2013 through 2017

Resource Measures

Police Services Costs per Capita

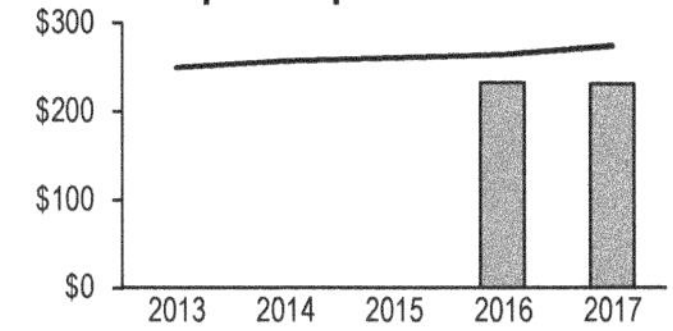

	2013	2014	2015	2016	2017
Raleigh				$232	$230
Average	$249	$256	$260	$263	$273

Total Police Services Personnel per 10,000 Population

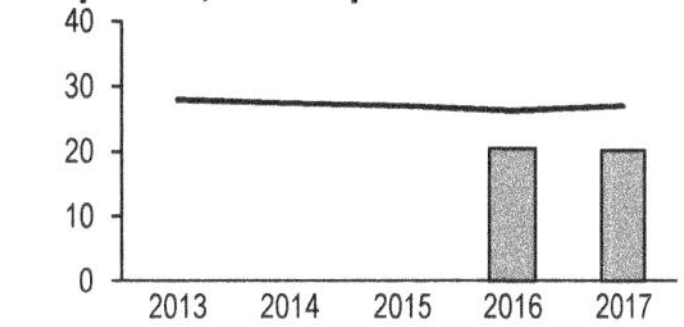

	2013	2014	2015	2016	2017
Raleigh				20.4	20.1
Average	27.9	27.3	26.9	26.2	26.9

Sworn Police Officers per 10,000 Population

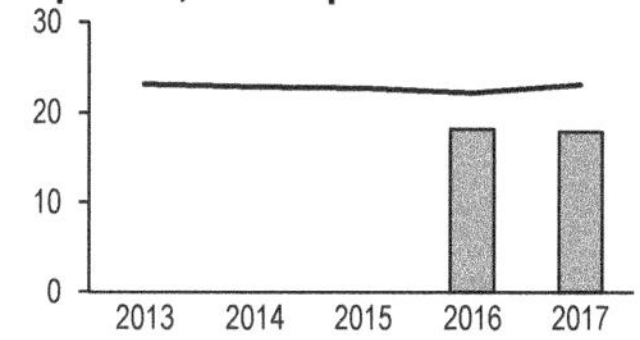

	2013	2014	2015	2016	2017
Raleigh				18.1	17.8
Average	23.1	22.8	22.6	22.1	23.0

Workload Measures

Calls Dispatched per 1,000 Population

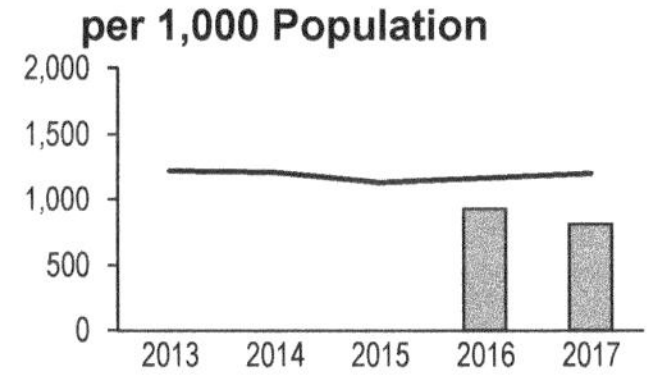

	2013	2014	2015	2016	2017
Raleigh				925	807
Average	1,220	1,213	1,134	1,166	1,203

Part I Crimes per 1,000 Population

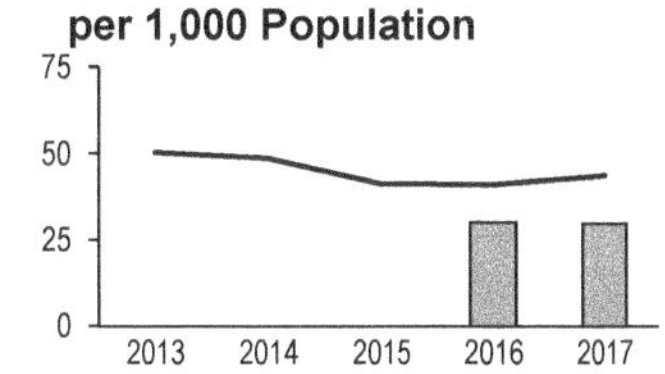

	2013	2014	2015	2016	2017
Raleigh				30.1	29.7
Average	50.5	48.8	41.4	41.1	43.8

Efficiency Measures

Police Services Cost per Call Dispatched

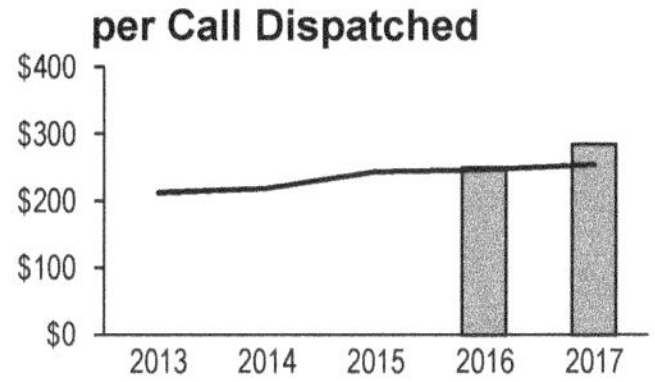

	2013	2014	2015	2016	2017
Raleigh				$251	$285
Average	$213	$219	$243	$247	$254

Calls Dispatched per Sworn Officer

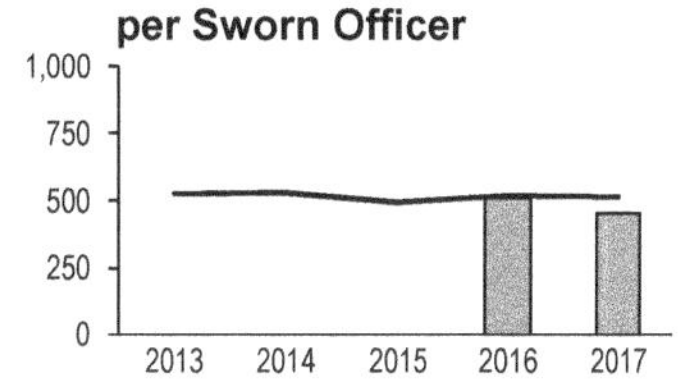

	2013	2014	2015	2016	2017
Raleigh				510	453
Average	528	532	496	521	516

Police Services Cost per Part I Case Cleared

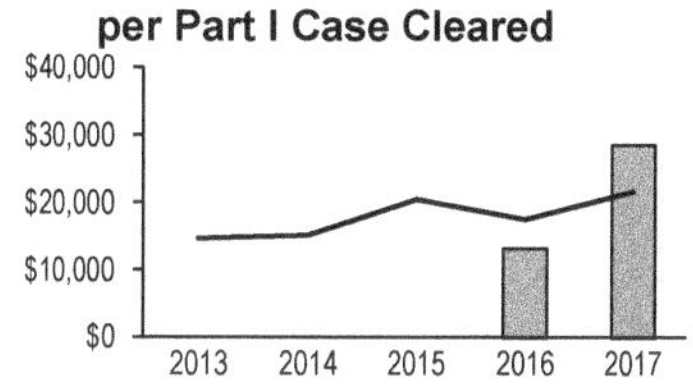

	2013	2014	2015	2016	2017
Raleigh				$13,291	$28,604
Average	$14,685	$15,183	$20,524	$17,593	$21,594

Part I Cases Cleared per Sworn Officer

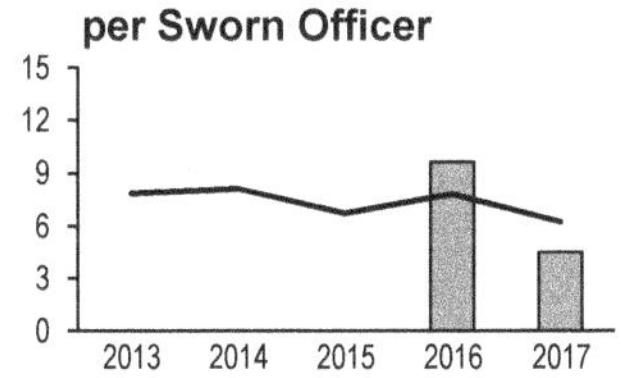

	2013	2014	2015	2016	2017
Raleigh				9.6	4.5
Average	7.9	8.1	6.7	7.8	6.2

Effectiveness Measures

Percentage of Part I Cases Cleared of Those Reported

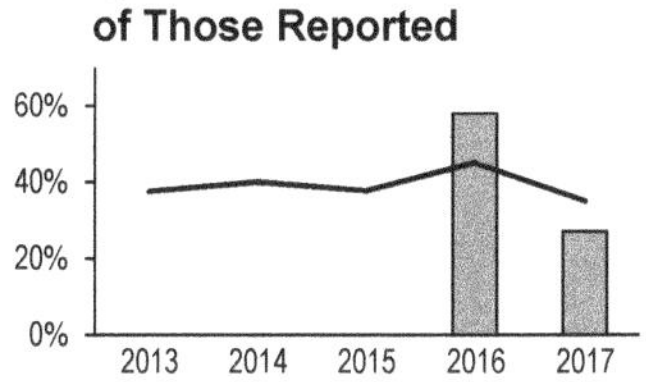

	2013	2014	2015	2016	2017
Raleigh				57.9%	27.1%
Average	37.5%	40.0%	37.6%	45.0%	35.0%

Response Time to High Priority Calls in Minutes

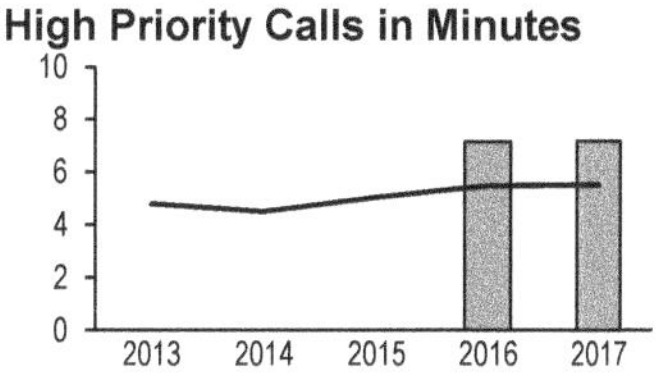

	2013	2014	2015	2016	2017
Raleigh				7.2	7.2
Average	4.8	4.5	5.0	5.5	5.5

Fiscal Year 2016–17

Explanatory Information

Service Level and Delivery

Salisbury's police department provides an array of police services, including patrol, investigations, traffic, canine, special response, bicycle patrol, drug enforcement, a school program, and other programs.

The city had eighty-one sworn officer positions authorized for the fiscal year, with an average length of service of 11.9 years. The police department is located in a two-story facility.

Uniformed officers work a variety of shift schedules. The most common schedule is one twelve-hour shift, with two days on and two off, three days on and two off, and then two days on and three off. A few officers work 10.5-hour shifts, with four days on and three off. This 10.5-hour shift serves as flex coverage during the day's heaviest call volume period and can be moved according to departmental need.

Sworn officers who serve in an on-call capacity are permitted to take their assigned vehicles to their residence up to a maximum of a thirty-mile radius from the police department. Sworn officers not serving in an on-call capacity who reside anywhere within Rowan County or those who live outside of Rowan County but within fifteen miles are able to have the benefit without charge of driving their assigned vehicle to their residence.

The police department was successful in clearing a total of 514 Part I cases in FY 2016–17.

The city defines high priority emergency calls as those involving crimes that are in progress or calls that are life-threatening or potentially life-threatening.

Conditions Affecting Service, Performance, and Costs

The average response time to high priority calls reflects the response time of the first arriving unit. Self-initiated calls with a response time of zero are included in the average response time to high priority calls.

Salisbury has increased special initiatives to reduce crime, such as through projects aimed at "hot spots" and aggressive prosecutions through Project Safe.

Municipal Profile

Population (OSBM 2016)	34,459
Land Area (Square Miles)	22.28
Persons per Square Mile	1,547
Median Family Income U.S. Census 2010	$40,192

Service Profile

FTE Positions—Sworn	81.0
FTE Positions—Other	7.0
Marked and Unmarked Patrol Vehicles	94
Part I Crimes Reported	
Homicide	7
Rape	17
Robbery	72
Assault	143
Burglary	371
Larceny	1,238
Auto Theft	87
Arson	13
TOTAL	1,948
Part II Crimes Reported	2,035
Part I Crimes Cleared	
Persons	102
Property	412
TOTAL	514
Reporting Format	IBR
Number of Calls Dispatched	37,459
Number of Traffic Accidents	1,965
Property Damage for Accidents	NA

Full Cost Profile

Cost Breakdown by Percentage	
Personal Services	65.5%
Operating Costs	22.6%
Capital Costs	11.8%
TOTAL	100.0%
Cost Breakdown in Dollars	
Personal Services	$5,839,628
Operating Costs	$2,017,778
Capital Costs	$1,052,828
TOTAL	$8,910,233

Key: Salisbury ▒ Benchmarking Average — Fiscal Years 2013 through 2017

Resource Measures

Police Services Costs per Capita

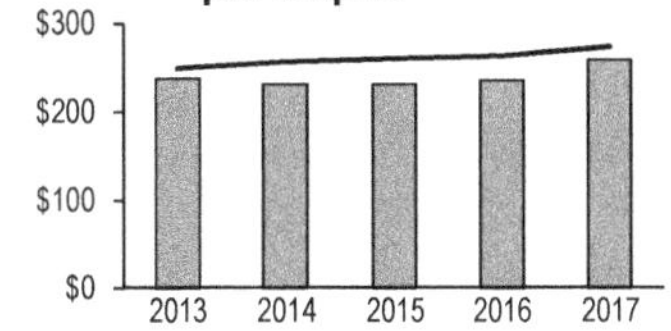

	2013	2014	2015	2016	2017
Salisbury	$238	$231	$232	$235	$259
Average	$249	$256	$260	$263	$273

Total Police Services Personnel per 10,000 Population

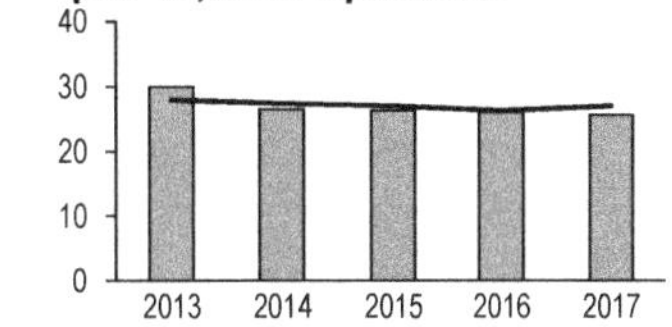

	2013	2014	2015	2016	2017
Salisbury	29.9	26.4	26.2	26.0	25.5
Average	27.9	27.3	26.9	26.2	26.9

Sworn Police Officers per 10,000 Population

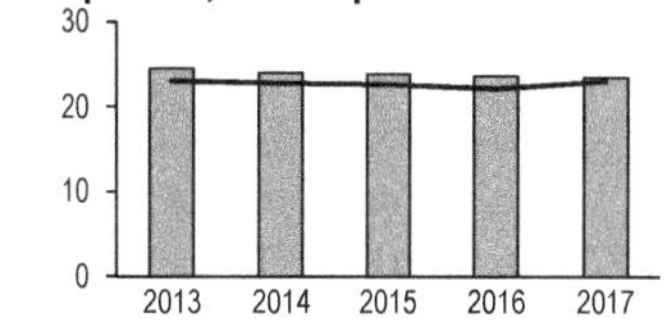

	2013	2014	2015	2016	2017
Salisbury	24.5	24.0	23.9	23.6	23.5
Average	23.1	22.8	22.6	22.1	23.0

Workload Measures

Calls Dispatched per 1,000 Population

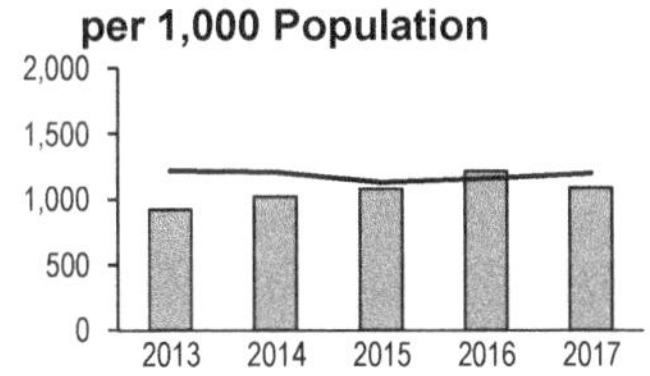

	2013	2014	2015	2016	2017
Salisbury	915	1,012	1,074	1,214	1,087
Average	1,220	1,213	1,134	1,166	1,203

Part I Crimes per 1,000 Population

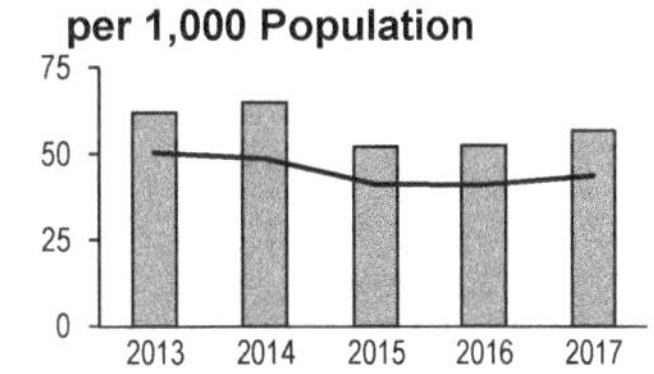

	2013	2014	2015	2016	2017
Salisbury	61.7	64.7	51.9	52.3	56.5
Average	50.5	48.8	41.4	41.1	43.8

Efficiency Measures

Police Services Cost per Call Dispatched

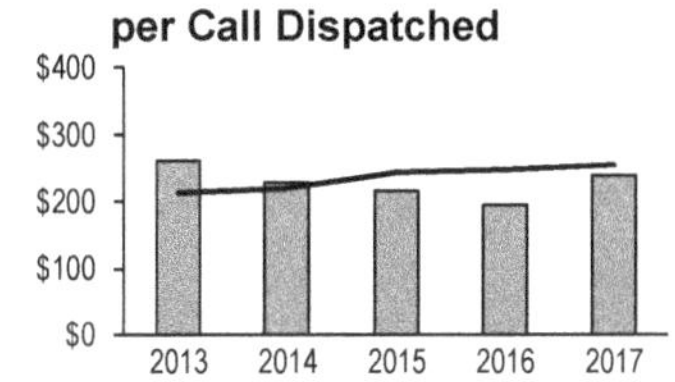

	2013	2014	2015	2016	2017
Salisbury	$260	$228	$216	$194	$238
Average	$213	$219	$243	$247	$254

Calls Dispatched per Sworn Officer

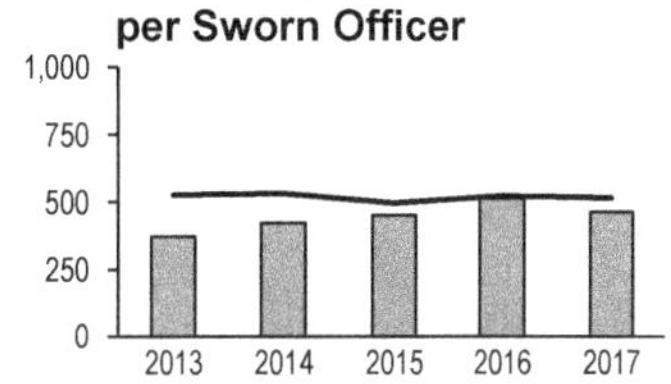

	2013	2014	2015	2016	2017
Salisbury	373	422	450	514	462
Average	528	532	496	521	516

Police Services Cost per Part I Case Cleared

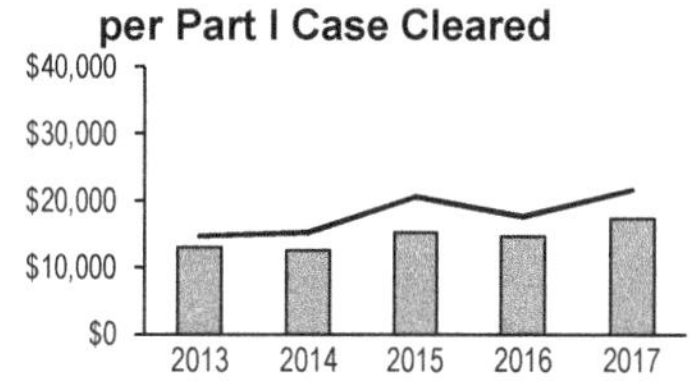

	2013	2014	2015	2016	2017
Salisbury	$13,023	$12,483	$15,211	$14,595	$17,335
Average	$14,685	$15,183	$20,524	$17,593	$21,594

Part I Cases Cleared per Sworn Officer

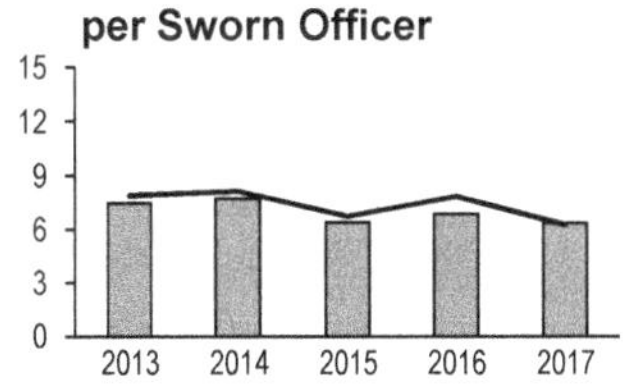

	2013	2014	2015	2016	2017
Salisbury	7.5	7.7	6.4	6.8	6.3
Average	7.9	8.1	6.7	7.8	6.2

Effectiveness Measures

Percentage of Part I Cases Cleared of Those Reported

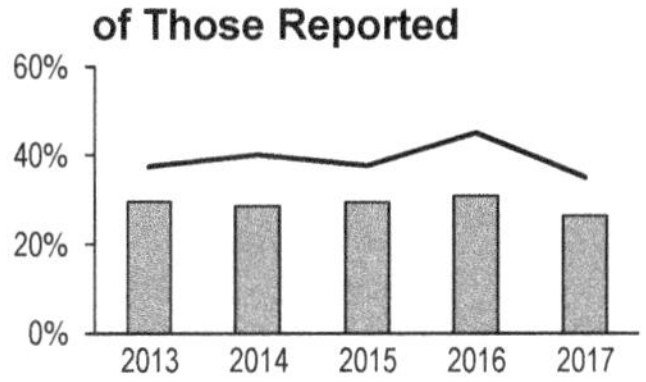

	2013	2014	2015	2016	2017
Salisbury	29.6%	28.6%	29.3%	30.8%	26.4%
Average	37.5%	40.0%	37.6%	45.0%	35.0%

Response Time to High Priority Calls in Minutes

	2013	2014	2015	2016	2017
Salisbury	3.3	2.5			
Average	4.8	4.5	5.0	5.5	5.5

Fiscal Year 2016–17

Explanatory Information

Service Level and Delivery

Wilson's police department provides an array of police services, including patrol, investigations, a telephone response unit, a forensics laboratory, a canine unit, a part-time mounted equine unit, a special response unit, street crimes, drug enforcement, and other services.

The city had 121 sworn officer positions authorized for the fiscal year, with an average length of service of 10.1 years. The main police department headquarters is located in downtown Wilson, housing administration, records, property, major case investigations, police information services, victim services, evidence, and recruitment and training. There are six substations.

Patrol officers work twelve-hour shifts, working fourteen days of a twenty-eight day cycle (168 hours). Shifts are either 7 a.m. to 7 p.m. or 7 p.m. to 7 a.m. and are rotated every two weeks. Department needs may cause shifts to vary. Investigators generally work eight-hour shifts five days per week. Shifts are 8 a.m. to 5 p.m.

Each patrol officer is assigned a vehicle and may take the vehicle home if he or she resides in the city. Officers living outside the city limits park their vehicles at businesses.

The police department was successful in clearing a total of 799 Part I cases in FY 2016–17.

Wilson defines high priority emergency calls as calls related to crimes in progress that require immediate response: murder, rape, robbery, burglary, arson/fire, and assaults.

Conditions Affecting Service, Performance, and Costs

The average response time to high priority calls reflects the response time of the first unit to arrive. Self-initiated calls with a response time of zero are not included in the average response time to high priority calls.

Municipal Profile

Population (OSBM 2016)	49,406
Land Area (Square Miles)	30.60
Persons per Square Mile	1,615
Median Family Income U.S. Census 2010	$43,442

Service Profile

FTE Positions—Sworn	121.0
FTE Positions—Other	16.0
Marked and Unmarked Patrol Vehicles	128
Part I Crimes Reported	
Homicide	6
Rape	14
Robbery	94
Assault	148
Burglary	484
Larceny	1,255
Auto Theft	134
Arson	6
TOTAL	2,141
Part II Crimes Reported	2,887
Part I Crimes Cleared	
Persons	167
Property	632
TOTAL	799
Reporting Format	UCR
Number of Calls Dispatched	99,227
Number of Traffic Accidents	2,596
Property Damage for Accidents	NA

Full Cost Profile

Cost Breakdown by Percentage	
Personal Services	66.8%
Operating Costs	26.0%
Capital Costs	7.2%
TOTAL	100.0%
Cost Breakdown in Dollars	
Personal Services	$10,688,875
Operating Costs	$4,167,202
Capital Costs	$1,150,124
TOTAL	$16,006,200

Key: Wilson ▒ Benchmarking Average — Fiscal Years 2013 through 2017

Resource Measures

Police Services Costs per Capita

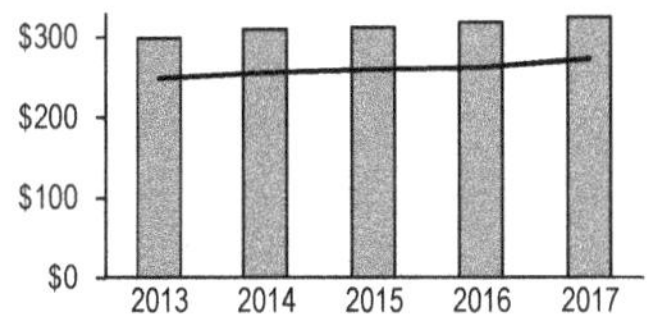

	2013	2014	2015	2016	2017
Wilson	$297	$309	$311	$317	$324
Average	$249	$256	$260	$263	$273

Total Police Services Personnel per 10,000 Population

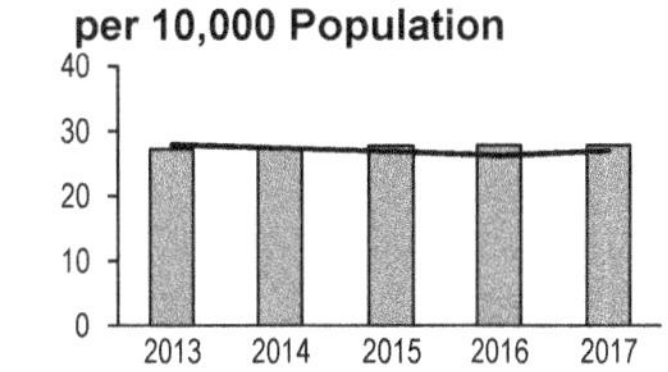

	2013	2014	2015	2016	2017
Wilson	27.1	27.3	27.6	27.8	27.7
Average	27.9	27.3	26.9	26.2	26.9

Sworn Police Officers per 10,000 Population

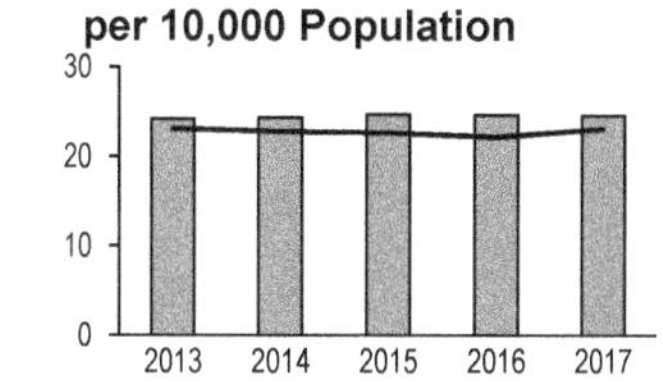

	2013	2014	2015	2016	2017
Wilson	24.1	24.2	24.6	24.5	24.5
Average	23.1	22.8	22.6	22.1	23.0

Workload Measures

Calls Dispatched per 1,000 Population

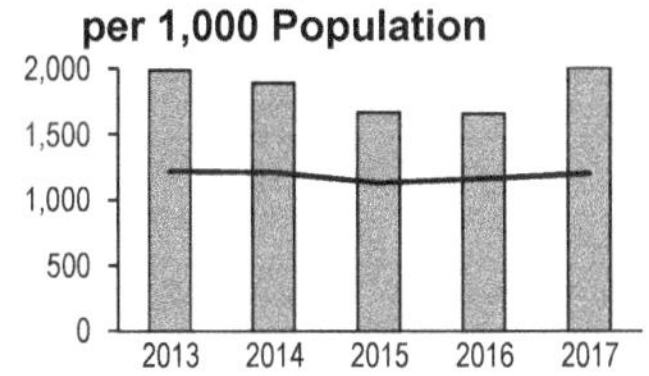

	2013	2014	2015	2016	2017
Wilson	1,988	1,891	1,666	1,659	2,008
Average	1,220	1,213	1,134	1,166	1,203

Part I Crimes per 1,000 Population

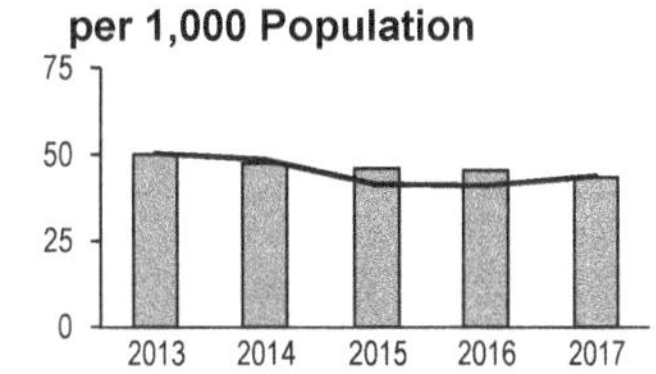

	2013	2014	2015	2016	2017
Wilson	50.0	47.4	45.8	45.3	43.3
Average	50.5	48.8	41.4	41.1	43.8

Efficiency Measures

Police Services Cost per Call Dispatched

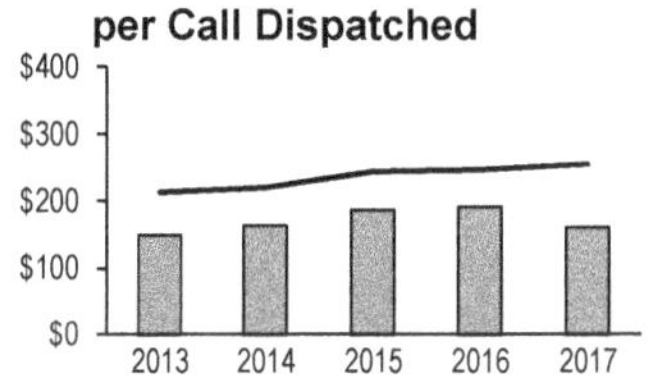

	2013	2014	2015	2016	2017
Wilson	$150	$164	$187	$191	$161
Average	$213	$219	$243	$247	$254

Calls Dispatched per Sworn Officer

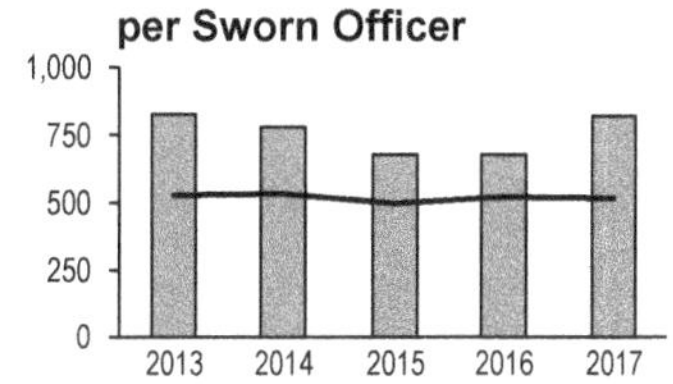

	2013	2014	2015	2016	2017
Wilson	826	780	678	677	820
Average	528	532	496	521	516

Police Services Cost per Part I Case Cleared

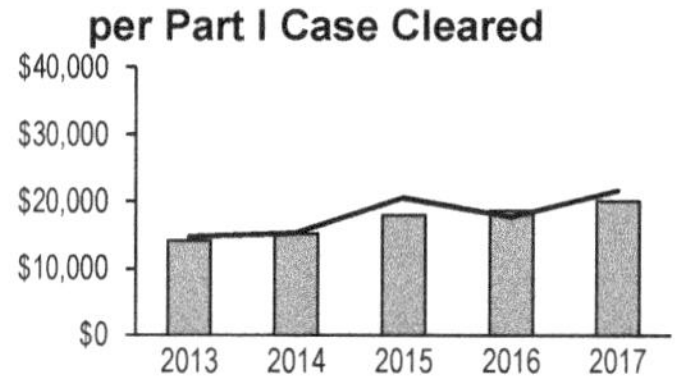

	2013	2014	2015	2016	2017
Wilson	$14,100	$15,136	$17,910	$18,555	$20,033
Average	$14,685	$15,183	$20,524	$17,593	$21,594

Part I Cases Cleared per Sworn Officer

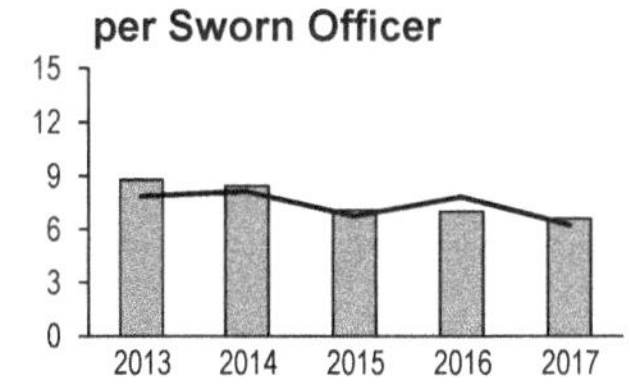

	2013	2014	2015	2016	2017
Wilson	8.8	8.4	7.1	7.0	6.6
Average	7.9	8.1	6.7	7.8	6.2

Effectiveness Measures

Percentage of Part I Cases Cleared of Those Reported

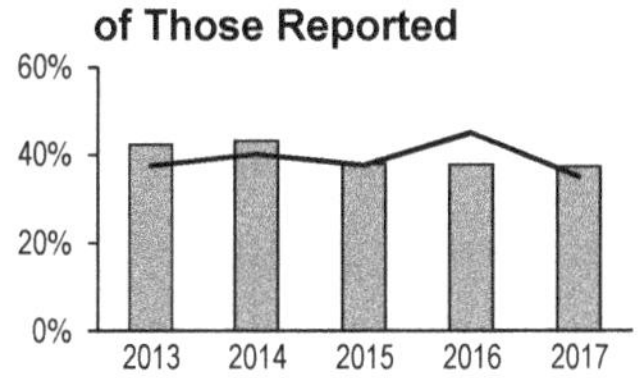

	2013	2014	2015	2016	2017
Wilson	42.2%	43.1%	37.9%	37.8%	37.3%
Average	37.5%	40.0%	37.6%	45.0%	35.0%

Response Time to High Priority Calls in Minutes

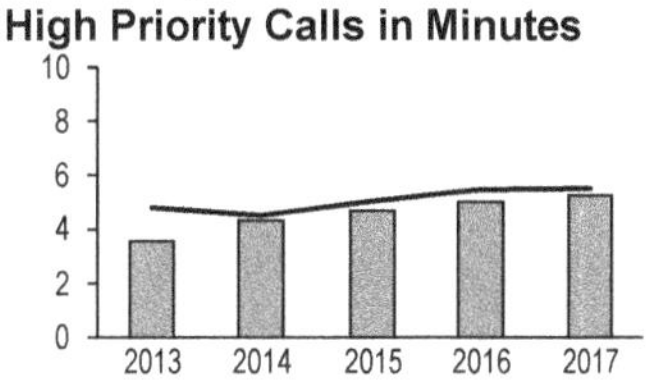

	2013	2014	2015	2016	2017
Wilson	3.6	4.3	4.7	5.0	5.3
Average	4.8	4.5	5.0	5.5	5.5

Fiscal Year 2016–17

Explanatory Information

Service Level and Delivery

Winston-Salem provides an array of police services to its citizens, including patrol, investigations, a traffic enforcement unit, a DWI Task Force, a telephone response unit, a canine unit, a special response unit, bicycle patrol, drug enforcement, a gang unit, and other crime prevention programs.

The city had 570 sworn officer positions authorized for the fiscal year, with an average length of service of 12.3 years. The police department occupies the public safety center. It houses the police department, emergency communications, and the fire department administration. The special investigations division occupies offices in leased space in another facility. A downtown bike patrol office is maintained in the central downtown area.

The department employs a forward-rotating schedule of five shifts. Officers work five days on and four days off. Shifts are ten hours in length. The majority of investigators work Monday through Friday from 8 a.m. to 5 p.m.

Patrol vehicles are assigned to individual officers. Officers residing within Forsyth County take their vehicles home. If officers reside outside of the county, they park their vehicles in a residential or business area within the city limits.

The police department was successful in clearing a total of 4,728 Part I crimes in FY 2016–17.

Winston-Salem defines highest priority emergency calls as those dealing with a significant threat of imminent injury to persons or with crimes against persons that are in progress or have just occurred and where the suspect is still there.

Conditions Affecting Service, Performance, and Costs

The average response time to high priority calls reflects the response time of the first arriving unit. Self-initiated calls with a response time of zero are included in the average response time to high priority calls.

The Winston-Salem Police Department does not investigate arsons, so arsons are not included in the crimes reported here. Arson investigations are handled by the Winston-Salem Fire Department.

Municipal Profile

Population (OSBM 2016)	240,603
Land Area (Square Miles)	132.55
Persons per Square Mile	1,815
Median Family Income U.S. Census 2010	$51,491

Service Profile

FTE Positions—Sworn	570.0
FTE Positions—Other	124.0
Marked and Unmarked Patrol Vehicles	473
Part I Crimes Reported	
Homicide	18
Rape	119
Robbery	536
Assault	1,666
Burglary	3,164
Larceny	8,816
Auto Theft	893
Arson	NA
TOTAL	15,212
Part II Crimes Reported	34,454
Part I Crimes Cleared	
Persons	1,026
Property	3,702
TOTAL	4,728
Reporting Format	IBR
Number of Calls Dispatched	225,958
Number of Traffic Accidents	10,573
Property Damage for Accidents	$33,018,707

Full Cost Profile

Cost Breakdown by Percentage	
Personal Services	75.6%
Operating Costs	15.3%
Capital Costs	9.1%
TOTAL	100.0%
Cost Breakdown in Dollars	
Personal Services	$53,625,076
Operating Costs	$10,872,147
Capital Costs	$6,448,002
TOTAL	$70,945,226

Key: Winston-Salem (bars) Benchmarking Average — (line) Fiscal Years 2013 through 2017

Resource Measures

Police Services Costs per Capita

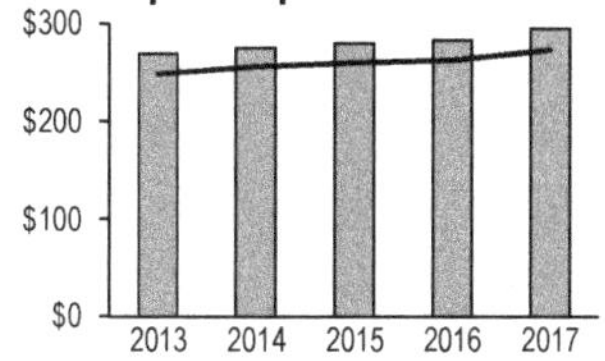

	2013	2014	2015	2016	2017
Winston-Salem	$269	$275	$280	$283	$295
Average	$249	$256	$260	$263	$273

Total Police Services Personnel per 10,000 Population

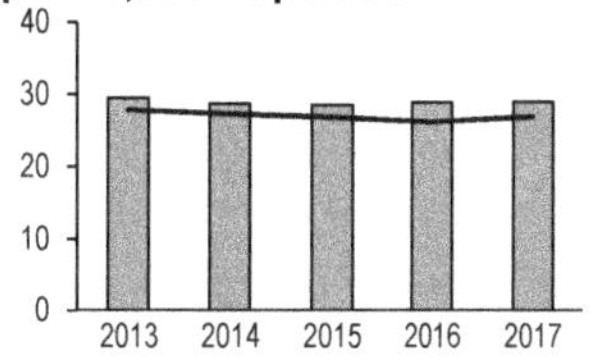

	2013	2014	2015	2016	2017
Winston-Salem	29.4	28.6	28.5	28.8	28.8
Average	27.9	27.3	26.9	26.2	26.9

Sworn Police Officers per 10,000 Population

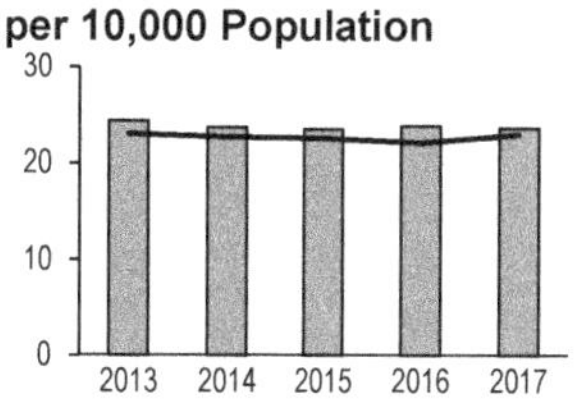

	2013	2014	2015	2016	2017
Winston-Salem	24.4	23.7	23.5	23.9	23.7
Average	23.1	22.8	22.6	22.1	23.0

Workload Measures

Calls Dispatched per 1,000 Population

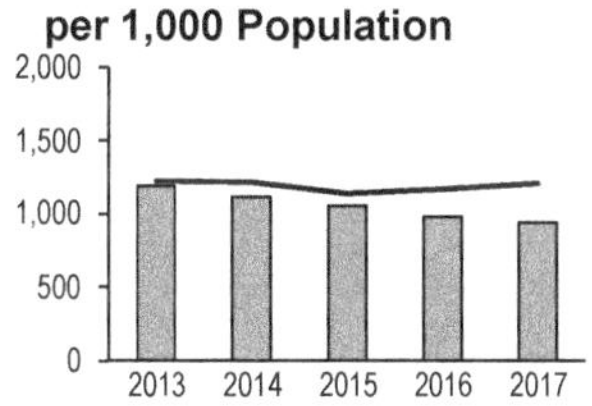

	2013	2014	2015	2016	2017
Winston-Salem	1,188	1,113	1,053	977	939
Average	1,220	1,213	1,134	1,166	1,203

Part I Crimes per 1,000 Population

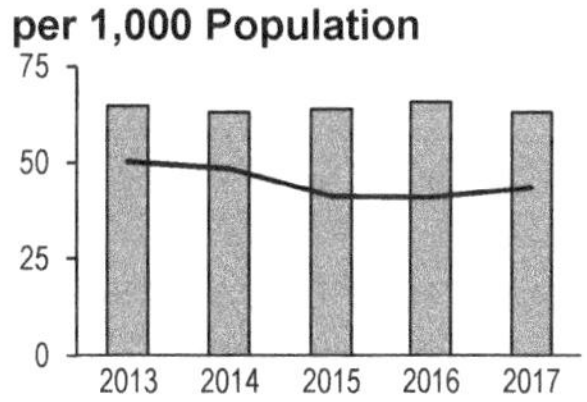

	2013	2014	2015	2016	2017
Winston-Salem	64.9	63.2	63.9	65.9	63.2
Average	50.5	48.8	41.4	41.1	43.8

Efficiency Measures

Police Services Cost per Call Dispatched

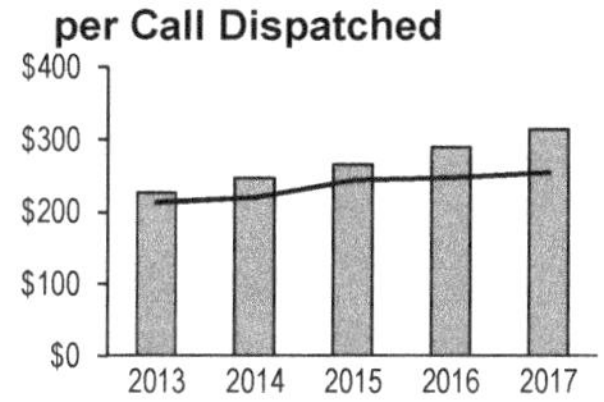

	2013	2014	2015	2016	2017
Winston-Salem	$226	$247	$266	$290	$314
Average	$213	$219	$243	$247	$254

Calls Dispatched per Sworn Officer

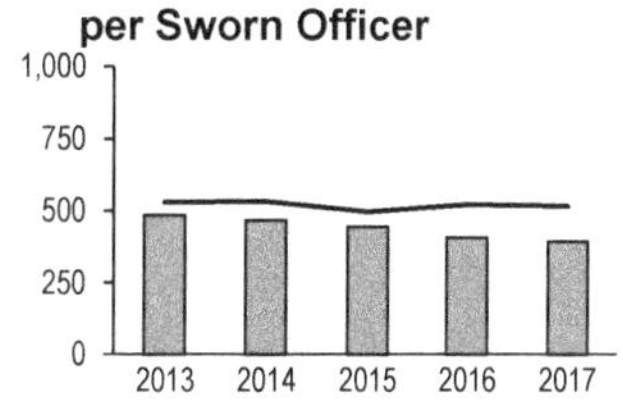

	2013	2014	2015	2016	2017
Winston-Salem	487	469	447	410	396
Average	528	532	496	521	516

Police Services Cost per Part I Case Cleared

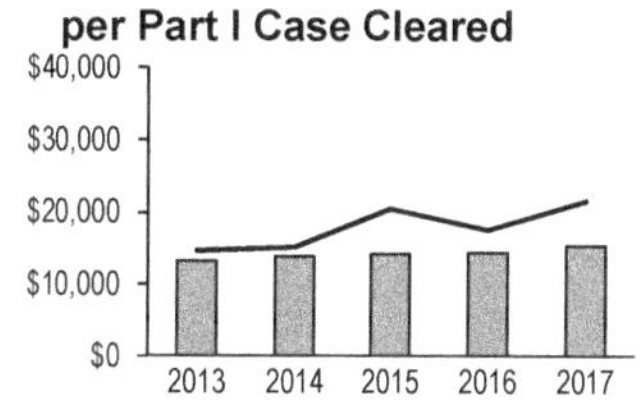

	2013	2014	2015	2016	2017
Winston-Salem	$13,193	$13,868	$14,160	$14,381	$15,330
Average	$14,685	$15,183	$20,524	$17,593	$21,594

Part I Cases Cleared per Sworn Officer

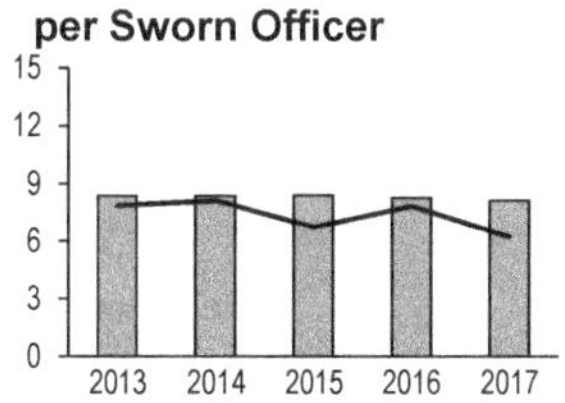

	2013	2014	2015	2016	2017
Winston-Salem	8.4	8.3	8.4	8.2	8.1
Average	7.9	8.1	6.7	7.8	6.2

Effectiveness Measures

Percentage of Part I Cases Cleared of Those Reported

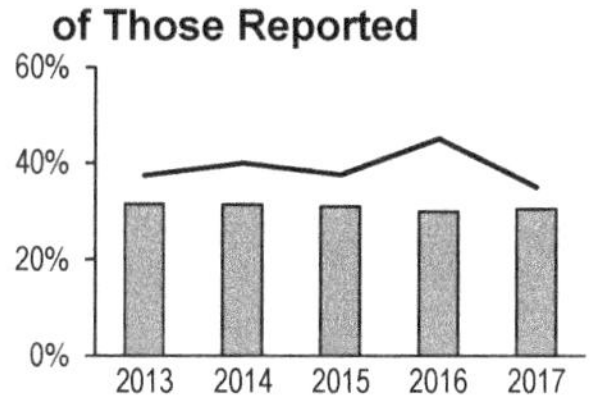

	2013	2014	2015	2016	2017
Winston-Salem	31.5%	31.3%	30.9%	29.9%	30.4%
Average	37.5%	40.0%	37.6%	45.0%	35.0%

Response Time to High Priority Calls in Minutes

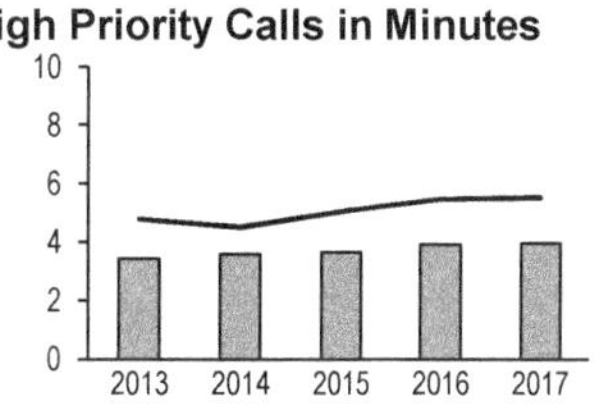

	2013	2014	2015	2016	2017
Winston-Salem	3.4	3.6	3.6	3.9	4.0
Average	4.8	4.5	5.0	5.5	5.5

UNC | SCHOOL OF GOVERNMENT
North Carolina Benchmarking Project

Performance and Cost Data

EMERGENCY COMMUNICATIONS

PERFORMANCE MEASURES FOR EMERGENCY COMMUNICATIONS

SERVICE DEFINITION

This service refers to the receipt and handling of 911 and other calls by an emergency communications center. Such a center must answer all calls, including those that come in over 911 lines and others that come in over regular phone lines. Some calls result in the dispatch of a police or other emergency response unit. Others do not.

NOTES ON PERFORMANCE MEASURES

1. Number of Calls Answered and Number of Calls Dispatched per 1,000 Population

These are used as measures of workload. All calls coming into a police emergency communications center must be answered; therefore, these measures assess service workload. Calls coming into a center also reflect the actual or existing, if not full potential, need for emergency communications services. Many calls coming into a center are dispatched. Others come in over regular telephone lines, and still others may be referred to the center by an external call-taker, such as a county emergency communications center.

2. Telecommunicators

Telecommunicators are the personnel who handle the calls in the communication centers. They may take calls, dispatch calls, or do both. Telecommunicators receive specialized training. They work on a shift schedule that generally allows twenty-four-hour-a-day, seven-day-a-week coverage.

3. Average Number of Seconds from Initial Ring to Answer and Percentage of Calls Answered within Twenty Seconds

These are effectiveness measures that assess how quickly telecommunicators answer calls.

4. Average Processing Time (Seconds)

This is an effectiveness measure, representing the average time in seconds between when the telecommunicator answers the telephone and when computer-aided dispatch (CAD) entry begins. This measure is often referred to as "talk time."

5. For Calls Dispatched, Average Number of Seconds from CAD Entry to Dispatch—Highest Priority Calls

Some calls result in the dispatch of a police or other emergency response unit to a life-threatening or other similar emergency situation. Other calls result in a dispatch to a serious—but not emergency—situation. Other calls do not result in a dispatch. This measure assesses dispatch time for high priority, emergency situations.

Emergency Communications

Summary of Key Dimensions of Service

City or Town	Population Served	Number of FTEs	Average Length of Service for Call Takers (in Years)	Total Incoming Calls Handled	Total E-911 Calls Handled	Total Dispatches	Outgoing Calls Other than Dispatches
Apex	46,688	11.3	14.7	48,231	3,749	41,917	13,193
Asheville	91,929	25.0	5.3	152,325	34,529	118,790	35,287
Concord	88,815	23.5	8.8	106,933	28,931	146,565	32,142
Greensboro	520,230	103.0	9.8	622,258	354,870	438,345	154,235
Greenville	87,989	17.0	8.1	106,537	29,394	85,416	18,593
Hickory	40,453	12.0	6.8	157,124	15,072	97,600	30,270
High Point	110,244	33.0	10.3	272,352	83,394	133,217	57,192
Raleigh	1,026,748	127.0	5.8	850,340	578,648	487,733	284,295
Winston-Salem	240,603	49.0	9.3	495,612	224,012	253,021	71,297

NOTES

The population served by the municipal emergency communications center may go beyond municipal boundaries up to the entire county in cases where the service is a consolidated center.

EXPLANATORY FACTORS

These are factors that the project found affected emergency communication performance and cost in one or more of the municipalities:

Types of emergency response units dispatched, such as police, fire, and EMS
Number and proportion of nonemergency calls received by center
Types of assistance or advice, such as medical, that telecommunicators provide over the phone
Technology available to telecommunication centers
City's definition of what constitutes an "emergency" and "highest priority" call
Service to city only or to city and outlying areas
Training of telecommunicators
Demographic makeup of community
Organizational configuration and staffing for service

Fiscal Year 2016–17

Explanatory Information

Service Level and Delivery

The Apex Emergency Communications Center is a division within the Apex Police Department. This center is a secondary public safety answering point within Wake County, using Raleigh computer-aided dispatch (CAD) as a remote position. The communications center dispatches calls for police, fire, public works, and utilities.

The town owns a 150-foot radio tower which is tied into the Wake County radio system. The system is an 800 MHz system tied into the state VIPER system for radio operations.

Apex's emergency communications center handled a total of 48,231 incoming calls in the fiscal year and dispatched 41,917 calls. The city defines highest priority emergency calls as those with immediate life or property risk or in-progress calls.

Conditions Affecting Service, Performance, and Costs

CAD entry for Apex does not begin immediately but is activated by operators.

Municipal Profile

Population (OSBM 2016)	46,688
Land Area (Square Miles)	20.61
Persons per Square Mile	2,265
Median Family Income U.S. Census 2010	$97,201
County	Wake

Service Profile

Primary or Secondary Answering Point	Secondary
Calls Dispatched	
Police	Yes
Fire	No
Other	Yes
FTE Positions	
Telecommunicators/Call-Takers	10.40
Other	0.85
Total Positions	11.25
Average Length of Service for Call-Takers	14.7 years
Total Incoming Calls	48,231
Total 911 Calls	3,749
Total Calls Dispatched	41,917
Outgoing Calls Other than Dispatch	13,193
Revenue from E-911 Fees	None

Full Cost Profile

Cost Breakdown by Percentage	
Personal Services	70.6%
Operating Costs	25.0%
Capital Costs	4.4%
TOTAL	100.0%
Cost Breakdown in Dollars	
Personal Services	$665,289
Operating Costs	$235,540
Capital Costs	$41,889
TOTAL	$942,718

Key: Apex ▒ Benchmarking Average — Fiscal Years 2013 through 2017

Resource Measures

Emergency Communications Services Costs per Capita

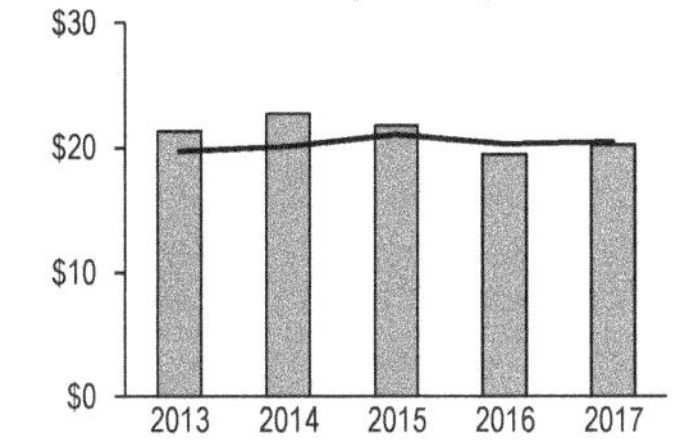

	2013	2014	2015	2016	2017
Apex	$21.32	$22.09	$21.77	$19.43	$20.19
Average	$19.68	$20.04	$21.03	$20.26	$20.40

Emergency Communications FTEs per 10,000 Population

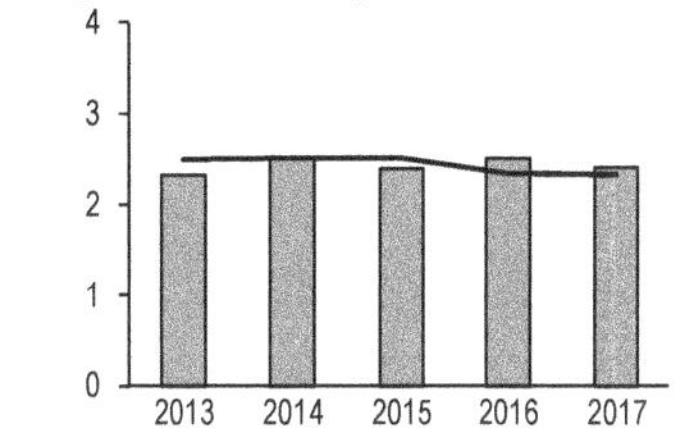

	2013	2014	2015	2016	2017
Apex	2.33	2.50	2.40	2.51	2.41
Average	2.49	2.51	2.51	2.33	2.32

Workload Measures

Total Calls Answered per 1,000 Population

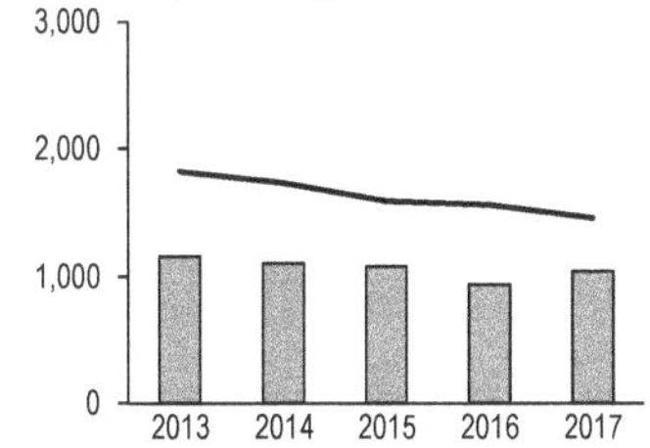

	2013	2014	2015	2016	2017
Apex	1,156	1,097	1,073	933	1,033
Average	1,823	1,732	1,592	1,560	1,457

Calls Dispatched per 1,000 Population

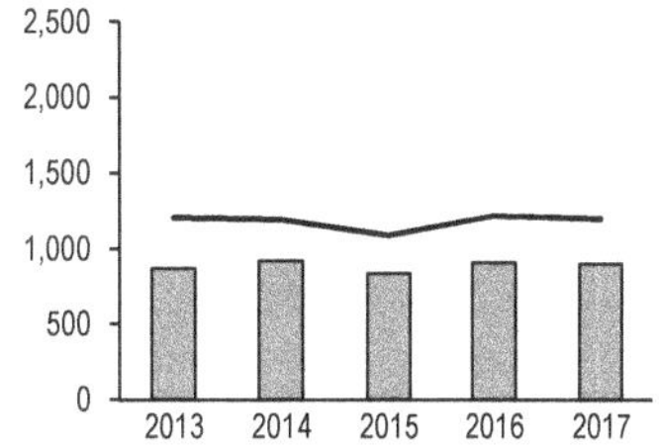

	2013	2014	2015	2016	2017
Apex	868	917	834	905	898
Average	1,207	1,195	1,090	1,217	1,200

E-911 Calls as a Percentage of All Incoming Calls

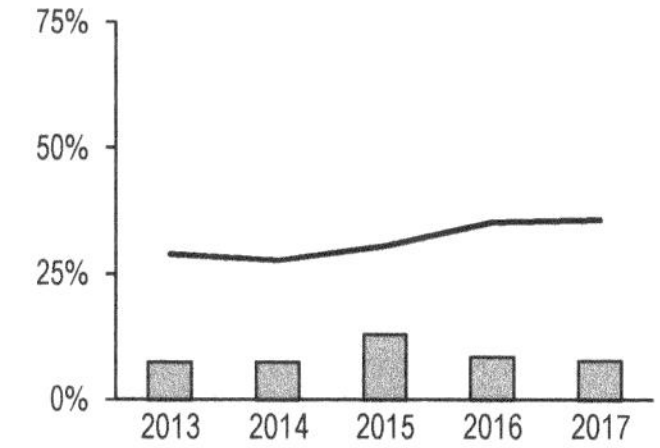

	2013	2014	2015	2016	2017
Apex	7.5%	7.5%	13.0%	8.6%	7.8%
Average	28.9%	27.7%	30.6%	35.3%	35.7%

Efficiency Measures

Calls Answered per Telecommunicator

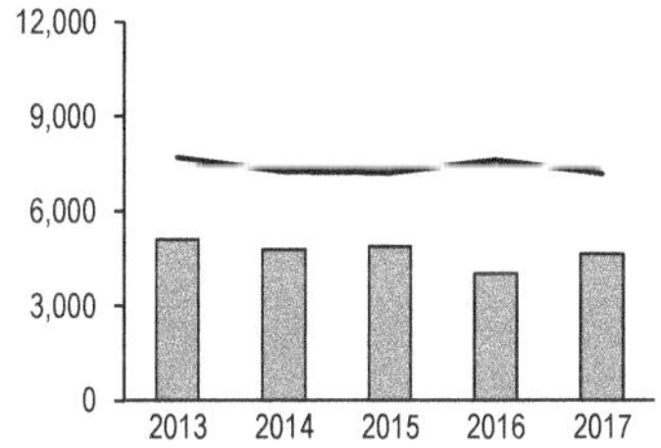

	2013	2014	2015	2016	2017
Apex	5,107	4,776	4,874	4,014	4,638
Average	7,694	7,244	7,204	7,614	7,178

Calls Dispatched per Telecommunicator

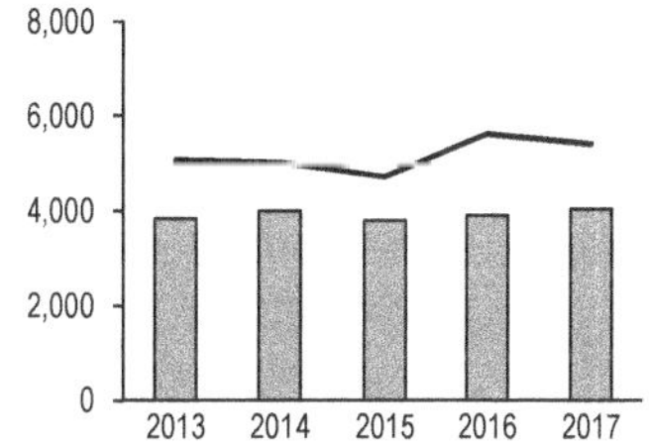

	2013	2014	2015	2016	2017
Apex	3,837	3,992	3,786	3,894	4,030
Average	5,084	5,033	4,724	5,628	5,410

Emergency Communications Cost per Call Dispatched

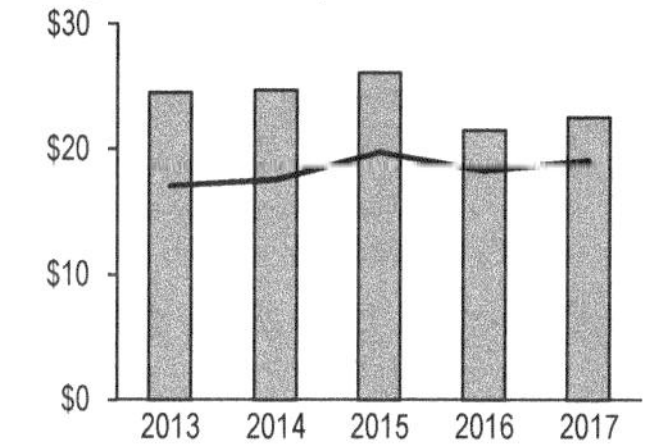

	2013	2014	2015	2016	2017
Apex	$24.55	$24.75	$26.11	$21.47	$22.49
Average	$17.03	$17.52	$19.67	$18.23	$19.06

Effectiveness Measures

Number of Seconds from Initial Ring to Answer

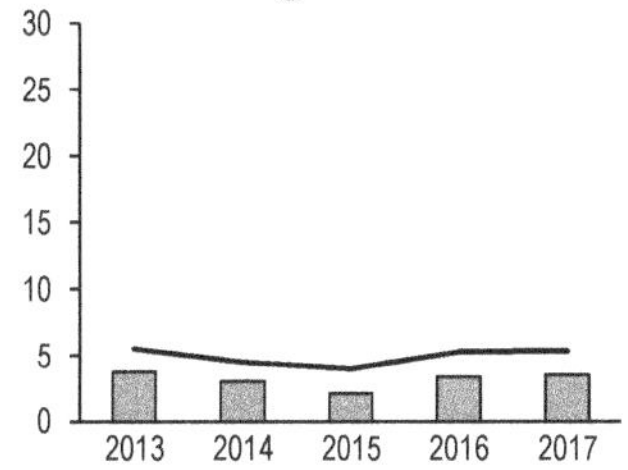

	2013	2014	2015	2016	2017
Apex	4	3	2	3	4
Average	6	5	4	5	5

Percent of E-911 Calls Answered within Twenty Seconds

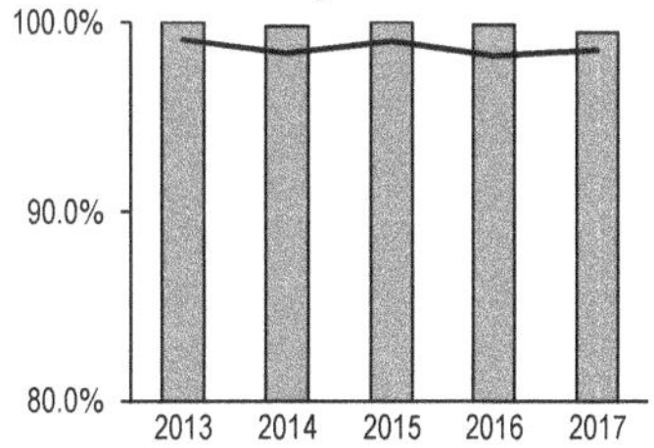

	2013	2014	2015	2016	2017
Apex	100.0%	99.8%	100.0%	99.9%	99.4%
Average	99.1%	98.3%	99.0%	98.2%	98.5%

Average Time in Seconds from CAD Entry to Dispatch for Priority One Calls

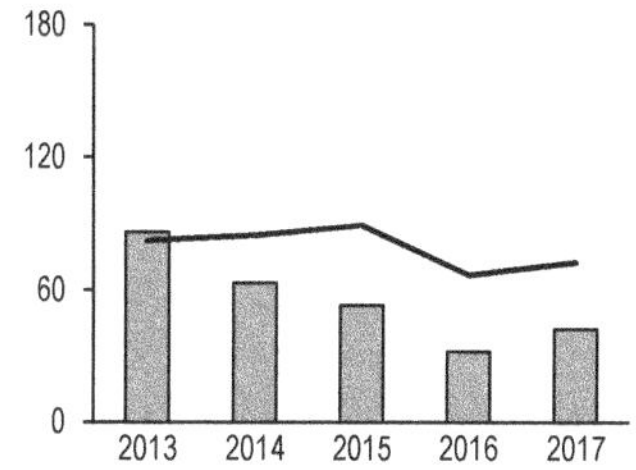

	2013	2014	2015	2016	2017
Apex	86	63	53	32	42
Average	82	84	89	67	72

Fiscal Year 2016–17

Explanatory Information

Service Level and Delivery

Asheville's Communication Unit handles emergency calls for police and other assistance calls coming into its center from the city. The center is organizationally located in the Support Services Division of the police department. The city handles adminstrative calls, requests for police response, and E-911 calls. The center is co-located with Buncombe County Emergency Operations Center and Buncombe County Sheriff's Office.

The communications center operates twenty-four hours a day, seven days a week, using four permanent "twelve hour" shifts. A work week consists of three twelve hour shifts and one eight hour shift. The communications center uses a call-taker for its E-911 emergency calls. Buncombe County takes such calls and directs them by computer to the city's communications center. Non-emergency calls, however, come directly into the city's communications center.

The city owns its communications infrastructure, consisting of three towers. One tower is used for repeated radio communications, while the other two towers are stand-alone sites which require officers/telecommunicators to manually switch channels. The city uses the Motorola Simulcast system.

Asheville's emergency communications center handled a total of 152,325 incoming calls in the fiscal year and dispatched 118,790 calls. The city defines highest priority emergency calls as crimes in progress and situations that are property- or life-threatening.

Conditions Affecting Service, Performance, and Costs

Computer-aided dispatch (CAD) entry is an immediate action beginning when a telecommunicator hits "new call" or "new event."

Asheville's community policing initiative encourages citizens to report criminal activity, and this has generated more calls over time. The wider use of cell phones has also made it easier for citizens to respond immediately, which has probably increased calls as well.

Asheville's Communication Unit has made an effort to better categorize high priority calls, which has helped reduce the time between the start of CAD entry and dispatch.

Municipal Profile

Population (OSBM 2016)	91,929
Land Area (Square Miles)	45.52
Persons per Square Mile	2,019
Median Family Income U.S. Census 2010	$53,350
County	Buncombe

Service Profile

Primary or Secondary Answering Point	Secondary
Calls Dispatched	
Police	Yes
Fire	No
Other	Yes
FTE Positions	
Telecommunicators/Call-Takers	24.0
Other	1.0
Total Positions	25.0
Average Length of Service for Call-Takers	5.3 years
Total Incoming Calls	152,325
Total 911 Calls	34,529
Total Calls Dispatched	118,790
Outgoing Calls Other than Dispatch	35,287
Revenue from E-911 Fees	None

Full Cost Profile

Cost Breakdown by Percentage	
Personal Services	57.8%
Operating Costs	40.6%
Capital Costs	1.6%
TOTAL	100.0%
Cost Breakdown in Dollars	
Personal Services	$1,210,494
Operating Costs	$850,673
Capital Costs	$33,823
TOTAL	$2,094,989

Key: Asheville ▒ Benchmarking Average — Fiscal Years 2013 through 2017

Resource Measures

Emergency Communications Services Costs per Capita

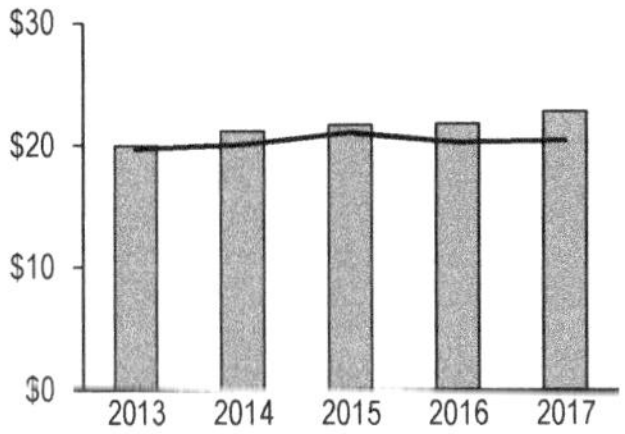

	2013	2014	2015	2016	2017
Asheville	$19.94	$21.16	$21.68	$21.78	$22.79
Average	$19.68	$20.04	$21.03	$20.26	$20.40

Emergency Communications FTEs per 10,000 Population

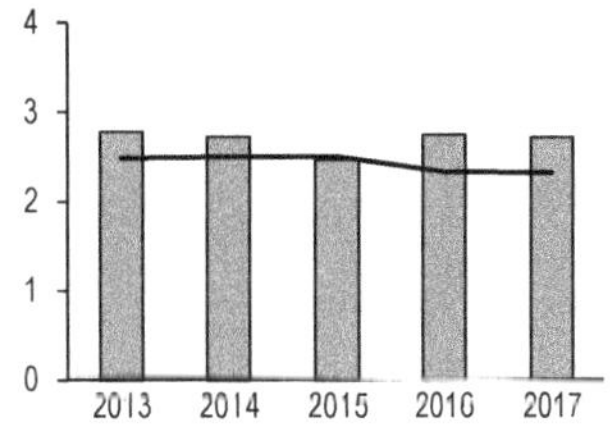

	2013	2014	2015	2016	2017
Asheville	2.78	2.73	2.47	2.75	2.72
Average	2.49	2.51	2.51	2.33	2.32

Workload Measures

Total Calls Answered per 1,000 Population

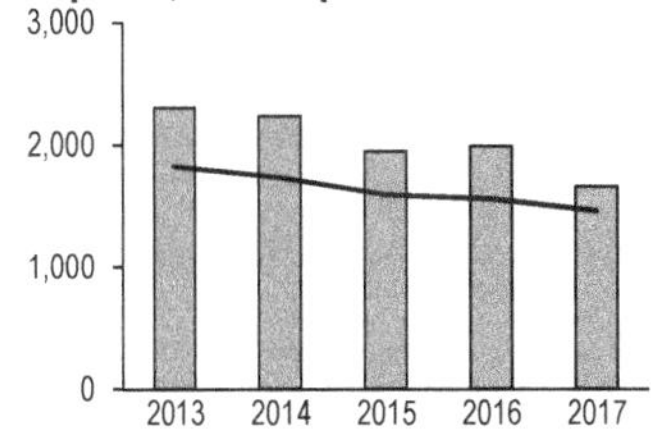

	2013	2014	2015	2016	2017
Asheville	2,301	2,236	1,945	1,991	1,657
Average	1,823	1,732	1,592	1,560	1,457

Calls Dispatched per 1,000 Population

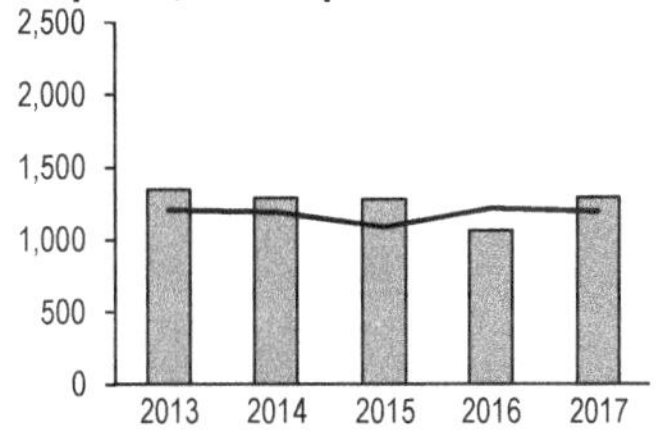

	2013	2014	2015	2016	2017
Asheville	1,344	1,289	1,278	1,064	1,292
Average	1,207	1,195	1,090	1,217	1,200

E-911 Calls as a Percentage of All Incoming Calls

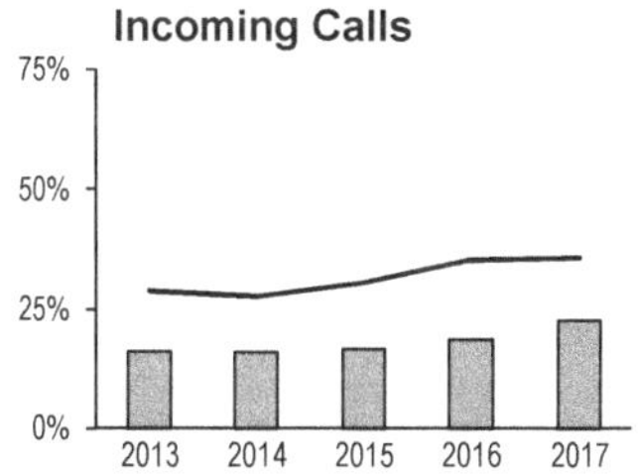

	2013	2014	2015	2016	2017
Asheville	16.1%	16.0%	16.6%	18.7%	22.7%
Average	28.9%	27.7%	30.6%	35.3%	35.7%

Efficiency Measures

Calls Answered per Telecommunicator

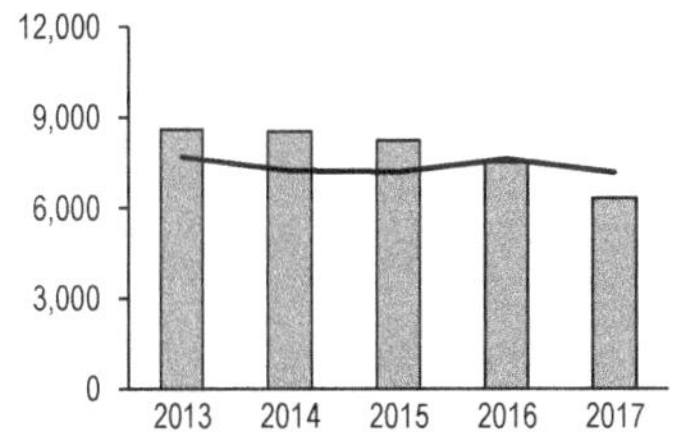

	2013	2014	2015	2016	2017
Asheville	8,623	8,555	8,265	7,541	6,347
Average	7,694	7,244	7,204	7,614	7,178

Calls Dispatched per Telecommunicator

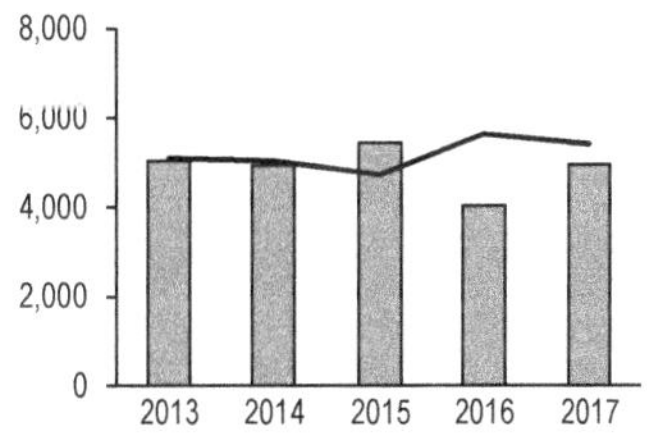

	2013	2014	2015	2016	2017
Asheville	5,036	4,933	5,432	4,032	4,950
Average	5,084	5,033	4,724	5,628	5,410

Emergency Communications Cost per Call Dispatched

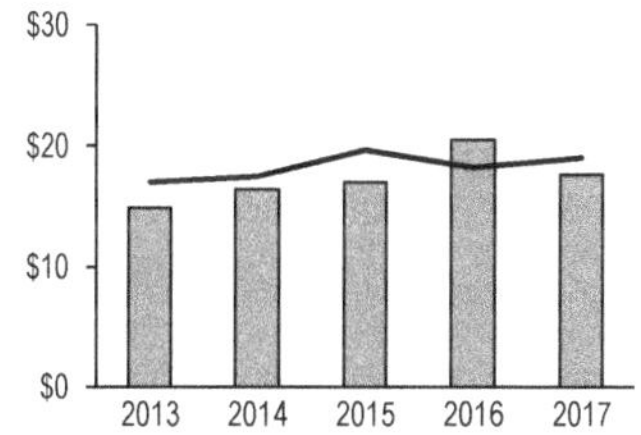

	2013	2014	2015	2016	2017
Asheville	$14.84	$16.42	$16.96	$20.46	$17.64
Average	$17.03	$17.52	$19.67	$18.23	$19.06

Effectiveness Measures

Number of Seconds from Initial Ring to Answer

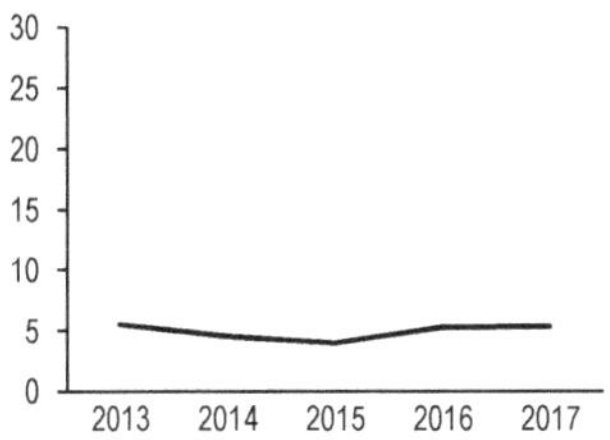

	2013	2014	2015	2016	2017
Asheville					
Average	6	5	4	5	5

Percent of E-911 Calls Answered within Twenty Seconds

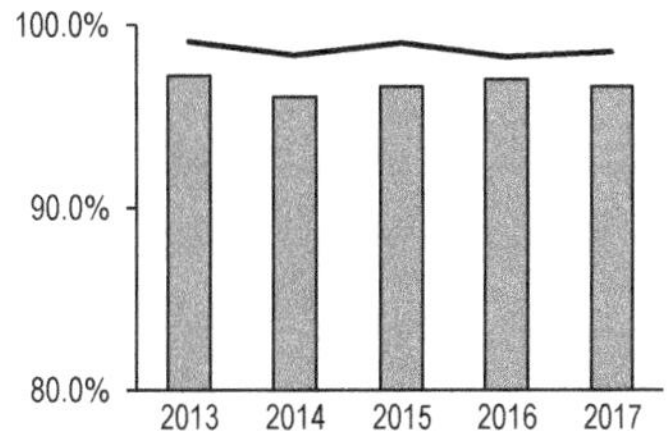

	2013	2014	2015	2016	2017
Asheville	97.2%	96.1%	96.6%	97.0%	96.6%
Average	99.1%	98.3%	99.0%	98.2%	98.5%

Average Time in Seconds from CAD Entry to Dispatch for Priority One Calls

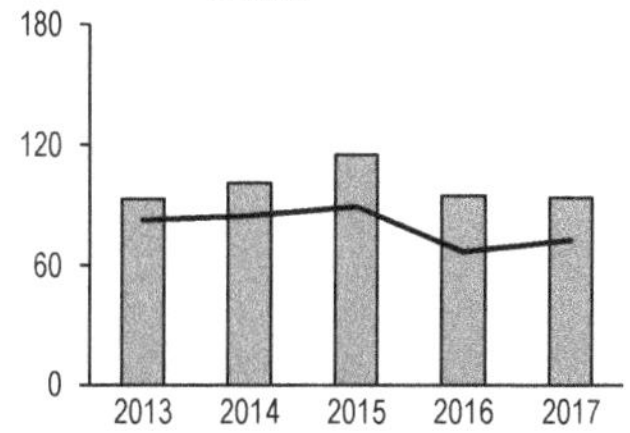

	2013	2014	2015	2016	2017
Asheville	93	101	115	94	94
Average	82	84	89	67	72

Fiscal Year 2016–17

Explanatory Information

Service Level and Delivery

Concord's emergency communications center handles E-911 and non-emergency calls for the city. The emergency communications function of the city is separate from the police and fire functions and does not answer or transfer administrative calls for those departments. The emergency communications center does answer calls for utility and other city departments after hours, which is reflected in the number of incoming calls.

The city uses an 800 MHz system, which is a twelve-channel, five-site system shared with Cabarrus County and the City of Kannapolis.

Concord's center handled a total of 106,933 calls in the fiscal year, dispatching 146,565 calls.

Conditions Affecting Service, Performance, and Costs

Municipal Profile

Population (OSBM 2016)	88,815
Land Area (Square Miles)	62.61
Persons per Square Mile	1,419
Median Family Income U.S. Census 2010	$63,643
County	Cabarrus

Service Profile

Primary or Secondary Answering Point	Primary
Calls Dispatched	
Police	Yes
Fire	Yes
Other	Yes
FTE Positions	
Telecommunicators/Call-Takers	21.5
Other	2.0
Total Positions	23.5
Average Length of Service for Call-Takers	8.8 years
Total Incoming Calls	106,933
Total 911 Calls	28,931
Total Calls Dispatched	146,565
Outgoing Calls Other than Dispatch	32,142
Revenue from E-911 Fees	None

Full Cost Profile

Cost Breakdown by Percentage	
Personal Services	83.4%
Operating Costs	15.3%
Capital Costs	1.3%
TOTAL	100.0%
Cost Breakdown in Dollars	
Personal Services	$1,270,088
Operating Costs	$233,765
Capital Costs	$19,942
TOTAL	$1,523,795

Concord — Emergency Communications

Key: Concord ▒ Benchmarking Average — Fiscal Years 2013 through 2017

Resource Measures

Emergency Communications Services Costs per Capita

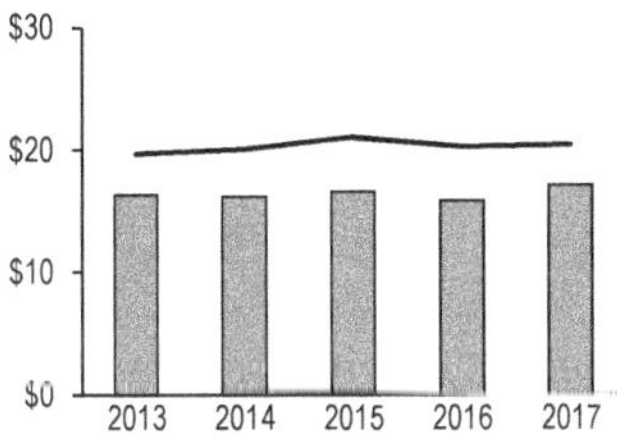

	2013	2014	2015	2016	2017
Concord	$16.37	$16.20	$16.62	$15.91	$17.16
Average	$19.68	$20.04	$21.03	$20.26	$20.40

Emergency Communications FTEs per 10,000 Population

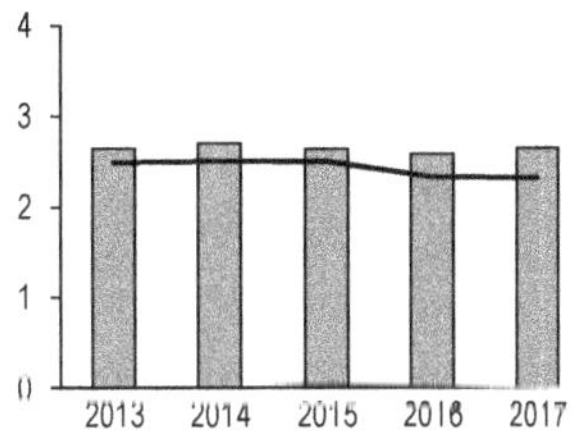

	2013	2014	2015	2016	2017
Concord	2.64	2.70	2.63	2.58	2.65
Average	2.49	2.51	2.51	2.33	2.32

Workload Measures

Total Calls Answered per 1,000 Population

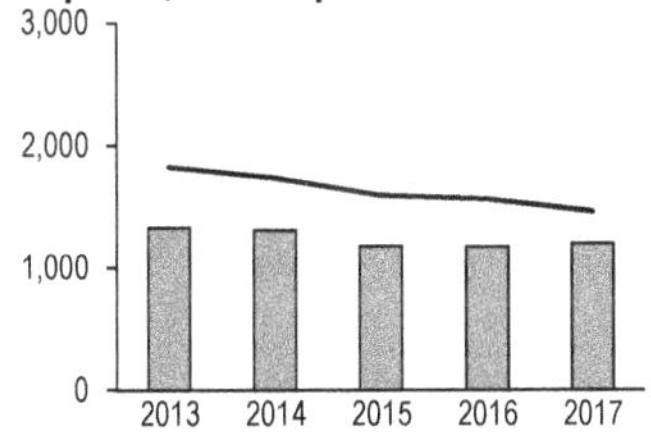

	2013	2014	2015	2016	2017
Concord	1,336	1,313	1,181	1,177	1,204
Average	1,823	1,732	1,592	1,560	1,457

Calls Dispatched per 1,000 Population

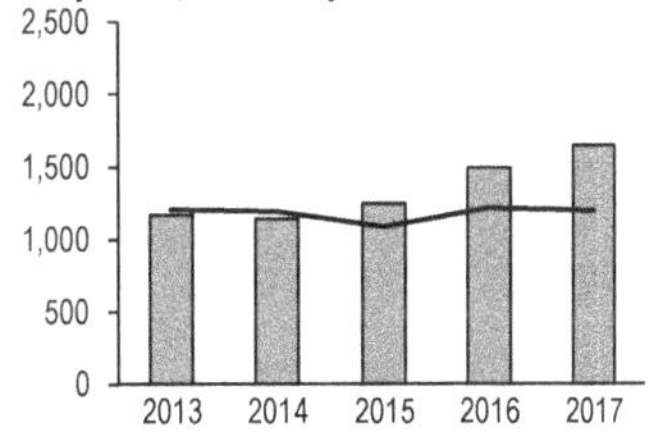

	2013	2014	2015	2016	2017
Concord	1,171	1,144	1,250	1,495	1,650
Average	1,207	1,195	1,090	1,217	1,200

E-911 Calls as a Percentage of All Incoming Calls

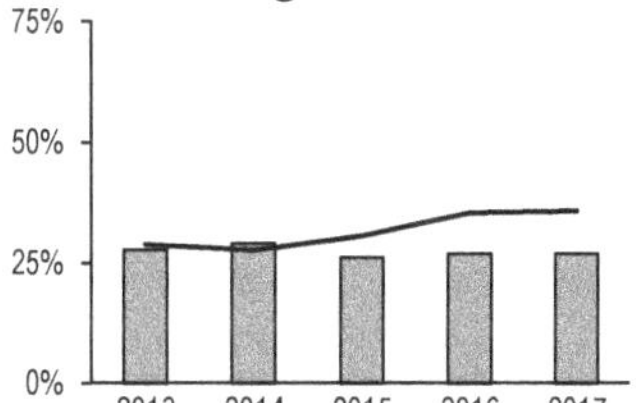

	2013	2014	2015	2016	2017
Concord	27.8%	29.2%	26.2%	27.0%	27.1%
Average	28.9%	27.7%	30.6%	35.3%	35.7%

Efficiency Measures

Calls Answered per Telecommunicator

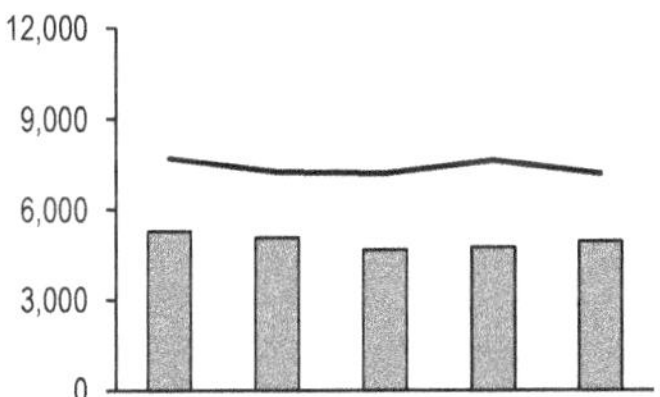

	2013	2014	2015	2016	2017
Concord	5,309	5,088	4,691	4,769	4,974
Average	7,694	7,244	7,204	7,614	7,178

Calls Dispatched per Telecommunicator

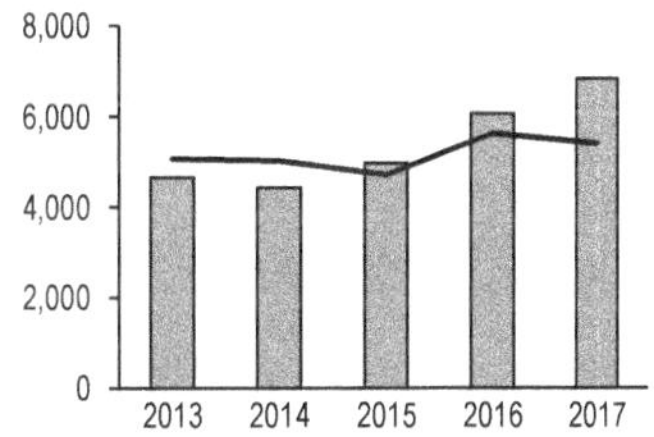

	2013	2014	2015	2016	2017
Concord	4,652	4,430	4,968	6,057	6,817
Average	5,084	5,033	4,724	5,628	5,410

Emergency Communications Cost per Call Dispatched

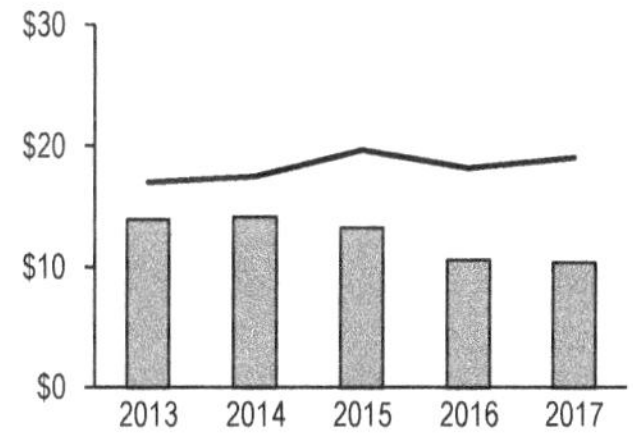

	2013	2014	2015	2016	2017
Concord	$13.98	$14.17	$13.30	$10.64	$10.40
Average	$17.03	$17.52	$19.67	$18.23	$19.06

Effectiveness Measures

Number of Seconds from Initial Ring to Answer

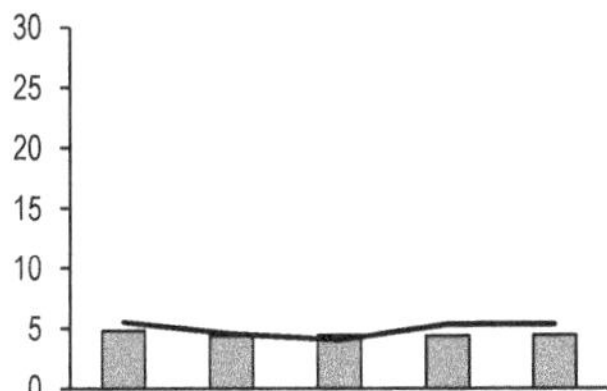

	2013	2014	2015	2016	2017
Concord	5	4	4	4	4
Average	6	5	4	5	5

Percent of E-911 Calls Answered within Twenty Seconds

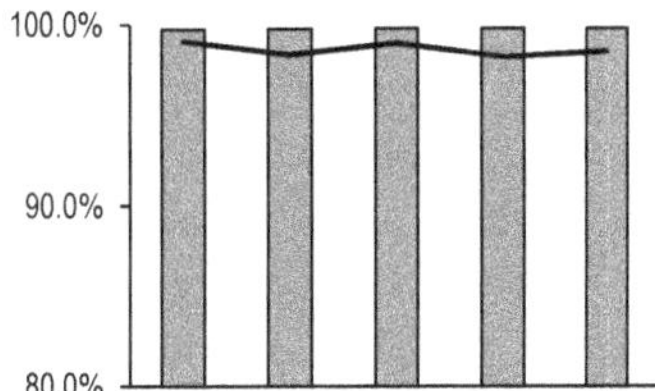

	2013	2014	2015	2016	2017
Concord	99.7%	99.8%	99.8%	99.8%	99.8%
Average	99.1%	98.3%	99.0%	98.2%	98.5%

Average Time in Seconds from CAD Entry to Dispatch for Priority One Calls

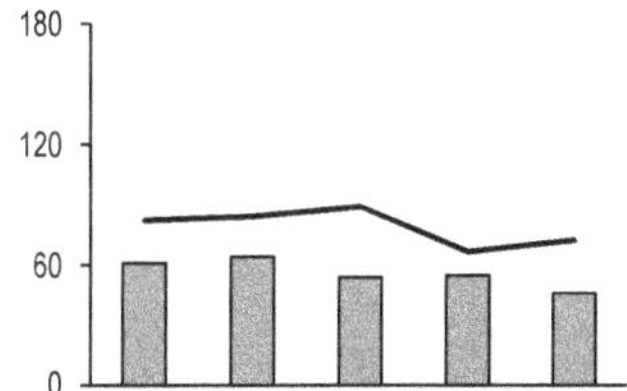

	2013	2014	2015	2016	2017
Concord	61	64	54	55	46
Average	82	84	89	67	72

Fiscal Year 2016–17

Explanatory Information

Service Level and Delivery

Guilford Metro 911 operates under an interlocal agreement between the City of Greensboro and Guilford County. The public safety answering point serves as a separate department providing emergency communications for the City of Greensboro, Guilford County, and Gibsonville (except for the City of High Point Police and Fire departments). The services include dispatch and call intake for all law agencies, fire agencies, and EMS. The consolidation process enabled the first update of all 911 equipment in ten years and the creation of a back-up E-911 center to improve disaster preparedness. These changes contributed to slightly higher operational costs.

Guilford Metro 911 uses a twenty-eight-channel Motorola SmartNet 800 MHz radio system. The system has five tower sites and is jointly owned with Guilford County.

Greensboro's communications center handled a total of 622,258 incoming calls in the fiscal year, dispatching 438,345 calls. The city defines highest priority emergency calls as call types that require the fastest response, such as shootings, robberies, and domestic violence.

Greensboro received $2,991,354 in E-911 revenues to support system operations.

Conditions Affecting Service, Performance, and Costs

Municipal Profile

Population (OSBM 2016)–Guilford County	520,230
Land Area (Square Miles)	649.42
Persons per Square Mile	801
Median Family Income	$52,752
U.S. Census 2010	
County	Guilford

Service Profile

Primary or Secondary Answering Point	Primary
Calls Dispatched	
Police	Yes
Fire	Yes
Other	Yes
FTE Positions	
Telecommunicators/Call-Takers	92.0
Other	11.0
Total Positions	103.0
Average Length of Service for Call-Takers	9.8 years
Total Incoming Calls	622,258
Total 911 Calls	354,870
Total Calls Dispatched	438,345
Outgoing Calls Other than Dispatch	154,235
Revenue from E-911 Fees	$2,991,354

Full Cost Profile

Cost Breakdown by Percentage	
Personal Services	81.4%
Operating Costs	18.6%
Capital Costs	0.0%
TOTAL	100.0%
Cost Breakdown in Dollars	
Personal Services	$6,378,494
Operating Costs	$1,460,979
Capital Costs	$0
TOTAL	$7,839,473

Key: Greensboro ▒ Benchmarking Average — Fiscal Years 2013 through 2017

Resource Measures

Emergency Communications Services Costs per Capita

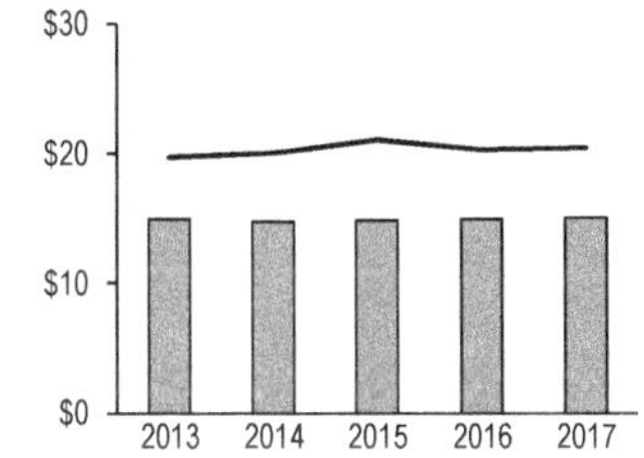

	2013	2014	2015	2016	2017
Greensboro	$14.89	$14.71	$14.82	$14.91	$15.07
Average	$19.68	$20.04	$21.03	$20.26	$20.40

Emergency Communications FTEs per 10,000 Population

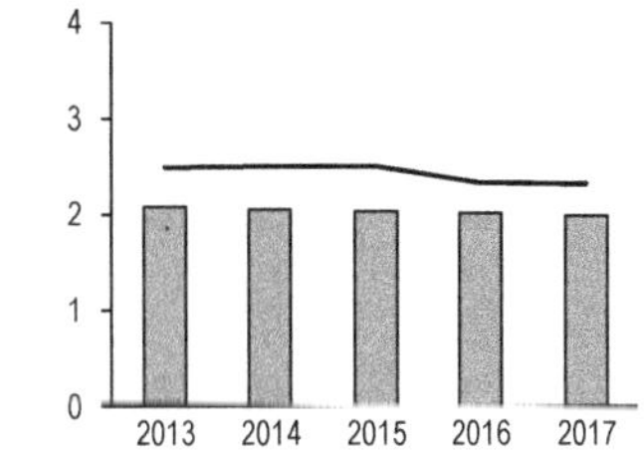

	2013	2014	2015	2016	2017
Greensboro	2.08	2.05	2.03	2.01	1.98
Average	2.49	2.51	2.51	2.33	2.32

Workload Measures

Total Calls Answered per 1,000 Population

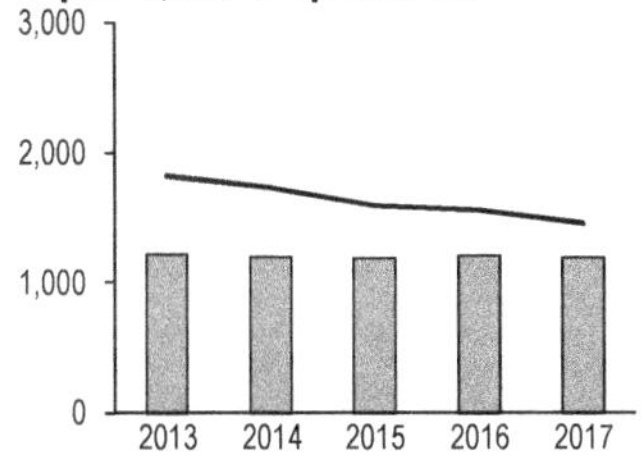

	2013	2014	2015	2016	2017
Greensboro	1,217	1,199	1,187	1,207	1,196
Average	1,823	1,732	1,592	1,560	1,457

Calls Dispatched per 1,000 Population

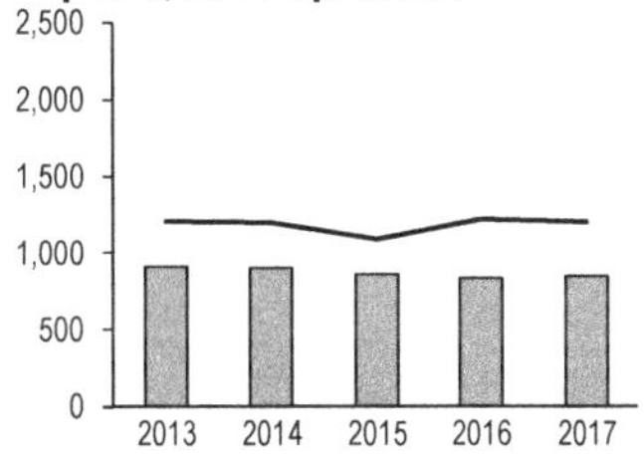

	2013	2014	2015	2016	2017
Greensboro	906	900	856	831	843
Average	1,207	1,195	1,090	1,217	1,200

E-911 Calls as a Percentage of All Incoming Calls

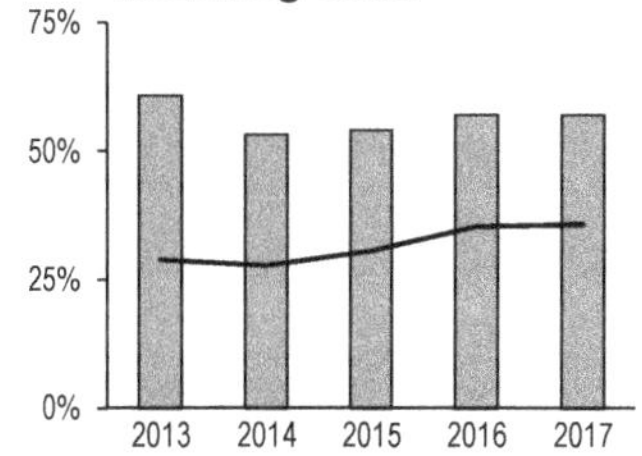

	2013	2014	2015	2016	2017
Greensboro	60.8%	53.3%	54.1%	57.1%	57.0%
Average	28.9%	27.7%	30.6%	35.3%	35.7%

Efficiency Measures

Calls Answered per Telecommunicator

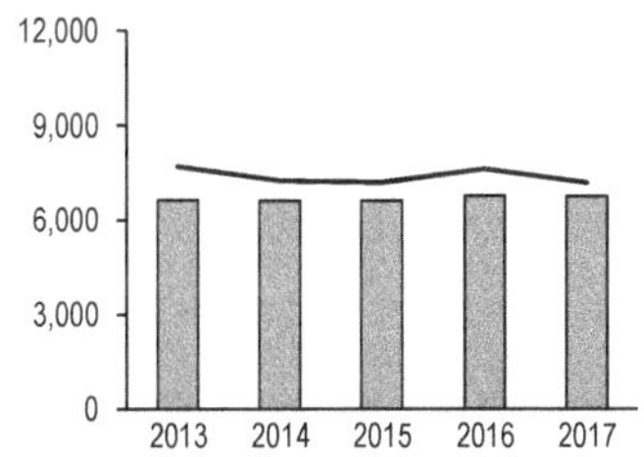

	2013	2014	2015	2016	2017
Greensboro	6,630	6,613	6,609	6,786	6,764
Average	7,694	7,244	7,204	7,614	7,178

Calls Dispatched per Telecommunicator

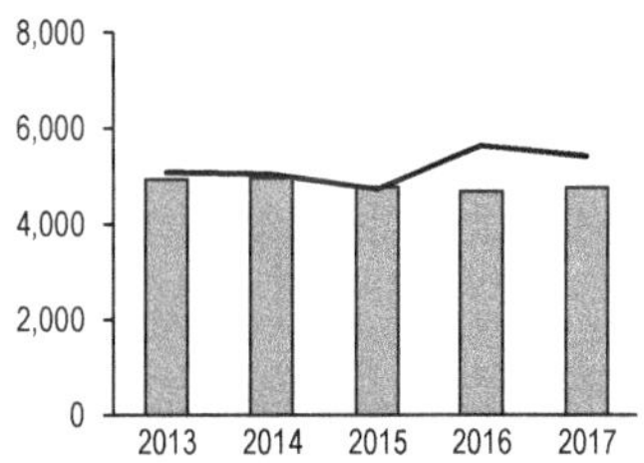

	2013	2014	2015	2016	2017
Greensboro	4,935	4,962	4,767	4,673	4,765
Average	5,084	5,033	4,724	5,628	5,410

Emergency Communications Cost per Call Dispatched

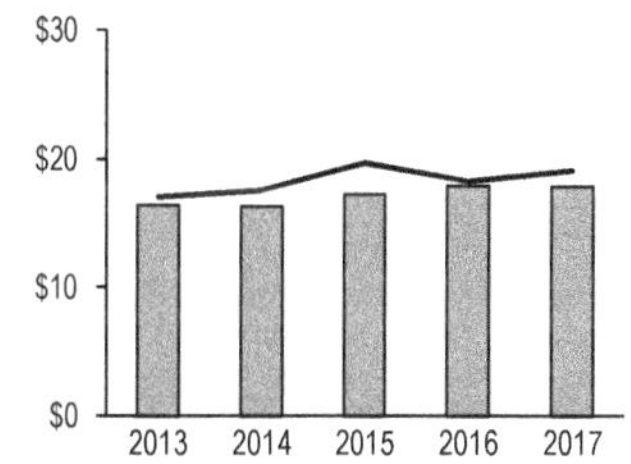

	2013	2014	2015	2016	2017
Greensboro	$16.43	$16.36	$17.31	$17.94	$17.88
Average	$17.03	$17.52	$19.67	$18.23	$19.06

Effectiveness Measures

Number of Seconds from Initial Ring to Answer

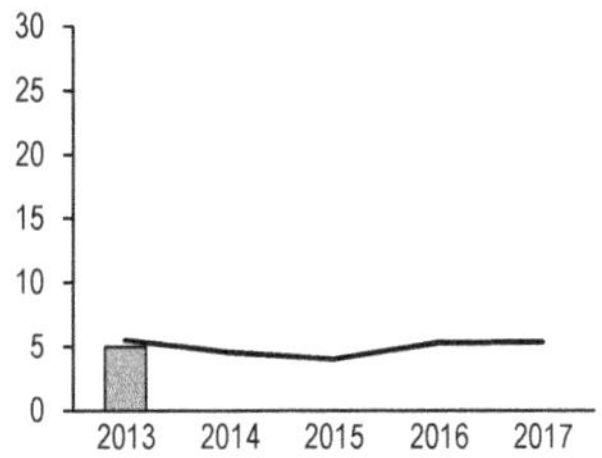

	2013	2014	2015	2016	2017
Greensboro	5				
Average	6	5	4	5	5

Percent of E-911 Calls Answered within Twenty Seconds

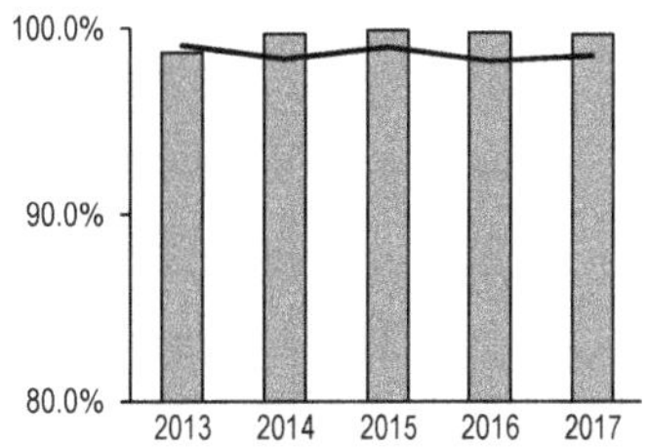

	2013	2014	2015	2016	2017
Greensboro	98.7%	99.7%	99.9%	99.7%	99.6%
Average	99.1%	98.3%	99.0%	98.2%	98.5%

Average Time in Seconds from CAD Entry to Dispatch for Priority One Calls

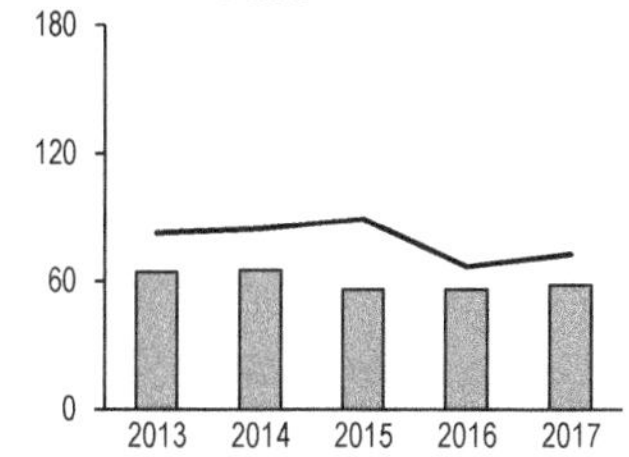

	2013	2014	2015	2016	2017
Greensboro	64	65	56	56	58
Average	82	84	89	67	72

Fiscal Year 2016–17

Explanatory Information

Service Level and Delivery

Greenville's emergency communications center is a secondary public safety answering point, with Pitt County being the primary answering point. Pitt County initially receives all 911 calls and dispatches fire and EMS calls inside the city limits. All 911 calls for police services are transferred to the Greenville Police Department emergency communications center for dispatch. Calls can also be made directly to the police department over a dedicated emergency line.

The city does not own its own communications system and infrastructure. Greenville operates on the VIPER system maintained by the North Carolina State Highway Patrol. This system is fully maintained and operated by the state. The system has one tower located within the city limits and fully supports communication interoperability among all law enforcement agencies in Pitt County and with Greenville Fire/Rescue and East Care medical transport.

Greenville's center took in 106,537 incoming calls in the fiscal year and dispatched 85,416 calls.

Conditions Affecting Service, Performance, and Costs

The emegency phone systems in Greenville and Pitt County were both changed during FY 2013–14. The city's tracking system lost two months of data on incoming calls, which could not be retrieved. The drop in calls answered is a data issue rather than a change in service over the prior year. The problem did not affect calls dispatched. The new system starting in FY 2014–15 is better able to more accurately track calls, particularly 911 calls.

Telecommunicators in Greenville are also tasked with overseeing public safety cameras through several large monitors. When needed, they are instructed to log events requiring a response as service calls. This video monitoring results in higher staffing needs in the emergency communications center.

Municipal Profile

Population (OSBM 2016)	87,989
Land Area (Square Miles)	35.41
Persons per Square Mile	2,485
Median Family Income U.S. Census 2010	$50,395
County	Pitt

Service Profile

Primary or Secondary Answering Point	Secondary
Calls Dispatched	
Police	Yes
Fire	No
Other	Yes
FTE Positions	
Telecommunicators/Call-Takers	16.0
Other	1.0
Total Positions	17.0
Average Length of Service for Call-Takers	8.1 years
Total Incoming Calls	106,537
Total 911 Calls	29,394
Total Calls Dispatched	85,416
Outgoing Calls Other than Dispatch	18,593
Revenue from E-911 Fees	None

Full Cost Profile

Cost Breakdown by Percentage	
Personal Services	65.6%
Operating Costs	27.1%
Capital Costs	7.4%
TOTAL	100.0%
Cost Breakdown in Dollars	
Personal Services	$1,257,062
Operating Costs	$518,638
Capital Costs	$141,409
TOTAL	$1,917,109

Key: Greenville ▒ Benchmarking Average — Fiscal Years 2013 through 2017

Resource Measures

Emergency Communications Services Costs per Capita

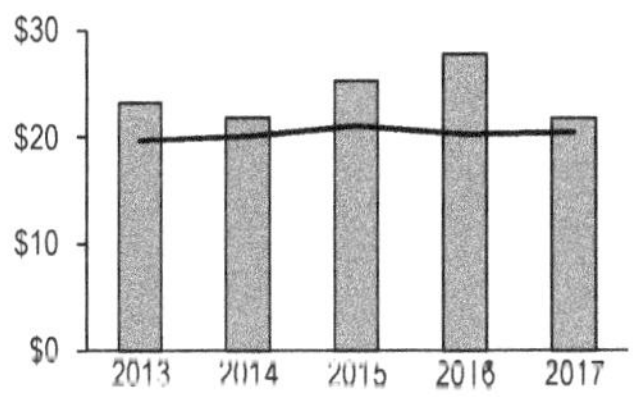

	2013	2014	2015	2016	2017
Greenville	$23.23	$21.86	$25.30	$27.81	$21.79
Average	$19.68	$20.04	$21.03	$20.26	$20.40

Emergency Communications FTEs per 10,000 Population

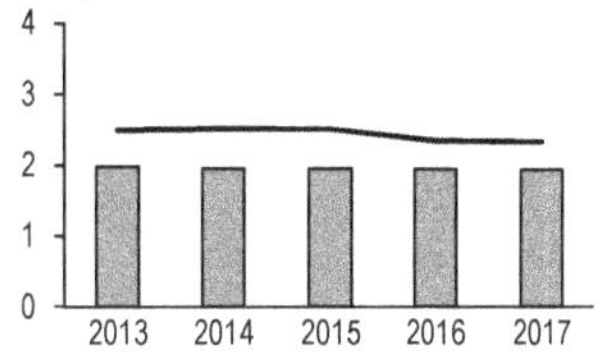

	2013	2014	2015	2016	2017
Greenville	1.97	1.95	1.94	1.93	1.93
Average	2.49	2.51	2.51	2.33	2.32

Workload Measures

Total Calls Answered per 1,000 Population

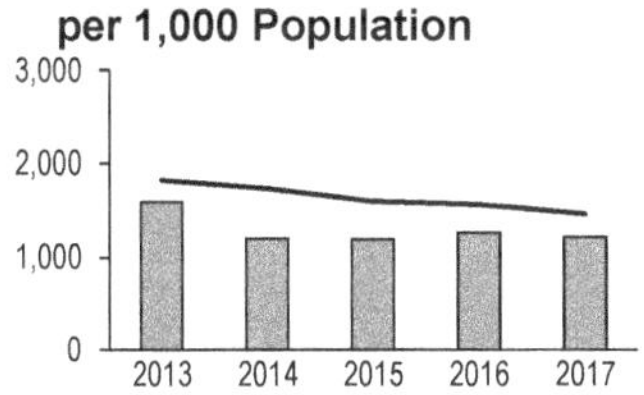

	2013	2014	2015	2016	2017
Greenville	1,589	1,196	1,191	1,259	1,211
Average	1,823	1,732	1,592	1,560	1,457

Calls Dispatched per 1,000 Population

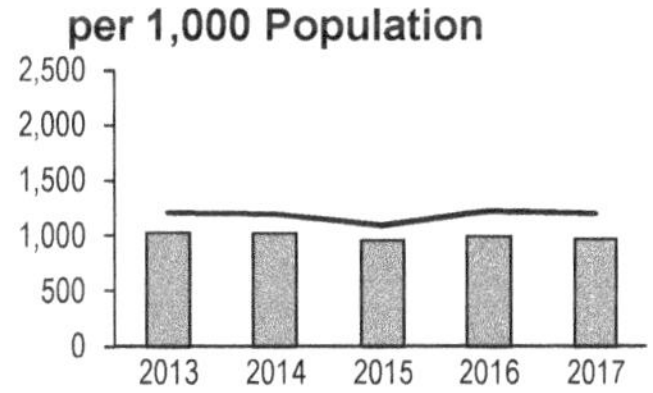

	2013	2014	2015	2016	2017
Greenville	1,031	1,023	964	993	971
Average	1,207	1,195	1,090	1,217	1,200

E-911 Calls as a Percentage of All Incoming Calls

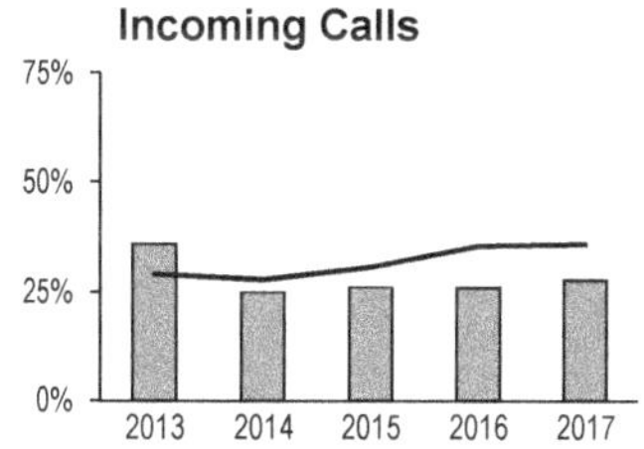

	2013	2014	2015	2016	2017
Greenville	35.8%	24.8%	26.0%	25.9%	27.6%
Average	28.9%	27.7%	30.6%	35.3%	35.7%

Efficiency Measures

Calls Answered per Telecommunicator

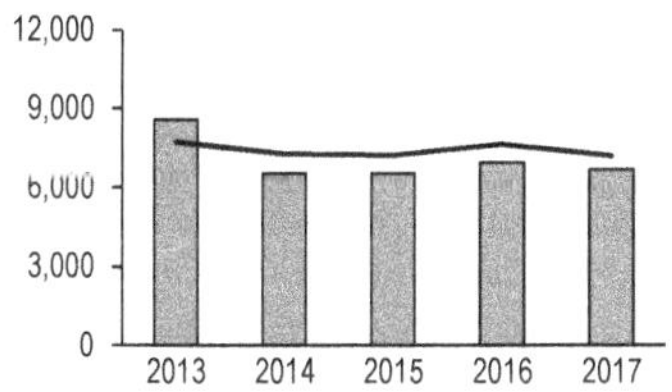

	2013	2014	2015	2016	2017
Greenville	8,555	6,522	6,510	6,921	6,659
Average	7,694	7,244	7,204	7,614	7,178

Calls Dispatched per Telecommunicator

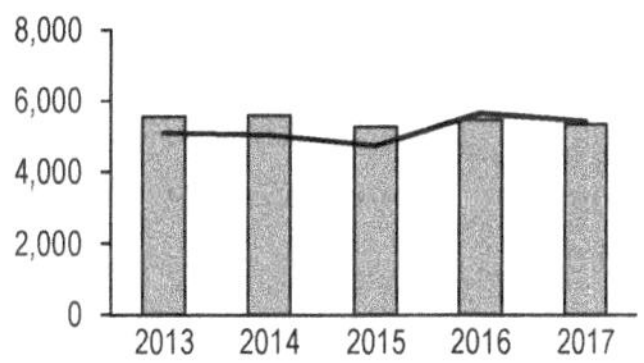

	2013	2014	2015	2016	2017
Greenville	5,552	5,577	5,266	5,459	5,339
Average	5,084	5,033	4,724	5,628	5,410

Emergency Communications Cost per Call Dispatched

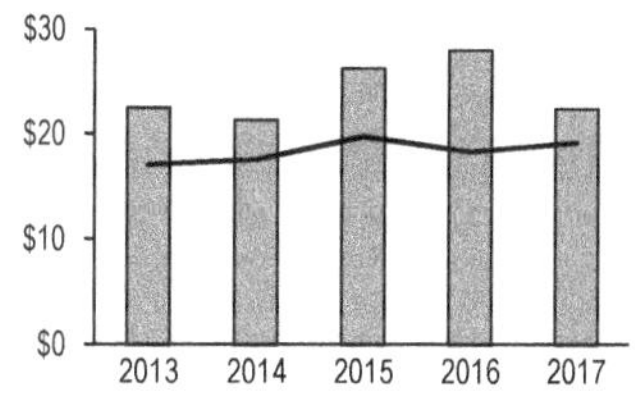

	2013	2014	2015	2016	2017
Greenville	$22.53	$21.37	$26.25	$28.01	$22.44
Average	$17.03	$17.52	$19.67	$18.23	$19.06

Effectiveness Measures

Number of Seconds from Initial Ring to Answer

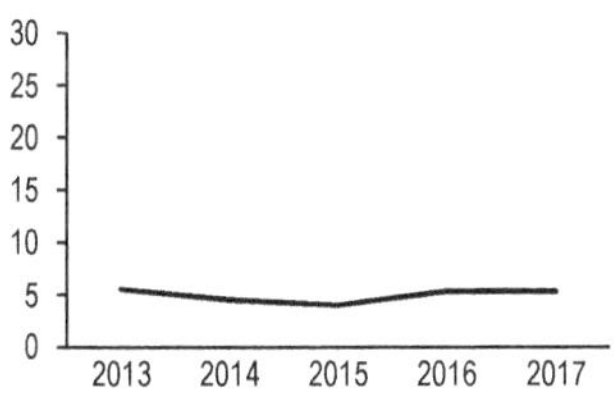

	2013	2014	2015	2016	2017
Greenville					
Average	6	5	4	5	5

Percent of E-911 Calls Answered within Twenty Seconds

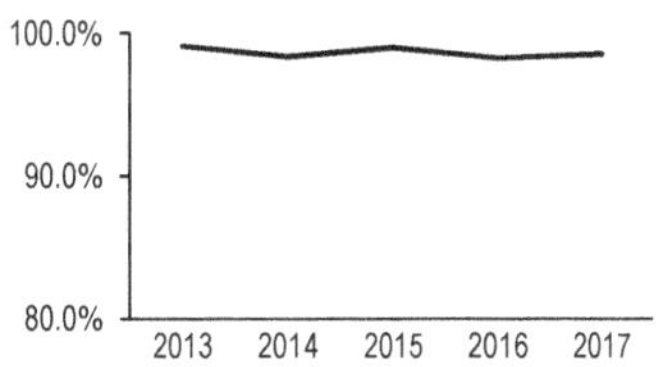

	2013	2014	2015	2016	2017
Greenville					
Average	99.1%	98.3%	99.0%	98.2%	98.5%

Average Time in Seconds from CAD Entry to Dispatch for Priority One Calls

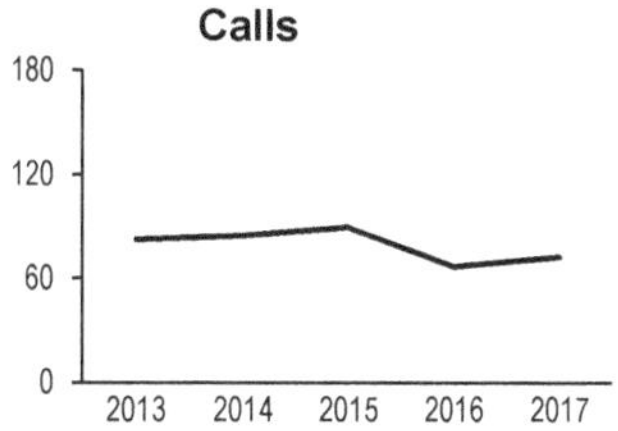

	2013	2014	2015	2016	2017
Greenville					
Average	82	84	89	67	72

Fiscal Year 2016–17

Explanatory Information

Service Level and Delivery

Hickory's emergency communications center is a secondary public safety answering point, with Catawba County being the primary answering point. Catwaba County initially receives all 911 calls and dispatches fire and EMS calls inside the city limits. All 911 calls for police services are transferred to the emergency communications center for dispatch. Any emergency calls for other city services are transferred to the emergency communications center between 3:30 p.m. and 7:00 a.m.

The city owns its communications system and infrastructure. It uses an Ericsson 800 MHz radio system. There is one 1,350-foot tower and antennas at two other sites. The system serves approximately 200 users in five city departments.

Hickory's communications center took in 157,124 incoming calls during the year. The center dispatched 97,600 calls during the year.

Hickory received $52,445 in E-911 revenues to support system operations.

Conditions Affecting Service, Performance, and Costs

Incoming calls in Hickory are down over time because of changes in how calls are routed. Several special units now have their own administrative phones, so calls no longer come through the emergency communications center. Additionally, the animal control unit's operations were moved out of the police department, so their calls are now being fed through code enforcement.

Municipal Profile

Population (OSBM 2016)	40,453
Land Area (Square Miles)	29.90
Persons per Square Mile	1,353
Median Family Income U.S. Census 2010	$54,093
County	Catawba

Service Profile

Primary or Secondary Answering Point	Secondary
Calls Dispatched	
Police	Yes
Fire	No
Other	No
FTE Positions	
Telecommunicators/Call-Takers	12.0
Other	0.0
Total Positions	12.0
Average Length of Service for Call-Takers	6.8 years
Total Incoming Calls	157,124
Total 911 Calls	15,072
Total Calls Dispatched	97,600
Outgoing Calls Other than Dispatch	30,270
Revenue from E-911 Fees	$52,445

Full Cost Profile

Cost Breakdown by Percentage	
Personal Services	74.9%
Operating Costs	23.3%
Capital Costs	1.9%
TOTAL	100.0%
Cost Breakdown in Dollars	
Personal Services	$609,372
Operating Costs	$189,240
Capital Costs	$15,229
TOTAL	$813,841

Key: Hickory ▒ Benchmarking Average — Fiscal Years 2013 through 2017

Resource Measures

Emergency Communications Services Costs per Capita

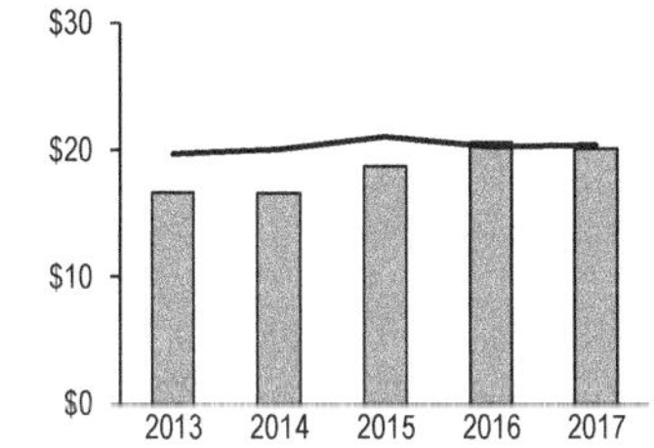

	2013	2014	2015	2016	2017
Hickory	$16.67	$16.67	$18.77	$20.62	$20.12
Average	$19.68	$20.04	$21.03	$20.26	$20.40

Emergency Communications FTEs per 10,000 Population

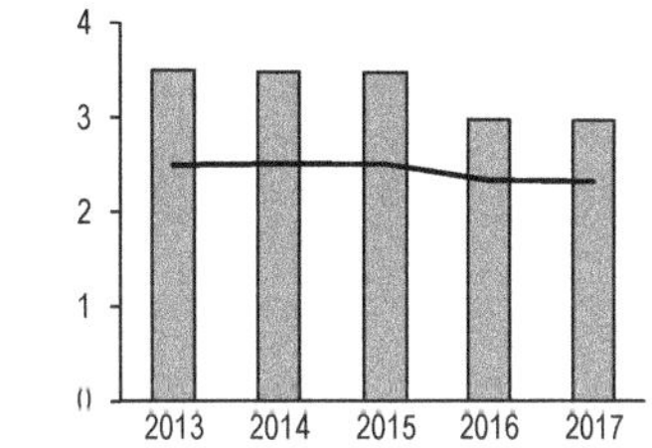

	2013	2014	2015	2016	2017
Hickory	3.50	3.48	3.47	2.97	2.97
Average	2.49	2.51	2.51	2.33	2.32

Workload Measures

Total Calls Answered per 1,000 Population

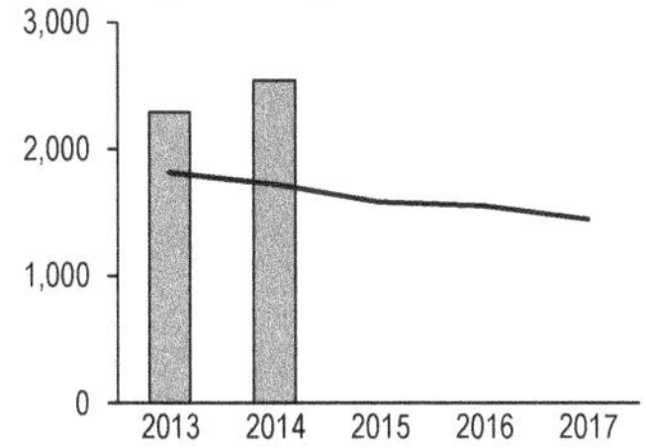

	2013	2014	2015	2016	2017
Hickory	2,291	2,543			
Average	1,823	1,732	1,592	1,560	1,457

Calls Dispatched per 1,000 Population

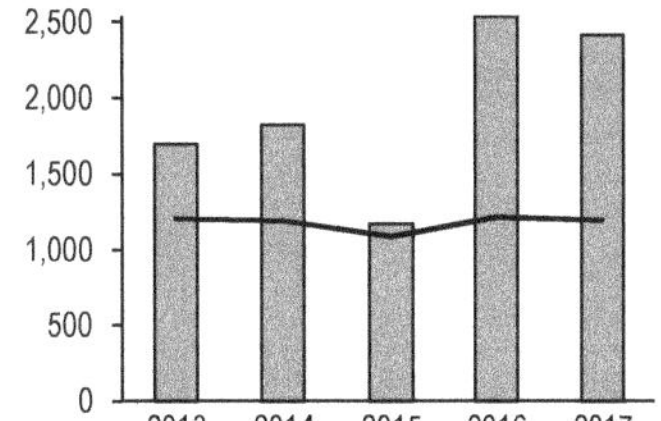

	2013	2014	2015	2016	2017
Hickory	1,697	1,825	1,172	2,535	2,413
Average	1,207	1,195	1,090	1,217	1,200

E-911 Calls as a Percentage of All Incoming Calls

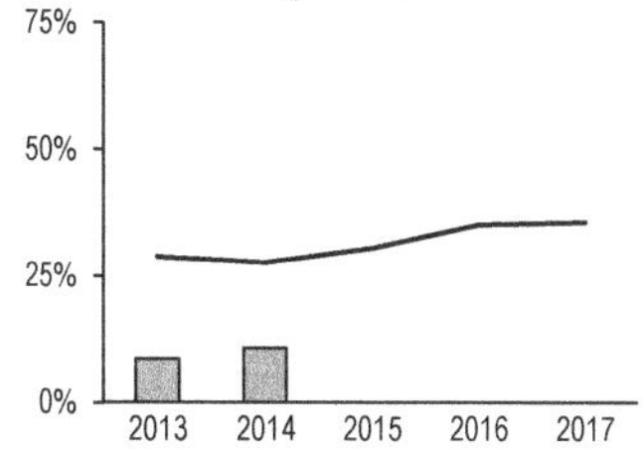

	2013	2014	2015	2016	2017
Hickory	8.5%	10.7%			
Average	28.9%	27.7%	30.6%	35.3%	35.7%

Efficiency Measures

Calls Answered per Telecommunicator

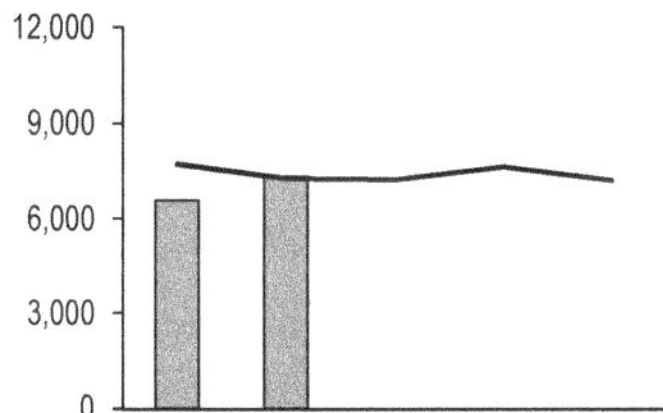

	2013	2014	2015	2016	2017
Hickory	6,553	7,306			
Average	7,694	7,244	7,204	7,614	7,178

Calls Dispatched per Telecommunicator

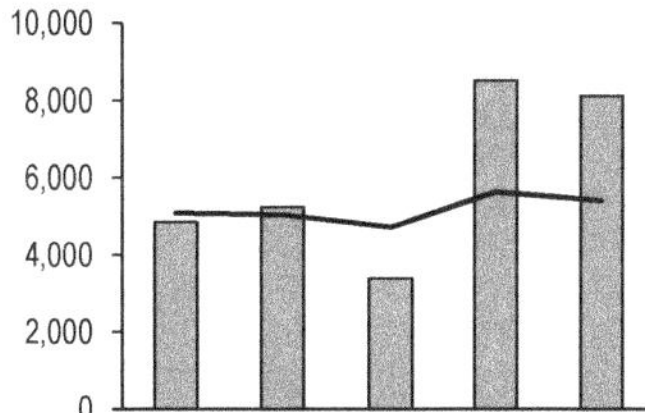

	2013	2014	2015	2016	2017
Hickory	4,852	5,243	3,377	8,525	8,133
Average	5,084	5,033	4,724	5,628	5,410

Emergency Communications Cost per Call Dispatched

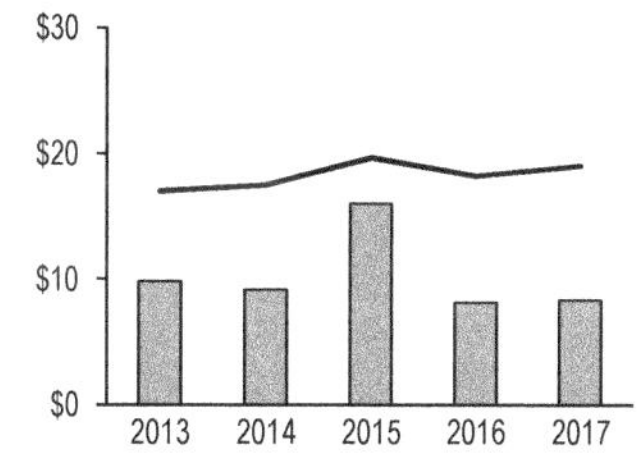

	2013	2014	2015	2016	2017
Hickory	$9.82	$9.13	$16.01	$8.13	$8.34
Average	$17.03	$17.52	$19.67	$18.23	$19.06

Effectiveness Measures

Number of Seconds from Initial Ring to Answer

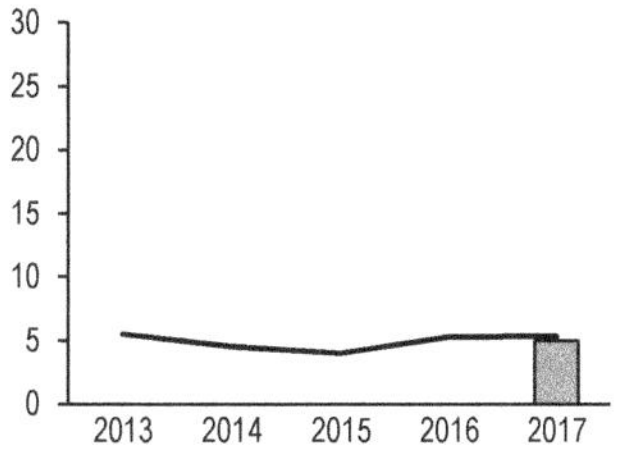

	2013	2014	2015	2016	2017
Hickory					5
Average	6	5	4	5	5

Percent of E-911 Calls Answered within Twenty Seconds

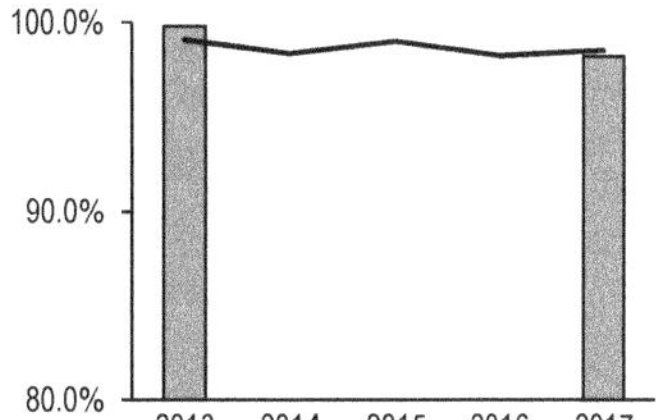

	2013	2014	2015	2016	2017
Hickory	99.8%				98.2%
Average	99.1%	98.3%	99.0%	98.2%	98.5%

Average Time in Seconds from CAD Entry to Dispatch for Priority One Calls

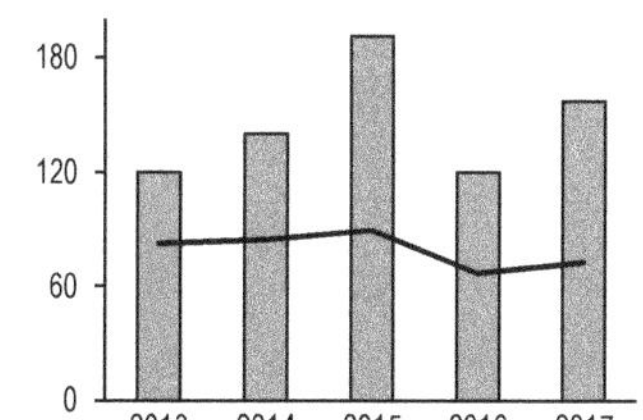

	2013	2014	2015	2016	2017
Hickory	120	140	191	120	157
Average	82	84	89	67	72

High Point — Emergency Communications

Fiscal Year 2016–17

Explanatory Information

Service Level and Delivery

High Point's emergency communications center is a civilian-staffed and city-managed department. The center functions as a primary public safety answering point, dispatching all police and fire calls within the city; medical calls are routed to Guilford County EMS.

The center has ten consoles, seven of which are dispatch positions. Operations are conducted by four teams of five telecommunicators and a supervisor. All telecommunicators are cross-trained in fire and police dispatch and function as call-takers and dispatchers. Personnel assigned to the center work rotating twelve-hour shifts.

The city of High Point owns its communications infrastructure. Communications utilizes an 800 MHz radio system that implements analog and digital talk groups. The city uses a Motorola SmartNet system with three towers.

High Point's center handled a total of 272,352 calls in the fiscal year, dispatching 133,217 calls. The city defines highest priority emergency calls as situations likely to result in loss of life, injury, or property damage and crimes in progress.

High Point received $534,373 in E-911 revenues to support system operations.

Conditions Affecting Service, Performance, and Costs

High Point was unable to provide data on certain measures, given a change in technology.

Municipal Profile

Population (OSBM 2016)	110,244
Land Area (Square Miles)	55.14
Persons per Square Mile	1,999
Median Family Income U.S. Census 2010	$49,720
County	Guilford

Service Profile

Primary or Secondary Answering Point	Primary
Calls Dispatched	
Police	Yes
Fire	Yes
Other	No
FTE Positions	
Telecommunicators/Call-Takers	30.0
Other	3.0
Total Positions	33.0
Average Length of Service for Call-Takers	10.3 years
Total Incoming Calls	272,352
Total 911 Calls	83,394
Total Calls Dispatched	133,217
Outgoing Calls Other than Dispatch	57,192
Revenue from E-911 Fees	$534,373

Full Cost Profile

Cost Breakdown by Percentage	
Personal Services	61.9%
Operating Costs	29.1%
Capital Costs	9.0%
TOTAL	100.0%
Cost Breakdown in Dollars	
Personal Services	$2,291,579
Operating Costs	$1,076,027
Capital Costs	$332,370
TOTAL	$3,699,976

High Point — Emergency Communications

Key: High Point ▒ Benchmarking Average — Fiscal Years 2013 through 2017

Resource Measures

Emergency Communications Services Costs per Capita

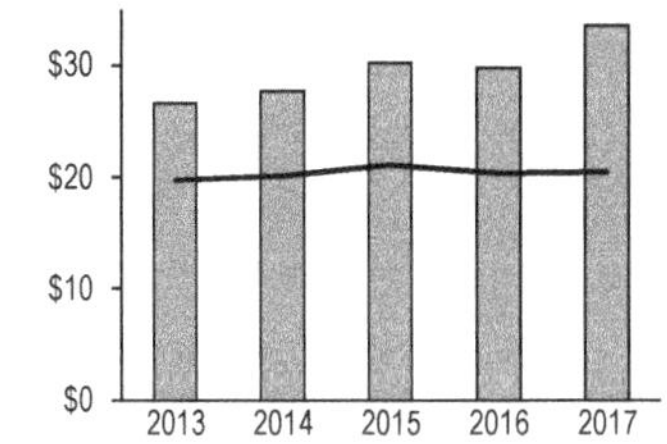

	2013	2014	2015	2016	2017
High Point	$26.62	$27.71	$30.22	$29.77	$33.56
Average	$19.68	$20.04	$21.03	$20.26	$20.40

Emergency Communications FTEs per 10,000 Population

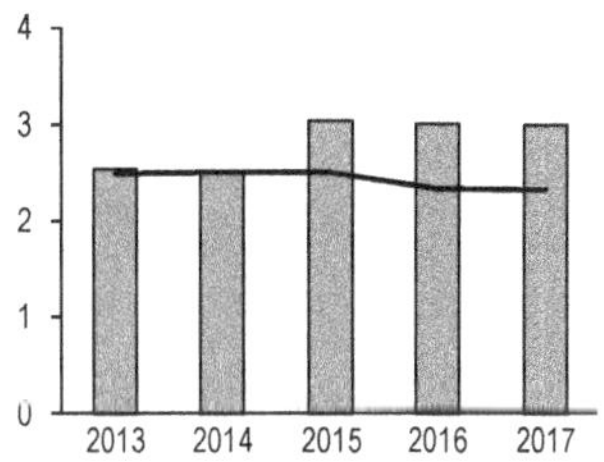

	2013	2014	2015	2016	2017
High Point	2.54	2.51	3.04	3.01	2.99
Average	2.49	2.51	2.51	2.33	2.32

Workload Measures

Total Calls Answered per 1,000 Population

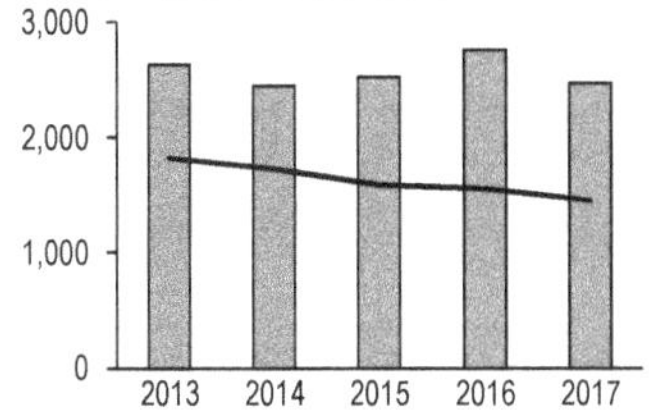

	2013	2014	2015	2016	2017
High Point	2,630	2,449	2,522	2,755	2,470
Average	1,823	1,732	1,592	1,560	1,457

Calls Dispatched per 1,000 Population

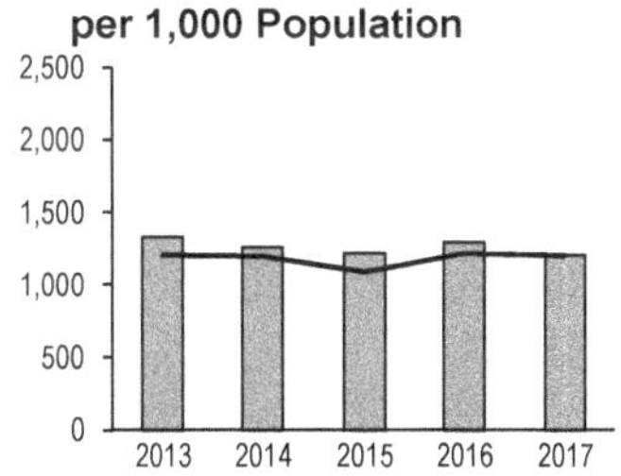

	2013	2014	2015	2016	2017
High Point	1,334	1,264	1,224	1,298	1,208
Average	1,207	1,195	1,090	1,217	1,200

E-911 Calls as a Percentage of All Incoming Calls

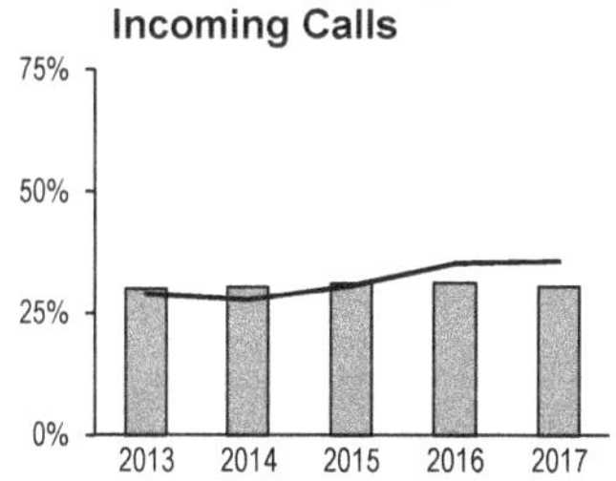

	2013	2014	2015	2016	2017
High Point	30.2%	30.5%	31.2%	31.4%	30.6%
Average	28.9%	27.7%	30.6%	35.3%	35.7%

Efficiency Measures

Calls Answered per Telecommunicator

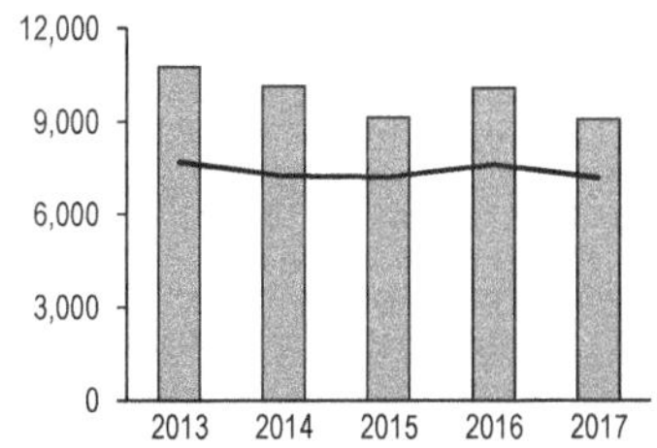

	2013	2014	2015	2016	2017
High Point	10,763	10,140	9,125	10,080	9,078
Average	7,694	7,244	7,204	7,614	7,178

Calls Dispatched per Telecommunicator

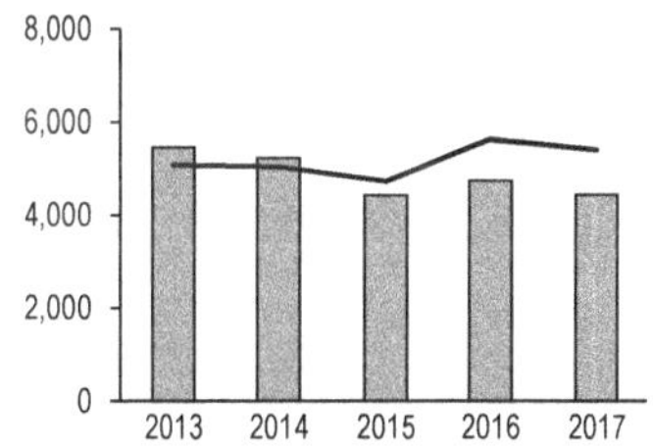

	2013	2014	2015	2016	2017
High Point	5,460	5,232	4,428	4,747	4,441
Average	5,084	5,033	4,724	5,628	5,410

Emergency Communications Cost per Call Dispatched

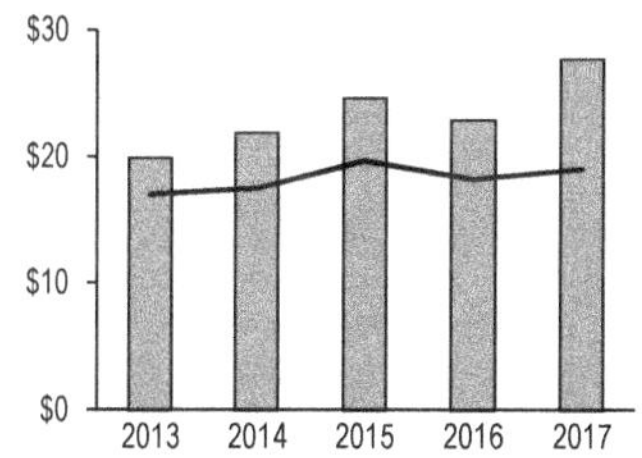

	2013	2014	2015	2016	2017
High Point	$19.95	$21.93	$24.70	$22.95	$27.77
Average	$17.03	$17.52	$19.67	$18.23	$19.06

Effectiveness Measures

Number of Seconds from Initial Ring to Answer

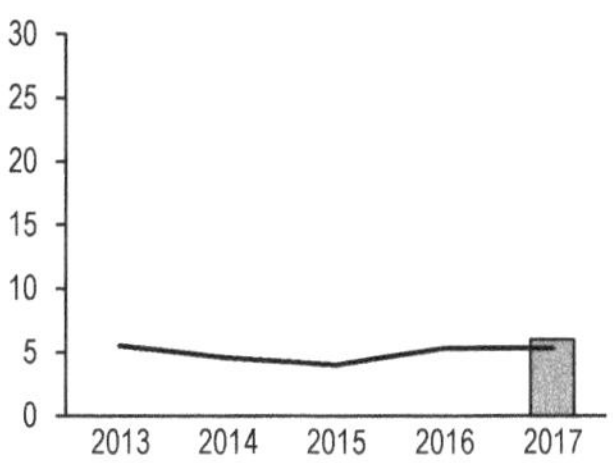

	2013	2014	2015	2016	2017
High Point					6
Average	6	5	4	5	5

Percent of E-911 Calls Answered within Twenty Seconds

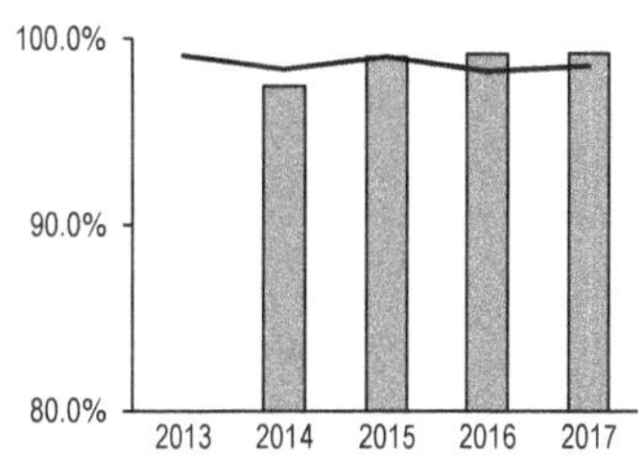

	2013	2014	2015	2016	2017
High Point		97.5%	99.0%	99.2%	99.2%
Average	99.1%	98.3%	99.0%	98.2%	98.5%

Average Time in Seconds from CAD Entry to Dispatch for Priority One Calls

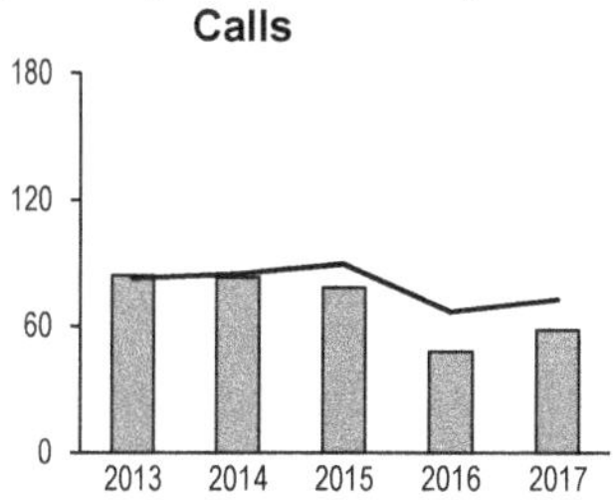

	2013	2014	2015	2016	2017
High Point	84	83	78	48	58
Average	82	84	89	67	72

Fiscal Year 2016–17

Explanatory Information

Service Level and Delivery
The Emergency Communications Center (ECC) is the answering and dispatch agency for all of Wake County. It provides dispatch services for forty-four law enforcement, fire, EMS, rescue, and public service agencies. The ECC takes 911 calls for the Wake County Sheriff's Department, but these calls are transferred to the Sheriff's telecommunicators.

The Town of Cary provides its own services for fire and police, but the ECC provides EMS call service for Cary.

The ECC uses a combination of city-owned and leased tower and transmitter sites. The system uses an 800 MHz system. Over 7,000 mobile and portable radios have been issued to public safety and non-public safety users within Wake County for use of the system.

The ECC handled a total of 850,340 incoming calls in the fiscal year, dispatching 487,733 calls. The ECC defines highest priority emergency calls as all fire and EMS calls and also police calls with a priority of "0" or "1" as defined by the police agency being dispatched.

Raleigh received $2,026,804 in E-911 revenues to support system operations.

Conditions Affecting Service, Performance, and Costs
Raleigh rejoined the Benchmarking Project in July 2016 with the first year of data showing for FY 2015–16.

At the start of FY 2015–16, the ECC switched from all positions being on automatic call distribution to specific positions utilizing the automatic system. This decreased answering efficiency, but it helped increase responder safety issues that were identified when all positions used the automatic system. Additionally during this year, the ECC had a one-fourth attrition rate, which impacted answering efficiencies as well.

Municipal Profile

Population (OSBM 2016)-Wake County	1,026,748
Land Area (Square Miles)	831.92
Persons per Square Mile	1,234
Median Family Income	$68,678
U.S. Census 2010	
County	Wake

Service Profile

Primary or Secondary Answering Point	Primary
Calls Dispatched	
Police	Yes
Fire	Yes
Other	Yes
FTE Positions	
Telecommunicators/Call-Takers	101.0
Other	26.0
Total Positions	127.0
Average Length of Service for Call-Takers	5.8 years
Total Incoming Calls	850,340
Total 911 Calls	578,648
Total Calls Dispatched	487,733
Outgoing Calls Other than Dispatch	284,295
Revenue from E-911 Fees	$2,026,804

Full Cost Profile

Cost Breakdown by Percentage	
Personal Services	68.2%
Operating Costs	29.9%
Capital Costs	1.9%
TOTAL	100.0%
Cost Breakdown in Dollars	
Personal Services	$8,037,137
Operating Costs	$3,517,723
Capital Costs	$225,818
TOTAL	$11,780,678

Key: Raleigh ▒ Benchmarking Average — Fiscal Years 2013 through 2017

Resource Measures

Emergency Communications Services Costs per Capita

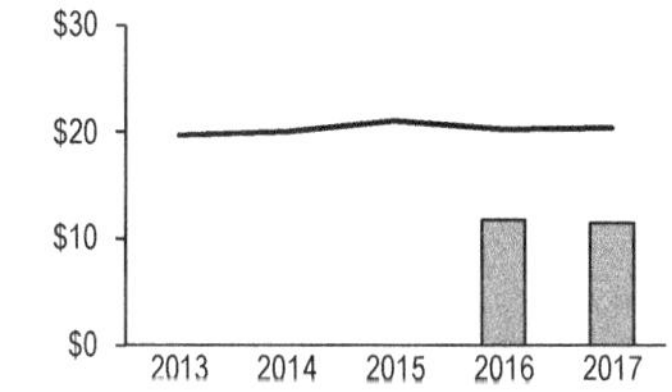

	2013	2014	2015	2016	2017
Raleigh				$11.80	$11.47
Average	$19.68	$20.04	$21.03	$20.26	$20.40

Emergency Communications FTEs per 10,000 Population

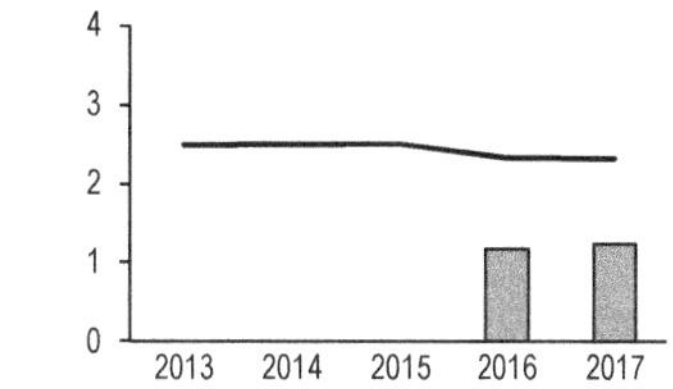

	2013	2014	2015	2016	2017
Raleigh				1.17	1.24
Average	2.49	2.51	2.51	2.33	2.32

Workload Measures

Total Calls Answered per 1,000 Population

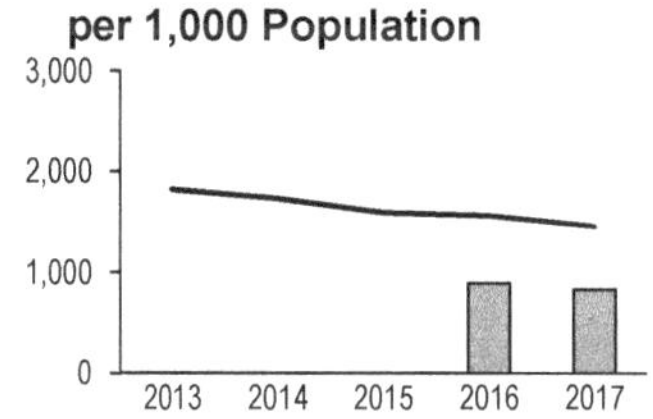

	2013	2014	2015	2016	2017
Raleigh				893	828
Average	1,823	1,732	1,592	1,560	1,457

Calls Dispatched per 1,000 Population

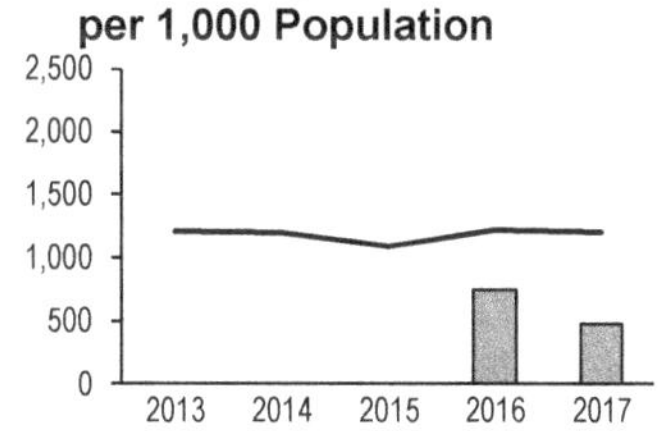

	2013	2014	2015	2016	2017
Raleigh				743	475
Average	1,207	1,195	1,090	1,217	1,200

E-911 Calls as a Percentage of All Incoming Calls

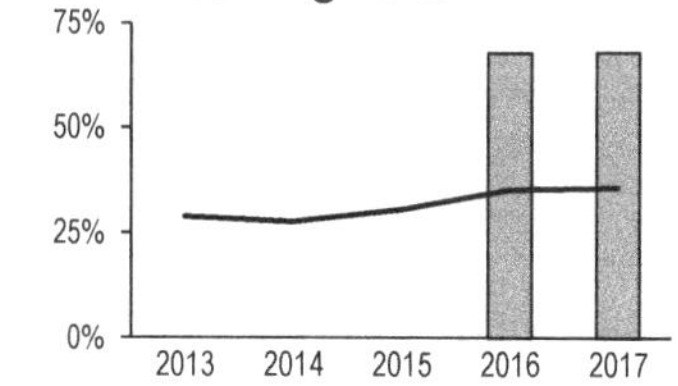

	2013	2014	2015	2016	2017
Raleigh				67.9%	68.0%
Average	28.9%	27.7%	30.6%	35.3%	35.7%

Efficiency Measures

Calls Answered per Telecommunicator

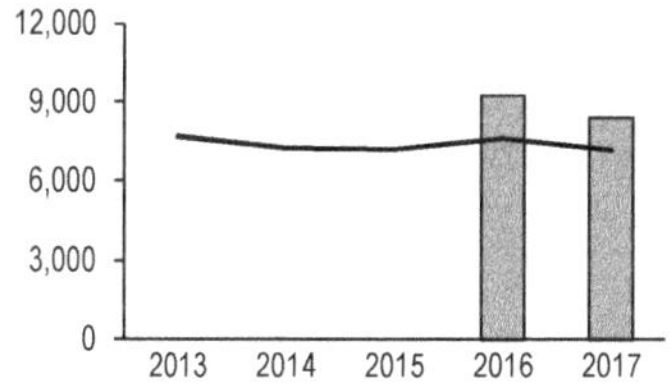

	2013	2014	2015	2016	2017
Raleigh				9,273	8,419
Average	7,694	7,244	7,204	7,614	7,178

Calls Dispatched per Telecommunicator

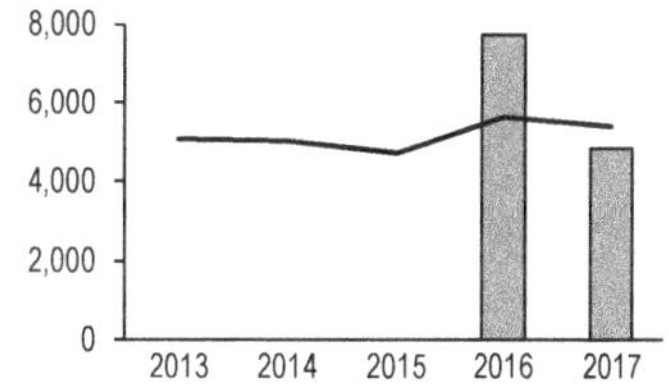

	2013	2014	2015	2016	2017
Raleigh				7,722	4,829
Average	5,084	5,033	4,724	5,628	5,410

Emergency Communications Cost per Call Dispatched

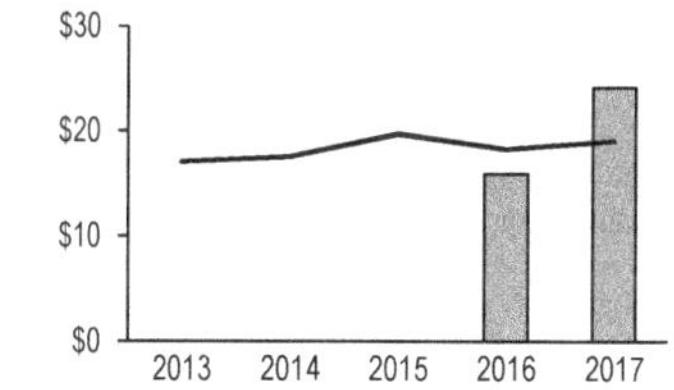

	2013	2014	2015	2016	2017
Raleigh				$15.88	$24.15
Average	$17.03	$17.52	$19.67	$18.23	$19.06

Effectiveness Measures

Number of Seconds from Initial Ring to Answer

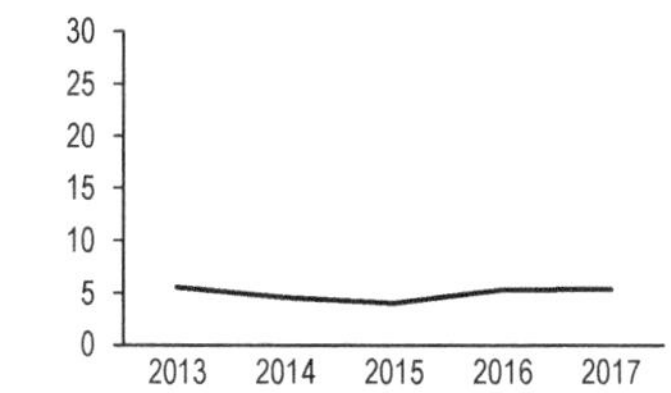

	2013	2014	2015	2016	2017
Raleigh					
Average	6	5	4	5	5

Percent of E-911 Calls Answered within Twenty Seconds

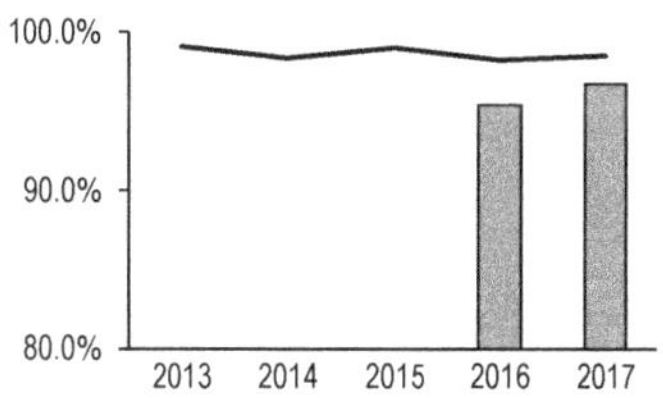

	2013	2014	2015	2016	2017
Raleigh				95.4%	96.7%
Average	99.1%	98.3%	99.0%	98.2%	98.5%

Average Time in Seconds from CAD Entry to Dispatch for Priority One Calls

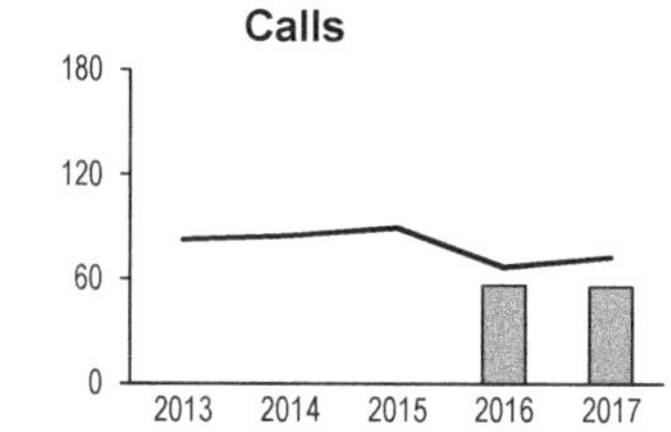

	2013	2014	2015	2016	2017
Raleigh				56	56
Average	82	84	89	67	72

Winston-Salem Emergency Communications

Fiscal Year 2016–17

Explanatory Information

Service Level and Delivery

Winston-Salem's Emergency Communications Division is part of the police department and handles 911 and non-emergency calls for police and fire. Calls received for EMS, the sheriff's office, county fire, and the highway patrol are transferred to the appropriate agency. All telecommunicators are hired and trained as call-takers and dispatchers.

The city owns the infrastructure but contracts with local vendors to provide telecommunications services. The City of Winston-Salem and Forsyth County implemented a voice radio system in October 2004. The Motorola ASTRO 800 MHz Trunked Simulcast system is made up of eight tower sites utilizing fifteen channels. The Winston-Salem Police Department uses a non-trunked 800 MHz system for the mobile data system, with one transmitter site using three channels.

Winston-Salem's center handled a total of 495,612 calls in the fiscal year, dispatching 253,021 calls. The city defines highest priority emergency calls as calls with a significant threat of imminent injury to persons or calls for crimes against persons that are in progress or have just occurred and the suspect is still there.

Winston-Salem received $454,636 in E-911 revenues to support system operations.

Conditions Affecting Service, Performance, and Costs

The Emergency Communications Division has been short fourteen operators from its authorized total during this fiscal year.

The system does not currently provide data on calls answered in the 20 second interval.

Municipal Profile

Population (OSBM 2016)	240,603
Land Area (Square Miles)	132.55
Persons per Square Mile	1,815
Median Family Income U.S. Census 2010	$51,491
County	Forsyth

Service Profile

Primary or Secondary Answering Point	Primary
Calls Dispatched	
Police	Yes
Fire	Yes
Other	No
FTE Positions	
Telecommunicators/Call-Takers	47.0
Other	2.0
Total Positions	49.0
Average Length of Service for Call-Takers	9.3 years
Total Incoming Calls	495,612
Total 911 Calls	224,012
Total Calls Dispatched	253,021
Outgoing Calls Other than Dispatch	71,297
Revenue from E-911 Fees	$454,636

Full Cost Profile

Cost Breakdown by Percentage	
Personal Services	72.7%
Operating Costs	22.9%
Capital Costs	4.4%
TOTAL	100.0%
Cost Breakdown in Dollars	
Personal Services	$3,758,322
Operating Costs	$1,184,249
Capital Costs	$227,388
TOTAL	$5,169,959

Winston-Salem — Emergency Communications

Key: Winston-Salem ▒ Benchmarking Average — Fiscal Years 2013 through 2017

Resource Measures

Emergency Communications Services Costs per Capita

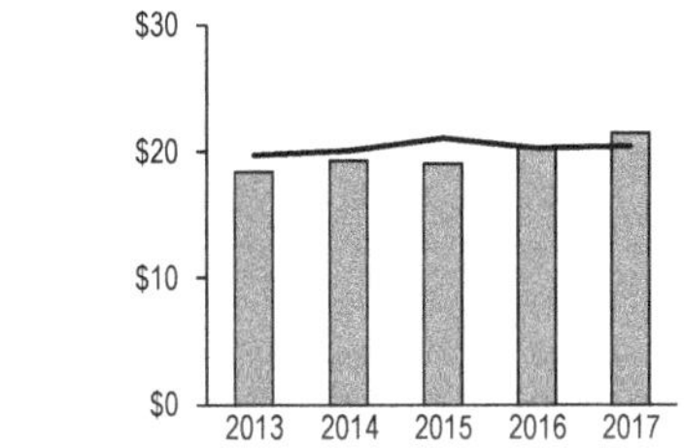

	2013	2014	2015	2016	2017
Winston-Salem	$18.44	$19.30	$19.07	$20.29	$21.49
Average	$19.68	$20.04	$21.03	$20.26	$20.40

Emergency Communications FTEs per 10,000 Population

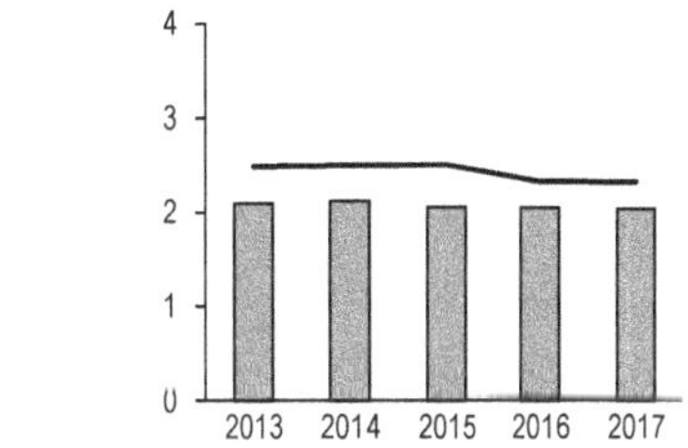

	2013	2014	2015	2016	2017
Winston-Salem	2.10	2.12	2.06	2.05	2.04
Average	2.49	2.51	2.51	2.33	2.32

Workload Measures

Total Calls Answered per 1,000 Population

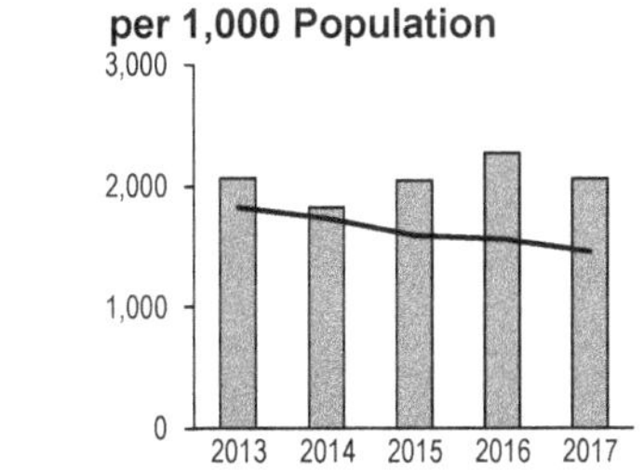

	2013	2014	2015	2016	2017
Winston-Salem	2,061	1,824	2,045	2,268	2,060
Average	1,823	1,732	1,592	1,560	1,457

Calls Dispatched per 1,000 Population

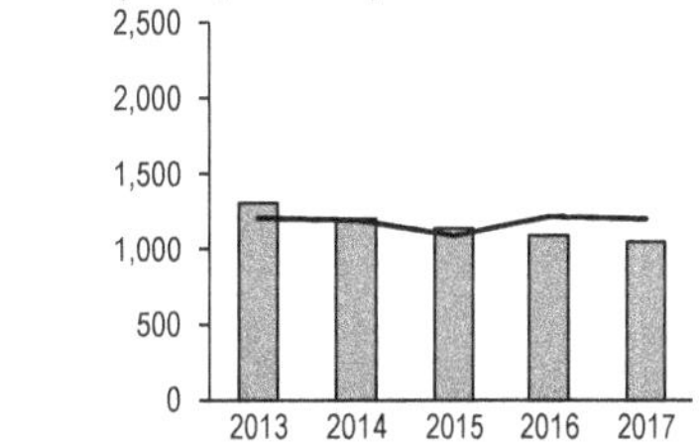

	2013	2014	2015	2016	2017
Winston-Salem	1,307	1,201	1,138	1,091	1,052
Average	1,207	1,195	1,090	1,217	1,200

E-911 Calls as a Percentage of All Incoming Calls

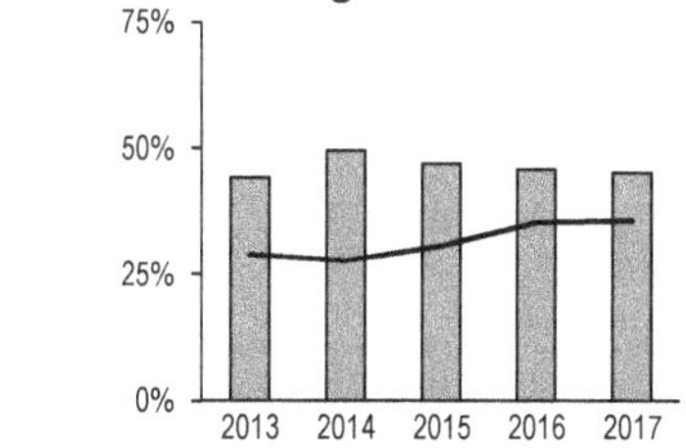

	2013	2014	2015	2016	2017
Winston-Salem	44.2%	49.5%	46.9%	45.8%	45.2%
Average	28.9%	27.7%	30.6%	35.3%	35.7%

Efficiency Measures

Calls Answered per Telecommunicator

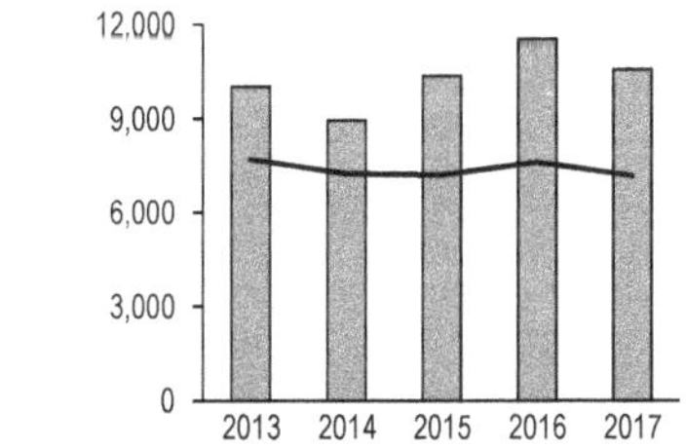

	2013	2014	2015	2016	2017
Winston-Salem	10,014	8,948	10,353	11,528	10,545
Average	7,694	7,244	7,204	7,614	7,178

Calls Dispatched per Telecommunicator

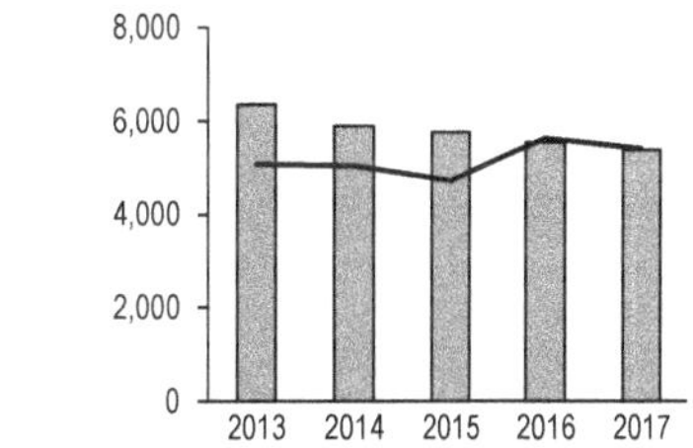

	2013	2014	2015	2016	2017
Winston-Salem	6,350	5,893	5,763	5,544	5,383
Average	5,084	5,033	4,724	5,628	5,410

Emergency Communications Cost per Call Dispatched

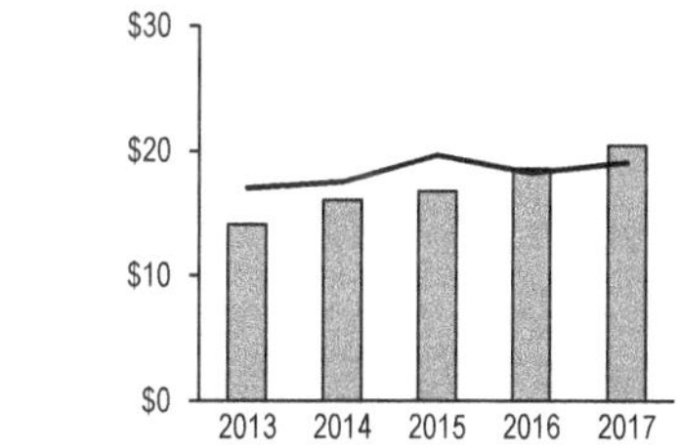

	2013	2014	2015	2016	2017
Winston-Salem	$14.11	$16.07	$16.75	$18.60	$20.43
Average	$17.03	$17.52	$19.67	$18.23	$19.06

Effectiveness Measures

Number of Seconds from Initial Ring to Answer

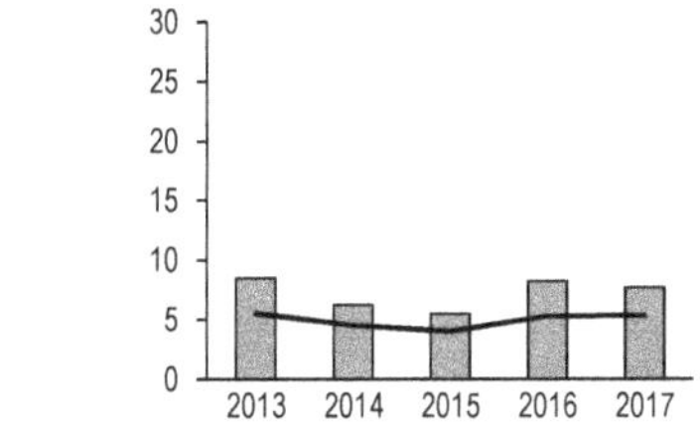

	2013	2014	2015	2016	2017
Winston-Salem	9	6	5	8	8
Average	6	5	4	5	5

Percent of E-911 Calls Answered within Twenty Seconds

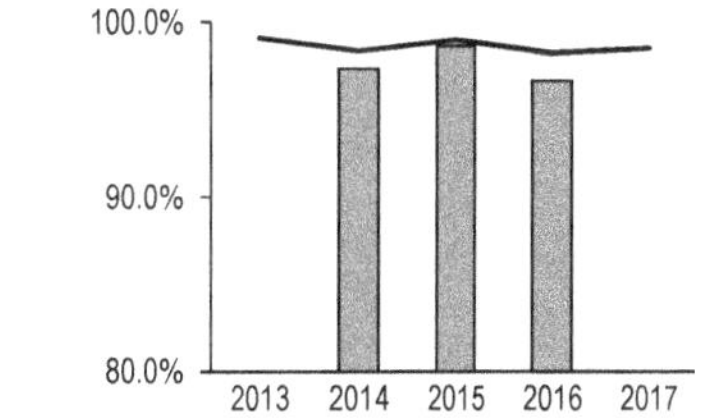

	2013	2014	2015	2016	2017
Winston-Salem		97.3%	98.6%	96.6%	
Average	99.1%	98.3%	99.0%	98.2%	98.5%

Average Time in Seconds from CAD Entry to Dispatch for Priority One Calls

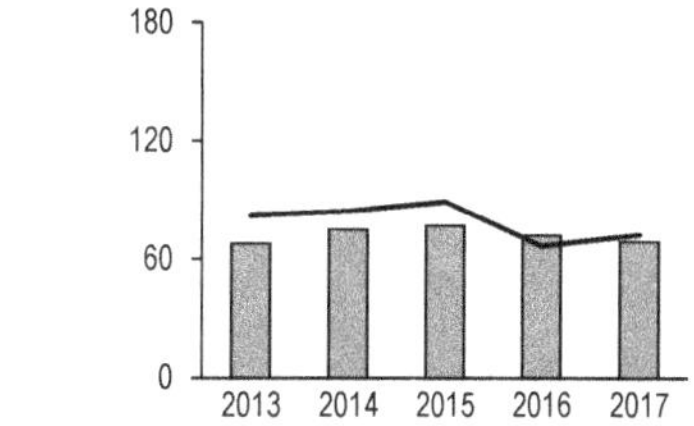

	2013	2014	2015	2016	2017
Winston-Salem	68	75	77	72	69
Average	82	84	89	67	72

SCHOOL OF GOVERNMENT
North Carolina Benchmarking Project

Performance and Cost Data

ASPHALT MAINTENANCE AND REPAIR

PERFORMANCE MEASURES FOR ASPHALT MAINTENANCE AND REPAIR

SERVICE DEFINITION

Asphalt Maintenance and Repair includes the activities of pothole repair, repaving, surface treatment, structure adjustments, milling, and utility cuts. It does not include reconstruction, handicap ramps, storm drainage, sidewalks, curb and gutter, right-of-way maintenance, street cleaning and sweeping, pavement marking, lane widening, unpaved street maintenance, or snow and ice removal.

NOTES ON PERFORMANCE MEASURES

1. Lane Miles Maintained

This measure refers to total lane miles that a municipality maintains, including state streets and municipal streets. The standard lane mile is 12 feet in width and 5,280 feet in length. Some jurisdictions do not track lane miles. Therefore, a methodology must be employed to calculate lane miles for participation.

2. Potholes and Utility Cuts per Lane Mile

Breaks in pavement due to potholes or to intentional utility cuts affect asphalt maintenance workload in the short term and long term because of breaks in the pavement integrity.

3. Cost of Road Treatment per Lane Mile

This is the cost of different types of asphalt treatment that a municipality may use to maintain or repair roads. Treatments include preservation work, such as crack or slurry sealing; resurfacing, which is typically one to two inches of new asphalt; and rehabilitation, which combines resurfacing with milling work to repair more damaged roads.

4. Cost of Asphalt Maintenance and Repair

Total cost of asphalt maintenance and repair represents the total direct, indirect, and capital costs taken from the accounting form. "Cost of maintenance" represents total cost from the accounting form minus cost of any treatment efforts by contract and municipal crews.

5. Percentage of Street Segments Rated 85 or Better and Below 45

Many municipalities use standard rating systems for assessing street pavement condition. These systems apply professionally determined criteria and embody scales that provide relatively objective ratings. These measures indicate the proportion of street segments that are rated 85 or better, which is good condition, and those rated below 45, which is poor condition, on the most recent street pavement assessment.

6. Percentage of Potholes Repaired within Twenty-Four Hours

Repair of potholes in a timely manner is important for maintaining pavement integrity and minimizing further damage to the street and vehicle traffic.

Asphalt Maintenance and Repair

Summary of Key Dimensions of Service

City or Town	Lane Miles Maintained	Total Lane Miles Treated by Type			Percent Treated			FTE Positions for City Staff
		Preservation	Resurfacing	Rehabilitation	Preservation	Resurfacing	Rehabilitation	
Apex	341.84	0.0	0.0	1.6	0.0%	0.0%	0.5%	14.5
Asheville	715.19	2.4	2.2	11.3	0.3%	0.3%	1.6%	17.1
Chapel Hill	333.40	0.0	0.8	11.8	0.0%	0.2%	3.5%	6.8
Charlotte	5,322.61	1.9	12.7	264.1	0.0%	0.2%	5.0%	119.0
Concord	711.91	0.0	31.3	28.5	0.0%	4.4%	4.0%	11.1
Goldsboro	162.74	0.0	4.8	2.4	0.0%	2.9%	1.5%	4.5
Greensboro	2,431.00	36.5	34.2	0.0	1.5%	1.4%	0.0%	51.0
Greenville	676.66	0.0	0.0	42.9	0.0%	0.0%	6.3%	6.0
Hickory	719.52	0.0	17.1	0.0	0.0%	2.4%	0.0%	7.0
High Point	1,321.00	0.0	8.0	23.3	0.0%	0.6%	1.8%	15.3
Raleigh	2,293.00	0.0	26.0	0.0	0.0%	1.1%	0.0%	48.0
Salisbury	345.50	1.3	1.0	5.8	0.4%	0.3%	1.7%	4.3
Wilson	695.37	12.5	6.0	0.0	1.8%	0.9%	0.0%	5.5
Winston-Salem	2,329.28	23.7	4.7	100.6	1.0%	0.2%	4.3%	44.5

EXPLANATORY FACTORS

These are factors that the project found affected asphalt maintenance and repair performance and cost in one or more of the municipalities:

Costs of materials in different cities
Weather conditions and terrain
Vehicle burden placed on streets
Age of street infrastructure
Depth of materials applied in repaving
Extent of contracting

Fiscal Year 2016–17

Explanatory Information

Service Level and Delivery

The Town of Apex's Streets Department was responsible for maintaining approximately 342 lane miles during the fiscal year. The Streets Department is part of the Public Works and Utilities Division for the town.

The town rehabilitated 1.6 lane miles during the year, which involves milling and resurfacing. This represented treatment of about 0.5 percent of total lane miles maintained.

The city reported that 56 percent of its lane miles were rated 85 or better on the pavement condition rating. The rating was performed by US Infrastructure of Carolina, Inc. using surveying in 2014.

The number of potholes reported for the fiscal year was 162. The town only repairs within one day those potholes which are considered large and dangerous. Smaller potholes are repaired when the streets crews can get to them.

The Streets Department also repaired thirty utility cuts and four maintenance patches.

Conditions Affecting Service, Performance, and Costs

Hurricane Matthew in Septermber 2016 had impacts on Apex which raised it to a Federal Emergency Management Agency (FEMA) event and response.

Municipal Profile

Population (OSBM 2016)	46,688
Land Area (Square Miles)	20.61
Persons per Square Mile	2,265
Topography	Flat; gently rolling
Climate	Temperate; little ice and snow

Service Profile

FTE Positions—Crews	12.00
FTE Positions—Other	2.50
Lane Miles Maintained	341.8
Lane Miles Treated	
Preservation	0.0
Resurfacing	0.0
Rehabilitation	1.6
TOTAL	1.6
Total Costs for All Treatment Types	$480,000
Potholes Repaired	162
Number of Utility Cuts	30
Number of Maintenance Patches (exclusive of potholes and utility cuts)	4
Average Cost per Ton of Hot Asphalt during Year	$112.87

Full Cost Profile

Cost Breakdown by Percentage	
Personal Services	16.8%
Operating Costs	80.3%
Capital Costs	2.9%
TOTAL	100.0%
Cost Breakdown in Dollars	
Personal Services	$283,586
Operating Costs	$1,358,606
Capital Costs	$49,566
TOTAL	$1,691,758

Key: Apex ▒ Benchmarking Average — Fiscal Years 2013 through 2017

Resource Measures

Asphalt Maintenance and Repair Services Costs per Capita

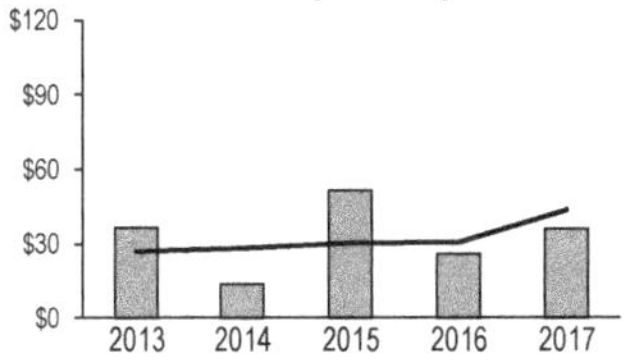

	2013	2014	2015	2016	2017
Apex	$36.72	$13.65	$51.70	$26.08	$36.24
Average	$27.05	$20.29	$30.38	$30.70	$43.66

Asphalt Maintenance and Repair FTEs per 10,000 Population

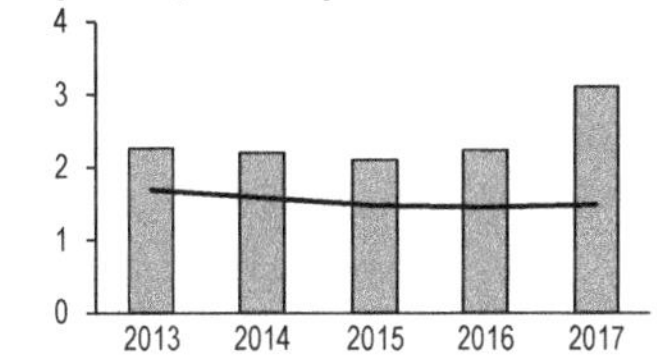

	2013	2014	2015	2016	2017
Apex	2.26	2.20	2.11	2.23	3.11
Average	1.70	1.60	1.49	1.46	1.49

Service Costs per Lane Mile of Road Maintained

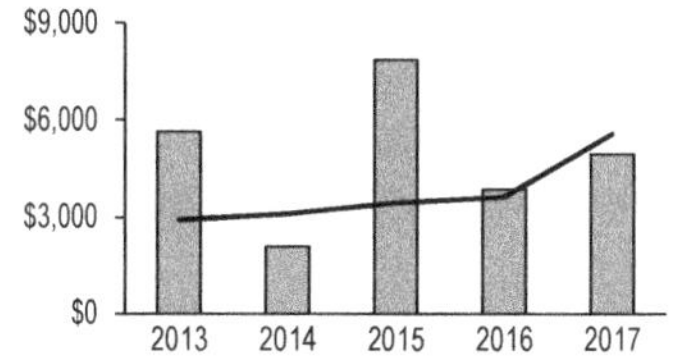

	2013	2014	2015	2016	2017
Apex	$5,643	$2,107	$7,868	$3,863	$4,949
Average	$2,923	$3,110	$3,452	$3,632	$5,582

Workload Measures

Number of Lane Miles Maintained per 1,000 Population

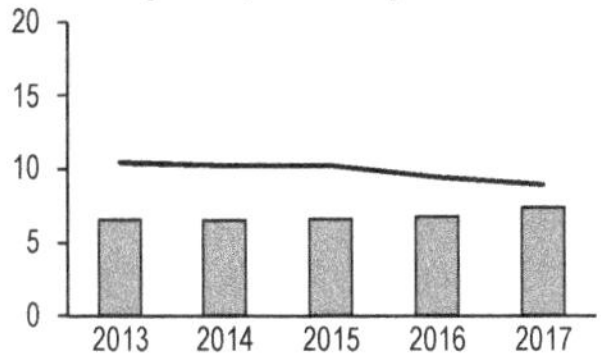

	2013	2014	2015	2016	2017
Apex	6.5	6.5	6.6	6.8	7.3
Average	10.4	10.2	10.2	9.5	8.9

Reported Potholes per Lane Mile Maintained

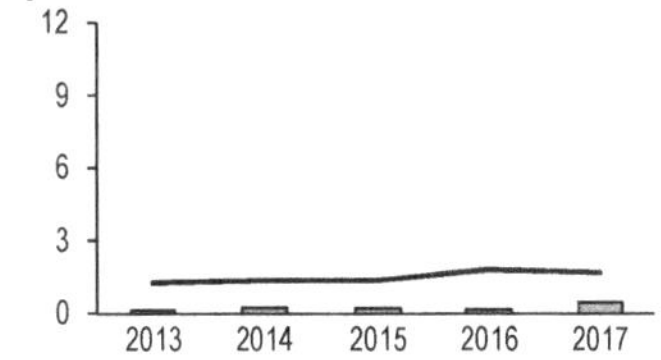

	2013	2014	2015	2016	2017
Apex	0.16	0.26	0.23	0.18	0.47
Average	1.26	1.35	1.34	1.78	1.67

Repaired Utility Cuts per Lane Mile Maintained

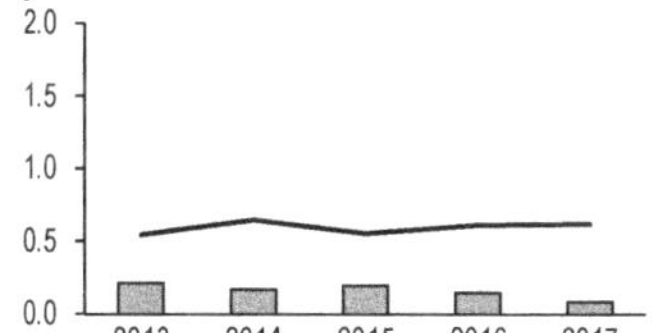

	2013	2014	2015	2016	2017
Apex	0.21	0.17	0.20	0.15	0.09
Average	0.54	0.64	0.55	0.61	0.62

Efficiency Measures

Cost of Maintenance per Lane Mile Maintained

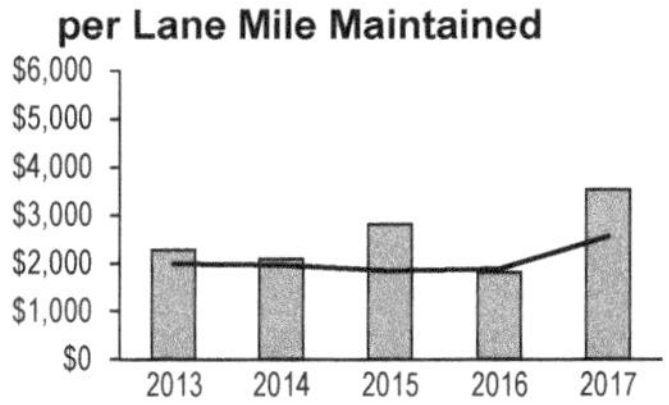

	2013	2014	2015	2016	2017
Apex	$2,287	$2,107	$2,827	$1,827	$3,545
Average	$2,005	$1,976	$1,852	$1,894	$2,564

Cost per Lane Mile for Preservation Treatment

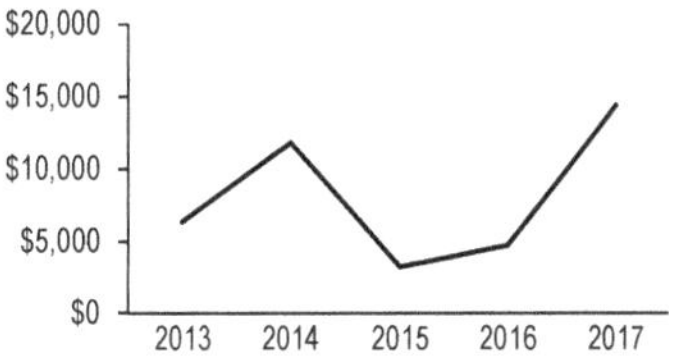

	2013	2014	2015	2016	2017
Apex					
Average	$6,371	$11,806	$3,214	$4,648	$14,370

Cost per Lane Mile for Resurfacing Treatment

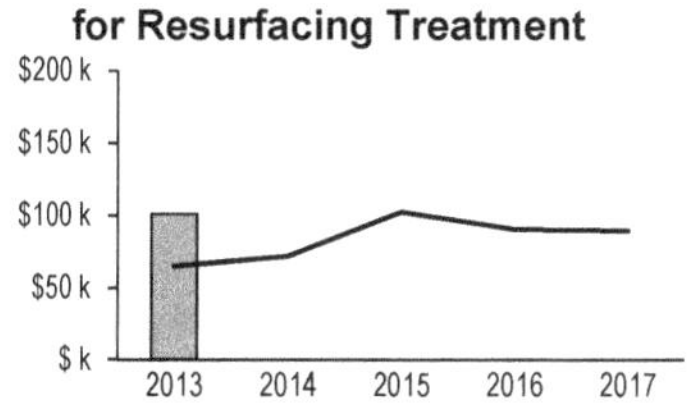

	2013	2014	2015	2016	2017
Apex	$101 k				
Average	$65 k	$72 k	$102 k	$90 k	$89 k

Cost per Lane Mile for Rehabilitation Treatment

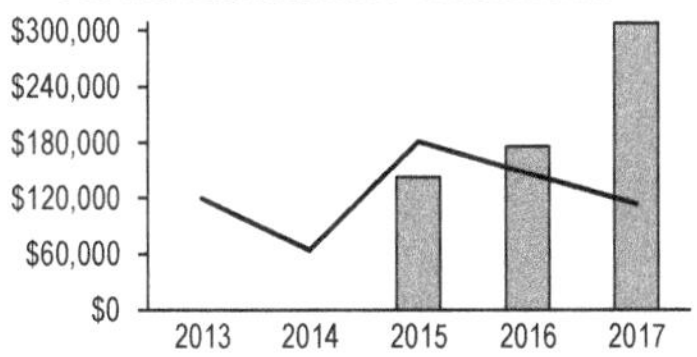

	2013	2014	2015	2016	2017
Apex			$142 k	$176 k	$308 k
Average	$119 k	$64 k	$181 k	$147 k	$113 k

Cost per Ton for Contract Resurfacing

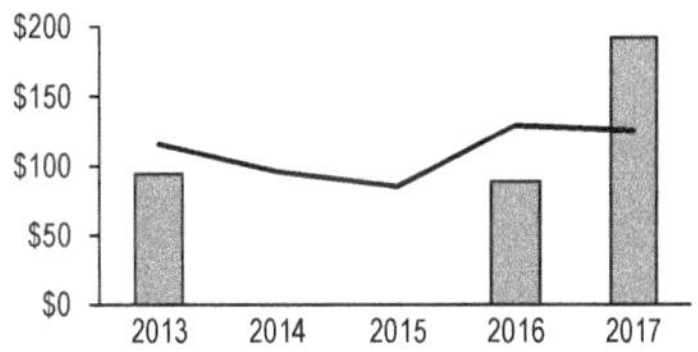

	2013	2014	2015	2016	2017
Apex	$94			$89	$192
Average	$116	$96	$86	$129	$125

Effectiveness Measures

Percent of Lane Miles Rated 85 or Better

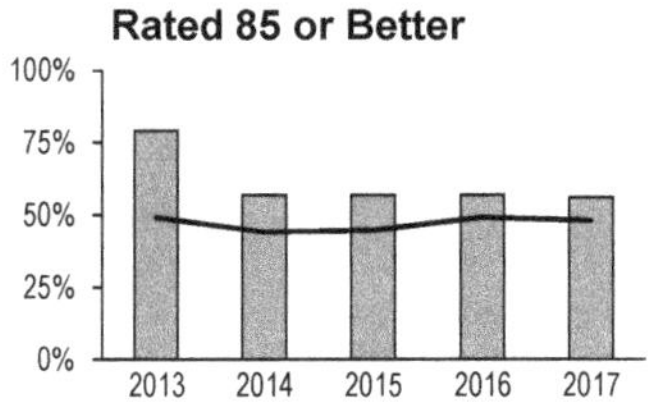

	2013	2014	2015	2016	2017
Apex	79%	57%	57%	57%	56%
Average	49%	44%	45%	49%	48%

Percent of Lane Miles Rated Below 45

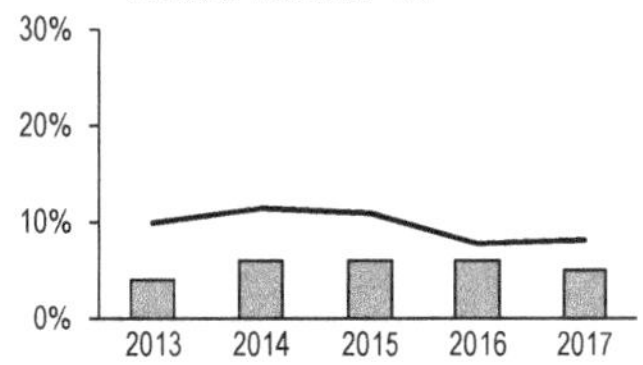

	2013	2014	2015	2016	2017
Apex	4.0%	6.0%	6.0%	6.0%	5.0%
Average	9.9%	11.4%	10.9%	7.7%	8.1%

Percentage of Potholes Repaired within 24 hours

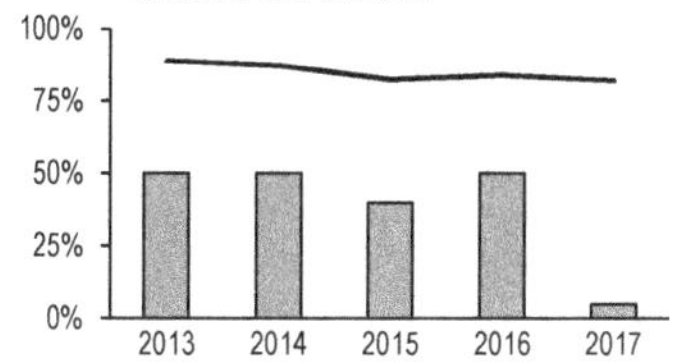

	2013	2014	2015	2016	2017
Apex	50%	50%	40%	50%	5%
Average	89%	87%	83%	84%	82%

Fiscal Year 2016–17

Explanatory Information

Service Level and Delivery

The City of Asheville was responsible for maintaining approximately 715 lane miles during the fiscal year. The city treated 15.8 lane miles during the year, equating to approximately 2.2 percent of total lane miles.

The city used contractors to use preservation treatment such as crack sealing or overlay methods on a total of 2.4 lane miles. Contract crews also resurfaced 2.2 lane miles during the year. Contract crews also did rehabilitation work on 9.13 lane miles, which includes milling and resurfacing. City crews also completed 2.13 lane miles of rehabilitation work as well.

The city reported that ten percent of its lane miles were rated 85 or above on its most recent street pavement condition rating. This rating was done by in-house staff using the Institute for Transportation Research and Education (ITRE) system.

The number of potholes reported for the year was 3,718. The percentage of potholes repaired within twenty-four hours was approximately 99 percent.

The city has a permitting system for any utility cuts that must be made either by city or contractor crews. A total of 1,697 utility cuts were repaired during the year.

Conditions Affecting Service, Performance, and Costs

Due to the somewhat harsher mountain weather in Asheville compared to the other benchmarking partners, problems with pavement, such as potholes, tend to be more common. The winter during the fiscal year was harsher than normal leading to more pavement damage than normally expected.

Municipal Profile

Population (OSBM 2016)	91,929
Land Area (Square Miles)	45.52
Persons per Square Mile	2,019
Topography	Hill, mountains
Climate	Moderate; ice and snow

Service Profile

FTE Positions—Crews	15.00
FTE Positions—Other	2.09
Lane Miles Maintained	715.2
Lane Miles Treated	
Preservation	2.4
Resurfacing	2.2
Rehabilitation	11.3
TOTAL	15.8
Total Costs for All Treatment Types	$2,427,596
Potholes Repaired	3,718
Number of Utility Cuts	1,697
Number of Maintenance Patches (exclusive of potholes and utility cuts)	11
Average Cost per Ton of Hot Asphalt during Year	$85.00

Full Cost Profile

Cost Breakdown by Percentage	
Personal Services	24.9%
Operating Costs	65.7%
Capital Costs	9.4%
TOTAL	100.0%
Cost Breakdown in Dollars	
Personal Services	$1,333,792
Operating Costs	$3,510,549
Capital Costs	$502,989
TOTAL	$5,347,330

Asheville

Asphalt Maintenance and Repair

Key: Asheville ▒ Benchmarking Average — Fiscal Years 2013 through 2017

Resource Measures

Asphalt Maintenance and Repair Services Costs per Capita

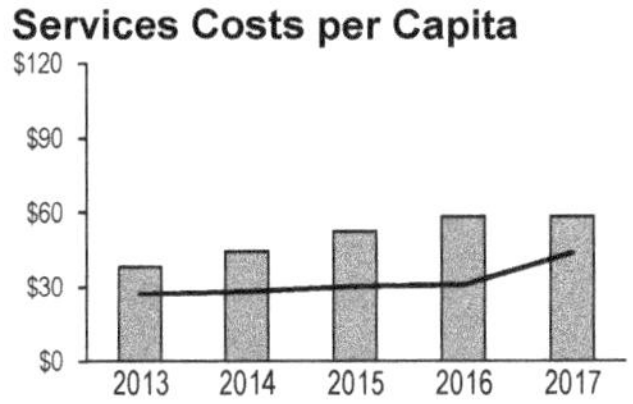

	2013	2014	2015	2016	2017
Asheville	$38.09	$44.15	$52.27	$58.07	$58.17
Average	$27.05	$28.29	$30.38	$30.70	$43.00

Asphalt Maintenance and Repair FTEs per 10,000 Population

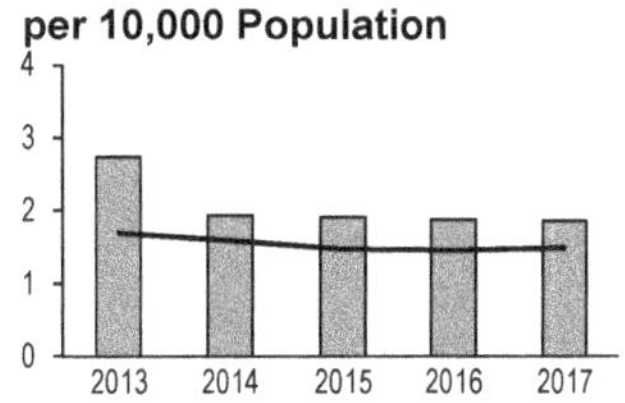

	2013	2014	2015	2016	2017
Asheville	2.74	1.94	1.91	1.88	1.86
Average	1.70	1.60	1.49	1.46	1.49

Service Costs per Lane Mile of Road Maintained

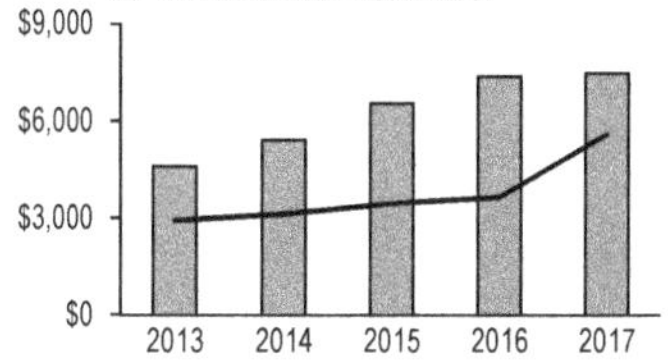

	2013	2014	2015	2016	2017
Asheville	$4,605	$5,426	$6,540	$7,390	$7,477
Average	$2,923	$3,110	$3,452	$3,632	$5,582

Workload Measures

Number of Lane Miles Maintained per 1,000 Population

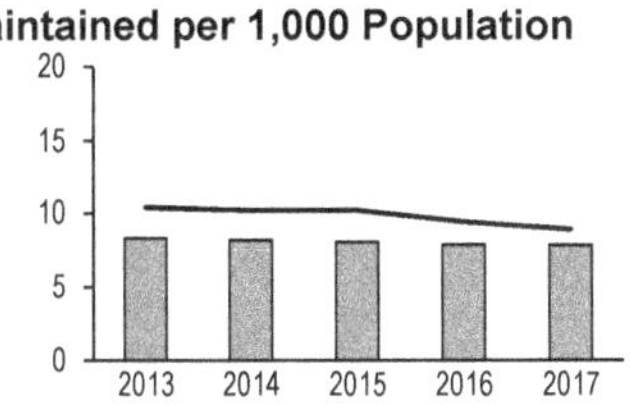

	2013	2014	2015	2016	2017
Asheville	8.3	8.1	8.0	7.9	7.8
Average	10.4	10.2	10.2	9.5	8.9

Reported Potholes per Lane Mile Maintained

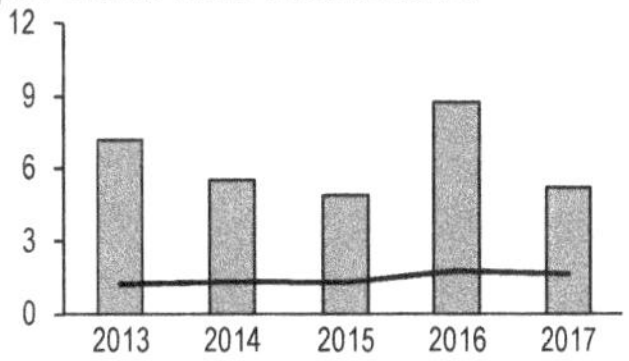

	2013	2014	2015	2016	2017
Asheville	7.14	5.52	4.88	8.72	5.20
Average	1.26	1.35	1.34	1.78	1.67

Repaired Utility Cuts per Lane Mile Maintained

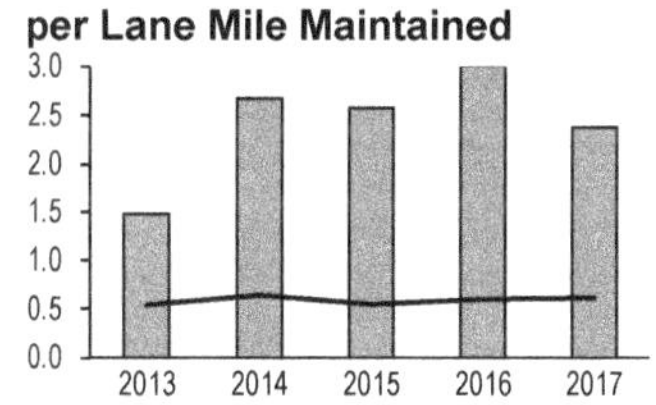

	2013	2014	2015	2016	2017
Asheville	1.47	2.67	2.57	3.01	2.37
Average	0.54	0.64	0.55	0.61	0.62

Efficiency Measures

Cost of Maintenance per Lane Mile Maintained

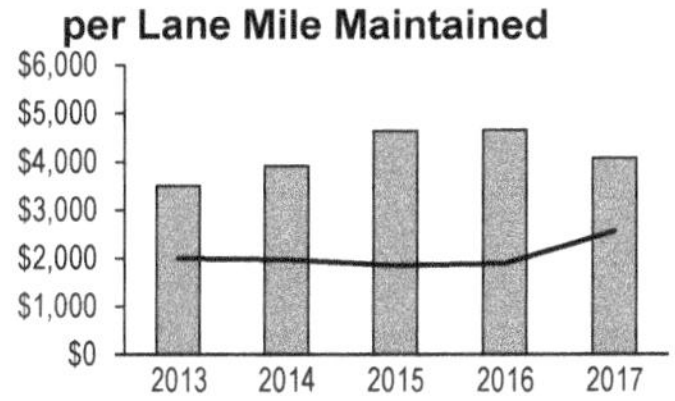

	2013	2014	2015	2016	2017
Asheville	$3,506	$3,911	$4,635	$4,664	$4,082
Average	$2,005	$1,976	$1,852	$1,894	$2,564

Cost per Lane Mile for Preservation Treatment

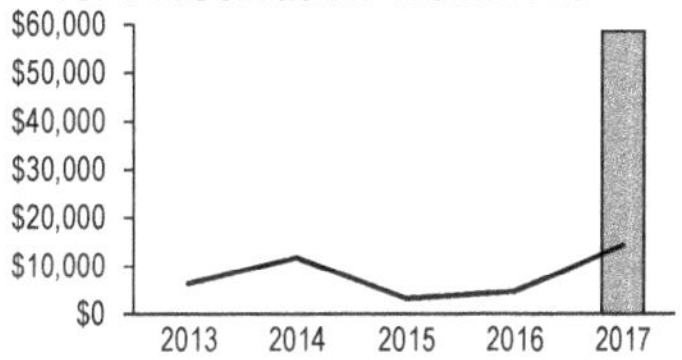

	2013	2014	2015	2016	2017
Asheville					$58,597
Average	$6,371	$11,806	$3,214	$4,648	$14,370

Cost per Lane Mile for Resurfacing Treatment

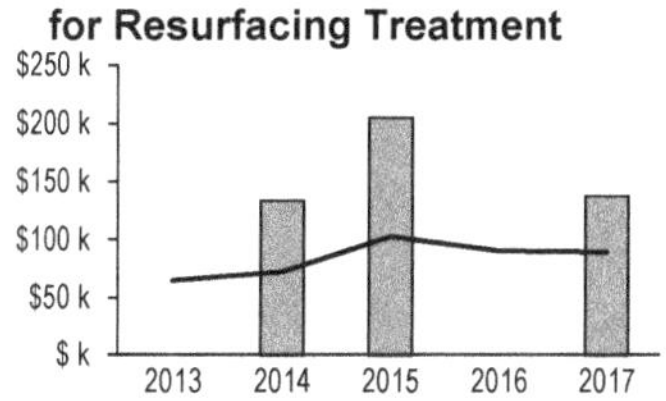

	2013	2014	2015	2016	2017
Asheville		$134 k	$205 k		$138 k
Average	$65 k	$72 k	$102 k	$90 k	$89 k

Cost per Lane Mile for Rehabilitation Treatment

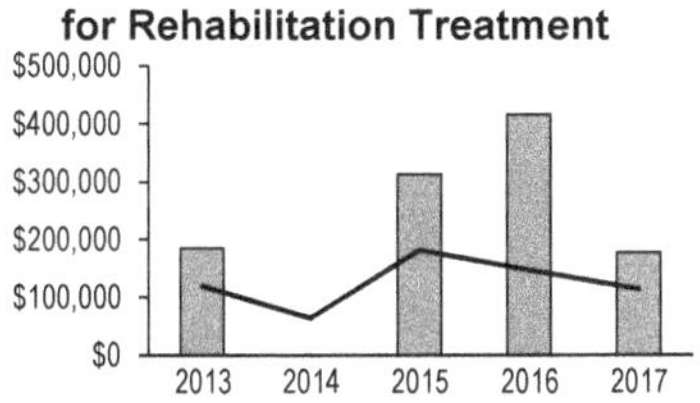

	2013	2014	2015	2016	2017
Asheville	$184 k		$313 k	$416 k	$176 k
Average	$119 k	$64 k	$181 k	$147 k	$113 k

Cost per Ton for Contract Resurfacing

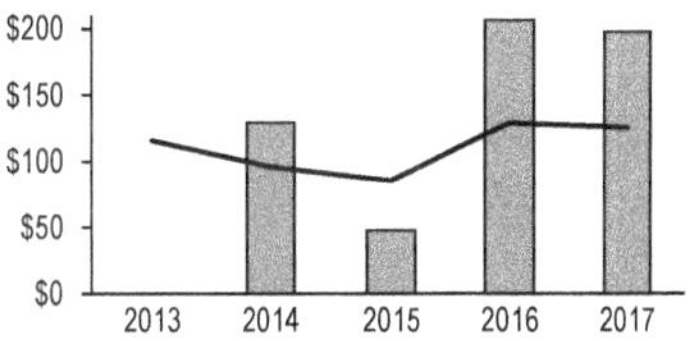

	2013	2014	2015	2016	2017
Asheville		$130	$48	$206	$197
Average	$116	$96	$86	$129	$125

Effectiveness Measures

Percent of Lane Miles Rated 85 or Better

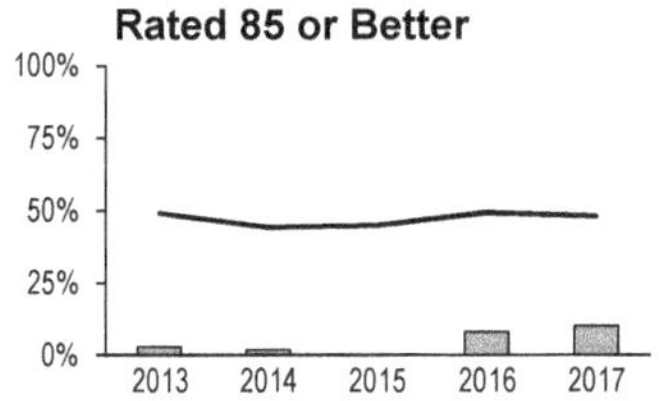

	2013	2014	2015	2016	2017
Asheville	3%	2%	0%	8%	10%
Average	49%	44%	45%	49%	48%

Percent of Lane Miles Rated Below 45

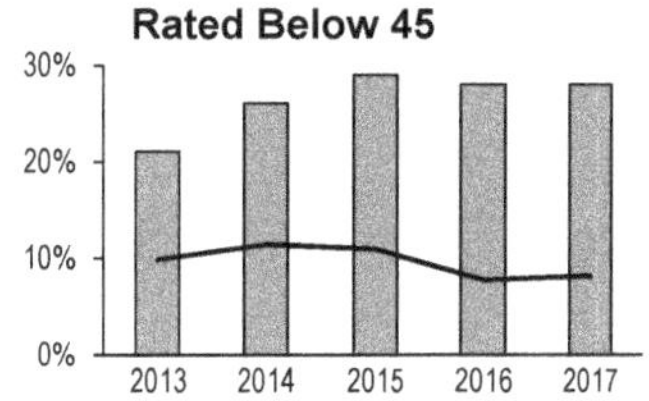

	2013	2014	2015	2016	2017
Asheville	21.0%	26.0%	29.0%	28.0%	28.0%
Average	9.9%	11.4%	10.9%	7.7%	8.1%

Percentage of Potholes Repaired within 24 hours

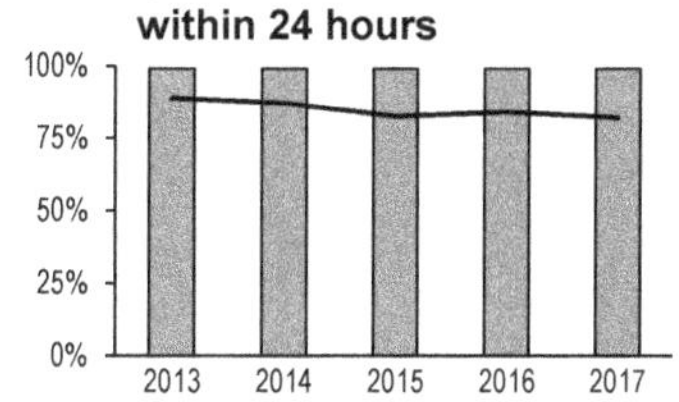

	2013	2014	2015	2016	2017
Asheville	99%	99%	99%	99%	99%
Average	89%	87%	83%	84%	82%

Fiscal Year 2016–17

Explanatory Information

Service Level and Delivery

Asphalt maintenance is performed by the Town of Chapel Hill Streets and Construction Services Division of the Public Works Department. The Town provides services in asphalt maintenance, sidewalk maintenance, storm debris cleanup, gravel road maintenance, snow and ice removal, and cleanup following special events. During the fiscal year the town was responsible for maintaining approximately 333 lane miles. During the year 12.6 lane miles were treated or about 3.8 percent of total lane miles.

Contract crews treated a total of 12.6 miles with 0.8 miles being just resurfacing and a further 11.8 lane miles being rehabilitation work, which requires milling before resurfacing. Contract crews used a total of 10,164 tons of asphalt with an average depth of 1.75 inches.

The town reported that 48 percent of its lane miles rated 85 or above on its most recent pavement condition rating conducted in 2016. The roads were rated by US Infrastructure of Carolina using the system relying on the Institute for Transportation Research and Education (ITRE) degradation curves.

The number of potholes reported for the year was sixty-three. Permit holders repaired sixty-five utility cuts during the year. A permit is required for any non-town entity cutting inside the right-of-way. The permit holder is responsible for all repairs. Because one permit can involve multiple cuts, the actual number of cuts is higher than the number listed. The Streets Inspector monitors the work and bills the responsible party. The Public Works Engineering Division inspects larger projects involving a water or sewer line replacement.

Conditions Affecting Service, Performance, and Costs

The Town of Chapel Hill began participation in the benchmarking project in July 2015, with FY 2014–15 being the first reporting year.

Though the FY 2015–16 Chapel Hill budget included $585,222 for annual resurfacing work, this funding was encumbered and carried forward into FY 2016–17 and is not reflected in the costs for this service area for that report year. A total of 5.5 lane miles were resurfaced using FY 2015–16 funds but at the beginning of FY 2016–17. These costs were reported in this year's benchmarking report.

Municipal Profile

Population (OSBM 2016)	59,852
Land Area (Square Miles)	21.21
Persons per Square Mile	2,822
Topography	Flat; gently rolling
Climate	Temperate; little ice and snow

Service Profile

FTE Positions—Crews	5.20
FTE Positions—Other	1.60
Lane Miles Maintained	333.4
Lane Miles Treated	
Preservation	0.0
Resurfacing	0.8
Rehabilitation	11.8
TOTAL	12.6
Total Costs for All Treatment Types	$1,528,127
Potholes Repaired	63
Number of Utility Cuts	65
Number of Maintenance Patches (exclusive of potholes and utility cuts)	NA
Registered Vehicles	
Registered Vehicles/Square Mile	
Average Cost per Ton of Hot Asphalt during Year	$60.00

Full Cost Profile

Cost Breakdown by Percentage	
Personal Services	17.0%
Operating Costs	72.8%
Capital Costs	10.2%
TOTAL	100.0%
Cost Breakdown in Dollars	
Personal Services	$453,548
Operating Costs	$1,939,607
Capital Costs	$271,293
TOTAL	$2,664,448

Chapel Hill — Asphalt Maintenance and Repair

Key: Chapel Hill ▒ Benchmarking Average — Fiscal Years 2013 through 2017

Resource Measures

Asphalt Maintenance and Repair Services Costs per Capita

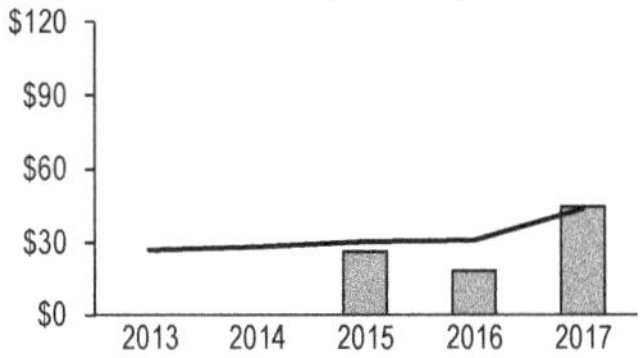

	2013	2014	2015	2016	2017
Chapel Hill			$26.21	$18.14	$44.52
Average	$27.05	$28.29	$30.38	$30.70	$43.66

Asphalt Maintenance and Repair FTEs per 10,000 Population

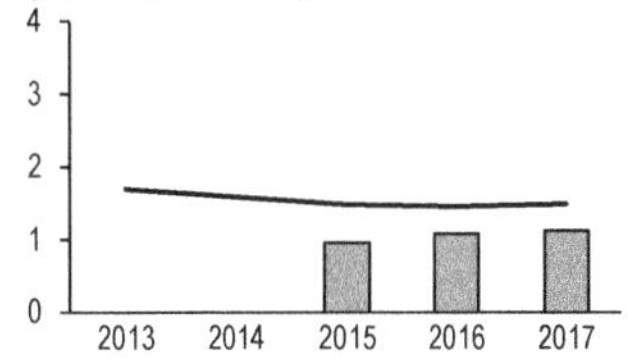

	2013	2014	2015	2016	2017
Chapel Hill			0.96	1.09	1.14
Average	1.70	1.60	1.49	1.46	1.49

Service Costs per Lane Mile of Road Maintained

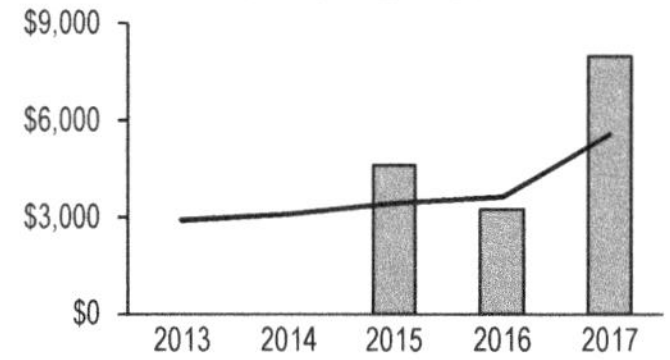

	2013	2014	2015	2016	2017
Chapel Hill			$4,615	$3,242	$7,992
Average	$2,923	$3,110	$3,452	$3,632	$5,582

Workload Measures

Number of Lane Miles Maintained per 1,000 Population

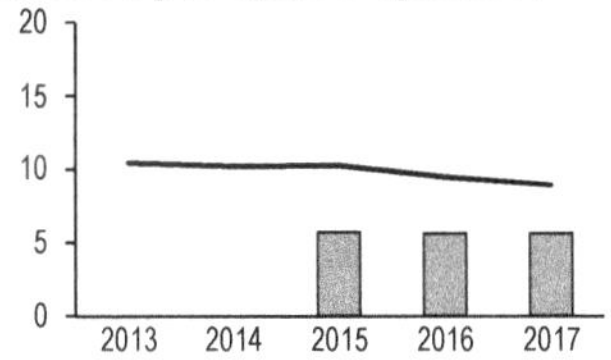

	2013	2014	2015	2016	2017
Chapel Hill			5.7	5.6	5.6
Average	10.4	10.2	10.2	9.5	8.9

Reported Potholes per Lane Mile Maintained

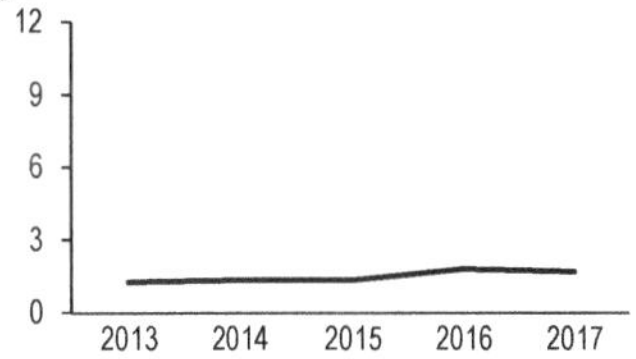

	2013	2014	2015	2016	2017
Chapel Hill					
Average	1.26	1.35	1.34	1.78	1.67

Repaired Utility Cuts per Lane Mile Maintained

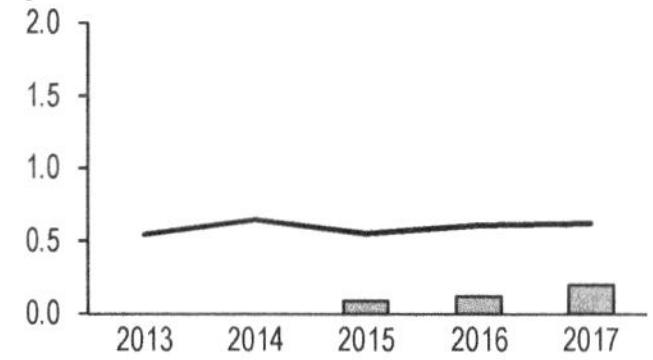

	2013	2014	2015	2016	2017
Chapel Hill			0.09	0.12	0.19
Average	0.54	0.64	0.55	0.61	0.62

Efficiency Measures

Cost of Maintenance per Lane Mile Maintained

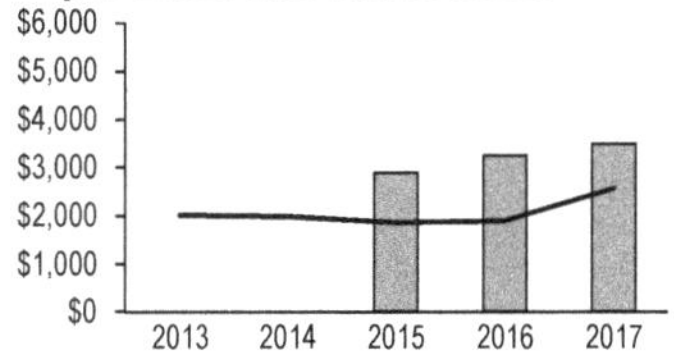

	2013	2014	2015	2016	2017
Chapel Hill			$2,880	$3,242	$3,479
Average	$2,005	$1,976	$1,852	$1,894	$2,564

Cost per Lane Mile for Preservation Treatment

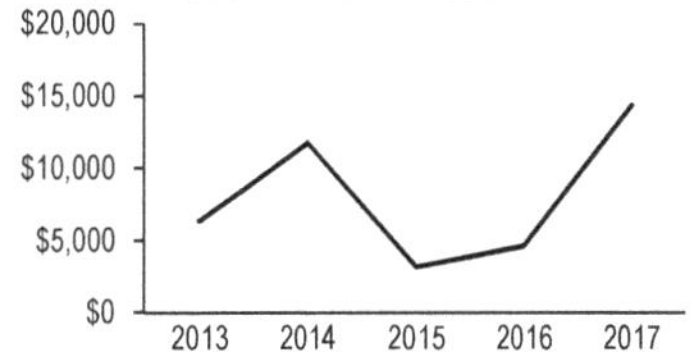

	2013	2014	2015	2016	2017
Chapel Hill					
Average	$6,371	$11,806	$3,214	$4,648	$14,370

Cost per Lane Mile for Resurfacing Treatment

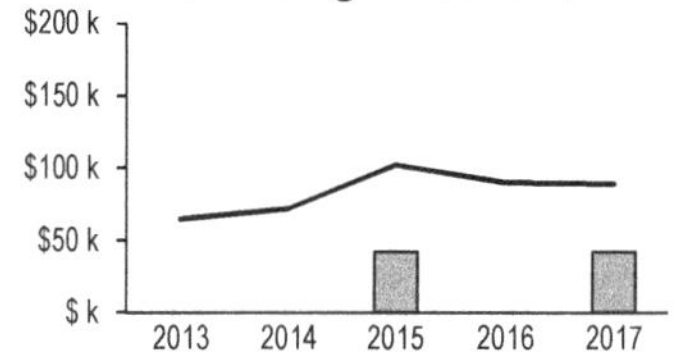

	2013	2014	2015	2016	2017
Chapel Hill			$42 k		$42 k
Average	$65 k	$72 k	$102 k	$90 k	$89 k

Cost per Lane Mile for Rehabilitation Treatment

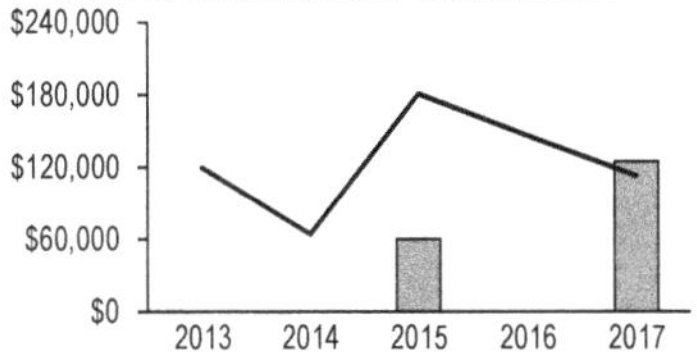

	2013	2014	2015	2016	2017
Chapel Hill			$60 k		$125 k
Average	$119 k	$64 k	$181 k	$147 k	$113 k

Cost per Ton for Contract Resurfacing

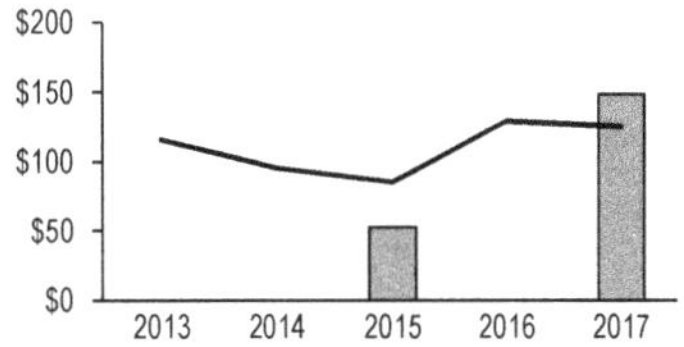

	2013	2014	2015	2016	2017
Chapel Hill			$52		$148
Average	$116	$96	$86	$129	$125

Effectiveness Measures

Percent of Lane Miles Rated 85 or Better

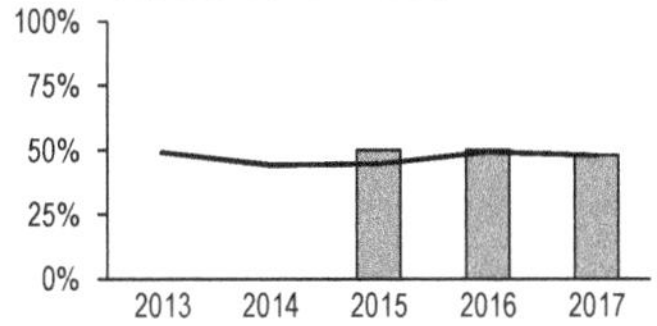

	2013	2014	2015	2016	2017
Chapel Hill			50%	50%	48%
Average	49%	44%	45%	49%	48%

Percent of Lane Miles Rated Below 45

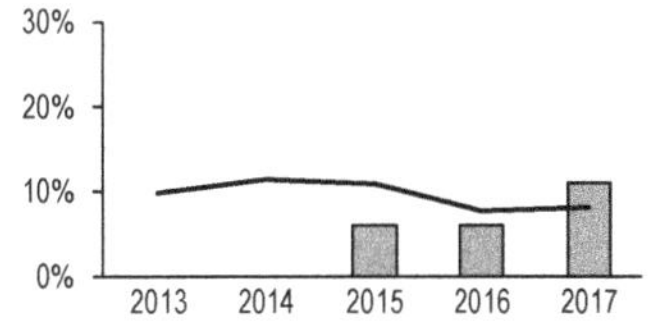

	2013	2014	2015	2016	2017
Chapel Hill			6.0%	6.0%	11.0%
Average	9.9%	11.4%	10.9%	7.7%	8.1%

Percentage of Potholes Repaired within 24 hours

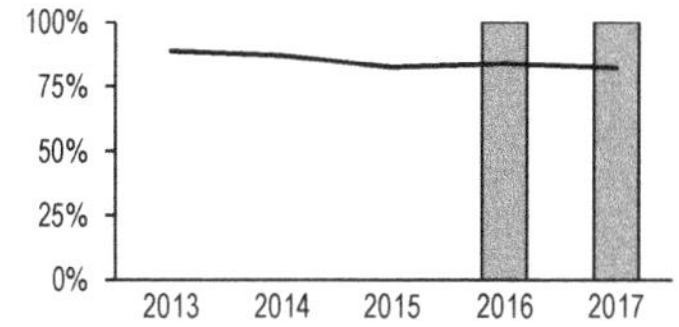

	2013	2014	2015	2016	2017
Chapel Hill				100%	100%
Average	89%	87%	83%	84%	82%

Fiscal Year 2016–17

Explanatory Information

Service Level and Delivery
The City of Charlotte Street Maintenance Division provides service in the areas of maintenance and repair of street drainage structures; sidewalks; storm debris clean-up; and specialty repair items such as brick walls, decorative pavers, fences, and guardrails. During the fiscal year, the city was responsible for maintaining approximately 5,323 lane miles and treated 278.7 lane miles, equating to approximately 5.2 percent of total lane miles.

Of the treatment work done during the year, 1.9 lane miles received preservation work, completed by city crews, such as crack sealing or thin overlays. Resurfacing work covered 12.7 lane miles and was done by contractors. Additionally, 244.3 lane miles were rehabilitated by contractors with milling followed by resurfacing. Contractors used a total of 162,810 tons of asphalt across the resurfacing and rehabilitation projects applied at an average depth of 1.14 inches. City crews completed a further 19.78 lane miles of rehabilitation work as well using 12,877 tons of asphalt applied at an average depth of 1.5 inches.

The city reported that 56.81 percent of its lane miles rated 85 or above on its most recent pavement condition rating conducted in 2017.

The number of potholes reported for the fiscal year was 1,183. The percentage of potholes repaired within twenty-four hours was 84 percent. A total of 3,821 utility cuts were also repaired during the year by contractors and the Street Maintenance Division.

Conditions Affecting Service, Performance, and Costs
Charlotte did not participate in the Benchmarking Project during FY 2014–15. No data are available for that year.

The Street Maintenance Division conducted a pilot in-house paving program during the fiscal year. This program resulted in additional paving expenses and personnel costs during the year.

Municipal Profile

Population (OSBM 2016)	830,258
Land Area (Square Miles)	305.48
Persons per Square Mile	2,718
Topography	Flat; gently rolling
Climate	Temperate; little ice and snow

Service Profile

FTE Positions—Crews	101.00
FTE Positions—Other	18.00
Lane Miles Maintained	5,322.6
Lane Miles Treated	
Preservation	1.9
Resurfacing	12.7
Rehabilitation	264.1
TOTAL	278.7
Total Costs for All Treatment Types	$18,283,947
Potholes Repaired	1,183
Number of Utility Cuts	3,821
Number of Maintenance Patches (exclusive of potholes and utility cuts)	NA
Registered Vehicles	
Registered Vehicles/Square Mile	
Average Cost per Ton of Hot Asphalt during Year	$45.05

Full Cost Profile

Cost Breakdown by Percentage	
Personal Services	18.1%
Operating Costs	69.2%
Capital Costs	12.7%
TOTAL	100.0%
Cost Breakdown in Dollars	
Personal Services	$6,463,284
Operating Costs	$24,714,695
Capital Costs	$4,529,099
TOTAL	$35,707,078

Key: Charlotte ▒ Benchmarking Average — Fiscal Years 2013 through 2017

Resource Measures

Asphalt Maintenance and Repair Services Costs per Capita

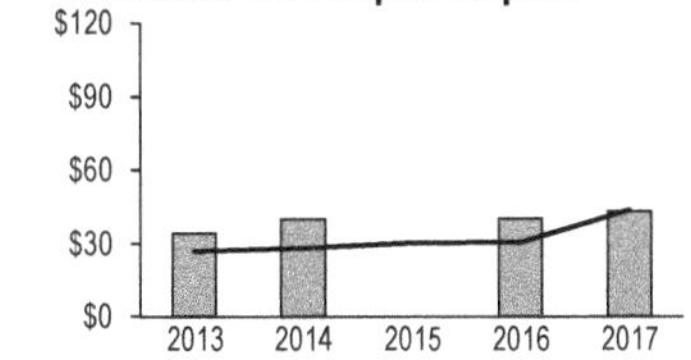

	2013	2014	2015	2016	2017
Charlotte	$34.07	$39.98		$40.02	$43.01
Average	$27.05	$28.20	$30.38	$30.70	$43.66

Asphalt Maintenance and Repair FTEs per 10,000 Population

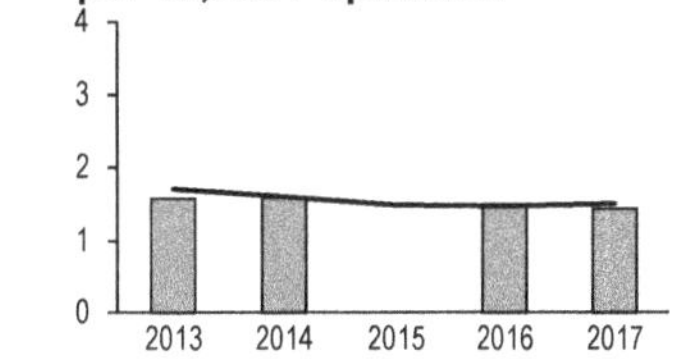

	2013	2014	2015	2016	2017
Charlotte	1.58	1.58		1.50	1.43
Average	1.70	1.60	1.49	1.46	1.49

Service Costs per Lane Mile of Road Maintained

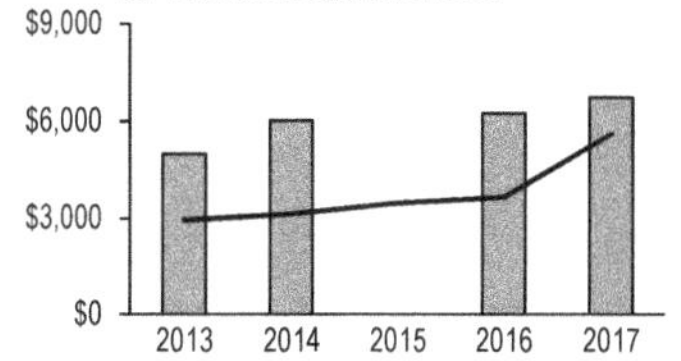

	2013	2014	2015	2016	2017
Charlotte	$4,957	$5,993		$6,199	$6,709
Average	$2,923	$3,110	$3,452	$3,632	$5,582

Workload Measures

Number of Lane Miles Maintained per 1,000 Population

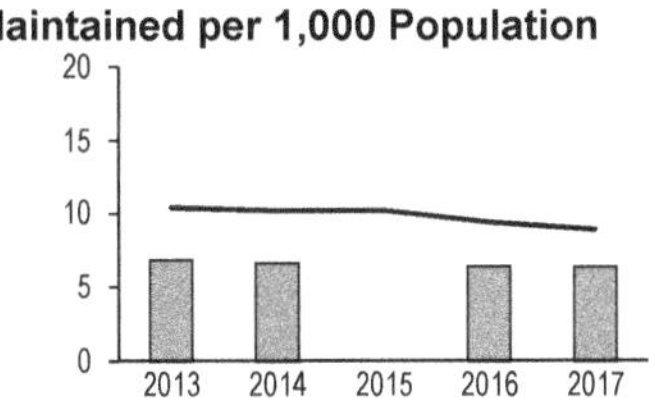

	2013	2014	2015	2016	2017
Charlotte	6.9	6.7		6.5	6.4
Average	10.4	10.2	10.2	9.5	8.9

Reported Potholes per Lane Mile Maintained

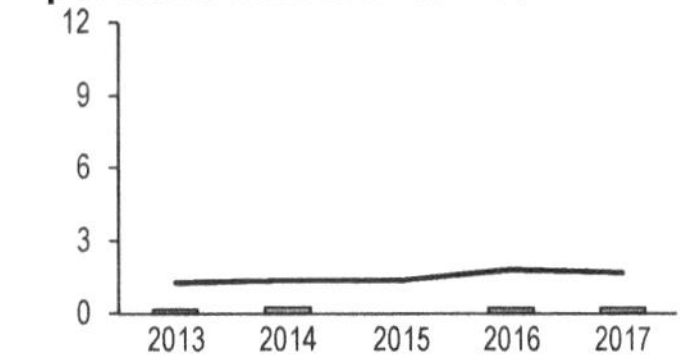

	2013	2014	2015	2016	2017
Charlotte	0.16	0.23		0.22	0.22
Average	1.26	1.35	1.34	1.78	1.67

Repaired Utility Cuts per Lane Mile Maintained

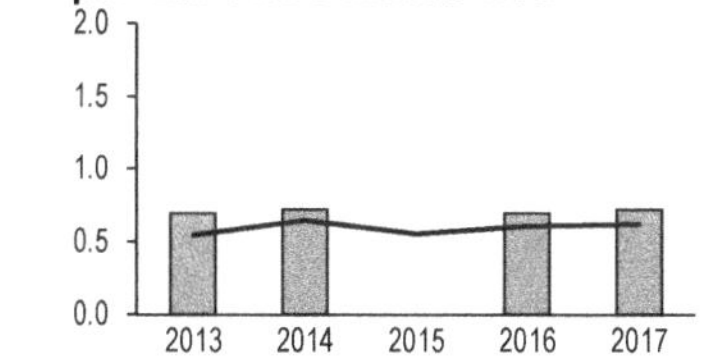

	2013	2014	2015	2016	2017
Charlotte	0.69	0.72		0.69	0.72
Average	0.54	0.64	0.55	0.61	0.62

Efficiency Measures

Cost of Maintenance per Lane Mile Maintained

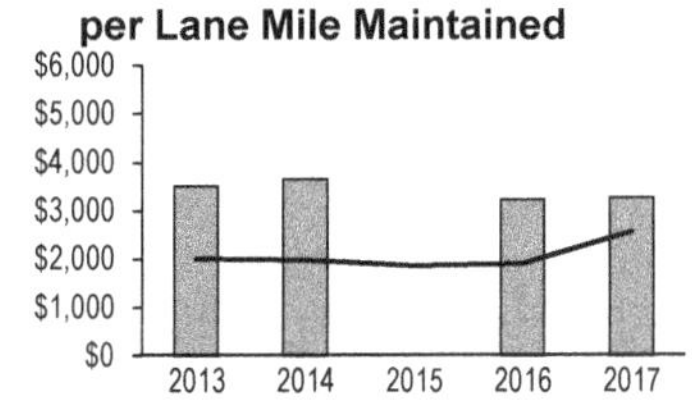

	2013	2014	2015	2016	2017
Charlotte	$3,517	$3,604		$3,237	$3,273
Average	$2,005	$1,976	$1,852	$1,894	$2,564

Cost per Lane Mile for Preservation Treatment

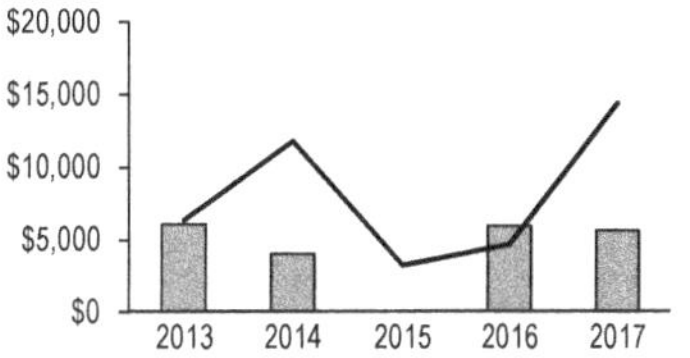

	2013	2014	2015	2016	2017
Charlotte	$6,042	$4,024		$5,915	$5,624
Average	$6,371	$11,806	$3,214	$4,648	$14,370

Cost per Lane Mile for Resurfacing Treatment

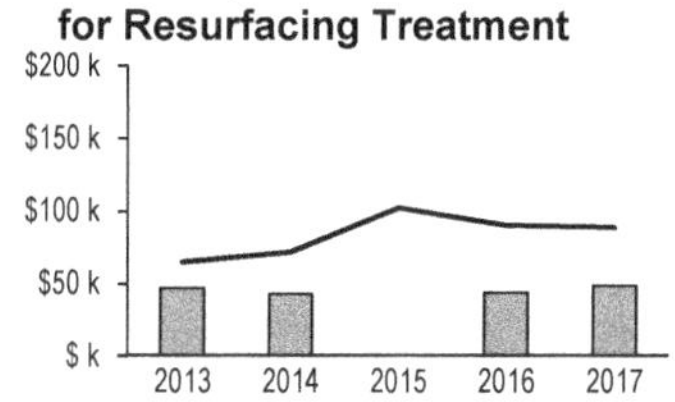

	2013	2014	2015	2016	2017
Charlotte	$47 k	$43 k		$44 k	$49 k
Average	$65 k	$72 k	$102 k	$90 k	$89 k

Cost per Lane Mile for Rehabilitation Treatment

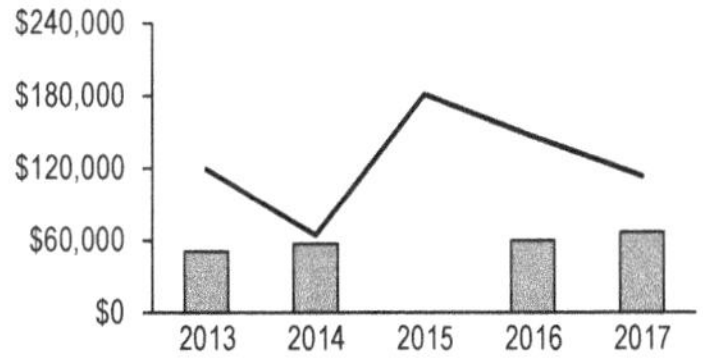

	2013	2014	2015	2016	2017
Charlotte	$51 k	$57 k		$60 k	$67 k
Average	$119 k	$64 k	$181 k	$147 k	$113 k

Cost per Ton for Contract Resurfacing

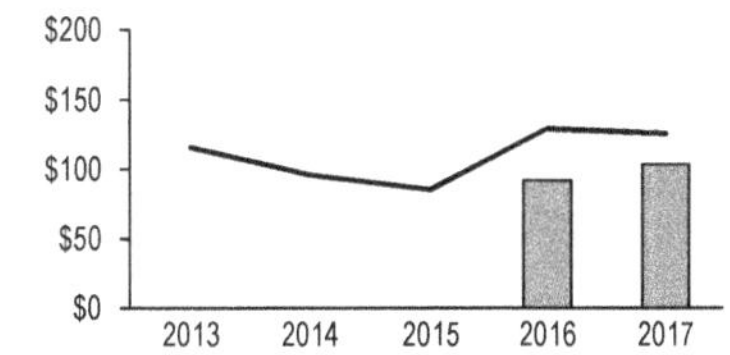

	2013	2014	2015	2016	2017
Charlotte				$92	$103
Average	$116	$96	$86	$129	$125

Effectiveness Measures

Percent of Lane Miles Rated 85 or Better

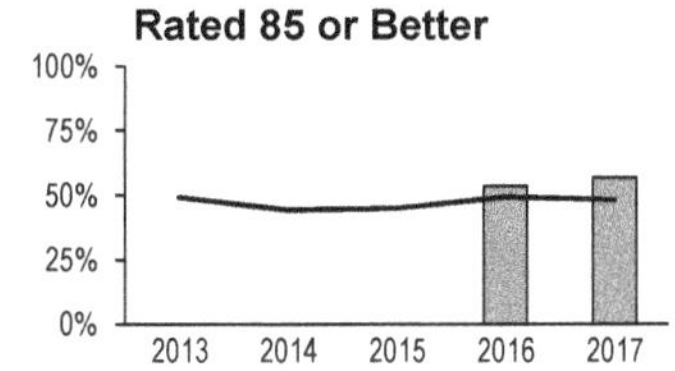

	2013	2014	2015	2016	2017
Charlotte				54%	57%
Average	49%	44%	45%	49%	48%

Percent of Lane Miles Rated Below 45

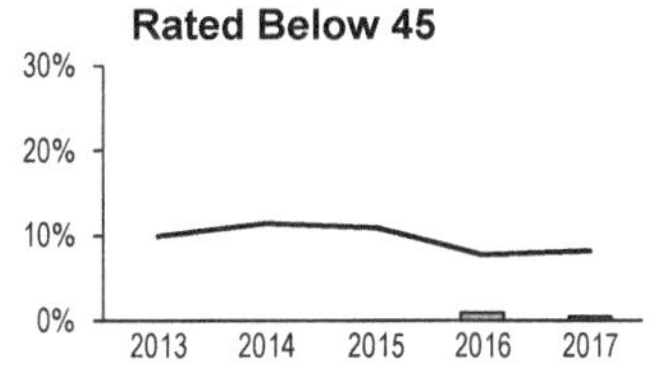

	2013	2014	2015	2016	2017
Charlotte				0.9%	0.5%
Average	9.9%	11.4%	10.9%	7.7%	8.1%

Percentage of Potholes Repaired within 24 hours

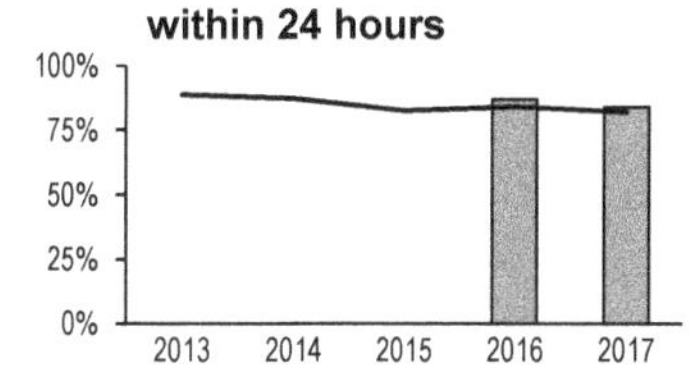

	2013	2014	2015	2016	2017
Charlotte				87%	84%
Average	89%	87%	83%	84%	82%

Fiscal Year 2016–17

Explanatory Information

Service Level and Delivery
The City of Concord was responsible for maintaining approximately 712 lane miles during the fiscal year. A total of 59.8 lane miles were treated during the year or about 8.4 percent of the total.

Contractors resurfaced 31.3 lane miles. Additionally contractors rehabilitated a further 28.5 lane miles, which first requires milling work before resurfacing. Contractors used a total of 36,165 tons of asphalt with an average depth of 3 inches.

The city reported that 43 percent of its lane miles rated 85 or above on its most recent pavement condition rating, conducted in 2017 using a city system based on North Carolina Department of Transportation ratings.

The number of potholes reported for the year was 112, including those reported by citizens and the city. The percentage of potholes repaired within twenty-four hours was 95. Concord also reported 209 utility cuts that were repaired and 60 maintenance patches for work other than potholes or utility cuts.

Conditions Affecting Service, Performance, and Costs
The costs associated with asphalt maintenance and resurfacing are influenced by competition among providers due to the location of three asphalt plants within the city limits.

The increase in roads rated below 45 percent increased in FY 2013–14 as a result of significant adverse winter weather taking a toll on streets around the city.

The drop in utility cuts with the rise in potholes in FY 2013–14 is due in part to better tracking and classification of repair work. Some repairs had previously been reported as utility cut repairs but were actually pothole repairs.

Municipal Profile

Population (OSBM 2016)	88,815
Land Area (Square Miles)	62.61
Persons per Square Mile	1,419
Topography	Flat; gently rolling
Climate	Temperate; little ice and snow

Service Profile

FTE Positions—Crews	8.70
FTE Positions—Other	2.35
Lane Miles Maintained	711.9
Lane Miles Treated	
Preservation	0.0
Resurfacing	31.3
Rehabilitation	28.5
TOTAL	59.8
Total Costs for All Treatment Types	$2,353,264
Potholes Repaired	112
Number of Utility Cuts	209
Number of Maintenance Patches (exclusive of potholes and utility cuts)	60
Registered Vehicles	
Registered Vehicles/Square Mile	
Average Cost per Ton of Hot Asphalt during Year	$65.00

Full Cost Profile

Cost Breakdown by Percentage	
Personal Services	17.9%
Operating Costs	76.4%
Capital Costs	5.6%
TOTAL	100.0%
Cost Breakdown in Dollars	
Personal Services	$644,155
Operating Costs	$2,745,462
Capital Costs	$202,421
TOTAL	$3,592,037

Key: Concord ▒ Benchmarking Average — Fiscal Years 2013 through 2017

Resource Measures

Asphalt Maintenance and Repair Services Costs per Capita

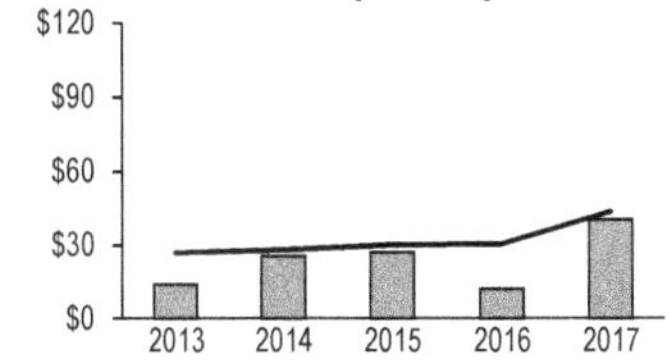

	2013	2014	2015	2016	2017
Concord	$13.86	$25.64	$27.24	$12.21	$40.44
Average	$27.05	$28.29	$30.38	$30.70	$43.66

Asphalt Maintenance and Repair FTEs per 10,000 Population

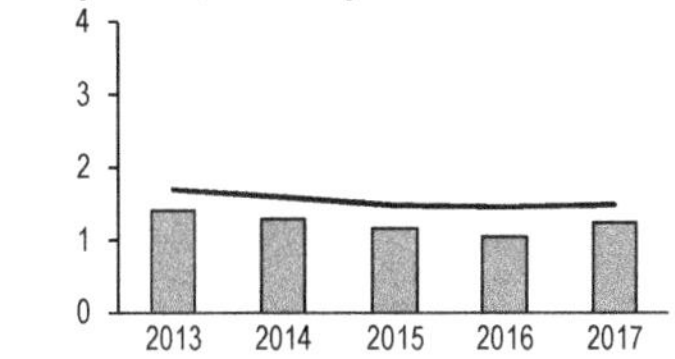

	2013	2014	2015	2016	2017
Concord	1.42	1.30	1.17	1.05	1.24
Average	1.70	1.60	1.49	1.46	1.49

Service Costs per Lane Mile of Road Maintained

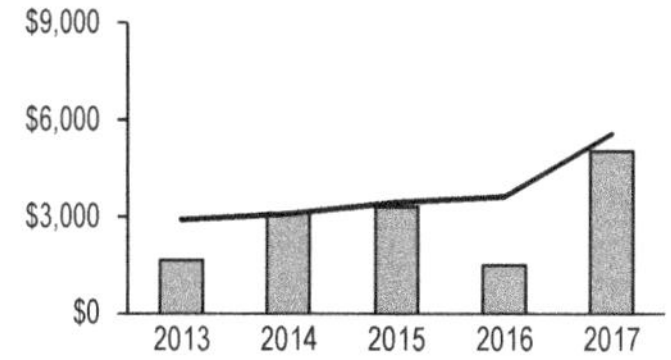

	2013	2014	2015	2016	2017
Concord	$1,677	$3,113	$3,331	$1,515	$5,046
Average	$2,923	$3,110	$3,452	$3,632	$5,582

Workload Measures

Number of Lane Miles Maintained per 1,000 Population

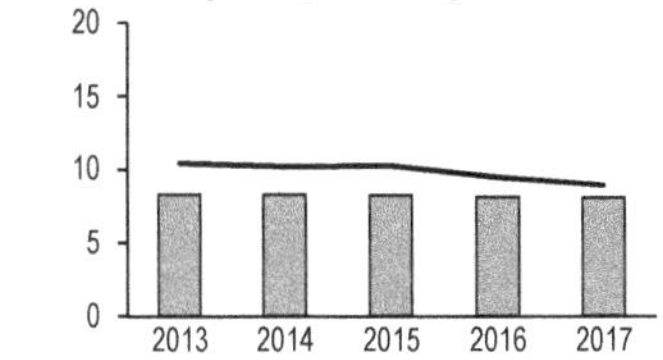

	2013	2014	2015	2016	2017
Concord	8.3	8.2	8.2	8.1	8.0
Average	10.4	10.2	10.2	9.5	8.9

Reported Potholes per Lane Mile Maintained

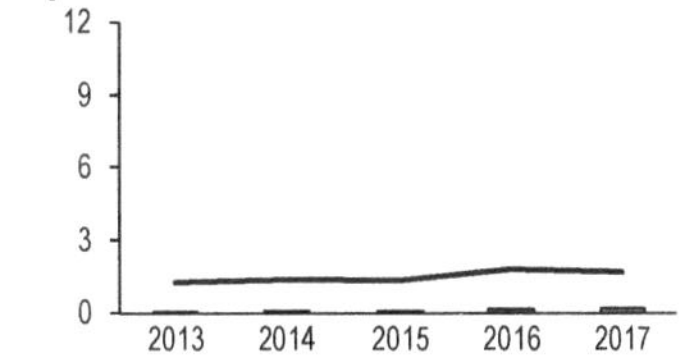

	2013	2014	2015	2016	2017
Concord	0.04	0.06	0.07	0.13	0.16
Average	1.26	1.35	1.34	1.78	1.67

Repaired Utility Cuts per Lane Mile Maintained

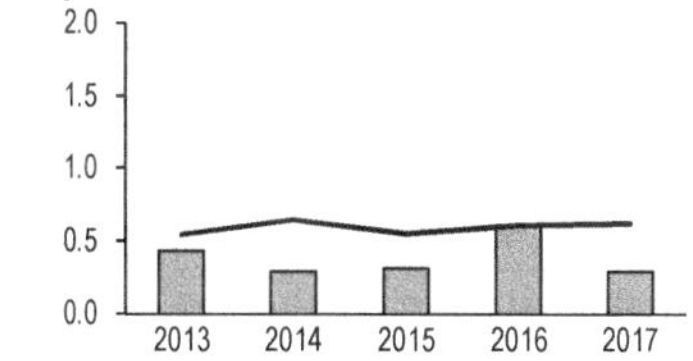

	2013	2014	2015	2016	2017
Concord	0.43	0.29	0.31	0.61	0.29
Average	0.54	0.64	0.55	0.61	0.62

Efficiency Measures

Cost of Maintenance per Lane Mile Maintained

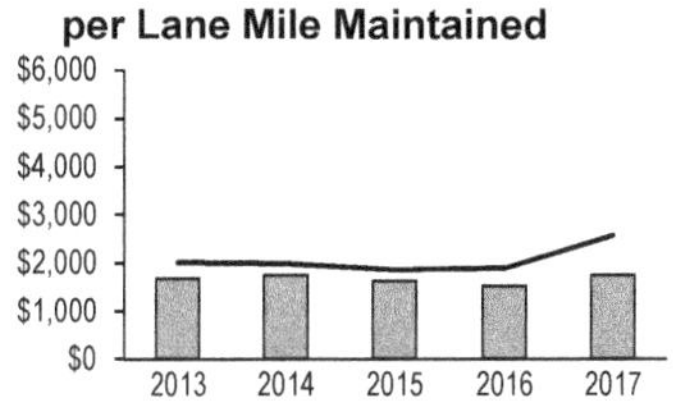

	2013	2014	2015	2016	2017
Concord	$1,677	$1,747	$1,620	$1,515	$1,740
Average	$2,005	$1,976	$1,852	$1,894	$2,564

Cost per Lane Mile for Preservation Treatment

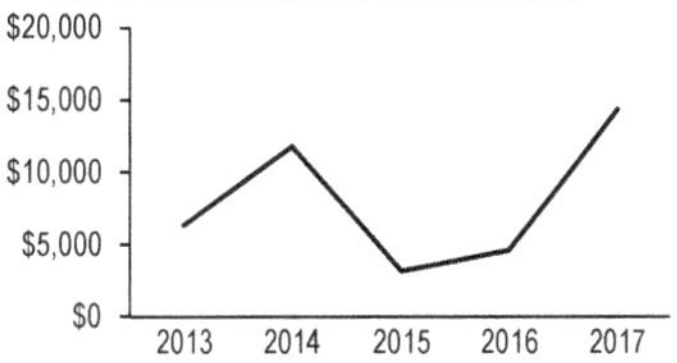

	2013	2014	2015	2016	2017
Concord					
Average	$6,371	$11,806	$3,214	$4,648	$14,370

Cost per Lane Mile for Resurfacing Treatment

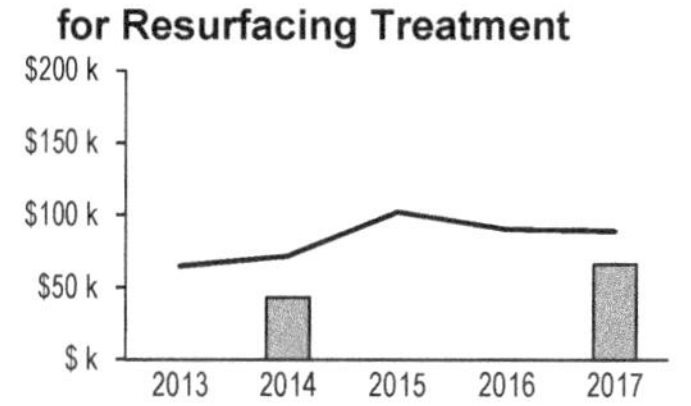

	2013	2014	2015	2016	2017
Concord		$44 k			$66 k
Average	$65 k	$72 k	$102 k	$90 k	$89 k

Cost per Lane Mile for Rehabilitation Treatment

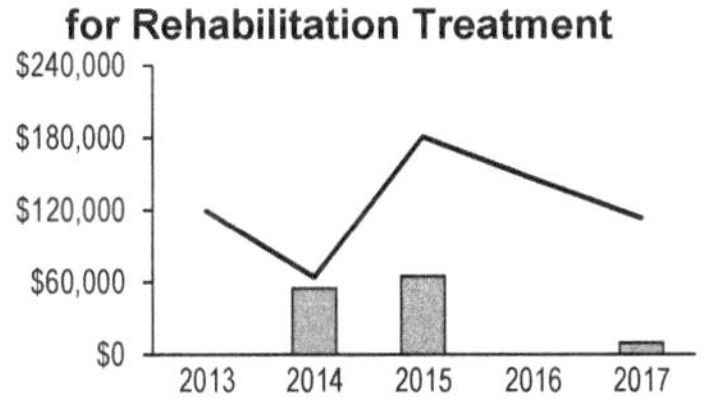

	2013	2014	2015	2016	2017
Concord		$55 k	$65 k		$10 k
Average	$119 k	$64 k	$181 k	$147 k	$113 k

Cost per Ton for Contract Resurfacing

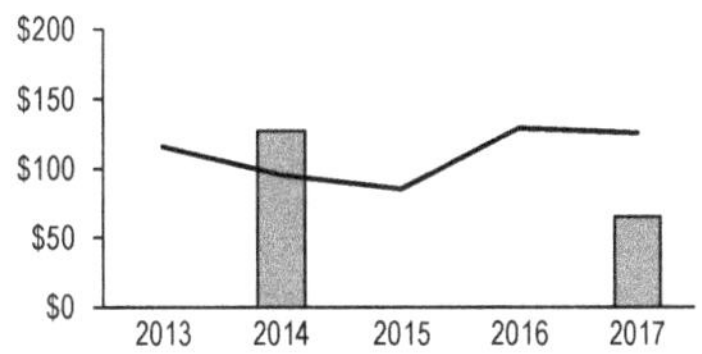

	2013	2014	2015	2016	2017
Concord		$127			$65
Average	$116	$96	$86	$129	$125

Effectiveness Measures

Percent of Lane Miles Rated 85 or Better

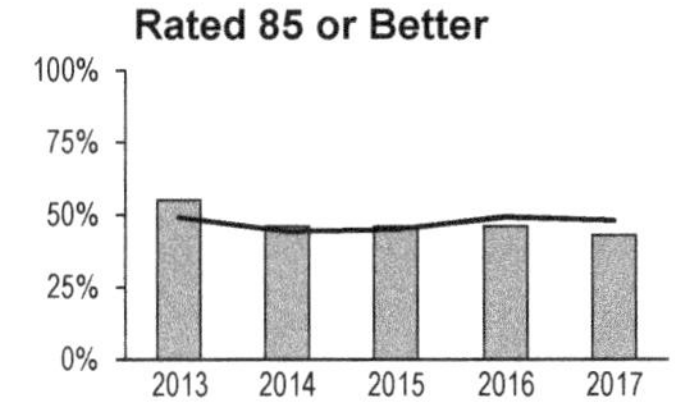

	2013	2014	2015	2016	2017
Concord	55%	46%	46%	46%	43%
Average	49%	44%	45%	49%	48%

Percent of Lane Miles Rated Below 45

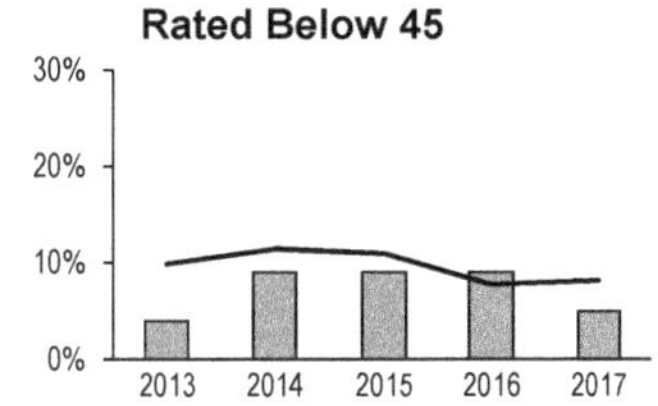

	2013	2014	2015	2016	2017
Concord	4.0%	9.0%	9.0%	9.0%	5.0%
Average	9.9%	11.4%	10.9%	7.7%	8.1%

Percentage of Potholes Repaired within 24 hours

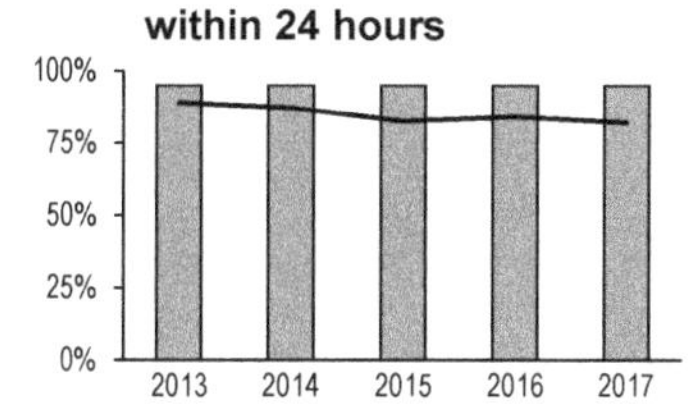

	2013	2014	2015	2016	2017
Concord	95%	95%	95%	95%	95%
Average	89%	87%	83%	84%	82%

Fiscal Year 2016–17

Explanatory Information

Service Level and Delivery

The City of Goldsboro was responsible for maintaining 163 lane miles during the fiscal year. Goldsboro treated a total of 7.2 lane miles during the year, equating to about 4.4 percent of total lane miles.

Of the treatment work done on Goldsboro's streets, 4.8 of the lane miles had resurfacing work done by contractors. A further 2.4 lane miles received rehabilitation work also done by contractors. Rehabilitation work requires milling work and is then followed by resurfacing. Contract crews used a total of 4,977 tons of asphalt with an average depth of 1.5 inches.

The number of potholes reported for the year was 654. The percentage of potholes repaired within twenty-four hours was estimated at 95 percent. The city has one person driving around the city every day looking for potholes that need to be repaired and fixing them on the spot. A total of 134 utility cuts were also repaired, with city crews repairing water and sewer cuts reported by the city's Distribution and Collections Divison.

Conditions Affecting Service, Performance, and Costs

The city of Goldsboro joined the Benchmarking Project in July 2017 with the first year of data showing for FY 2016–17.

Hurricane Matthew in October 2016 impacted asphalt work significantly. Crews were diverted to recovery efforts such as tree removal. Additionally, fifty-one sink holes developed over the year in roads due to storm water infrastructure failures under the asphalt surfaces.

Municipal Profile

Population (OSBM 2016)	34,793
Land Area (Square Miles)	29.35
Persons per Square Mile	1,186
Topography	Flat
Climate	Temperate; little ice and snow

Service Profile

FTE Positions—Crews	3.00
FTE Positions—Other	1.50
Lane Miles Maintained	162.7
Lane Miles Treated	
Preservation	0.0
Resurfacing	4.8
Rehabilitation	2.4
TOTAL	7.2
Total Costs for All Treatment Types	$302,218
Potholes Repaired	654
Number of Utility Cuts	134
Number of Maintenance Patches (exclusive of potholes and utility cuts)	NA
Registered Vehicles	
Registered Vehicles/Square Mile	
Average Cost per Ton of Hot Asphalt during Year	$80.00

Full Cost Profile

Cost Breakdown by Percentage	
Personal Services	34.7%
Operating Costs	53.5%
Capital Costs	11.8%
TOTAL	100.0%
Cost Breakdown in Dollars	
Personal Services	$457,199
Operating Costs	$705,035
Capital Costs	$155,012
TOTAL	$1,317,246

Key: Goldsboro ▒ Benchmarking Average — Fiscal Years 2013 through 2017

Resource Measures

Asphalt Maintenance and Repair Services Costs per Capita

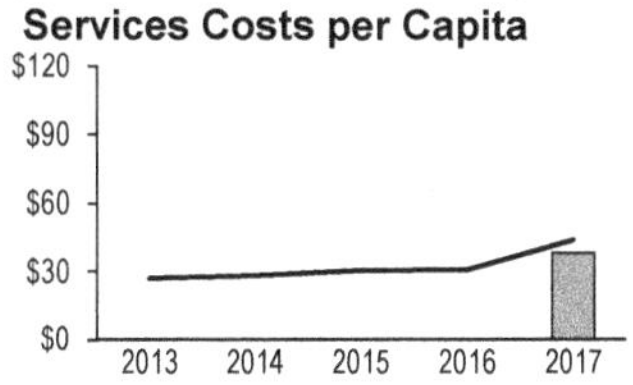

	2013	2014	2015	2016	2017
Goldsboro					$37.86
Average	$27.05	$28.29	$30.38	$30.70	$43.66

Asphalt Maintenance and Repair FTEs per 10,000 Population

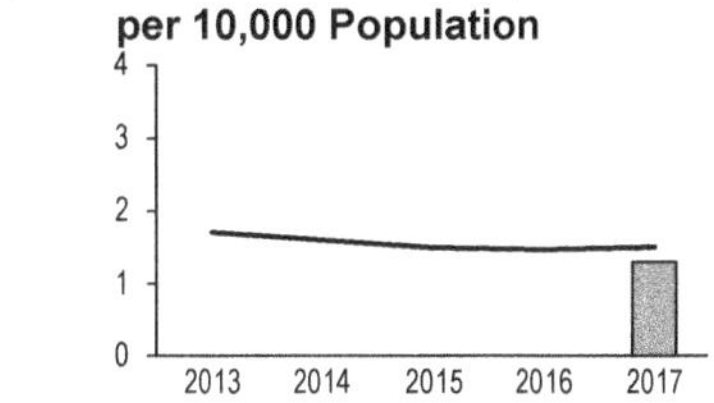

	2013	2014	2015	2016	2017
Goldsboro					1.29
Average	1.70	1.60	1.49	1.46	1.49

Service Costs per Lane Mile of Road Maintained

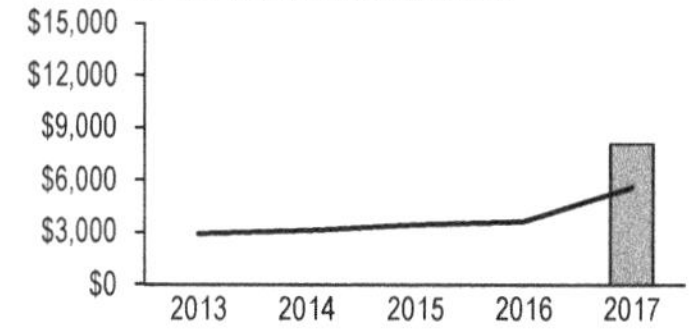

	2013	2014	2015	2016	2017
Goldsboro					$8,094
Average	$2,923	$3,110	$3,452	$3,632	$5,582

Workload Measures

Number of Lane Miles Maintained per 1,000 Population

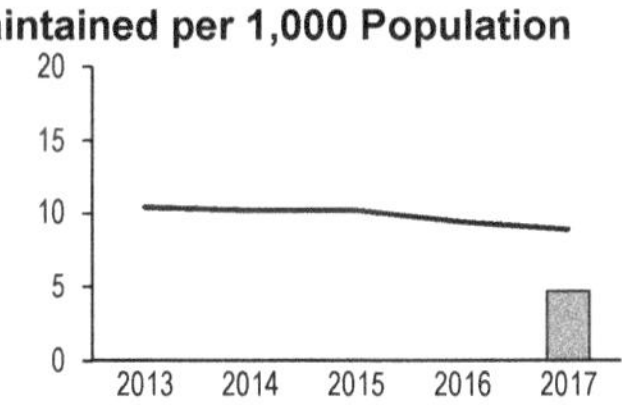

	2013	2014	2015	2016	2017
Goldsboro					4.7
Average	10.4	10.2	10.2	9.5	8.9

Reported Potholes per Lane Mile Maintained

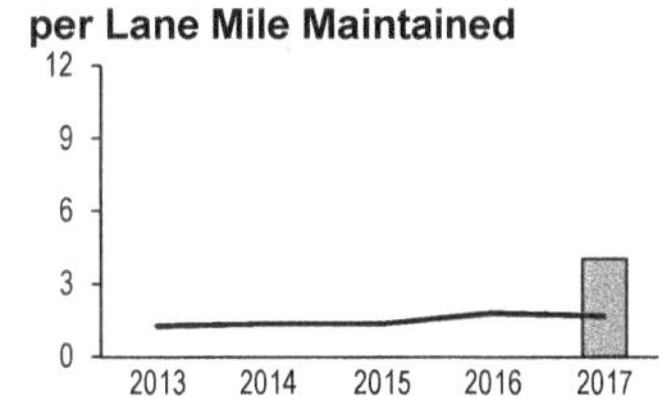

	2013	2014	2015	2016	2017
Goldsboro					4.02
Average	1.26	1.35	1.34	1.78	1.67

Repaired Utility Cuts per Lane Mile Maintained

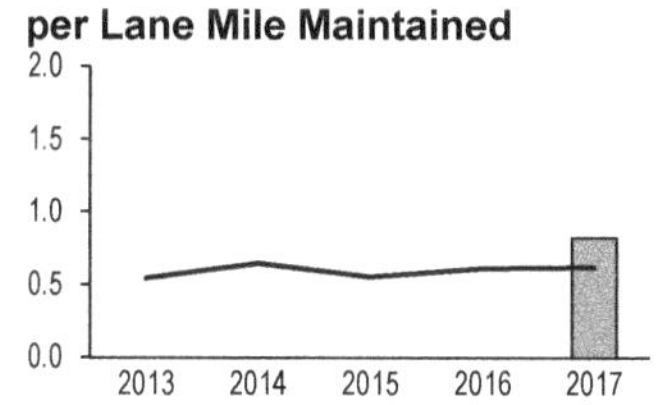

	2013	2014	2015	2016	2017
Goldsboro					0.82
Average	0.54	0.64	0.55	0.61	0.62

Efficiency Measures

Cost of Maintenance per Lane Mile Maintained

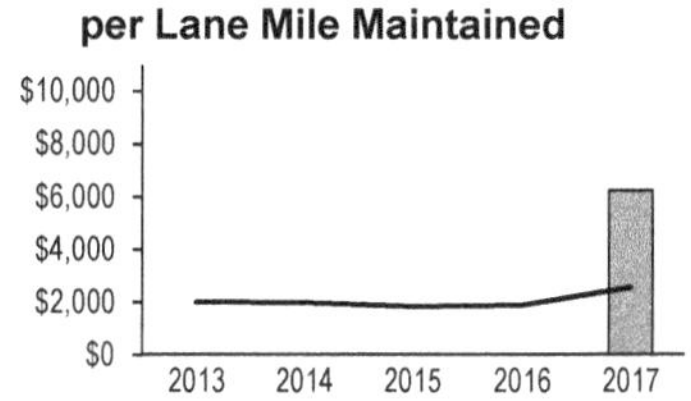

	2013	2014	2015	2016	2017
Goldsboro					$6,237
Average	$2,005	$1,976	$1,852	$1,894	$2,564

Cost per Lane Mile for Preservation Treatment

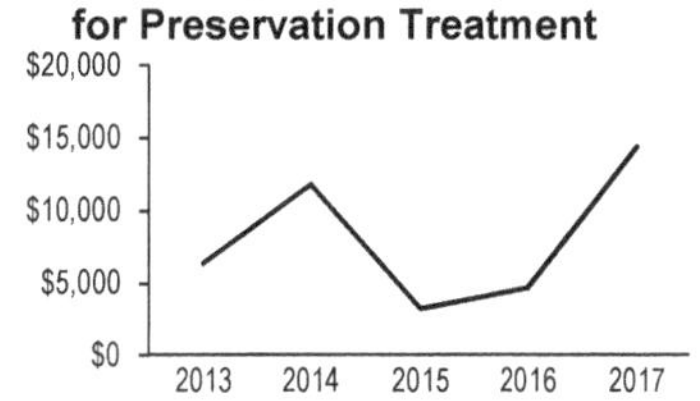

	2013	2014	2015	2016	2017
Goldsboro					
Average	$6,371	$11,806	$3,214	$4,648	$14,370

Cost per Lane Mile for Resurfacing Treatment

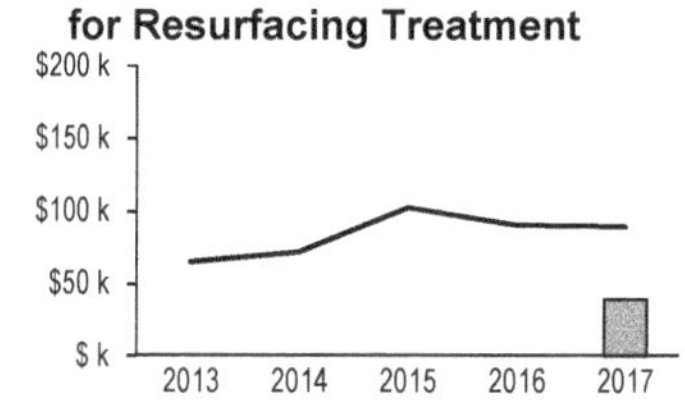

	2013	2014	2015	2016	2017
Goldsboro					$39 k
Average	$65 k	$72 k	$102 k	$90 k	$89 k

Cost per Lane Mile for Rehabilitation Treatment

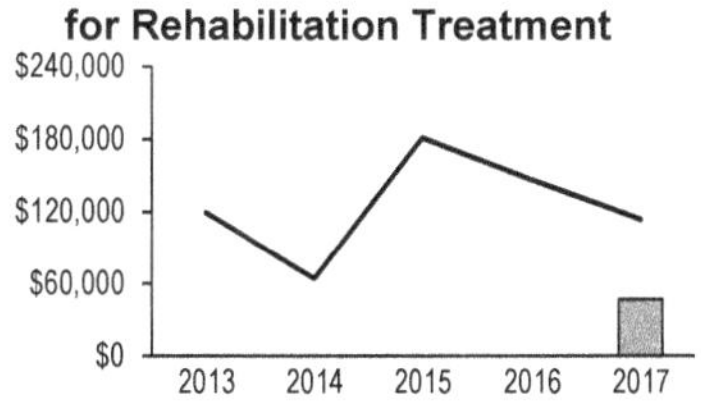

	2013	2014	2015	2016	2017
Goldsboro					$47 k
Average	$119 k	$64 k	$181 k	$147 k	$113 k

Cost per Ton for Contract Resurfacing

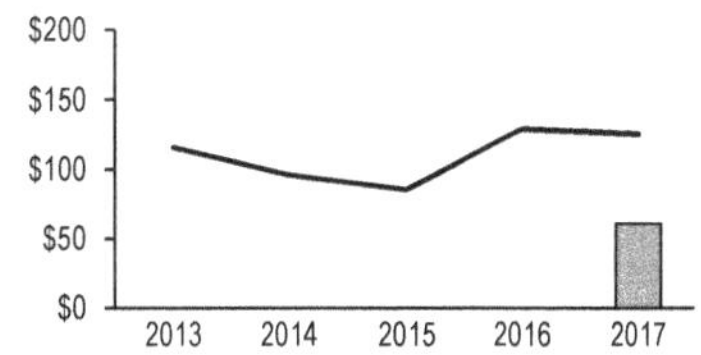

	2013	2014	2015	2016	2017
Goldsboro					$61
Average	$116	$96	$86	$129	$125

Effectiveness Measures

Percent of Lane Miles Rated 85 or Better

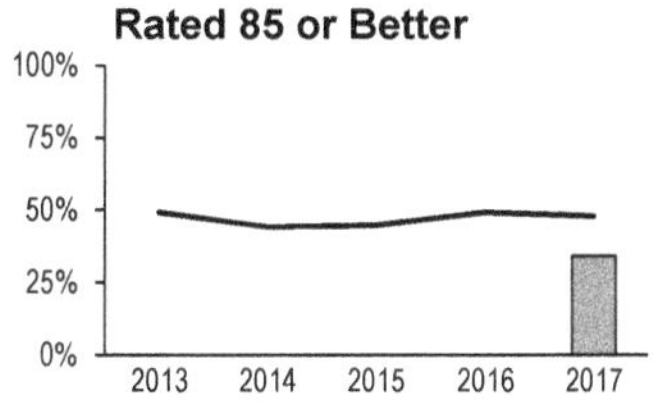

	2013	2014	2015	2016	2017
Goldsboro					34%
Average	49%	44%	45%	49%	48%

Percent of Lane Miles Rated Below 45

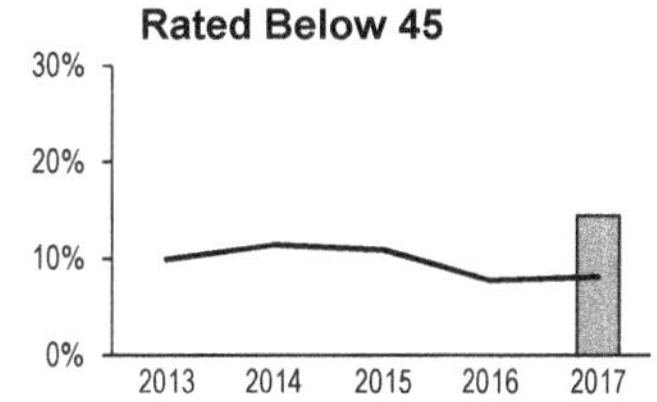

	2013	2014	2015	2016	2017
Goldsboro					14.4%
Average	9.9%	11.4%	10.9%	7.7%	8.1%

Percentage of Potholes Repaired within 24 hours

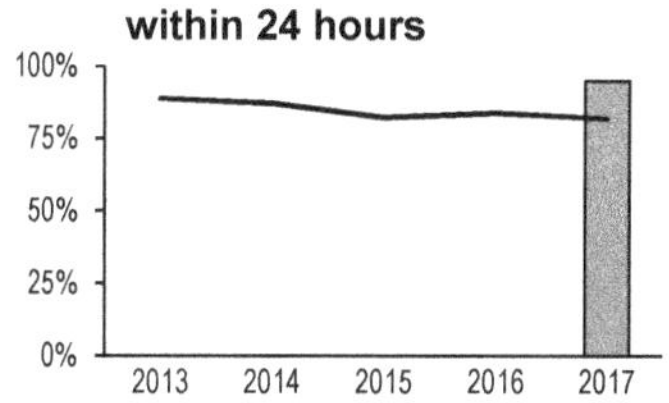

	2013	2014	2015	2016	2017
Goldsboro					95%
Average	89%	87%	83%	84%	82%

Fiscal Year 2016–17

Explanatory Information

Service Level and Delivery

The City of Greensboro was responsible for maintaining 2,431 lane miles during the fiscal year. Greensboro treated a total of 70.7 lane miles during the year, equating to about 2.9 percent of total lane miles.

Of the treatment work done on Greensboro's streets, 36.5 of the lane miles had preservation work such as crack sealing or thin overlays performed. All of this preservation work was done by city crews. Resurfacing work was done on 34.2 lane miles by contract crews. This resurfacing work required a total of 30,000 tons of asphalt and used an average resurfacing depth of 1.5 inches.

The number of potholes reported for the year was 3,812. The percentage of potholes repaired within twenty-four hours was 62 percent. A total of 438 utility cuts were also repaired, with city crews repairing water and sewer cuts but private contractors repairing others after getting permits from the city. A further eighty-eight maintenance patches were completed beyond potholes and utility cuts.

Conditions Affecting Service, Performance, and Costs

Changes in tracking software have improved the accuracy of potholes reported and asphalt used.

Municipal Profile

Population (OSBM 2016)	284,343
Land Area (Square Miles)	128.72
Persons per Square Mile	2,209
Topography	Flat; gently rolling
Climate	Temperate; little ice and snow

Service Profile

FTE Positions—Crews	45.00
FTE Positions—Other	6.00
Lane Miles Maintained	2,431.0
Lane Miles Treated	
Preservation	36.5
Resurfacing	34.2
Rehabilitation	0.0
TOTAL	70.7
Total Costs for All Treatment Types	$3,821,400
Potholes Repaired	3,812
Number of Utility Cuts	438
Number of Maintenance Patches (exclusive of potholes and utility cuts)	88
Registered Vehicles	
Registered Vehicles/Square Mile	
Average Cost per Ton of Hot Asphalt during Year	$56.78

Full Cost Profile

Cost Breakdown by Percentage	
Personal Services	25.9%
Operating Costs	74.1%
Capital Costs	0.0%
TOTAL	100.0%
Cost Breakdown in Dollars	
Personal Services	$2,299,336
Operating Costs	$6,579,462
Capital Costs	$0
TOTAL	$8,878,798

Key: Greensboro ▒ Benchmarking Average — Fiscal Years 2013 through 2017

Resource Measures

Asphalt Maintenance and Repair Services Costs per Capita

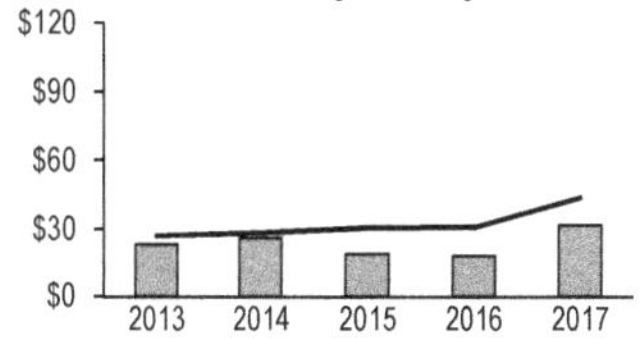

	2013	2014	2015	2016	2017
Greensboro	$22.98	$25.82	$18.73	$17.78	$31.23
Average	$27.05	$28.29	$30.38	$30.70	$43.66

Asphalt Maintenance and Repair FTEs per 10,000 Population

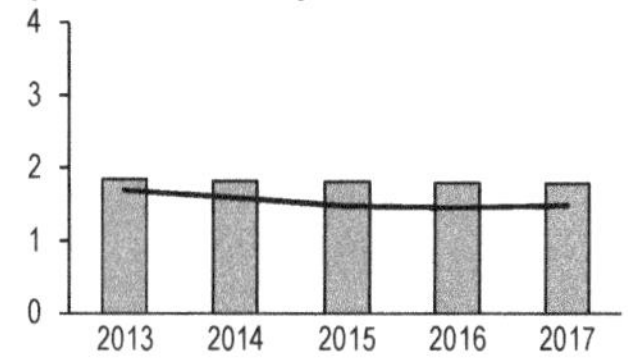

	2013	2014	2015	2016	2017
Greensboro	1.85	1.83	1.82	1.80	1.79
Average	1.70	1.60	1.49	1.46	1.49

Service Costs per Lane Mile of Road Maintained

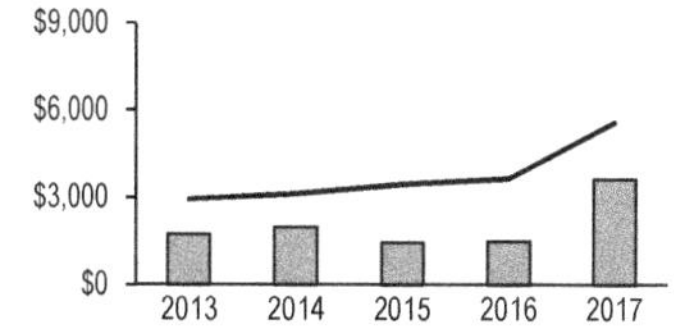

	2013	2014	2015	2016	2017
Greensboro	$1,740	$1,981	$1,447	$1,498	$3,652
Average	$2,923	$3,110	$3,452	$3,632	$5,582

Workload Measures

Number of Lane Miles Maintained per 1,000 Population

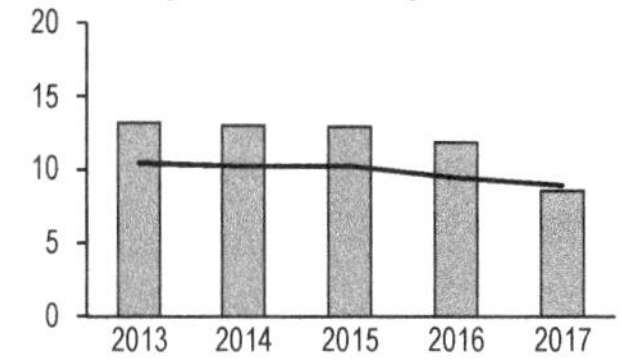

	2013	2014	2015	2016	2017
Greensboro	13.2	13.0	12.9	11.9	8.5
Average	10.4	10.2	10.2	9.5	8.9

Reported Potholes per Lane Mile Maintained

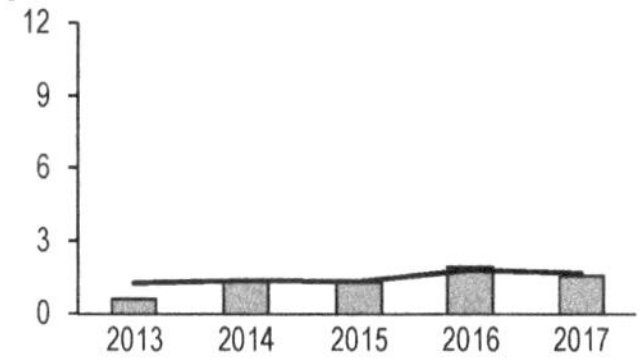

	2013	2014	2015	2016	2017
Greensboro	0.61	1.32	1.30	1.93	1.57
Average	1.26	1.35	1.34	1.78	1.67

Repaired Utility Cuts per Lane Mile Maintained

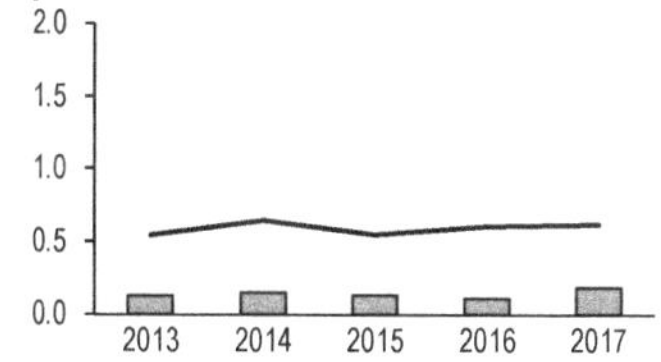

	2013	2014	2015	2016	2017
Greensboro	0.12	0.15	0.13	0.11	0.18
Average	0.54	0.64	0.55	0.61	0.62

Efficiency Measures

Cost of Maintenance per Lane Mile Maintained

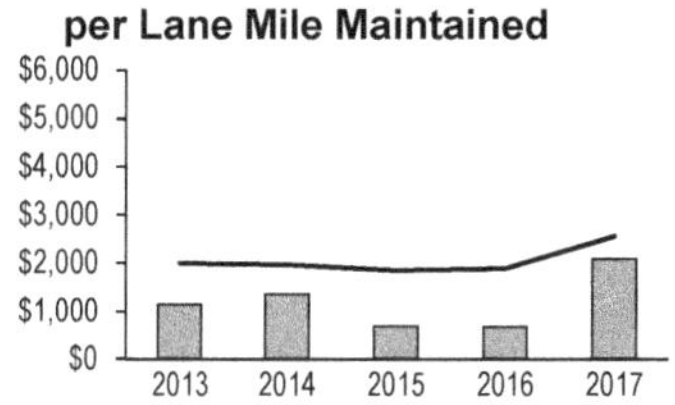

	2013	2014	2015	2016	2017
Greensboro	$1,142	$1,359	$676	$657	$2,080
Average	$2,005	$1,976	$1,852	$1,894	$2,564

Cost per Lane Mile for Preservation Treatment

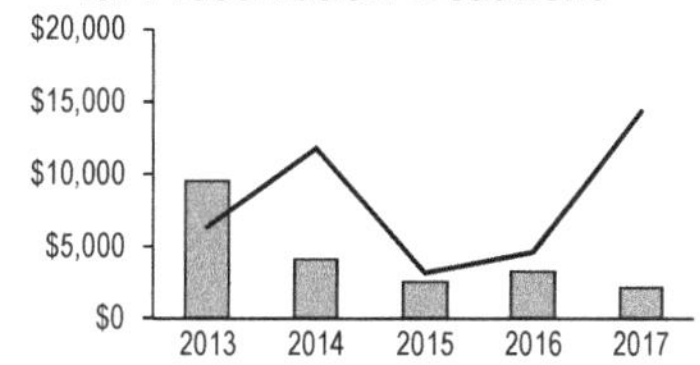

	2013	2014	2015	2016	2017
Greensboro	$9,519	$4,123	$2,560	$3,282	$2,148
Average	$6,371	$11,806	$3,214	$4,648	$14,370

Cost per Lane Mile for Resurfacing Treatment

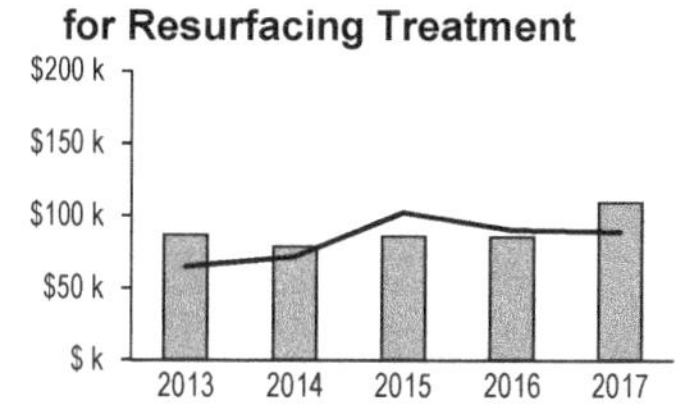

	2013	2014	2015	2016	2017
Greensboro	$87 k	$79 k	$86 k	$85 k	$109 k
Average	$65 k	$72 k	$102 k	$90 k	$89 k

Cost per Lane Mile for Rehabilitation Treatment

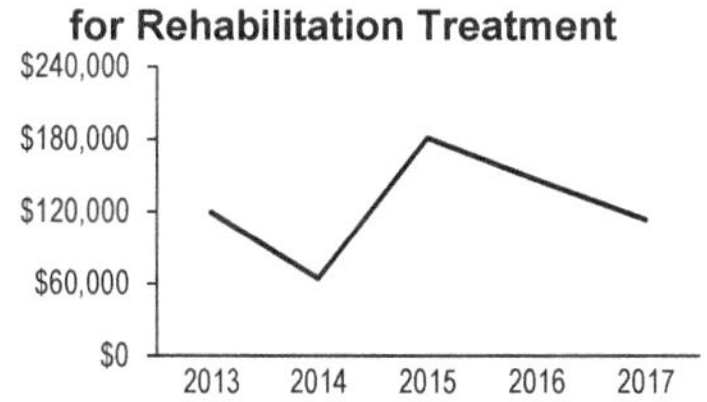

	2013	2014	2015	2016	2017
Greensboro					
Average	$119 k	$64 k	$181 k	$147 k	$113 k

Cost per Ton for Contract Resurfacing

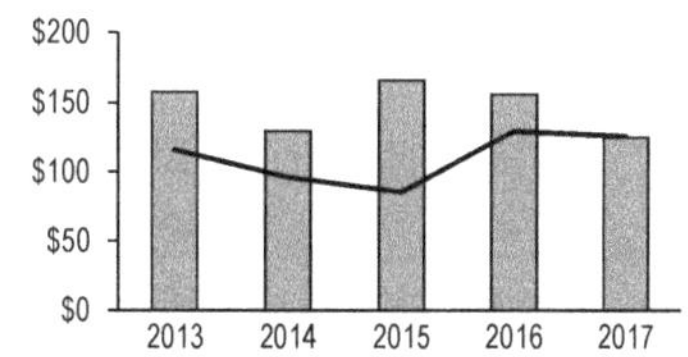

	2013	2014	2015	2016	2017
Greensboro	$157	$129	$166	$155	$125
Average	$116	$96	$86	$129	$125

Effectiveness Measures

Percent of Lane Miles Rated 85 or Better

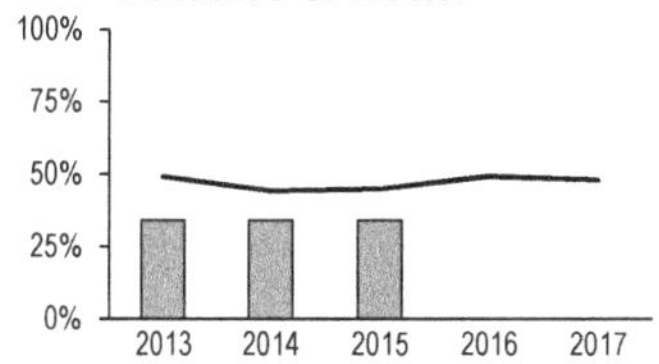

	2013	2014	2015	2016	2017
Greensboro	34%	34%	34%		
Average	49%	44%	45%	49%	48%

Percent of Lane Miles Rated Below 45

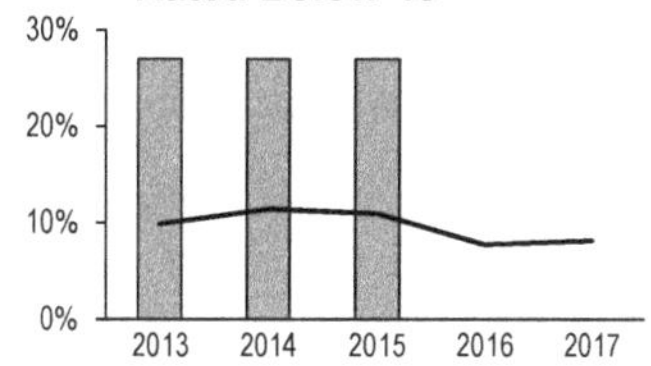

	2013	2014	2015	2016	2017
Greensboro	27.0%	27.0%	27.0%		
Average	9.9%	11.4%	10.9%	7.7%	8.1%

Percentage of Potholes Repaired within 24 hours

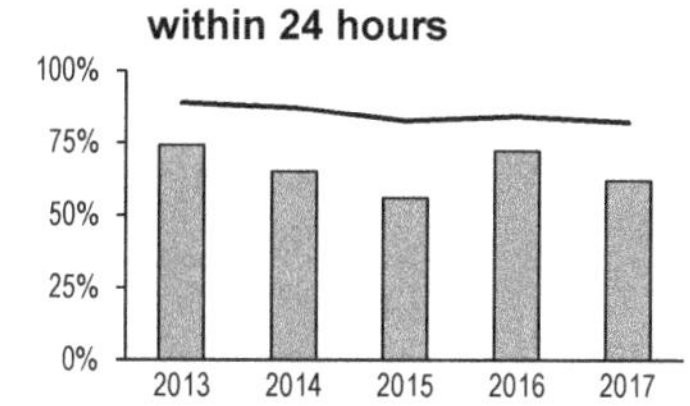

	2013	2014	2015	2016	2017
Greensboro	74%	65%	56%	72%	62%
Average	89%	87%	83%	84%	82%

Fiscal Year 2016–17

Explanatory Information

Service Level and Delivery

The City of Greenville was responsible for maintaining approximately 677 lane miles during the fiscal year, all city streets. During the year, Greenville reported that 42.9 lane miles were given some form of treatment, equating to 6.3 percent of total lane miles. Contract crews treated 42.9 lane miles with rehabilitation which includes milling along with resurfacing. .

Greenville reported that 46 percent of lane miles were rated 85 or better on its most recent pavement condition rating, conducted in 2014 by a consultant.

Conditions Affecting Service, Performance, and Costs

Greenville did a special pilot project using a proprietary material for lane preservation work during FY 2013–14. This material is applied at a high rate over the asphalt service to be treated resulting in higher costs per lane mile for preservation work. The project will be evaluated over time to determine if the higher cost produces improved performance.

The number of potholes, utility cuts, and maintenance patching was not available for some of the last few years.

Municipal Profile

Population (OSBM 2016)	87,989
Land Area (Square Miles)	35.41
Persons per Square Mile	2,485
Topography	Flat
Climate	Temperate; little ice and snow

Service Profile

FTE Positions—Crews	4.00
FTE Positions—Other	2.00
Lane Miles Maintained	676.7
Lane Miles Treated	
Preservation	0.0
Resurfacing	0.0
Rehabilitation	42.9
TOTAL	42.9
Total Costs for All Treatment Types	$7,600,000
Potholes Repaired	1,200
Number of Utility Cuts	107
Number of Maintenance Patches (exclusive of potholes and utility cuts)	NA
Average Cost per Ton of Hot Asphalt during Year	$81.50

Full Cost Profile

Cost Breakdown by Percentage	
Personal Services	5.5%
Operating Costs	94.0%
Capital Costs	0.5%
TOTAL	100.0%
Cost Breakdown in Dollars	
Personal Services	$464,257
Operating Costs	$8,006,457
Capital Costs	$45,136
TOTAL	$8,515,850

Key: Greenville ▒ Benchmarking Average — Fiscal Years 2013 through 2017

Resource Measures

Asphalt Maintenance and Repair Services Costs per Capita

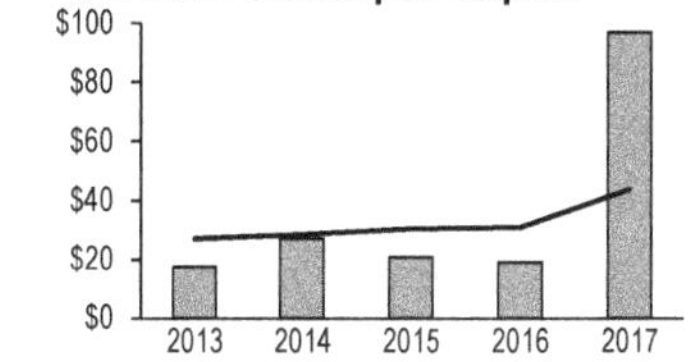

	2013	2014	2015	2016	2017
Greenville	$17.64	$27.08	$20.77	$19.01	$96.78
Average	$27.05	$28.29	$30.38	$30.70	$43.66

Asphalt Maintenance and Repair FTEs per 10,000 Population

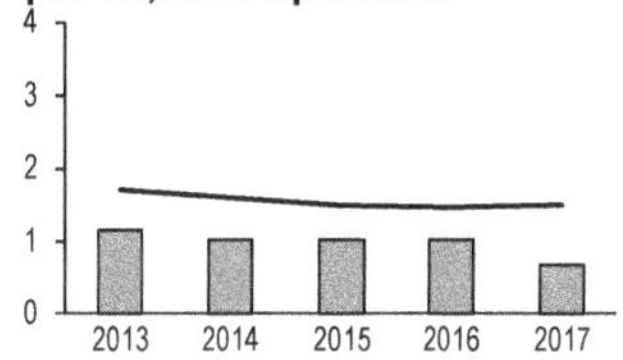

	2013	2014	2015	2016	2017
Greenville	1.16	1.03	1.03	1.03	0.68
Average	1.70	1.60	1.40	1.46	1.49

Service Costs per Lane Mile of Road Maintained

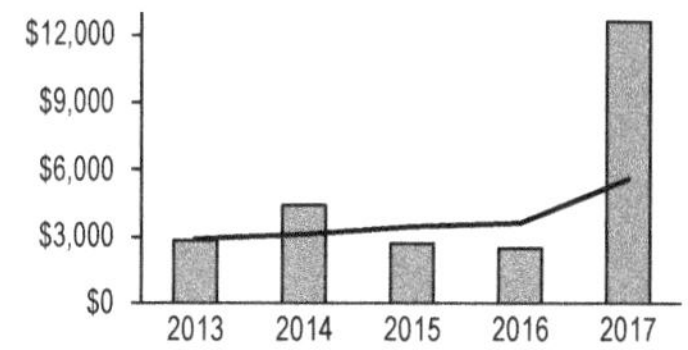

	2013	2014	2015	2016	2017
Greenville	$2,828	$4,397	$2,691	$2,479	$12,585
Average	$2,923	$3,110	$3,452	$3,632	$5,582

Workload Measures

Number of Lane Miles Maintained per 1,000 Population

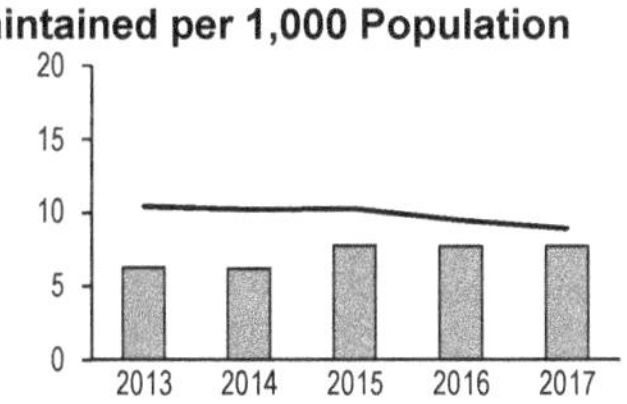

	2013	2014	2015	2016	2017
Greenville	6.2	6.2	7.7	7.7	7.7
Average	10.4	10.2	10.2	9.5	8.9

Reported Potholes per Lane Mile Maintained

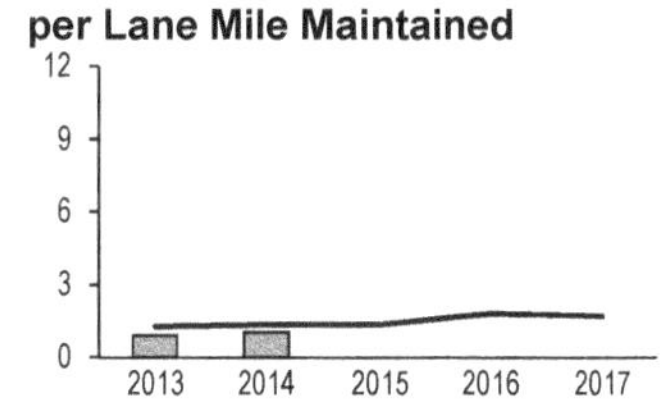

	2013	2014	2015	2016	2017
Greenville	0.90	1.02			
Average	1.26	1.35	1.34	1.78	1.67

Repaired Utility Cuts per Lane Mile Maintained

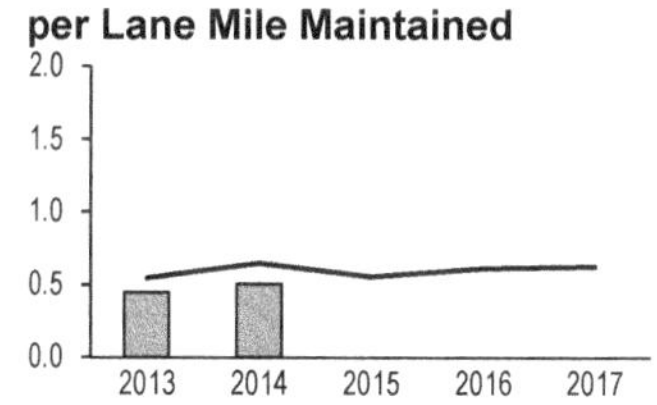

	2013	2014	2015	2016	2017
Greenville	0.44	0.50			
Average	0.54	0.64	0.55	0.61	0.62

Efficiency Measures

Cost of Maintenance per Lane Mile Maintained

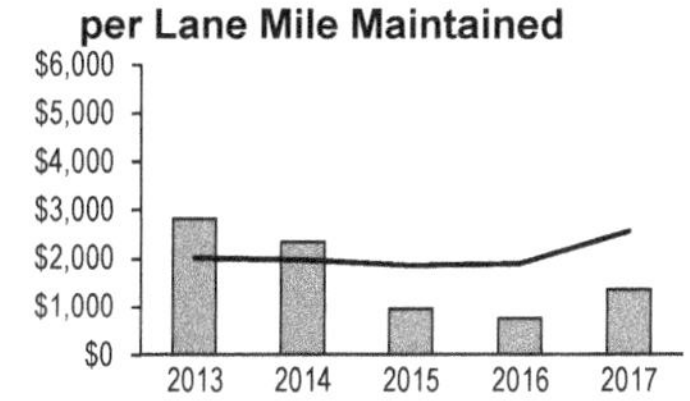

	2013	2014	2015	2016	2017
Greenville	$2,821	$2,338	$960	$748	$1,353
Average	$2,005	$1,976	$1,852	$1,894	$2,564

Cost per Lane Mile for Preservation Treatment

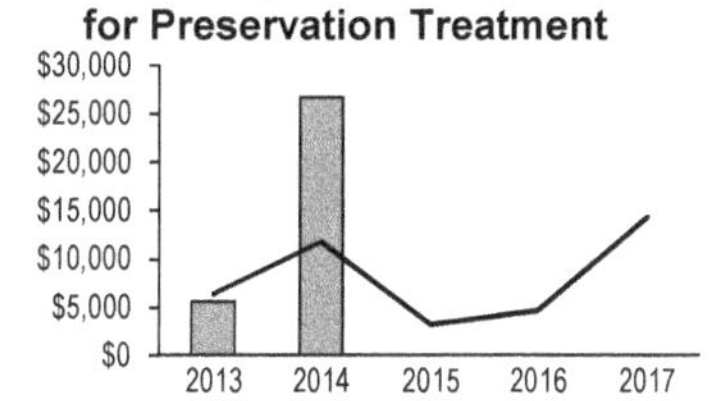

	2013	2014	2015	2016	2017
Greenville	$5,507	$26,603			
Average	$6,371	$11,806	$3,214	$4,648	$14,370

Cost per Lane Mile for Resurfacing Treatment

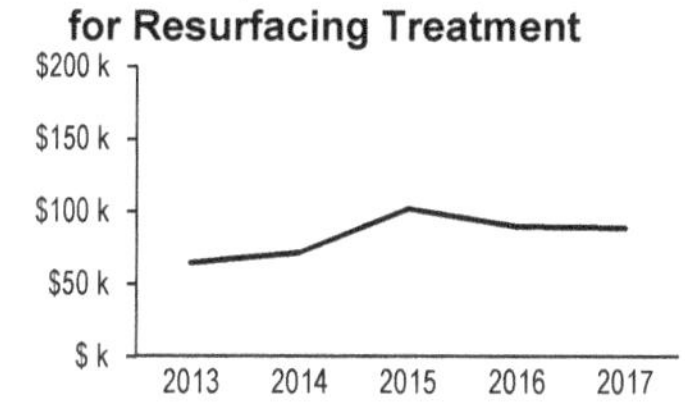

	2013	2014	2015	2016	2017
Greenville					
Average	$65 k	$72 k	$102 k	$90 k	$89 k

Cost per Lane Mile for Rehabilitation Treatment

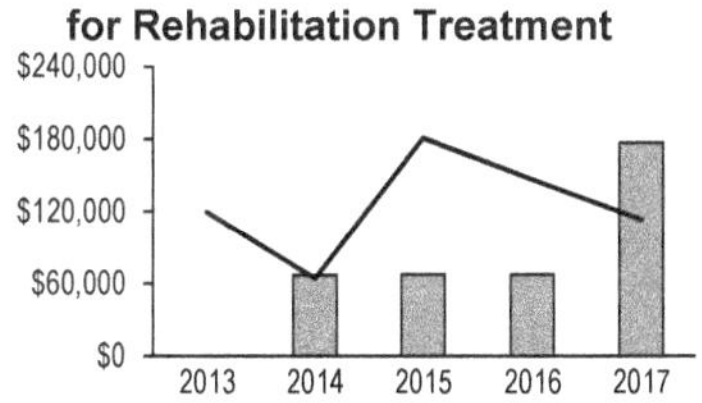

	2013	2014	2015	2016	2017
Greenville		$67 k	$68 k	$68 k	$177 k
Average	$119 k	$64 k	$181 k	$147 k	$113 k

Cost per Ton for Contract Resurfacing

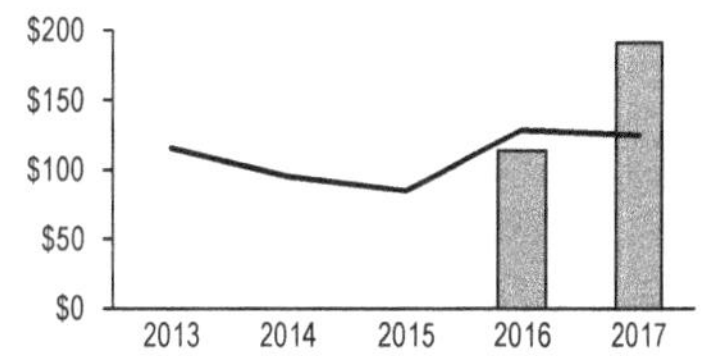

	2013	2014	2015	2016	2017
Greenville				$114	$191
Average	$116	$96	$86	$129	$125

Effectiveness Measures

Percent of Lane Miles Rated 85 or Better

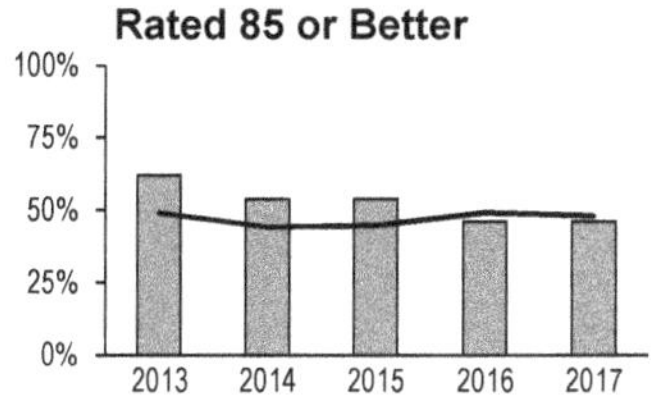

	2013	2014	2015	2016	2017
Greenville	62%	54%	54%	46%	46%
Average	49%	44%	45%	49%	48%

Percent of Lane Miles Rated Below 45

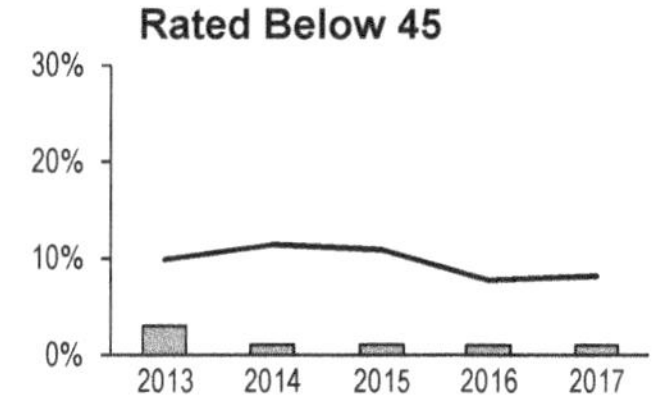

	2013	2014	2015	2016	2017
Greenville	3.0%	1.1%	1.1%	1.0%	1.0%
Average	9.9%	11.4%	10.9%	7.7%	8.1%

Percentage of Potholes Repaired within 24 hours

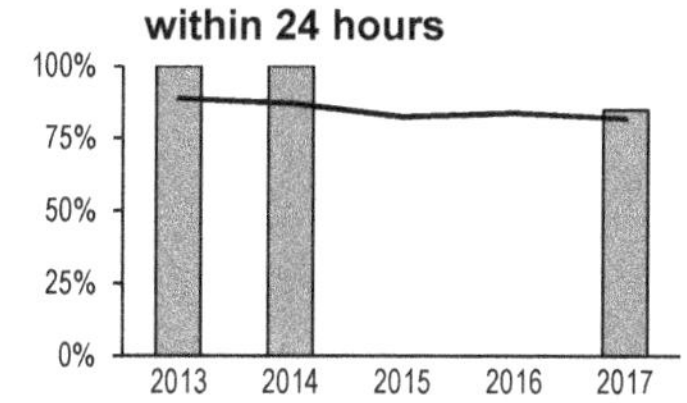

	2013	2014	2015	2016	2017
Greenville	100%	100%			85%
Average	89%	87%	83%	84%	82%

Fiscal Year 2016–17

Explanatory Information

Service Level and Delivery

The City of Hickory was responsible for maintaining approximately 720 lane miles during the fiscal year, including 238.8 lane miles of state roads. The city treated a total of 17.1 lane miles with resurfacing, equating to 2.4 percent of total lane miles.

The city resurfaced 17.1 lane miles using contractors. A total of 7,750 tons of asphalt were used by the contractors. The average resurfacing depth used was 1.5 inches and required 9,937 tons of asphalt.

The city reported that 37 percent of its lane miles rated 85 or above on its most recent pavement condition rating, conducted in 2017. The city used the Institute for Transportation Research and Education (ITRE) to conduct its rating system.

The number of potholes reported for the year was 322, including self-reported and citizen-reported potholes. The percentage of potholes repaired within twenty-four hours was 92 percent.

Conditions Affecting Service, Performance, and Costs

Municipal Profile

Population (OSBM 2016)	40,453
Land Area (Square Miles)	29.90
Persons per Square Mile	1,353
Topography	Gently rolling
Climate	Temperate; some ice and snow

Service Profile

FTE Positions—Crews	6.00
FTE Positions—Other	1.00
Lane Miles Maintained	719.5
Lane Miles Treated	
Preservation	0.0
Resurfacing	17.1
Rehabilitation	0.0
TOTAL	17.1
Total Costs for All Treatment Types	$760,195
Potholes Repaired	322
Number of Utility Cuts	NA
Number of Maintenance Patches (exclusive of potholes and utility cuts)	NA
Registered Vehicles	
Registered Vehicles/Square Mile	
Average Cost per Ton of Hot Asphalt during Year	$76.50

Full Cost Profile

Cost Breakdown by Percentage	
Personal Services	15.6%
Operating Costs	83.0%
Capital Costs	1.4%
TOTAL	100.0%
Cost Breakdown in Dollars	
Personal Services	$272,041
Operating Costs	$1,446,213
Capital Costs	$25,097
TOTAL	$1,743,351

Hickory — Asphalt Maintenance and Repair

Key: Hickory ▒ Benchmarking Average — Fiscal Years 2013 through 2017

Resource Measures

Asphalt Maintenance and Repair Services Costs per Capita

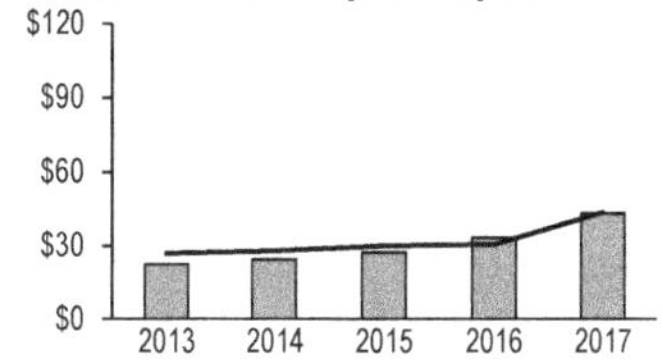

	2013	2014	2015	2016	2017
Hickory	$22.16	$24.18	$27.01	$33.22	$43.10
Average	$27.05	$28.20	$30.38	$30.70	$43.66

Asphalt Maintenance and Repair FTEs per 10,000 Population

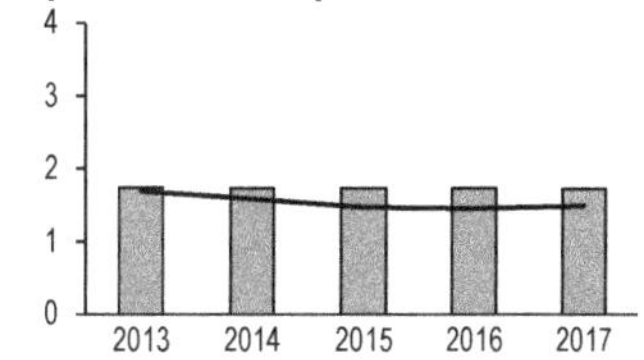

	2013	2014	2015	2016	2017
Hickory	1.75	1.74	1.74	1.73	1.73
Average	1.70	1.60	1.49	1.46	1.49

Service Costs per Lane Mile of Road Maintained

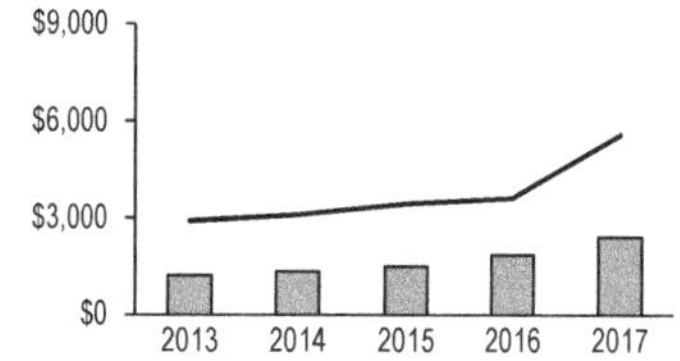

	2013	2014	2015	2016	2017
Hickory	$1,234	$1,353	$1,515	$1,862	$2,423
Average	$2,923	$3,110	$3,452	$3,632	$5,582

Workload Measures

Number of Lane Miles Maintained per 1,000 Population

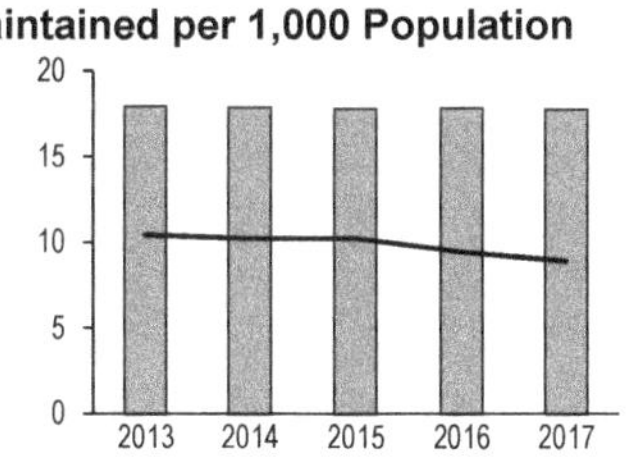

	2013	2014	2015	2016	2017
Hickory	18.0	17.9	17.8	17.8	17.8
Average	10.4	10.2	10.2	9.5	8.9

Reported Potholes per Lane Mile Maintained

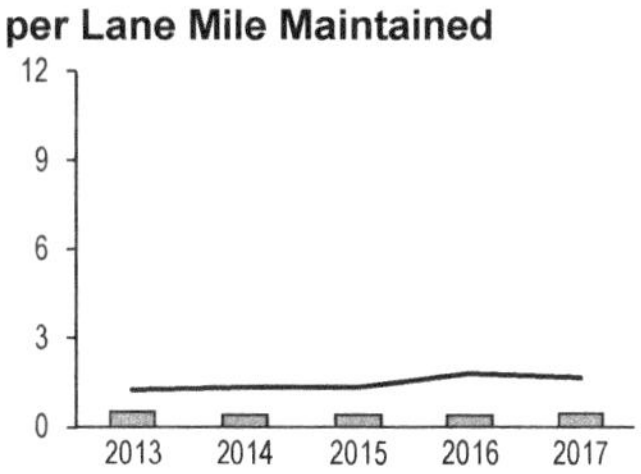

	2013	2014	2015	2016	2017
Hickory	0.51	0.41	0.41	0.38	0.45
Average	1.26	1.35	1.34	1.78	1.67

Repaired Utility Cuts per Lane Mile Maintained

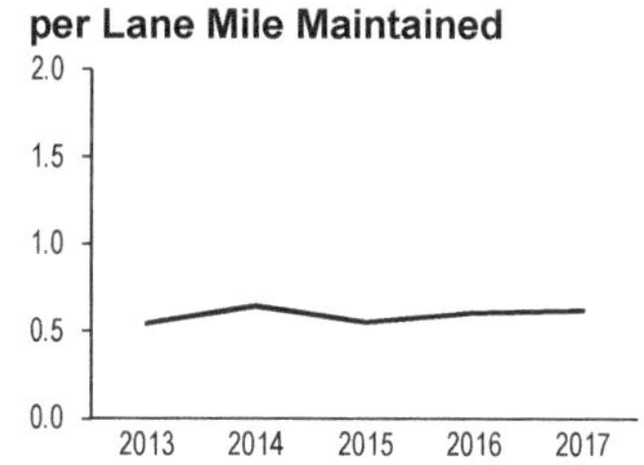

	2013	2014	2015	2016	2017
Hickory					
Average	0.54	0.64	0.55	0.61	0.62

Efficiency Measures

Cost of Maintenance per Lane Mile Maintained

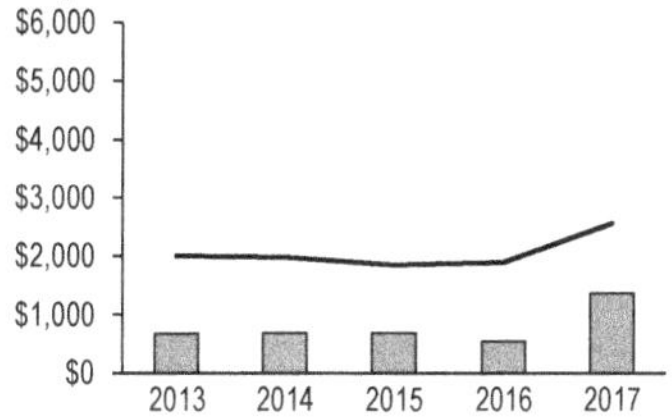

	2013	2014	2015	2016	2017
Hickory	$678	$685	$690	$545	$1,366
Average	$2,005	$1,976	$1,852	$1,894	$2,564

Cost per Lane Mile for Preservation Treatment

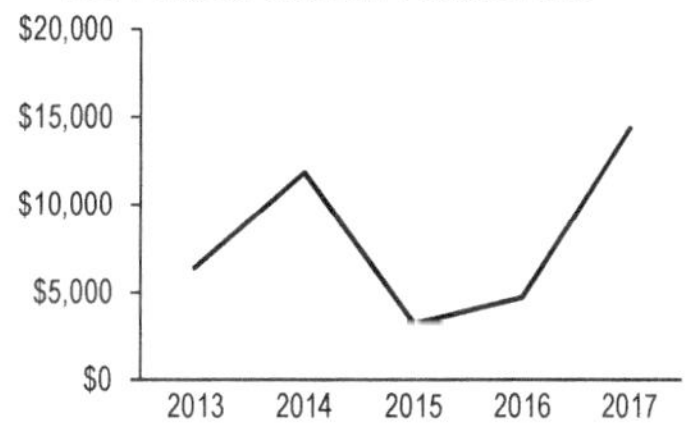

	2013	2014	2015	2016	2017
Hickory					
Average	$6,371	$11,806	$3,214	$4,648	$14,370

Cost per Lane Mile for Resurfacing Treatment

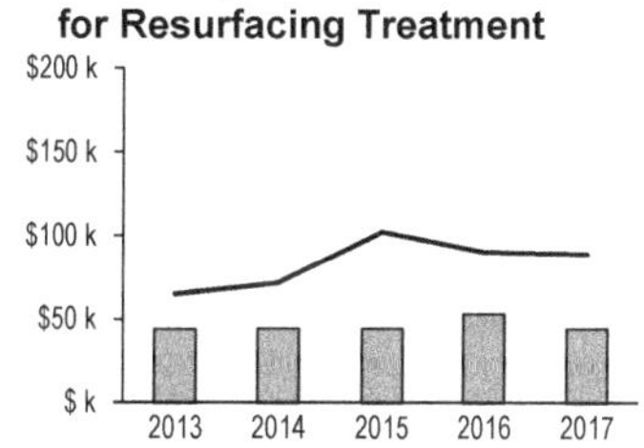

	2013	2014	2015	2016	2017
Hickory	$44 k	$44 k	$44 k	$53 k	$44 k
Average	$65 k	$72 k	$102 k	$90 k	$89 k

Cost per Lane Mile for Rehabilitation Treatment

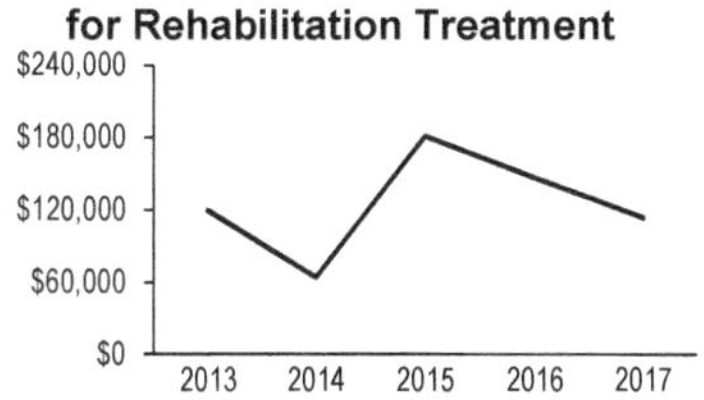

	2013	2014	2015	2016	2017
Hickory					
Average	$119 k	$64 k	$181 k	$147 k	$113 k

Cost per Ton for Contract Resurfacing

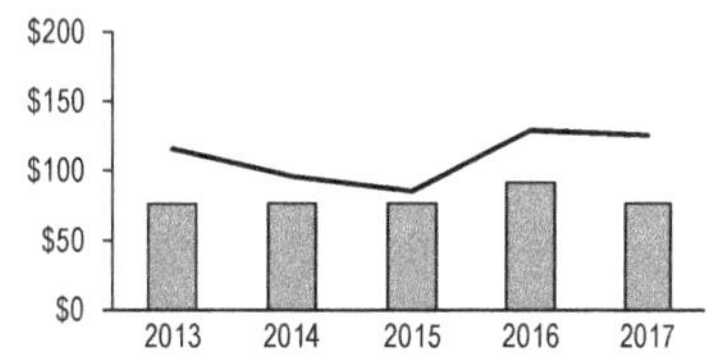

	2013	2014	2015	2016	2017
Hickory	$76	$77	$77	$92	$77
Average	$116	$96	$86	$129	$125

Effectiveness Measures

Percent of Lane Miles Rated 85 or Better

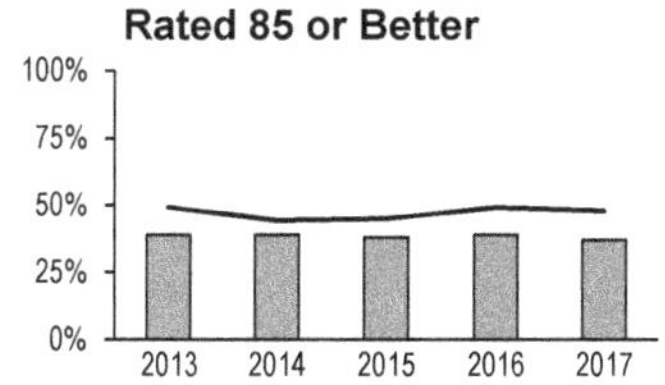

	2013	2014	2015	2016	2017
Hickory	39%	39%	38%	39%	37%
Average	49%	44%	45%	49%	48%

Percent of Lane Miles Rated Below 45

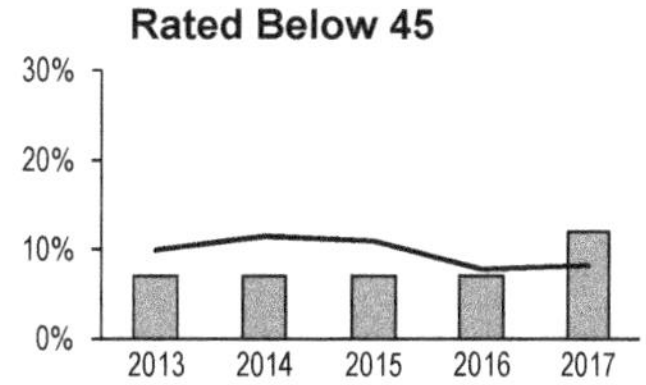

	2013	2014	2015	2016	2017
Hickory	7.0%	7.0%	7.0%	7.0%	12.0%
Average	9.9%	11.4%	10.9%	7.7%	8.1%

Percentage of Potholes Repaired within 24 hours

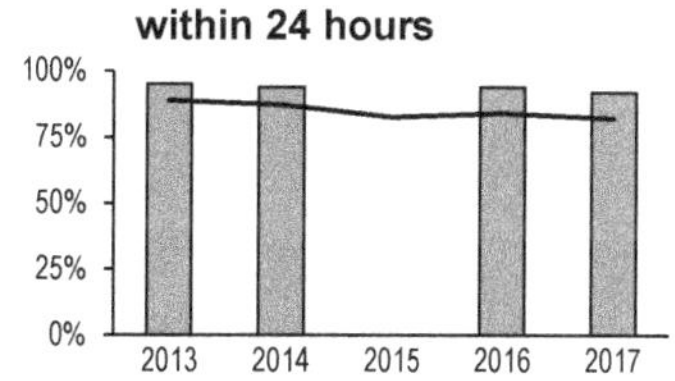

	2013	2014	2015	2016	2017
Hickory	95%	94%		94%	92%
Average	89%	87%	83%	84%	82%

High Point

Asphalt Maintenance

Fiscal Year 2016–17

Explanatory Information

Service Level and Delivery

The City of High Point was responsible for maintaining 1,321 lane miles during the fiscal year, which includes 340 lane miles of state roads. The city treated 31.3 lane miles by various methods, equating to 2.4 percent of total lane miles.

City crews resurfaced eight lane miles using 5,576 tons of asphalt. Contract crews rehabilitated 23.3 lane miles which includes resurfacing preceded by milling work. A total of 17,126 tons of asphalt were used by the contracting crews. The average resurfacing depth was two inches for the city and contract crew work.

The city reported that 47 percent of its street segments rated 85 or above on its most recent pavement condition rating, conducted in 2014. The rating was done by a consultant using the Institute for Transportation Research and Education (ITRE) rating system.

The number of potholes reported for the year was 1,338, including self-reported and citizen-reported potholes. The percentage of potholes repaired within twenty-four hours was 95 percent.

A total of 324 utility cuts were made in the streets during the year. The Streets Division places asphalt in water-sewer utility cuts after the utility forces backfill and compacts. Material, equipment, and personnel costs are tracked for this repair. Funds are transferred from the Water-Sewer Mains Division to recover applicable expenses associated with patching.

Conditions Affecting Service, Performance, and Costs

Improvements in FY 2013–14 in the measurement and tracking of road segments in High Point have produced an estimate of fewer lane miles than in prior years. Rather than an actual drop in lane miles, the lower reported mileage reflects a more accurate tracking. The relative decrease in reported lane miles means that some of the performance measures saw an increase, which was due to this improvement in measurement rather than actual changes.

Municipal Profile

Population (OSBM 2016)	110,244
Land Area (Square Miles)	55.14
Persons per Square Mile	1,999
Topography	Flat; gently rolling
Climate	Temperate; little ice and snow

Service Profile

FTE Positions—Crews	14.00
FTE Positions—Other	1.25
Lane Miles Maintained	1,321.0
Lane Miles Treated	
Preservation	0.0
Resurfacing	8.0
Rehabilitation	23.3
TOTAL	31.3
Total Costs for All Treatment Types	$2,330,733
Potholes Repaired	1,338
Number of Utility Cuts	324
Number of Maintenance Patches (exclusive of potholes and utility cuts)	89
Average Cost per Ton of Hot Asphalt during Year	$55.00

Full Cost Profile

Cost Breakdown by Percentage	
Personal Services	18.4%
Operating Costs	75.9%
Capital Costs	5.8%
TOTAL	100.0%
Cost Breakdown in Dollars	
Personal Services	$719,197
Operating Costs	$2,971,418
Capital Costs	$226,427
TOTAL	$3,917,042

Key: High Point ▒ Benchmarking Average — Fiscal Years 2013 through 2017

Resource Measures

Asphalt Maintenance and Repair Services Costs per Capita

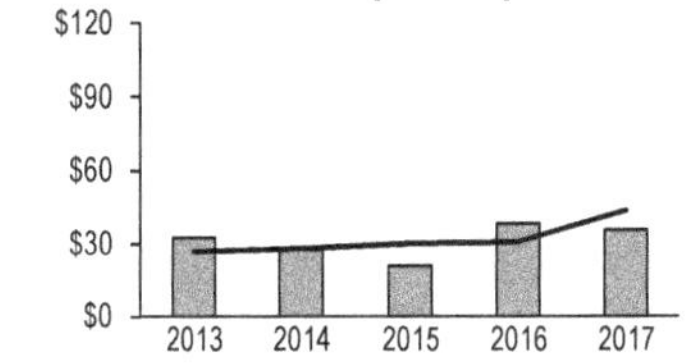

	2013	2014	2015	2016	2017
High Point	$32.28	$27.31	$20.61	$38.04	$35.53
Average	$27.05	$28.29	$30.30	$30.70	$43.66

Asphalt Maintenance and Repair FTEs per 10,000 Population

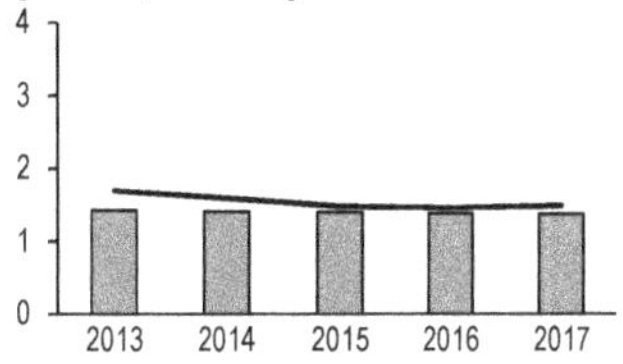

	2013	2014	2015	2016	2017
High Point	1.43	1.42	1.40	1.39	1.38
Average	1.70	1.60	1.49	1.48	1.49

Service Costs per Lane Mile of Road Maintained

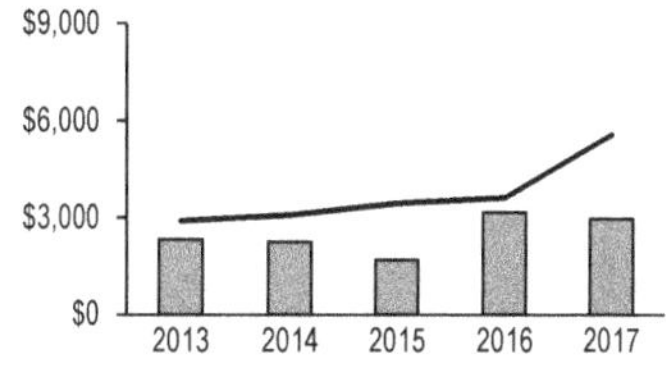

	2013	2014	2015	2016	2017
High Point	$2,323	$2,244	$1,697	$3,165	$2,965
Average	$2,923	$3,110	$3,452	$3,632	$5,582

Workload Measures

Number of Lane Miles Maintained per 1,000 Population

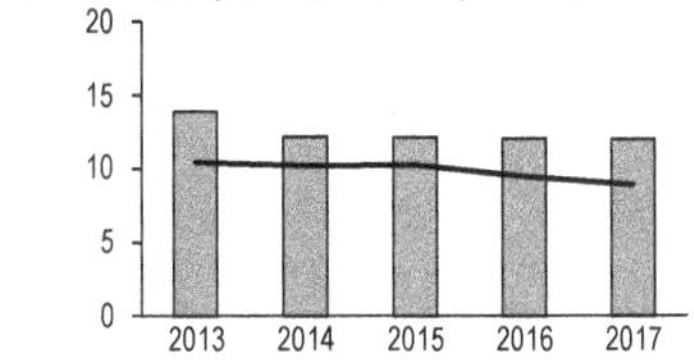

	2013	2014	2015	2016	2017
High Point	13.9	12.2	12.1	12.0	12.0
Average	10.4	10.2	10.2	9.5	8.9

Reported Potholes per Lane Mile Maintained

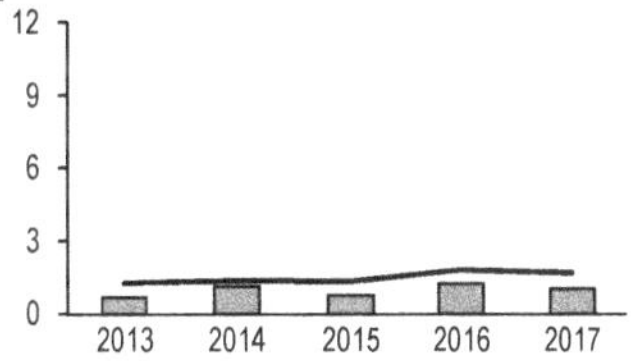

	2013	2014	2015	2016	2017
High Point	0.66	1.13	0.73	1.21	1.01
Average	1.26	1.35	1.34	1.78	1.67

Repaired Utility Cuts per Lane Mile Maintained

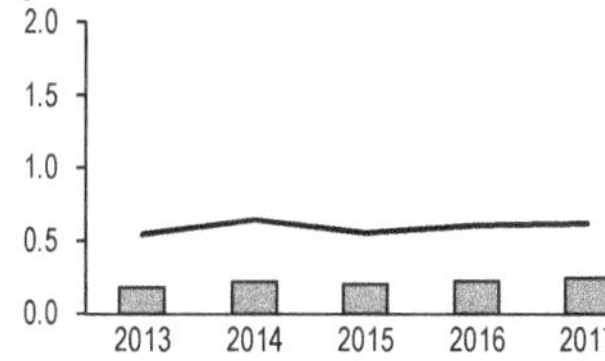

	2013	2014	2015	2016	2017
High Point	0.18	0.22	0.20	0.22	0.25
Average	0.54	0.64	0.55	0.61	0.62

Efficiency Measures

Cost of Maintenance per Lane Mile Maintained

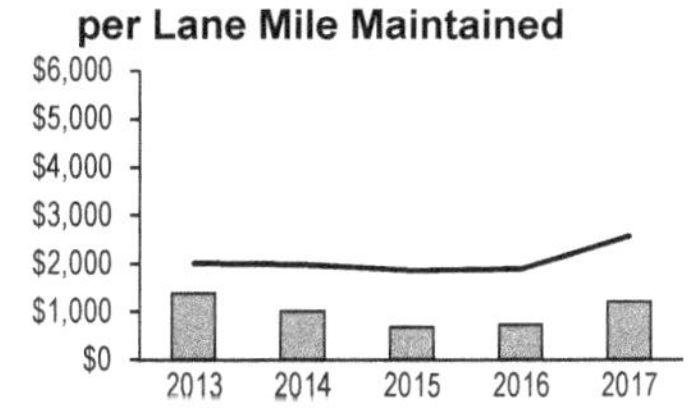

	2013	2014	2015	2016	2017
High Point	$1,375	$1,004	$667	$717	$1,201
Average	$2,005	$1,976	$1,852	$1,894	$2,564

Cost per Lane Mile for Preservation Treatment

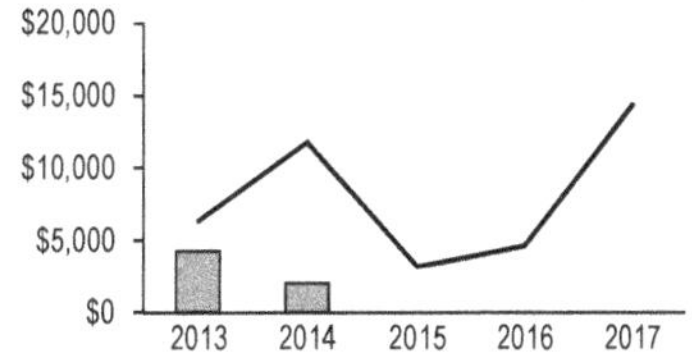

	2013	2014	2015	2016	2017
High Point	$4,243	$2,016			
Average	$6,371	$11,806	$3,214	$4,648	$14,370

Cost per Lane Mile for Resurfacing Treatment

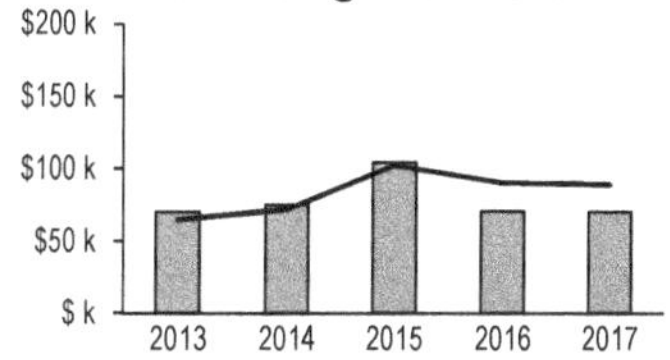

	2013	2014	2015	2016	2017
High Point	$70 k	$75 k	$104 k	$70 k	$70 k
Average	$65 k	$72 k	$102 k	$90 k	$89 k

Cost per Lane Mile for Rehabilitation Treatment

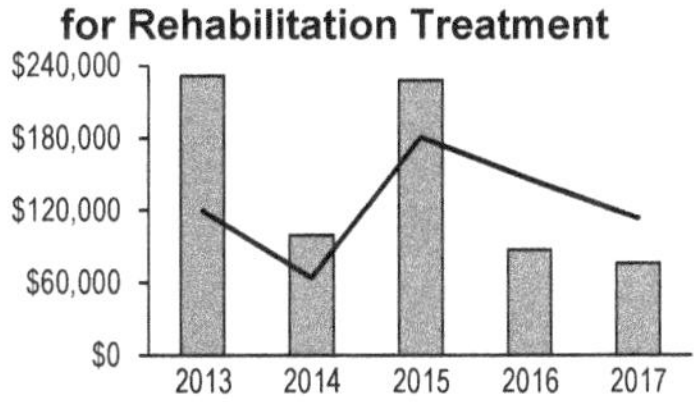

	2013	2014	2015	2016	2017
High Point	$232 k	$100 k	$228 k	$87 k	$76 k
Average	$119 k	$64 k	$181 k	$147 k	$113 k

Cost per Ton for Contract Resurfacing

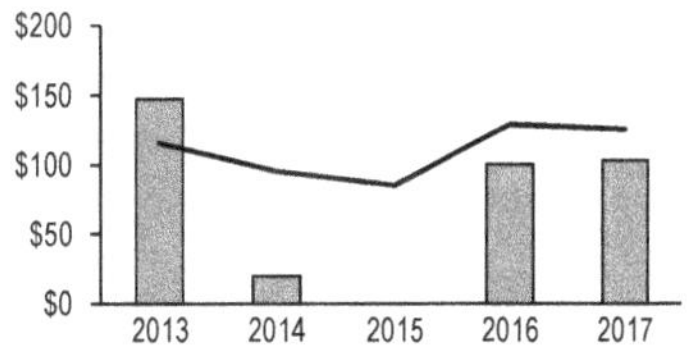

	2013	2014	2015	2016	2017
High Point	$148	$20		$101	$103
Average	$116	$96	$86	$129	$125

Effectiveness Measures

Percent of Lane Miles Rated 85 or Better

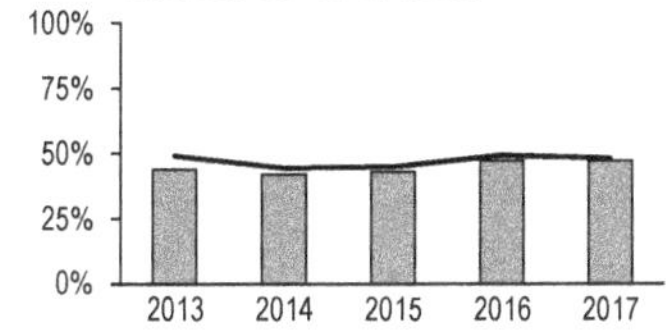

	2013	2014	2015	2016	2017
High Point	44%	42%	43%	47%	47%
Average	49%	44%	45%	49%	48%

Percent of Lane Miles Rated Below 45

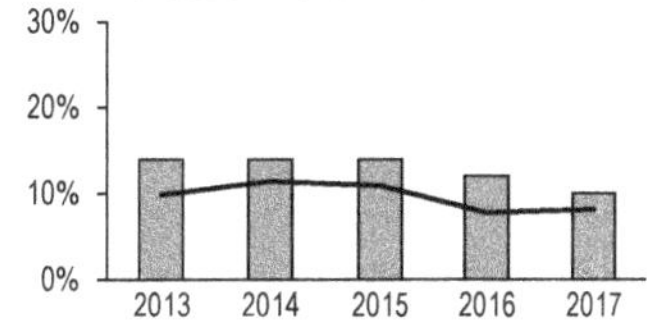

	2013	2014	2015	2016	2017
High Point	14.0%	14.0%	14.0%	12.0%	10.0%
Average	9.9%	11.4%	10.9%	7.7%	8.1%

Percentage of Potholes Repaired within 24 hours

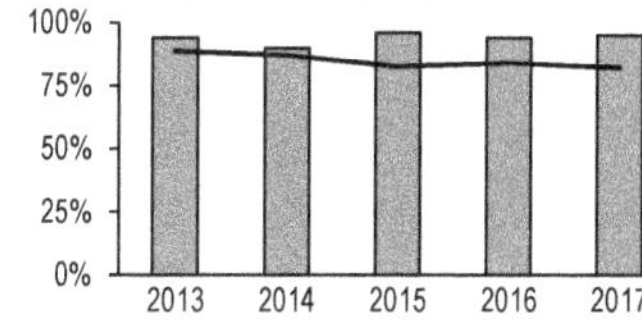

	2013	2014	2015	2016	2017
High Point	94%	90%	96%	94%	95%
Average	89%	87%	83%	84%	82%

Raleigh — Asphalt Maintenance

Fiscal Year 2016–17

Explanatory Information

Service Level and Delivery

The City of Raleigh's Department of Transportation has the responsibility for street maintenance. During the year the city was responsible for maintaining approximately 2,293 lane miles.

The city used contractors to resurface 26 lane miles (1.1 percent of total lane miles). The contractors used a total of 37,952 tons of asphalt laid to an average depth of 1.5 to 2 inches.

The city reported that 70 percent of its lane miles rated 85 or above on its most recent pavement condition rating, conducted in 2016. The city used city staff conducting a windshield survey following the Institute for Transportation Research and Education (ITRE) rating system.

The number of potholes reported for the year was 5,506. A total of 1,031 utility cuts were also made, with the city repairing all of these.

Conditions Affecting Service, Performance, and Costs

Raleigh rejoined the Benchmarking Project in July 2016 with the first year of data showing for FY 2015–16.

Municipal Profile

Population (OSBM 2016)	448,706
Land Area (Square Miles)	145.57
Persons per Square Mile	3,083
Topography	Flat; gently rolling
Climate	Temperate; little ice and snow

Service Profile

FTE Positions—Crews	40.00
FTE Positions—Other	8.00
Lane Miles Maintained	2,293.0
Lane Miles Treated	
Preservation	0.0
Resurfacing	26.0
Rehabilitation	0.0
TOTAL	26.0
Total Costs for All Treatment Types	$6,785,390
Potholes Repaired	5,506
Number of Utility Cuts	1,031
Number of Maintenance Patches (exclusive of potholes and utility cuts)	NA
Average Cost per Ton of Hot Asphalt during Year	$61.00

Full Cost Profile

Cost Breakdown by Percentage	
Personal Services	20.4%
Operating Costs	70.5%
Capital Costs	9.1%
TOTAL	100.0%
Cost Breakdown in Dollars	
Personal Services	$2,623,999
Operating Costs	$9,092,709
Capital Costs	$1,173,216
TOTAL	$12,889,924

Key: Raleigh ▒ Benchmarking Average — Fiscal Years 2013 through 2017

Resource Measures

Asphalt Maintenance and Repair Services Costs per Capita

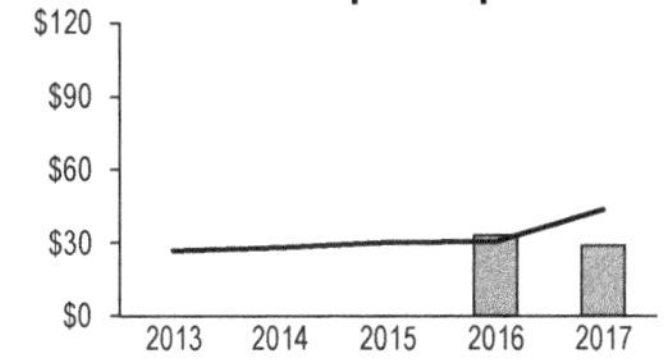

	2013	2014	2015	2016	2017
Raleigh				$32.95	$28.73
Average	$27.05	$28.29	$30.38	$30.70	$43.66

Asphalt Maintenance and Repair FTEs per 10,000 Population

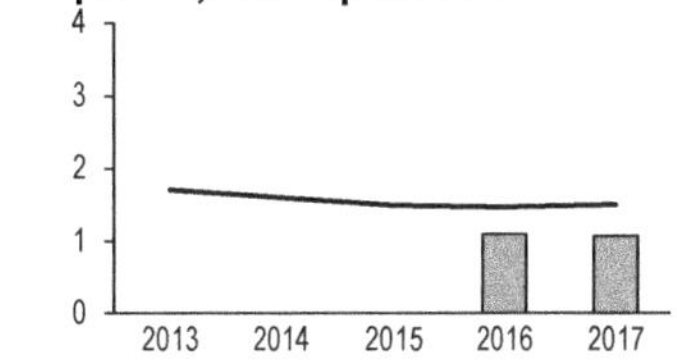

	2013	2014	2015	2016	2017
Raleigh				1.09	1.07
Average	1.70	1.60	1.49	1.46	1.49

Service Costs per Lane Mile of Road Maintained

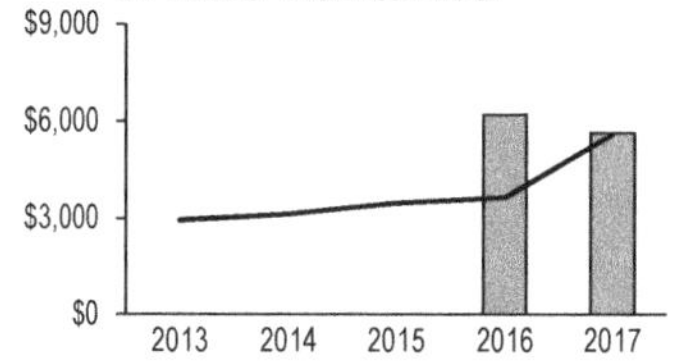

	2013	2014	2015	2016	2017
Raleigh				$6,180	$5,621
Average	$2,923	$3,110	$3,452	$3,632	$5,582

Workload Measures

Number of Lane Miles Maintained per 1,000 Population

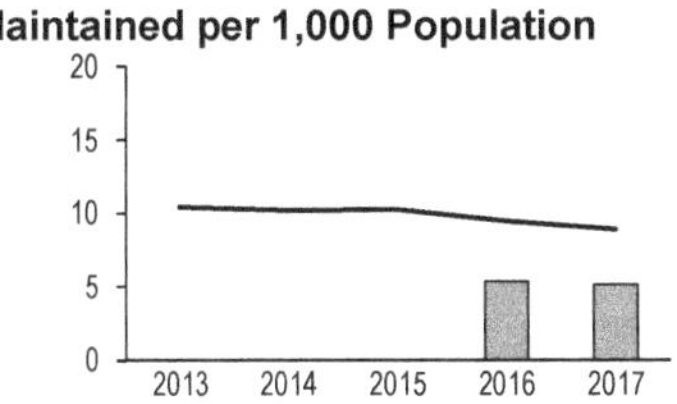

	2013	2014	2015	2016	2017
Raleigh				5.3	5.1
Average	10.4	10.2	10.2	9.5	8.9

Reported Potholes per Lane Mile Maintained

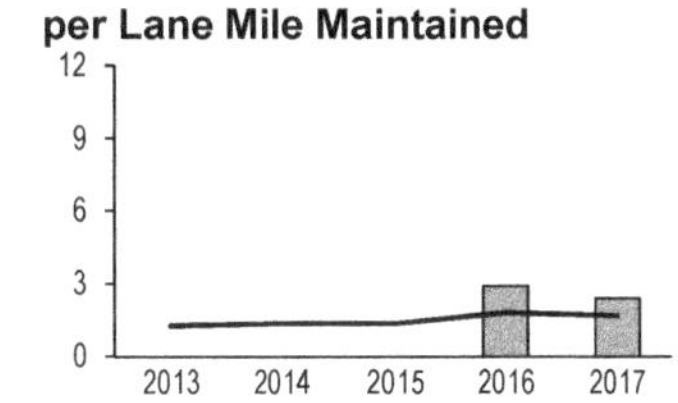

	2013	2014	2015	2016	2017
Raleigh				2.91	2.40
Average	1.26	1.35	1.34	1.78	1.67

Repaired Utility Cuts per Lane Mile Maintained

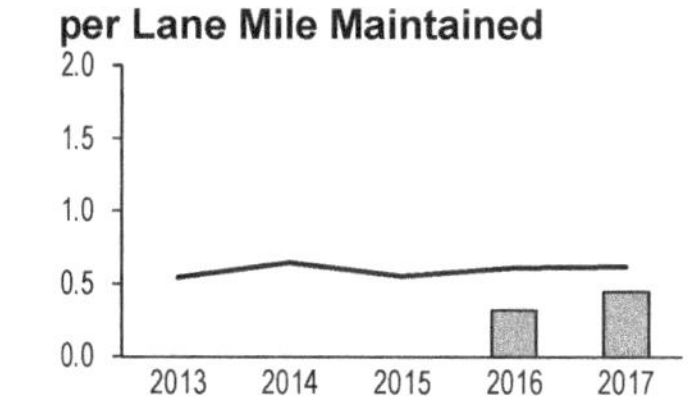

	2013	2014	2015	2016	2017
Raleigh				0.32	0.45
Average	0.54	0.64	0.55	0.61	0.62

Efficiency Measures

Cost of Maintenance per Lane Mile Maintained

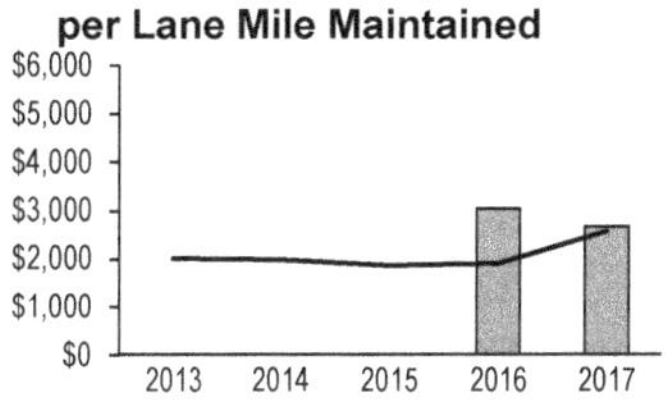

	2013	2014	2015	2016	2017
Raleigh				$3,030	$2,662
Average	$2,005	$1,976	$1,852	$1,894	$2,564

Cost per Lane Mile for Preservation Treatment

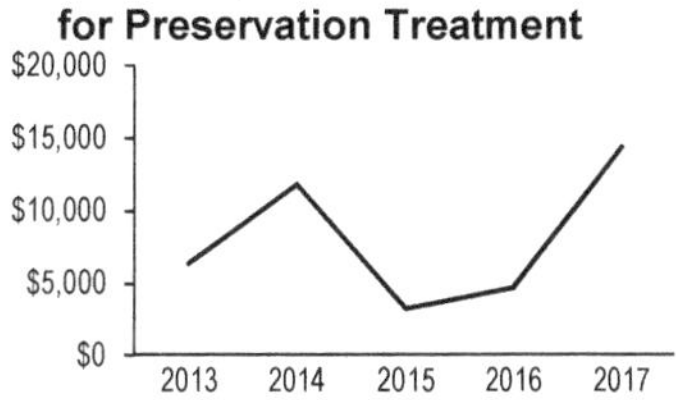

	2013	2014	2015	2016	2017
Raleigh					
Average	$6,371	$11,806	$3,214	$4,648	$14,370

Cost per Lane Mile for Resurfacing Treatment

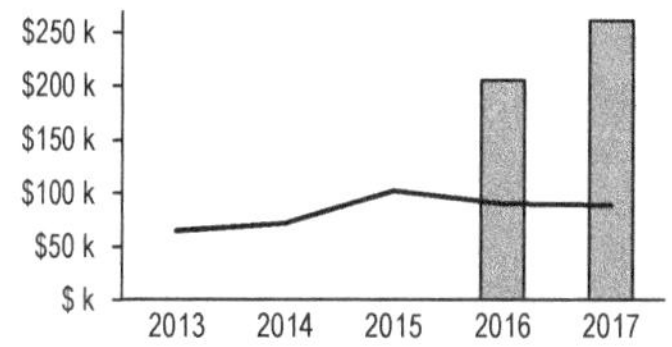

	2013	2014	2015	2016	2017
Raleigh				$206 k	$261 k
Average	$65 k	$72 k	$102 k	$90 k	$89 k

Cost per Lane Mile for Rehabilitation Treatment

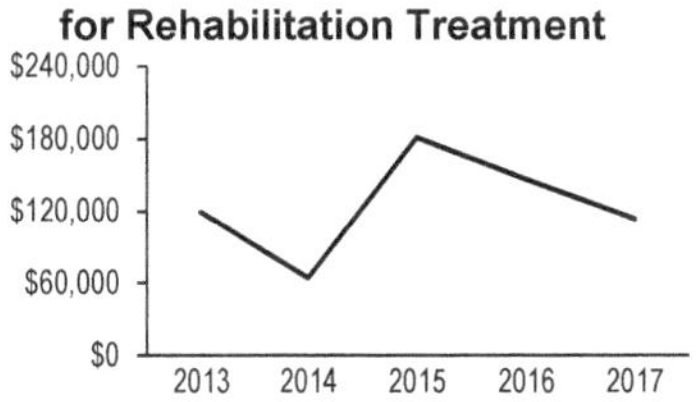

	2013	2014	2015	2016	2017
Raleigh					
Average	$119 k	$64 k	$181 k	$147 k	$113 k

Cost per Ton for Contract Resurfacing

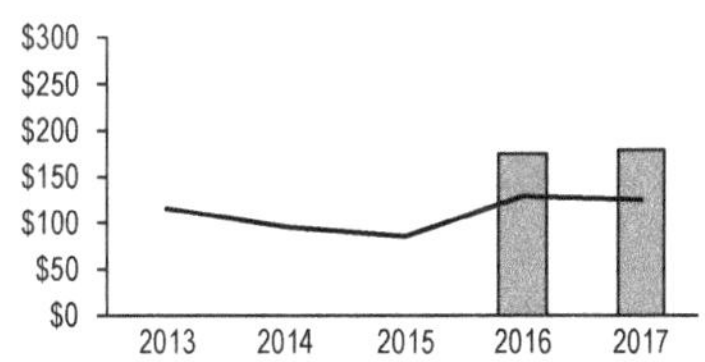

	2013	2014	2015	2016	2017
Raleigh				$175	$179
Average	$116	$96	$86	$129	$125

Effectiveness Measures

Percent of Lane Miles Rated 85 or Better

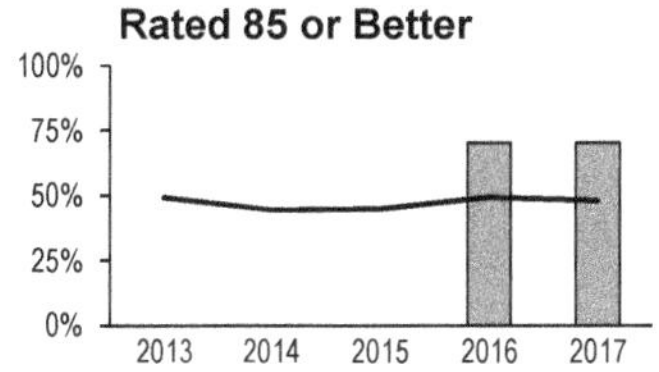

	2013	2014	2015	2016	2017
Raleigh				70%	70%
Average	49%	44%	45%	49%	48%

Percent of Lane Miles Rated Below 45

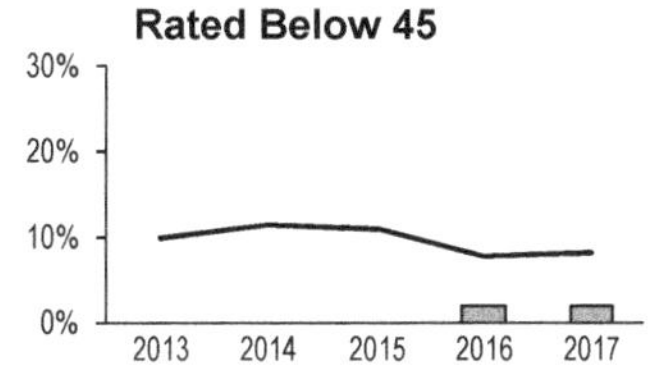

	2013	2014	2015	2016	2017
Raleigh				2.0%	2.0%
Average	9.9%	11.4%	10.9%	7.7%	8.1%

Percentage of Potholes Repaired within 24 hours

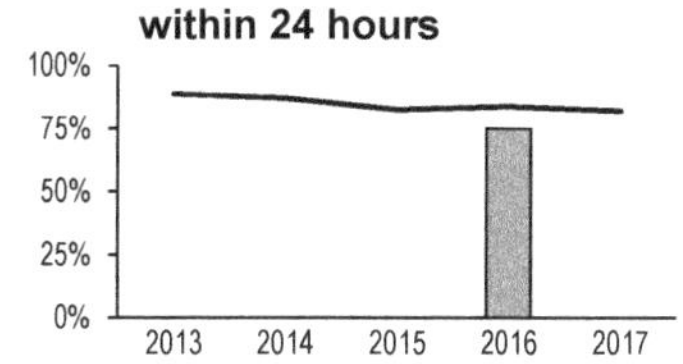

	2013	2014	2015	2016	2017
Raleigh				75%	
Average	89%	87%	83%	84%	82%

Fiscal Year 2016–17

Explanatory Information

Service Level and Delivery

The City of Salisbury was responsible for maintaining approximately 345 lane miles during the fiscal year. The city treated a total of 8.1 lane miles, or 2.3 percent of total lane miles.

City crews treated a total of 1.3 lane miles with preservation methods which includes crack sealing or thin seal overlays. Contractors resurfaced 1.04 lane miles and a further 5.8 lane miles received rehabilitation, which involves milling before resurfacing. The contractors used a total of 4,738 tons of asphalt, and the average resurfacing depth used by the contractors was 1.5 inches.

The city reported that 67 percent of its lane miles rated 85 or above on its most recent pavement condition rating, conducted in 2010. The city used a consultant for the rating, who relied on the Institute for Transportation Research and Education (ITRE) rating system.

The number of potholes reported for the year was 366. The percentage of potholes repaired within twenty-four hours was 100 percent. A total of sixty-three utility cuts were also made, with the city repairing all of these. Additionally, 109 maintenance patches were done, which are not included in the pothole or utility cut numbers.

Conditions Affecting Service, Performance, and Costs

Municipal Profile

Population (OSBM 2016)	34,459
Land Area (Square Miles)	22.28
Persons per Square Mile	1,547
Topography	Flat; gently rolling
Climate	Temperate; little ice and snow

Service Profile

FTE Positions—Crews	4.00
FTE Positions—Other	0.25
Lane Miles Maintained	345.5
Lane Miles Treated	
Preservation	1.3
Resurfacing	1.0
Rehabilitation	5.8
TOTAL	8.1
Total Costs for All Treatment Types	$519,825
Potholes Repaired	366
Number of Utility Cuts	63
Number of Maintenance Patches (exclusive of potholes and utility cuts)	109
Average Cost per Ton of Hot Asphalt during Year	$91.00

Full Cost Profile

Cost Breakdown by Percentage	
Personal Services	8.1%
Operating Costs	45.9%
Capital Costs	46.0%
TOTAL	100.0%
Cost Breakdown in Dollars	
Personal Services	$106,165
Operating Costs	$602,420
Capital Costs	$604,036
TOTAL	$1,312,621

Salisbury Asphalt Maintenance and Repair

Key: Salisbury ▒ Benchmarking Average — Fiscal Years 2013 through 2017

Resource Measures

Asphalt Maintenance and Repair Services Costs per Capita

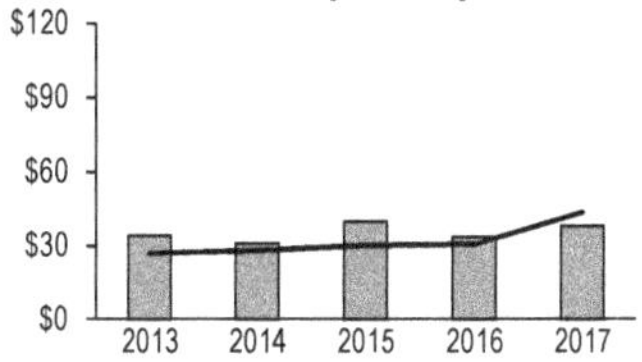

	2013	2014	2015	2016	2017
Salisbury	$34.15	$30.98	$40.01	$33.76	$38.09
Average	$27.05	$28.29	$30.38	$30.70	$43.66

Asphalt Maintenance and Repair FTEs per 10,000 Population

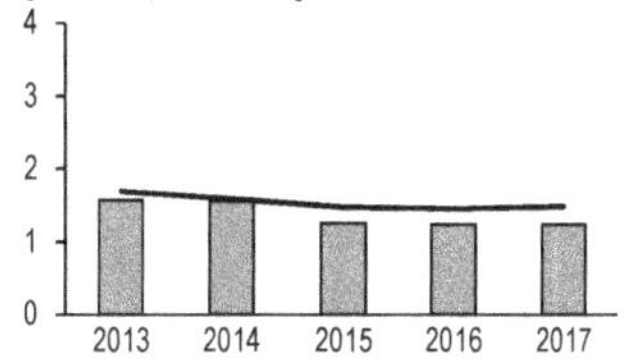

	2013	2014	2015	2016	2017
Salisbury	1.57	1.56	1.25	1.24	1.23
Average	1.70	1.60	1.49	1.46	1.49

Service Costs per Lane Mile of Road Maintained

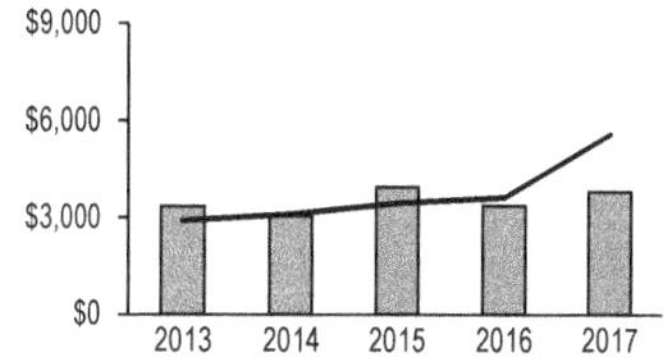

	2013	2014	2015	2016	2017
Salisbury	$3,336	$3,031	$3,941	$3,353	$3,799
Average	$2,923	$3,110	$3,452	$3,632	$5,582

Workload Measures

Number of Lane Miles Maintained per 1,000 Population

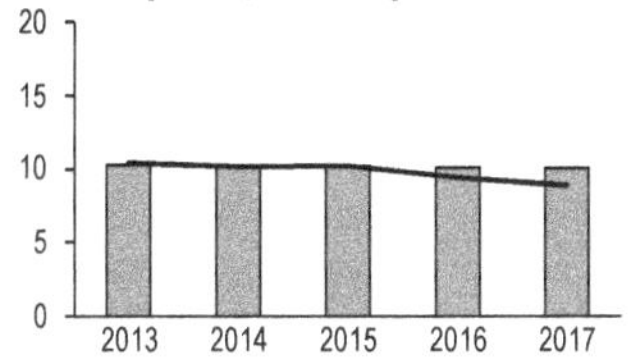

	2013	2014	2015	2016	2017
Salisbury	10.2	10.2	10.2	10.1	10.0
Average	10.4	10.2	10.2	9.5	8.9

Reported Potholes per Lane Mile Maintained

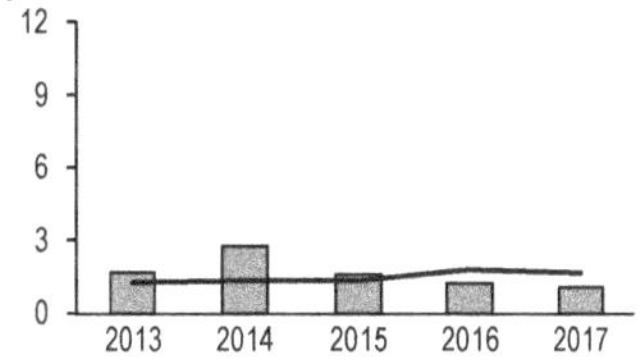

	2013	2014	2015	2016	2017
Salisbury	1.66	2.75	1.59	1.23	1.06
Average	1.26	1.35	1.34	1.78	1.67

Repaired Utility Cuts per Lane Mile Maintained

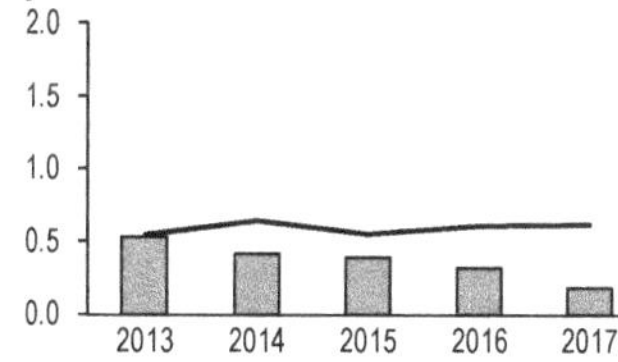

	2013	2014	2015	2016	2017
Salisbury	0.53	0.41	0.39	0.32	0.18
Average	0.54	0.64	0.55	0.61	0.62

Efficiency Measures

Cost of Maintenance per Lane Mile Maintained

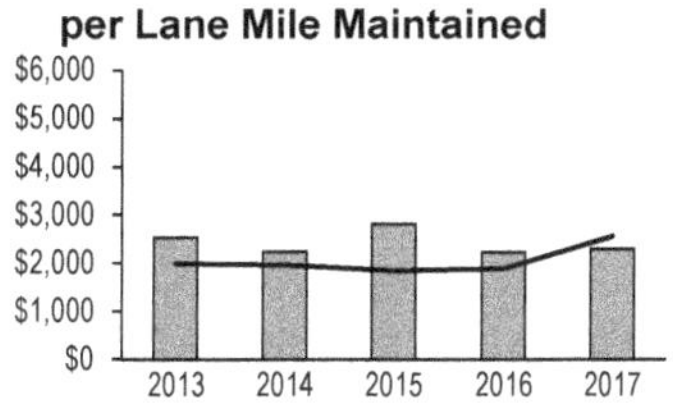

	2013	2014	2015	2016	2017
Salisbury	$2,537	$2,242	$2,811	$2,236	$2,295
Average	$2,005	$1,976	$1,852	$1,894	$2,564

Cost per Lane Mile for Preservation Treatment

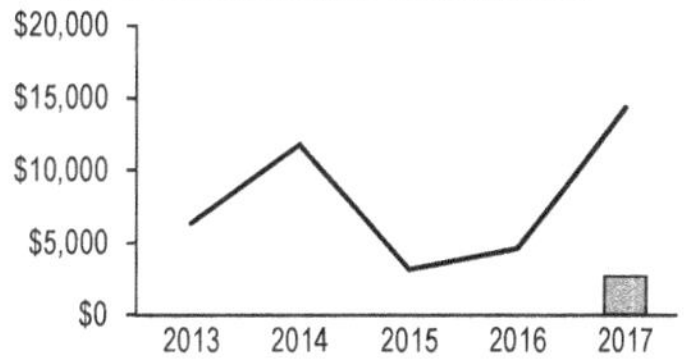

	2013	2014	2015	2016	2017
Salisbury					$2,704
Average	$6,371	$11,806	$3,214	$4,648	$14,370

Cost per Lane Mile for Resurfacing Treatment

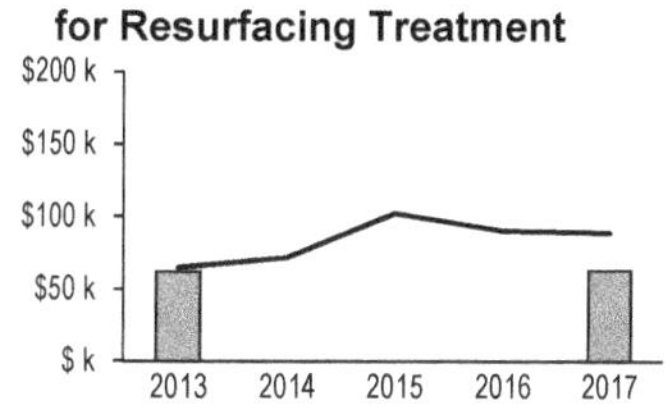

	2013	2014	2015	2016	2017
Salisbury	$62 k				$63 k
Average	$65 k	$72 k	$102 k	$90 k	$89 k

Cost per Lane Mile for Rehabilitation Treatment

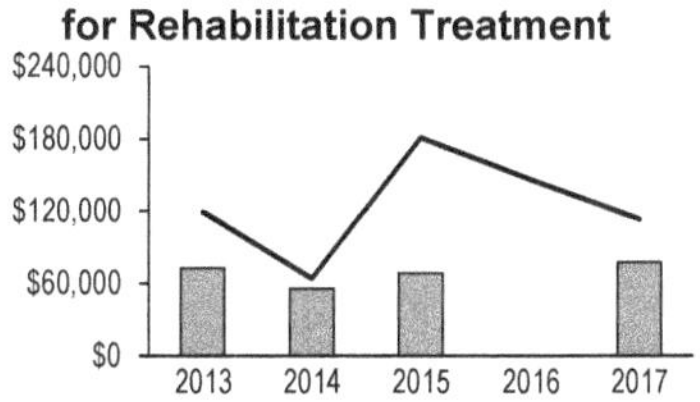

	2013	2014	2015	2016	2017
Salisbury	$73 k	$56 k	$69 k		$78 k
Average	$119 k	$64 k	$181 k	$147 k	$113 k

Cost per Ton for Contract Resurfacing

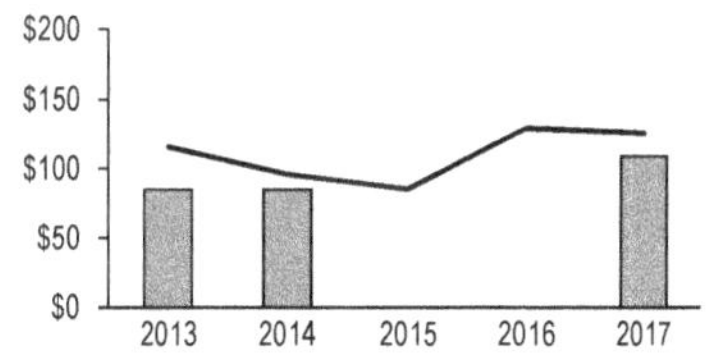

	2013	2014	2015	2016	2017
Salisbury	$85	$85			$109
Average	$116	$96	$86	$129	$125

Effectiveness Measures

Percent of Lane Miles Rated 85 or Better

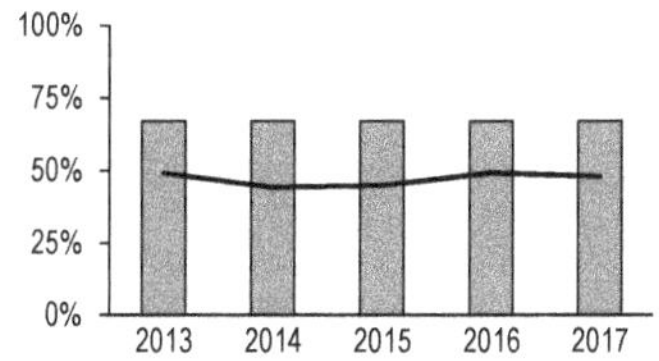

	2013	2014	2015	2016	2017
Salisbury	67%	67%	67%	67%	67%
Average	49%	44%	45%	49%	48%

Percent of Lane Miles Rated Below 45

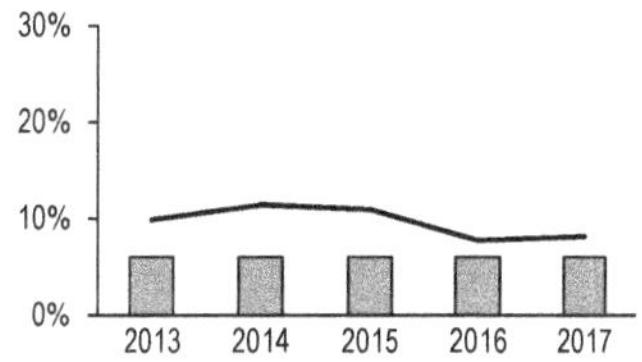

	2013	2014	2015	2016	2017
Salisbury	6.0%	6.0%	6.0%	6.0%	6.0%
Average	9.9%	11.4%	10.9%	7.7%	8.1%

Percentage of Potholes Repaired within 24 hours

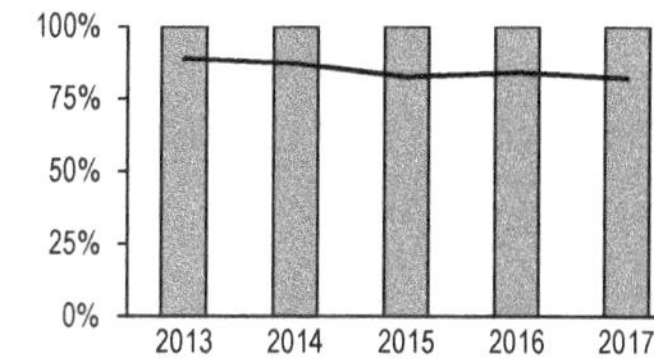

	2013	2014	2015	2016	2017
Salisbury	100%	100%	100%	100%	100%
Average	89%	87%	83%	84%	82%

Fiscal Year 2016–17

Explanatory Information

Service Level and Delivery

The City of Wilson was responsible for maintaining approximately 695 lane miles of city streets during the year. The city treated a total of 18.5 lane miles during the year, or 2.7 percent of the total lane miles maintained.

Contract crews treated 6.0 lane miles with resurfacing. City crews performed preservation work on 5.5 lane miles and contractors did preservation work on an additional 7.0 lane miles. Preservation techniques include methods such as crack sealing or thin overlays.

The city reported that 54 percent of its lane miles rated 85 or above on its most recent pavement condition rating, conducted in 2014. The city relied on a consultant for the rating, who used a customized rating based on the Institute for Transportation Research and Education (ITRE) system.

The number of potholes reported for the year was 1,652. The percentage of potholes repaired within twenty-four hours was 90 percent. Repairs to 1,142 utility cuts were also made during the year.

Conditions Affecting Service, Performance, and Costs

The cost of asphalt and maintenance materials is directly related to fluctuations in the price of petroleum.

Municipal Profile

Population (OSBM 2016)	49,406
Land Area (Square Miles)	30.60
Persons per Square Mile	1,615
Topography	Flat
Climate	Temperate; little ice and snow

Service Profile

FTE Positions—Crews	5.00
FTE Positions—Other	0.50
Lane Miles Maintained	695.4
Lane Miles Treated	
Preservation	12.5
Resurfacing	6.0
Rehabilitation	0.0
TOTAL	18.5
Total Costs for All Treatment Types	$663,958
Potholes Repaired	1,652
Number of Utility Cuts	1,142
Number of Maintenance Patches (exclusive of potholes and utility cuts)	890
Average Cost per Ton of Hot Asphalt during Year	$78.00

Full Cost Profile

Cost Breakdown by Percentage	
Personal Services	22.4%
Operating Costs	71.7%
Capital Costs	5.9%
TOTAL	100.0%
Cost Breakdown in Dollars	
Personal Services	$402,246
Operating Costs	$1,285,715
Capital Costs	$106,348
TOTAL	$1,794,308

Wilson

Asphalt Maintenance and Repair

Key: Wilson ▒ Benchmarking Average — Fiscal Years 2013 through 2017

Resource Measures

Asphalt Maintenance and Repair Services Costs per Capita

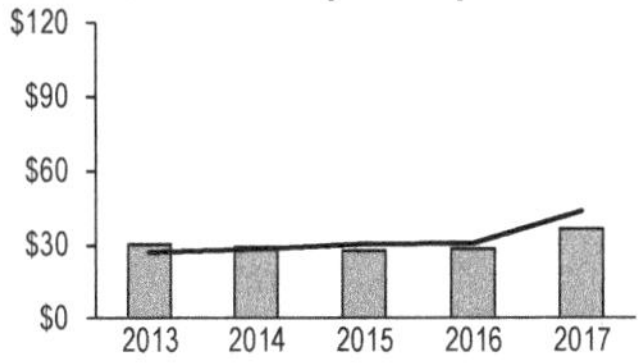

	2013	2014	2015	2016	2017
Wilson	$30.25	$28.98	$27.48	$28.44	$36.32
Average	$27.05	$28.29	$30.38	$30.70	$43.66

Asphalt Maintenance and Repair FTEs per 10,000 Population

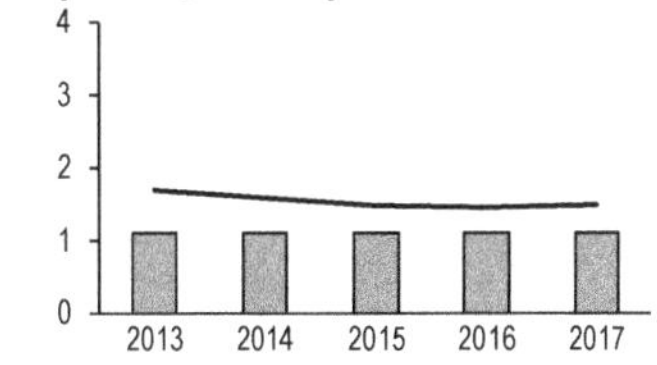

	2013	2014	2015	2016	2017
Wilson	1.11	1.12	1.12	1.11	1.11
Average	1.70	1.60	1.49	1.46	1.49

Service Costs per Lane Mile of Road Maintained

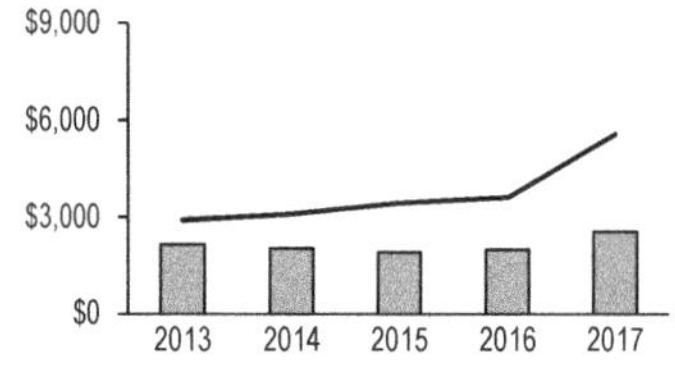

	2013	2014	2015	2016	2017
Wilson	$2,171	$2,049	$1,945	$2,019	$2,580
Average	$2,923	$3,110	$3,452	$3,632	$5,582

Workload Measures

Number of Lane Miles Maintained per 1,000 Population

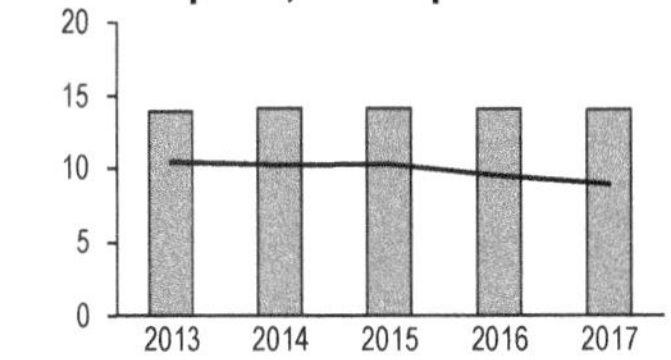

	2013	2014	2015	2016	2017
Wilson	13.9	14.1	14.1	14.1	14.1
Average	10.4	10.2	10.2	9.5	8.9

Reported Potholes per Lane Mile Maintained

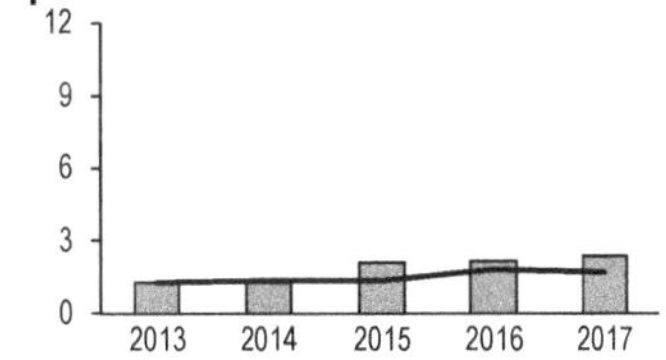

	2013	2014	2015	2016	2017
Wilson	1.29	1.28	2.11	2.15	2.38
Average	1.26	1.35	1.34	1.78	1.67

Repaired Utility Cuts per Lane Mile Maintained

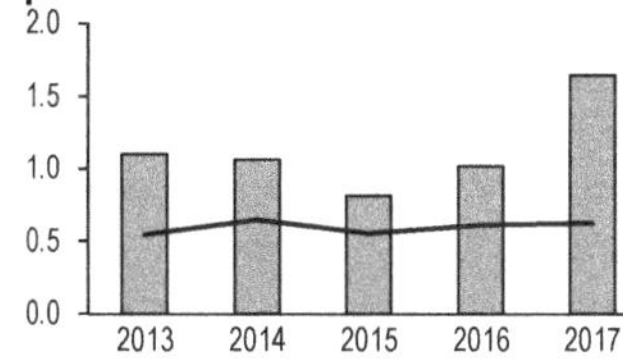

	2013	2014	2015	2016	2017
Wilson	1.10	1.06	0.81	1.01	1.64
Average	0.54	0.64	0.55	0.61	0.62

Efficiency Measures

Cost of Maintenance per Lane Mile Maintained

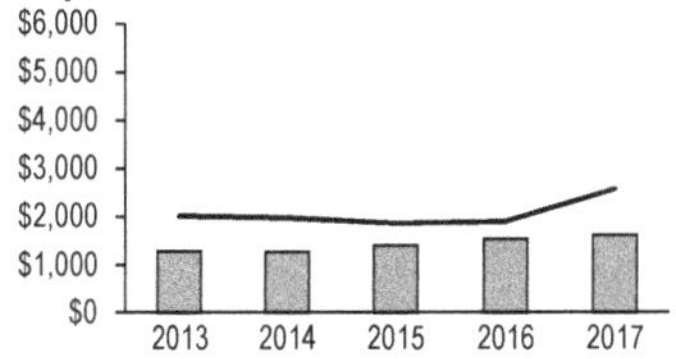

	2013	2014	2015	2016	2017
Wilson	$1,298	$1,278	$1,410	$1,540	$1,620
Average	$2,005	$1,976	$1,852	$1,894	$2,564

Cost per Lane Mile for Preservation Treatment

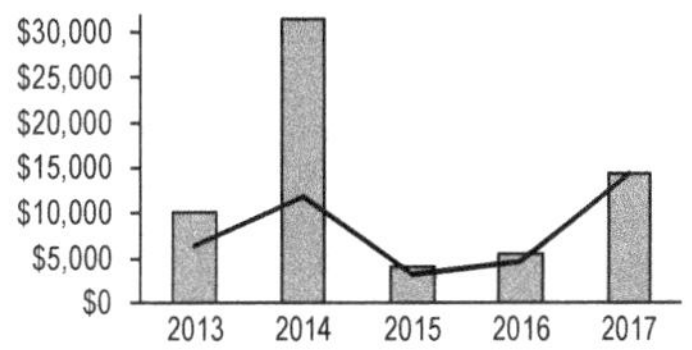

	2013	2014	2015	2016	2017
Wilson	$10,066	$31,387	$4,077	$5,500	$14,360
Average	$6,371	$11,806	$3,214	$4,648	$14,370

Cost per Lane Mile for Resurfacing Treatment

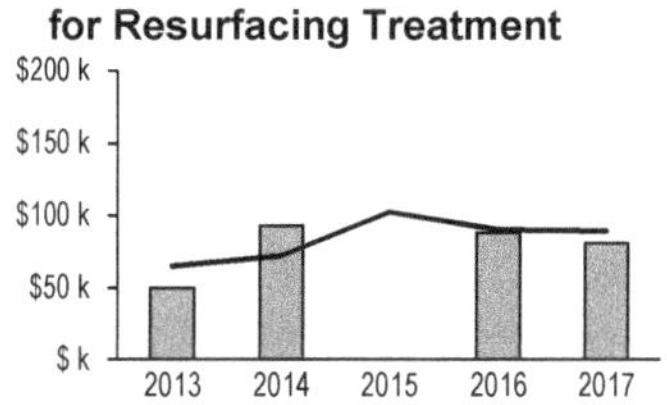

	2013	2014	2015	2016	2017
Wilson	$50 k	$93 k		$88 k	$81 k
Average	$65 k	$72 k	$102 k	$90 k	$89 k

Cost per Lane Mile for Rehabilitation Treatment

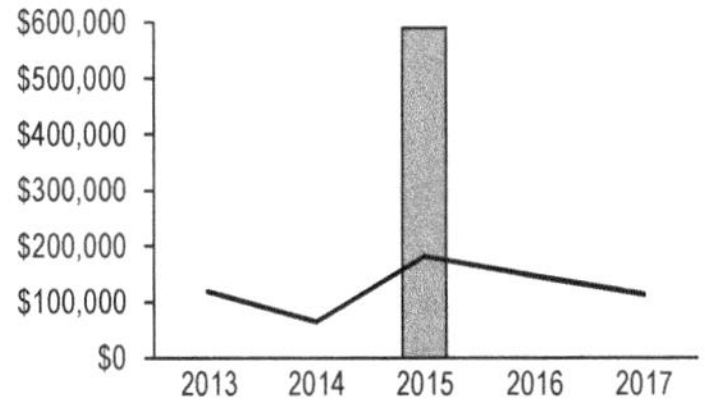

	2013	2014	2015	2016	2017
Wilson			$590 k		
Average	$119 k	$64 k	$181 k	$147 k	$113 k

Cost per Ton for Contract Resurfacing

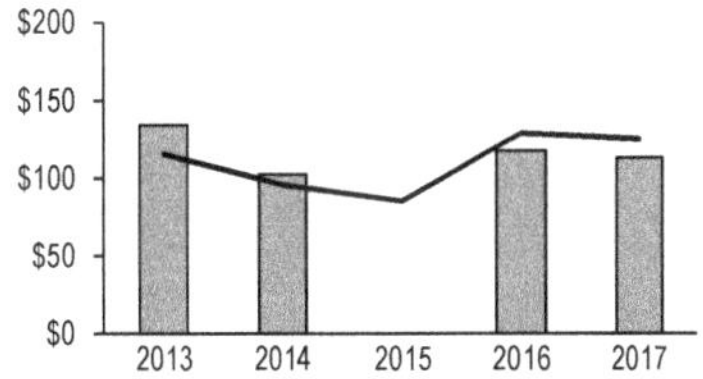

	2013	2014	2015	2016	2017
Wilson	$134	$103		$118	$113
Average	$116	$96	$86	$129	$125

Effectiveness Measures

Percent of Lane Miles Rated 85 or Better

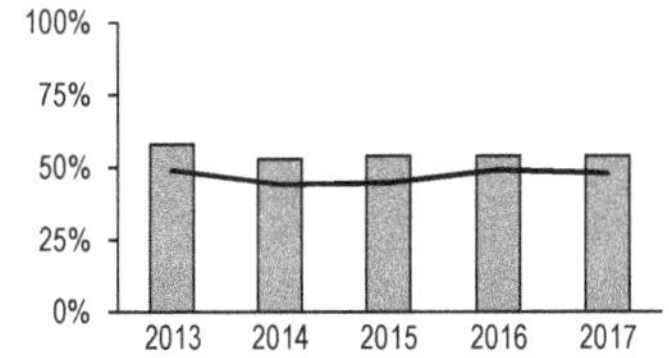

	2013	2014	2015	2016	2017
Wilson	58%	53%	54%	54%	54%
Average	49%	44%	45%	49%	48%

Percent of Lane Miles Rated Below 45

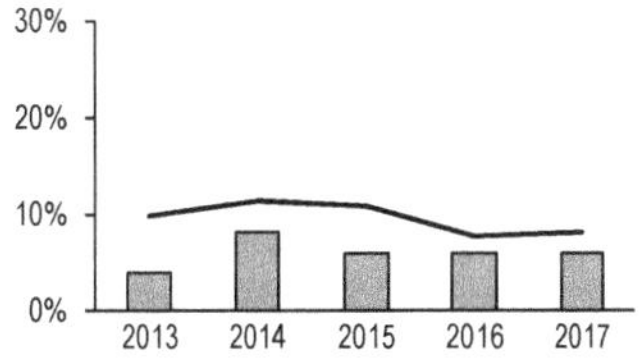

	2013	2014	2015	2016	2017
Wilson	4.0%	8.2%	6.0%	6.0%	6.0%
Average	9.9%	11.4%	10.9%	7.7%	8.1%

Percentage of Potholes Repaired within 24 hours

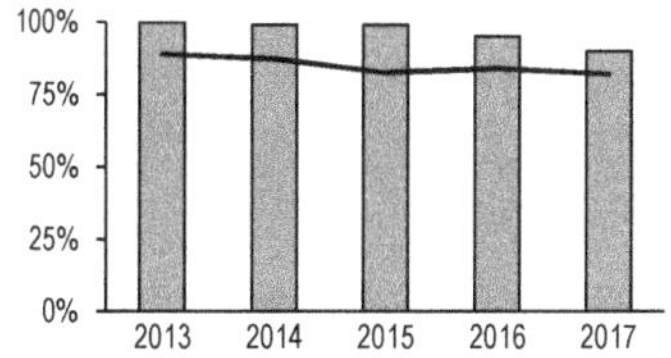

	2013	2014	2015	2016	2017
Wilson	100%	99%	99%	95%	90%
Average	89%	87%	83%	84%	82%

Fiscal Year 2016–17

Explanatory Information

Service Level and Delivery

The City of Winston-Salem was responsible for maintaining approximately 2,329.2 lane miles of city streets during the fiscal year. The city treated 129.0 lane miles or 5.5 percent of the total lane miles.

The city used a variety of treatment methods for repair of roads by both city crews and contractors. A total of about 23.7 lane miles were treated with preservation methods such as crack sealing or thin overlays. Contract crews did 18.39 lane miles of preservation work and city crews did a further 5.28 lane miles. City crews resurfaced about 4.7 lane miles using a total of 3,482 tons of asphalt. Finally, 100.6 lane miles were rehabilitated by contract crews with milling followed by resurfacing. A total of 77,299 tons of asphalt were used by contracted crews for this work.

The city reported that 55 percent of its lane miles rated 85 or above on its most recent pavement condition rating, conducted in 2017. The city used the Pavement Tracking System (PTS).

The city reported 2,499 potholes for the year. The percentage of potholes repaired within twenty-four hours was estimated at 65 percent. City policy is to repair potholes within twenty-four hours, but the lower response level is a result of calls on weekends and sick or vacation time of repair crews.

Conditions Affecting Service, Performance, and Costs

Winston-Salem's Department of Transportation had considerable staff changes which caused work delays in some areas. Multiple winter weather events also impacted roadway conditions significantly.

Municipal Profile

Population (OSBM 2016)	240,603
Land Area (Square Miles)	132.55
Persons per Square Mile	1,815
Topography	Gently rolling
Climate	Temperate; some ice and snow

Service Profile

FTE Positions—Crews	39.50
FTE Positions—Other	5.00
Lane Miles Maintained	2,329.3
Lane Miles Treated	
Preservation	23.7
Resurfacing	4.7
Rehabilitation	100.6
TOTAL	129.0
Total Costs for All Treatment Types	$7,697,088
Potholes Repaired	2,499
Number of Utility Cuts	517
Number of Maintenance Patches (exclusive of potholes and utility cuts)	75
Average Cost per Ton of Hot Asphalt during Year	$60.00

Full Cost Profile

Cost Breakdown by Percentage	
Personal Services	10.7%
Operating Costs	87.1%
Capital Costs	2.2%
TOTAL	100.0%
Cost Breakdown in Dollars	
Personal Services	$1,060,264
Operating Costs	$8,640,525
Capital Costs	$220,598
TOTAL	$9,921,387

Winston-Salem — Asphalt Maintenance and Repair

Key: Winston-Salem ▒ Benchmarking Average — Fiscal Years 2013 through 2017

Resource Measures

Asphalt Maintenance and Repair Services Costs per Capita

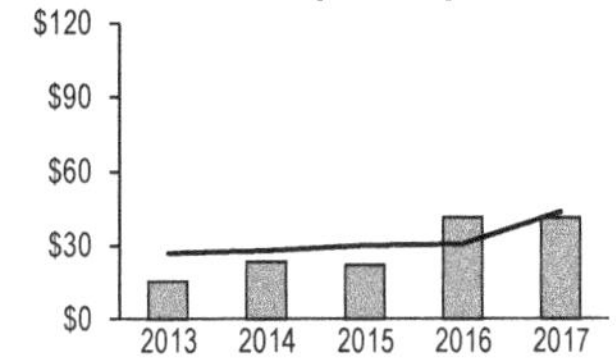

	2013	2014	2015	2016	2017
Winston-Salem	$15.31	$23.42	$22.14	$41.38	$41.24
Average	$27.06	$28.29	$30.38	$30.70	$43.66

Asphalt Maintenance and Repair FTEs per 10,000 Population

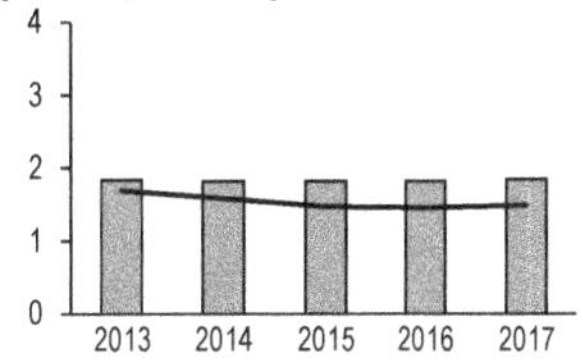

	2013	2014	2015	2016	2017
Winston-Salem	1.84	1.83	1.83	1.82	1.85
Average	1.70	1.60	1.49	1.46	1.49

Service Costs per Lane Mile of Road Maintained

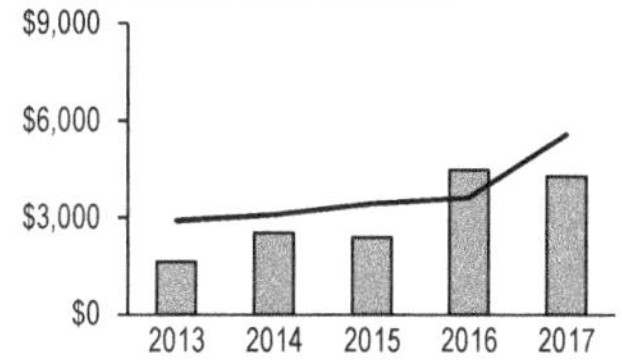

	2013	2014	2015	2016	2017
Winston-Salem	$1,635	$2,522	$2,385	$4,455	$4,259
Average	$2,923	$3,110	$3,452	$3,632	$5,582

Workload Measures

Number of Lane Miles Maintained per 1,000 Population

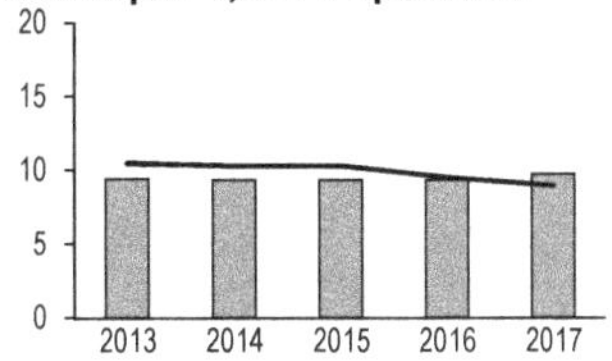

	2013	2014	2015	2016	2017
Winston-Salem	9.4	9.3	9.3	9.3	9.7
Average	10.4	10.2	10.2	9.5	8.9

Reported Potholes per Lane Mile Maintained

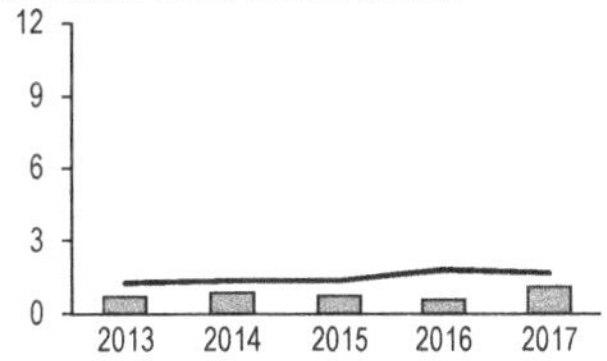

	2013	2014	2015	2016	2017
Winston-Salem	0.68	0.84	0.70	0.55	1.07
Average	1.26	1.35	1.34	1.78	1.67

Repaired Utility Cuts per Lane Mile Maintained

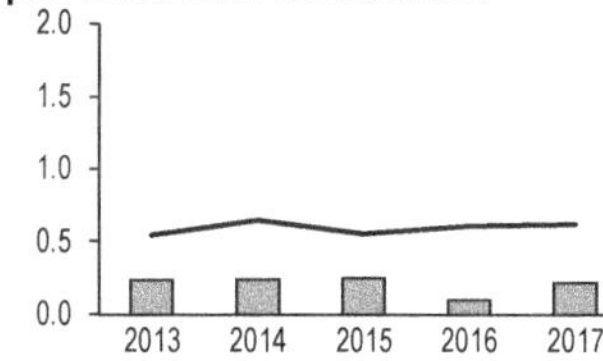

	2013	2014	2015	2016	2017
Winston-Salem	0.24	0.24	0.25	0.10	0.22
Average	0.54	0.64	0.55	0.61	0.62

Efficiency Measures

Cost of Maintenance per Lane Mile Maintained

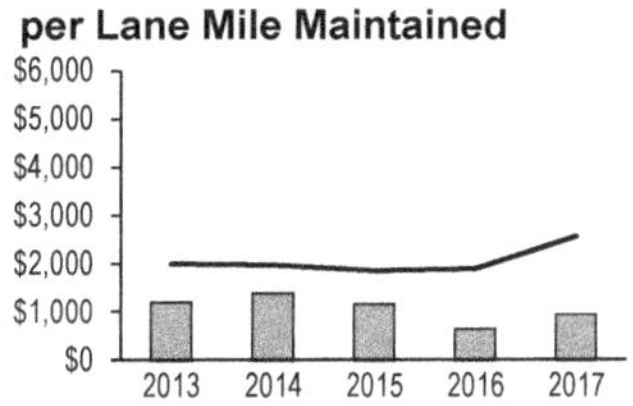

	2013	2014	2015	2016	2017
Winston-Salem	$1,217	$1,404	$1,179	$652	$955
Average	$2,005	$1,976	$1,852	$1,894	$2,564

Cost per Lane Mile for Preservation Treatment

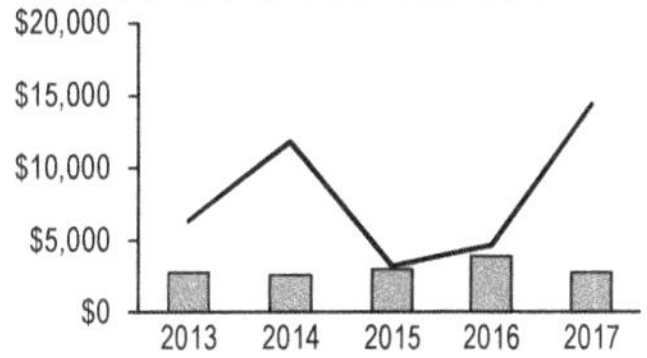

	2013	2014	2015	2016	2017
Winston-Salem	$2,759	$2,591	$3,004	$3,095	$2,701
Average	$6,371	$11,806	$3,214	$4,648	$14,370

Cost per Lane Mile for Resurfacing Treatment

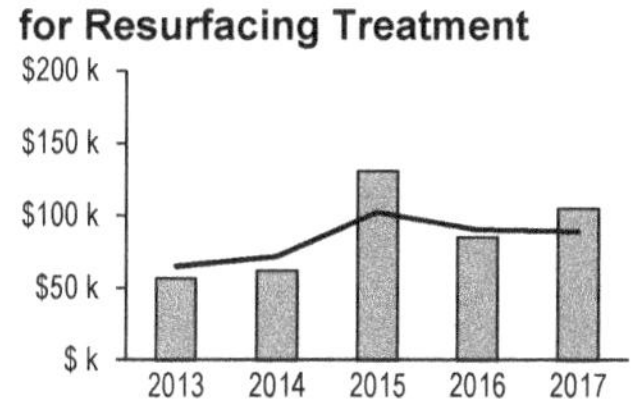

	2013	2014	2015	2016	2017
Winston-Salem	$57 k	$62 k	$131 k	$85 k	$105 k
Average	$65 k	$72 k	$102 k	$90 k	$89 k

Cost per Lane Mile for Rehabilitation Treatment

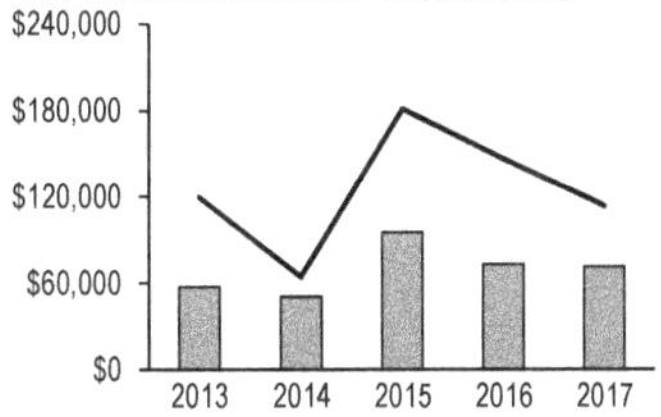

	2013	2014	2015	2016	2017
Winston-Salem	$57 k	$50 k	$95 k	$73 k	$71 k
Average	$119 k	$64 k	$181 k	$147 k	$113 k

Cost per Ton for Contract Resurfacing

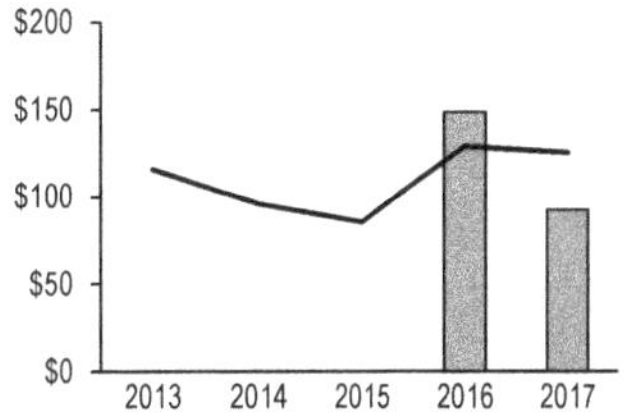

	2013	2014	2015	2016	2017
Winston-Salem				$148	$92
Average	$116	$96	$86	$129	$125

Effectiveness Measures

Percent of Lane Miles Rated 85 or Better

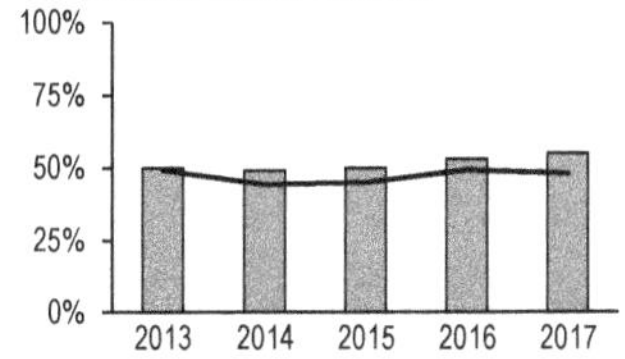

	2013	2014	2015	2016	2017
Winston-Salem	50%	49%	50%	53%	55%
Average	49%	44%	45%	49%	48%

Percent of Lane Miles Rated Below 45

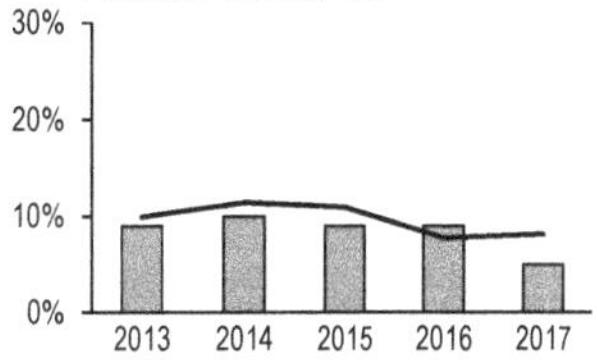

	2013	2014	2015	2016	2017
Winston-Salem	9.0%	10.0%	9.0%	9.0%	5.0%
Average	9.9%	11.4%	10.9%	7.7%	8.1%

Percentage of Potholes Repaired within 24 hours

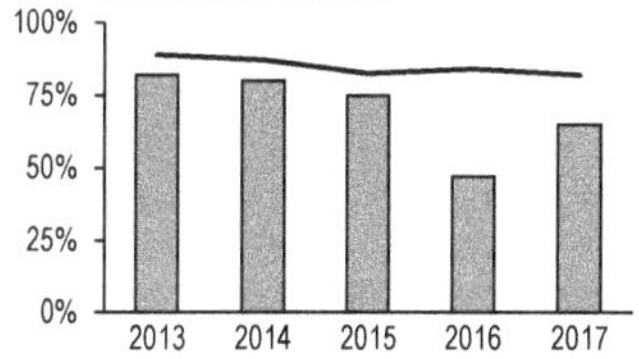

	2013	2014	2015	2016	2017
Winston-Salem	82%	80%	75%	47%	65%
Average	89%	87%	83%	84%	82%

UNC | SCHOOL OF GOVERNMENT
North Carolina Benchmarking Project

Performance and Cost Data

FIRE SERVICES

UNC | SCHOOL OF GOVERNMENT
North Carolina Benchmarking Project

PERFORMANCE MEASURES FOR FIRE SERVICES

SERVICE DEFINITION

Fire Services refers to activities and programs relating to the prevention and suppression of fires, responses to calls for service, rescue service (if provided), fire inspections (if provided), responses to hazardous materials calls (if provided), and fire education services. The services provided by fire departments vary from city to city, but the common goal remains the same: to protect the lives and property of the community served.

NOTES ON PERFORMANCE MEASURES

1. Number of Actual Fires per 1,000 Population

The total number of actual fires includes all types of fires, including structural fires.

2. Fire Inspections Completed per 1,000 Population

Fire inspections include Level I, II, and III inspections.

3. Number of Fire Department Responses per 1,000 Population

Responses include those to fires, medical emergencies, false alarms, and other types of situations that result in mobilization of fire equipment and personnel.

4. Cost per Fire Department Response

The cost represents the total cost of fire services and is calculated using a full cost accounting model that captures direct, indirect, and capital costs. Response is as defined above.

5. Number of Inspections Completed per Fire Inspector FTE

One full-time equivalent (FTE) position equals 2,080 hours of work per year. Any combination of employees providing 2,080 hours of work per year is counted as one FTE.

6. Average Turnout and Travel Time for First Unit Dispatched under "Priority One" Situations

Fast response is a critical determinant in how successful fire responders will be. Response time is calculated by adding both the turnout time (the time the dispatch is received until the first unit is out the door) and the travel time (the time the first unit is out the door until the unit arrives on the scene).

7. Percentage of Full Responses within Eight Minutes

The speed of fire department responses can be judged both by the time for the first unit arriving and also by how long it takes a full complement of trucks and personnel to respond to an emergency. The percentage within eight minutes takes into account travel time.

8. Percentage of Fires Confined to Object or Room of Origin

Containment of fires to as small an area as possible limits total damages. The degree of containment depends on how quickly the fire department is called and also is an effectiveness measure that is reported to the state.

9. Percentage of Fires for Which Cause Is Determined

Investigation of the causes of fires can be an important part of prevention and suppression efforts. While the cause of all fires cannot always be determined, being able to identify causes is important if lessons are to be learned from the investigations.

10. Percentage of Fire Code Violations "Cleared" by Correction or Imposition of Penalty within Ninety Days

Fire code violations are violations of state and local laws and regulations as found through fire inspections. The violators are given time to correct the violation before a penalty is imposed. This is an effectiveness measure that provides an indication of timeliness of follow-up.

11. Percentage of Cases with Lost Pulse Where Pulse Is Recovered at Time of Transfer for Transport

Fire departments frequently are the first responders to medical calls, including cases where an individual has no pulse either at the time of arrival or during the response. This effectiveness measure reports the percentage of these cases where the patient has recovered a pulse by the time responsibility for care has been transferred to emergency responders who will transport the patient to a hospital. Many patients cannot be saved, and recovery of pulse does not guarantee survival at the hospital.

Fire Services

Summary of Key Dimensions of Service

City or Town	Population Served	Land Area Served (in Square Miles)	Value of Property in Service Area (in Billions)	Total Number of Fire Department Responses	Fire Code Violations Found	Number of Community Fire Stations	Number of Fire Services FTEs	ISO* Rating
Apex	50,412	63.8	$5.9	3,009	1,911	4	74	3—town 6—outlying
Asheville	91,929	45.5	$11.4	18,793	7,695	12	262	3
Chapel Hill	60,416	22.8	$7.6	4,655	1,173	5	97	2
Charlotte	845,880	313.2	$93.3	123,149	45,067	41 + 1 airport	1,166	1
Concord	92,367	69.1	$10.1	11,560	3,976	10 + 1 airport	207	2
Goldsboro	34,793	29.3	$2.4	2,840	823	5	83	3
Greensboro	293,233	139.8	$26.4	38,395	12,581	25	584	1
Greenville	88,394	36.9	$6.0	18,087	3,822	6	159	3
Hickory	45,507	42.8	$5.0	6,720	3,981	6 + 1 airport	134	3
High Point	119,857	67.1	$9.9	14,662	1,297	14	234	1
Raleigh	448,706	145.6	$53.6	40,891	23,998	28	621	1
Salisbury	34,459	22.3	$2.8	5,994	2,691	5	75	2
Wilson	49,406	30.6	$4.3	4,453	4,626	5	97	2
Winston-Salem	240,603	132.5	$20.4	26,901	8,693	19	353	2

NOTES

*ISO—Insurance Service Office

EXPLANATORY FACTORS

These are factors that the project found affected fire services performance and cost in one or more of the municipalities:

Population and area served
Value of property area protected in service area
Number of engine companies
Number of fire department responses
Fire code violations
ISO rating
Age of housing stock

Fiscal Year 2016–17

Explanatory Information

Service Level and Delivery

The mission of the Apex Fire Department is to protect life, property, and the environment from fire, medical emergencies, natural disasters, and other emergencies for those who live, work, and travel in and through the town and surrounding area. In addition to the town, the fire department serves an additional forty-nine square miles in surrounding fire districts.

The fire department uses a shift schedule with one twenty-four-hour shift on schedule and one off every three days, followed by a four-day break. On average, shift personnel work ten to eleven days per twenty-eight-day cycle.

The area within the Town of Apex has an ISO rating of 3, while the surrounding fire districts served have an ISO rating of 6. The rating was done during 2013 and was an upgrade from the prior rating for both areas.

The Apex Fire Department conducted 1,644 fire maintenance, construction, and reinspections during the fiscal year. The fire department handles all inspections within town limits and coordinates with the Wake County Fire Marshal for joint inspections in the extra-territorial jurisdiction for new construction, fire alarms, and sprinkler reviews and inspections. Apex has a fire marshal and one inspector.

All fire investigations in Apex are handled by the Wake County Fire Marshal. Apex assists in investigations but does not provide the investigative reports.

Conditions Affecting Service, Performance, and Costs

Municipal Profile

Service Population	50,412
Land Area (Square Miles)	63.81
Persons per Square Mile	790
Median Family Income U.S. Census 2010	$97,201

Service Profile

FTE Positions—Firefighters	66.0
FTE Positions—Other	8.0
Fire Stations	4
First-Line Fire Apparatus	
Pumpers	3
Aerial Trucks	1
Quints	1
Squads	0
Rescue	1
Other	6
Fire Department Responses	3,009
Responses for Fires	127
Structural Fires Reported	29
Inspections Completed for Maintenance, Construction, and Reinspections	1,644
Fire Code Violations Reported	1,911
Estimated Fire Loss (millions)	$0.65
Amount of Property Protected in Service Area (millions)	$5,942
Number of Fire Education Programs or Events	108

Full Cost Profile

Cost Breakdown by Percentage	
Personal Services	69.0%
Operating Costs	18.8%
Capital Costs	12.2%
TOTAL	100.0%
Cost Breakdown in Dollars	
Personal Services	$5,518,543
Operating Costs	$1,504,013
Capital Costs	$976,877
TOTAL	$7,999,433

Key: Apex ▒ Benchmarking Average — Fiscal Years 2013 through 2017

Resource Measures

Fire Services Costs per Capita

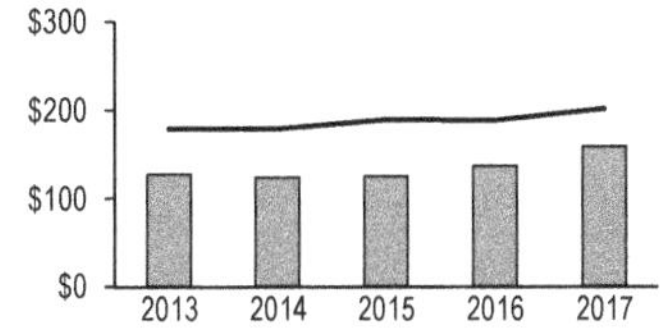

	2013	2014	2015	2016	2017
Apex	$127	$123	$125	$137	$159
Average	$179	$179	$189	$188	$201

Fire Services Total FTEs per 10,000 Population

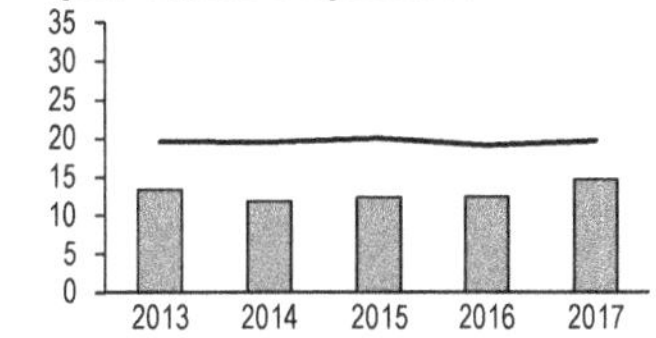

	2013	2014	2015	2016	2017
Apex	13.3	11.9	12.3	12.4	14.7
Average	19.7	19.6	20.1	19.2	19.7

Fire Services Cost per Thousand Dollars of Property Protected

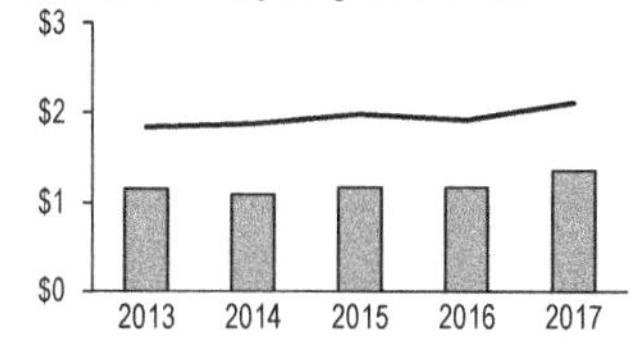

	2013	2014	2015	2016	2017
Apex	$1.14	$1.08	$1.16	$1.16	$1.35
Average	$1.84	$1.87	$1.98	$1.91	$2.11

Workload Measures

Actual Fires per 1,000 Population

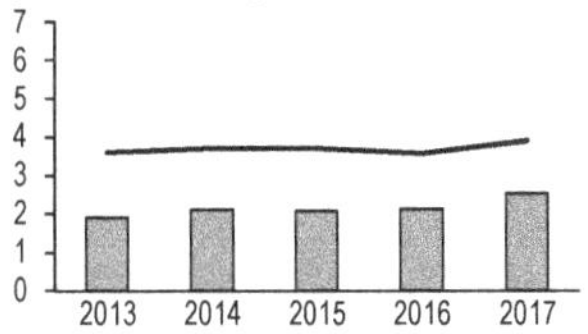

	2013	2014	2015	2016	2017
Apex	1.89	2.10	2.06	2.12	2.52
Average	3.60	3.70	3.70	3.57	3.90

Fire Department Responses per 1,000 Population

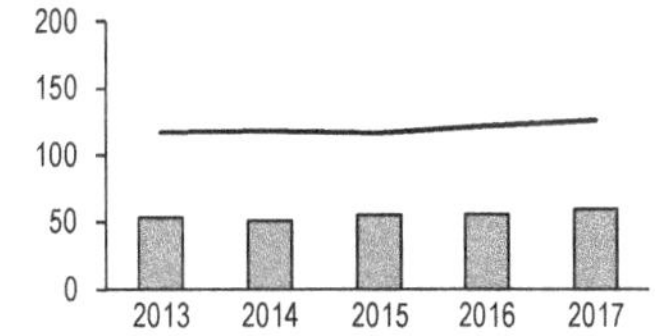

	2013	2014	2015	2016	2017
Apex	53	51	55	56	60
Average	117	118	117	122	126

Fire Inspections Completed per 1,000 Population

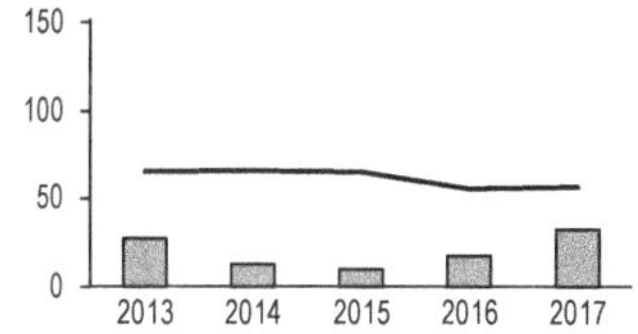

	2013	2014	2015	2016	2017
Apex	28	13	10	18	33
Average	65	65	65	55	56

Efficiency Measures

Fire Services Cost per Fire Department Response

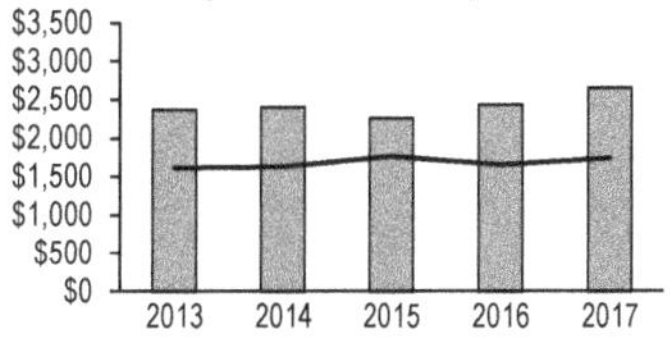

	2013	2014	2015	2016	2017
Apex	$2,376	$2,411	$2,282	$2,443	$2,659
Average	$1,619	$1,627	$1,766	$1,659	$1,735

Inspections Completed per Inspector FTE

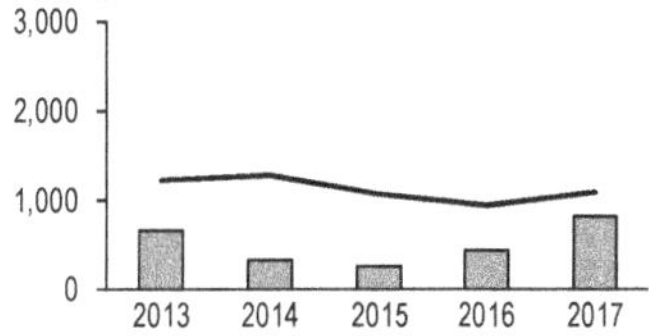

	2013	2014	2015	2016	2017
Apex	663	333	265	445	822
Average	1,224	1,280	1,067	943	1,090

Effectiveness Measures

Average Response Time to Priority One Calls in Minutes

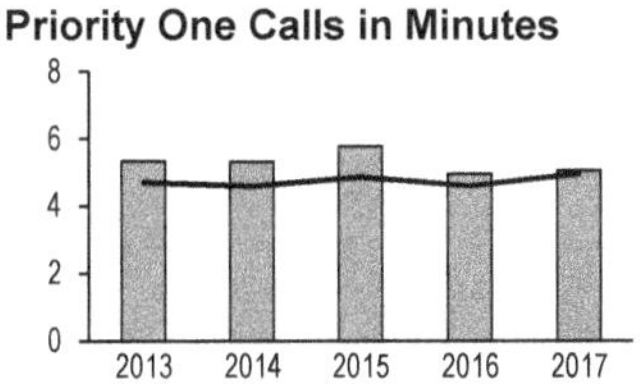

	2013	2014	2015	2016	2017
Apex	5.3	5.3	5.8	5.0	5.1
Average	4.7	4.6	4.8	4.6	4.9

Percentage of Fire Code Violations Cleared within 90 Days

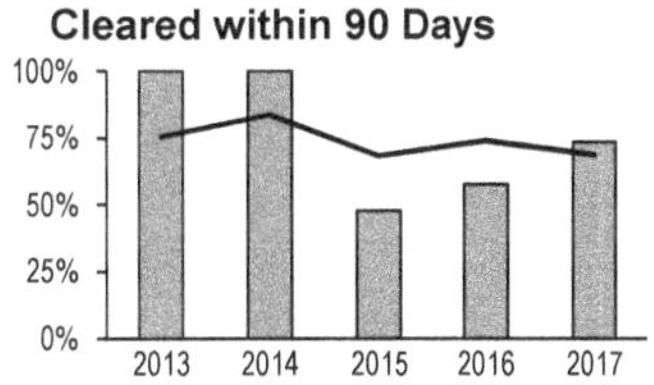

	2013	2014	2015	2016	2017
Apex	100%	100%	48%	57%	73%
Average	75%	84%	68%	74%	69%

Percentage of Fires Confined to Rooms or Objects Involved on Arrival

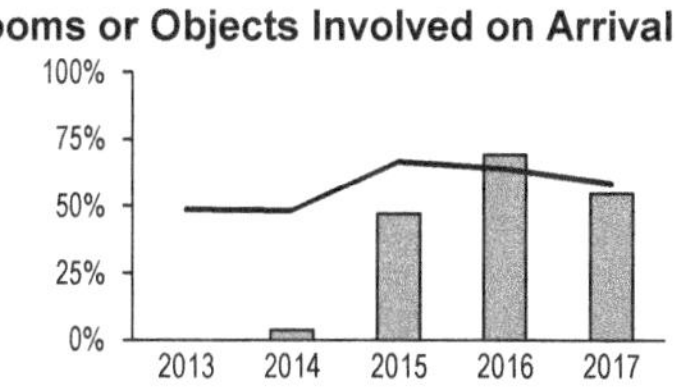

	2013	2014	2015	2016	2017
Apex	0%	4%	47%	69%	55%
Average	49%	48%	67%	64%	58%

Percentage of Fires for Which Cause Was Determined

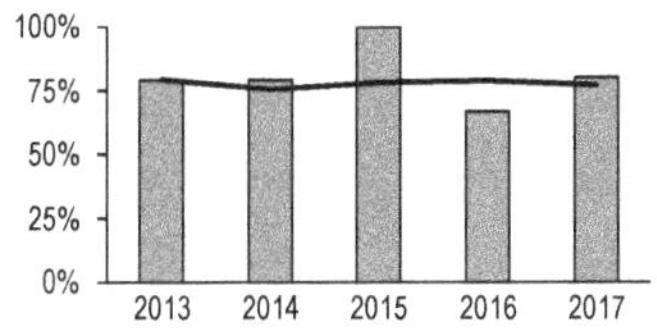

	2013	2014	2015	2016	2017
Apex	79%	79%	100%	67%	80%
Average	79%	75%	78%	79%	77%

Percentage of Full Response within 8 Minutes Travel Time

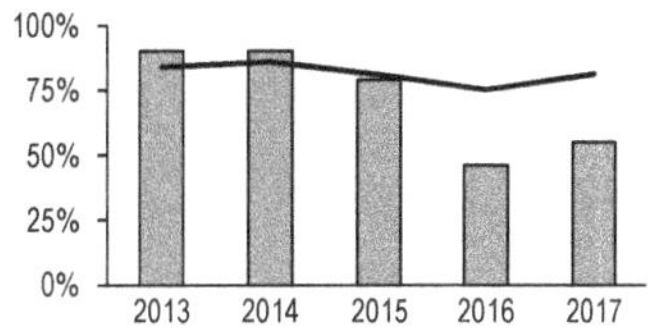

	2013	2014	2015	2016	2017
Apex	90%	90%	79%	46%	55%
Average	84%	86%	81%	75%	81%

Percentage of Lost Pulse Cases Recovered Pulse at Transfer of Care

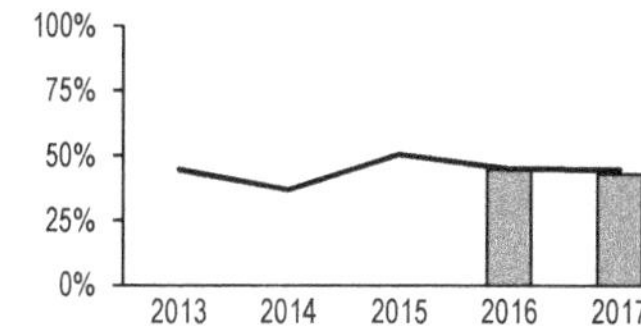

	2013	2014	2015	2016	2017
Apex				44.4%	42.9%
Average	44.7%	36.8%	50.3%	44.9%	44.5%

Fiscal Year 2016–17

Explanatory Information

Service Level and Delivery

The mission of the Asheville Fire Department is to protect the lives, property, and environment of all people within Asheville by preventing the occurrence and minimizing the adverse effects of fires, accidents, and all other emergencies.

The fire department contains the following divisions: emergency response, technical services, and fire marshal.

The fire department uses a modified shift schedule that includes twenty-four hours on duty and twenty-four hours off duty, averaging fifty-six hours per week. The work schedule is as follows: twenty-four hours on, twenty-four hours off; twenty-four hours on, forty-eight hours off; twenty-four hours on, twenty-four hours off; twenty-four hours on, ninety-six hours off. This works out to an average work week of fifty-six hours.

The city has an ISO rating of 3, as rated in 2012. The Asheville Fire Department has been accredited since 2005.

The fire and rescue department conducted 8,022 fire maintenance, construction, and reinspections during the fiscal year. The fire marshal's office is comprised of two sections. One section is responsible for existing construction and another for new construction. Deputy fire marshals (DFMs) are responsible for conducting periodic fire prevention inspections inside the corporate limits of the City of Asheville, as required by the N.C. Office of the State Fire Marshal. The Asheville city council adopted a fee schedule for periodic fire inspections. These fees are based on a cost recovery basis. Each DFM conducts fire inspections of every commercial premise located within Asheville. Most personnel work a day shift, while several work a twenty-four-hour shift. These DFMs are liaisons to the other divisions on matters regarding code enforcement, fire investigations, and pre-incident planning.

Conditions Affecting Service, Performance, and Costs

Municipal Profile

Service Population	91,929
Land Area (Square Miles)	45.52
Persons per Square Mile	2,019
Median Family Income U.S. Census 2010	$53,350

Service Profile

FTE Positions—Firefighters	236.0
FTE Positions—Other	25.5
Fire Stations	12
First-Line Fire Apparatus	
Pumpers	9
Aerial Trucks	3
Quints	2
Squads	1
Rescue	1
Other	1
Fire Department Responses	18,793
Responses for Fires	451
Structural Fires Reported	57
Inspections Completed for Maintenance, Construction, and Reinspections	8,022
Fire Code Violations Reported	7,695
Estimated Fire Loss (millions)	$5.85
Amount of Property Protected in Service Area (millions)	$11,391
Number of Fire Education Programs or Events	622

Full Cost Profile

Cost Breakdown by Percentage	
Personal Services	71.3%
Operating Costs	18.3%
Capital Costs	10.3%
TOTAL	100.0%
Cost Breakdown in Dollars	
Personal Services	$20,857,688
Operating Costs	$5,359,030
Capital Costs	$3,025,473
TOTAL	$29,242,191

Asheville — Fire Services

Key: Asheville ▒ Benchmarking Average — Fiscal Years 2013 through 2017

Resource Measures

Fire Services Costs per Capita

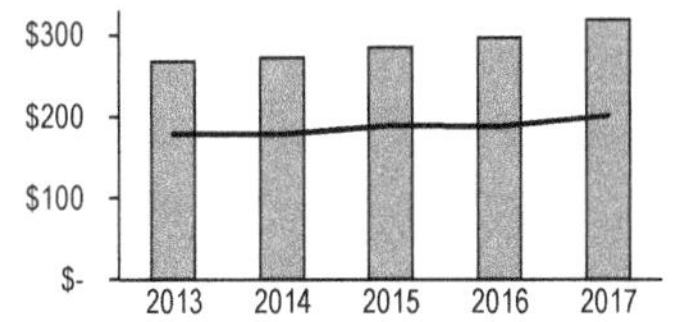

	2013	2014	2015	2016	2017
Asheville	$266.76	$271.42	$283.73	$296	$318
Average	$179	$179	$189	$188	$201

Fire Services Total FTEs per 10,000 Population

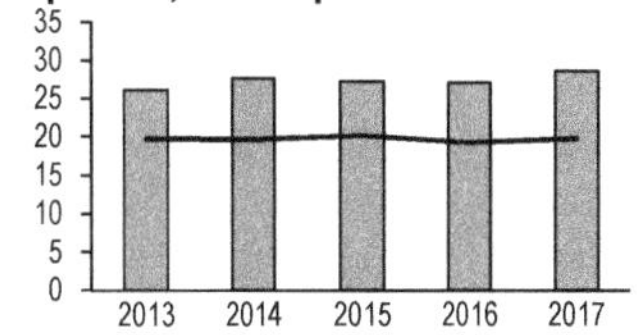

	2013	2014	2015	2016	2017
Asheville	26.1	27.5	27.2	27.0	28.4
Average	19.7	19.6	20.1	19.2	19.7

Fire Services Cost per Thousand Dollars of Property Protected

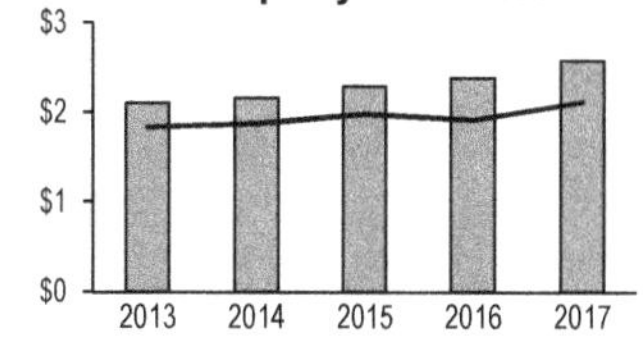

	2013	2014	2015	2016	2017
Asheville	$2.10	$2.15	$2.28	$2.37	$2.57
Average	$1.84	$1.87	$1.98	$1.91	$2.11

Workload Measures

Actual Fires per 1,000 Population

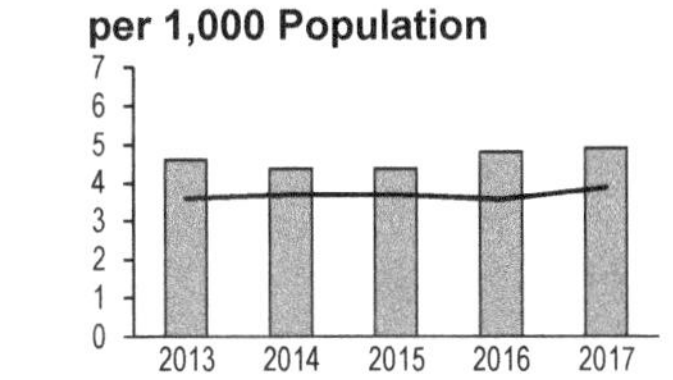

	2013	2014	2015	2016	2017
Asheville	4.60	4.37	4.37	4.79	4.91
Average	3.60	3.70	3.70	3.57	3.90

Fire Department Responses per 1,000 Population

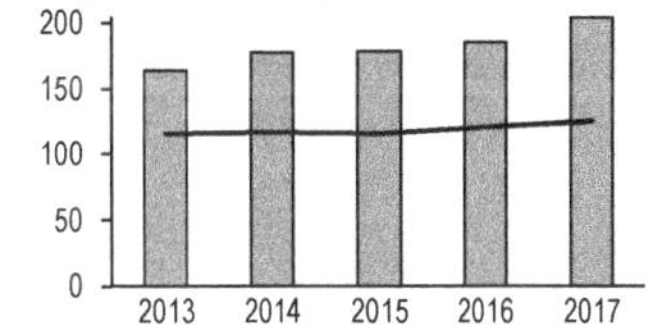

	2013	2014	2015	2016	2017
Asheville	164	178	178	185	204
Average	117	118	117	122	126

Fire Inspections Completed per 1,000 Population

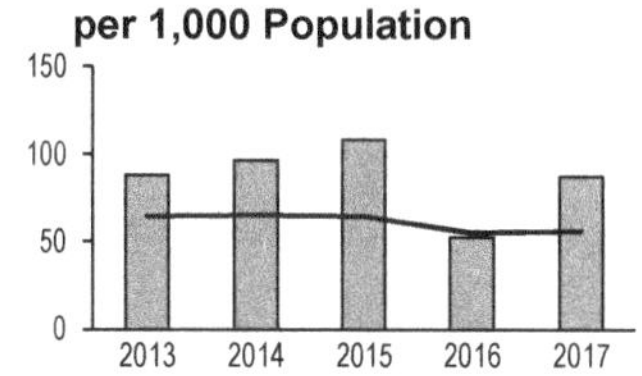

	2013	2014	2015	2016	2017
Asheville	88	96	108	52	87
Average	65	65	65	55	56

Efficiency Measures

Fire Services Cost per Fire Department Response

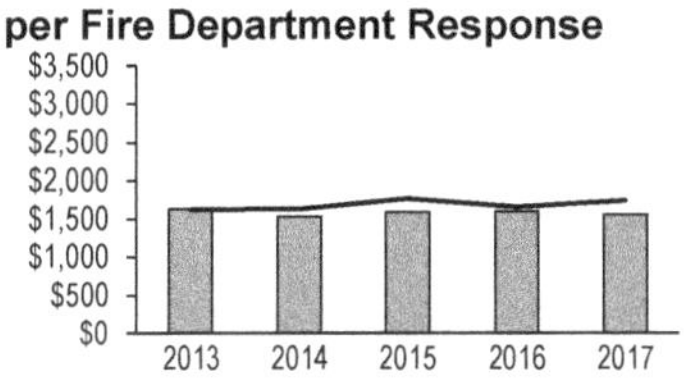

	2013	2014	2015	2016	2017
Asheville	$1,629	$1,528	$1,591	$1,597	$1,556
Average	$1,619	$1,627	$1,766	$1,659	$1,735

Inspections Completed per Inspector FTE

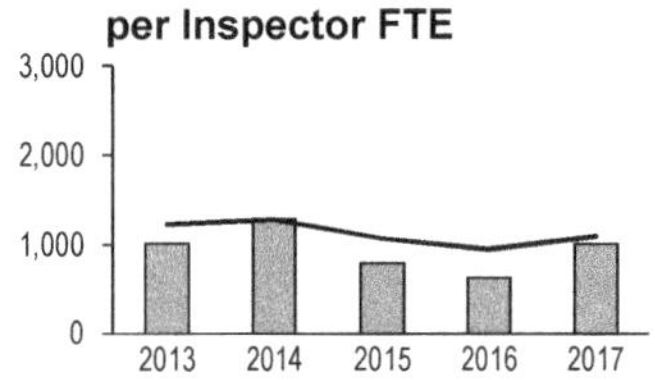

	2013	2014	2015	2016	2017
Asheville	1,010	1,286	787	624	1,003
Average	1,224	1,280	1,067	943	1,090

Effectiveness Measures

Average Response Time to Priority One Calls in Minutes

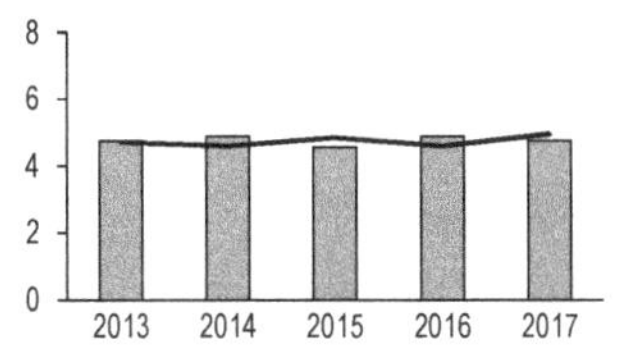

	2013	2014	2015	2016	2017
Asheville	4.7	4.9	4.6	4.9	4.7
Average	4.7	4.6	4.8	4.6	4.9

Percentage of Fire Code Violations Cleared within 90 Days

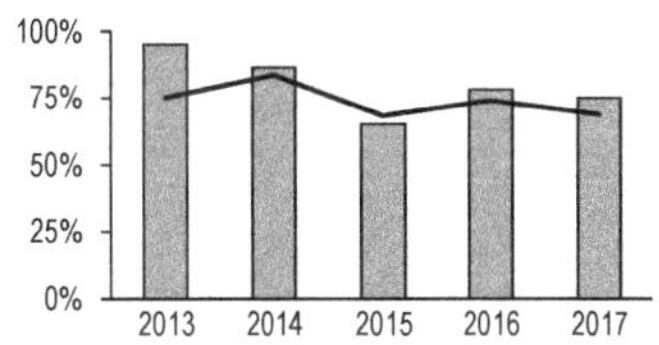

	2013	2014	2015	2016	2017
Asheville	95%	86%	65%	78%	75%
Average	75%	84%	68%	74%	69%

Percentage of Fires Confined to Rooms or Objects Involved on Arrival

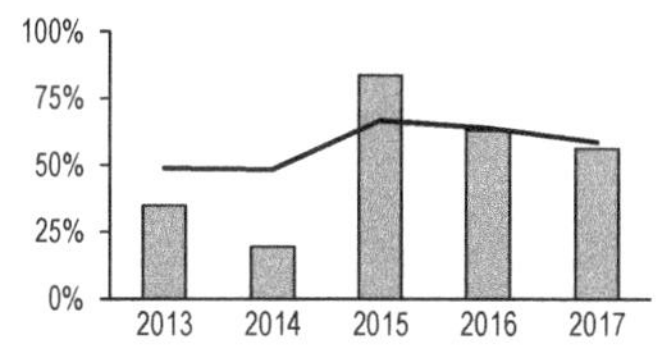

	2013	2014	2015	2016	2017
Asheville	35%	20%	84%	63%	56%
Average	49%	48%	67%	64%	58%

Percentage of Fires for Which Cause Was Determined

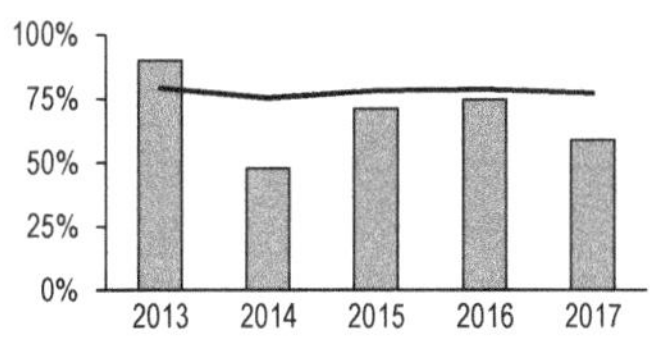

	2013	2014	2015	2016	2017
Asheville	90%	48%	71%	75%	59%
Average	79%	75%	78%	79%	77%

Percentage of Full Response within 8 Minutes Travel Time

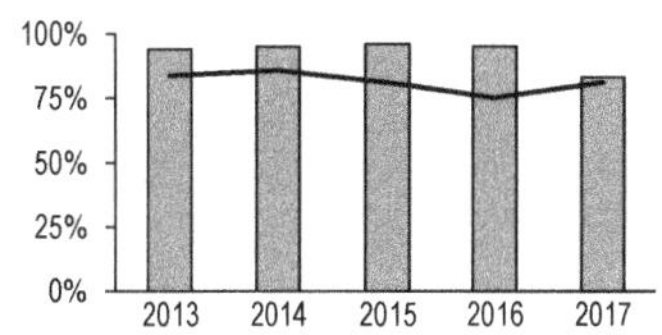

	2013	2014	2015	2016	2017
Asheville	94%	95%	96%	95%	83%
Average	84%	86%	81%	75%	81%

Percentage of Lost Pulse Cases Recovered Pulse at Transfer of Care

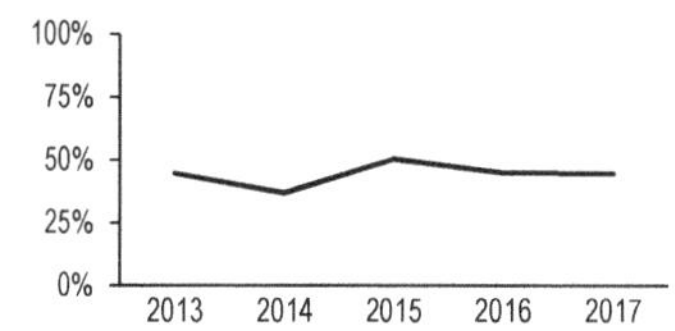

	2013	2014	2015	2016	2017
Asheville					
Average	44.7%	36.8%	50.3%	44.9%	44.5%

Fiscal Year 2016–17

Explanatory Information

Service Level and Delivery
The Town of Chapel Hill's Fire Department mission is to minimize the risk of fire and other hazards to the life and property of the citizens of Chapel Hill. To accomplish this mission, the department provides response to and mitigation of fires, medical emergencies, hazardous materials incidents, and other emergencies as they arise.

The fire department is organized into three divisions: operations, administration, and life safety. Operations and life safety are administered by a deputy chief with support staff. Administration consists of the fire chief and support staff.

The fire department works a 3/4 system where personnel are on duty for 24 hours starting at 7 a.m. The town has five community stations with six primary vehicles for response.

The town has an ISO rating of 2 received in 2016, which was an upgrade from the year before.

The fire department conducted 1,780 fire maintenance, construction, and reinspections during the fiscal year. Fire inspections are performed by fire inspectors and are designed to be completed in accordance with the State of North Carolina's inspection schedule. Initial inspections may generate findings for reinspection. The Town of Chapel Hill has implemented a tablet-based fire inspection system to more efficiently manage the inspection process as well as initiate the fire inspection fee schedule and billing system. The department counts malls as one inspection per occupancy and one per building structure. High rises have one inspection per building plus one per commercial occupancy. Multi-structure apartment complexes have just one inspection per complex.

Conditions Affecting Service, Performance, and Costs
The Town of Chapel Hill began participation in the benchmarking project in July 2015, with FY 2014–15 being the first reporting year.

Municipal Profile

Service Population	60,416
Land Area (Square Miles)	22.81
Persons per Square Mile	2,649
Median Family Income U.S. Census 2010	$61,405

Service Profile

FTE Positions—Firefighters	79.0
FTE Positions—Other	18.0
Fire Stations	5
First-Line Fire Apparatus	
Pumpers	3
Aerial Trucks	1
Quints	1
Squads	0
Rescue	1
Other	0
Fire Department Responses	4,655
Responses for Fires	131
Structural Fires Reported	34
Inspections Completed for Maintenance, Construction, and Reinspections	1,780
Fire Code Violations Reported	1,173
Estimated Fire Loss (millions)	$0.68
Amount of Property Protected in Service Area (millions)	$7,586
Number of Fire Education	285
Programs or Events	NA

Full Cost Profile

Cost Breakdown by Percentage	
Personal Services	67.7%
Operating Costs	21.7%
Capital Costs	10.6%
TOTAL	100.0%
Cost Breakdown in Dollars	
Personal Services	$7,660,600
Operating Costs	$2,457,346
Capital Costs	$1,202,629
TOTAL	$11,320,575

Key: Chapel Hill ▒ Benchmarking Average — Fiscal Years 2013 through 2017

Resource Measures

Fire Services Costs per Capita

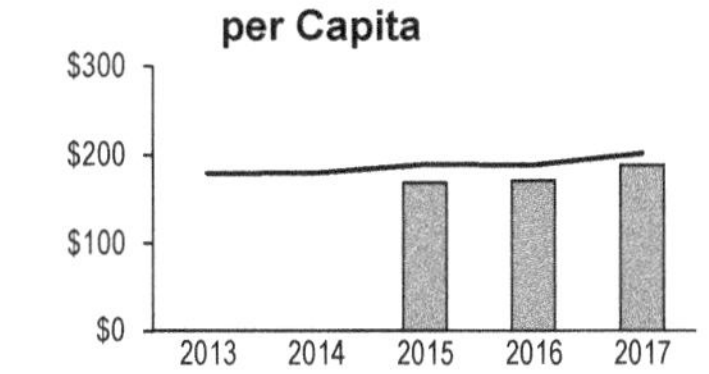

	2013	2014	2015	2016	2017
Chapel Hill			$167	$170	$187
Average	$179	$179	$189	$188	$201

Fire Services Total FTEs per 10,000 Population

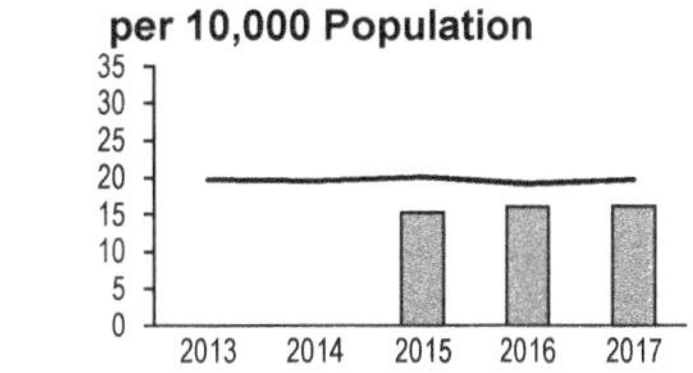

	2013	2014	2015	2016	2017
Chapel Hill			15.3	16.0	16.1
Average	19.7	19.6	20.1	19.2	19.7

Fire Services Cost per Thousand Dollars of Property Protected

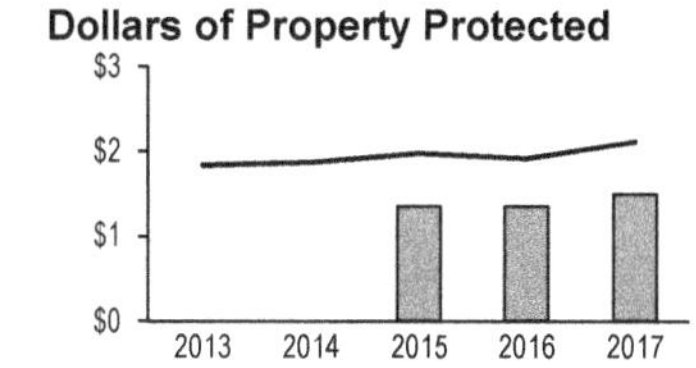

	2013	2014	2015	2016	2017
Chapel Hill			$1.35	$1.35	$1.49
Average	$1.84	$1.87	$1.98	$1.91	$2.11

Workload Measures

Actual Fires per 1,000 Population

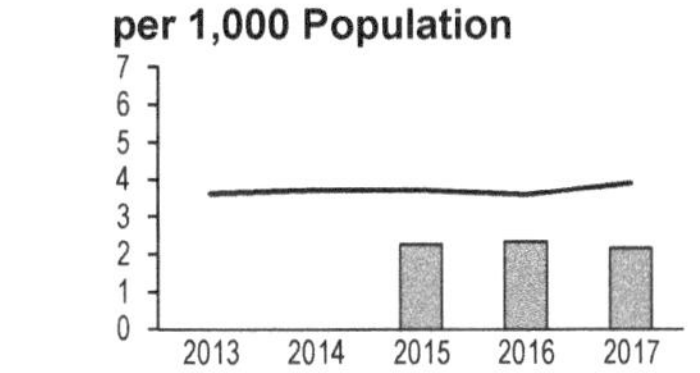

	2013	2014	2015	2016	2017
Chapel Hill			2.27	2.33	2.17
Average	3.60	3.70	3.70	3.57	3.90

Fire Department Responses per 1,000 Population

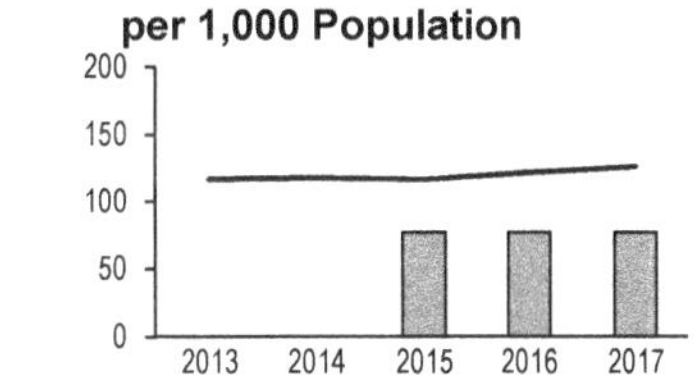

	2013	2014	2015	2016	2017
Chapel Hill			77	77	77
Average	117	118	117	122	126

Fire Inspections Completed per 1,000 Population

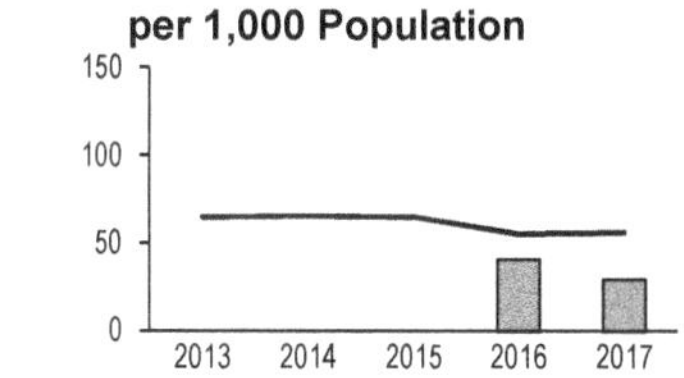

	2013	2014	2015	2016	2017
Chapel Hill				41	29
Average	65	65	65	55	56

Efficiency Measures

Fire Services Cost per Fire Department Response

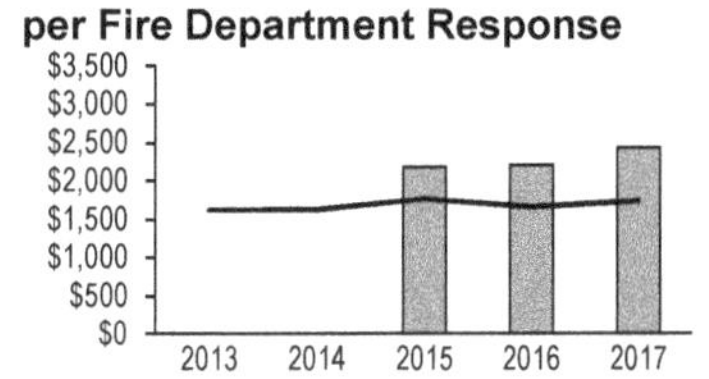

	2013	2014	2015	2016	2017
Chapel Hill			$2,176	$2,203	$2,432
Average	$1,619	$1,627	$1,766	$1,659	$1,735

Inspections Completed per Inspector FTE

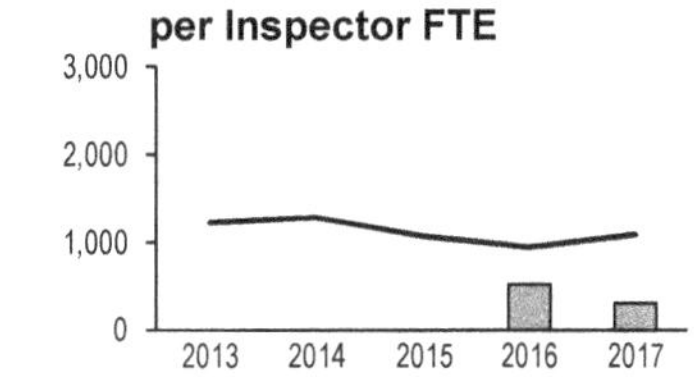

	2013	2014	2015	2016	2017
Chapel Hill				517	310
Average	1,224	1,280	1,067	943	1,090

Effectiveness Measures

Average Response Time to Priority One Calls in Minutes

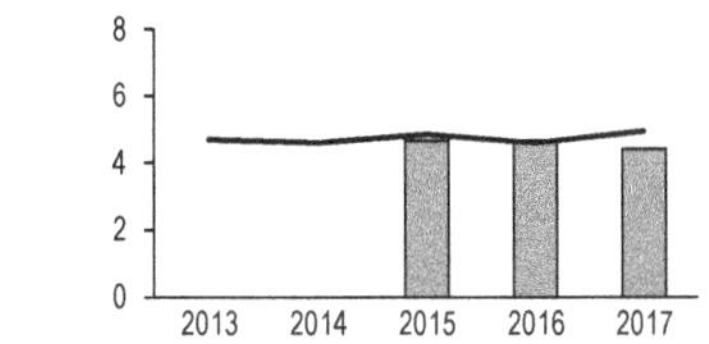

	2013	2014	2015	2016	2017
Chapel Hill			4.7	4.7	4.4
Average	4.7	4.6	4.8	4.6	4.9

Percentage of Fire Code Violations Cleared within 90 Days

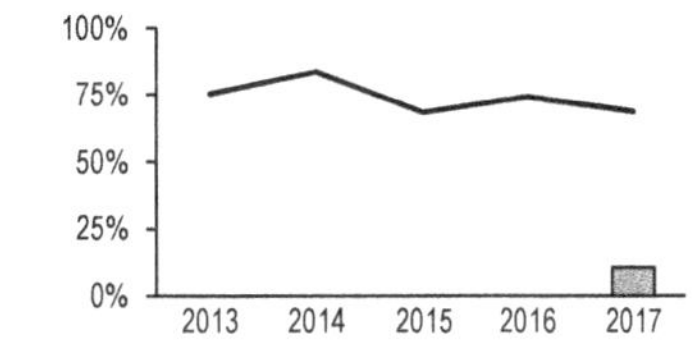

	2013	2014	2015	2016	2017
Chapel Hill					11%
Average	75%	84%	68%	74%	69%

Percentage of Fires Confined to Rooms or Objects Involved on Arrival

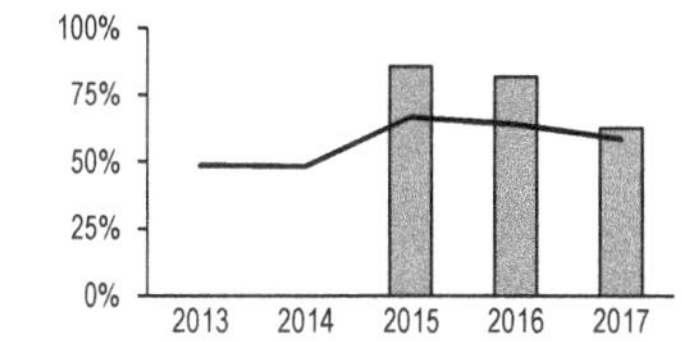

	2013	2014	2015	2016	2017
Chapel Hill			86%	82%	63%
Average	49%	48%	67%	64%	58%

Percentage of Fires for Which Cause Was Determined

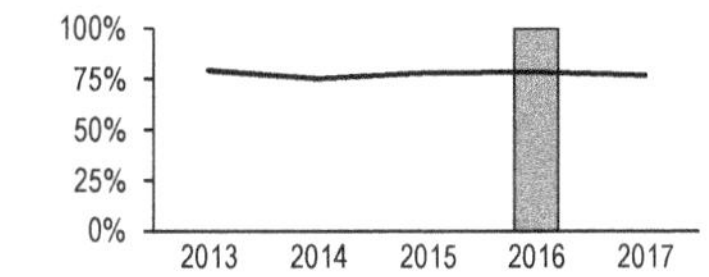

	2013	2014	2015	2016	2017
Chapel Hill				100%	
Average	79%	75%	78%	79%	77%

Percentage of Full Response within 8 Minutes Travel Time

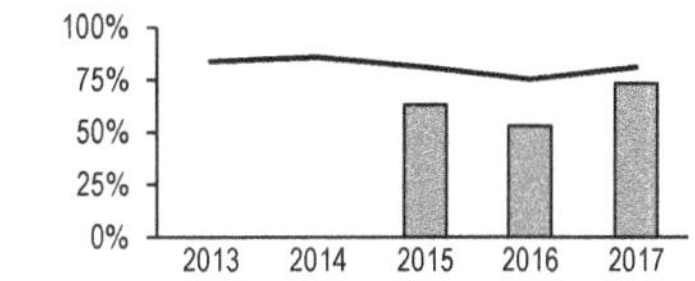

	2013	2014	2015	2016	2017
Chapel Hill			63%	53%	73%
Average	84%	86%	81%	75%	81%

Percentage of Lost Pulse Cases Recovered Pulse at Transfer of Care

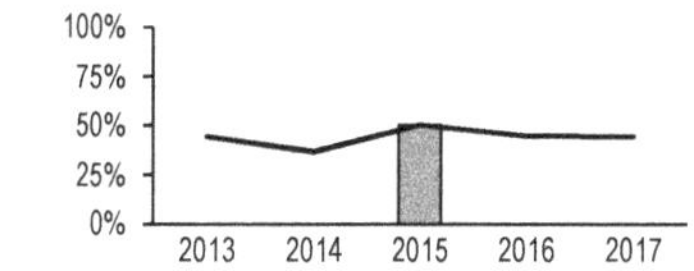

	2013	2014	2015	2016	2017
Chapel Hill			50.0%		
Average	44.7%	36.8%	50.3%	44.9%	44.5%

Fiscal Year 2016–17

Explanatory Information

Service Level and Delivery
The mission of the Charlotte Fire Department is to minimize the risk of fire and other hazards to the life and property of the citizens of Charlotte. To accomplish this mission, the department provides response to and mitigation of fires, medical emergencies, hazardous materials incidents, aircraft emergencies, technical rescues, and other emergencies as they arise. These services are provided immediately to any person who has a need anywhere within the corporate limits of Charlotte.

The divisions of the Charlotte Fire Department are operations (A, B, C), training, administration, communications, logistics, fire prevention, and fire investigation.

The city uses a modified twenty-four-hour/forty-eight-hour shift schedule, using four twenty-four-hour shifts in a twelve-day cycle. The cycle is on one day, off one day, on one day, off two days, on one day, off one day, on one day, off four days. In addition, firefighters receive a Kelley day (ten hours) off and a Kelley night (fourteen hours) off every seven weeks to maintain the number of hours worked per week at fifty-two.

The city has an ISO rating of 1, the highest level possible. The Charlotte Fire Department has been accredited since 2000.

The fire department conducted 37,447 fire maintenance, construction, and reinspections during the fiscal year. All inspections are performed by certified fire inspectors who are employees of the Fire Prevention Bureau. The inspectors handle certificate of occupancy inspections, permit inspections and issuances, regular code enforcement inspections, and reinspections. The Bureau currently uses separate inspections on each building of an apartment complex.

Conditions Affecting Service, Performance, and Costs
Charlotte did not participate in the Benchmarking Project during FY 2014–15. No data are available for that year.

Charlotte staffs a fire station at the airport in addition to forty-one community fire stations.

Municipal Profile

Service Population	845,880
Land Area (Square Miles)	313.24
Persons per Square Mile	2,700
Median Family Income U.S. Census 2010	$61,405

Service Profile

FTE Positions—Firefighters	1034.0
FTE Positions—Other	132.0
Fire Stations	42
First-Line Fire Apparatus	
Pumpers	42
Aerial Trucks	0
Quints	16
Squads	0
Rescue	2
Other	36
Fire Department Responses	123,149
Responses for Fires	2,550
Structural Fires Reported	775
Inspections Completed for Maintenance, Construction, and Reinspections	37,447
Fire Code Violations Reported	45,067
Estimated Fire Loss (millions)	$1,040.53
Amount of Property Protected in Service Area (millions)	$93,264
Number of Fire Education Programs or Events	2,254

Full Cost Profile

Cost Breakdown by Percentage	
Personal Services	66.5%
Operating Costs	21.7%
Capital Costs	11.8%
TOTAL	100.0%
Cost Breakdown in Dollars	
Personal Services	$104,043,645
Operating Costs	$20,646,267
Capital Costs	$70,167,286
TOTAL	$194,857,198

Key: Charlotte ▒ Benchmarking Average — Fiscal Years 2013 through 2017

Resource Measures

Fire Services Costs per Capita

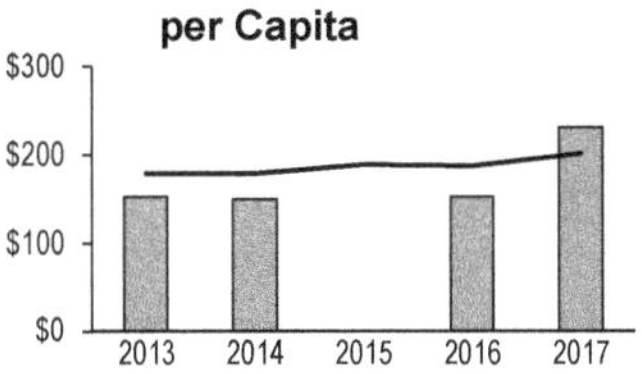

	2013	2014	2015	2016	2017
Charlotte	$152	$149		$152	$230
Average	$179	$179	$189	$188	$201

Fire Services Total FTEs per 10,000 Population

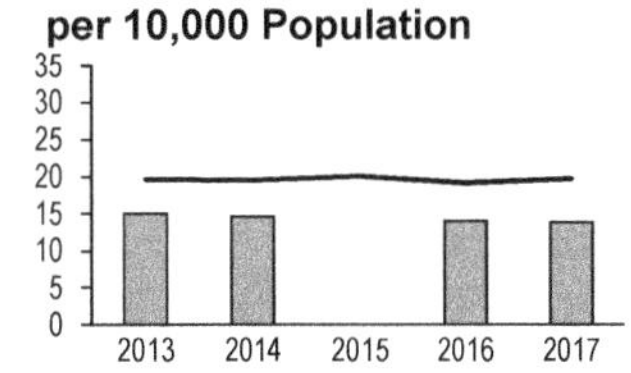

	2013	2014	2015	2016	2017
Charlotte	15.0	14.6		14.0	13.8
Average	19.7	19.6	20.1	19.2	19.7

Fire Services Cost per Thousand Dollars of Property Protected

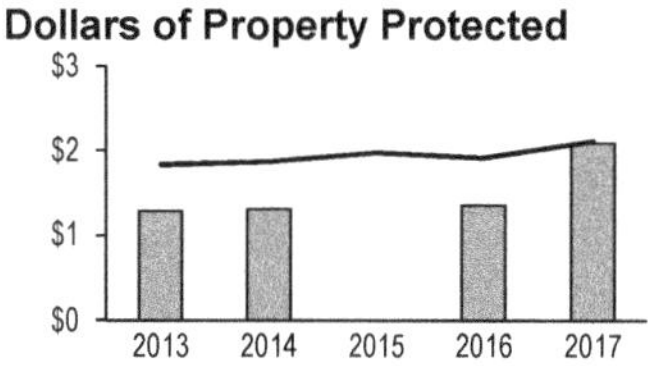

	2013	2014	2015	2016	2017
Charlotte	$1.29	$1.31		$1.36	$2.09
Average	$1.84	$1.87	$1.98	$1.91	$2.11

Workload Measures

Actual Fires per 1,000 Population

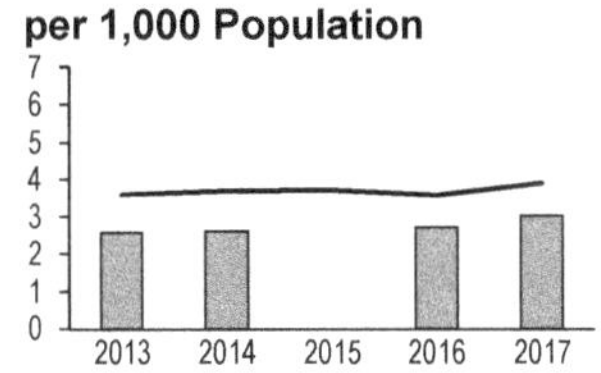

	2013	2014	2015	2016	2017
Charlotte	2.57	2.60		2.70	3.01
Average	3.60	3.70	3.70	3.57	3.90

Fire Department Responses per 1,000 Population

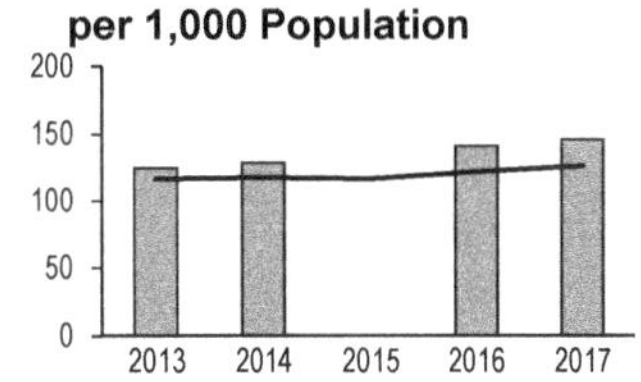

	2013	2014	2015	2016	2017
Charlotte	125	129		141	146
Average	117	118	117	122	126

Fire Inspections Completed per 1,000 Population

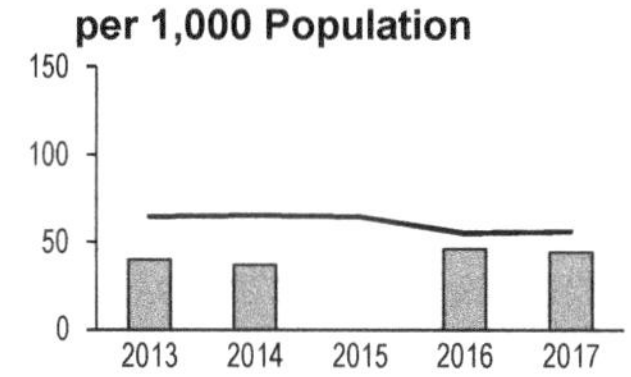

	2013	2014	2015	2016	2017
Charlotte	40	37		46	44
Average	65	65	65	55	56

Efficiency Measures

Fire Services Cost per Fire Department Response

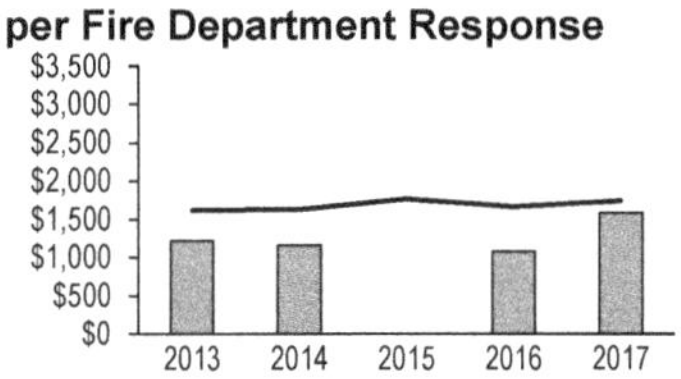

	2013	2014	2015	2016	2017
Charlotte	$1,219	$1,161		$1,078	$1,582
Average	$1,619	$1,627	$1,766	$1,659	$1,735

Inspections Completed per Inspector FTE

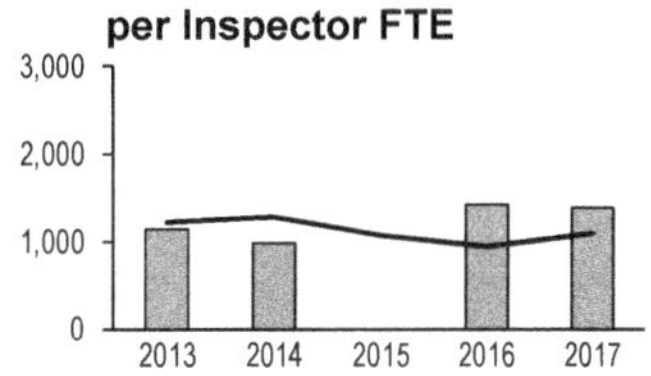

	2013	2014	2015	2016	2017
Charlotte	1,146	984		1,421	1,387
Average	1,224	1,280	1,067	943	1,090

Effectiveness Measures

Average Response Time to Priority One Calls in Minutes

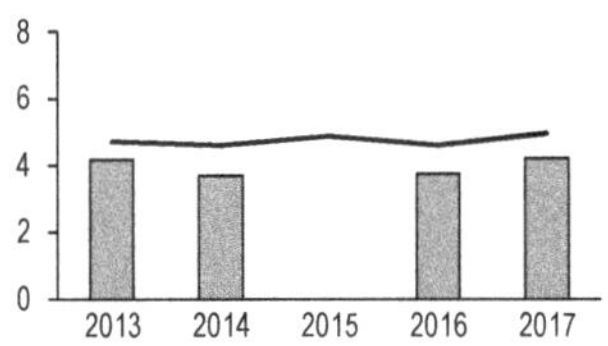

	2013	2014	2015	2016	2017
Charlotte	4.2	3.7		3.7	4.2
Average	4.7	4.6	4.8	4.6	4.9

Percentage of Fire Code Violations Cleared within 90 Days

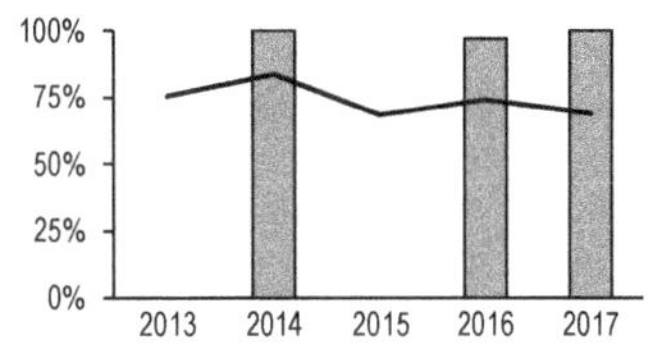

	2013	2014	2015	2016	2017
Charlotte		100%		97%	100%
Average	75%	84%	68%	74%	69%

Percentage of Fires Confined to Rooms or Objects Involved on Arrival

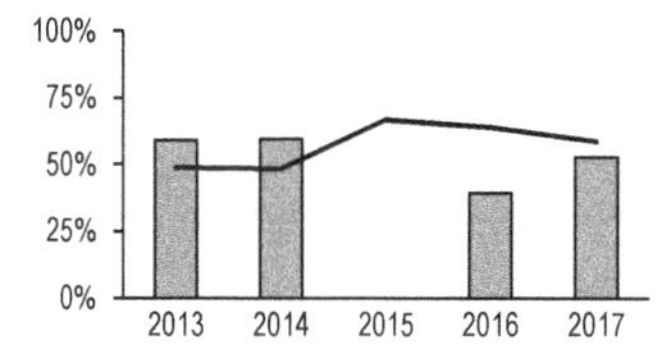

	2013	2014	2015	2016	2017
Charlotte	59%	59%		39%	53%
Average	49%	48%	67%	64%	58%

Percentage of Fires for Which Cause Was Determined

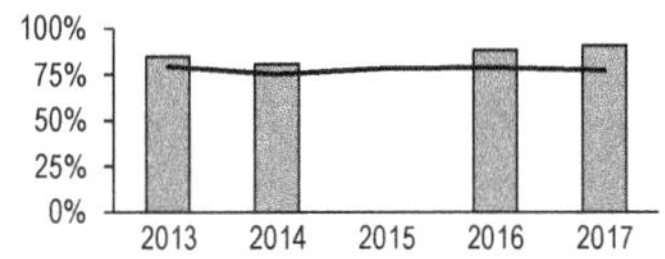

	2013	2014	2015	2016	2017
Charlotte	85%	81%		89%	91%
Average	79%	75%	78%	79%	77%

Percentage of Full Response within 8 Minutes Travel Time

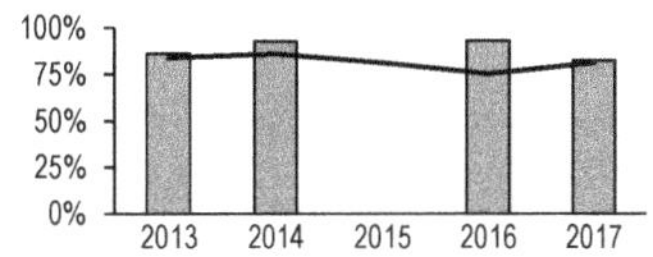

	2013	2014	2015	2016	2017
Charlotte	86%	93%		93%	82%
Average	84%	86%	81%	75%	81%

Percentage of Lost Pulse Cases Recovered Pulse at Transfer of Care

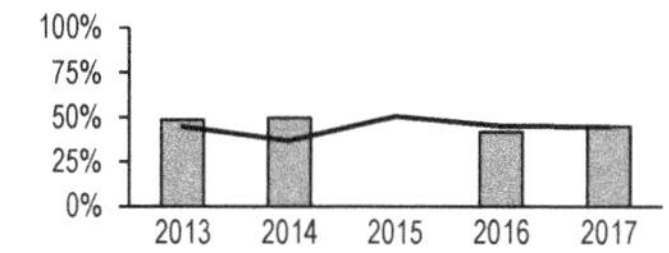

	2013	2014	2015	2016	2017
Charlotte	48.4%	49.5%		41.7%	44.7%
Average	44.7%	36.8%	50.3%	44.9%	44.5%

Fiscal Year 2016–17

Explanatory Information

Service Level and Delivery

The City of Concord Fire Department is committed to providing a positive work environment to enable the department and its personnel to strive for and achieve excellence in fire protection services.

The department is committed to the following: providing leadership through a management/employee team organizational concept that is dedicated to modern-day management principles and practices; providing the citizens with the best possible modern-day fire protection and life safety services in a courteous, professional, and cost-effective manner; providing equal opportunity for all employees to excel in their job performance and career development; striving to continually increase the public's awareness through fire prevention activities, public education, and community-based services; maintaining and striving to improve on an open, informative flow of correct information so that all employees and employee teams reach their goals and objectives; subscribing to departmental values of honesty, professionalism, teamwork, loyalty, dedication, and commitment to serving the public; and planning for change to develop and prepare the department to always strive for excellence.

The fire department in Concord contains the following divisions: administration, suppression, operations, training and career development, fire-risk management, and emergency management.

The fire department utilizes a shift schedule that includes twenty-four hours on and forty-eight hours off.

The city has an ISO rating of 2, as rated in 2013. This represented an improvement from the prior rating.

The fire department conducted 8,834 fire maintenance, construction, and reinspections during the fiscal year. Inspections are conducted by the Fire-Risk Management Division. Each inspector has an assigned area of the city and a specific number of inspections to complete. Each occupancy is counted separately in the inspections number. An apartment complex would be considered as one occupancy. Reinspections are conducted within forty-five days to confirm corrections.

Conditions Affecting Service, Performance, and Costs

Concord staffs a fire station at the airport in addition to ten community fire stations.

Municipal Profile

Service Population	92,367
Land Area (Square Miles)	69.06
Persons per Square Mile	1,337
Median Family Income U.S. Census 2010	$63,643

Service Profile

FTE Positions—Firefighters	189.0
FTE Positions—Other	18.0
Fire Stations	11
First-Line Fire Apparatus	
Pumpers	9
Aerial Trucks	3
Quints	0
Squads	0
Rescue	1
Other	11
Fire Department Responses	11,560
Responses for Fires	270
Structural Fires Reported	43
Inspections Completed for Maintenance, Construction, and Reinspections	8,834
Fire Code Violations Reported	3,976
Estimated Fire Loss (millions)	$1.95
Amount of Property Protected in Service Area (millions)	$10,092
Number of Fire Education Programs or Events	545

Full Cost Profile

Cost Breakdown by Percentage	
Personal Services	67.2%
Operating Costs	20.8%
Capital Costs	12.0%
TOTAL	100.0%
Cost Breakdown in Dollars	
Personal Services	$13,459,689
Operating Costs	$4,164,782
Capital Costs	$2,404,782
TOTAL	$20,029,253

Key: Concord ▒ Benchmarking Average — Fiscal Years 2013 through 2017

Resource Measures

Fire Services Costs per Capita

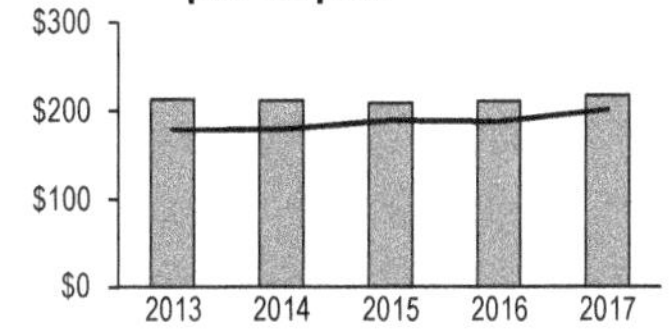

	2013	2014	2015	2016	2017
Concord	$213	$211	$209	$211	$217
Average	$179	$179	$189	$188	$201

Fire Services Total FTEs per 10,000 Population

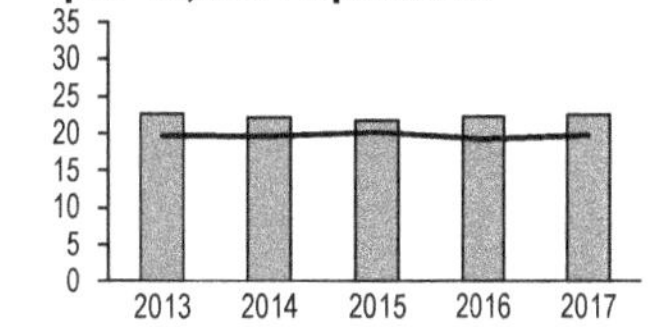

	2013	2014	2015	2016	2017
Concord	22.5	22.1	21.6	22.1	22.4
Average	19.7	19.6	20.1	19.2	19.7

Fire Services Cost per Thousand Dollars of Property Protected

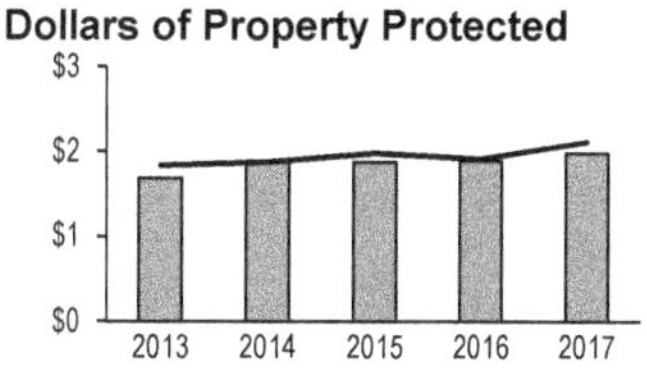

	2013	2014	2015	2016	2017
Concord	$1.69	$1.89	$1.88	$1.89	$1.98
Average	$1.84	$1.87	$1.98	$1.91	$2.11

Workload Measures

Actual Fires per 1,000 Population

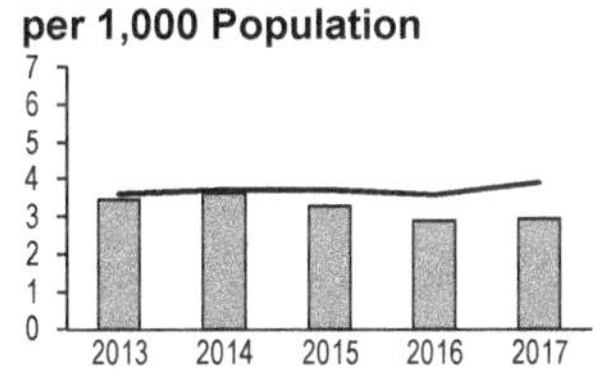

	2013	2014	2015	2016	2017
Concord	3.45	3.62	3.27	2.88	2.92
Average	3.60	3.70	3.70	3.57	3.90

Fire Department Responses per 1,000 Population

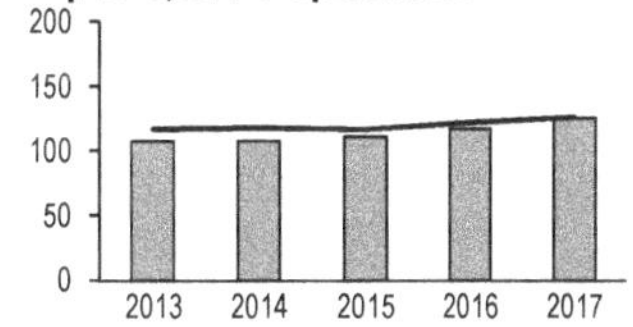

	2013	2014	2015	2016	2017
Concord	107	107	111	117	125
Average	117	118	117	122	126

Fire Inspections Completed per 1,000 Population

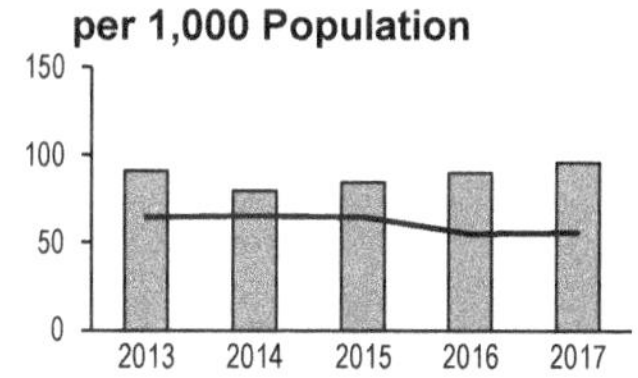

	2013	2014	2015	2016	2017
Concord	91	80	84	90	96
Average	65	65	65	55	56

Efficiency Measures

Fire Services Cost per Fire Department Response

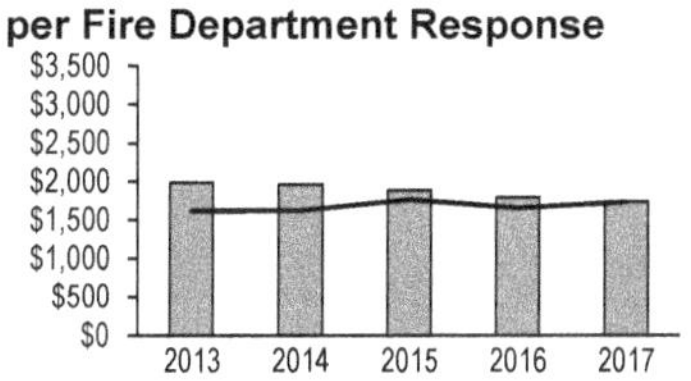

	2013	2014	2015	2016	2017
Concord	$1,984	$1,963	$1,883	$1,797	$1,733
Average	$1,619	$1,627	$1,766	$1,659	$1,735

Inspections Completed per Inspector FTE

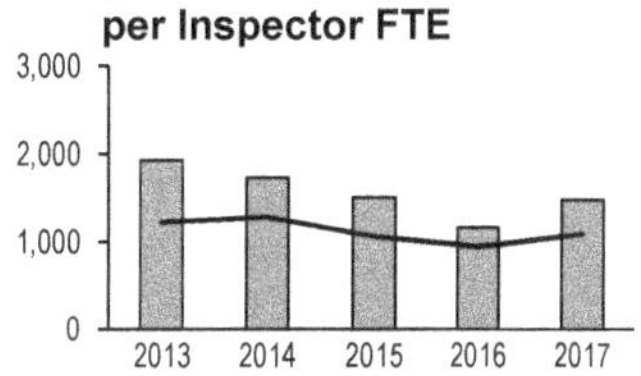

	2013	2014	2015	2016	2017
Concord	1,926	1,727	1,500	1,163	1,472
Average	1,224	1,280	1,067	943	1,090

Effectiveness Measures

Average Response Time to Priority One Calls in Minutes

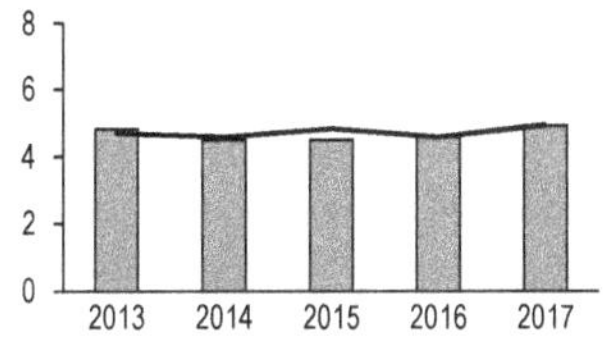

	2013	2014	2015	2016	2017
Concord	4.8	4.5	4.5	4.6	4.9
Average	4.7	4.6	4.8	4.6	4.9

Percentage of Fire Code Violations Cleared within 90 Days

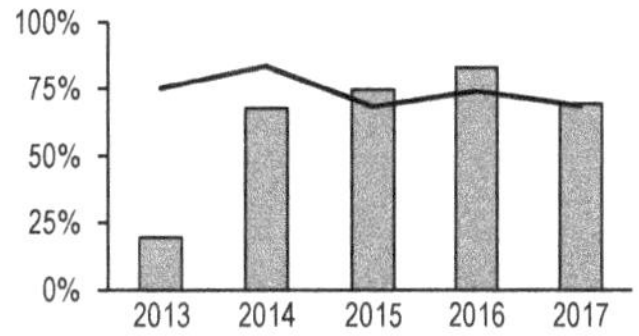

	2013	2014	2015	2016	2017
Concord	20%	68%	75%	83%	69%
Average	75%	84%	68%	74%	69%

Percentage of Fires Confined to Rooms or Objects Involved on Arrival

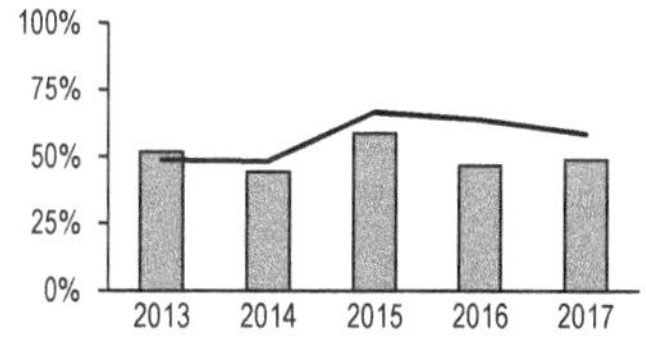

	2013	2014	2015	2016	2017
Concord	52%	44%	59%	47%	49%
Average	49%	48%	67%	64%	58%

Percentage of Fires for Which Cause Was Determined

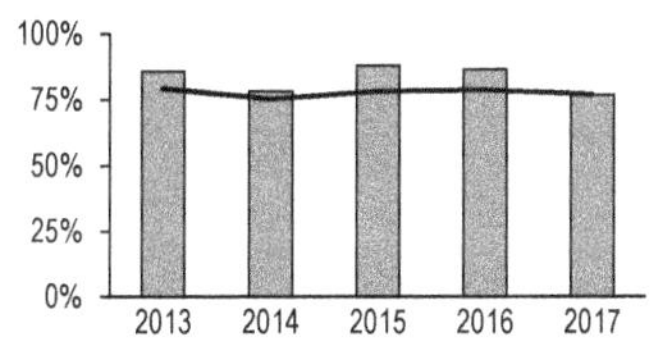

	2013	2014	2015	2016	2017
Concord	86%	78%	88%	86%	77%
Average	79%	75%	78%	79%	77%

Percentage of Full Response within 8 Minutes Travel Time

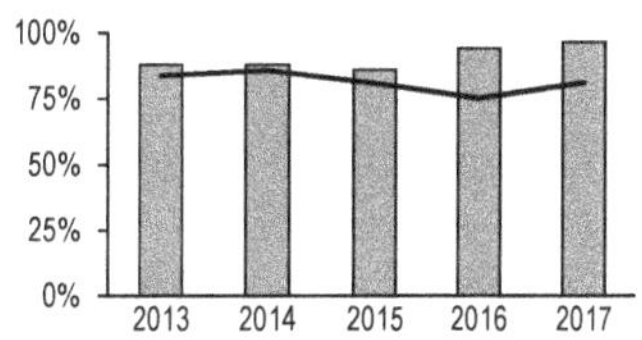

	2013	2014	2015	2016	2017
Concord	88%	88%	86%	94%	97%
Average	84%	86%	81%	75%	81%

Percentage of Lost Pulse Cases Recovered Pulse at Transfer of Care

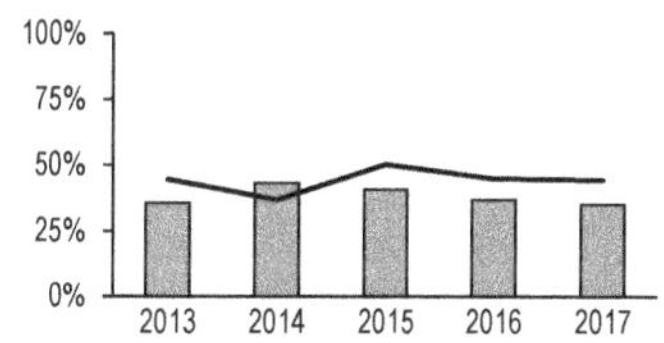

	2013	2014	2015	2016	2017
Concord	35.6%	43.3%	40.9%	37.0%	35.2%
Average	44.7%	36.8%	50.3%	44.9%	44.5%

Fiscal Year 2016–17

Explanatory Information

Service Level and Delivery
The mission of the Goldsboro Fire Department is to protect lives, the environment, and property by providing prompt, skillful, and cost-effective fire protection, EMS, and life safety service. The Department maintains a receptive and ethical work environment which is conducive to the development of innovative and creative solutions by employees to meet the ever-changing needs of the community.

The fire department utilizes a shift schedule that includes alternates twenty-four hours on and twenty-four hours off for five days followed by four days off. This works out to fifty-six hour work weeks with shifts starting and ending at 8 a.m.

The city has an ISO rating of 3 as rated in 2010.

The fire department in Goldsboro conducted 1,421 fire maintenance, construction, and reinspections during the fiscal year. General inspections are performed according to the mandated inspection schedule, which is based on occupancy type established in the International Fire Code. Maintenance fire inspections are assigned by the fire marshal to the fire inspectors, fire company inspectors, and the fire marshal. The fire inspector or fire marshal perform all site plan reviews, fumigation, tent inspections, construction inspections for fire suppression and sprinklers, tanks, and fire alarm systems.

Conditions Affecting Service, Performance, and Costs
The city of Goldsboro joined the Benchmarking Project in July 2017 with the first year of data showing for FY 2016–17.

Municipal Profile

Service Population	34,793
Land Area (Square Miles)	29.35
Persons per Square Mile	1,185
Median Family Income U.S. Census 2010	$52,752

Service Profile

FTE Positions—Firefighters	74.5
FTE Positions—Other	8.1
Fire Stations	5
First-Line Fire Apparatus	
Pumpers	4
Aerial Trucks	1
Quints	1
Squads	0
Rescue	0
Other	1
Fire Department Responses	2,840
Responses for Fires	212
Structural Fires Reported	48
Inspections Completed for Maintenance, Construction, and Reinspections	1,421
Fire Code Violations Reported	823
Estimated Fire Loss (millions)	$1.39
Amount of Property Protected in Service Area (millions)	$2,392
Number of Fire Education Programs or Events	156

Full Cost Profile

Cost Breakdown by Percentage	
Personal Services	82.9%
Operating Costs	16.7%
Capital Costs	0.4%
TOTAL	100.0%
Cost Breakdown in Dollars	
Personal Services	$5,266,421
Operating Costs	$1,060,024
Capital Costs	$22,740
TOTAL	$6,349,185

Goldsboro — Fire Services

Key: Goldsboro ▒ Benchmarking Average — Fiscal Years 2013 through 2017

Resource Measures

Fire Services Costs per Capita

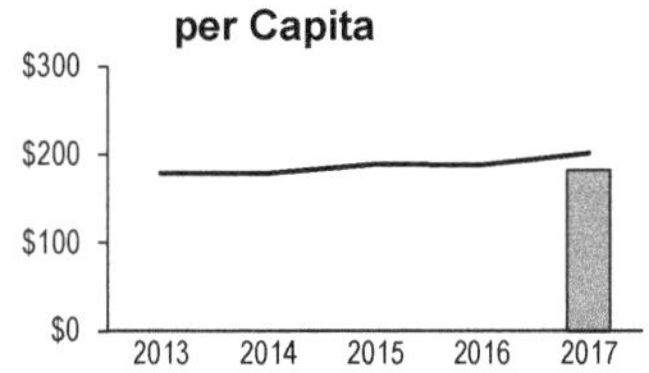

	2013	2014	2015	2016	2017
Goldsboro					$182
Average	$179	$179	$189	$188	$201

Fire Services Total FTEs per 10,000 Population

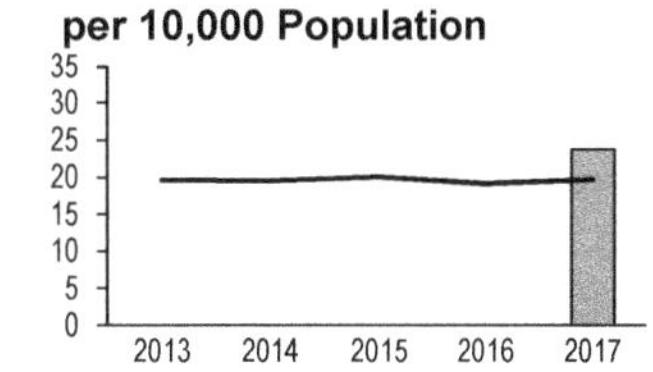

	2013	2014	2015	2016	2017
Goldsboro					23.7
Average	19.7	19.6	20.1	19.2	19.7

Fire Services Cost per Thousand Dollars of Property Protected

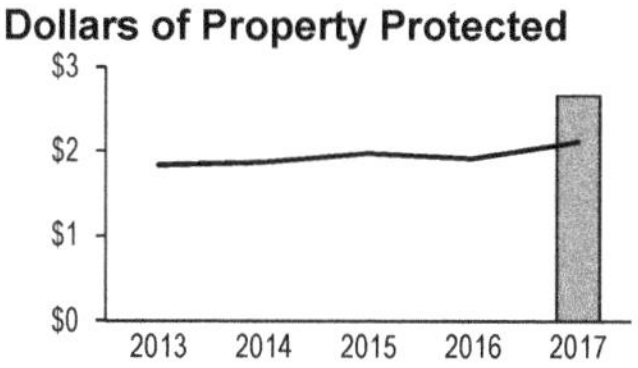

	2013	2014	2015	2016	2017
Goldsboro					$2.65
Average	$1.84	$1.87	$1.98	$1.91	$2.11

Workload Measures

Actual Fires per 1,000 Population

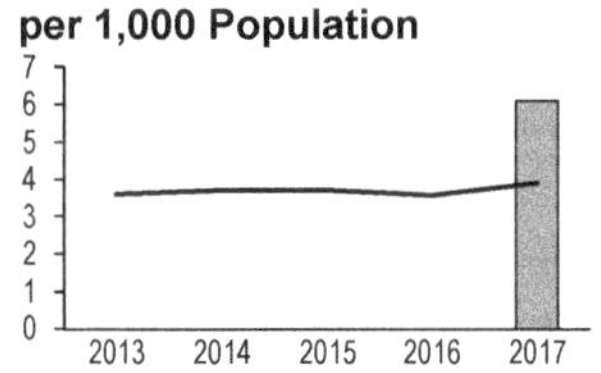

	2013	2014	2015	2016	2017
Goldsboro					6.09
Average	3.60	3.70	3.70	3.57	3.90

Fire Department Responses per 1,000 Population

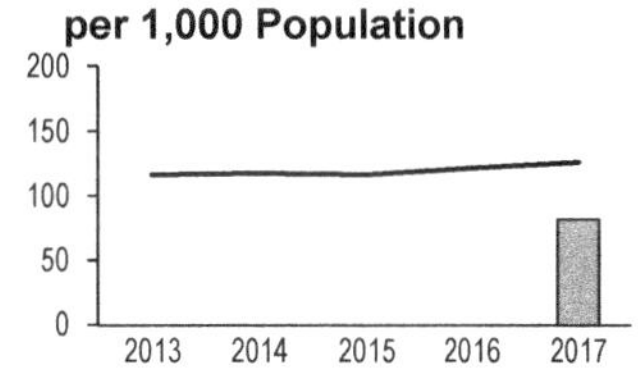

	2013	2014	2015	2016	2017
Goldsboro					82
Average	117	118	117	122	126

Fire Inspections Completed per 1,000 Population

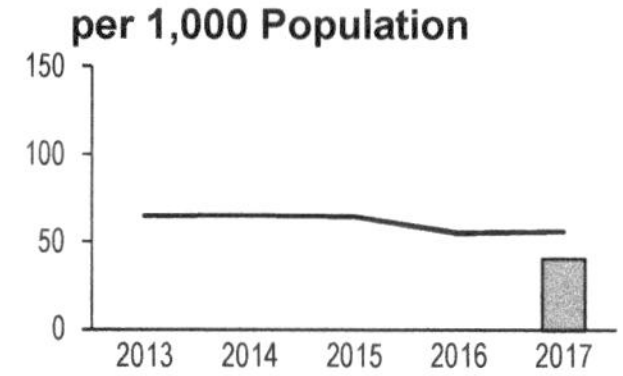

	2013	2014	2015	2016	2017
Goldsboro					41
Average	65	65	65	55	56

Efficiency Measures

Fire Services Cost per Fire Department Response

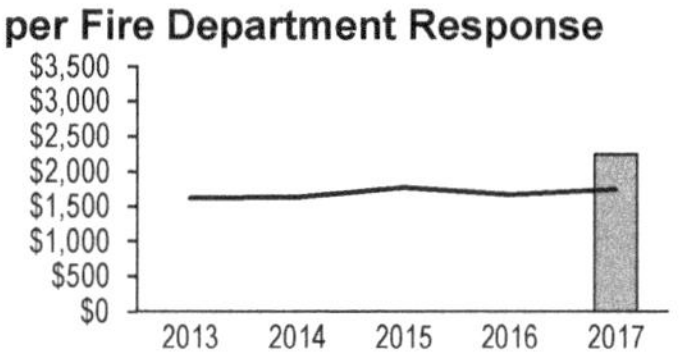

	2013	2014	2015	2016	2017
Goldsboro					$2,236
Average	$1,619	$1,627	$1,766	$1,659	$1,735

Inspections Completed per Inspector FTE

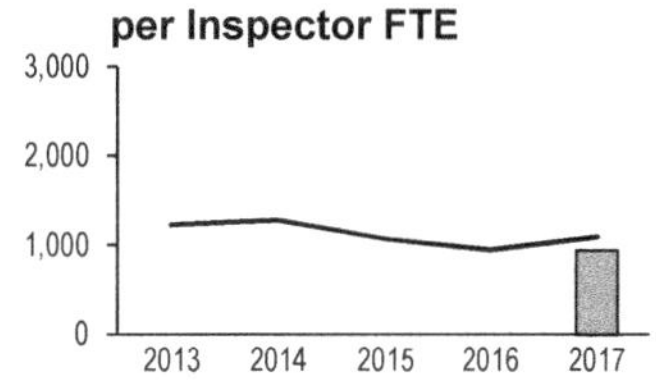

	2013	2014	2015	2016	2017
Goldsboro					947
Average	1,224	1,280	1,067	943	1,090

Effectiveness Measures

Average Response Time to Priority One Calls in Minutes

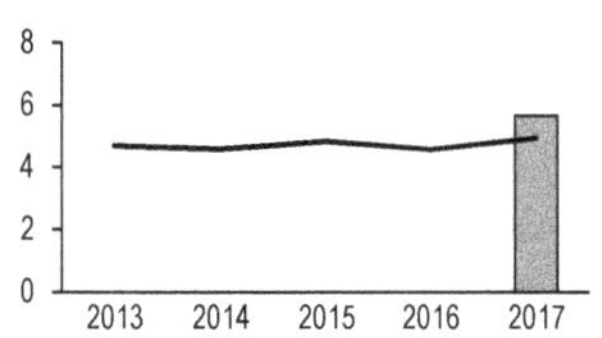

	2013	2014	2015	2016	2017
Goldsboro					5.7
Average	4.7	4.6	4.8	4.6	4.9

Percentage of Fire Code Violations Cleared within 90 Days

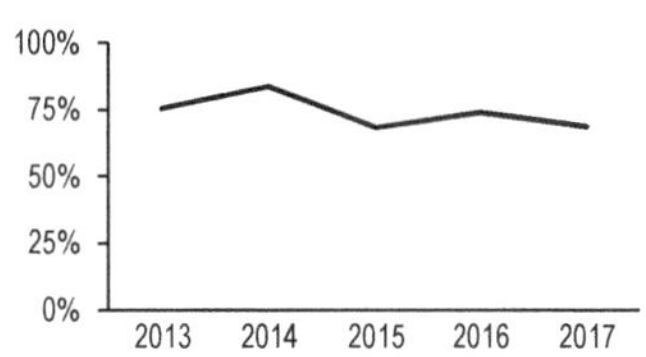

	2013	2014	2015	2016	2017
Goldsboro					
Average	75%	84%	68%	74%	69%

Percentage of Fires Confined to Rooms or Objects Involved on Arrival

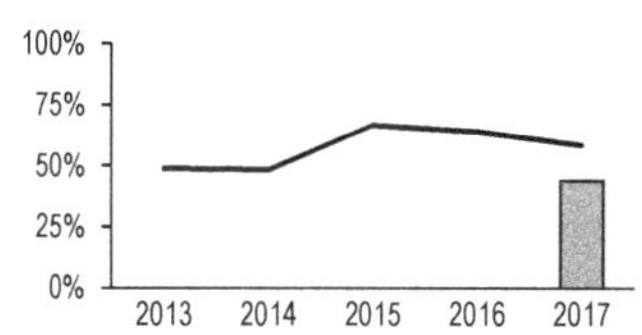

	2013	2014	2015	2016	2017
Goldsboro					44%
Average	49%	48%	67%	64%	58%

Percentage of Fires for Which Cause Was Determined

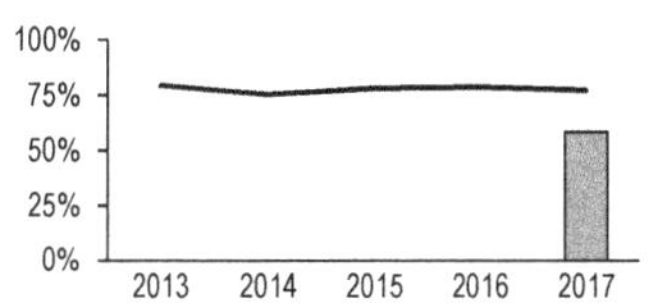

	2013	2014	2015	2016	2017
Goldsboro					58%
Average	79%	75%	78%	79%	77%

Percentage of Full Response within 8 Minutes Travel Time

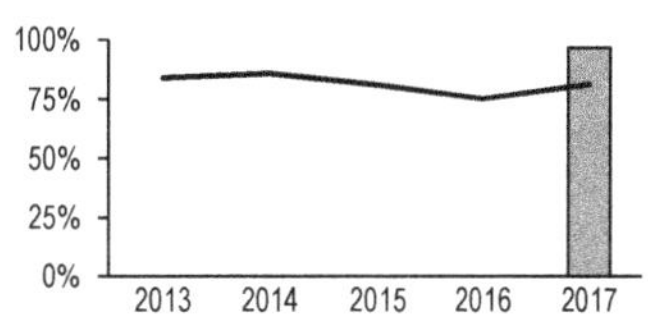

	2013	2014	2015	2016	2017
Goldsboro					97%
Average	84%	86%	81%	75%	81%

Percentage of Lost Pulse Cases Recovered Pulse at Transfer of Care

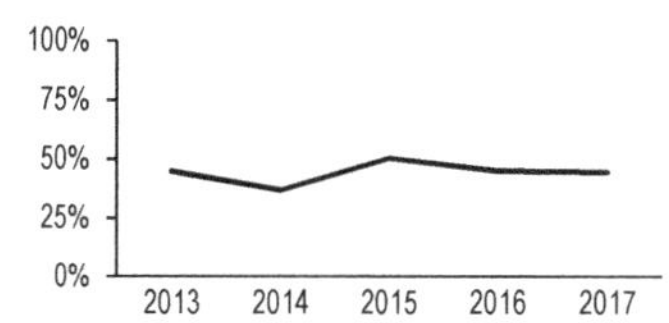

	2013	2014	2015	2016	2017
Goldsboro					
Average	44.7%	36.8%	50.3%	44.9%	44.5%

Fiscal Year 2016–17

Explanatory Information

Service Level and Delivery

The mission of the Greensboro Fire Department is to provide the public the best possible service in a courteous, professional, and cost-effective manner; to provide leadership through a well-defined management team committed to the departmental management philosophy; to provide equal opportunity for all employees in job performance and career development; to enhance public awareness through education, activities, and services; to maintain an open, informative flow of information so that all municipal departments may reach their goals and objectives; and to subscribe to honesty, integrity, and fairness.

The fire department contains two branches: emergency services and support services.

The fire department utilizes a shift schedule that includes twenty-four hours on and forty-eight hours off. For Fair Labor Standards Act (FLSA) purposes, the department utilizes a twenty-seven-day cycle.

The city has an ISO rating of 1, the highest rating possible, as rated in 2012. The Greensboro Fire Department has been accredited since 1997.

The fire department in Greensboro conducted 10,176 fire maintenance, construction, and reinspections during the fiscal year. General inspections are performed according to the mandated inspection schedule, which is based on occupancy type established in the International Fire Code. Complaints are addressed within twenty-four hours and are handled twenty-four hours a day as shift personnel are available. Inspectors generally work in districts and work in specialized areas, including educational, institutional, high rise, privilege licenses, and certificates of compliance. Apartment complexes are assigned one file number for the entire complex.

Conditions Affecting Service, Performance, and Costs

Municipal Profile

Service Population	293,233
Land Area (Square Miles)	139.82
Persons per Square Mile	2,097
Median Family Income U.S. Census 2010	$52,752

Service Profile

FTE Positions—Firefighters	523.0
FTE Positions—Other	61.0
Fire Stations	25
First-Line Fire Apparatus	
Pumpers	24
Aerial Trucks	0
Quints	11
Squads	0
Rescue	1
Other	0
Fire Department Responses	38,395
Responses for Fires	1,236
Structural Fires Reported	290
Inspections Completed for Maintenance, Construction, and Reinspections	10,176
Fire Code Violations Reported	12,581
Estimated Fire Loss (millions)	$4.21
Amount of Property Protected in Service Area (millions)	$26,415
Number of Fire Education Programs or Events	589

Full Cost Profile

Cost Breakdown by Percentage	
Personal Services	80.1%
Operating Costs	19.9%
Capital Costs	0.0%
TOTAL	100.0%
Cost Breakdown in Dollars	
Personal Services	$42,321,990
Operating Costs	$10,505,556
Capital Costs	$0
TOTAL	$52,827,546

Greensboro — Fire Services

Key: Greensboro ▒ Benchmarking Average — Fiscal Years 2013 through 2017

Resource Measures

Fire Services Costs per Capita

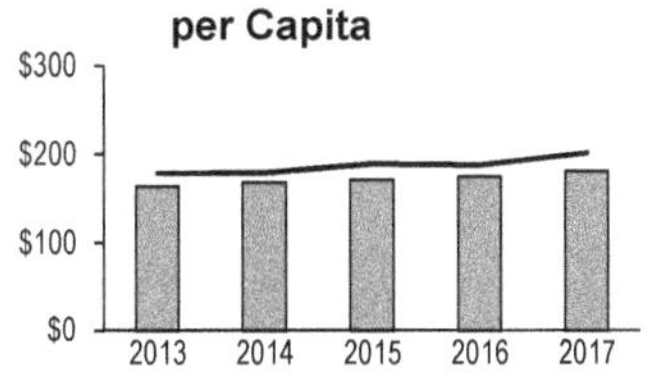

	2013	2014	2015	2016	2017
Greensboro	$164	$168	$171	$175	$180
Average	$179	$179	$189	$188	$201

Fire Services Total FTEs per 10,000 Population

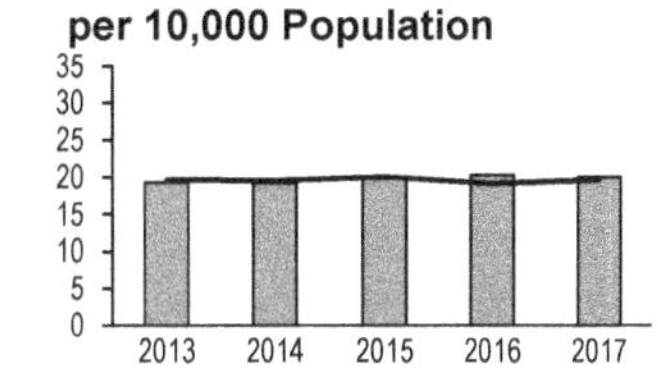

	2013	2014	2015	2016	2017
Greensboro	19.3	19.2	19.8	20.2	19.9
Average	19.7	19.6	20.1	19.2	19.7

Fire Services Cost per Thousand Dollars of Property Protected

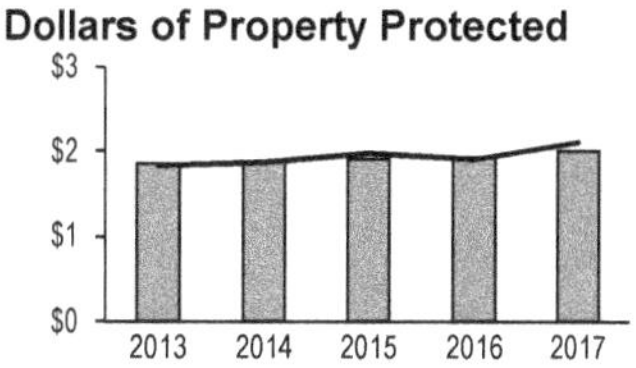

	2013	2014	2015	2016	2017
Greensboro	$1.85	$1.87	$1.90	$1.93	$2.00
Average	$1.84	$1.87	$1.98	$1.91	$2.11

Workload Measures

Actual Fires per 1,000 Population

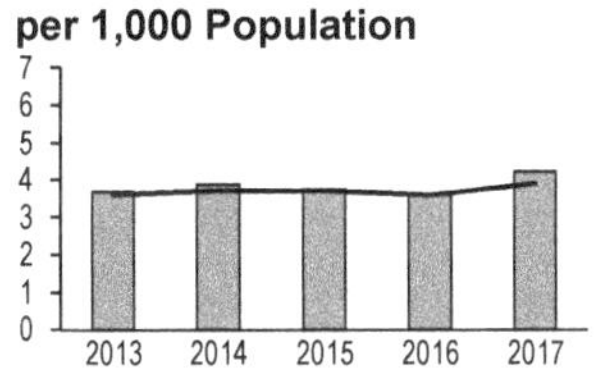

	2013	2014	2015	2016	2017
Greensboro	3.66	3.87	3.73	3.58	4.22
Average	3.60	3.70	3.70	3.57	3.90

Fire Department Responses per 1,000 Population

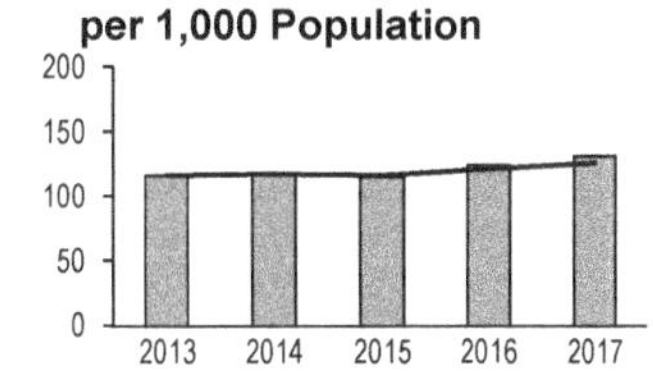

	2013	2014	2015	2016	2017
Greensboro	116	118	115	124	131
Average	117	118	117	122	126

Fire Inspections Completed per 1,000 Population

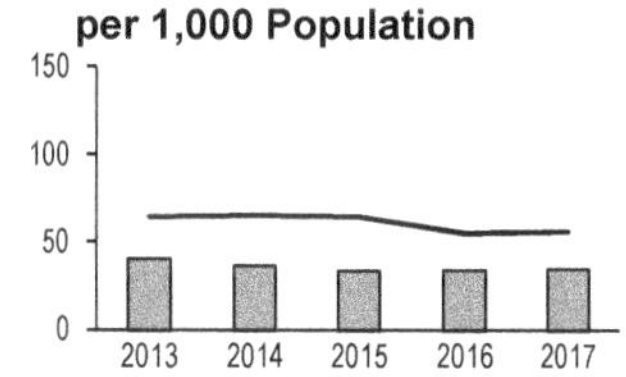

	2013	2014	2015	2016	2017
Greensboro	41	37	34	34	35
Average	65	65	65	55	56

Efficiency Measures

Fire Services Cost per Fire Department Response

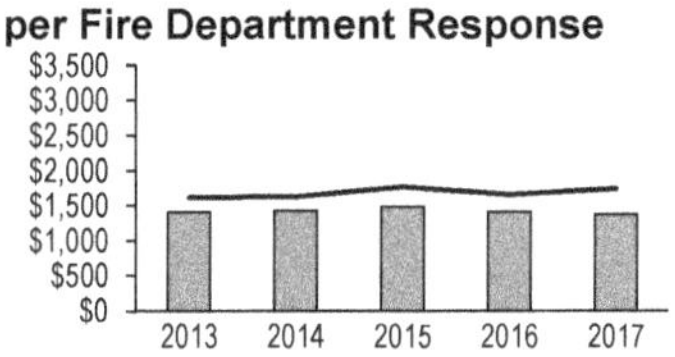

	2013	2014	2015	2016	2017
Greensboro	$1,410	$1,428	$1,482	$1,406	$1,376
Average	$1,619	$1,627	$1,766	$1,659	$1,735

Inspections Completed per Inspector FTE

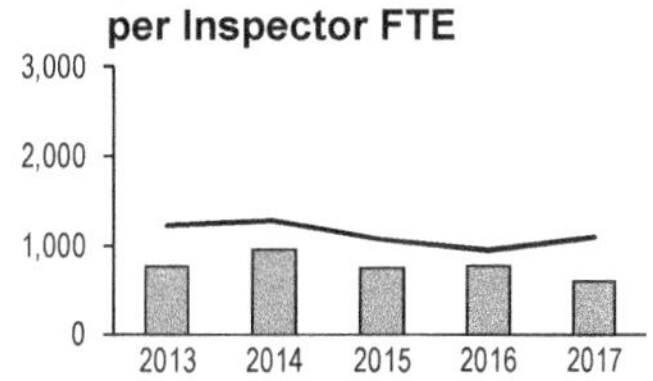

	2013	2014	2015	2016	2017
Greensboro	767	954	747	768	599
Average	1,224	1,280	1,067	943	1,090

Effectiveness Measures

Average Response Time to Priority One Calls in Minutes

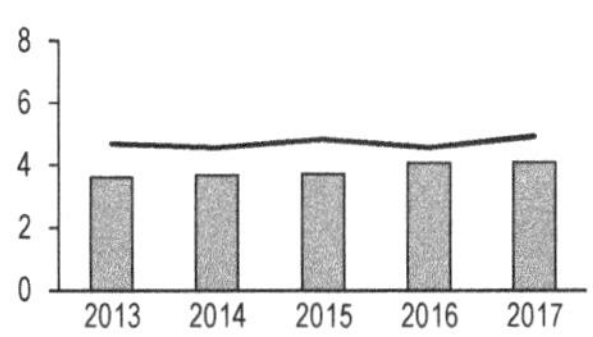

	2013	2014	2015	2016	2017
Greensboro	3.6	3.7	3.7	4.1	4.1
Average	4.7	4.6	4.8	4.6	4.9

Percentage of Fire Code Violations Cleared within 90 Days

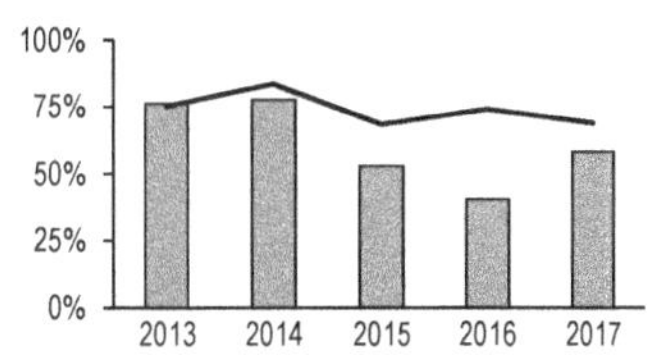

	2013	2014	2015	2016	2017
Greensboro	76%	78%	53%	40%	58%
Average	75%	84%	68%	74%	69%

Percentage of Fires Confined to Rooms or Objects Involved on Arrival

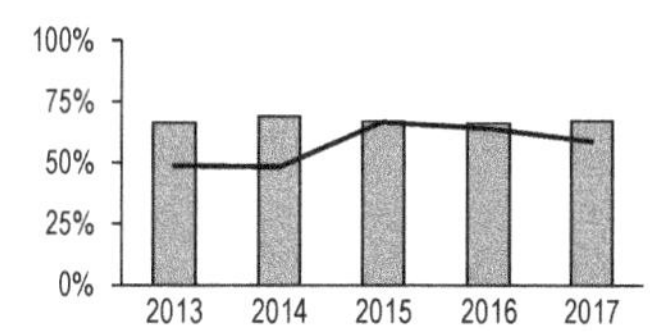

	2013	2014	2015	2016	2017
Greensboro	66%	69%	67%	66%	67%
Average	49%	48%	67%	64%	58%

Percentage of Fires for Which Cause Was Determined

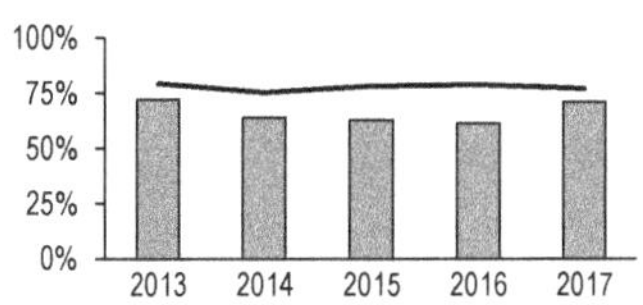

	2013	2014	2015	2016	2017
Greensboro	72%	64%	63%	61%	71%
Average	79%	75%	78%	79%	77%

Percentage of Full Response within 8 Minutes Travel Time

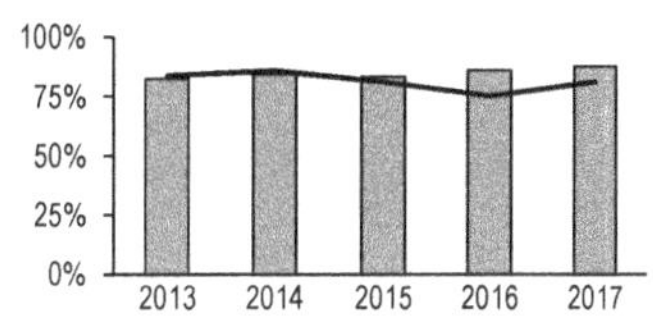

	2013	2014	2015	2016	2017
Greensboro	82%	84%	83%	86%	88%
Average	84%	86%	81%	75%	81%

Percentage of Lost Pulse Cases Recovered Pulse at Transfer of Care

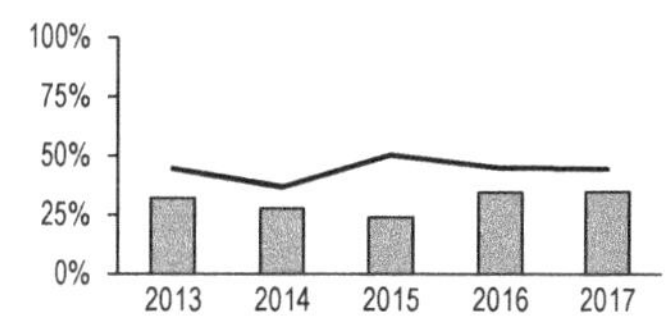

	2013	2014	2015	2016	2017
Greensboro	32.1%	27.6%	24.0%	34.5%	34.8%
Average	44.7%	36.8%	50.3%	44.9%	44.5%

Fiscal Year 2016–17

Explanatory Information

Service Level and Delivery
The primary goals of the Greenville Fire and Rescue Department are to prevent fires and save lives and property by providing emergency response services for fires or medical emergencies. The city provides fire services in areas beyond the city boundaries covering thirty-two square miles.

Emergency personnel work a 24.25-hour shift followed by 47.75 hours off.

The city has an ISO rating of 3, as rated in 2015.

The fire department in Greenville conducted 2,347 fire maintenance, construction, and reinspections during the fiscal year. The Life Safety Services Division handles all inspection-related matters following the International Fire Code.

Conditions Affecting Service, Performance, and Costs
Greenville is the only city in the benchmarking project that has emergency medical services transports (EMS) provided through the city fire department. In the other jurisdictions, EMS transports are provided by county departments.

Complications with data tracking prevented Greenville from being able to submit numbers on fire incidents and several other measures for previous fiscal years.

Municipal Profile

Service Population	88,394
Land Area (Square Miles)	36.91
Persons per Square Mile	2,395
Median Family Income U.S. Census 2010	$50,395

Service Profile

FTE Positions—Firefighters	142.0
FTE Positions—Other	17.0
Fire Stations	6
First-Line Fire Apparatus	
Pumpers	1
Aerial Trucks	1
Quints	4
Squads	0
Rescue	1
Other	1
Fire Department Responses	18,087
Responses for Fires	329
Structural Fires Reported	97
Inspections Completed for Maintenance, Construction, and Reinspections	2,347
Fire Code Violations Reported	3,822
Estimated Fire Loss (millions)	$3.71
Amount of Property Protected in Service Area (millions)	$6,038
Number of Fire Education Programs or Events	205

Full Cost Profile

Cost Breakdown by Percentage	
Personal Services	68.7%
Operating Costs	22.4%
Capital Costs	9.0%
TOTAL	100.0%
Cost Breakdown in Dollars	
Personal Services	$11,877,240
Operating Costs	$3,866,779
Capital Costs	$1,550,323
TOTAL	$17,294,342

Key: Greenville ▒ Benchmarking Average — Fiscal Years 2013 through 2017

Resource Measures

Fire Services Costs per Capita

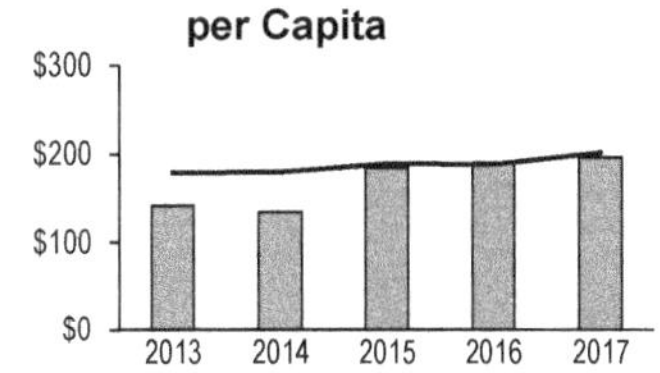

	2013	2014	2015	2016	2017
Greenville	$141	$134	$184	$190	$196
Average	$179	$179	$189	$188	$201

Fire Services Total FTEs per 10,000 Population

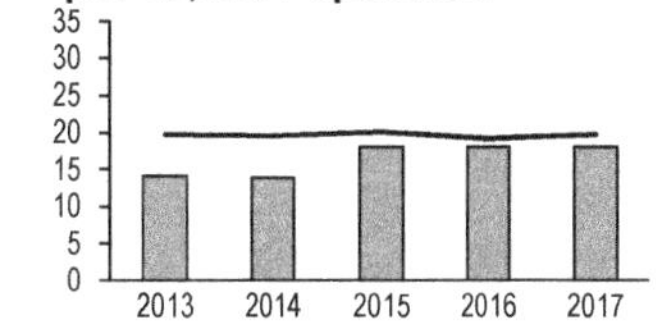

	2013	2014	2015	2016	2017
Greenville	14.1	13.8	18.0	18.0	18.0
Average	19.7	19.6	20.1	19.2	19.7

Fire Services Cost per Thousand Dollars of Property Protected

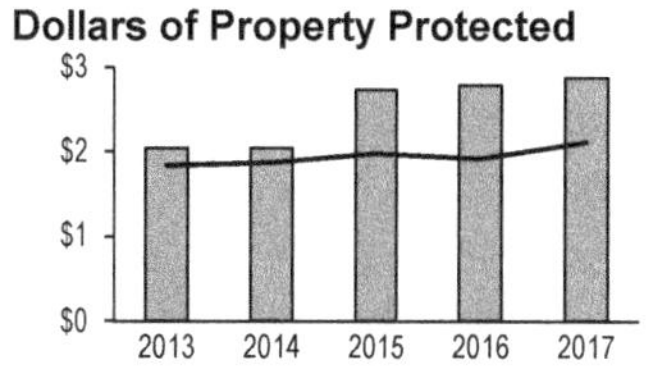

	2013	2014	2015	2016	2017
Greenville	$2.03	$2.03	$2.73	$2.77	$2.86
Average	$1.84	$1.87	$1.98	$1.91	$2.11

Workload Measures

Actual Fires per 1,000 Population

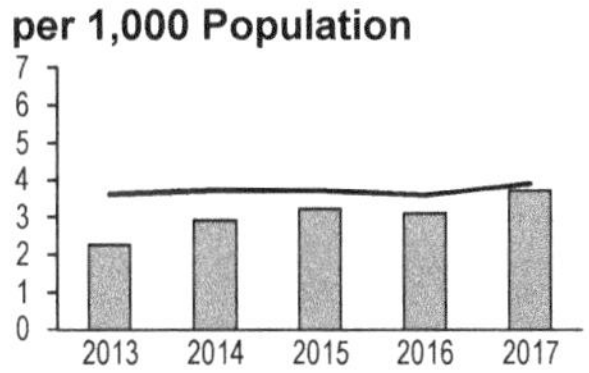

	2013	2014	2015	2016	2017
Greenville	2.26	2.91	3.22	3.11	3.72
Average	3.60	3.70	3.70	3.57	3.90

Fire Department Responses per 1,000 Population

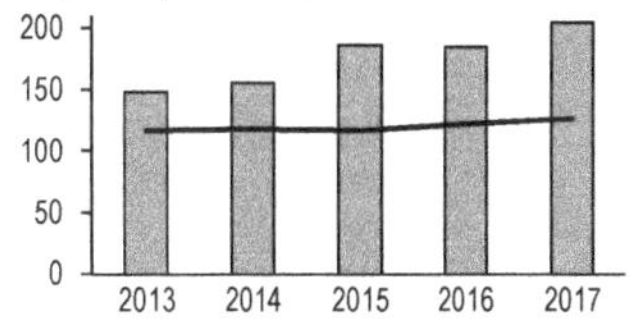

	2013	2014	2015	2016	2017
Greenville	148	156	186	185	205
Average	117	118	117	122	126

Fire Inspections Completed per 1,000 Population

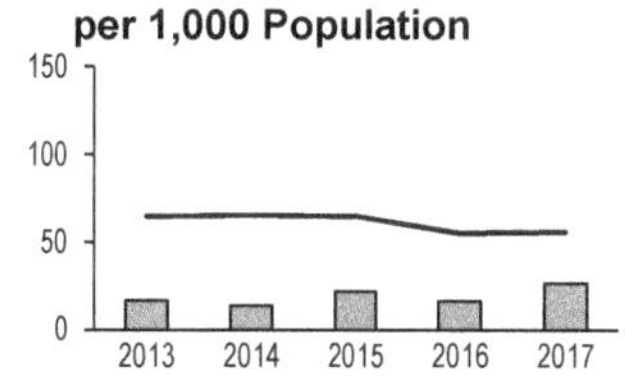

	2013	2014	2015	2016	2017
Greenville	17	14	22	16	27
Average	65	65	65	55	56

Efficiency Measures

Fire Services Cost per Fire Department Response

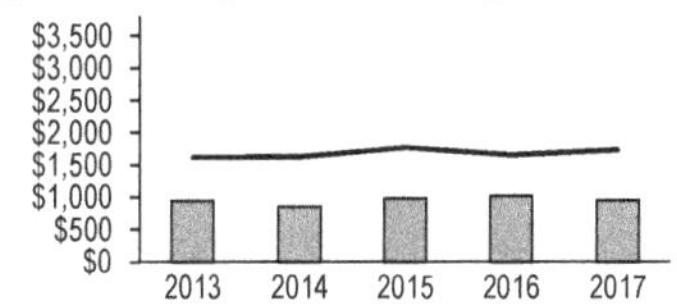

	2013	2014	2015	2016	2017
Greenville	$949	$860	$986	$1,027	$956
Average	$1,619	$1,627	$1,766	$1,659	$1,735

Inspections Completed per Inspector FTE

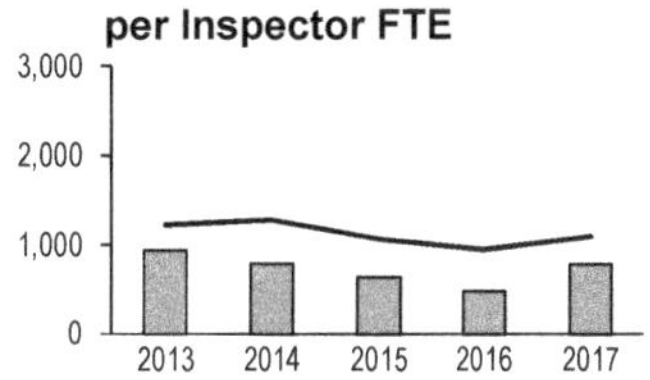

	2013	2014	2015	2016	2017
Greenville	941	790	641	481	782
Average	1,224	1,280	1,067	943	1,090

Effectiveness Measures

Average Response Time to Priority One Calls in Minutes

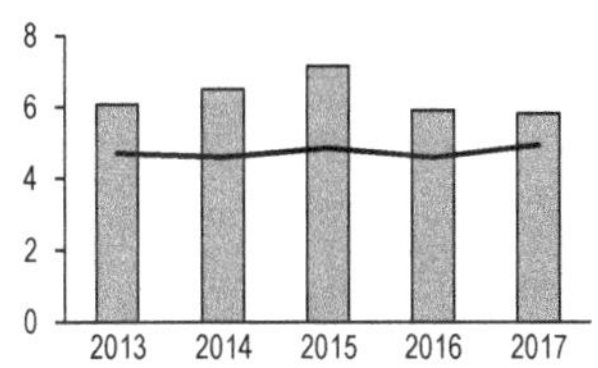

	2013	2014	2015	2016	2017
Greenville	6.1	6.5	7.2	5.9	5.8
Average	4.7	4.6	4.8	4.6	4.9

Percentage of Fire Code Violations Cleared within 90 Days

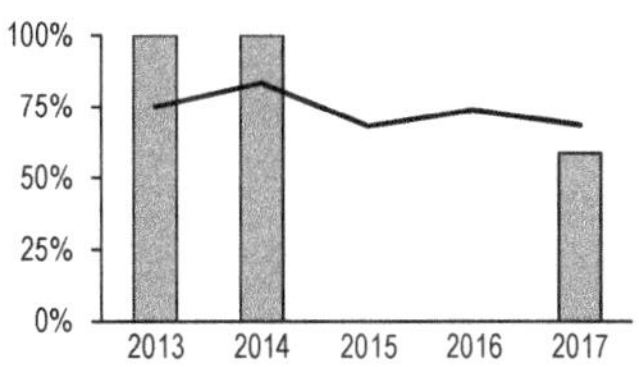

	2013	2014	2015	2016	2017
Greenville	100%	100%			59%
Average	75%	84%	68%	74%	69%

Percentage of Fires Confined to Rooms or Objects Involved on Arrival

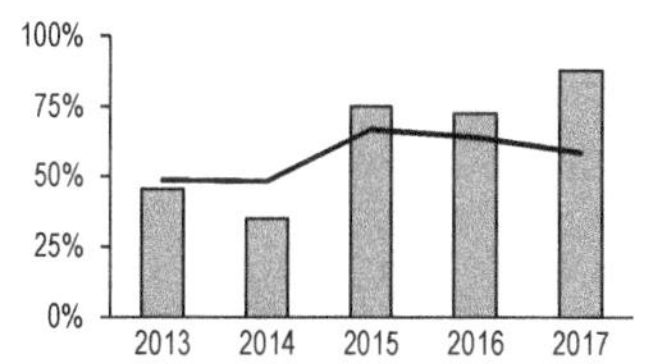

	2013	2014	2015	2016	2017
Greenville	45%	35%	75%	72%	88%
Average	49%	48%	67%	64%	58%

Percentage of Fires for Which Cause Was Determined

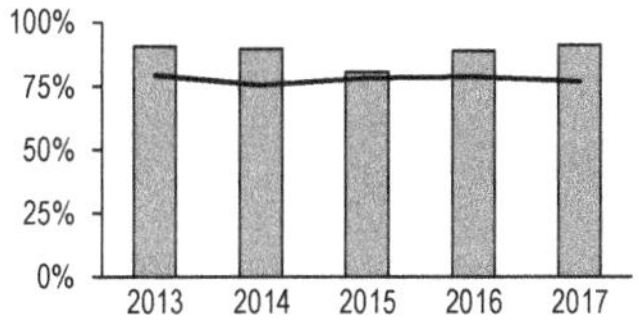

	2013	2014	2015	2016	2017
Greenville	91%	89%	80%	89%	91%
Average	79%	75%	78%	79%	77%

Percentage of Full Response within 8 Minutes Travel Time

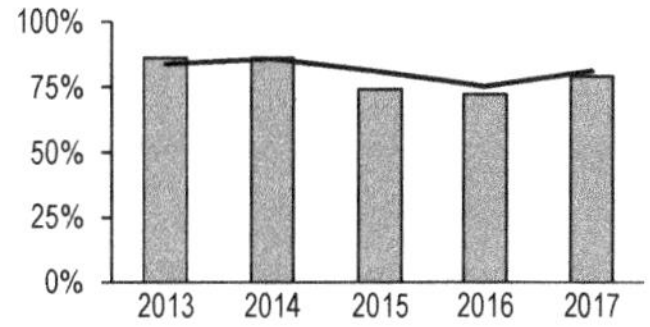

	2013	2014	2015	2016	2017
Greenville	86%	86%	74%	72%	79%
Average	84%	86%	81%	75%	81%

Percentage of Lost Pulse Cases Recovered Pulse at Transfer of Care

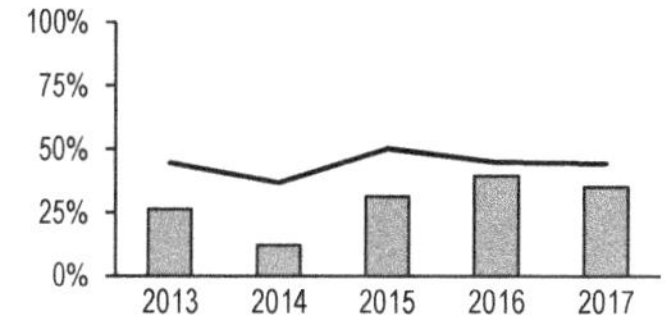

	2013	2014	2015	2016	2017
Greenville	26.4%	12.0%	31.3%	39.4%	35.2%
Average	44.7%	36.8%	50.3%	44.9%	44.5%

Fiscal Year 2016–17

Explanatory Information

Service Level and Delivery
The goal of the Hickory Fire Department is to provide high quality emergency services, education, and prevention that protect the community through professional coworkers focused on customer service, compassion, commitment, and innovation. The city provides fire coverage for an area of 13 square miles beyond city boundaries.

The fire department contains the following divisions: administration, fire and life safety, training, maintenance, and fire suppression.

Fire suppression personnel work a twenty-four-hour shift with forty-eight hours off between shifts. The twenty-four-hour shift begins at 8 a.m.

The city has an ISO rating of 3, as rated in 2005.

The fire department in Hickory conducted 5,210 fire maintenance, construction, and reinspections during the fiscal year. Fire prevention inspectors are assigned Level I, Level II, and Level III inspections. They also review construction and fire protection plans and inspect the installation of fire protection systems. The inspectors also accompany building inspectors during certificate of occupancy inspections and are responsible for conducting fire investigations, fire hydrant flow tests, occupancy and site visits, and other activities as assigned.

Conditions Affecting Service, Performance, and Costs
Hickory has a fire station staffed at the regional airport in addition to the six community fire stations.

Municipal Profile

Service Population	45,507
Land Area (Square Miles)	42.82
Persons per Square Mile	1,063
Median Family Income U.S. Census 2010	$54,093

Service Profile

FTE Positions—Firefighters	114.2
FTE Positions—Other	19.8
Fire Stations	7
First-Line Fire Apparatus	
Pumpers	7
Aerial Trucks	2
Quints	0
Squads	0
Rescue	1
Other	2
Fire Department Responses	6,720
Responses for Fires	210
Structural Fires Reported	38
Inspections Completed for Maintenance, Construction, and Reinspections	5,210
Fire Code Violations Reported	3,981
Estimated Fire Loss (millions)	$2.29
Amount of Property Protected in Service Area (millions)	$5,001
Number of Fire Education Programs or Events	472

Full Cost Profile

Cost Breakdown by Percentage	
Personal Services	79.2%
Operating Costs	16.8%
Capital Costs	4.0%
TOTAL	100.0%
Cost Breakdown in Dollars	
Personal Services	$8,277,136
Operating Costs	$1,752,501
Capital Costs	$417,988
TOTAL	$10,447,625

Key: Hickory ▒ Benchmarking Average — Fiscal Years 2013 through 2017

Resource Measures

Fire Services Costs per Capita

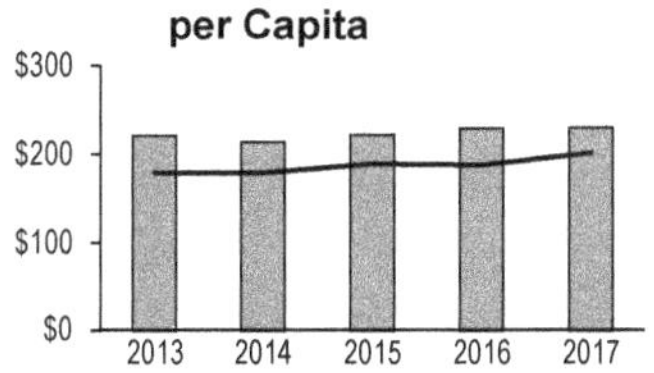

	2013	2014	2015	2016	2017
Hickory	$221	$214	$222	$229	$230
Average	$179	$179	$189	$188	$201

Fire Services Total FTEs per 10,000 Population

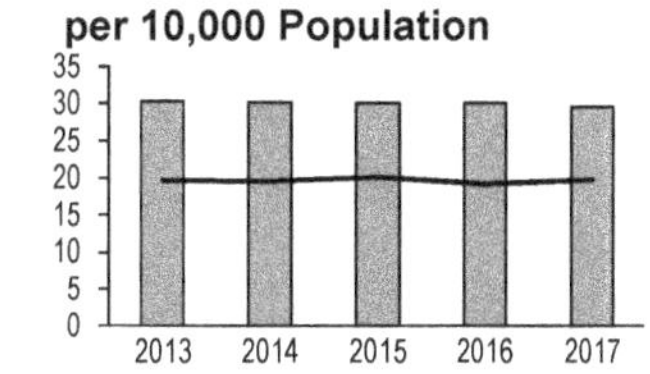

	2013	2014	2015	2016	2017
Hickory	30.2	30.1	30.0	30.0	29.4
Average	19.7	19.6	20.1	19.2	19.7

Fire Services Cost per Thousand Dollars of Property Protected

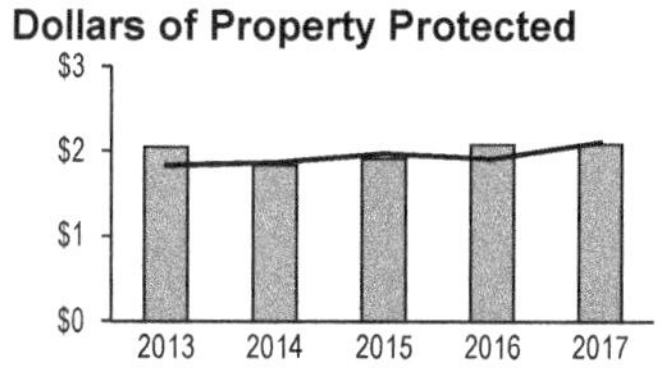

	2013	2014	2015	2016	2017
Hickory	$2.05	$1.84	$1.92	$2.08	$2.09
Average	$1.84	$1.87	$1.98	$1.91	$2.11

Workload Measures

Actual Fires per 1,000 Population

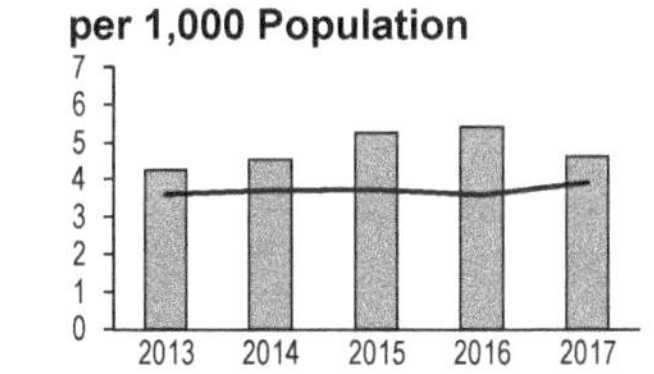

	2013	2014	2015	2016	2017
Hickory	4.26	4.53	5.25	5.40	4.61
Average	3.60	3.70	3.70	3.57	3.90

Fire Department Responses per 1,000 Population

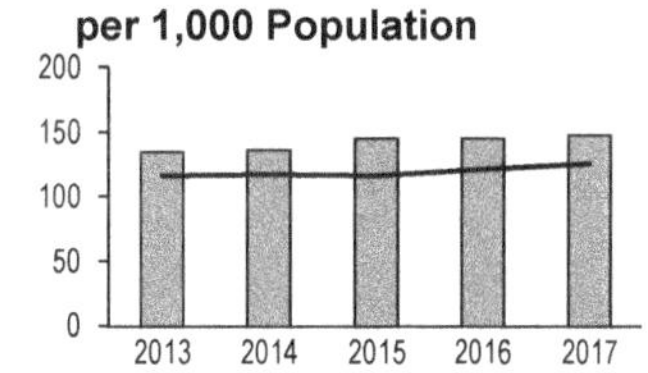

	2013	2014	2015	2016	2017
Hickory	135	137	145	146	148
Average	117	118	117	122	126

Fire Inspections Completed per 1,000 Population

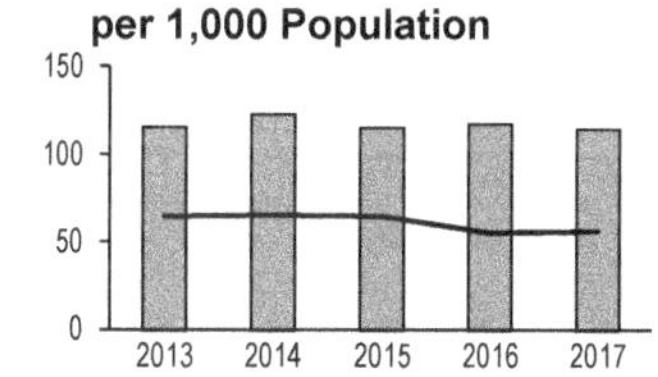

	2013	2014	2015	2016	2017
Hickory	116	123	115	118	114
Average	65	65	65	55	56

Efficiency Measures

Fire Services Cost per Fire Department Response

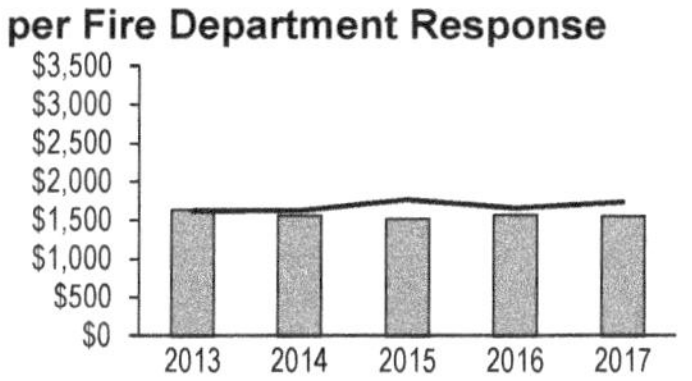

	2013	2014	2015	2016	2017
Hickory	$1,637	$1,565	$1,524	$1,575	$1,555
Average	$1,619	$1,627	$1,766	$1,659	$1,735

Inspections Completed per Inspector FTE

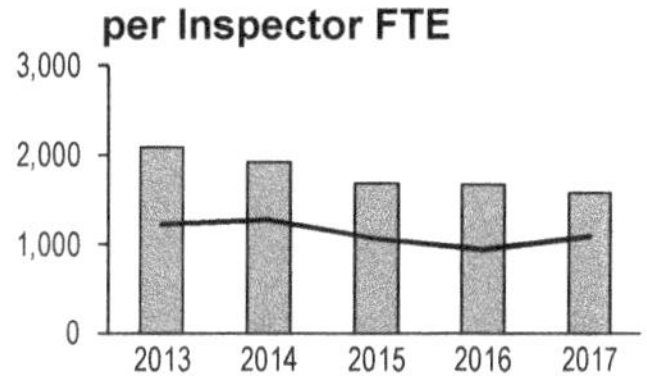

	2013	2014	2015	2016	2017
Hickory	2,086	1,918	1,686	1,667	1,579
Average	1,224	1,280	1,067	943	1,090

Effectiveness Measures

Average Response Time to Priority One Calls in Minutes

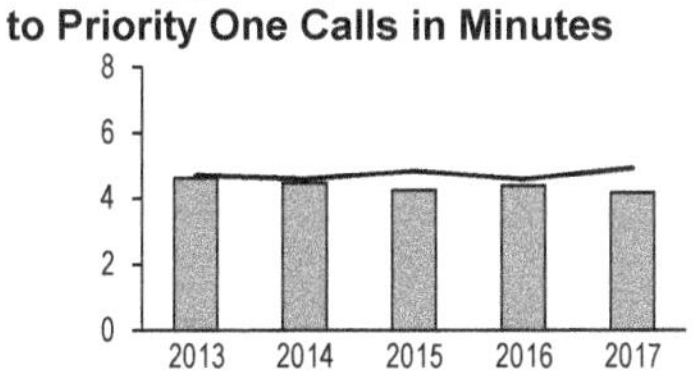

	2013	2014	2015	2016	2017
Hickory	4.6	4.5	4.3	4.4	4.2
Average	4.7	4.6	4.8	4.6	4.9

Percentage of Fire Code Violations Cleared within 90 Days

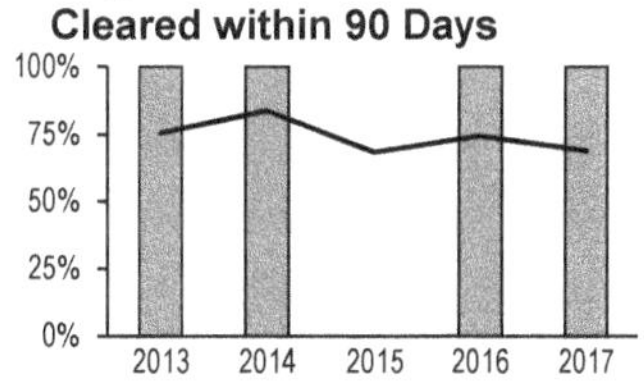

	2013	2014	2015	2016	2017
Hickory	100%	100%		100%	100%
Average	75%	84%	68%	74%	69%

Percentage of Fires Confined to Rooms or Objects Involved on Arrival

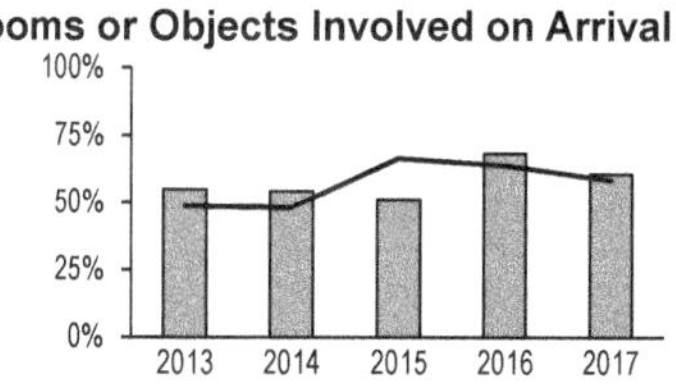

	2013	2014	2015	2016	2017
Hickory	55%	54%	51%	68%	61%
Average	49%	48%	67%	64%	58%

Percentage of Fires for Which Cause Was Determined

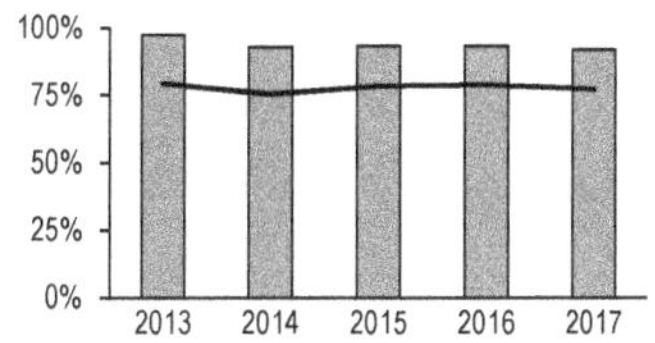

	2013	2014	2015	2016	2017
Hickory	97%	93%	93%	93%	92%
Average	79%	75%	78%	79%	77%

Percentage of Full Response within 8 Minutes Travel Time

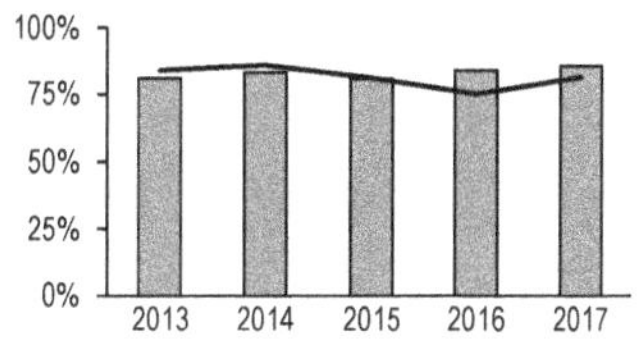

	2013	2014	2015	2016	2017
Hickory	81%	83%	81%	84%	85%
Average	84%	86%	81%	75%	81%

Percentage of Lost Pulse Cases Recovered Pulse at Transfer of Care

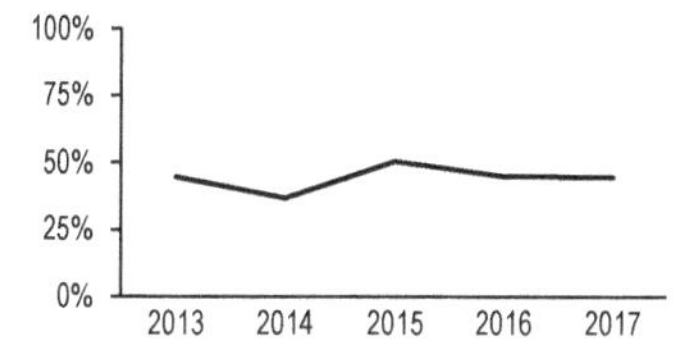

	2013	2014	2015	2016	2017
Hickory					
Average	44.7%	36.8%	50.3%	44.9%	44.5%

High Point Fire Services

Fiscal Year 2016–17

Explanatory Information

Service Level and Delivery

The High Point Fire Department provides the following functions: firefighting, emergency medical response, rescue response, hazardous material technician response, inspection, fleet/vehicle maintenance, departmental technical services, and public life safety education and community relations.

The fire department contains the following divisions: administration, operations, and technical services.

Firefighters work three rotating shifts. A shift cycle alternates three twenty-four-hour shifts on duty with one twenty-four-hour break between each scheduled shift day. This is then followed by a four-day break. This averages to a fifty-six-hour work week over a twenty-seven-day period.

The city has an ISO rating of 1, as rated in 2015. This is the highest rating possible. The High Point Fire Department became accredited in 2016.

The fire department in High Point conducted 8,104 fire maintenance, construction, and reinspections during the fiscal year. All Level I inspections are conducted by fire suppression personnel. They are responsible for making the first inspection on an occupancy as well as conducting the first reinspection for that occupancy within thirty days. If code violations are not corrected, the case is turned over to fire prevention personnel for follow-up. All Level II and Level III inspections are conducted by fire prevention staff. All reinspections are conducted on thirty-day cycles.

Conditions Affecting Service, Performance, and Costs

Municipal Profile

Service Population	119,857
Land Area (Square Miles)	67.14
Persons per Square Mile	1,785
Median Family Income U.S. Census 2010	$49,720

Service Profile

FTE Positions—Firefighters	210.0
FTE Positions—Other	24.0
Fire Stations	14
First-Line Fire Apparatus	
Pumpers	14
Aerial Trucks	4
Quints	0
Squads	0
Rescue	1
Other	10
Fire Department Responses	14,662
Responses for Fires	534
Structural Fires Reported	123
Inspections Completed for Maintenance, Construction, and Reinspections	8,104
Fire Code Violations Reported	1,297
Estimated Fire Loss (millions)	$3.03
Amount of Property Protected in Service Area (millions)	$9,904
Number of Fire Education Programs or Events	219

Full Cost Profile

Cost Breakdown by Percentage	
Personal Services	70.6%
Operating Costs	18.6%
Capital Costs	10.8%
TOTAL	100.0%
Cost Breakdown in Dollars	
Personal Services	$17,396,716
Operating Costs	$4,578,001
Capital Costs	$2,656,888
TOTAL	$24,631,605

High Point

Fire Services

Key: High Point ▒ Benchmarking Average — Fiscal Years 2013 through 2017

Resource Measures

Fire Services Costs per Capita

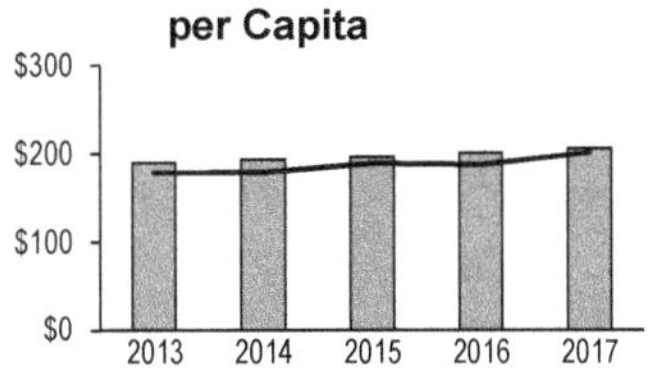

	2013	2014	2015	2016	2017
High Point	$190	$193	$196	$200	$206
Average	$179	$179	$189	$188	$201

Fire Services Total FTEs per 10,000 Population

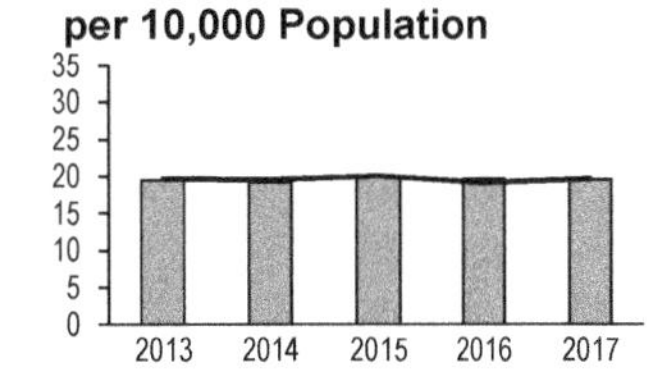

	2013	2014	2015	2016	2017
High Point	19.5	19.1	19.8	19.6	19.5
Average	19.7	19.6	20.1	19.2	19.7

Fire Services Cost per Thousand Dollars of Property Protected

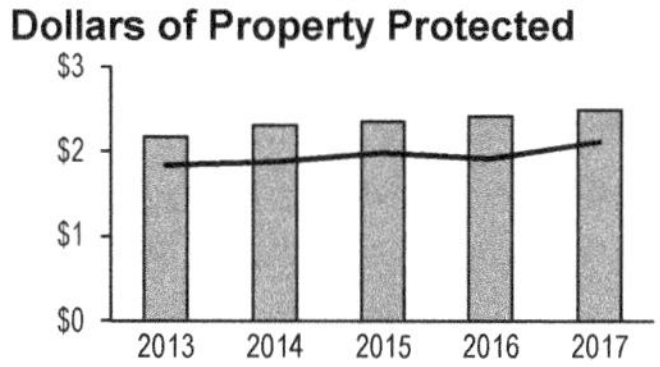

	2013	2014	2015	2016	2017
High Point	$2.17	$2.30	$2.35	$2.41	$2.49
Average	$1.84	$1.87	$1.98	$1.91	$2.11

Workload Measures

Actual Fires per 1,000 Population

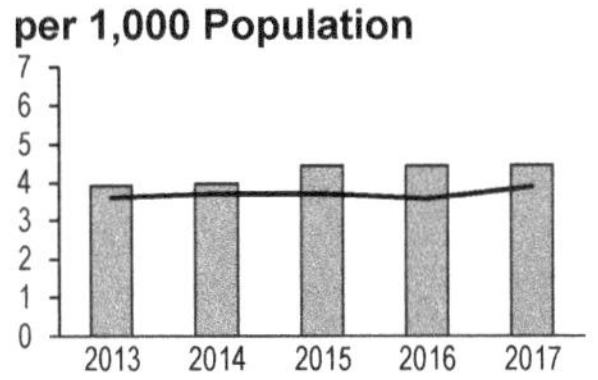

	2013	2014	2015	2016	2017
High Point	3.93	3.96	4.43	4.44	4.46
Average	3.60	3.70	3.70	3.57	3.90

Fire Department Responses per 1,000 Population

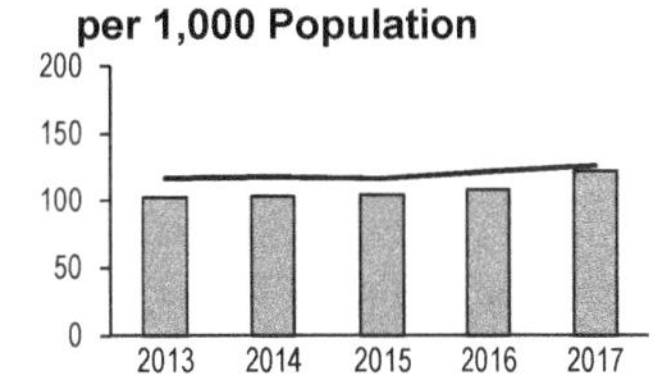

	2013	2014	2015	2016	2017
High Point	103	104	105	109	122
Average	117	118	117	122	126

Fire Inspections Completed per 1,000 Population

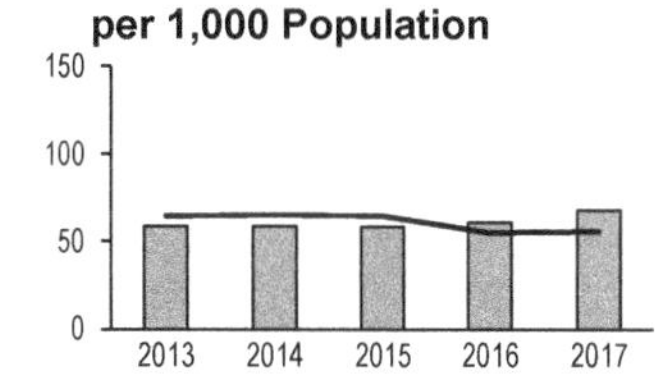

	2013	2014	2015	2016	2017
High Point	58	59	58	61	68
Average	65	65	65	55	56

Efficiency Measures

Fire Services Cost per Fire Department Response

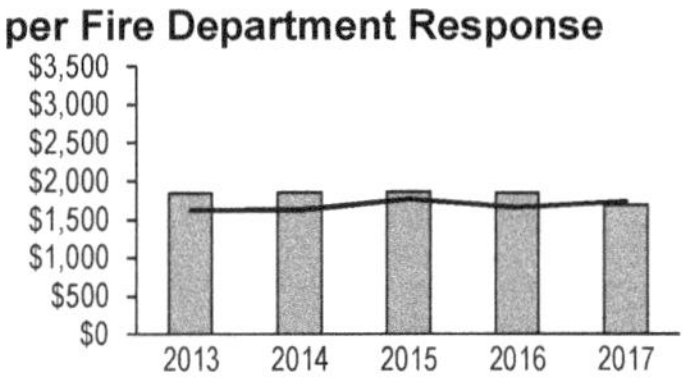

	2013	2014	2015	2016	2017
High Point	$1,840	$1,852	$1,861	$1,842	$1,680
Average	$1,619	$1,627	$1,766	$1,659	$1,735

Inspections Completed per Inspector FTE

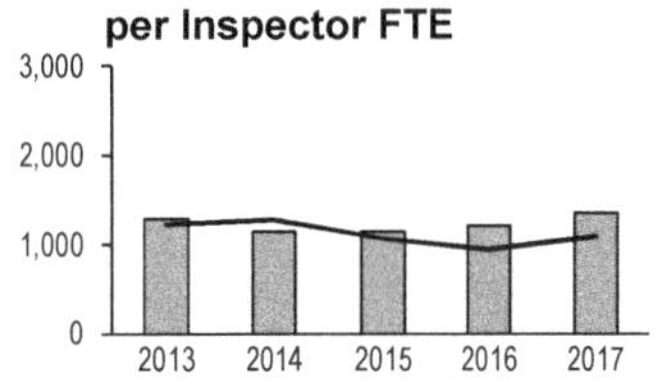

	2013	2014	2015	2016	2017
High Point	1,288	1,141	1,142	1,204	1,351
Average	1,224	1,280	1,067	943	1,090

Effectiveness Measures

Average Response Time to Priority One Calls in Minutes

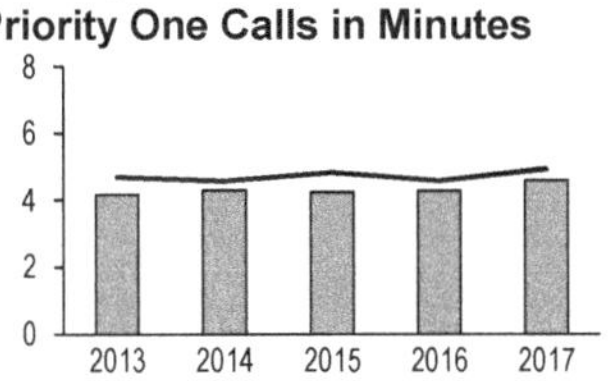

	2013	2014	2015	2016	2017
High Point	4.2	4.3	4.3	4.3	4.6
Average	4.7	4.6	4.8	4.6	4.9

Percentage of Fire Code Violations Cleared within 90 Days

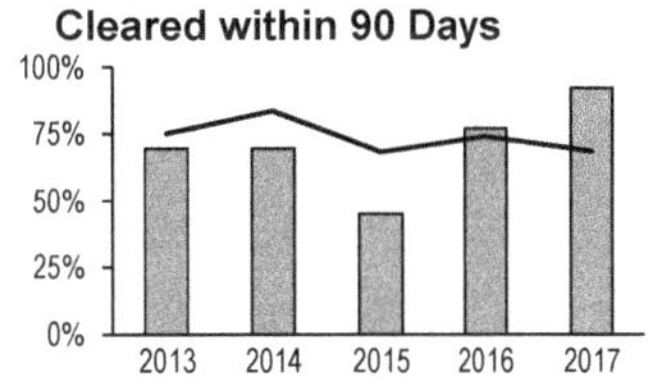

	2013	2014	2015	2016	2017
High Point	69%	70%	45%	77%	92%
Average	75%	84%	68%	74%	69%

Percentage of Fires Confined to Rooms or Objects Involved on Arrival

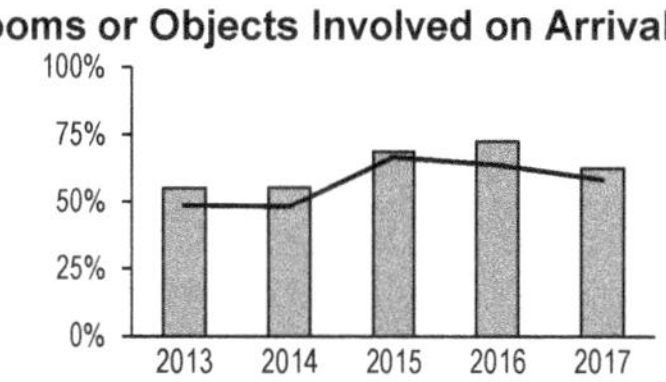

	2013	2014	2015	2016	2017
High Point	55%	55%	69%	72%	62%
Average	49%	48%	67%	64%	58%

Percentage of Fires for Which Cause Was Determined

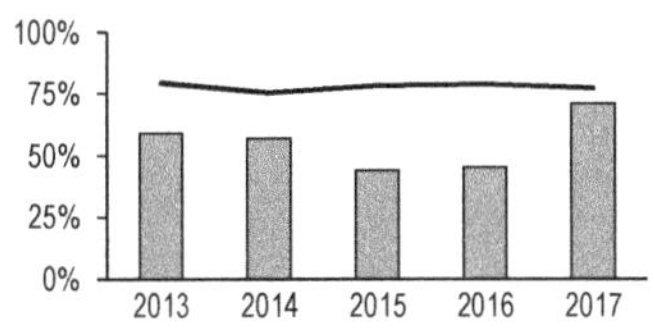

	2013	2014	2015	2016	2017
High Point	59%	57%	44%	45%	71%
Average	79%	75%	78%	79%	77%

Percentage of Full Response within 8 Minutes Travel Time

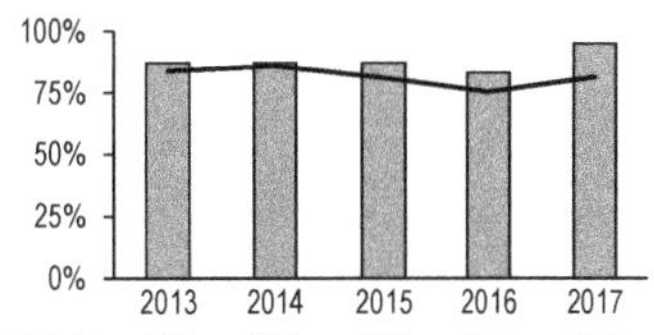

	2013	2014	2015	2016	2017
High Point	87%	87%	87%	83%	95%
Average	84%	86%	81%	75%	81%

Percentage of Lost Pulse Cases Recovered Pulse at Transfer of Care

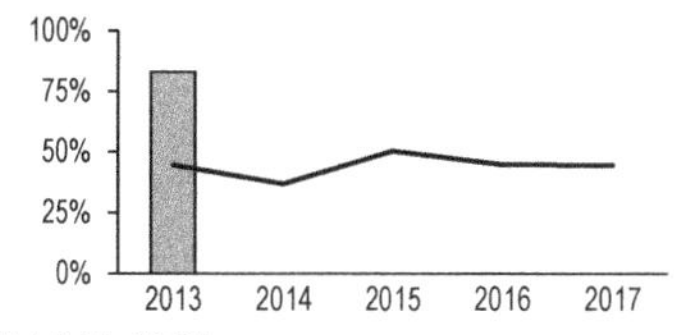

	2013	2014	2015	2016	2017
High Point	82.9%				
Average	44.7%	36.8%	50.3%	44.9%	44.5%

Fiscal Year 2016–17

Explanatory Information

Service Level and Delivery
The Raleigh Fire Department provides the following services in carrying out its mission: fire protection, emergency medical first response, extrication, confined space and high angle rescue, hazardous materials response, fire inspections, and fire education.

The fire department is broken into five primary function areas. The Office of the Fire Chief provides administrative services and oversight; the Office of the Fire Marshal is the enforcement, educational, and informational arm; the Operations Division responds to and manages incidents and special events; the Support Services Division supplies and maintains infrastructure, equipment, clothing, and apparatus; and the Training Divison recruits, hires, trains, and manages career development.

The shift schedule for the fire department is a nine-day cycle as follows: five twenty-four-hour days alternating on and off followed by four days off.

The city received an ISO rating of 1 in 2016. This is the highest rating possible.

The fire department in Raleigh conducted 23,228 fire maintenance, construction, and reinspections during the fiscal year. Fire inspections are scheduled by the Office of the Fire Marshal through an automated process based on a priority basis and consistent with section 106 of the NC State Fire Code. Other inspections are scheduled as requested for special events, operational permits, and special requests. Apartment complexes are counted as one inspection per building and high rises are considered as one inspection with one file.

Conditions Affecting Service, Performance, and Costs
Raleigh rejoined the Benchmarking Project in July 2016 with the first year of data showing for FY 2015–16.

Municipal Profile

Service Population	448,706
Land Area (Square Miles)	145.56
Persons per Square Mile	3,083
Median Family Income U.S. Census 2010	$68,678

Service Profile

FTE Positions—Firefighters	551.0
FTE Positions—Other	70.0
Fire Stations	28
First-Line Fire Apparatus	
Pumpers	27
Aerial Trucks	9
Quints	0
Squads	2
Rescue	1
Other	0
Fire Department Responses	40,891
Responses for Fires	1,188
Structural Fires Reported	224
Inspections Completed for Maintenance, Construction, and Reinspections	23,228
Fire Code Violations Reported	23,998
Estimated Fire Loss (millions)	$74.22
Amount of Property Protected in Service Area (millions)	$53,578
Number of Fire Education Programs or Events	775

Full Cost Profile

Cost Breakdown by Percentage	
Personal Services	72.5%
Operating Costs	17.4%
Capital Costs	10.1%
TOTAL	100.0%
Cost Breakdown in Dollars	
Personal Services	$50,113,871
Operating Costs	$11,995,763
Capital Costs	$6,969,952
TOTAL	$69,079,586

Key: Raleigh ▒ Benchmarking Average — Fiscal Years 2013 through 2017

Resource Measures

Fire Services Costs per Capita

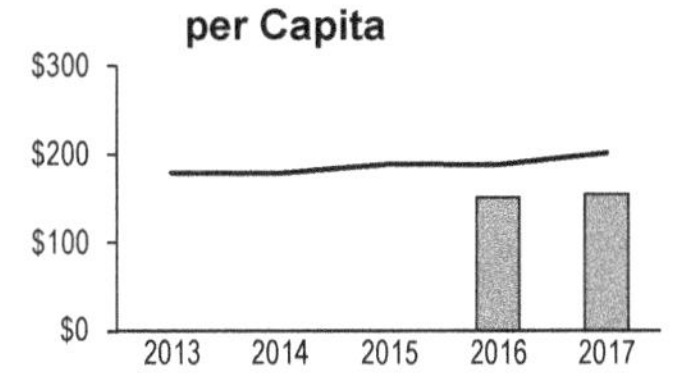

	2013	2014	2015	2016	2017
Raleigh				$151	$154
Average	$179	$179	$189	$188	$201

Fire Services Total FTEs per 10,000 Population

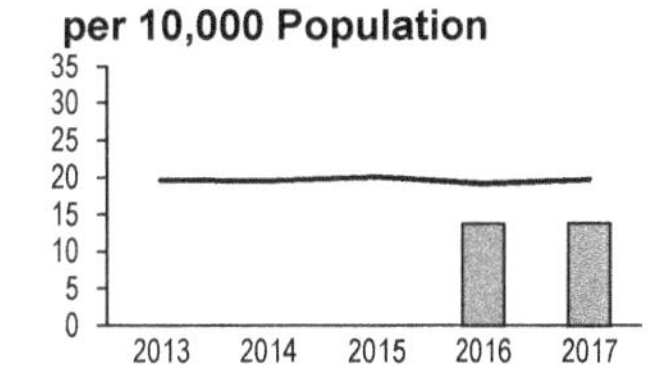

	2013	2014	2015	2016	2017
Raleigh				13.8	13.8
Average	19.7	19.6	20.1	19.2	19.7

Fire Services Cost per Thousand Dollars of Property Protected

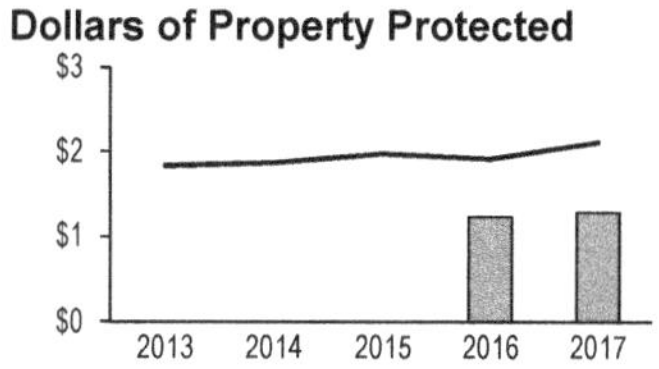

	2013	2014	2015	2016	2017
Raleigh				$1.24	$1.29
Average	$1.84	$1.87	$1.98	$1.91	$2.11

Workload Measures

Actual Fires per 1,000 Population

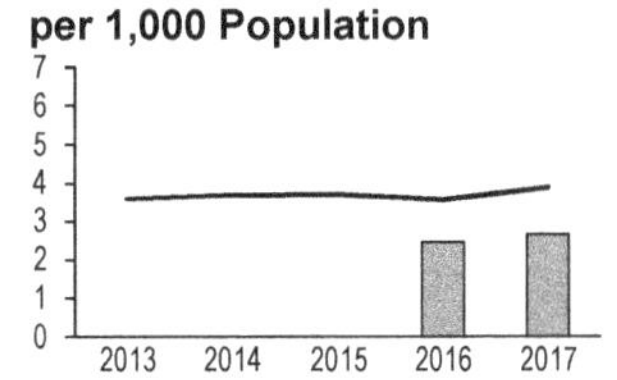

	2013	2014	2015	2016	2017
Raleigh				2.45	2.65
Average	3.60	3.70	3.70	3.57	3.90

Fire Department Responses per 1,000 Population

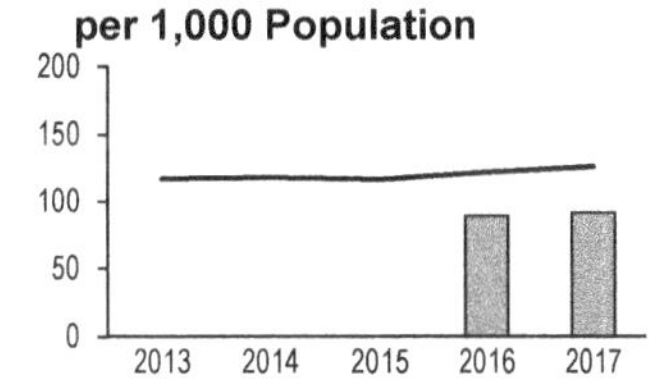

	2013	2014	2015	2016	2017
Raleigh				89	91
Average	117	118	117	122	126

Fire Inspections Completed per 1,000 Population

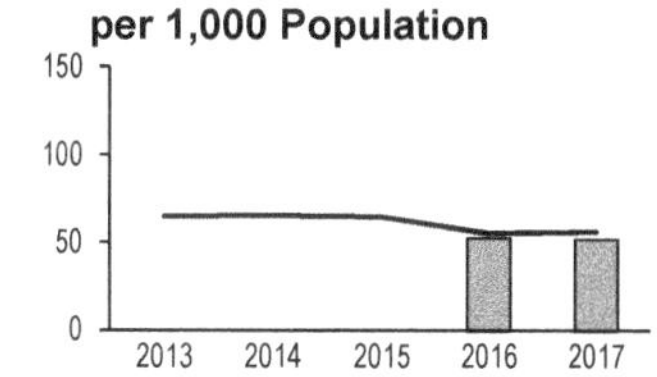

	2013	2014	2015	2016	2017
Raleigh				53	52
Average	65	65	65	55	56

Efficiency Measures

Fire Services Cost per Fire Department Response

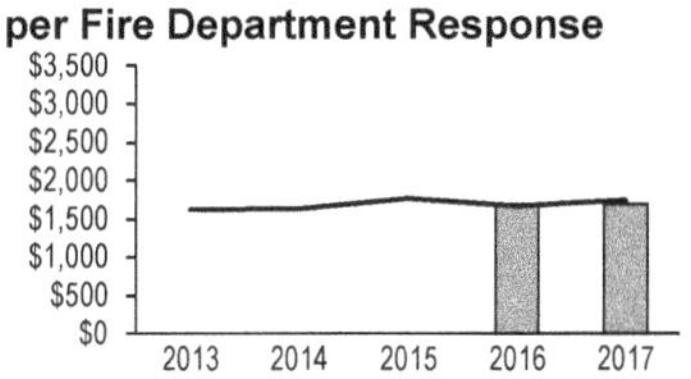

	2013	2014	2015	2016	2017
Raleigh				$1,690	$1,689
Average	$1,619	$1,627	$1,766	$1,659	$1,735

Inspections Completed per Inspector FTE

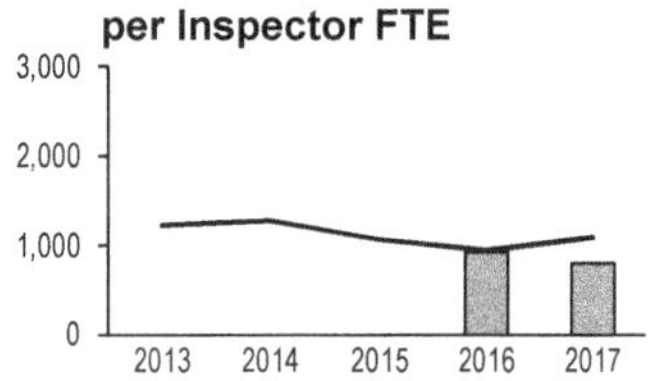

	2013	2014	2015	2016	2017
Raleigh				926	801
Average	1,224	1,280	1,067	943	1,090

Effectiveness Measures

Average Response Time to Priority One Calls in Minutes

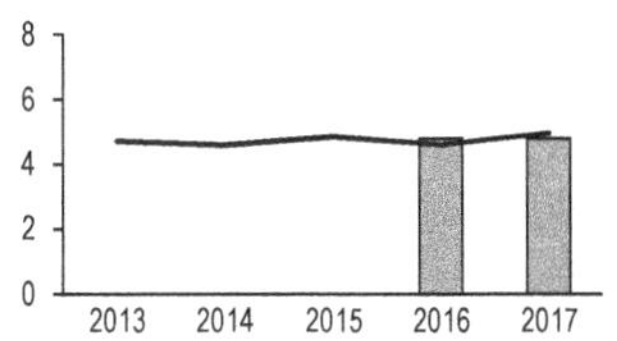

	2013	2014	2015	2016	2017
Raleigh				4.8	4.8
Average	4.7	4.6	4.8	4.6	4.9

Percentage of Fire Code Violations Cleared within 90 Days

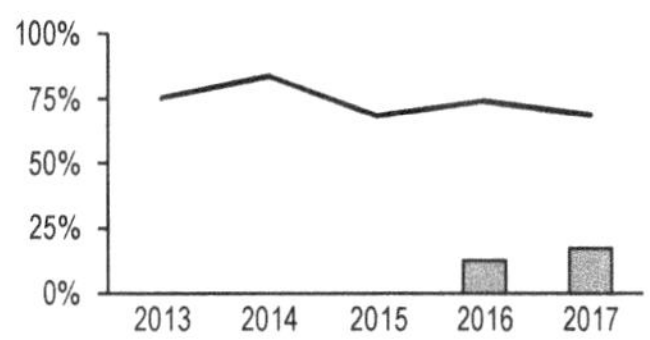

	2013	2014	2015	2016	2017
Raleigh				13%	17%
Average	75%	84%	68%	74%	69%

Percentage of Fires Confined to Rooms or Objects Involved on Arrival

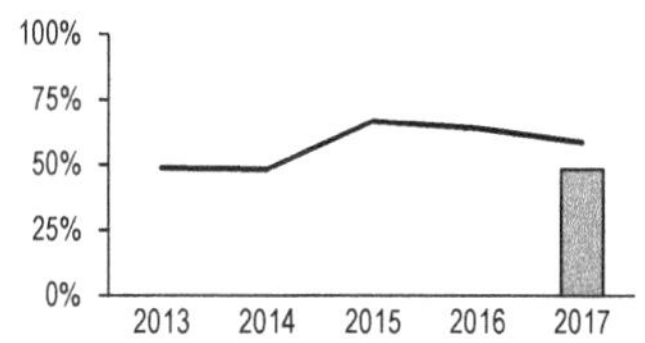

	2013	2014	2015	2016	2017
Raleigh					48%
Average	49%	48%	67%	64%	58%

Percentage of Fires for Which Cause Was Determined

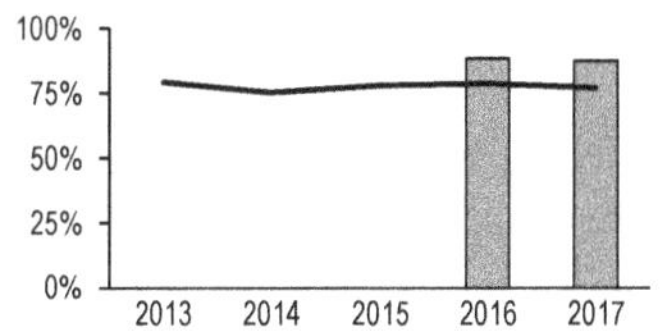

	2013	2014	2015	2016	2017
Raleigh				88%	87%
Average	79%	75%	78%	79%	77%

Percentage of Full Response within 8 Minutes Travel Time

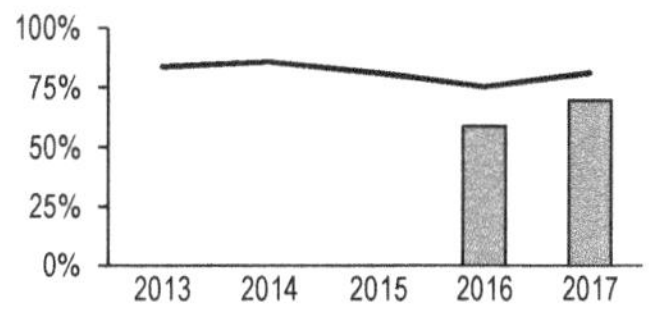

	2013	2014	2015	2016	2017
Raleigh				59%	70%
Average	84%	86%	81%	75%	81%

Percentage of Lost Pulse Cases Recovered Pulse at Transfer of Care

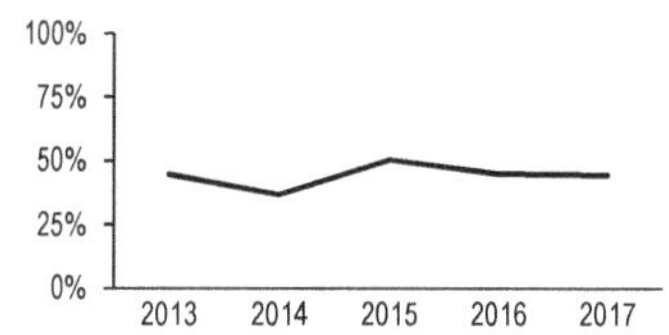

	2013	2014	2015	2016	2017
Raleigh					
Average	44.7%	36.8%	50.3%	44.9%	44.5%

Fiscal Year 2016–17

Explanatory Information

Service Level and Delivery

The purpose of the Salisbury Fire Department is to provide capable, well-trained personnel and necessary equipment to suppress fires and effectively manage hazardous chemical accidents that may occur in the community related to transportation or industry; to provide rescue services as needed and basic life support through the updated First Responder Program; and to work toward a more fire-safe community through loss prevention activities, including inspections, code enforcement, minimum housing activities, and public education programs.

The fire department contains the following divisions: fire control, loss prevention, training, and logistics.

The shift schedule for the fire department is twenty-four hours on and forty-eight hours off for three cycles. There are three shifts. Captains and firefighters get a twenty-four-hour Kelley day plus four hours off for any twenty-eight-day cycle exceeding 212 hours worked. The city has some part-time personnel working to fill vacant spots on the shifts due to Kelley days. Salisbury now is a quint system of deployment and duty. The quint trucks combine the duties of an engine and a truck company into a single company.

The city has an ISO rating of 2, as rated in 2008.

The fire department in Salisbury conducted 1,751 fire maintenance, construction, and reinspections during the fiscal year. The city follows or exceeds the state guidelines for frequency of inspections for all occupancies. Apartment buildings have one file number. Reinspections are performed at thirty-day intervals. Fees are assessed at the third inspection.

Conditions Affecting Service, Performance, and Costs

Municipal Profile

Service Population	34,459
Land Area (Square Miles)	22.28
Persons per Square Mile	1,547
Median Family Income U.S. Census 2010	$40,192

Service Profile

FTE Positions—Firefighters	67.0
FTE Positions—Other	8.0
Fire Stations	5
First-Line Fire Apparatus	
Pumpers	2
Aerial Trucks	2
Quints	2
Squads	0
Rescue	0
Other	3
Fire Department Responses	5,994
Responses for Fires	172
Structural Fires Reported	60
Inspections Completed for Maintenance, Construction, and Reinspections	1,751
Fire Code Violations Reported	2,691
Estimated Fire Loss (millions)	$1.44
Amount of Property Protected in Service Area (millions)	$2,803
Number of Fire Education Programs or Events	85

Full Cost Profile

Cost Breakdown by Percentage	
Personal Services	68.8%
Operating Costs	16.8%
Capital Costs	14.4%
TOTAL	100.0%
Cost Breakdown in Dollars	
Personal Services	$4,857,613
Operating Costs	$1,188,606
Capital Costs	$1,013,454
TOTAL	$7,059,673

Key: Salisbury ▒ Benchmarking Average — Fiscal Years 2013 through 2017

Resource Measures

Fire Services Costs per Capita

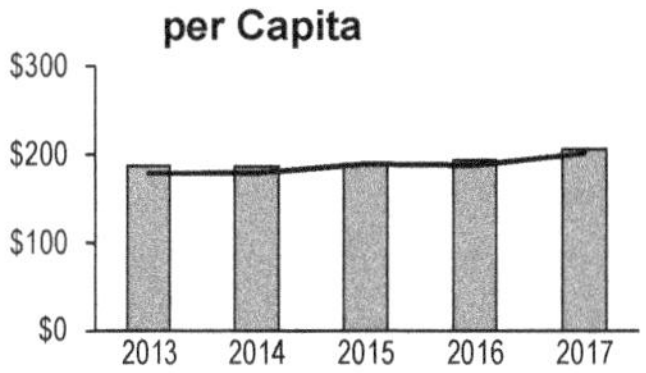

	2013	2014	2015	2016	2017
Salisbury	$186	$185	$188	$193	$205
Average	$179	$179	$189	$188	$201

Fire Services Total FTEs per 10,000 Population

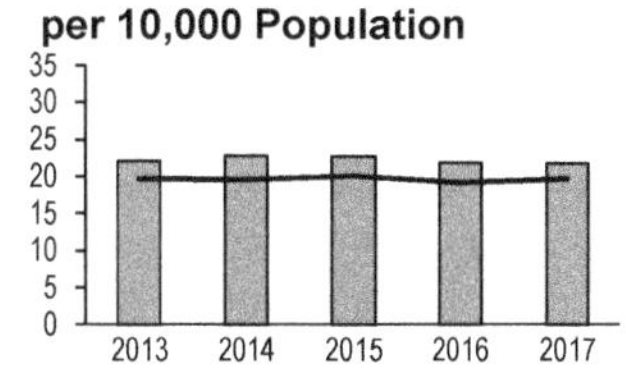

	2013	2014	2015	2016	2017
Salisbury	22.1	22.8	22.7	21.9	21.8
Average	19.7	19.6	20.1	19.2	19.7

Fire Services Cost per Thousand Dollars of Property Protected

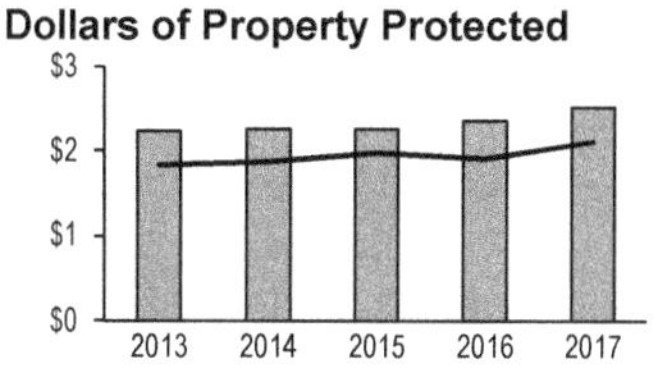

	2013	2014	2015	2016	2017
Salisbury	$2.24	$2.26	$2.26	$2.36	$2.52
Average	$1.84	$1.87	$1.98	$1.91	$2.11

Workload Measures

Actual Fires per 1,000 Population

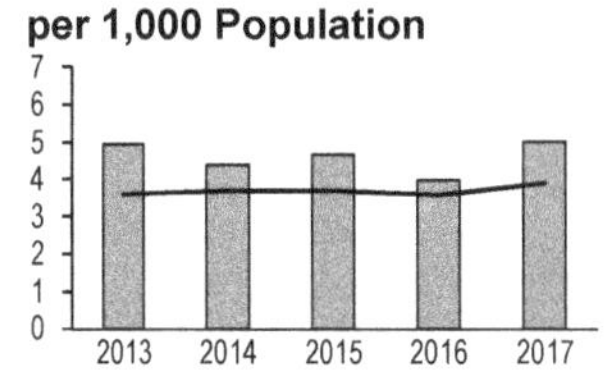

	2013	2014	2015	2016	2017
Salisbury	4.93	4.39	4.65	3.97	4.99
Average	3.60	3.70	3.70	3.57	3.90

Fire Department Responses per 1,000 Population

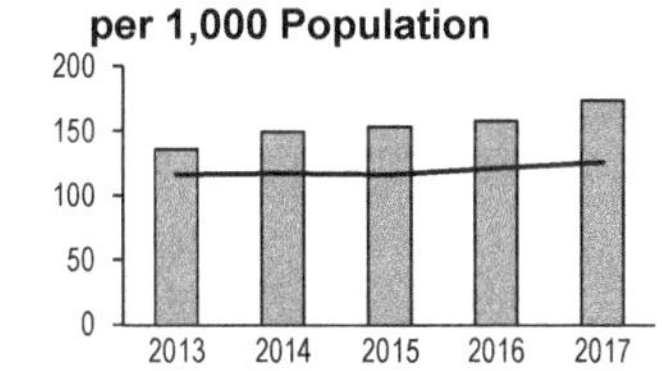

	2013	2014	2015	2016	2017
Salisbury	136	149	153	158	174
Average	117	118	117	122	126

Fire Inspections Completed per 1,000 Population

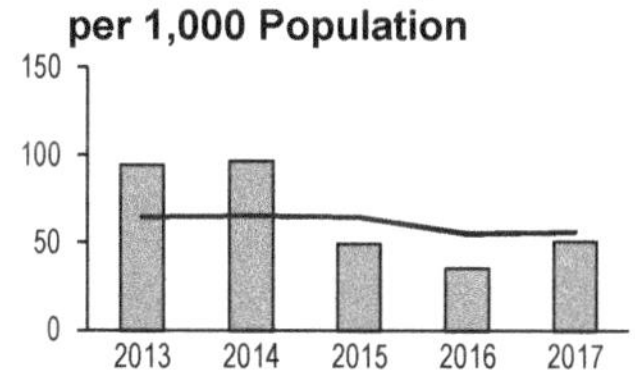

	2013	2014	2015	2016	2017
Salisbury	95	97	49	36	51
Average	65	65	65	55	56

Efficiency Measures

Fire Services Cost per Fire Department Response

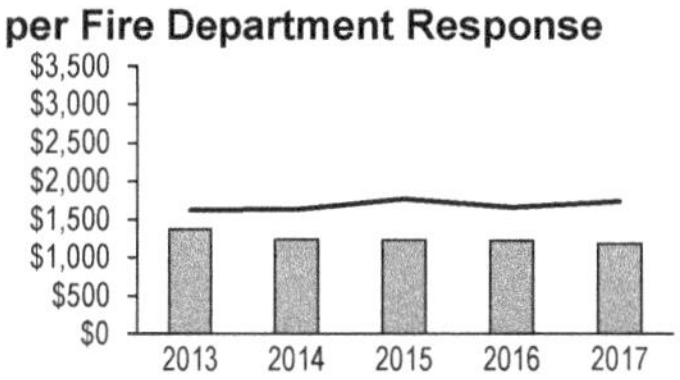

	2013	2014	2015	2016	2017
Salisbury	$1,368	$1,240	$1,228	$1,219	$1,178
Average	$1,619	$1,627	$1,766	$1,659	$1,735

Inspections Completed per Inspector FTE

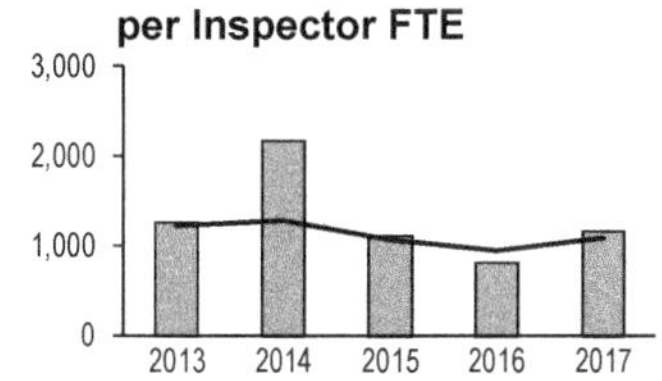

	2013	2014	2015	2016	2017
Salisbury	1,265	2,172	1,117	816	1,167
Average	1,224	1,280	1,067	943	1,090

Effectiveness Measures

Average Response Time to Priority One Calls in Minutes

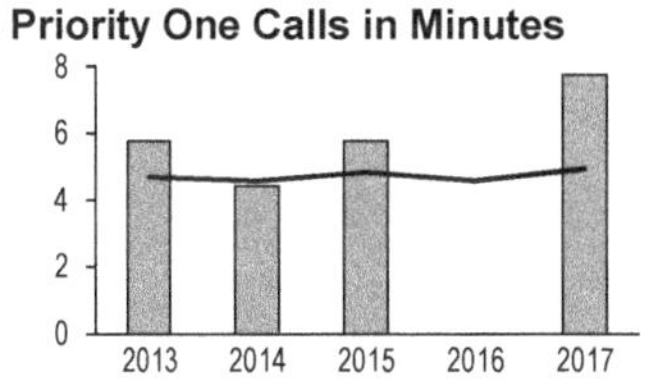

	2013	2014	2015	2016	2017
Salisbury	5.8	4.4	5.8		7.8
Average	4.7	4.6	4.8	4.6	4.9

Percentage of Fire Code Violations Cleared within 90 Days

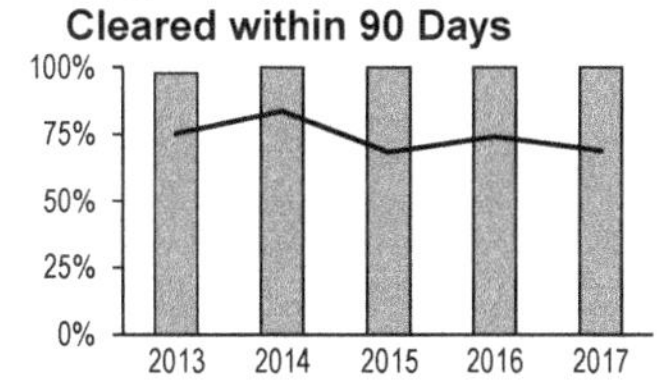

	2013	2014	2015	2016	2017
Salisbury	98%	100%	100%	100%	100%
Average	75%	84%	68%	74%	69%

Percentage of Fires Confined to Rooms or Objects Involved on Arrival

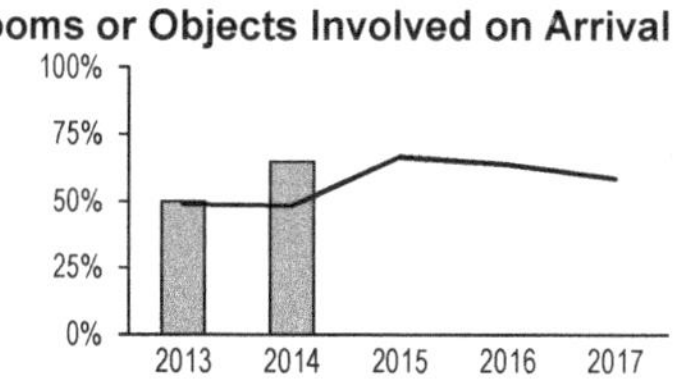

	2013	2014	2015	2016	2017
Salisbury	50%	65%			
Average	49%	48%	67%	64%	58%

Percentage of Fires for Which Cause Was Determined

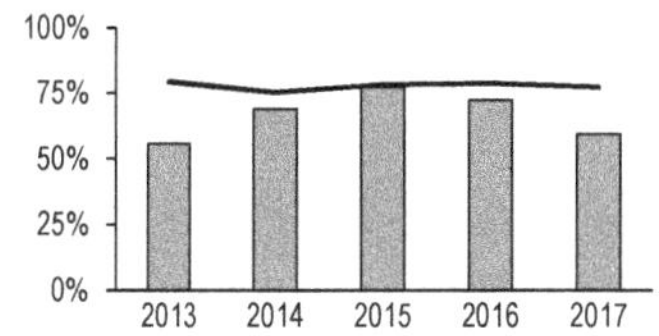

	2013	2014	2015	2016	2017
Salisbury	56%	69%	77%	72%	59%
Average	79%	75%	78%	79%	77%

Percentage of Full Response within 8 Minutes Travel Time

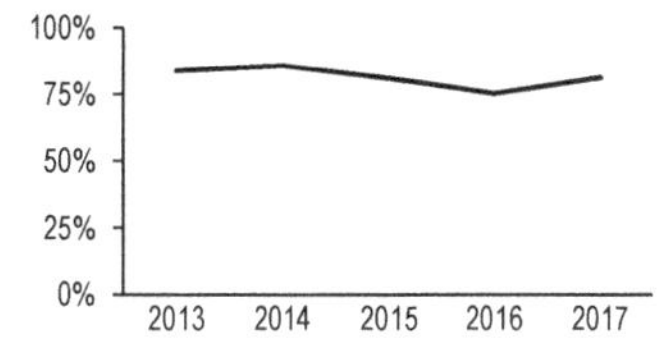

	2013	2014	2015	2016	2017
Salisbury					
Average	84%	86%	81%	75%	81%

Percentage of Lost Pulse Cases Recovered Pulse at Transfer of Care

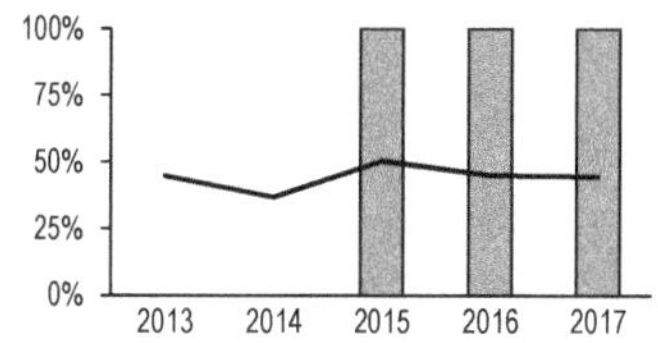

	2013	2014	2015	2016	2017
Salisbury			100.0%	100.0%	100.0%
Average	44.7%	36.8%	50.3%	44.9%	44.5%

Fiscal Year 2016–17

Explanatory Information

Service Level and Delivery

Wilson Fire/Rescue Services is a public safety organization whose mission is to assist the public in the protection of life and property by minimizing the impact of fire, medical emergencies, and potential disasters or events that affect the community and the environment.

Wilson Fire/Rescue Services has two major divisions. Operations handles emergency responses and equipment maintenance. Support Services handles fire prevention and education, facility maintenance, IM/GIS, and budget.

Firefighters work twenty-four hours on and twenty-four hours off. Each work cycle consists of three twenty-four-hour shifts with a day off between shifts. A four-day break is then provided before the cycle repeats itself.

The city has an ISO rating of 2, as rated in 2005. The Wilson Fire Department has been accredited since 2002.

The fire department in Wilson conducted 3,521 fire maintenance, construction, and reinspections during the fiscal year. Fire inspections are conducted by the Fire Prevention Bureau on a daily basis. Each inspector is assigned a district in which he or she handles all inspections. A charge is made on the third reinspection.

Conditions Affecting Service, Performance, and Costs

Municipal Profile

Service Population	49,406
Land Area (Square Miles)	30.60
Persons per Square Mile	1,615
Median Family Income	$43,442
U.S. Census 2010	

Service Profile

FTE Positions—Firefighters	81.0
FTE Positions—Other	16.0
Fire Stations	5
First-Line Fire Apparatus	
Pumpers	4
Aerial Trucks	1
Quints	1
Squads	0
Rescue	0
Other	1
Fire Department Responses	4,453
Responses for Fires	238
Structural Fires Reported	69
Inspections Completed for Maintenance, Construction, and Reinspections	3,521
Fire Code Violations Reported	4,626
Estimated Fire Loss (millions)	$1.95
Amount of Property Protected in Service Area (millions)	$4,267
Number of Fire Education Programs or Events	790

Full Cost Profile

Cost Breakdown by Percentage	
Personal Services	72.5%
Operating Costs	17.9%
Capital Costs	9.6%
TOTAL	100.0%
Cost Breakdown in Dollars	
Personal Services	$7,780,972
Operating Costs	$1,923,554
Capital Costs	$1,026,134
TOTAL	$10,730,660

Key: Wilson ▒ Benchmarking Average — Fiscal Years 2013 through 2017

Resource Measures

Fire Services Costs per Capita

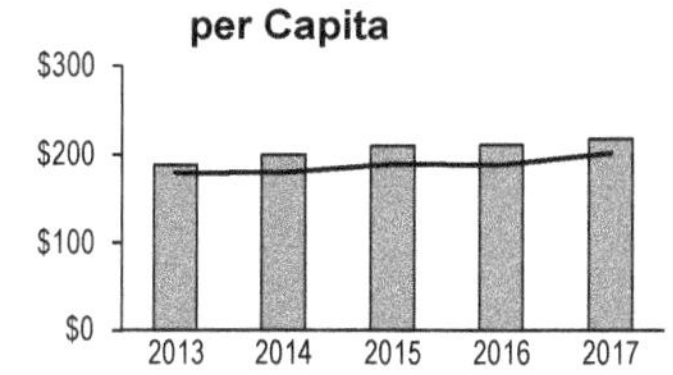

	2013	2014	2015	2016	2017
Wilson	$187	$199	$209	$211	$217
Average	$179	$179	$189	$188	$201

Fire Services Total FTEs per 10,000 Population

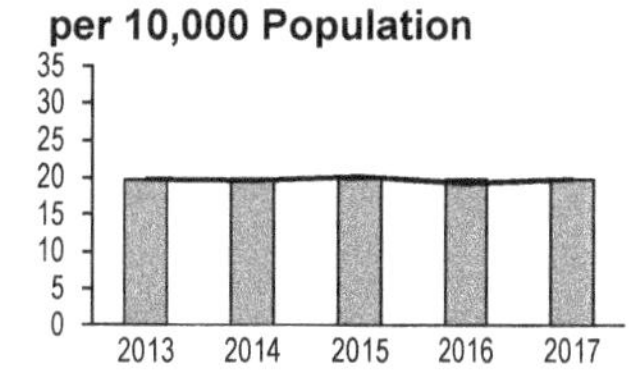

	2013	2014	2015	2016	2017
Wilson	19.6	19.8	19.7	19.7	19.6
Average	19.7	19.6	20.1	19.2	19.7

Fire Services Cost per Thousand Dollars of Property Protected

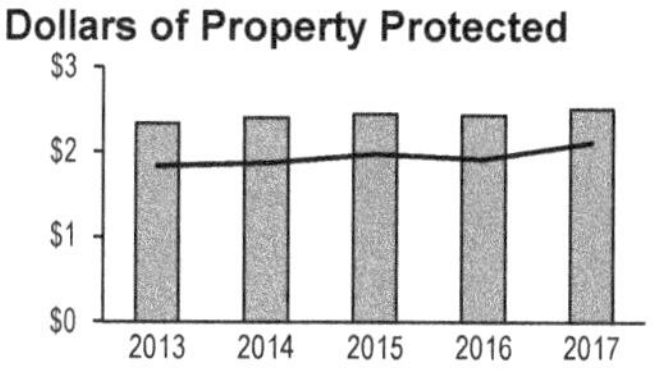

	2013	2014	2015	2016	2017
Wilson	$2.34	$2.41	$2.45	$2.44	$2.51
Average	$1.84	$1.87	$1.98	$1.91	$2.11

Workload Measures

Actual Fires per 1,000 Population

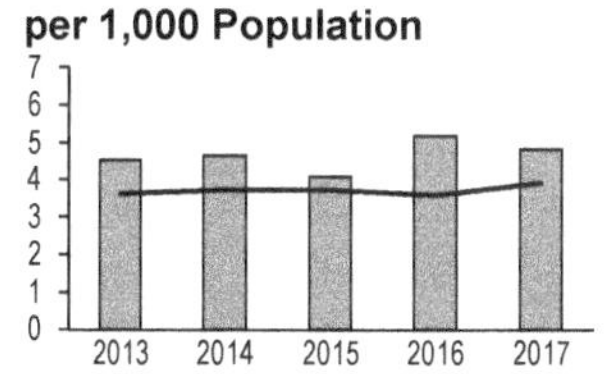

	2013	2014	2015	2016	2017
Wilson	4.53	4.64	4.06	5.17	4.82
Average	3.60	3.70	3.70	3.57	3.90

Fire Department Responses per 1,000 Population

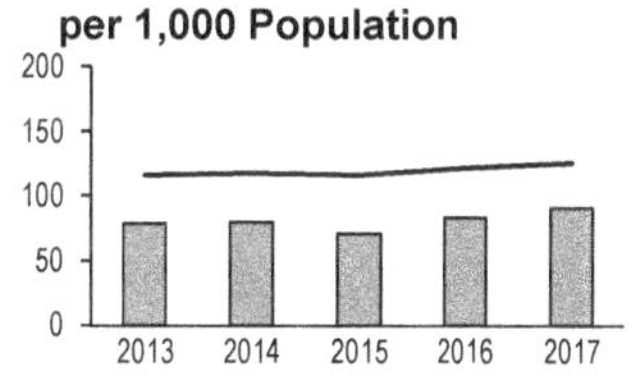

	2013	2014	2015	2016	2017
Wilson	78	79	71	83	90
Average	117	118	117	122	126

Fire Inspections Completed per 1,000 Population

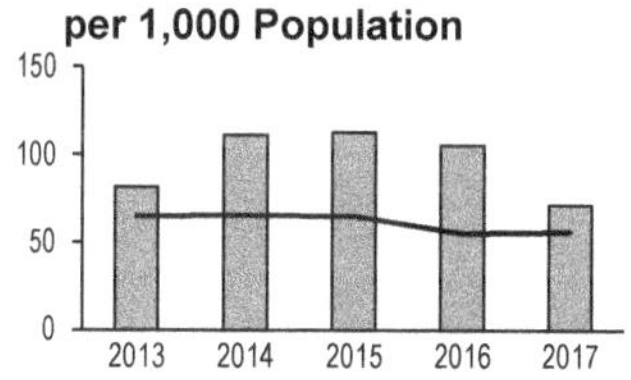

	2013	2014	2015	2016	2017
Wilson	82	111	113	105	71
Average	65	65	65	55	56

Efficiency Measures

Fire Services Cost per Fire Department Response

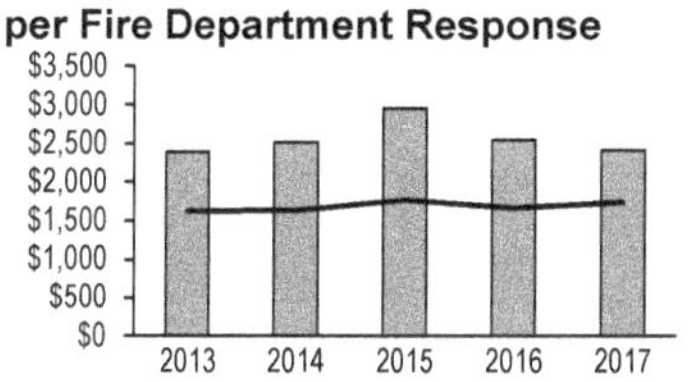

	2013	2014	2015	2016	2017
Wilson	$2,309	$2,511	$2,966	$2,643	$2,410
Average	$1,619	$1,627	$1,766	$1,659	$1,735

Inspections Completed per Inspector FTE

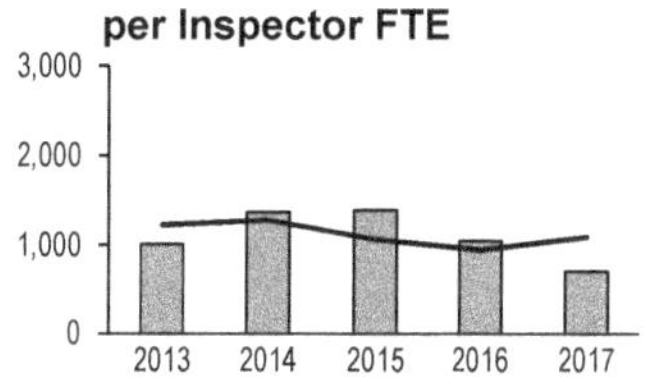

	2013	2014	2015	2016	2017
Wilson	1,008	1,366	1,385	1,041	704
Average	1,224	1,280	1,067	943	1,090

Effectiveness Measures

Average Response Time to Priority One Calls in Minutes

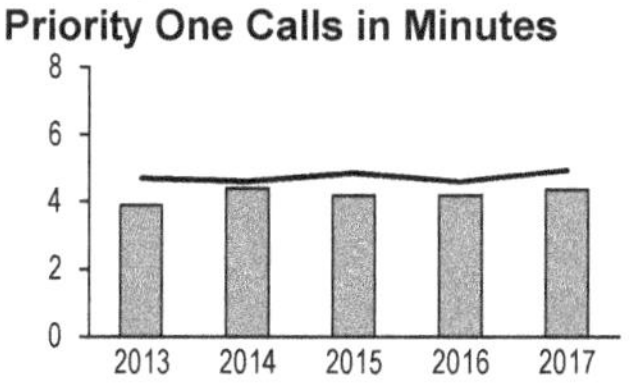

	2013	2014	2015	2016	2017
Wilson	3.9	4.4	4.2	4.2	4.4
Average	4.7	4.6	4.8	4.6	4.9

Percentage of Fire Code Violations Cleared within 90 Days

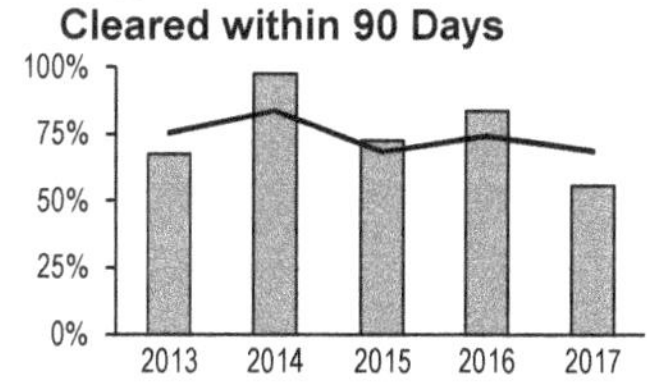

	2013	2014	2015	2016	2017
Wilson	67%	97%	73%	83%	56%
Average	75%	84%	68%	74%	69%

Percentage of Fires Confined to Rooms or Objects Involved on Arrival

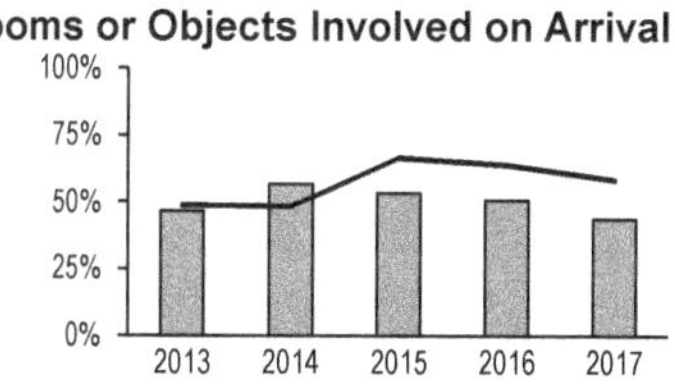

	2013	2014	2015	2016	2017
Wilson	46%	57%	53%	51%	43%
Average	49%	48%	67%	64%	58%

Percentage of Fires for Which Cause Was Determined

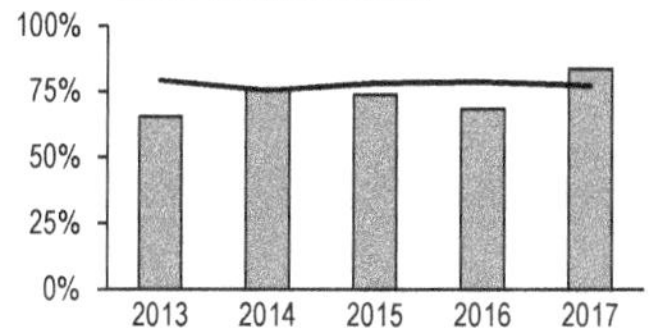

	2013	2014	2015	2016	2017
Wilson	65%	76%	74%	68%	84%
Average	79%	75%	78%	79%	77%

Percentage of Full Response within 8 Minutes Travel Time

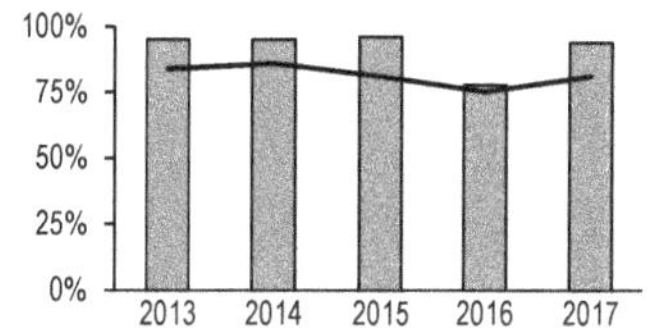

	2013	2014	2015	2016	2017
Wilson	95%	95%	96%	78%	94%
Average	84%	86%	81%	75%	81%

Percentage of Lost Pulse Cases Recovered Pulse at Transfer of Care

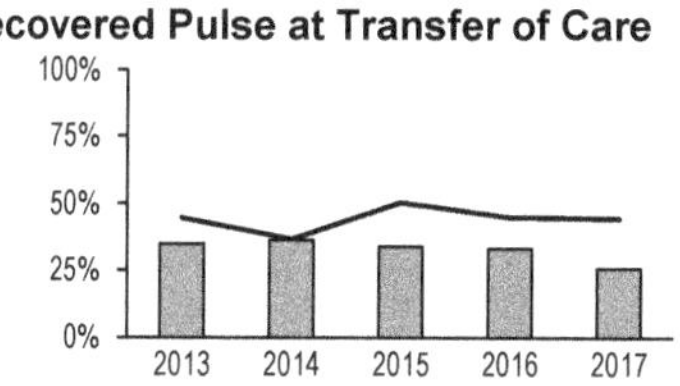

	2013	2014	2015	2016	2017
Wilson	34.9%	36.4%	34.0%	33.3%	25.8%
Average	44.7%	36.8%	50.3%	44.9%	44.5%

Winston-Salem — Fire Services

Fiscal Year 2016–17

Explanatory Information

Service Level and Delivery

The mission of the Winston-Salem Fire Department is to protect the lives and property of all people within Winston-Salem by reducing the occurrence and minimizing the effects of fires.

The Winston-Salem Fire Department contains the following six divisions: fire suppression, vehicle maintenance, planning, community education, fire prevention, and administration.

Fire suppression personnel work a twenty-one-day cycle with an average of fifty-six hours per week.

The city has an ISO rating of 2, as rated in 2015.

The fire department in Winston-Salem conducted 9,324 fire maintenance, construction, and reinspections during the fiscal year. The fire department inspection program includes inspections that (1) ensure reasonable life safety conditions within a structure; (2) identify fire hazards; and (3) determine the proper installation, operation, and maintenance of fire protection features, systems, and appliances within buildings. The fire department inspection program involves both the Fire Prevention Bureau and the fire engine companies. Similar to the Fire Prevention Bureau, all fire stations have inspection responsibilities and conduct building inspections within their assigned territories. Each business within the city limits is inspected annually and receives as many return visits as necessary for fire code compliance.

Conditions Affecting Service, Performance, and Costs

Winston-Salem has a high number of inspections per inspector full-time equivalent (FTE) when compared to the other jurisdictions due to the fact that many inspections are performed by fire company personnel. The city defines an inspection as a site interior and/or exterior survey of a building, operation, event, condition, and/or activity for the purpose of verifying fire and building code compliance.

Winston-Salem made a policy change for medical call responses, which lowered the total number of incidents the fire department responded to during FY 2013–14. The city worked through the dispatch protocol to eliminate certain "non-life threatening" calls, which lowered the number of medical calls.

Municipal Profile

Service Population	240,603
Land Area (Square Miles)	132.55
Persons per Square Mile	1,815
Median Family Income U.S. Census 2010	$51,491

Service Profile

FTE Positions—Firefighters	324.0
FTE Positions—Other	29.0
Fire Stations	19
First-Line Fire Apparatus	
Pumpers	18
Aerial Trucks	5
Quints	0
Squads	0
Rescue	2
Other	13
Fire Department Responses	26,901
Responses for Fires	836
Structural Fires Reported	238
Inspections Completed for Maintenance, Construction, and Reinspections	9,324
Fire Code Violations Reported	8,693
Estimated Fire Loss (millions)	$4.77
Amount of Property Protected in Service Area (millions)	$20,370
Number of Fire Education Programs or Events	547

Full Cost Profile

Cost Breakdown by Percentage	
Personal Services	80.1%
Operating Costs	12.6%
Capital Costs	7.3%
TOTAL	100.0%
Cost Breakdown in Dollars	
Personal Services	$26,983,361
Operating Costs	$4,248,855
Capital Costs	$2,469,120
TOTAL	$33,701,336

Key: Winston-Salem ▒ Benchmarking Average — Fiscal Years 2013 through 2017

Resource Measures

Fire Services Costs per Capita

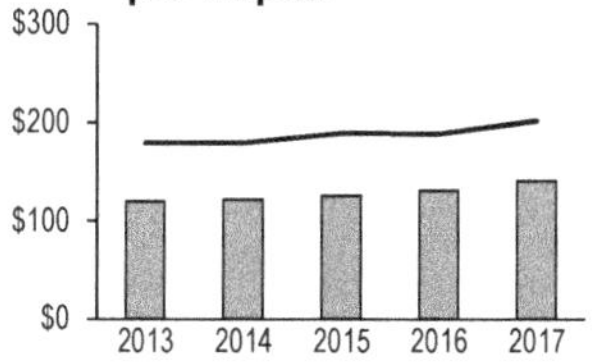

	2013	2014	2015	2016	2017
Winston-Salem	$119	$121	$125	$130	$140
Average	$179	$179	$189	$188	$201

Fire Services Total FTEs per 10,000 Population

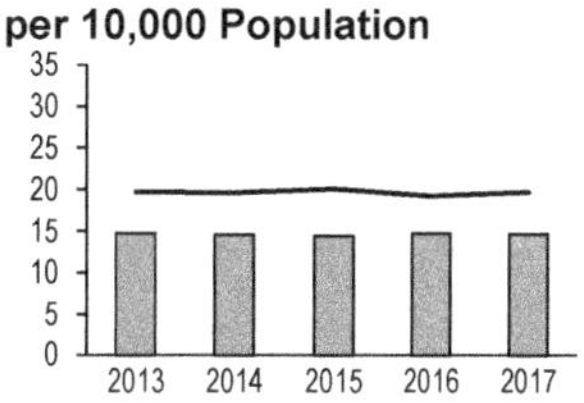

	2013	2014	2015	2016	2017
Winston-Salem	14.7	14.6	14.4	14.8	14.7
Average	19.7	19.6	20.1	19.2	19.7

Fire Services Cost per Thousand Dollars of Property Protected

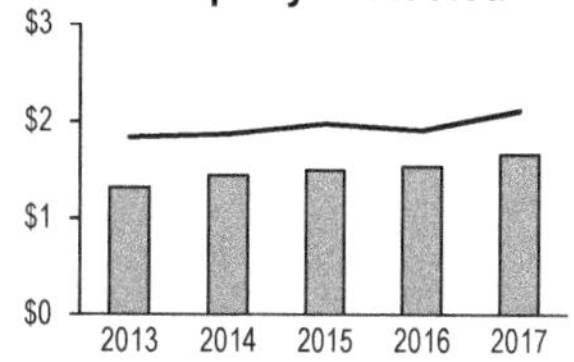

	2013	2014	2015	2016	2017
Winston-Salem	$1.31	$1.43	$1.49	$1.52	$1.65
Average	$1.84	$1.87	$1.98	$1.91	$2.11

Workload Measures

Actual Fires per 1,000 Population

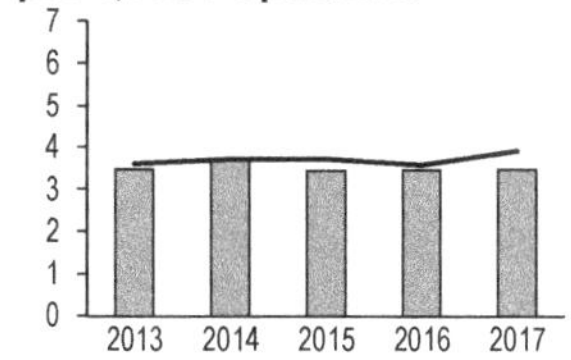

	2013	2014	2015	2016	2017
Winston-Salem	3.48	3.69	3.44	3.47	3.47
Average	3.60	3.70	3.70	3.57	3.90

Fire Department Responses per 1,000 Population

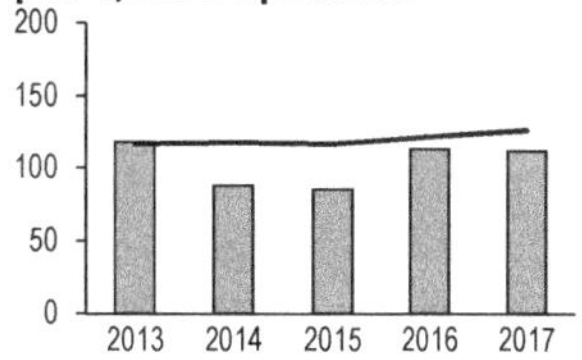

	2013	2014	2015	2016	2017
Winston-Salem	118	88	85	113	112
Average	117	118	117	122	126

Fire Inspections Completed per 1,000 Population

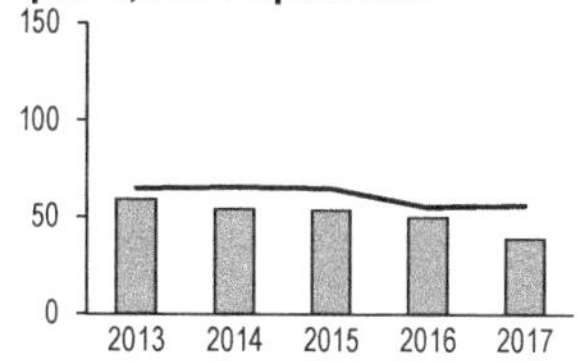

	2013	2014	2015	2016	2017
Winston-Salem	59	54	53	49	39
Average	65	65	65	55	56

Efficiency Measures

Fire Services Cost per Fire Department Response

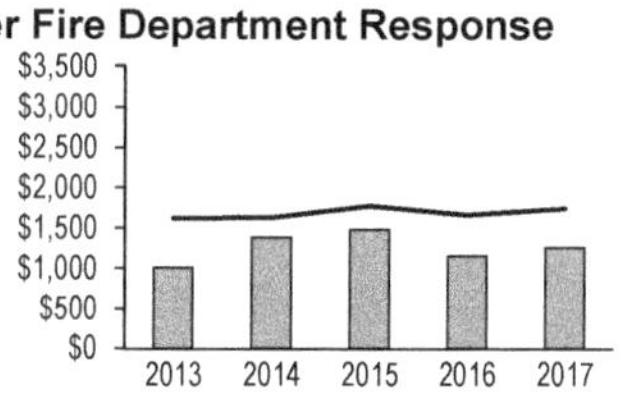

	2013	2014	2015	2016	2017
Winston-Salem	$1,009	$1,377	$1,473	$1,140	$1,253
Average	$1,619	$1,627	$1,766	$1,659	$1,735

Inspections Completed per Inspector FTE

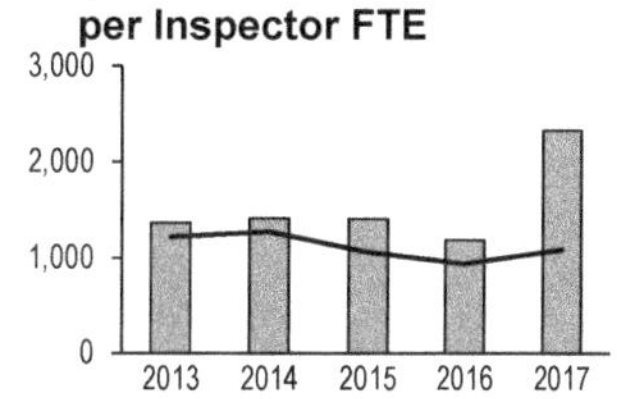

	2013	2014	2015	2016	2017
Winston-Salem	1,368	1,411	1,404	1,182	2,331
Average	1,224	1,280	1,067	943	1,090

Effectiveness Measures

Average Response Time to Priority One Calls in Minutes

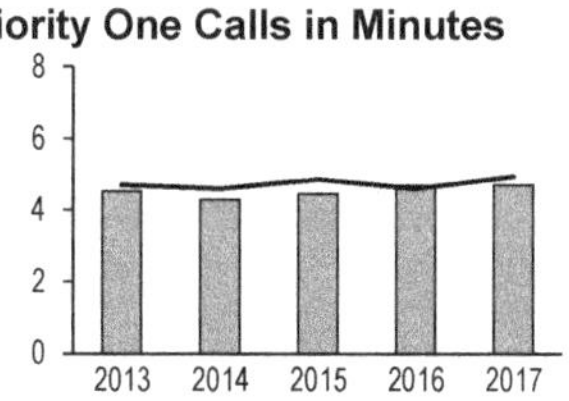

	2013	2014	2015	2016	2017
Winston-Salem	4.5	4.3	4.5	4.7	4.7
Average	4.7	4.6	4.8	4.6	4.9

Percentage of Fire Code Violations Cleared within 90 Days

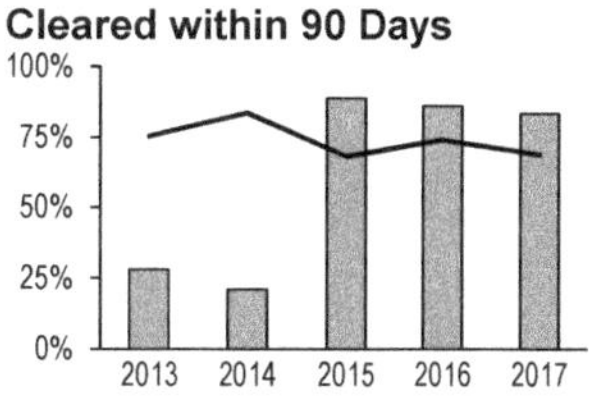

	2013	2014	2015	2016	2017
Winston-Salem	28%	21%	89%	86%	83%
Average	75%	84%	68%	74%	69%

Percentage of Fires Confined to Rooms or Objects Involved on Arrival

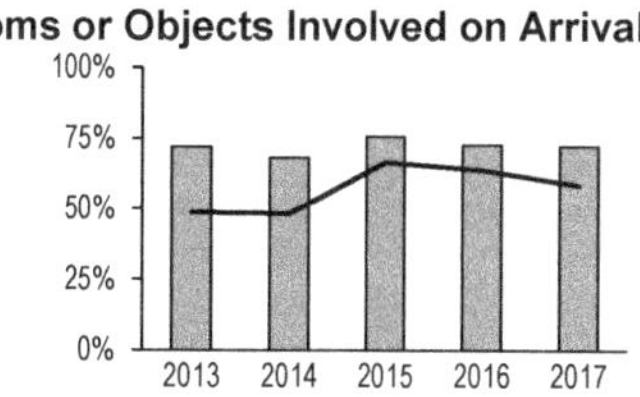

	2013	2014	2015	2016	2017
Winston-Salem	72%	68%	76%	73%	72%
Average	49%	48%	67%	64%	58%

Percentage of Fires for Which Cause Was Determined

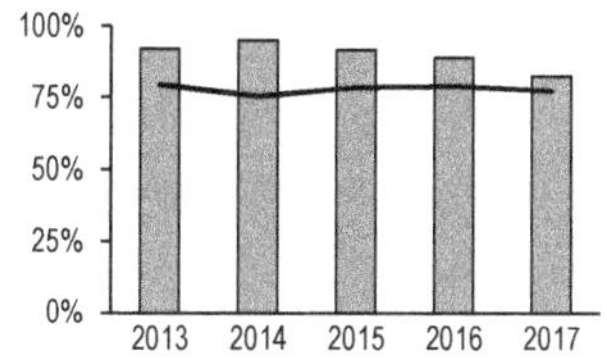

	2013	2014	2015	2016	2017
Winston-Salem	92%	95%	91%	89%	82%
Average	79%	75%	78%	79%	77%

Percentage of Full Response within 8 Minutes Travel Time

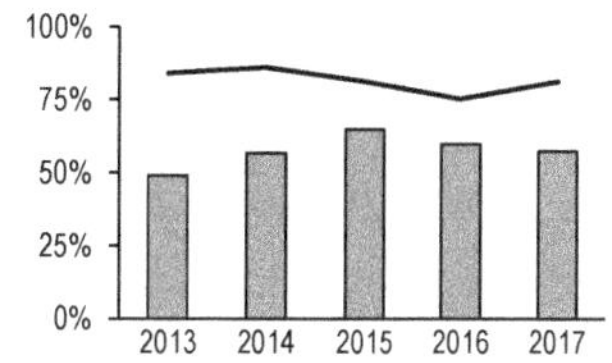

	2013	2014	2015	2016	2017
Winston-Salem	49%	57%	65%	60%	57%
Average	84%	86%	81%	75%	81%

Percentage of Lost Pulse Cases Recovered Pulse at Transfer of Care

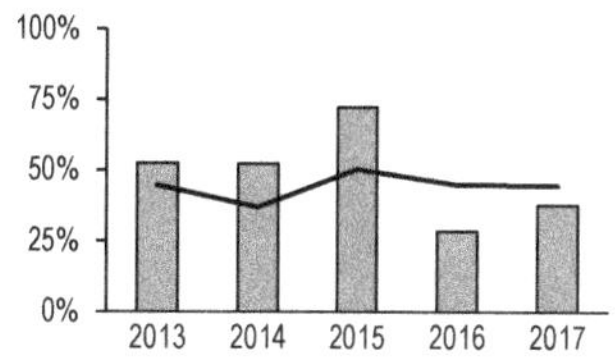

	2013	2014	2015	2016	2017
Winston-Salem	52.4%	52.2%	72.2%	28.6%	37.7%
Average	44.7%	36.8%	50.3%	44.9%	44.5%

UNC | SCHOOL OF GOVERNMENT
North Carolina Benchmarking Project

Performance and Cost Data

BUILDING INSPECTIONS

UNC | SCHOOL OF GOVERNMENT
North Carolina Benchmarking Project

PERFORMANCE MEASURES FOR BUILDING INSPECTIONS

SERVICE DEFINITION

Building inspection services refers to permit issuance and inspections for building, electrical, mechanical (including heating and cooling), and plumbing work on new residential and commercial construction or additions and alterations to enforce the North Carolina State Building Code and related local building regulations. The inspection process includes the receipt of permit applications, review of plans and specifications, issuance of permits, and follow-up field inspections to ensure compliance. Excluded are the enforcement of zoning and subdivision regulations, fire codes, minimum housing codes, erosion and sedimentation control regulations, watershed regulations, historic preservation ordinances, and other development regulations or plans.

NOTES ON PERFORMANCE MEASURES

1. Building Inspections per 1,000 Population

Building inspections are those required by the North Carolina State Building Code for general building, electrical, mechanical (including heating and cooling), and plumbing work associated with construction projects. Inspections include reinspections. They do not include non–building code inspections or consultation visits.

2. Value of Total Building Permits as Percentage of Tax Base of Area Served

When a building permit is issued, the dollar amount of the work specified in the contract(s) authorizing the work is recorded as the value of the building permit. Tax base refers to the taxable valuation used for levying the fiscal year property tax for the area served.

3. Value of Commercial Permits as Percentage of Tax Base of Area Served

Commercial building permits are issued for construction of business, manufacturing, institutional, and other nonresidential buildings or improvements. Tax base is defined above.

4. Cost per Building Inspection and Inspections per Day per Inspector

Building inspections are defined above. Cost is determined using the project's full cost accounting model, including direct, indirect, and capital costs. An inspector full-time equivalent (FTE) is calculated using a work year of 235 days. Inspector FTEs include permanent, temporary, part-time, and full-time inspectors.

5. Value of Building Permits per FTE

Value of building permits is defined above. Inspectors must be certified by the state to enforce the state building code and be able to review plans and conduct inspections to enforce that code. Inspector FTEs exclude supervisors, who may be certified but who spend less than 50 percent of their time performing inspections. Inspector FTEs also exclude support personnel who are not certified.

6. Number of Plan Reviews per Reviewer FTE

The state building code requires that plans and specifications for most commercial and residential construction be reviewed before permits are issued for such construction. Reviewer FTEs are calculated using a 2,080-hour work year, the actual number of plan reviews conducted during the fiscal year, and the number of plan reviewers.

7. Percentage of Inspection Responses within One Working Day of Request

A request for inspection may be made by phone, in person, or in writing. A response refers to at least beginning an inspection, regardless of whether approval of the work occurs. The majority of inspections are completed the same day as initiated. A response to a request within one working day means that the inspection is initiated before the end of the workday following the day on which the request is made.

8. Percentage of Inspections That Are Reinspections

A reinspection occurs when a building inspector must inspect work that has previously been inspected. A reinspection can occur due to problems found in the original inspection or for other reasons.

Building Inspections

Summary of Key Dimensions of Service

City or Town	Area Served (in Square Miles)	Population Growth from 2010 to 2016	Building Inspections by Trade					Number of Plan Reviewers	Building Inspector FTEs	Total Staff FTEs
			Building	Electrical	Mechanical	Plumbing	Total			
Apex	36.2	24.5%	16,737	11,342	9,320	10,430	47,829	3.0	7.0	15.0
Asheville	45.8	10.2%	16,080	8,455	5,020	6,510	36,065	5.0	15.0	25.0
Chapel Hill	27.5	4.6%	3,374	2,512	2,959	1,823	11,056	2.0	7.0	13.5
Goldsboro	57.7	-4.5%	1,978	2,618	1,872	1,054	7,522	1.0	4.0	8.0
Greensboro	133.8	5.4%	22,472	17,190	15,507	15,646	70,815	4.5	16.0	30.0
Greenville	67.3	4.0%	4,414	3,941	3,557	2,597	14,509	1.0	5.0	10.0
High Point	55.4	5.6%	8,079	7,183	5,271	3,592	24,125	3.0	12.0	20.0
Raleigh	144.8	11.1%	31,146	39,923	30,024	22,049	123,142	15.0	46.0	81.0
Wilson	55.2	0.5%	2,440	2,280	1,905	986	7,611	1.0	4.0	7.0
Winston-Salem	396.0	4.8%	16,944	14,493	18,230	12,133	61,800	4.0	16.0	37.4

EXPLANATORY FACTORS

These are factors that the project found affected building inspection performance and cost in one or more of the municipalities:

Rate of growth and development in city
Size and complexity of construction projects
Geographic area served by county building inspections
Inspectors' enforcement of local development regulations
Emphasis given to plan review in each jurisdiction
Inspector specialization
Organization of the building inspection function

Fiscal Year 2016–17

Explanatory Information

Service Level and Delivery

The Town of Apex provides building inspection services though the Building Inspections and Permits Department. The department is organized into two major divisions, building inspections and engineering. The department provides inspections for all of Apex and just over twenty-one square miles of area in its extra-territorial jurisdiction (ETJ).

All building inspectors in Apex serve each of the major trades. The department enforces the North Carolina State Building Code.

The department has a goal of having all inspectors fully qualified for the technical, administrative, and customer service aspects of their job. Training is accomplished primarily by offsite seminars and conferences offered by state-approved sponsors.

Apex has a standard that all inspection requests recorded by a permit technician or the permit office voicemail by 3 a.m. are to be performed on the next business day. Due to high workload during the latter part of the fiscal year, the city was not able to always meet this standard of service.

Total revenue received from inspection fees amounted to $3,197,855 for the fiscal year.

Conditions Affecting Service, Performance, and Costs

The population served is calculated by adding the population of Apex with the population of the ETJ. The tax base served is calculated by adding the tax base of Apex with the tax base of the ETJ. The population and the tax base of the ETJ are calculated by taking the population and tax base per square mile of Wake County and multiplying them by the square miles of the ETJ.

Apex does not track multi-family as a category of reporting for inspections or plan reviews. Instead, townhomes are included with residential, and condos and apartments are included with commercial.

Municipal Profile

Population Served	64,744
Land Area Inspected (Square Miles)	36.16
Persons per Square Mile	1,790
Estimated Tax Base in Service Area (billions)	$7.60
Median Family Income U.S. Census 2010	$97,201

Service Profile

FTE Inspectors	
Building	0.0
Electrical	0.0
Mechanical	0.0
Plumbing	0.0
All Trades	7.0
Total Inspectors	7.0
FTE Plan Reviewers	3.0
Other FTE Positions	5.0
Total of All Positions	15.0
Number of Inspections by Type	
Building	16,737
Electrical	11,342
Mechanical	9,320
Plumbing	10,430
TOTAL	47,829
Building Permit Values	
Residential	$234,889,624
Multi-Family	with other categories
Commercial	$49,068,381
TOTAL	$283,958,005
Inspection Fee Revenue	$3,197,855

Full Cost Profile

Cost Breakdown by Percentage	
Personal Services	71.0%
Operating Costs	24.0%
Capital Costs	4.9%
TOTAL	100.0%
Cost Breakdown in Dollars	
Personal Services	$1,349,244
Operating Costs	$456,676
Capital Costs	$93,419
TOTAL	$1,899,339

Key: Apex ▒ Benchmarking Average — Fiscal Years 2013 through 2017

Resource Measures

Building Inspections Services Costs per Capita

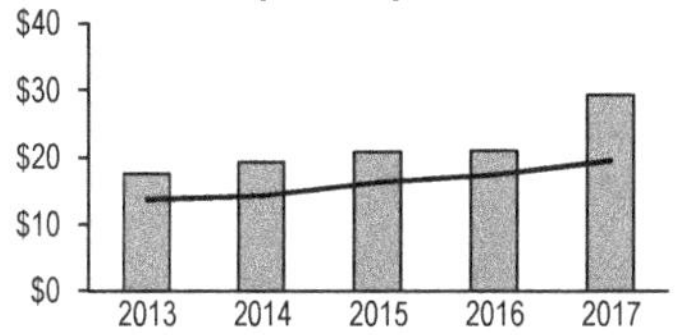

	2013	2014	2015	2016	2017
Apex	$17.57	$19.29	$20.82	$21.07	$29.34
Average	$13.80	$14.33	$16.31	$17.40	$19.55

Building Inspections Services FTEs per 10,000 Population

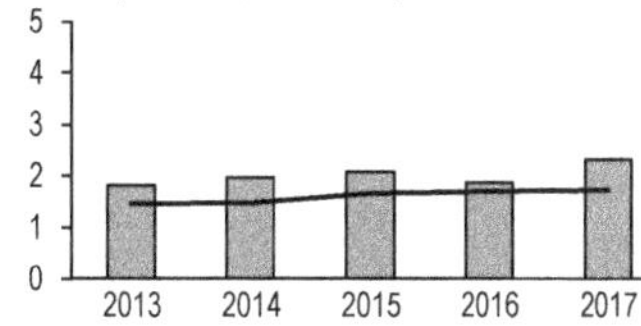

	2013	2014	2015	2016	2017
Apex	1.81	1.96	2.08	1.87	2.32
Average	1.46	1.48	1.66	1.70	1.72

Building Inspections Services Cost per Million Dollars of Tax Base

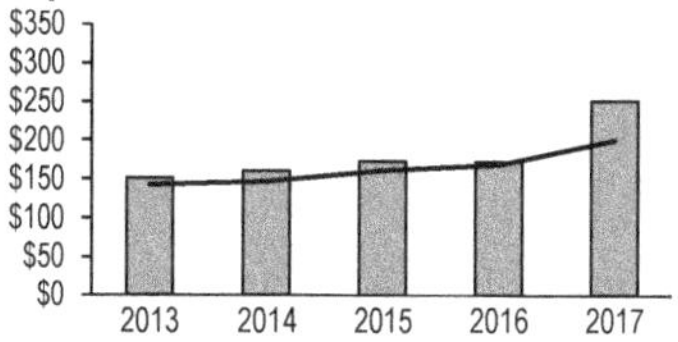

	2013	2014	2015	2016	2017
Apex	$150	$160	$172	$172	$250
Average	$143	$148	$161	$169	$200

Workload Measures

Inspections per 1,000 Population in Service Area

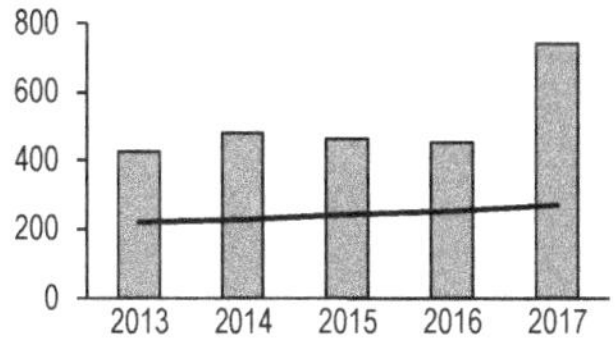

	2013	2014	2015	2016	2017
Apex	425	479	461	450	739
Average	221	229	243	253	270

Inspections per Square Mile in Service Area

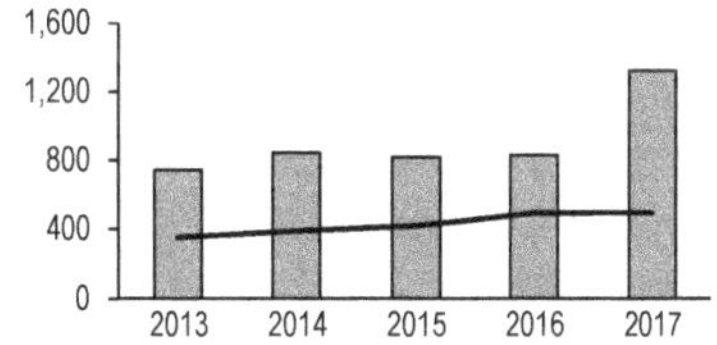

	2013	2014	2015	2016	2017
Apex	743	843	817	828	1,323
Average	353	389	421	495	497

Value of Building Permits as Percentage of Tax Base of Area Served

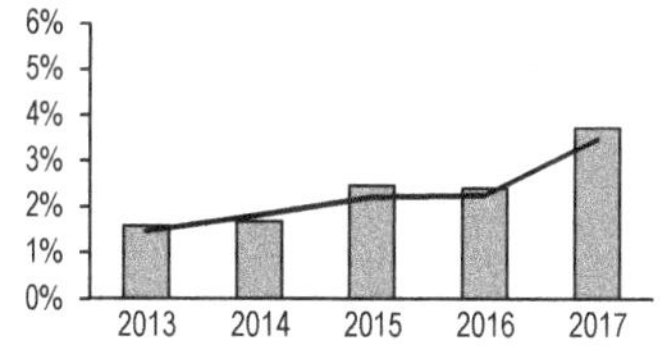

	2013	2014	2015	2016	2017
Apex	1.57%	1.67%	2.45%	2.39%	3.73%
Average	1.47%	1.82%	2.21%	2.25%	3.48%

Value of Commercial Permits as Percentage of Tax Base of Area Served

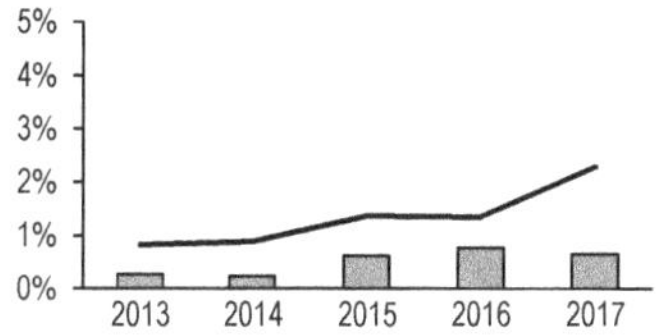

	2013	2014	2015	2016	2017
Apex	0.27%	0.24%	0.62%	0.77%	0.65%
Average	0.83%	0.89%	1.36%	1.35%	2.28%

Value of Building Permits per Inspector FTE in Millions of Dollars

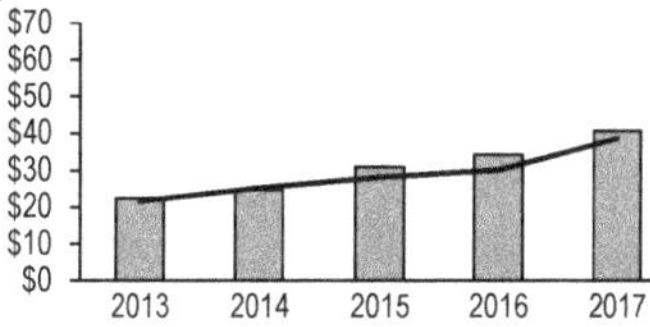

	2013	2014	2015	2016	2017
Apex	$22.3	$24.7	$30.9	$34.1	$40.6
Average	$21.5	$25.2	$28.0	$29.9	$38.7

Efficiency Measures

Building Services Cost per Inspection—All Types

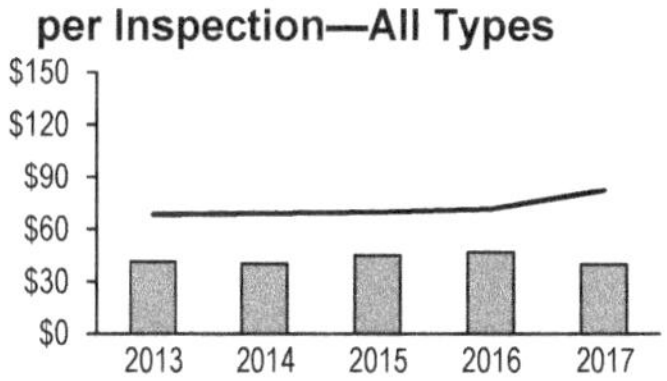

	2013	2014	2015	2016	2017
Apex	$41.38	$40.28	$45.13	$46.84	$39.71
Average	$68.41	$68.71	$69.65	$71.57	$82.35

Inspections per Day per Inspector FTE

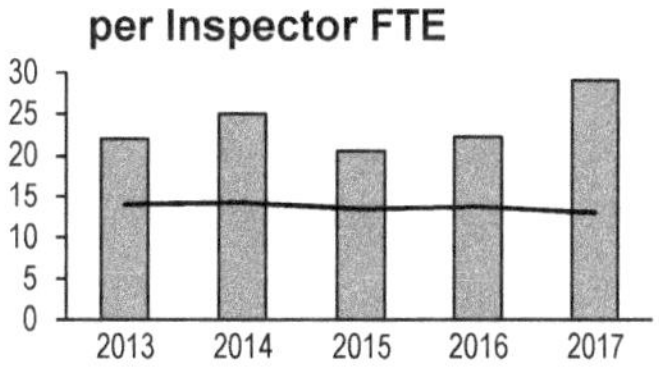

	2013	2014	2015	2016	2017
Apex	22.0	25.0	20.5	22.2	29.1
Average	13.9	14.2	13.3	13.7	13.0

Plan Reviews per Year per Reviewer FTE

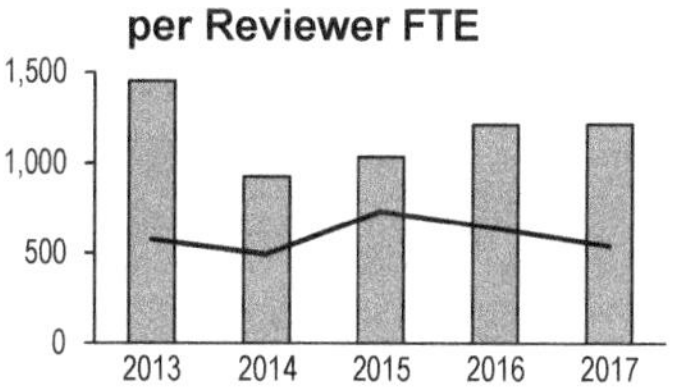

	2013	2014	2015	2016	2017
Apex	1,452	926	1,034	1,213	1,217
Average	573	492	729	636	538

Effectiveness Measures

Percentage of Inspection Responses within One Working Day of Request

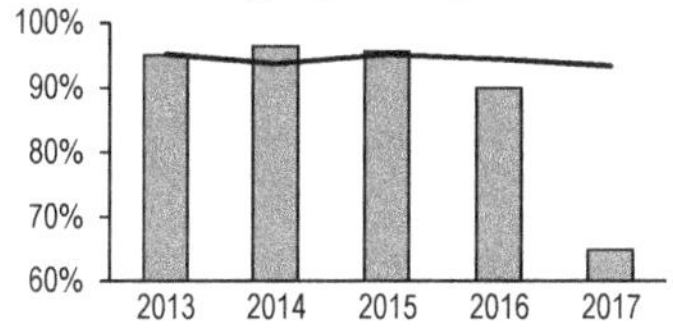

	2013	2014	2015	2016	2017
Apex	95.0%	96.4%	95.6%	90.0%	65.0%
Average	95.1%	93.7%	95.1%	94.4%	93.4%

Percentage of Inspections That Are Reinspections

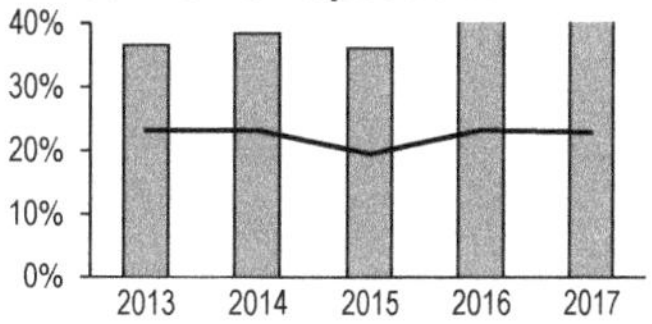

	2013	2014	2015	2016	2017
Apex	36.6%	38.4%	36.0%	45.0%	44.4%
Average	23.1%	23.1%	19.4%	23.1%	22.8%

Fiscal Year 2016–17

Explanatory Information

Service Level and Delivery

The City of Asheville Building Safety Division provides building inspection and permitting services to all areas within the Asheville city limits.

Inspectors include those who function in all trades and those who are certified in one of the following four trades: building, electrical, plumbing, or mechanical. The Building Safety Division enforces the North Carolina State Building Code and the Asheville Minimum Housing Code. The costs and the positions associated with enforcing the housing code are excluded from the project's performance and cost data.

The division has a goal of twelve training days per inspector per year. Inspectors are required to obtain certification in their primary trade plus two others. A career ladder encourages inspectors to work toward obtaining Level III certification in their primary trade and Level II certification in two other trades. Training is a high priority for the department, with an emphasis on code consistency. Training for contractors and designers also is a high priority for the department.

Asheville's policy is that all inspection requests received by phone before 4:30 p.m. and online by 6:00 p.m. will be performed the following business day.

Total revenue received from inspection fees amounted to $4.2 million for the fiscal year. The fee schedule separates fees for each type of permit, with specific fees depending on type of work, cost, square footage, and other factors. One free reinspection is granted per trade per project. Additional inspections are provided for a fee of $75 that must be paid prior to the inspection.

Conditions Affecting Service, Performance, and Costs

The city has many old and historic buildings that are difficult to renovate and bring into compliance with the state code. The city also has days during which snow and ice impact service delivery for this city function.

Municipal Profile

Population Served	91,929
Land Area Inspected (Square Miles)	45.79
Persons per Square Mile	2,008
Estimated Tax Base in Service Area (billions)	$11.39
Median Family Income U.S. Census 2010	$53,350

Service Profile

FTE Inspectors	
Building	0.0
Electrical	0.0
Mechanical	0.0
Plumbing	0.0
All Trades	15.0
Total Inspectors	15.0
FTE Plan Reviewers	5.0
Other FTE Positions	5.0
Total of All Positions	25.0
Number of Inspections by Type	
Building	16,080
Electrical	8,455
Mechanical	5,020
Plumbing	6,510
TOTAL	36,065
Building Permit Values	
Residential	$116,778,700
Multi-Family	$51,271,440
Commercial	$488,879,216
TOTAL	$656,929,356
Inspection Fee Revenue	$4,169,666

Full Cost Profile

Cost Breakdown by Percentage	
Personal Services	70.1%
Operating Costs	25.0%
Capital Costs	4.9%
TOTAL	100.0%
Cost Breakdown in Dollars	
Personal Services	$2,288,824
Operating Costs	$816,623
Capital Costs	$160,462
TOTAL	$3,265,909

Key: Asheville ▒ Benchmarking Average — Fiscal Years 2013 through 2017

Resource Measures

Building Inspections Services Costs per Capita

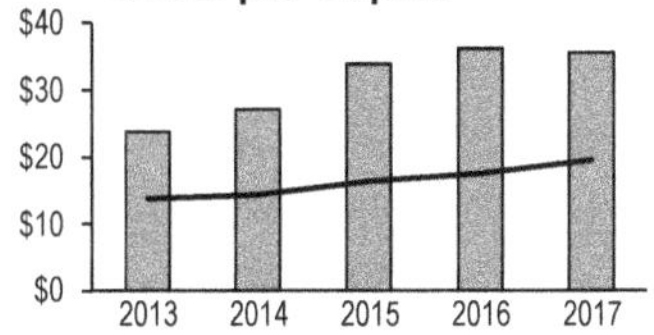

	2013	2014	2015	2016	2017
Asheville	$23.71	$27.04	$33.90	$36.13	$35.53
Average	$13.80	$14.33	$16.31	$17.48	$19.55

Building Inspections Services FTEs per 10,000 Population

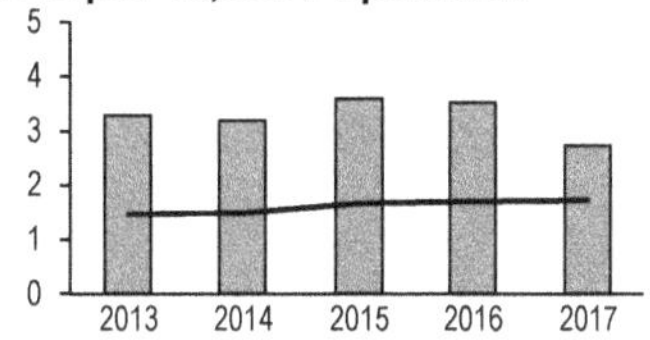

	2013	2014	2015	2016	2017
Asheville	3.28	3.18	3.59	3.52	2.72
Average	1.46	1.48	1.66	1.70	1.72

Building Inspections Services Cost per Million Dollars of Tax Base

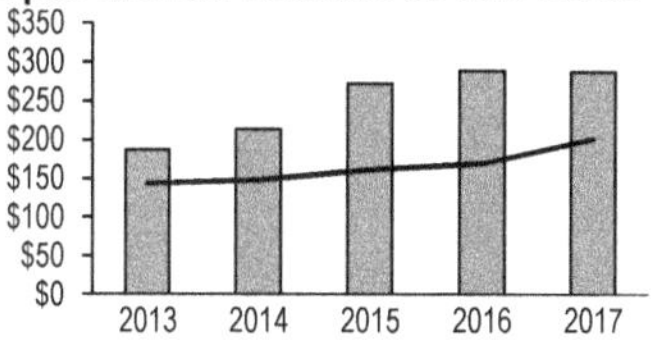

	2013	2014	2015	2016	2017
Asheville	$186	$213	$271	$288	$287
Average	$143	$148	$161	$169	$200

Workload Measures

Inspections per 1,000 Population in Service Area

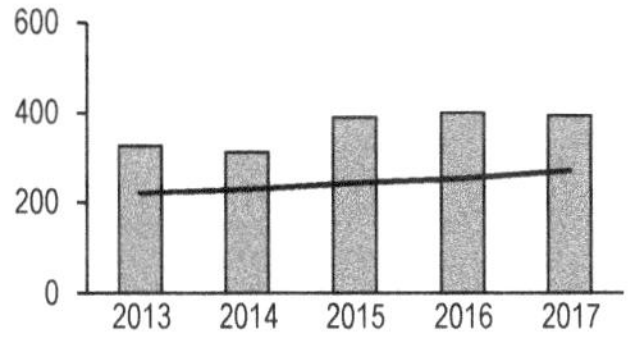

	2013	2014	2015	2016	2017
Asheville	325	311	388	400	392
Average	221	229	243	253	270

Inspections per Square Mile in Service Area

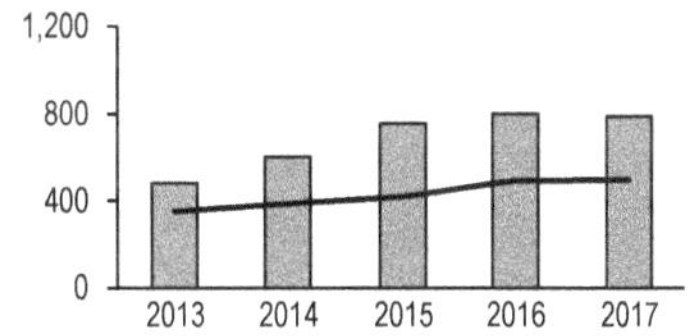

	2013	2014	2015	2016	2017
Asheville	478	599	755	800	788
Average	353	389	421	495	497

Value of Building Permits as Percentage of Tax Base of Area Served

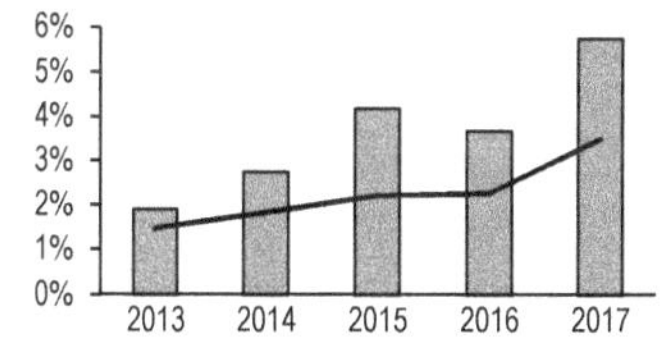

	2013	2014	2015	2016	2017
Asheville	1.91%	2.74%	4.19%	3.68%	5.77%
Average	1.47%	1.82%	2.21%	2.25%	3.48%

Value of Commercial Permits as Percentage of Tax Base of Area Served

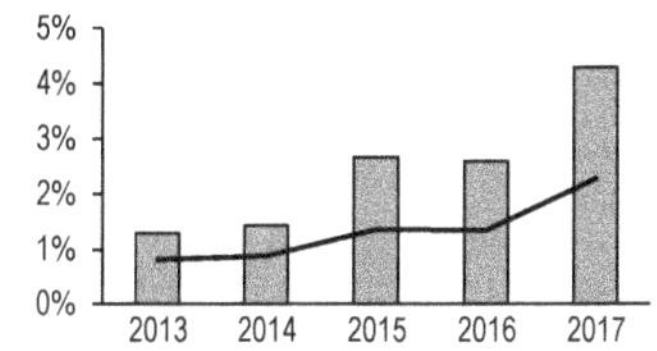

	2013	2014	2015	2016	2017
Asheville	1.29%	1.43%	2.67%	2.59%	4.29%
Average	0.83%	0.89%	1.36%	1.35%	2.28%

Value of Building Permits per Inspector FTE in Millions of Dollars

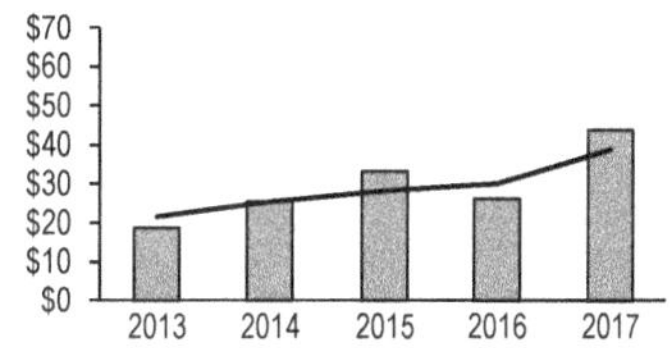

	2013	2014	2015	2016	2017
Asheville	$18.8	$25.5	$33.4	$26.2	$43.8
Average	$21.5	$25.2	$28.0	$29.9	$38.7

Efficiency Measures

Building Services Cost per Inspection—All Types

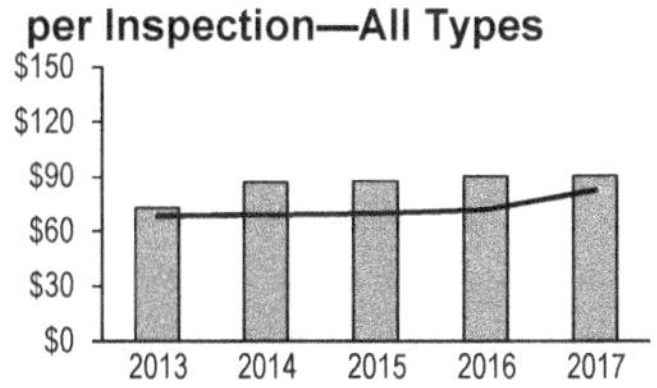

	2013	2014	2015	2016	2017
Asheville	$72.87	$86.83	$87.47	$90.26	$90.56
Average	$68.41	$68.71	$69.65	$71.57	$82.35

Inspections per Day per Inspector FTE

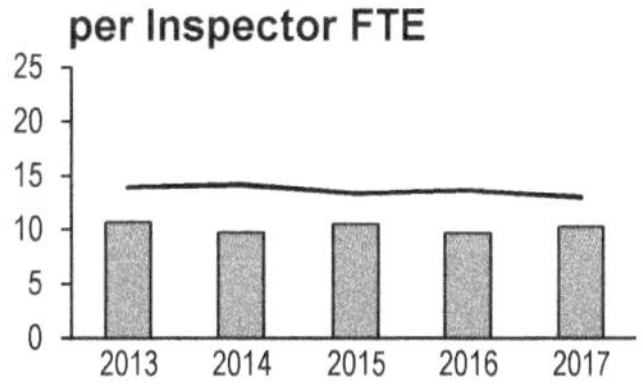

	2013	2014	2015	2016	2017
Asheville	10.7	9.7	10.5	9.7	10.2
Average	13.9	14.2	13.3	13.7	13.0

Plan Reviews per Year per Reviewer FTE

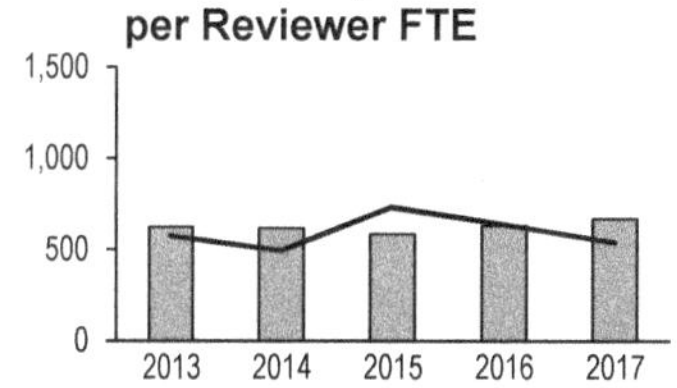

	2013	2014	2015	2016	2017
Asheville	622	616	585	630	669
Average	573	492	729	636	538

Effectiveness Measures

Percentage of Inspection Responses within One Working Day of Request

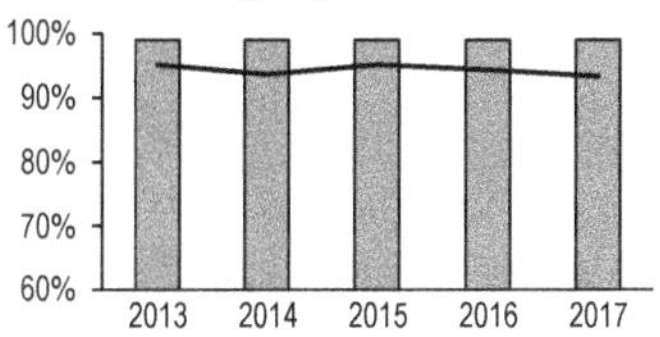

	2013	2014	2015	2016	2017
Asheville	99.0%	99.0%	99.0%	99.0%	99.0%
Average	95.1%	93.7%	95.1%	94.4%	93.4%

Percentage of Inspections That Are Reinspections

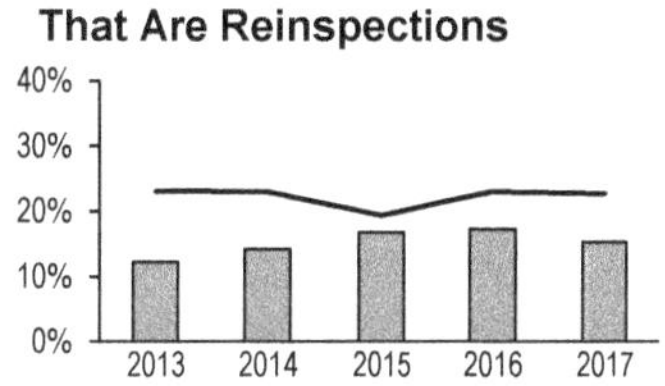

	2013	2014	2015	2016	2017
Asheville	12.3%	14.2%	16.8%	17.2%	15.3%
Average	23.1%	23.1%	19.4%	23.1%	22.8%

Chapel Hill

Building Inspections

Fiscal Year 2016–17

Explanatory Information

Service Level and Delivery

The Town of Chapel Hill provides building inspection services within its corporate limits and extra-territorial jurisdiction (ETJ) through its Permits and Inspections Division within the Office of Planning and Sustainability. The division is a full-service entity, meeting all requirements mandated by the N.C. General Statutes.

Inspectors have a main discipline in one of the building trades and usually perform Level 3 inspections, plus they perform inspections in other disciplines when needed. On occasion retired part-time inspectors are brought in to help with overloads and the need for plan review in field inspections.

Total revenue received from inspection fees amounted to $1.1 million for the fiscal year. The fee schedule separates fees for each type of permit, with specific fees depending on a minimum amount, square footage, and other factors. There is a fee for reinspections.

Conditions Affecting Service, Performance, and Costs

The Town of Chapel Hill began participation in the benchmarking project in July 2015, with FY 2014–15 being the first reporting year.

Although data for the earlier years are not shown here, Chapel Hill has noted an uptick in permits and construction over prior years. There has particularly been an increase in larger and more complex projects requiring staff attention.

The population served is calculated by adding the population of Chapel Hill with the population of the ETJ. The tax base served is calculated by adding the tax base of Chapel Hill with the tax base of the ETJ. The population and the tax base of the ETJ are calculated by taking the population and tax base per square mile of Orange County and multiplying them by the square miles of the ETJ.

Municipal Profile

Population Served	62,036
Land Area Inspected (Square Miles)	27.50
Persons per Square Mile	2,256
Estimated Tax Base in Service Area (billions)	$7.78
Median Family Income U.S. Census 2010	$61,405

Service Profile

FTE Inspectors	
Building	3.0
Electrical	0.0
Mechanical	2.0
Plumbing	0.0
All Trades	2.0
Total Inspectors	7.0
FTE Plan Reviewers	2.0
Other FTE Positions	4.5
Total of All Positions	13.5
Number of Inspections by Type	
Building	3,374
Electrical	2,512
Mechanical	2,959
Plumbing	1,823
TOTAL	11,056
Building Permit Values	
Residential	$65,572,342
Multi-Family	included with commercial
Commercial	$85,774,181
TOTAL	$151,346,523
Inspection Fee Revenue	$1,061,783

Full Cost Profile

Cost Breakdown by Percentage	
Personal Services	68.1%
Operating Costs	26.7%
Capital Costs	5.3%
TOTAL	100.0%
Cost Breakdown in Dollars	
Personal Services	$1,124,564
Operating Costs	$440,739
Capital Costs	$87,157
TOTAL	$1,652,461

Chapel Hill — Building Inspections

Key: Chapel Hill ▒ Benchmarking Average — Fiscal Years 2013 through 2017

Resource Measures

Building Inspections Services Costs per Capita

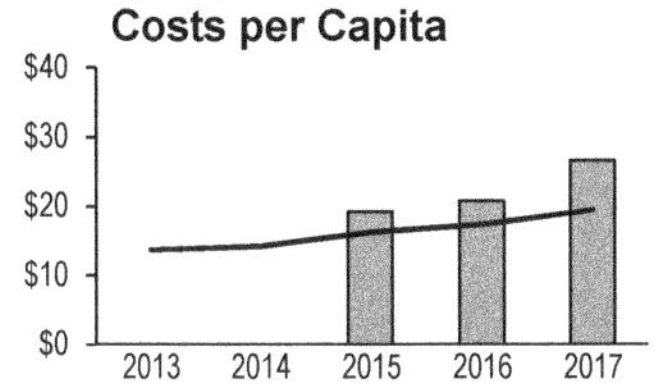

	2013	2014	2015	2016	2017
Chapel Hill			$19.17	$20.78	$26.64
Average	$13.80	$14.33	$16.31	$17.48	$19.55

Building Inspections Services FTEs per 10,000 Population

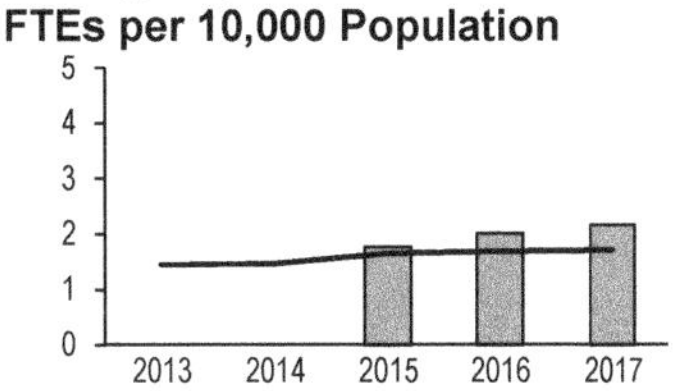

	2013	2014	2015	2016	2017
Chapel Hill			1.78	2.02	2.18
Average	1.46	1.48	1.66	1.70	1.72

Building Inspections Services Cost per Million Dollars of Tax Base

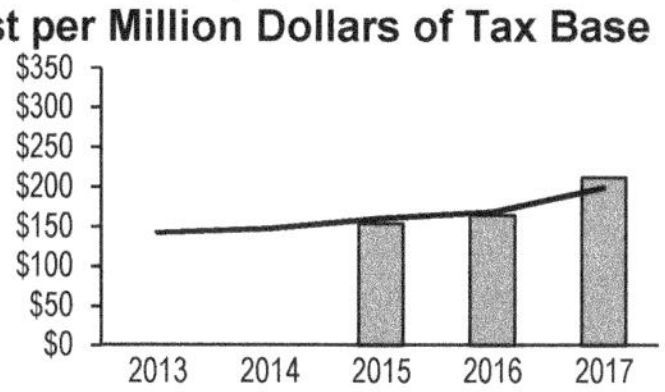

	2013	2014	2015	2016	2017
Chapel Hill			$154	$165	$212
Average	$143	$148	$161	$169	$200

Workload Measures

Inspections per 1,000 Population in Service Area

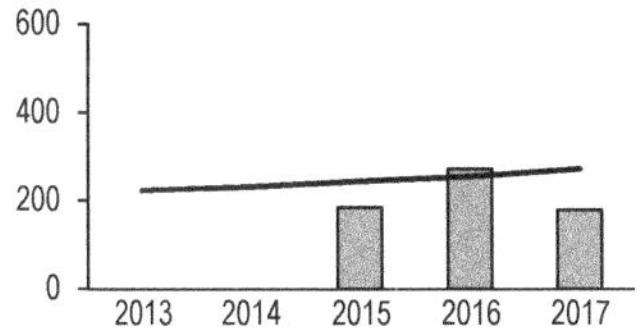

	2013	2014	2015	2016	2017
Chapel Hill			184	270	178
Average	221	229	243	253	270

Inspections per Square Mile in Service Area

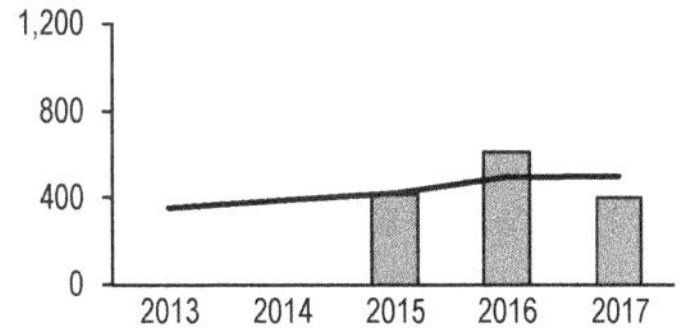

	2013	2014	2015	2016	2017
Chapel Hill			414	609	402
Average	353	389	421	495	497

Value of Building Permits as Percentage of Tax Base of Area Served

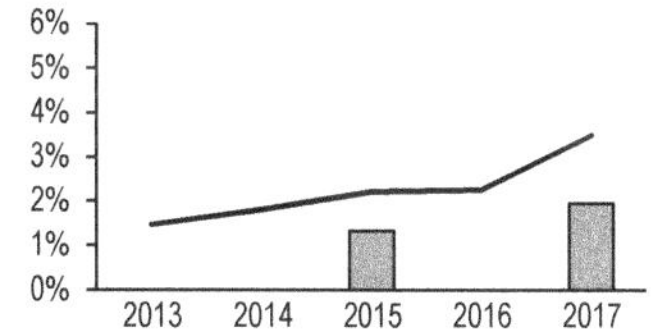

	2013	2014	2015	2016	2017
Chapel Hill			1.32%		1.95%
Average	1.47%	1.82%	2.21%	2.25%	3.48%

Value of Commercial Permits as Percentage of Tax Base of Area Served

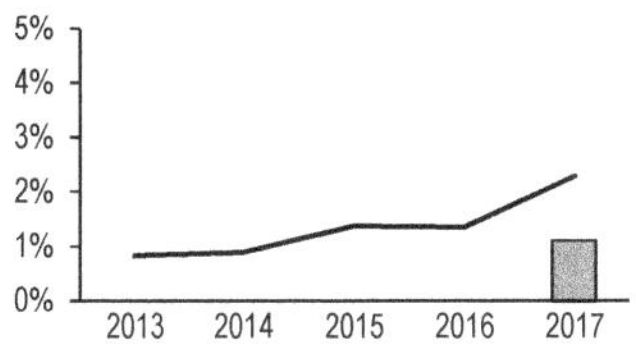

	2013	2014	2015	2016	2017
Chapel Hill					1.10%
Average	0.83%	0.89%	1.36%	1.35%	2.28%

Value of Building Permits per Inspector FTE in Millions of Dollars

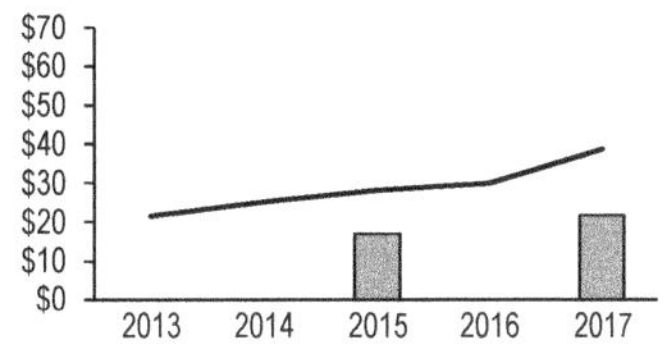

	2013	2014	2015	2016	2017
Chapel Hill			$16.9		$21.6
Average	$21.5	$25.2	$28.0	$29.9	$38.7

Efficiency Measures

Building Services Cost per Inspection—All Types

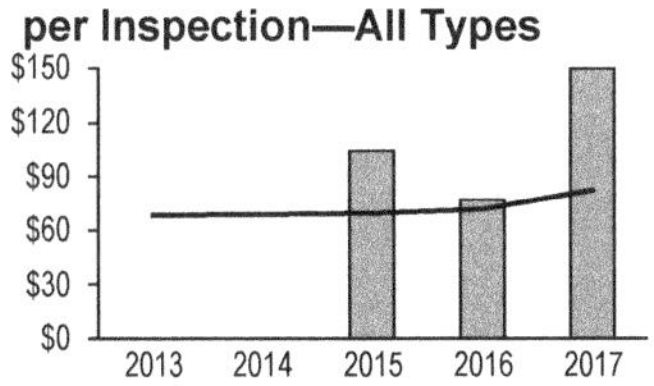

	2013	2014	2015	2016	2017
Chapel Hill			$104.21	$76.95	$149.46
Average	$68.41	$68.71	$69.65	$71.57	$82.35

Inspections per Day per Inspector FTE

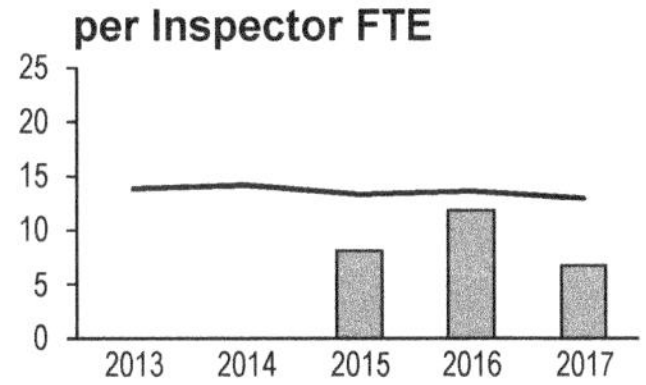

	2013	2014	2015	2016	2017
Chapel Hill			8.1	11.8	6.7
Average	13.9	14.2	13.3	13.7	13.0

Plan Reviews per Year per Reviewer FTE

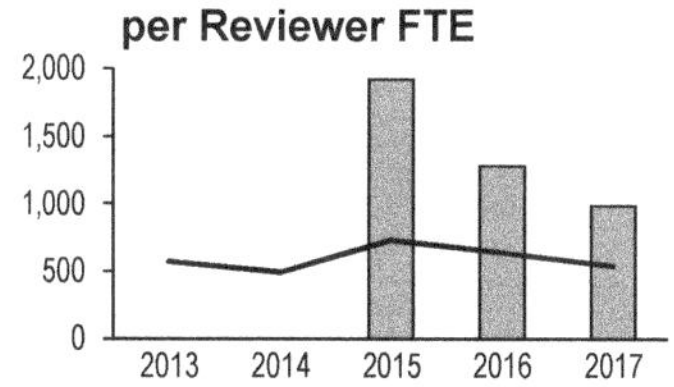

	2013	2014	2015	2016	2017
Chapel Hill			1,921	1,281	985
Average	573	492	729	636	538

Effectiveness Measures

Percentage of Inspection Responses within One Working Day of Request

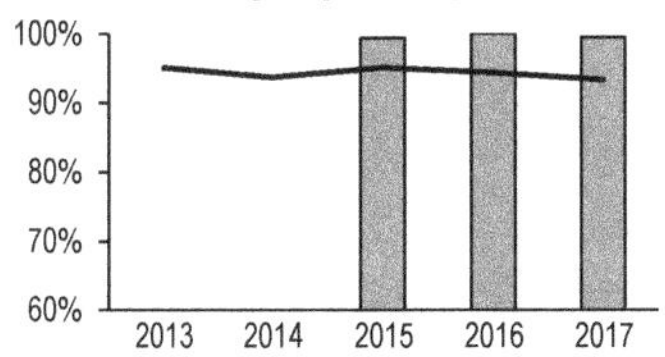

	2013	2014	2015	2016	2017
Chapel Hill			99.3%	100.0%	99.4%
Average	95.1%	93.7%	95.1%	94.4%	93.4%

Percentage of Inspections That Are Reinspections

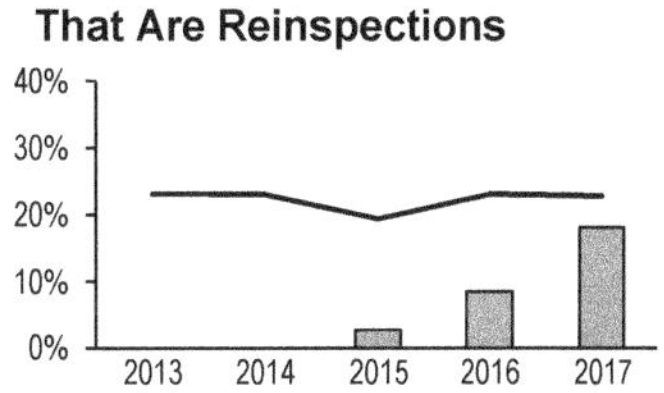

	2013	2014	2015	2016	2017
Chapel Hill			2.7%	8.5%	18.1%
Average	23.1%	23.1%	19.4%	23.1%	22.8%

Fiscal Year 2016–17

Explanatory Information

Service Level and Delivery

Goldboro Inspections is a separate department which operates independently of the Wayne County inspections function. Goldsboro performs all residential and commericial inspections within the city limits and the extra-territorial jurisdiction areas. The Department performs single phase inspections for commercial and residential properties.

Inspectors for the city are trade-specific. Inspectors are required to take at least six hours of trade specific training each year in addition to thirty hours of state mandated training.

All requests for inspections have a goal of a response within twenty-four hours. Initial inspections do not have a fee. Re-inspections are charged $75 for the first time and $125 for each subsequent time. The lack of a charge for initial inspections means that only a small amount of revenue is collected for inspections.

Conditions Affecting Service, Performance, and Costs

The city of Goldsboro joined the Benchmarking Project in July 2017 with the first year of data showing for FY 2016–17.

Goldsboro combines residential and multi-family when reporting dollar value of permits.

The city of Goldsboro had a noticeably higher level of residential and building permits for FY 2016–17 due to recovery work following Hurricane Matthew in October 2016.

Municipal Profile

Population Served	41,339
Land Area Inspected (Square Miles)	57.65
Persons per Square Mile	717
Estimated Tax Base in Service Area (billions)	$2.82
Median Family Income U.S. Census 2010	$52,752

Service Profile

FTE Inspectors	
Building	1.0
Electrical	1.0
Mechanical	1.0
Plumbing	1.0
All Trades	0.0
Total Inspectors	4.0
FTE Plan Reviewers	1.0
Other FTE Positions	3.0
Total of All Positions	8.0
Number of Inspections by Type	
Building	1,978
Electrical	2,618
Mechanical	1,872
Plumbing	1,054
TOTAL	7,522
Building Permit Values	
Residential	$20,000,000
Multi-Family	included with residential
Commercial	$91,000,000
TOTAL	$111,000,000
Inspection Fee Revenue	$6,550

Full Cost Profile

Cost Breakdown by Percentage	
Personal Services	61.0%
Operating Costs	36.7%
Capital Costs	2.3%
TOTAL	100.0%
Cost Breakdown in Dollars	
Personal Services	$540,285
Operating Costs	$324,445
Capital Costs	$20,329
TOTAL	$885,059

Goldsboro Building Inspections

Key: Goldsboro ▒ Benchmarking Average — Fiscal Years 2013 through 2017

Resource Measures

Building Inspections Services Costs per Capita

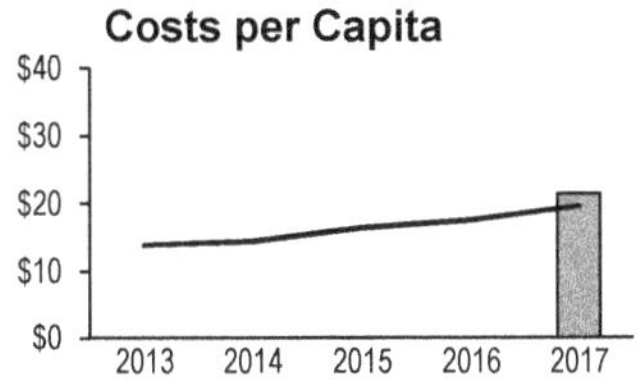

	2013	2014	2015	2016	2017
Goldsboro					$21.41
Average	$13.80	$14.33	$16.31	$17.48	$19.55

Building Inspections Services FTEs per 10,000 Population

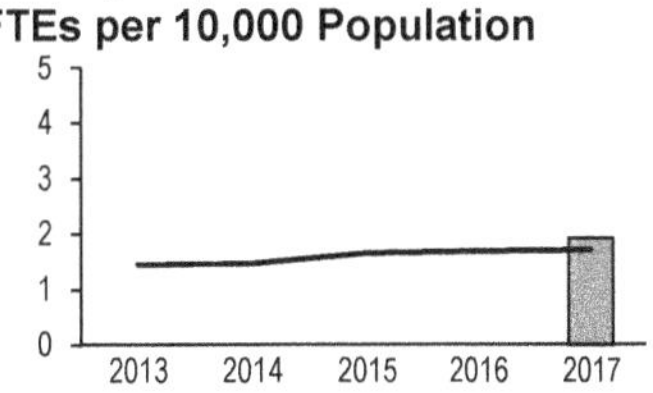

	2013	2014	2015	2016	2017
Goldsboro					1.94
Average	1.46	1.48	1.66	1.70	1.72

Building Inspections Services Cost per Million Dollars of Tax Base

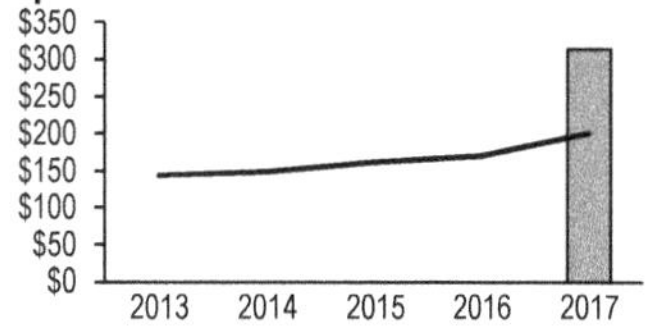

	2013	2014	2015	2016	2017
Goldsboro					$314
Average	$143	$148	$161	$169	$200

Workload Measures

Inspections per 1,000 Population in Service Area

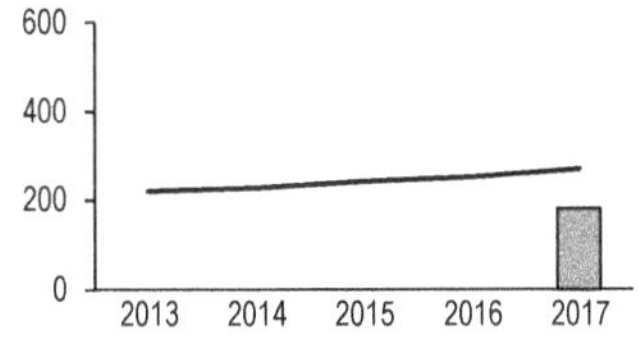

	2013	2014	2015	2016	2017
Goldsboro					182
Average	221	229	243	253	270

Inspections per Square Mile in Service Area

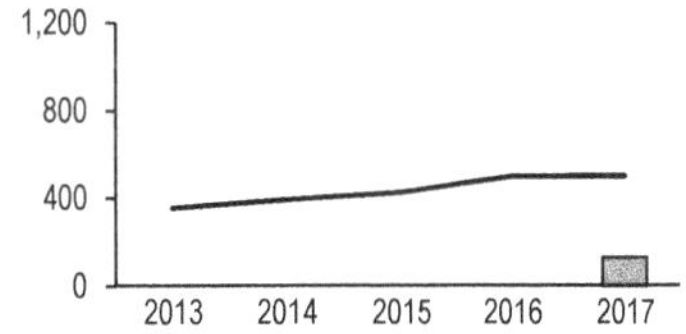

	2013	2014	2015	2016	2017
Goldsboro					130
Average	353	389	421	495	497

Value of Building Permits as Percentage of Tax Base of Area Served

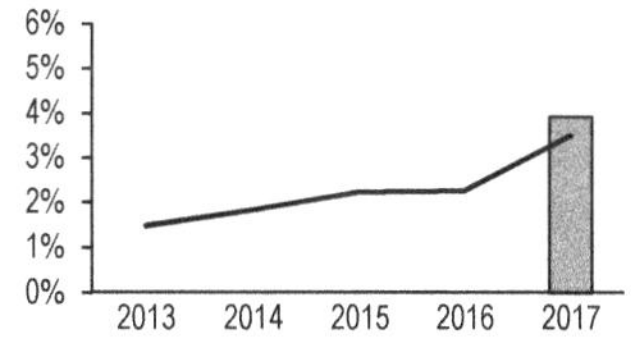

	2013	2014	2015	2016	2017
Goldsboro					3.94%
Average	1.47%	1.82%	2.21%	2.25%	3.48%

Value of Commercial Permits as Percentage of Tax Base of Area Served

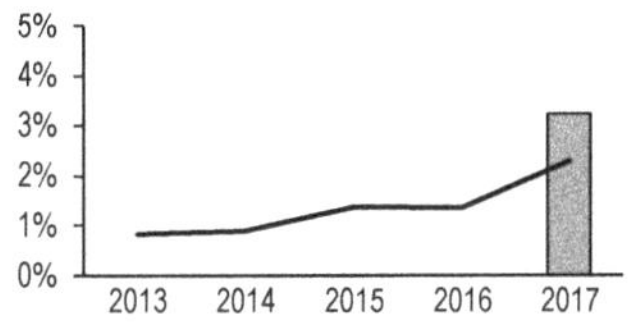

	2013	2014	2015	2016	2017
Goldsboro					3.23%
Average	0.83%	0.89%	1.36%	1.35%	2.28%

Value of Building Permits per Inspector FTE in Millions of Dollars

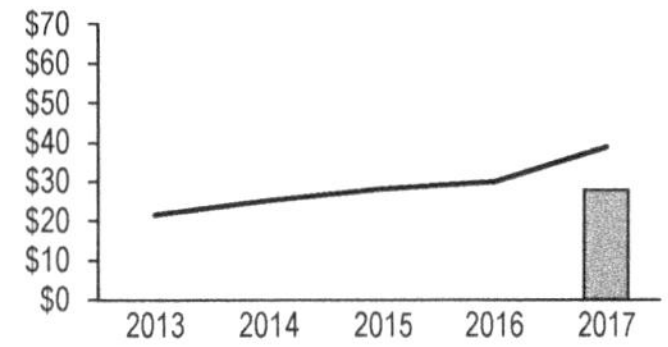

	2013	2014	2015	2016	2017
Goldsboro					$27.8
Average	$21.5	$25.2	$28.0	$29.9	$38.7

Efficiency Measures

Building Services Cost per Inspection—All Types

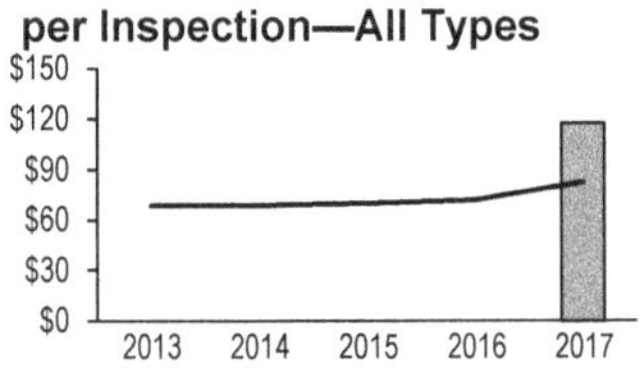

	2013	2014	2015	2016	2017
Goldsboro					$117.66
Average	$68.41	$68.71	$69.65	$71.57	$82.35

Inspections per Day per Inspector FTE

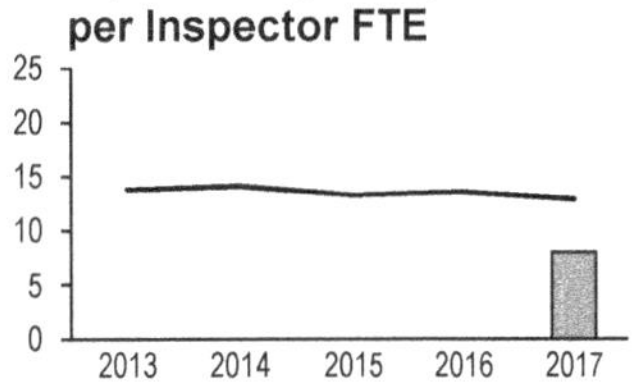

	2013	2014	2015	2016	2017
Goldsboro					8.0
Average	13.9	14.2	13.3	13.7	13.0

Plan Reviews per Year per Reviewer FTE

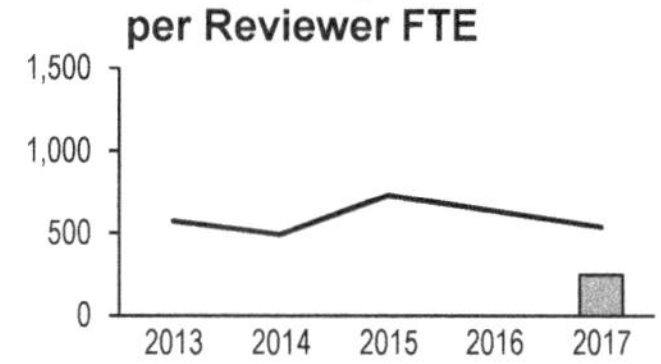

	2013	2014	2015	2016	2017
Goldsboro					249
Average	573	492	729	636	538

Effectiveness Measures

Percentage of Inspection Responses within One Working Day of Request

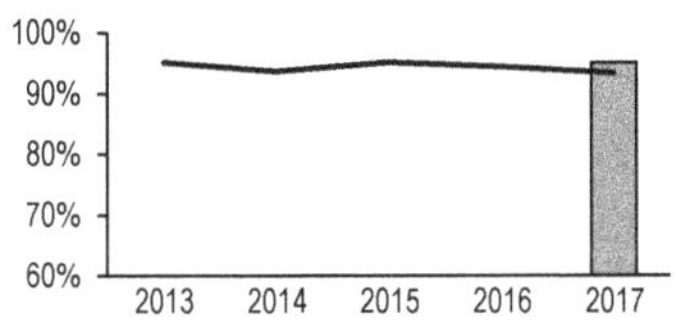

	2013	2014	2015	2016	2017
Goldsboro					95.0%
Average	95.1%	93.7%	95.1%	94.4%	93.4%

Percentage of Inspections That Are Reinspections

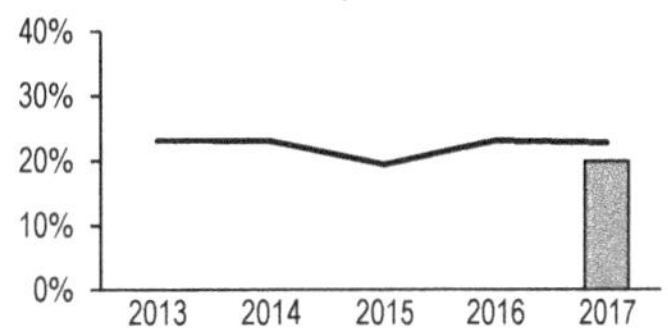

	2013	2014	2015	2016	2017
Goldsboro					19.9%
Average	23.1%	23.1%	19.4%	23.1%	22.8%

Fiscal Year 2016–17

Explanatory Information

Service Level and Delivery
Inspections is a division of the Engineering and Inspections Department of the City of Greensboro. The inspections division consists of plans review, building inspections, plumbing inspections, mechanical inspections, electrical inspections, and local code enforcement. The city services the incorporated portion of the city but not the extra-territorial jurisdiction areas.

Trade inspectors are required to attain a Level III certification of their primary building trade within two years. Mechanical and plumbing inspectors are required to attain a secondary certification. Local ordinance inspectors are required to attain a Level I certification. All certified inspectors are required to take and pass a law and administrative course.

All requests for inspections are responded to within forty-eight hours or less. Nearly all requests are called into the city's automated system or entered via its website.

Total revenue received from inspection fees amounted to $3.2 million for the fiscal year. If a request for inspection is made and the job is not ready or corrections have not been made, a $45 fee for each reinspection is assessed.

Conditions Affecting Service, Performance, and Costs
The broad downturn in the economy had reduced building activity and the number of requests for inspections in the earlier years.

Municipal Profile

Population Served	284,343
Land Area Inspected (Square Miles)	133.81
Persons per Square Mile	2,125
Estimated Tax Base in Service Area (billions)	$25.61
Median Family Income U.S. Census 2010	$52,752

Service Profile

FTE Inspectors	
Building	5.0
Electrical	5.0
Mechanical	3.0
Plumbing	3.0
All Trades	0.0
Total Inspectors	16.0
FTE Plan Reviewers	4.5
Other FTE Positions	9.5
Total of All Positions	30.0
Number of Inspections by Type	
Building	22,472
Electrical	17,190
Mechanical	15,507
Plumbing	15,646
TOTAL	70,815
Building Permit Values	
Residential	$156,574,946
Multi-Family	$176,938,468
Commercial	$406,877,710
TOTAL	$740,391,124
Inspection Fee Revenue	$3,205,224

Full Cost Profile

Cost Breakdown by Percentage	
Personal Services	78.8%
Operating Costs	21.2%
Capital Costs	0.0%
TOTAL	100.0%
Cost Breakdown in Dollars	
Personal Services	$2,373,781
Operating Costs	$640,103
Capital Costs	$0
TOTAL	$3,013,884

Greensboro — Building Inspections

Key: Greensboro ▒ Benchmarking Average — Fiscal Years 2013 through 2017

Resource Measures

Building Inspections Services Costs per Capita

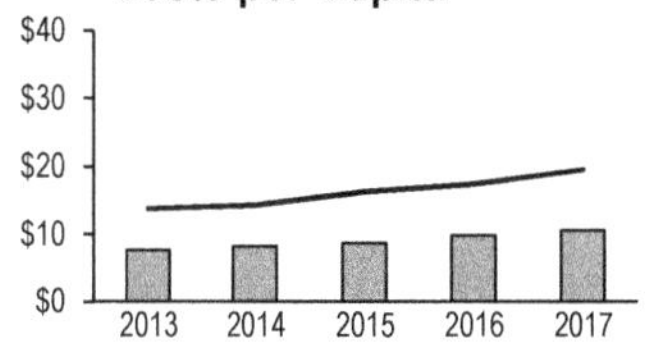

	2013	2014	2015	2016	2017
Greensboro	$7.65	$8.21	$8.69	$9.80	$10.60
Average	$13.80	$14.33	$16.31	$17.48	$19.55

Building Inspections Services FTEs per 10,000 Population

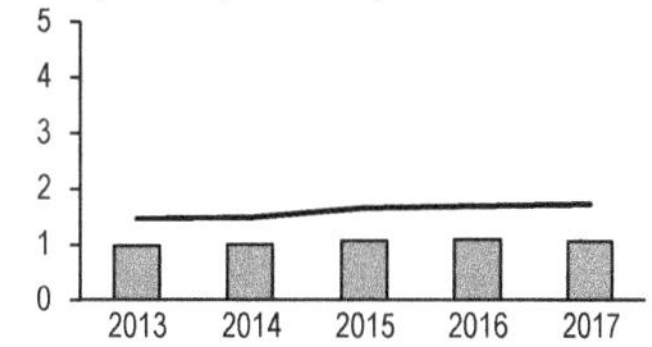

	2013	2014	2015	2016	2017
Greensboro	0.98	1.00	1.07	1.10	1.06
Average	1.46	1.48	1.66	1.70	1.72

Building Inspections Services Cost per Million Dollars of Tax Base

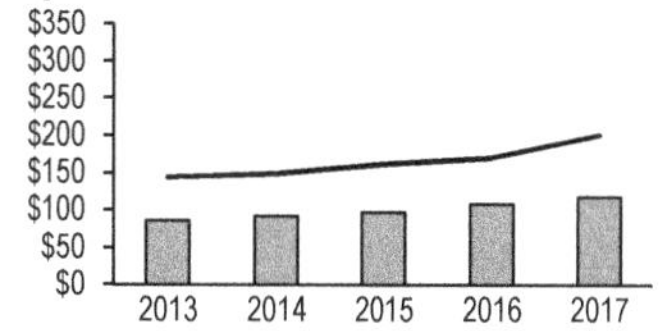

	2013	2014	2015	2016	2017
Greensboro	$86	$92	$97	$108	$118
Average	$143	$148	$161	$169	$200

Workload Measures

Inspections per 1,000 Population in Service Area

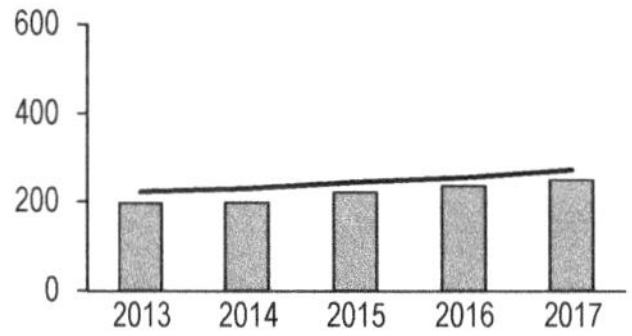

	2013	2014	2015	2016	2017
Greensboro	195	197	220	234	249
Average	221	229	243	253	270

Inspections per Square Mile in Service Area

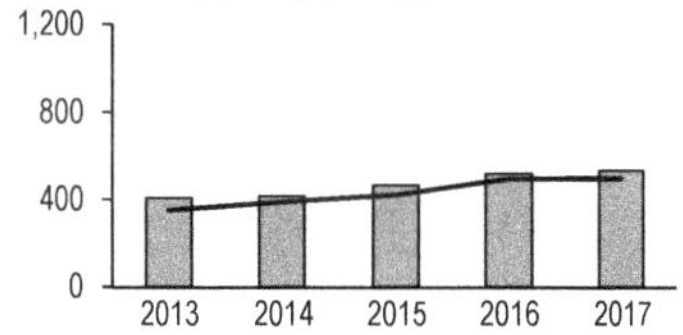

	2013	2014	2015	2016	2017
Greensboro	404	412	464	516	529
Average	353	389	421	495	497

Value of Building Permits as Percentage of Tax Base of Area Served

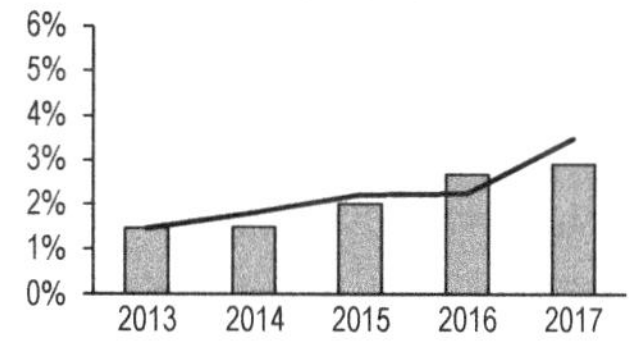

	2013	2014	2015	2016	2017
Greensboro	1.47%	1.50%	2.00%	2.66%	2.89%
Average	1.47%	1.82%	2.21%	2.25%	3.48%

Value of Commercial Permits as Percentage of Tax Base of Area Served

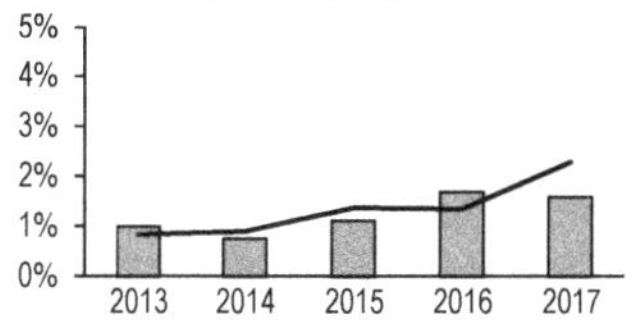

	2013	2014	2015	2016	2017
Greensboro	1.00%	0.76%	1.11%	1.69%	1.59%
Average	0.83%	0.89%	1.36%	1.35%	2.28%

Value of Building Permits per Inspector FTE in Millions of Dollars

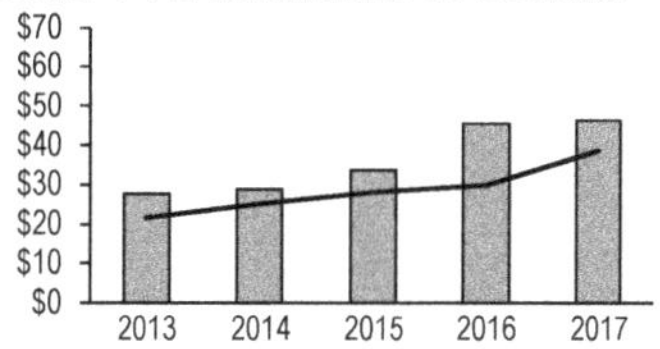

	2013	2014	2015	2016	2017
Greensboro	$27.5	$28.8	$33.6	$45.4	$46.3
Average	$21.5	$25.2	$28.0	$29.9	$38.7

Efficiency Measures

Building Services Cost per Inspection—All Types

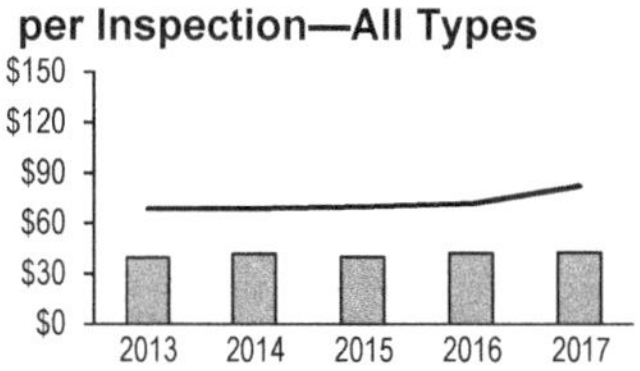

	2013	2014	2015	2016	2017
Greensboro	$39.20	$41.71	$39.52	$41.90	$42.56
Average	$68.41	$68.71	$69.65	$71.57	$82.35

Inspections per Day per Inspector FTE

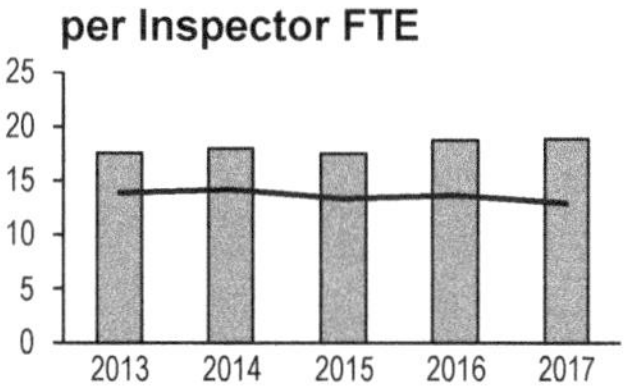

	2013	2014	2015	2016	2017
Greensboro	17.6	18.0	17.5	18.8	18.8
Average	13.9	14.2	13.3	13.7	13.0

Plan Reviews per Year per Reviewer FTE

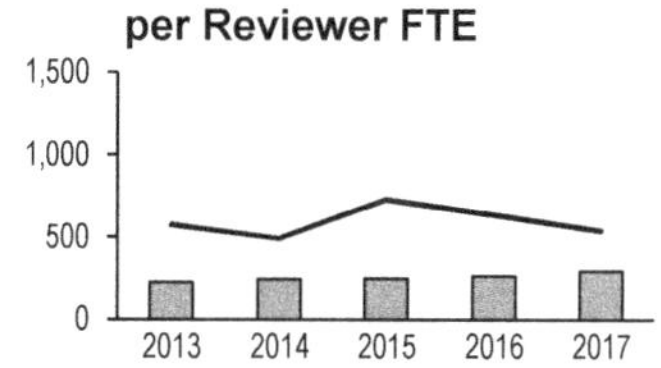

	2013	2014	2015	2016	2017
Greensboro	225	245	248	265	293
Average	573	492	729	636	538

Effectiveness Measures

Percentage of Inspection Responses within One Working Day of Request

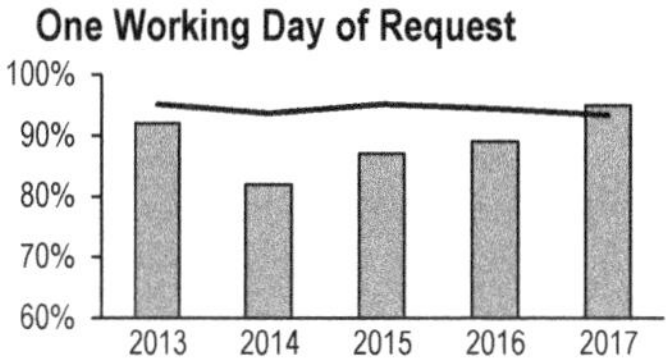

	2013	2014	2015	2016	2017
Greensboro	92.0%	82.0%	87.0%	89.0%	95.0%
Average	95.1%	93.7%	95.1%	94.4%	93.4%

Percentage of Inspections That Are Reinspections

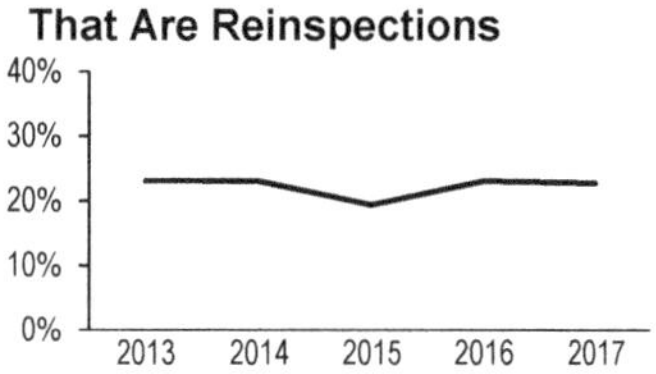

	2013	2014	2015	2016	2017
Greensboro					
Average	23.1%	23.1%	19.4%	23.1%	22.8%

Fiscal Year 2016–17

Explanatory Information

Service Level and Delivery

The City of Greenville provides detailed inspections services within city limits and its extra-territorial jurisdiction (ETJ). The city provides building, plumbing, electrical, and mechanical code enforcement services.

Total revenue received from inspection fees amounted to $1.3 million for the fiscal year. Inspection and permit fees depend on the type of construction or work, value of construction, and other factors.

Conditions Affecting Service, Performance, and Costs

The population served is calculated by adding the population of Greenville with the population of the ETJ. The tax base served is calculated by adding the tax base of Greenville with the tax base of the ETJ. The population and the tax base of the ETJ are calculated by taking the population and tax base per square mile of Pitt County and multiplying them by the square miles of the ETJ.

Plan reviews are being done by inspectors as the plan review position has been cut from the budget.

The earlier downturn in the economy over the past several years had decreased the demand for inspections services.

Municipal Profile

Population Served	96,423
Land Area Inspected (Square Miles)	67.34
Persons per Square Mile	1,432
Estimated Tax Base in Service Area (billions)	$6.59
Median Family Income U.S. Census 2010	$50,395

Service Profile

FTE Inspectors	
Building	0.0
Electrical	0.0
Mechanical	0.0
Plumbing	0.0
All Trades	5.0
Total Inspectors	5.0
FTE Plan Reviewers	1.0
Other FTE Positions	4.0
Total of All Positions	10.0
Number of Inspections by Type	
Building	4,414
Electrical	3,941
Mechanical	3,557
Plumbing	2,597
TOTAL	14,509
Building Permit Values	
Residential	$59,996,989
Multi-Family	$55,187,409
Commercial	$203,861,657
TOTAL	$319,046,055
Inspection Fee Revenue	$1,384,401

Full Cost Profile

Cost Breakdown by Percentage	
Personal Services	75.2%
Operating Costs	20.0%
Capital Costs	4.8%
TOTAL	100.0%
Cost Breakdown in Dollars	
Personal Services	$741,498
Operating Costs	$196,849
Capital Costs	$47,374
TOTAL	$985,721

Key: Greenville ▒ Benchmarking Average — Fiscal Years 2013 through 2017

Resource Measures

Building Inspections Services Costs per Capita

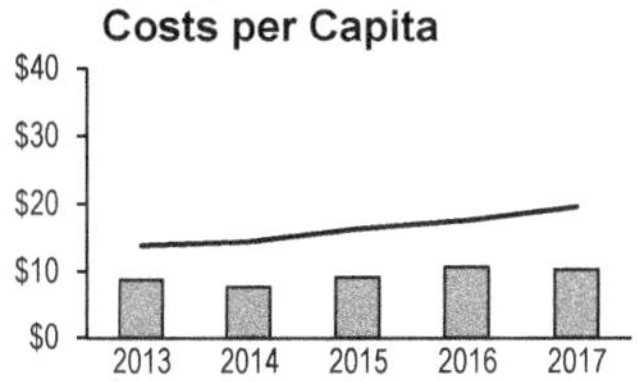

	2013	2014	2015	2016	2017
Greenville	$8.64	$7.58	$9.04	$10.58	$10.22
Average	$13.80	$14.33	$16.31	$17.48	$19.55

Building Inspections Services FTEs per 10,000 Population

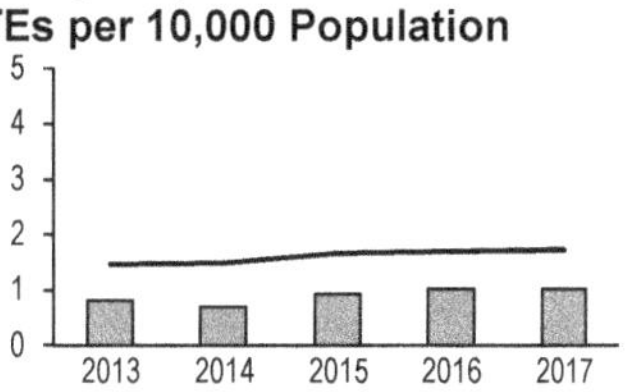

	2013	2014	2015	2016	2017
Greenville	0.83	0.70	0.94	1.04	1.04
Average	1.46	1.48	1.66	1.70	1.72

Building Inspections Services Cost per Million Dollars of Tax Base

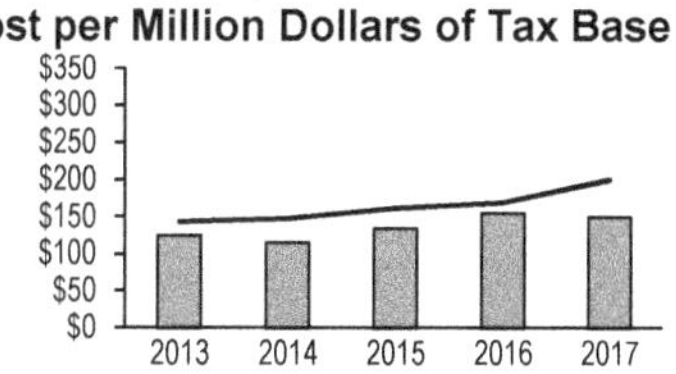

	2013	2014	2015	2016	2017
Greenville	$125	$115	$134	$155	$150
Average	$143	$148	$161	$169	$200

Workload Measures

Inspections per 1,000 Population in Service Area

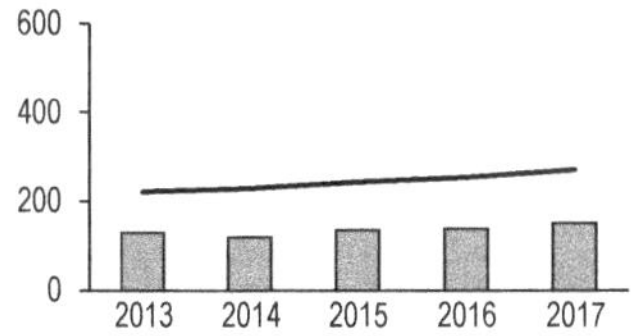

	2013	2014	2015	2016	2017
Greenville	130	120	136	138	150
Average	221	229	243	253	270

Inspections per Square Mile in Service Area

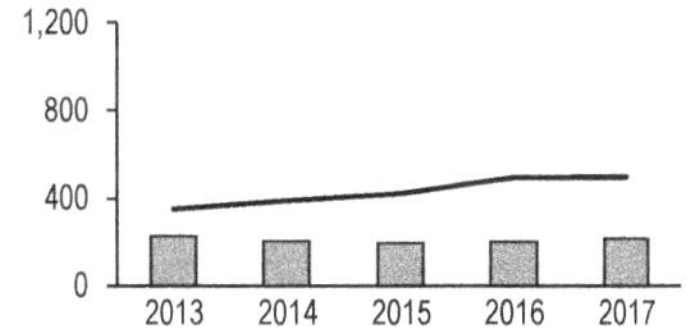

	2013	2014	2015	2016	2017
Greenville	228	204	195	200	215
Average	353	389	421	495	497

Value of Building Permits as Percentage of Tax Base of Area Served

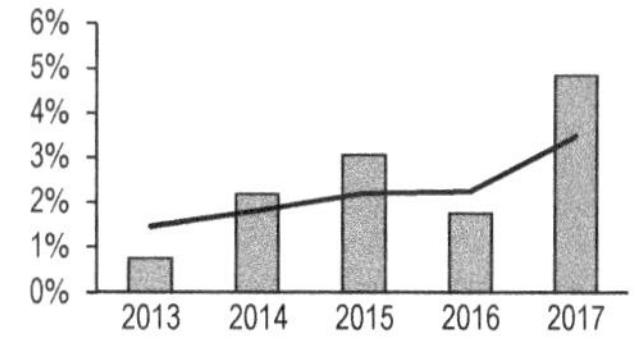

	2013	2014	2015	2016	2017
Greenville	0.74%	2.17%	3.05%	1.74%	4.84%
Average	1.47%	1.82%	2.21%	2.25%	3.48%

Value of Commercial Permits as Percentage of Tax Base of Area Served

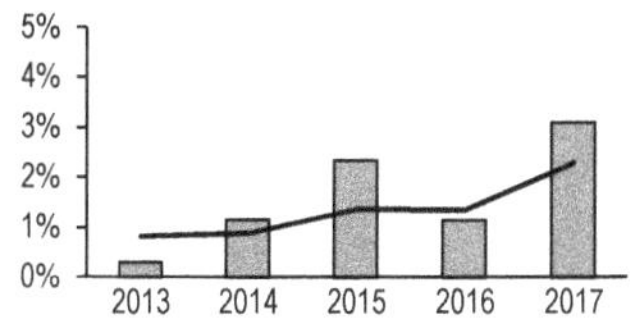

	2013	2014	2015	2016	2017
Greenville	0.30%	1.16%	2.33%	1.14%	3.09%
Average	0.83%	0.89%	1.36%	1.35%	2.28%

Value of Building Permits per Inspector FTE in Millions of Dollars

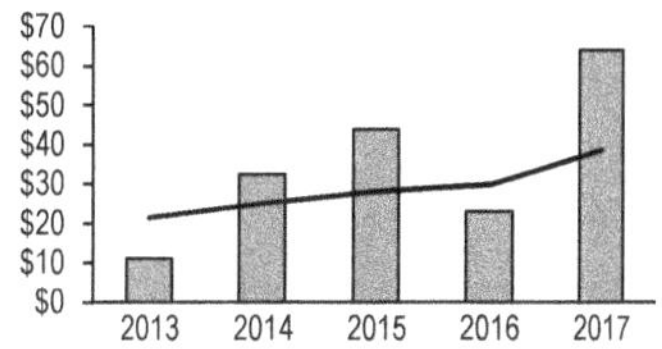

	2013	2014	2015	2016	2017
Greenville	$11.1	$32.6	$43.8	$23.0	$63.8
Average	$21.5	$25.2	$28.0	$29.9	$38.7

Efficiency Measures

Building Services Cost per Inspection—All Types

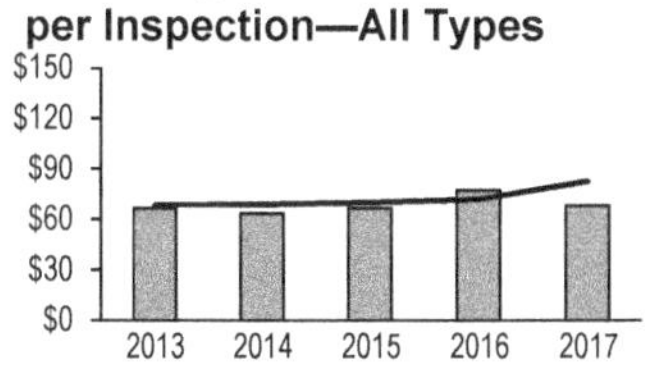

	2013	2014	2015	2016	2017
Greenville	$66.44	$63.30	$66.57	$76.87	$67.94
Average	$68.41	$68.71	$69.65	$71.57	$82.35

Inspections per Day per Inspector FTE

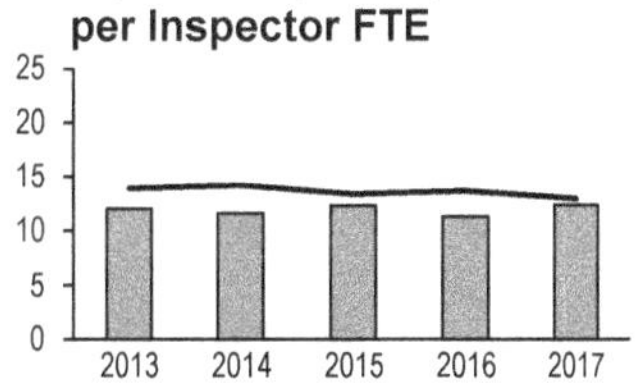

	2013	2014	2015	2016	2017
Greenville	12.0	11.6	12.3	11.3	12.3
Average	13.9	14.2	13.3	13.7	13.0

Plan Reviews per Year per Reviewer FTE

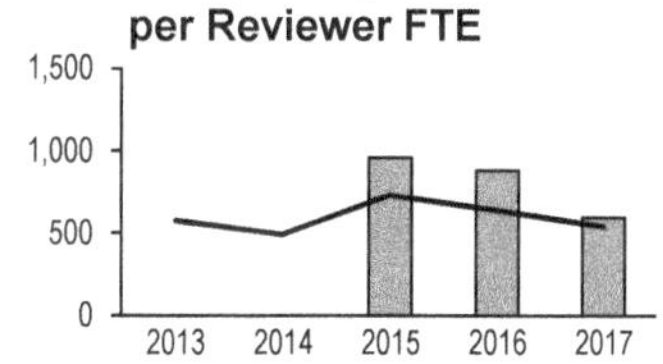

	2013	2014	2015	2016	2017
Greenville			957	879	593
Average	573	492	729	636	538

Effectiveness Measures

Percentage of Inspection Responses within One Working Day of Request

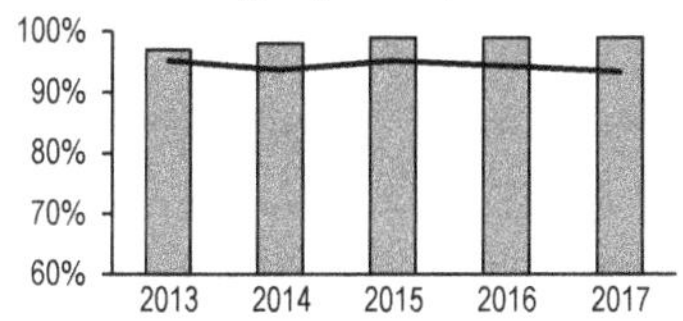

	2013	2014	2015	2016	2017
Greenville	97.0%	98.0%	99.0%	99.0%	99.0%
Average	95.1%	93.7%	95.1%	94.4%	93.4%

Percentage of Inspections That Are Reinspections

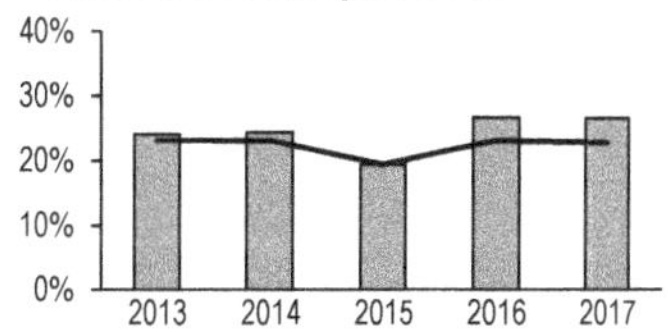

	2013	2014	2015	2016	2017
Greenville	24.1%	24.4%	19.4%	26.6%	26.5%
Average	23.1%	23.1%	19.4%	23.1%	22.8%

Fiscal Year 2016–17

Explanatory Information

Service Level and Delivery

The inspections department of High Point provides building, plumbing, electrical, and mechanical code enforcement services to the incorporated area of the city in addition to a small portion of the rural/suburban extra-territorial jurisdiction (ETJ) within Guilford County.

Fire inspections and permit records are maintained by the inspections department, but fire inspections are performed by fire marshals. The department also has a local codes division, which enforces zoning, housing, public nuisance, and vehicle codes. This staff was not included in this report.

Inspectors are required to complete a level of training prior to receiving individual assignments. Prior to completing the required training, employees must work under the direct supervision of their supervisor or assigned employees. Training includes formal classroom and on-the-job training in code enforcement, technical codes, related state and local code laws, safety, and personnel regulations. All inspection requests received by midnight are inspected the next business day.

Total revenue received from inspection fees amounted to $1,040,885 for the fiscal year. Inspection and permit fees depend on the type of construction or work, value of construction, and other factors.

Conditions Affecting Service, Performance, and Costs

The population served is calculated by adding the population of High Point with the population of the ETJ. The tax base served is calculated by adding the tax base of High Point with the tax base of the ETJ. The population and the tax base of the ETJ are calculated by taking the population and tax base per square mile of Guilford County and multiplying them by the square miles of the ETJ.

Reinspection data was not available for FY 2016–17.

The earlier broad downturn in the economy had reduced building activity and the number of requests for inspections.

Municipal Profile

Population Served	110,244
Land Area Inspected (Square Miles)	55.40
Persons per Square Mile	1,990
Estimated Tax Base in Service Area (billions)	$9.31
Median Family Income U.S. Census 2010	$49,720

Service Profile

FTE Inspectors	
Building	0.0
Electrical	0.0
Mechanical	0.0
Plumbing	0.0
All Trades	12.0
Total Inspectors	12.0
FTE Plan Reviewers	3.0
Other FTE Positions	5.0
Total of All Positions	20.0
Number of Inspections by Type	
Building	8,079
Electrical	7,183
Mechanical	5,271
Plumbing	3,592
TOTAL	24,125
Building Permit Values	
Residential	$25,714,577
Multi-Family	$88,160
Commercial	$118,339,335
TOTAL	$144,142,072
Inspection Fee Revenue	$1,040,885

Full Cost Profile

Cost Breakdown by Percentage	
Personal Services	73.1%
Operating Costs	23.2%
Capital Costs	3.7%
TOTAL	100.0%
Cost Breakdown in Dollars	
Personal Services	$1,478,287
Operating Costs	$470,225
Capital Costs	$74,909
TOTAL	$2,023,421

Key: High Point ▒ Benchmarking Average — Fiscal Years 2013 through 2017

Resource Measures

Building Inspections Services Costs per Capita

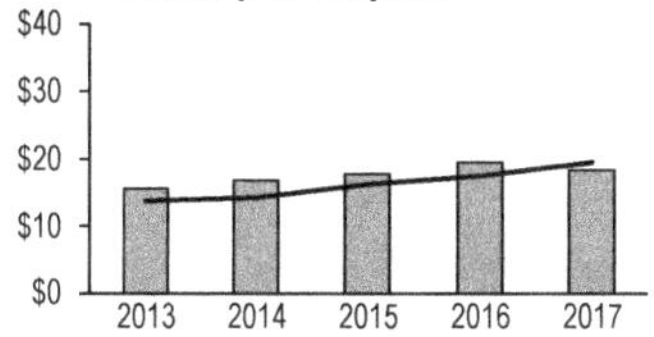

	2013	2014	2015	2016	2017
High Point	$15.64	$16.81	$17.85	$19.51	$18.35
Average	$13.80	$14.33	$16.31	$17.40	$19.55

Building Inspections Services FTEs per 10,000 Population

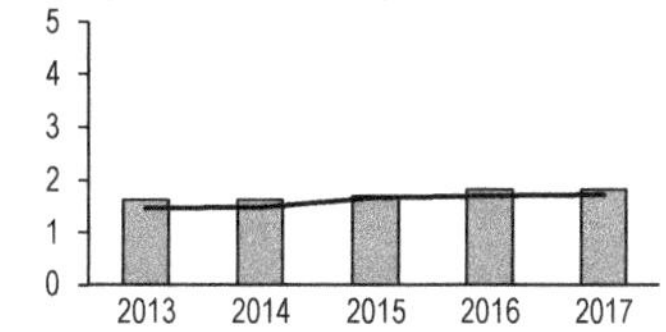

	2013	2014	2015	2016	2017
High Point	1.62	1.63	1.70	1.82	1.81
Average	1.46	1.48	1.66	1.70	1.72

Building Inspections Services Cost per Million Dollars of Tax Base

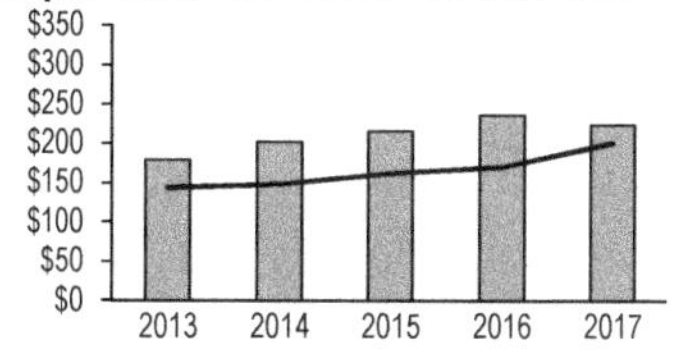

	2013	2014	2015	2016	2017
High Point	$179	$202	$216	$236	$224
Average	$143	$148	$161	$169	$200

Workload Measures

Inspections per 1,000 Population in Service Area

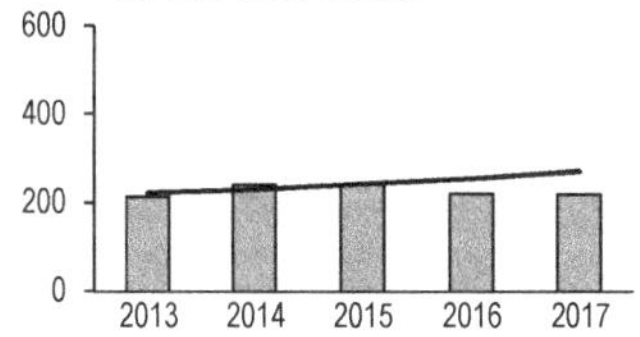

	2013	2014	2015	2016	2017
High Point	213	240	243	221	219
Average	221	229	243	253	270

Inspections per Square Mile in Service Area

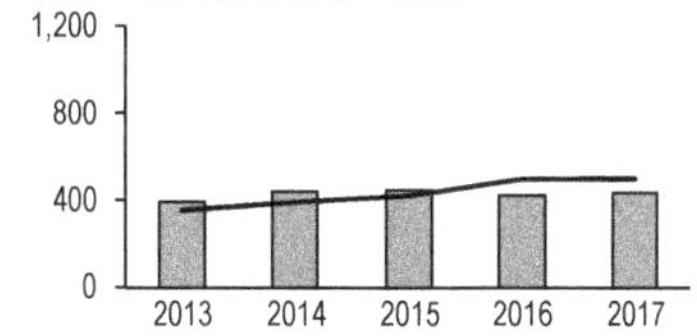

	2013	2014	2015	2016	2017
High Point	393	441	447	423	435
Average	353	389	421	495	497

Value of Building Permits as Percentage of Tax Base of Area Served

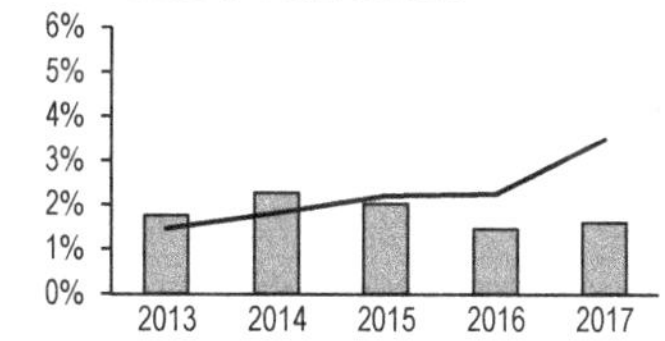

	2013	2014	2015	2016	2017
High Point	1.75%	2.25%	2.01%	1.44%	1.60%
Average	1.47%	1.82%	2.21%	2.25%	3.48%

Value of Commercial Permits as Percentage of Tax Base of Area Served

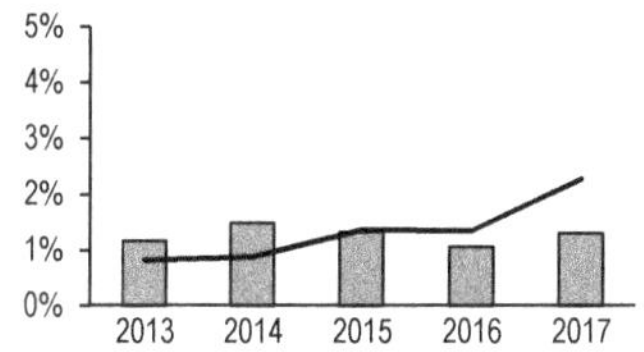

	2013	2014	2015	2016	2017
High Point	1.17%	1.50%	1.34%	1.07%	1.31%
Average	0.83%	0.89%	1.36%	1.35%	2.28%

Value of Building Permits per Inspector FTE in Millions of Dollars

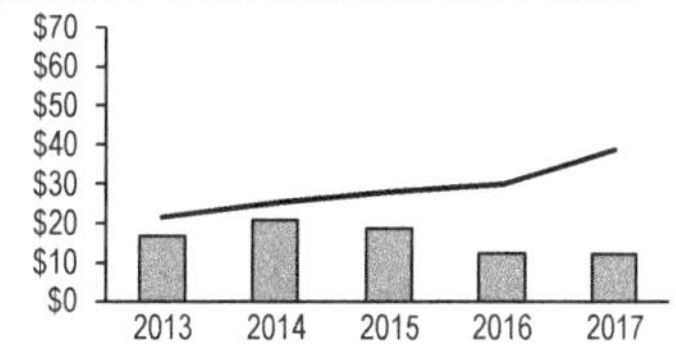

	2013	2014	2015	2016	2017
High Point	$16.7	$20.7	$18.6	$12.2	$12.0
Average	$21.5	$25.2	$28.0	$29.9	$38.7

Efficiency Measures

Building Services Cost per Inspection—All Types

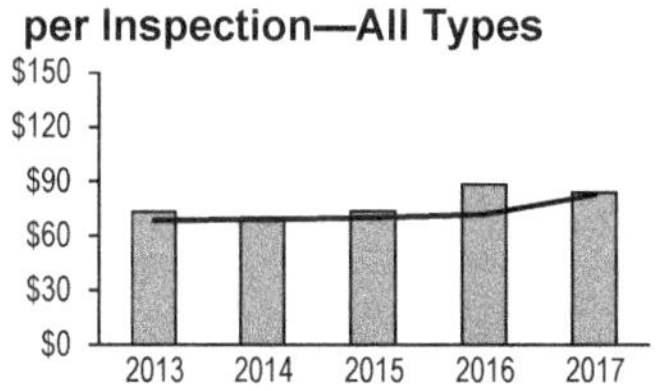

	2013	2014	2015	2016	2017
High Point	$73.31	$70.04	$73.58	$88.39	$83.87
Average	$68.41	$68.71	$69.65	$71.57	$82.35

Inspections per Day per Inspector FTE

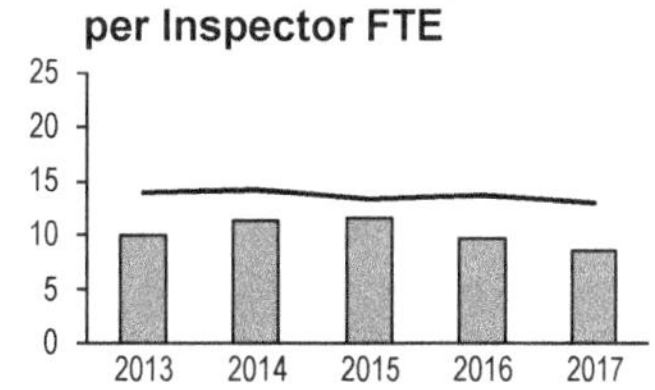

	2013	2014	2015	2016	2017
High Point	9.9	11.3	11.5	9.6	8.6
Average	13.9	14.2	13.3	13.7	13.0

Plan Reviews per Year per Reviewer FTE

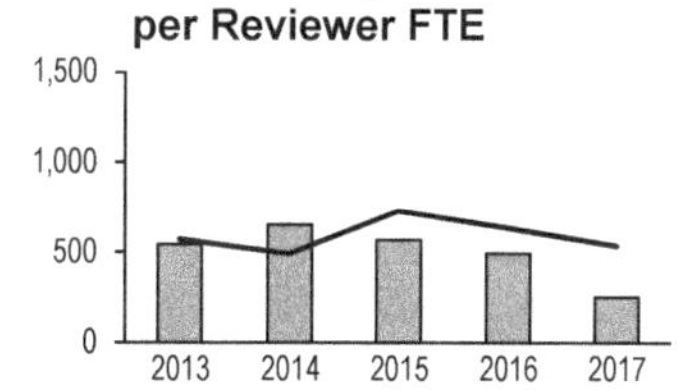

	2013	2014	2015	2016	2017
High Point	544	653	568	494	253
Average	573	492	729	636	538

Effectiveness Measures

Percentage of Inspection Responses within One Working Day of Request

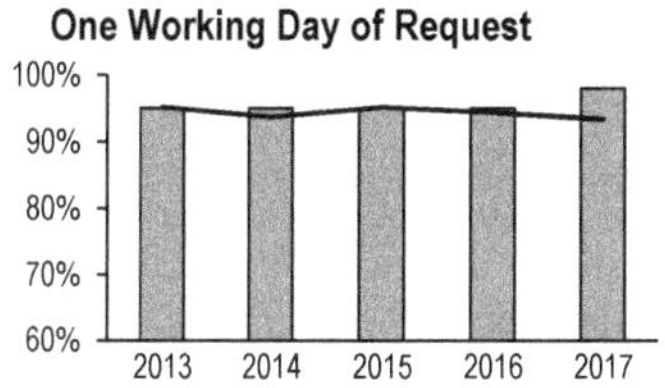

	2013	2014	2015	2016	2017
High Point	95.0%	95.0%	95.0%	95.0%	98.0%
Average	95.1%	93.7%	95.1%	94.4%	93.4%

Percentage of Inspections That Are Reinspections

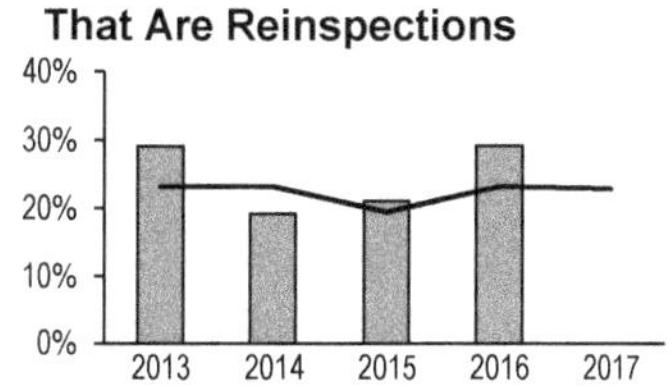

	2013	2014	2015	2016	2017
High Point	29.0%	19.1%	21.0%	29.1%	
Average	23.1%	23.1%	19.4%	23.1%	22.8%

Fiscal Year 2016–17

Explanatory Information

Service Level and Delivery

The City of Raleigh conducts building inspections through its Building and Safety Division of the Development Services Department. The Development Services Department serves the entire jurisdictional territory of the City of Raleigh.

Inspection services are currently provided by inspectors specializing in each of the major service trades as well as inspectors who cover all trades. A staff of plan reviewers and support specialists further the work in the Division.

It is the policy of the inspection work team to respond to an inspection request within twenty-four hours for each type of construction. Most inspections are completed within one day of a request.

Total revenue received from inspection fees was $7.7 million for the fiscal year. Inspection and permit fees depend on the type of construction or work, the value of construction, and other factors. Reinspections are not charged for the first time. Reinspections of the same inspection item that has failed for a second time are subject to a reinspection fee.

Conditions Affecting Service, Performance, and Costs

Raleigh rejoined the Benchmarking Project in July 2016 with the first year of data showing for FY 2015–16.

The permit value of multi-family building projects is included in the totals for commercial projects.

Municipal Profile

Population Served	448,706
Land Area Inspected (Square Miles)	144.80
Persons per Square Mile	3,099
Estimated Tax Base in Service Area (billions)	$53.58
Median Family Income U.S. Census 2010	$68,678

Service Profile

FTE Inspectors	
Building	8.0
Electrical	10.0
Mechanical	8.0
Plumbing	7.0
All Trades	13.0
Total Inspectors	46.0
FTE Plan Reviewers	15.0
Other FTE Positions	20.0
Total of All Positions	81.0
Number of Inspections by Type	
Building	31,146
Electrical	39,923
Mechanical	30,024
Plumbing	22,049
TOTAL	123,142
Building Permit Values	
Residential	$780,486,896
Multi-Family	with commercial
Commercial	$2,051,860,672
TOTAL	$2,832,347,568
Inspection Fee Revenue	$7,733,763

Full Cost Profile

Cost Breakdown by Percentage	
Personal Services	77.4%
Operating Costs	12.6%
Capital Costs	10.0%
TOTAL	100.0%
Cost Breakdown in Dollars	
Personal Services	$6,006,003
Operating Costs	$977,760
Capital Costs	$779,996
TOTAL	$7,763,759

Key: Raleigh ▒ Benchmarking Average — Fiscal Years 2013 through 2017

Resource Measures

Building Inspections Services Costs per Capita

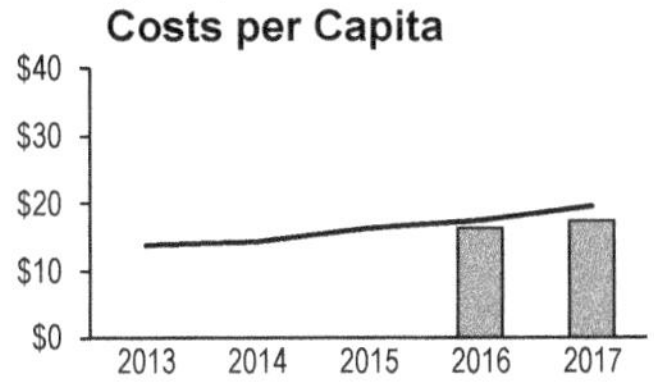

	2013	2014	2015	2016	2017
Raleigh				$16.32	$17.30
Average	$13.80	$14.33	$16.31	$17.48	$19.55

Building Inspections Services FTEs per 10,000 Population

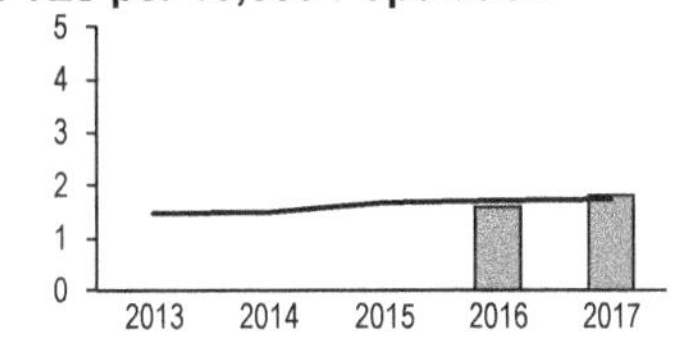

	2013	2014	2015	2016	2017
Raleigh				1.59	1.81
Average	1.46	1.48	1.66	1.70	1.72

Building Inspections Services Cost per Million Dollars of Tax Base

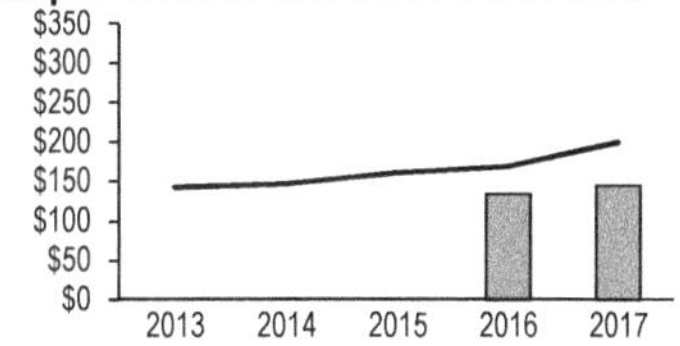

	2013	2014	2015	2016	2017
Raleigh				$134	$145
Average	$143	$148	$161	$169	$200

Workload Measures

Inspections per 1,000 Population in Service Area

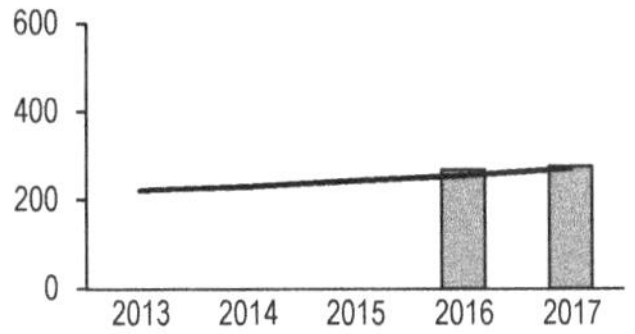

	2013	2014	2015	2016	2017
Raleigh				266	274
Average	221	229	243	253	270

Inspections per Square Mile in Service Area

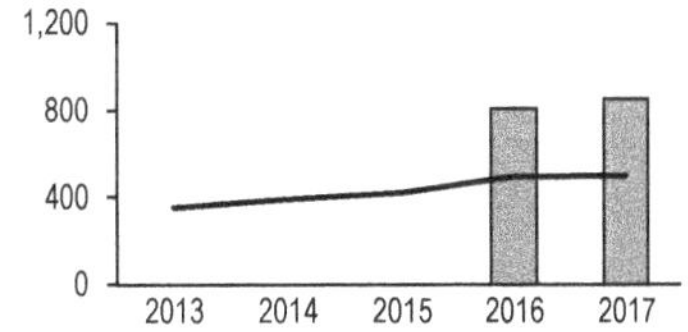

	2013	2014	2015	2016	2017
Raleigh				808	850
Average	353	389	421	495	497

Value of Building Permits as Percentage of Tax Base of Area Served

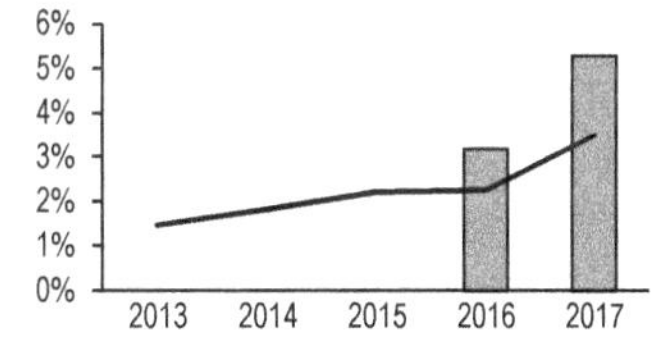

	2013	2014	2015	2016	2017
Raleigh				3.18%	5.29%
Average	1.47%	1.82%	2.21%	2.25%	3.48%

Value of Commercial Permits as Percentage of Tax Base of Area Served

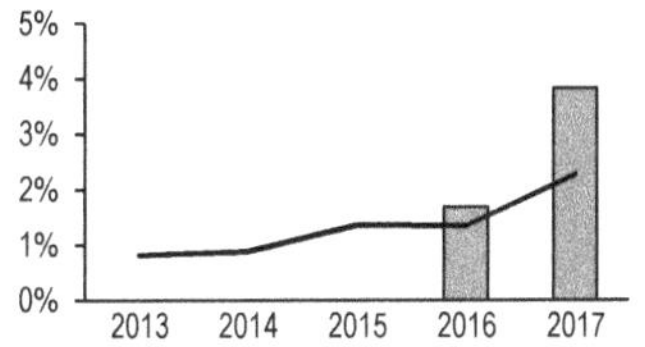

	2013	2014	2015	2016	2017
Raleigh				1.68%	3.83%
Average	0.83%	0.89%	1.36%	1.35%	2.28%

Value of Building Permits per Inspector FTE in Millions of Dollars

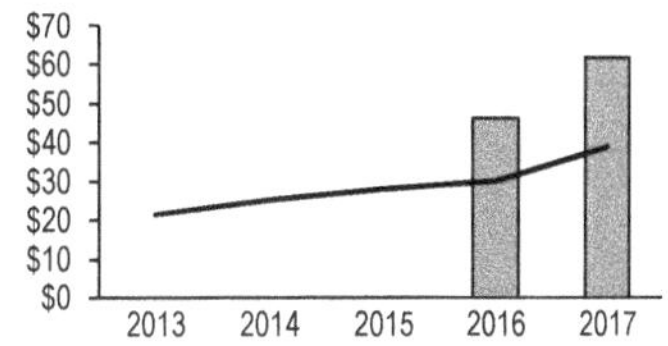

	2013	2014	2015	2016	2017
Raleigh				$46.0	$61.6
Average	$21.5	$25.2	$28.0	$29.9	$38.7

Efficiency Measures

Building Services Cost per Inspection—All Types

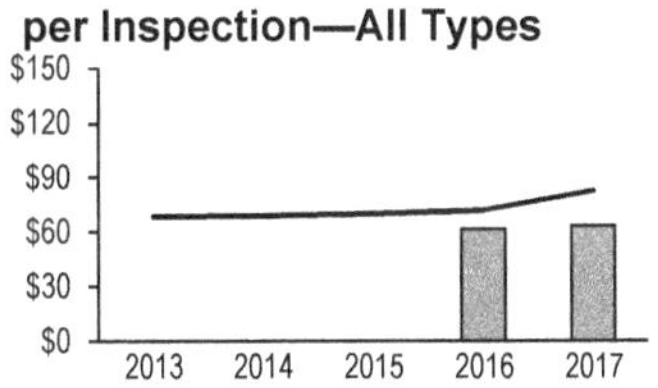

	2013	2014	2015	2016	2017
Raleigh				$61.30	$63.05
Average	$68.41	$68.71	$69.65	$71.57	$82.35

Inspections per Day per Inspector FTE

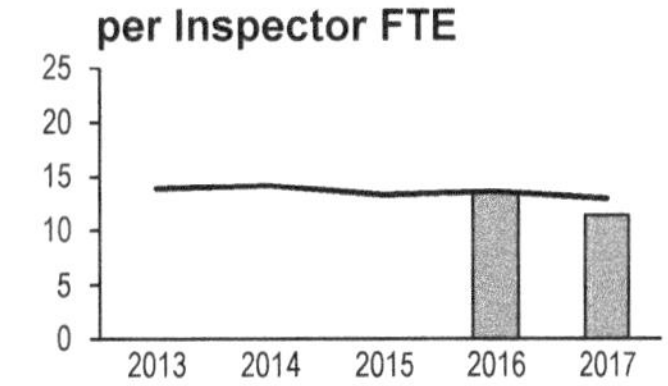

	2013	2014	2015	2016	2017
Raleigh				13.5	11.4
Average	13.9	14.2	13.3	13.7	13.0

Plan Reviews per Year per Reviewer FTE

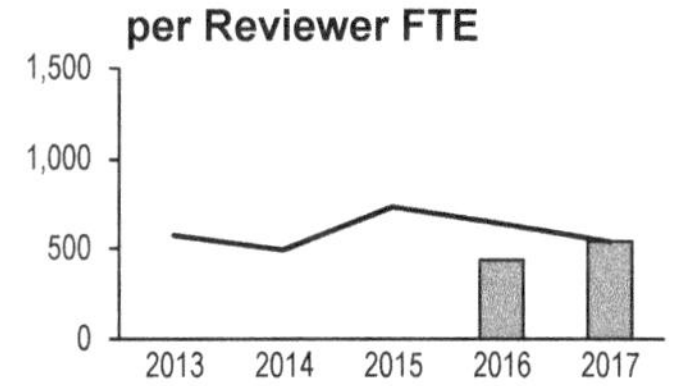

	2013	2014	2015	2016	2017
Raleigh				439	542
Average	573	492	729	636	538

Effectiveness Measures

Percentage of Inspection Responses within One Working Day of Request

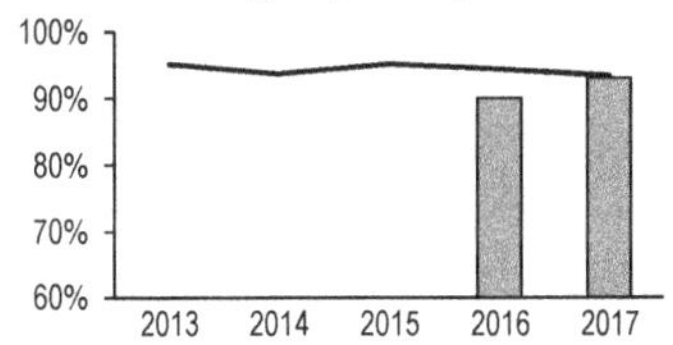

	2013	2014	2015	2016	2017
Raleigh				90.0%	93.0%
Average	95.1%	93.7%	95.1%	94.4%	93.4%

Percentage of Inspections That Are Reinspections

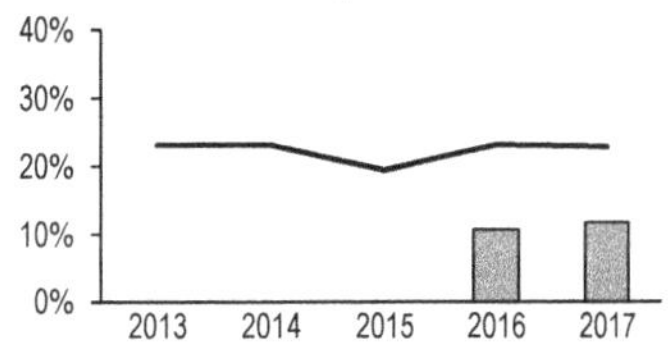

	2013	2014	2015	2016	2017
Raleigh				10.7%	11.8%
Average	23.1%	23.1%	19.4%	23.1%	22.8%

Fiscal Year 2016–17

Explanatory Information

Service Level and Delivery

The City of Wilson's inspection team serves the area within the city's corporate limits and the extra-territorial zoning jurisdiction (ETJ) that is approximately one mile beyond city limits.

Inspection services are currently provided by three inspectors, one field supervisor, and the inspections divisions manager. Two permit technicians provide support to this function. For commercial jobs, each inspector is assigned a primary inspection field. For residential jobs, inspectors hold certificates in all trade areas. Fire inspections are typically handled by certified inspectors in the fire department but are occasionally conducted by building inspectors who have fire inspection certification.

It is the policy of the inspection work team to respond to an inspection request on the same working day if the request is made prior to 8:30 a.m. and to respond to an inspection request by the following working day if the request is made after 8:30 a.m. Most inspections are completed on the same day the request is made.

Total revenue received from inspection fees was $537,289 for the fiscal year. Inspection and permit fees depend on the type of construction or work, the value of construction, and other factors. A reinspection fee is assessed when making an inspection for the same trade that had been previously rejected.

Conditions Affecting Service, Performance, and Costs

The population served is calculated by adding the population of Wilson with the population of the ETJ. The tax base served is calculated by adding the tax base of Wilson with the tax base of the ETJ. The population and the tax base of the ETJ are calculated by taking the population and tax base per square mile of Wilson County and multiplying them by the square miles of the ETJ.

The broad downturn in the economy had reduced building activity and the number of requests for inspections.

Municipal Profile

Population Served	54,566
Land Area Inspected (Square Miles)	55.18
Persons per Square Mile	989
Estimated Tax Base in Service Area (billions)	$4.70
Median Family Income U.S. Census 2010	$43,442

Service Profile

FTE Inspectors	
Building	0.0
Electrical	0.0
Mechanical	0.0
Plumbing	0.0
All Trades	4.0
Total Inspectors	4.0
FTE Plan Reviewers	1.0
Other FTE Positions	2.0
Total of All Positions	7.0
Number of Inspections by Type	
Building	2,440
Electrical	2,280
Mechanical	1,905
Plumbing	986
TOTAL	7,611
Building Permit Values	
Residential	$15,879,332
Multi-Family	$2,780,000
Commercial	$127,197,868
TOTAL	$145,857,200
Inspection Fee Revenue	$537,289

Full Cost Profile

Cost Breakdown by Percentage	
Personal Services	75.3%
Operating Costs	17.9%
Capital Costs	6.8%
TOTAL	100.0%
Cost Breakdown in Dollars	
Personal Services	$598,684
Operating Costs	$142,171
Capital Costs	$53,746
TOTAL	$794,600

Key: Wilson ▒ Benchmarking Average — Fiscal Years 2013 through 2017

Resource Measures

Building Inspections Services Costs per Capita

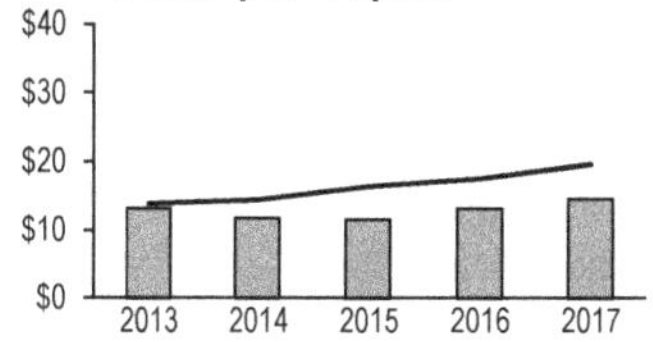

	2013	2014	2015	2016	2017
Wilson	$13.19	$11.78	$11.52	$13.19	$14.56
Average	$13.80	$14.33	$16.31	$17.48	$19.55

Building Inspections Services FTEs per 10,000 Population

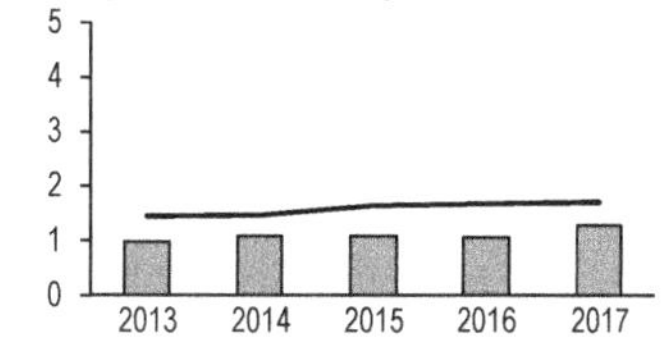

	2013	2014	2015	2016	2017
Wilson	0.97	1.09	1.09	1.07	1.28
Average	1.46	1.48	1.66	1.70	1.72

Building Inspections Services Cost per Million Dollars of Tax Base

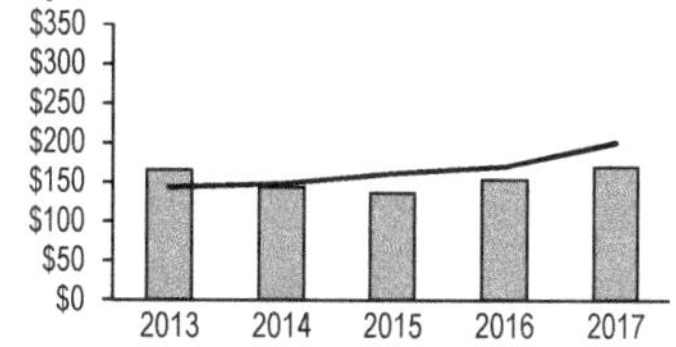

	2013	2014	2015	2016	2017
Wilson	$165	$143	$135	$153	$169
Average	$143	$148	$161	$169	$200

Workload Measures

Inspections per 1,000 Population in Service Area

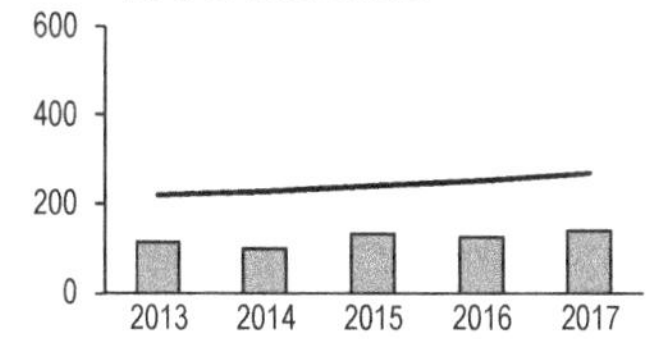

	2013	2014	2015	2016	2017
Wilson	114	101	133	126	139
Average	221	229	243	253	270

Inspections per Square Mile in Service Area

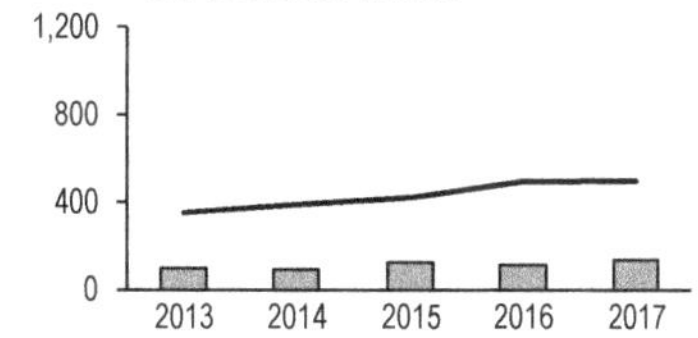

	2013	2014	2015	2016	2017
Wilson	99	95	125	114	138
Average	353	389	421	495	497

Value of Building Permits as Percentage of Tax Base of Area Served

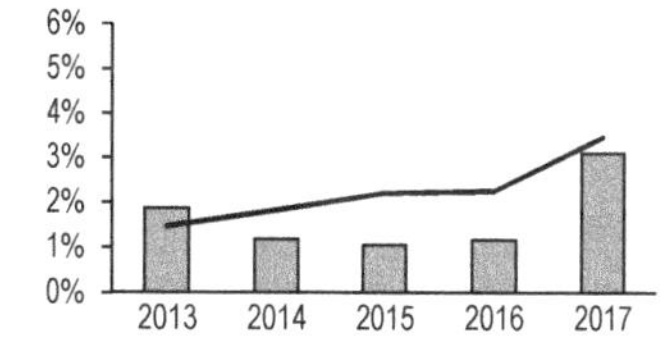

	2013	2014	2015	2016	2017
Wilson	1.87%	1.18%	1.05%	1.17%	3.10%
Average	1.47%	1.82%	2.21%	2.25%	3.48%

Value of Commercial Permits as Percentage of Tax Base of Area Served

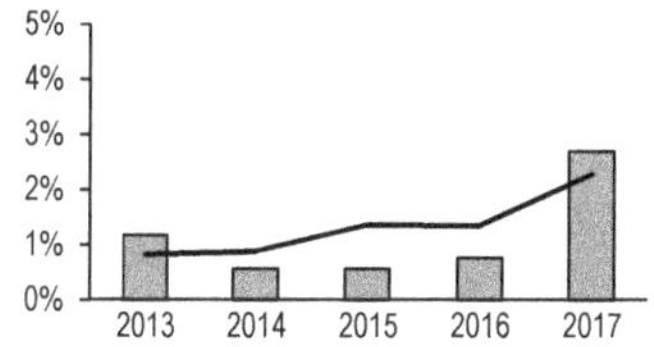

	2013	2014	2015	2016	2017
Wilson	1.19%	0.58%	0.58%	0.78%	2.70%
Average	0.83%	0.89%	1.36%	1.35%	2.28%

Value of Building Permits per Inspector FTE in Millions of Dollars

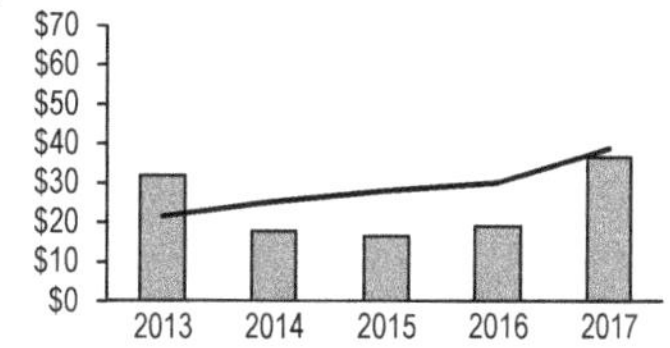

	2013	2014	2015	2016	2017
Wilson	$31.9	$17.8	$16.5	$18.9	$36.5
Average	$21.5	$25.2	$28.0	$29.9	$38.7

Efficiency Measures

Building Services Cost per Inspection—All Types

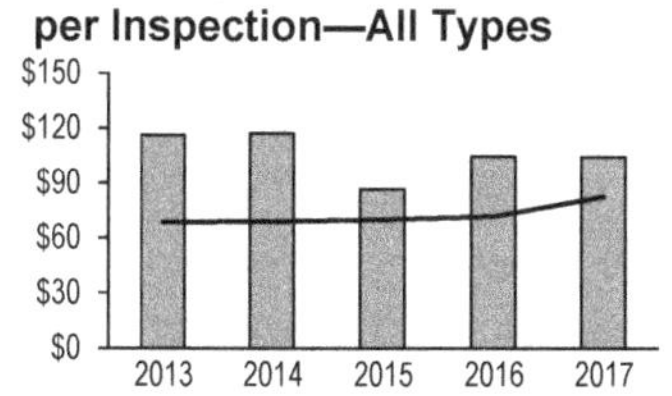

	2013	2014	2015	2016	2017
Wilson	$116.09	$117.19	$86.64	$104.80	$104.40
Average	$68.41	$68.71	$69.65	$71.57	$82.35

Inspections per Day per Inspector FTE

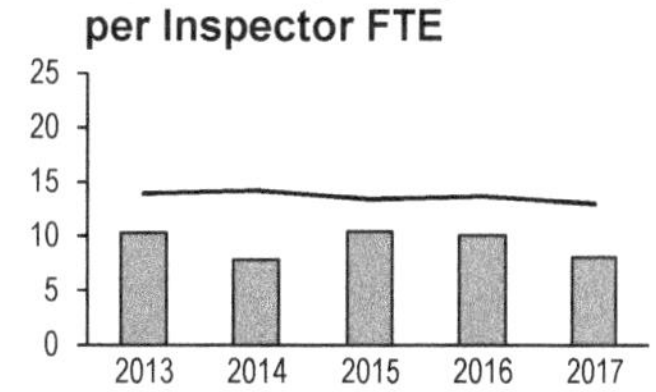

	2013	2014	2015	2016	2017
Wilson	10.3	7.8	10.4	10.0	8.1
Average	13.9	14.2	13.3	13.7	13.0

Plan Reviews per Year per Reviewer FTE

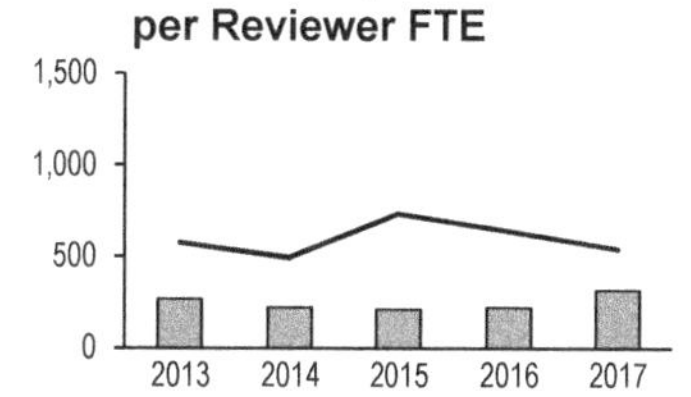

	2013	2014	2015	2016	2017
Wilson	265	221	211	222	313
Average	573	492	729	636	538

Effectiveness Measures

Percentage of Inspection Responses within One Working Day of Request

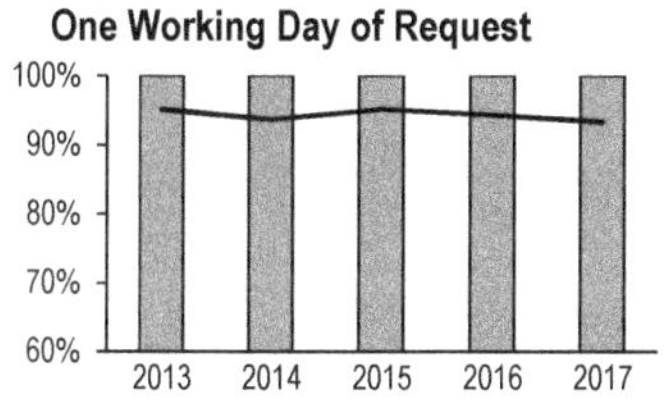

	2013	2014	2015	2016	2017
Wilson	100.0%	100.0%	100.0%	100.0%	100.0%
Average	95.1%	93.7%	95.1%	94.4%	93.4%

Percentage of Inspections That Are Reinspections

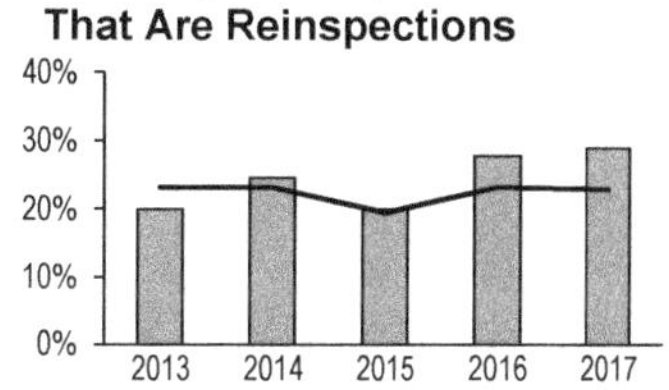

	2013	2014	2015	2016	2017
Wilson	19.9%	24.5%	19.9%	27.7%	28.8%
Average	23.1%	23.1%	19.4%	23.1%	22.8%

Fiscal Year 2016–17

Explanatory Information

Service Level and Delivery

The Inspections Division is a combined program for Winston-Salem and Forsyth County, providing building inspections services for all areas of the county, with the exception of the Town of Kernersville.

Inspectors are certified in one of the following four trades: building, electrical, mechanical, or plumbing. Inspectors drive to and from inspection sites in city-owned vehicles. Besides the North Carolina State Building Code, the Inspections Division enforces zoning codes and soil and sedimentation control regulations. Full-time equivalent positions and costs for these responsibilities are excluded from the project's figures for building inspections.

It is the policy of the Inspections Division to respond to inspection requests within one working day; 90 percent of the time it achieves this goal.

Total revenue received from inspection fees amounted to $4.05 million for the fiscal year. Inspection and permit fees depend on the type of construction or work, value of the construction, and other factors. An extra trip charge of $40 is assessed for each reinspection due to a second and subsequent failed inspection on each permit.

Conditions Affecting Service, Performance, and Costs

Municipal Profile

Population Served	344,826
Land Area Inspected (Square Miles)	396.00
Persons per Square Mile	871
Estimated Tax Base in Service Area (billions)	$30.22
Median Family Income U.S. Census 2010	$51,491

Service Profile

FTE Inspectors	
Building	4.0
Electrical	4.0
Mechanical	5.0
Plumbing	3.0
All Trades	0.0
Total Inspectors	16.0
FTE Plan Reviewers	4.0
Other FTE Positions	17.4
Total of All Positions	37.4
Number of Inspections by Type	
Building	16,944
Electrical	14,493
Mechanical	18,230
Plumbing	12,133
TOTAL	61,800
Building Permit Values	
Residential	$219,863,802
Multi-Family	with residential
Commercial	$303,558,718
TOTAL	$523,422,520
Inspection Fee Revenue	$4,051,110

Full Cost Profile

Cost Breakdown by Percentage	
Personal Services	63.0%
Operating Costs	31.5%
Capital Costs	5.5%
TOTAL	100.0%
Cost Breakdown in Dollars	
Personal Services	$2,502,739
Operating Costs	$1,251,134
Capital Costs	$220,504
TOTAL	$3,974,377

Winston-Salem — Building Inspections

Key: Winston-Salem ▒ Benchmarking Average — Fiscal Years 2013 through 2017

Resource Measures

Building Inspections Services Costs per Capita

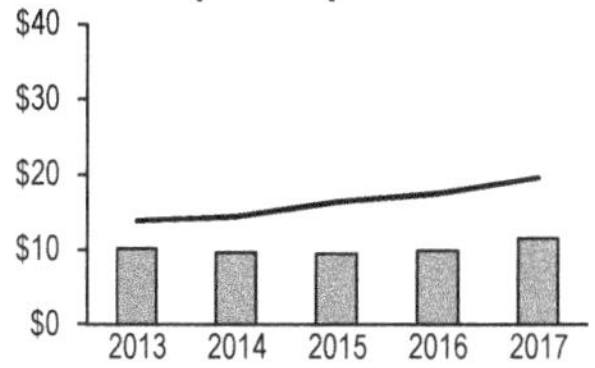

	2013	2014	2015	2016	2017
Winston-Salem	$10.20	$9.62	$9.52	$9.93	$11.53
Average	$13.80	$14.33	$16.31	$17.40	$19.55

Building Inspections Services FTEs per 10,000 Population

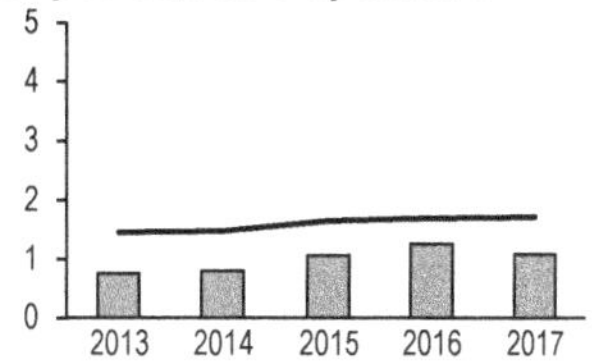

	2013	2014	2015	2016	2017
Winston-Salem	0.76	0.80	1.06	1.26	1.08
Average	1.46	1.48	1.66	1.70	1.72

Building Inspections Services Cost per Million Dollars of Tax Base

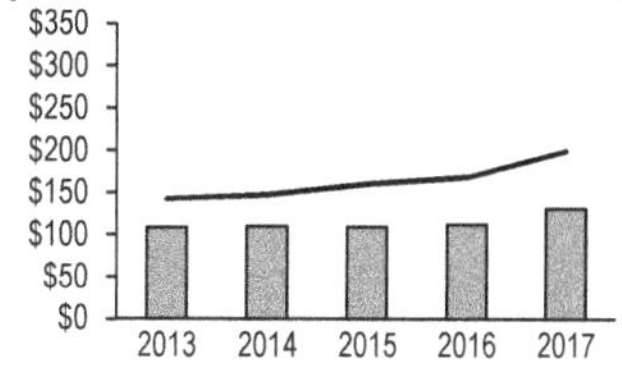

	2013	2014	2015	2016	2017
Winston-Salem	$109	$110	$109	$112	$131
Average	$143	$148	$161	$169	$200

Workload Measures

Inspections per 1,000 Population in Service Area

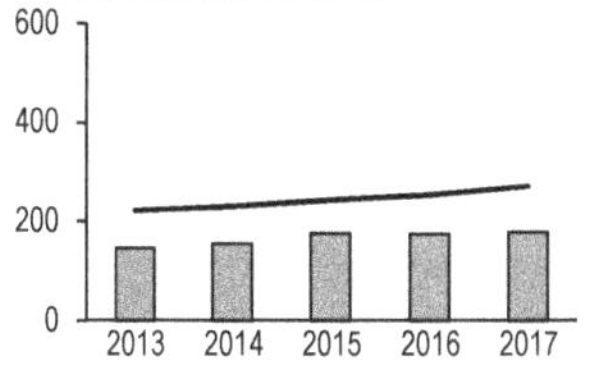

	2013	2014	2015	2016	2017
Winston-Salem	147	156	176	175	179
Average	221	229	243	253	270

Inspections per Square Mile in Service Area

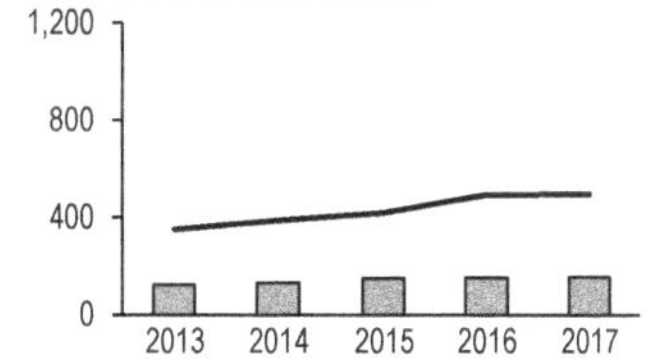

	2013	2014	2015	2016	2017
Winston-Salem	124	133	151	152	156
Average	353	389	421	495	497

Value of Building Permits as Percentage of Tax Base of Area Served

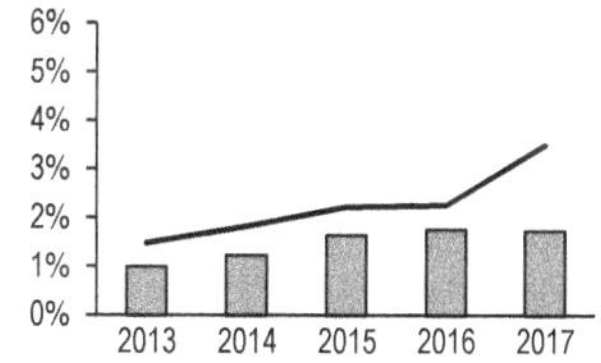

	2013	2014	2015	2016	2017
Winston-Salem	0.99%	1.24%	1.64%	1.77%	1.73%
Average	1.47%	1.82%	2.21%	2.25%	3.48%

Value of Commercial Permits as Percentage of Tax Base of Area Served

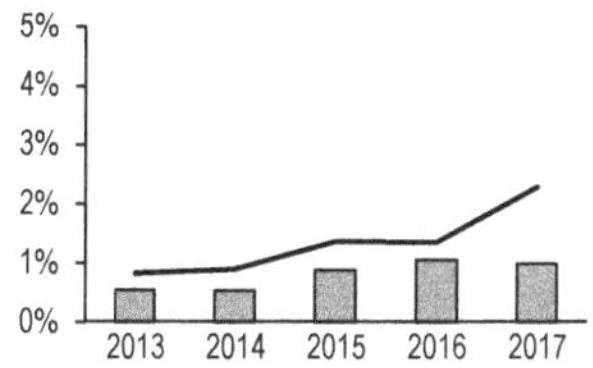

	2013	2014	2015	2016	2017
Winston-Salem	0.56%	0.56%	0.89%	1.06%	1.00%
Average	0.83%	0.89%	1.36%	1.35%	2.28%

Value of Building Permits per Inspector FTE in Millions of Dollars

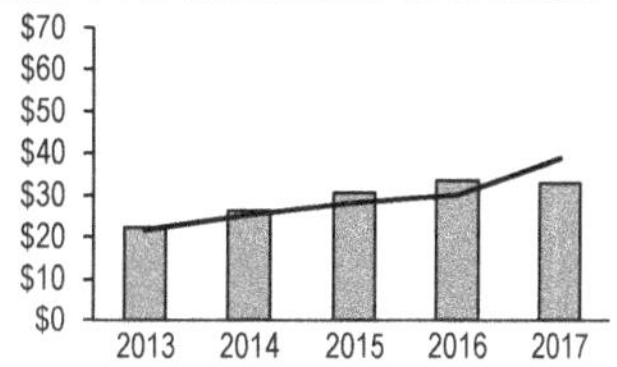

	2013	2014	2015	2016	2017
Winston-Salem	$22.2	$26.1	$30.5	$33.4	$32.7
Average	$21.5	$25.2	$28.0	$29.9	$38.7

Efficiency Measures

Building Services Cost per Inspection—All Types

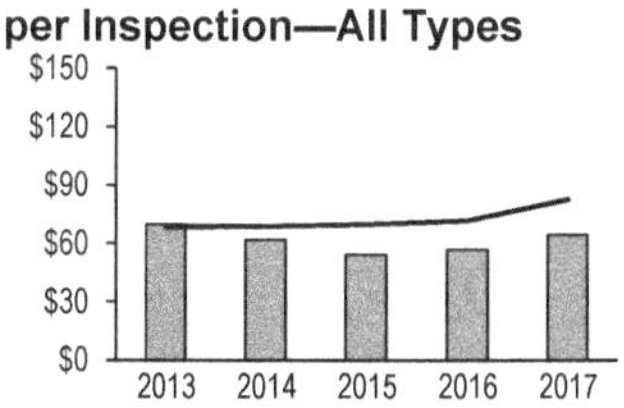

	2013	2014	2015	2016	2017
Winston-Salem	$69.57	$61.64	$54.09	$56.83	$64.31
Average	$68.41	$68.71	$69.65	$71.57	$82.35

Inspections per Day per Inspector FTE

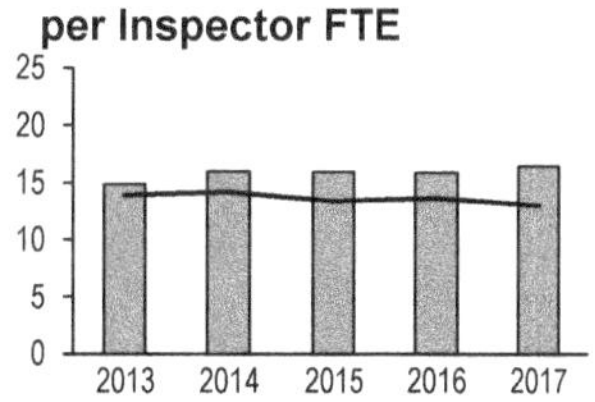

	2013	2014	2015	2016	2017
Winston-Salem	14.9	16.0	15.9	15.9	16.4
Average	13.9	14.2	13.3	13.7	13.0

Plan Reviews per Year per Reviewer FTE

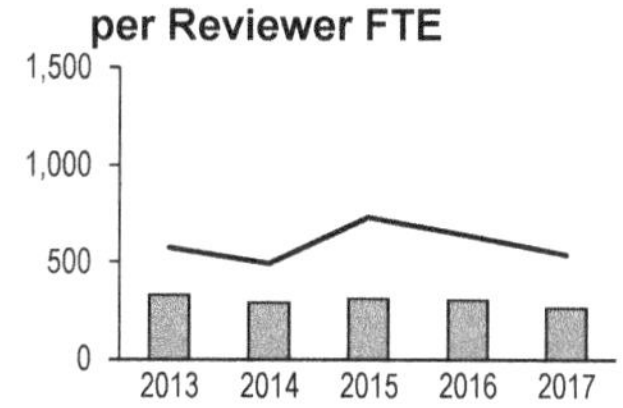

	2013	2014	2015	2016	2017
Winston-Salem	331	290	312	304	266
Average	573	492	729	636	538

Effectiveness Measures

Percentage of Inspection Responses within One Working Day of Request

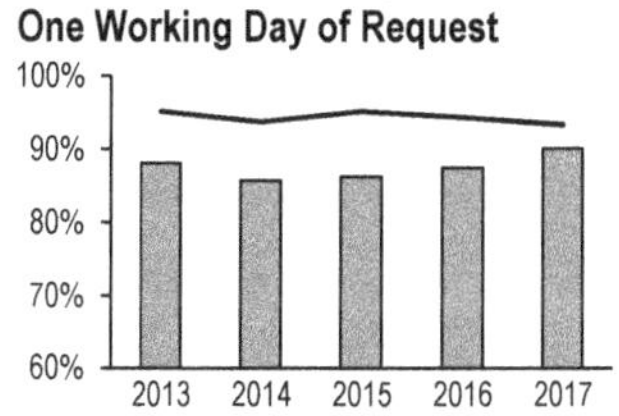

	2013	2014	2015	2016	2017
Winston-Salem	88.0%	85.7%	86.2%	87.4%	90.1%
Average	95.1%	93.7%	95.1%	94.4%	93.4%

Percentage of Inspections That Are Reinspections

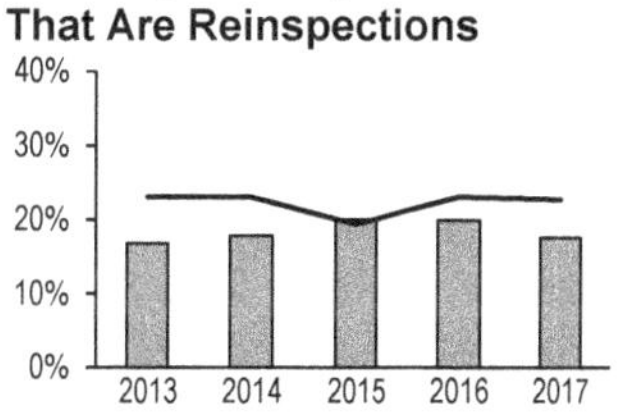

	2013	2014	2015	2016	2017
Winston-Salem	16.8%	17.9%	20.0%	20.0%	17.6%
Average	23.1%	23.1%	19.4%	23.1%	22.8%

SCHOOL OF GOVERNMENT
North Carolina Benchmarking Project

Performance and Cost Data

FLEET MAINTENANCE

UNC | SCHOOL OF GOVERNMENT
North Carolina Benchmarking Project

PERFORMANCE MEASURES FOR FLEET MAINTENANCE

SERVICE DEFINITION

Fleet maintenance represents the scheduled and unscheduled maintenance of rolling stock performed by the central garage and contractual work assigned by the central garage. This includes preventive, predictive, corrective, and breakdown maintenance. Excluded from this definition are rolling stock not maintained by the central garage and the broader activities of fleet services, such as rolling stock replacement and disposal, fuel station operation, and pool vehicle management.

NOTES ON PERFORMANCE MEASURES

1. Number of Vehicle Equivalent Units (VEUs) per Technician FTE

Vehicle Equivalent Units (VEUs) are a weighted measure of the maintenance effort associated with different classes of vehicles. A normal-use car is considered equal to one VEU. Vehicles such as fire trucks or police cars have higher VEUs, reflecting greater expected levels of maintenance effort. The number of VEUs in a municipality is determined by taking the number of rolling stock units in different classes of vehicles and multiplying them by a class weight for that category of vehicle. Vehicle categories include cars; light, medium, and heavy vehicles; trailed equipment; off-road/construction/tractor units; and buses. The number of full-time equivalent (FTE) positions for technicians is the number of employees directly involved in providing the maintenance services for the municipality's rolling stock as approved in the annual operating budget for the fiscal year.

2. Number of Preventive Maintenances Completed In-House per Technician FTE

The number of preventive maintenance jobs (PMs) completed in-house is the total number completed for the fiscal year ending June 30 that are done by the municipality's staff. The number of FTE positions for technicians is the same as defined above.

3. Cost per Work Order

This measure represents the total cost of fleet maintenance and is calculated using the full cost accounting model that captures direct, indirect, and capital costs. Work orders include the total number of work orders produced, including those related to contractual work, for the fiscal year ending June 30.

4. Cost per Vehicle Equivalent Unit (VEU)

This measure represents the total cost of fleet maintenance and is calculated using the full cost accounting model that captures direct, indirect, and capital costs. VEUs are calculated as defined above for the fiscal year ending June 30.

5. Hours Billed as a Percentage of Total Hours
The total number of billable hours includes all hours for technicians available for work during the fiscal year. Billable hours are calculated by multiplying 2,080 (hours in a normal working year) by the number of FTE positions for technicians as defined above. However, this number of FTEs is adjusted for vacancies. Hours billed represents actual hours billed during the fiscal year by the central garage to departments, divisions, and programs.

6. Preventive Maintenances (PMs) as a Percentage of All Work Orders
This measure is based on the total number of PMs (done in-house or by outside contractors) completed during the fiscal year divided by the total number of work orders (including contractual work) completed during the fiscal year for that jurisdiction.

7. Percentage of PMs Completed on Schedule
Based on the total number of PMs as defined above, this measure represents the percentage of PMs completed as scheduled as defined by the respective jurisdiction's standards.

8. Percentage of Work Orders Completed within Twenty-Four Hours
Based on the total number of work orders as defined above, this measure represents the percentage of work orders completed during the fiscal year within twenty-four hours of being received.

9. Percentage of Rolling Stock Available per Day
Based on the total number of rolling stock units as defined above, this measure represents the average percentage of rolling stock available for use per working day of the jurisdiction.

10. Percentage of Work Orders Requiring Repeat Repair within Thirty Days
Based on the total number of work orders as defined above, this measure represents the percentage of work orders (completed work on a unit of rolling stock) requiring repeat repair for the same problem within thirty days.

Fleet Maintenance

Summary of Key Dimensions of Service

City or Town	Number of Rolling Stock Maintained	Average Age of Rolling Stock (in Years)	Number of Work Orders	Number of Preventive Maintenances	Number of Work Bays	Authorized Technician FTEs	Labor Rate (per Hour)	Parts Inventory Turnover per Year	Fund Type
Apex	416	6.7	2,313	1,411	6	4.3	NA	4.0	General Fund
Asheville	883	7.2	5,256	1,428	16	9.0	$60.00	1.0	General Fund
Chapel Hill	422	7.1	2,187	1,128	8	5.5	$90.00	3.0	Internal Service
Charlotte	3,960	7.0	32,694	10,970	90	70.8	$75.00	4.7	General Fund
Concord	916	7.9	3,939	1,807	8	8.0	$60.00	14.2	General Fund
Goldsboro	360	11.8	3,819	1,020	11	8.0	$13.50	NA	General Fund
Greensboro	1,666	7.4	11,951	4,602	34	31.0	$52.00	2.6	Internal Service
Greenville	696	6.8	5,976	2,441	12	13.0	$60.00	2.2	Internal Service
Hickory	516	13.3	5,023	1,278	14	5.0	$56.00	6.0	Internal Service
High Point	1,018	4.2	4,644	2,193	18	10.0	$64.00	5.0	Internal Service
Raleigh	2,633	6.3	13,843	9,108	51	49.0	Heavy&Lead Mech - $65, Motor Mech - $55, Welder - $40, Auto Specialist - $40, Auto Tire-$40, PM Tech - $27	2.7	Internal Service
Salisbury	522	12.0	5,077	2,004	17	10.0	NA	2.0	General Fund
Wilson	822	11.2	7,413	1,555	15	11.0	$44.00	3.1	General Fund
Winston-Salem	1,883	8.8	8,403	7,159	31	18.0	$50.00	2.2	Internal Service

EXPLANATORY FACTORS

These are factors that the project found affected fleet maintenance performance and cost in one or more of the municipalities:

Number of vehicles maintained
Types of vehicles maintained
Fleet replacement plan
Average age of vehicles by type
Average miles driven for each type of vehicle
Preventive maintenance classification system
Preventive maintenance schedule

Fiscal Year 2016–17

Explanatory Information

Service Level and Delivery
Fleet Services is a division of the Facility and Fleet Services Department in the Town of Apex. The activities for this operation are accounted for in the general fund.

The town does not charge departments for labor but does track time technicians spend on work orders. There is no charge to departments for parts or sublet work. Parts inventory turned over approximately four times during the fiscal year.

The following services were contracted out:

- transmission repairs
- extended repair order work
- major engine repairs
- body work
- EMS ambulance body service work
- electric line truck repairs
- major hydraulic cylinder repairs
- fire truck pump repairs.

Conditions Affecting Service, Performance, and Costs
Vehicle Equivalent Units (VEUs) are a weighted measure of the maintenance effort associated with different classes of vehicles. A normal-use car is considered equal to one VEU. Vehicles such as fire trucks or police cars have higher VEUs, reflecting greater expected levels of maintenance.

The measure "hours billed as a percentage of total hours" is based on a work year of 2,080 hours and only counts those positions that were filled. It should be noted that technicians have responsibilities that do not result in billable hours and they take normal vacation and sick leave. Therefore this percentage should not be expected to be near 100 percent.

In Apex the preventive maintenance (PM) completion standard for "percentage of PMs completed as scheduled" is within thirty days of the scheduled date or within mileage parameters.

In addition to rolling stock, Apex's fleet services has maintenance responsibilities for other pieces of equipment, including asphalt rollers, whacker and roller tamps, portable generators, ballfield conditioners, various types of ATVs, weedeaters, lawnmowers, chainsaws, sump pumps, water pumps, snow plows, flail mowers, boat motors, light towers, and stump grinders.

The Apex Fleet Services supervisor provides technician support on an as needed basis.

Municipal Profile

Population (OSBM 2016)	46,688
Land Area (Square Miles)	20.61
Persons per Square Mile	2,265

Service Profile

FTE Positions—Technician		4.3
FTE Positions—Other		1.5
Work Bays		6
Rolling Stock Maintained	No.	Average Age
Cars—Normal Usage	12	6.0 Years
Cars—Severe Usage	83	4.0 Years
Motorcycles	2	6.0 Years
Light Utility Vehicles	5	5.0 Years
Light Vehicles	112	5.0 Years
Medium Vehicles	31	7.0 Years
Heavy—Sanitation	0	NA
Heavy—Sewer	3	4.5 Years
Heavy—Fire Apparatus	11	8.0 Years
Heavy—Other	22	7.0 Years
Trailed Equipment	80	10.0 Years
Off-Road/Construction/Tractors	55	9.0 Years
Buses	0	NA
TOTAL	416	
Vehicle Equivalent Units (VEUs)		1,189
Average Rolling Stock Units Available per Day		405
Hours Billed		7,696
Work Orders		2,313
Repeat Repairs within 30 Days		40
Work Orders Completed within 24 hours		1,850
Preventive Maintenance Jobs (PMs)		1,411
PMs Completed as Scheduled		1,411

Full Cost Profile

Cost Breakdown by Percentage	
Personal Services	43.4%
Operating Costs	49.8%
Capital Costs	6.8%
TOTAL	100.0%
Cost Breakdown in Dollars	
Personal Services	$413,361
Operating Costs	$473,627
Capital Costs	$64,730
TOTAL	$951,718

Key: Apex ▒ Benchmarking Average — Fiscal Years 2013 through 2017

Resource Measures

Fleet Maintenance Services Cost per Capita

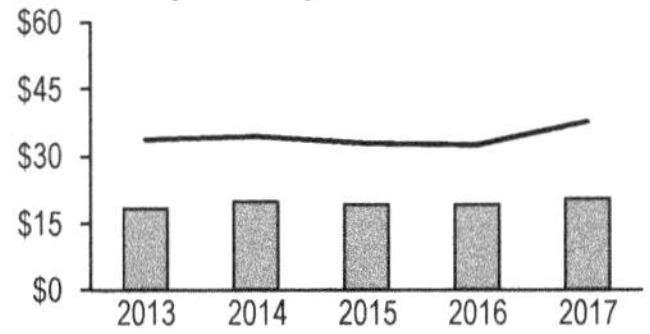

	2013	2014	2015	2016	2017
Apex	$18.13	$19.75	$19.12	$18.99	$20.38
Average	$33.64	$34.39	$32.91	$32.46	$37.72

Fleet Maintenance FTEs per 10,000 Population

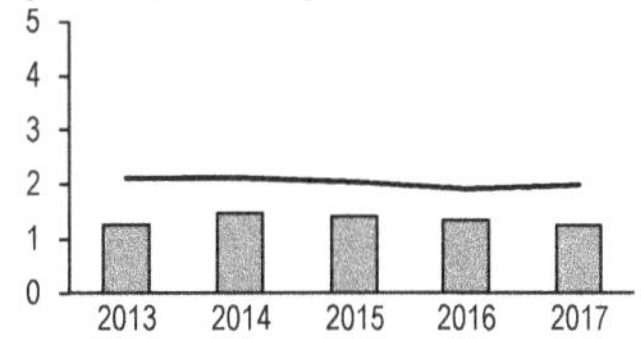

	2013	2014	2015	2016	2017
Apex	1.26	1.47	1.41	1.34	1.24
Average	2.11	2.12	2.05	1.92	1.99

Fleet Maintenance FTEs per 100 Municipal Employees

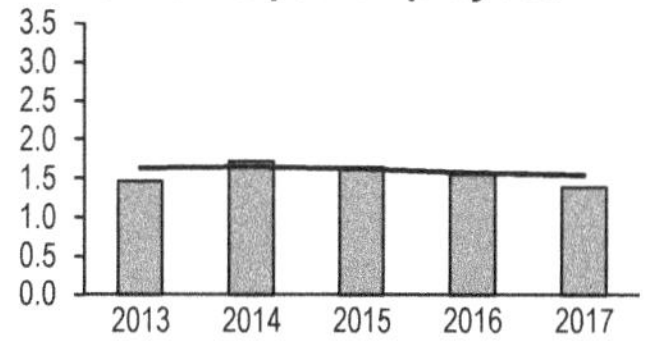

	2013	2014	2015	2016	2017
Apex	1.47	1.72	1.65	1.55	1.39
Average	1.64	1.66	1.63	1.58	1.55

Workload Measures

Number of Vehicle Equivalent Units (VEUs) per Technician FTE

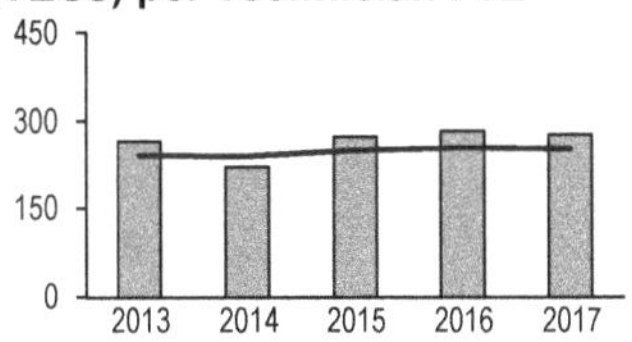

	2013	2014	2015	2016	2017
Apex	266	221	273	284	277
Average	240	239	249	252	251

Preventive Maintenances (PMs) Completed In-House per Tech FTE

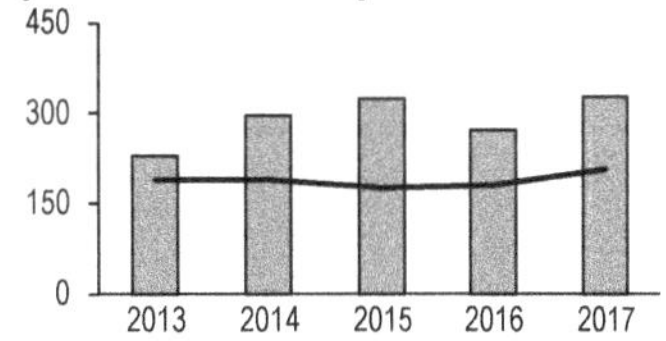

	2013	2014	2015	2016	2017
Apex	229	297	325	273	328
Average	189	189	175	179	206

Efficiency Measures

Fleet Maintenance Cost per Work Order

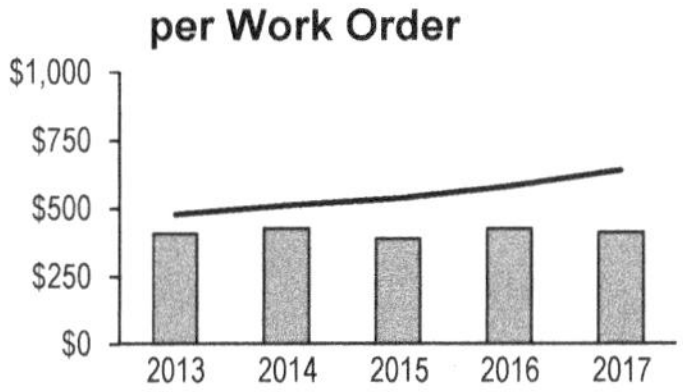

	2013	2014	2015	2016	2017
Apex	$405	$425	$388	$425	$411
Average	$477	$510	$535	$581	$639

Fleet Maintenance Cost per Vehicle Equivalent Unit (VEU)

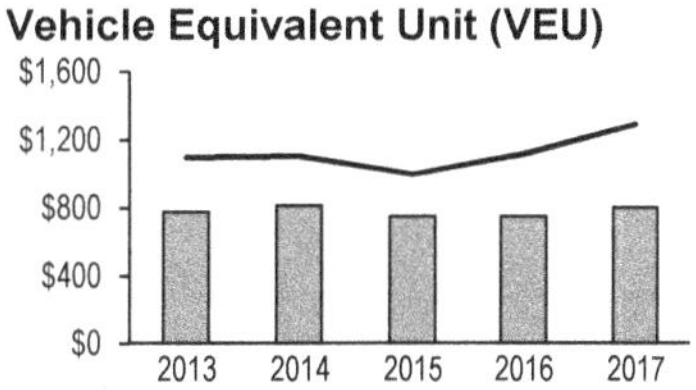

	2013	2014	2015	2016	2017
Apex	$775	$812	$747	$749	$800
Average	$1,096	$1,103	$994	$1,114	$1,289

Hours Billed as a Percentage of Total Hours

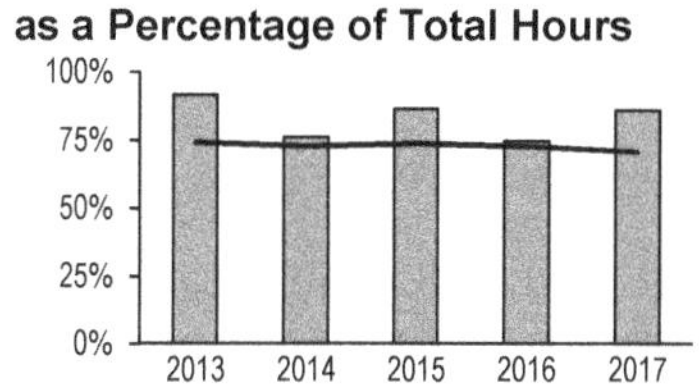

	2013	2014	2015	2016	2017
Apex	92%	76%	86%	74%	86%
Average	74%	73%	74%	73%	71%

Effectiveness Measures

Preventive Maintenances (PMs) as a Percentage of All Work Orders

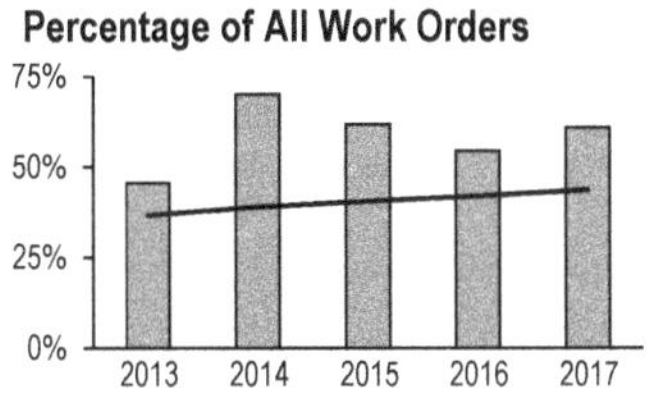

	2013	2014	2015	2016	2017
Apex	46%	70%	62%	54%	61%
Average	37%	39%	40%	42%	44%

Percentage of Preventive Maintenances (PMs) Completed as Scheduled

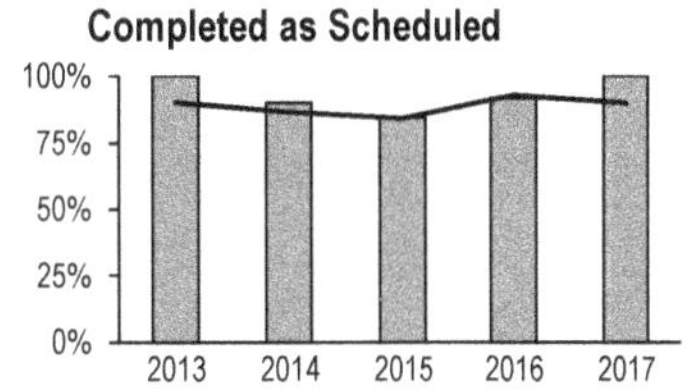

	2013	2014	2015	2016	2017
Apex	100%	90%	85%	92%	100%
Average	90%	87%	84%	93%	90%

Percentage of Work Orders Completed within 24 Hours

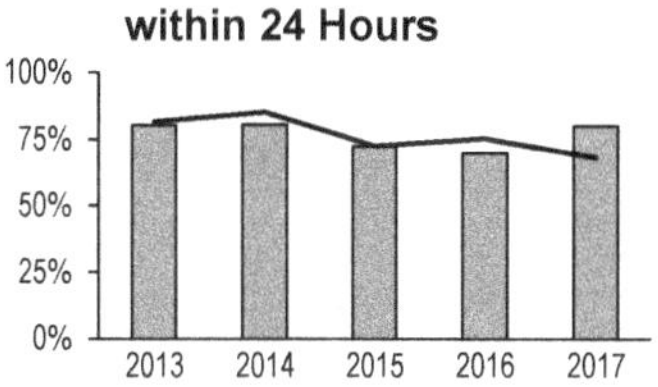

	2013	2014	2015	2016	2017
Apex	80%	81%	72%	70%	80%
Average	81%	85%	72%	75%	68%

Percentage of Rolling Stock Available per Day

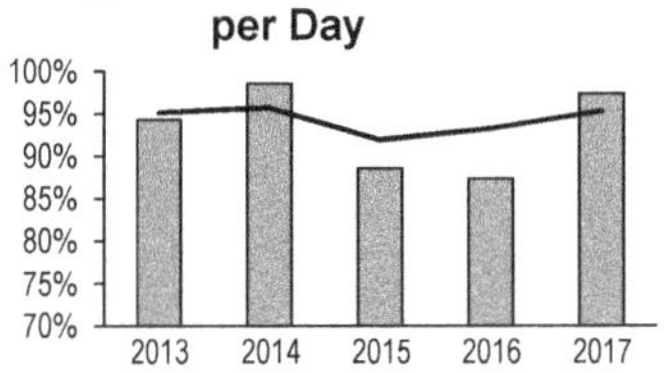

	2013	2014	2015	2016	2017
Apex	94%	99%	89%	87%	97%
Average	95%	96%	92%	93%	95%

Percentage of Work Orders Requiring Repeat Repair within 30 Days

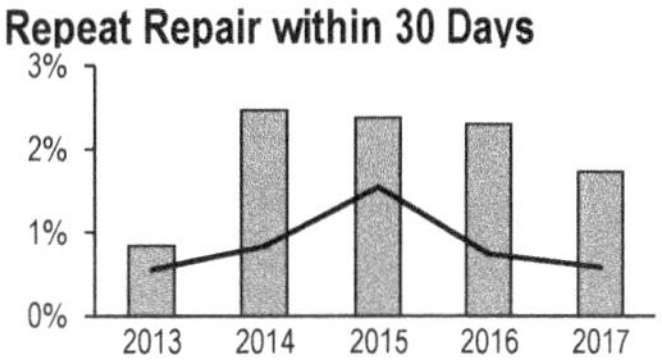

	2013	2014	2015	2016	2017
Apex	0.84%	2.47%	2.38%	2.30%	1.73%
Average	0.55%	0.83%	1.54%	0.74%	0.58%

Fiscal Year 2016–17

Explanatory Information

Service Level and Delivery
Fleet Management is a division of the Asheville General Services Department, consisting of the fleet maintenance garage and a fueling station. The activities for this operation are accounted for in the general fund.

Charges for maintenance services are charged at a $60-an-hour labor rate, a 30 percent markup on parts stocked, a 5 percent markup on parts immediately installed, and a 5 percent markup on sublet work.

The following services were contracted out:

- major automatic and manual transmission repairs
- front-end alignments
- major emergency generator repairs
- aerial inspections
- paint and body repairs
- tire repairs on trucks over one ton
- major hydraulic cylinder repairs.

Conditions Affecting Service, Performance, and Costs
Vehicle Equivalent Units (VEUs) are a weighted measure of the maintenance effort associated with different classes of vehicles. A normal-use car is considered equal to one VEU. Vehicles such as fire trucks or police cars have higher VEUs, reflecting greater expected levels of maintenance.

The measure "hours billed as a percentage of total hours" is based on a work year of 2,080 hours and only counts those positions that were filled. It should be noted that technicians have responsibilities that do not result in billable hours and they take normal vacation, sick leave, and time for training. Therefore this percentage should not be expected to be near 100 percent.

In addition to rolling stock, Asheville's fleet services has maintenance responsibilities for other pieces of equipment, including snow plows, sand spreaders, a curb builder, and other city equipment.

Municipal Profile

Population (OSBM 2016)	91,929
Land Area (Square Miles)	45.52
Persons per Square Mile	2,019

Service Profile

FTE Positions—Technician	9.0
FTE Positions—Other	7.0
Work Bays	16

Rolling Stock Maintained	No.	Average Age
Cars—Normal Usage	67	6.0 Years
Cars—Severe Usage	268	4.9 Years
Motorcycles	4	3.5 Years
Light Utility Vehicles	13	9.2 Years
Light Vehicles	148	6.3 Years
Medium Vehicles	80	8.3 Years
Heavy—Sanitation	22	5.0 Years
Heavy—Sewer	3	8.2 Years
Heavy—Fire Apparatus	27	15.7 Years
Heavy—Other	29	7.6 Years
Trailed Equipment	117	10.4 Years
Off-Road/Construction/Tractors	79	9.7 Years
Buses	26	5.6 Years
TOTAL	883	

Vehicle Equivalent Units (VEUs)	2,966
Average Rolling Stock Units Available per Day	862
Hours Billed	8,537
Work Orders	5,256
Repeat Repairs within 30 Days	73
Work Orders Completed within 24 hours	134
Preventive Maintenance Jobs (PMs)	1,428
PMs Completed as Scheduled	NA

Full Cost Profile

Cost Breakdown by Percentage	
Personal Services	29.9%
Operating Costs	65.7%
Capital Costs	4.4%
TOTAL	100.0%

Cost Breakdown in Dollars	
Personal Services	$908,638
Operating Costs	$1,999,651
Capital Costs	$133,531
TOTAL	$3,041,819

Asheville — Fleet Maintenance

Key: Asheville ▒ Benchmarking Average — Fiscal Years 2013 through 2017

Resource Measures

Fleet Maintenance Services Cost per Capita

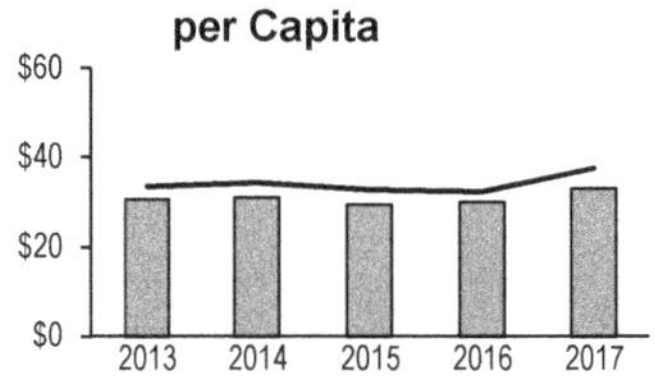

	2013	2014	2015	2016	2017
Asheville	$30.74	$31.07	$29.57	$30.14	$33.09
Average	$33.64	$34.39	$32.91	$32.46	$37.72

Fleet Maintenance FTEs per 10,000 Population

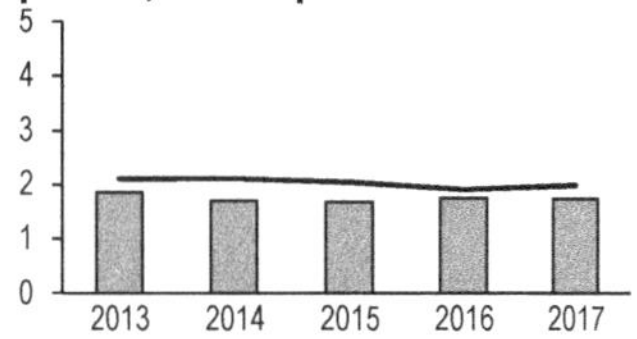

	2013	2014	2015	2016	2017
Asheville	1.86	1.70	1.68	1.76	1.74
Average	2.11	2.12	2.05	1.92	1.99

Fleet Maintenance FTEs per 100 Municipal Employees

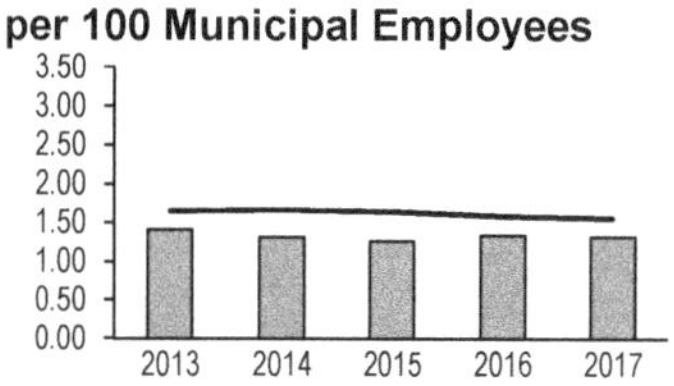

	2013	2014	2015	2016	2017
Asheville	1.41	1.31	1.26	1.33	1.32
Average	1.64	1.66	1.63	1.58	1.55

Workload Measures

Number of Vehicle Equivalent Units (VEUs) per Technician FTE

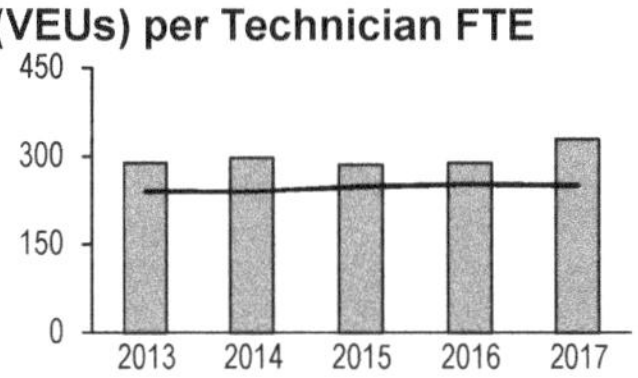

	2013	2014	2015	2016	2017
Asheville	289	298	287	290	330
Average	240	239	249	252	251

Preventive Maintenances (PMs) Completed In-House per Tech FTE

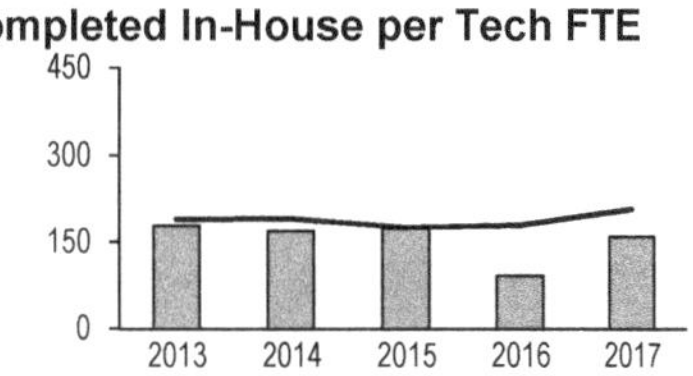

	2013	2014	2015	2016	2017
Asheville	177	168	173	92	159
Average	189	189	175	179	206

Efficiency Measures

Fleet Maintenance Cost per Work Order

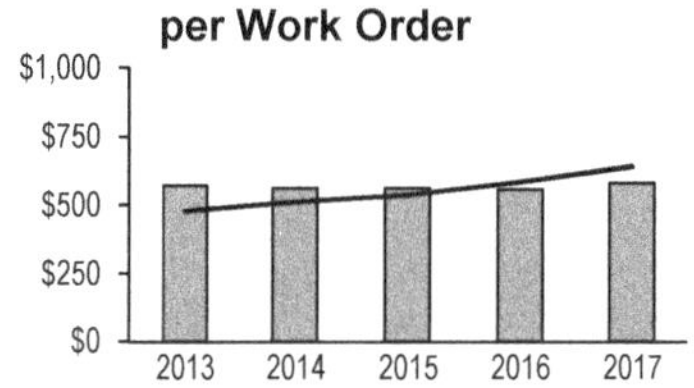

	2013	2014	2015	2016	2017
Asheville	$571	$560	$560	$555	$579
Average	$477	$510	$535	$581	$639

Fleet Maintenance Cost per Vehicle Equivalent Unit (VEU)

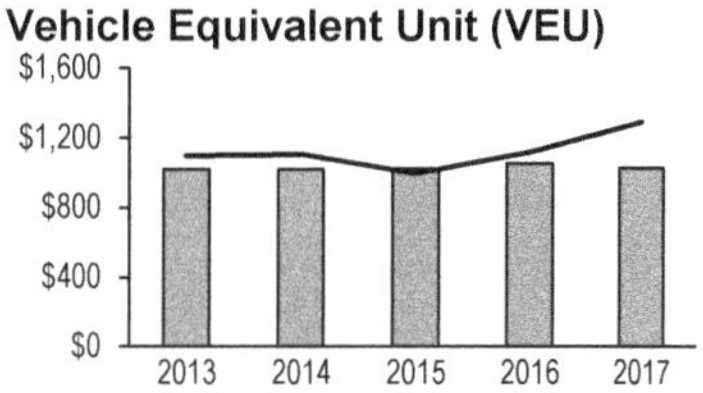

	2013	2014	2015	2016	2017
Asheville	$1,019	$1,018	$1,023	$1,051	$1,026
Average	$1,096	$1,103	$994	$1,114	$1,289

Hours Billed as a Percentage of Total Hours

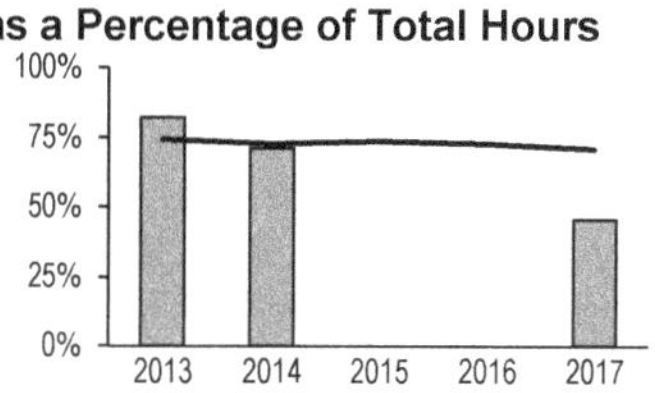

	2013	2014	2015	2016	2017
Asheville	82%	71%			46%
Average	74%	73%	74%	73%	71%

Effectiveness Measures

Preventive Maintenances (PMs) as a Percentage of All Work Orders

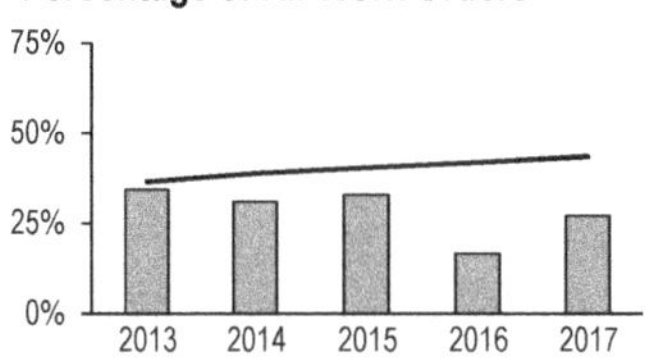

	2013	2014	2015	2016	2017
Asheville	34%	31%	33%	17%	27%
Average	37%	39%	40%	42%	44%

Percentage of Preventive Maintenances (PMs) Completed as Scheduled

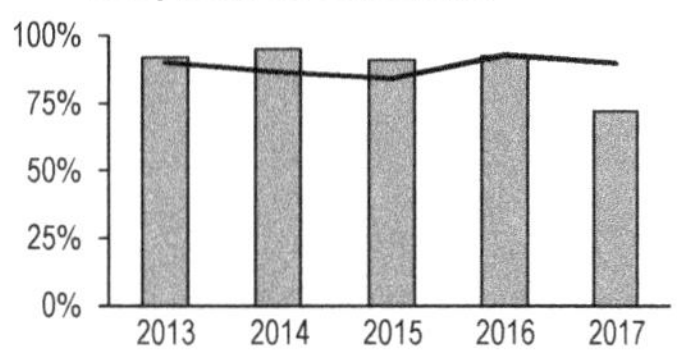

	2013	2014	2015	2016	2017
Asheville	92%	95%	91%	92%	72%
Average	90%	87%	84%	93%	90%

Percentage of Work Orders Completed within 24 Hours

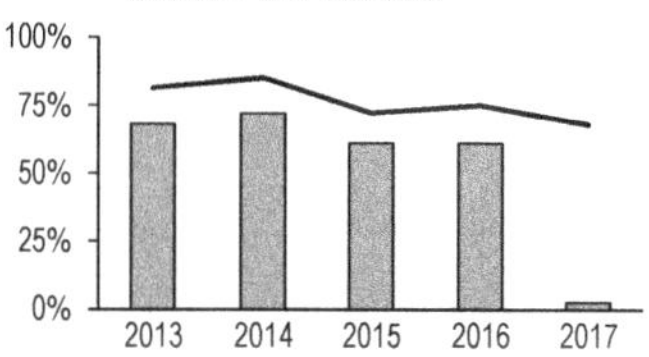

	2013	2014	2015	2016	2017
Asheville	68%	72%	61%	61%	3%
Average	81%	85%	72%	75%	68%

Percentage of Rolling Stock Available per Day

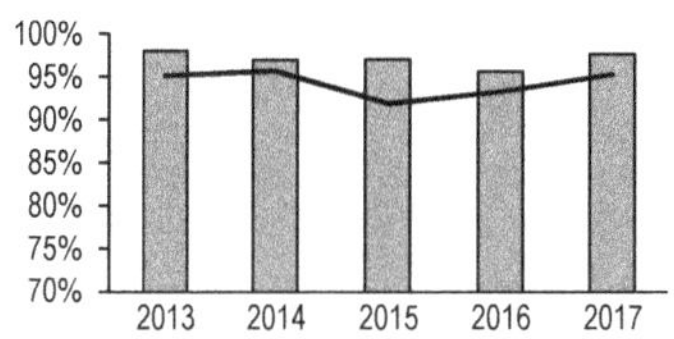

	2013	2014	2015	2016	2017
Asheville	98%	97%	97%	96%	98%
Average	95%	96%	92%	93%	95%

Percentage of Work Orders Requiring Repeat Repair within 30 Days

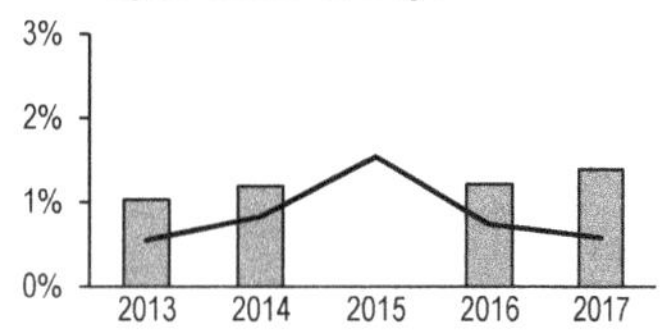

	2013	2014	2015	2016	2017
Asheville	1.03%	1.19%		1.22%	1.39%
Average	0.55%	0.83%	1.54%	0.74%	0.58%

Fiscal Year 2016–17

Explanatory Information

Service Level and Delivery
The Town of Chapel Hill provides fleet maintenance through the Fleet Management Program in the Public Works Department Administration Division. The program is operated as an internal service fund charging departments for services.

A labor rate of $90 per hour is charged for maintenance work. Additionally, a parts markup of 20 percent is applied to the cost of parts and a 10 percent markup is charged for overseeing sublet work.

The town contracted out some maintenance services during the fiscal year, including towing, body work, lift truck inspections, and parts inventory. The overall turnover in parts was estimated at three times per year.

Conditions Affecting Service, Performance, and Costs
The Town of Chapel Hill began participation in the benchmarking project in July 2015, with FY 2014–15 being the first reporting year.

Chapel Hill improved its tracking of repeat repairs to more closely follow the benchmarking directions of repairs to the same component as opposed to repairs to address the same complaint.

Vehicle Equivalent Units (VEUs) are a weighted measure of the maintenance effort associated with different classes of vehicles. A normal-use car is considered equal to one VEU. Vehicles such as fire trucks or police cars have higher VEUs, reflecting greater expected levels of maintenance.

The measure "hours billed as a percentage of total hours" is based on a work year of 2,080 hours and only counts those positions that were filled. It should be noted that technicians have responsibilities that do not result in billable hours and they take normal vacation and sick leave. Therefore, this percentage should not be expected to be near 100 percent. There was a large degree of turnover in the shop during the prior year with a full complement only reached at the start of FY 2015–16.

In Chapel Hill the preventive maintenance (PM) completion standard for "percentage of PMs completed as scheduled" includes varying standards depending on the work but must occur within thirty days of the scheduled date, within the scheduled month, or within mileage parameters.

In addition to rolling stock, Chapel Hill's fleet services had maintenance responsibilities for generators, light towers, mowers, weed wackers, leaf blowers, leaf vacuum machines, and sign towers.

Municipal Profile

Population (OSBM 2016)	59,852
Land Area (Square Miles)	21.21
Persons per Square Mile	2,822

Service Profile

FTE Positions—Technician	5.50
FTE Positions—Other	2.25
Work Bays	8

Rolling Stock Maintained	No.	Average Age
Cars—Normal Usage	123	6.0 Years
Cars—Severe Usage	64	5.5 Years
Motorcycles	0	NA
Light Utility Vehicles	5	7.8 Years
Light Vehicles	26	6.2 Years
Medium Vehicles	84	6.8 Years
Heavy—Sanitation	24	6.4 Years
Heavy—Sewer	1	8.4 Years
Heavy—Fire Apparatus	13	9.4 Years
Heavy—Other	21	7.2 Years
Trailed Equipment	37	11.7 Years
Off-Road/Construction/Tractors	24	11.5 Years
Buses	0	NA
TOTAL	422	

Vehicle Equivalent Units (VEUs)	1,525
Average Rolling Stock Units Available per Day	383
Hours Billed	9,724
Work Orders	2,187
Repeat Repairs within 30 Days	17
Work Orders Completed within 24 hours	1,905
Preventive Maintenance Jobs (PMs)	1,128
PMs Completed as Scheduled	1,038

Full Cost Profile

Cost Breakdown by Percentage	
Personal Services	31.6%
Operating Costs	55.2%
Capital Costs	13.2%
TOTAL	100.0%

Cost Breakdown in Dollars	
Personal Services	$567,811
Operating Costs	$993,017
Capital Costs	$236,904
TOTAL	$1,797,732

Key: Chapel Hill ▒ Benchmarking Average — Fiscal Years 2013 through 2017

Resource Measures

Fleet Maintenance Services Cost per Capita

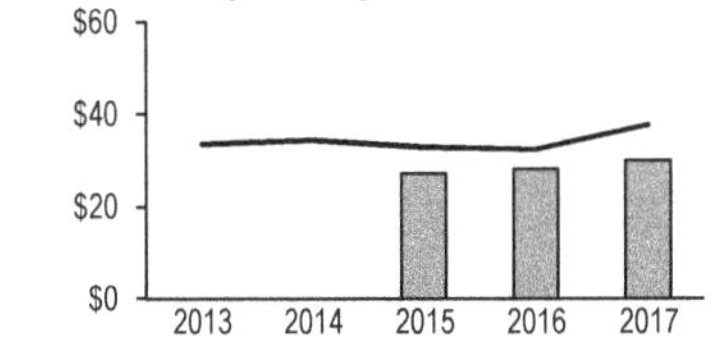

	2013	2014	2015	2016	2017
Chapel Hill			$27.20	$28.25	$30.04
Average	$33.64	$34.39	$32.91	$32.46	$37.72

Fleet Maintenance FTEs per 10,000 Population

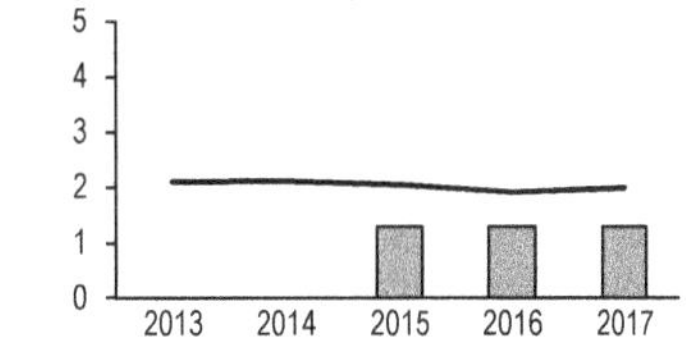

	2013	2014	2015	2016	2017
Chapel Hill			1.30	1.30	1.29
Average	2.11	2.12	2.05	1.92	1.99

Fleet Maintenance FTEs per 100 Municipal Employees

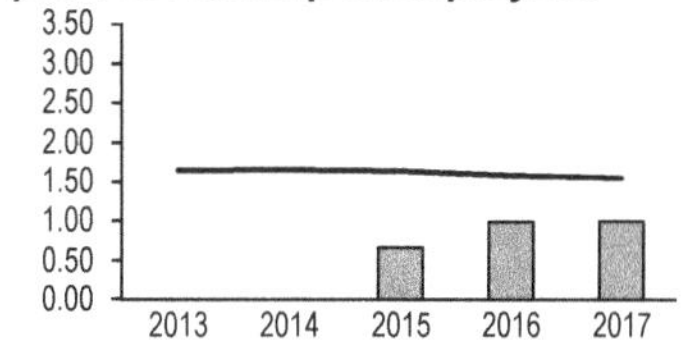

	2013	2014	2015	2016	2017
Chapel Hill			0.67	0.99	1.00
Average	1.64	1.66	1.63	1.58	1.55

Workload Measures

Number of Vehicle Equivalent Units (VEUs) per Technician FTE

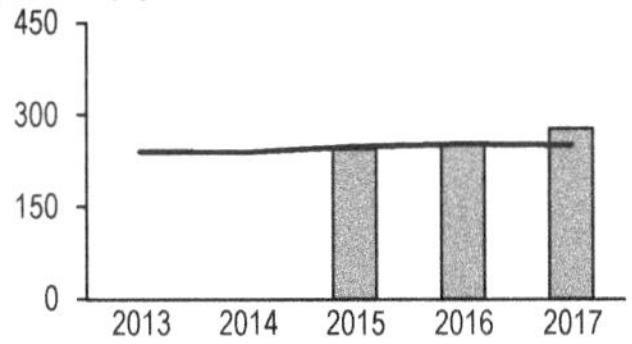

	2013	2014	2015	2016	2017
Chapel Hill			243	252	277
Average	240	239	249	252	251

Preventive Maintenances (PMs) Completed In-House per Tech FTE

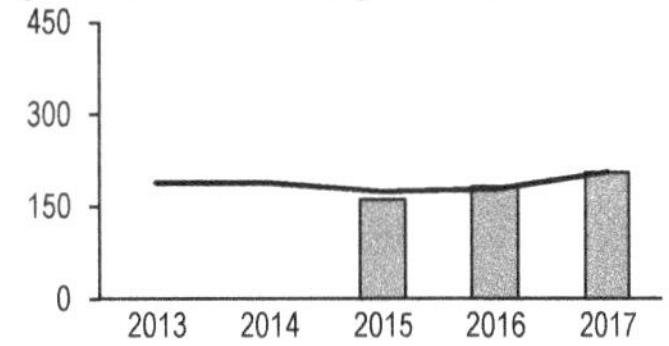

	2013	2014	2015	2016	2017
Chapel Hill			160	182	205
Average	189	189	175	179	206

Efficiency Measures

Fleet Maintenance Cost per Work Order

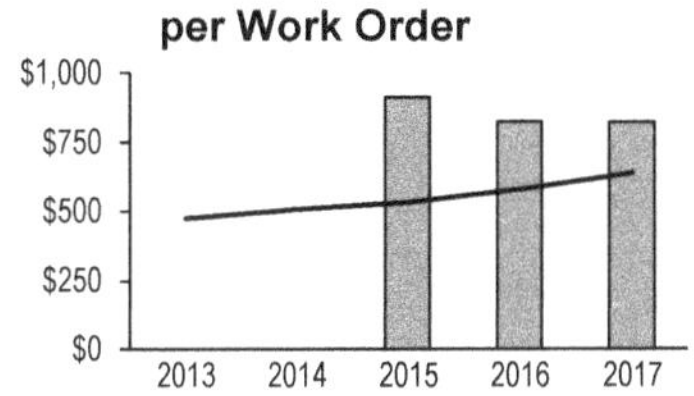

	2013	2014	2015	2016	2017
Chapel Hill			$911	$824	$822
Average	$477	$510	$535	$581	$639

Fleet Maintenance Cost per Vehicle Equivalent Unit (VEU)

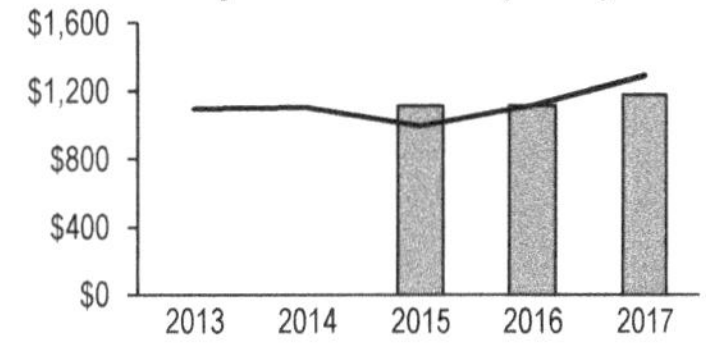

	2013	2014	2015	2016	2017
Chapel Hill			$1,113	$1,114	$1,179
Average	$1,096	$1,103	$994	$1,114	$1,289

Hours Billed as a Percentage of Total Hours

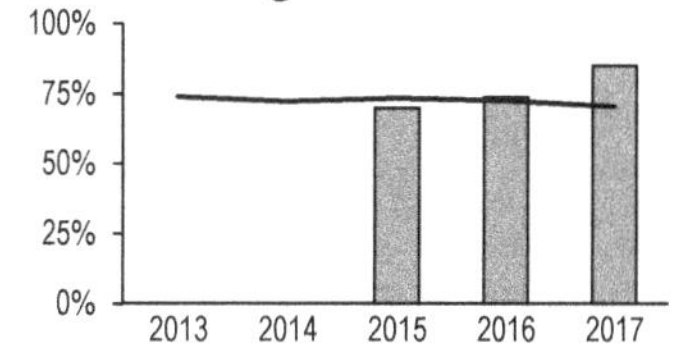

	2013	2014	2015	2016	2017
Chapel Hill			70%	74%	85%
Average	74%	73%	74%	73%	71%

Effectiveness Measures

Preventive Maintenances (PMs) as a Percentage of All Work Orders

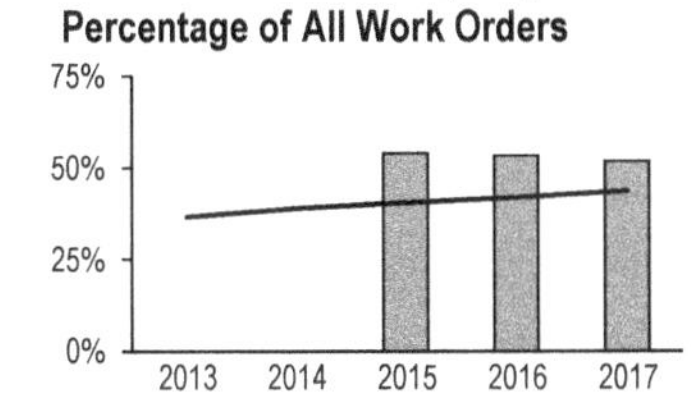

	2013	2014	2015	2016	2017
Chapel Hill			54%	53%	52%
Average	37%	39%	40%	42%	44%

Percentage of Preventive Maintenances (PMs) Completed as Scheduled

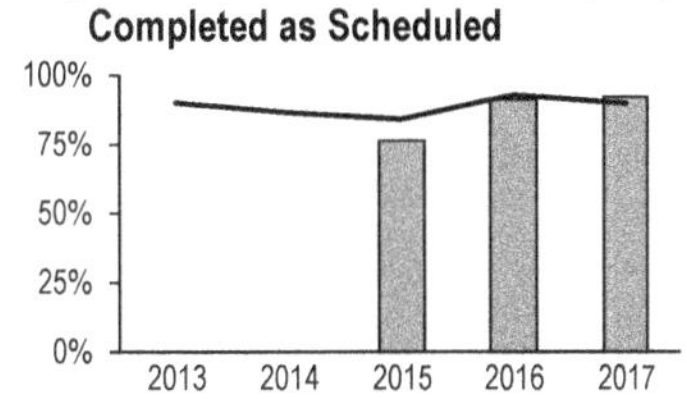

	2013	2014	2015	2016	2017
Chapel Hill			76%	91%	92%
Average	90%	87%	84%	93%	90%

Percentage of Work Orders Completed within 24 Hours

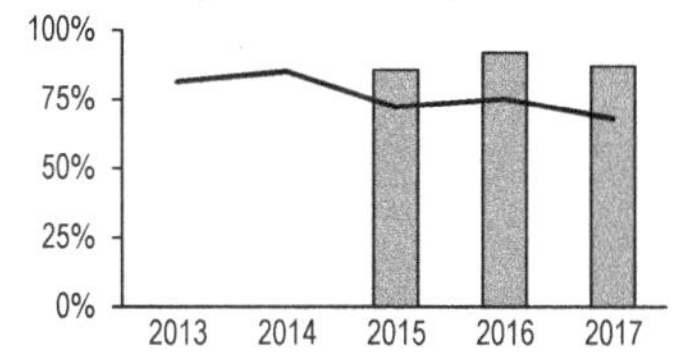

	2013	2014	2015	2016	2017
Chapel Hill			86%	92%	87%
Average	81%	85%	72%	75%	68%

Percentage of Rolling Stock Available per Day

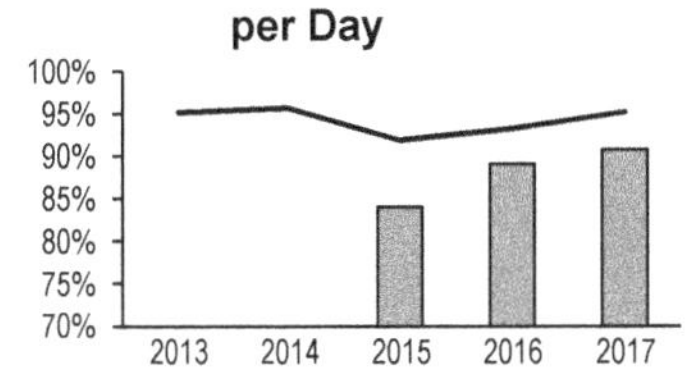

	2013	2014	2015	2016	2017
Chapel Hill			84%	89%	91%
Average	95%	96%	92%	93%	95%

Percentage of Work Orders Requiring Repeat Repair within 30 Days

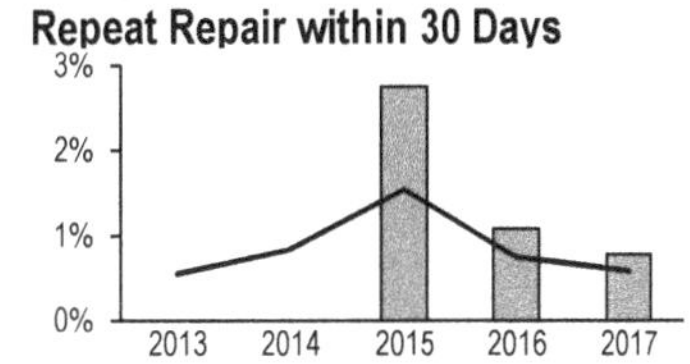

	2013	2014	2015	2016	2017
Chapel Hill			2.75%	1.08%	0.78%
Average	0.55%	0.83%	1.54%	0.74%	0.58%

Fiscal Year 2016–17

Explanatory Information

Service Level and Delivery

The City of Charlotte and the County of Mecklenburg merged fleet maintenance services under a city-operated program beginning July 1, 2009. The data reported here are inclusive of both fleets. The services are provided by Charlotte's Equipment Management Division, which is part of Business Support Services. All activities for this operation are accounted for in the general fund. The Equipment Management Division currently charges an administrative fee per unit to compensate for the overhead of administrative staff, including tags and title work, specification writing, and fleet analysis.

Charges for maintenance services included a $75-per-hour labor rate, a 17.6 percent markup charge on parts sold, and an 18.4 percent markup charge on sublet work. Part caps are negotiated individually, based on very special and specific needs. All sublet transactions are subject to a $500 cap.

The following services were contracted out during the year: accident repair, body work, spring repairs, front-end alignment, glass replacement, fuel system repair, engine overhauls, transmission overhauls, towing, some tire service, police car preparation, heavy tire replacement and repair, some light-vehicle preventive maintenance, painting/graphic installation, and radio/computer installation or removal.

Conditions Affecting Service, Performance, and Costs

Charlotte did not participate in the Benchmarking Project during FY 2014–15. No data are available for that year.

Vehicle Equivalent Units (VEUs) are a weighted measure of the maintenance effort associated with different classes of vehicles. A normal-use car is considered equal to one VEU.

The measure "hours billed as a percentage of total hours" is based on a work year of 2,080 hours and only counts those positions that were filled. Technicians have responsibilities that do not result in billable hours and they take normal vacation and sick leave. Therefore this percentage should not be expected to be near 100 percent.

In Charlotte the preventive maintenance (PM) completion standard for "percentage of PMs completed as scheduled" is within thirty days of the scheduled date and mileage parameters.

The city provides motorpool services. These include reservations, tracking, cleaning, parking, and check-in.

In addition to rolling stock, Charlotte's fleet services had maintenance responsibilities for generators, mowers, weedwhackers, compressors, saws, blowers, fans, asphalt-tar/kettles, edgers, snow plows, spreaders, tamps, mixers, chippers, posthole diggers, grinders, pressure washers, and other city equipment.

The measure Fleet personnel per 100 municipal employees includes county employees due to the joint operations of Fleet.

Municipal Profile

Population (OSBM 2016)	830,258
Land Area (Square Miles)	305.48
Persons per Square Mile	2,718

Service Profile

FTE Positions—Technician	70.75
FTE Positions—Other	48.3
Work Bays	90

Rolling Stock Maintained	No.	Average Age
Cars—Normal Usage	438	6.0 Years
Cars—Severe Usage	791	3.3 Years
Motorcycles	79	4.3 Years
Light Utility Vehicles	79	5.5 Years
Light Vehicles	1,292	6.3 Years
Medium Vehicles	138	10.0 Years
Heavy—Sanitation	151	5.5 Years
Heavy—Sewer	32	6.9 Years
Heavy—Fire Apparatus	102	8.0 Years
Heavy—Other	134	8.9 Years
Trailed Equipment	368	11.9 Years
Off-Road/Construction/Tractors	354	13.2 Years
Buses	2	9.3 Years
TOTAL	3,960	

Vehicle Equivalent Units (VEUs)	12,460
Average Rolling Stock Units Available per Day	3,281
Hours Billed	139,360
Work Orders	32,694
Repeat Repairs within 30 Days	5
Work Orders Completed within 24 hours	17,223
Preventive Maintenance Jobs (PMs)	10,970
PMs Completed as Scheduled	NA

Full Cost Profile

Cost Breakdown by Percentage	
Personal Services	39.1%
Operating Costs	59.3%
Capital Costs	1.6%
TOTAL	100.0%

Cost Breakdown in Dollars	
Personal Services	$8,854,783
Operating Costs	$13,405,461
Capital Costs	$362,742
TOTAL	$22,622,986

Key: Charlotte ▒ Benchmarking Average — Fiscal Years 2013 through 2017

Resource Measures

Fleet Maintenance Services Cost per Capita

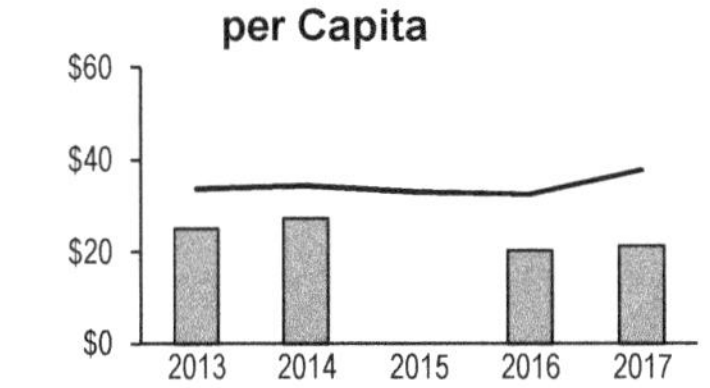

	2013	2014	2015	2016	2017
Charlotte	$25.20	$27.44		$20.51	$21.47
Average	$33.64	$34.39	$32.91	$32.46	$37.72

Fleet Maintenance FTEs per 10,000 Population

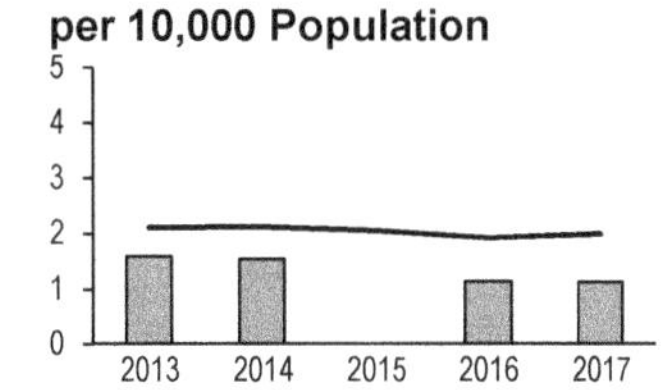

	2013	2014	2015	2016	2017
Charlotte	1.59	1.55		1.14	1.13
Average	2.11	2.12	2.05	1.92	1.99

Fleet Maintenance FTEs per 100 Municipal Employees

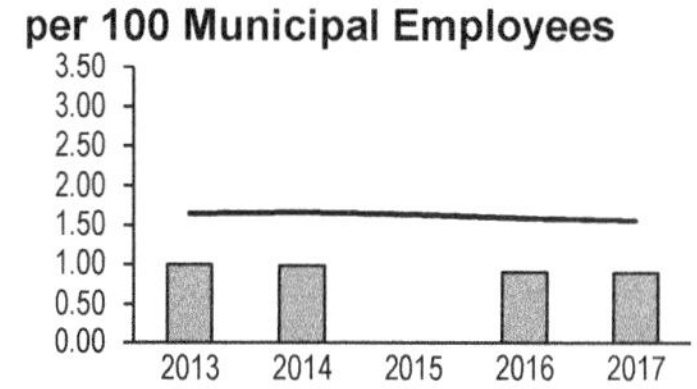

	2013	2014	2015	2016	2017
Charlotte	1.00	0.99		0.90	0.90
Average	1.64	1.66	1.63	1.58	1.55

Charlotte includes county employees too.

Workload Measures

Number of Vehicle Equivalent Units (VEUs) per Technician FTE

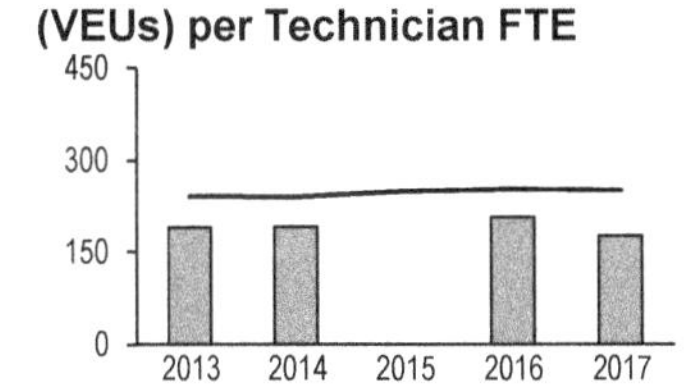

	2013	2014	2015	2016	2017
Charlotte	190	191		206	176
Average	240	239	249	252	251

Preventive Maintenances (PMs) Completed In-House per Tech FTE

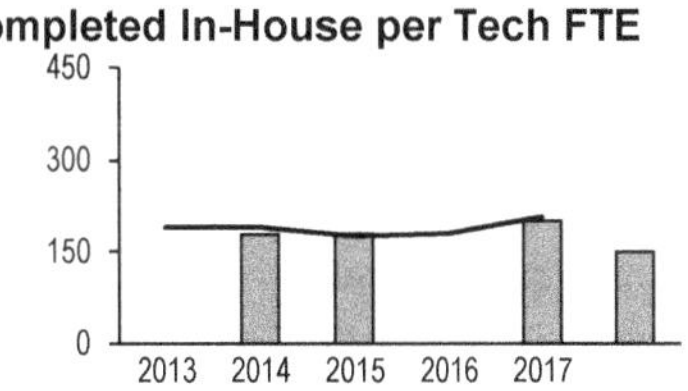

	2013	2014	2015	2016	2017	
Charlotte		178	179		200	150
Average	189	189	175	179	206	

Efficiency Measures

Fleet Maintenance Cost per Work Order

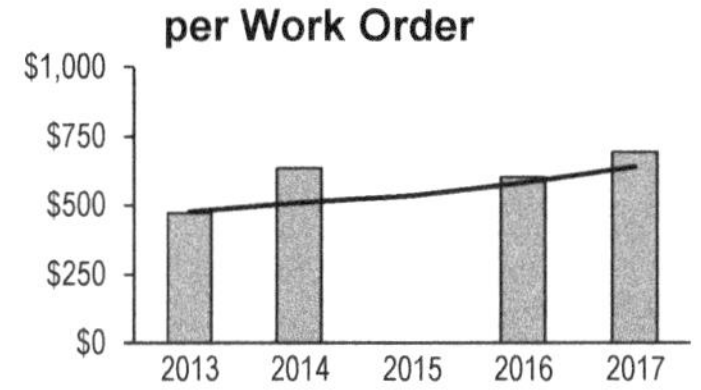

	2013	2014	2015	2016	2017
Charlotte	$471	$633		$601	$692
Average	$477	$510	$535	$581	$639

Fleet Maintenance Cost per Vehicle Equivalent Unit (VEU)

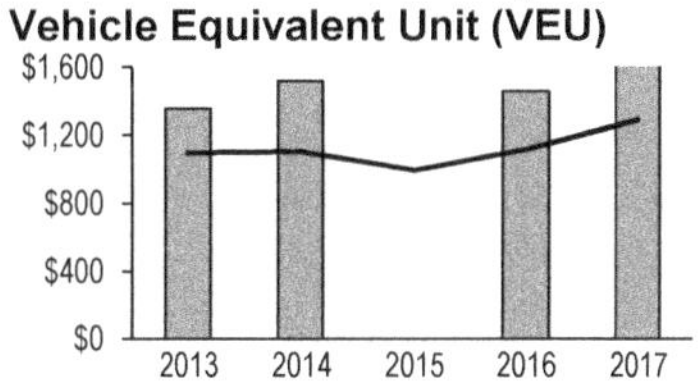

	2013	2014	2015	2016	2017
Charlotte	$1,357	$1,516		$1,456	$1,816
Average	$1,096	$1,103	$994	$1,114	$1,289

Hours Billed as a Percentage of Total Hours

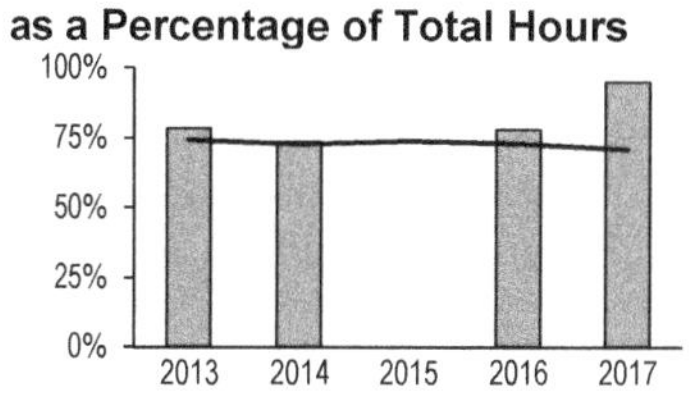

	2013	2014	2015	2016	2017
Charlotte	78%	74%		78%	95%
Average	74%	73%	74%	73%	71%

Effectiveness Measures

Preventive Maintenances (PMs) as a Percentage of All Work Orders

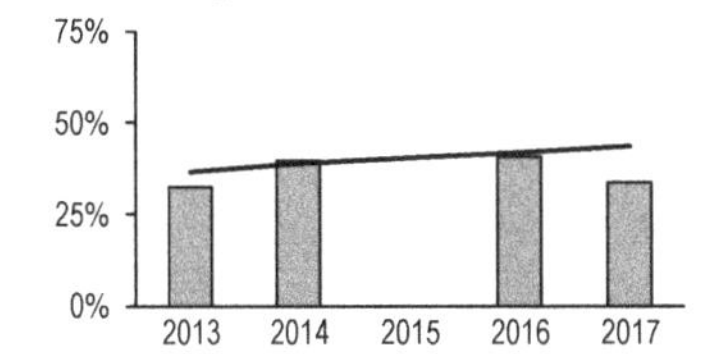

	2013	2014	2015	2016	2017
Charlotte	32%	40%		41%	34%
Average	37%	39%	40%	42%	44%

Percentage of Preventive Maintenances (PMs) Completed as Scheduled

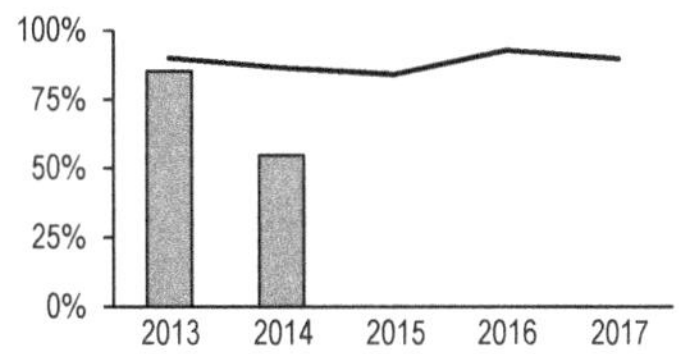

	2013	2014	2015	2016	2017
Charlotte	85%	55%			
Average	90%	87%	84%	93%	90%

Percentage of Work Orders Completed within 24 Hours

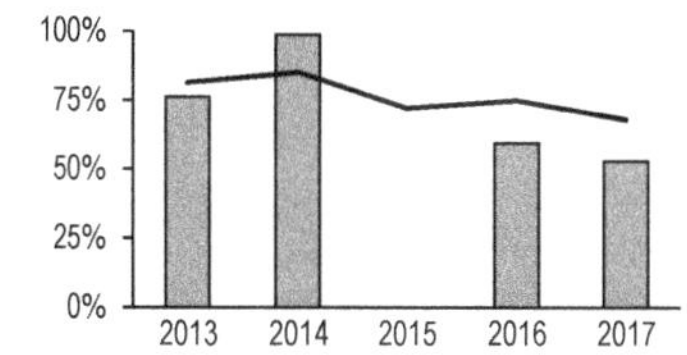

	2013	2014	2015	2016	2017
Charlotte	76%	99%		59%	53%
Average	81%	85%	72%	75%	68%

Percentage of Rolling Stock Available per Day

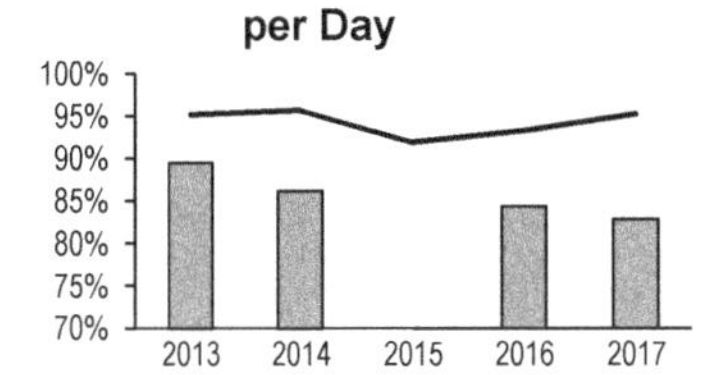

	2013	2014	2015	2016	2017
Charlotte	90%	86%		84%	83%
Average	95%	96%	92%	93%	95%

Percentage of Work Orders Requiring Repeat Repair within 30 Days

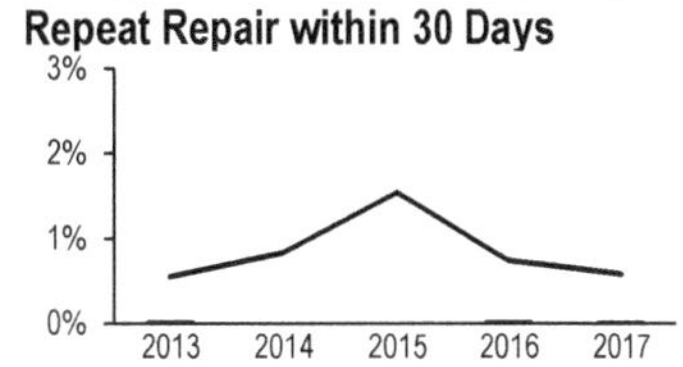

	2013	2014	2015	2016	2017
Charlotte	0.02%			0.02%	0.02%
Average	0.55%	0.83%	1.54%	0.74%	0.58%

Fiscal Year 2016–17

Explanatory Information

Service Level and Delivery

Concord's Fleet Department operates as a separate city department through an internal service fund, charging other departments for services rendered.

A labor rate of $60 per hour is charged for all maintenance services. There is a 25 percent markup charge for parts and a 10 percent markup on sublet work.

The following services were contracted out:

- body repairs
- aerial device repairs
- front-end alignments.

Conditions Affecting Service, Performance, and Costs

Vehicle Equivalent Units (VEUs) are a weighted measure of the maintenance effort associated with different classes of vehicles. A normal-use car is considered equal to one VEU. Vehicles such as fire trucks or police cars have higher VEUs, reflecting greater expected levels of maintenance.

The measure "hours billed as a percentage of total hours" is based on a work year of 2,080 hours and only counts those positions that were filled. It should be noted that technicians have responsibilities that do not result in billable hours and they take normal vacation and sick leave. Therefore this percentage should not be expected to be near 100 percent.

In Concord, the preventive maintenance (PM) completion standard for "percentage of PMs completed as scheduled" is within thirty days of the scheduled date.

In addition to rolling stock, Concord's fleet services has maintenance responsibilities for generators, mowers, weedeaters, chainsaws, chop saws, leaf blowers, tamps, pumps, power washers, and other city equipment.

A drop in repeat repairs was driven by an analysis that showed that a large portion of comebacks were due to A/C and charging system issues. Better equipment was purchased for these repairs and a master mechanic was hired to do most of the A/C repair work, leading to lower repeat repairs.

Municipal Profile

Population (OSBM 2016)	88,815
Land Area (Square Miles)	62.61
Persons per Square Mile	1,419

Service Profile

FTE Positions—Technician		8.00
FTE Positions—Other		6.0
Work Bays		8
Rolling Stock Maintained	No.	Average Age
Cars—Normal Usage	10	10.5 Years
Cars—Severe Usage	189	4.4 Years
Motorcycles	2	2.3 Years
Light Utility Vehicles	58	9.7 Years
Light Vehicles	236	7.1 Years
Medium Vehicles	46	7.8 Years
Heavy—Sanitation	12	5.3 Years
Heavy—Sewer	3	9.6 Years
Heavy—Fire Apparatus	23	11.8 Years
Heavy—Other	60	7.9 Years
Trailed Equipment	164	11.8 Years
Off-Road/Construction/Tractors	98	8.5 Years
Buses	15	7.1 Years
TOTAL	916	
Vehicle Equivalent Units (VEUs)		2,782
Average Rolling Stock Units Available per Day		903
Hours Billed		10,056
Work Orders		3,939
Repeat Repairs within 30 Days		17
Work Orders Completed within 24 hours		3,861
Preventive Maintenance Jobs (PMs)		1,807
PMs Completed as Scheduled		1,683

Full Cost Profile

Cost Breakdown by Percentage	
Personal Services	41.9%
Operating Costs	53.7%
Capital Costs	4.4%
TOTAL	100.0%
Cost Breakdown in Dollars	
Personal Services	$925,997
Operating Costs	$1,187,775
Capital Costs	$97,818
TOTAL	$2,211,590

Key: Concord ▒ Benchmarking Average — Fiscal Years 2013 through 2017

Resource Measures

Fleet Maintenance Services Cost per Capita

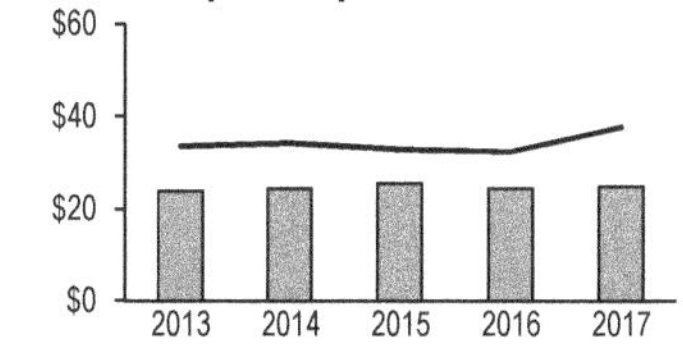

	2013	2014	2015	2016	2017
Concord	$23.94	$24.45	$25.66	$24.55	$24.90
Average	$33.64	$34.39	$32.91	$32.46	$37.72

Fleet Maintenance FTEs per 10,000 Population

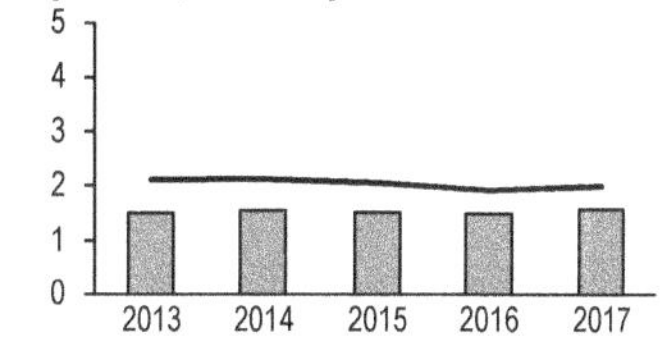

	2013	2014	2015	2016	2017
Concord	1.50	1.56	1.52	1.49	1.58
Average	2.11	2.12	2.05	1.92	1.99

Fleet Maintenance FTEs per 100 Municipal Employees

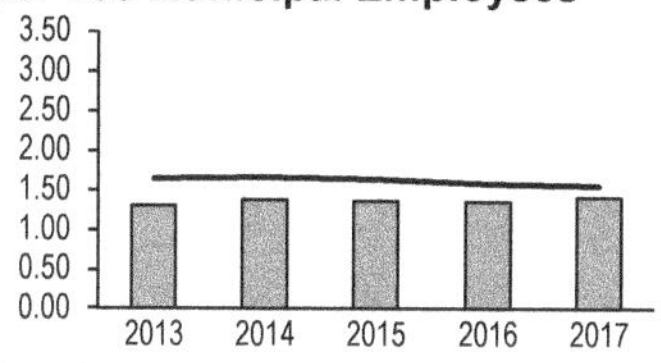

	2013	2014	2015	2016	2017
Concord	1.31	1.38	1.37	1.35	1.41
Average	1.64	1.66	1.63	1.58	1.55

Workload Measures

Number of Vehicle Equivalent Units (VEUs) per Technician FTE

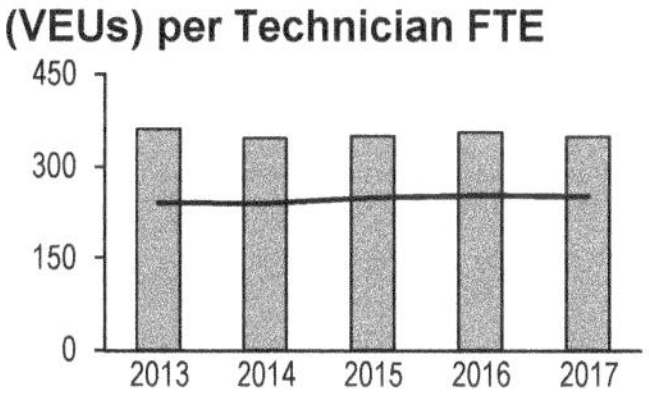

	2013	2014	2015	2016	2017
Concord	359	346	348	354	348
Average	240	239	249	252	251

Preventive Maintenances (PMs) Completed In-House per Tech FTE

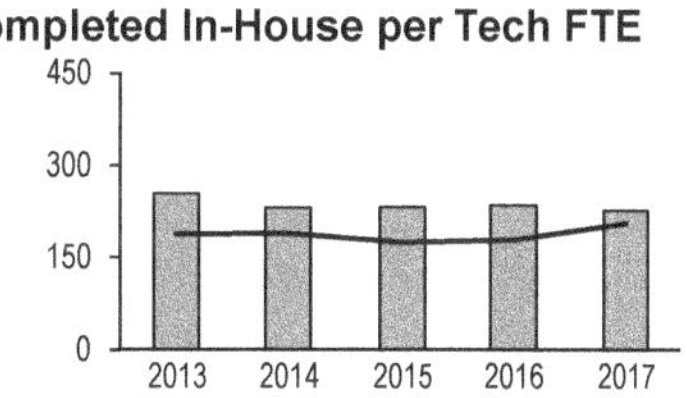

	2013	2014	2015	2016	2017
Concord	253	230	230	234	226
Average	189	189	175	179	206

Efficiency Measures

Fleet Maintenance Cost per Work Order

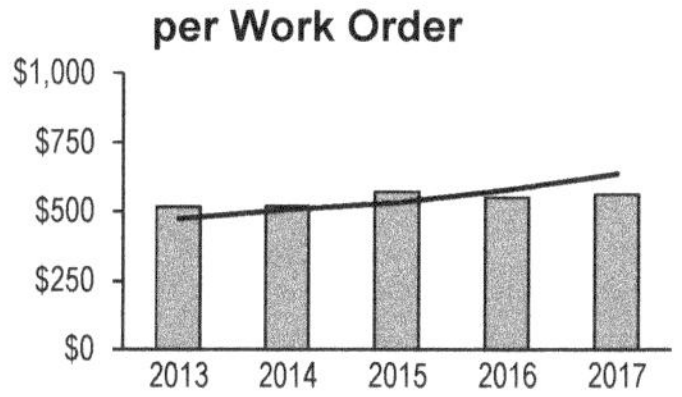

	2013	2014	2015	2016	2017
Concord	$516	$519	$573	$552	$561
Average	$477	$510	$535	$581	$639

Fleet Maintenance Cost per Vehicle Equivalent Unit (VEU)

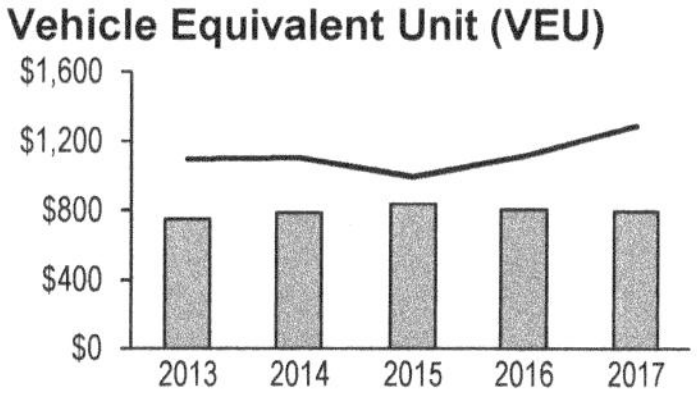

	2013	2014	2015	2016	2017
Concord	$748	$786	$839	$805	$795
Average	$1,096	$1,103	$994	$1,114	$1,289

Hours Billed as a Percentage of Total Hours

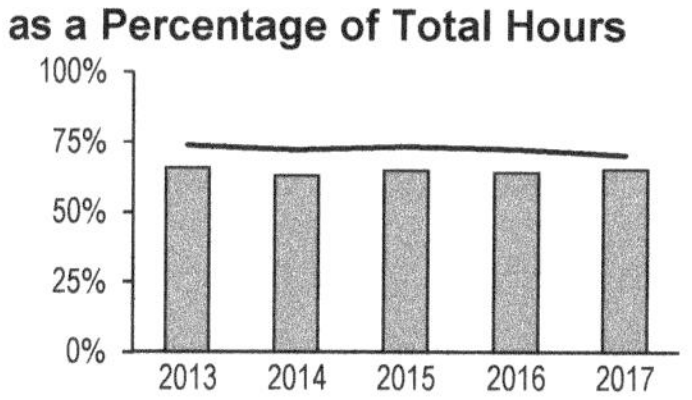

	2013	2014	2015	2016	2017
Concord	66%	63%	65%	64%	65%
Average	74%	73%	74%	73%	71%

Effectiveness Measures

Preventive Maintenances (PMs) as a Percentage of All Work Orders

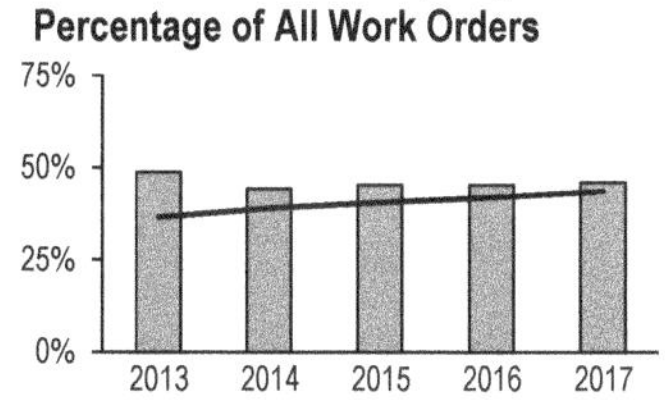

	2013	2014	2015	2016	2017
Concord	49%	44%	45%	45%	46%
Average	37%	39%	40%	42%	44%

Percentage of Preventive Maintenances (PMs) Completed as Scheduled

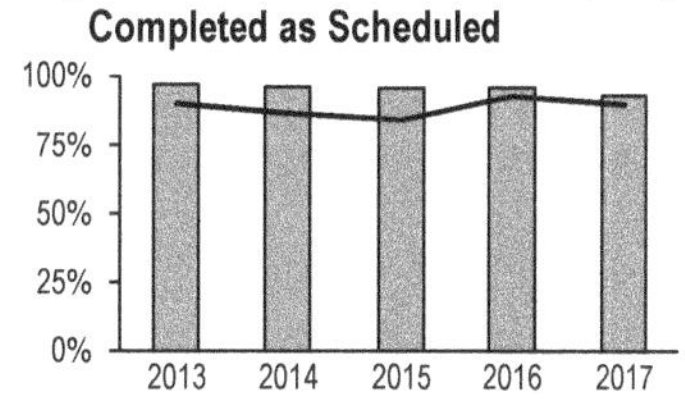

	2013	2014	2015	2016	2017
Concord	97%	96%	96%	96%	93%
Average	90%	87%	84%	93%	90%

Percentage of Work Orders Completed within 24 Hours

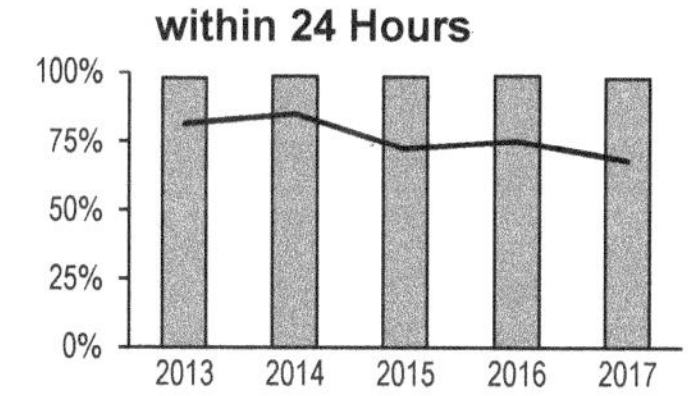

	2013	2014	2015	2016	2017
Concord	98%	99%	98%	99%	98%
Average	81%	85%	72%	75%	68%

Percentage of Rolling Stock Available per Day

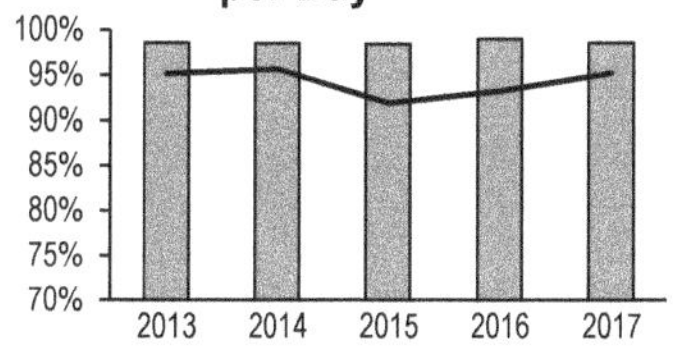

	2013	2014	2015	2016	2017
Concord	99%	99%	98%	99%	99%
Average	95%	96%	92%	93%	95%

Percentage of Work Orders Requiring Repeat Repair within 30 Days

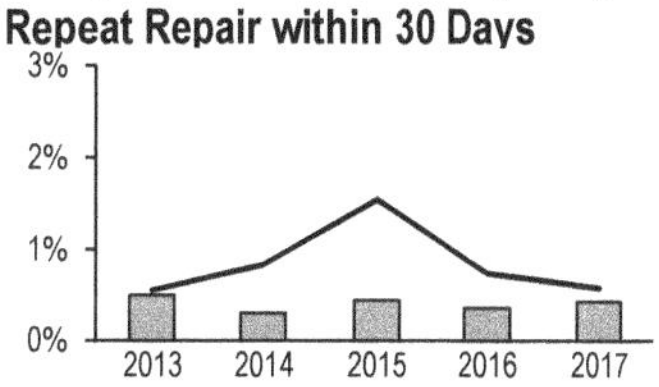

	2013	2014	2015	2016	2017
Concord	0.50%	0.31%	0.44%	0.36%	0.43%
Average	0.55%	0.83%	1.54%	0.74%	0.58%

Fiscal Year 2016–17

Explanatory Information

Service Level and Delivery
Goldsboro's fleet maintenance operation is housed within the Garage Division of the Public Works Department. The Division is funded out of the city's General Fund.

The labor rate for the fiscal year was $13.50 an hour. No markup charges are placed on parts or sublet work performed by the Garage Division.

The following services were contracted out:

- body work
- engine repairs requiring specialized tools
- engine diagnostics
- wheel alignments
- hydraulics.

Conditions Affecting Service, Performance, and Costs
The city of Goldsboro joined the Benchmarking Project in July 2017, with the first year of data showing for FY 2016–17.

Vehicle Equivalent Units (VEUs) are a weighted measure of the maintenance effort associated with different classes of vehicles. A normal-use car is considered equal to one VEU. Vehicles such as fire trucks or police cars have higher VEUs, reflecting greater expected levels of maintenance.

The measure "hours billed as a percentage of total hours" is based on a work year of 2,080 hours and only counts those positions that were filled. It should be noted that technicians have responsibilities that do not result in billable hours and they take normal vacation and sick leave. Therefore this percentage should not be expected to be near 100 percent.

In Goldsboro, the preventive maintenance (PM) completion standard for "percentage of PMs completed as scheduled" uses scheduled dates within the calendar month or within thirty days of schedule.

In addition to rolling stock, Goldsboro's Garage Division has maintenance responsibilities for portable generators, mowers, blowers, weed wackers, pressure washers, and other equipment.

Municipal Profile

Population (OSBM 2016)	34,793
Land Area (Square Miles)	29.35
Persons per Square Mile	1,186

Service Profile

FTE Positions—Technician		8.0
FTE Positions—Other		2.0
Work Bays		11
Rolling Stock Maintained	No.	Average Age
Cars—Normal Usage	11	16.0 Years
Cars—Severe Usage	107	12.0 Years
Motorcycles	0	na
Light Utility Vehicles	3	6.0 Years
Light Vehicles	56	6.0 Years
Medium Vehicles	36	12.0 Years
Heavy—Sanitation	14	4.0 Years
Heavy—Sewer	3	4.0 Years
Heavy—Fire Apparatus	10	14.0 Years
Heavy—Other	46	18.0 Years
Trailed Equipment	52	12.0 Years
Off-Road/Construction/Tractors	21	16.0 Years
Buses	1	3.0 Years
TOTAL	360	
Vehicle Equivalent Units (VEUs)		1,362
Average Rolling Stock Units Available per Day		353
Hours Billed		4,371
Work Orders		3,819
Repeat Repairs within 30 Days		1
Work Orders Completed within 24 hours		1,527
Preventive Maintenance Jobs (PMs)		1,020
PMs Completed as Scheduled		1,020

Full Cost Profile

Cost Breakdown by Percentage	
Personal Services	21.5%
Operating Costs	75.7%
Capital Costs	2.8%
TOTAL	100.0%
Cost Breakdown in Dollars	
Personal Services	$566,257
Operating Costs	$1,990,769
Capital Costs	$72,717
TOTAL	$2,629,743

Key: Goldsboro ▩ Benchmarking Average — Fiscal Years 2013 through 2017

Resource Measures

Fleet Maintenance Services Cost per Capita

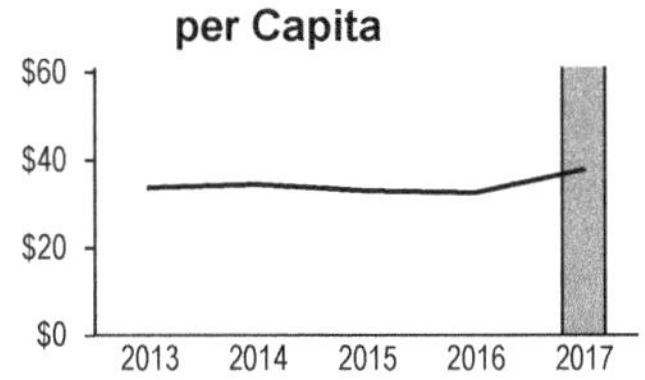

	2013	2014	2015	2016	2017
Goldsboro					$75.58
Average	$33.64	$34.39	$32.91	$32.46	$37.72

Fleet Maintenance FTEs per 10,000 Population

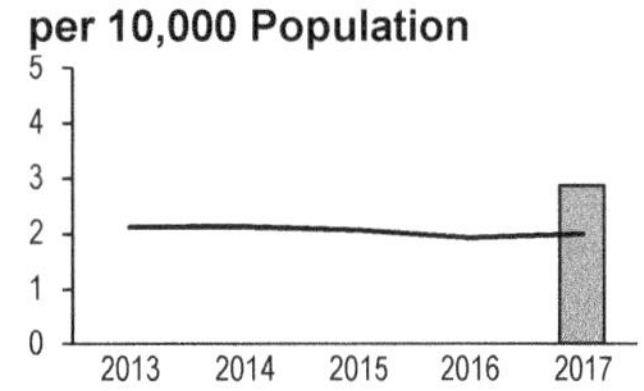

	2013	2014	2015	2016	2017
Goldsboro					2.87
Average	2.11	2.12	2.05	1.92	1.99

Fleet Maintenance FTEs per 100 Municipal Employees

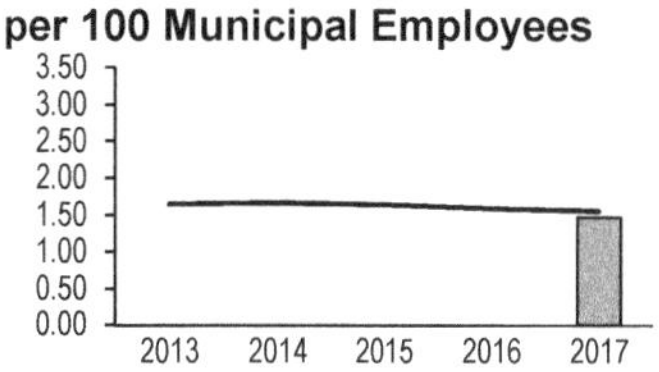

	2013	2014	2015	2016	2017
Goldsboro					1.47
Average	1.64	1.66	1.63	1.58	1.55

Workload Measures

Number of Vehicle Equivalent Units (VEUs) per Technician FTE

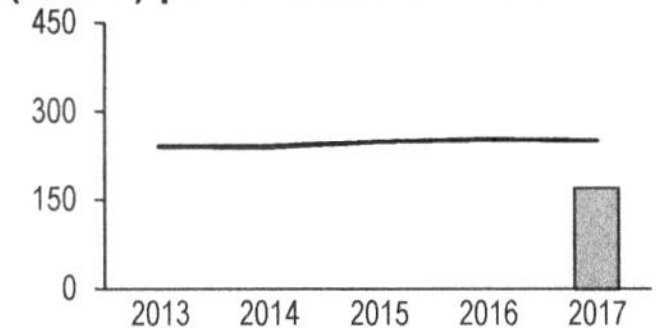

	2013	2014	2015	2016	2017
Goldsboro					170
Average	240	239	249	252	251

Preventive Maintenances (PMs) Completed In-House per Tech FTE

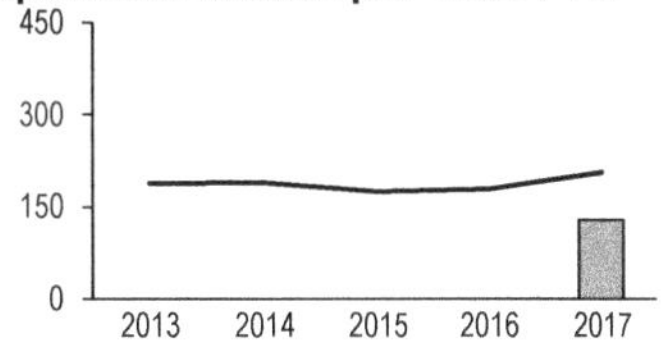

	2013	2014	2015	2016	2017
Goldsboro					128
Average	189	189	175	179	206

Efficiency Measures

Fleet Maintenance Cost per Work Order

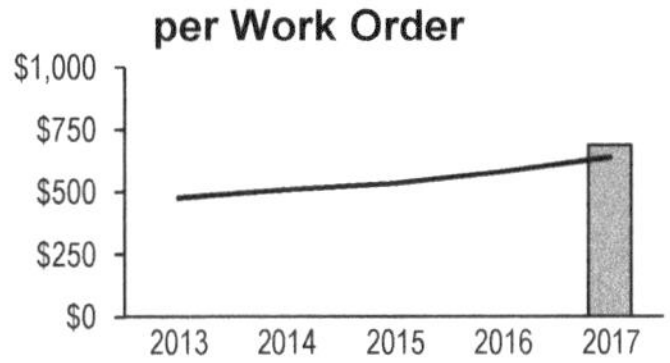

	2013	2014	2015	2016	2017
Goldsboro					$689
Average	$477	$510	$535	$581	$639

Fleet Maintenance Cost per Vehicle Equivalent Unit (VEU)

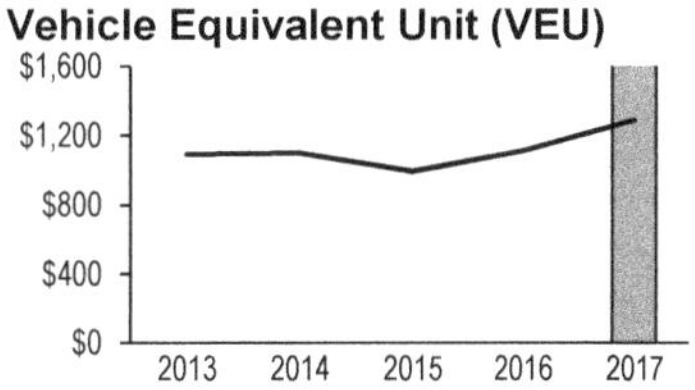

	2013	2014	2015	2016	2017
Goldsboro					$1,931
Average	$1,096	$1,103	$994	$1,114	$1,289

Hours Billed as a Percentage of Total Hours

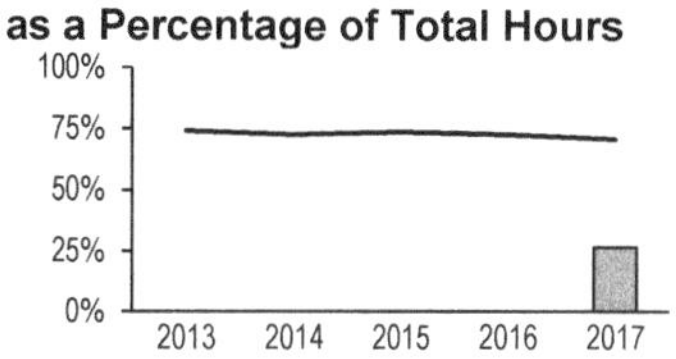

	2013	2014	2015	2016	2017
Goldsboro					27%
Average	74%	73%	74%	73%	71%

Effectiveness Measures

Preventive Maintenances (PMs) as a Percentage of All Work Orders

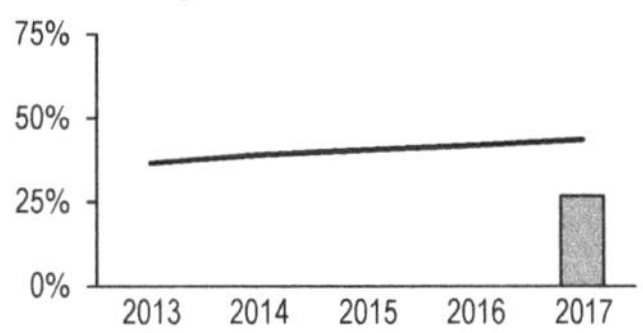

	2013	2014	2015	2016	2017
Goldsboro					27%
Average	37%	39%	40%	42%	44%

Percentage of Preventive Maintenances (PMs) Completed as Scheduled

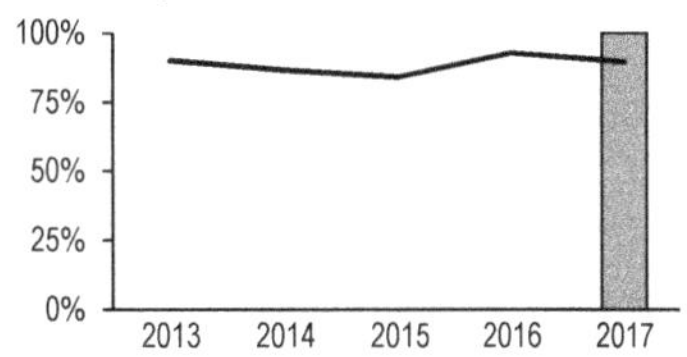

	2013	2014	2015	2016	2017
Goldsboro					100%
Average	90%	87%	84%	93%	90%

Percentage of Work Orders Completed within 24 Hours

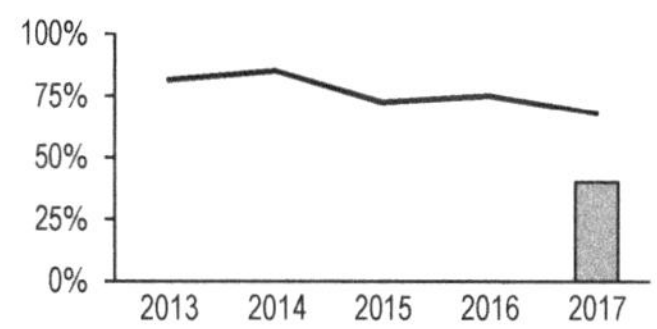

	2013	2014	2015	2016	2017
Goldsboro					40%
Average	81%	85%	72%	75%	68%

Percentage of Rolling Stock Available per Day

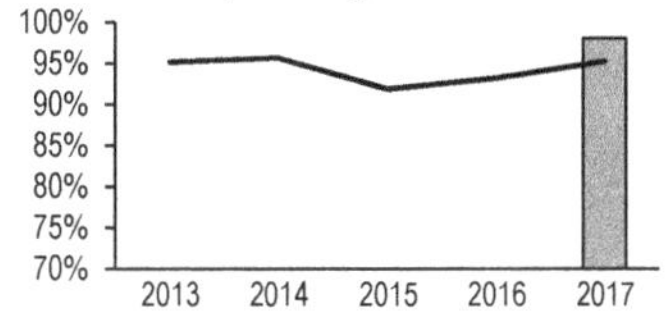

	2013	2014	2015	2016	2017
Goldsboro					98%
Average	95%	96%	92%	93%	95%

Percentage of Work Orders Requiring Repeat Repair within 30 Days

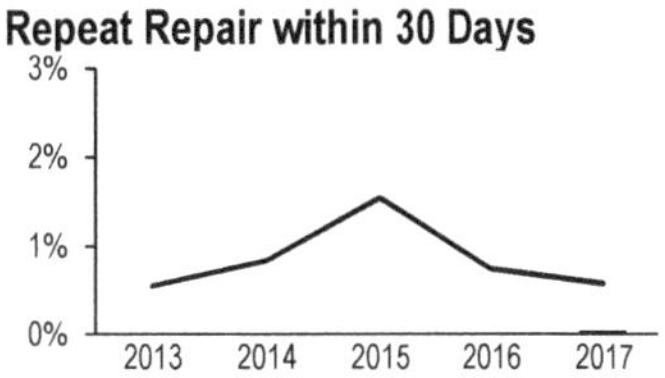

	2013	2014	2015	2016	2017
Goldsboro					0.03%
Average	0.55%	0.83%	1.54%	0.74%	0.58%

Explanatory Information

Service Level and Delivery

Greensboro's fleet maintenance operation is housed within the Equipment Services Division of the Finance Department. The division consists of four sections: administration, services, parts, and tires. All activities for this operation are accounted for in an internal service fund, with other departments and programs charged for its maintenance services on a cost recovery basis.

The labor rate for the fiscal year was $52 an hour. Charges included a 25 percent markup for parts sold and a 5 percent markup for sublet work.

The following services were contracted out:

- body work
- glass repair
- upholstery repair
- most automotive and light-duty oil changes
- other repairs when workload exceeded in-house capacity.

Conditions Affecting Service, Performance, and Costs

Vehicle Equivalent Units (VEUs) are a weighted measure of the maintenance effort associated with different classes of vehicles. A normal-use car is considered equal to one VEU. Vehicles such as fire trucks or police cars have higher VEUs, reflecting greater expected levels of maintenance.

The measure "hours billed as a percentage of total hours" is based on a work year of 2,080 hours and only counts those positions that were filled. It should be noted that technicians have responsibilities that do not result in billable hours and they take normal vacation and sick leave. Therefore this percentage should not be expected to be near 100 percent.

In Greensboro, the preventive maintenance (PM) completion standard for "percentage of PMs completed as scheduled" uses mileage parameters and scheduled dates within the calendar month or within thirty days of schedule.

In addition to rolling stock, Greensboro's fleet services has maintenance responsibilities for generators, saws, blowers, various police equipment, asphalt pavers, sprayers, hydraulic hammers, a motor mixer, pumps, snow plows, spreaders, and other equipment.

In Greensboro, maintenance on fire vehicles is performed by mechanics in the fire department. The work performed is not counted here.

Municipal Profile

Population (OSBM 2016)	284,343
Land Area (Square Miles)	128.72
Persons per Square Mile	2,209

Service Profile

FTE Positions—Technician	31.0
FTE Positions—Other	18.0
Work Bays	34

Rolling Stock Maintained	No.	Average Age
Cars—Normal Usage	200	5.0 Years
Cars—Severe Usage	301	4.0 Years
Motorcycles	8	3.0 Years
Light Utility Vehicles	36	10.0 Years
Light Vehicles	446	8.0 Years
Medium Vehicles	58	7.0 Years
Heavy—Sanitation	98	4.0 Years
Heavy—Sewer	8	6.0 Years
Heavy—Fire Apparatus	0	NA
Heavy—Other	170	8.0 Years
Trailed Equipment	234	12.0 Years
Off-Road/Construction/Tractors	102	10.0 Years
Buses	5	16.0 Years
TOTAL	1,666	

Vehicle Equivalent Units (VEUs)	5,417
Average Rolling Stock Units Available per Day	1,545
Hours Billed	45,934
Work Orders	11,951
Repeat Repairs within 30 Days	28
Work Orders Completed within 24 hours	11,114
Preventive Maintenance Jobs (PMs)	4,602
PMs Completed as Scheduled	4,602

Full Cost Profile

Cost Breakdown by Percentage	
Personal Services	44.7%
Operating Costs	55.3%
Capital Costs	0.0%
TOTAL	100.0%

Cost Breakdown in Dollars	
Personal Services	$3,456,512
Operating Costs	$4,284,502
Capital Costs	$0
TOTAL	$7,741,014

Key: Greensboro ▒ Benchmarking Average — Fiscal Years 2013 through 2017

Resource Measures

Fleet Maintenance Services Cost per Capita

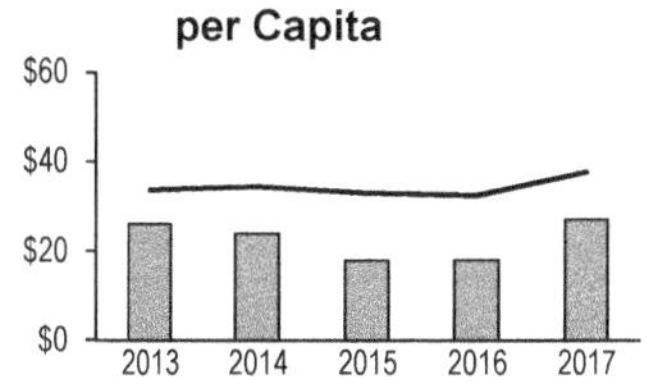

	2013	2014	2015	2016	2017
Greensboro	$26.18	$24.03	$18.07	$18.22	$27.22
Average	$33.64	$34.39	$32.91	$32.46	$37.72

Fleet Maintenance FTEs per 10,000 Population

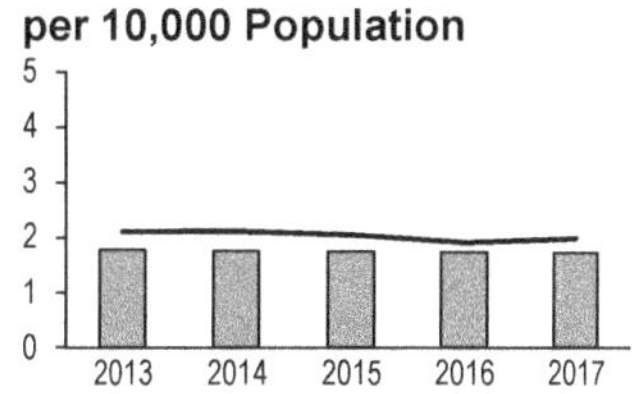

	2013	2014	2015	2016	2017
Greensboro	1.78	1.76	1.74	1.73	1.72
Average	2.11	2.12	2.05	1.92	1.99

Fleet Maintenance FTEs per 100 Municipal Employees

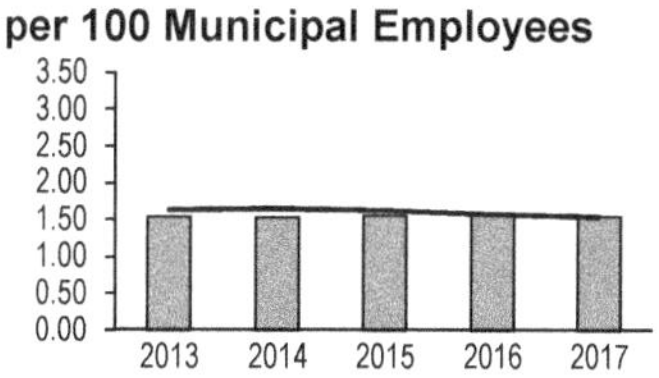

	2013	2014	2015	2016	2017
Greensboro	1.54	1.54	1.56	1.60	1.56
Average	1.64	1.66	1.63	1.58	1.55

Workload Measures

Number of Vehicle Equivalent Units (VEUs) per Technician FTE

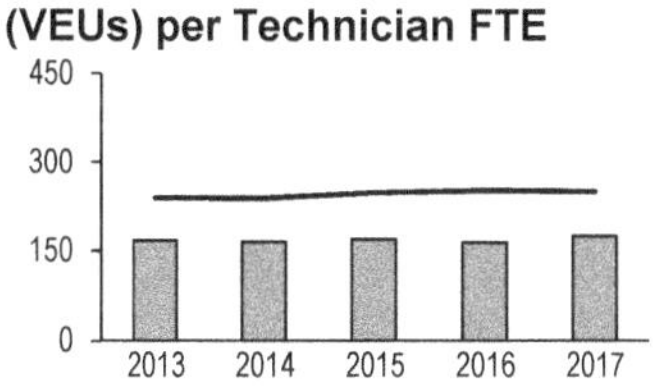

	2013	2014	2015	2016	2017
Greensboro	167	165	170	165	175
Average	240	239	249	252	251

Preventive Maintenances (PMs) Completed In-House per Tech FTE

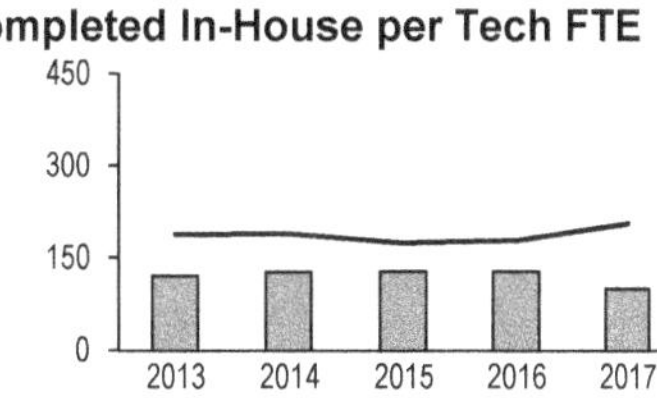

	2013	2014	2015	2016	2017
Greensboro	121	127	128	128	100
Average	189	189	175	179	206

Efficiency Measures

Fleet Maintenance Cost per Work Order

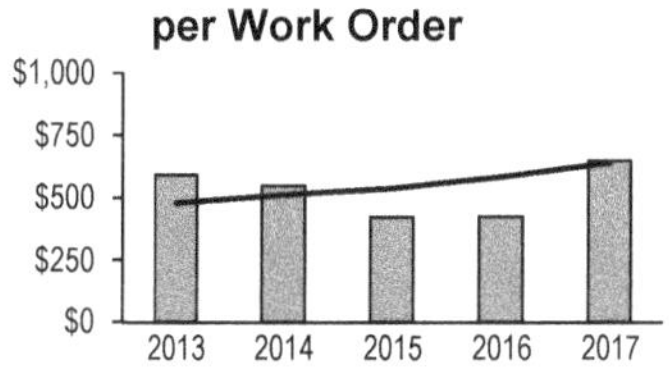

	2013	2014	2015	2016	2017
Greensboro	$591	$547	$420	$422	$648
Average	$477	$510	$535	$581	$639

Fleet Maintenance Cost per Vehicle Equivalent Unit (VEU)

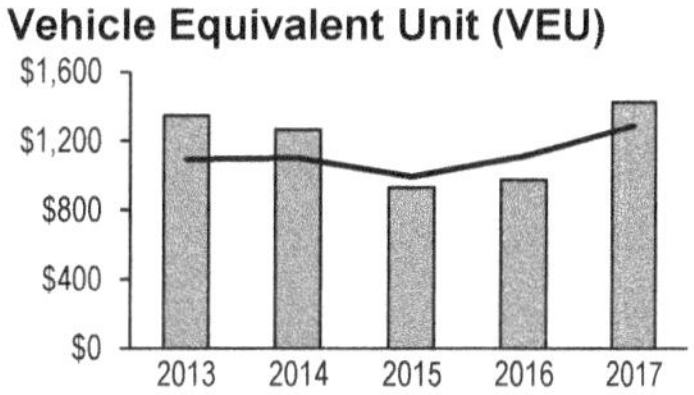

	2013	2014	2015	2016	2017
Greensboro	$1,348	$1,268	$933	$979	$1,429
Average	$1,096	$1,103	$994	$1,114	$1,289

Hours Billed as a Percentage of Total Hours

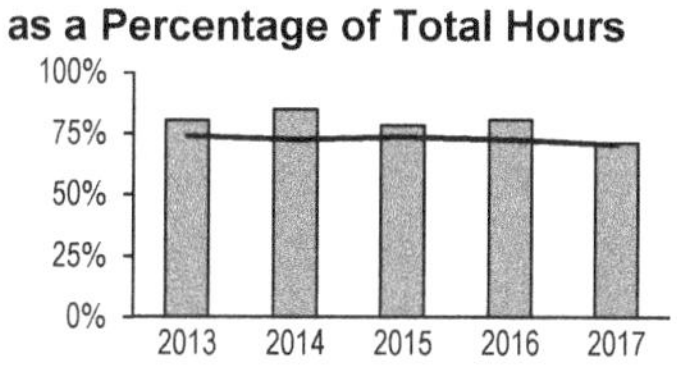

	2013	2014	2015	2016	2017
Greensboro	80%	85%	78%	81%	71%
Average	74%	73%	74%	73%	71%

Effectiveness Measures

Preventive Maintenances (PMs) as a Percentage of All Work Orders

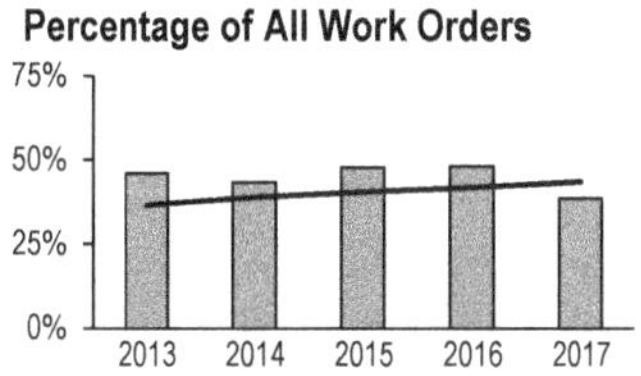

	2013	2014	2015	2016	2017
Greensboro	46%	43%	48%	48%	39%
Average	37%	39%	40%	42%	44%

Percentage of Preventive Maintenances (PMs) Completed as Scheduled

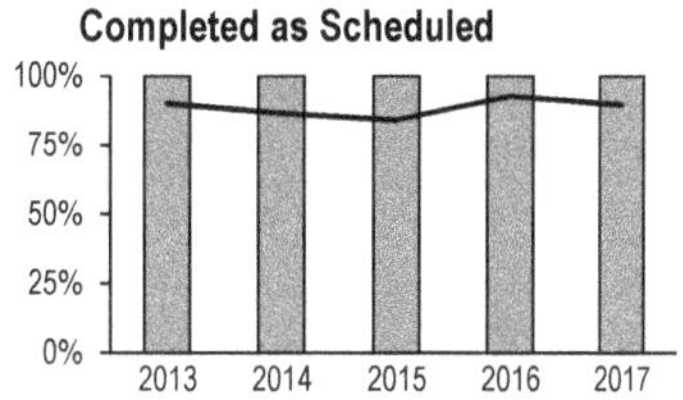

	2013	2014	2015	2016	2017
Greensboro	100%	100%	100%	100%	100%
Average	90%	87%	84%	93%	90%

Percentage of Work Orders Completed within 24 Hours

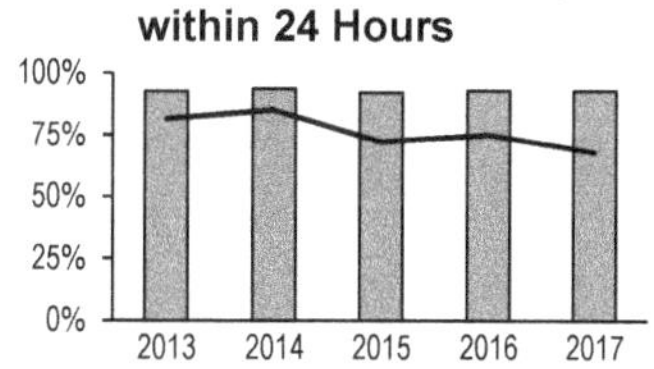

	2013	2014	2015	2016	2017
Greensboro	93%	94%	92%	93%	93%
Average	81%	85%	72%	75%	68%

Percentage of Rolling Stock Available per Day

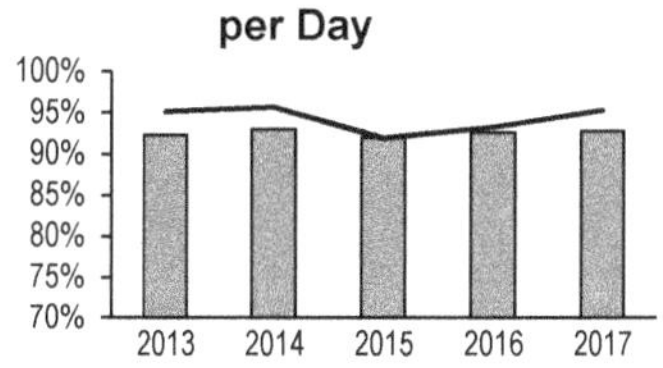

	2013	2014	2015	2016	2017
Greensboro	92%	93%	92%	93%	93%
Average	95%	96%	92%	93%	95%

Percentage of Work Orders Requiring Repeat Repair within 30 Days

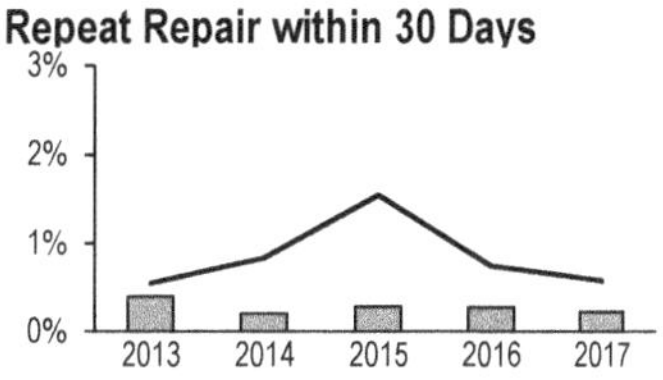

	2013	2014	2015	2016	2017
Greensboro	0.40%	0.21%	0.29%	0.28%	0.23%
Average	0.55%	0.83%	1.54%	0.74%	0.58%

Fiscal Year 2016–17

Explanatory Information

Service Level and Delivery

The Fleet Division is a part of Greenville's Public Works Department. All activities for this operation are accounted for as part of an internal service fund.

The division charges the Transit and Sanitation departments a $60-per-hour labor rate for maintenance services and has a 15 percent markup on parts and a 15 percent markup on sublet work.

The following services were contracted out:

- alignments
- major body and paint repair
- two-way radio installs
- emergency light installs
- exhaust repair
- glass repair or replacement
- transmission overhaul
- major engine repair
- warranty repairs
- towing.

Conditions Affecting Service, Performance, and Costs

Vehicle Equivalent Units (VEUs) are a weighted measure of the maintenance effort associated with different classes of vehicles. A normal-use car is considered equal to one VEU. Vehicles such as fire trucks or police cars have higher VEUs, reflecting greater expected levels of maintenance.

In Greenville, the preventive maintenance (PM) completion standard for "percentage of PMs completed as scheduled" is within thirty days of the scheduled date or mileage parameters.

In addition to rolling stock, Greenville's fleet division has maintenance responsibilities for generators, lawnmowers, blowers, weedeaters, light towers, tampers, chainsaws, golf carts, utility carts, bush hogs, sprayers, fog machines, tractors, salt spreaders, leaf vacuums, concrete saws, an asphalt melter, rollers, a stump grinder, trail mowers, and other equipment.

Municipal Profile

Population (OSBM 2016)	87,989
Land Area (Square Miles)	35.41
Persons per Square Mile	2,485

Service Profile

FTE Positions—Technician		13.0
FTE Positions—Other		5.0
Work Bays		12
Rolling Stock Maintained	No.	Average Age
Cars—Normal Usage	32	7.0 Years
Cars—Severe Usage	168	5.0 Years
Motorcycles	7	3.3 Years
Light Utility Vehicles	64	NA
Light Vehicles	195	7.8 Years
Medium Vehicles	35	4.5 Years
Heavy—Sanitation	40	3.1 Years
Heavy—Sewer	1	2.1 Years
Heavy—Fire Apparatus	11	9.1 Years
Heavy—Other	33	5.8 Years
Trailed Equipment	62	13.0 Years
Off-Road/Construction/Tractors	34	19.0 Years
Buses	14	8.5 Years
TOTAL	696	
Vehicle Equivalent Units (VEUs)		2,370
Average Rolling Stock Units Available per Day		668
Hours Billed		23,244
Work Orders		5,976
Repeat Repairs within 30 Days		NA
Work Orders Completed within 24 hours		NA
Preventive Maintenance Jobs (PMs)		2,441
PMs Completed as Scheduled		NA

Full Cost Profile

Cost Breakdown by Percentage	
Personal Services	69.0%
Operating Costs	22.6%
Capital Costs	8.3%
TOTAL	100.0%

Cost Breakdown in Dollars	
Personal Services	$1,501,801
Operating Costs	$492,693
Capital Costs	$180,963
TOTAL	$2,175,457

Key: Greenville ▒ Benchmarking Average — Fiscal Years 2013 through 2017

Resource Measures

Fleet Maintenance Services Cost per Capita

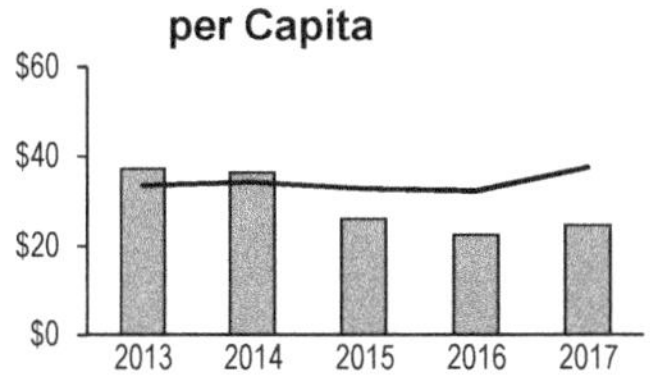

	2013	2014	2015	2016	2017
Greenville	$37.41	$36.55	$26.23	$22.69	$24.72
Average	$33.64	$34.39	$32.91	$32.46	$37.72

Fleet Maintenance FTEs per 10,000 Population

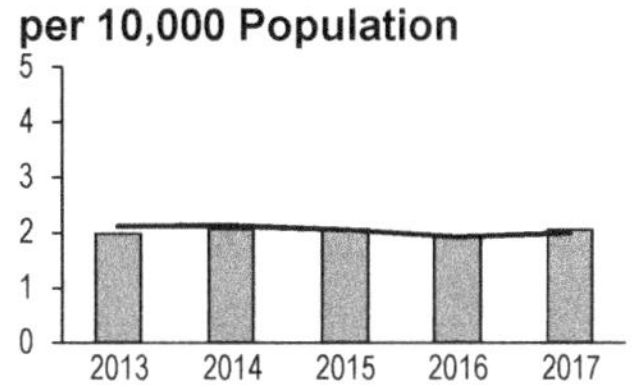

	2013	2014	2015	2016	2017
Greenville	1.97	2.06	2.06	1.93	2.05
Average	2.11	2.12	2.05	1.92	1.99

Fleet Maintenance FTEs per 100 Municipal Employees

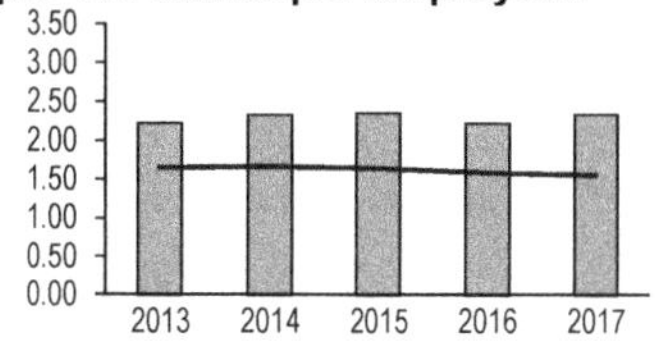

	2013	2014	2015	2016	2017
Greenville	2.22	2.33	2.35	2.22	2.34
Average	1.64	1.66	1.63	1.58	1.55

Workload Measures

Number of Vehicle Equivalent Units (VEUs) per Technician FTE

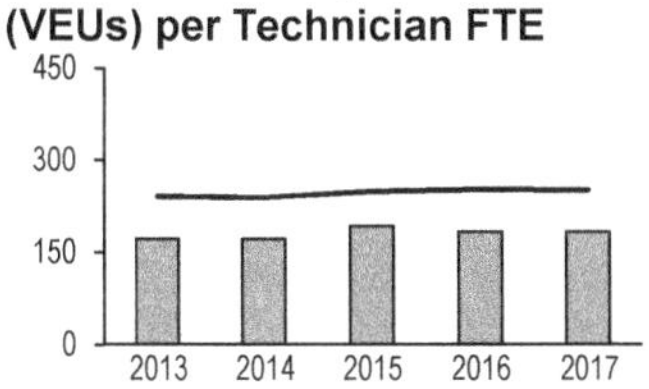

	2013	2014	2015	2016	2017
Greenville	171	170	191	182	182
Average	240	239	249	252	251

Preventive Maintenances (PMs) Completed In-House per Tech FTE

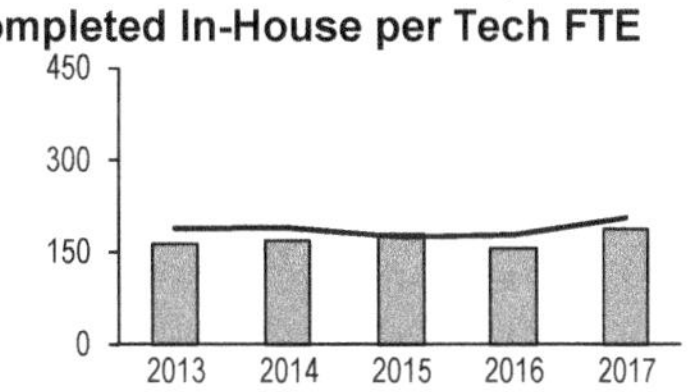

	2013	2014	2015	2016	2017
Greenville	164	168	179	157	188
Average	189	189	175	179	206

Efficiency Measures

Fleet Maintenance Cost per Work Order

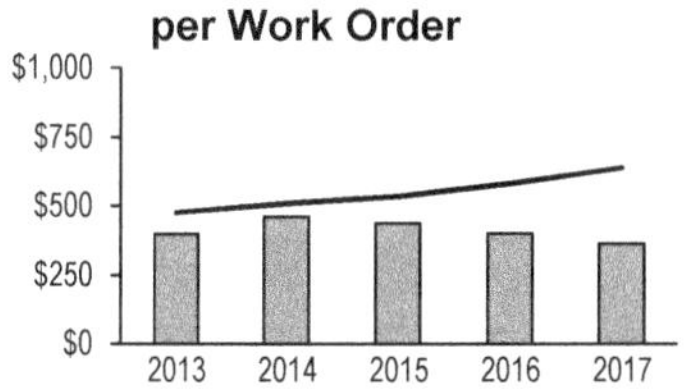

	2013	2014	2015	2016	2017
Greenville	$398	$461	$439	$402	$364
Average	$477	$510	$535	$581	$639

Fleet Maintenance Cost per Vehicle Equivalent Unit (VEU)

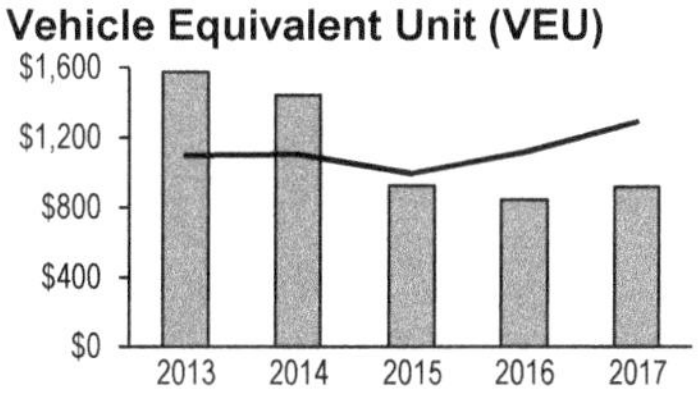

	2013	2014	2015	2016	2017
Greenville	$1,571	$1,440	$923	$844	$918
Average	$1,096	$1,103	$994	$1,114	$1,289

Hours Billed as a Percentage of Total Hours

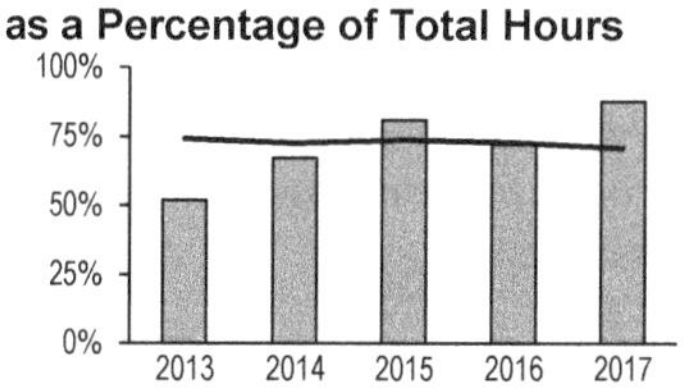

	2013	2014	2015	2016	2017
Greenville	52%	67%	81%	72%	88%
Average	74%	73%	74%	73%	71%

Effectiveness Measures

Preventive Maintenances (PMs) as a Percentage of All Work Orders

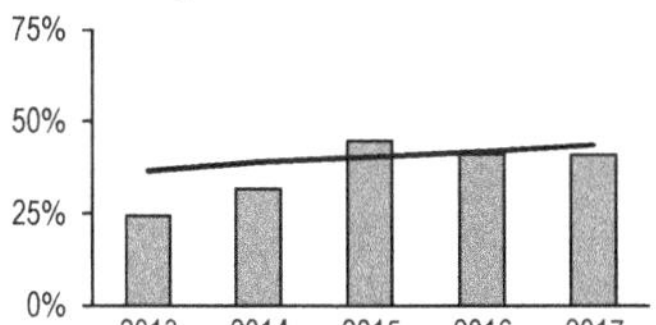

	2013	2014	2015	2016	2017
Greenville	24%	32%	45%	41%	41%
Average	37%	39%	40%	42%	44%

Percentage of Preventive Maintenances (PMs) Completed as Scheduled

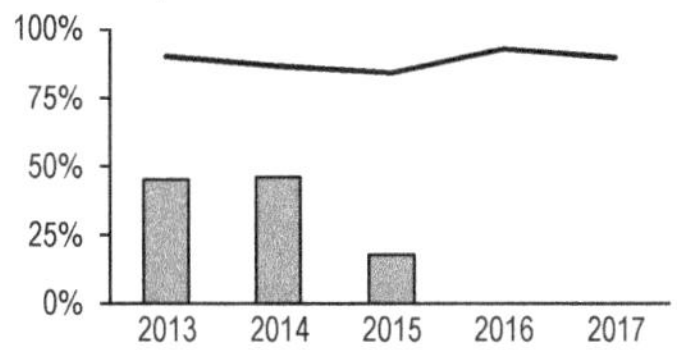

	2013	2014	2015	2016	2017
Greenville	45%	46%	18%		
Average	90%	87%	84%	93%	90%

Percentage of Work Orders Completed within 24 Hours

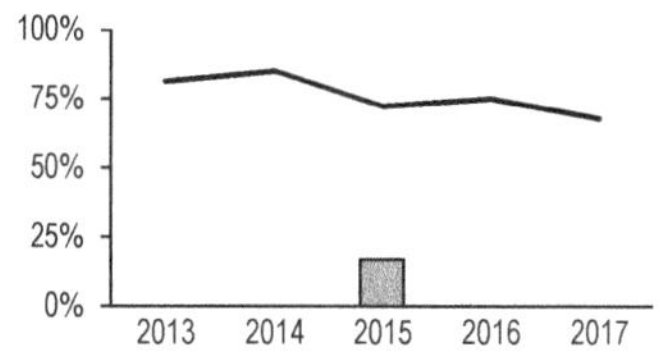

	2013	2014	2015	2016	2017
Greenville			17%		
Average	81%	85%	72%	75%	68%

Percentage of Rolling Stock Available per Day

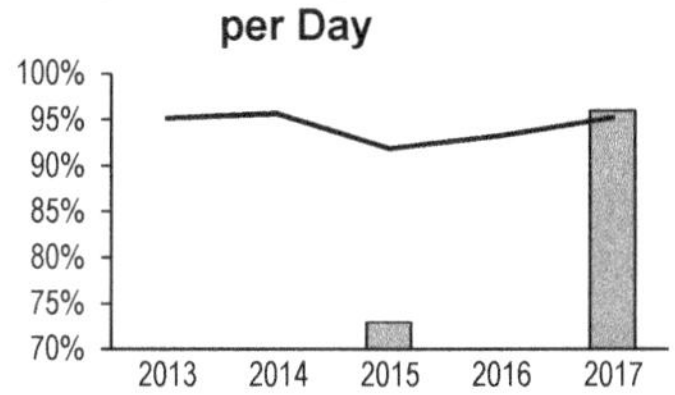

	2013	2014	2015	2016	2017
Greenville			73%		96%
Average	95%	96%	92%	93%	95%

Percentage of Work Orders Requiring Repeat Repair within 30 Days

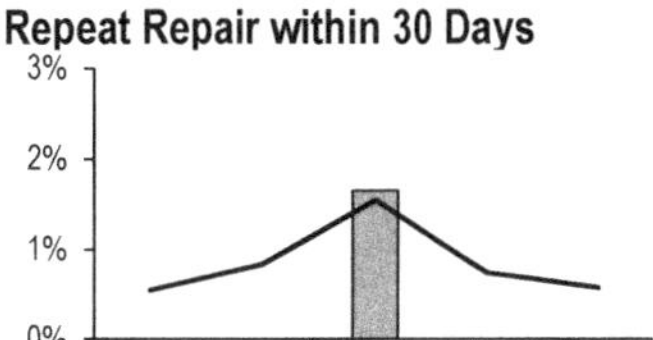

	2013	2014	2015	2016	2017
Greenville			1.65%		
Average	0.55%	0.83%	1.54%	0.74%	0.58%

Fiscal Year 2016–17

Explanatory Information

Service Level and Delivery

Fleet Maintenance is a division of Hickory's Public Services Department and consists of a garage office, a parts warehouse, a welding shop, a maintenance shop, a fleet wash station, a fuel station, and a compressed natural gas station. All activities for this operation are accounted for in an internal service fund.

The division charges a $56-per-hour labor rate for maintenance services and a 25 percent markup charge on parts sold. There is no markup charge for sublet work.

The following services were contracted out:

- alignments
- body work
- large wrecker service
- special machine work
- starter/alternator repair
- glass repair or replacement
- transmission repairs.

Conditions Affecting Service, Performance, and Costs

Vehicle Equivalent Units (VEUs) are a weighted measure of the maintenance effort associated with different classes of vehicles. A normal-use car is considered equal to one VEU. Vehicles such as fire trucks or police cars have higher VEUs, reflecting greater expected levels of maintenance.

The measure "hours billed as a percentage of total hours" is based on a work year of 2,080 hours and only counts those positions that were filled. It should be noted that technicians have responsibilities that do not result in billable hours and they take normal vacation and sick leave. Therefore this percentage should not be expected to be near 100 percent.

In Hickory, the preventive maintenance (PM) completion standard for "percentage of PMs completed as scheduled" is within thirty days of the scheduled date.

In addition to rolling stock, Hickory's fleet services has maintenance responsibilities for electronic signs, saws, weedeaters, sewer machines, hole piercing tools, boring machines, pumps, mowers, edgers, a sand blaster, pressure washers, blowers, mules, spreaders, generators, tamps, vacuums, airport equipment, grinders, a fleet wash station, a compressed natural gas fuel station, a gasoline and diesel fuel station, and other equipment.

In Hickory, maintenance on fire vehicles is performed by mechanics in the fire department. The work performed is not counted here.

Municipal Profile

Population (OSBM 2016)	40,453
Land Area (Square Miles)	29.90
Persons per Square Mile	1,353

Service Profile

FTE Positions—Technician	5.0
FTE Positions—Other	4.0
Work Bays	14

Rolling Stock Maintained	No.	Average Age
Cars—Normal Usage	18	11.4 Years
Cars—Severe Usage	126	7.1 Years
Motorcycles	0	NA
Light Utility Vehicles	8	6.5 Years
Light Vehicles	90	9.5 Years
Medium Vehicles	32	15.1 Years
Heavy—Sanitation	28	10.3 Years
Heavy—Sewer	6	9.5 Years
Heavy—Fire Apparatus	0	NA
Heavy—Other	19	16.7 Years
Trailed Equipment	54	9.9 Years
Off-Road/Construction/Tractors	135	23.6 Years
Buses	0	NA
TOTAL	516	

Vehicle Equivalent Units (VEUs)	1,812
Average Rolling Stock Units Available per Day	483
Hours Billed	10,495
Work Orders	5,023
Repeat Repairs within 30 Days	9
Work Orders Completed within 24 hours	4,521
Preventive Maintenance Jobs (PMs)	1,278
PMs Completed as Scheduled	NA

Full Cost Profile

Cost Breakdown by Percentage	
Personal Services	34.7%
Operating Costs	64.6%
Capital Costs	0.7%
TOTAL	100.0%

Cost Breakdown in Dollars	
Personal Services	$586,315
Operating Costs	$1,091,467
Capital Costs	$11,158
TOTAL	$1,688,940

Key: Hickory ▒ Benchmarking Average — Fiscal Years 2013 through 2017

Resource Measures

Fleet Maintenance Services Cost per Capita

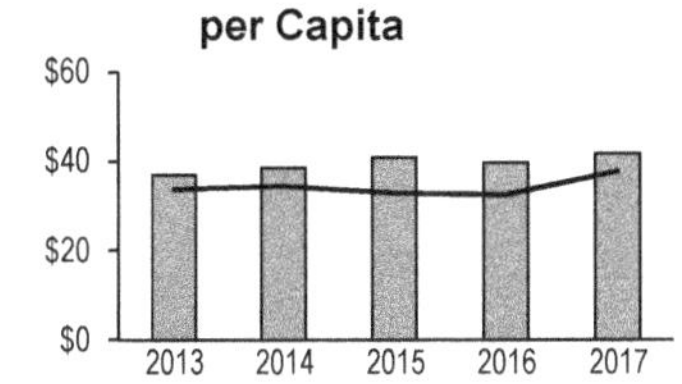

	2013	2014	2015	2016	2017
Hickory	$37.00	$38.64	$40.84	$39.78	$41.75
Average	$33.64	$34.39	$32.91	$32.46	$37.72

Fleet Maintenance FTEs per 10,000 Population

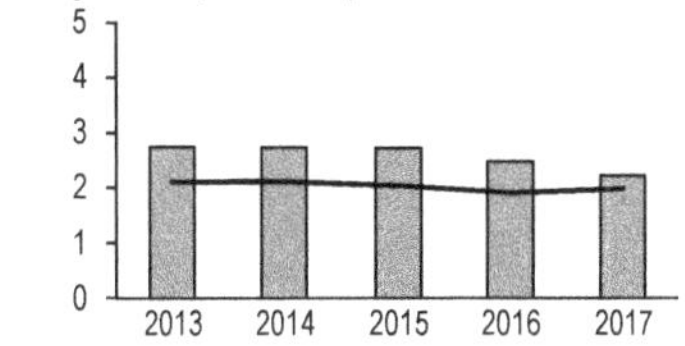

	2013	2014	2015	2016	2017
Hickory	2.75	2.73	2.73	2.48	2.22
Average	2.11	2.12	2.05	1.92	1.99

Fleet Maintenance FTEs per 100 Municipal Employees

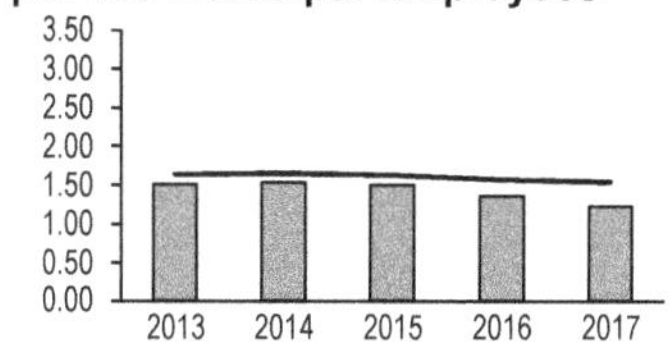

	2013	2014	2015	2016	2017
Hickory	1.51	1.53	1.50	1.36	1.22
Average	1.64	1.66	1.63	1.58	1.55

Workload Measures

Number of Vehicle Equivalent Units (VEUs) per Technician FTE

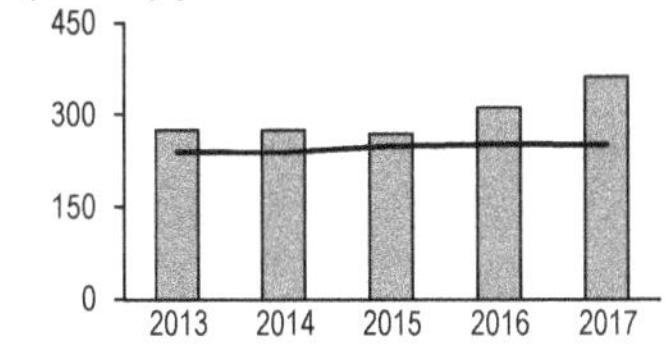

	2013	2014	2015	2016	2017
Hickory	275	275	269	312	362
Average	240	239	249	252	251

Preventive Maintenances (PMs) Completed In-House per Tech FTE

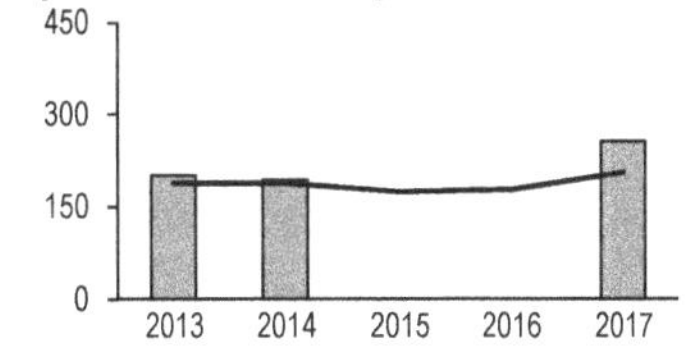

	2013	2014	2015	2016	2017
Hickory	201	193			256
Average	189	189	175	179	206

Efficiency Measures

Fleet Maintenance Cost per Work Order

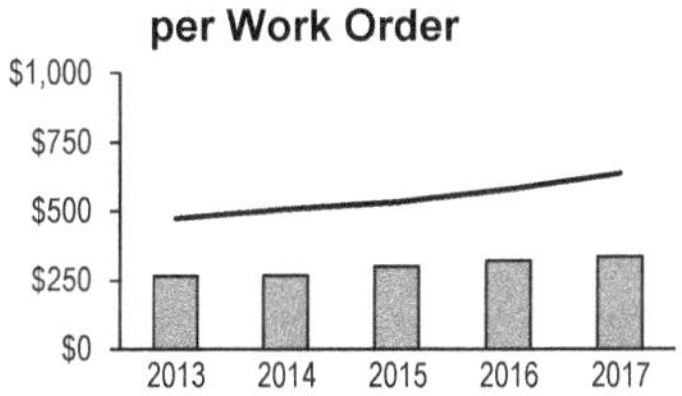

	2013	2014	2015	2016	2017
Hickory	$268	$270	$301	$322	$336
Average	$477	$510	$535	$581	$639

Fleet Maintenance Cost per Vehicle Equivalent Unit (VEU)

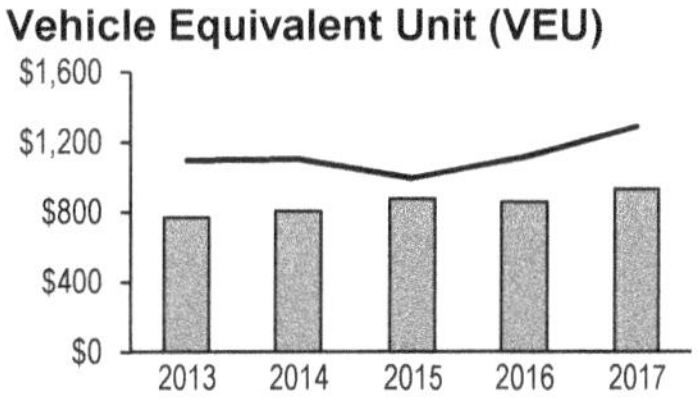

	2013	2014	2015	2016	2017
Hickory	$768	$806	$876	$857	$932
Average	$1,096	$1,103	$994	$1,114	$1,289

Hours Billed as a Percentage of Total Hours

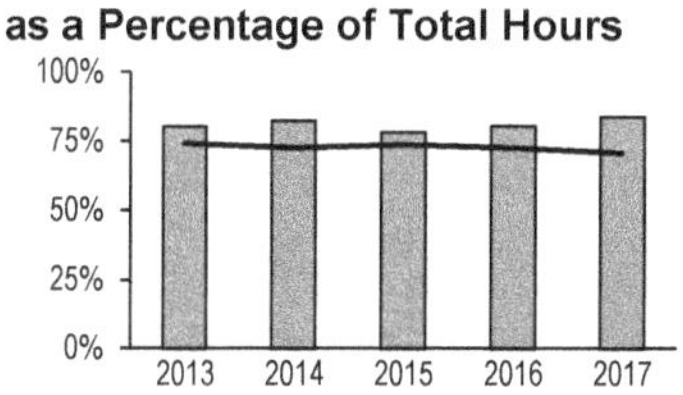

	2013	2014	2015	2016	2017
Hickory	81%	83%	78%	81%	84%
Average	74%	73%	74%	73%	71%

Effectiveness Measures

Preventive Maintenances (PMs) as a Percentage of All Work Orders

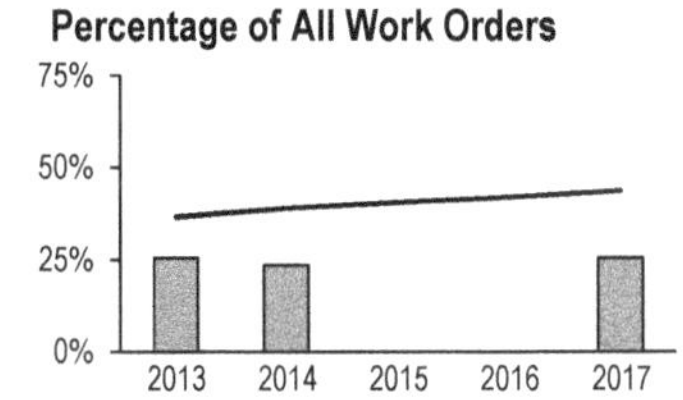

	2013	2014	2015	2016	2017
Hickory	25%	23%			25%
Average	37%	39%	40%	42%	44%

Percentage of Preventive Maintenances (PMs) Completed as Scheduled

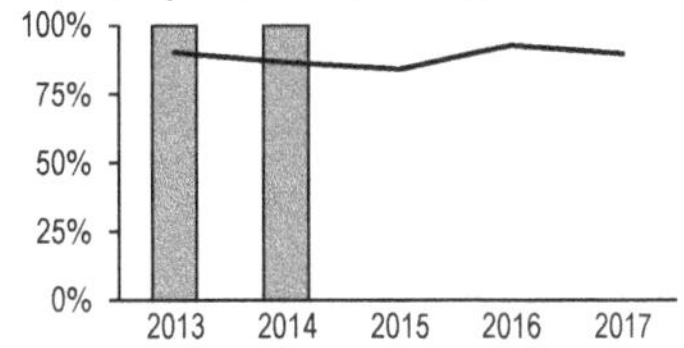

	2013	2014	2015	2016	2017
Hickory	100%	100%			
Average	90%	87%	84%	93%	90%

Percentage of Work Orders Completed within 24 Hours

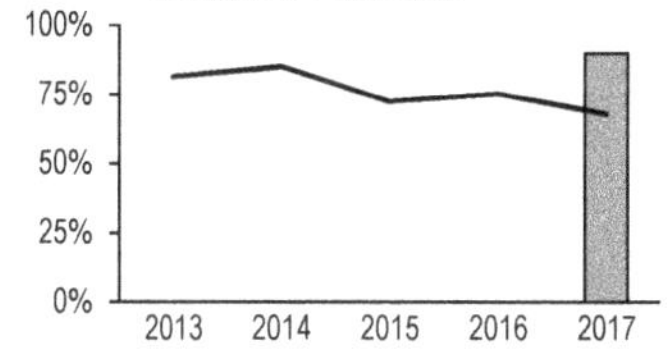

	2013	2014	2015	2016	2017
Hickory					90%
Average	81%	85%	72%	75%	68%

Percentage of Rolling Stock Available per Day

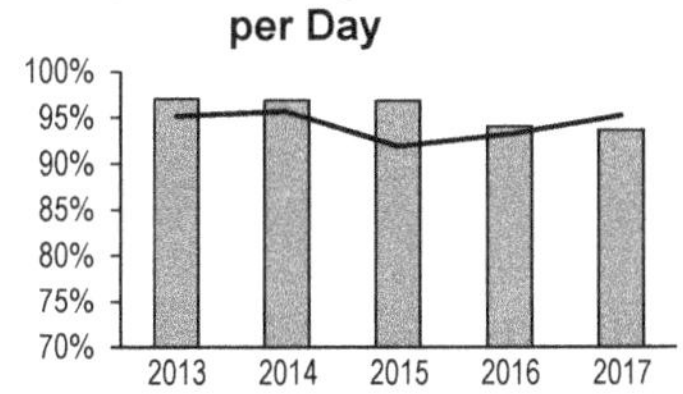

	2013	2014	2015	2016	2017
Hickory	97%	97%	97%	94%	94%
Average	95%	96%	92%	93%	95%

Percentage of Work Orders Requiring Repeat Repair within 30 Days

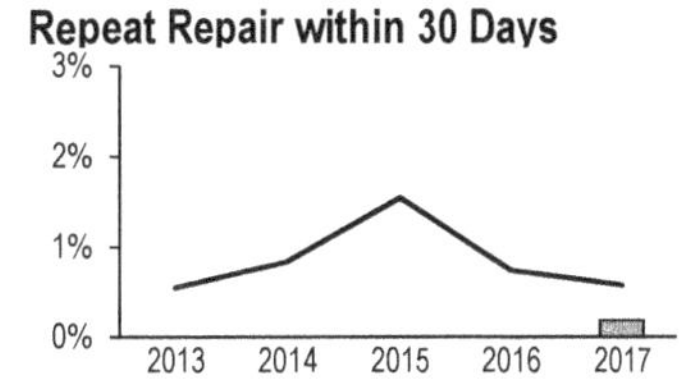

	2013	2014	2015	2016	2017
Hickory					0.18%
Average	0.55%	0.83%	1.54%	0.74%	0.58%

Fiscal Year 2016–17

Explanatory Information

Service Level and Delivery

High Point's Fleet Maintenance Department consists of a director, administrative staff, support staff, and technicians. All activities in this operation are accounted for in an internal service fund, where costs are recovered through maintenance and service charges to other city departments.

Labor is billed at $64 per hour. There is no markup charge on parts sold or sublet work. Parts inventory turned over five times during the fiscal year.

The following services were contracted out:

- body work
- windshield/glass replacements
- front-end alignment
- mufflers/exhaust systems
- after-hours towing
- car washes
- refurbishing special equipment
- upholstery repairs
- hydraulic cylinder and pump rebuilds
- 50 percent of engine and transmission overhauls
- tire repairs for heavy equipment
- maintenance and repairs covered under manufacturer warranty.

Conditions Affecting Service, Performance, and Costs

Vehicle Equivalent Units (VEUs) are a weighted measure of the maintenance effort associated with different classes of vehicles. A normal-use car is considered equal to one VEU. Vehicles such as fire trucks or police cars have higher VEUs, reflecting greater expected levels of maintenance.

In High Point, the preventive maintenance (PM) completion standard for "percentage of PMs completed as scheduled" is within certain mileage parameters or every three months, whichever comes first.

Municipal Profile

Population (OSBM 2016)	110,244
Land Area (Square Miles)	55.14
Persons per Square Mile	1,999

Service Profile

FTE Positions—Technician	10.0
FTE Positions—Other	9.0
Work Bays	18

Rolling Stock Maintained	No.	Average Age
Cars—Normal Usage	26	6.0 Years
Cars—Severe Usage	240	4.0 Years
Motorcycles	4	3.0 Years
Light Utility Vehicles	26	4.0 Years
Light Vehicles	298	5.0 Years
Medium Vehicles	27	5.0 Years
Heavy—Sanitation	32	6.0 Years
Heavy—Sewer	3	3.0 Years
Heavy—Fire Apparatus	25	NA
Heavy—Other	61	7.0 Years
Trailed Equipment	136	NA
Off-Road/Construction/Tractors	140	6.0 Years
Buses	0	NA
TOTAL	1,018	

Vehicle Equivalent Units (VEUs)	3,311
Average Rolling Stock Units Available per Day	1,007
Hours Billed	14,560
Work Orders	4,644
Repeat Repairs within 30 Days	18
Work Orders Completed within 24 hours	NA
Preventive Maintenance Jobs (PMs)	2,193
PMs Completed as Scheduled	1,973

Full Cost Profile

Cost Breakdown by Percentage	
Personal Services	29.4%
Operating Costs	60.6%
Capital Costs	10.0%
TOTAL	100.0%

Cost Breakdown in Dollars	
Personal Services	$1,244,606
Operating Costs	$2,570,950
Capital Costs	$424,696
TOTAL	$4,240,252

Key: High Point ▒ Benchmarking Average — Fiscal Years 2013 through 2017

Resource Measures

Fleet Maintenance Services Cost per Capita

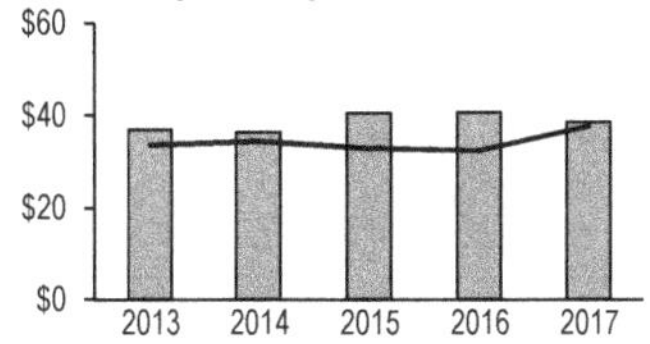

	2013	2014	2015	2016	2017
High Point	$36.75	$36.24	$40.35	$40.49	$38.46
Average	$33.64	$34.39	$32.91	$32.46	$37.72

Fleet Maintenance FTEs per 10,000 Population

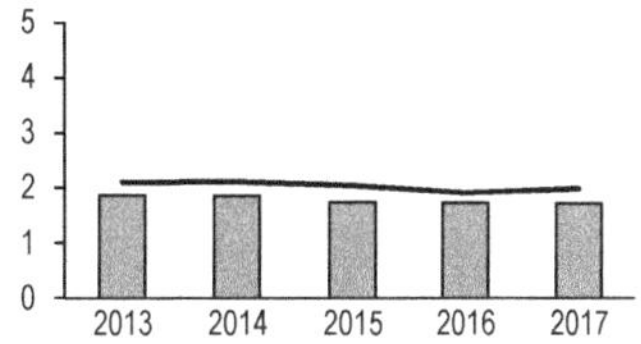

	2013	2014	2015	2016	2017
High Point	1.88	1.86	1.75	1.73	1.72
Average	2.11	2.12	2.05	1.92	1.99

Fleet Maintenance FTEs per 100 Municipal Employees

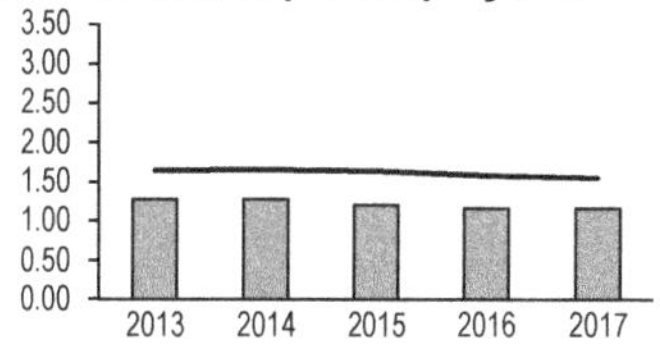

	2013	2014	2015	2016	2017
High Point	1.28	1.28	1.20	1.16	1.16
Average	1.64	1.66	1.63	1.58	1.55

Workload Measures

Number of Vehicle Equivalent Units (VEUs) per Technician FTE

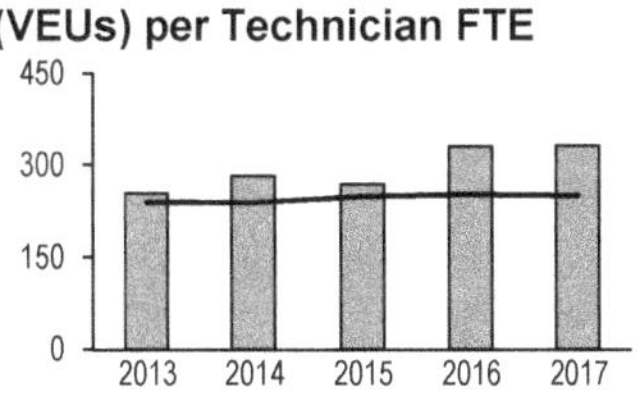

	2013	2014	2015	2016	2017
High Point	253	281	267	331	331
Average	240	239	249	252	251

Preventive Maintenances (PMs) Completed In-House per Tech FTE

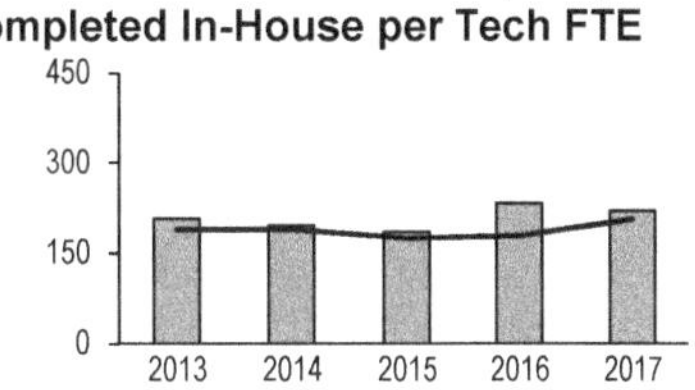

	2013	2014	2015	2016	2017
High Point	207	195	184	233	219
Average	189	189	175	179	206

Efficiency Measures

Fleet Maintenance Cost per Work Order

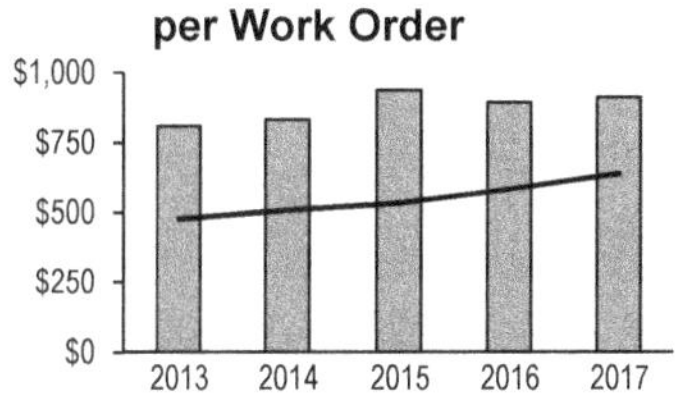

	2013	2014	2015	2016	2017
High Point	$809	$832	$937	$893	$913
Average	$477	$510	$535	$581	$639

Fleet Maintenance Cost per Vehicle Equivalent Unit (VEU)

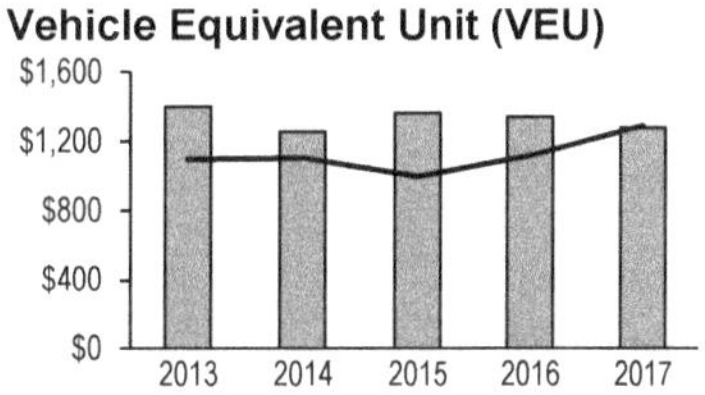

	2013	2014	2015	2016	2017
High Point	$1,403	$1,260	$1,365	$1,343	$1,281
Average	$1,096	$1,103	$994	$1,114	$1,289

Hours Billed as a Percentage of Total Hours

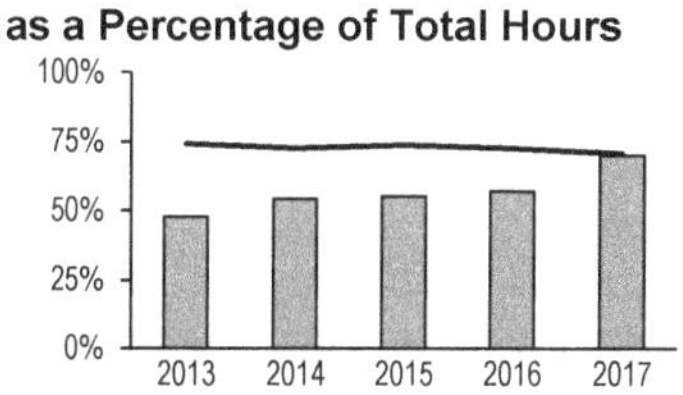

	2013	2014	2015	2016	2017
High Point	48%	54%	55%	57%	70%
Average	74%	73%	74%	73%	71%

Effectiveness Measures

Preventive Maintenances (PMs) as a Percentage of All Work Orders

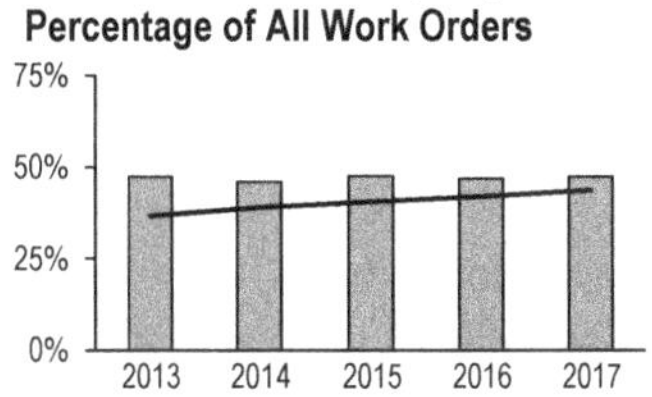

	2013	2014	2015	2016	2017
High Point	47%	46%	47%	47%	47%
Average	37%	39%	40%	42%	44%

Percentage of Preventive Maintenances (PMs) Completed as Scheduled

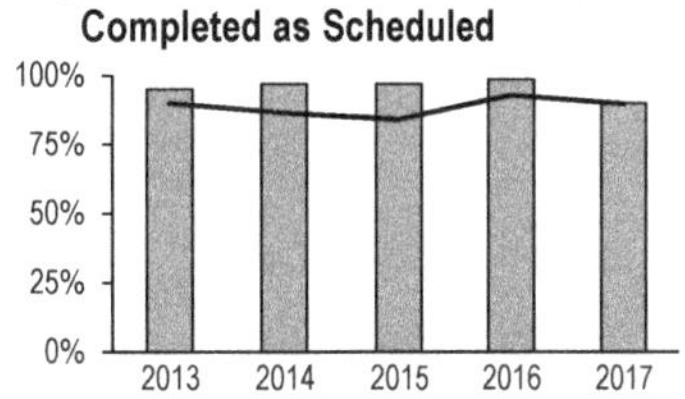

	2013	2014	2015	2016	2017
High Point	95%	97%	97%	98%	90%
Average	90%	87%	84%	93%	90%

Percentage of Work Orders Completed within 24 Hours

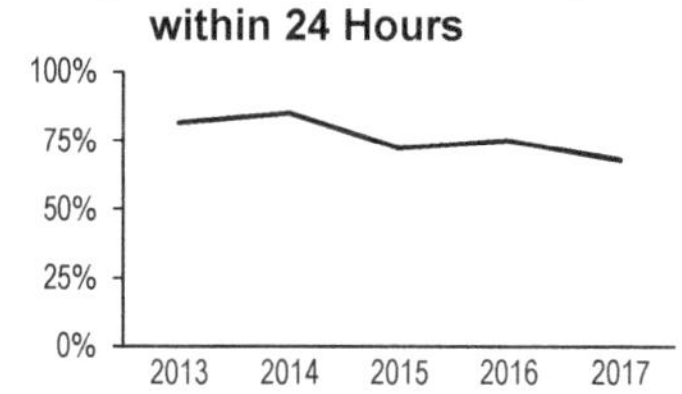

	2013	2014	2015	2016	2017
High Point					
Average	81%	85%	72%	75%	68%

Percentage of Rolling Stock Available per Day

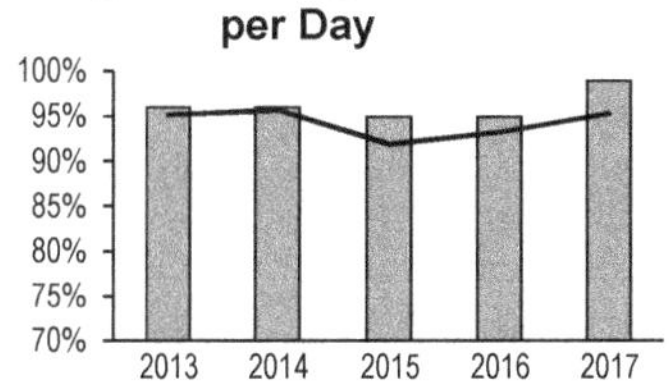

	2013	2014	2015	2016	2017
High Point	96%	96%	95%	95%	99%
Average	95%	96%	92%	93%	95%

Percentage of Work Orders Requiring Repeat Repair within 30 Days

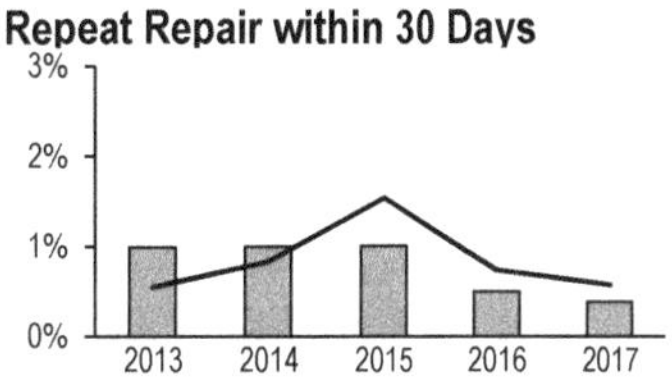

	2013	2014	2015	2016	2017
High Point	0.99%	1.00%	1.01%	0.50%	0.39%
Average	0.55%	0.83%	1.54%	0.74%	0.58%

Fiscal Year 2016–17

Explanatory Information

Service Level and Delivery
The Vehicle Fleet Service Divsion is under the Engineering Services Department for the City of Raleigh. The Division provides maintenance and repair services for all city vehicles and motorized equipment except for Fire Department vehicles and city buses, which are handled by their own department. The city operates three separate locations to sevice vehicles. The Division also handles replacement of new vehicles and equipment, managing fuel operations, and the city motor pool. The Division is run as an internal service fund for the City.

Varying labor rates are used for different types of worker ranging from $27 per hour for preventative maintenance technicians up to $65 for heavy equipment mechanics. A markup of 25 percent is added for parts and a 15 percent markup is added for sublet work.

The following services were contracted out:

- body work
- painting of new vehicles
- transmission work and overhauls
- some engine replacements
- spring work
- natural gas tank inspections
- onsite lubrication services for refuse vehicles
- towing.

Conditions Affecting Service, Performance, and Costs
Raleigh rejoined the Benchmarking Project in July 2016 with the first year of data showing for FY 2015–16.

Vehicle Equivalent Units (VEUs) are a weighted measure of the maintenance effort associated with different classes of vehicles. A normal-use car is considered equal to one VEU. Vehicles such as fire trucks or police cars have higher VEUs, reflecting greater expected levels of maintenance.

In Raleigh, the preventive maintenance (PM) completion standard for "percentage of PMs completed as scheduled" is 45 days and a 30 percent variance for meters, which could be miles or hours.

In addition to maintenance responsibilities for the city's rolling stock, the Division also has responsibility for equipment, including pumps, weed eaters, concrete saws, mowers, blowers, compressors, light towers, scissor lifts, vacuums, pipe saws, flashing light arrows, chippers, spray washes, line markers, leaf vacuums, outboard motors, spreaders, generators, paint sprayers, grass trimmers, yard waste handlers, power rodders, golf carts, forklifts, and other city equipment.

Municipal Profile

Population (OSBM 2016)	448,706
Land Area (Square Miles)	145.57
Persons per Square Mile	3,083

Service Profile

FTE Positions—Technician	49.0
FTE Positions—Other	28.0
Work Bays	51

Rolling Stock Maintained	No.	Average Age
Cars—Normal Usage	206	6.1 Years
Cars—Severe Usage	444	4.4 Years
Motorcycles	10	4.2 Years
Light Utility Vehicles	98	6.8 Years
Light Vehicles	864	5.6 Years
Medium Vehicles	139	6.9 Years
Heavy—Sanitation	110	4.2 Years
Heavy—Sewer	23	5.8 Years
Heavy—Fire Apparatus	0	NA
Heavy—Other	132	6.6 Years
Trailed Equipment	394	9.4 Years
Off-Road/Construction/Tractors	192	8.3 Years
Buses	21	9.6 Years
TOTAL	2,633	

Vehicle Equivalent Units (VEUs)	7,684
Average Rolling Stock Units Available per Day	2,549
Hours Billed	53,945
Work Orders	13,843
Repeat Repairs within 30 Days	133
Work Orders Completed within 24 hours	6,981
Preventive Maintenance Jobs (PMs)	9,108
PMs Completed as Scheduled	5,775

Full Cost Profile

Cost Breakdown by Percentage	
Personal Services	23.7%
Operating Costs	72.9%
Capital Costs	3.4%
TOTAL	100.0%

Cost Breakdown in Dollars	
Personal Services	$4,763,309
Operating Costs	$14,642,003
Capital Costs	$675,543
TOTAL	$20,080,855

Raleigh — Fleet Maintenance

Key: Raleigh ▒ Benchmarking Average — Fiscal Years 2013 through 2017

Resource Measures

Fleet Maintenance Services Cost per Capita

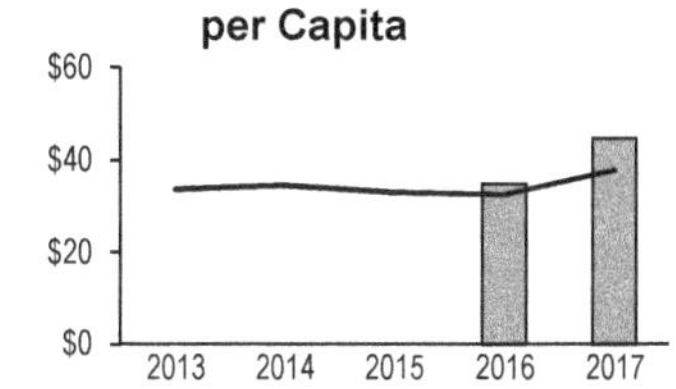

Raleigh				$34.93	$44.75
Average	$33.64	$34.39	$32.91	$32.46	$37.72

Fleet Maintenance FTEs per 10,000 Population

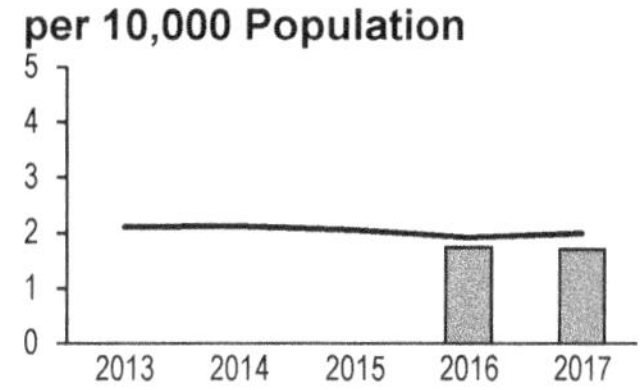

Raleigh				1.75	1.72
Average	2.11	2.12	2.05	1.92	1.99

Fleet Maintenance FTEs per 100 Municipal Employees

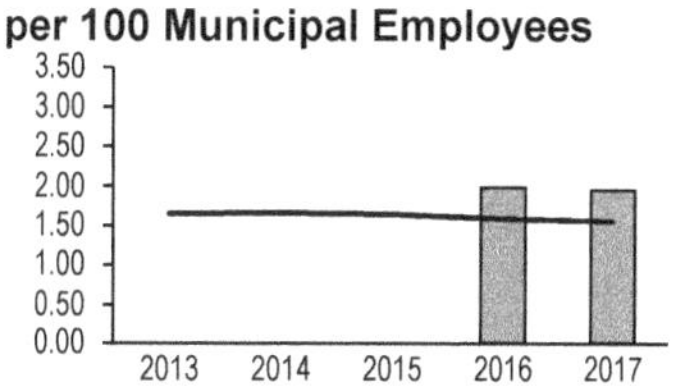

Raleigh				1.98	1.95
Average	1.64	1.66	1.63	1.58	1.55

Workload Measures

Number of Vehicle Equivalent Units (VEUs) per Technician FTE

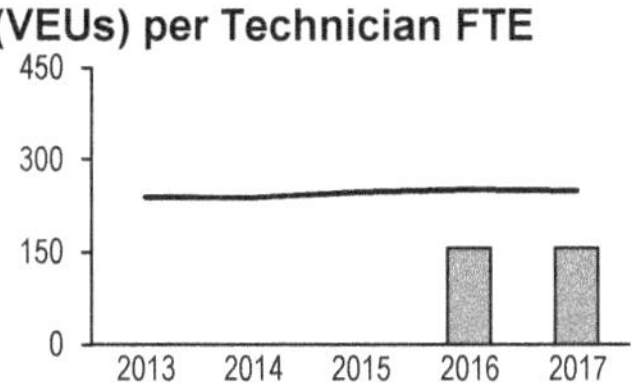

Raleigh				157	157
Average	240	239	249	252	251

Preventive Maintenances (PMs) Completed In-House per Tech FTE

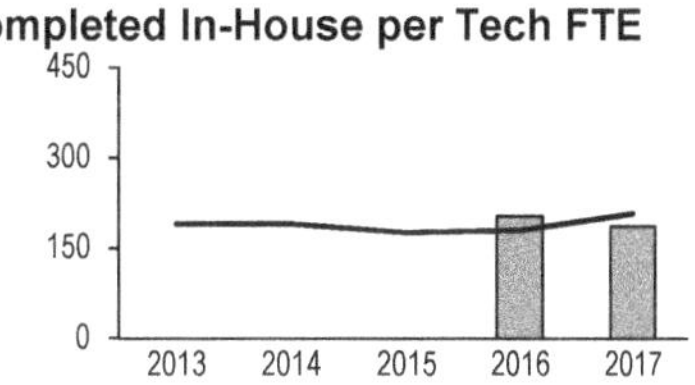

Raleigh				202	186
Average	189	189	175	179	206

Efficiency Measures

Fleet Maintenance Cost per Work Order

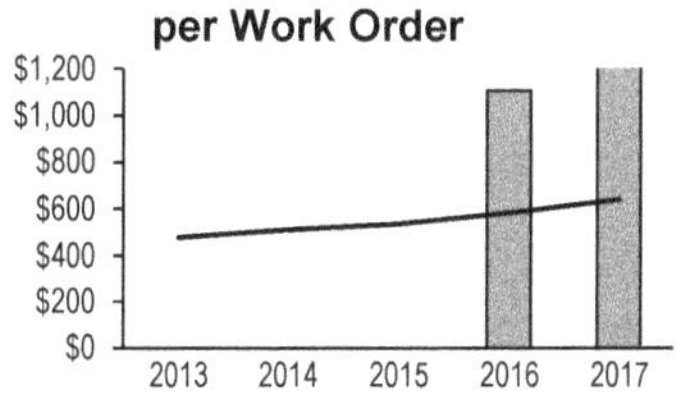

Raleigh				$1,106	$1,451
Average	$477	$510	$535	$581	$639

Fleet Maintenance Cost per Vehicle Equivalent Unit (VEU)

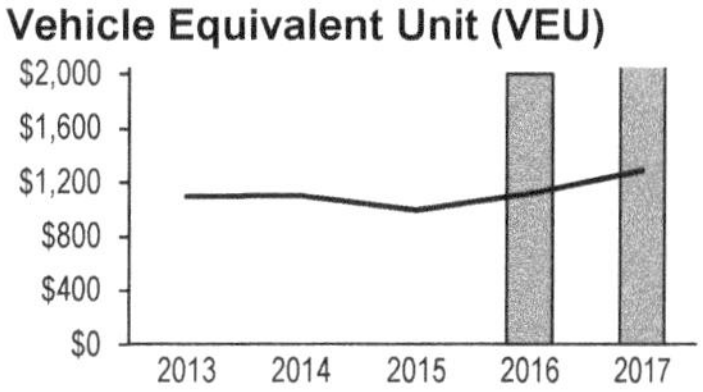

Raleigh				$2,003	$2,613
Average	$1,096	$1,103	$994	$1,114	$1,289

Hours Billed as a Percentage of Total Hours

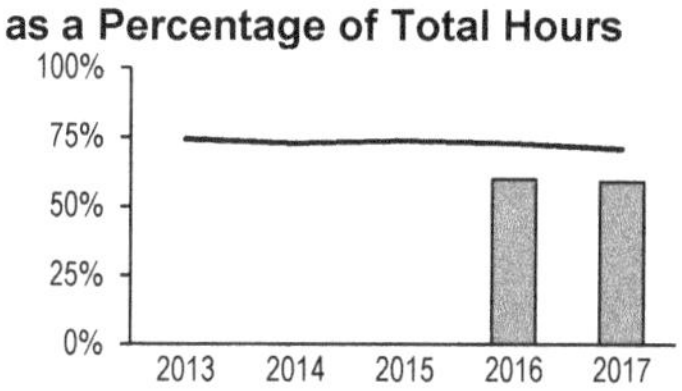

Raleigh				60%	59%
Average	74%	73%	74%	73%	71%

Effectiveness Measures

Preventive Maintenances (PMs) as a Percentage of All Work Orders

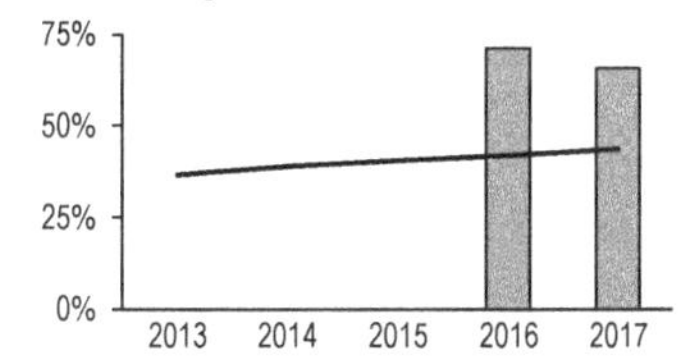

Raleigh				71%	66%
Average	37%	39%	40%	42%	44%

Percentage of Preventive Maintenances (PMs) Completed as Scheduled

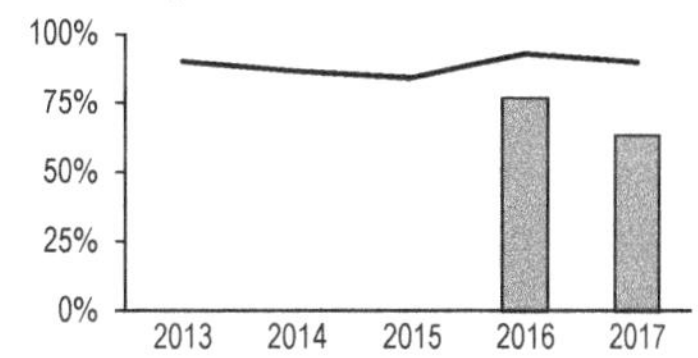

Raleigh				77%	63%
Average	90%	87%	84%	93%	90%

Percentage of Work Orders Completed within 24 Hours

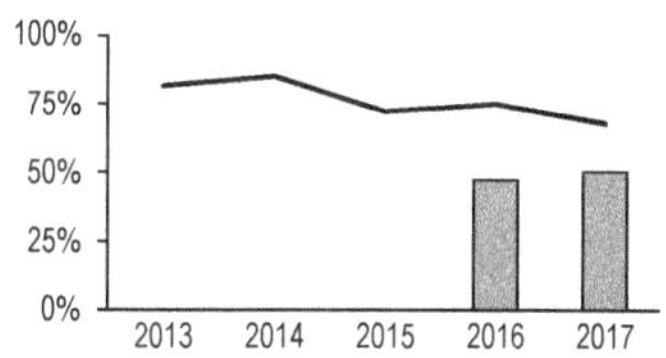

Raleigh				47%	50%
Average	81%	85%	72%	75%	68%

Percentage of Rolling Stock Available per Day

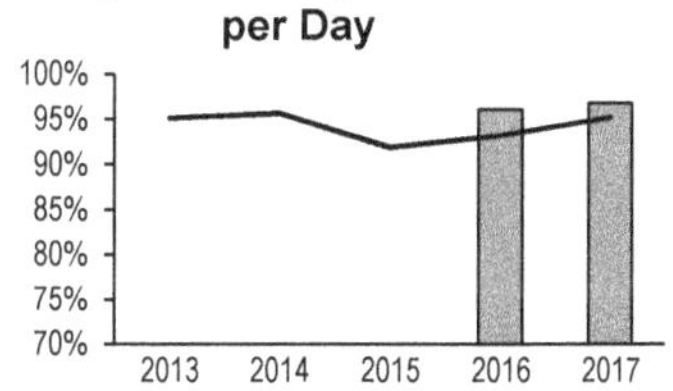

Raleigh				96%	97%
Average	95%	96%	92%	93%	95%

Percentage of Work Orders Requiring Repeat Repair within 30 Days

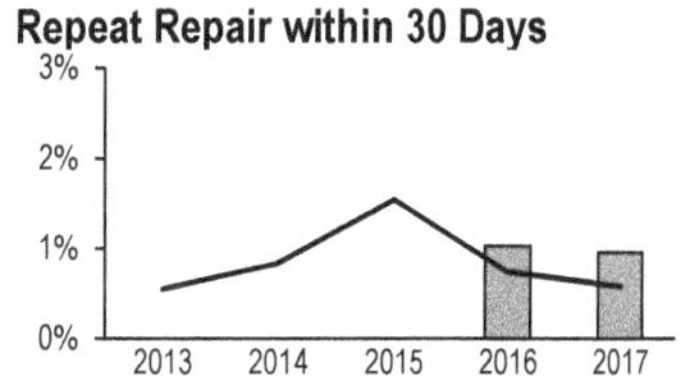

Raleigh				1.03%	0.96%
Average	0.55%	0.83%	1.54%	0.74%	0.58%

Fiscal Year 2016–17

Explanatory Information

Service Level and Delivery
Fleet Maintenance is a division of the Public Services Department and operates the fleet and transit shops. All activities in this operation are accounted for in Salisbury's general fund.

There is no markup on any parts sold or sublet work performed on city vehicles. However, for work done on vehicles owned by other local governments, such as the county, the city charges for labor and includes a markup on parts and sublet work.

The following services were contracted out:

- body work
- exhaust system repairs
- towing.

Conditions Affecting Service, Performance, and Costs
Vehicle Equivalent Units (VEUs) are a weighted measure of the maintenance effort associated with different classes of vehicles. A normal-use car is considered equal to one VEU. Vehicles such as fire trucks or police cars have higher VEUs, reflecting greater expected levels of maintenance.

In Salisbury, the preventive maintenance (PM) completion standard for "percentage of PMs completed as scheduled" is within thirty days of scheduled maintenance or within defined mileage parameters.

In addition to maintenance responsibilities for the city's rolling stock, the fleet maintenance division also maintains vehicles for Rowan County and two trolleys for downtown Salisbury. The division also has responsibility for equipment, including generators, water pumps, hydraulic power units, mowers, tamps, weedwhackers, jack hammers, rescue equipment, air compressors, sidewalk sweepers, thermo plastic equipment, hydraulic hammers, pavement saws, chain saws, and other city equipment.

During the fiscal year Salisbury had a higher employee turnover in fleet maintenance than usual. Repeat repairs were up due to the higher turnover along with a number of warranty repairs and new equipment installation responsibilities.

Municipal Profile

Population (OSBM 2016)	34,459
Land Area (Square Miles)	22.28
Persons per Square Mile	1,547

Service Profile

FTE Positions—Technician	10.0
FTE Positions—Other	4.0
Work Bays	17

Rolling Stock Maintained	No.	Average Age
Cars—Normal Usage	4	14.8 Years
Cars—Severe Usage	105	6.4 Years
Motorcycles	0	NA
Light Utility Vehicles	9	9.8 Years
Light Vehicles	136	12.3 Years
Medium Vehicles	30	13.6 Years
Heavy—Sanitation	14	9.1 Years
Heavy—Sewer	3	13.3 Years
Heavy—Fire Apparatus	12	20.4 Years
Heavy—Other	28	13.0 Years
Trailed Equipment	98	16.5 Years
Off-Road/Construction/Tractors	74	11.5 Years
Buses	9	12.2 Years
TOTAL	522	

Vehicle Equivalent Units (VEUs)	1,709
Average Rolling Stock Units Available per Day	498
Hours Billed	NA
Work Orders	5,077
Repeat Repairs within 30 Days	16
Work Orders Completed within 24 hours	NA
Preventive Maintenance Jobs (PMs)	2,004
PMs Completed as Scheduled	1,942

Full Cost Profile

Cost Breakdown by Percentage	
Personal Services	50.2%
Operating Costs	46.4%
Capital Costs	3.4%
TOTAL	100.0%

Cost Breakdown in Dollars	
Personal Services	$838,074
Operating Costs	$773,469
Capital Costs	$56,654
TOTAL	$1,668,198

Key: Salisbury ▒ Benchmarking Average — Fiscal Years 2013 through 2017

Resource Measures

Fleet Maintenance Services Cost per Capita

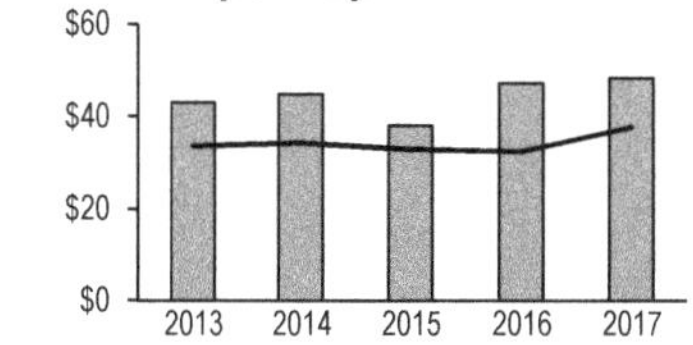

	2013	2014	2015	2016	2017
Salisbury	$43.13	$44.93	$38.01	$47.19	$48.41
Average	$33.64	$34.39	$32.91	$32.46	$37.72

Fleet Maintenance FTEs per 10,000 Population

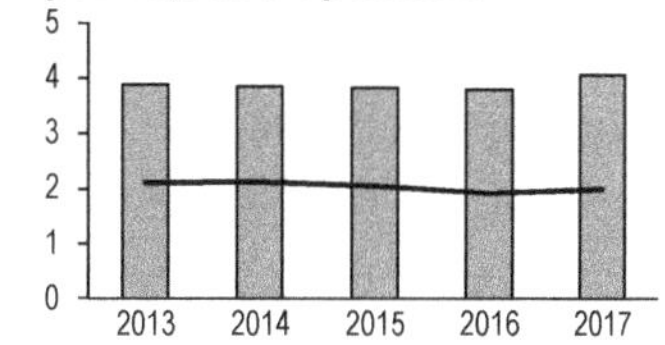

	2013	2014	2015	2016	2017
Salisbury	3.89	3.85	3.83	3.79	4.06
Average	2.11	2.12	2.05	1.92	1.99

Fleet Maintenance FTEs per 100 Municipal Employees

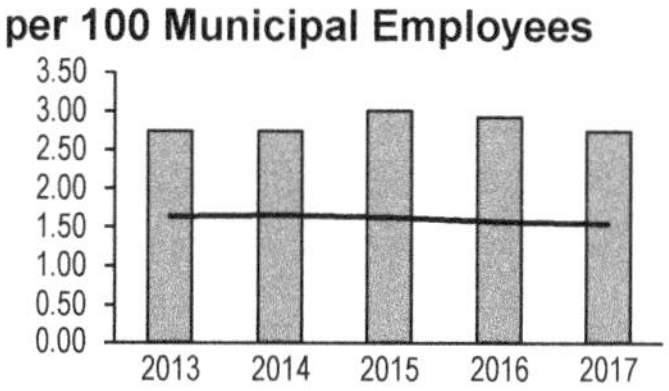

	2013	2014	2015	2016	2017
Salisbury	2.73	2.73	3.00	2.91	2.73
Average	1.64	1.66	1.63	1.58	1.55

Workload Measures

Number of Vehicle Equivalent Units (VEUs) per Technician FTE

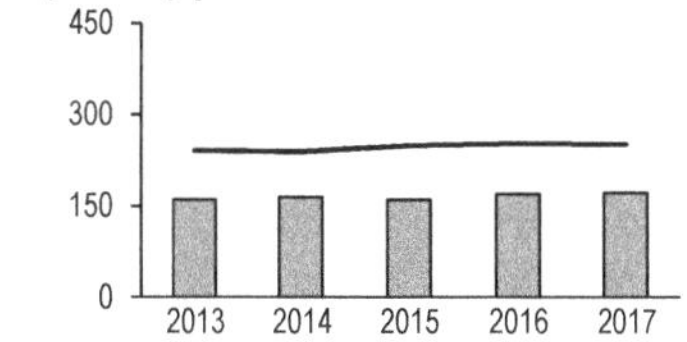

	2013	2014	2015	2016	2017
Salisbury	160	163	160	169	171
Average	240	239	249	252	251

Preventive Maintenances (PMs) Completed In-House per Tech FTE

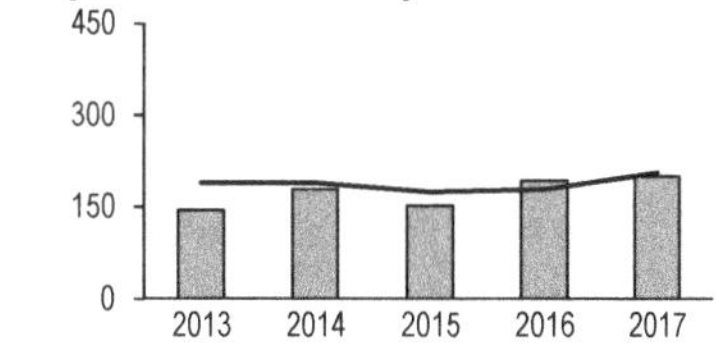

	2013	2014	2015	2016	2017
Salisbury	144	179	151	192	200
Average	189	189	175	179	206

Efficiency Measures

Fleet Maintenance Cost per Work Order

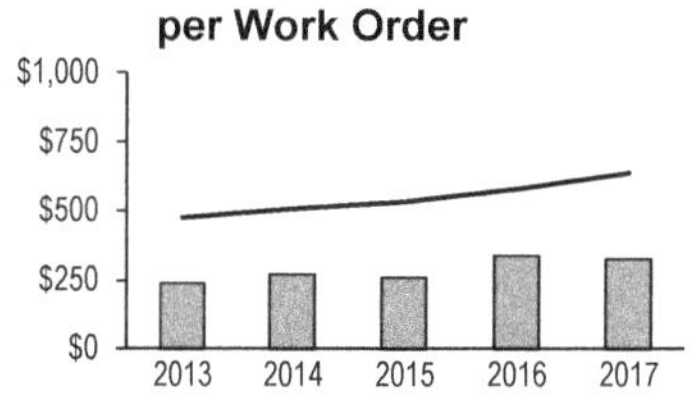

	2013	2014	2015	2016	2017
Salisbury	$240	$272	$260	$341	$329
Average	$477	$510	$535	$581	$639

Fleet Maintenance Cost per Vehicle Equivalent Unit (VEU)

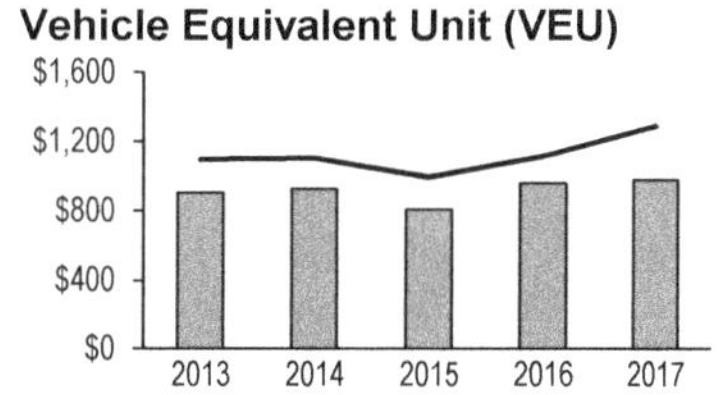

	2013	2014	2015	2016	2017
Salisbury	$902	$928	$808	$959	$976
Average	$1,096	$1,103	$994	$1,114	$1,289

Hours Billed as a Percentage of Total Hours

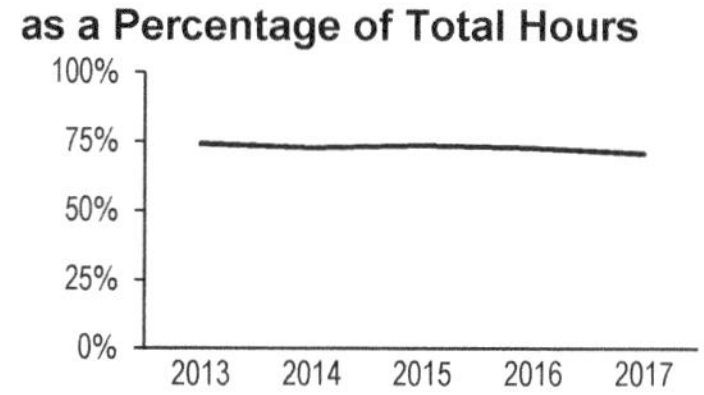

	2013	2014	2015	2016	2017
Salisbury					
Average	74%	73%	74%	73%	71%

Effectiveness Measures

Preventive Maintenances (PMs) as a Percentage of All Work Orders

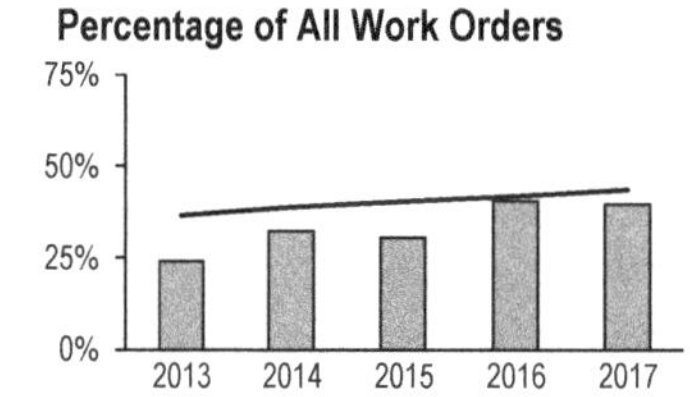

	2013	2014	2015	2016	2017
Salisbury	24%	32%	30%	40%	39%
Average	37%	39%	40%	42%	44%

Percentage of Preventive Maintenances (PMs) Completed as Scheduled

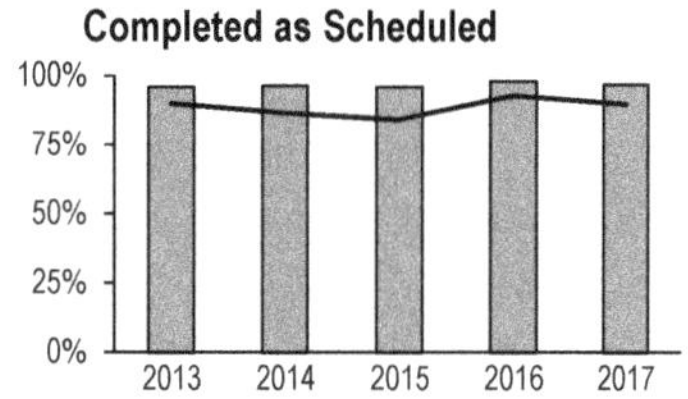

	2013	2014	2015	2016	2017
Salisbury	96%	96%	96%	98%	97%
Average	90%	87%	84%	93%	90%

Percentage of Work Orders Completed within 24 Hours

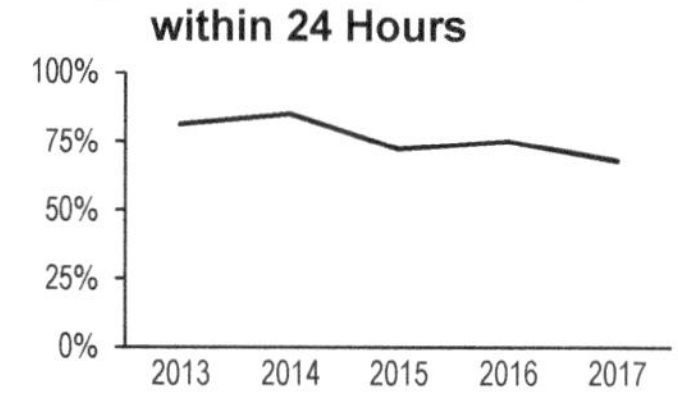

	2013	2014	2015	2016	2017
Salisbury					
Average	81%	85%	72%	75%	68%

Percentage of Rolling Stock Available per Day

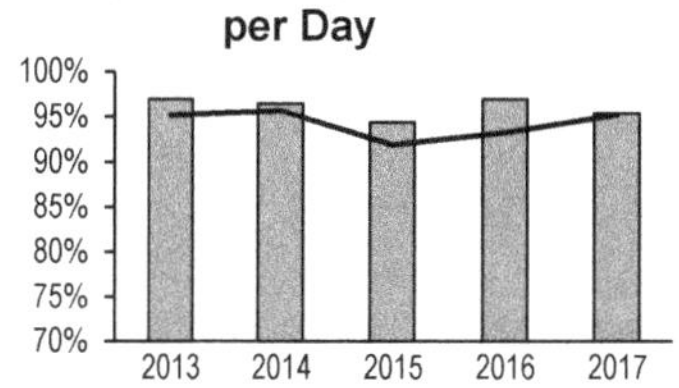

	2013	2014	2015	2016	2017
Salisbury	97%	96%	94%	97%	95%
Average	95%	96%	92%	93%	95%

Percentage of Work Orders Requiring Repeat Repair within 30 Days

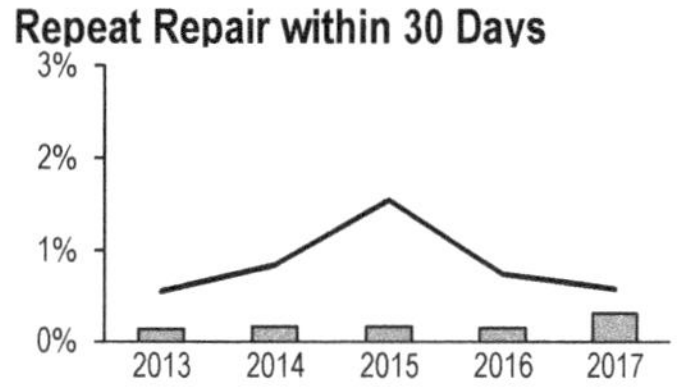

	2013	2014	2015	2016	2017
Salisbury	0.13%	0.16%	0.16%	0.15%	0.32%
Average	0.55%	0.83%	1.54%	0.74%	0.58%

Fiscal Year 2016–17

Explanatory Information

Service Level and Delivery

Wilson's Fleet Maintenance Division is housed within the Department of Public Services. All activities in this operation are accounted for in the general fund.

Charges for maintenance services included a $44-per-hour labor rate, a 25 percent markup charge on parts sold, and a 5 percent markup charge on sublet work.

The following services were contracted out:

- body repairs
- paint work
- wrecker service
- radiator repairs
- alignment
- muffler repairs.

Conditions Affecting Service, Performance, and Costs

Vehicle Equivalent Units (VEUs) are a weighted measure of the maintenance effort associated with different classes of vehicles. A normal-use car is considered equal to one VEU. Vehicles such as fire trucks or police cars have higher VEUs, reflecting greater expected levels of maintenance.

The measure "hours billed as a percentage of total hours" is based on a work year of 2,080 hours and only counts those positions that were filled. It should be noted that technicians have responsibilities that do not result in billable hours and they take normal vacation and sick leave. Therefore this percentage should not be expected to be near 100 percent.

In Wilson, the preventive maintenance (PM) completion standard for "percentage of PMs completed as scheduled" varies, including both calendar and mileage standards.

In addition to rolling stock, Wilson's fleet services has maintenance responsibilities for generators, mowers, tamps, leaf machines, water pumps, and other city equipment.

Municipal Profile

Population (OSBM 2016)	49,406
Land Area (Square Miles)	30.60
Persons per Square Mile	1,615

Service Profile

FTE Positions—Technician	11.0
FTE Positions—Other	5.0
Work Bays	15

Rolling Stock Maintained	No.	Average Age
Cars—Normal Usage	24	13.7 Years
Cars—Severe Usage	112	7.0 Years
Motorcycles	3	3.0 Years
Light Utility Vehicles	5	3.0 Years
Light Vehicles	194	9.0 Years
Medium Vehicles	59	12.0 Years
Heavy—Sanitation	31	8.5 Years
Heavy—Sewer	5	10.6 Years
Heavy—Fire Apparatus	9	15.3 Years
Heavy—Other	53	11.5 Years
Trailed Equipment	150	14.0 Years
Off-Road/Construction/Tractors	172	14.0 Years
Buses	5	12.0 Years
TOTAL	822	

Vehicle Equivalent Units (VEUs)	2,752
Average Rolling Stock Units Available per Day	789
Hours Billed	18,154
Work Orders	7,413
Repeat Repairs within 30 Days	37
Work Orders Completed within 24 hours	6,375
Preventive Maintenance Jobs (PMs)	1,555
PMs Completed as Scheduled	1,399

Full Cost Profile

Cost Breakdown by Percentage	
Personal Services	34.3%
Operating Costs	61.2%
Capital Costs	4.5%
TOTAL	100.0%

Cost Breakdown in Dollars	
Personal Services	$1,256,578
Operating Costs	$2,246,327
Capital Costs	$165,110
TOTAL	$3,668,015

Key: Wilson ▒ Benchmarking Average — Fiscal Years 2013 through 2017

Resource Measures

Fleet Maintenance Services Cost per Capita

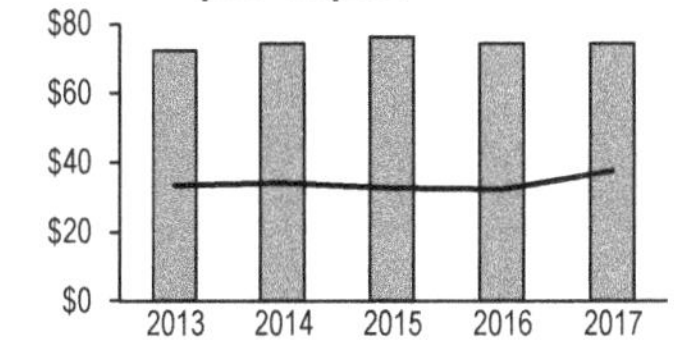

	2013	2014	2015	2016	2017
Wilson	$72.24	$74.31	$76.14	$74.36	$74.24
Average	$33.64	$34.39	$32.91	$32.46	$37.72

Fleet Maintenance FTEs per 10,000 Population

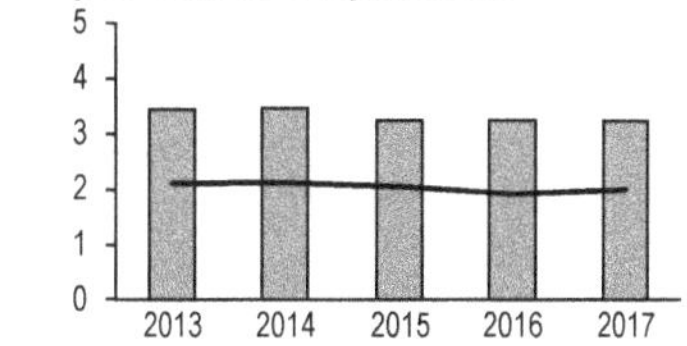

	2013	2014	2015	2016	2017
Wilson	3.44	3.46	3.25	3.24	3.24
Average	2.11	2.12	2.05	1.92	1.99

Fleet Maintenance FTEs per 100 Municipal Employees

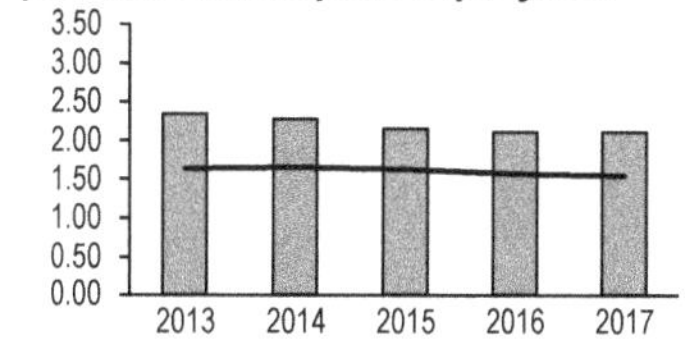

	2013	2014	2015	2016	2017
Wilson	2.34	2.27	2.15	2.11	2.11
Average	1.64	1.66	1.63	1.58	1.55

Workload Measures

Number of Vehicle Equivalent Units (VEUs) per Technician FTE

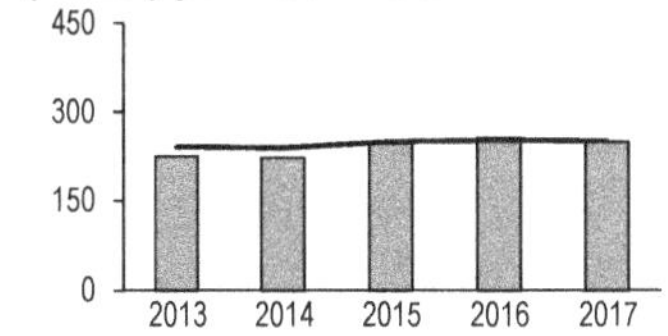

	2013	2014	2015	2016	2017
Wilson	226	223	248	257	250
Average	240	239	249	252	251

Preventive Maintenances (PMs) Completed In-House per Tech FTE

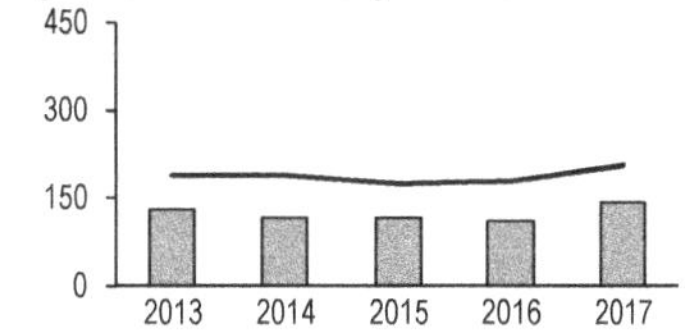

	2013	2014	2015	2016	2017
Wilson	130	115	115	110	141
Average	189	189	175	179	206

Efficiency Measures

Fleet Maintenance Cost per Work Order

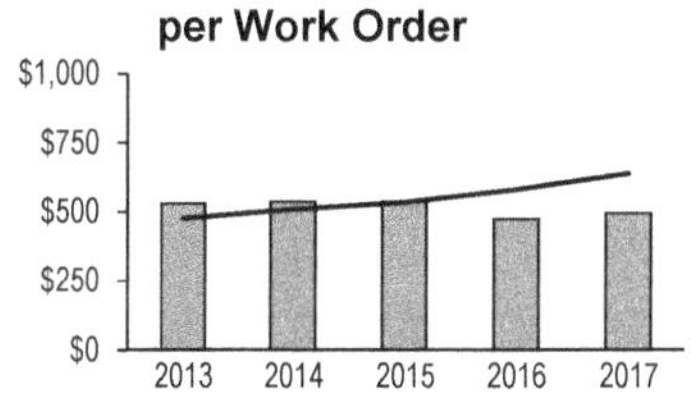

	2013	2014	2015	2016	2017
Wilson	$531	$536	$536	$475	$495
Average	$477	$510	$535	$581	$639

Fleet Maintenance Cost per Vehicle Equivalent Unit (VEU)

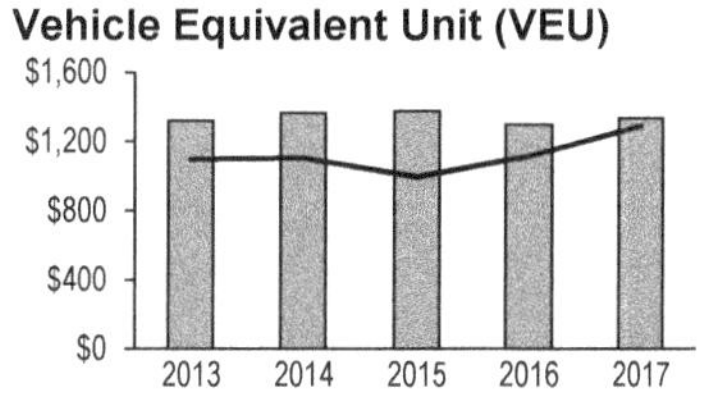

	2013	2014	2015	2016	2017
Wilson	$1,320	$1,364	$1,375	$1,298	$1,333
Average	$1,096	$1,103	$994	$1,114	$1,289

Hours Billed as a Percentage of Total Hours

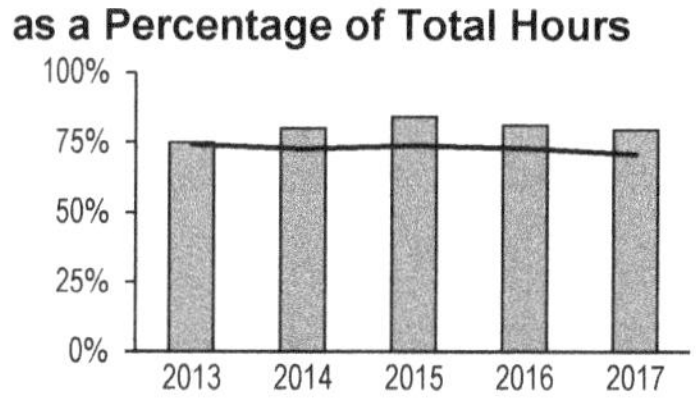

	2013	2014	2015	2016	2017
Wilson	75%	80%	84%	81%	79%
Average	74%	73%	74%	73%	71%

Effectiveness Measures

Preventive Maintenances (PMs) as a Percentage of All Work Orders

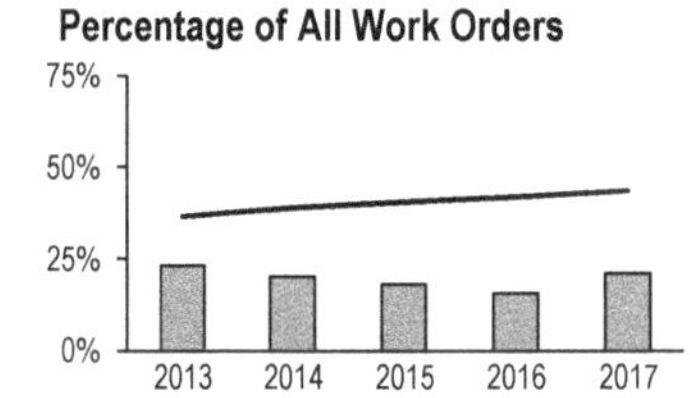

	2013	2014	2015	2016	2017
Wilson	23%	20%	18%	16%	21%
Average	37%	39%	40%	42%	44%

Percentage of Preventive Maintenances (PMs) Completed as Scheduled

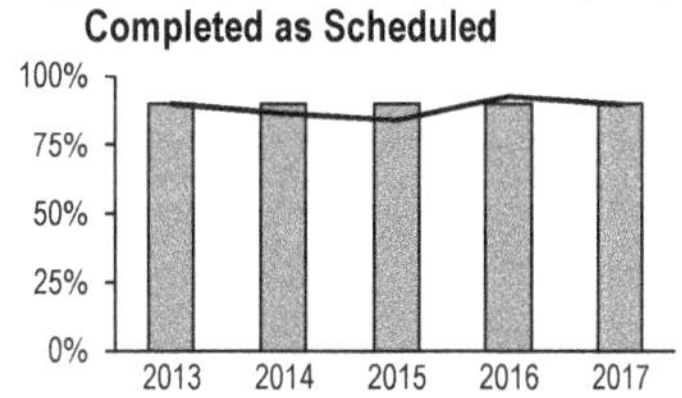

	2013	2014	2015	2016	2017
Wilson	90%	90%	90%	90%	90%
Average	90%	87%	84%	93%	90%

Percentage of Work Orders Completed within 24 Hours

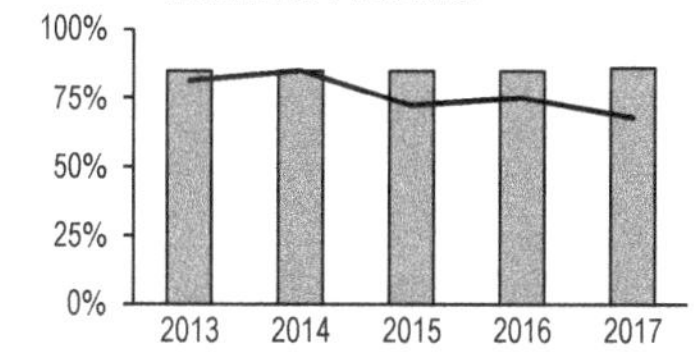

	2013	2014	2015	2016	2017
Wilson	85%	85%	85%	85%	86%
Average	81%	85%	72%	75%	68%

Percentage of Rolling Stock Available per Day

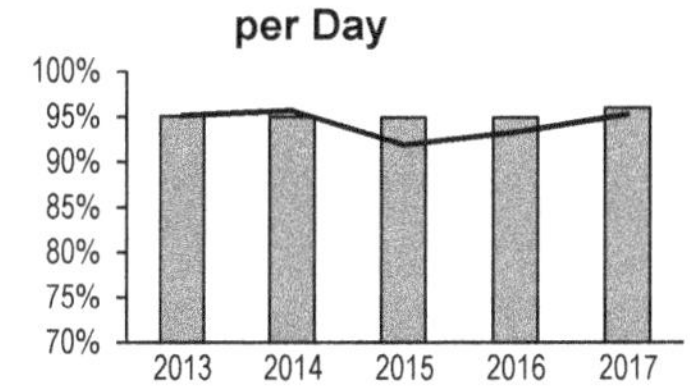

	2013	2014	2015	2016	2017
Wilson	95%	95%	95%	95%	96%
Average	95%	96%	92%	93%	95%

Percentage of Work Orders Requiring Repeat Repair within 30 Days

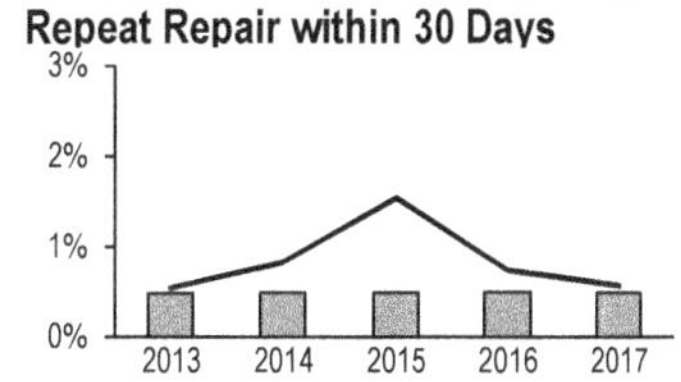

	2013	2014	2015	2016	2017
Wilson	0.49%	0.50%	0.50%	0.50%	0.50%
Average	0.55%	0.83%	1.54%	0.74%	0.58%

Fiscal Year 2016–17

Explanatory Information

Service Level and Delivery
Fleet Services is a division of the Property and Facilities Management Department, consisting of eight units: vehicle maintenance administration, contract monitoring administration, heavy equipment, service station, vehicle leasing, parts, light equipment, and tire shop. All activities in this operation are accounted for in an internal service fund.

Charges for maintenance services included a $50-per-hour labor rate, a 26 percent markup charge for parts sold, and a 13 percent markup charge for sublet work.

The following services were contracted out:

- body work
- welding
- hydraulic cylinder and pump repair
- glass repair
- towing
- transmission repair.

Conditions Affecting Service, Performance, and Costs
Vehicle Equivalent Units (VEUs) are a weighted measure of the maintenance effort associated with different classes of vehicles. A normal-use car is considered equal to one VEU. Vehicles such as fire trucks or police cars have higher VEUs, reflecting greater expected levels of maintenance.

The measure "hours billed as a percentage of total hours" is based on a work year of 2,080 hours and only counts those positions that were filled. It should be noted that technicians have responsibilities that do not result in billable hours and they take normal vacation and sick leave. Therefore this percentage should not be expected to be near 100 percent. Winston-Salem indicated that seventeen technician FTEs were actually working during the fiscal year for this calculation.

Results for the measures "percentage of PMs completed as scheduled" and "percentage of work orders requiring repeat repairs within 30 days" were not available.

In addition to rolling stock, Winston-Salem's Fleet Services has maintenance responsibilities for mowers, weedeaters, water pumps, chain saws, whacker tamps, pavement stripers, tractor implements, leaf blowers, power trimmers, salt spreaders, snow plows, and other city equipment.

In Winston-Salem, maintenance on fire vehicles is performed by mechanics in the fire department. The work performed is not counted here.

Municipal Profile

Population (OSBM 2016)	240,603
Land Area (Square Miles)	132.55
Persons per Square Mile	1,815

Service Profile

FTE Positions—Technician	18.0
FTE Positions—Other	13.0
Work Bays	31

Rolling Stock Maintained	No.	Average Age
Cars—Normal Usage	290	7.1 Years
Cars—Severe Usage	463	5.0 Years
Motorcycles	13	NA
Light Utility Vehicles	10	NA
Light Vehicles	425	7.8 Years
Medium Vehicles	142	9.9 Years
Heavy—Sanitation	60	4.2 Years
Heavy—Sewer	6	7.8 Years
Heavy—Fire Apparatus	0	NA
Heavy—Other	63	5.4 Years
Trailed Equipment	153	20.3 Years
Off-Road/Construction/Tractors	258	14.8 Years
Buses	0	NA
TOTAL	1,883	

Vehicle Equivalent Units (VEUs)	5,434
Average Rolling Stock Units Available per Day	1,861
Hours Billed	24,185
Work Orders	8,403
Repeat Repairs within 30 Days	NA
Work Orders Completed within 24 hours	5,637
Preventive Maintenance Jobs (PMs)	7,159
PMs Completed as Scheduled	NA

Full Cost Profile

Cost Breakdown by Percentage	
Personal Services	27.1%
Operating Costs	71.2%
Capital Costs	1.7%
TOTAL	100.0%

Cost Breakdown in Dollars	
Personal Services	$1,506,467
Operating Costs	$3,953,735
Capital Costs	$92,114
TOTAL	$5,552,316

Key: Winston-Salem ▒ Benchmarking Average — Fiscal Years 2013 through 2017

Resource Measures

Fleet Maintenance Services Cost per Capita

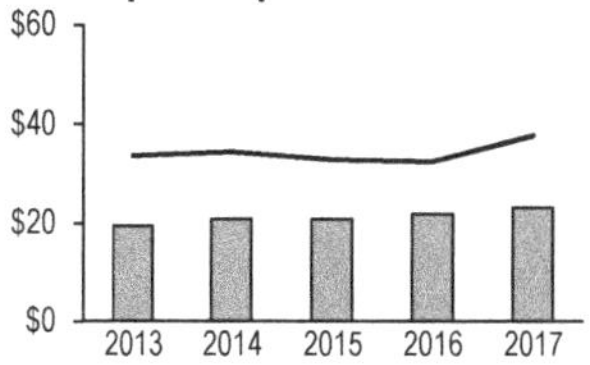

	2013	2014	2015	2016	2017
Winston-Salem	$19.35	$20.85	$20.78	$21.87	$23.08
Average	$33.64	$34.39	$32.91	$32.46	$37.72

Fleet Maintenance FTEs per 10,000 Population

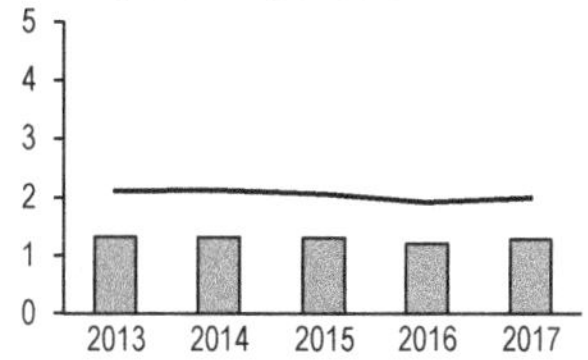

	2013	2014	2015	2016	2017
Winston-Salem	1.33	1.32	1.30	1.21	1.29
Average	2.11	2.12	2.05	1.92	1.99

Fleet Maintenance FTEs per 100 Municipal Employees

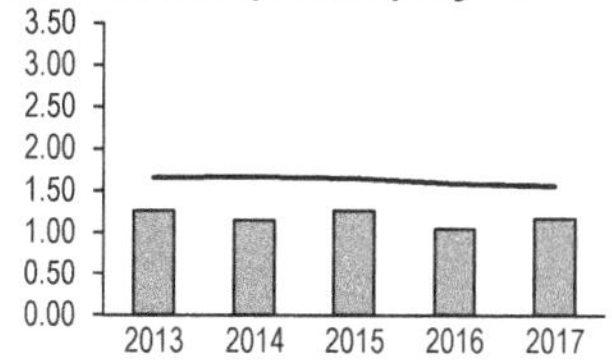

	2013	2014	2015	2016	2017
Winston-Salem	1.25	1.14	1.25	1.04	1.16
Average	1.64	1.66	1.63	1.58	1.55

Workload Measures

Number of Vehicle Equivalent Units (VEUs) per Technician FTE

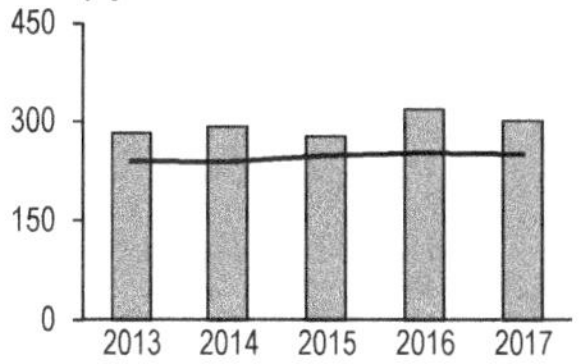

	2013	2014	2015	2016	2017
Winston-Salem	283	293	278	320	302
Average	240	239	249	252	251

Preventive Maintenances (PMs) Completed In-House per Tech FTE

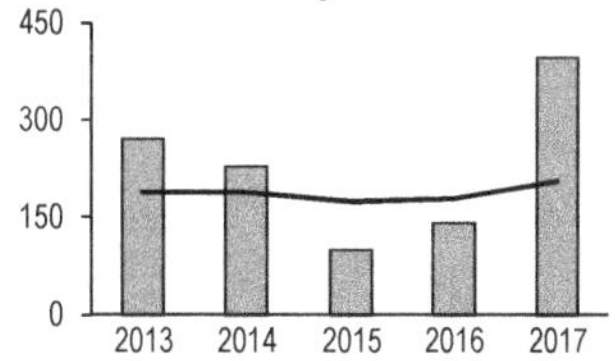

	2013	2014	2015	2016	2017
Winston-Salem	271	229	100	142	398
Average	189	189	175	179	206

Efficiency Measures

Fleet Maintenance Cost per Work Order

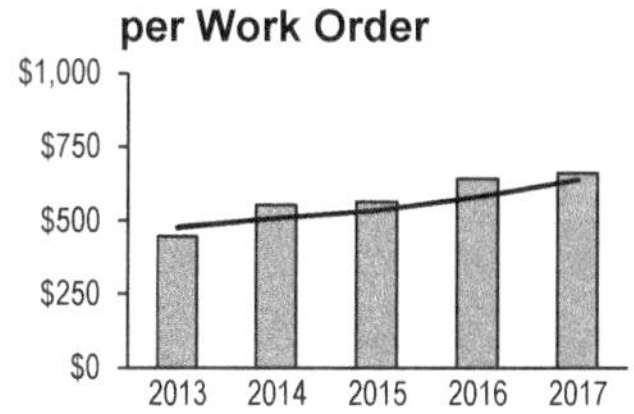

	2013	2014	2015	2016	2017
Winston-Salem	$446	$552	$563	$642	$661
Average	$477	$510	$535	$581	$639

Fleet Maintenance Cost per Vehicle Equivalent Unit (VEU)

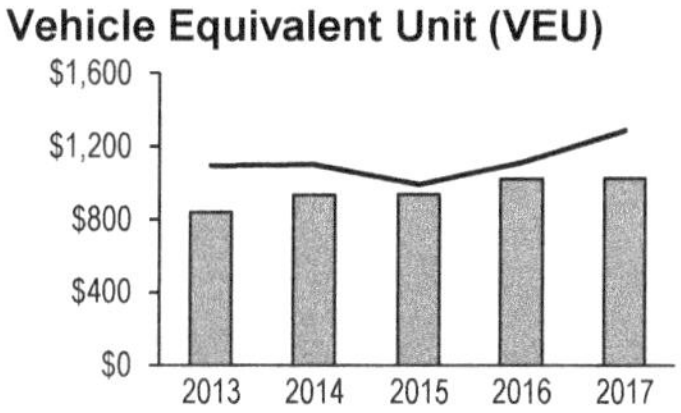

	2013	2014	2015	2016	2017
Winston-Salem	$839	$931	$935	$1,021	$1,022
Average	$1,096	$1,103	$994	$1,114	$1,289

Hours Billed as a Percentage of Total Hours

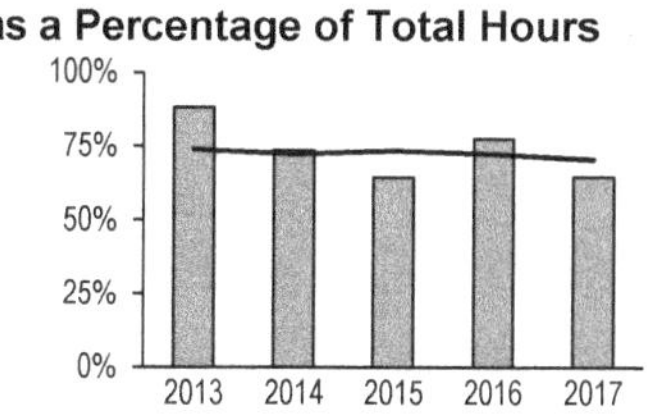

	2013	2014	2015	2016	2017
Winston-Salem	88%	73%	64%	77%	65%
Average	74%	73%	74%	73%	71%

Effectiveness Measures

Preventive Maintenances (PMs) as a Percentage of All Work Orders

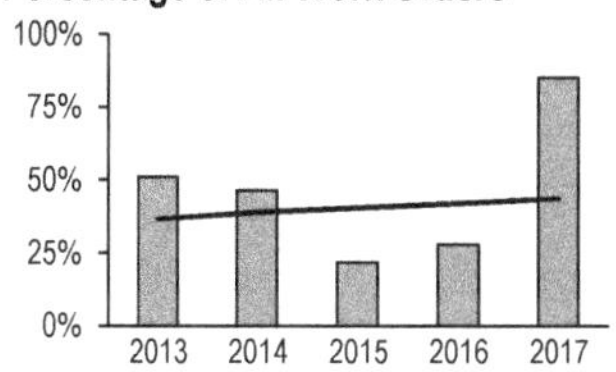

	2013	2014	2015	2016	2017
Winston-Salem	51%	46%	22%	28%	85%
Average	37%	39%	40%	42%	44%

Percentage of Preventive Maintenances (PMs) Completed as Scheduled

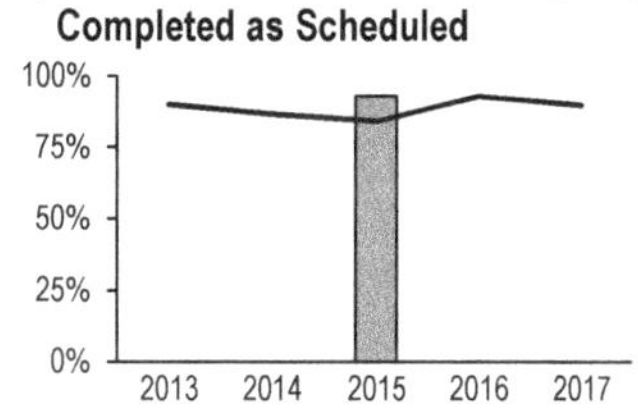

	2013	2014	2015	2016	2017
Winston-Salem			93%		
Average	90%	87%	84%	93%	90%

Percentage of Work Orders Completed within 24 Hours

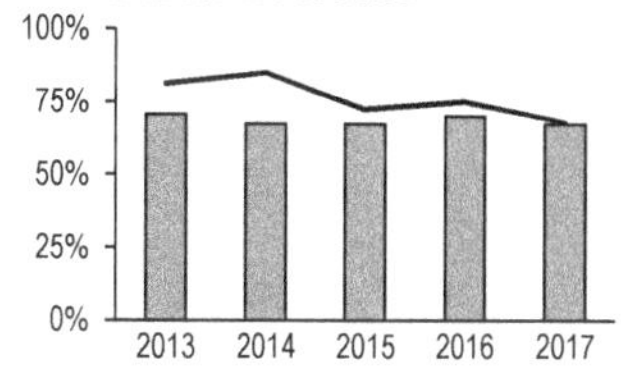

	2013	2014	2015	2016	2017
Winston-Salem	70%	67%	67%	70%	67%
Average	81%	85%	72%	75%	68%

Percentage of Rolling Stock Available per Day

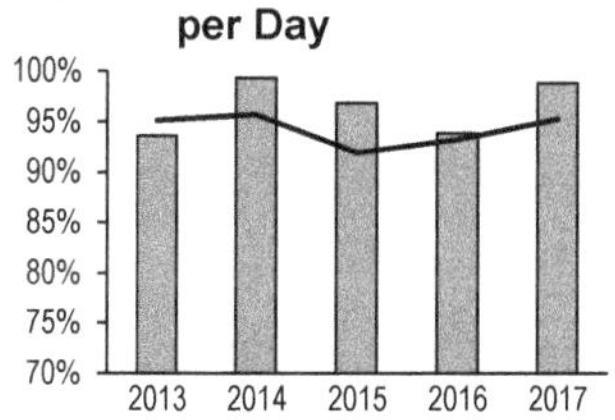

	2013	2014	2015	2016	2017
Winston-Salem	94%	99%	97%	94%	99%
Average	95%	96%	92%	93%	95%

Percentage of Work Orders Requiring Repeat Repair within 30 Days

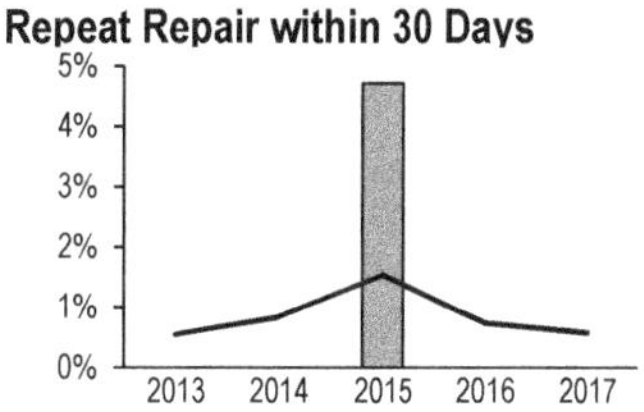

	2013	2014	2015	2016	2017
Winston-Salem			4.71%		
Average	0.55%	0.83%	1.54%	0.74%	0.58%

UNC SCHOOL OF GOVERNMENT
North Carolina Benchmarking Project

Performance and Cost Data

CENTRAL HUMAN RESOURCES

UNC | SCHOOL OF GOVERNMENT
North Carolina Benchmarking Project

PERFORMANCE MEASURES FOR CENTRAL HUMAN RESOURCES

SERVICE DEFINITION

Central human resources represents an internal support service. It is characterized by various functions related to the daily management of human capital or personnel, including compensation analysis; position classification; benefits administration; management of employee training and development; employee relations; position control; employee performance evaluations; recruitment and selection; occupational health, wellness, and safety programs; administration of the Human Resources Information System (HRIS); and general administration of the central human resources office. Excluded from the counts here are staff who may be assisting with certain human resource functions but who are not in the central human resources department, such as employees who might be assigned to individual departments. Also excluded from this service area is risk financing, including general liability insurance and workers' compensation.

NOTES ON PERFORMANCE MEASURES

1. Total Workforce FTEs per 10,000 Population

The number of full-time equivalent (FTE) positions includes all permanent full-time and permanent part-time employees budgeted for the municipality. One FTE equates to 2,080 hours of work per year. Any combination of employees providing 2,080 hours of annual work equals one FTE.

2. Number of Applications Received per 100 Employees

Human resources is responsible for the recruitment and selection of applicants to fill new or vacant positions.

3. Number of Position Requisitions per 100 Employees

Position requisitions are submitted to the human resources office by departments seeking to fill vacant positions.

4. Cost per Employee

This measure represents the total cost of human resources for the fiscal year ending June 30 and is calculated using the project's full cost accounting model, which captures direct, indirect, and capital costs. Cost per employee is the primary measure of cost efficiency for this service area.

5. Ratio of Human Resources Staff to Total Workforce

This is a calculation of human resource FTEs divided by the total number of employees in the permanent municipal workforce, including full- and part-time staff.

6. Probationary Period Completion Rate (New Hires)

Most organizations require that new employees complete a probationary employment period, typically lasting three to eighteen months from the hire date, depending on the job classification. This effectiveness measure is calculated by dividing the total number of employees that completed the probationary period by the number of employees eligible to complete the probationary period during the fiscal year.

7. Employee Total Turnover Rate

The employee turnover rate is calculated by dividing the total number of separated staff during the fiscal year by the total number of authorized positions.

8. Employee Voluntary Turnover Rate

The employee voluntary turnover rate is calculated by dividing the number of voluntarily separated staff during the fiscal year by the total number of authorized positions. Voluntary separations include retirements and resignations.

9. Percentage of Grievances Resolved at Department Level

Most jurisdictions have a process in place for handling formal grievances filed by employees. This effectiveness measure is calculated by dividing the number of formal grievances that were resolved within the respective department (prior to going to a higher level or third party for resolution) by the total number of grievances filed during the fiscal year.

10. Average Number of Days from Position Post Date to Hire Date

This includes the number of working days from the date a job is posted to the hire date (first day of employment). It includes only recruitments for permanent full-time and part-time positions that were completed during the fiscal year. This measure excludes recruitment of temporary workers.

Central Human Resources

Summary of Key Dimensions of Service

City or Town	Total Number of Authorized Municipal Positions	Average Length of Service (in Years)	Number of Position Requisitions	Number of Employment Applications Processed	Number of Retirees Serviced	Probationary Period	Turnover Rate	Number of HR FTEs
Apex	417	7.7	161	4,012	32	6 & 12 months	12.2%	4.0
Asheville	1,213	8.7	256	11,843	210	6 months	12.5%	19.6
Chapel Hill	775	11.0	81	10,515	50	6 & 12 months	11.6%	7.0
Charlotte	7,590	10.5	663	52,960	NA	6 & 12 months	8.2%	40.0
Concord	993	10.3	190	6,604	294	6 & 12 months	10.4%	11.0
Goldsboro	680	11.0	93	3,378	23	6 & 12 months	6.9%	5.0
Greensboro	3,148	10.5	417	26,979	1,663	6 & 12 months	1.5%	36.0
Greenville	769	11.1	222	7,434	245	6 & 12 months	10.8%	9.0
Hickory	736	9.9	102	4,083	110	12 months	10.6%	7.0
High Point	1,637	10.8	392	7,085	81	12 months	8.2%	12.0
Raleigh	3,950	10.0	557	24,519	NA	6 & 12 months	10.9%	42.0
Salisbury	512	8.0	92	1,581	67	6 & 12 months	14.5%	6.0
Wilson	760	13.3	70	1,906	240	12 months	10.1%	5.5
Winston-Salem	2,676	11.1	569	28,435	474	6 & 12 months	13.7%	15.0

NOTES

For municipalities with varying probationary periods, typically fire and/or police personnel have longer probationary periods.

EXPLANATORY FACTORS

These are factors that the project found affected human resources performance and cost in one or more of the municipalities:

Decentralization of HR functions
Personnel policies
External economic climate
Unemployment rate
Extent of contracting out for services
Departmental discretion regarding vacancies
Hiring freezes
State and/or federal mandates

Fiscal Year 2016–17

Explanatory Information

Service Level and Delivery
The Human Resources Department for Apex provides a comprehensive assortment of services, including occupational health and wellness, benefits, recruitment and selection, compensation, employee relations, and training and development programs.

One employee compensation study was completed during the fiscal year covering eighty-seven postions. The Town of Apex tries to study one-third of the job classifications every three years and uses a consultant to assist in this process.

The town's probationary period for new employees is six months for general employees and twelve months for sworn police, fire, and EMS personnel.

Conditions Affecting Service, Performance, and Costs

Municipal Profile

Population (OSBM 2016)	46,688
Land Area (Square Miles)	20.61
Persons per Square Mile	2,265
Median Family Income U.S. Census 2010	$97,201
County Unemployment Rate (2016) U.S. Bureau of Labor Statistics	4.2%

Service Profile

Central HR FTE Positions	
Administration	1.0
Generalist/Specialist	2.0
Staff Support/Clerical	1.00
Total Authorized Workforce	417.0
Authorized FTEs	416.4
Average Length of Service (Months)	92
Number of Position Requisitions	161
Employment Applications Processed	4,012
Length of Probationary Employment Period	6 & 12 months
Compensation Studies Completed	1
Positions Studied	87
Employee Turnover	
Voluntary Separations	46
Involuntary Separations	5
TOTAL SEPARATIONS	51
Formal Grievances Filed by Employees	2
Equal Employment Opportunity Commission (EEOC) Complaints Filed	0

Full Cost Profile

Cost Breakdown by Percentage	
Personal Services	64.0%
Operating Costs	34.2%
Capital Costs	1.7%
TOTAL	100.0%
Cost Breakdown in Dollars	
Personal Services	$357,311
Operating Costs	$191,004
Capital Costs	$9,620
TOTAL	$557,935

Key: Apex ▒ Benchmarking Average — Fiscal Years 2013through 2017

Resource Measures

Human Resources Services Cost per Capita

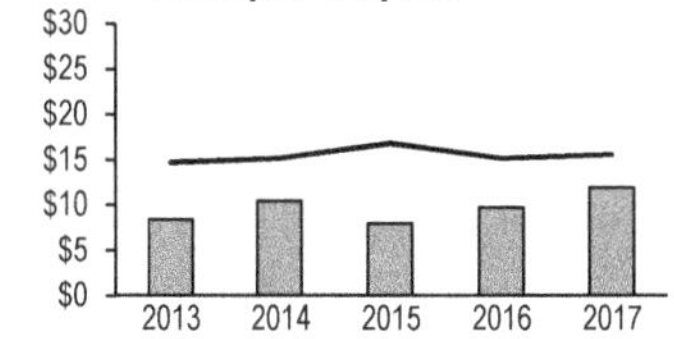

	2013	2014	2015	2016	2017
Apex	$8.36	$10.46	$7.94	$9.73	$11.95
Average	$14.68	$15.20	$16.80	$15.16	$15.62

Human Resources FTEs per 10,000 Population

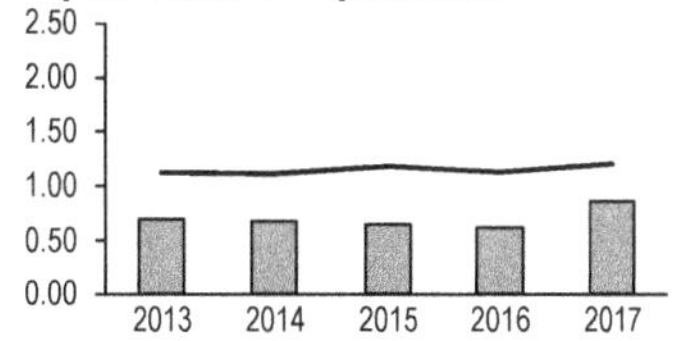

	2013	2014	2015	2016	2017
Apex	0.69	0.67	0.64	0.61	0.86
Average	1.12	1.11	1.18	1.13	1.20

Workload Measures

Total Municipal FTEs per 10,000 Population

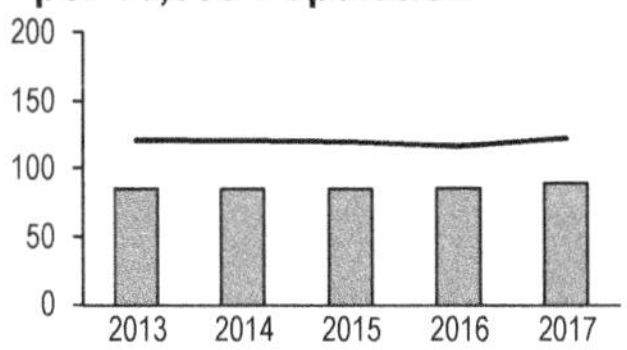

	2013	2014	2015	2016	2017
Apex	85	85	85	86	89
Average	121	120	119	116	122

Applications Processed per 100 Municipal Employees

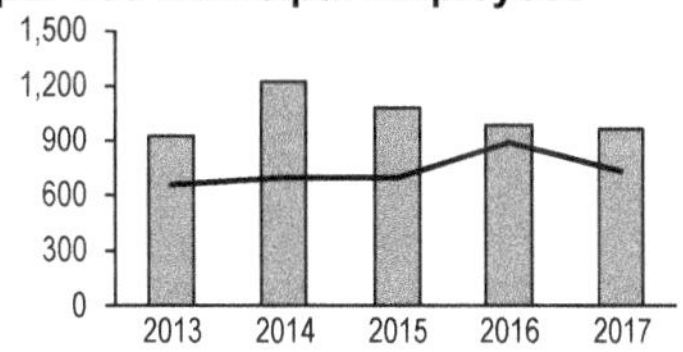

	2013	2014	2015	2016	2017
Apex	925	1,221	1,078	982	962
Average	655	693	695	884	729

Position Requisitions per 100 Municipal Employees

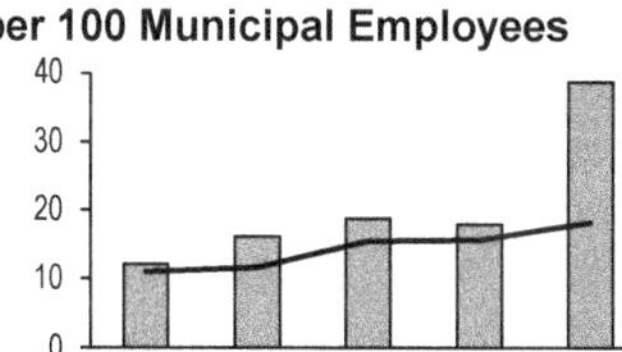

	2013	2014	2015	2016	2017
Apex	12.1	16.0	18.7	17.9	38.6
Average	11.0	11.6	15.4	15.6	18.2

Efficiency Measures

Human Resources Cost per Municipal Employee

	2013	2014	2015	2016	2017
Apex	$978	$1,226	$932	$1,128	$1,338
Average	$1,210	$1,271	$1,346	$1,281	$1,272

Ratio of Human Resources Staff to 100 Municipal Employees

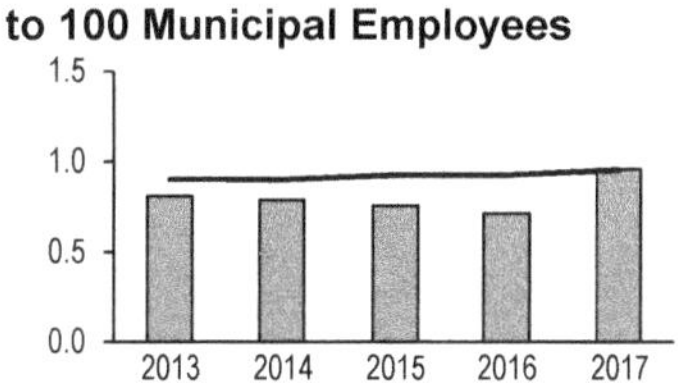

	2013	2014	2015	2016	2017
Apex	0.81	0.79	0.76	0.71	0.96
Average	0.90	0.90	0.93	0.93	0.95

Effectiveness Measures

Probationary Period Completion Rate (New Hires)

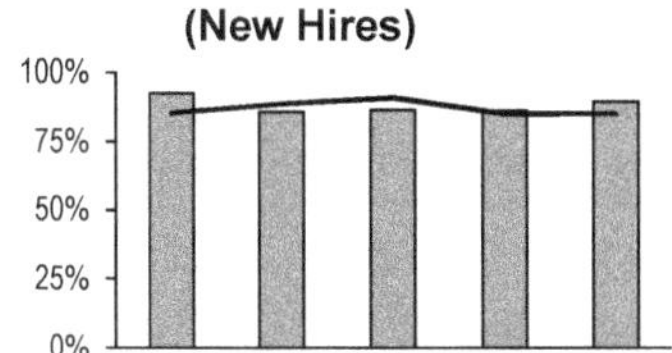

	2013	2014	2015	2016	2017
Apex	93%	86%	86%	86%	89%
Average	85%	88%	91%	85%	85%

Employee Turnover Rate (All Separations)

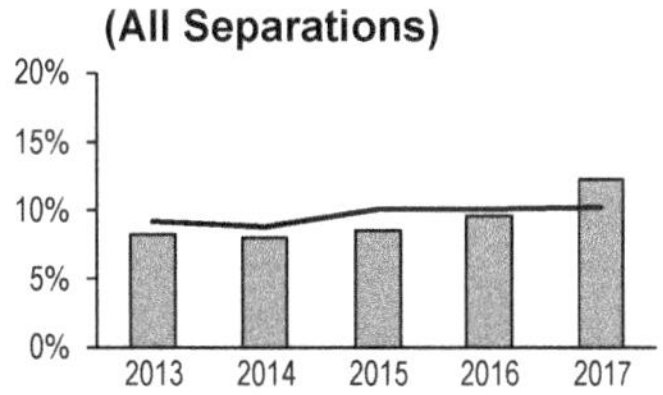

	2013	2014	2015	2016	2017
Apex	8.2%	8.0%	8.5%	9.6%	12.2%
Average	9.2%	8.8%	10.1%	10.0%	10.2%

Employee Turnover Rate (Voluntary Separations)

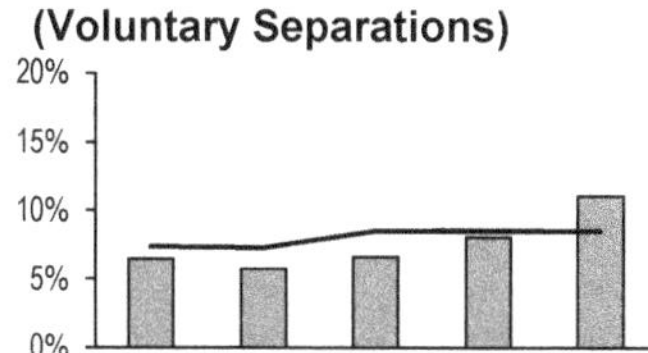

	2013	2014	2015	2016	2017
Apex	6.5%	5.7%	6.6%	8.0%	11.0%
Average	7.4%	7.3%	8.5%	8.5%	8.5%

Percentage of Grievances Resolved at Department Level

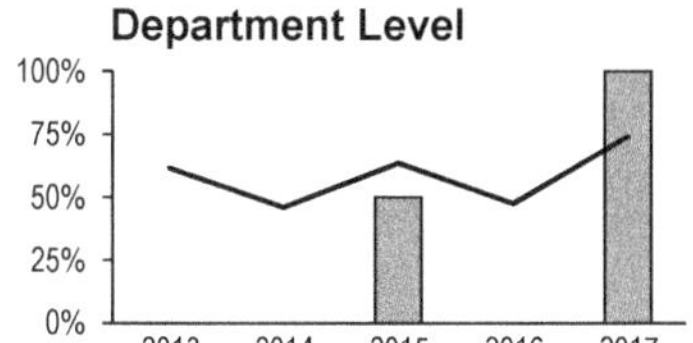

	2013	2014	2015	2016	2017
Apex			50%		100%
Average	61%	46%	64%	48%	74%

Average Days from Post Date to Hire Date (First Day of Employment)

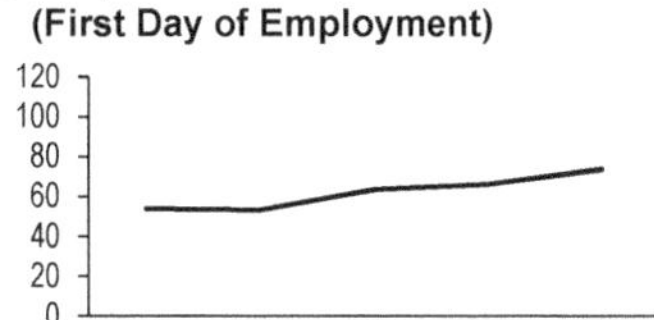

	2013	2014	2015	2016	2017
Apex					
Average	54	53	64	66	74

Fiscal Year 2016–17

Explanatory Information

Service Level and Delivery

The Human Resources Department provides a comprehensive assortment of services, including occupational health and wellness, benefits, recruitment and selection, compensation, employee relations, and youth development programs.

Three employee compensation studies were conducted during the year covering a total of thirty-nine positions.

The city's probationary period for new employees is six months.

Conditions Affecting Service, Performance, and Costs

The city's data include the following positions (and related costs) as part of the city's Human Resources Department: health services supervisor, registered nurse, and administrative staff.

Employee relations issues are resolved through the city's administration.

All advertising costs for vacant positions are now paid for out of the Human Resources budget, with the exception of industry-specific websites or publications specifically requested by the individual departments.

Municipal Profile

Population (OSBM 2016)	91,929
Land Area (Square Miles)	45.52
Persons per Square Mile	2,019
Median Family Income U.S. Census 2010	$53,350
County Unemployment Rate (2016) U.S. Bureau of Labor Statistics	3.8%

Service Profile

Central HR FTE Positions	
Administration	5.00
Generalist/Specialist	9.00
Staff Support/Clerical	5.60
Total Authorized Workforce	1,213.0
Authorized FTEs	1,205.0
Average Length of Service (Months)	104.718
Number of Position Requisitions	256
Employment Applications Processed	11,843
Length of Probationary Employment Period	6 months
Compensation Studies Completed	3
Positions Studied	39
Employee Turnover	
Voluntary Separations	155
Involuntary Separations	8
TOTAL SEPARATIONS	163
Formal Grievances Filed by Employees	10
Equal Employment Opportunity Commission (EEOC) Complaints Filed	0

Full Cost Profile

Cost Breakdown by Percentage	
Personal Services	62.3%
Operating Costs	34.3%
Capital Costs	3.4%
TOTAL	100.0%
Cost Breakdown in Dollars	
Personal Services	$1,685,092
Operating Costs	$926,903
Capital Costs	$92,742
TOTAL	$2,704,737

Key: Asheville ▒ Benchmarking Average — Fiscal Years 2013through 2017

Resource Measures

Human Resources Services Cost per Capita

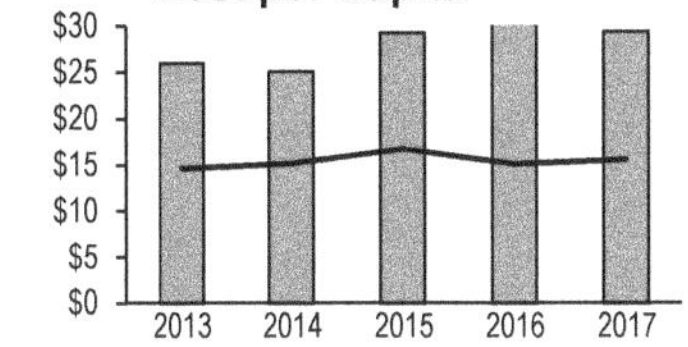

	2013	2014	2015	2016	2017
Asheville	$26.04	$25.12	$29.28	$30.93	$29.42
Average	$14.68	$15.20	$16.80	$15.16	$15.62

Human Resources FTEs per 10,000 Population

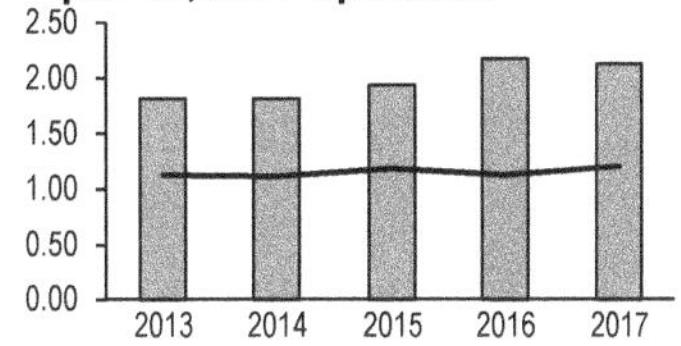

	2013	2014	2015	2016	2017
Asheville	1.82	1.82	1.94	2.18	2.13
Average	1.12	1.11	1.18	1.13	1.20

Workload Measures

Total Municipal FTEs per 10,000 Population

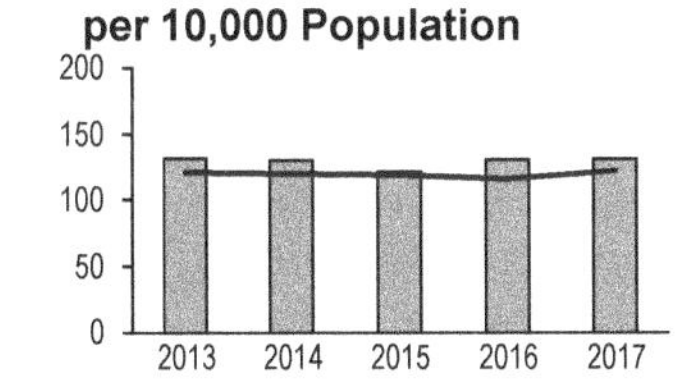

	2013	2014	2015	2016	2017
Asheville	131	130	121	131	131
Average	121	120	119	116	122

Applications Processed per 100 Municipal Employees

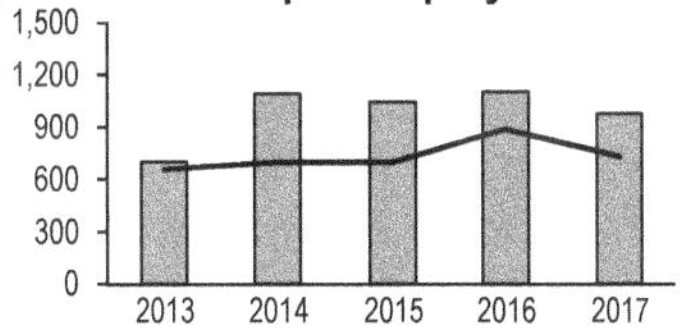

	2013	2014	2015	2016	2017
Asheville	697	1,090	1,042	1,100	976
Average	655	693	695	884	729

Position Requisitions per 100 Municipal Employees

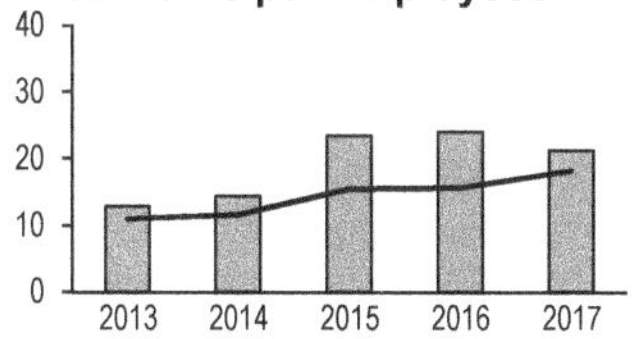

	2013	2014	2015	2016	2017
Asheville	12.7	14.3	23.3	23.9	21.1
Average	11.0	11.6	15.4	15.6	18.2

Efficiency Measures

Human Resources Cost per Municipal Employee

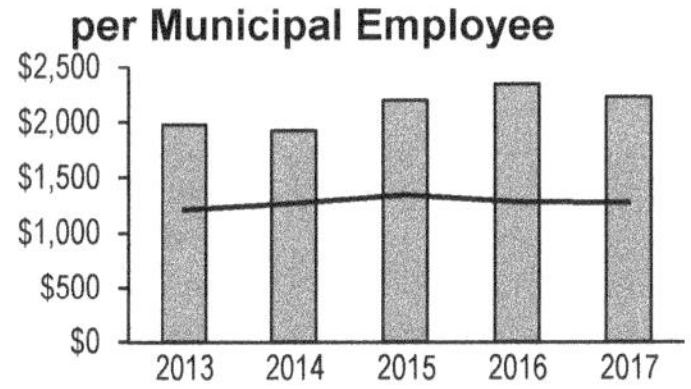

	2013	2014	2015	2016	2017
Asheville	$1,981	$1,929	$2,198	$2,345	$2,230
Average	$1,210	$1,271	$1,346	$1,281	$1,272

Ratio of Human Resources Staff to 100 Municipal Employees

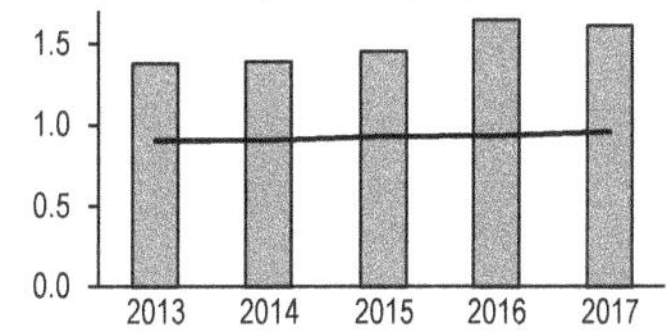

	2013	2014	2015	2016	2017
Asheville	1.38	1.39	1.46	1.65	1.62
Average	0.90	0.90	0.93	0.93	0.95

Effectiveness Measures

Probationary Period Completion Rate (New Hires)

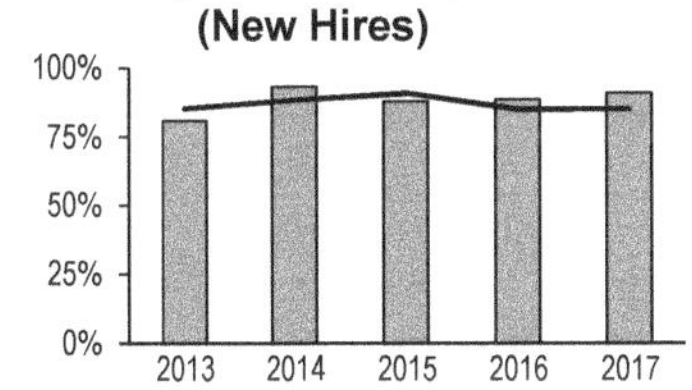

	2013	2014	2015	2016	2017
Asheville	81%	93%	88%	88%	91%
Average	85%	88%	91%	85%	85%

Employee Turnover Rate (All Separations)

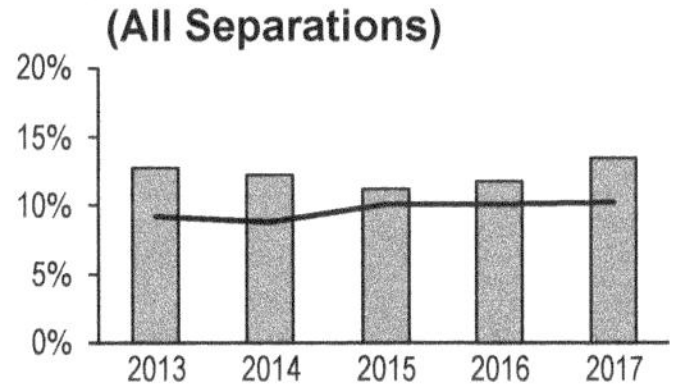

	2013	2014	2015	2016	2017
Asheville	12.7%	12.2%	11.2%	11.8%	13.4%
Average	9.2%	8.8%	10.1%	10.0%	10.2%

Employee Turnover Rate (Voluntary Separations)

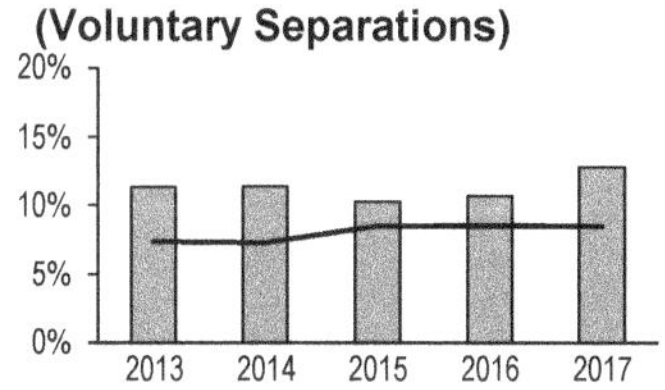

	2013	2014	2015	2016	2017
Asheville	11.3%	11.3%	10.3%	10.7%	12.8%
Average	7.4%	7.3%	8.5%	8.5%	8.5%

Percentage of Grievances Resolved at Department Level

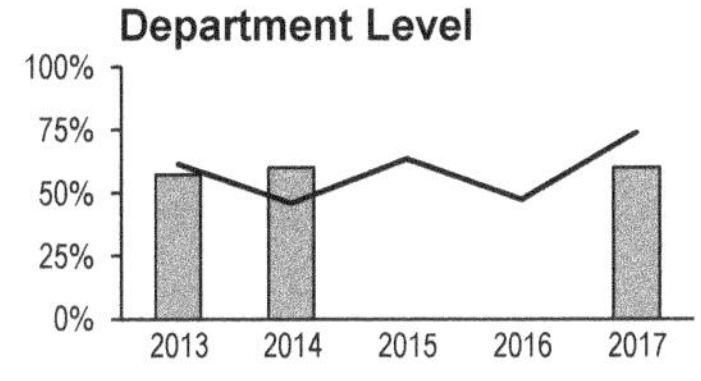

	2013	2014	2015	2016	2017
Asheville	57%	60%	0%	0%	60%
Average	61%	46%	64%	48%	74%

Average Days from Post Date to Hire Date (First Day of Employment)

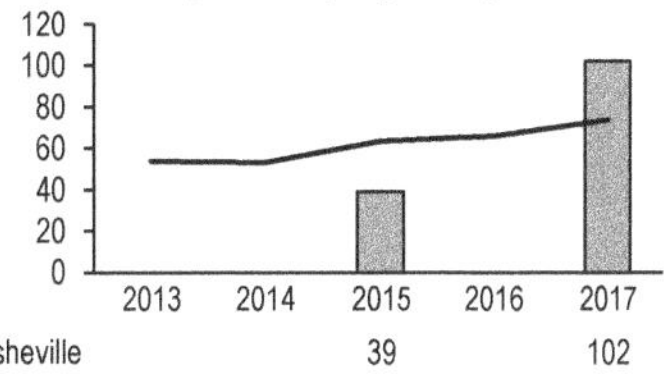

	2013	2014	2015	2016	2017
Asheville			39		102
Average	54	53	64	66	74

Fiscal Year 2016–17

Explanatory Information

Service Level and Delivery
The Town of Chapel Hill's Human Resource Development Department is organized into one centralized HR department using a specialist structure with several departmental HR liasons who facilitate communication of Town processes and procedures, benefits paperwork, and predisciplinary conferences. The department ensures standard operating procedures are followed and coordinates departmental interviews for job openings.

The town provides an employee assistance program at no cost to town staff. Chapel Hill also provides some life insurance coverage and short and long-term disability at no cost to employees. The town has an on-site wellness clinic staffed with a nurse practioner and registered nurse. The town also offers a variety of other wellness programs at reduced cost such as gym membership, nutrionists, and Weight Watchers.

During the fiscal year, one compensation study was conducted covering ninety-five positions. There were 10,515 applications processed electronically or online.

The town's probationary period for most new employees is six months. Department heads and police personnel serve a twelve-month period.

Conditions Affecting Service, Performance, and Costs
The Town of Chapel Hill began participation in the benchmarking project in July 2015, with FY 2014–15 being the first reporting year.

Municipal Profile

Population (OSBM 2016)	59,852
Land Area (Square Miles)	21.21
Persons per Square Mile	2,822
Median Family Income U.S. Census 2010	$61,405
County Unemployment Rate (2016) U.S. Bureau of Labor Statistics	4.3%

Service Profile

Central HR FTE Positions	
Administration	2.0
Generalist/Specialist	4.0
Staff Support/Clerical	1.0
Total Authorized Workforce	775.0
Authorized FTEs	765.00
Average Length of Service (Months)	132.5
Number of Position Requisitions	81
Employment Applications Processed	10,515
Length of Probationary Employment Period	6 & 12 months
Compensation Studies Completed	1
Positions Studied	95
Employee Turnover	
Voluntary Separations	71
Involuntary Separations	11
TOTAL SEPARATIONS	82
Formal Grievances Filed by Employees	7
Equal Employment Opportunity Commission (EEOC) Complaints Filed	5

Full Cost Profile

Cost Breakdown by Percentage	
Personal Services	41.4%
Operating Costs	58.1%
Capital Costs	0.5%
TOTAL	100.0%
Cost Breakdown in Dollars	
Personal Services	$610,741
Operating Costs	$857,507
Capital Costs	$7,069
TOTAL	$1,475,317

Key: Chapel Hill ▒ Benchmarking Average — Fiscal Years 2013through 2017

Resource Measures

Human Resources Services Cost per Capita

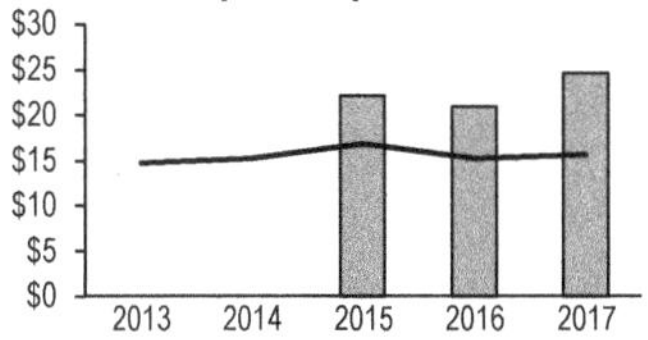

	2013	2014	2015	2016	2017
Chapel Hill			$22.20	$20.98	$24.65
Average	$14.68	$15.20	$16.80	$15.16	$15.62

Human Resources FTEs per 10,000 Population

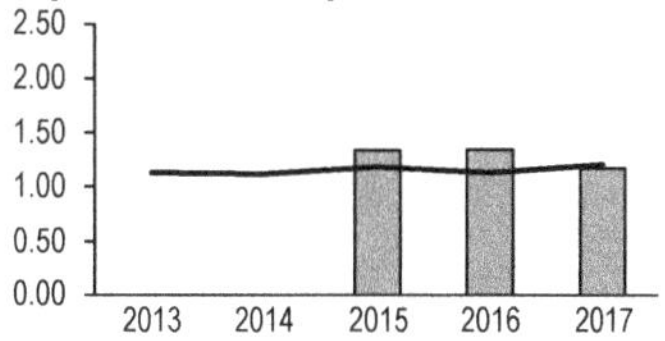

	2013	2014	2015	2016	2017
Chapel Hill			1.34	1.34	1.17
Average	1.12	1.11	1.18	1.13	1.20

Workload Measures

Total Municipal FTEs per 10,000 Population

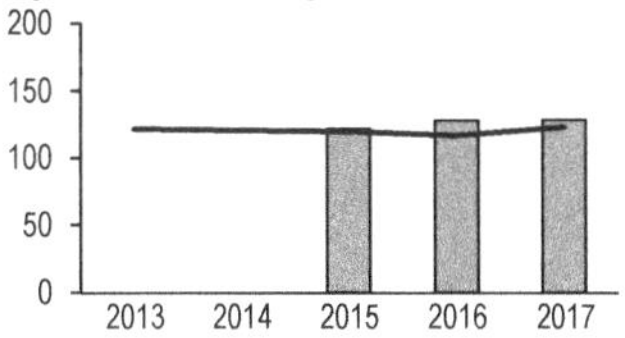

	2013	2014	2015	2016	2017
Chapel Hill			121	128	128
Average	121	120	119	116	122

Applications Processed per 100 Municipal Employees

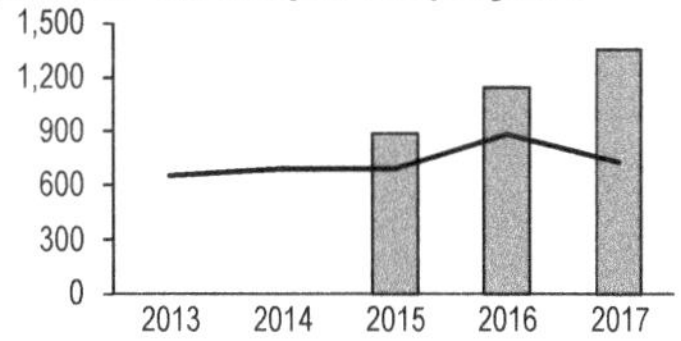

	2013	2014	2015	2016	2017
Chapel Hill			889	1,148	1,357
Average	655	693	695	884	729

Position Requisitions per 100 Municipal Employees

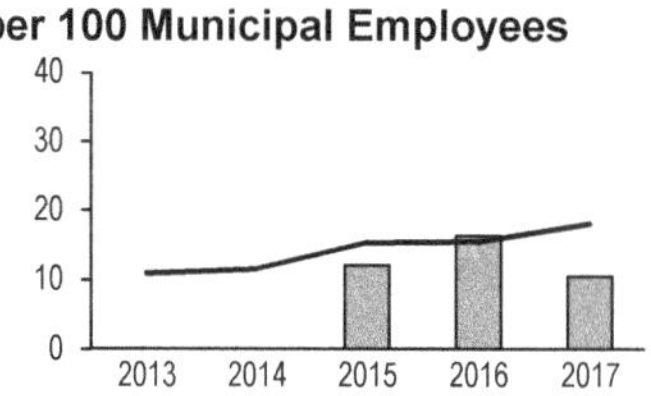

	2013	2014	2015	2016	2017
Chapel Hill			12.0	16.4	10.5
Average	11.0	11.6	15.4	15.6	18.2

Efficiency Measures

Human Resources Cost per Municipal Employee

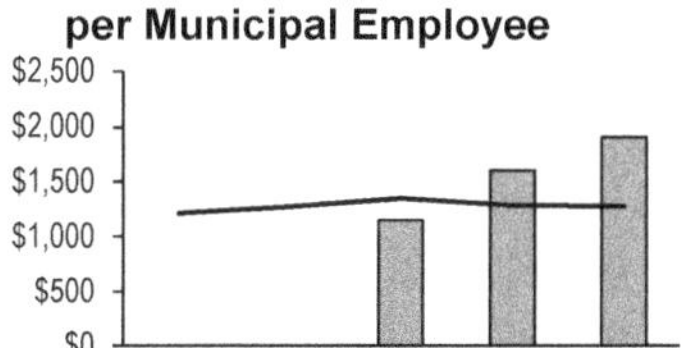

	2013	2014	2015	2016	2017
Chapel Hill			$1,149	$1,599	$1,904
Average	$1,210	$1,271	$1,346	$1,281	$1,272

Ratio of Human Resources Staff to 100 Municipal Employees

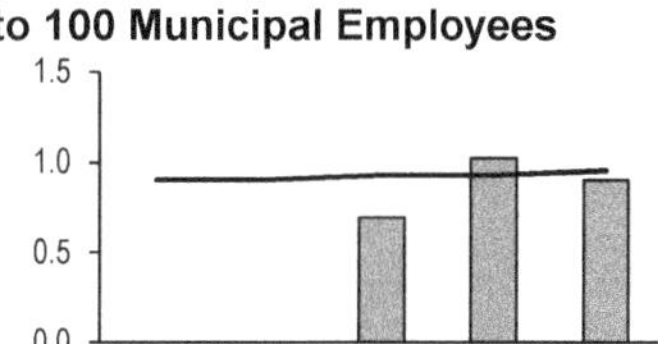

	2013	2014	2015	2016	2017
Chapel Hill			0.69	1.02	0.90
Average	0.90	0.90	0.93	0.93	0.95

Effectiveness Measures

Probationary Period Completion Rate (New Hires)

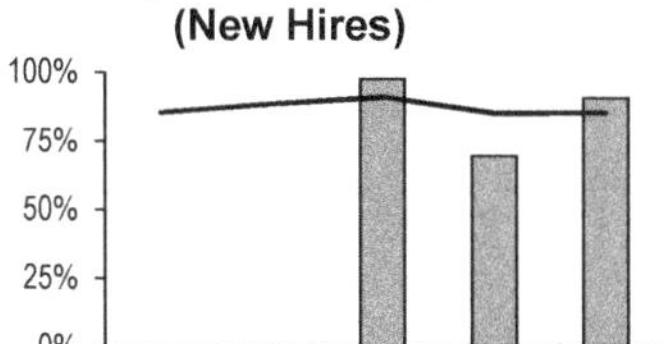

	2013	2014	2015	2016	2017
Chapel Hill			98%	69%	90%
Average	85%	88%	91%	85%	85%

Employee Turnover Rate (All Separations)

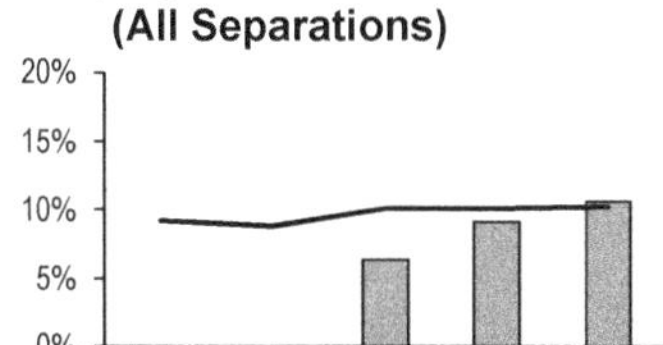

	2013	2014	2015	2016	2017
Chapel Hill			6.3%	9.1%	10.6%
Average	9.2%	8.8%	10.1%	10.0%	10.2%

Employee Turnover Rate (Voluntary Separations)

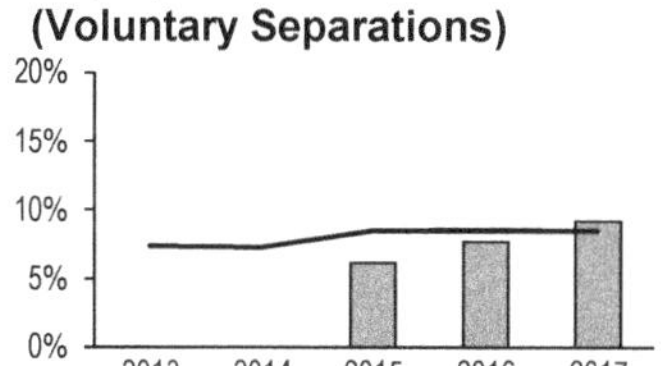

	2013	2014	2015	2016	2017
Chapel Hill			6.1%	7.7%	9.2%
Average	7.4%	7.3%	8.5%	8.5%	8.5%

Percentage of Grievances Resolved at Department Level

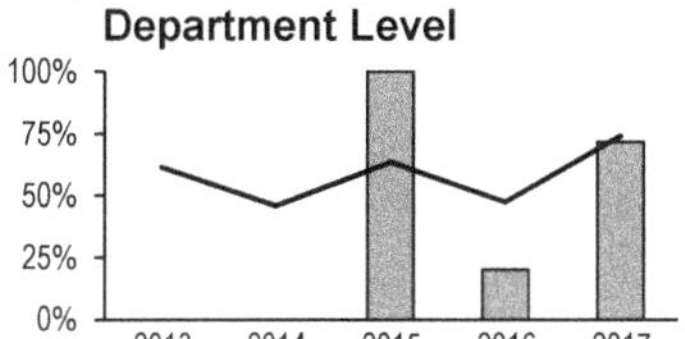

	2013	2014	2015	2016	2017
Chapel Hill			100%	20%	71%
Average	61%	46%	64%	48%	74%

Average Days from Post Date to Hire Date (First Day of Employment)

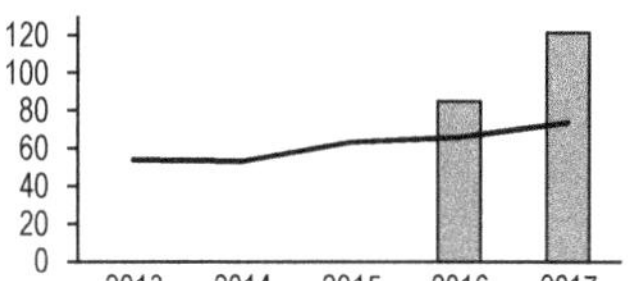

	2013	2014	2015	2016	2017
Chapel Hill				85	121
Average	54	53	64	66	74

Fiscal Year 2016–17

Explanatory Information

Service Level and Delivery

Charlotte's Human Resources Business Unit is organized into five core services: benefits, compensations, business unit services, HRMS/payroll, and organizational development and learning. These functional areas perform a variety of strategic, tactical, and transactional services. Some of the transactional services are outsourced.

During the fiscal year, three compensation studies were conducted covering two positions. Surveys were done on the basis of national, regional, and other larger city comparisons.

There were 52,960 employment applications processed electronically or online. All applicants (except sworn police and fire positions) must use the PeopleSoft online job application software for each position for which they wish to apply.

The city is self-insured for medical and dental insurance, and third-party administrators are retained to administer the plans. The wellness program, Wellness Works, includes a number of programs, such as tobacco cessation, annual flu shots, blood pressure screenings, onsite education programs, and weight loss programs. The city partners with Provant to administer health coaching and health risk assessments. New in 2011, the city offered a premium differential to employees who take a health screening, complete a health assessment, and engage with a health coach on an ongoing basis.

Conditions Affecting Service, Performance, and Costs

Charlotte did not participate in the Benchmarking Project during FY 2014–15. No data are available for that year.

Charlotte has a very robust wellness program. Many resources are devoted to the success of this program. There are wellness ambassadors in every department in the city.

The payroll function in many cities is located in finance; it resides in Human Resources in Charlotte.

Municipal Profile

Population (OSBM 2016)	830,258
Land Area (Square Miles)	305.48
Persons per Square Mile	2,718
Median Family Income U.S. Census 2010	$61,405
County Unemployment Rate (2016) U.S. Bureau of Labor Statistics	4.7%

Service Profile

Central HR FTE Positions	
Administration	3.0
Generalist/Specialist	34.0
Staff Support/Clerical	3.0
Total Authorized Workforce	7,590.0
Authorized FTEs	7,582.8
Average Length of Service (Months)	126.42
Number of Position Requisitions	663
Employment Applications Processed	52,960
Length of Probationary Employment Period	6 & 12 months
Compensation Studies Completed	3
Positions Studied	2
Employee Turnover	
Voluntary Separations	564
Involuntary Separations	89
TOTAL SEPARATIONS	653
Formal Grievances Filed by Employees	8
Equal Employment Opportunity Commission (EEOC) Complaints Filed	11

Full Cost Profile

Cost Breakdown by Percentage	
Personal Services	70.1%
Operating Costs	29.7%
Capital Costs	0.2%
TOTAL	100.0%
Cost Breakdown in Dollars	
Personal Services	$3,661,607
Operating Costs	$1,551,617
Capital Costs	$7,900
TOTAL	$5,221,124

Charlotte — Central Human Resources

Key: Charlotte ▒ Benchmarking Average — Fiscal Years 2013through 2017

Resource Measures

Human Resources Services Cost per Capita

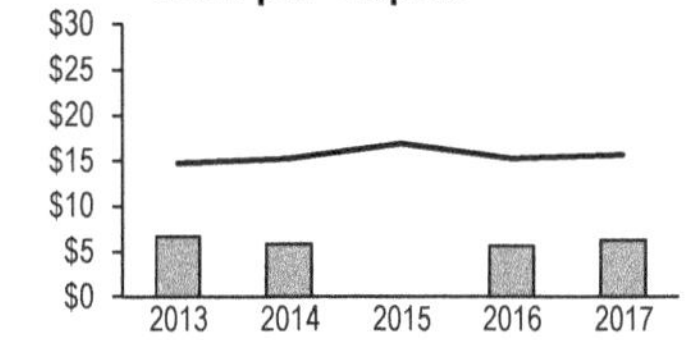

	2013	2014	2015	2016	2017
Charlotte	$6.72	$5.87		$5.68	$6.29
Average	$14.68	$15.20	$16.80	$15.16	$15.62

Human Resources FTEs per 10,000 Population

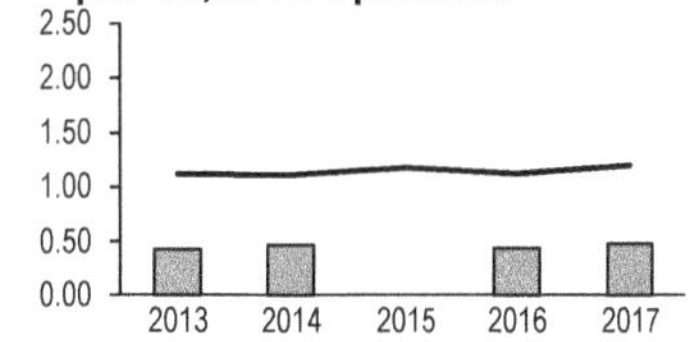

	2013	2014	2015	2016	2017
Charlotte	0.43	0.47		0.44	0.48
Average	1.12	1.11	1.18	1.13	1.20

Workload Measures

Total Municipal FTEs per 10,000 Population

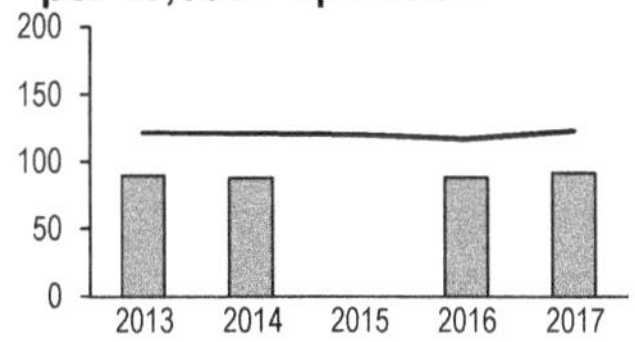

	2013	2014	2015	2016	2017
Charlotte	89	88		88	91
Average	121	120	119	116	122

Applications Processed per 100 Municipal Employees

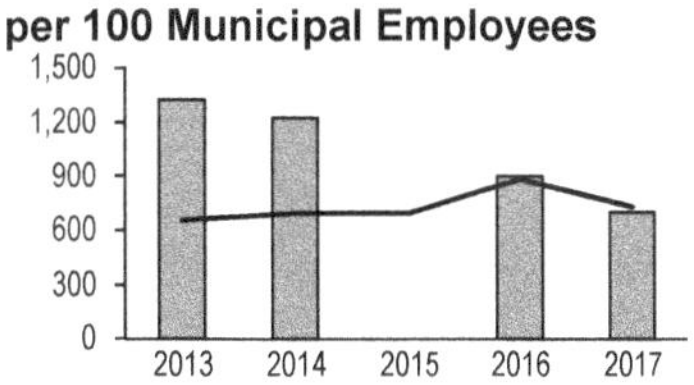

	2013	2014	2015	2016	2017
Charlotte	1,322	1,221		895	698
Average	655	693	695	884	729

Position Requisitions per 100 Municipal Employees

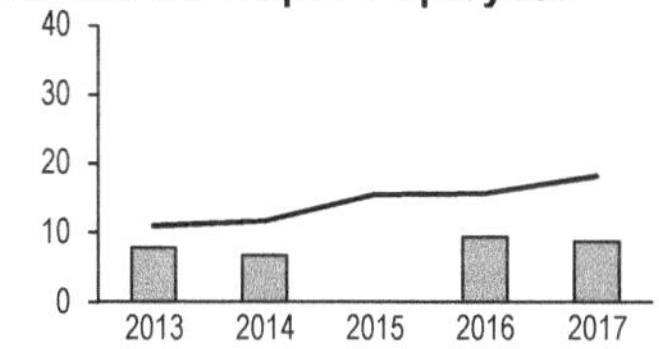

	2013	2014	2015	2016	2017
Charlotte	7.8	6.7		9.4	8.7
Average	11.0	11.6	15.4	15.6	18.2

Efficiency Measures

Human Resources Cost per Municipal Employee

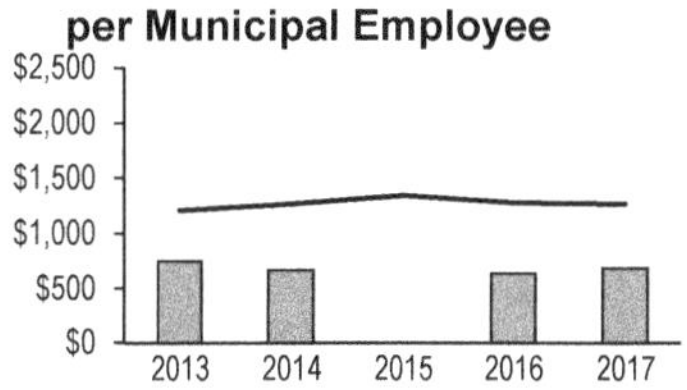

	2013	2014	2015	2016	2017
Charlotte	$750	$670		$643	$688
Average	$1,210	$1,271	$1,346	$1,281	$1,272

Ratio of Human Resources Staff to 100 Municipal Employees

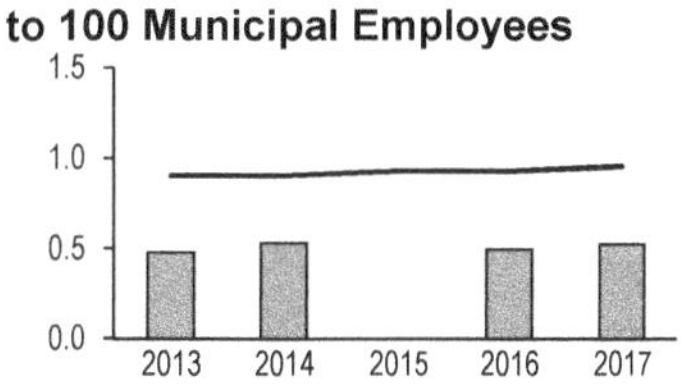

	2013	2014	2015	2016	2017
Charlotte	0.48	0.54		0.50	0.53
Average	0.90	0.90	0.93	0.93	0.95

Effectiveness Measures

Probationary Period Completion Rate (New Hires)

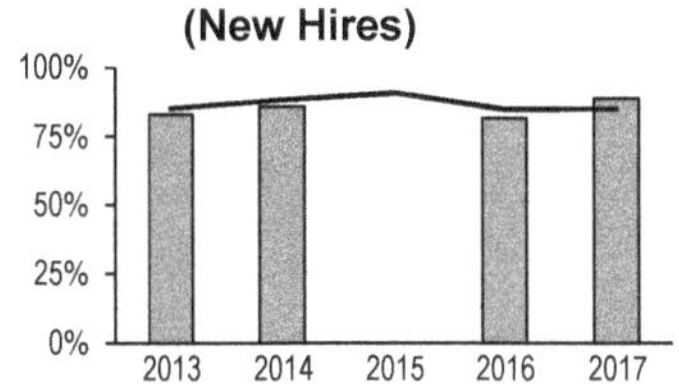

	2013	2014	2015	2016	2017
Charlotte	83%	86%		82%	89%
Average	85%	88%	91%	85%	85%

Employee Turnover Rate (All Separations)

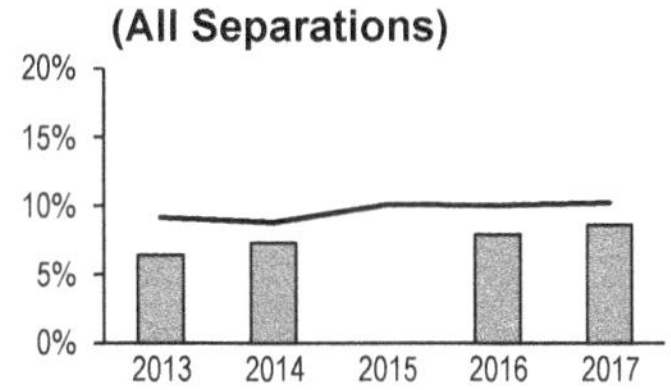

	2013	2014	2015	2016	2017
Charlotte	6.4%	7.3%		7.9%	8.6%
Average	9.2%	8.8%	10.1%	10.0%	10.2%

Employee Turnover Rate (Voluntary Separations)

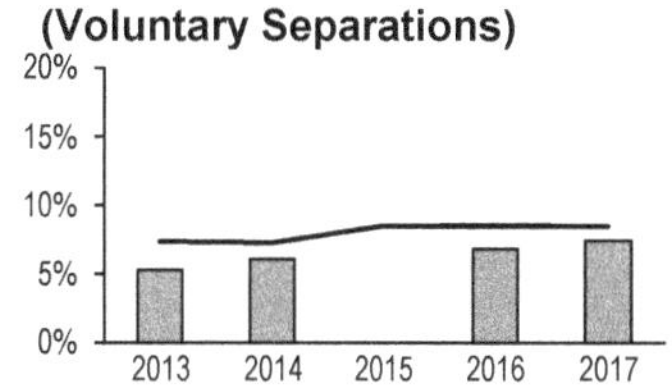

	2013	2014	2015	2016	2017
Charlotte	5.3%	6.1%		6.8%	7.4%
Average	7.4%	7.3%	8.5%	8.5%	8.5%

Percentage of Grievances Resolved at Department Level

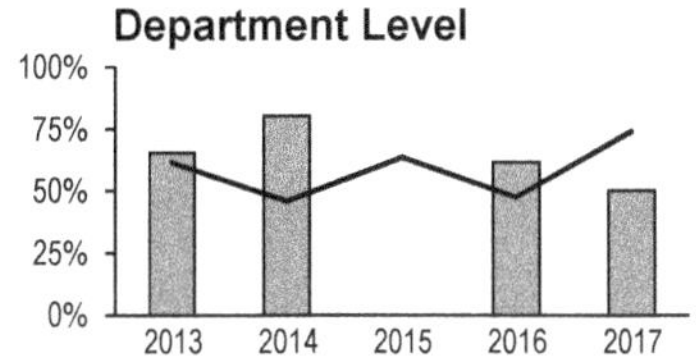

	2013	2014	2015	2016	2017
Charlotte	65%	80%		62%	50%
Average	61%	46%	64%	48%	74%

Average Days from Post Date to Hire Date (First Day of Employment)

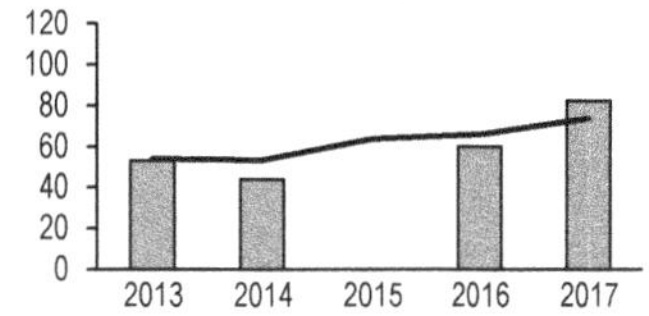

	2013	2014	2015	2016	2017
Charlotte	53	44		60	82
Average	54	53	64	66	74

Fiscal Year 2016–17

Explanatory Information

Service Level and Delivery

The Human Resources Department for the City of Concord is responsible for the following functions: departmental management, policy design and administration, classification and compensation design and administration, benefits plan design and administration, employee relations, grievance and disciplinary actions, and employee rewards.

The department conducted one compensation study during the most recent year covering forty-four positions.

The city's probationary period for new employees is six months for non–public safety employees and twelve months for public safety employees.

Conditions Affecting Service, Performance, and Costs

Municipal Profile

Population (OSBM 2016)	88,815
Land Area (Square Miles)	62.61
Persons per Square Mile	1,419
Median Family Income U.S. Census 2010	$63,643
County Unemployment Rate (2016) U.S. Bureau of Labor Statistics	4.5%

Service Profile

Central HR FTE Positions	
Administration	4.0
Generalist/Specialist	6.0
Staff Support/Clerical	1.0
Total Authorized Workforce	993.0
Authorized FTEs	979.1
Average Length of Service (Months)	123.24
Number of Position Requisitions	190
Employment Applications Processed	6,604
Length of Probationary Employment Period	6 & 12 months
Compensation Studies Completed	1
Positions Studied	44
Employee Turnover	
Voluntary Separations	89
Involuntary Separations	14
TOTAL SEPARATIONS	103
Formal Grievances Filed by Employees	6
Equal Employment Opportunity Commission (EEOC) Complaints Filed	3

Full Cost Profile

Cost Breakdown by Percentage	
Personal Services	51.2%
Operating Costs	46.7%
Capital Costs	2.1%
TOTAL	100.0%
Cost Breakdown in Dollars	
Personal Services	$817,088
Operating Costs	$746,424
Capital Costs	$33,759
TOTAL	$1,597,271

Key: Concord ▒ Benchmarking Average — Fiscal Years 2013through 2017

Resource Measures

Human Resources Services Cost per Capita

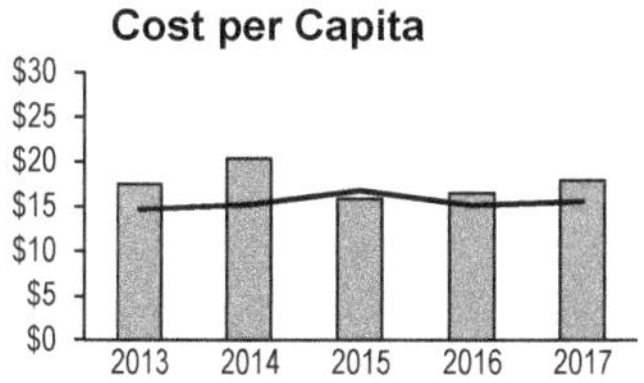

	2013	2014	2015	2016	2017
Concord	$17.54	$20.42	$15.85	$16.51	$17.98
Average	$14.68	$15.20	$16.80	$15.16	$15.62

Human Resources FTEs per 10,000 Population

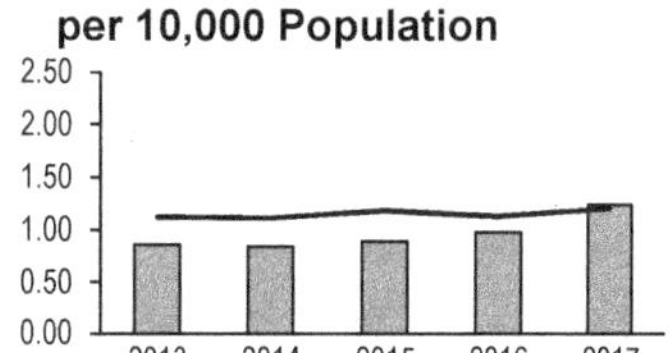

	2013	2014	2015	2016	2017
Concord	0.86	0.84	0.89	0.98	1.24
Average	1.12	1.11	1.18	1.13	1.20

Workload Measures

Total Municipal FTEs per 10,000 Population

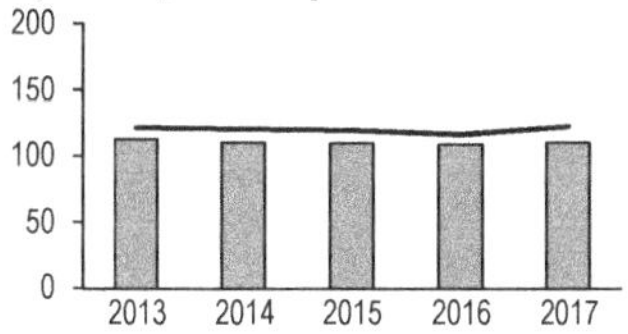

	2013	2014	2015	2016	2017
Concord	112	110	109	108	110
Average	121	120	119	116	122

Applications Processed per 100 Municipal Employees

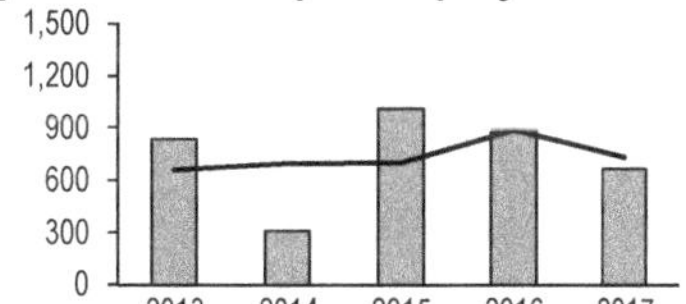

	2013	2014	2015	2016	2017
Concord	835	311	1,017	876	665
Average	655	693	695	884	729

Position Requisitions per 100 Municipal Employees

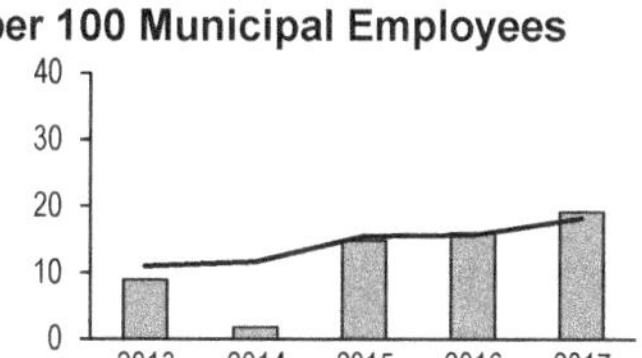

	2013	2014	2015	2016	2017
Concord	9.0	1.8	14.8	15.9	19.1
Average	11.0	11.6	15.4	15.6	18.2

Efficiency Measures

Human Resources Cost per Municipal Employee

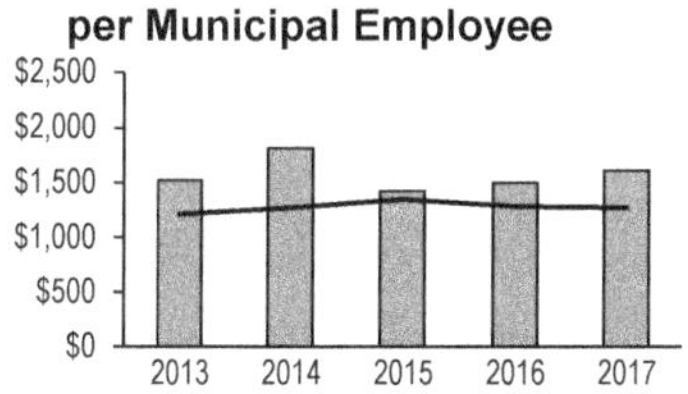

	2013	2014	2015	2016	2017
Concord	$1,523	$1,811	$1,424	$1,498	$1,609
Average	$1,210	$1,271	$1,346	$1,281	$1,272

Ratio of Human Resources Staff to 100 Municipal Employees

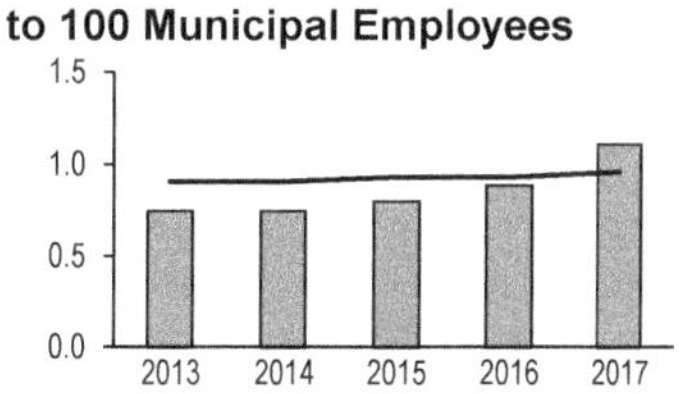

	2013	2014	2015	2016	2017
Concord	0.75	0.75	0.80	0.89	1.11
Average	0.90	0.90	0.93	0.93	0.95

Effectiveness Measures

Probationary Period Completion Rate (New Hires)

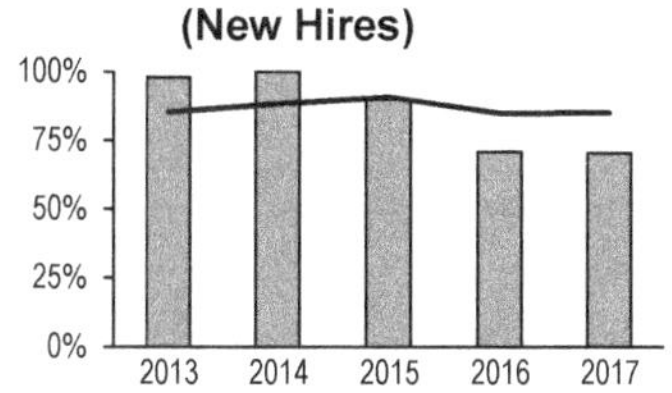

	2013	2014	2015	2016	2017
Concord	98%	100%	90%	71%	70%
Average	85%	88%	91%	85%	85%

Employee Turnover Rate (All Separations)

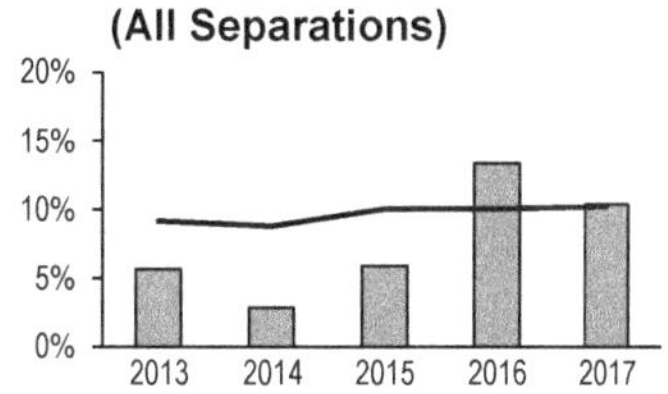

	2013	2014	2015	2016	2017
Concord	5.7%	2.9%	5.9%	13.3%	10.4%
Average	9.2%	8.8%	10.1%	10.0%	10.2%

Employee Turnover Rate (Voluntary Separations)

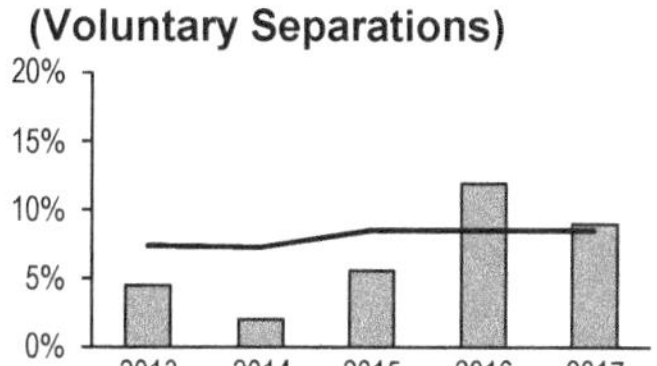

	2013	2014	2015	2016	2017
Concord	4.5%	2.0%	5.6%	11.9%	9.0%
Average	7.4%	7.3%	8.5%	8.5%	8.5%

Percentage of Grievances Resolved at Department Level

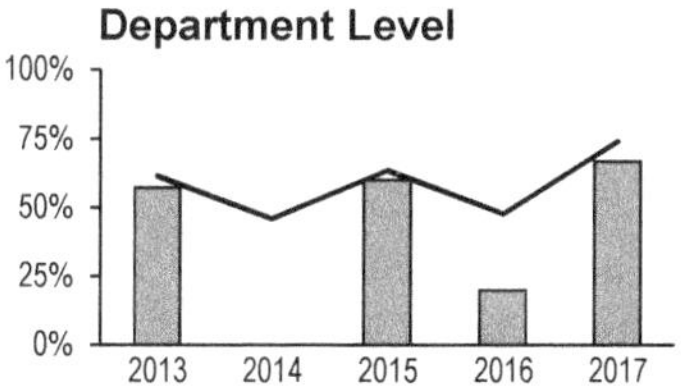

	2013	2014	2015	2016	2017
Concord	57%		60%	20%	67%
Average	61%	46%	64%	48%	74%

Average Days from Post Date to Hire Date (First Day of Employment)

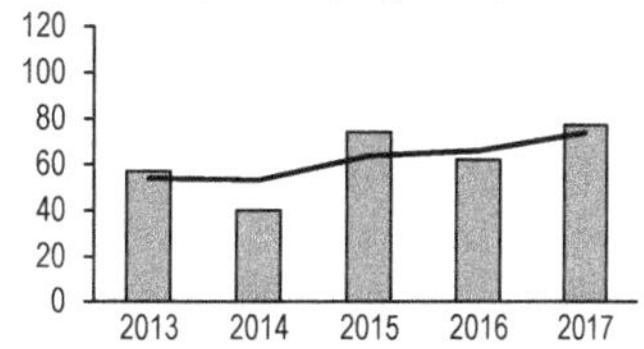

	2013	2014	2015	2016	2017
Concord	57	40	74	62	77
Average	54	53	64	66	74

Goldsboro

Central Human Resources

Fiscal Year 2016–17

Explanatory Information

Service Level and Delivery

The mission of the Human Resources Department for the City of Goldsboro is to provide services that promote a work environment that is characterized by fair treatment of staff, open communications, personal accountabiltiy, trust, and mutual respect. The Department provides a comprehensive array of services that includes employee selection and recruitment, salary and compensation, benefits, professional development, employee relations, employee health/wellness, and compliance with federal and state safety regulations.

The city's probationary period for new employees is six months for non–public safety employees and twelve months for public safety employees.

During the fiscal year, the city conducted three compensation studies covering ten positions.

Conditions Affecting Service, Performance, and Costs

The city of Goldsboro joined the Benchmarking Project in July 2017, with the first year of data showing for FY 2016–17.

Municipal Profile

Population (OSBM 2016)	34,793
Land Area (Square Miles)	29.35
Persons per Square Mile	1,186
Median Family Income U.S. Census 2010	$33,879
County Unemployment Rate (2016) U.S. Bureau of Labor Statistics	5.8%

Service Profile

Central HR FTE Positions	
Administration	1.0
Generalist/Specialist	3.0
Staff Support/Clerical	1.0
Total Authorized Workforce	680.0
Authorized FTEs	530.0
Average Length of Service (Months)	132
Number of Position Requisitions	93
Employment Applications Processed	3,378
Length of Probationary Employment Period	6 & 12 months
Compensation Studies Completed	3
Positions Studied	10
Employee Turnover	
Voluntary Separations	45
Involuntary Separations	2
TOTAL SEPARATIONS	47
Formal Grievances Filed by Employees	NA
Equal Employment Opportunity Commission (EEOC) Complaints Filed	1

Full Cost Profile

Cost Breakdown by Percentage	
Personal Services	63.1%
Operating Costs	36.0%
Capital Costs	0.9%
TOTAL	100.0%
Cost Breakdown in Dollars	
Personal Services	$367,535
Operating Costs	$209,839
Capital Costs	$5,215
TOTAL	$582,589

Key: Goldsboro ▒ Benchmarking Average — Fiscal Years 2013through 2017

Resource Measures

Human Resources Services Cost per Capita

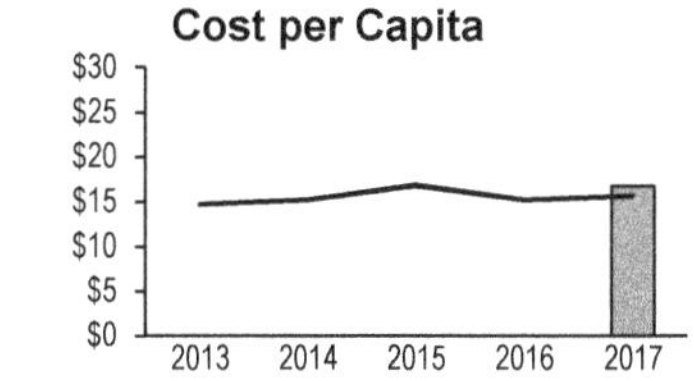

	2013	2014	2015	2016	2017
Goldsboro					$16.74
Average	$14.68	$15.20	$16.80	$15.16	$15.62

Human Resources FTEs per 10,000 Population

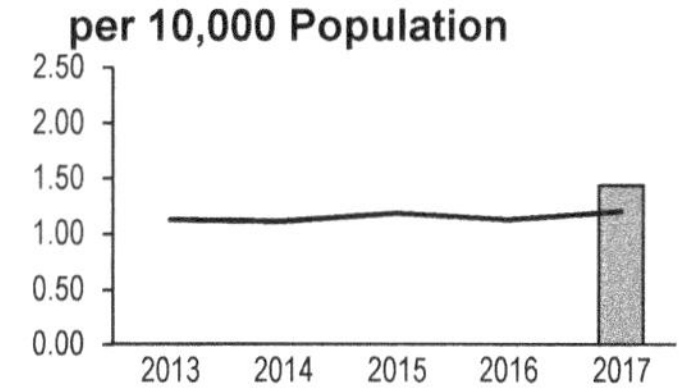

	2013	2014	2015	2016	2017
Goldsboro					1.44
Average	1.12	1.11	1.18	1.13	1.20

Workload Measures

Total Municipal FTEs per 10,000 Population

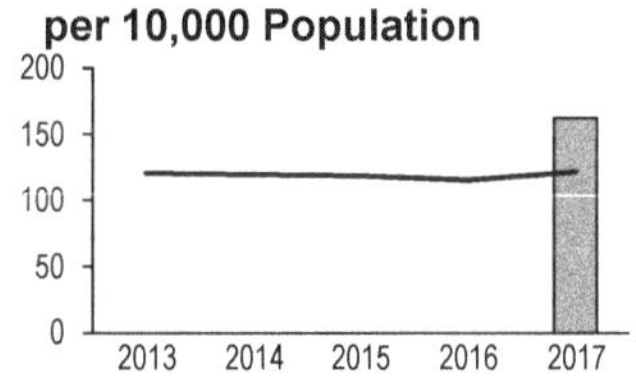

	2013	2014	2015	2016	2017
Goldsboro					162
Average	121	120	119	116	122

Applications Processed per 100 Municipal Employees

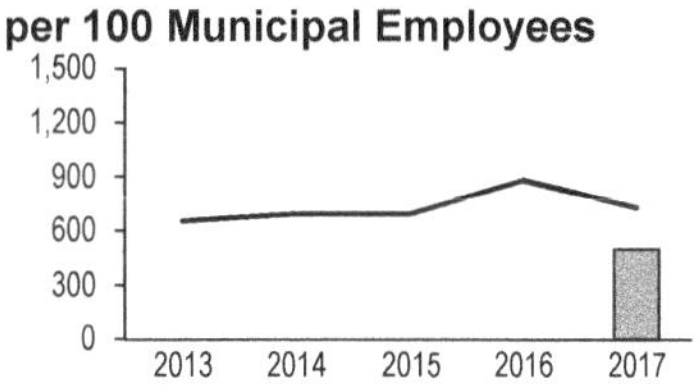

	2013	2014	2015	2016	2017
Goldsboro					497
Average	655	693	695	884	729

Position Requisitions per 100 Municipal Employees

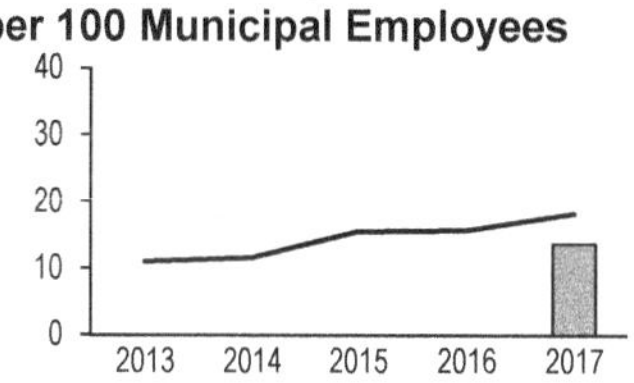

	2013	2014	2015	2016	2017
Goldsboro					13.7
Average	11.0	11.6	15.4	15.6	18.2

Efficiency Measures

Human Resources Cost per Municipal Employee

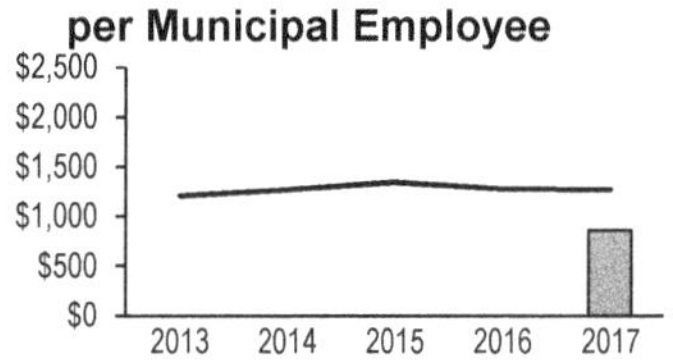

	2013	2014	2015	2016	2017
Goldsboro					$857
Average	$1,210	$1,271	$1,346	$1,281	$1,272

Ratio of Human Resources Staff to 100 Municipal Employees

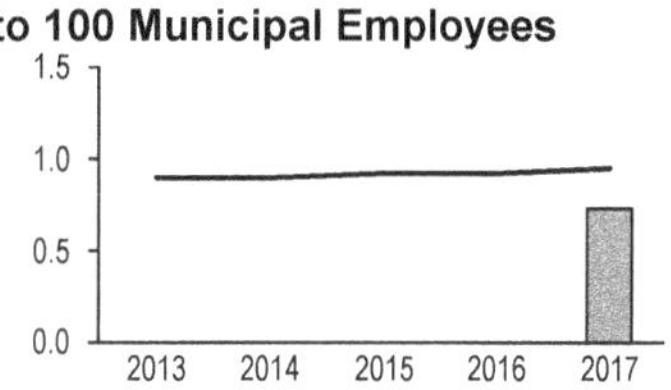

	2013	2014	2015	2016	2017
Goldsboro					0.74
Average	0.90	0.90	0.93	0.93	0.95

Effectiveness Measures

Probationary Period Completion Rate (New Hires)

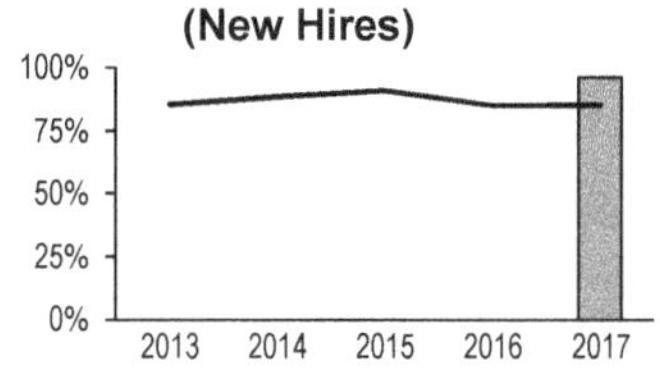

	2013	2014	2015	2016	2017
Goldsboro					96%
Average	85%	88%	91%	85%	85%

Employee Turnover Rate (All Separations)

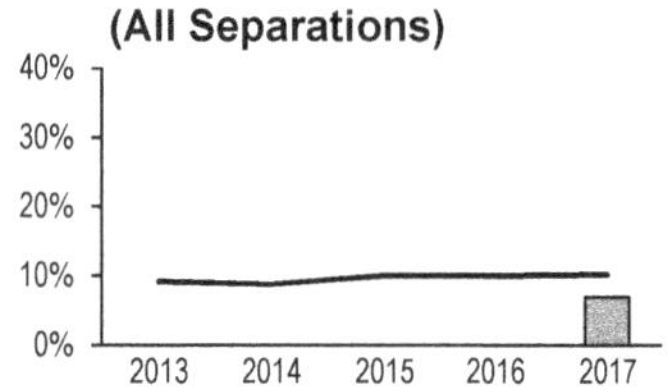

	2013	2014	2015	2016	2017
Goldsboro					6.9%
Average	9.2%	8.8%	10.1%	10.0%	10.2%

Employee Turnover Rate (Voluntary Separations)

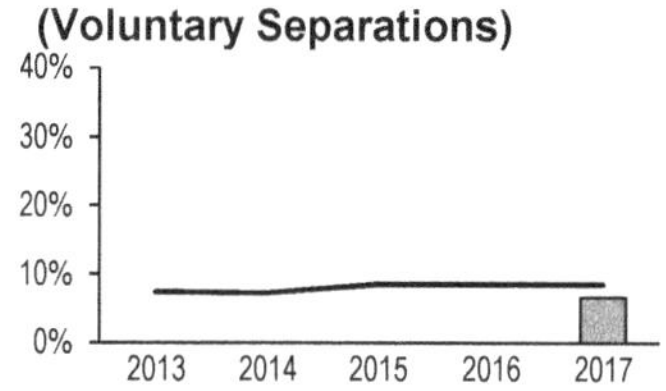

	2013	2014	2015	2016	2017
Goldsboro					6.6%
Average	7.4%	7.3%	8.5%	8.5%	8.5%

Percentage of Grievances Resolved at Department Level

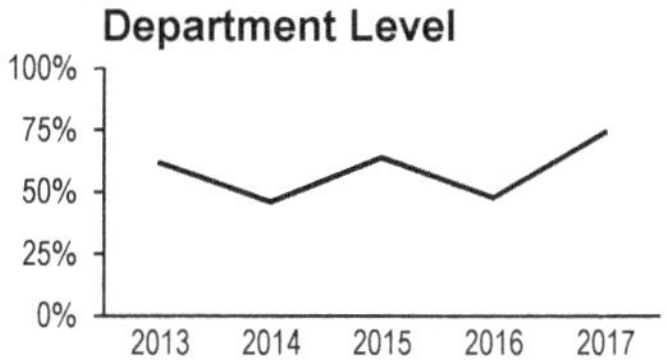

	2013	2014	2015	2016	2017
Goldsboro					
Average	61%	46%	64%	48%	74%

Average Days from Post Date to Hire Date (First Day of Employment)

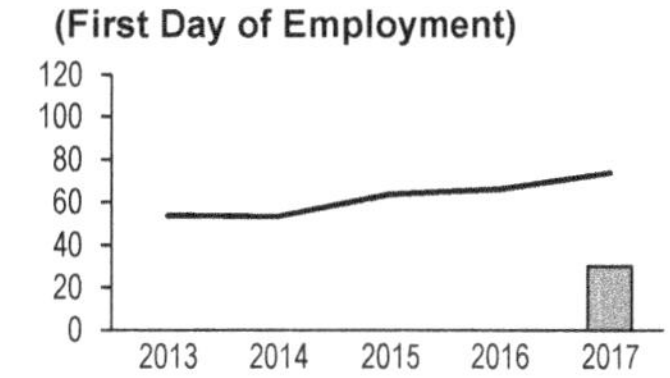

	2013	2014	2015	2016	2017
Goldsboro					30
Average	54	53	64	66	74

Fiscal Year 2016–17

Explanatory Information

Service Level and Delivery

The Human Resources Department for the City of Greensboro provides comprehensive personnel services, including recruitment and selection, compensation, benefits, employee relations, safety, and occupational health and wellness. The total number of full-time equivalent (FTE) positions includes staff from the Training Division, which is housed in a separate department from Human Resources. The HR department has a staff attorney who is able to provide legal consultation on a variety of issues confronting the HR department.

The city conducted one compensation study for the year covering 120 positions.

The city's probationary period for new employees is six months for non–public safety employees and twelve months for public safety employees.

Conditions Affecting Service, Performance, and Costs

Municipal Profile

Population (OSBM 2016)	284,343
Land Area (Square Miles)	128.72
Persons per Square Mile	2,209
Median Family Income U.S. Census 2010	$52,752
County Unemployment Rate (2016) U.S. Bureau of Labor Statistics	5.2%

Service Profile

Central HR FTE Positions	
Administration	6.0
Generalist/Specialist	27.0
Staff Support/Clerical	3.0
Total Authorized Workforce	3,148.0
Authorized FTEs	3,115.0
Average Length of Service (Months)	125.4
Number of Position Requisitions	417
Employment Applications Processed	26,979
Length of Probationary Employment Period	6 & 12 months
Compensation Studies Completed	1
Positions Studied	120
Employee Turnover	
Voluntary Separations	37
Involuntary Separations	10
TOTAL SEPARATIONS	47
Formal Grievances Filed by Employees	12
Equal Employment Opportunity Commission (EEOC) Complaints Filed	2

Full Cost Profile

Cost Breakdown by Percentage	
Personal Services	73.1%
Operating Costs	26.9%
Capital Costs	0.0%
TOTAL	100.0%
Cost Breakdown in Dollars	
Personal Services	$2,615,603
Operating Costs	$962,501
Capital Costs	$0
TOTAL	$3,578,104

Key: Greensboro ▒ Benchmarking Average — Fiscal Years 2013through 2017

Resource Measures

Human Resources Services Cost per Capita

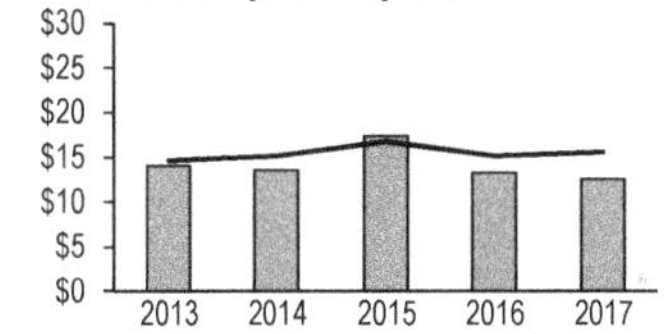

	2013	2014	2015	2016	2017
Greensboro	$14.11	$13.58	$17.39	$13.28	$12.58
Average	$14.68	$15.20	$16.80	$15.16	$15.62

Human Resources FTEs per 10,000 Population

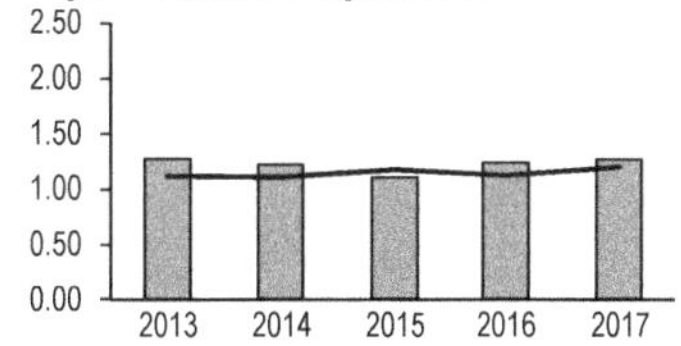

	2013	2014	2015	2016	2017
Greensboro	1.27	1.22	1.10	1.24	1.27
Average	1.12	1.11	1.18	1.13	1.20

Workload Measures

Total Municipal FTEs per 10,000 Population

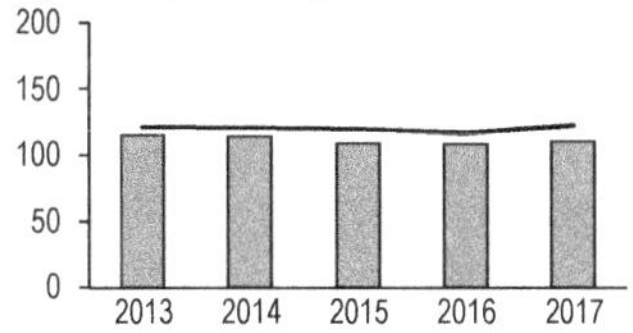

	2013	2014	2015	2016	2017
Greensboro	115	114	108	108	110
Average	121	120	119	116	122

Applications Processed per 100 Municipal Employees

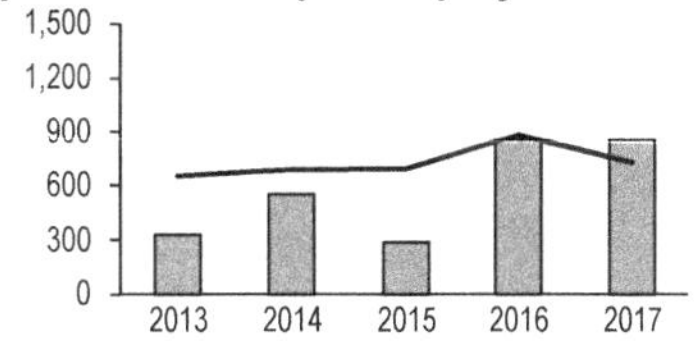

	2013	2014	2015	2016	2017
Greensboro	332	553	288	855	857
Average	655	693	695	884	729

Position Requisitions per 100 Municipal Employees

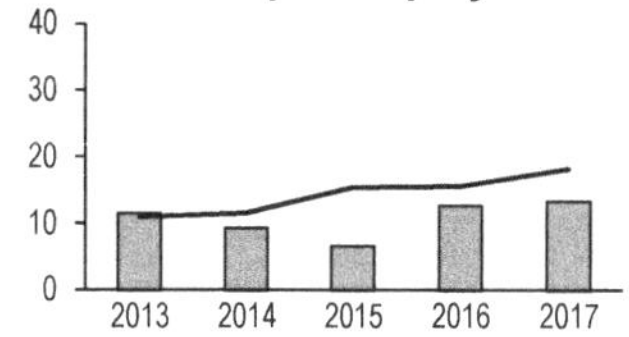

	2013	2014	2015	2016	2017
Greensboro	11.5	9.2	6.5	12.6	13.2
Average	11.0	11.6	15.4	15.6	18.2

Efficiency Measures

Human Resources Cost per Municipal Employee

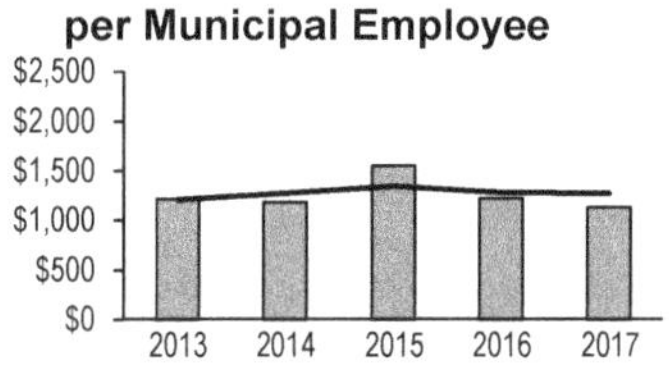

	2013	2014	2015	2016	2017
Greensboro	$1,222	$1,188	$1,555	$1,226	$1,137
Average	$1,210	$1,271	$1,346	$1,281	$1,272

Ratio of Human Resources Staff to 100 Municipal Employees

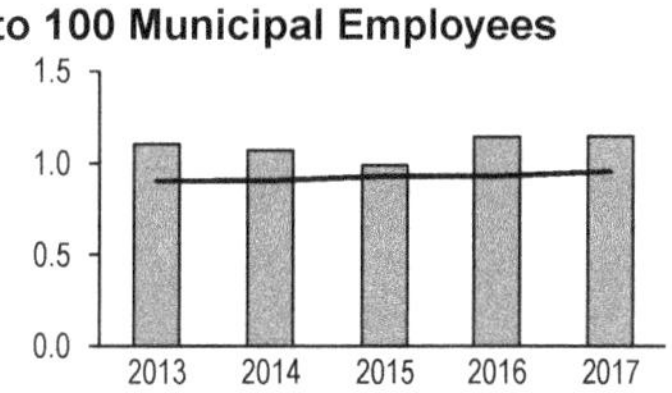

	2013	2014	2015	2016	2017
Greensboro	1.10	1.07	0.99	1.14	1.14
Average	0.90	0.90	0.93	0.93	0.95

Effectiveness Measures

Probationary Period Completion Rate (New Hires)

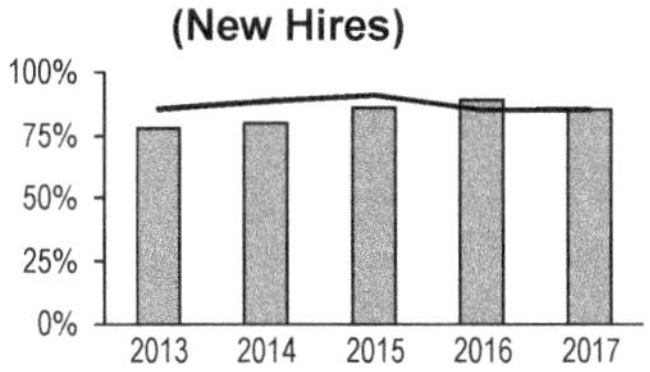

	2013	2014	2015	2016	2017
Greensboro	78%	80%	86%	89%	85%
Average	85%	88%	91%	85%	85%

Employee Turnover Rate (All Separations)

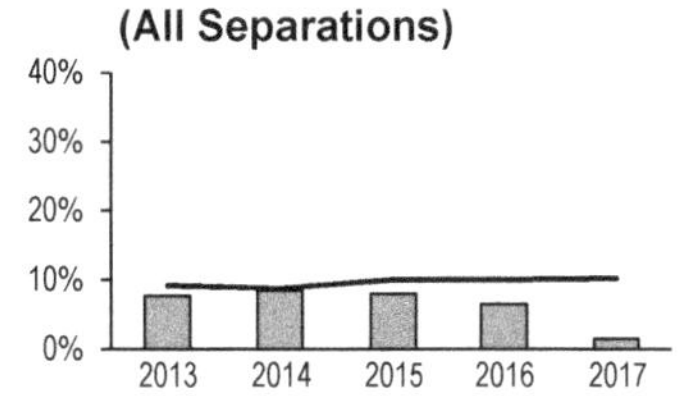

	2013	2014	2015	2016	2017
Greensboro	7.7%	8.5%	8.0%	6.5%	1.5%
Average	9.2%	8.8%	10.1%	10.0%	10.2%

Employee Turnover Rate (Voluntary Separations)

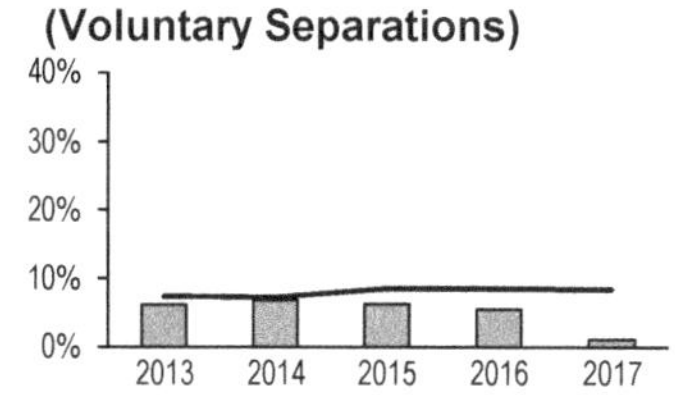

	2013	2014	2015	2016	2017
Greensboro	6.2%	6.8%	6.3%	5.6%	1.2%
Average	7.4%	7.3%	8.5%	8.5%	8.5%

Percentage of Grievances Resolved at Department Level

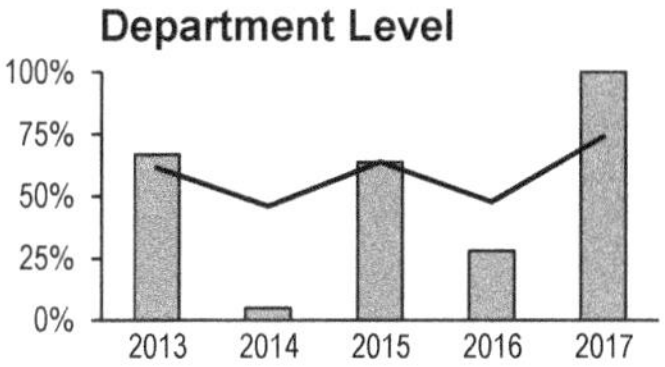

	2013	2014	2015	2016	2017
Greensboro	67%	5%	64%	28%	100%
Average	61%	46%	64%	48%	74%

Average Days from Post Date to Hire Date (First Day of Employment)

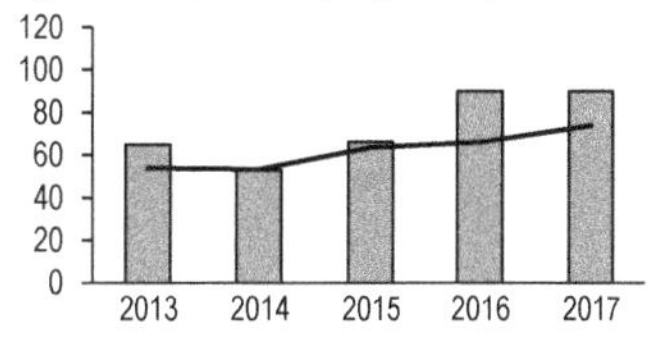

	2013	2014	2015	2016	2017
Greensboro	65	53	66	90	90
Average	54	53	64	66	74

Fiscal Year 2016–17

Explanatory Information

Service Level and Delivery

The Human Resources Department for the City of Greenville is responsible for recruitment and selection, salary and benefits administration, position classification, employee relations, affirmative action and equal employment opportunity, training and development, risk administration, and safety.

The city's probationary period is twelve months for all law enforcement personnel and employees in a trainee status, such as fire/rescue trainees. All other employees serve a six-month probationary period.

Nearly all employment applications are processed online. The Human Resources Department screens applications to ensure that applicants meet the position minimum qualifications. Applications are only accepted for positions that are open for recruitment.

Greenville has a voluntary wellness program focusing on education, fitness, mental health, nutrition, weight management, personal health, and personal safety. A safety specialist provides technical safety and occupational illness and injury prevention training.

A formal grievance by an employee in Greenville requires a written notice appealing a disciplinary action given to a supervisor . The grievance process is an internal one, moving up the chain of command with specific timeframes for responses and appeals to the next level.

Conditions Affecting Service, Performance, and Costs

Municipal Profile

Population (OSBM 2016)	87,989
Land Area (Square Miles)	35.41
Persons per Square Mile	2,485
Median Family Income U.S. Census 2010	$50,395
County Unemployment Rate (2016) U.S. Bureau of Labor Statistics	5.5%

Service Profile

Central HR FTE Positions	
Administration	3.0
Generalist/Specialist	3.0
Staff Support/Clerical	3.0
Total Authorized Workforce	769.0
Authorized FTEs	764.75
Average Length of Service (Months)	133
Number of Position Requisitions	222
Employment Applications Processed	7,434
Length of Probationary Employment Period	6 & 12 months
Compensation Studies Completed	0
Positions Studied	0
Employee Turnover	
Voluntary Separations	77
Involuntary Separations	6
TOTAL SEPARATIONS	83
Formal Grievances Filed by Employees	4
Equal Employment Opportunity Commission (EEOC) Complaints Filed	2

Full Cost Profile

Cost Breakdown by Percentage	
Personal Services	59.4%
Operating Costs	40.1%
Capital Costs	0.5%
TOTAL	100.0%
Cost Breakdown in Dollars	
Personal Services	$836,299
Operating Costs	$563,698
Capital Costs	$7,050
TOTAL	$1,407,048

Key: Greenville ▒ Benchmarking Average — Fiscal Years 2013through 2017

Resource Measures

Human Resources Services Cost per Capita

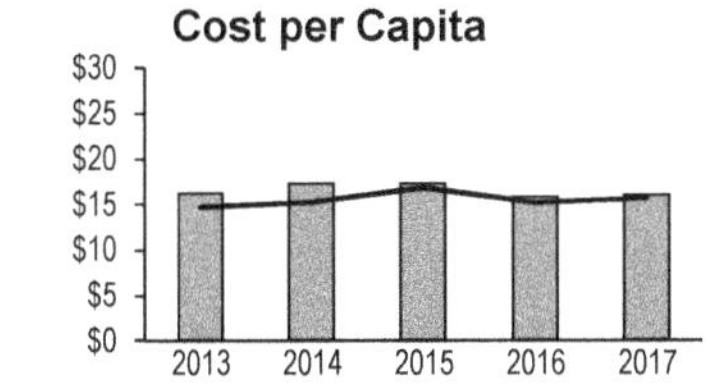

	2013	2014	2015	2016	2017
Greenville	$16.19	$17.24	$17.29	$15.76	$15.99
Average	$14.68	$15.20	$16.80	$15.16	$15.62

Human Resources FTEs per 10,000 Population

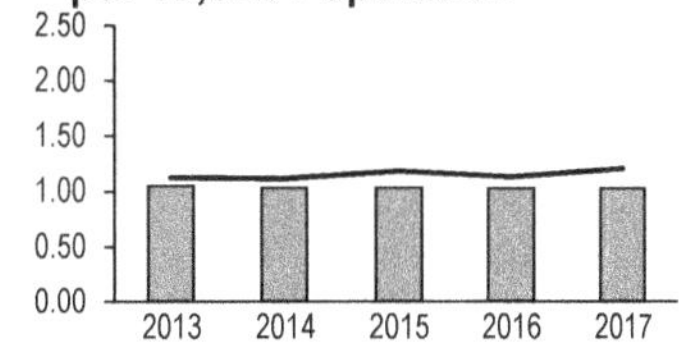

	2013	2014	2015	2016	2017
Greenville	1.04	1.03	1.03	1.02	1.02
Average	1.12	1.11	1.18	1.13	1.20

Workload Measures

Total Municipal FTEs per 10,000 Population

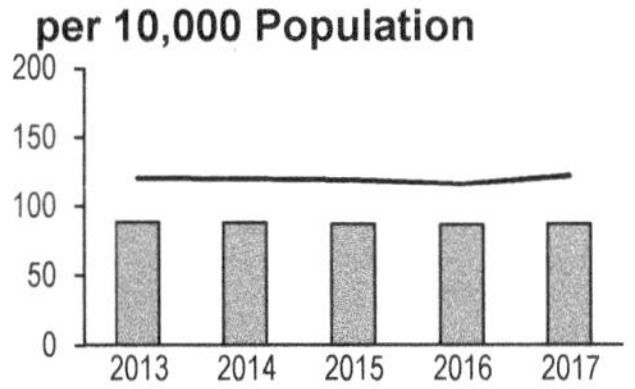

	2013	2014	2015	2016	2017
Greenville	88	88	87	86	87
Average	121	120	119	116	122

Applications Processed per 100 Municipal Employees

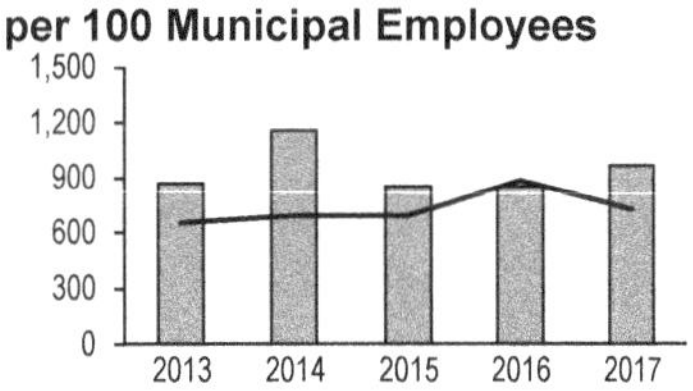

	2013	2014	2015	2016	2017
Greenville	869	1,157	851	851	967
Average	655	693	695	884	729

Position Requisitions per 100 Municipal Employees

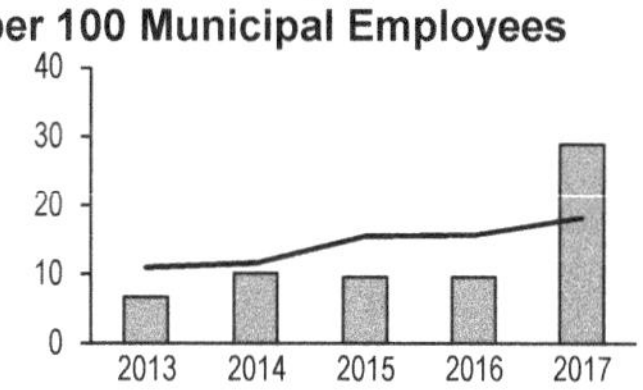

	2013	2014	2015	2016	2017
Greenville	6.7	10.1	9.5	9.5	28.9
Average	11.0	11.6	15.4	15.6	18.2

Efficiency Measures

Human Resources Cost per Municipal Employee

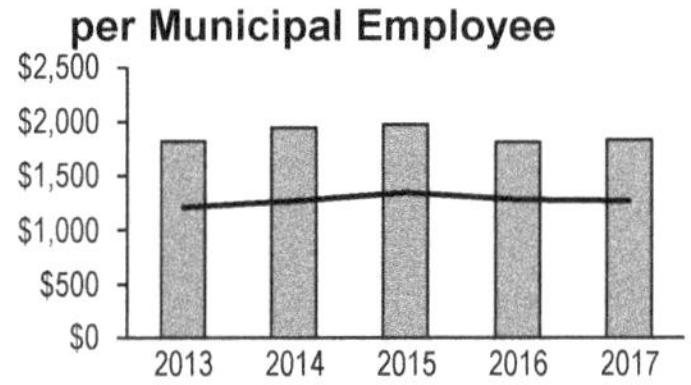

	2013	2014	2015	2016	2017
Greenville	$1,823	$1,948	$1,976	$1,812	$1,830
Average	$1,210	$1,271	$1,346	$1,281	$1,272

Ratio of Human Resources Staff to 100 Municipal Employees

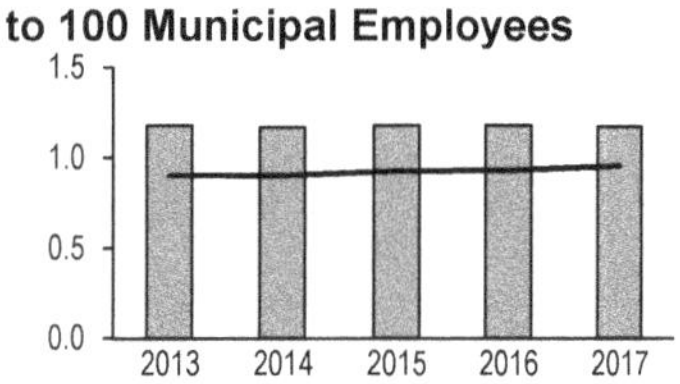

	2013	2014	2015	2016	2017
Greenville	1.18	1.17	1.18	1.18	1.17
Average	0.90	0.90	0.93	0.93	0.95

Effectiveness Measures

Probationary Period Completion Rate (New Hires)

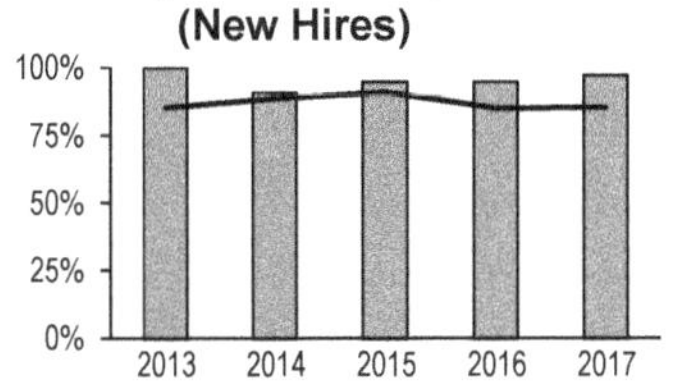

	2013	2014	2015	2016	2017
Greenville	100%	91%	95%	95%	97%
Average	85%	88%	91%	85%	85%

Employee Turnover Rate (All Separations)

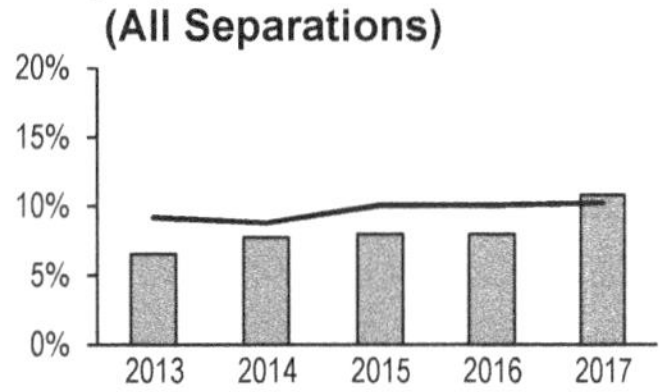

	2013	2014	2015	2016	2017
Greenville	6.5%	7.8%	8.0%	8.0%	10.8%
Average	9.2%	8.8%	10.1%	10.0%	10.2%

Employee Turnover Rate (Voluntary Separations)

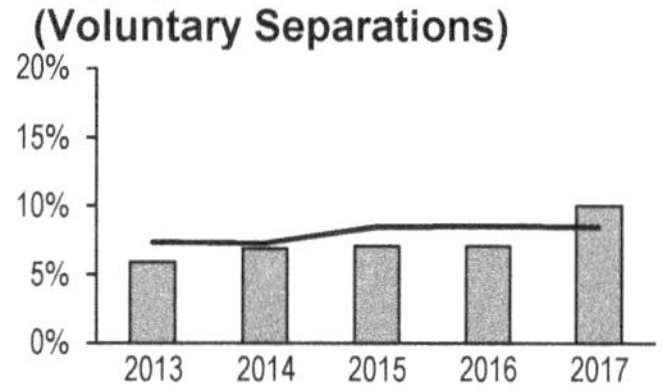

	2013	2014	2015	2016	2017
Greenville	5.9%	6.9%	7.1%	7.1%	10.0%
Average	7.4%	7.3%	8.5%	8.5%	8.5%

Percentage of Grievances Resolved at Department Level

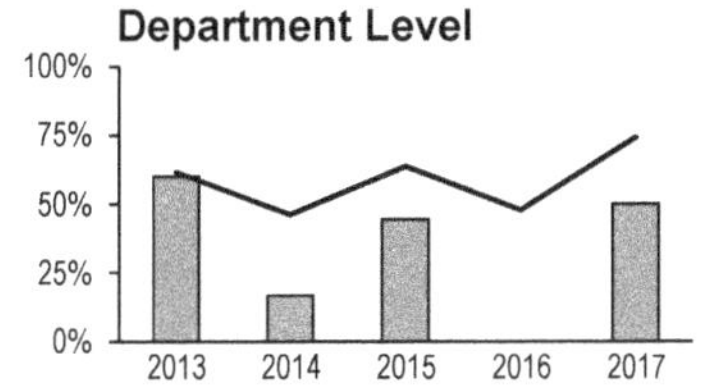

	2013	2014	2015	2016	2017
Greenville	60%	17%	44%		50%
Average	61%	46%	64%	48%	74%

Average Days from Post Date to Hire Date (First Day of Employment)

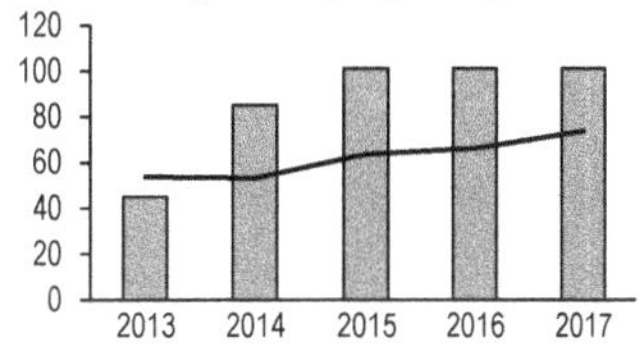

	2013	2014	2015	2016	2017
Greenville	45	85	101	101	101
Average	54	53	64	66	74

Hickory — Central Human Resources

Fiscal Year 2016–17

Explanatory Information

Service Level and Delivery

The human resources function for the City of Hickory contains a director, an organizational development coordinator, a city nurse, two human resources analysts (one oversees benefits administration and the other oversees general employment), and one clerical position. Risk management is a division of the human resources function, which includes a risk manager and a clerical support position.

The city's probationary period is twelve months for all new city employees. The city conducted three compensation studies during the fiscal year for eight different positions.

Conditions Affecting Service, Performance, and Costs

Municipal Profile

Population (OSBM 2016)	40,453
Land Area (Square Miles)	29.90
Persons per Square Mile	1,353
Median Family Income U.S. Census 2010	$54,093
County Unemployment Rate (2016) U.S. Bureau of Labor Statistics	4.7%

Service Profile

Central HR FTE Positions	
Administration	1.00
Generalist/Specialist	4.0
Staff Support/Clerical	2.00
Total Authorized Workforce	736.0
Authorized FTEs	736.0
Average Length of Service (Months)	118.66
Number of Position Requisitions	102
Employment Applications Processed	4,083
Length of Probationary Employment Period	12 months
Compensation Studies Completed	3
Positions Studied	8
Employee Turnover	
Voluntary Separations	70
Involuntary Separations	8
TOTAL SEPARATIONS	78
Formal Grievances Filed by Employees	7
Equal Employment Opportunity Commission (EEOC) Complaints Filed	1

Full Cost Profile

Cost Breakdown by Percentage	
Personal Services	72.2%
Operating Costs	27.0%
Capital Costs	0.8%
TOTAL	100.0%
Cost Breakdown in Dollars	
Personal Services	$357,768
Operating Costs	$133,717
Capital Costs	$3,879
TOTAL	$495,364

Key: Hickory ▒ Benchmarking Average — Fiscal Years 2013through 2017

Resource Measures

Human Resources Services Cost per Capita

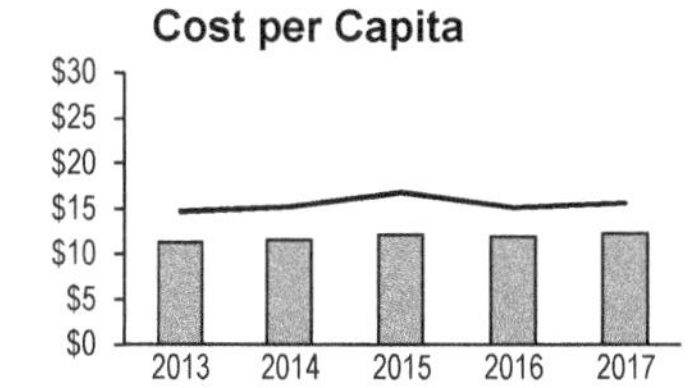

	2013	2014	2015	2016	2017
Hickory	$11.29	$11.56	$12.12	$11.92	$12.25
Average	$14.68	$15.20	$16.80	$15.16	$15.62

Human Resources FTEs per 10,000 Population

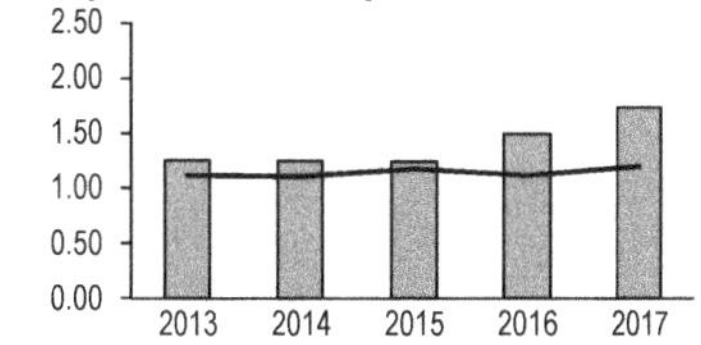

	2013	2014	2015	2016	2017
Hickory	1.25	1.24	1.24	1.49	1.73
Average	1.12	1.11	1.18	1.13	1.20

Workload Measures

Total Municipal FTEs per 10,000 Population

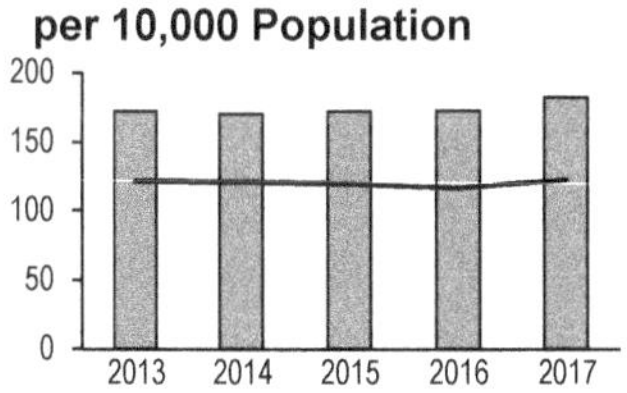

	2013	2014	2015	2016	2017
Hickory	172	170	172	172	182
Average	121	120	119	116	122

Applications Processed per 100 Municipal Employees

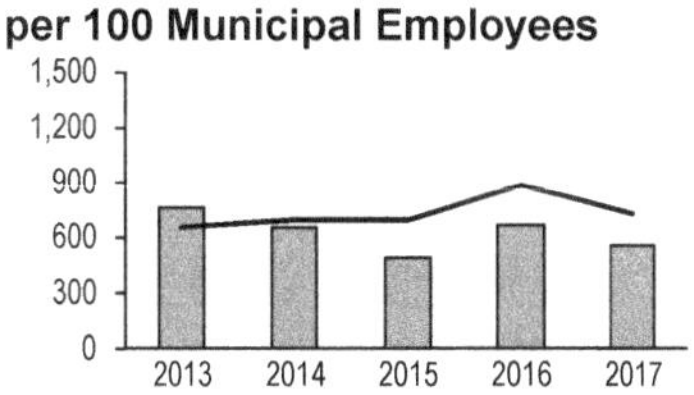

	2013	2014	2015	2016	2017
Hickory	759	654	489	667	555
Average	655	693	695	884	729

Position Requisitions per 100 Municipal Employees

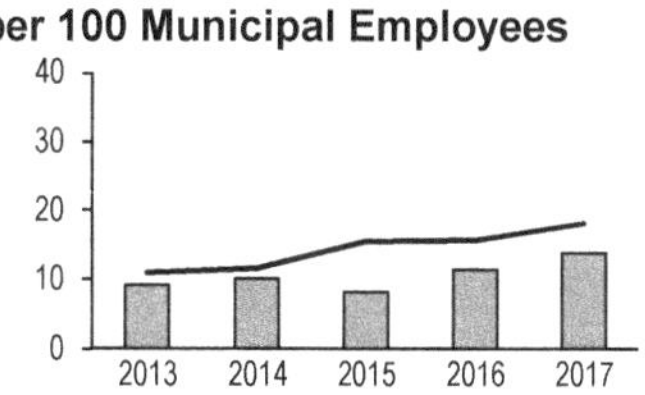

	2013	2014	2015	2016	2017
Hickory	9.2	10.1	8.2	11.4	13.9
Average	11.0	11.6	15.4	15.6	18.2

Efficiency Measures

Human Resources Cost per Municipal Employee

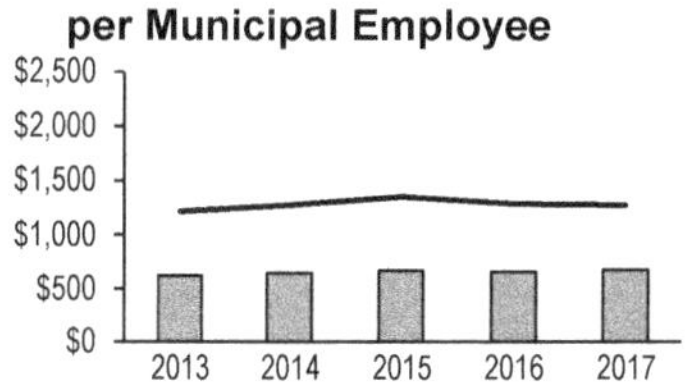

	2013	2014	2015	2016	2017
Hickory	$620	$645	$667	$654	$673
Average	$1,210	$1,271	$1,346	$1,281	$1,272

Ratio of Human Resources Staff to 100 Municipal Employees

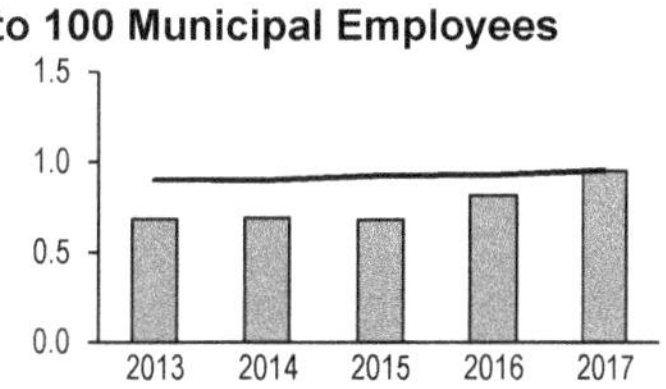

	2013	2014	2015	2016	2017
Hickory	0.69	0.69	0.68	0.82	0.95
Average	0.90	0.90	0.93	0.93	0.95

Effectiveness Measures

Probationary Period Completion Rate (New Hires)

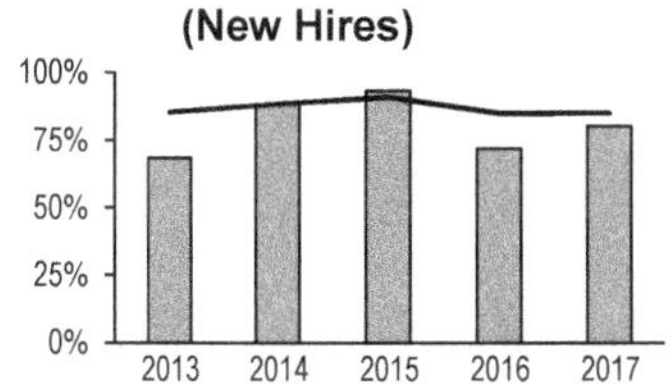

	2013	2014	2015	2016	2017
Hickory	68%	88%	93%	72%	80%
Average	85%	88%	91%	85%	85%

Employee Turnover Rate (All Separations)

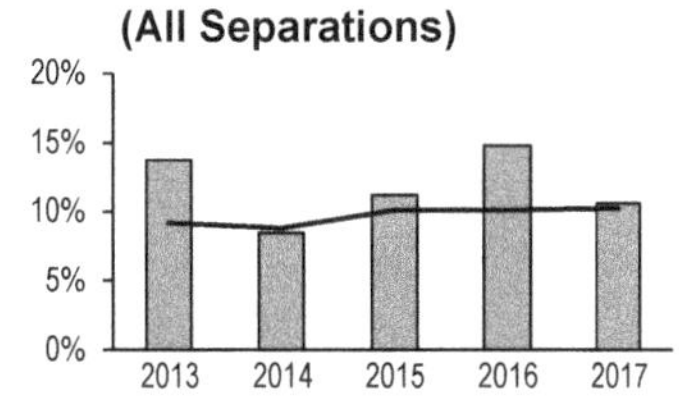

	2013	2014	2015	2016	2017
Hickory	13.7%	8.5%	11.2%	14.8%	10.6%
Average	9.2%	8.8%	10.1%	10.0%	10.2%

Employee Turnover Rate (Voluntary Separations)

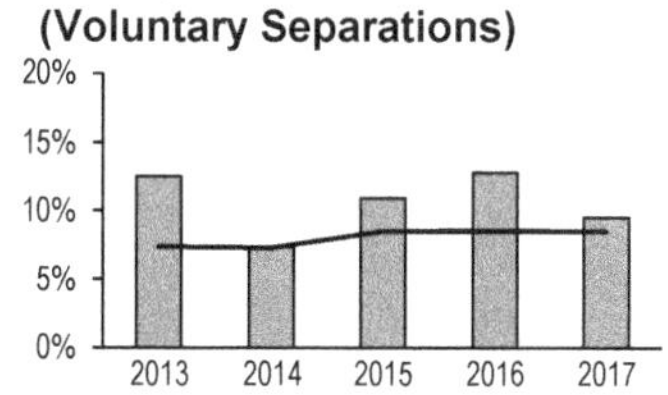

	2013	2014	2015	2016	2017
Hickory	12.5%	7.4%	10.9%	12.8%	9.5%
Average	7.4%	7.3%	8.5%	8.5%	8.5%

Percentage of Grievances Resolved at Department Level

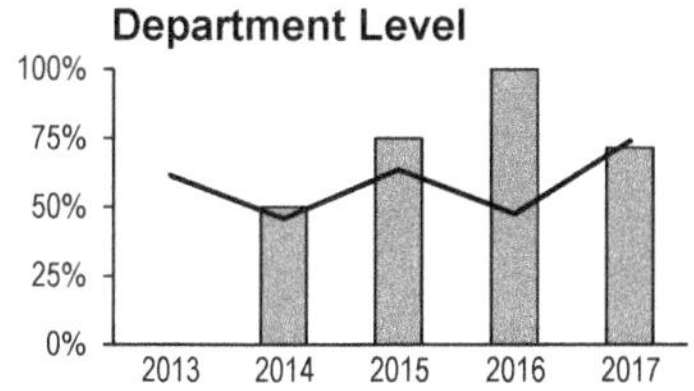

	2013	2014	2015	2016	2017
Hickory		50%	75%	100%	71%
Average	61%	46%	64%	48%	74%

Average Days from Post Date to Hire Date (First Day of Employment)

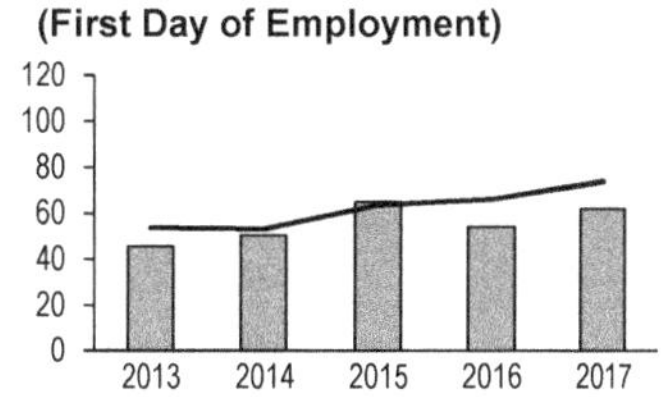

	2013	2014	2015	2016	2017
Hickory	46	50	65	54	62
Average	54	53	64	66	74

Explanatory Information

Service Level and Delivery

The City of High Point Human Resources Department is organized into two divisions. The Administrative Division's organizational objectives consist of personnel and fringe benefits budgeting; workforce planning; recruitment, selection, and EEO, ADA, FMLA, FLSA, and HIPAA compliance; fringe benefit competitiveness and cost containment; employee benefits education and awareness; maintaining a competitive and equitable salary and classification plan; offering professional training opportunities for employees; development of intervention strategies to address workplace problems; and facilitation services to employee groups. The HR Department spends a good of time processing the bi-weekly payroll and administers a rewards and recognition program and performance management. The director of human resources reports directly to the city manager.

The Safety and Health Division's organizational objectives consist of assisting city departments in providing a safe work environment, promoting a healthier workforce through job fitness assessments and wellness programs, coordination of the city's substance abuse program, workers' compensation cost containment and compliance with OSHA, HIPAA, EPA, and DOT regulations; and compliance with North Carolina workers' compensation regulations.

One compensation study was conducted during the most recent fiscal year, covering 516 positions.

The city's probationary period is twelve months for new employees. Department directors may extend probationary periods for up to ninety additional days if approved by the human resources director.

Conditions Affecting Service, Performance, and Costs

Municipal Profile

Population (OSBM 2016)	110,244
Land Area (Square Miles)	55.14
Persons per Square Mile	1,999
Median Family Income U.S. Census 2010	$49,720
County Unemployment Rate (2016) U.S. Bureau of Labor Statistics	5.2%

Service Profile

Central HR FTE Positions	
Administration	5.0
Generalist/Specialist	6.0
Staff Support/Clerical	1.0
Total Authorized Workforce	1,637.0
Authorized FTEs	1,481.0
Average Length of Service (Months)	129
Number of Position Requisitions	392
Employment Applications Processed	7,085
Length of Probationary Employment Period	12 months
Compensation Studies Completed	1
Positions Studied	516
Employee Turnover	
Voluntary Separations	108
Involuntary Separations	26
TOTAL SEPARATIONS	134
Formal Grievances Filed by Employees	12
Equal Employment Opportunity Commission (EEOC) Complaints Filed	1

Full Cost Profile

Cost Breakdown by Percentage	
Personal Services	65.3%
Operating Costs	33.7%
Capital Costs	1.0%
TOTAL	100.0%
Cost Breakdown in Dollars	
Personal Services	$1,052,518
Operating Costs	$544,376
Capital Costs	$16,102
TOTAL	$1,612,996

High Point — Central Human Resources

Key: High Point ▒ Benchmarking Average — Fiscal Years 2013through 2017

Resource Measures

Human Resources Services Cost per Capita

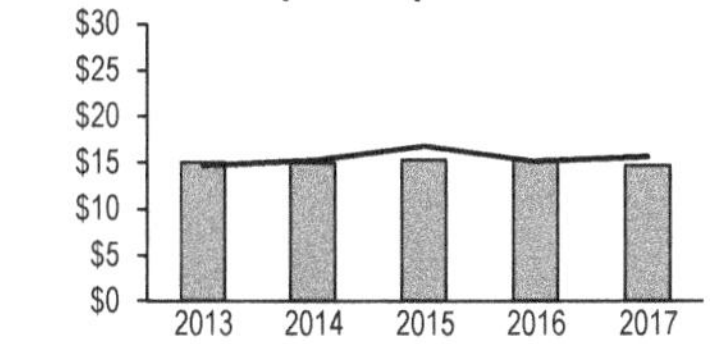

	2013	2014	2015	2016	2017
High Point	$14.97	$14.94	$15.26	$15.19	$14.63
Average	$14.68	$15.20	$16.80	$15.16	$15.62

Human Resources FTEs per 10,000 Population

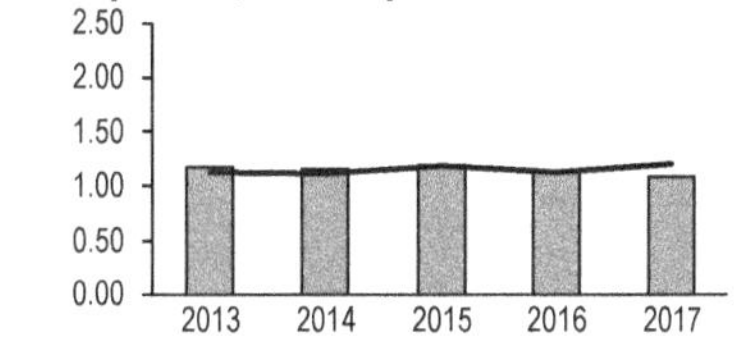

	2013	2014	2015	2016	2017
High Point	1.17	1.16	1.20	1.14	1.09
Average	1.12	1.11	1.18	1.13	1.20

Workload Measures

Total Municipal FTEs per 10,000 Population

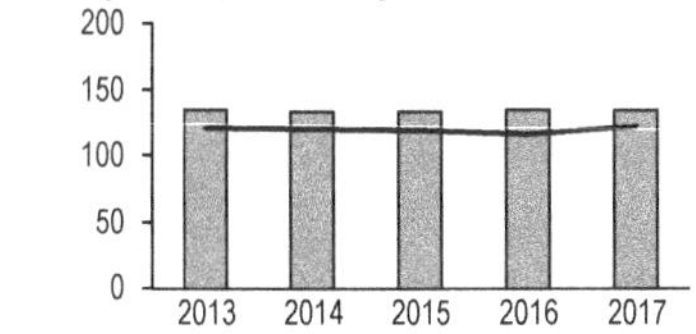

	2013	2014	2015	2016	2017
High Point	135	133	133	135	134
Average	121	120	119	116	122

Applications Processed per 100 Municipal Employees

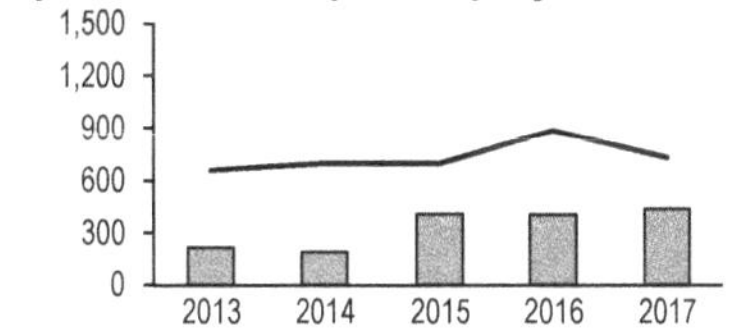

	2013	2014	2015	2016	2017
High Point	214	189	405	400	433
Average	655	693	695	884	729

Position Requisitions per 100 Municipal Employees

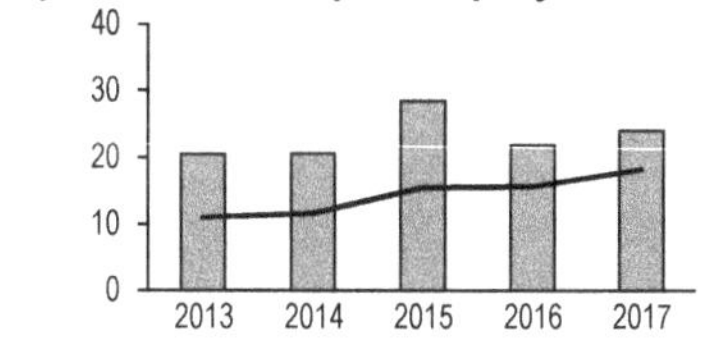

	2013	2014	2015	2016	2017
High Point	20.3	20.5	28.4	21.7	23.9
Average	11.0	11.6	15.4	15.6	18.2

Efficiency Measures

Human Resources Cost per Municipal Employee

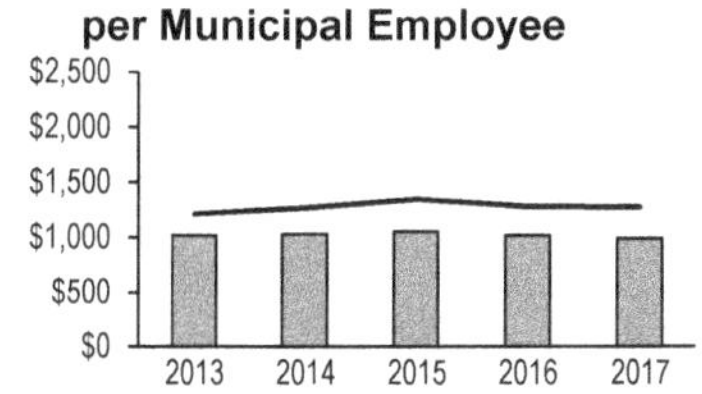

	2013	2014	2015	2016	2017
High Point	$1,019	$1,029	$1,051	$1,019	$985
Average	$1,210	$1,271	$1,346	$1,281	$1,272

Ratio of Human Resources Staff to 100 Municipal Employees

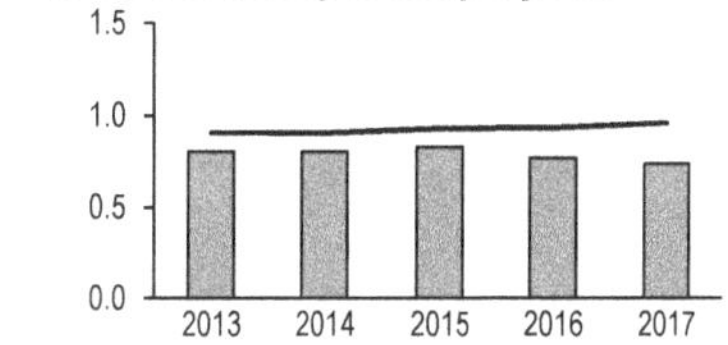

	2013	2014	2015	2016	2017
High Point	0.80	0.80	0.82	0.76	0.73
Average	0.90	0.90	0.93	0.93	0.95

Effectiveness Measures

Probationary Period Completion Rate (New Hires)

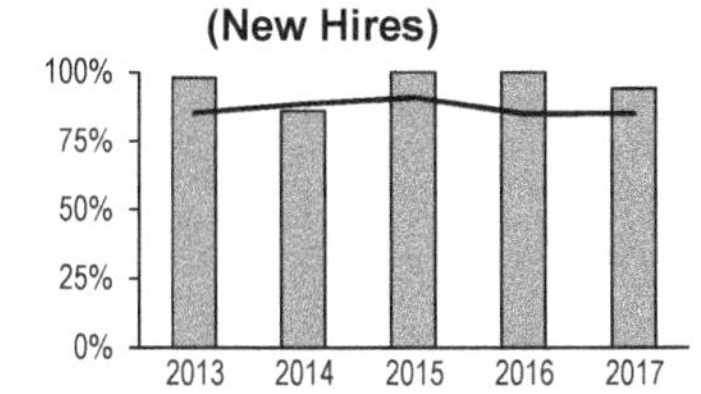

	2013	2014	2015	2016	2017
High Point	98%	86%	100%	100%	94%
Average	85%	88%	91%	85%	85%

Employee Turnover Rate (All Separations)

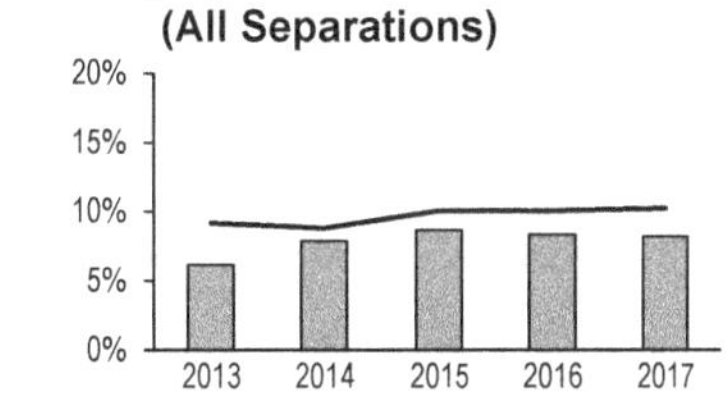

	2013	2014	2015	2016	2017
High Point	6.1%	7.9%	8.6%	8.3%	8.2%
Average	9.2%	8.8%	10.1%	10.0%	10.2%

Employee Turnover Rate (Voluntary Separations)

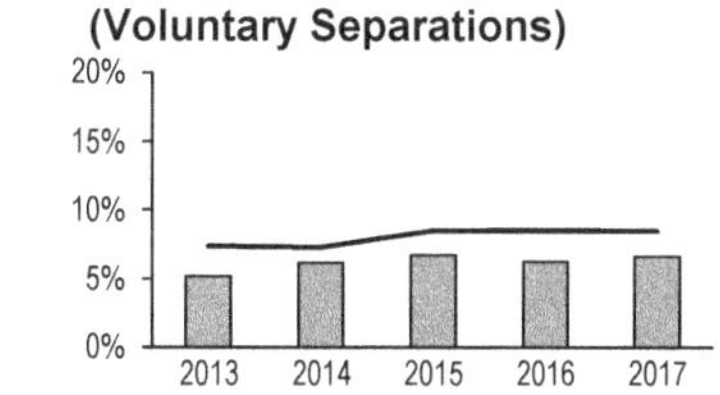

	2013	2014	2015	2016	2017
High Point	5.2%	6.1%	6.7%	6.2%	6.6%
Average	7.4%	7.3%	8.5%	8.5%	8.5%

Percentage of Grievances Resolved at Department Level

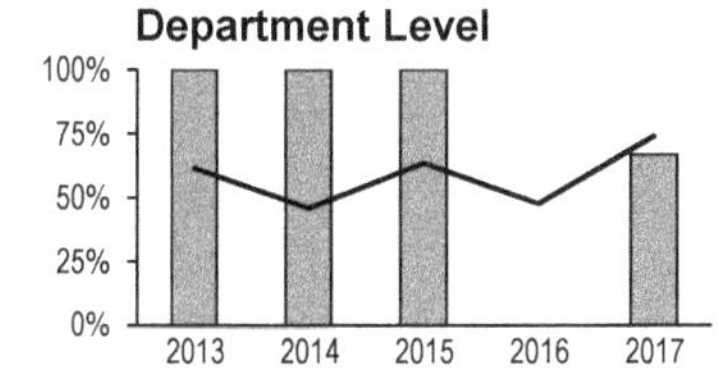

	2013	2014	2015	2016	2017
High Point	100%	100%	100%	0%	67%
Average	61%	46%	64%	48%	74%

Average Days from Post Date to Hire Date (First Day of Employment)

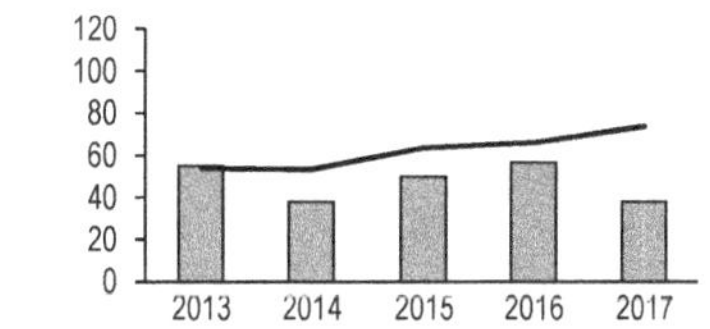

	2013	2014	2015	2016	2017
High Point	55	38	50	57	38
Average	54	53	64	66	74

Fiscal Year 2016–17

Explanatory Information

Service Level and Delivery

The City of Raleigh's Human Resource Department is organized around work units covering benefits, which includes employee health and wellness; employee training and organizational development; talent acquisition, compensation and HRIS; and safety. In addition, the Department has three business partners who align with the city's assistant city managers.

The City's probationary period for law enforcement officers is twelve months from the date of employement or successful completion of field training. For firefighters, the probationary period is from the date of employment to six months after graduation from the academy. For all other employees, the probation period lasts six months from the date of employment.

Five compensation studies covering 3,950 positions were conducted during the fiscal year. A market review of benchmark jobs was conducted for comparison.

All applications for employment must be completed electronically. HR conducts an initial scan based on minimum qualifications and secondarily by screening questions developed by the hiring manager.

Conditions Affecting Service, Performance, and Costs

Raleigh rejoined the Benchmarking Project in July 2016, with the first year of data showing for FY 2015–16.

Municipal Profile

Population (OSBM 2016)	448,706
Land Area (Square Miles)	145.57
Persons per Square Mile	3,083
Median Family Income U.S. Census 2010	$68,678
County Unemployment Rate (2016) U.S. Bureau of Labor Statistics	4.2%

Service Profile

Central HR FTE Positions	
Administration	17.0
Generalist/Specialist	4.0
Staff Support/Clerical	21.0
Total Authorized Workforce	3,950.0
Authorized FTEs	3,950.0
Average Length of Service (Months)	119.4
Number of Position Requisitions	557
Employment Applications Processed	24,519
Length of Probationary Employment Period	6 & 12 months
Compensation Studies Completed	5
Positions Studied	3,950
Employee Turnover	
Voluntary Separations	130
Involuntary Separations	301
TOTAL SEPARATIONS	431
Formal Grievances Filed by Employees	13
Equal Employment Opportunity Commission (EEOC) Complaints Filed	2

Full Cost Profile

Cost Breakdown by Percentage	
Personal Services	66.4%
Operating Costs	32.1%
Capital Costs	1.5%
TOTAL	100.0%
Cost Breakdown in Dollars	
Personal Services	$2,970,869
Operating Costs	$1,438,083
Capital Costs	$65,396
TOTAL	$4,474,348

Key: Raleigh ▒ Benchmarking Average — Fiscal Years 2013through 2017

Resource Measures

Human Resources Services Cost per Capita

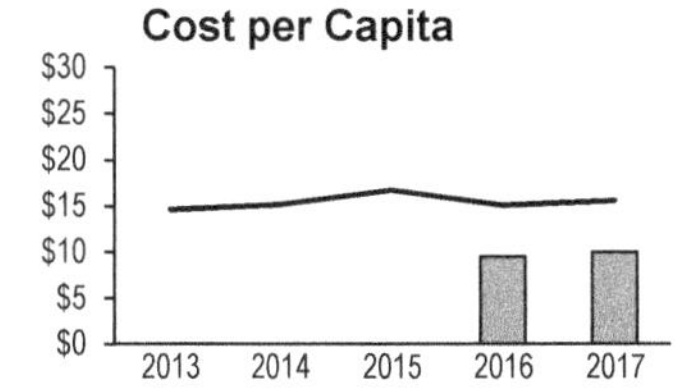

	2013	2014	2015	2016	2017
Raleigh				$9.52	$9.97
Average	$14.68	$15.20	$16.80	$15.16	$15.62

Human Resources FTEs per 10,000 Population

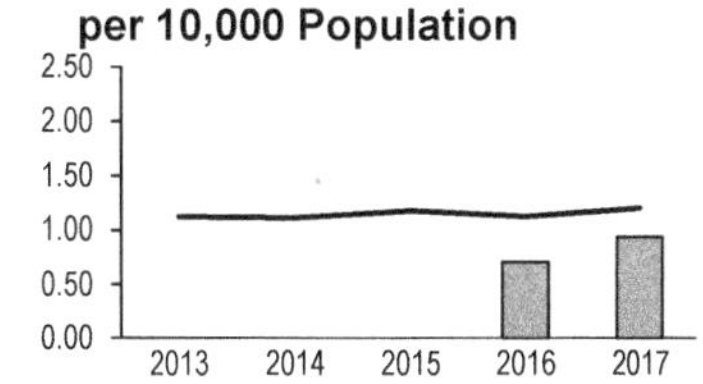

	2013	2014	2015	2016	2017
Raleigh				0.70	0.94
Average	1.12	1.11	1.18	1.13	1.20

Workload Measures

Total Municipal FTEs per 10,000 Population

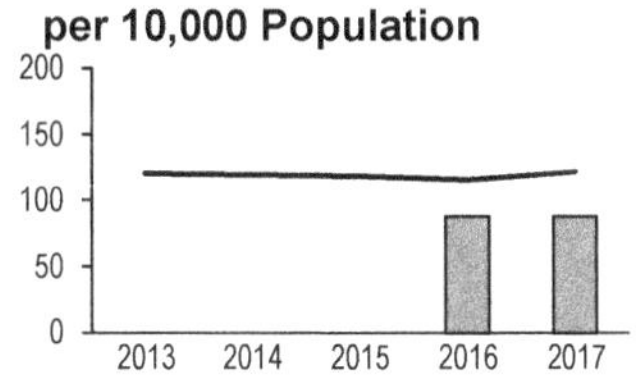

	2013	2014	2015	2016	2017
Raleigh				88	88
Average	121	120	119	116	122

Applications Processed per 100 Municipal Employees

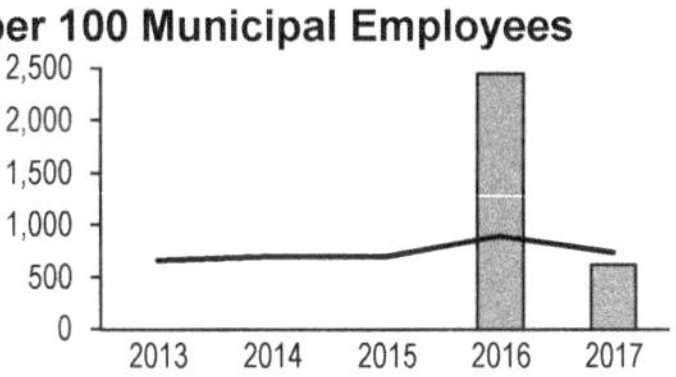

	2013	2014	2015	2016	2017
Raleigh				2,447	621
Average	655	693	695	884	729

Position Requisitions per 100 Municipal Employees

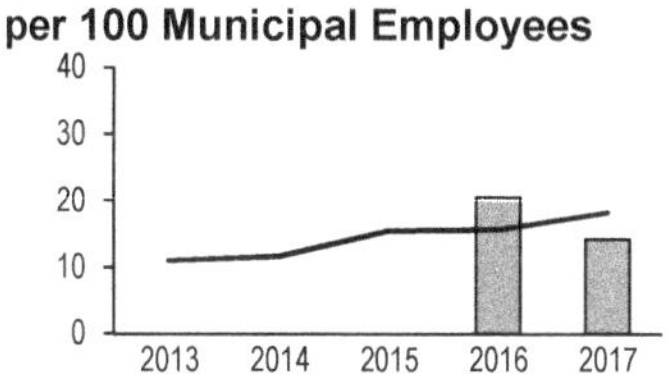

	2013	2014	2015	2016	2017
Raleigh				20.5	14.1
Average	11.0	11.6	15.4	15.6	18.2

Efficiency Measures

Human Resources Cost per Municipal Employee

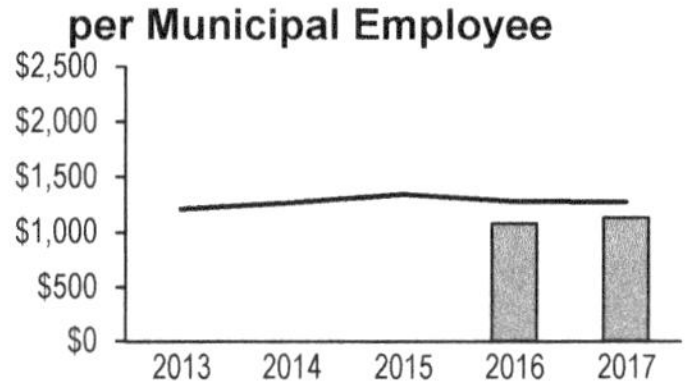

	2013	2014	2015	2016	2017
Raleigh				$1,080	$1,133
Average	$1,210	$1,271	$1,346	$1,281	$1,272

Ratio of Human Resources Staff to 100 Municipal Employees

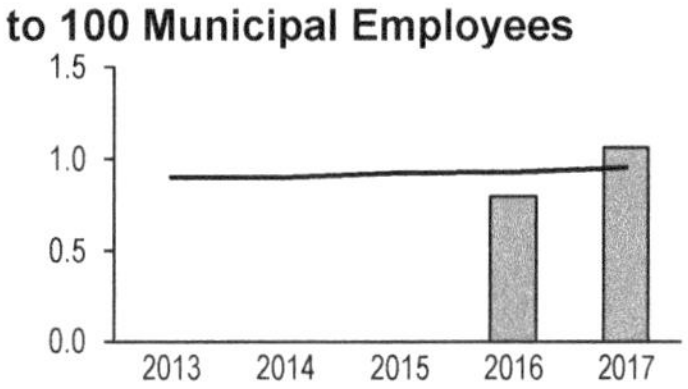

	2013	2014	2015	2016	2017
Raleigh				0.80	1.06
Average	0.90	0.90	0.93	0.93	0.95

Effectiveness Measures

Probationary Period Completion Rate (New Hires)

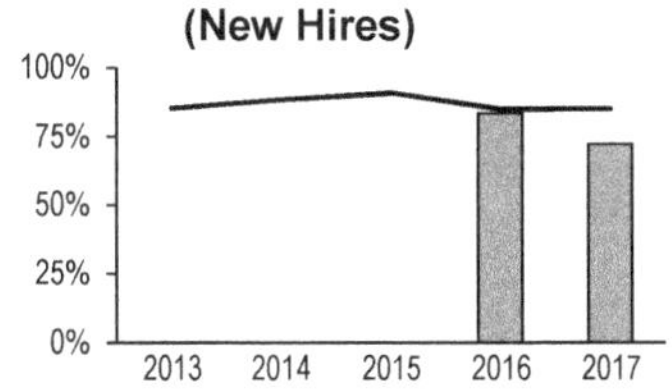

	2013	2014	2015	2016	2017
Raleigh				83%	72%
Average	85%	88%	91%	85%	85%

Employee Turnover Rate (All Separations)

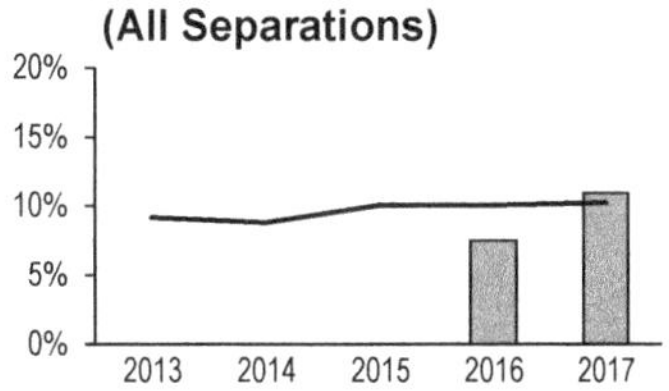

	2013	2014	2015	2016	2017
Raleigh				7.5%	10.9%
Average	9.2%	8.8%	10.1%	10.0%	10.2%

Employee Turnover Rate (Voluntary Separations)

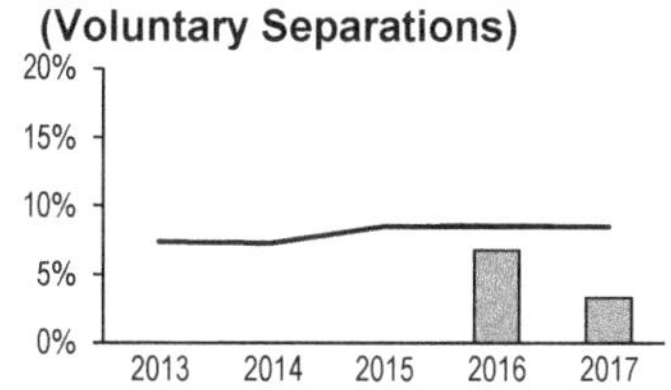

	2013	2014	2015	2016	2017
Raleigh				6.7%	3.3%
Average	7.4%	7.3%	8.5%	8.5%	8.5%

Percentage of Grievances Resolved at Department Level

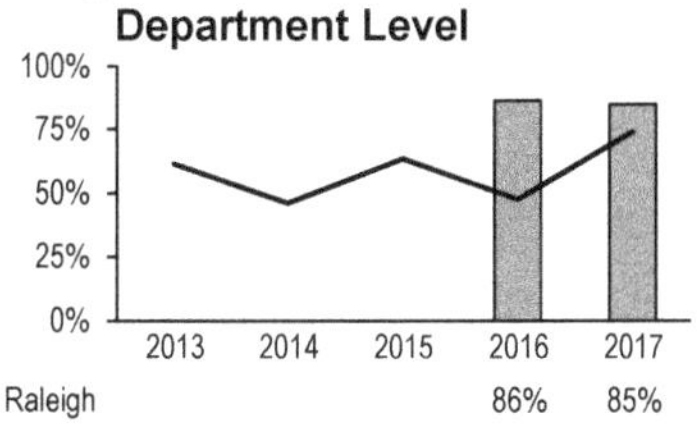

	2013	2014	2015	2016	2017
Raleigh				86%	85%
Average	61%	46%	64%	48%	74%

Average Days from Post Date to Hire Date (First Day of Employment)

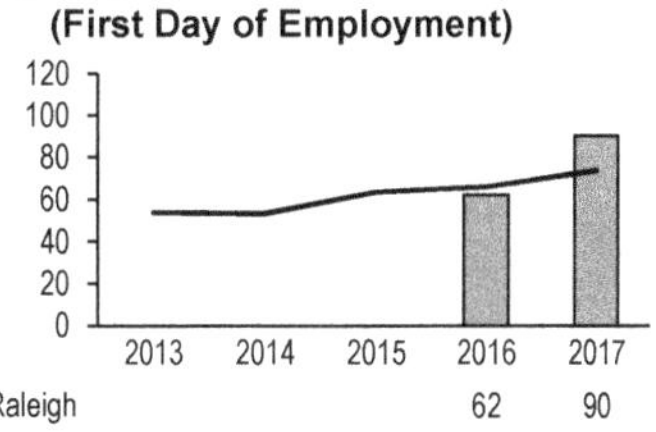

	2013	2014	2015	2016	2017
Raleigh				62	90
Average	54	53	64	66	74

Fiscal Year 2016–17

Explanatory Information

Service Level and Delivery

The City of Salisbury's Human Resources Department operates as an internal support service reporting directly to the Assistant City Manager for Human Resources. Human Resources handles the daily management of human capital while also helping to support community functions such as the Human Relations Council and the Salisbury Youth Council. The human resources function in Salisbury is a centralized unit with six staff members.

The Human Resources Department has been the lead agency in the development of customer service provisions identified by the city council as the top priority for the city.

The city's probationary period for new general employees is six months and twelve months for police and fire employees.

Two compensation studies covering four positions were conducted during the fiscal year.

Conditions Affecting Service, Performance, and Costs

Municipal Profile

Population (OSBM 2016)	34,459
Land Area (Square Miles)	22.28
Persons per Square Mile	1,547
Median Family Income U.S. Census 2010	$40,192
County Unemployment Rate (2016) U.S. Bureau of Labor Statistics	5.5%

Service Profile

Central HR FTE Positions	
Administration	1.0
Generalist/Specialist	4.0
Staff Support/Clerical	1.0
Total Authorized Workforce	512.0
Authorized FTEs	478.8
Average Length of Service (Months)	96
Number of Position Requisitions	92
Employment Applications Processed	1,581
Length of Probationary Employment Period	6 & 12 months
Compensation Studies Completed	2
Positions Studied	4
Employee Turnover	
Voluntary Separations	60
Involuntary Separations	14
TOTAL SEPARATIONS	74
Formal Grievances Filed by Employees	8
Equal Employment Opportunity Commission (EEOC) Complaints Filed	1

Full Cost Profile

Cost Breakdown by Percentage	
Personal Services	71.2%
Operating Costs	28.5%
Capital Costs	0.3%
TOTAL	100.0%
Cost Breakdown in Dollars	
Personal Services	$444,311
Operating Costs	$177,608
Capital Costs	$1,889
TOTAL	$623,808

Key: Salisbury ▒ Benchmarking Average — Fiscal Years 2013through 2017

Resource Measures

Human Resources Services Cost per Capita

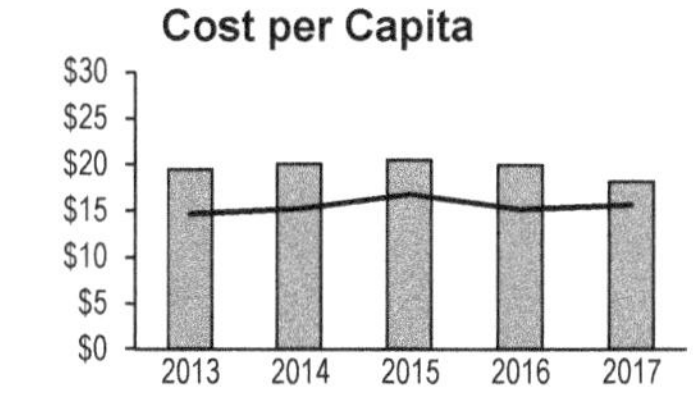

	2013	2014	2015	2016	2017
Salisbury	$19.45	$20.09	$20.46	$19.96	$18.10
Average	$14.68	$15.20	$16.80	$15.16	$15.62

Human Resources FTEs per 10,000 Population

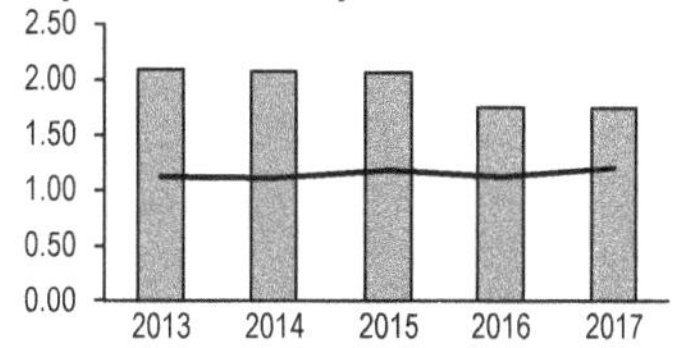

	2013	2014	2015	2016	2017
Salisbury	2.09	2.08	2.06	1.75	1.74
Average	1.12	1.11	1.18	1.13	1.20

Workload Measures

Total Municipal FTEs per 10,000 Population

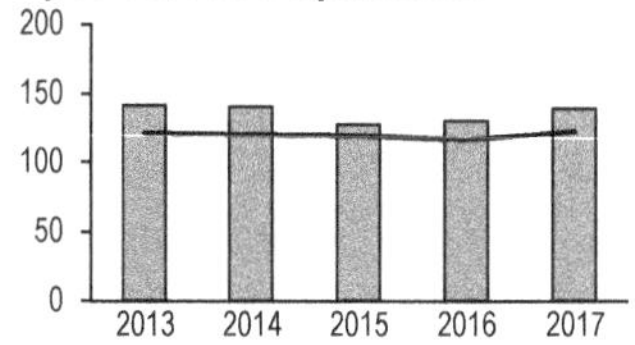

	2013	2014	2015	2016	2017
Salisbury	141	140	128	130	139
Average	121	120	119	116	122

Applications Processed per 100 Municipal Employees

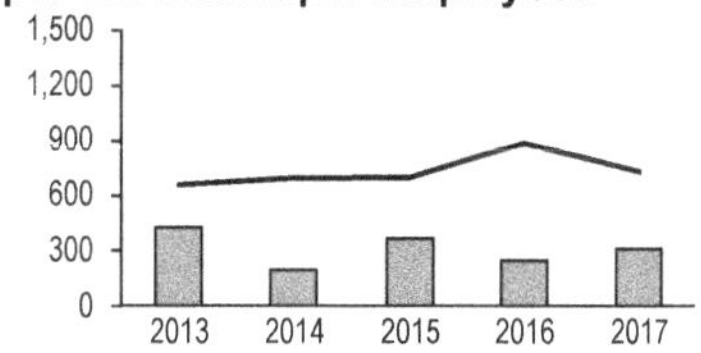

	2013	2014	2015	2016	2017
Salisbury	424	194	366	247	309
Average	655	693	695	884	729

Position Requisitions per 100 Municipal Employees

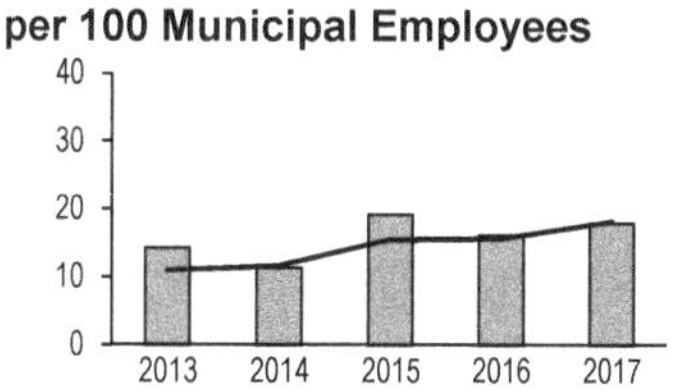

	2013	2014	2015	2016	2017
Salisbury	14.3	11.3	19.2	16.1	18.0
Average	11.0	11.6	15.4	15.6	18.2

Efficiency Measures

Human Resources Cost per Municipal Employee

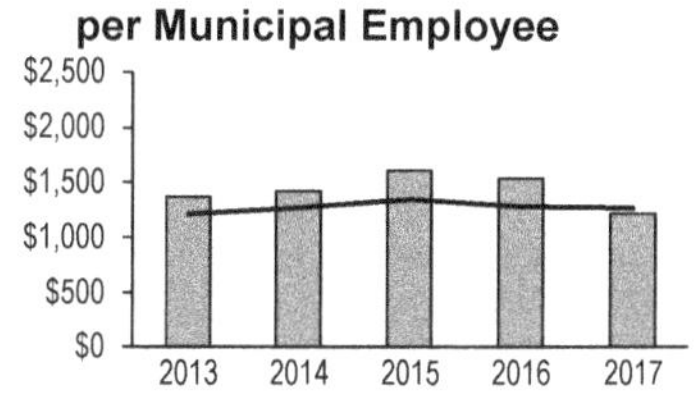

	2013	2014	2015	2016	2017
Salisbury	$1,366	$1,423	$1,605	$1,534	$1,218
Average	$1,210	$1,271	$1,346	$1,281	$1,272

Ratio of Human Resources Staff to 100 Municipal Employees

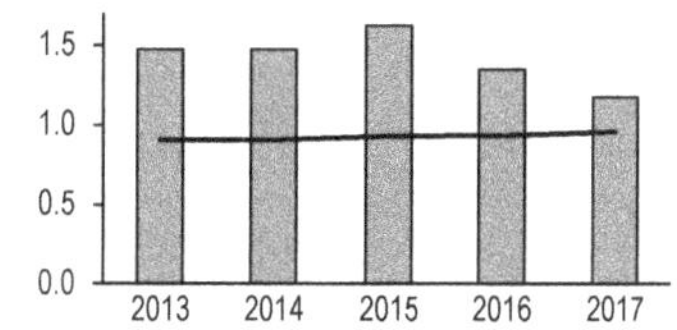

	2013	2014	2015	2016	2017
Salisbury	1.47	1.47	1.62	1.35	1.17
Average	0.90	0.90	0.93	0.93	0.95

Effectiveness Measures

Probationary Period Completion Rate (New Hires)

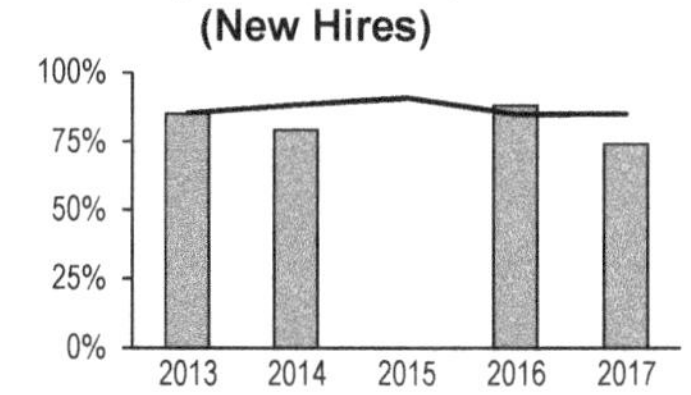

	2013	2014	2015	2016	2017
Salisbury	85%	79%		88%	74%
Average	85%	88%	91%	85%	85%

Employee Turnover Rate (All Separations)

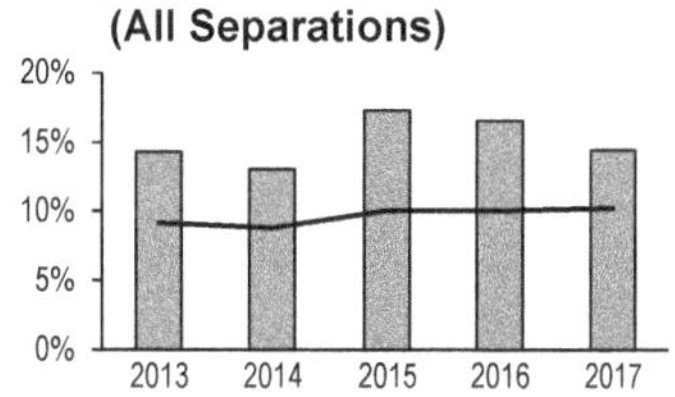

	2013	2014	2015	2016	2017
Salisbury	14.3%	13.0%	17.3%	16.6%	14.5%
Average	9.2%	8.8%	10.1%	10.0%	10.2%

Employee Turnover Rate (Voluntary Separations)

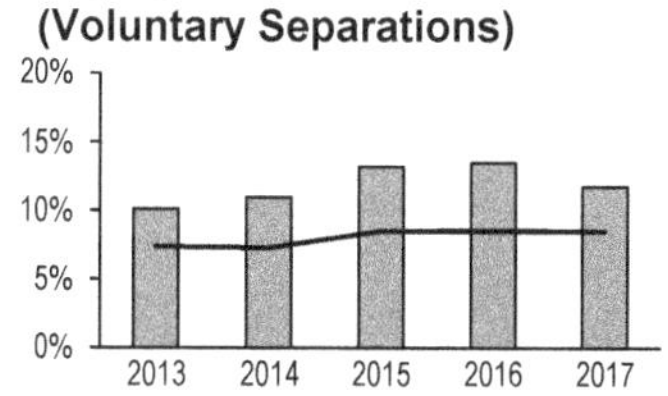

	2013	2014	2015	2016	2017
Salisbury	10.1%	10.9%	13.2%	13.5%	11.7%
Average	7.4%	7.3%	8.5%	8.5%	8.5%

Percentage of Grievances Resolved at Department Level

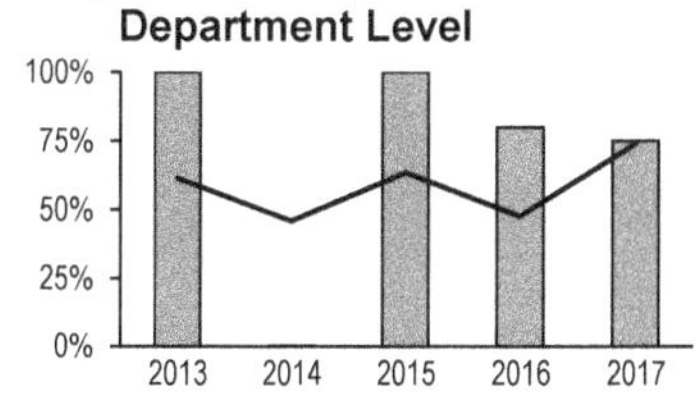

	2013	2014	2015	2016	2017
Salisbury	100%	0%	100%	80%	75%
Average	61%	46%	64%	48%	74%

Average Days from Post Date to Hire Date (First Day of Employment)

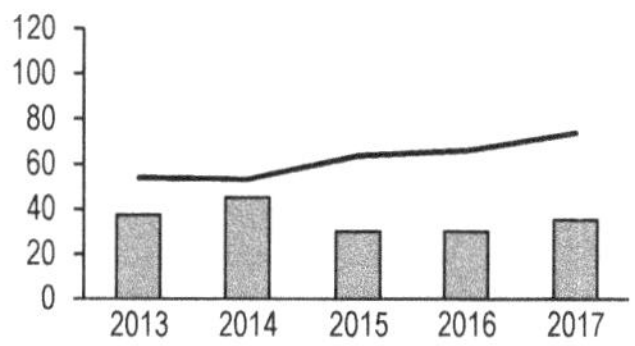

	2013	2014	2015	2016	2017
Salisbury	38	45	30	30	35
Average	54	53	64	66	74

Fiscal Year 2016–17

Explanatory Information

Service Level and Delivery

The City of Wilson has a centralized Human Resources Department that includes policy development and implementation, classification and pay administration, recruitment and selection, benefits administration, and employee relations. The safety and health program is a function of the Risk Management Division under another department. Occupational health needs are met through a contract with the Wilson Medical Center.

The city conducted one compensation study during the fiscal year covering fourteen positions.

The city's probationary period is twelve months for new city employees.

Conditions Affecting Service, Performance, and Costs

Municipal Profile

Population (OSBM 2016)	49,406
Land Area (Square Miles)	30.60
Persons per Square Mile	1,615
Median Family Income U.S. Census 2010	$43,442
County Unemployment Rate (2016) U.S. Bureau of Labor Statistics	8.1%

Service Profile

Central HR FTE Positions	
Administration	0.5
Generalist/Specialist	3.0
Staff Support/Clerical	2.0
Total Authorized Workforce	760.0
Authorized FTEs	751.0
Average Length of Service (Months)	159
Number of Position Requisitions	70
Employment Applications Processed	1,906
Length of Probationary Employment Period	12 months
Compensation Studies Completed	1
Positions Studied	14
Employee Turnover	
Voluntary Separations	62
Involuntary Separations	15
TOTAL SEPARATIONS	77
Formal Grievances Filed by Employees	6
Equal Employment Opportunity Commission (EEOC) Complaints Filed	1

Full Cost Profile

Cost Breakdown by Percentage	
Personal Services	73.1%
Operating Costs	24.6%
Capital Costs	2.4%
TOTAL	100.0%
Cost Breakdown in Dollars	
Personal Services	$467,373
Operating Costs	$157,017
Capital Costs	$15,064
TOTAL	$639,454

Key: Wilson ▒ Benchmarking Average — Fiscal Years 2013through 2017

Resource Measures

Human Resources Services Cost per Capita

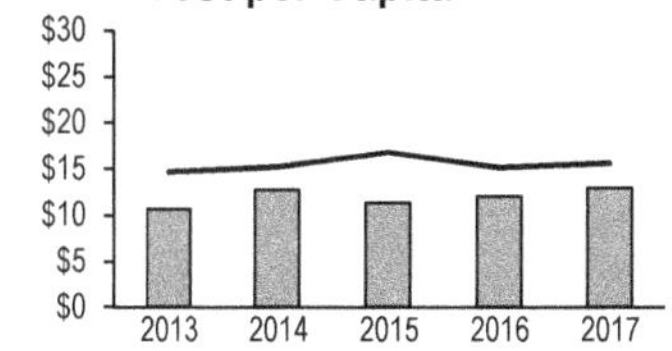

	2013	2014	2015	2016	2017
Wilson	$10.64	$12.71	$11.34	$12.02	$12.94
Average	$14.68	$15.20	$16.80	$15.16	$15.62

Human Resources FTEs per 10,000 Population

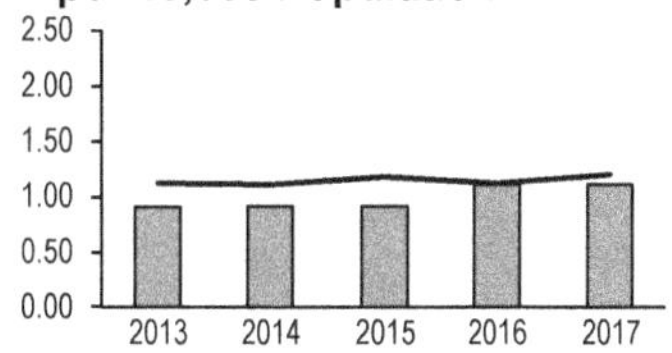

	2013	2014	2015	2016	2017
Wilson	0.91	0.92	0.91	1.11	1.11
Average	1.12	1.11	1.18	1.13	1.20

Workload Measures

Total Municipal FTEs per 10,000 Population

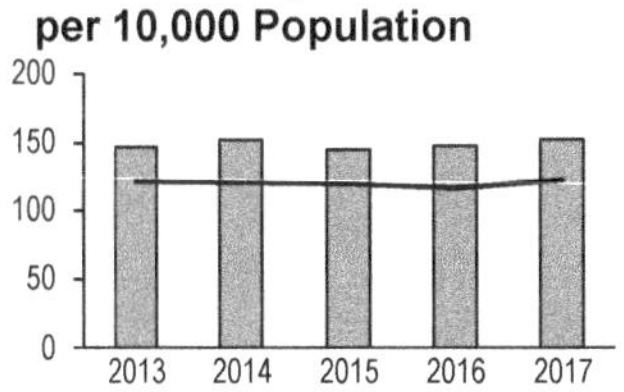

	2013	2014	2015	2016	2017
Wilson	146	152	145	147	152
Average	121	120	119	116	122

Applications Processed per 100 Municipal Employees

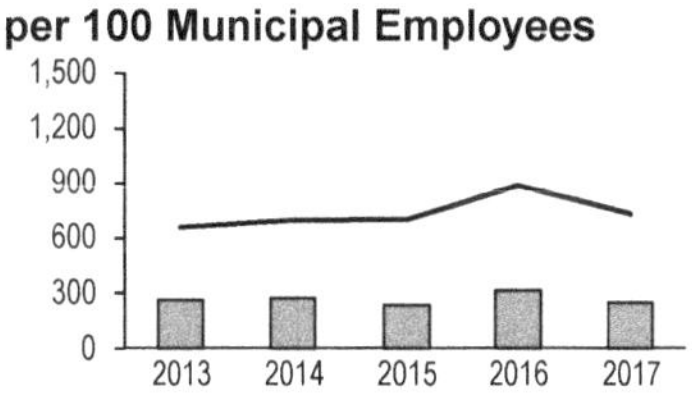

	2013	2014	2015	2016	2017
Wilson	264	274	236	315	251
Average	655	693	695	884	729

Position Requisitions per 100 Municipal Employees

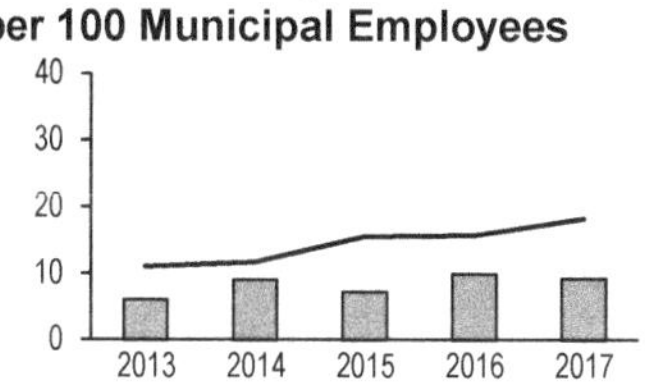

	2013	2014	2015	2016	2017
Wilson	6.1	9.1	7.2	9.9	9.2
Average	11.0	11.6	15.4	15.6	18.2

Efficiency Measures

Human Resources Cost per Municipal Employee

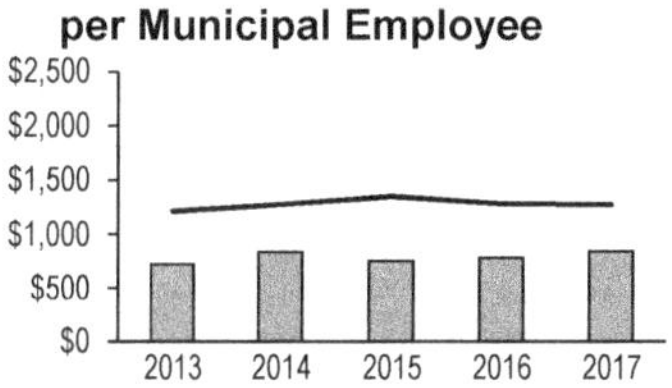

	2013	2014	2015	2016	2017
Wilson	$724	$832	$750	$781	$841
Average	$1,210	$1,271	$1,346	$1,281	$1,272

Ratio of Human Resources Staff to 100 Municipal Employees

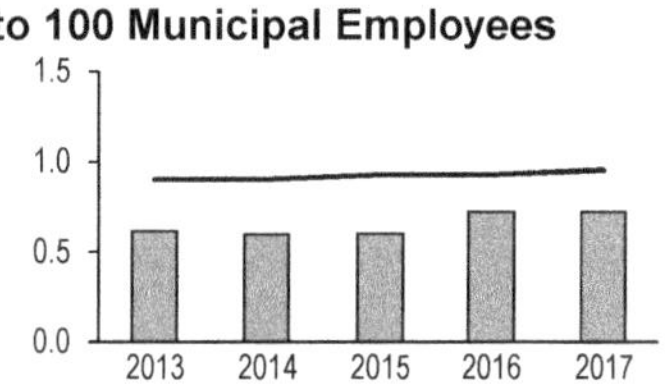

	2013	2014	2015	2016	2017
Wilson	0.62	0.60	0.60	0.72	0.72
Average	0.90	0.90	0.93	0.93	0.95

Effectiveness Measures

Probationary Period Completion Rate (New Hires)

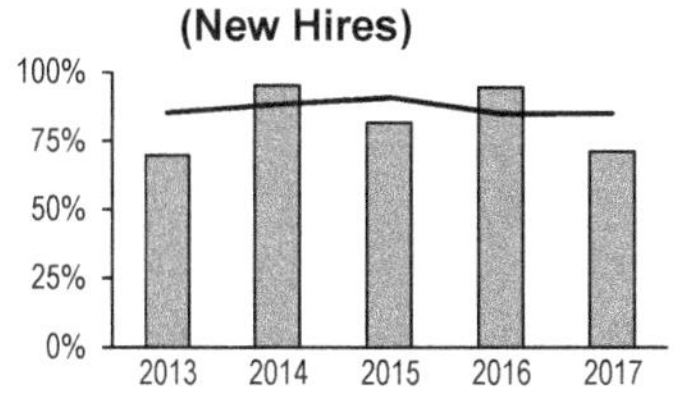

	2013	2014	2015	2016	2017
Wilson	70%	95%	82%	94%	71%
Average	85%	88%	91%	85%	85%

Employee Turnover Rate (All Separations)

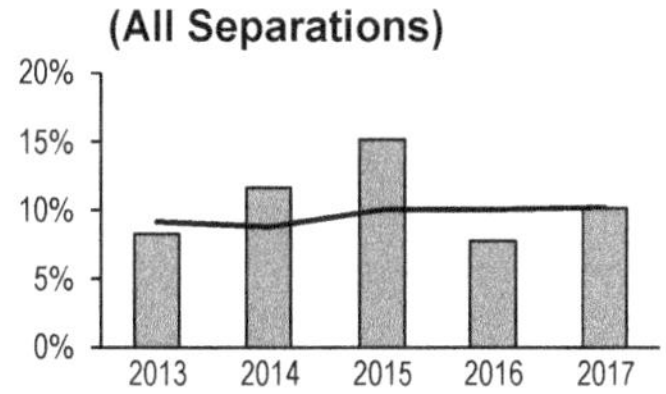

	2013	2014	2015	2016	2017
Wilson	8.3%	11.6%	15.2%	7.8%	10.1%
Average	9.2%	8.8%	10.1%	10.0%	10.2%

Employee Turnover Rate (Voluntary Separations)

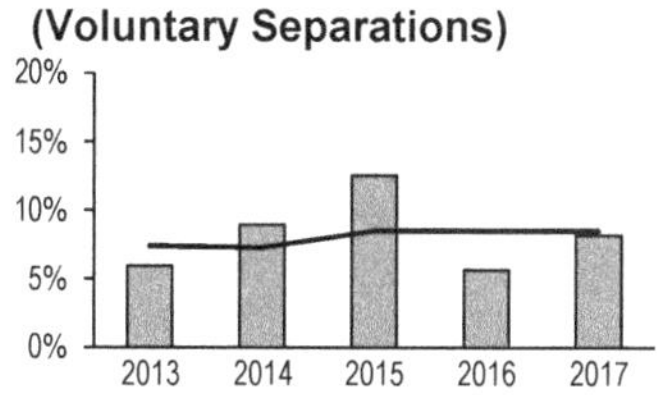

	2013	2014	2015	2016	2017
Wilson	5.9%	8.9%	12.5%	5.7%	8.2%
Average	7.4%	7.3%	8.5%	8.5%	8.5%

Percentage of Grievances Resolved at Department Level

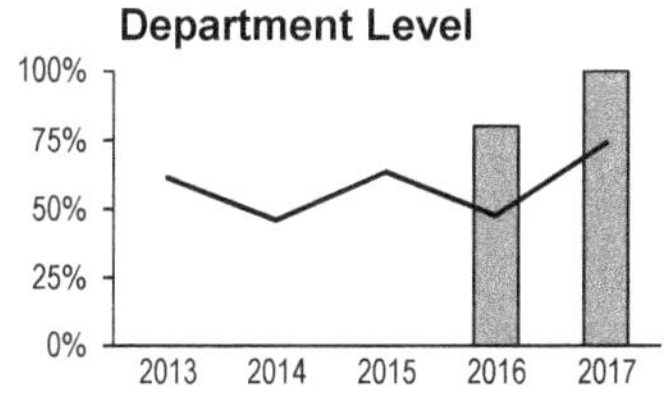

	2013	2014	2015	2016	2017
Wilson	0%			80%	100%
Average	61%	46%	64%	48%	74%

Average Days from Post Date to Hire Date (First Day of Employment)

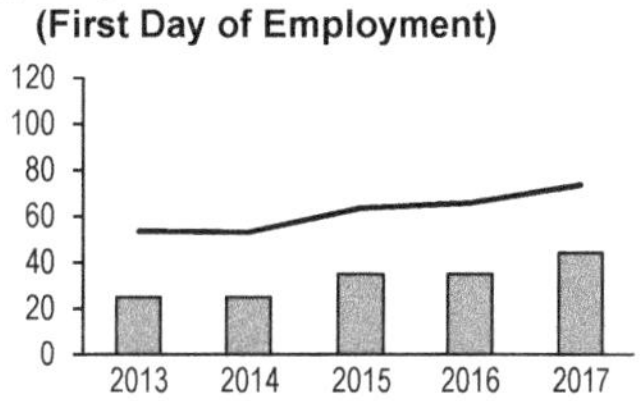

	2013	2014	2015	2016	2017
Wilson	25	25	35	35	44
Average	54	53	64	66	74

Fiscal Year 2016–17

Explanatory Information

Service Level and Delivery

The human resources function is housed under two separate departments: Human Resources (HR) and Finance. The finance department is responsible for benefits administration and employee safety. The human resources department has three separate sections: general human resources management, employee health, and employee training.

The city conducted one compensation study during the fiscal year covering 199 positions.

Winston-Salem began having employees go through a probationary period in FY 2015–16 for the first time. The city's probationary period for new general employees is six months and twelve months for police and fire personnel. No data are available for the measure "probationary period completion rate (new hires)" before FY 2015–16.

Conditions Affecting Service, Performance, and Costs

Winston-Salem now requires all job applications to be submitted online. This process has made it substantially easier to apply for jobs, pushing up the number of applications.

The city has two health insurance plans: a basic plan and the Basic Plus Plan, which has richer benefits and more expensive premiums for employees. The city offers a dental reimbursement plan instead of a dental insurance plan.

The City Attorney's Office handles all Equal Employment Opportunity Commission (EEOC) charges.

Winston-Salem's HR department manually calculates the time from post date to hire by subtracting the "approved for posting date" from the actual hire date as noted in the department's system. Certain current policies can effectively stretch this time period, which accounts for the long time reported in the length of time to hire new employees. For example, graduates from the fire academy may sometimes require five months before all evaluations are completed.

Municipal Profile

Population (OSBM 2016)	240,603
Land Area (Square Miles)	132.55
Persons per Square Mile	1,815
Median Family Income U.S. Census 2010	$51,491
County Unemployment Rate (2016) U.S. Bureau of Labor Statistics	4.9%

Service Profile

Central HR FTE Positions	
Administration	3.0
Generalist/Specialist	9.0
Staff Support/Clerical	3.0
Total Authorized Workforce	2,676.0
Authorized FTEs	2,575.0
Average Length of Service (Months)	133
Number of Position Requisitions	569
Employment Applications Processed	28,435
Length of Probationary Employment Period	6 & 12 months
Compensation Studies Completed	1
Positions Studied	199
Employee Turnover	
Voluntary Separations	325
Involuntary Separations	57
TOTAL SEPARATIONS	382
Formal Grievances Filed by Employees	87
Equal Employment Opportunity Commission (EEOC) Complaints Filed	6

Full Cost Profile

Cost Breakdown by Percentage	
Personal Services	37.0%
Operating Costs	59.6%
Capital Costs	3.5%
TOTAL	100.0%
Cost Breakdown in Dollars	
Personal Services	$1,349,252
Operating Costs	$2,175,619
Capital Costs	$125,992
TOTAL	$3,650,863

Key: Winston-Salem ▒ Benchmarking Average — Fiscal Years 2013through 2017

Resource Measures

Human Resources Services Cost per Capita

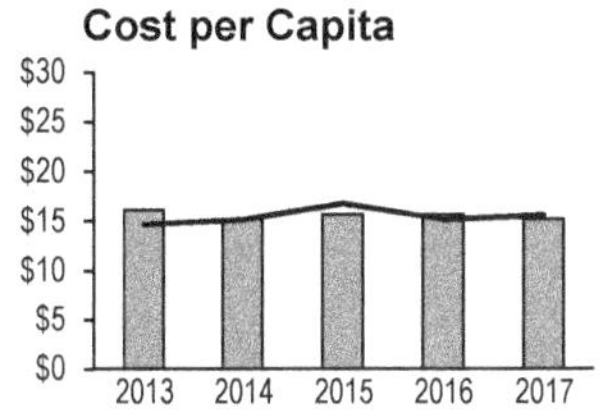

	2013	2014	2015	2016	2017
Winston-Salem	$16.13	$15.20	$15.62	$15.65	$15.17
Average	$14.68	$15.20	$16.80	$15.16	$15.62

Human Resources FTEs per 10,000 Population

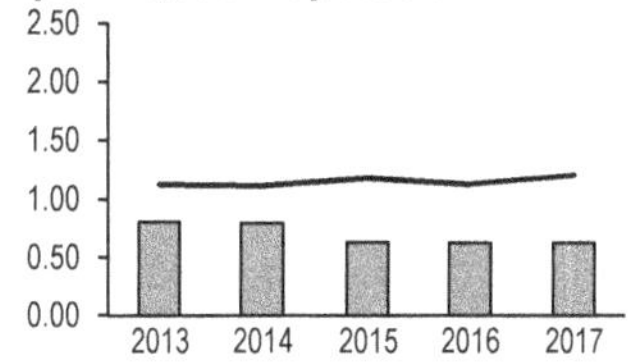

	2013	2014	2015	2016	2017
Winston-Salem	0.81	0.80	0.63	0.63	0.62
Average	1.12	1.11	1.18	1.13	1.20

Workload Measures

Total Municipal FTEs per 10,000 Population

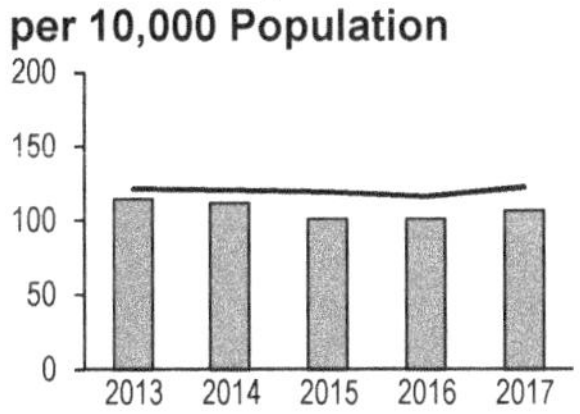

	2013	2014	2015	2016	2017
Winston-Salem	115	112	101	101	107
Average	121	120	119	116	122

Applications Processed per 100 Municipal Employees

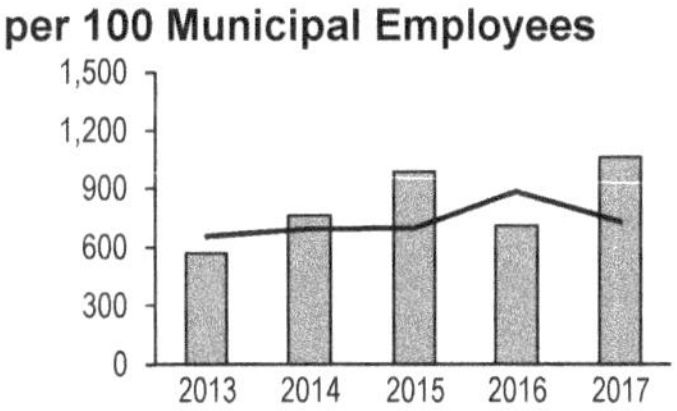

	2013	2014	2015	2016	2017
Winston-Salem	567	763	989	709	1,063
Average	655	693	695	884	729

Position Requisitions per 100 Municipal Employees

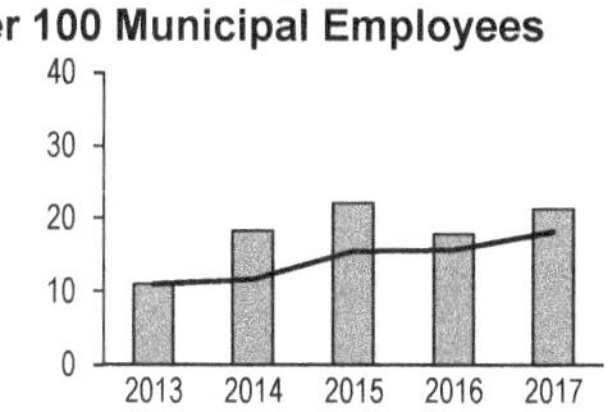

	2013	2014	2015	2016	2017
Winston-Salem	11.0	18.3	22.0	17.9	21.3
Average	11.0	11.6	15.4	15.6	18.2

Efficiency Measures

Human Resources Cost per Municipal Employee

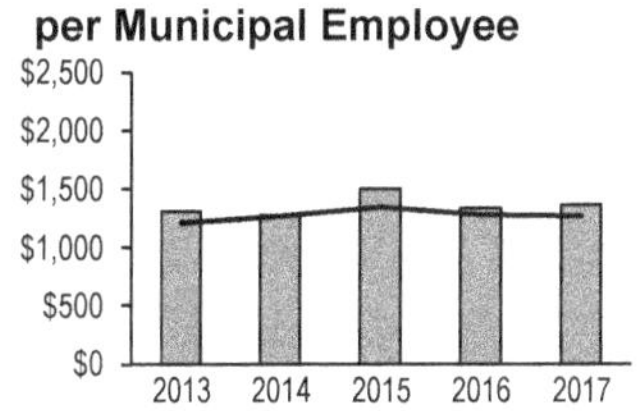

	2013	2014	2015	2016	2017
Winston-Salem	$1,308	$1,274	$1,502	$1,338	$1,364
Average	$1,210	$1,271	$1,346	$1,281	$1,272

Ratio of Human Resources Staff to 100 Municipal Employees

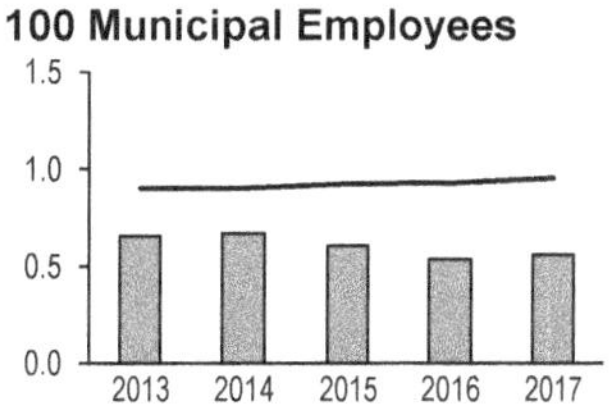

	2013	2014	2015	2016	2017
Winston-Salem	0.65	0.67	0.61	0.54	0.56
Average	0.90	0.90	0.93	0.93	0.95

Effectiveness Measures

Probationary Period Completion Rate (New Hires)

	2013	2014	2015	2016	2017
Winston-Salem				86%	91%
Average	85%	88%	91%	85%	85%

Employee Turnover Rate (All Separations)

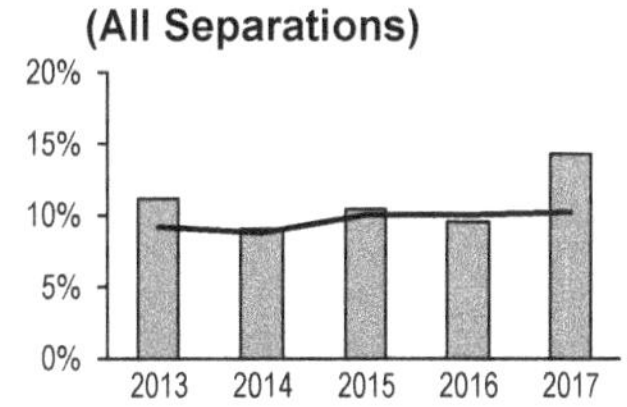

	2013	2014	2015	2016	2017
Winston-Salem	11.2%	9.0%	10.4%	9.6%	14.3%
Average	9.2%	8.8%	10.1%	10.0%	10.2%

Employee Turnover Rate (Voluntary Separations)

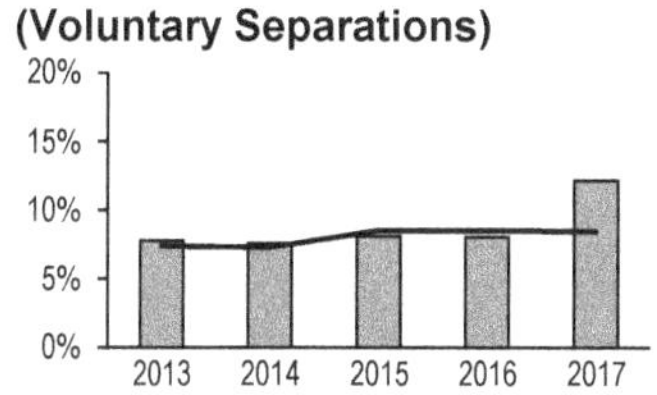

	2013	2014	2015	2016	2017
Winston-Salem	7.8%	7.6%	8.1%	8.1%	12.1%
Average	7.4%	7.3%	8.5%	8.5%	8.5%

Percentage of Grievances Resolved at Department Level

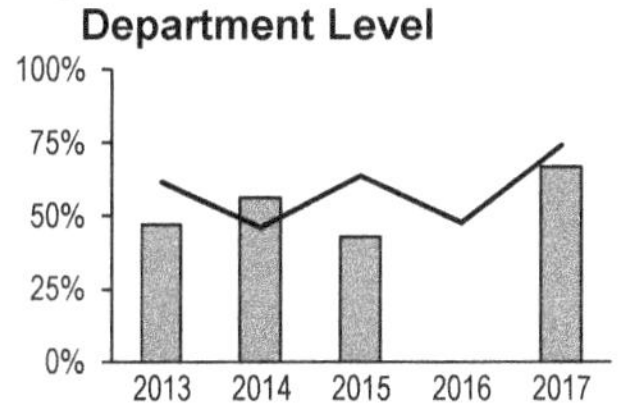

	2013	2014	2015	2016	2017
Winston-Salem	47%	56%	43%		67%
Average	61%	46%	64%	48%	74%

Average Days from Post Date to Hire Date (First Day of Employment)

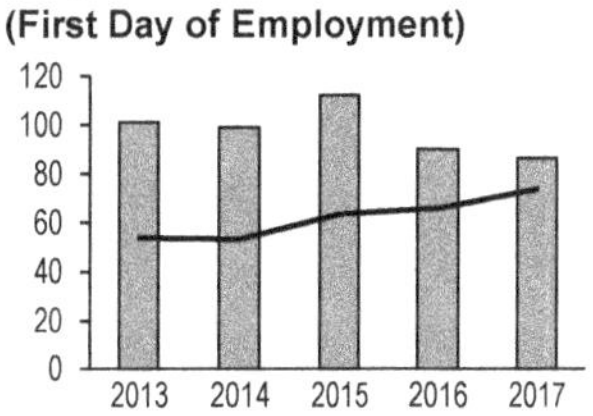

	2013	2014	2015	2016	2017
Winston-Salem	101	99	112	90	86
Average	54	53	64	66	74

UNC | SCHOOL OF GOVERNMENT
North Carolina Benchmarking Project

Performance and Cost Data

WATER SERVICES

UNC | SCHOOL OF GOVERNMENT
North Carolina Benchmarking Project

PERFORMANCE MEASURES FOR WATER SERVICES

SERVICE DEFINITION

This service area includes the collection, treatment, distribution, and billing related to drinking water services. It includes reservoirs where appropriate, pumping stations, pipes to and from treatment plants, storage tanks, and treatment plants. Activities and costs include the operation, maintenance, and installation of infrastructure. Also included are costs and activities associated with the installation, upkeep, and reading of meters; billing and collection costs for drinking water services; and administrative activities such as planning, engineering, and testing. Excluded are reclaimed water, sewer collection, and wastewater treatment services.

NOTES ON PERFORMANCE MEASURES

1. Thousands of Gallons Billed Water per Meter

This workload measure captures the amount of water provided per meter in the system. Water that does not make it to customer taps is not included.

2. Miles of Main Line Pipe per Square Mile of Service Area

The amount of pipe per square mile shows the density of the pipe infrastructure to be maintained relative to the geographic size of the area served.

3. Total Cost per Thousand Gallons of Billed Water

This efficiency measure shows the total system costs per 1,000 gallons of water that is actually billed to customers.

4. Million Gallons of Billed Water per All Staff FTEs

Large numbers of staff are required including treatment staff, line maintenance staff, meter readers, billing staff, and others to bring drinking water to customer taps. Based on all staff who help support the delivery of drinking water to customers, this efficiency measure shows how much billable water is produced per full-time equivalent (FTE) staff member.

5. Billed Water as a Percentage of Finished Water

Not all water produced at treatment plants makes it to customer meters. Some water is lost through leaks or breaks in the system. Other water is unbilled but authorized for uses such as fighting fires or flushing lines. This efficiency measure shows the percentage of water produced that makes it to customer taps.

6. Percentage of Existing Pipeline Renewed

Replacement or rehabilitation of existing pipeline is needed to ensure that the distribution infrastructure can continue to function. This effectiveness measure shows the percentage of existing water lines that are renewed each year.

7. Percentage of Bills Not Collected
Collection of water bills sent to customers is necessary to ensure revenues for system operation. Adjustments to bills reflecting water loss adjustments are not included in the amount of billings.

8. Peak Daily Demand as a Percentage of Treatment Capacity
A water system needs sufficient capacity to meet not only average demands, but also peak demands. This measure looks at peak historical demand relative to the water system treatment capacity in a day.

9. Breaks and Leaks per Mile of Main Line Pipe
Breaks or leaks in water distribution lines mean the loss of treated water.

10. Customer Complaints about Water Quality per Thousand Meters
Concerns for the adequacy of water are matched with the quality of the water delivered to customers. This effectiveness measure assesses customers' perceptions about their water quality.

Water Services

Summary of Key Dimensions of Service

City or Town	Estimated Residential Population in Service Area	Service Area (in Square Miles)	Average Daily Demand for Water (in MGD)	Operating Treatment Plants	Total Treatment Capacity for Finished Water (in MGD)	Miles of Water Main Lines	Number of Water Meters	Water System FTE Positions
Apex	49,541	22.0	3.6	Shared with Cary	Shared with Cary	277.0	15,958	24.0
Asheville	124,300	183.0	20.2	3	43.5	1,694.9	60,916	155.0
Charlotte	989,410	546.0	106.8	3	242.0	4,314.0	290,633	395.0
Concord	88,815	142.8	12.0	2	24.0	717.4	39,835	80.0
Goldsboro	35,792	25.0	5.0	1	12.0	274.0	13,495	24.0
Greensboro	285,344	148.0	34.5	2	54.0	1,502.8	104,958	155.5
Hickory	99,530	326.0	12.5	1	32.0	935.5	29,481	60.0
High Point	112,201	65.0	12.3	1	24.0	616.0	43,241	63.4
Raleigh	561,428	299.0	52.0	2	102.0	2,388.0	188,844	328.0
Salisbury	53,600	47.5	9.6	1	25.0	422.0	19,466	40.0
Wilson	52,500	40.0	8.7	2	22.0	428.0	22,386	43.0
Winston-Salem	368,946	393.0	35.9	3	91.0	2,322.5	127,823	171.0

NOTES

MGD stands for millions of gallons per day.

EXPLANATORY FACTORS

These are factors that the project found affected water services performance and cost in one or more of the municipalities:

Topography
Water quality of source water
Size of service area
Population density
Age of infrastructure
Growth of population and businesses

Apex — Water Services

Fiscal Year 2016–17

Explanatory Information

Service Level and Delivery

The Town of Apex Water Distribution Division is housed within the Department of Public Works. It consists of repairs, preventive maintenance, meter installation and replacement, and testing. The town is co-owner of the Cary/Apex water treatment facility, which draws raw water from Jordan Lake. The Town of Cary provides the operational staff for the treatment plant, but Apex shares in the costs of operation and capital.

Apex bases replacement of water lines on customer complaints, frequency of repairs, street rehabilitation needs, age and material of pipes, and flow concerns.

Currently, most water meters are read by automatic means. Replacement of meters is based on a combination of factors, as is water line replacement.

Conditions Affecting Service, Performance, and Costs

The costs of water services as captured here do not include debt service but do capture depreciation.

Municipal Profile

Estimated Service Population	49,541
Service Land Area (Square Miles)	22.0
Persons per Square Mile	2,252
Topography	Flat; gently rolling
Climate	Temperate; little ice and snow
Median Family Income U.S. Census 2010	$97,201

Service Profile

FTE Staff Positions	
Treatment Plant	0.0
Line Crews	14.0
Meter Readers	4.0
Billing/Collection	4.0
Other	2.0
Total	24.0
Number of Treatment Plants	NA
Total Treatment Capacity	NA
Average Daily Demand	3.6 MGD
Miles of Main Line Pipe	277
Average Age of Main Line Pipe	16 years
Number of Breaks/Leaks	77
Number of Water Meters	15,958
Percent of Meters Read Automatically	99.0%
Total Revenues Collected	$11,763,555

Full Cost Profile

Cost Breakdown by Percentage	
Personal Services	17.2%
Operating Costs	51.4%
Capital Costs	31.4%
TOTAL	100.0%
Cost Breakdown in Dollars	
Personal Services	$1,042,262
Operating Costs	$3,121,208
Capital Costs	$1,903,098
TOTAL	$6,066,568

Key: Apex ▒ Benchmarking Average — Fiscal Years 2013 through 2017

Resource Measures

Water Services Cost per Capita

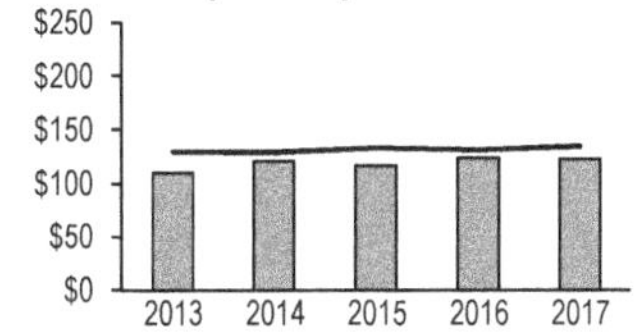

	2013	2014	2015	2016	2017
Apex	$110	$120	$117	$124	$122
Average	$130	$129	$133	$131	$135

Water Services FTEs per 10,000 Population

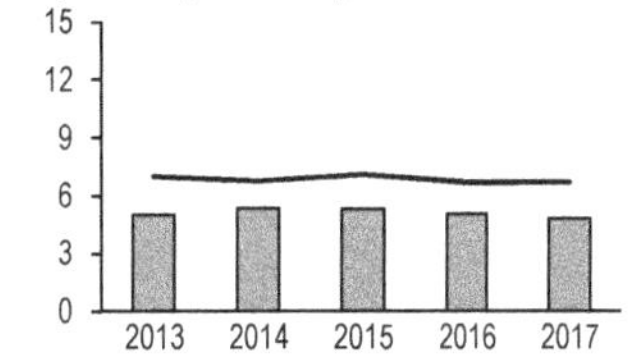

	2013	2014	2015	2016	2017
Apex	5.0	5.4	5.3	5.0	4.8
Average	7.0	6.8	7.1	6.7	6.7

Water Services Cost per Meter

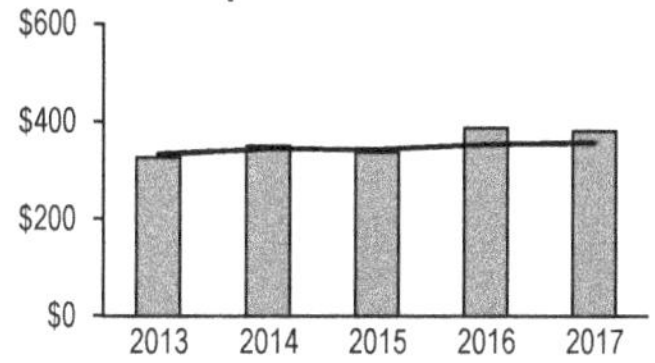

	2013	2014	2015	2016	2017
Apex	$327	$349	$336	$387	$380
Average	$333	$344	$344	$354	$356

Workload Measures

Thousands of Gallons of Billed Water per Meter

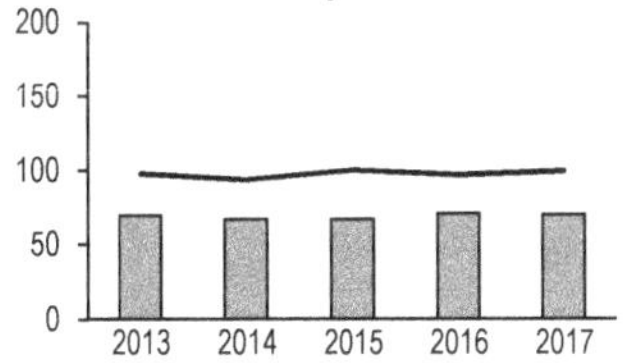

	2013	2014	2015	2016	2017
Apex	69.4	67.0	67.0	70.8	70.0
Average	98.2	93.9	100.5	97.3	100.0

Miles of Main Line Pipe per Square Mile of Service Area

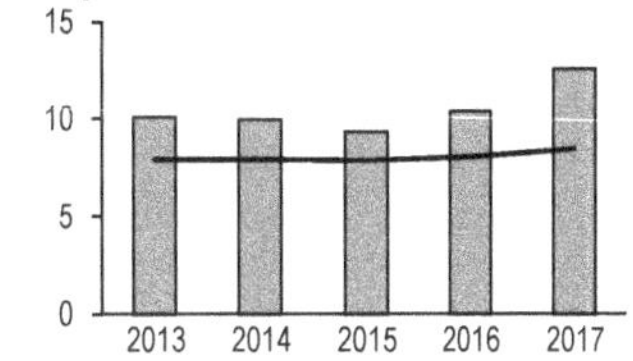

	2013	2014	2015	2016	2017
Apex	10.1	10.0	9.4	10.4	12.6
Average	7.9	7.9	7.9	8.1	8.5

Efficiency Measures

Total Cost per Thousand Gallons of Billed Water

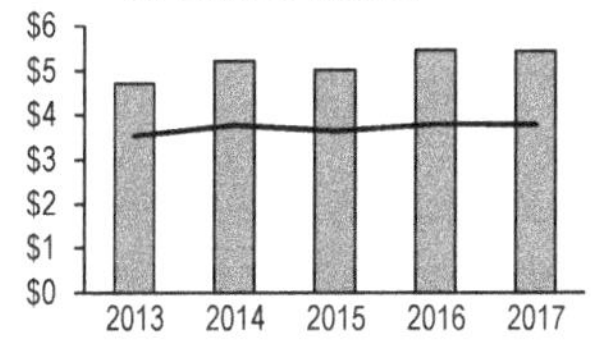

	2013	2014	2015	2016	2017
Apex	$4.70	$5.21	$5.01	$5.47	$5.43
Average	$3.53	$3.78	$3.64	$3.79	$3.78

Million Gallons of Billed Water per Water Services FTEs

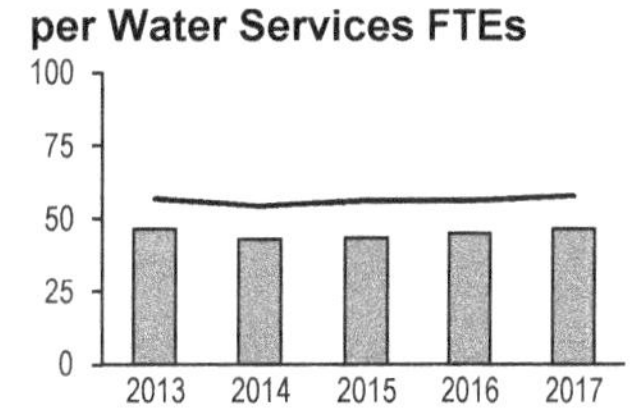

	2013	2014	2015	2016	2017
Apex	46.6	43.1	43.5	44.9	46.6
Average	56.8	54.3	56.2	56.2	57.8

Billed Water as a Percentage of Finished Water

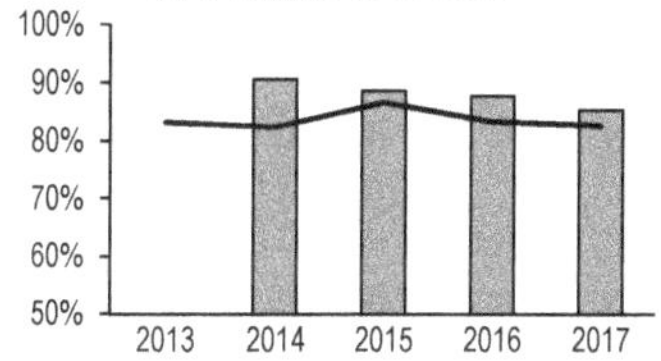

	2013	2014	2015	2016	2017
Apex		91%	89%	88%	85%
Average	83%	82%	87%	83%	83%

Effectiveness Measures

Percentage of Existing Pipeline Replaced or Rehabbed

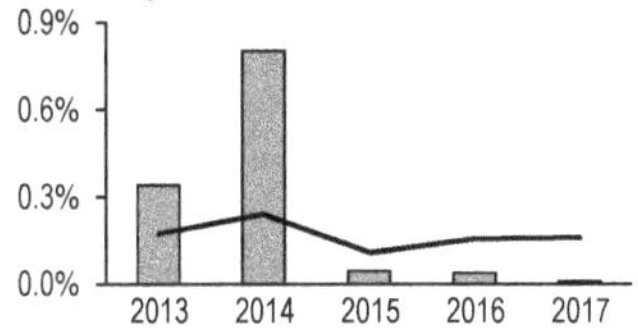

	2013	2014	2015	2016	2017
Apex	0.3%	0.8%	0.0%	0.0%	0.0%
Average	0.2%	0.2%	0.1%	0.2%	0.2%

Percentage of Water Bills Not Collected

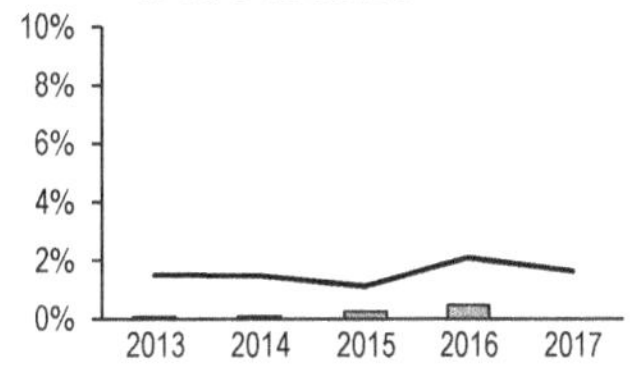

	2013	2014	2015	2016	2017
Apex	0.06%	0.10%	0.24%	0.46%	0.00%
Average	1.49%	1.47%	1.12%	2.09%	1.62%

Peak Daily Demand as a Percentage of Treatment Capacity

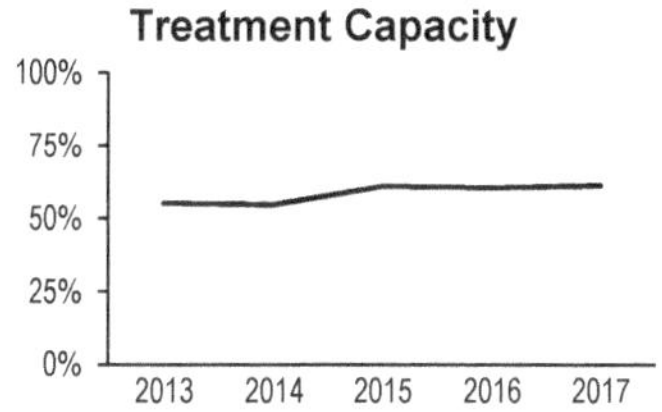

	2013	2014	2015	2016	2017
Apex					
Average	55%	55%	61%	60%	61%

Breaks and Leaks per Mile of Main Line Pipe

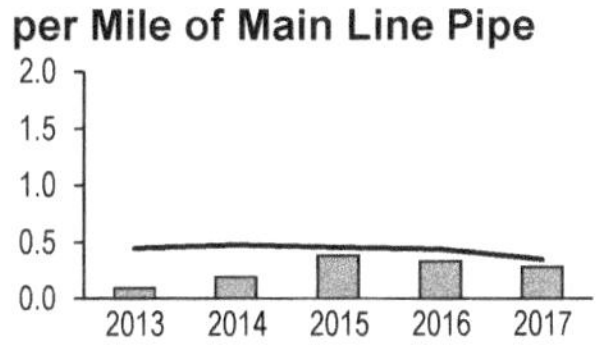

	2013	2014	2015	2016	2017
Apex	0.10	0.20	0.38	0.33	0.28
Average	0.45	0.48	0.45	0.44	0.35

Customer Complaints about Water Quality per 1,000 Meters

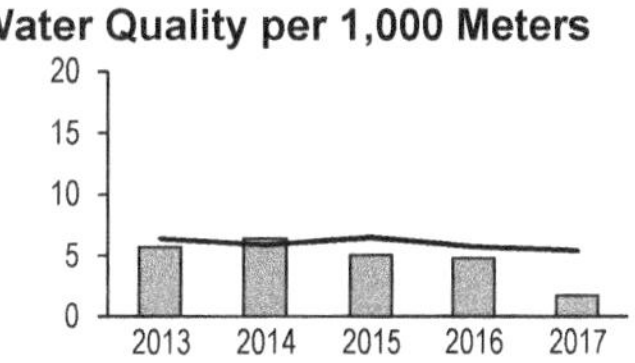

	2013	2014	2015	2016	2017
Apex	5.67	6.35	5.00	4.73	1.69
Average	6.37	5.83	6.45	5.70	5.37

Fiscal Year 2016–17

Explanatory Information

Service Level and Delivery

The City of Asheville Water Resources Department is a publicly owned water utility that produces and supplies water for residential, business, industrial, and wholesale bulk customers. The utility serves the city of Asheville, approximately 27 percent of Buncombe County, and approximately 2 percent of Henderson County. Approximately 124,000 people are served over a 183-square-mile area.

Asheville has three water treatment plants drawing from a city reservoir, the Mills River, and may also take water from the French Broad River as needed. The estimated safe yield for water is 35 million gallons per day.

Asheville has an asset management program in place to assist with identifying replacement and refurbishment needs. The goal is for water main lines to be replaced every eighty years.

Currently almost 99 percent of water meters are read by various automatic systems, including radio-read and touch-read meters. The goal is to replace all meters in the next few years with radio-read meters.

Conditions Affecting Service, Performance, and Costs

The costs of water services as captured here do not include debt service but do capture depreciation.

The topography and climate in Asheville create a number of problems for water systems operation. The mountainous terrain makes it difficult to install water lines. The utility has fifty-three pressure zones, ranging from 20 to 643 psi, with an average from 180 to 200 psi. Colder temperatures can also make maintenance harder to complete and lead to breaks due to freezing. Due to the Sullivan Acts, Asheville is not allowed to refuse water line installation in any areas of Buncombe County or to charge differential rates.

The number of breaks and leaks in the system has been declining. The Water Resources Department has worked actively to better identify situations with repeated leaks in time and, when identified, to replace pipe for a more permanent solution. These efforts with the help of an engineering firm have led to an approximately ten percent reduction in water losses.

Municipal Profile

Estimated Service Population	124,300
Service Land Area (Square Miles)	183.0
Persons per Square Mile	679
Topography	Hilly, mountains
Climate	Moderate; ice and snow
Median Family Income U.S. Census 2010	$53,350

Service Profile

FTE Staff Positions	
Treatment Plant	43.0
Line Crews	47.0
Meter Readers	2.0
Billing/Collection	23.0
Other	40.0
Total	155.0
Number of Treatment Plants	3
Total Treatment Capacity	43.5 MGD
Average Daily Demand	20.2 MGD
Miles of Main Line Pipe	1,695
Average Age of Main Line Pipe	56 years
Number of Breaks/Leaks	998
Number of Water Meters	60,916
Percent of Meters Read Automatically	98.7%
Total Revenues Collected	$42,881,610

Full Cost Profile

Cost Breakdown by Percentage	
Personal Services	34.6%
Operating Costs	35.3%
Capital Costs	30.1%
TOTAL	100.0%
Cost Breakdown in Dollars	
Personal Services	$9,266,451
Operating Costs	$9,468,836
Capital Costs	$8,062,413
TOTAL	$26,797,701

Asheville — Water Services

Key: Asheville ▒ Benchmarking Average — Fiscal Years 2013 through 2017

Resource Measures

Water Services Cost per Capita

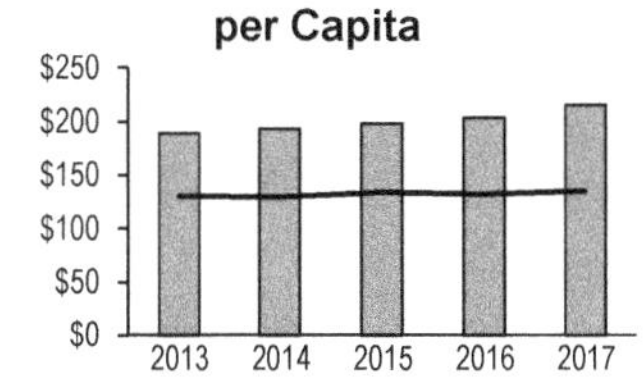

	2013	2014	2015	2016	2017
Asheville	$189	$193	$198	$203	$216
Average	$130	$129	$133	$131	$135

Water Services FTEs per 10,000 Population

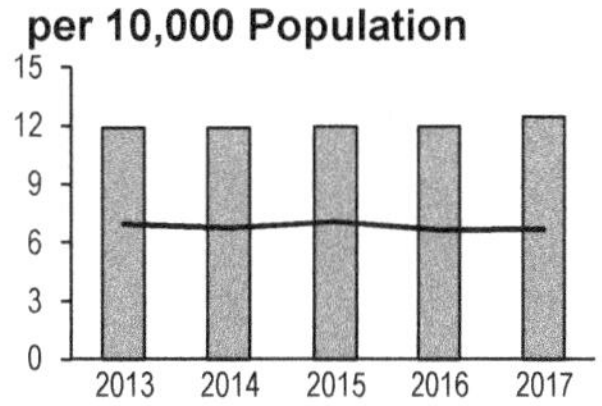

	2013	2014	2015	2016	2017
Asheville	11.9	11.9	12.0	12.0	12.5
Average	7.0	6.8	7.1	6.7	6.7

Water Services Cost per Meter

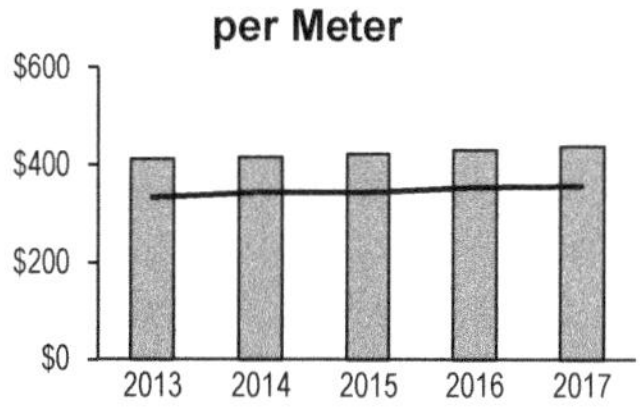

	2013	2014	2015	2016	2017
Asheville	$413	$417	$423	$431	$440
Average	$333	$344	$344	$354	$356

Workload Measures

Thousands of Gallons of Billed Water per Meter

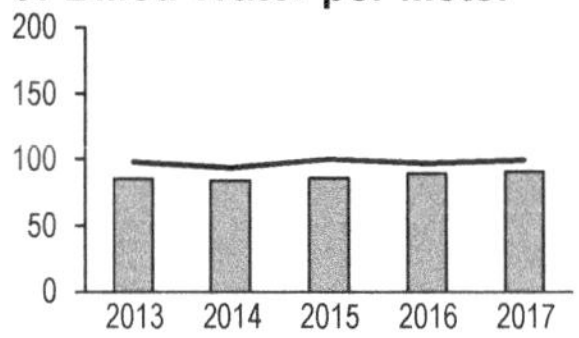

	2013	2014	2015	2016	2017
Asheville	85.0	84.0	85.6	89.2	90.6
Average	98.2	93.9	100.5	97.3	100.0

Miles of Main Line Pipe per Square Mile of Service Area

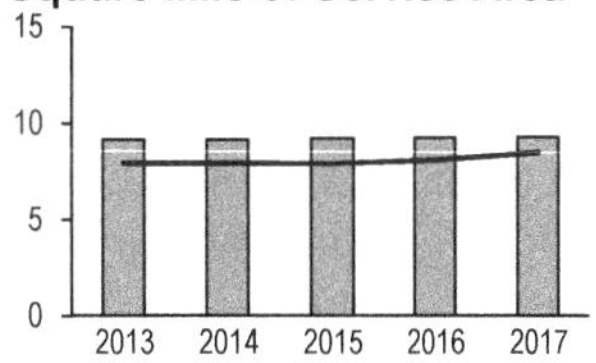

	2013	2014	2015	2016	2017
Asheville	9.1	9.1	9.2	9.2	9.3
Average	7.9	7.9	7.9	8.1	8.5

Efficiency Measures

Total Cost per Thousand Gallons of Billed Water

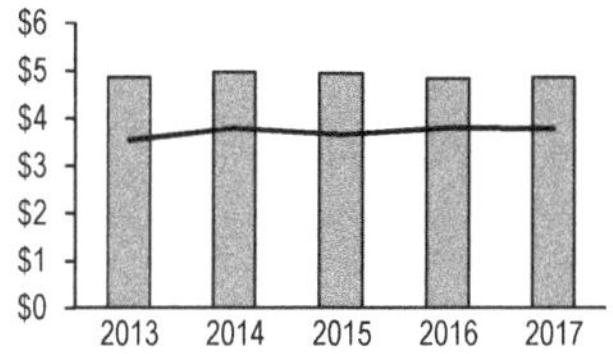

	2013	2014	2015	2016	2017
Asheville	$4.86	$4.97	$4.95	$4.83	$4.86
Average	$3.53	$3.78	$3.64	$3.79	$3.78

Million Gallons of Billed Water per Water Services FTEs

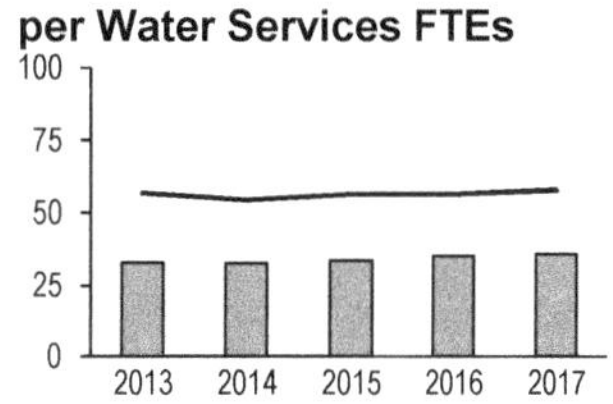

	2013	2014	2015	2016	2017
Asheville	32.7	32.6	33.5	35.1	35.6
Average	56.8	54.3	56.2	56.2	57.8

Billed Water as a Percentage of Finished Water

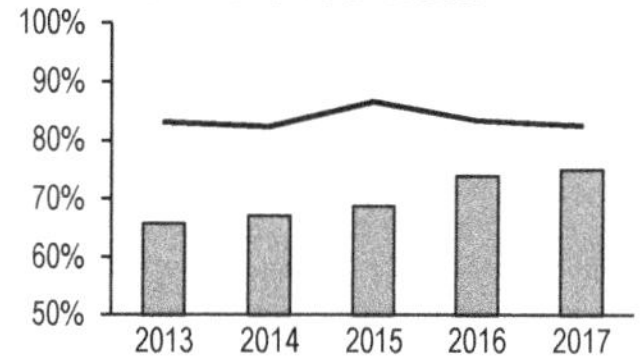

	2013	2014	2015	2016	2017
Asheville	66%	67%	69%	74%	75%
Average	83%	82%	87%	83%	83%

Effectiveness Measures

Percentage of Existing Pipeline Replaced or Rehabbed

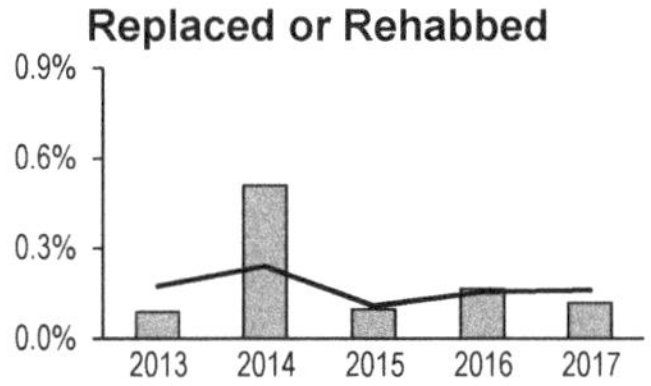

	2013	2014	2015	2016	2017
Asheville	0.1%	0.5%	0.1%	0.2%	0.1%
Average	0.2%	0.2%	0.1%	0.2%	0.2%

Percentage of Water Bills Not Collected

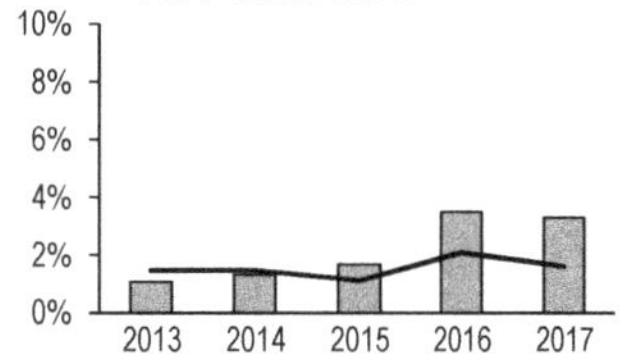

	2013	2014	2015	2016	2017
Asheville	1.08%	1.32%	1.67%	3.49%	3.29%
Average	1.49%	1.47%	1.12%	2.09%	1.62%

Peak Daily Demand as a Percentage of Treatment Capacity

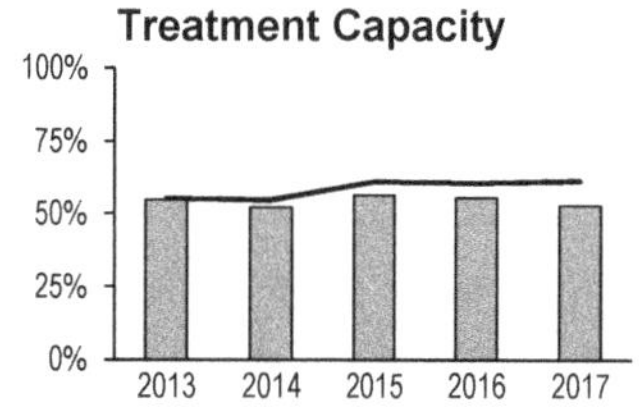

	2013	2014	2015	2016	2017
Asheville	55%	52%	56%	55%	53%
Average	55%	55%	61%	60%	61%

Breaks and Leaks per Mile of Main Line Pipe

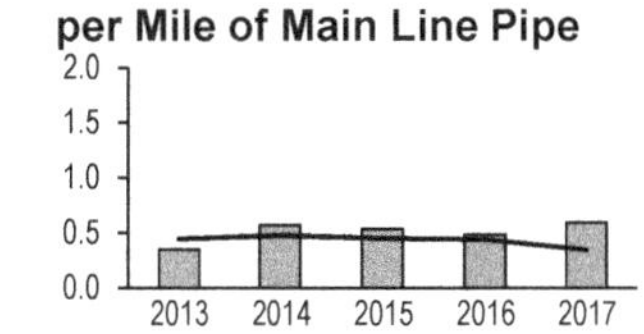

	2013	2014	2015	2016	2017
Asheville	0.35	0.57	0.53	0.48	0.59
Average	0.45	0.48	0.45	0.44	0.35

Customer Complaints about Water Quality per 1,000 Meters

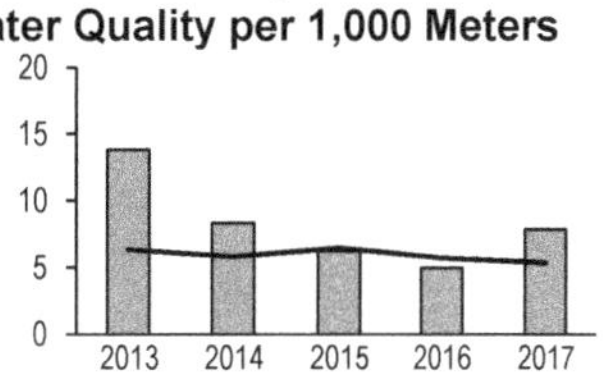

	2013	2014	2015	2016	2017
Asheville	13.81	8.33	6.20	4.93	7.86
Average	6.37	5.83	6.45	5.70	5.37

Charlotte — Water Services

Fiscal Year 2016–17

Explanatory Information

Service Level and Delivery

Charlotte-Mecklenburg Utilities (CMU) is a combined water and sewer operation. The utility is a consolidated business unit of Mecklenburg County and the City of Charlotte. The utility is an official City of Charlotte Key Business Unit, Charlotte's term for city departments.

The area served is generally considered to be Mecklenburg County but also includes a small number of metered drinking water interconnections with the City of Concord and the counties of Union in North Carolina and Lancaster and York in South Carolina. The service area covers approximately 546 square miles and serves over 989,000 people.

Source water for the system is drawn from two impounded lakes on the Catawba River, Lake Norman and Mountain Island Lake, which are operated by Duke Energy. The combined estimated safe yield is between 376 and 503 million gallons per day. The system operates three treatment plants with a combined treatment capacity of 242 million gallons per day. The treatment plants are conventional facilities using rapid mix, flocculation, settling, filtration, and chemical application.

The estimated average age of main line pipes in the system is twenty-nine years. CMU's replacement policy for pipe is based on flow and quality standards.

All meters are now read automatically. CMU uses a system that allows vans traveling the city to read meters as they drive by. The replacement standard is every fifteen years for water meters.

Conditions Affecting Service, Performance, and Costs

Charlotte did not participate in the Benchmarking Project during FY 2014–15. No data are available for that year.

The costs of water services as captured here do not include debt service but do capture depreciation.

The reduction in reported leaks and breaks over time is in large part due to improvements in tracking and data reporting. CMU staff worked on improving how the work order system is used to determine the number of leaks or breaks in the water system.

Municipal Profile

Estimated Service Population	989,410
Service Land Area (Square Miles)	546.0
Persons per Square Mile	1,812
Topography	Flat; gently rolling
Climate	Temperate; little ice and snow
Median Family Income U.S. Census 2010	$61,405

Service Profile

FTE Staff Positions	
Treatment Plant	66.0
Line Crews	151.0
Meter Readers	4.0
Billing/Collection	12.0
Other	162.0
Total	395.0
Number of Treatment Plants	3
Total Treatment Capacity	242.0 MGD
Average Daily Demand	106.8 MGD
Miles of Main Line Pipe	4,314
Average Age of Main Line Pipe	30 years
Number of Breaks/Leaks	1,054
Number of Water Meters	290,633
Percent of Meters Read Automatically	100.0%
Total Revenues Collected	$175,112,767

Full Cost Profile

Cost Breakdown by Percentage	
Personal Services	24.8%
Operating Costs	32.4%
Capital Costs	42.9%
TOTAL	100.0%
Cost Breakdown in Dollars	
Personal Services	$25,262,622
Operating Costs	$33,029,765
Capital Costs	$43,726,528
TOTAL	$102,018,915

Key: Charlotte ▒ Benchmarking Average — Fiscal Years 2013 through 2017

Resource Measures

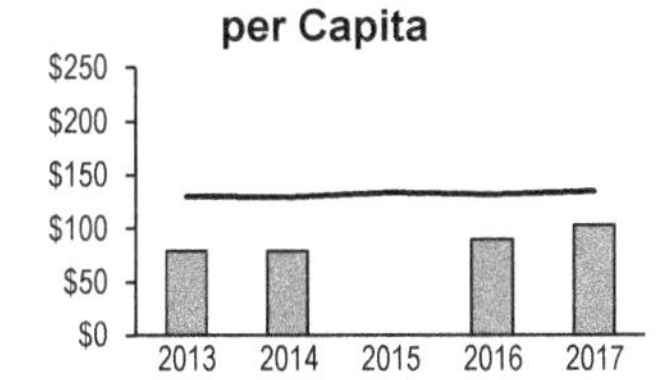

	2013	2014	2015	2016	2017
Charlotte	$79	$79		$90	$103
Average	$130	$129	$133	$131	$135

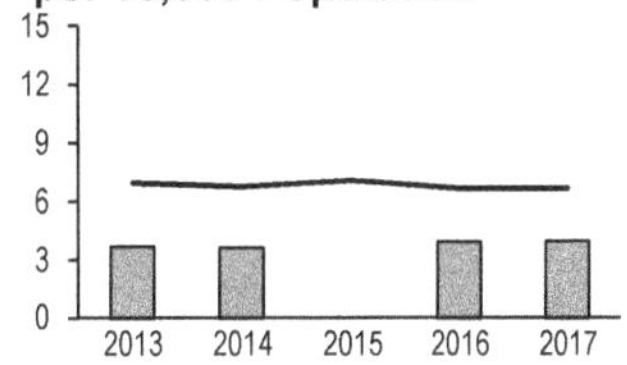

	2013	2014	2015	2016	2017
Charlotte	3.7	3.7		3.9	4.0
Average	7.0	6.8	7.1	6.7	6.7

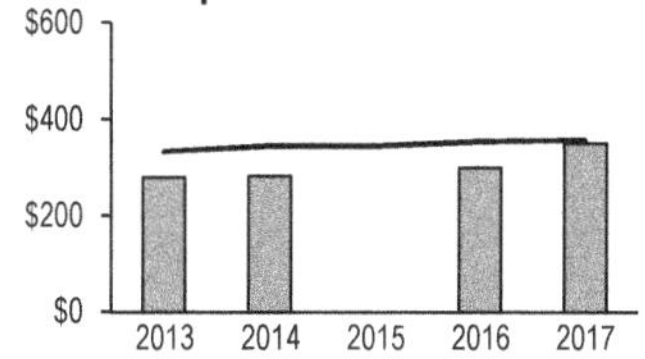

	2013	2014	2015	2016	2017
Charlotte	$280	$282		$300	$351
Average	$333	$344	$344	$354	$356

Workload Measures

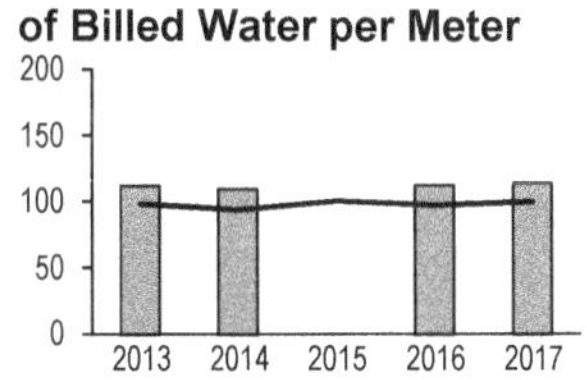

	2013	2014	2015	2016	2017
Charlotte	112.1	109.6		112.3	113.7
Average	98.2	93.9	100.5	97.3	100.0

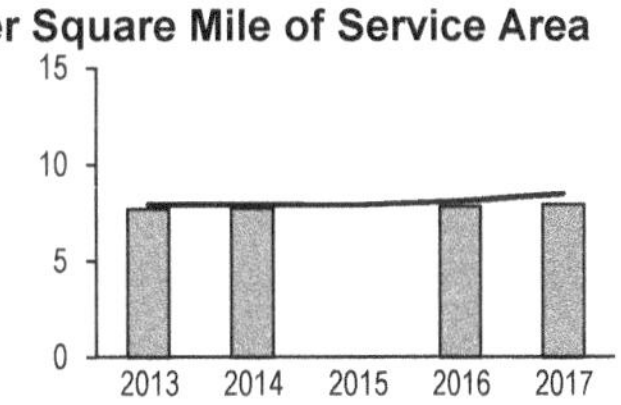

	2013	2014	2015	2016	2017
Charlotte	7.7	7.7		7.8	7.9
Average	7.9	7.9	7.9	8.1	8.5

Efficiency Measures

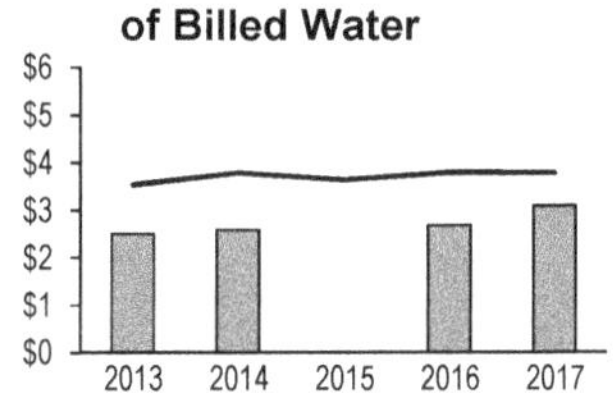

	2013	2014	2015	2016	2017
Charlotte	$2.50	$2.58		$2.67	$3.09
Average	$3.53	$3.78	$3.64	$3.79	$3.78

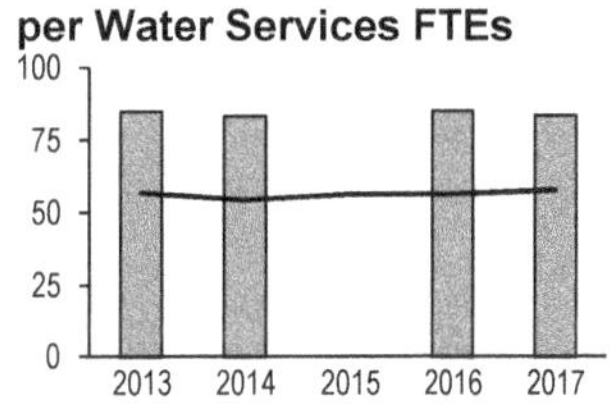

	2013	2014	2015	2016	2017
Charlotte	85.2	83.5		85.2	83.6
Average	56.8	54.3	56.2	56.2	57.8

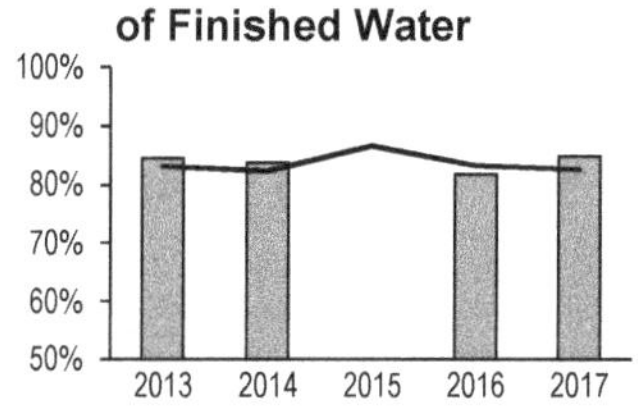

	2013	2014	2015	2016	2017
Charlotte	84%	84%		82%	85%
Average	83%	82%	87%	83%	83%

Effectiveness Measures

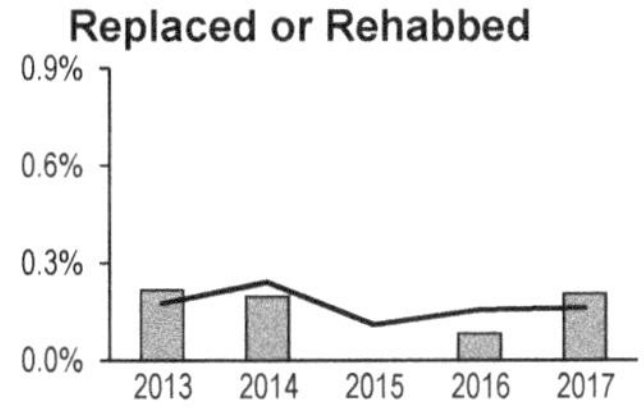

	2013	2014	2015	2016	2017
Charlotte	0.2%	0.2%		0.1%	0.2%
Average	0.2%	0.2%	0.1%	0.2%	0.2%

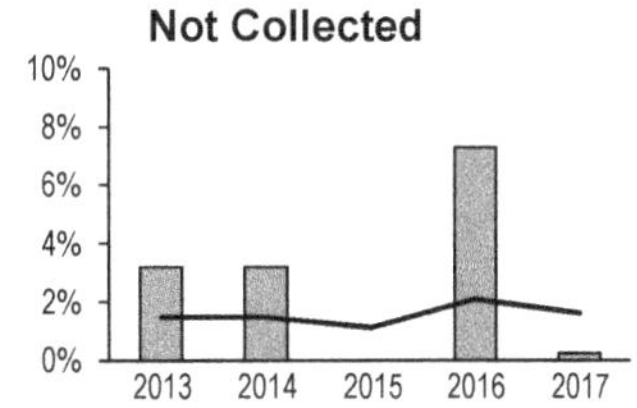

	2013	2014	2015	2016	2017
Charlotte	3.20%	3.20%		7.29%	0.24%
Average	1.49%	1.47%	1.12%	2.09%	1.62%

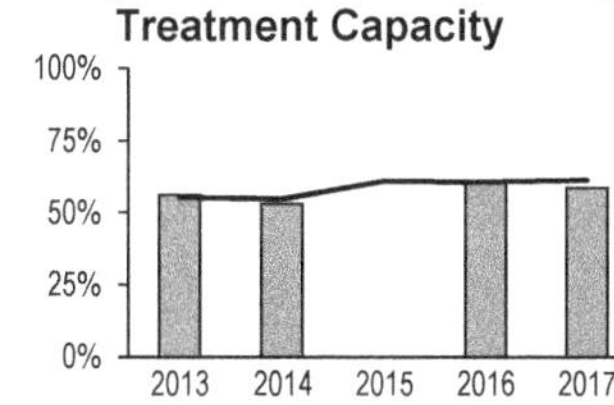

	2013	2014	2015	2016	2017
Charlotte	56%	53%		60%	58%
Average	55%	55%	61%	60%	61%

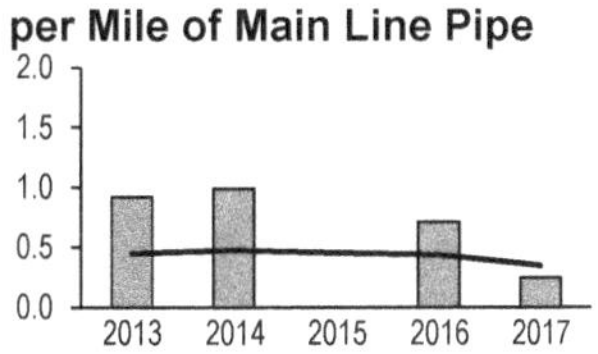

	2013	2014	2015	2016	2017
Charlotte	0.92	0.99		0.71	0.24
Average	0.45	0.48	0.45	0.44	0.35

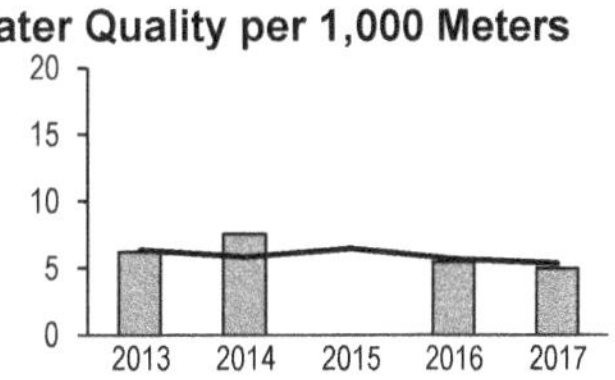

	2013	2014	2015	2016	2017
Charlotte	6.21	7.55		5.45	4.98
Average	6.37	5.83	6.45	5.70	5.37

Fiscal Year 2016–17

Explanatory Information

Service Level and Delivery
The City of Concord Water Resources Department is a water-only utility. The department has three divisions, one for operations and maintenance and one for each of two treatment plants. Meter reading, billing, and collections are handled by the city Finance Department.

Concord's system serves approximately 89,000 people and covers the City of Concord, the Town of Midland, and approximately one-fourth of Cabarrus County. Water sources for the system are Lake Fisher, owned by the city, and Lakes Howell and Concord, reservoirs owned by the Water and Sewer Authority of Cabarrus County. The combined estimated safe yield is 24 million gallons per day.

The city operates two treatment plants with a combined treatment capacity of 24 million gallons per day. Concord has emergency connections with the City of Charlotte and the City of Kannapolis and sells small amounts of water to the Town of Harrisburg and the Town of Midland.

The estimated average age of main line pipes in the system is thirty-five years. Water meters are read monthly with all being read using automatic means. The replacement standard for water meters is fifteen years.

Conditions Affecting Service, Performance, and Costs
The costs of water services as captured here do not include debt service but do capture depreciation.

Municipal Profile

Estimated Service Population	88,815
Service Land Area (Square Miles)	142.8
Persons per Square Mile	622
Topography	Flat; gently rolling
Climate	Temperate; little ice and snow
Median Family Income U.S. Census 2010	$63,643

Service Profile

FTE Staff Positions	
Treatment Plant	32.0
Line Crews	24.0
Meter Readers	4.0
Billing/Collection	13.0
Other	7.0
Total	80.0
Number of Treatment Plants	2
Total Treatment Capacity	24.0 MGD
Average Daily Demand	12.0 MGD
Miles of Main Line Pipe	717
Average Age of Main Line Pipe	35 years
Number of Breaks/Leaks	271
Number of Water Meters	39,835
Percent of Meters Read Automatically	100.0%
Total Revenues Collected	$23,379,274

Full Cost Profile

Cost Breakdown by Percentage	
Personal Services	31.2%
Operating Costs	45.2%
Capital Costs	23.6%
TOTAL	100.0%
Cost Breakdown in Dollars	
Personal Services	$4,922,769
Operating Costs	$7,117,831
Capital Costs	$3,712,497
TOTAL	$15,753,097

Key: Concord ▒ Benchmarking Average — Fiscal Years 2013 through 2017

Resource Measures

Water Services Cost per Capita

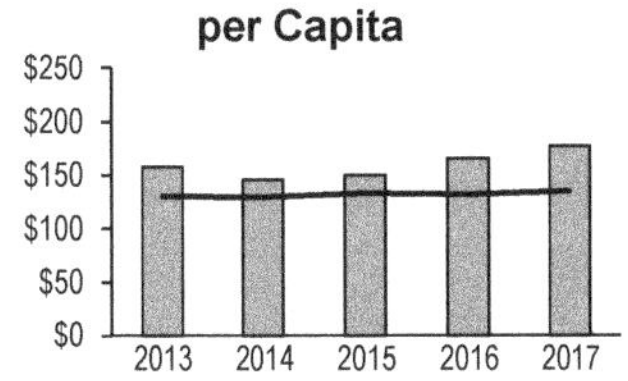

	2013	2014	2015	2016	2017
Concord	$158	$146	$150	$166	$177
Average	$130	$129	$133	$131	$135

Water Services FTEs per 10,000 Population

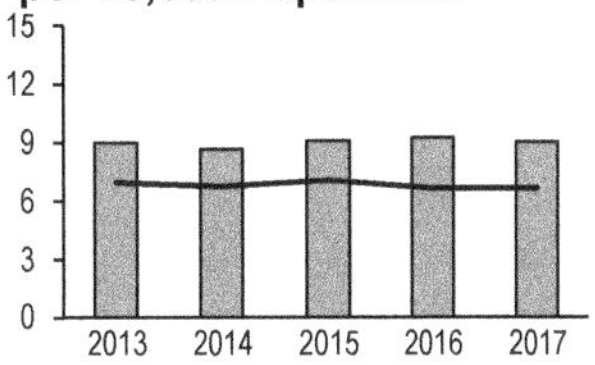

	2013	2014	2015	2016	2017
Concord	9.0	8.7	9.1	9.2	9.0
Average	7.0	6.8	7.1	6.7	6.7

Water Services Cost per Meter

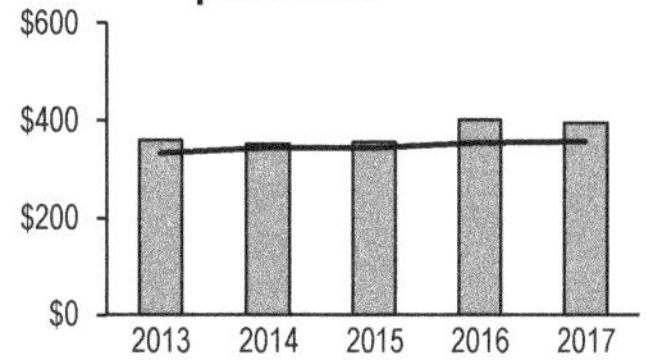

	2013	2014	2015	2016	2017
Concord	$360	$351	$356	$401	$395
Average	$333	$344	$344	$354	$356

Workload Measures

Thousands of Gallons of Billed Water per Meter

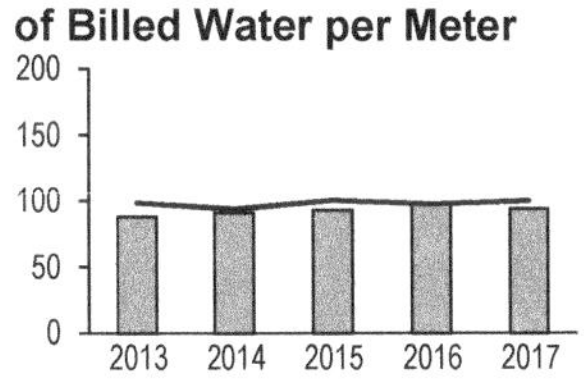

	2013	2014	2015	2016	2017
Concord	88.4	91.2	93.2	97.4	94.0
Average	98.2	93.9	100.5	97.3	100.0

Miles of Main Line Pipe per Square Mile of Service Area

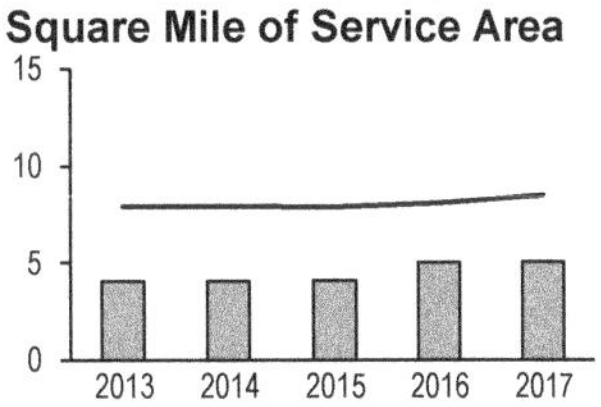

	2013	2014	2015	2016	2017
Concord	4.0	4.1	4.1	5.0	5.0
Average	7.9	7.9	7.9	8.1	8.5

Efficiency Measures

Total Cost per Thousand Gallons of Billed Water

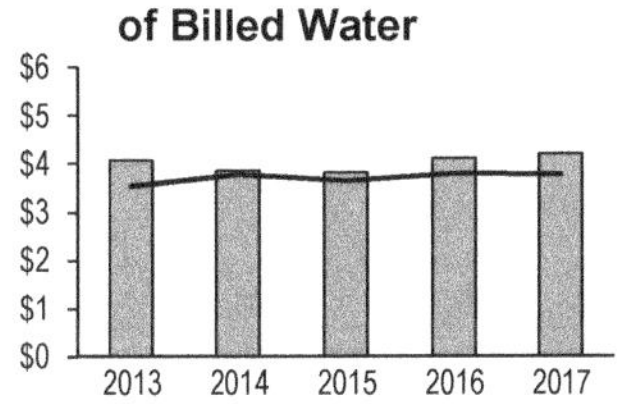

	2013	2014	2015	2016	2017
Concord	$4.07	$3.86	$3.82	$4.12	$4.21
Average	$3.53	$3.78	$3.64	$3.79	$3.78

Million Gallons of Billed Water per Water Services FTEs

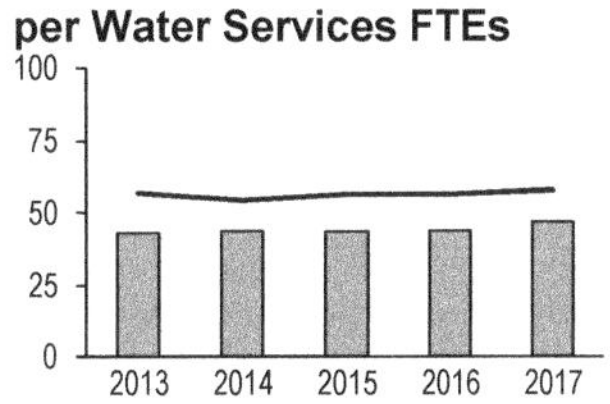

	2013	2014	2015	2016	2017
Concord	43.1	43.7	43.4	43.6	46.8
Average	56.8	54.3	56.2	56.2	57.8

Billed Water as a Percentage of Finished Water

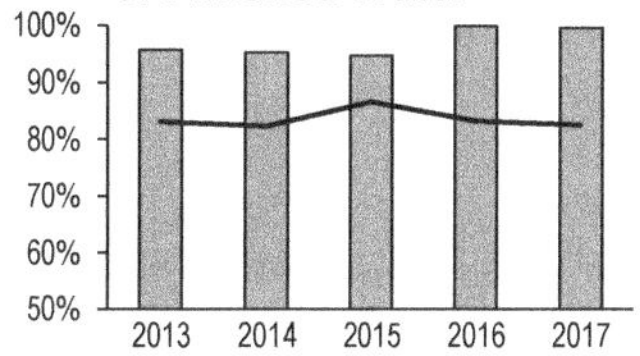

	2013	2014	2015	2016	2017
Concord	96%	95%	95%	100%	100%
Average	83%	82%	87%	83%	83%

Effectiveness Measures

Percentage of Existing Pipeline Replaced or Rehabbed

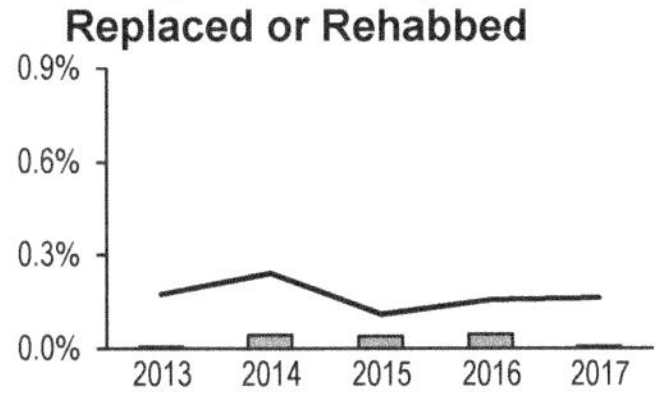

	2013	2014	2015	2016	2017
Concord	0.0%	0.0%	0.0%	0.0%	0.0%
Average	0.2%	0.2%	0.1%	0.2%	0.2%

Percentage of Water Bills Not Collected

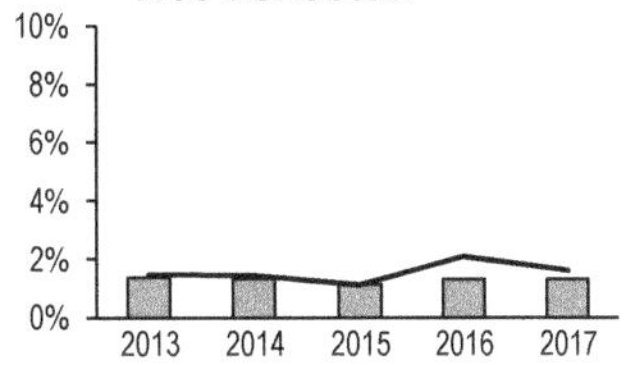

	2013	2014	2015	2016	2017
Concord	1.37%	1.34%	1.13%	1.31%	1.31%
Average	1.49%	1.47%	1.12%	2.09%	1.62%

Peak Daily Demand as a Percentage of Treatment Capacity

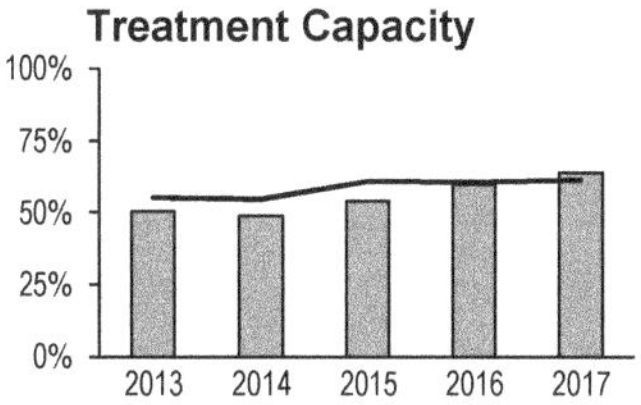

	2013	2014	2015	2016	2017
Concord	50%	49%	54%	60%	64%
Average	55%	55%	61%	60%	61%

Breaks and Leaks per Mile of Main Line Pipe

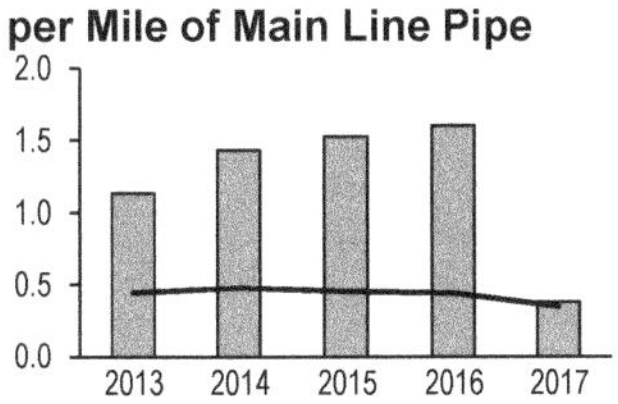

	2013	2014	2015	2016	2017
Concord	1.13	1.43	1.52	1.60	0.38
Average	0.45	0.48	0.45	0.44	0.35

Customer Complaints about Water Quality per 1,000 Meters

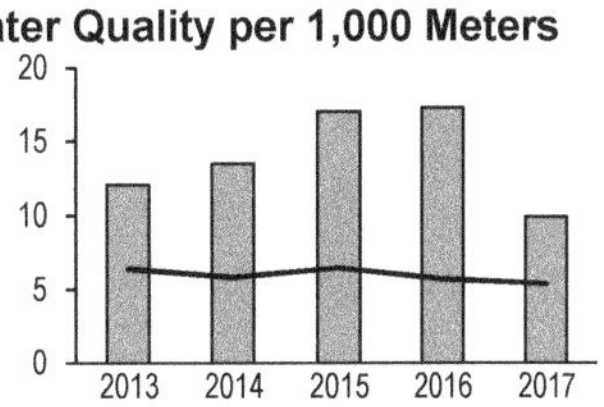

	2013	2014	2015	2016	2017
Concord	12.07	13.50	17.01	17.26	9.89
Average	6.37	5.83	6.45	5.70	5.37

Fiscal Year 2016–17

Explanatory Information

Service Level and Delivery

Goldsboro's drinking water services are a joint responsibility between the Public Works and Public Utilities Departments. Both departments are overseen by the Public Works Director. Public Works is responsible for the collection and distribution system lines. Public Utilities is responsible for the operations of the water treatment plant, the water reclamation facility, and pump stations.

The Goldsboro system serves approximately 36,000 people in an area covering twenty-five square miles. Water is collected from the Neuse River. The system also has an emergency option to collect from the Littler River but this option has not been needed for several years. The estimated safe yield of the system is 6 million gallons per day based on an analysis performed by consultants. The system has emergency connections with Eastern Wayne, Belfast-Patetown, Fork Town, and Southern Wayne Sanitary Districts.

The city runs one treatment plant with a capacity of 12 million gallons per day. The plant uses traditional surface water treatment consisting of coagualation, flocculation, sedimentation, filtration, and disinfection.

The estimated average age of main line pipes in the system is seventy-five years. Goldsboro handles pipe placement by focusing on breaks in the system.

Water meters are read and billed monthly. All meters are currently read by manual means but the City is converting to an advanced metering infrastructure (AMI) system.

Conditions Affecting Service, Performance, and Costs

The city of Goldsboro joined the Benchmarking Project in July 2017 with the first year of data showing for FY 2016–17.

The costs of water services as captured here do not include debt service but do capture depreciation.

Hurricane Matthew in October 2016 put stress on the water system due to the extensive flooding.

Municipal Profile

Estimated Service Population	35,792
Service Land Area (Square Miles)	25.0
Persons per Square Mile	1,432
Topography	Flat
Climate	Temperate; little ice and snow
Median Family Income U.S. Census 2010	$33,879

Service Profile

FTE Staff Positions	
Treatment Plant	11.0
Line Crews	5.0
Meter Readers	6.0
Billing/Collection	2.0
Other	0.0
Total	22.0
Number of Treatment Plants	1
Total Treatment Capacity	12.0 MGD
Average Daily Demand	5.0 MGD
Miles of Main Line Pipe	274
Average Age of Main Line Pipe	75 years
Number of Breaks/Leaks	327
Number of Water Meters	13,495
Percent of Meters Read Automatically	0.0%
Total Revenues Collected	NA

Full Cost Profile

Cost Breakdown by Percentage	
Personal Services	13.5%
Operating Costs	80.0%
Capital Costs	6.5%
TOTAL	100.0%
Cost Breakdown in Dollars	
Personal Services	$661,129
Operating Costs	$3,915,373
Capital Costs	$317,541
TOTAL	$4,894,043

Goldsboro   Water Services

Key: Goldsboro ▒   Benchmarking Average —   Fiscal Years 2013 through 2017

Resource Measures

Water Services Cost per Capita

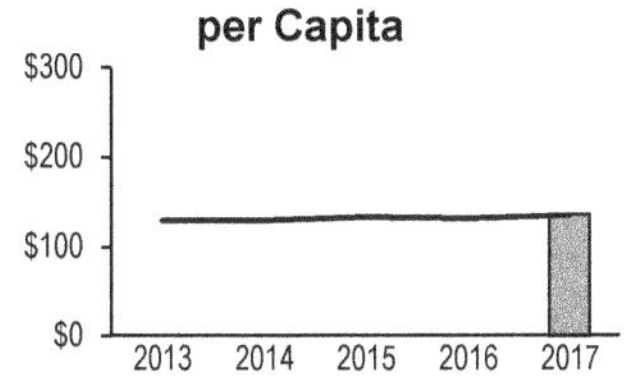

	2013	2014	2015	2016	2017
Goldsboro					$137
Average	$130	$129	$133	$131	$135

Water Services FTEs per 10,000 Population

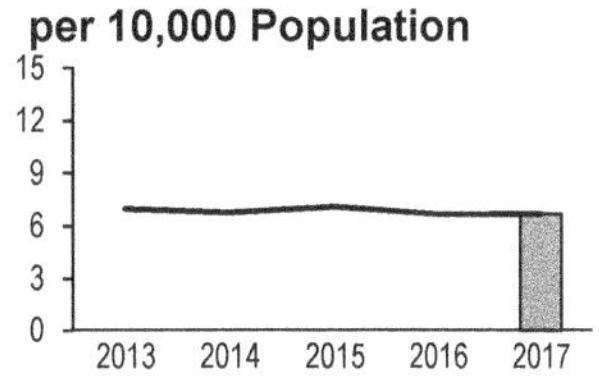

	2013	2014	2015	2016	2017
Goldsboro					6.7
Average	7.0	6.8	7.1	6.7	6.7

Water Services Cost per Meter

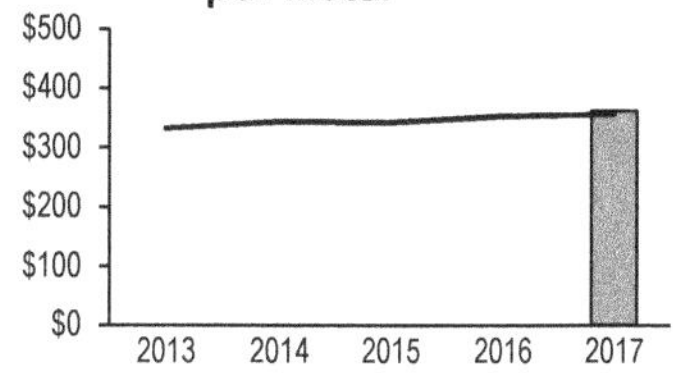

	2013	2014	2015	2016	2017
Goldsboro					$363
Average	$333	$344	$344	$354	$356

Workload Measures

Thousands of Gallons of Billed Water per Meter

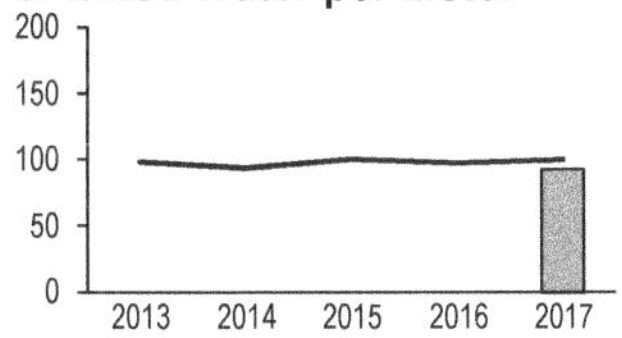

	2013	2014	2015	2016	2017
Goldsboro					92.6
Average	98.2	93.9	100.5	97.3	100.0

Miles of Main Line Pipe per Square Mile of Service Area

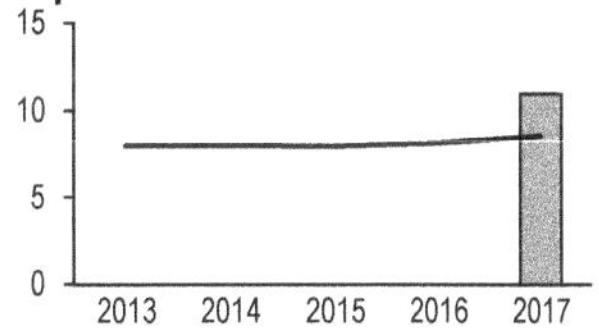

	2013	2014	2015	2016	2017
Goldsboro					11.0
Average	7.9	7.9	7.9	8.1	8.5

Efficiency Measures

Total Cost per Thousand Gallons of Billed Water

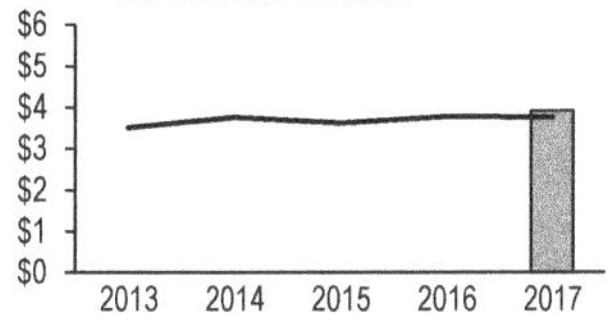

	2013	2014	2015	2016	2017
Goldsboro					$3.91
Average	$3.53	$3.78	$3.64	$3.79	$3.78

Million Gallons of Billed Water per Water Services FTEs

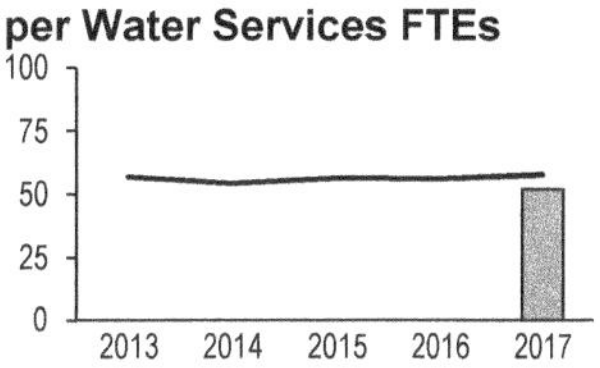

	2013	2014	2015	2016	2017
Goldsboro					52.1
Average	56.8	54.3	56.2	56.2	57.8

Billed Water as a Percentage of Finished Water

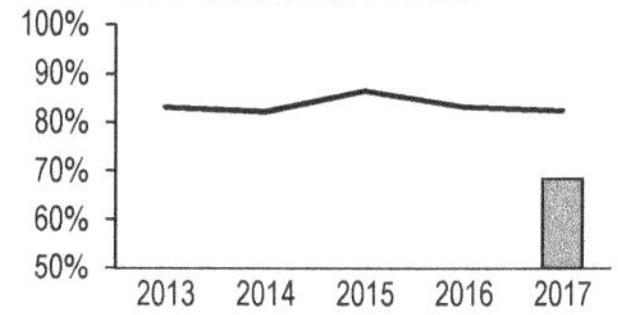

	2013	2014	2015	2016	2017
Goldsboro					68%
Average	83%	82%	87%	83%	83%

Effectiveness Measures

Percentage of Existing Pipeline Replaced or Rehabbed

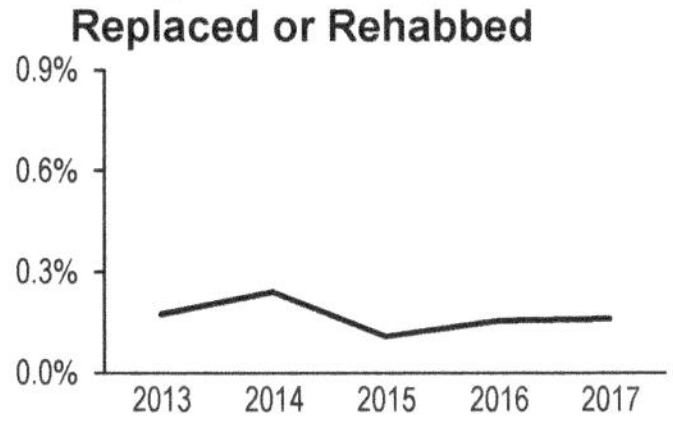

	2013	2014	2015	2016	2017
Goldsboro					0.0%
Average	0.2%	0.2%	0.1%	0.2%	0.2%

Percentage of Water Bills Not Collected

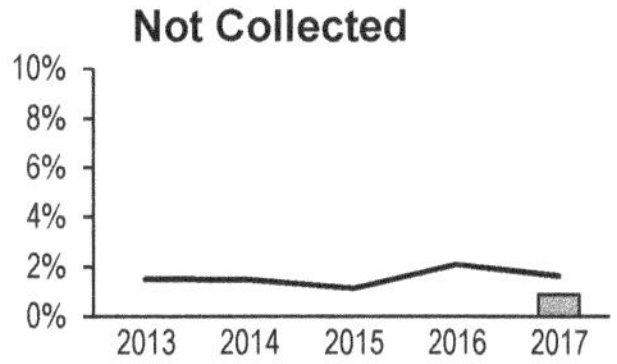

	2013	2014	2015	2016	2017
Goldsboro					0.88%
Average	1.49%	1.47%	1.12%	2.09%	1.62%

Peak Daily Demand as a Percentage of Treatment Capacity

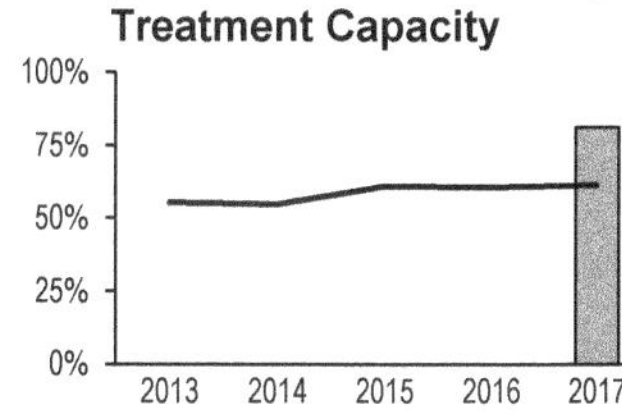

	2013	2014	2015	2016	2017
Goldsboro					81%
Average	55%	55%	61%	60%	61%

Breaks and Leaks per Mile of Main Line Pipe

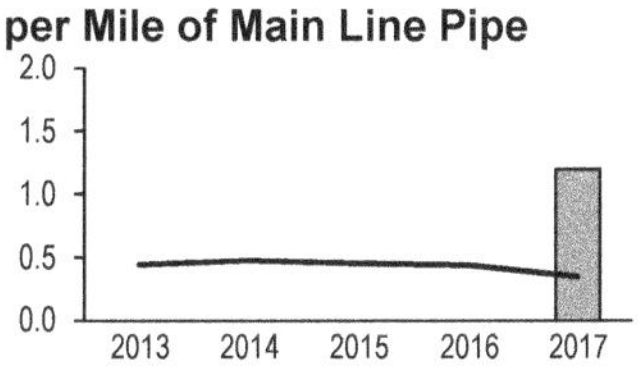

	2013	2014	2015	2016	2017
Goldsboro					1.19
Average	0.45	0.48	0.45	0.44	0.35

Customer Complaints about Water Quality per 1,000 Meters

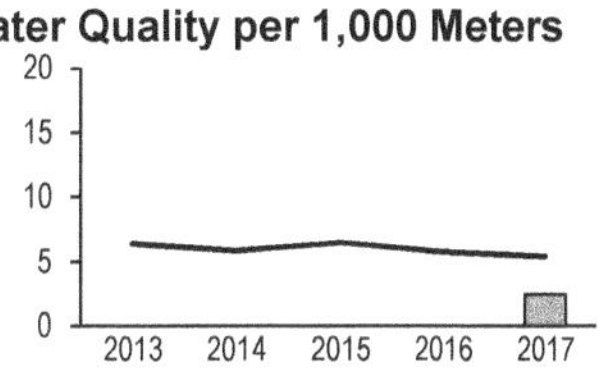

	2013	2014	2015	2016	2017
Goldsboro					2.45
Average	6.37	5.83	6.45	5.70	5.37

Greensboro — Water Services

Fiscal Year 2016–17

Explanatory Information

Service Level and Delivery
Greensboro's drinking water is provided by the Water Supply Division, which is part of the Water Resources Department, which also includes wastewater and stormwater services. The water system serves approximately 285,000 people in an area covering about 148 square miles. In addition to City of Greensboro residents, the system serves many addresses in Guilford County in areas adjacent to the city limits.

Water sources for the system are three city-owned reservoirs in the Haw River basin, which is part of the Upper Cape Fear River basin. The estimated safe yield of the system is 42 million gallons per day, based on a fifty-year estimate as certified by engineers. The system has emergency connections with High Point, Burlington, Reidsville, and Winston-Salem.

The city runs two treatment plants with a combined capacity of 54 million gallons. Both plants use conventional surface water treatment.

The estimated average age of main line pipes in the system is thirty-nine years. Greensboro has begun a spending program on water line rehabilitation and plans to increase funding for this activity for the next several years.

Water meters are read and billed monthly. All meters are read automatically using a radio system.

Conditions Affecting Service, Performance, and Costs
Greensboro has a very high collection rate for water bills. The city has a lien law, so only a small portion of billed amounts goes unpaid. The lien law was changed during FY 2010–11 so that it now only includes owners and not tenants.

Greensboro has a large public education program to encourage water conservation.

The costs of water services as captured here do not include debt service but do capture depreciation.

Water complaints in Greensboro rose in part due to a change in the method of disinfection being used, which led some customers to call the city in FY 2013–14. The change in the disinfection method also led to additional flushing of water lines and, consequently, some water could not be billed.

Municipal Profile

Estimated Service Population	285,344
Service Land Area (Square Miles)	148.0
Persons per Square Mile	1,928
Topography	Flat; gently rolling
Climate	Temperate; little ice and snow
Median Family Income U.S. Census 2010	$52,752

Service Profile

FTE Staff Positions	
Treatment Plant	51.0
Line Crews	66.0
Meter Readers	14.0
Billing/Collection	7.0
Other	17.5
Total	155.5
Number of Treatment Plants	2
Total Treatment Capacity	54.0 MGD
Average Daily Demand	34.5 MGD
Miles of Main Line Pipe	1,503
Average Age of Main Line Pipe	39 years
Number of Breaks/Leaks	302
Number of Water Meters	104,958
Percent of Meters Read Automatically	100.0%
Total Revenues Collected	$54,492,399

Full Cost Profile

Cost Breakdown by Percentage	
Personal Services	20.5%
Operating Costs	79.5%
Capital Costs	0.0%
TOTAL	100.0%
Cost Breakdown in Dollars	
Personal Services	$6,168,661
Operating Costs	$23,960,539
Capital Costs	$0
TOTAL	$30,129,200

Key: Greensboro ▒ Benchmarking Average — Fiscal Years 2013 through 2017

Resource Measures

Water Services Cost per Capita

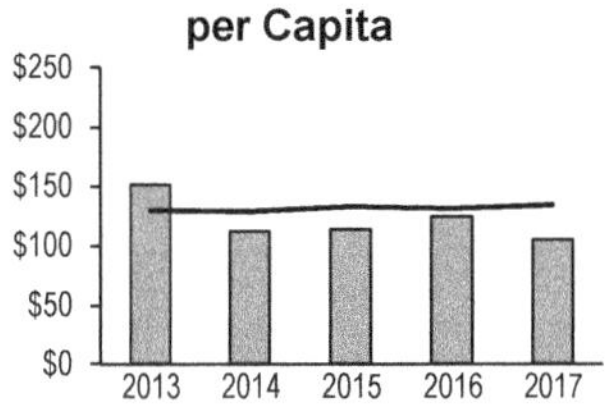

	2013	2014	2015	2016	2017
Greensboro	$152	$113	$114	$125	$106
Average	$130	$129	$133	$131	$135

Water Services FTEs per 10,000 Population

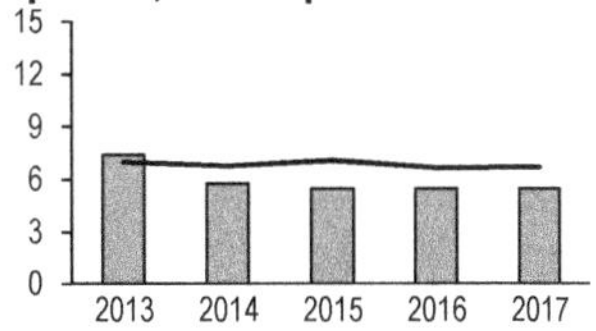

	2013	2014	2015	2016	2017
Greensboro	7.4	5.8	5.5	5.4	5.4
Average	7.0	6.8	7.1	6.7	6.7

Water Services Cost per Meter

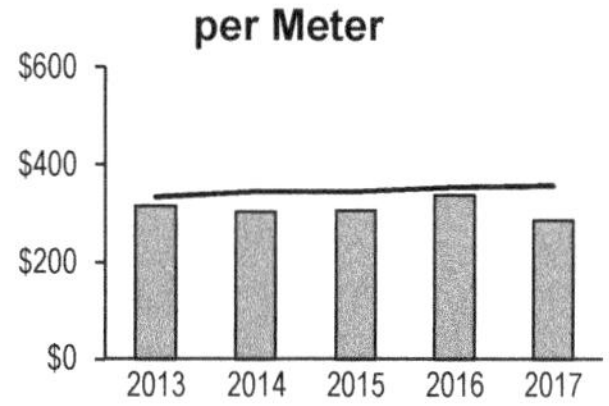

	2013	2014	2015	2016	2017
Greensboro	$317	$304	$307	$338	$287
Average	$333	$344	$344	$354	$356

Workload Measures

Thousands of Gallons of Billed Water per Meter

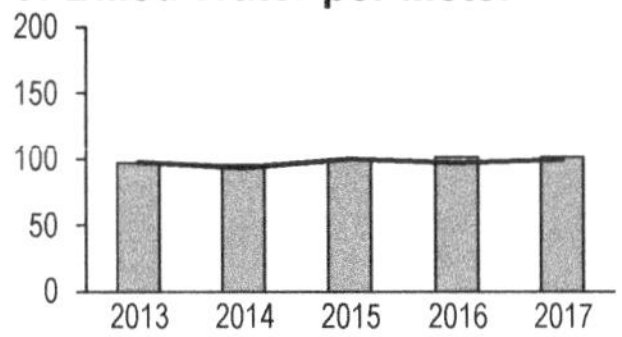

	2013	2014	2015	2016	2017
Greensboro	97.1	95.8	99.9	101.6	101.5
Average	98.2	93.9	100.5	97.3	100.0

Miles of Main Line Pipe per Square Mile of Service Area

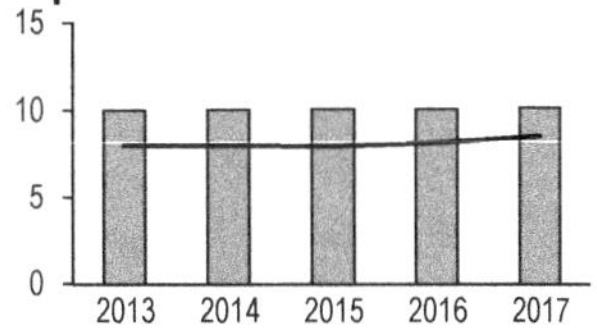

	2013	2014	2015	2016	2017
Greensboro	10.0	10.0	10.1	10.1	10.2
Average	7.9	7.9	7.9	8.1	8.5

Efficiency Measures

Total Cost per Thousand Gallons of Billed Water

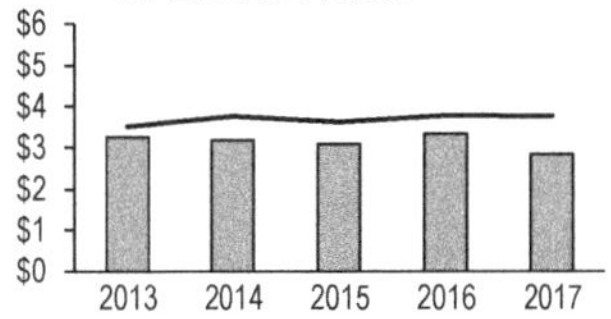

	2013	2014	2015	2016	2017
Greensboro	$3.26	$3.18	$3.08	$3.33	$2.83
Average	$3.53	$3.78	$3.64	$3.79	$3.78

Million Gallons of Billed Water per Water Services FTEs

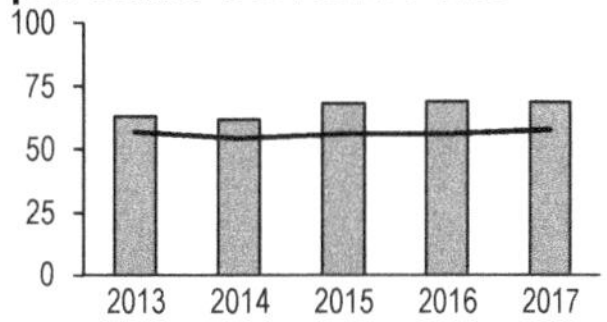

	2013	2014	2015	2016	2017
Greensboro	63.0	61.7	68.0	68.9	68.5
Average	56.8	54.3	56.2	56.2	57.8

Billed Water as a Percentage of Finished Water

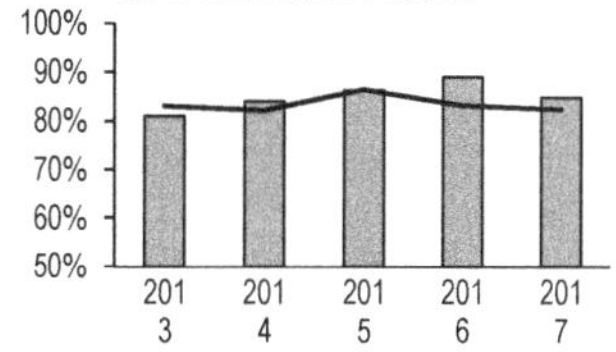

	2013	2014	2015	2016	2017
Greensboro	81%	84%	86%	89%	85%
Average	83%	82%	87%	83%	83%

Effectiveness Measures

Percentage of Existing Pipeline Replaced or Rehabbed

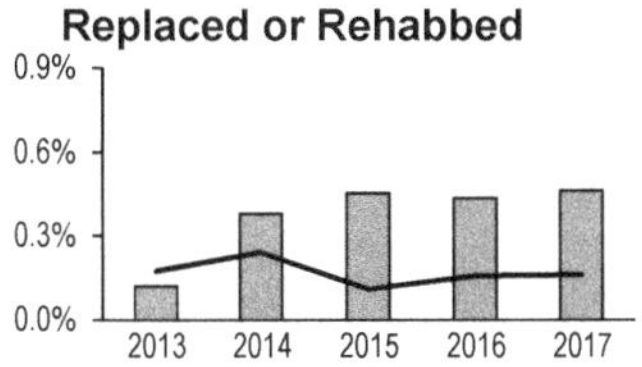

	2013	2014	2015	2016	2017
Greensboro	0.1%	0.4%	0.5%	0.4%	0.5%
Average	0.2%	0.2%	0.1%	0.2%	0.2%

Percentage of Water Bills Not Collected

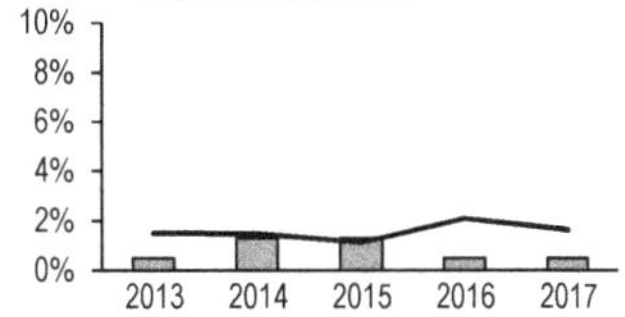

	2013	2014	2015	2016	2017
Greensboro	0.50%	1.28%	1.28%	0.50%	0.50%
Average	1.49%	1.47%	1.12%	2.09%	1.62%

Peak Daily Demand as a Percentage of Treatment Capacity

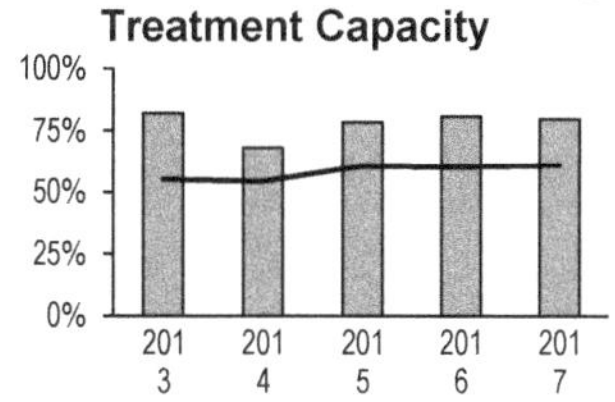

	2013	2014	2015	2016	2017
Greensboro	82%	68%	78%	81%	80%
Average	55%	55%	61%	60%	61%

Breaks and Leaks per Mile of Main Line Pipe

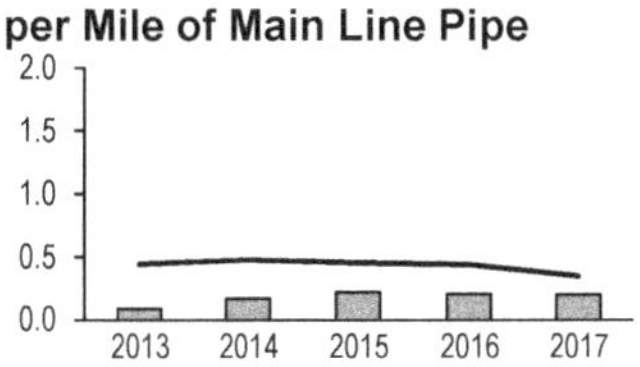

	2013	2014	2015	2016	2017
Greensboro	0.09	0.17	0.22	0.20	0.20
Average	0.45	0.48	0.45	0.44	0.35

Customer Complaints about Water Quality per 1,000 Meters

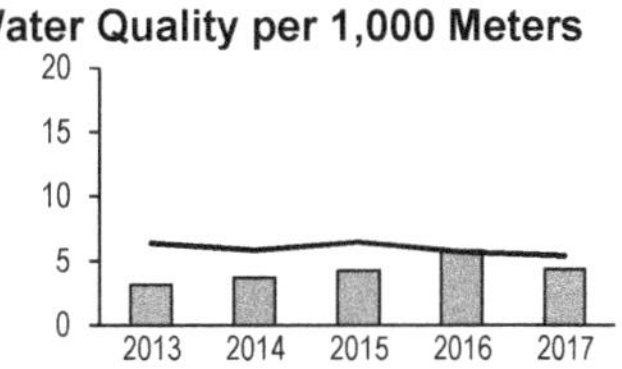

	2013	2014	2015	2016	2017
Greensboro	3.15	3.67	4.24	5.80	4.32
Average	6.37	5.83	6.45	5.70	5.37

Fiscal Year 2016–17

Explanatory Information

Service Level and Delivery

Water services in Hickory are provided by a combined water distribution division under the Public Services Department. The water system services an area covering roughly 305 square miles and approximately 100,000 people. Water is provided for the city of Hickory and also for the towns of Hildenbran, Brookford, and Catawba; the Sherrill's Ford, Mountain View, and Cooksville communities of Catawba County; and the Bethlehem, Sugarloaf, and Highway 16 communities of Alexander County.

Source water is from the Catawba River basin, with an estimated safe yield of 54 million gallons per day. Hickory sells water to the systems in Conover, Claremont, and Icard Township. The system has one treatment plant with a capacity of 32 million gallons per day.

Water meters are read monthly. Hickory's replacement standard for water meters is twenty years. About 14.8 percent of water meters in the system are read by automatic means.

Conditions Affecting Service, Performance, and Costs

The costs of water services as captured here do not include debt service but do capture depreciation.

Municipal Profile

Estimated Service Population	99,530
Service Land Area (Square Miles)	326.0
Persons per Square Mile	305
Topography	Flat; gently rolling
Climate	Temperate; some ice and snow
Median Family Income U.S. Census 2010	$54,093

Service Profile

FTE Staff Positions	
Treatment Plant	12.0
Line Crews	35.0
Meter Readers	6.0
Billing/Collection	5.0
Other	2.0
Total	60.0
Number of Treatment Plants	1
Total Treatment Capacity	32.0 MGD
Average Daily Demand	12.5 MGD
Miles of Main Line Pipe	936
Average Age of Main Line Pipe	40 years
Number of Breaks/Leaks	189
Number of Water Meters	29,481
Percent of Meters Read Automatically	14.8%
Total Revenues Collected	$14,879,540

Full Cost Profile

Cost Breakdown by Percentage	
Personal Services	30.7%
Operating Costs	50.7%
Capital Costs	18.6%
TOTAL	100.0%
Cost Breakdown in Dollars	
Personal Services	$2,435,873
Operating Costs	$4,026,032
Capital Costs	$1,475,063
TOTAL	$7,936,968

Key: Hickory ▒ Benchmarking Average — Fiscal Years 2013 through 2017

Resource Measures

Water Services Cost per Capita

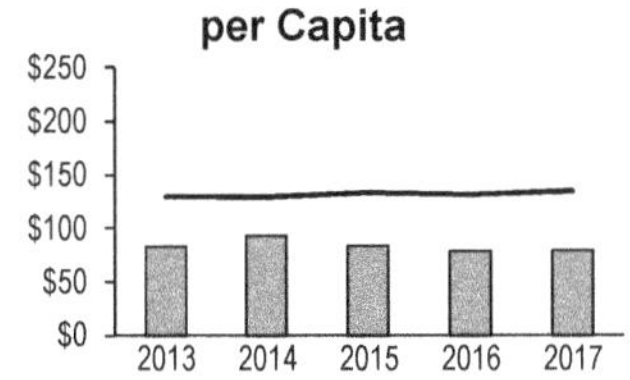

	2013	2014	2015	2016	2017
Hickory	$84	$94	$84	$79	$80
Average	$130	$129	$133	$131	$135

Water Services FTEs per 10,000 Population

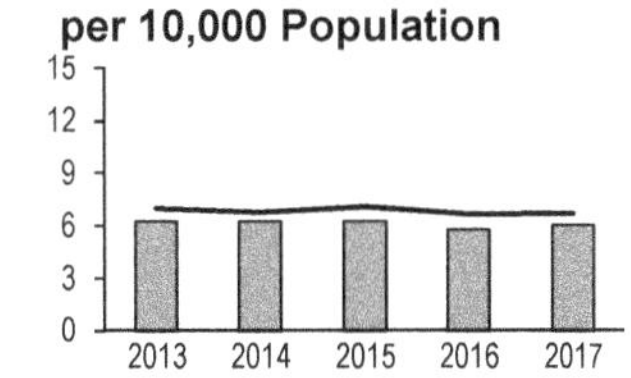

	2013	2014	2015	2016	2017
Hickory	6.3	6.3	6.3	5.8	6.0
Average	7.0	6.8	7.1	6.7	6.7

Water Services Cost per Meter

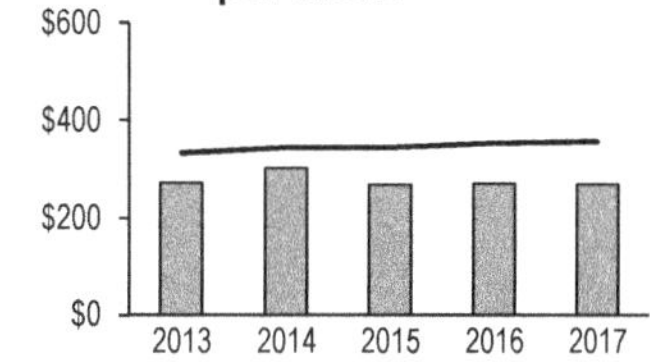

	2013	2014	2015	2016	2017
Hickory	$271	$302	$268	$270	$269
Average	$333	$344	$344	$354	$356

Workload Measures

Thousands of Gallons of Billed Water per Meter

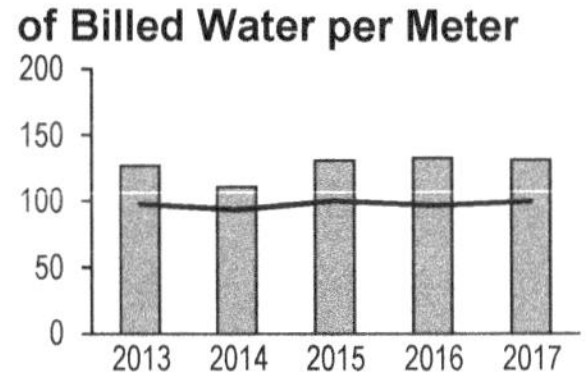

	2013	2014	2015	2016	2017
Hickory	127.0	111.0	130.8	133.0	131.5
Average	98.2	93.9	100.5	97.3	100.0

Miles of Main Line Pipe per Square Mile of Service Area

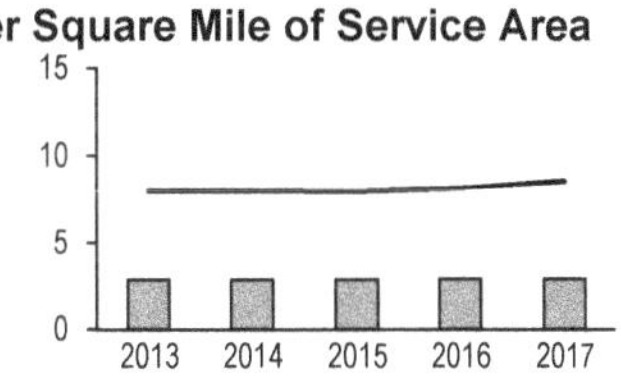

	2013	2014	2015	2016	2017
Hickory	2.8	2.8	2.8	2.9	2.9
Average	7.9	7.9	7.9	8.1	8.5

Efficiency Measures

Total Cost per Thousand Gallons of Billed Water

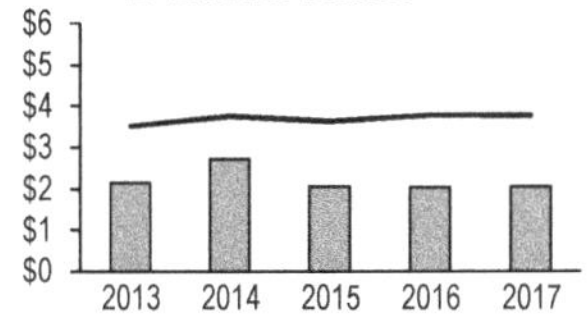

	2013	2014	2015	2016	2017
Hickory	$2.14	$2.72	$2.05	$2.03	$2.05
Average	$3.53	$3.78	$3.64	$3.79	$3.78

Million Gallons of Billed Water per Water Services FTEs

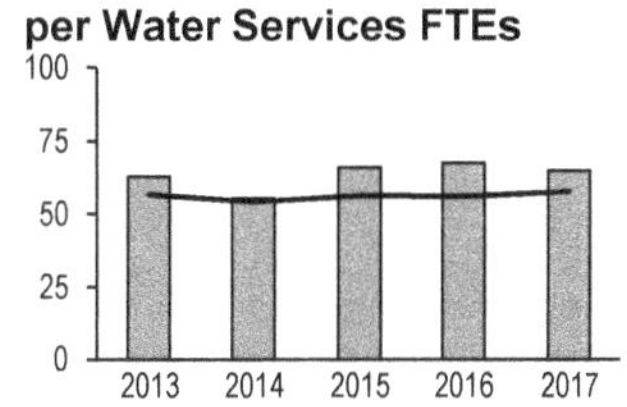

	2013	2014	2015	2016	2017
Hickory	62.6	55.2	65.7	67.3	64.6
Average	56.8	54.3	56.2	56.2	57.8

Billed Water as a Percentage of Finished Water

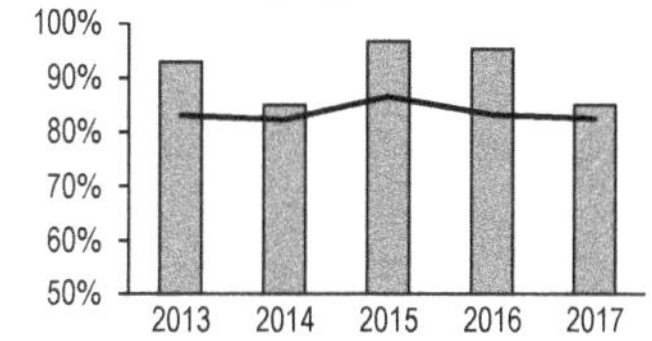

	2013	2014	2015	2016	2017
Hickory	93%	85%	97%	95%	85%
Average	83%	82%	87%	83%	83%

Effectiveness Measures

Percentage of Existing Pipeline Replaced or Rehabbed

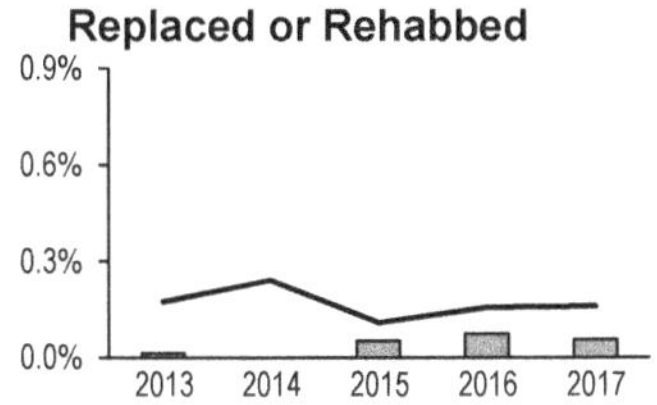

	2013	2014	2015	2016	2017
Hickory	0.0%	0.0%	0.1%	0.1%	0.1%
Average	0.2%	0.2%	0.1%	0.2%	0.2%

Percentage of Water Bills Not Collected

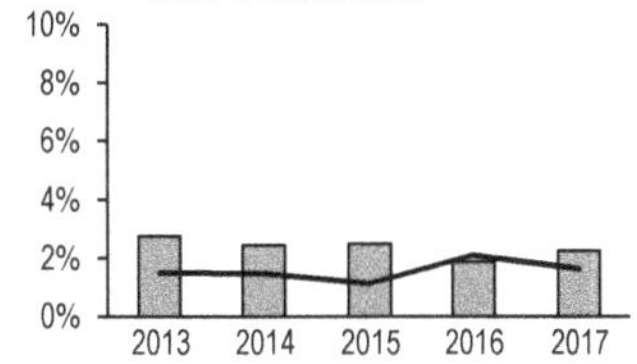

	2013	2014	2015	2016	2017
Hickory	2.73%	2.44%	2.47%	1.86%	2.24%
Average	1.49%	1.47%	1.12%	2.09%	1.62%

Peak Daily Demand as a Percentage of Treatment Capacity

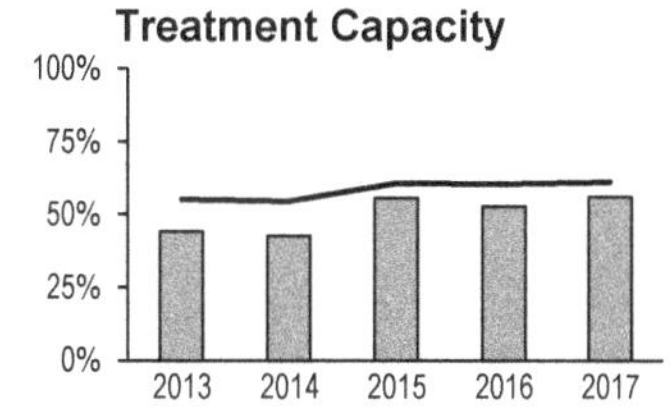

	2013	2014	2015	2016	2017
Hickory	44%	43%	55%	53%	56%
Average	55%	55%	61%	60%	61%

Breaks and Leaks per Mile of Main Line Pipe

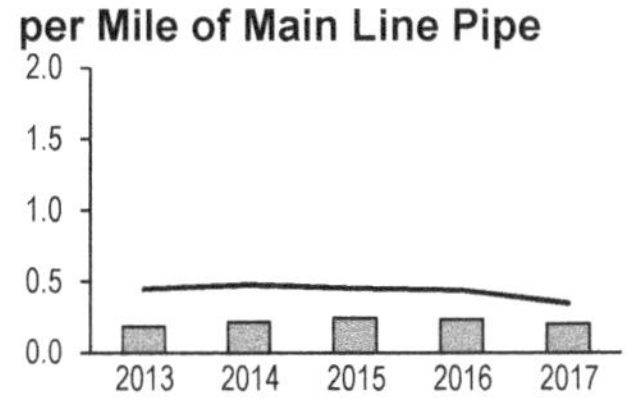

	2013	2014	2015	2016	2017
Hickory	0.19	0.22	0.24	0.23	0.20
Average	0.45	0.48	0.45	0.44	0.35

Customer Complaints about Water Quality per 1,000 Meters

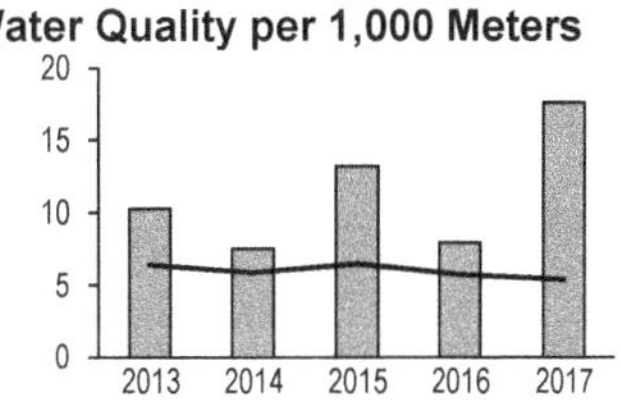

	2013	2014	2015	2016	2017
Hickory	10.26	7.53	13.22	7.94	17.57
Average	6.37	5.83	6.45	5.70	5.37

Fiscal Year 2016–17

Explanatory Information

Service Level and Delivery
The City of High Point's drinking water services are part of a combined Water/Sewer Division under the Public Services Department. The system covers sixty-five square miles and serves approximately 112,000 people.

Water sources for the system are two city-owned reservoirs located in the Deep River basin and the Piedmont Triad Regional Water Authority. The estimated safe yield of the system is 22 million gallons per day. The system has one treatment plant and uses an upflow clarification process and a super "U" pulsator with a treatment capacity of 24 million gallons per day.

Water meters are read monthly. Approximately one-third of meters are read by automatic means. The city has a standard to replace water meters every ten years on average.

Conditions Affecting Service, Performance, and Costs
High Point has a very high collection rate for water bills. The city participates in the State of North Carolina's debt set-off program. The program is in place to garnish a person's state tax return if he or she does not pay his or her bill. In addition, High Point performs a credit check with Equifax based on the customer's payment history.

The costs of water services as captured here do not include debt service but do capture depreciation.

High Point is a partner in the Piedmont Triad Regional Water Authority. It received several millions gallons per day through the partnership. This has changed the High Point system from a single-pressure zone system to a double-pressure zone system.

Municipal Profile

Estimated Service Population	112,201
Service Land Area (Square Miles)	65.0
Persons per Square Mile	1,726
Topography	Flat; gently rolling
Climate	Temperate; little ice and snow
Median Family Income U.S. Census 2010	$49,720

Service Profile

FTE Staff Positions	
Treatment Plant	13.0
Line Crews	26.8
Meter Readers	5.0
Billing/Collection	6.0
Other	12.6
Total	63.4
Number of Treatment Plants	1
Total Treatment Capacity	24.0 MGD
Average Daily Demand	12.3 MGD
Miles of Main Line Pipe	616
Average Age of Main Line Pipe	43 years
Number of Breaks/Leaks	194
Number of Water Meters	43,241
Percent of Meters Read Automatically	34.5%
Total Revenues Collected	$19,021,500

Full Cost Profile

Cost Breakdown by Percentage	
Personal Services	29.9%
Operating Costs	38.2%
Capital Costs	31.9%
TOTAL	100.0%
Cost Breakdown in Dollars	
Personal Services	$3,778,629
Operating Costs	$4,828,090
Capital Costs	$4,035,249
TOTAL	$12,641,968

Key: High Point ▒ Benchmarking Average — Fiscal Years 2013 through 2017

Resource Measures

Water Services Cost per Capita

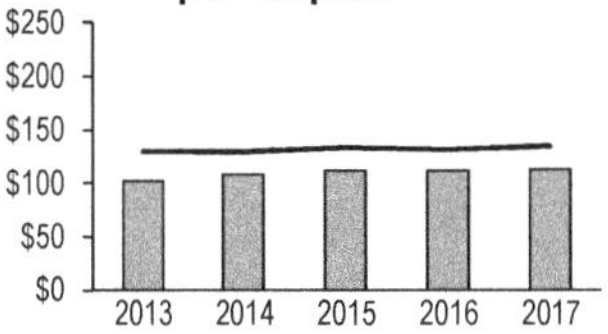

	2013	2014	2015	2016	2017
High Point	$102	$108	$111	$111	$113
Average	$130	$129	$133	$131	$135

Water Services FTEs per 10,000 Population

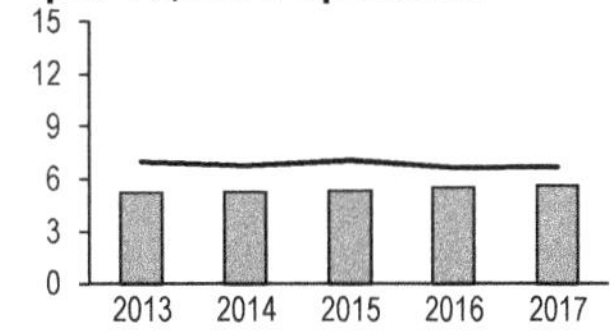

	2013	2014	2015	2016	2017
High Point	5.2	5.3	5.3	5.5	5.7
Average	7.0	6.8	7.1	6.7	6.7

Water Services Cost per Meter

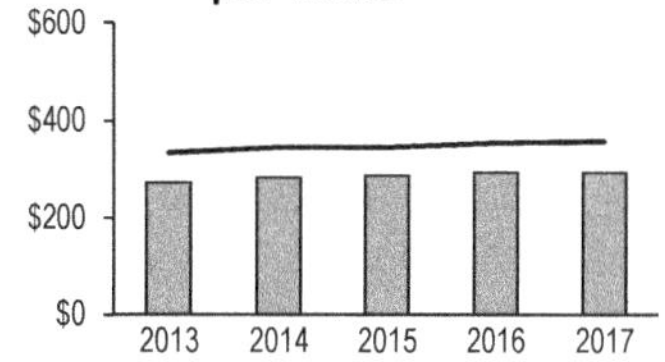

	2013	2014	2015	2016	2017
High Point	$271	$282	$286	$292	$292
Average	$333	$344	$344	$354	$356

Workload Measures

Thousands of Gallons of Billed Water per Meter

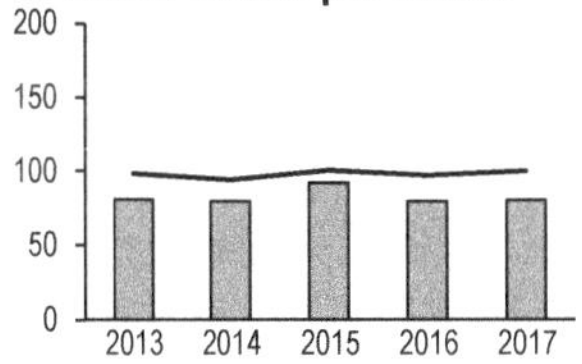

	2013	2014	2015	2016	2017
High Point	80.5	79.2	92.0	79.3	80.0
Average	98.2	93.9	100.5	97.3	100.0

Miles of Main Line Pipe per Square Mile of Service Area

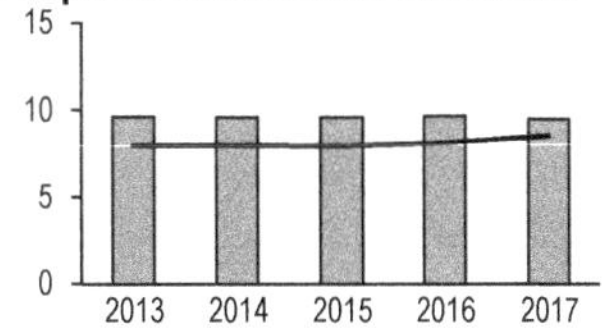

	2013	2014	2015	2016	2017
High Point	9.6	9.6	9.6	9.6	9.5
Average	7.9	7.9	7.9	8.1	8.5

Efficiency Measures

Total Cost per Thousand Gallons of Billed Water

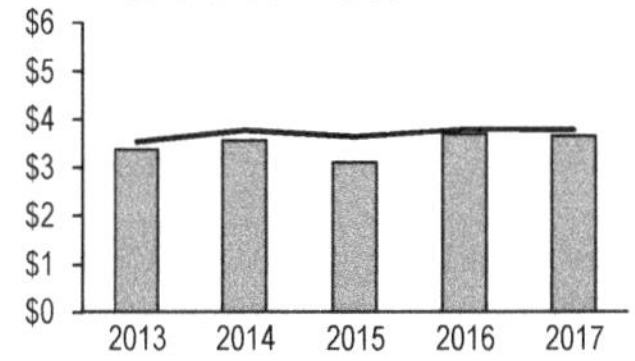

	2013	2014	2015	2016	2017
High Point	$3.37	$3.56	$3.11	$3.69	$3.65
Average	$3.53	$3.78	$3.64	$3.79	$3.78

Million Gallons of Billed Water per Water Services FTEs

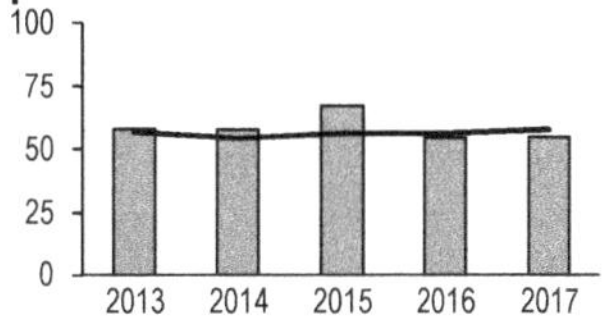

	2013	2014	2015	2016	2017
High Point	57.9	57.7	67.0	54.4	54.6
Average	56.8	54.3	56.2	56.2	57.8

Billed Water as a Percentage of Finished Water

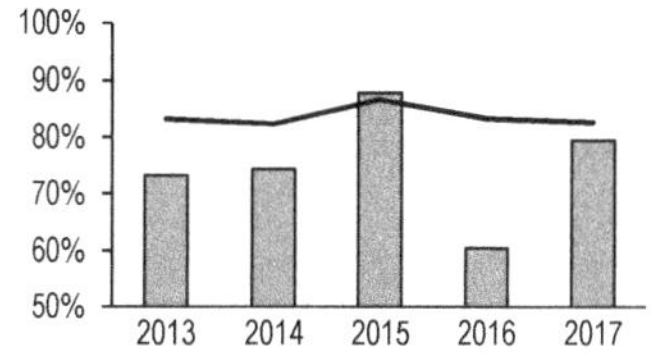

	2013	2014	2015	2016	2017
High Point	73%	74%	88%	60%	80%
Average	83%	82%	87%	83%	83%

Effectiveness Measures

Percentage of Existing Pipeline Replaced or Rehabbed

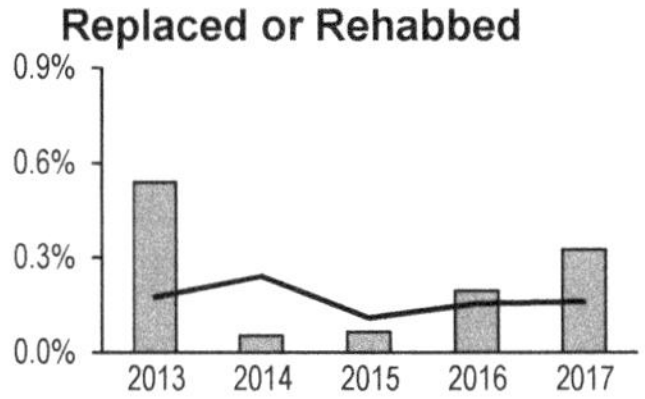

	2013	2014	2015	2016	2017
High Point	0.5%	0.1%	0.1%	0.2%	0.3%
Average	0.2%	0.2%	0.1%	0.2%	0.2%

Percentage of Water Bills Not Collected

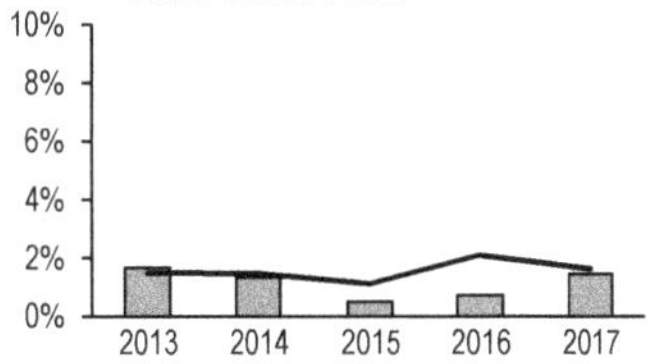

	2013	2014	2015	2016	2017
High Point	1.67%	1.35%	0.50%	0.73%	1.46%
Average	1.49%	1.47%	1.12%	2.09%	1.62%

Peak Daily Demand as a Percentage of Treatment Capacity

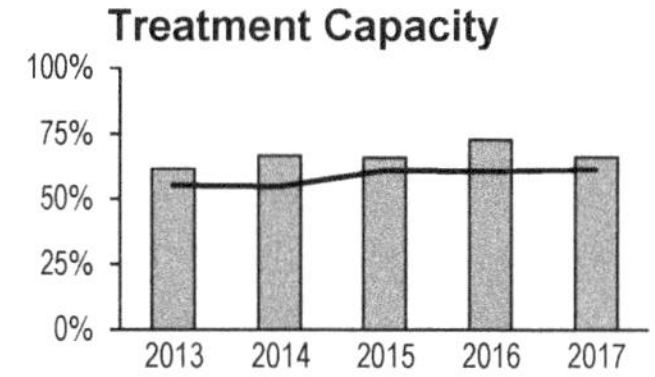

	2013	2014	2015	2016	2017
High Point	61%	67%	66%	73%	66%
Average	55%	55%	61%	60%	61%

Breaks and Leaks per Mile of Main Line Pipe

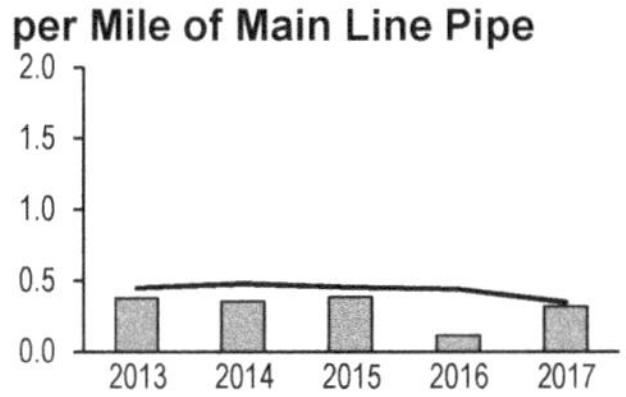

	2013	2014	2015	2016	2017
High Point	0.37	0.35	0.38	0.12	0.31
Average	0.45	0.48	0.45	0.44	0.35

Customer Complaints about Water Quality per 1,000 Meters

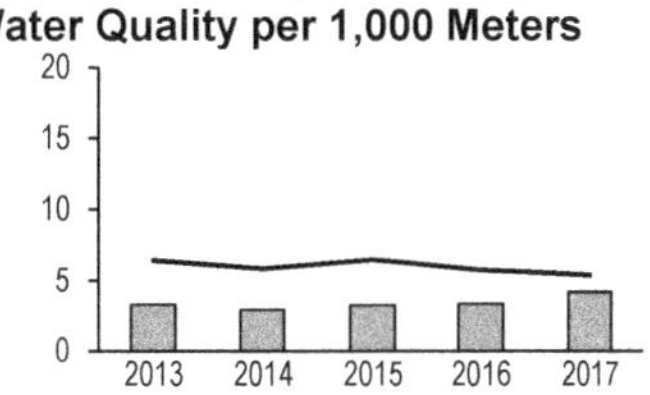

	2013	2014	2015	2016	2017
High Point	3.30	2.94	3.22	3.35	4.16
Average	6.37	5.83	6.45	5.70	5.37

Fiscal Year 2016–17

Explanatory Information

Service Level and Delivery
Public Utilities is a department within the City of Raleigh. It is a combined enterprise system that provides drinking water services to the City of Raleigh and several towns, including Garner, Rolesville, Knightdale, Wake Forest, Wendell, and Zebulon. Approximately 561,000 people live in the service area of roughly 299 square miles.

The water system collects its water from Falls Lake located in the Neuse River watershed and from Lake Wheeler and Lake Benson, which are in the Swift Creek watershed. The estimated 50-year safe yield of the system is 77.3 million gallons per day.

Public Utilities operates two treatment plants with a total permitted treatment capacity of 102 million gallons per day. Both plants are surface water treatment plants. One plant uses a conventional treatment process with the addition of settled water ozone. The second plant uses raw water ozone, a super pulsator, a two-stage filter process, and ultraviolet disinfection prior to clearwell storage.

Water meters are read once per month. Currently, nearly all meters are read by automatic means. The standard for meter replacement is fifteen years.

Conditions Affecting Service, Performance, and Costs
Raleigh rejoined the Benchmarking Project in July 2016 with the first year of data showing for FY 2015–16.

The costs of water services as captured here do not include debt service but do capture depreciation.

Municipal Profile

Estimated Service Population	561,428
Service Land Area (Square Miles)	299.0
Persons per Square Mile	1,878
Topography	Flat; gently rolling
Climate	Temperate; little ice and snow
Median Family Income U.S. Census 2010	$68,678

Service Profile

FTE Staff Positions	
Treatment Plant	53.0
Line Crews	86.0
Meter Readers	2.0
Billing/Collection	28.0
Other	159.0
Total	328.0
Number of Treatment Plants	2
Total Treatment Capacity	102.0 MGD
Average Daily Demand	52.0 MGD
Miles of Main Line Pipe	2,388
Average Age of Main Line Pipe	42 years
Number of Breaks/Leaks	NA
Number of Water Meters	188,844
Percent of Meters Read Automatically	NA
Total Revenues Collected	$105,910,331

Full Cost Profile

Cost Breakdown by Percentage	
Personal Services	25.7%
Operating Costs	43.7%
Capital Costs	30.6%
TOTAL	100.0%
Cost Breakdown in Dollars	
Personal Services	$17,293,487
Operating Costs	$29,351,440
Capital Costs	$20,590,947
TOTAL	$67,235,873

Key: Raleigh ▒ Benchmarking Average — Fiscal Years 2013 through 2017

Resource Measures

Water Services Cost per Capita

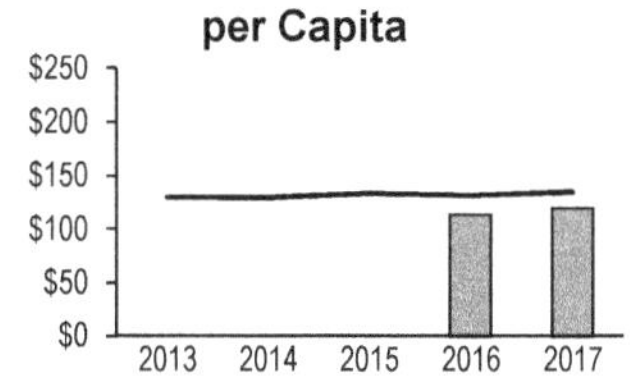

	2013	2014	2015	2016	2017
Raleigh				$114	$120
Average	$130	$129	$133	$131	$135

Water Services FTEs per 10,000 Population

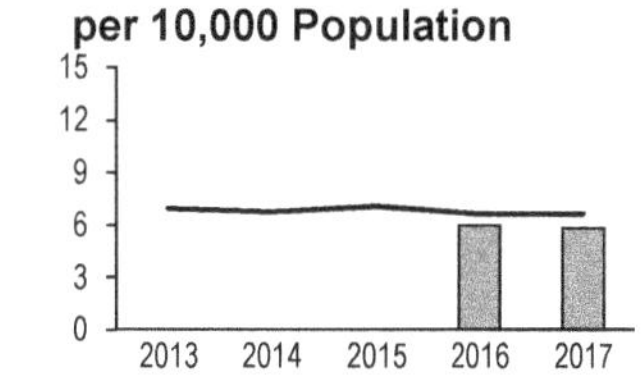

	2013	2014	2015	2016	2017
Raleigh				6.0	5.8
Average	7.0	6.8	7.1	6.7	6.7

Water Services Cost per Meter

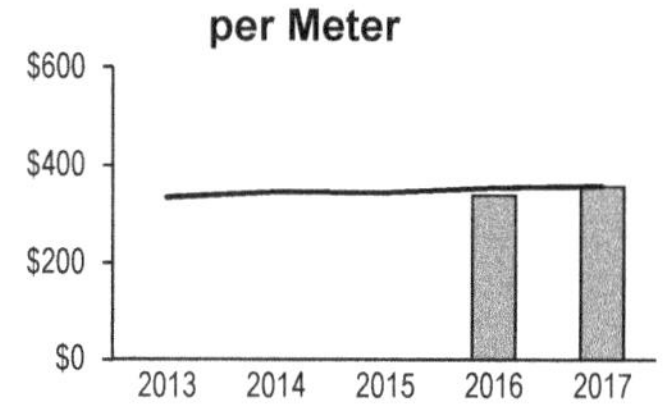

	2013	2014	2015	2016	2017
Raleigh				$337	$356
Average	$333	$344	$344	$354	$356

Workload Measures

Thousands of Gallons of Billed Water per Meter

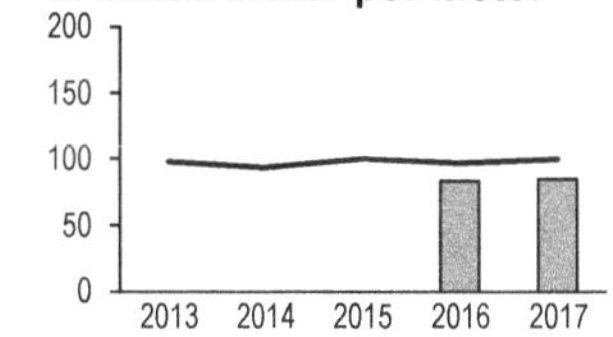

	2013	2014	2015	2016	2017
Raleigh				83.2	84.5
Average	98.2	93.9	100.5	97.3	100.0

Miles of Main Line Pipe per Square Mile of Service Area

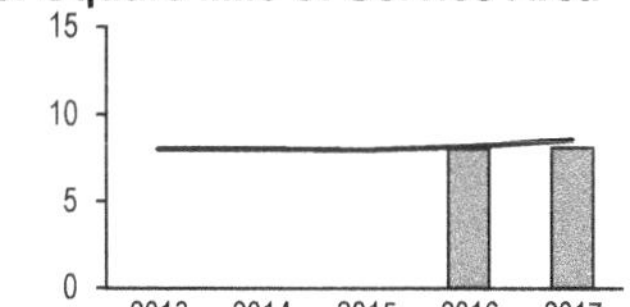

	2013	2014	2015	2016	2017
Raleigh				7.9	8.0
Average	7.9	7.9	7.9	8.1	8.5

Efficiency Measures

Total Cost per Thousand Gallons of Billed Water

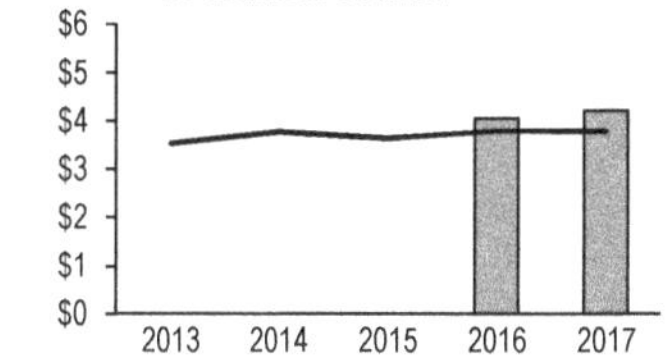

	2013	2014	2015	2016	2017
Raleigh				$4.06	$4.21
Average	$3.53	$3.78	$3.64	$3.79	$3.78

Million Gallons of Billed Water per Water Services FTEs

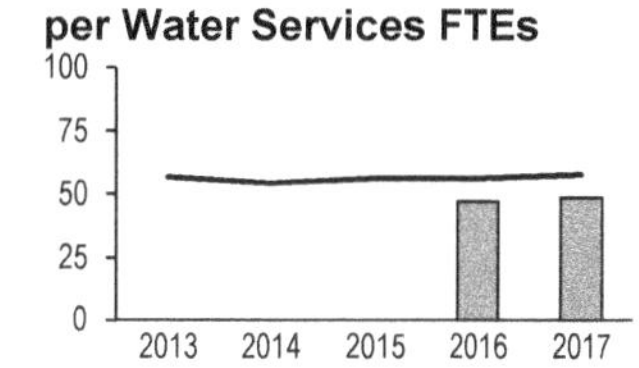

	2013	2014	2015	2016	2017
Raleigh				47.0	48.6
Average	56.8	54.3	56.2	56.2	57.8

Billed Water as a Percentage of Finished Water

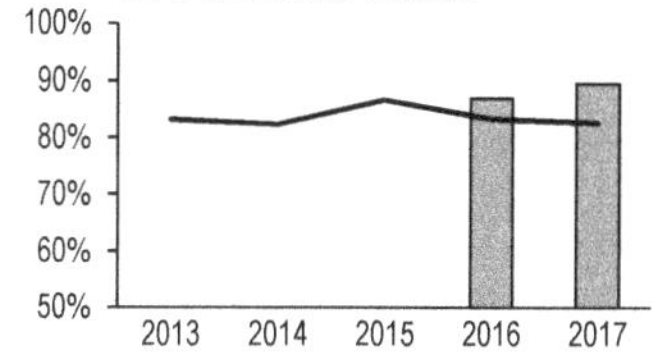

	2013	2014	2015	2016	2017
Raleigh				87%	89%
Average	83%	82%	87%	83%	83%

Effectiveness Measures

Percentage of Existing Pipeline Replaced or Rehabbed

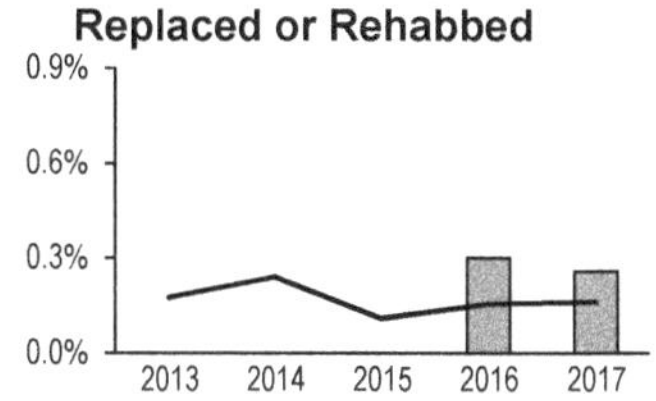

	2013	2014	2015	2016	2017
Raleigh				0.3%	0.3%
Average	0.2%	0.2%	0.1%	0.2%	0.2%

Percentage of Water Bills Not Collected

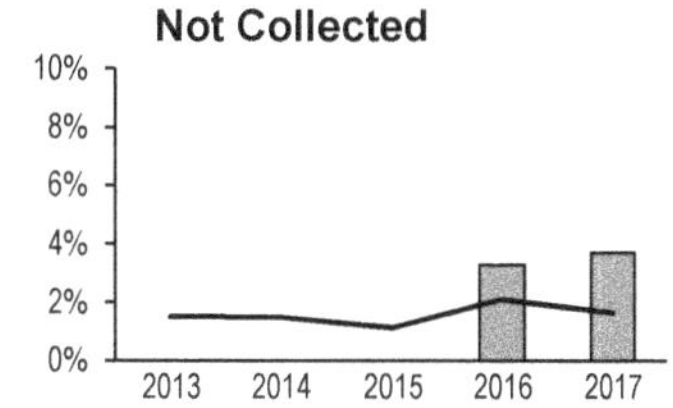

	2013	2014	2015	2016	2017
Raleigh				3.28%	3.70%
Average	1.49%	1.47%	1.12%	2.09%	1.62%

Peak Daily Demand as a Percentage of Treatment Capacity

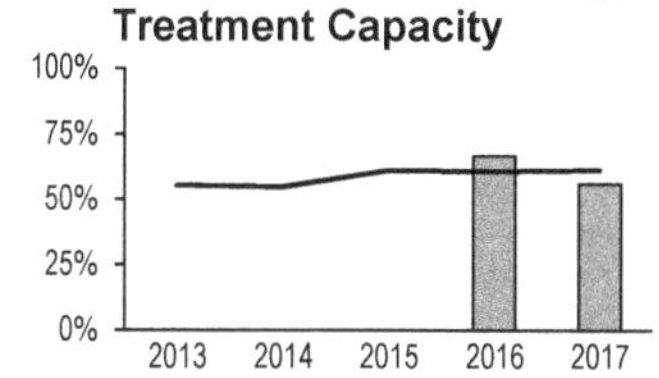

	2013	2014	2015	2016	2017
Raleigh				67%	56%
Average	55%	55%	61%	60%	61%

Breaks and Leaks per Mile of Main Line Pipe

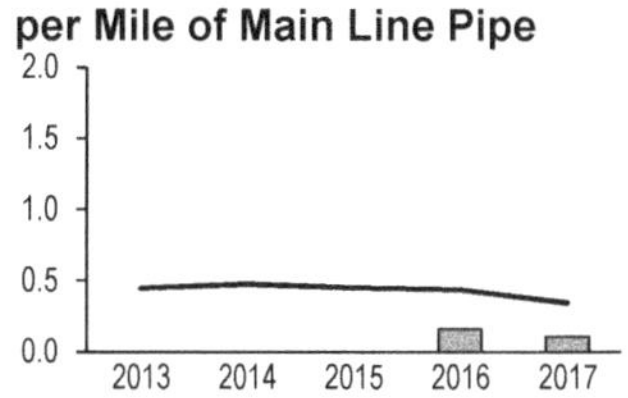

	2013	2014	2015	2016	2017
Raleigh				0.16	0.11
Average	0.45	0.48	0.45	0.44	0.35

Customer Complaints about Water Quality per 1,000 Meters

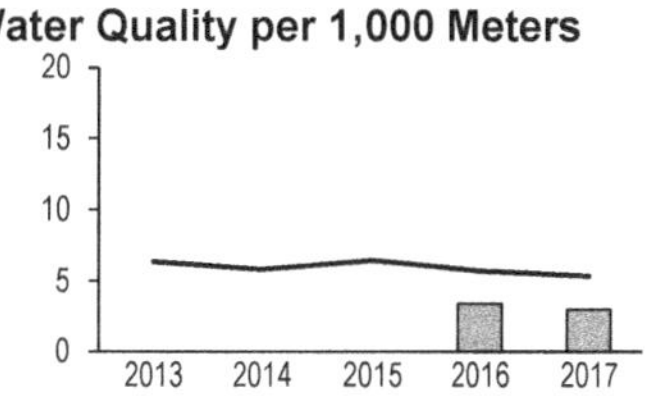

	2013	2014	2015	2016	2017
Raleigh				3.40	3.00
Average	6.37	5.83	6.45	5.70	5.37

Fiscal Year 2016–17

Explanatory Information

Service Level and Delivery

The City of Salisbury provides water service through an enterprise fund department. This department is known as Salisbury-Rowan Utilities. The system covers 47.5 square miles and covers much of Rowan County. Approximately 53,600 people are served. In the late 1990s and early 2000s, Salisbury assumed ownership of the water and sewer systems of the towns of Spencer, Granite Quarry, and Rockwell, followed by China Grove in 2011. Rowan County turned over its water assets to Salisbury in 2004. Salisbury also sells bulk water to the towns of East Spencer, China Grove, Landis, and to the City of Kannapolis.

The water source for the system is the Yadkin River. The estimated safe yield for the system is 108 million gallons per day. The system has one treatment plant with a capacity of 25 million gallons per day. The plant uses an Actiflo pre-treatment process followed by a conventional sedimentation and filtration treatment process.

Water meters are read once per month. Currently, approximately 31 percent of meters are read by automatic means. The standard for meter replacement is fifteen years.

Conditions Affecting Service, Performance, and Costs

The costs of water services as captured here do not include debt service but do capture depreciation.

Municipal Profile

Estimated Service Population	53,600
Service Land Area (Square Miles)	47.5
Persons per Square Mile	1,128
Topography	Flat; gently rolling
Climate	Temperate; little ice and snow
Median Family Income U.S. Census 2010	$40,192

Service Profile

FTE Staff Positions	
Treatment Plant	9.0
Line Crews	11.0
Meter Readers	6.0
Billing/Collection	6.0
Other	8.0
Total	40.0
Number of Treatment Plants	1
Total Treatment Capacity	25.0 MGD
Average Daily Demand	9.6 MGD
Miles of Main Line Pipe	422
Average Age of Main Line Pipe	50 years
Number of Breaks/Leaks	143
Number of Water Meters	19,466
Percent of Meters Read Automatically	30.8%
Total Revenues Collected	$13,262,032

Full Cost Profile

Cost Breakdown by Percentage	
Personal Services	28.3%
Operating Costs	39.0%
Capital Costs	32.7%
TOTAL	100.0%
Cost Breakdown in Dollars	
Personal Services	$2,171,690
Operating Costs	$2,995,073
Capital Costs	$2,513,619
TOTAL	$7,680,382

Key: Salisbury ▒ Benchmarking Average — Fiscal Years 2013 through 2017

Resource Measures

Water Services Cost per Capita

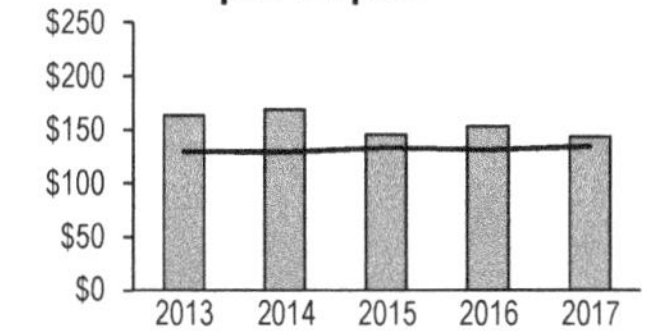

	2013	2014	2015	2016	2017
Salisbury	$163	$168	$145	$153	$143
Average	$130	$129	$133	$131	$135

Water Services FTEs per 10,000 Population

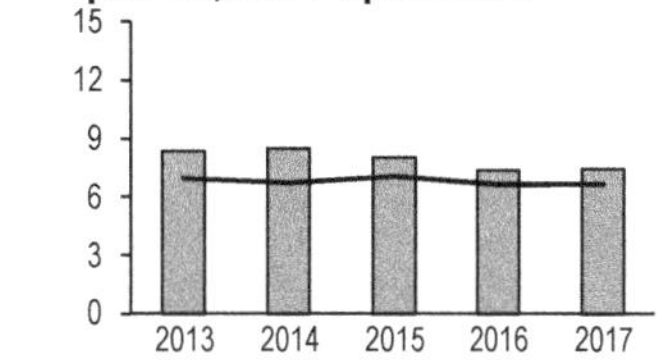

	2013	2014	2015	2016	2017
Salisbury	8.4	8.5	8.1	7.4	7.5
Average	7.0	6.8	7.1	6.7	6.7

Water Services Cost per Meter

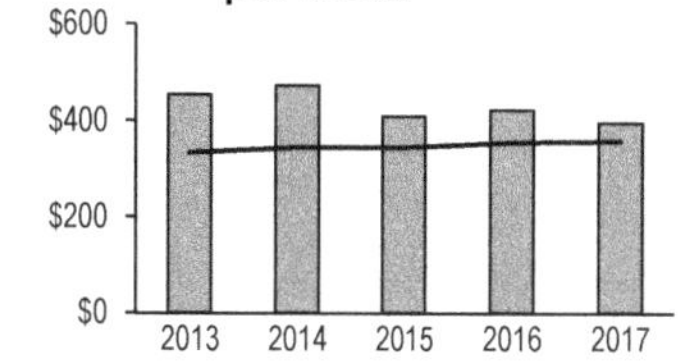

	2013	2014	2015	2016	2017
Salisbury	$453	$471	$407	$421	$395
Average	$333	$344	$344	$354	$356

Workload Measures

Thousands of Gallons of Billed Water per Meter

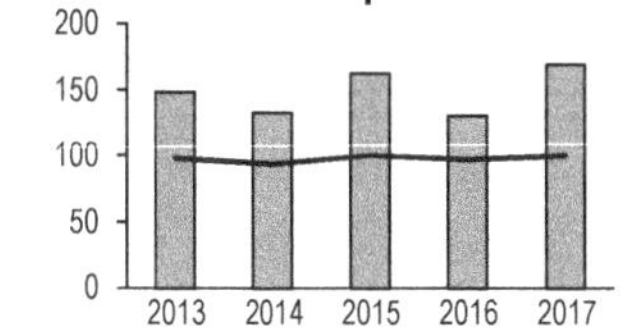

	2013	2014	2015	2016	2017
Salisbury	148.6	132.8	162.3	130.4	169.0
Average	98.2	93.9	100.5	97.3	100.0

Miles of Main Line Pipe per Square Mile of Service Area

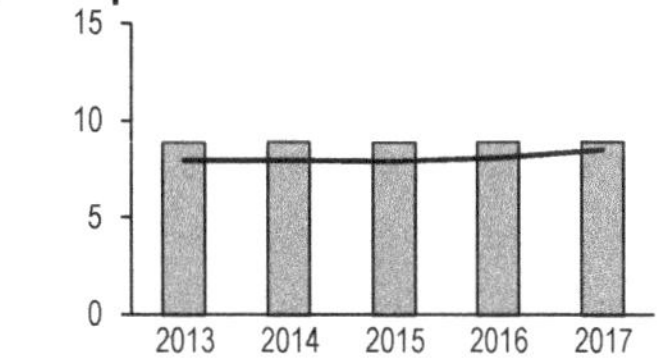

	2013	2014	2015	2016	2017
Salisbury	8.9	8.9	8.9	8.9	8.9
Average	7.9	7.9	7.9	8.1	8.5

Efficiency Measures

Total Cost per Thousand Gallons of Billed Water

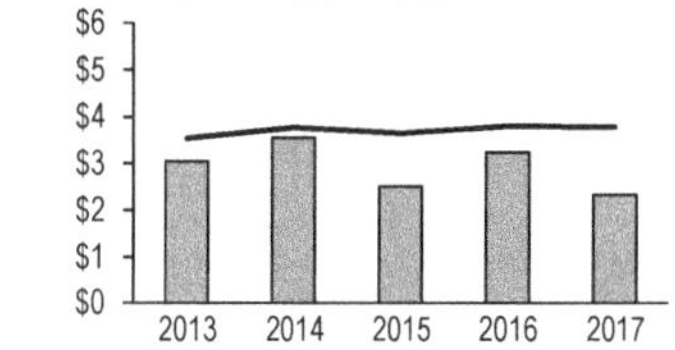

	2013	2014	2015	2016	2017
Salisbury	$3.05	$3.55	$2.51	$3.23	$2.33
Average	$3.53	$3.78	$3.64	$3.79	$3.78

Million Gallons of Billed Water per Water Services FTEs

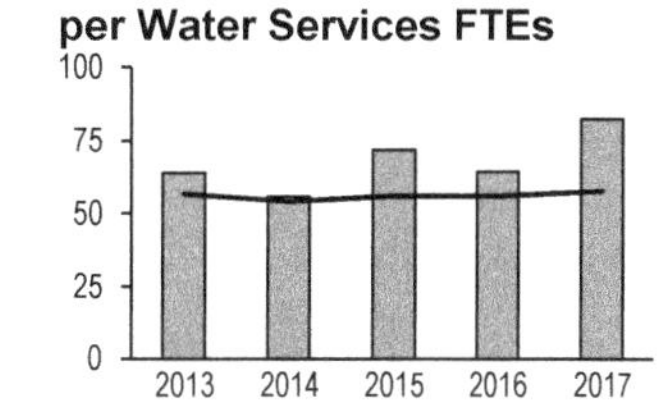

	2013	2014	2015	2016	2017
Salisbury	63.9	55.8	71.7	64.3	82.3
Average	56.8	54.3	56.2	56.2	57.8

Billed Water as a Percentage of Finished Water

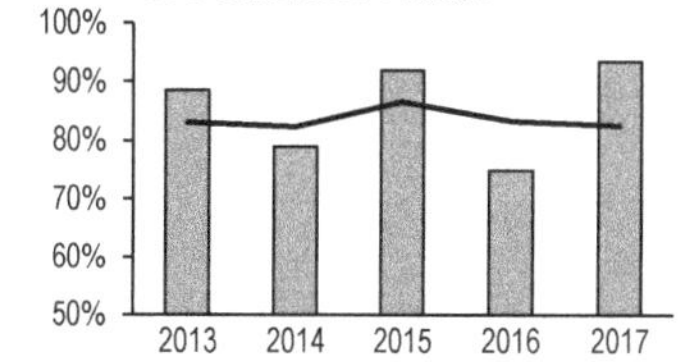

	2013	2014	2015	2016	2017
Salisbury	89%	79%	92%	75%	93%
Average	83%	82%	87%	83%	83%

Effectiveness Measures

Percentage of Existing Pipeline Replaced or Rehabbed

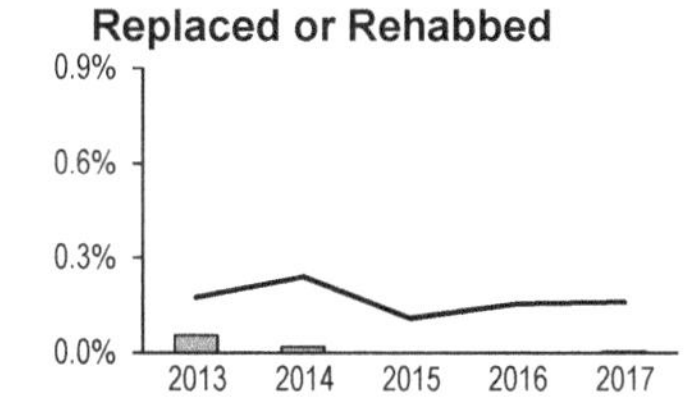

	2013	2014	2015	2016	2017
Salisbury	0.1%	0.0%	0.0%	0.0%	0.0%
Average	0.2%	0.2%	0.1%	0.2%	0.2%

Percentage of Water Bills Not Collected

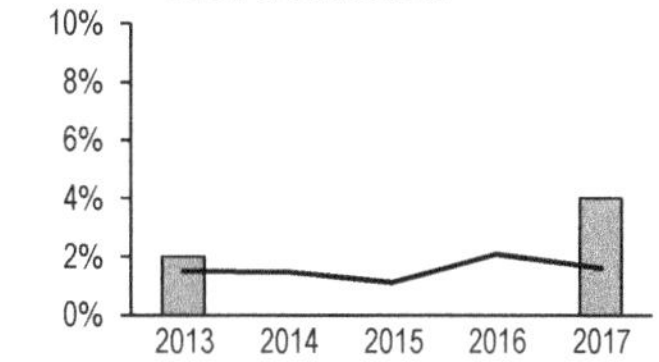

	2013	2014	2015	2016	2017
Salisbury	2.00%				4.00%
Average	1.49%	1.47%	1.12%	2.09%	1.62%

Peak Daily Demand as a Percentage of Treatment Capacity

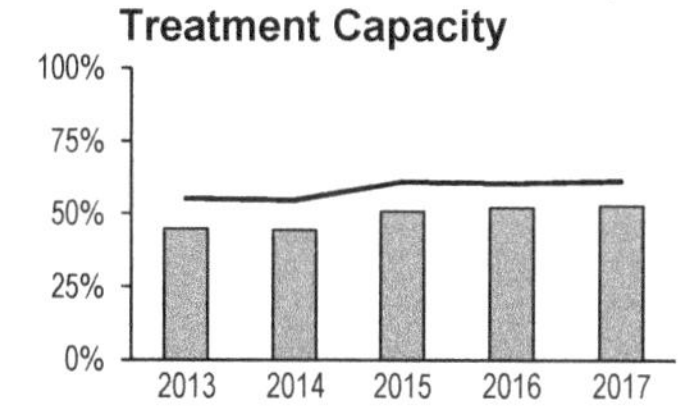

	2013	2014	2015	2016	2017
Salisbury	45%	44%	51%	52%	53%
Average	55%	55%	61%	60%	61%

Breaks and Leaks per Mile of Main Line Pipe

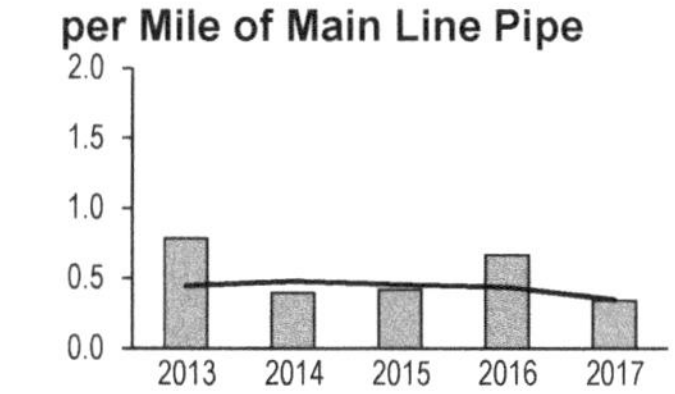

	2013	2014	2015	2016	2017
Salisbury	0.78	0.39	0.42	0.66	0.34
Average	0.45	0.48	0.45	0.44	0.35

Customer Complaints about Water Quality per 1,000 Meters

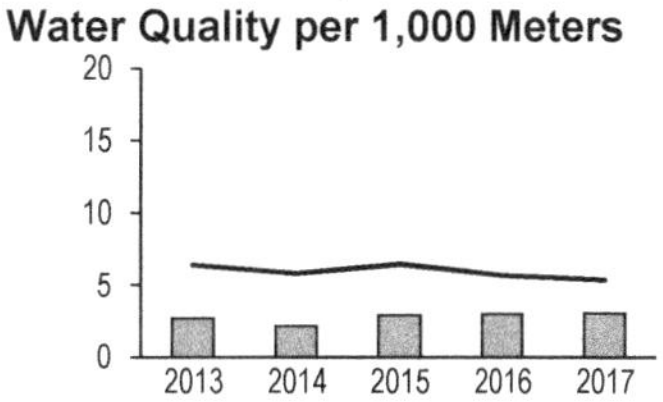

	2013	2014	2015	2016	2017
Salisbury	2.70	2.17	2.95	3.03	3.08
Average	6.37	5.83	6.45	5.70	5.37

Fiscal Year 2016–17

Explanatory Information

Service Level and Delivery

Water services in Wilson are handled by a combined water/sewer division under the Department of Public Works. Billing services are handled by the Wilson Finance Department. The water system serves approximately 52,500 people over forty square miles.

Source water for the system comes from four city-owned reservoirs. Water is also pumped from two different reservoirs in the Neuse River basin. The estimated safe yield for the system is 29 million gallons per day.

The system has two treatment plants with a combined treatment capacity of 22 million gallons per day. The plants use conventional surface water treatment with flocculation, sedimentation, and filtration.

Water meters are read once per month in Wilson. Approximately half of the water meters in the system are read by automatic remote means using a radio system by Itron.

Conditions Affecting Service, Performance, and Costs

The costs of water services as captured here do not include debt service but do capture depreciation. Large capital improvements are being made to the Buckhorn Lake Dam and Wastewater Projects, which have been required to meet advanced nutrient removal.

Due to better mapping accuracy, the reported service area decreased from 99 square miles in earlier years. The improved mapping more precisely defined which areas were in the service area and excluded broader areas that were previously included in the area calculations. This apparent jump in the miles of pipe per square mile in FY 2012–13 is a result of this improved accuracy of the area served and not due to the laying of more pipe.

Municipal Profile

Estimated Service Population	52,500
Service Land Area (Square Miles)	40.0
Persons per Square Mile	1,313
Topography	Flat; gently rolling
Climate	Temperate; little ice and snow
Median Family Income U.S. Census 2010	$43,442

Service Profile

FTE Staff Positions	
Treatment Plant	18.0
Line Crews	20.0
Meter Readers	2.0
Billing/Collection	2.0
Other	1.0
Total	43.0
Number of Treatment Plants	2
Total Treatment Capacity	22.0 MGD
Average Daily Demand	8.7 MGD
Miles of Main Line Pipe	428
Average Age of Main Line Pipe	45 years
Number of Breaks/Leaks	43
Number of Water Meters	22,386
Percent of Meters Read Automatically	50.0%
Total Revenues Collected	$12,109,000

Full Cost Profile

Cost Breakdown by Percentage	
Personal Services	28.1%
Operating Costs	48.3%
Capital Costs	23.6%
TOTAL	100.0%
Cost Breakdown in Dollars	
Personal Services	$3,148,839
Operating Costs	$5,402,149
Capital Costs	$2,644,330
TOTAL	$11,195,318

Key: Wilson ▒ Benchmarking Average — Fiscal Years 2013 through 2017

Resource Measures

Water Services Cost per Capita

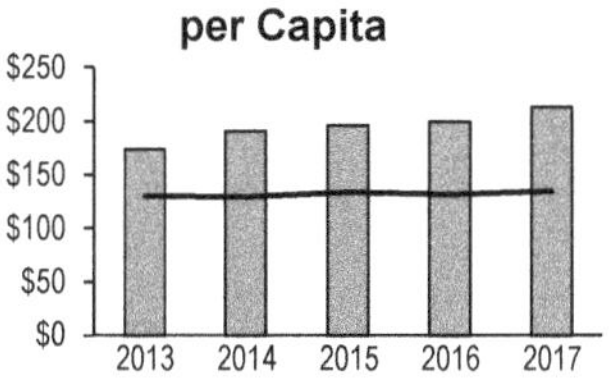

	2013	2014	2015	2016	2017
Wilson	$174	$191	$196	$200	$213
Average	$130	$129	$133	$131	$135

Water Services FTEs per 10,000 Population

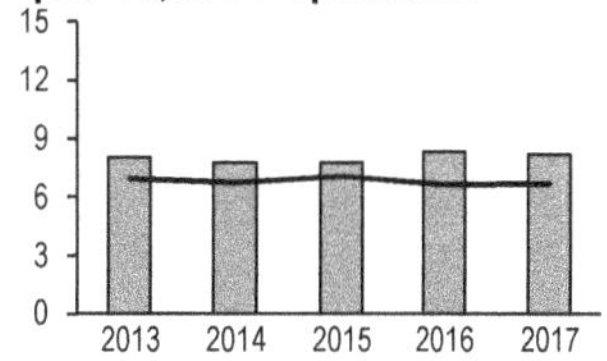

	2013	2014	2015	2016	2017
Wilson	8.0	7.8	7.8	8.3	8.2
Average	7.0	6.8	7.1	6.7	6.7

Water Services Cost per Meter

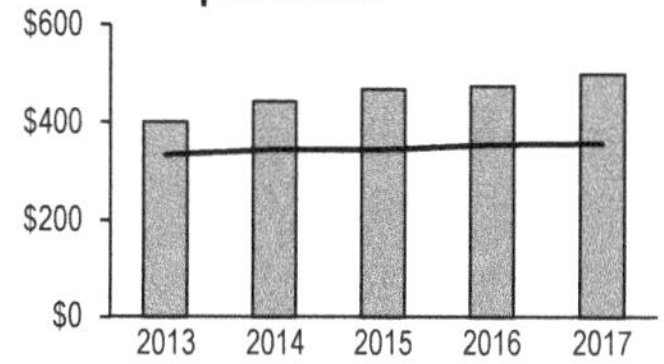

	2013	2014	2015	2016	2017
Wilson	$401	$444	$468	$475	$500
Average	$333	$344	$344	$354	$356

Workload Measures

Thousands of Gallons of Billed Water per Meter

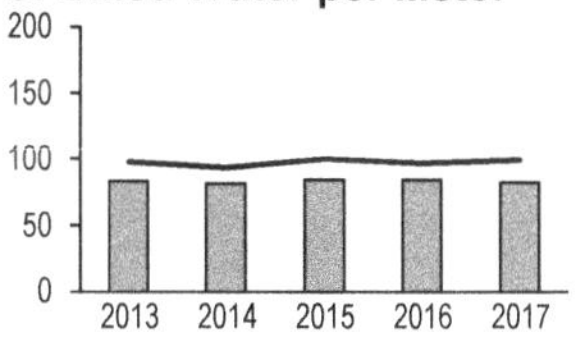

	2013	2014	2015	2016	2017
Wilson	83.1	81.6	84.2	84.1	82.2
Average	98.2	93.9	100.5	97.3	100.0

Miles of Main Line Pipe per Square Mile of Service Area

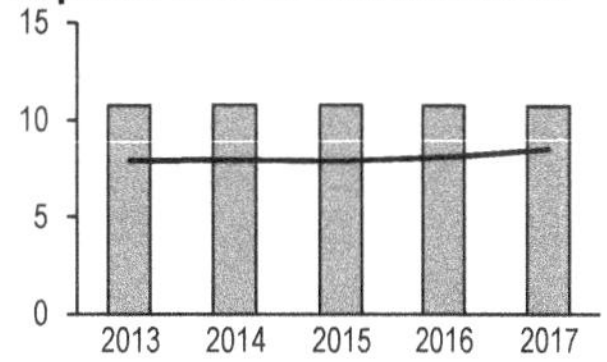

	2013	2014	2015	2016	2017
Wilson	10.7	10.8	10.8	10.7	10.7
Average	7.9	7.9	7.9	8.1	8.5

Efficiency Measures

Total Cost per Thousand Gallons of Billed Water

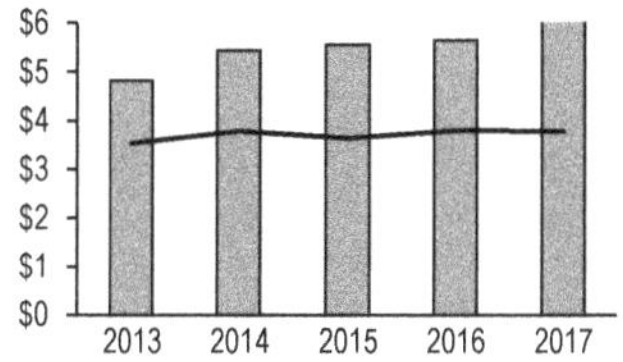

	2013	2014	2015	2016	2017
Wilson	$4.83	$5.44	$5.56	$5.65	$6.08
Average	$3.53	$3.78	$3.64	$3.79	$3.78

Million Gallons of Billed Water per Water Services FTEs

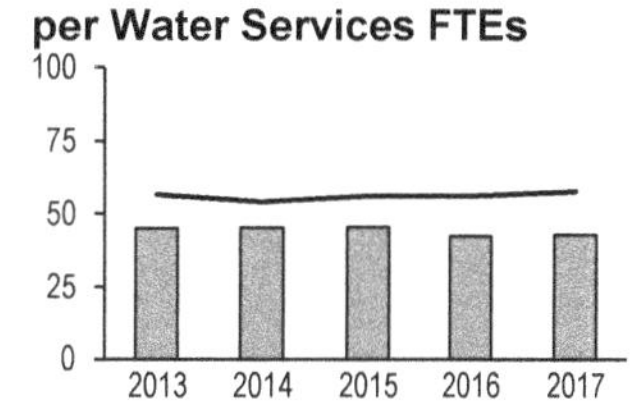

	2013	2014	2015	2016	2017
Wilson	45.0	45.3	45.5	42.4	42.8
Average	56.8	54.3	56.2	56.2	57.8

Billed Water as a Percentage of Finished Water

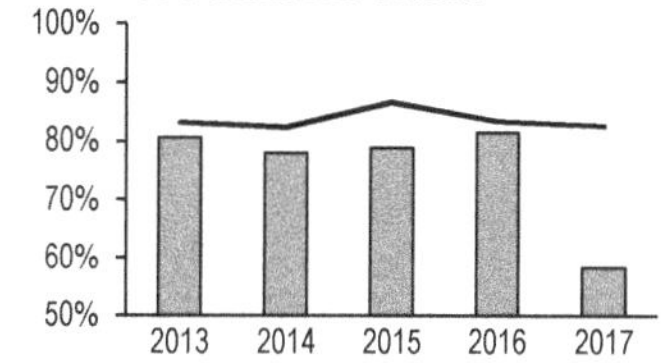

	2013	2014	2015	2016	2017
Wilson	80%	78%	79%	81%	58%
Average	83%	82%	87%	83%	83%

Effectiveness Measures

Percentage of Existing Pipeline Replaced or Rehabbed

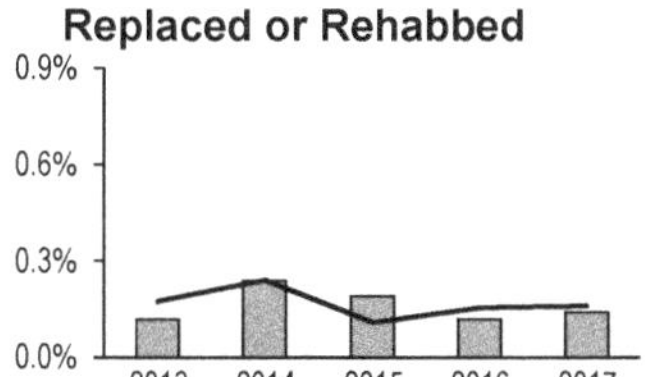

	2013	2014	2015	2016	2017
Wilson	0.1%	0.2%	0.2%	0.1%	0.1%
Average	0.2%	0.2%	0.1%	0.2%	0.2%

Percentage of Water Bills Not Collected

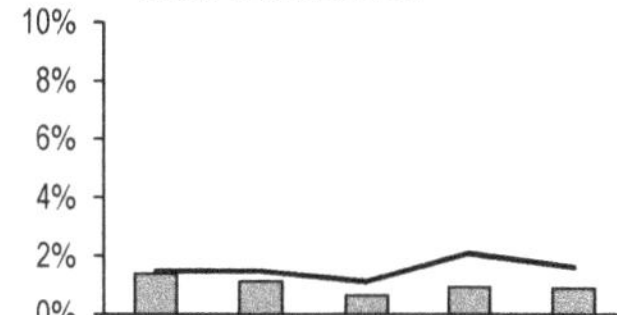

	2013	2014	2015	2016	2017
Wilson	1.39%	1.13%	0.64%	0.92%	0.89%
Average	1.49%	1.47%	1.12%	2.09%	1.62%

Peak Daily Demand as a Percentage of Treatment Capacity

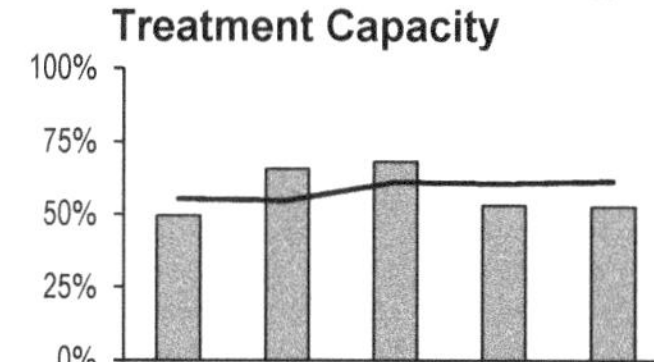

	2013	2014	2015	2016	2017
Wilson	50%	65%	68%	53%	53%
Average	55%	55%	61%	60%	61%

Breaks and Leaks per Mile of Main Line Pipe

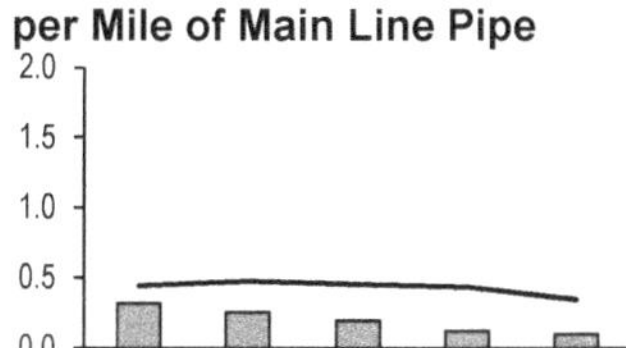

	2013	2014	2015	2016	2017
Wilson	0.32	0.25	0.19	0.12	0.10
Average	0.45	0.48	0.45	0.44	0.35

Customer Complaints about Water Quality per 1,000 Meters

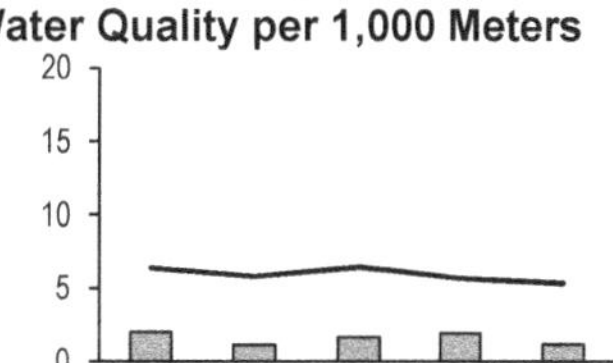

	2013	2014	2015	2016	2017
Wilson	2.03	1.17	1.66	1.94	1.21
Average	6.37	5.83	6.45	5.70	5.37

Fiscal Year 2016–17

Explanatory Information

Service Level and Delivery

The Winston-Salem and Forsyth County Utilities Division operates a combined water and sewer system that covers the city and most of the remaining population of Forsyth County. Approximately 369,000 people are served in an area covering roughly 393 square miles.

The system has an eleven-member utility commission that was created by an interlocal agreement between the City of Winston-Salem and Forsyth County. The commission sets policy for publicly owned water, wastewater, and solid waste disposal facilities. The commission is also charged with the responsibility for long-range planning, authorizing funding for projects, operation and maintenance of facilities, and setting policies and rate structures. The commission is not authorized to issue bonds to finance capital improvements.

Water sources for the system are drawn from two separate points on the Yadkin River. The city also uses Salem Lake as a water source. The estimated safe yield for the system is 100 million gallons per day.

The city uses three treatment plants with daily treatment capacity of 91 million gallons. The plants all use conventional treatment employing coagulation, flocculation, and sedimentation followed by rapid sand filtration and then chlorine treatment for disinfection.

The system has 2,323 miles of pipeline. The replacement goal for pipes is seventy-five years.

Water meters are read both monthly and bi-monthly depending on the account type. Currently the system has a small number of meters read by automatic means, totaling approximately 13 percent. The replacement standard for water meters is approximately every ten years. The goal is to have completely switched to automatically read meters within ten years.

Conditions Affecting Service, Performance, and Costs

The costs of water services as captured here do not include debt service but do capture depreciation.

Municipal Profile

Estimated Service Population	368,946
Service Land Area (Square Miles)	393.0
Persons per Square Mile	939
Topography	Gently rolling
Climate	Temperate; some ice and snow
Median Family Income U.S. Census 2010	$51,491

Service Profile

FTE Staff Positions	
Treatment Plant	53.0
Line Crews	74.0
Meter Readers	15.0
Billing/Collection	9.0
Other	20.0
Total	171.0
Number of Treatment Plants	3
Total Treatment Capacity	91.0 MGD
Average Daily Demand	35.9 MGD
Miles of Main Line Pipe	2,323
Average Age of Main Line Pipe	75 years
Number of Breaks/Leaks	476
Number of Water Meters	127,823
Percent of Meters Read Automatically	13.4%
Total Revenues Collected	$59,212,174

Full Cost Profile

Cost Breakdown by Percentage	
Personal Services	25.9%
Operating Costs	37.6%
Capital Costs	36.5%
TOTAL	100.0%
Cost Breakdown in Dollars	
Personal Services	$8,212,249
Operating Costs	$11,917,777
Capital Costs	$11,558,959
TOTAL	$31,688,985

Key: Winston-Salem ▒ Benchmarking Average — Fiscal Years 2013 through 2017

Resource Measures

Water Services Cost per Capita

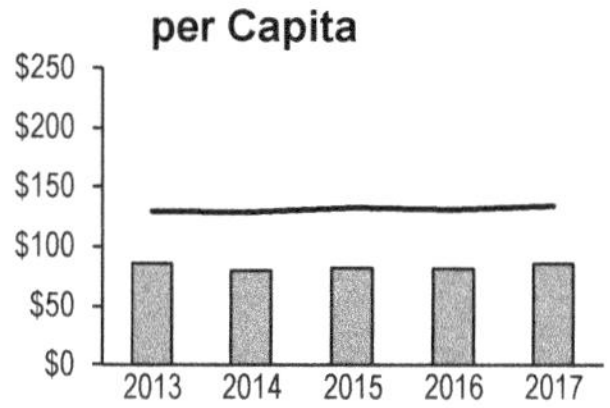

	2013	2014	2015	2016	2017
Winston-Salem	$86	$80	$82	$82	$86
Average	$130	$129	$133	$131	$135

Water Services FTEs per 10,000 Population

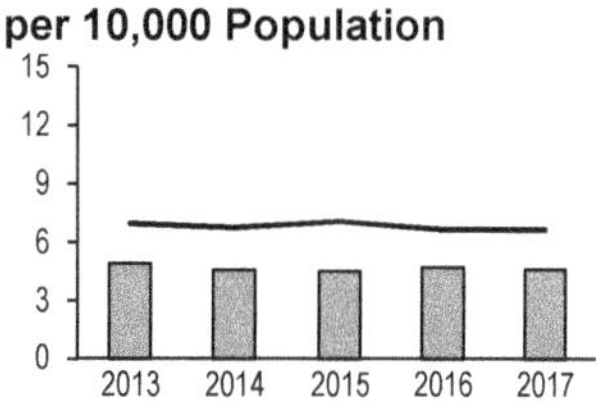

	2013	2014	2015	2016	2017
Winston-Salem	4.9	4.6	4.5	4.7	4.6
Average	7.0	6.8	7.1	6.7	6.7

Water Services Cost per Meter

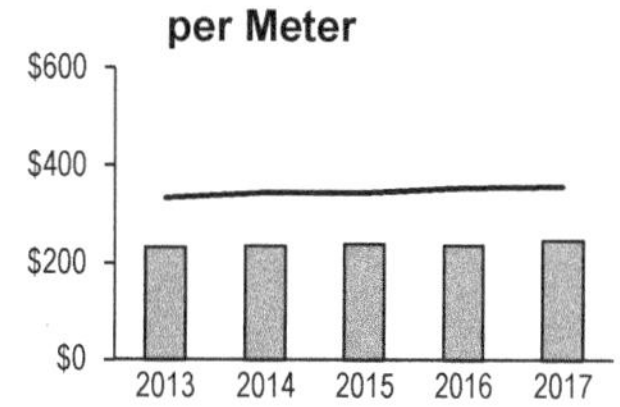

	2013	2014	2015	2016	2017
Winston-Salem	$233	$235	$240	$237	$248
Average	$333	$344	$344	$354	$356

Workload Measures

Thousands of Gallons of Billed Water per Meter

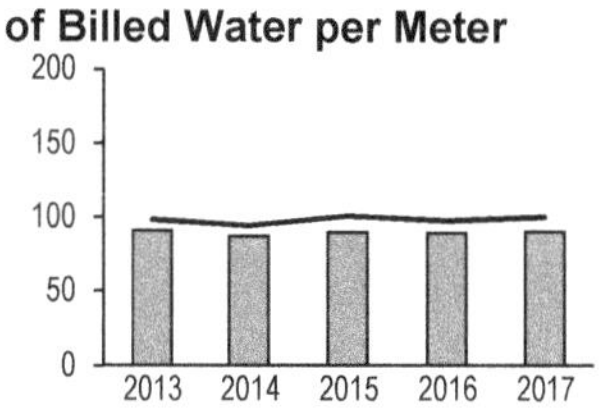

	2013	2014	2015	2016	2017
Winston-Salem	90.8	87.1	89.6	88.9	89.7
Average	98.2	93.9	100.5	97.3	100.0

Miles of Main Line Pipe per Square Mile of Service Area

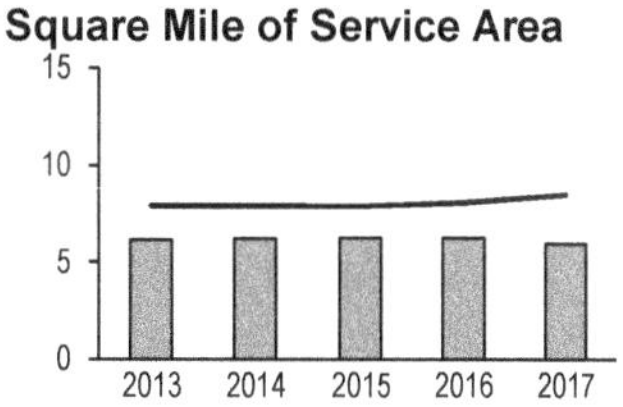

	2013	2014	2015	2016	2017
Winston-Salem	6.1	6.2	6.2	6.2	5.9
Average	7.9	7.9	7.9	8.1	8.5

Efficiency Measures

Total Cost per Thousand Gallons of Billed Water

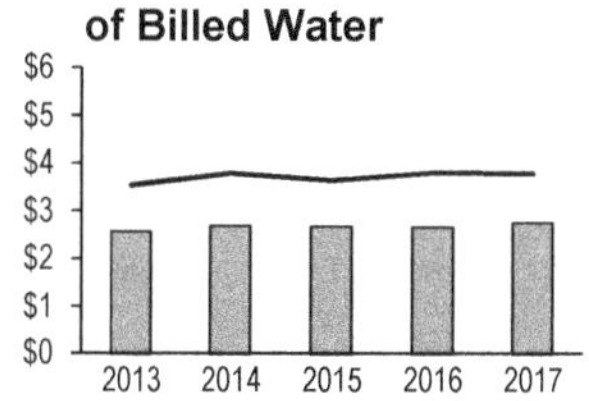

	2013	2014	2015	2016	2017
Winston-Salem	$2.57	$2.70	$2.68	$2.66	$2.76
Average	$3.53	$3.78	$3.64	$3.79	$3.78

Million Gallons of Billed Water per Water Services FTEs

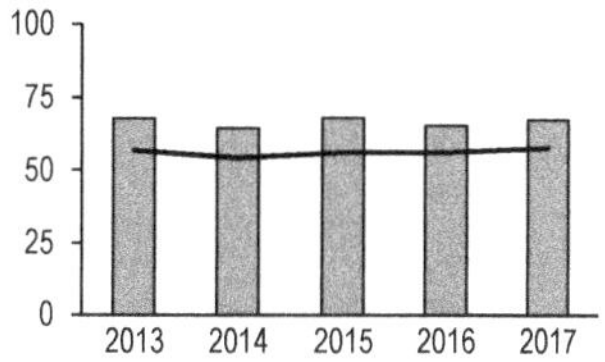

	2013	2014	2015	2016	2017
Winston-Salem	67.6	64.2	67.8	65.1	67.1
Average	56.8	54.3	56.2	56.2	57.8

Billed Water as a Percentage of Finished Water

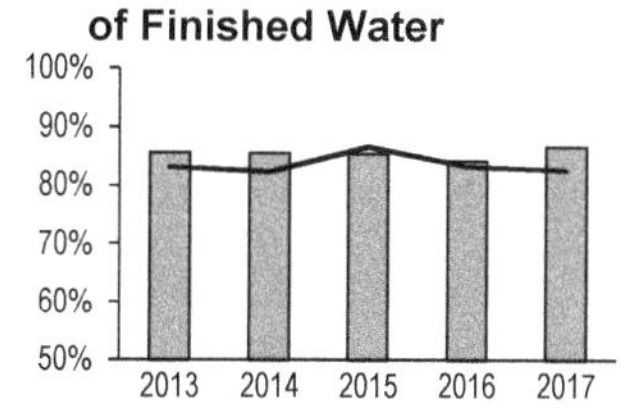

	2013	2014	2015	2016	2017
Winston-Salem	86%	86%	85%	84%	87%
Average	83%	82%	87%	83%	83%

Effectiveness Measures

Percentage of Existing Pipeline Replaced or Rehabbed

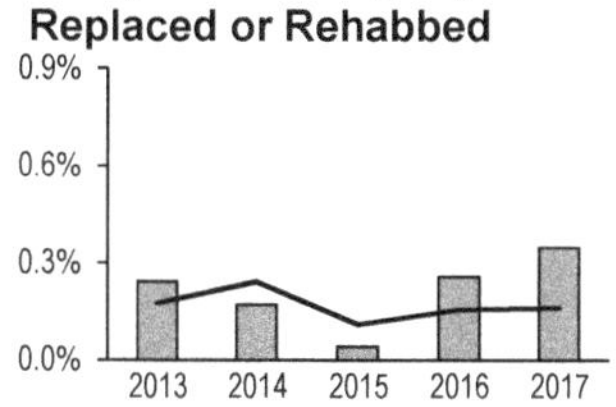

	2013	2014	2015	2016	2017
Winston-Salem	0.2%	0.2%	0.0%	0.3%	0.3%
Average	0.2%	0.2%	0.1%	0.2%	0.2%

Percentage of Water Bills Not Collected

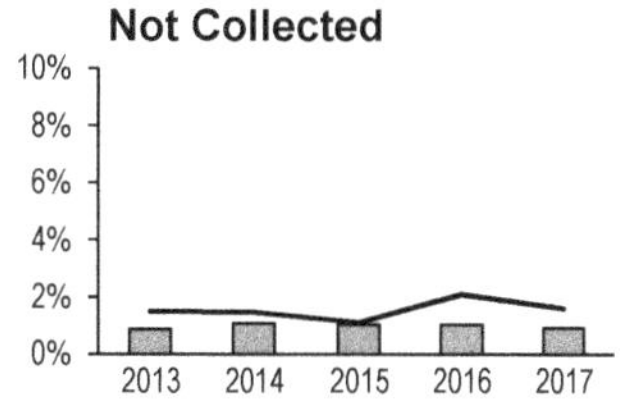

	2013	2014	2015	2016	2017
Winston-Salem	0.87%	1.08%	1.02%	1.02%	0.91%
Average	1.49%	1.47%	1.12%	2.09%	1.62%

Peak Daily Demand as a Percentage of Treatment Capacity

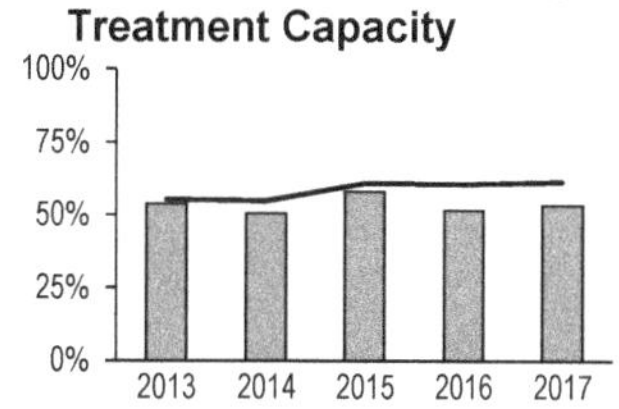

	2013	2014	2015	2016	2017
Winston-Salem	54%	50%	58%	51%	53%
Average	55%	55%	61%	60%	61%

Breaks and Leaks per Mile of Main Line Pipe

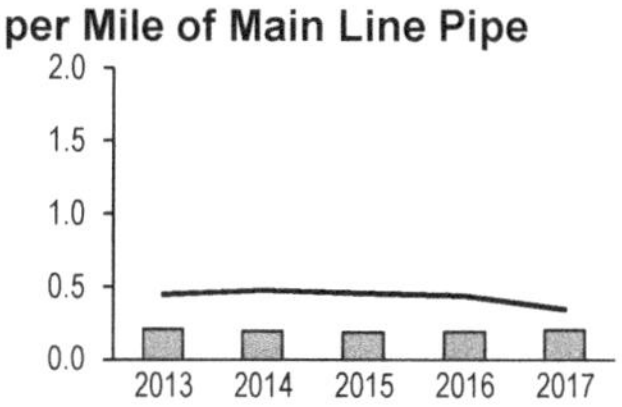

	2013	2014	2015	2016	2017
Winston-Salem	0.21	0.20	0.19	0.19	0.20
Average	0.45	0.48	0.45	0.44	0.35

Customer Complaints about Water Quality per 1,000 Meters

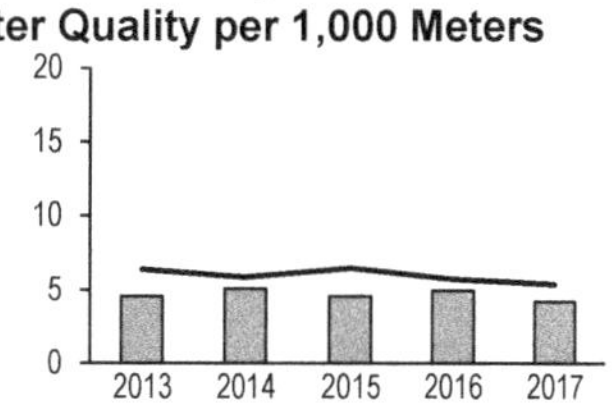

	2013	2014	2015	2016	2017
Winston-Salem	4.55	5.07	4.56	4.93	4.21
Average	6.37	5.83	6.45	5.70	5.37

SCHOOL OF GOVERNMENT
North Carolina Benchmarking Project

Performance and Cost Data

WASTEWATER SERVICES

UNC | SCHOOL OF GOVERNMENT
North Carolina Benchmarking Project

PERFORMANCE MEASURES FOR WASTEWATER SERVICES

SERVICE DEFINITION

Wastewater Services includes the collection, treatment, wastewater discharge, solids disposal, and billing related to sewer services. This service area includes the collection system after leaving the customer's outlet, lift stations, pretreatment, and treatment plants. Activities and costs include the operation, maintenance, and installation of infrastructure. Also included are costs and activities associated with billing and collection for sewer services and administrative activities such as planning, engineering, and testing. This includes wastewater treated for reuse at the plant site and for other purposes. Excluded are potable water systems and stormwater systems.

NOTES ON PERFORMANCE MEASURES

1. Volume of Sewage per Account

This workload measure captures the amount of wastewater generated and received at the treatment plant relative to the number of customers.

2. Miles of Sewer Main Line Pipe per Square Mile of Service Area

The amount of sewer main line pipe per square mile shows the density of the pipe infrastructure to be maintained relative to the geographic size of the area served.

3. Number of Lift Stations per Thousand Accounts

This workload measure provides some idea of the amount of reliance on pumping in a system to supplement gravity-fed delivery. Lift stations also generate additional maintenance workload.

4. Cost per Thousand Gallons of Collected and Treated Wastewater

This efficiency measure shows total system costs relative to the volume of wastewater reaching treatment plants. Some wastewater does not make it to treatment plants.

5. Wastewater Volume in Millions of Gallons per FTE

This efficiency measure captures the number of workers the system is using relative to the volume of wastewater treated.

6. Customer Accounts per FTE

The number of customer accounts relative to the number of workers is another efficiency measure showing how many customers are being served per worker.

7. Percentage of Bills Collected
Collection of wastewater bills sent to customers is necessary to ensure revenues for system operation. Bills not collected reflect potential lost revenue to the system, but some loss is unavoidable.

8. Average Daily Treatment as a Percent of Permitted Capacity
A wastewater system needs sufficient capacity to meet not only average demands, but also peak demands. This measure looks at average daily demand relative to the wastewater system treatment capacity in a day. Some excess capacity is needed to allow for daily service variations and also to plan for future expansion needs.

9. Percent of Existing Main Line Pipe Rehabilitated or Replaced
As the wastewater systems age, pipe needs to be replaced to ensure that service will not be interrupted. This effectiveness measure captures the amount of current stock being replaced or rehabilitated during a given year.

10. Overflows Per 100 Miles of Main Line Pipe
Sanitary system overflows may be due to blockages or breaks in pipe. Keeping these breaks to a low level is an important measure of the effectiveness of preventive maintenance and system upkeep. Overflows, if large enough, may also represent a public health concern.

11. Sewer Backups per 100 Miles of Main Line Pipe
Backups in sewer pipes are another measure of potential maintenance concerns, not to mention being a public health concern. Backups may also be a sign of insufficient maintenance.

12. Billed Sewer Effluents as a Percent of Treated Effluent
The volume of wastewater that is billed for relative to the volume received at the treatment plant is an effectiveness measure that points to potential losses in the collection system. Some loss is inevitable in sewer systems, and not all drinking water billed for is used in such a way that it should make it back to the wastewater treatment plant. But comparisons may reveal excessive infiltration or leakage.

Wastewater Services

Summary of Key Dimensions of Service

City or Town	Estimated Residential Population in Service Area	Service Area (in Square Miles)	Operating Treatment Plants	Average Daily Flow of Wastewater at Plants (in MGD)	Total Treatment Capacity for Wastewater (in MGD)	Miles of Gravity and Forced Main Lines	Number of Wastewater Accounts	Sewer System FTE Positions
Apex	49,541	22.0	1 + 1 jointly operated with Cary	2.8	9.7	263.9	16,399	24.5
Charlotte	989,410	546.0	7	78.8	123.2	4,301.5	256,297	451.0
Concord	88,815	105.7	0	NA	NA	562.8	34,897	44.0
Goldsboro	35,792	25.0	1	9.6	14.2	251.0	NA	26.0
Greensboro	285,344	148.0	2	32.6	56.0	1,492.8	101,828	152.5
Hickory	37,478	65.0	5	5.2	16.9	540.0	15,542	44.0
High Point	112,201	77.6	2	15.6	34.2	673.0	40,469	91.6
Raleigh	561,428	299.0	3	50.1	65.2	2,425.0	170,437	324.0
Salisbury	52,500	45.5	2	8.3	12.5	429.9	16,588	56.0
Wilson	53,600	35.0	1	9.0	14.0	365.0	20,441	61.0
Winston-Salem	352,025	320.0	2	32.1	51.0	1,762.3	98,300	175.0

NOTES

MGD stands for millions of gallons per day.

EXPLANATORY FACTORS

These are factors that the project found affected wastewater services performance and cost in one or more of the municipalities:

Topography
Size of service area
Population density
Age of infrastructure
Growth of population and businesses

Fiscal Year 2016–17

Explanatory Information

Service Level and Delivery

Wastewater services for the Town of Apex are managed by the Water Reclamation and Wastewater Collections Division under the Department of Public Works. The system covers the area within the municipal limits.

Apex has one treatment plant, which uses bar screens, grit removal, biological nutrient removal (BNR), oxidation ditches, secondary clarifiers, sand filters, ultraviolet disinfection, aerobic sludge digestion, and rotary drum sludge dewatering as part of its treatment process. The Apex wastewater system has nutrient limits in place which restrict what can be discharged from the plant to protect water quality. Apex uses land application for biosolids resulting from treatment and also dries some biosolids as fertilizer pellets. Apex also pays for one-third of the operation of a separate treatment plant which is jointly owned with the Town of Cary.

The town's system had no regulatory violations for the fiscal year.

Conditions Affecting Service, Performance, and Costs

The costs of wastewater or sewer services as captured here do not include debt service but do capture depreciation of capital.

Municipal Profile

Estimated Service Population	49,541
Service Land Area (Square Miles)	22.0
Persons per Square Mile	2,252
Topography	Flat; gently rolling
Climate	Temperate; little ice and snow
Median Family Income U.S. Census 2010	$97,201

Service Profile

Total FTE Staff Positions	24.5
Treatment Plant	7.5
Line Crews	13.0
Billing/Collection	2.0
Other	2.0
Number of Treatment Plants	2
Total Treatment Capacity	9.7 MGD
Average Daily Flow	2.8 MGD
River Basin into Which System Discharges	Neuse
Miles of Gravity Main Line Pipe	224
Miles of Forced Main Line Pipe	40
Average Age of Main Line Pipe	16 years
Blocks in Sewer Mains	59
Number of System Breaks	31
Sanitary System Overflows	0
Number of Customer Accounts	16,399
Total Revenues Collected	$13,863,093

Full Cost Profile

Cost Breakdown by Percentage	
Personal Services	17.8%
Operating Costs	40.2%
Capital Costs	42.0%
TOTAL	100.0%
Cost Breakdown in Dollars	
Personal Services	$1,537,155
Operating Costs	$3,476,936
Capital Costs	$3,631,459
TOTAL	$8,645,550

Key: Apex ▒ Benchmarking Average — Fiscal Years 2013 through 2017

Resource Measures

Wastewater Services Cost per Capita

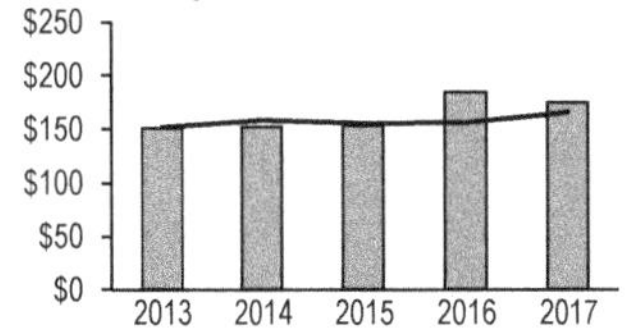

	2013	2014	2015	2016	2017
Apex	$151	$152	$153	$184	$175
Average	$152	$159	$156	$157	$166

Waterwater Services FTEs per 10,000 Population

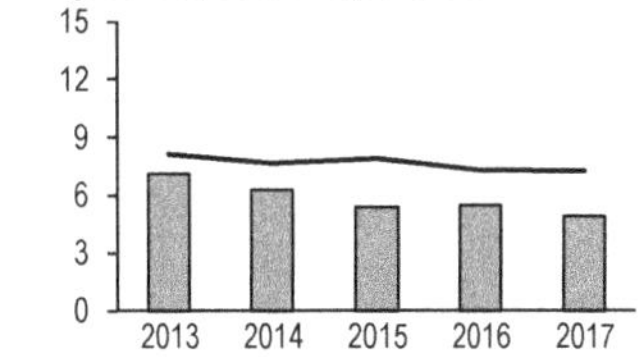

	2013	2014	2015	2016	2017
Apex	7.1	6.3	5.4	5.5	4.9
Average	8.1	7.7	7.9	7.3	7.3

Waterwaste Services Cost per Customer Account

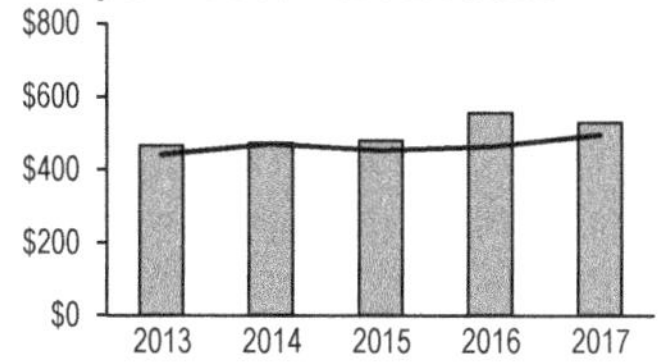

	2013	2014	2015	2016	2017
Apex	$464	$471	$479	$554	$527
Average	$440	$470	$452	$463	$494

Workload Measures

Thousands of Gallons of Wastewater per Account

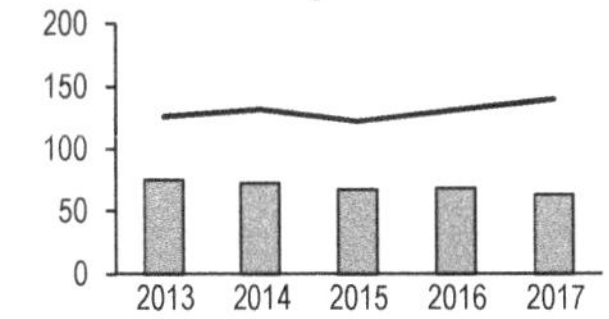

	2013	2014	2015	2016	2017
Apex	75.0	72.8	67.6	68.6	63.6
Average	125.7	131.5	122.1	130.9	139.8

Miles of Sewer Main Line Pipe per Square Mile of Service Area

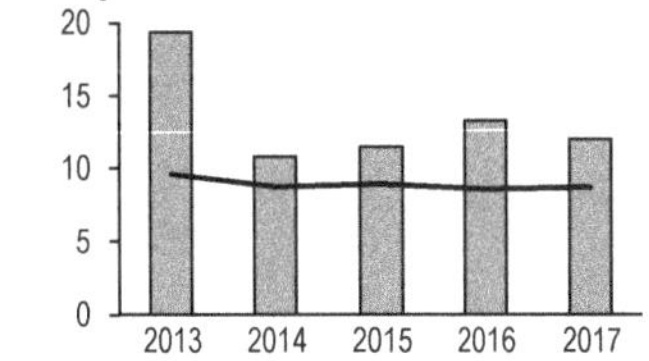

	2013	2014	2015	2016	2017
Apex	19.3	10.8	11.5	13.3	12.0
Average	9.6	8.8	8.9	8.6	8.7

Number of Lift Stations per 1,000 Accounts

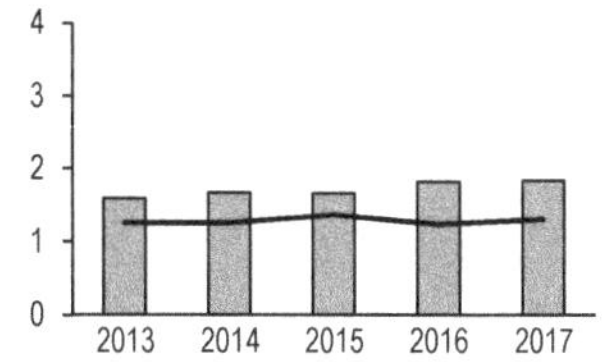

	2013	2014	2015	2016	2017
Apex	1.59	1.66	1.66	1.82	1.83
Average	1.25	1.26	1.37	1.23	1.31

Efficiency Measures

Total Cost per 1,000 Gallons of Treated Wastewater

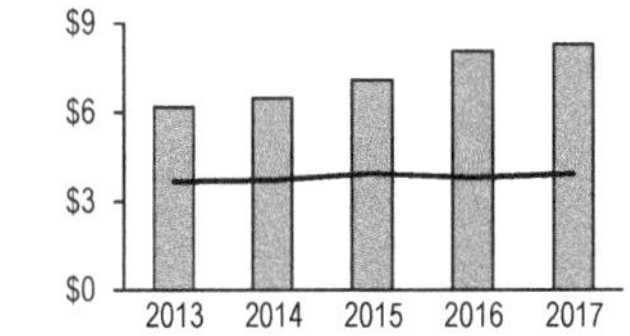

	2013	2014	2015	2016	2017
Apex	$6.19	$6.47	$7.09	$8.07	$8.29
Average	$3.67	$3.71	$3.94	$3.80	$3.92

Million Gallons of Wastewater per Wastewater Services FTE

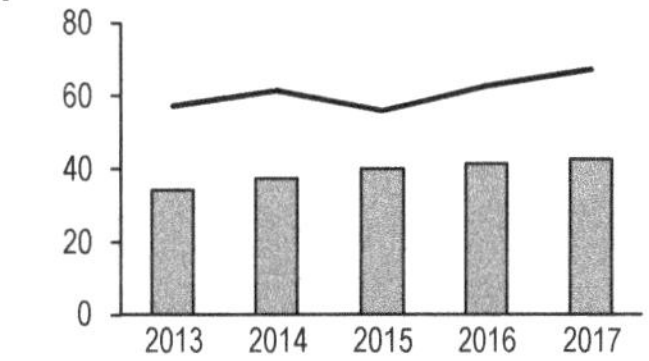

	2013	2014	2015	2016	2017
Apex	34.3	37.3	39.9	41.5	42.6
Average	57.2	61.4	55.9	62.6	67.2

Customer Accounts per Wastewater Services FTE

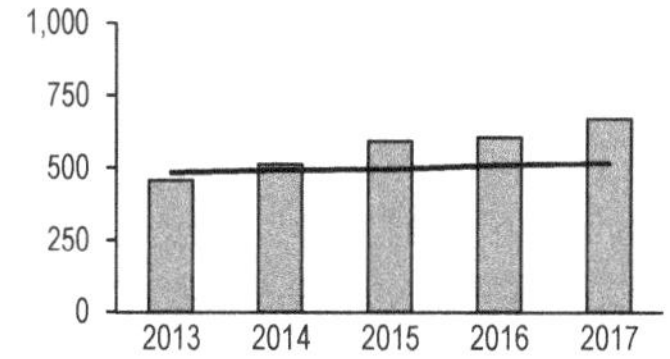

	2013	2014	2015	2016	2017
Apex	457	513	591	605	669
Average	483	491	494	510	515

Effectiveness Measures

Percentage of Wastewater Bills Not Collected

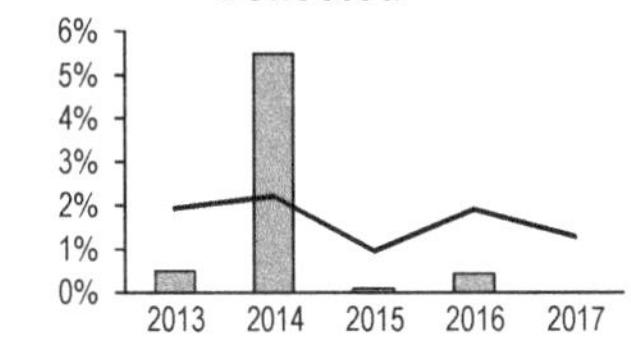

	2013	2014	2015	2016	2017
Apex	0.50%	5.48%	0.10%	0.44%	0.00%
Average	1.93%	2.21%	0.96%	1.90%	1.29%

Average Daily Treatment as a Percentage of Capacity

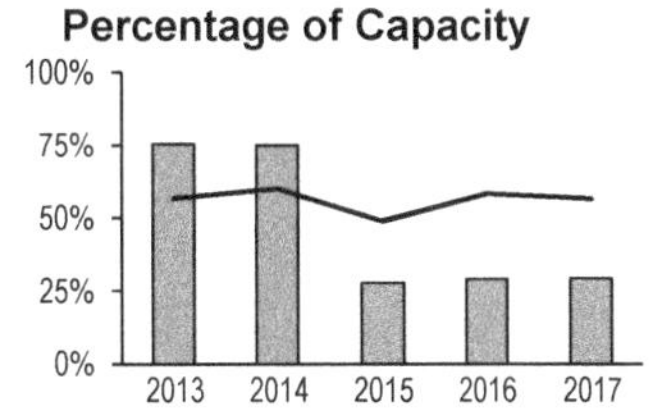

	2013	2014	2015	2016	2017
Apex	75.6%	75.0%	27.6%	29.1%	29.3%
Average	56.6%	60.0%	48.9%	58.1%	56.5%

Percent of Main Line Rehabbed or Replaced

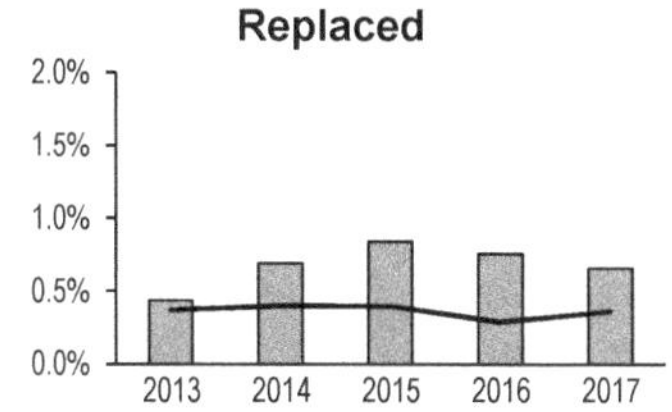

	2013	2014	2015	2016	2017
Apex	0.44%	0.69%	0.84%	0.76%	0.65%
Average	0.37%	0.40%	0.40%	0.29%	0.36%

Overflows per 100 Miles of Main Line Pipe

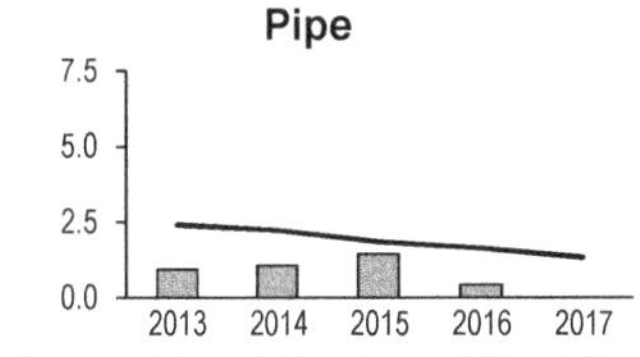

	2013	2014	2015	2016	2017
Apex	0.94	1.06	1.45	0.42	0.00
Average	2.41	2.23	1.85	1.64	1.33

Backups per 100 Miles of Main Line Pipe

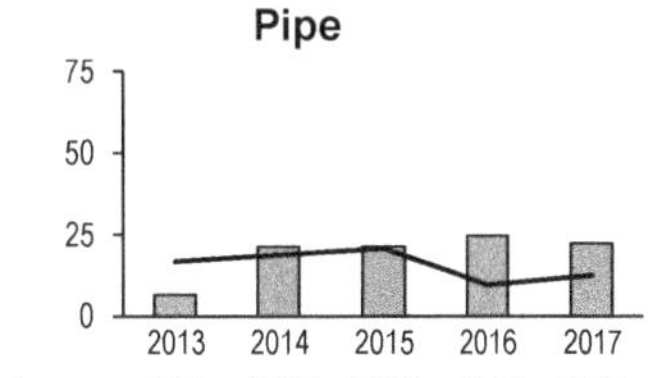

	2013	2014	2015	2016	2017
Apex	6.61	21.25	21.33	24.64	22.36
Average	16.84	18.71	20.70	9.52	12.45

Billed Wastewater as a Percent of Treated Effluent

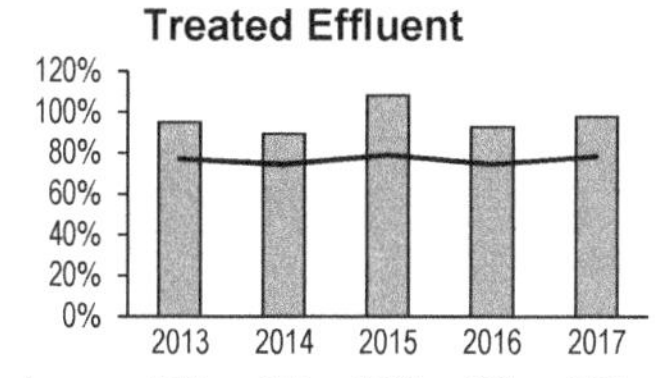

	2013	2014	2015	2016	2017
Apex	95%	90%	108%	93%	98%
Average	77%	74%	79%	75%	78%

Fiscal Year 2016–17

Explanatory Information

Service Level and Delivery

Wastewater collection and treatment is handled by Charlotte Water (CLTWater). This is a combined water and sewer utility which is a consolidated business unit for Mecklenburg County and the City of Charlotte. The department is run as an official City of Charlotte department. The service area corresponds roughly to the boundaries of Mecklenburg County.

There are seven wastewater treatment plants owned and operated by Charlotte Water. Each of CLTWater's treatment plants applies primary, secondary, and advanced treatment to the waste stream. The system does have regulatory limits in place on nutrient loads, which can be discharged in order to protect water quality. In addition to the treatment of wastewater, the system handles biosolids, most of which are applied to land (unless non-conforming) and then are taken to the landfill.

The system had one regulatory violation connected to treatment issues and 103 regulatory violations connected to the collection portion of the system during the year, all involving sanitary system overflows.

Conditions Affecting Service, Performance, and Costs

Charlotte did not participate in the Benchmarking Project during FY 2014–15. No data are available for that year.

The costs of wastewater or sewer services as captured here do not include debt service but do capture depreciation of capital.

Municipal Profile

Estimated Service Population	989,410
Service Land Area (Square Miles)	546
Persons per Square Mile	1,812
Topography	Flat; gently rolling
Climate	Temperate; little ice and snow
Median Family Income U.S. Census 2010	$61,405

Service Profile

Total FTE Staff Positions	451.0
Treatment Plant	125.0
Line Crews	152.0
Billing/Collection	12.0
Other	162.0
Number of Treatment Plants	7
Total Treatment Capacity	123.2 MGD
Average Daily Flow	78.8 MGD
River Basin into Which System Discharges	Cabarrus & Yadkin
Miles of Gravity Main Line Pipe	4,167
Miles of Forced Main Line Pipe	135
Average Age of Main Line Pipe	32 years
Blocks in Sewer Mains	137
Number of System Breaks	308
Sanitary System Overflows	103
Number of Customer Accounts	256,297
Total Revenues Collected	$235,176,309

Full Cost Profile

Cost Breakdown by Percentage	
Personal Services	18.1%
Operating Costs	34.3%
Capital Costs	47.7%
TOTAL	100.0%
Cost Breakdown in Dollars	
Personal Services	$29,137,634
Operating Costs	$55,350,994
Capital Costs	$76,906,891
TOTAL	$161,395,519

Key: Charlotte ▒ Benchmarking Average — Fiscal Years 2013 through 2017

Resource Measures

Wastewater Services Cost per Capita

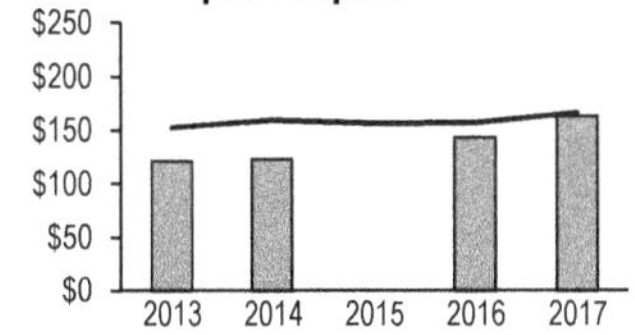

	2013	2014	2015	2016	2017
Charlotte	$121	$123		$144	$163
Average	$152	$159	$156	$157	$166

Waterwater Services FTEs per 10,000 Population

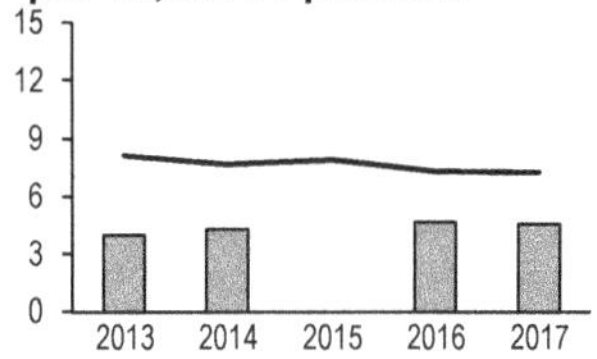

	2013	2014	2015	2016	2017
Charlotte	4.0	4.3		4.7	4.6
Average	8.1	7.7	7.9	7.3	7.3

Waterwaste Services Cost per Customer Account

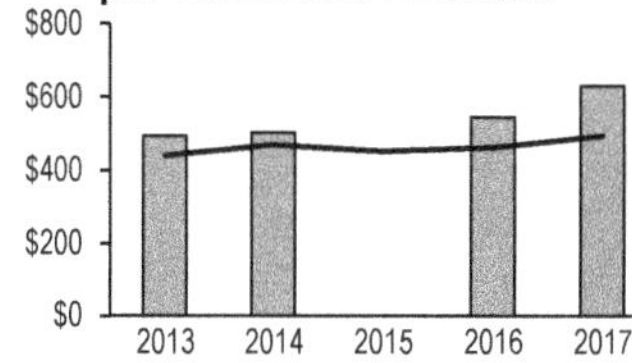

	2013	2014	2015	2016	2017
Charlotte	$492	$502		$544	$630
Average	$440	$470	$452	$463	$494

Workload Measures

Thousands of Gallons of Wastewater per Account

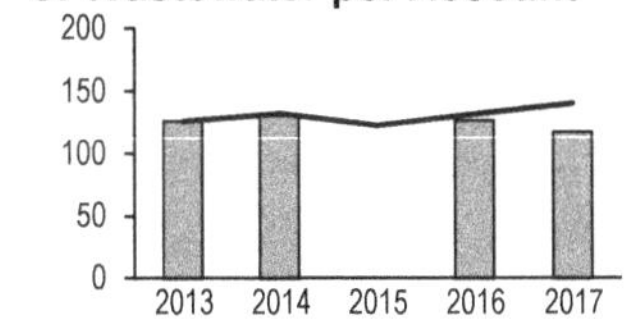

	2013	2014	2015	2016	2017
Charlotte	125.7	130.6		126.6	117.5
Average	125.7	131.5	122.1	130.9	139.8

Miles of Sewer Main Line Pipe per Square Mile of Service Area

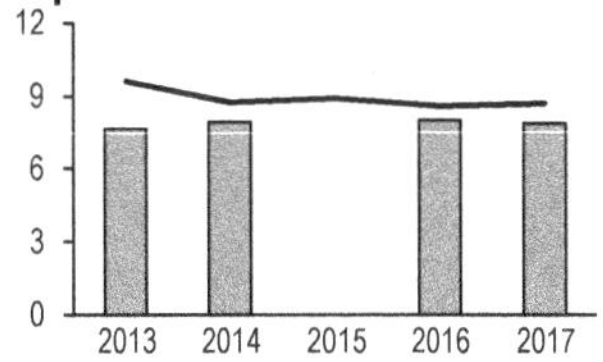

	2013	2014	2015	2016	2017
Charlotte	7.6	7.9		8.0	7.9
Average	9.6	8.8	8.9	8.6	8.7

Number of Lift Stations per 1,000 Accounts

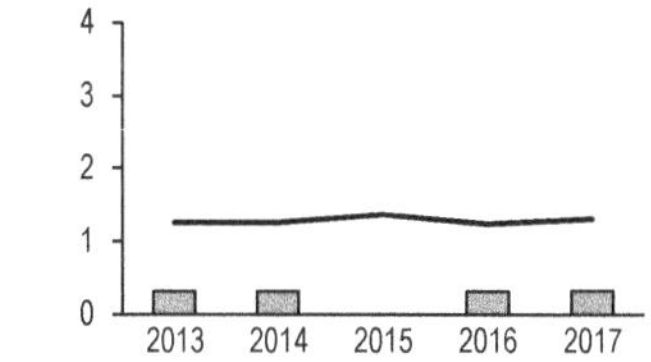

	2013	2014	2015	2016	2017
Charlotte	0.31	0.31		0.32	0.32
Average	1.25	1.26	1.37	1.23	1.31

Efficiency Measures

Total Cost per 1,000 Gallons of Treated Wastewater

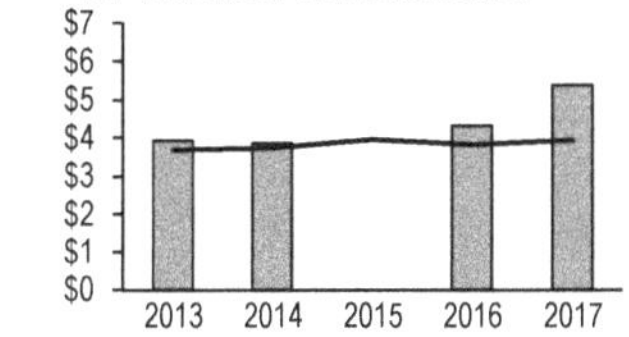

	2013	2014	2015	2016	2017
Charlotte	$3.91	$3.84		$4.30	$5.36
Average	$3.67	$3.71	$3.94	$3.80	$3.92

Million Gallons of Wastewater per Wastewater Services FTE

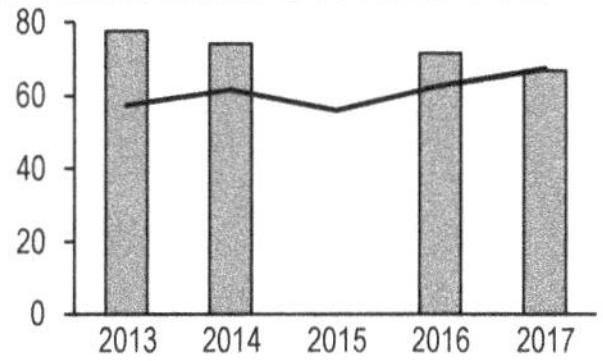

	2013	2014	2015	2016	2017
Charlotte	77.6	74.1		71.5	66.8
Average	57.2	61.4	55.9	62.6	67.2

Customer Accounts per Wastewater Services FTE

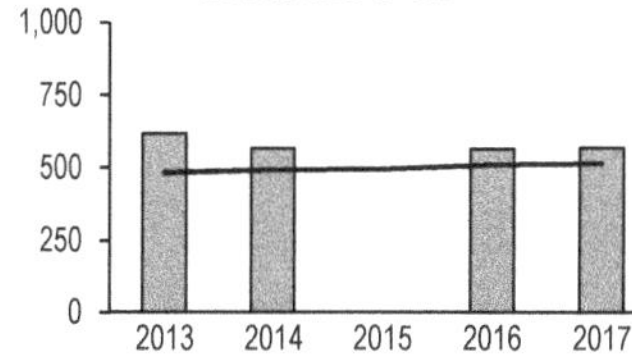

	2013	2014	2015	2016	2017
Charlotte	617	568		565	568
Average	483	491	494	510	515

Effectiveness Measures

Percentage of Wastewater Bills Not Collected

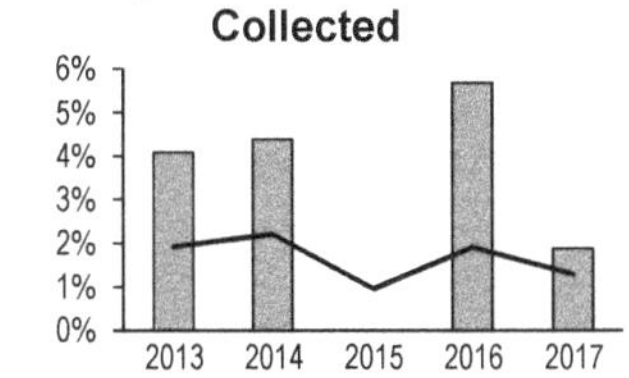

	2013	2014	2015	2016	2017
Charlotte	4.09%	4.38%		5.67%	1.88%
Average	1.93%	2.21%	0.96%	1.90%	1.29%

Average Daily Treatment as a Percentage of Capacity

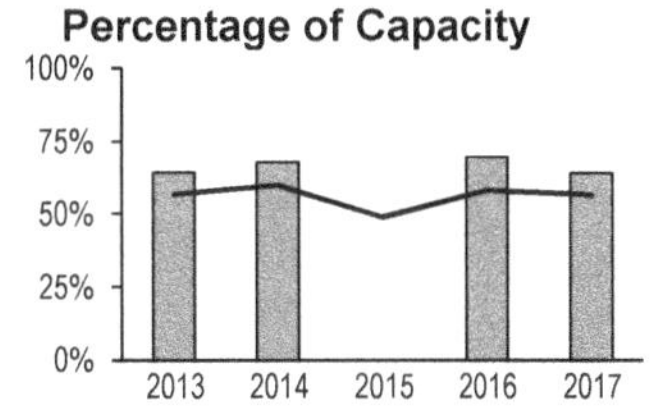

	2013	2014	2015	2016	2017
Charlotte	64.1%	67.6%		69.4%	64.0%
Average	56.6%	60.0%	48.9%	58.1%	56.5%

Percent of Main Line Rehabbed or Replaced

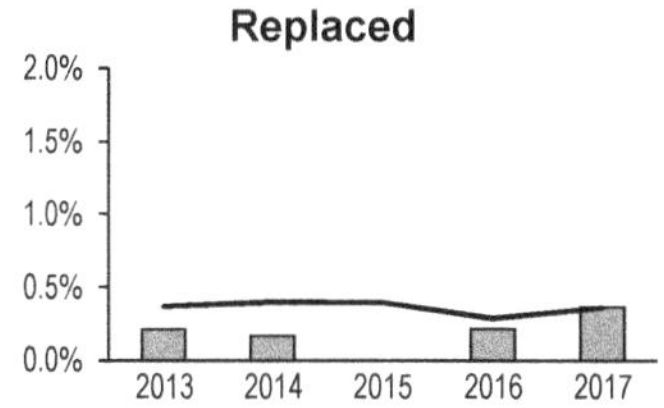

	2013	2014	2015	2016	2017
Charlotte	0.21%	0.17%		0.22%	0.37%
Average	0.37%	0.40%	0.40%	0.29%	0.36%

Overflows per 100 Miles of Main Line Pipe

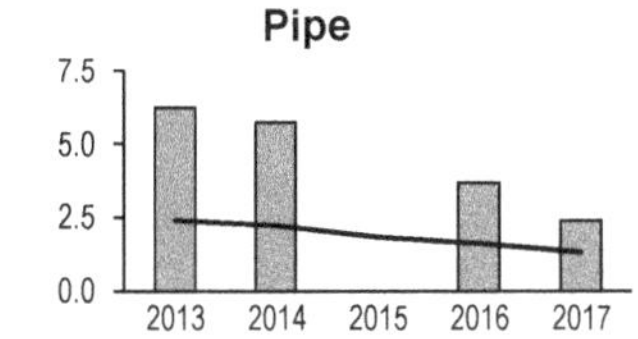

	2013	2014	2015	2016	2017
Charlotte	6.24	5.72		3.67	2.39
Average	2.41	2.23	1.85	1.64	1.33

Backups per 100 Miles of Main Line Pipe

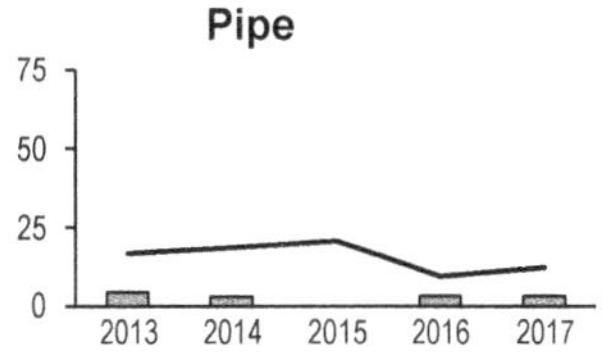

	2013	2014	2015	2016	2017
Charlotte	4.51	3.08		3.25	3.18
Average	16.84	18.71	20.70	9.52	12.45

Billed Wastewater as a Percent of Treated Effluent

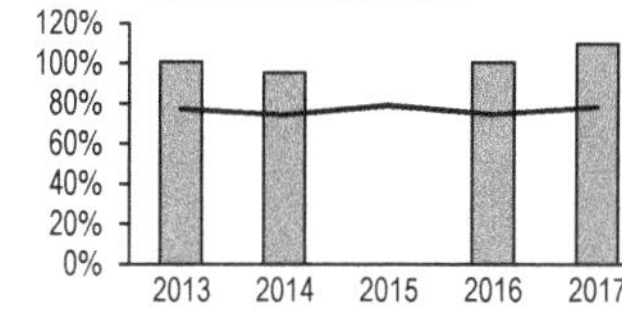

	2013	2014	2015	2016	2017
Charlotte	101%	95%		100%	110%
Average	77%	74%	79%	75%	78%

Concord

Wastewater Services

Fiscal Year 2016–17

Explanatory Information

Service Level and Delivery

The City of Concord has a wastewater department that focuses on the inspection, maintenance, and repair of the wastewater collection system. Concord does not have its own treatment plant, making it unique among the benchmarking partner cities. Instead, treatment is handled by the Water and Sewer Authority of Cabarrus County, a regional sytem. All treatment and disposal of wastewater and biosolids are handled by the regional authority using two treatment plants.

The Concord wastewater collection system had three violations on the collection portion of the system involving sanitary system overflows.

Conditions Affecting Service, Performance, and Costs

The costs of wastewater or sewer services as captured here do not include debt service but do capture depreciation of capital.

Municipal Profile

Estimated Service Population	88,815
Service Land Area (Square Miles)	105.7
Persons per Square Mile	840
Topography	Flat; gently rolling
Climate	Temperate; little ice and snow
Median Family Income U.S. Census 2010	$63,643

Service Profile

Total FTE Staff Positions	44.0
Treatment Plant	NA
Line Crews	27.0
Billing/Collection	13.0
Other	4.0
Number of Treatment Plants	0
Total Treatment Capacity	NA
Average Daily Flow	NA
River Basin into Which System Discharges	Yadkin-Pee Dee
Miles of Gravity Main Line Pipe	550
Miles of Forced Main Line Pipe	13
Average Age of Main Line Pipe	40 years
Blocks in Sewer Mains	3
Number of System Breaks	16
Sanitary System Overflows	8
Number of Customer Accounts	34,897
Total Revenues Collected	$16,481,555

Full Cost Profile

Cost Breakdown by Percentage	
Personal Services	17.2%
Operating Costs	60.4%
Capital Costs	22.4%
TOTAL	100.0%
Cost Breakdown in Dollars	
Personal Services	$2,373,521
Operating Costs	$8,322,689
Capital Costs	$3,091,811
TOTAL	$13,788,021

Concord — Wastewater Services

Key: Concord ▒ Benchmarking Average — Fiscal Years 2013 through 2017

Resource Measures

Wastewater Services Cost per Capita

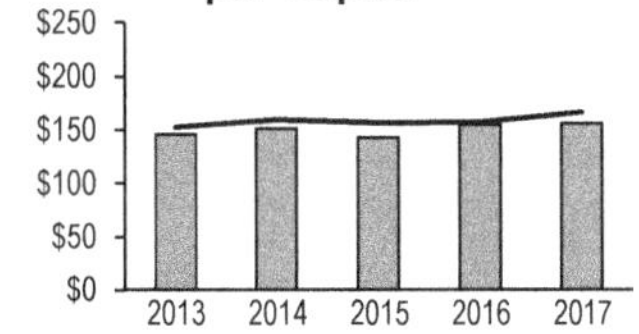

	2013	2014	2015	2016	2017
Concord	$145	$151	$142	$155	$155
Average	$152	$159	$156	$157	$166

Waterwater Services FTEs per 10,000 Population

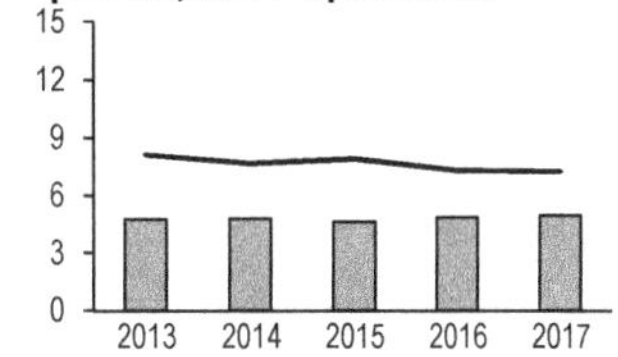

	2013	2014	2015	2016	2017
Concord	4.7	4.8	4.6	4.8	5.0
Average	8.1	7.7	7.9	7.3	7.3

Waterwaste Services Cost per Customer Account

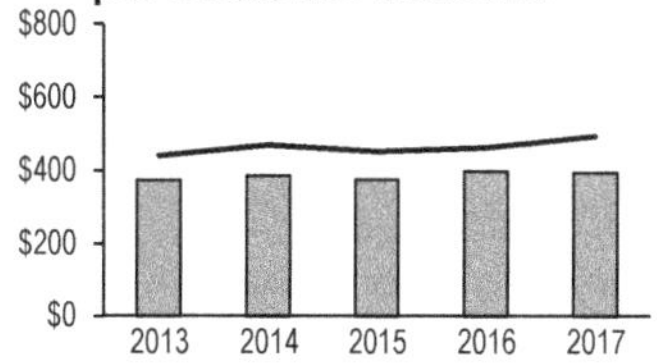

	2013	2014	2015	2016	2017
Concord	$374	$386	$375	$398	$395
Average	$440	$470	$452	$463	$494

Workload Measures

Thousands of Gallons of Wastewater per Account

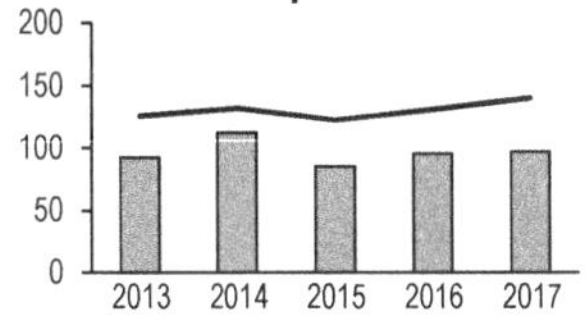

	2013	2014	2015	2016	2017
Concord	91.8	112.0	84.8	95.0	96.3
Average	125.7	131.5	122.1	130.9	139.8

Miles of Sewer Main Line Pipe per Square Mile of Service Area

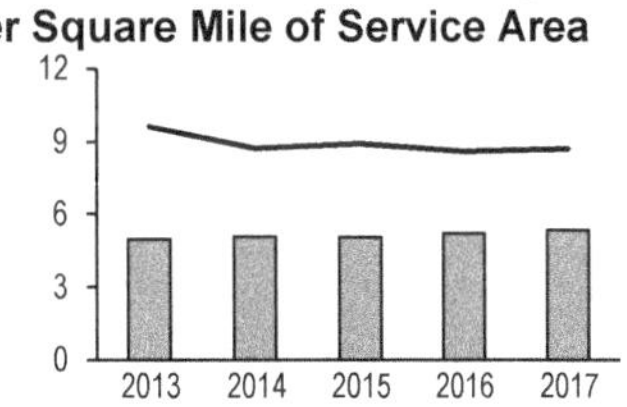

	2013	2014	2015	2016	2017
Concord	5.0	5.0	5.0	5.2	5.3
Average	9.6	8.8	8.9	8.6	8.7

Number of Lift Stations per 1,000 Accounts

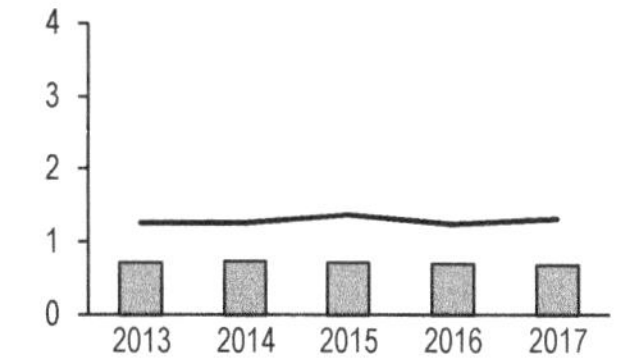

	2013	2014	2015	2016	2017
Concord	0.72	0.74	0.72	0.70	0.69
Average	1.25	1.26	1.37	1.23	1.31

Efficiency Measures

Total Cost per 1,000 Gallons of Treated Wastewater

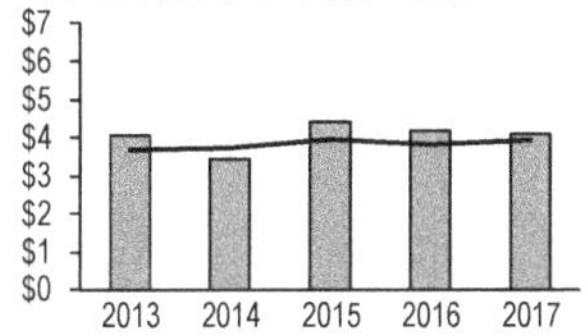

	2013	2014	2015	2016	2017
Concord	$4.08	$3.44	$4.43	$4.19	$4.10
Average	$3.67	$3.71	$3.94	$3.80	$3.92

Million Gallons of Wastewater per Wastewater Services FTE

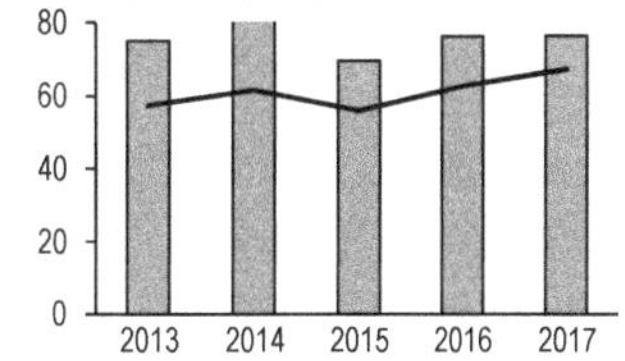

	2013	2014	2015	2016	2017
Concord	75.0	91.3	69.6	76.2	76.4
Average	57.2	61.4	55.9	62.6	67.2

Customer Accounts per Wastewater Services FTE

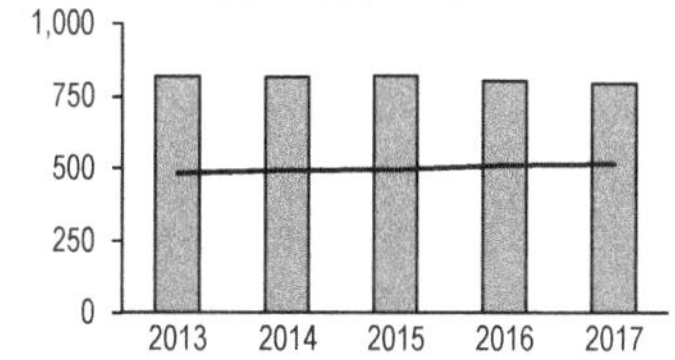

	2013	2014	2015	2016	2017
Concord	817	815	820	802	793
Average	483	491	494	510	515

Effectiveness Measures

Percentage of Wastewater Bills Not Collected

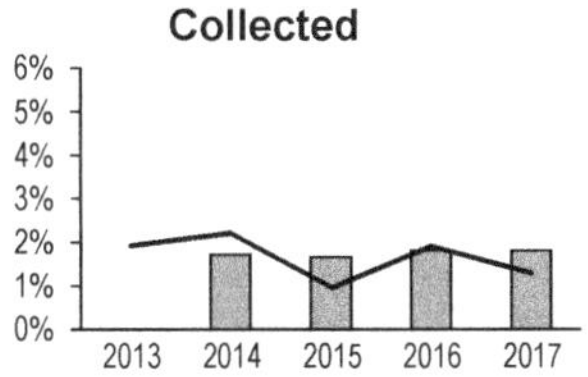

	2013	2014	2015	2016	2017
Concord		1.72%	1.65%	1.81%	1.81%
Average	1.93%	2.21%	0.96%	1.90%	1.29%

Average Daily Treatment as a Percentage of Capacity

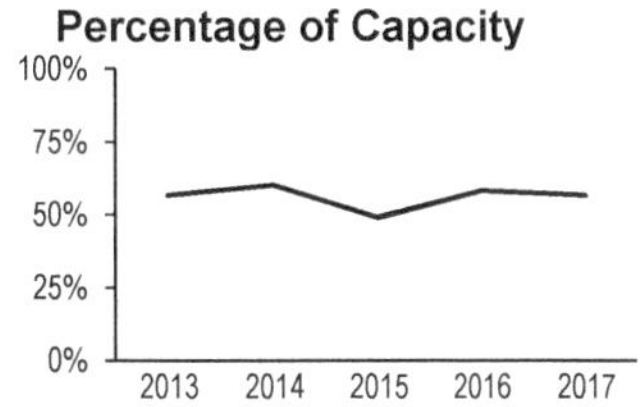

	2013	2014	2015	2016	2017
Concord					
Average	56.6%	60.0%	48.9%	58.1%	56.5%

Percent of Main Line Rehabbed or Replaced

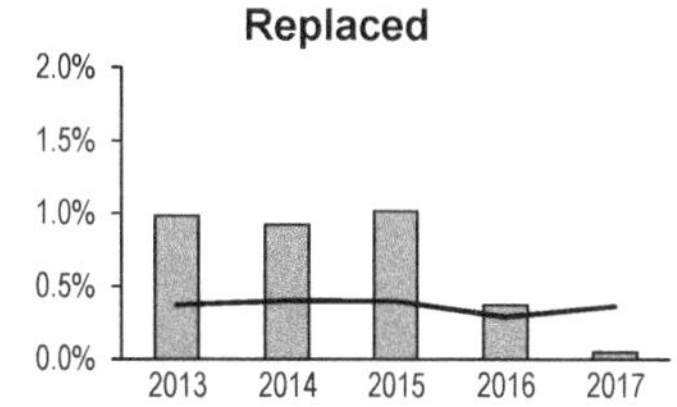

	2013	2014	2015	2016	2017
Concord	0.98%	0.92%	1.01%	0.37%	0.05%
Average	0.37%	0.40%	0.40%	0.29%	0.36%

Overflows per 100 Miles of Main Line Pipe

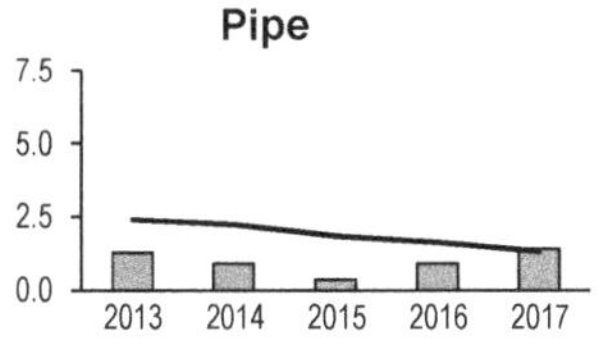

	2013	2014	2015	2016	2017
Concord	1.29	0.90	0.36	0.92	1.42
Average	2.41	2.23	1.85	1.64	1.33

Backups per 100 Miles of Main Line Pipe

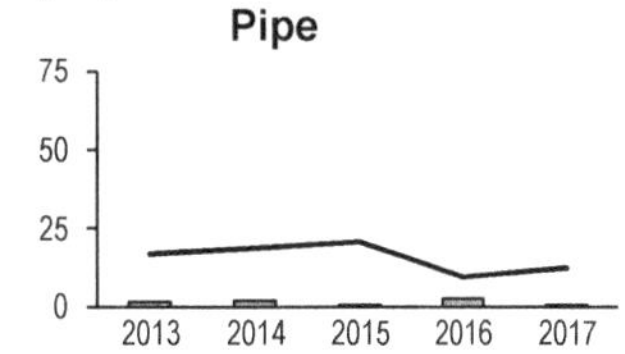

	2013	2014	2015	2016	2017
Concord	1.66	1.99	0.54	2.75	0.53
Average	16.84	18.71	20.70	9.52	12.45

Billed Wastewater as a Percent of Treated Effluent

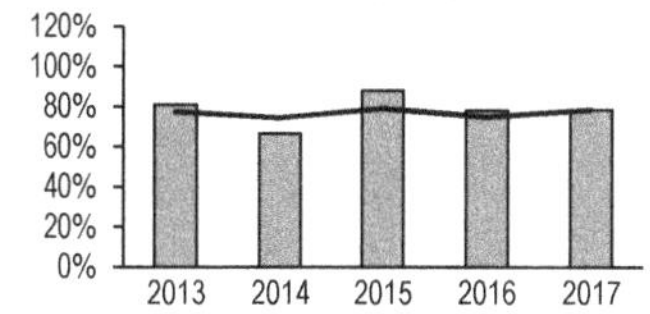

	2013	2014	2015	2016	2017
Concord	81%	66%	88%	78%	78%
Average	77%	74%	79%	75%	78%

Fiscal Year 2016–17

Explanatory Information

Service Level and Delivery

Wastewater treatment in Goldsboro is a joint responsibility between the Public Works and Public Utilities Departments. The Public Works Director oversees both departments. The Public Works Department is responsible for the collection and distribution system lines. The Public Utilities Department is responsible for the operation of the water treatment plant, the water reclamation facility, and pump stations.

The sewer system covers the city of Goldsboro and receives wastewater from neighboring systems in Wayne County. Wastewater treatment is done by one plant with a total treatment capacity of 14.2 million gallons per day. The plant uses advanced biological processes to remove pollutants from the water. Besides removing oxygen consuming wastes, the facility is able to remove nutrients such as nitrogen and phosphorus to very low levels. The system has nutrient regulatory limits in place that restrict what can be discharged in order to protect water quality. All biosolids produced by the Goldsboro treatment plant are dewatered and then composted.

During the fiscal year, the system had two regulatory violations connected to the treatment portion of the system and no violations connected to the collection portion of the system.

Conditions Affecting Service, Performance, and Costs

The city of Goldsboro joined the Benchmarking Project in July 2017 with the first year of data showing for FY 2016–17.

The costs of wastewater or sewer services as captured here do not include debt service but do capture depreciation of capital.

Hurricane Matthew in October 2016 put stress on the wastewater system in Goldsboro due to the extensive flooding.

Municipal Profile

Estimated Service Population	35,792
Service Land Area (Square Miles)	25
Persons per Square Mile	1,432
Topography	Flat; gently rolling
Climate	Temperate; little ice and snow
Median Family Income U.S. Census 2010	$33,879

Service Profile

Total FTE Staff Positions	26.0
Treatment Plant	19.0
Line Crews	5.0
Billing/Collection	2.0
Other	0.0
Number of Treatment Plants	1
Total Treatment Capacity	14.2 MGD
Average Daily Flow	9.6 MGD
River Basin into Which System Discharges	Neuse
Miles of Gravity Main Line Pipe	225
Miles of Forced Main Line Pipe	26
Average Age of Main Line Pipe	75 years
Blocks in Sewer Mains	0
Number of System Breaks	14
Sanitary System Overflows	0
Number of Customer Accounts	NA
Total Revenues Collected	NA

Full Cost Profile

Cost Breakdown by Percentage	
Personal Services	15.0%
Operating Costs	84.3%
Capital Costs	0.6%
TOTAL	100.0%
Cost Breakdown in Dollars	
Personal Services	$1,226,233
Operating Costs	$6,874,316
Capital Costs	$51,043
TOTAL	$8,151,592

Key: Goldsboro ▒ Benchmarking Average — Fiscal Years 2013 through 2017

Resource Measures

Wastewater Services Cost per Capita

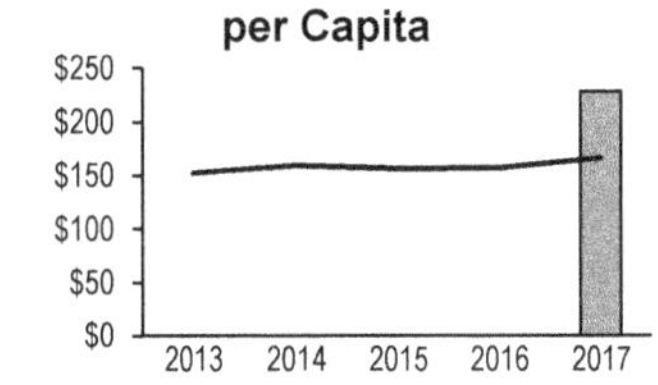

	2013	2014	2015	2016	2017
Goldsboro					$228
Average	$152	$159	$156	$157	$166

Waterwater Services FTEs per 10,000 Population

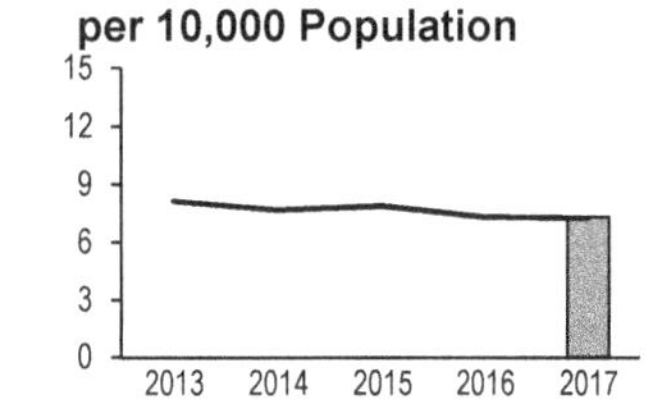

	2013	2014	2015	2016	2017
Goldsboro					7.3
Average	8.1	7.7	7.9	7.3	7.3

Waterwaste Services Cost per Customer Account

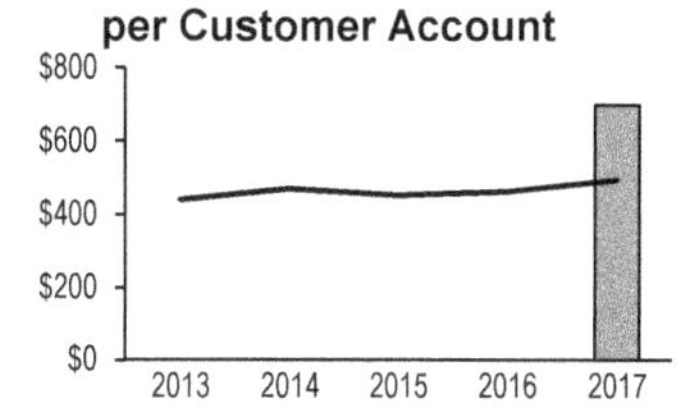

	2013	2014	2015	2016	2017
Goldsboro					$700
Average	$440	$470	$452	$463	$494

Workload Measures

Thousands of Gallons of Wastewater per Account

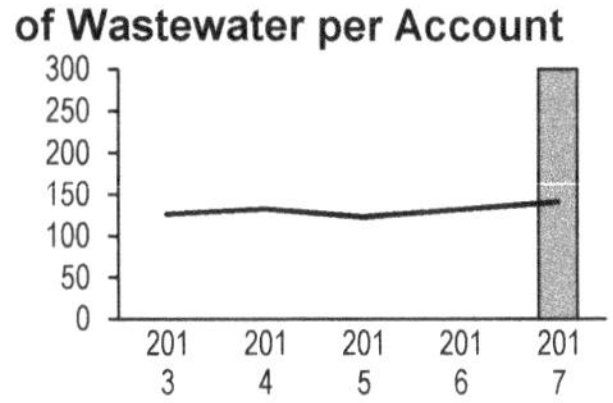

	2013	2014	2015	2016	2017
Goldsboro					299.3
Average	125.7	131.5	122.1	130.9	139.8

Miles of Sewer Main Line Pipe per Square Mile of Service Area

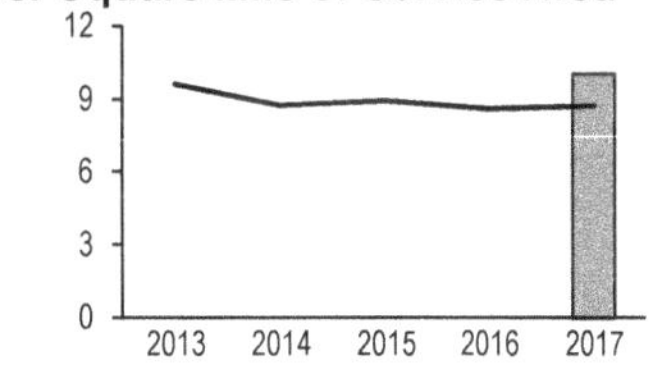

	2013	2014	2015	2016	2017
Goldsboro					10.0
Average	9.6	8.8	8.9	8.6	8.7

Number of Lift Stations per 1,000 Accounts

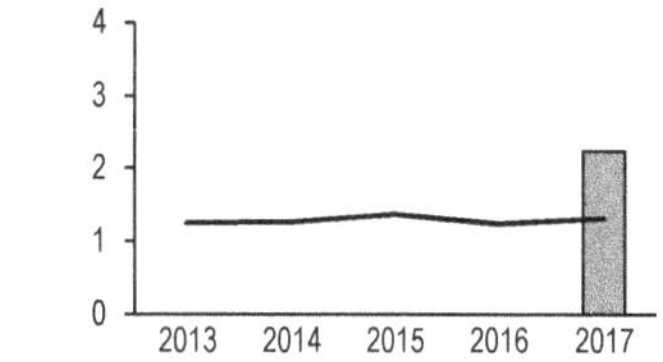

	2013	2014	2015	2016	2017
Goldsboro					2.23
Average	1.25	1.26	1.37	1.23	1.31

Efficiency Measures

Total Cost per 1,000 Gallons of Treated Wastewater

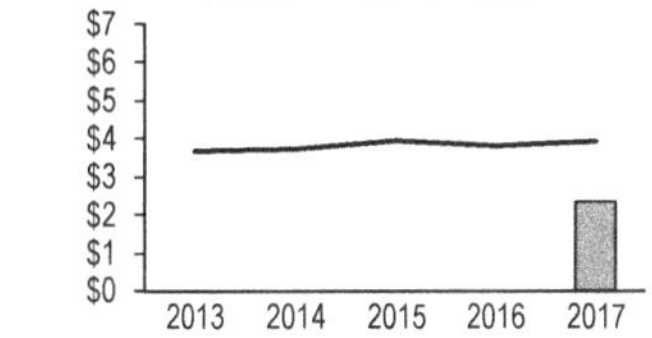

	2013	2014	2015	2016	2017
Goldsboro					$2.34
Average	$3.67	$3.71	$3.94	$3.80	$3.92

Million Gallons of Wastewater per Wastewater Services FTE

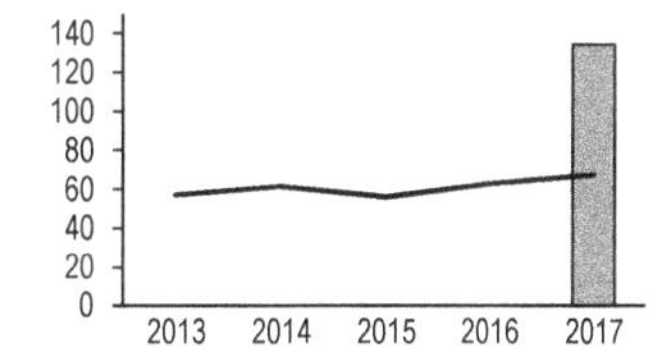

	2013	2014	2015	2016	2017
Goldsboro					134.0
Average	57.2	61.4	55.9	62.6	67.2

Customer Accounts per Wastewater Services FTE

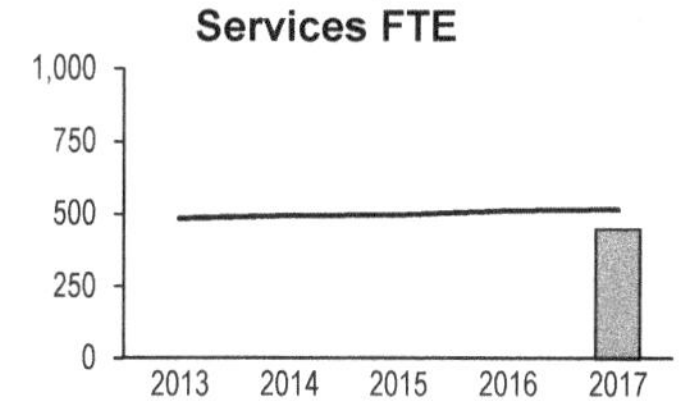

	2013	2014	2015	2016	2017
Goldsboro					448
Average	483	491	494	510	515

Effectiveness Measures

Percentage of Wastewater Bills Not Collected

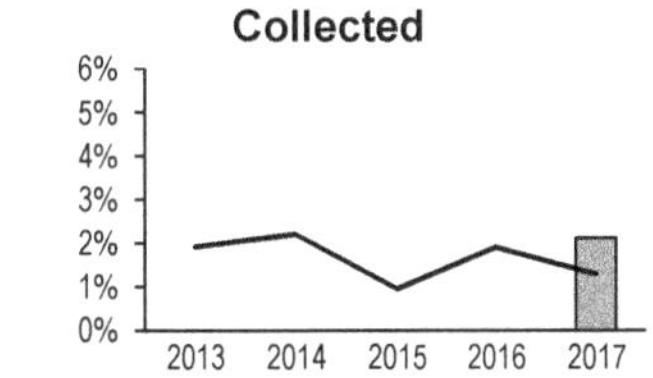

	2013	2014	2015	2016	2017
Goldsboro					2.11%
Average	1.93%	2.21%	0.96%	1.90%	1.29%

Average Daily Treatment as a Percentage of Capacity

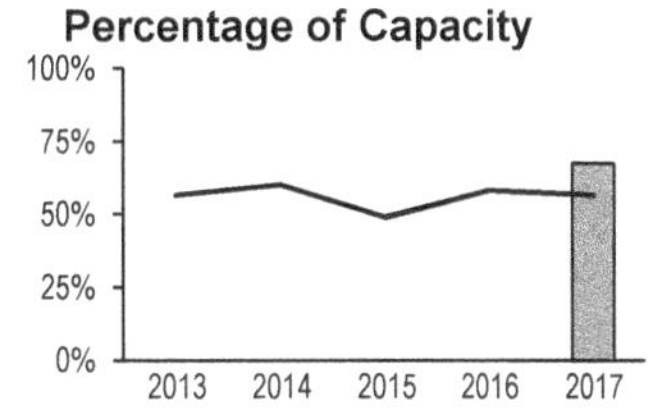

	2013	2014	2015	2016	2017
Goldsboro					67.3%
Average	56.6%	60.0%	48.9%	58.1%	56.5%

Percent of Main Line Rehabbed or Replaced

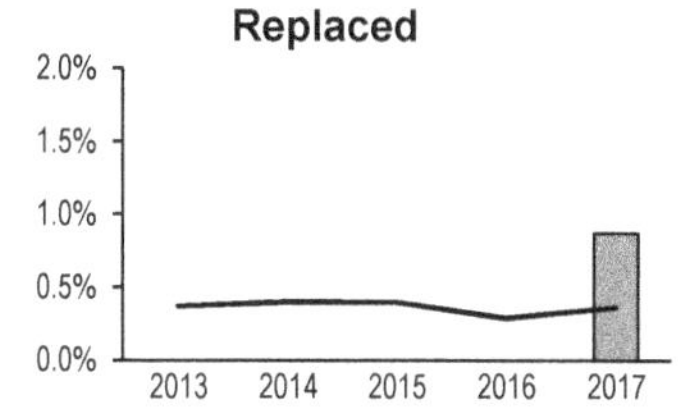

	2013	2014	2015	2016	2017
Goldsboro					0.87%
Average	0.37%	0.40%	0.40%	0.29%	0.36%

Overflows per 100 Miles of Main Line Pipe

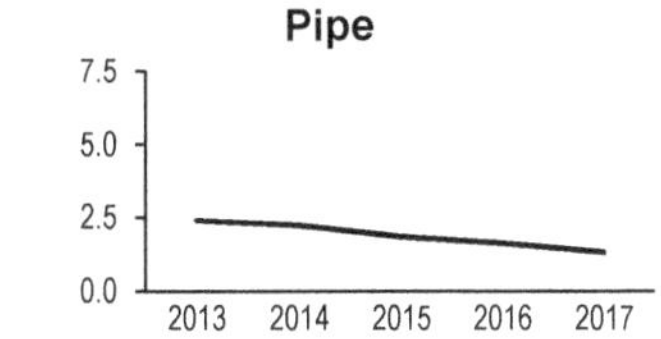

	2013	2014	2015	2016	2017
Goldsboro					0.00
Average	2.41	2.23	1.85	1.64	1.33

Backups per 100 Miles of Main Line Pipe

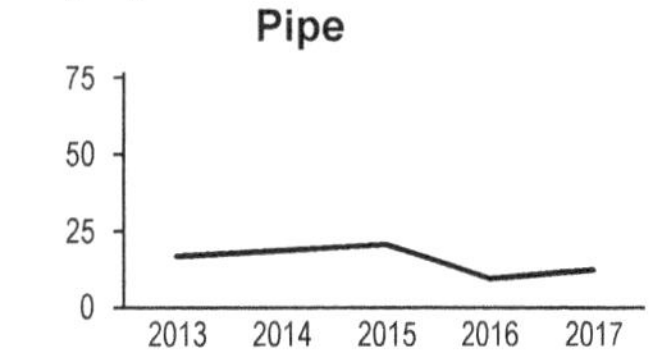

	2013	2014	2015	2016	2017
Goldsboro					0.00
Average	16.84	18.71	20.70	9.52	12.45

Billed Wastewater as a Percent of Treated Effluent

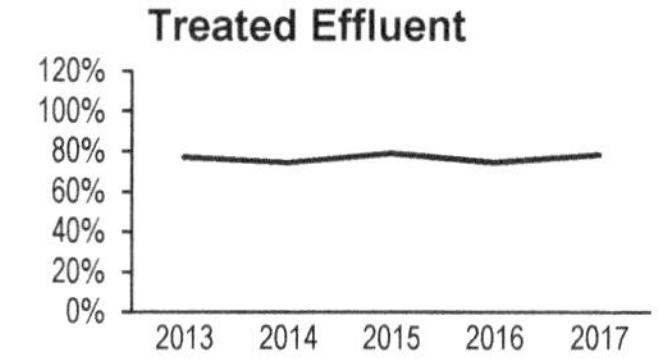

	2013	2014	2015	2016	2017
Goldsboro					
Average	77%	74%	79%	75%	78%

Fiscal Year 2016–17

Explanatory Information

Service Level and Delivery

Wastewater treatment in Greensboro is handled by the Water Reclamation Division. This is part of the Water Resources Department, which also includes stormwater and drinking water services. The director of water resources reports to the city manager. Services are provided to most of the City of Greensboro and to some addresses outside city limits within Guilford County.

Wastewater treatment in Greensboro is handled by two treatment plants. These plants use advanced tertiary treatment. The system has nutrient regulatory limits in place that restrict what can be discharged in order to protect water quality. All biosolids produced by the Greensboro treatment plants are incinerated.

During the fiscal year, the system had fourteen regulatory violations connected to the treatment portion of the system. The increase in these violations was largely due to construction to increase capacity at the treatment plants during the year.
Five violations connected to the collection portion of the system for sainitary system overflows were also experienced.

Conditions Affecting Service, Performance, and Costs

The costs of wastewater or sewer services as captured here do not include debt service but do capture depreciation of capital.

During FY 2015–16 a conversion to a new database used for tracking operations was undertaken. Some data were not available. The performance measure "Backups per 100 miles of main line pipe" could not be calculated.

The full implementation of a new asset management system designed for utilities took place in FY 2016–17 Work orders are now assigned and tracked by more specific types of duties which resulted in an increase in certain metrics over prior years.

Construction to increase capacity at the treatment plants led to several wastewater regulatory violations during the year.

Municipal Profile

Estimated Service Population	285,344
Service Land Area (Square Miles)	148
Persons per Square Mile	1,928
Topography	Flat; gently rolling
Climate	Temperate; little ice and snow
Median Family Income U.S. Census 2010	$52,752

Service Profile

Total FTE Staff Positions	152.5
Treatment Plant	51.0
Line Crews	77.0
Billing/Collection	7.0
Other	17.5
Number of Treatment Plants	2
Total Treatment Capacity	56.0 MGD
Average Daily Flow	32.6 MGD
River Basin into Which System Discharges	Cape Fear
Miles of Gravity Main Line Pipe	1,424
Miles of Forced Main Line Pipe	69
Average Age of Main Line Pipe	40 years
Blocks in Sewer Mains	823
Number of System Breaks	50
Sanitary System Overflows	7
Number of Customer Accounts	101,828
Total Revenues Collected	$59,269,089

Full Cost Profile

Cost Breakdown by Percentage	
Personal Services	25.9%
Operating Costs	74.1%
Capital Costs	0.0%
TOTAL	100.0%
Cost Breakdown in Dollars	
Personal Services	$7,076,410
Operating Costs	$20,255,043
Capital Costs	$0
TOTAL	$27,331,453

Greensboro — Wastewater Services

Key: Greensboro ▒ Benchmarking Average — Fiscal Years 2013 through 2017

Resource Measures

Wastewater Services Cost per Capita

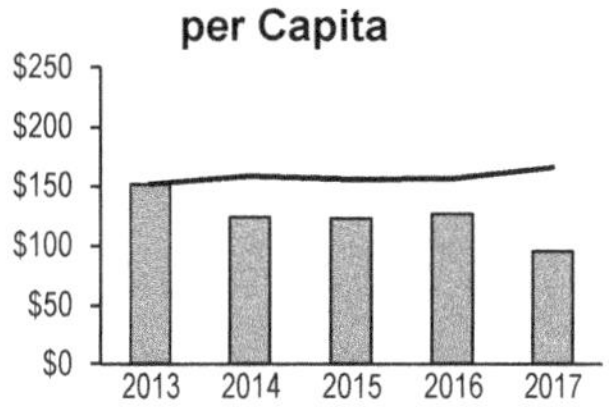

	2013	2014	2015	2016	2017
Greensboro	$152	$124	$123	$127	$96
Average	$152	$159	$156	$157	$166

Waterwater Services FTEs per 10,000 Population

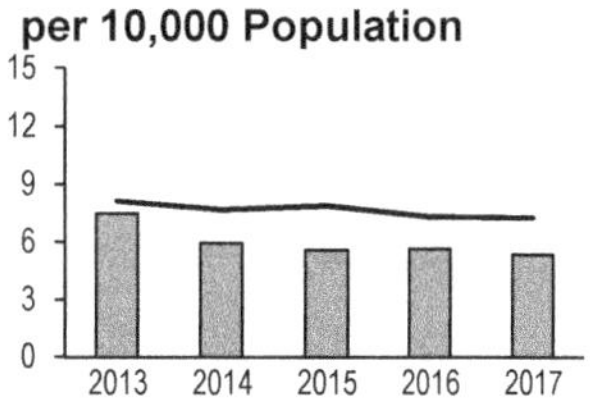

	2013	2014	2015	2016	2017
Greensboro	7.5	5.9	5.6	5.7	5.3
Average	8.1	7.7	7.9	7.3	7.3

Waterwaste Services Cost per Customer Account

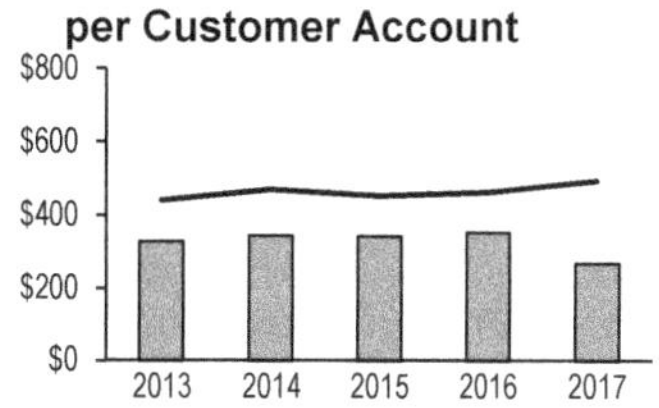

	2013	2014	2015	2016	2017
Greensboro	$329	$345	$343	$353	$268
Average	$440	$470	$452	$463	$494

Workload Measures

Thousands of Gallons of Wastewater per Account

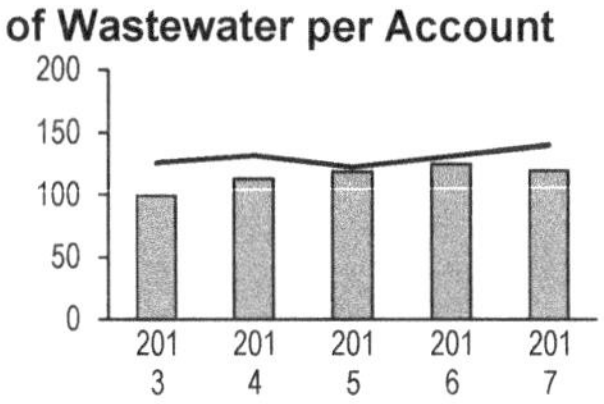

	2013	2014	2015	2016	2017
Greensboro	98.6	112.6	118.2	124.9	119.3
Average	125.7	131.5	122.1	130.9	139.8

Miles of Sewer Main Line Pipe per Square Mile of Service Area

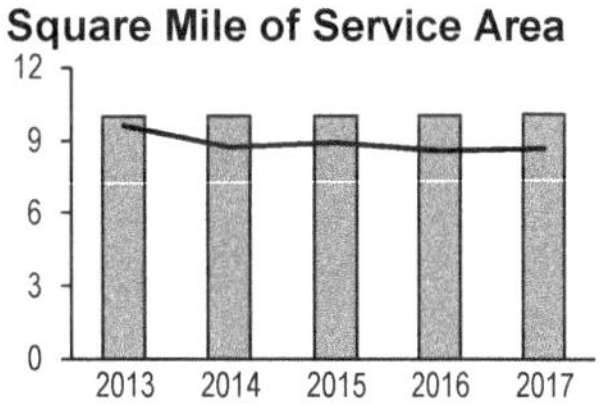

	2013	2014	2015	2016	2017
Greensboro	10.0	10.0	10.0	10.0	10.1
Average	9.6	8.8	8.9	8.6	8.7

Number of Lift Stations per 1,000 Accounts

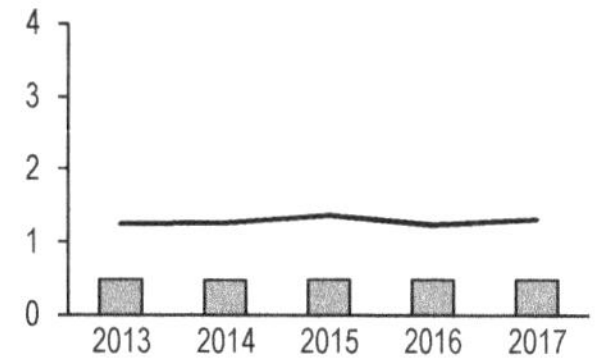

	2013	2014	2015	2016	2017
Greensboro	0.48	0.48	0.49	0.48	0.48
Average	1.25	1.26	1.37	1.23	1.31

Efficiency Measures

Total Cost per 1,000 Gallons of Treated Wastewater

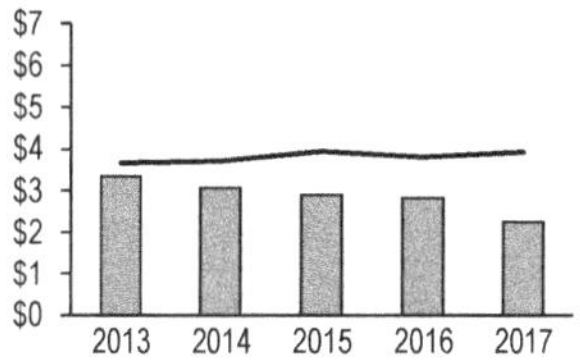

	2013	2014	2015	2016	2017
Greensboro	$3.34	$3.06	$2.90	$2.82	$2.25
Average	$3.67	$3.71	$3.94	$3.80	$3.92

Million Gallons of Wastewater per Wastewater Services FTE

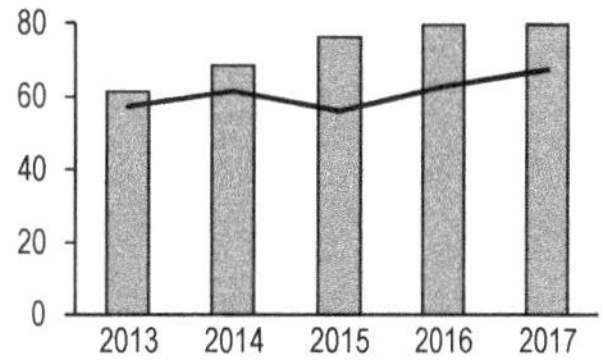

	2013	2014	2015	2016	2017
Greensboro	61.1	68.4	76.0	79.4	79.6
Average	57.2	61.4	55.9	62.6	67.2

Customer Accounts per Wastewater Services FTE

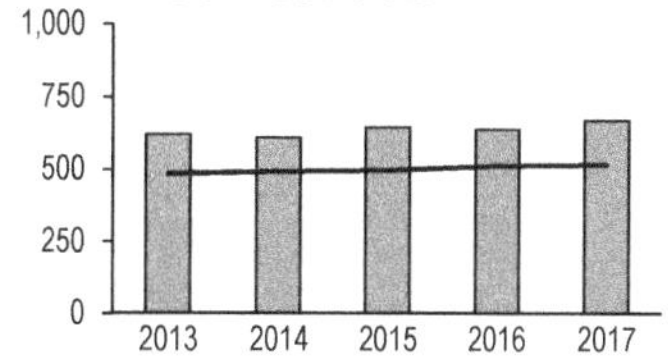

	2013	2014	2015	2016	2017
Greensboro	619	607	643	636	668
Average	483	491	494	510	515

Effectiveness Measures

Percentage of Wastewater Bills Not Collected

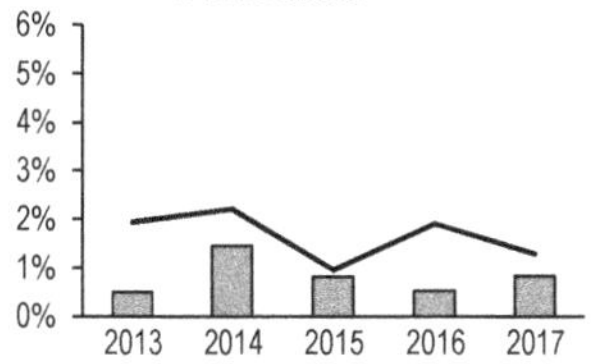

	2013	2014	2015	2016	2017
Greensboro	0.50%	1.44%	0.81%	0.53%	0.82%
Average	1.93%	2.21%	0.96%	1.90%	1.29%

Average Daily Treatment as a Percentage of Capacity

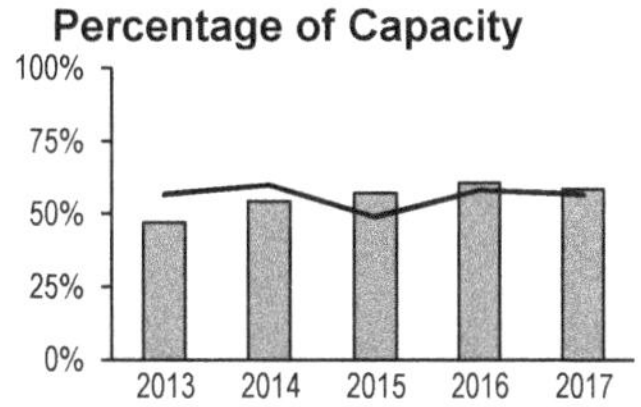

	2013	2014	2015	2016	2017
Greensboro	47.0%	54.1%	57.1%	60.5%	58.3%
Average	56.6%	60.0%	48.9%	58.1%	56.5%

Percent of Main Line Rehabbed or Replaced

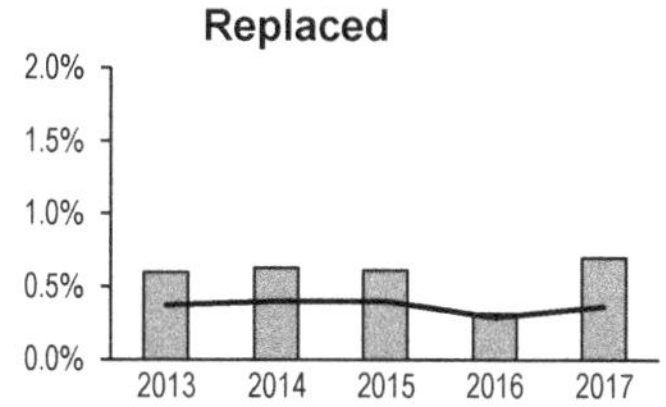

	2013	2014	2015	2016	2017
Greensboro	0.60%	0.63%	0.61%	0.32%	0.70%
Average	0.37%	0.40%	0.40%	0.29%	0.36%

Overflows per 100 Miles of Main Line Pipe

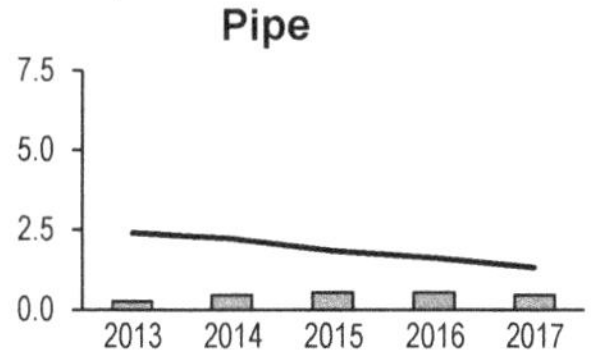

	2013	2014	2015	2016	2017
Greensboro	0.27	0.47	0.54	0.54	0.47
Average	2.41	2.23	1.85	1.64	1.33

Backups per 100 Miles of Main Line Pipe

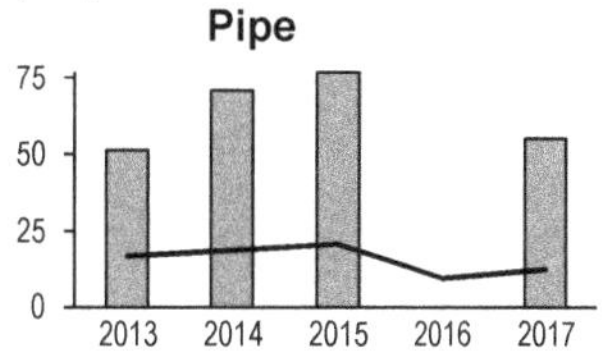

	2013	2014	2015	2016	2017
Greensboro	51.28	70.82	76.74		55.13
Average	16.84	18.71	20.70	9.52	12.45

Billed Wastewater as a Percent of Treated Effluent

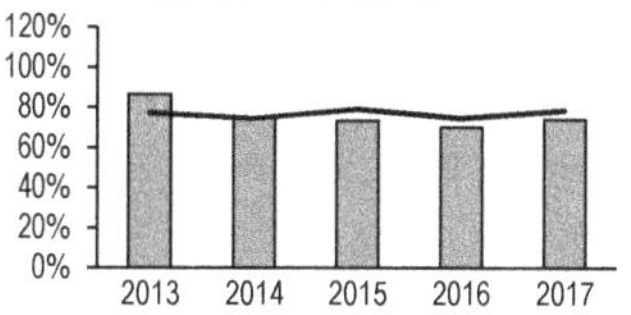

	2013	2014	2015	2016	2017
Greensboro	86%	75%	73%	70%	74%
Average	77%	74%	79%	75%	78%

Fiscal Year 2016–17

Explanatory Information

Service Level and Delivery
Wastewater is handled by the City of Hickory's Collection Division, which is part of Public Utilities under the Public Services Department. The service area covers the City of Hickory and several adjoining areas in Catawba County.

The system relies on three treatment plants to handle wastewater. One plant uses activated sludge biological nutrient removal (BNR), the second uses oxidation ditch activated sludge BNR, and the third uses conventional activated sludge. The entire system does not have nutrient limits in place at this time. Biosolids generated are handled as Class A compost.

The system in Hickory had five regulatory violations connected to the treatment portion of the system and four violations connected to the collection portion of the system during the fiscal year connected to sanitary system overflows.

Conditions Affecting Service, Performance, and Costs
The costs of wastewater or sewer services as captured here do not include debt service but do capture depreciation of capital.

Municipal Profile

Estimated Service Population	37,478
Service Land Area (Square Miles)	65.0
Persons per Square Mile	577
Topography	Gently rolling
Climate	Temperate; some ice and snow
Median Family Income U.S. Census 2010	$54,093

Service Profile

Total FTE Staff Positions	44.0
Treatment Plant	29.0
Line Crews	10.0
Billing/Collection	2.5
Other	2.5
Number of Treatment Plants	5
Total Treatment Capacity	16.9 MGD
Average Daily Flow	5.2 MGD
River Basin into Which System Discharges	Catawba
Miles of Gravity Main Line Pipe	497
Miles of Forced Main Line Pipe	43
Average Age of Main Line Pipe	45 years
Blocks in Sewer Mains	87
Number of System Breaks	8
Sanitary System Overflows	4
Number of Customer Accounts	15,542
Total Revenues Collected	$9,804,112

Full Cost Profile

Cost Breakdown by Percentage	
Personal Services	35.6%
Operating Costs	39.1%
Capital Costs	25.2%
TOTAL	100.0%
Cost Breakdown in Dollars	
Personal Services	$2,572,372
Operating Costs	$2,824,767
Capital Costs	$1,822,787
TOTAL	$7,219,926

Hickory — Wastewater Services

Key: Hickory ▒ Benchmarking Average — Fiscal Years 2013 through 2017

Resource Measures

Wastewater Services Cost per Capita

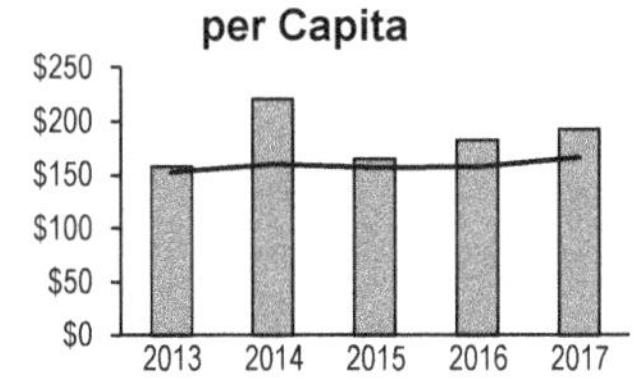

	2013	2014	2015	2016	2017
Hickory	$158	$221	$165	$183	$193
Average	$152	$159	$156	$157	$166

Waterwater Services FTEs per 10,000 Population

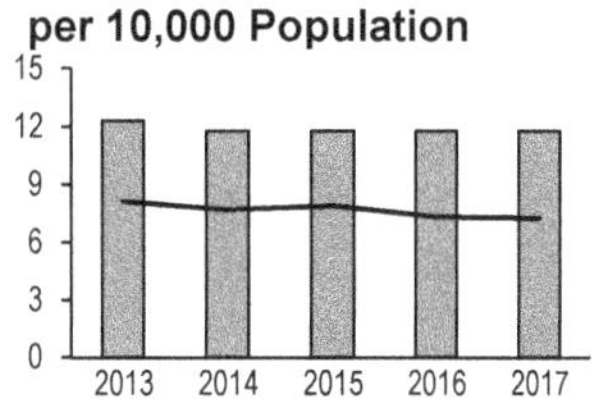

	2013	2014	2015	2016	2017
Hickory	12.3	11.7	11.7	11.7	11.7
Average	8.1	7.7	7.9	7.3	7.3

Waterwaste Services Cost per Customer Account

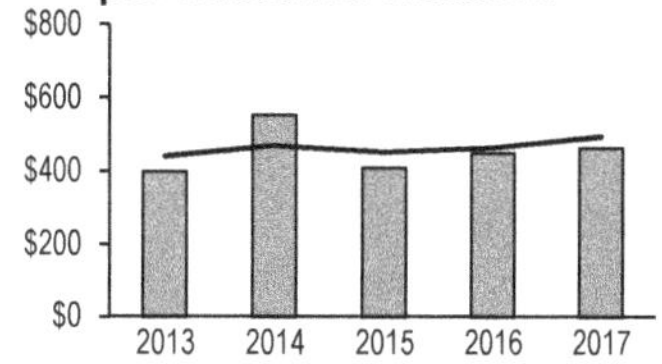

	2013	2014	2015	2016	2017
Hickory	$399	$553	$410	$450	$465
Average	$440	$470	$452	$463	$494

Workload Measures

Thousands of Gallons of Wastewater per Account

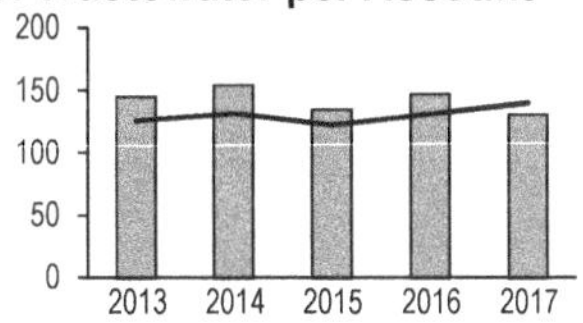

	2013	2014	2015	2016	2017
Hickory	145.3	154.2	134.7	147.3	131.0
Average	125.7	131.5	122.1	130.9	139.8

Miles of Sewer Main Line Pipe per Square Mile of Service Area

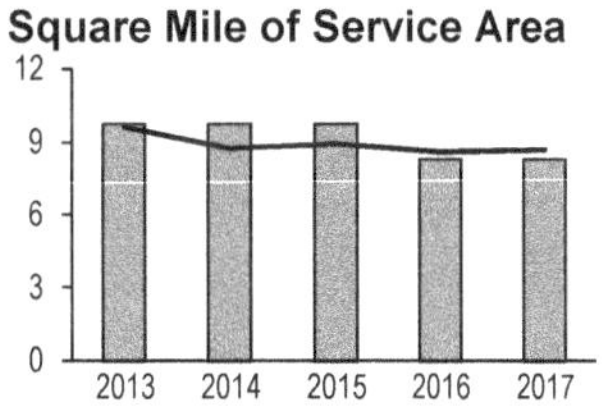

	2013	2014	2015	2016	2017
Hickory	9.8	9.8	9.8	8.3	8.3
Average	9.6	8.8	8.9	8.6	8.7

Number of Lift Stations per 1,000 Accounts

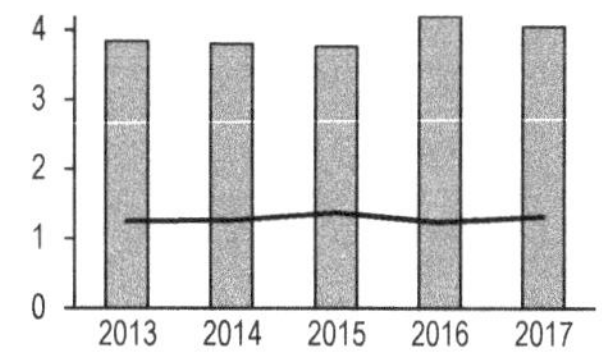

	2013	2014	2015	2016	2017
Hickory	3.83	3.80	3.77	4.20	4.05
Average	1.25	1.26	1.37	1.23	1.31

Efficiency Measures

Total Cost per 1,000 Gallons of Treated Wastewater

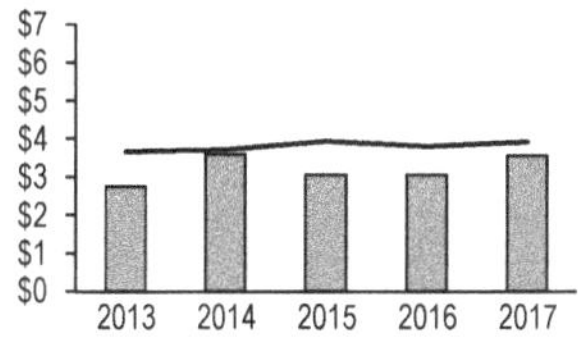

	2013	2014	2015	2016	2017
Hickory	$2.74	$3.59	$3.04	$3.05	$3.55
Average	$3.67	$3.71	$3.94	$3.80	$3.92

Million Gallons of Wastewater per Wastewater Services FTE

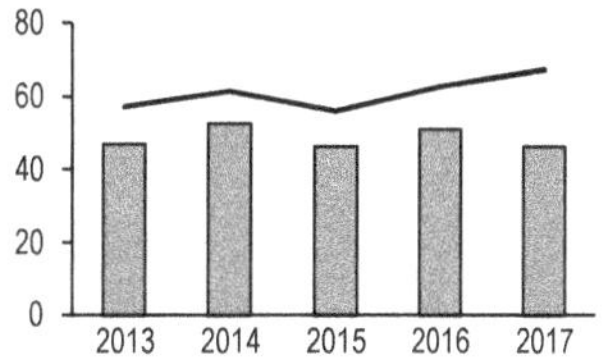

	2013	2014	2015	2016	2017
Hickory	47.0	52.5	46.3	51.0	46.3
Average	57.2	61.4	55.9	62.6	67.2

Customer Accounts per Wastewater Services FTE

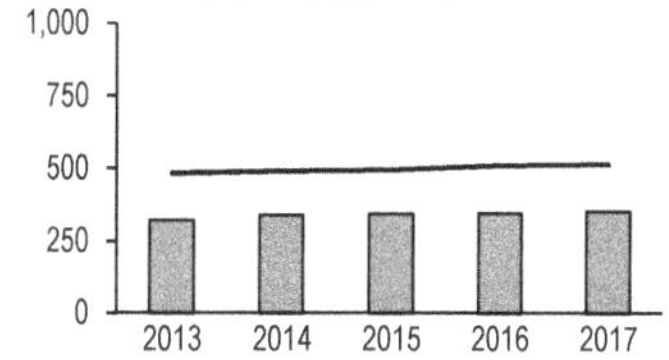

	2013	2014	2015	2016	2017
Hickory	323	341	344	346	353
Average	483	491	494	510	515

Effectiveness Measures

Percentage of Wastewater Bills Not Collected

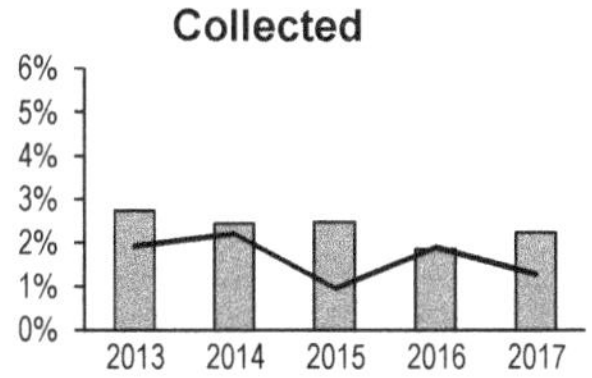

	2013	2014	2015	2016	2017
Hickory	2.73%	2.44%	2.47%	1.86%	2.24%
Average	1.93%	2.21%	0.96%	1.90%	1.29%

Average Daily Treatment as a Percentage of Capacity

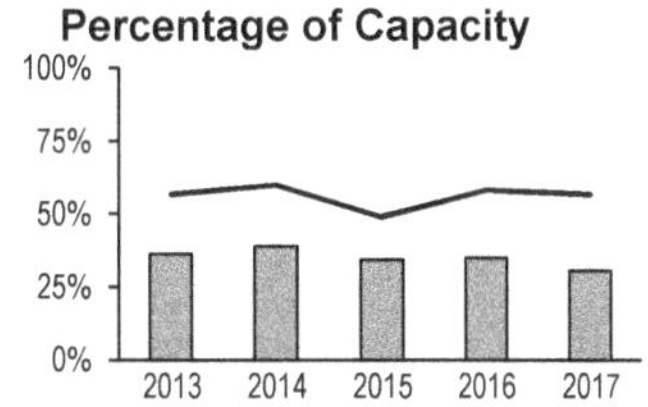

	2013	2014	2015	2016	2017
Hickory	36.2%	38.8%	34.1%	34.8%	30.6%
Average	56.6%	60.0%	48.9%	58.1%	56.5%

Percent of Main Line Rehabbed or Replaced

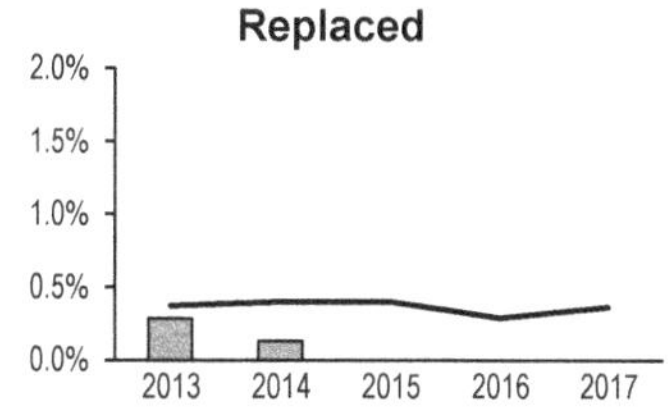

	2013	2014	2015	2016	2017
Hickory	0.28%	0.13%	0.00%	0.00%	0.00%
Average	0.37%	0.40%	0.40%	0.29%	0.36%

Overflows per 100 Miles of Main Line Pipe

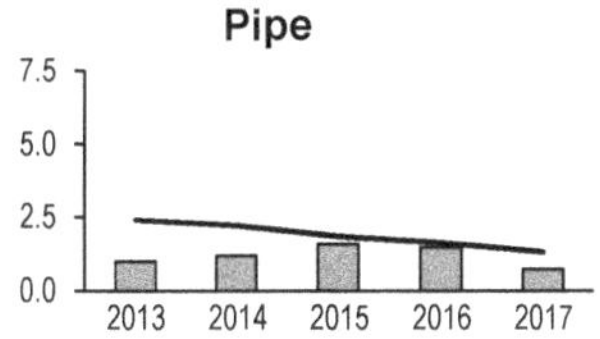

	2013	2014	2015	2016	2017
Hickory	1.00	1.20	1.60	1.48	0.74
Average	2.41	2.23	1.85	1.64	1.33

Backups per 100 Miles of Main Line Pipe

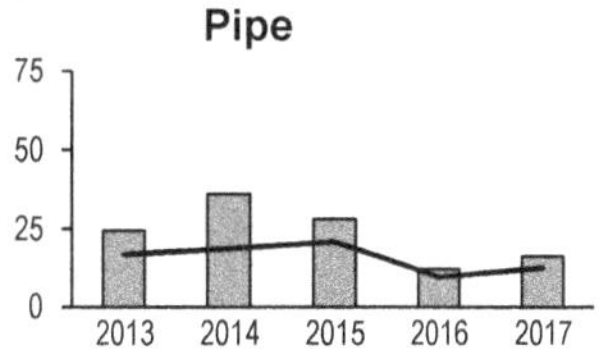

	2013	2014	2015	2016	2017
Hickory	24.40	36.00	28.00	12.04	16.11
Average	16.84	18.71	20.70	9.52	12.45

Billed Wastewater as a Percent of Treated Effluent

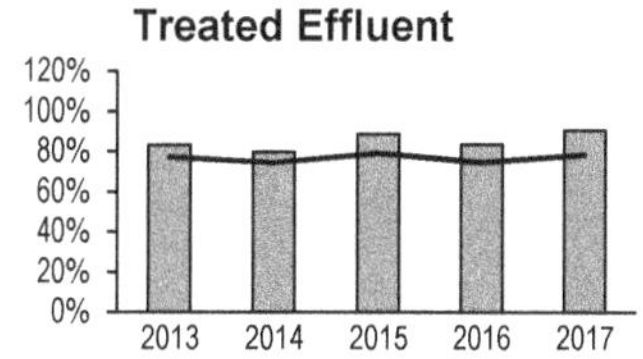

	2013	2014	2015	2016	2017
Hickory	83%	80%	89%	83%	91%
Average	77%	74%	79%	75%	78%

Fiscal Year 2016–17

Explanatory Information

Service Level and Delivery

The City of High Point wastewater system is part of the combined Water/Sewer Division under the Public Services Department. The system covers the City of High Point and several adjoining areas in Guilford and Davidson counties.

Wastewater is treated at two treatment plants. One plant uses biological nutrient removal, while the second plant uses extended aeration with chemical phosphorous removal. The system has regulatory nutrient limits in place that are designed to protect water quality in local waters. Biosolids left over after treatment are primarily handled by incineration, with landfill disposal as a backup.

During the fiscal year, the sytem had three regulatory violations connected to the treatment portion of the system and four violations connected to the collection portion of the system.

Conditions Affecting Service, Performance, and Costs

The costs of wastewater or sewer service as captured here do not include debt services but do capture depreciation of capital.

Municipal Profile

Estimated Service Population	112,201
Service Land Area (Square Miles)	77.6
Persons per Square Mile	1,446
Topography	Flat; gently rolling
Climate	Temperate; little ice and snow
Median Family Income U.S. Census 2010	$49,720

Service Profile

Total FTE Staff Positions	91.6
Treatment Plant	30.0
Line Crews	35.3
Billing/Collection	6.0
Other	20.3
Number of Treatment Plants	2
Total Treatment Capacity	34.2 MGD
Average Daily Flow	15.6 MGD
River Basin into Which System Discharges	Yadkin-Pee Dee and Cape Fear
Miles of Gravity Main Line Pipe	657
Miles of Forced Main Line Pipe	16
Average Age of Main Line Pipe	45 years
Blocks in Sewer Mains	115
Number of System Breaks	62
Sanitary System Overflows	14
Number of Customer Accounts	40,469
Total Revenues Collected	$31,557,557

Full Cost Profile

Cost Breakdown by Percentage	
Personal Services	30.5%
Operating Costs	32.6%
Capital Costs	36.9%
TOTAL	100.0%
Cost Breakdown in Dollars	
Personal Services	$6,310,886
Operating Costs	$6,751,468
Capital Costs	$7,623,297
TOTAL	$20,685,651

Key: High Point ▒ Benchmarking Average — Fiscal Years 2013 through 2017

Resource Measures

Wastewater Services Cost per Capita

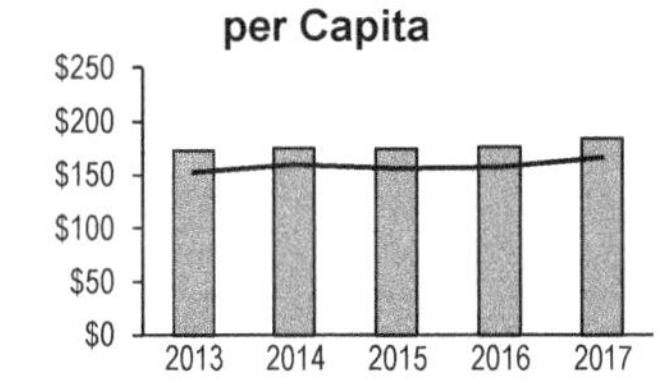

	2013	2014	2015	2016	2017
High Point	$173	$175	$175	$177	$184
Average	$152	$159	$156	$157	$166

Waterwater Services FTEs per 10,000 Population

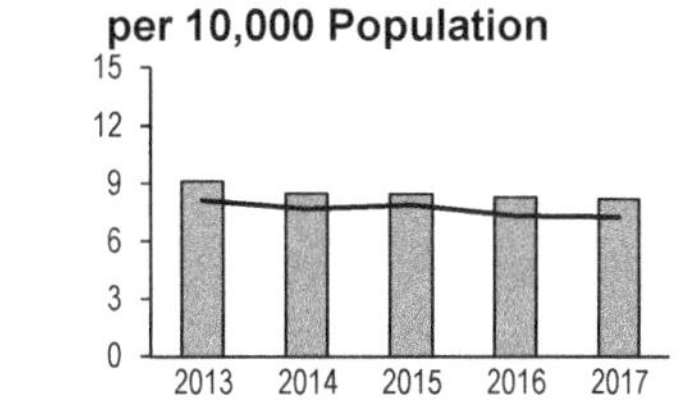

	2013	2014	2015	2016	2017
High Point	9.1	8.5	8.4	8.3	8.2
Average	8.1	7.7	7.9	7.3	7.3

Waterwaste Services Cost per Customer Account

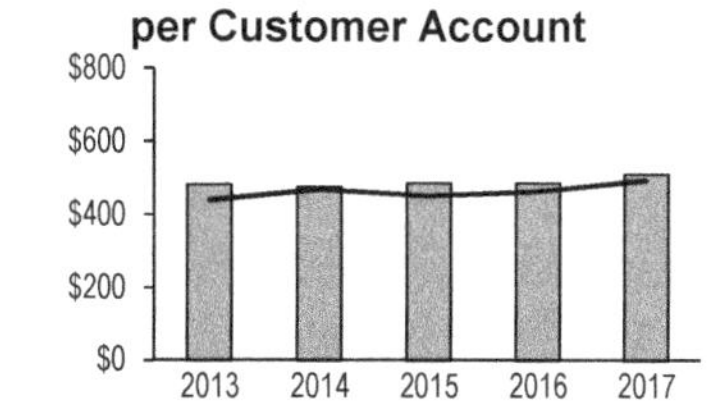

	2013	2014	2015	2016	2017
High Point	$484	$477	$487	$487	$511
Average	$440	$470	$452	$463	$494

Workload Measures

Thousands of Gallons of Wastewater per Account

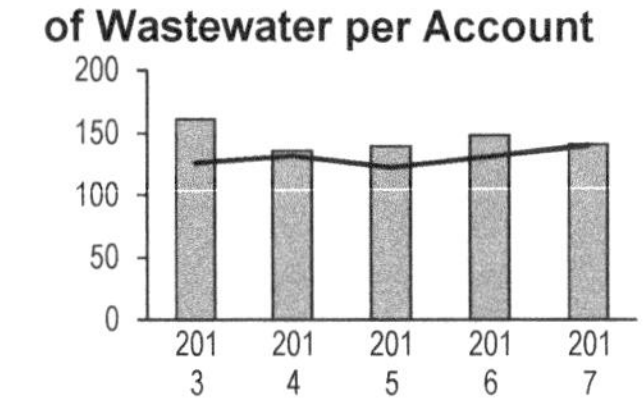

	2013	2014	2015	2016	2017
High Point	160.8	135.4	138.9	148.0	140.4
Average	125.7	131.5	122.1	130.9	139.8

Miles of Sewer Main Line Pipe per Square Mile of Service Area

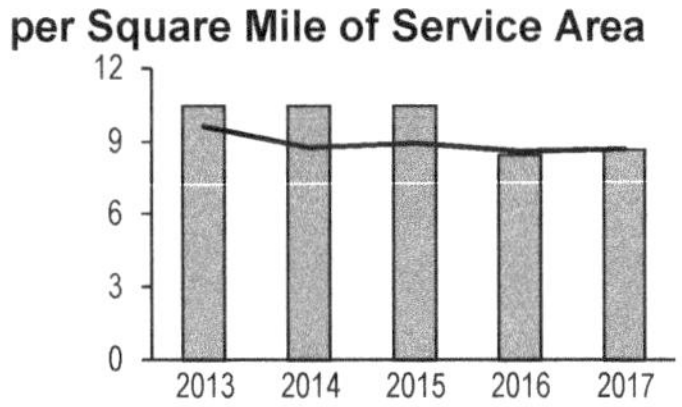

	2013	2014	2015	2016	2017
High Point	10.5	10.5	10.5	8.5	8.7
Average	9.6	8.8	8.9	8.6	8.7

Number of Lift Stations per 1,000 Accounts

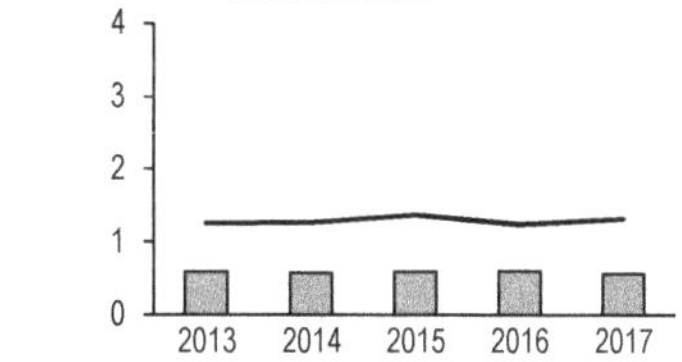

	2013	2014	2015	2016	2017
High Point	0.59	0.57	0.59	0.60	0.57
Average	1.25	1.26	1.37	1.23	1.31

Efficiency Measures

Total Cost per 1,000 Gallons of Treated Wastewater

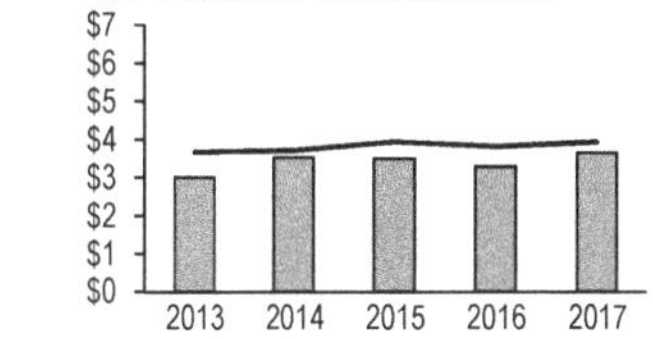

	2013	2014	2015	2016	2017
High Point	$3.01	$3.52	$3.50	$3.29	$3.64
Average	$3.67	$3.71	$3.94	$3.80	$3.92

Million Gallons of Wastewater per Wastewater Services FTE

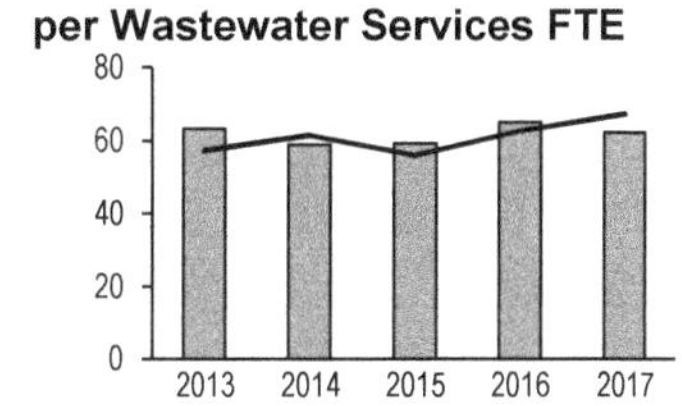

	2013	2014	2015	2016	2017
High Point	63.1	58.8	59.2	64.8	62.0
Average	57.2	61.4	55.9	62.6	67.2

Customer Accounts per Wastewater Services FTE

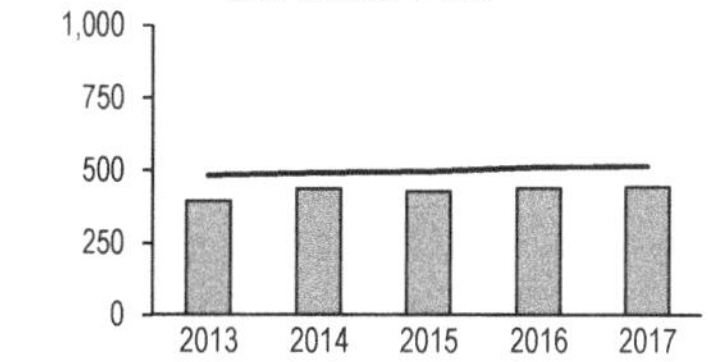

	2013	2014	2015	2016	2017
High Point	392	435	426	438	442
Average	483	491	494	510	515

Effectiveness Measures

Percentage of Wastewater Bills Not Collected

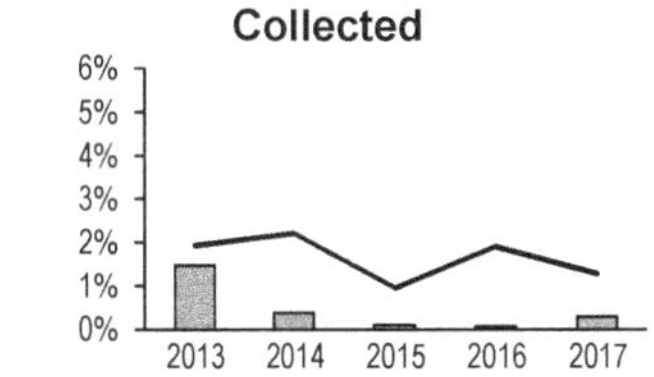

	2013	2014	2015	2016	2017
High Point	1.48%	0.38%	0.10%	0.08%	0.29%
Average	1.93%	2.21%	0.96%	1.90%	1.29%

Average Daily Treatment as a Percentage of Capacity

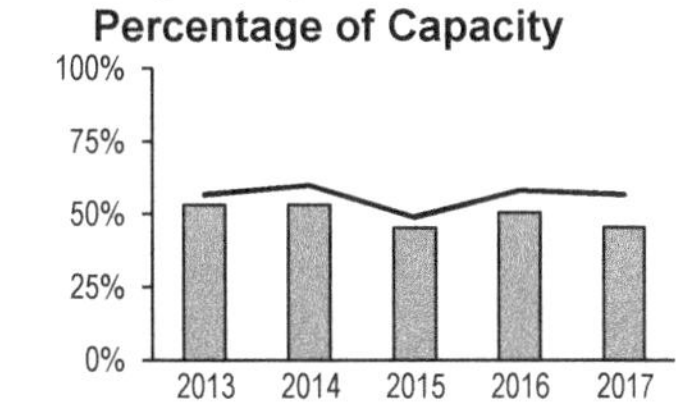

	2013	2014	2015	2016	2017
High Point	53.0%	53.0%	45.2%	50.4%	45.5%
Average	56.6%	60.0%	48.9%	58.1%	56.5%

Percent of Main Line Rehabbed or Replaced

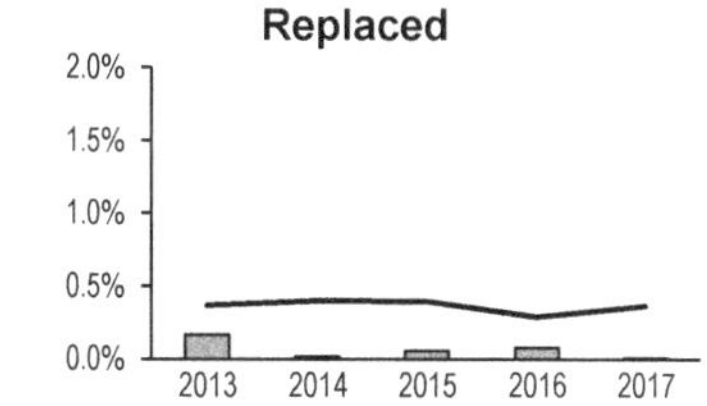

	2013	2014	2015	2016	2017
High Point	0.16%	0.02%	0.05%	0.08%	0.01%
Average	0.37%	0.40%	0.40%	0.29%	0.36%

Overflows per 100 Miles of Main Line Pipe

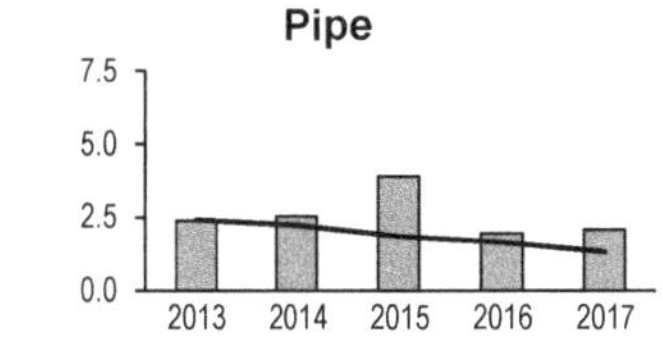

	2013	2014	2015	2016	2017
High Point	2.39	2.53	3.88	1.93	2.08
Average	2.41	2.23	1.85	1.64	1.33

Backups per 100 Miles of Main Line Pipe

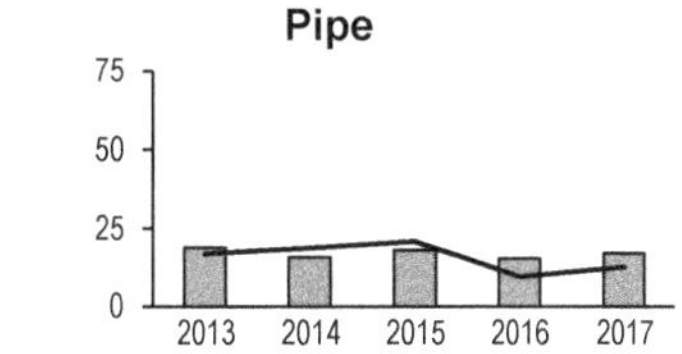

	2013	2014	2015	2016	2017
High Point	18.81	15.80	18.05	15.48	17.09
Average	16.84	18.71	20.70	9.52	12.45

Billed Wastewater as a Percent of Treated Effluent

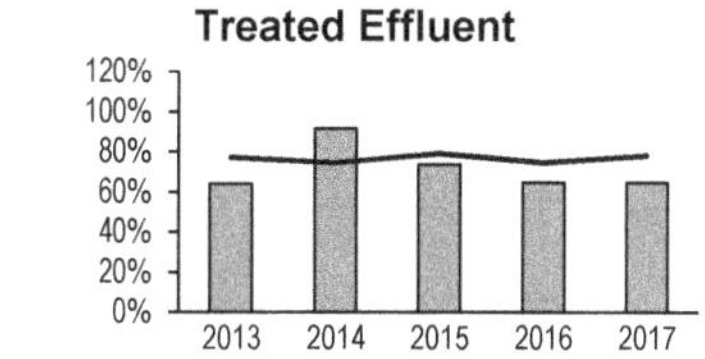

	2013	2014	2015	2016	2017
High Point	64%	91%	74%	65%	65%
Average	77%	74%	79%	75%	78%

Fiscal Year 2016–17

Explanatory Information

Service Level and Delivery

Public Utilities is a department within the City of Raleigh. It is a combined enterprise system which provides drinking water and sewage treatment services to the City of Raleigh and several towns, including Garner, Rolesville, Knightdale, Wake Forest, Wendell, and Zebulon. The City of Raleigh also provides wastewater collection for the Towns of Middlesex, Clayton, Apex, and for Johnston County. Approximately 561,000 people live in the service area of roughly 299 square miles.

Wastewater is treated at three plants. The total combined treatment capacity at the three plants is 65 million gallons per day. The plants use primary, secondary, and tertiary treatment along with a BNR process combined with reclaimed water distribution and biosolids treatment and land application.

The system had no regulatory violations connected to the treatment portion of the wastewater system and one regulatory violation during the fiscal year for issues connected to collections related to sanitary system overflows.

Conditions Affecting Service, Performance, and Costs

Raleigh rejoined the Benchmarking Project in July 2016 with the first year of data showing for FY 2015–16.

The costs of wastewater or sewer services as captured here do not include debt service but do capture depreciation of capital.

Raleigh's percent of wastewater bills not collected was below zero as as there was a high amount of due bills collected from prior years exceeding the amount that was due for the current fiscal year.

Municipal Profile

Estimated Service Population	561,428
Service Land Area (Square Miles)	299.0
Persons per Square Mile	1,878
Topography	Flat; gently rolling
Climate	Temperate; little ice and snow
Median Family Income U.S. Census 2010	$68,678

Service Profile

Total FTE Staff Positions	324.0
Treatment Plant	55.0
Line Crews	118.0
Billing/Collection	56.0
Other	95.0
Number of Treatment Plants	3
Total Treatment Capacity	65.2 MGD
Average Daily Flow	50.1 MGD
River Basin into Which System Discharges	Neuse
Miles of Gravity Main Line Pipe	2,300
Miles of Forced Main Line Pipe	125
Average Age of Main Line Pipe	30 years
Blocks in Sewer Mains	25
Number of System Breaks	220
Sanitary System Overflows	25
Number of Customer Accounts	170,437
Total Revenues Collected	$125,032,333

Full Cost Profile

Cost Breakdown by Percentage	
Personal Services	22.4%
Operating Costs	45.3%
Capital Costs	32.3%
TOTAL	100.0%
Cost Breakdown in Dollars	
Personal Services	$14,976,717
Operating Costs	$30,212,629
Capital Costs	$21,532,236
TOTAL	$66,721,582

Key: Raleigh ▒ Benchmarking Average — Fiscal Years 2013 through 2017

Resource Measures

Wastewater Services Cost per Capita

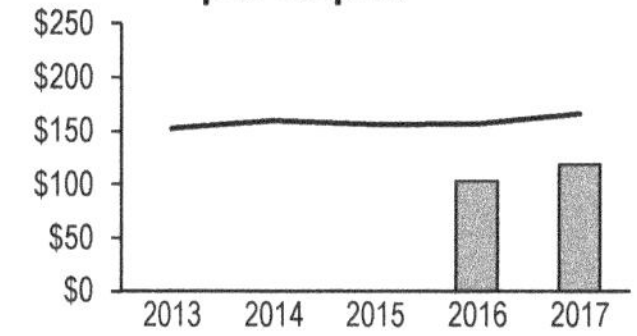

	2013	2014	2015	2016	2017
Raleigh				$104	$119
Average	$152	$159	$156	$157	$166

Waterwater Services FTEs per 10,000 Population

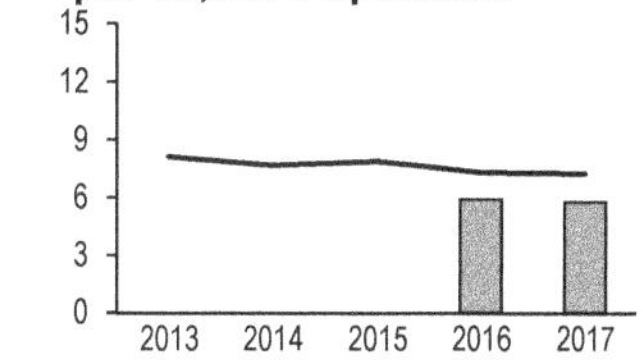

	2013	2014	2015	2016	2017
Raleigh				5.9	5.8
Average	8.1	7.7	7.9	7.3	7.3

Waterwaste Services Cost per Customer Account

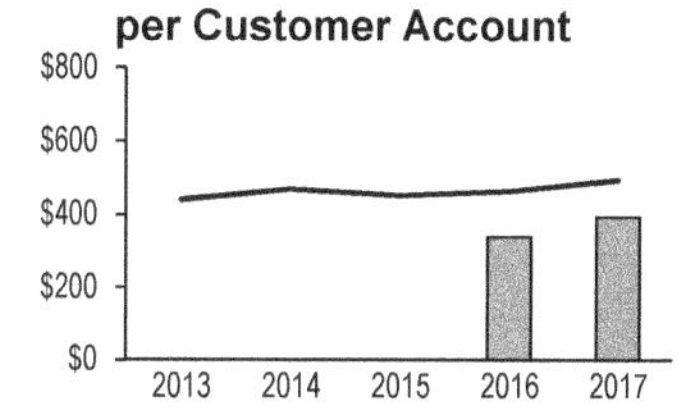

	2013	2014	2015	2016	2017
Raleigh				$337	$391
Average	$440	$470	$452	$463	$494

Workload Measures

Thousands of Gallons of Wastewater per Account

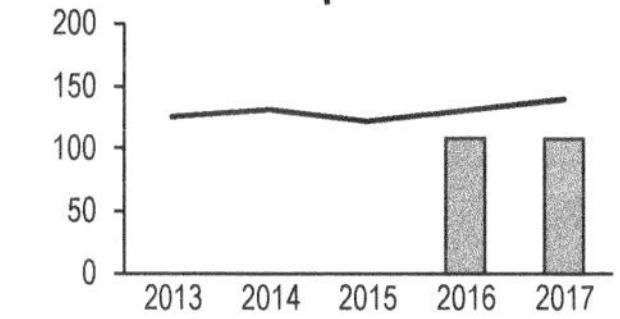

	2013	2014	2015	2016	2017
Raleigh				107.9	107.3
Average	125.7	131.5	122.1	130.9	139.8

Miles of Sewer Main Line Pipe per Square Mile of Service Area

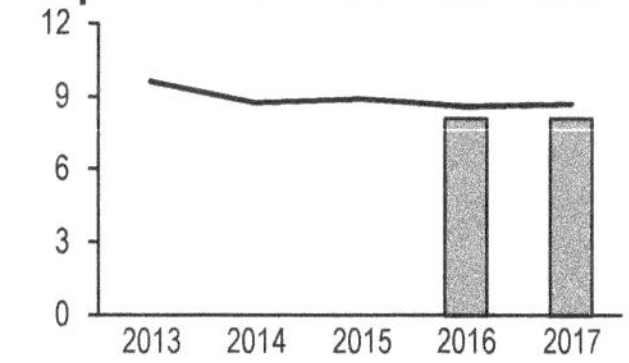

	2013	2014	2015	2016	2017
Raleigh				8.1	8.1
Average	9.6	8.8	8.9	8.6	8.7

Number of Lift Stations per 1,000 Accounts

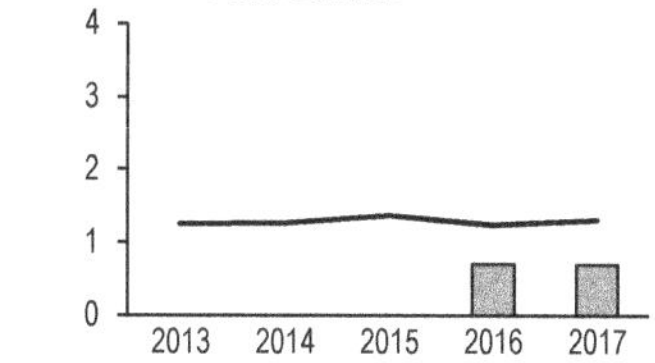

	2013	2014	2015	2016	2017
Raleigh				0.70	0.69
Average	1.25	1.26	1.37	1.23	1.31

Efficiency Measures

Total Cost per 1,000 Gallons of Treated Wastewater

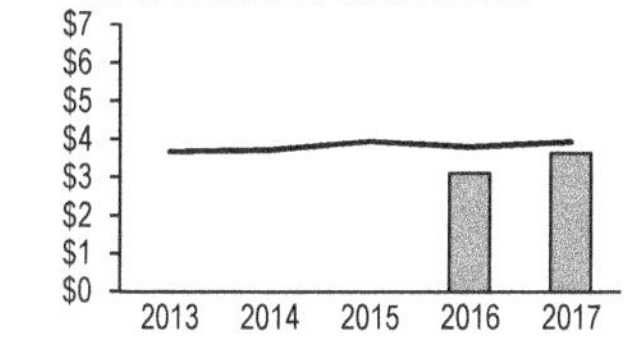

	2013	2014	2015	2016	2017
Raleigh				$3.12	$3.65
Average	$3.67	$3.71	$3.94	$3.80	$3.92

Million Gallons of Wastewater per Wastewater Services FTE

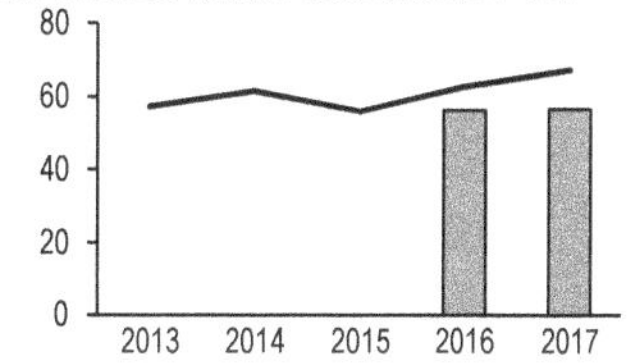

	2013	2014	2015	2016	2017
Raleigh				56.2	56.4
Average	57.2	61.4	55.9	62.6	67.2

Customer Accounts per Wastewater Services FTE

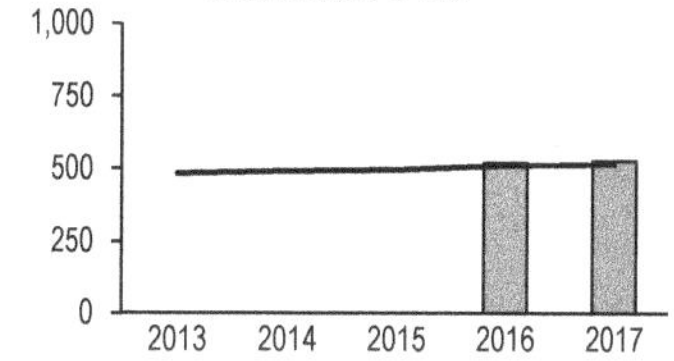

	2013	2014	2015	2016	2017
Raleigh				520	526
Average	483	491	494	510	515

Effectiveness Measures

Percentage of Wastewater Bills Not Collected

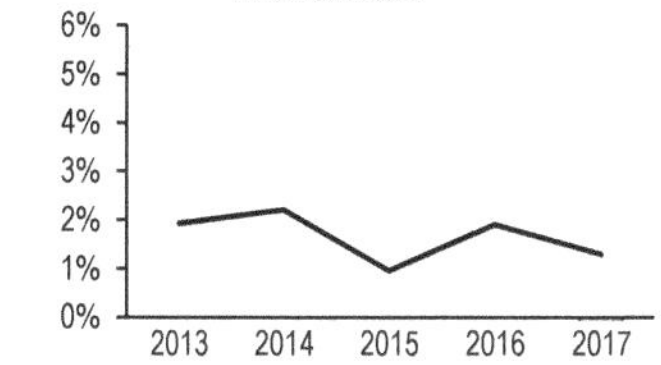

	2013	2014	2015	2016	2017
Raleigh					-0.98%
Average	1.93%	2.21%	0.96%	1.90%	1.29%

Average Daily Treatment as a Percentage of Capacity

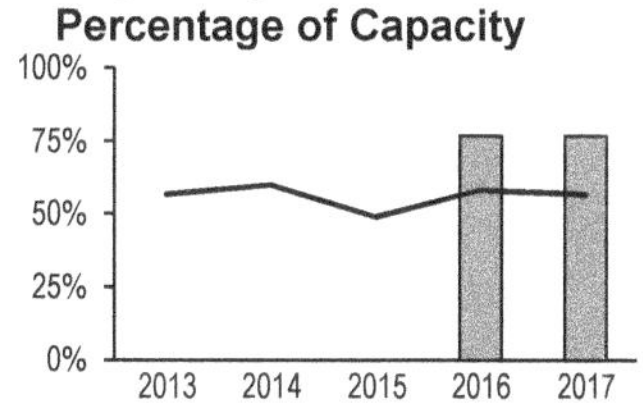

	2013	2014	2015	2016	2017
Raleigh				76.8%	76.9%
Average	56.6%	60.0%	48.9%	58.1%	56.5%

Percent of Main Line Rehabbed or Replaced

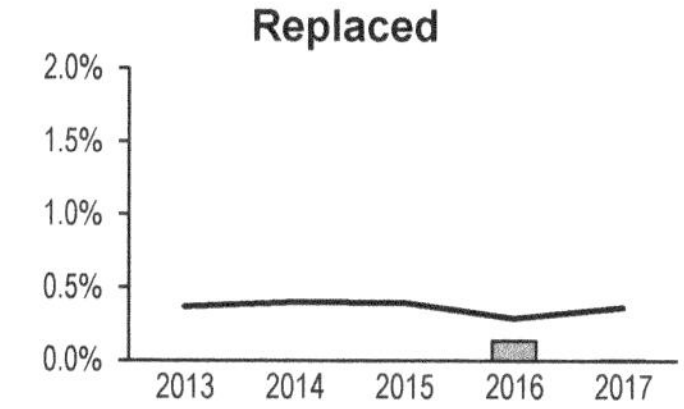

	2013	2014	2015	2016	2017
Raleigh				0.13%	0.00%
Average	0.37%	0.40%	0.40%	0.29%	0.36%

Overflows per 100 Miles of Main Line Pipe

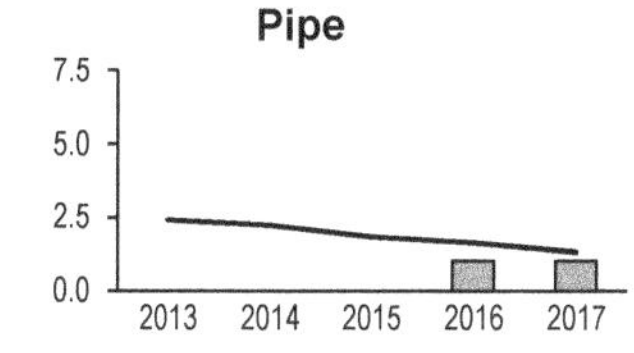

	2013	2014	2015	2016	2017
Raleigh				1.03	1.03
Average	2.41	2.23	1.85	1.64	1.33

Backups per 100 Miles of Main Line Pipe

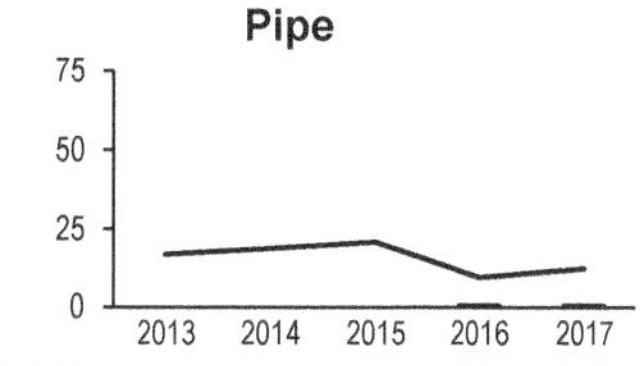

	2013	2014	2015	2016	2017
Raleigh				1.03	1.03
Average	16.84	18.71	20.70	9.52	12.45

Billed Wastewater as a Percent of Treated Effluent

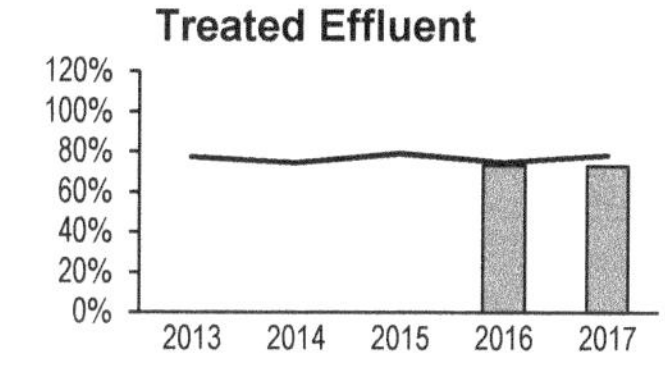

	2013	2014	2015	2016	2017
Raleigh				74%	73%
Average	77%	74%	79%	75%	78%

Salisbury

Wastewater Services

Fiscal Year 2016–17

Explanatory Information

Service Level and Delivery

The City of Salisbury provides water and sewer service through a combined enterprise fund department known as Salisbury-Rowan Utilities. The system covers Salisbury and much of Rowan County as well.

Wastewater is treated at two plants. Both plants use a biological activated sludge process for treatment. The treatment process includes mechanical bar screens, grit removal chambers, primary and secondary clarifiers, aeration basins, and liquid chlorine disinfection. The system does not currently have nutrient regulatory limits. Biosolids produced as a result of treatment are applied to farmland in Rowan County.

The system had no regulatory violations during the fiscal year for issues related to treatment and two violations connected to collections related to sanitary system overflows.

Conditions Affecting Service, Performance, and Costs

The costs of wastewater or sewer services as captured here do not include debt service but do capture depreciation of capital.

Municipal Profile

Estimated Service Population	52,500
Service Land Area (Square Miles)	45.5
Persons per Square Mile	1,154
Topography	Flat; gently rolling
Climate	Temperate; little ice and snow
Median Family Income U.S. Census 2010	$40,192

Service Profile

Total FTE Staff Positions	56.0
Treatment Plant	21.0
Line Crews	14.0
Billing/Collection	6.0
Other	15.0
Number of Treatment Plants	2
Total Treatment Capacity	12.5 MGD
Average Daily Flow	8.3 MGD
River Basin into Which System Discharges	Yadkin
Miles of Gravity Main Line Pipe	400
Miles of Forced Main Line Pipe	30
Average Age of Main Line Pipe	45 years
Blocks in Sewer Mains	27
Number of System Breaks	11
Sanitary System Overflows	2
Number of Customer Accounts	16,588
Total Revenues Collected	$12,750,626

Full Cost Profile

Cost Breakdown by Percentage	
Personal Services	36.5%
Operating Costs	37.9%
Capital Costs	25.5%
TOTAL	100.0%
Cost Breakdown in Dollars	
Personal Services	$3,595,381
Operating Costs	$3,731,595
Capital Costs	$2,513,619
TOTAL	$9,840,595

Key: Salisbury ▒ Benchmarking Average — Fiscal Years 2013 through 2017

Resource Measures

Wastewater Services Cost per Capita

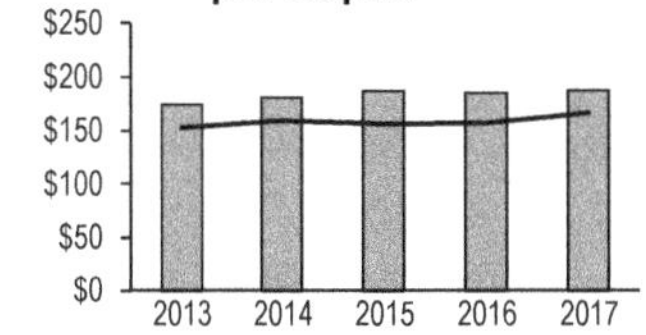

	2013	2014	2015	2016	2017
Salisbury	$175	$181	$187	$185	$187
Average	$152	$159	$156	$157	$166

Waterwater Services FTEs per 10,000 Population

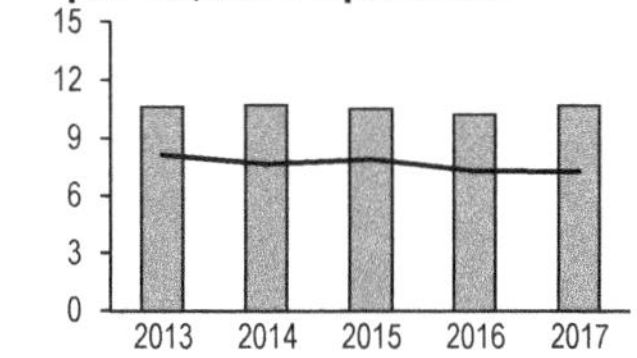

	2013	2014	2015	2016	2017
Salisbury	10.6	10.7	10.5	10.2	10.7
Average	8.1	7.7	7.9	7.3	7.3

Waterwaste Services Cost per Customer Account

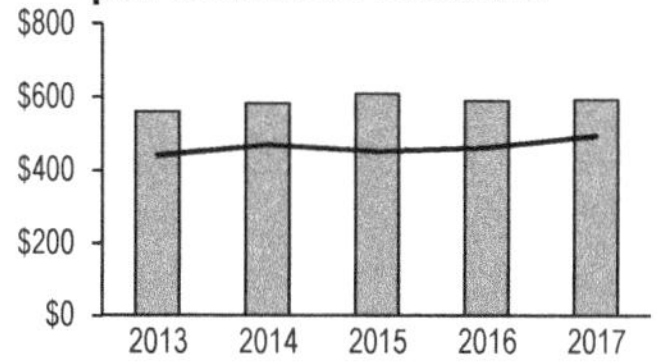

	2013	2014	2015	2016	2017
Salisbury	$559	$582	$608	$589	$593
Average	$440	$470	$452	$463	$494

Workload Measures

Thousands of Gallons of Wastewater per Account

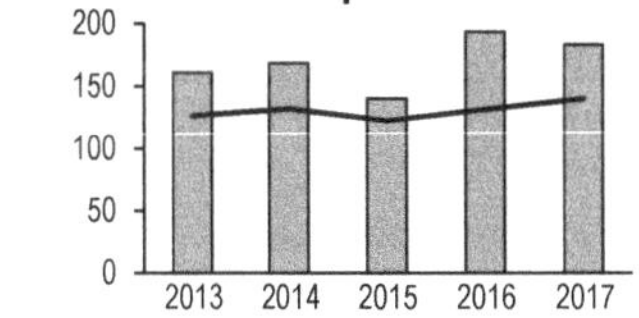

	2013	2014	2015	2016	2017
Salisbury	160.0	168.0	139.5	192.9	182.7
Average	125.7	131.5	122.1	130.9	139.8

Miles of Sewer Main Line Pipe per Square Mile of Service Area

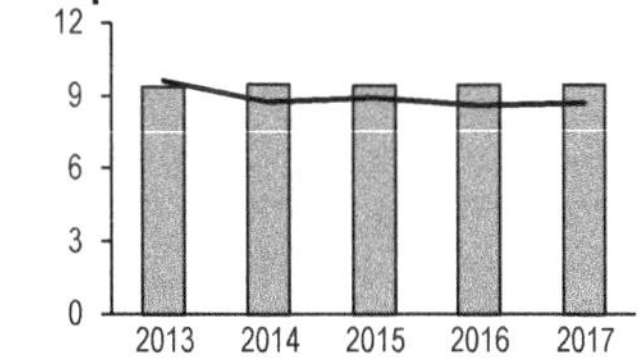

	2013	2014	2015	2016	2017
Salisbury	9.4	9.5	9.4	9.4	9.4
Average	9.6	8.8	8.9	8.6	8.7

Number of Lift Stations per 1,000 Accounts

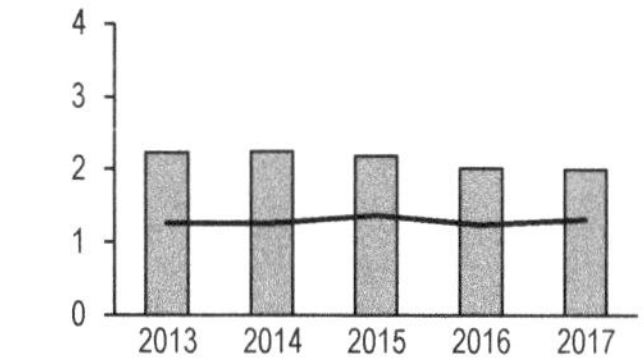

	2013	2014	2015	2016	2017
Salisbury	2.22	2.24	2.18	2.00	1.99
Average	1.25	1.26	1.37	1.23	1.31

Efficiency Measures

Total Cost per 1,000 Gallons of Treated Wastewater

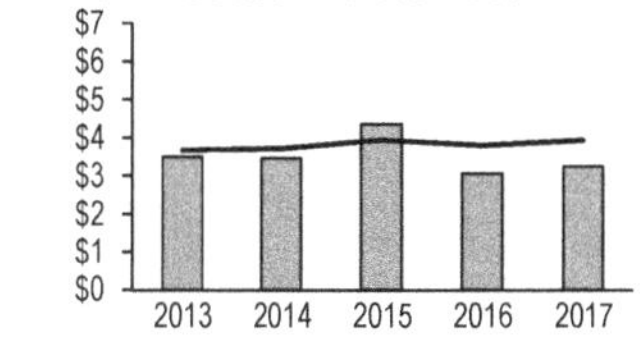

	2013	2014	2015	2016	2017
Salisbury	$3.49	$3.47	$4.35	$3.06	$3.25
Average	$3.67	$3.71	$3.94	$3.80	$3.92

Million Gallons of Wastewater per Wastewater Services FTE

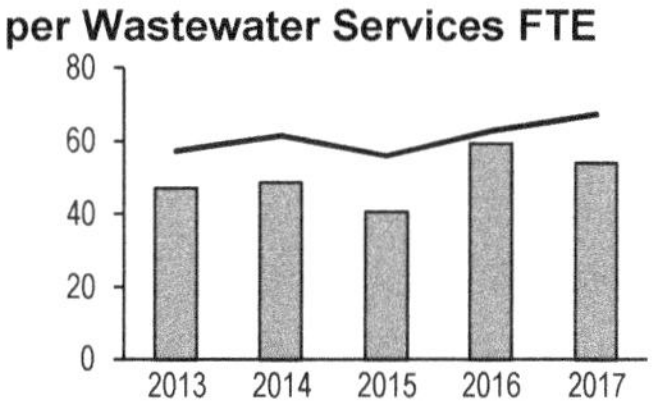

	2013	2014	2015	2016	2017
Salisbury	47.1	48.7	40.8	59.3	54.1
Average	57.2	61.4	55.9	62.6	67.2

Customer Accounts per Wastewater Services FTE

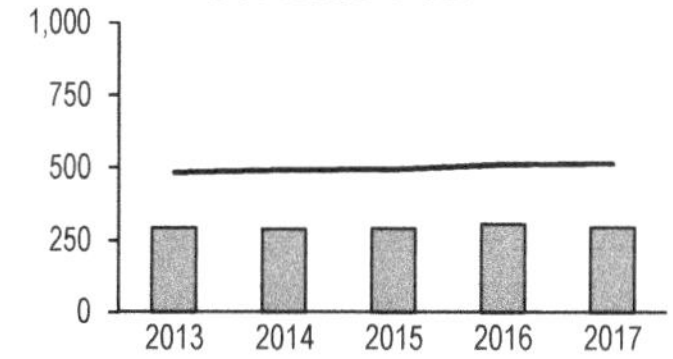

	2013	2014	2015	2016	2017
Salisbury	295	290	292	308	296
Average	483	491	494	510	515

Effectiveness Measures

Percentage of Wastewater Bills Not Collected

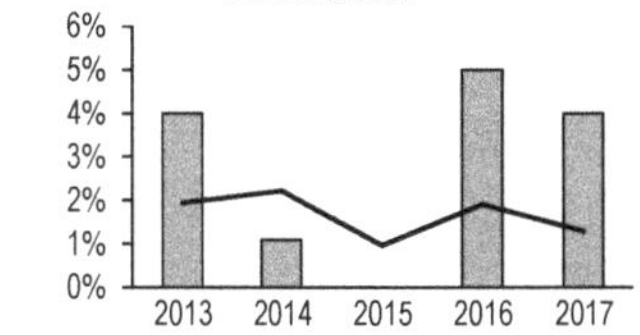

	2013	2014	2015	2016	2017
Salisbury	4.00%	1.09%		5.00%	4.00%
Average	1.93%	2.21%	0.96%	1.90%	1.29%

Average Daily Treatment as a Percentage of Capacity

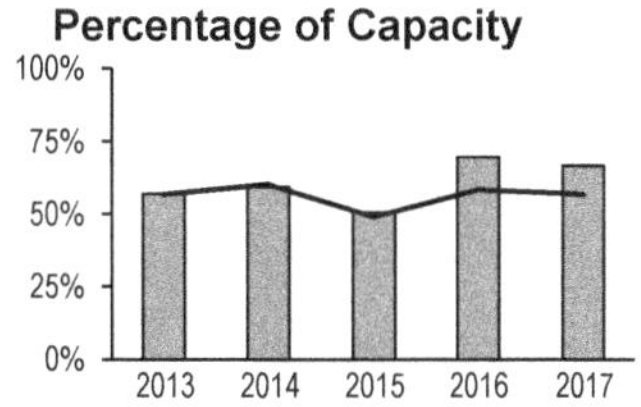

	2013	2014	2015	2016	2017
Salisbury	56.8%	59.2%	50.4%	69.6%	66.4%
Average	56.6%	60.0%	48.9%	58.1%	56.5%

Percent of Main Line Rehabbed or Replaced

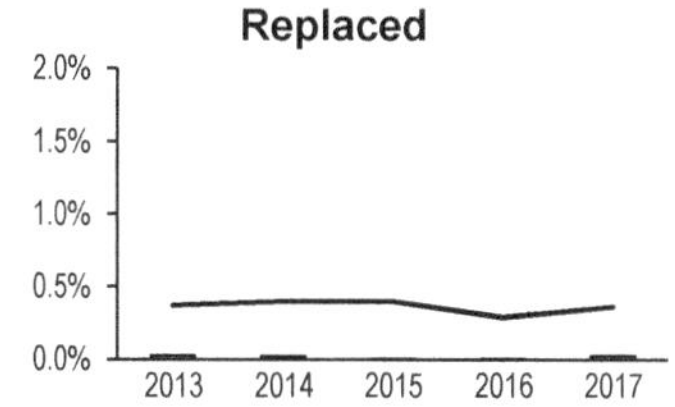

	2013	2014	2015	2016	2017
Salisbury	0.03%	0.02%	0.01%	0.00%	0.03%
Average	0.37%	0.40%	0.40%	0.29%	0.36%

Overflows per 100 Miles of Main Line Pipe

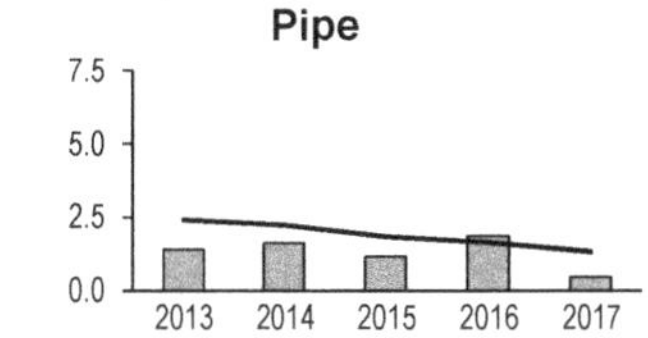

	2013	2014	2015	2016	2017
Salisbury	1.41	1.63	1.17	1.86	0.47
Average	2.41	2.23	1.85	1.64	1.33

Backups per 100 Miles of Main Line Pipe

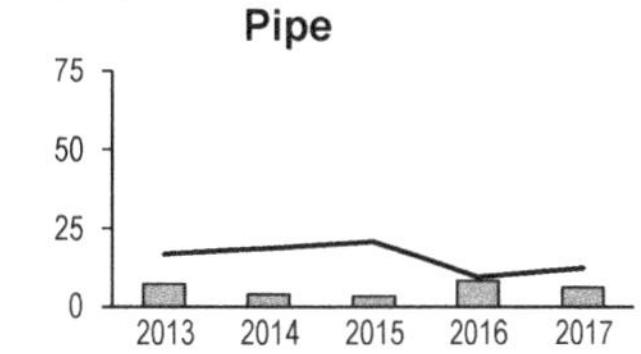

	2013	2014	2015	2016	2017
Salisbury	7.31	3.97	3.50	8.38	6.28
Average	16.84	18.71	20.70	9.52	12.45

Billed Wastewater as a Percent of Treated Effluent

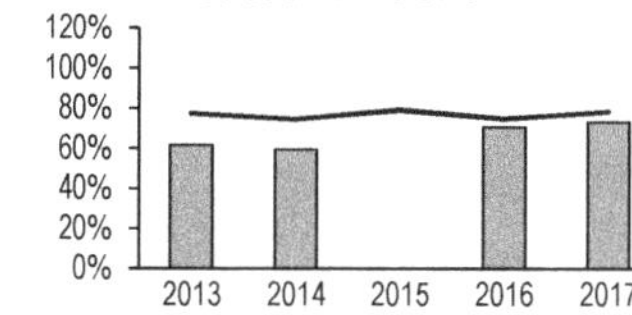

	2013	2014	2015	2016	2017
Salisbury	62%	59%		71%	73%
Average	77%	74%	79%	75%	78%

Fiscal Year 2016–17

Explanatory Information

Service Level and Delivery
Wastewater in Wilson is handled by the Water Reclamation and Wastewater Collection Division, which is part of Water Resources in the Public Services Department. Billing for large customers is handled by Water Resources, but residential customer billing is handled by the Customer Services Division in the Finance Department. The system covers the City of Wilson and several small adjoining areas outside the city in Wilson County.

Waterwater treatment is handled by one plant. The treatment plant uses advanced five-stage biological nutrient removal with deep-bed filters with methanol and biological and chemical phosphorous reduction. The system had very stringent nutrient limits in place to protect water quality in the Neuse River basin. The system produced Class A and B biosolids, with most of this solid waste being composted. A small portion is applied on city land or other permitted farmland.

The system had no reported regulatory violations for either the treatment or collection portion of the system during the fiscal year.

Conditions Affecting Service, Performance, and Costs
The costs of wastewater or sewer services as captured here do not include debt service but do capture depreciation of capital.

Large capital improvements are being made to the Buckhorn Lake Dam and Wastewater Projects, which have been required to meet advanced nutrient removal standards.

Municipal Profile

Estimated Service Population	53,600
Service Land Area (Square Miles)	35
Persons per Square Mile	1,531
Topography	Flat
Climate	Temperate; little ice and snow
Median Family Income U.S. Census 2010	$43,442

Service Profile

Total FTE Staff Positions	61.0
Treatment Plant	31.0
Line Crews	27.0
Billing/Collection	2.0
Other	1.0
Number of Treatment Plants	1
Total Treatment Capacity	14.0 MGD
Average Daily Flow	9.0 MGD
River Basin into Which System Discharges	Neuse
Miles of Gravity Main Line Pipe	355
Miles of Forced Main Line Pipe	10
Average Age of Main Line Pipe	44 years
Blocks in Sewer Mains	7
Number of System Breaks	7
Sanitary System Overflows	9
Number of Customer Accounts	20,441
Total Revenues Collected	$13,164,000

Full Cost Profile

Cost Breakdown by Percentage	
Personal Services	34.7%
Operating Costs	42.1%
Capital Costs	23.2%
TOTAL	100.0%
Cost Breakdown in Dollars	
Personal Services	$4,225,234
Operating Costs	$5,128,118
Capital Costs	$2,832,924
TOTAL	$12,186,275

Key: Wilson ▒ Benchmarking Average — Fiscal Years 2013 through 2017

Resource Measures

Wastewater Services Cost per Capita

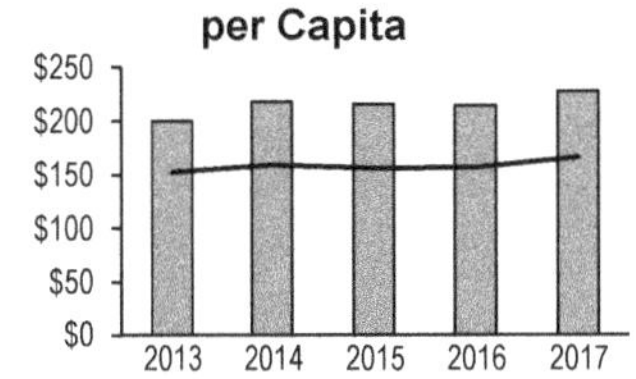

	2013	2014	2015	2016	2017
Wilson	$200	$218	$215	$214	$227
Average	$152	$159	$156	$157	$166

Waterwater Services FTEs per 10,000 Population

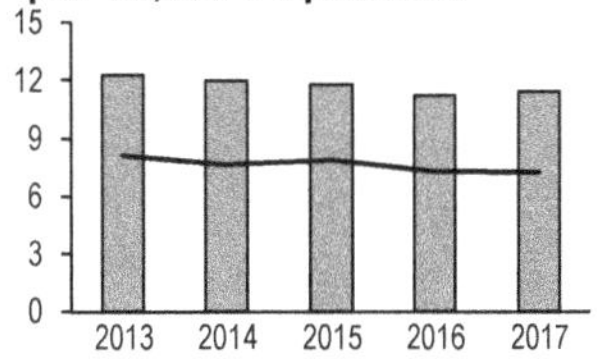

	2013	2014	2015	2016	2017
Wilson	12.2	11.9	11.8	11.2	11.4
Average	8.1	7.7	7.9	7.3	7.3

Waterwaste Services Cost per Customer Account

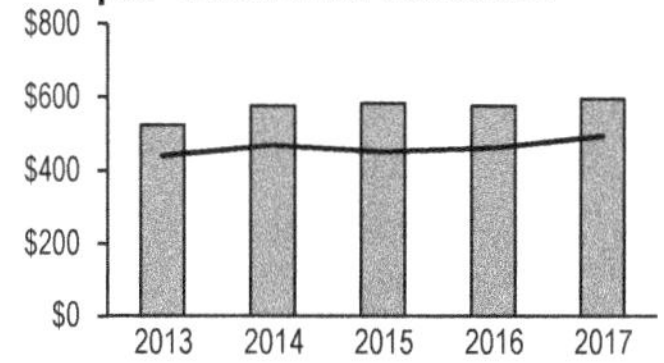

	2013	2014	2015	2016	2017
Wilson	$524	$577	$584	$577	$596
Average	$440	$470	$452	$463	$494

Workload Measures

Thousands of Gallons of Wastewater per Account

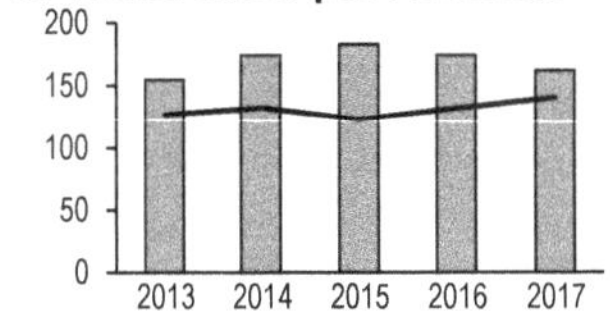

	2013	2014	2015	2016	2017
Wilson	154.2	173.3	182.4	173.7	161.2
Average	125.7	131.5	122.1	130.9	139.8

Miles of Sewer Main Line Pipe per Square Mile of Service Area

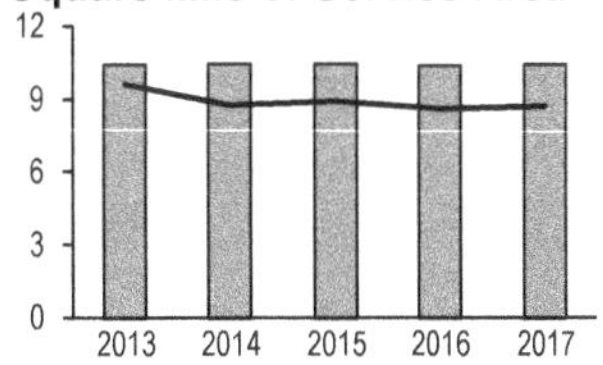

	2013	2014	2015	2016	2017
Wilson	10.4	10.4	10.4	10.4	10.4
Average	9.6	8.8	8.9	8.6	8.7

Number of Lift Stations per 1,000 Accounts

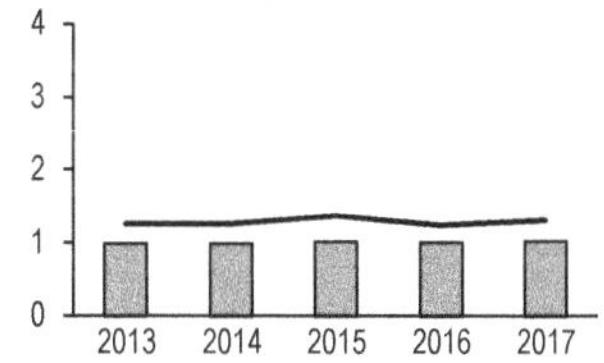

	2013	2014	2015	2016	2017
Wilson	0.99	0.99	1.01	1.01	1.03
Average	1.25	1.26	1.37	1.23	1.31

Efficiency Measures

Total Cost per 1,000 Gallons of Treated Wastewater

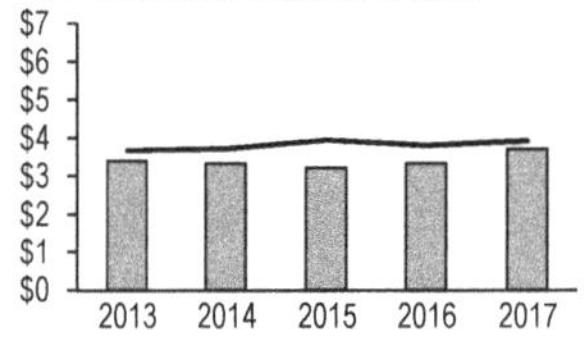

	2013	2014	2015	2016	2017
Wilson	$3.40	$3.33	$3.20	$3.32	$3.70
Average	$3.67	$3.71	$3.94	$3.80	$3.92

Million Gallons of Wastewater per Wastewater Services FTE

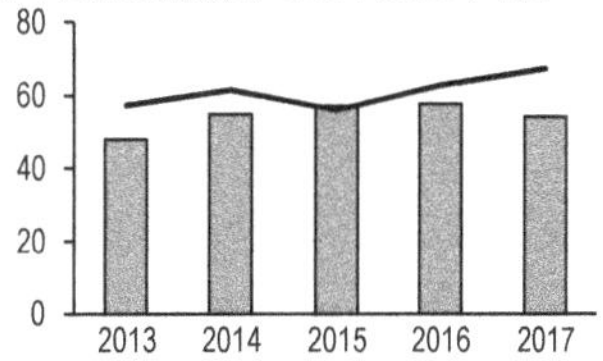

	2013	2014	2015	2016	2017
Wilson	48.0	54.8	57.1	57.6	54.0
Average	57.2	61.4	55.9	62.6	67.2

Customer Accounts per Wastewater Services FTE

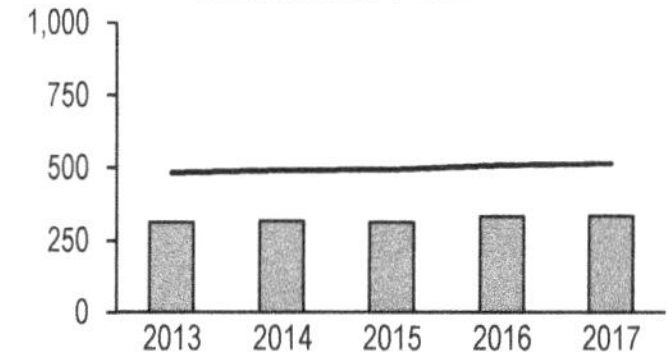

	2013	2014	2015	2016	2017
Wilson	311	316	313	331	335
Average	483	491	494	510	515

Effectiveness Measures

Percentage of Wastewater Bills Not Collected

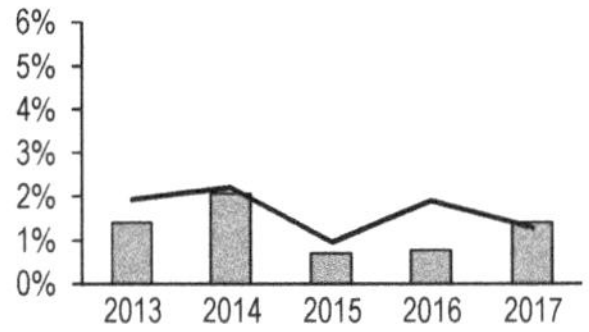

	2013	2014	2015	2016	2017
Wilson	1.40%	2.07%	0.70%	0.78%	1.41%
Average	1.93%	2.21%	0.96%	1.90%	1.29%

Average Daily Treatment as a Percentage of Capacity

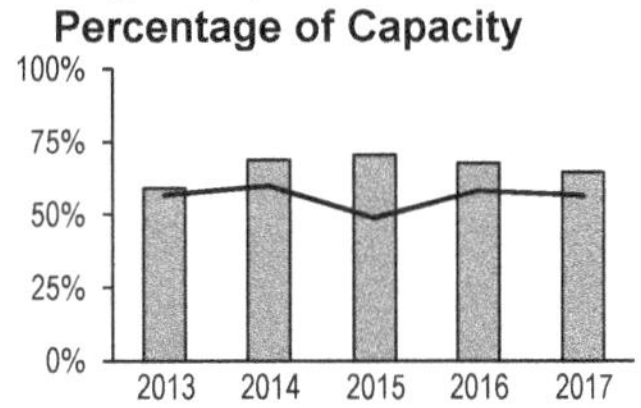

	2013	2014	2015	2016	2017
Wilson	59.1%	68.6%	70.4%	67.6%	64.5%
Average	56.6%	60.0%	48.9%	58.1%	56.5%

Percent of Main Line Rehabbed or Replaced

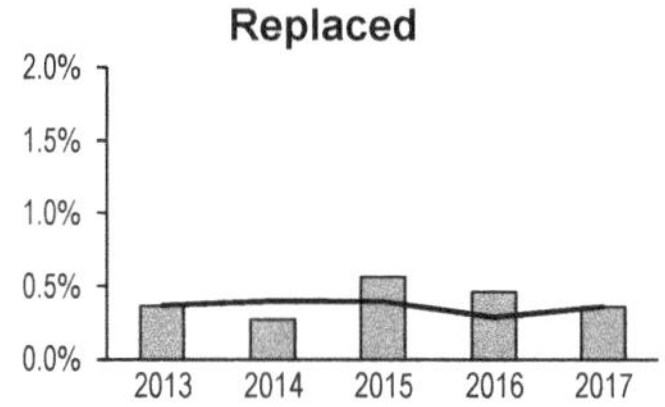

	2013	2014	2015	2016	2017
Wilson	0.36%	0.27%	0.56%	0.46%	0.36%
Average	0.37%	0.40%	0.40%	0.29%	0.36%

Overflows per 100 Miles of Main Line Pipe

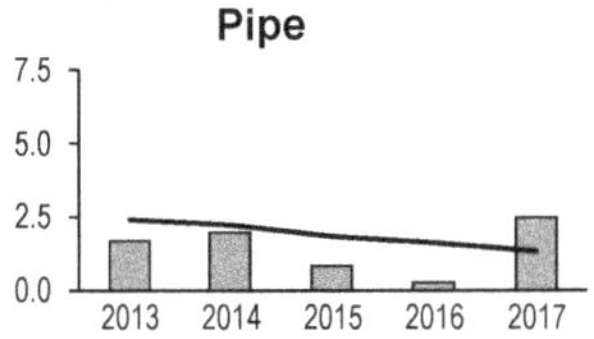

	2013	2014	2015	2016	2017
Wilson	1.69	1.97	0.85	0.28	2.47
Average	2.41	2.23	1.85	1.64	1.33

Backups per 100 Miles of Main Line Pipe

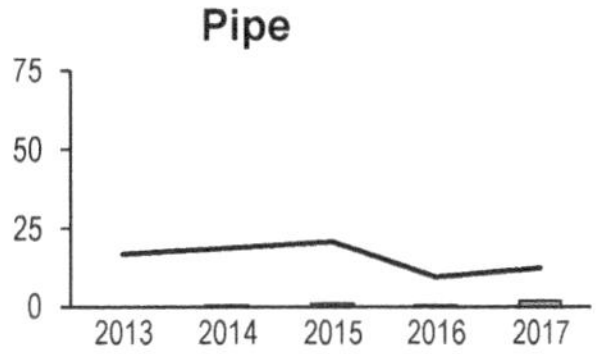

	2013	2014	2015	2016	2017
Wilson		0.56	1.13	0.57	1.92
Average	16.84	18.71	20.70	9.52	12.45

Billed Wastewater as a Percent of Treated Effluent

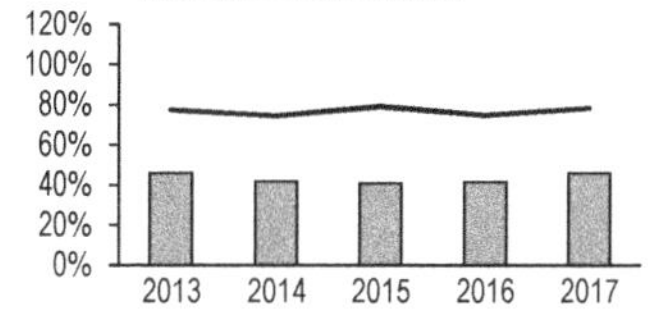

	2013	2014	2015	2016	2017
Wilson	46%	42%	41%	42%	46%
Average	77%	74%	79%	75%	78%

Winston-Salem — Wastewater Services

Fiscal Year 2016–17

Explanatory Information

Service Level and Delivery

The Winston-Salem and Forsyth County Utilities Division operates a combined water and sewer system that covers the city and most of the remaining population of Forsyth County. The system also serves several adjoining areas in Davie and Davidson counties. Beyond water and wastewater, the Utilities Division also handles solid waste disposal. Operations are divided among several divisions by function.

The system has two separate treatment plants. The plants use conventional activated sludge with anaerobic digestion for treatment. The system currently does not have regulatory nutrient limits in place. Biosolids produced are disposed after first using thermal drying with subsequent reuse as a soil amendment.

During the fiscal year, the system had no regulatory violations connected to the treatment portion of the system and eighty-six reported violations for the collection portion of the system connected to sanitary system overflows.

Conditions Affecting Service, Performance, and Costs

The costs of wastewater or sewer services as captured here do not include debt service but do capture depreciation of capital.

The city has used improvements in its GIS mapping systems and incident records to change the process by which the Division ranks and proactively cleans pipes. This process is expected to lower the number of breaks and overflows.

Municipal Profile

Estimated Service Population	352,025
Service Land Area (Square Miles)	320
Persons per Square Mile	1,100
Topography	Gently rolling
Climate	Temperate; some ice and snow
Median Family Income U.S. Census 2010	$51,491

Service Profile

Total FTE Staff Positions	175.0
Treatment Plant	83.0
Line Crews	65.0
Billing/Collection	8.0
Other	19.0
Number of Treatment Plants	2
Total Treatment Capacity	51.0 MGD
Average Daily Flow	32.1 MGD
River Basin into Which System Discharges	Yadkin
Miles of Gravity Main Line Pipe	1,726
Miles of Forced Main Line Pipe	36
Average Age of Main Line Pipe	50 years
Blocks in Sewer Mains	235
Number of System Breaks	52
Sanitary System Overflows	62
Number of Customer Accounts	98,300
Total Revenues Collected	$52,721,393

Full Cost Profile

Cost Breakdown by Percentage	
Personal Services	26.1%
Operating Costs	35.8%
Capital Costs	38.1%
TOTAL	100.0%
Cost Breakdown in Dollars	
Personal Services	$9,295,769
Operating Costs	$12,721,005
Capital Costs	$13,546,548
TOTAL	$35,563,322

Winston-Salem — Wastewater Services

Key: Winston-Salem ▒ Benchmarking Average — Fiscal Years 2013 through 2017

Resource Measures

Wastewater Services Cost per Capita

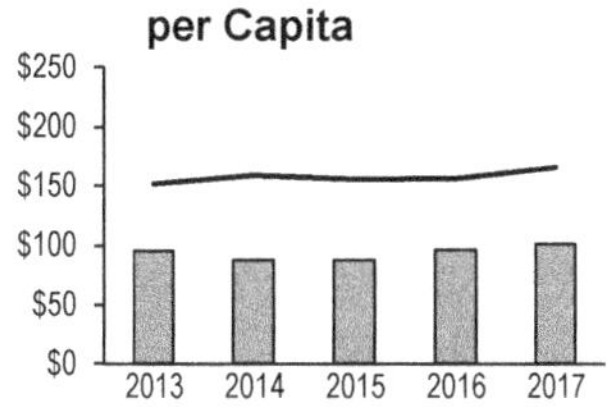

	2013	2014	2015	2016	2017
Winston-Salem	$95	$87	$87	$96	$101
Average	$152	$159	$156	$157	$166

Waterwater Services FTEs per 10,000 Population

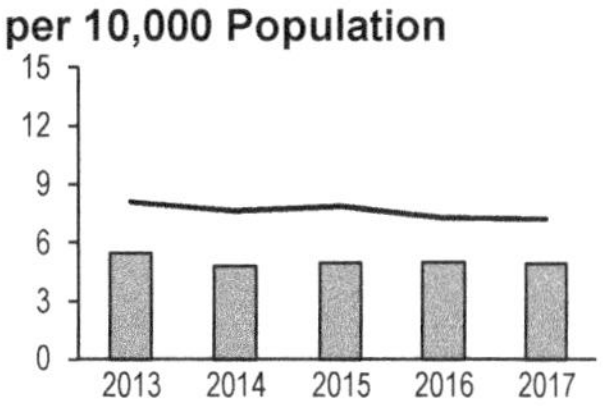

	2013	2014	2015	2016	2017
Winston-Salem	5.5	4.8	5.0	5.0	5.0
Average	8.1	7.7	7.9	7.3	7.3

Waterwaste Services Cost per Customer Account

	2013	2014	2015	2016	2017
Winston-Salem	$339	$336	$333	$346	$362
Average	$440	$470	$452	$463	$494

Workload Measures

Thousands of Gallons of Wastewater per Account

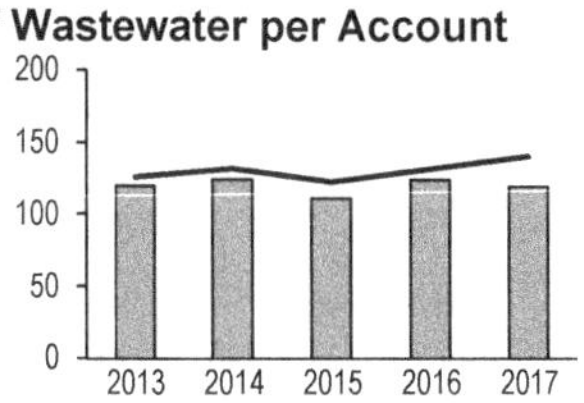

	2013	2014	2015	2016	2017
Winston-Salem	120.0	124.3	110.8	124.0	119.1
Average	125.7	131.5	122.1	130.9	139.8

Miles of Sewer Main Line Pipe per Square Mile of Service Area

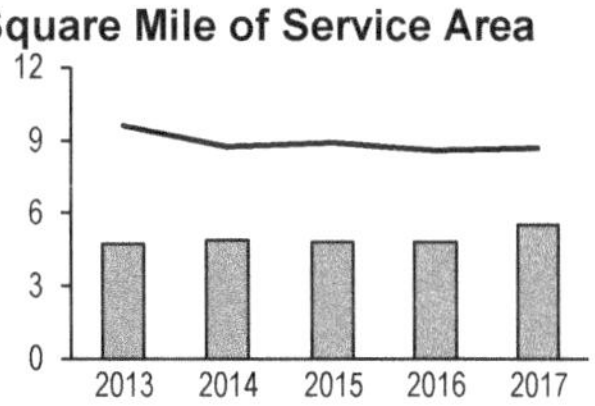

	2013	2014	2015	2016	2017
Winston-Salem	4.7	4.9	4.8	4.8	5.5
Average	9.6	8.8	8.9	8.6	8.7

Number of Lift Stations per 1,000 Accounts

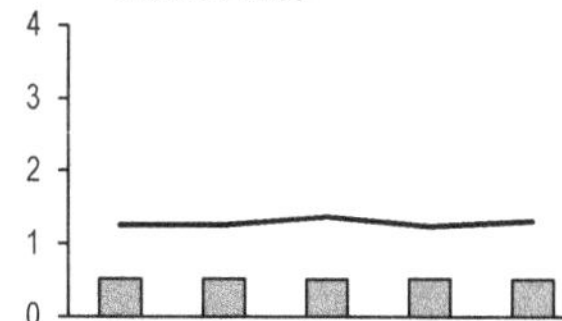

	2013	2014	2015	2016	2017
Winston-Salem	0.52	0.51	0.51	0.51	0.51
Average	1.25	1.26	1.37	1.23	1.31

Efficiency Measures

Total Cost per 1,000 Gallons of Treated Wastewater

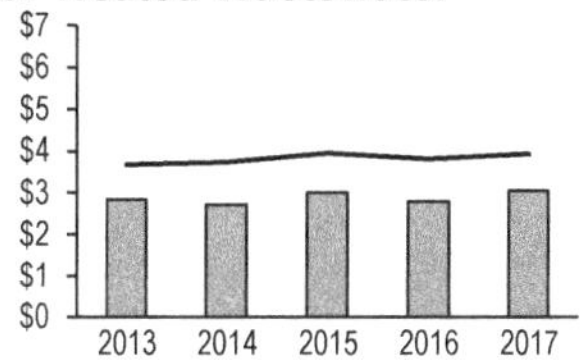

	2013	2014	2015	2016	2017
Winston-Salem	$2.82	$2.71	$3.00	$2.79	$3.04
Average	$3.67	$3.71	$3.94	$3.80	$3.92

Million Gallons of Wastewater per Wastewater Services FTE

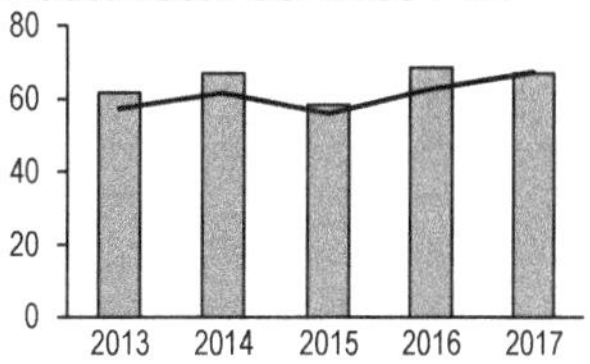

	2013	2014	2015	2016	2017
Winston-Salem	61.6	66.9	58.3	68.5	66.9
Average	57.2	61.4	55.9	62.6	67.2

Customer Accounts per Wastewater Services FTE

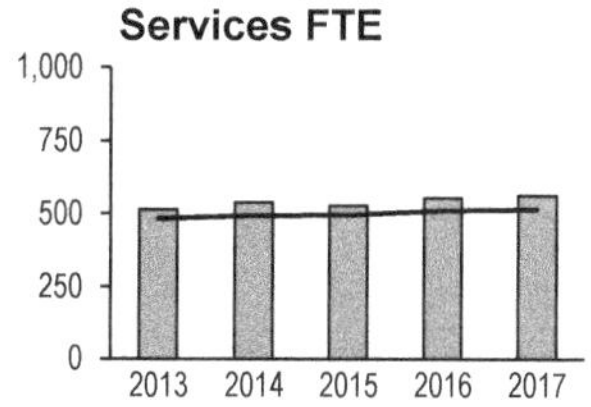

	2013	2014	2015	2016	2017
Winston-Salem	513	538	526	553	562
Average	483	491	494	510	515

Effectiveness Measures

Percentage of Wastewater Bills Not Collected

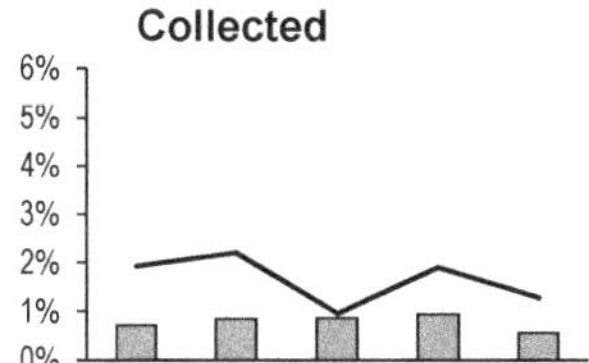

	2013	2014	2015	2016	2017
Winston-Salem	0.71%	0.85%	0.86%	0.94%	0.56%
Average	1.93%	2.21%	0.96%	1.90%	1.29%

Average Daily Treatment as a Percentage of Capacity

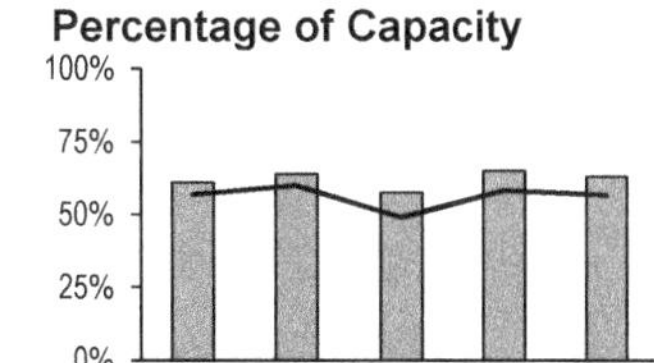

	2013	2014	2015	2016	2017
Winston-Salem	60.9%	63.6%	57.3%	64.8%	62.9%
Average	56.6%	60.0%	48.9%	58.1%	56.5%

Percent of Main Line Rehabbed or Replaced

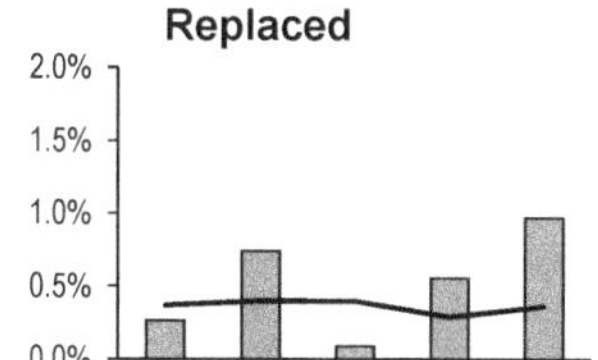

	2013	2014	2015	2016	2017
Winston-Salem	0.27%	0.74%	0.09%	0.55%	0.97%
Average	0.37%	0.40%	0.40%	0.29%	0.36%

Overflows per 100 Miles of Main Line Pipe

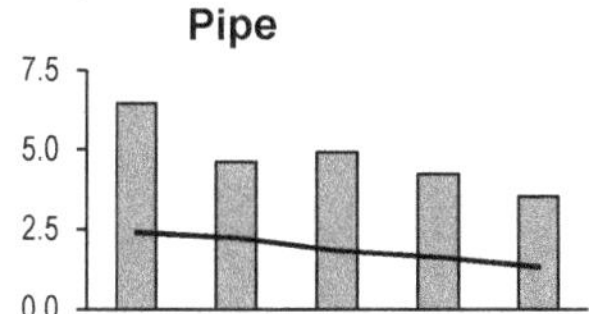

	2013	2014	2015	2016	2017
Winston-Salem	6.44	4.60	4.91	4.23	3.52
Average	2.41	2.23	1.85	1.64	1.33

Backups per 100 Miles of Main Line Pipe

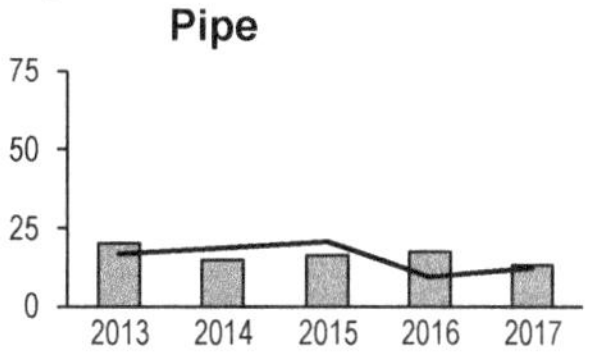

	2013	2014	2015	2016	2017
Winston-Salem	20.19	14.88	16.34	17.54	13.34
Average	16.84	18.71	20.70	9.52	12.45

Billed Wastewater as a Percent of Treated Effluent

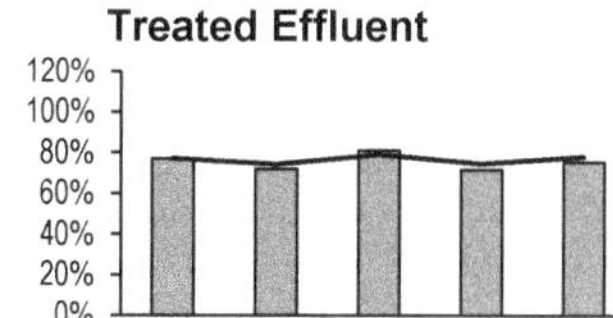

	2013	2014	2015	2016	2017
Winston-Salem	77%	72%	81%	71%	75%
Average	77%	74%	79%	75%	78%

UNC | SCHOOL OF GOVERNMENT
North Carolina Benchmarking Project

Performance and Cost Data

CORE PARKS AND RECREATION

SCHOOL OF GOVERNMENT
North Carolina Benchmarking Project

PERFORMANCE MEASURES FOR CORE PARKS AND RECREATION SERVICES

SERVICE DEFINITION

Parks and Recreation includes both passive and active recreation opportunities maintained and operated by a local government. For the purposes of this benchmarking effort, this includes core operational functions such as parks, multi-purpose recreation facilities, athletic facilities, greenways, and trails. This also includes programs and events.

However, Parks and Recreation departments frequently may include a variety of other activities and facilities. To support reasonable comparisons, this service benchmarking excludes these secondary recreational activities, including performance venues, museums, historic sites, golf courses, marinas/boat ramps, and professional stadiums. Also excluded are other non-recreational activities sometimes performed by parks and recreation departments, such as care of cemeteries; maintenance of rights-of-way along city streets; maintenance of facilities owned by a municipality but not parks-related; and maintenance of city lots. The dollars and people associated with these secondary and non-park activities are excluded.

Parks and Recreation does offer an important difference from many of the other services provided by local governments. Much of the objective of this service area is to provide facilities for use by citizens. Use of many of these facilities is not easily tracked. Many of the measures shown for this service area are accordingly measures of facility availability rather than the traditional workload type of measures seen in other service areas.

NOTES ON PERFORMANCE MEASURES

1. Land Acres of All Municipal Parks per 10,000 Population

This resource measure captures the amount of park land that is available relative to the population in the communities.

2. Recreation Centers per 10,000 Population

Recreation centers provide space for a variety of indoor recreational activities. This measure shows the number of centers relative to the population.

3. Swimming Pools per 10,000 Population

Indoor and outdoor pools are a desirable recreational facility. This resource measure captures the number of pools relative to the population.

4. Athletic Fields per 10,000 Population

Outdoor athletic fields are used for organized and informal recreation. This measure counts the number of formal athletic fields, including rectangular fields such as those for football and soccer, diamond fields as for baseball, and non-designated fields which can be used for multiple activities. The count includes both natural grass and artificial-surface fields, where available.

5. Playgrounds per 10,000 Population
Formal playgrounds include a variety of fixed equipment, such as swings, jungle gyms, slides, and other apparatus. This measure captures these playgrounds relative to the population.

6. Miles of Trails per 10,000 Population
Outdoor trails of all types represent an important type of active recreation. This measure captures the total miles of trails in a community relative to the population. The miles total includes paved and unpaved trails and covers various types of trail, such as those for walking, bike riding, and equestrian riding.

7. Total Core Parks and Recreation Costs
This efficiency measure represents the level of spending relative to the park acreage in a community. Although funds may be spent on facilities and activities, this measure provides some comparison on the intensity of spending.

8. Acres of Park Maintained per Maintenance Full-Time Equivalent (FTE)
This efficiency measure compares the amount of acres in the park system relative to the number of FTEs used by a jurisdiction to provide maintenance.

9. Volunteer Hours in FTEs as a Percent of Paid Staff FTEs
Volunteers represent an important resource to help support Parks and Recreation activities. This efficiency measure compares the estimated amount of volunteer labor relative to the paid staff in order to provide a measure of the benefit these volunteers bring to a community.

10. Revenue Gained as a Percent of Total Core Parks and Recreation Costs
Parks and Recreation is a service that is primarily supported by general funding from a local government budget. But gaining additional revenues in the form of user fees, grants, donations, and sponsorships helps to leverage spending and provide services. This effectiveness measure shows how much revenue has been raised from these other sources relative to the total costs reported.

11. Acts of Vandalism per 10,000 Population
Vandalism damages parks and recreation facilities, making them unavailable or less useful to citizens. This effectiveness measure compares the number of acts of vandalism relative to the population to indicate the extent of this problem.

Core Parks and Recreation

Summary of Key Dimensions of Service

City or Town	Municipal Population as of July 2016	Core Parks and Recreation FTEs	Number of Parks	Park Land Acreage	Number of Recreation and Senior Centers	Number of Playgrounds	Number of Athletic Fields	Miles of Trails
Apex	46,688	40.0	11	558.0	1	11	27	14.0
Asheville	91,929	132.7	47	869.0	13	24	27	5.5
Chapel Hill	59,852	76.8	31	1,114.0	2	11	16	23.6
Concord	88,815	33.4	9	226.0	3	14	22	10.7
Goldsboro	34,793	46.4	11	168.8	3	37	15	5.1
Greensboro	284,343	161.0	342	10,907.0	12	108	79	88.2
Greenville	87,989	129.3	26	1,460.9	8	17	24	7.8
Hickory	40,453	59.0	26	515.0	8	40	25	12.0
High Point	110,244	138.1	46	2,058.0	7	35	54	23.5
Raleigh	448,706	717.2	175	6,164.3	41	96	113	146.3
Salisbury	34,459	13.0	28	518.0	4	18	12	16.9
Wilson	49,406	68.0	28	400.0	4	25	26	14.5
Winston-Salem	240,603	200.2	79	3,852.0	17	45	97	23.3

EXPLANATORY FACTORS

These are some factors that the project found affected core parks and recreation services performance and cost in one or more of the municipalities:

Youth Population
Total Acreage
Miles of Trails
Number of Facilities

Fiscal Year 2016–17

Explanatory Information

Service Level and Delivery

The Town of Apex provides recreation services through the separate Parks, Recreation, and Cultural Resources Department. The city has priority use agreements with the Wake County School System in exchange for maintenance of areas used by the town.

The town has eleven separate parks and sites. These parks cover 558 land acres; most of this area is currently developed. The city has fourteen miles of trails; about three-fourths of them are paved.

In addition to the core parks and recreational facilities, Apex has a performing arts center. The operation of this other facility is not included in the Core Parks and Recreation comparisons reported here. This facility is not included here in dollars or staff as part of core parks and recreation facilities and activities.

Conditions Affecting Service, Performance, and Costs

Parks and Recreation is a new service area for the benchmarking project beginning with the FY 2012–13 reporting year.

Municipal Profile

Population (OSBM 2016)	46,688
Land Area (Square Miles)	20.61
Persons per Square Mile	2,265
Topography	Flat; gently rolling
Climate	Temperate; little ice and snow

Service Profile

Parks and Recreation Staff	
Administrative Position FTEs	5.0
Maintenance Staff FTEs	20.8
Program and Facility FTEs	11.2
Other Staff FTEs	3.0
TOTAL	40.0
Number of Parks and Sites	11
Total Land Acreage in Parks	558.0
Miles of Trails in Parks	14.0
Recreational Facilities	
Indoor and Outdoor Pools	0
Recreation Centers	1
Outdoor Basketball Courts	6
Outdoor Tennis Courts	15
Playgrounds	11
Diamond Fields	13
Rectangular Fields	12
Other Athletic Fields	2
Picnic Shelters	18
Parks and Recreation Revenues	
User Fees	$877,344
Grants	$34,000
Sponsorships	$12,100
Donations	$54,792

Full Cost Profile

Cost Breakdown by Percentage	
Personal Services	44.8%
Operating Costs	43.5%
Capital Costs	11.6%
TOTAL	100.0%
Cost Breakdown in Dollars	
Personal Services	$1,914,111
Operating Costs	$1,859,073
Capital Costs	$496,580
TOTAL	$4,269,764

Key: Apex ▒ Benchmarking Average — Fiscal Years 2013 through 2017

Resource Measures

Core Parks and Recreation Services per Capita

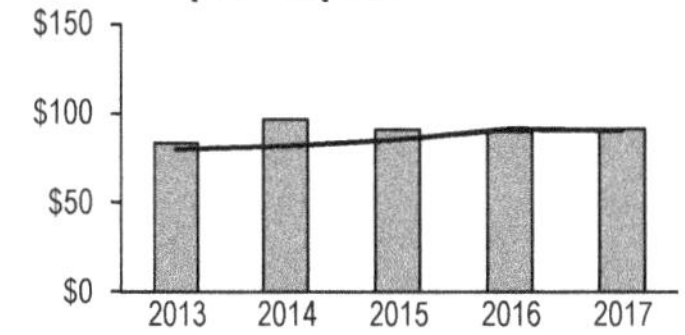

	2013	2014	2015	2016	2017
Apex	$83	$97	$91	$90	$91
Average	$80	$82	$85	$91	$91

Core Parks and Recreation Staff per 10,000 Population

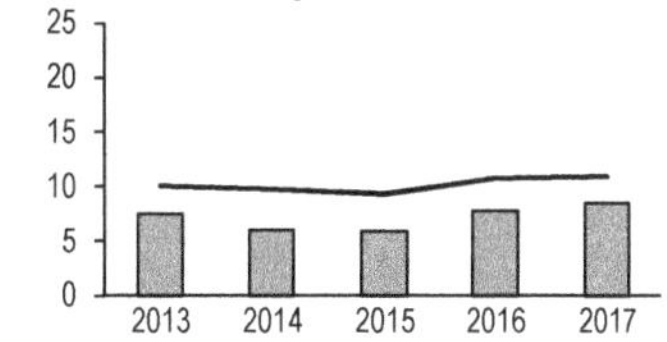

	2013	2014	2015	2016	2017
Apex	7.5	6.1	6.0	7.8	8.6
Average	10.1	9.8	9.3	10.8	10.9

Facilities Measures

Land Acres of Parks per 10,000 Population

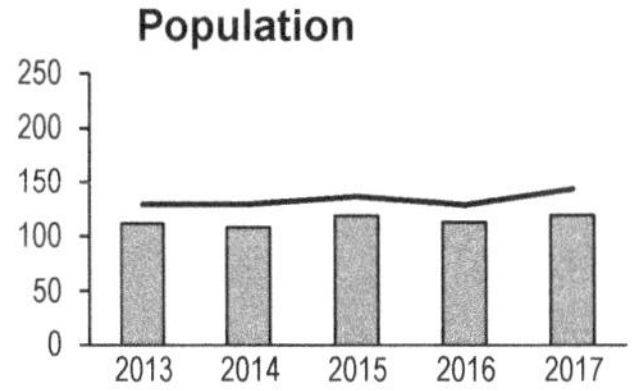

	2013	2014	2015	2016	2017
Apex	111.40	108.25	118.53	113.09	119.52
Average	129.38	129.25	136.59	128.88	143.58

Recreation Centers per 10,000 Population

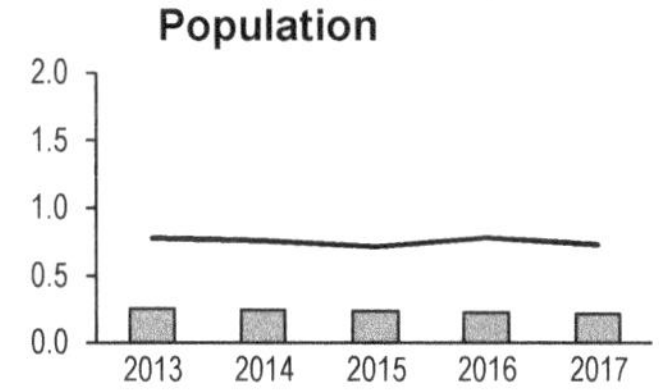

	2013	2014	2015	2016	2017
Apex	0.25	0.24	0.23	0.22	0.21
Average	0.77	0.75	0.71	0.77	0.72

Swimming Pools per 10,000 Population

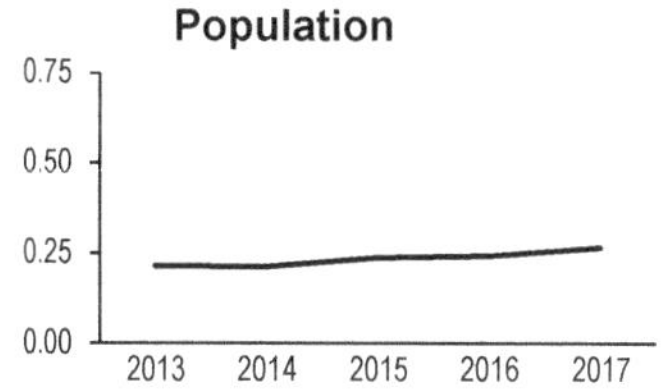

	2013	2014	2015	2016	2017
Apex	0.00	0.00	0.00	0.00	0.00
Average	0.22	0.21	0.24	0.24	0.27

Athletic Fields per 10,000 Population

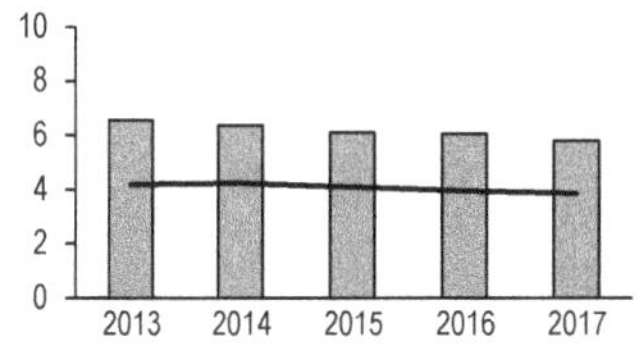

	2013	2014	2015	2016	2017
Apex	6.54	6.35	6.09	6.03	5.78
Average	4.18	4.23	4.08	3.94	3.85

Playgrounds per 10,000 Population

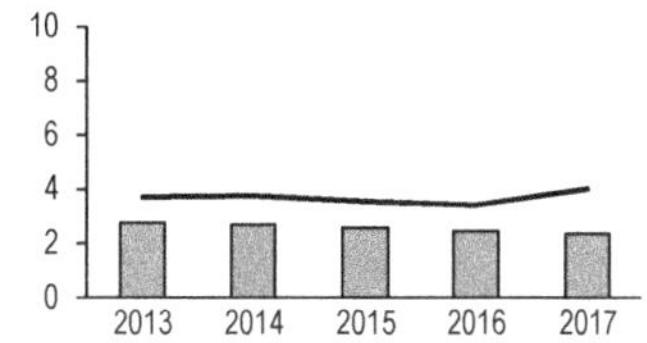

	2013	2014	2015	2016	2017
Apex	2.77	2.69	2.58	2.46	2.36
Average	3.70	3.76	3.54	3.41	4.01

Miles of Land Trails per 10,000 Population

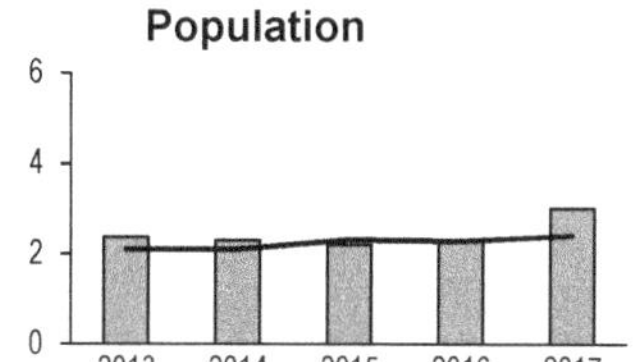

	2013	2014	2015	2016	2017
Apex	2.36	2.29	2.20	2.30	3.00
Average	2.11	2.10	2.32	2.29	2.41

Efficiency Measures

Total Core Parks and Recreation Costs per Acre

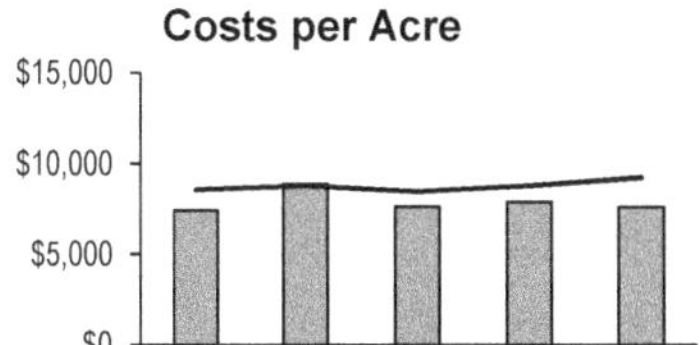

	2013	2014	2015	2016	2017
Apex	$7,493	$8,934	$7,697	$7,949	$7,652
Average	$8,582	$8,783	$8,478	$8,783	$9,233

Acres of Park Maintained per Maintenance FTE

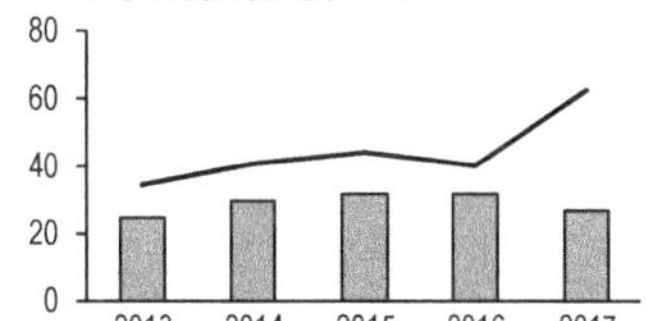

	2013	2014	2015	2016	2017
Apex	24.6	29.5	31.6	31.6	26.8
Average	34.3	40.5	43.9	39.9	62.5

Volunteer Hours in FTEs as a Percent of Paid Staff FTEs

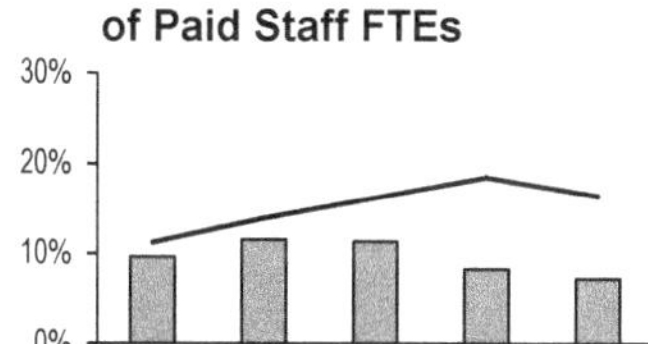

	2013	2014	2015	2016	2017
Apex	9.6%	11.5%	11.3%	8.2%	7.2%
Average	11.2%	13.9%	16.2%	18.4%	16.4%

Effectiveness Measures

Revenue Gained as a Percent of Total Core Costs

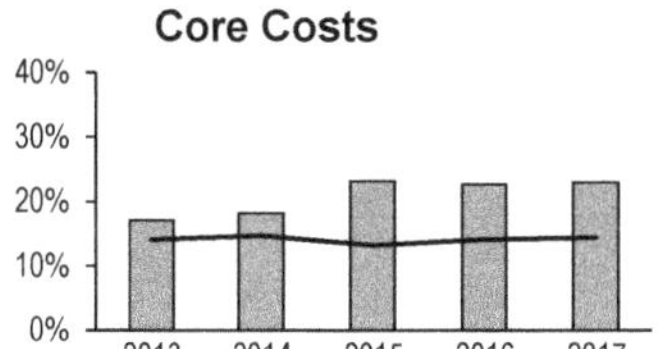

	2013	2014	2015	2016	2017
Apex	17.1%	18.2%	23.2%	22.7%	22.9%
Average	14.1%	14.7%	13.2%	14.1%	14.4%

Acts of Vandalism at Parks Facilities per 10,000 Population

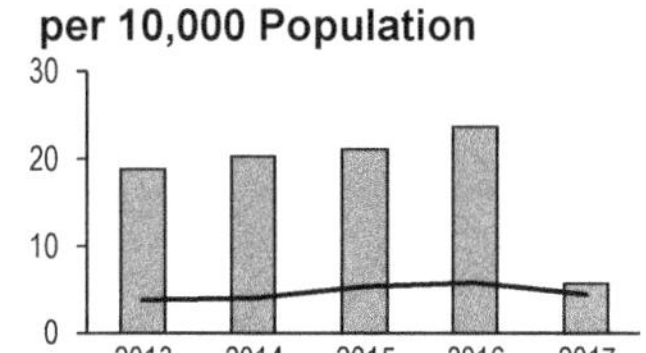

	2013	2014	2015	2016	2017
Apex	18.86	20.28	21.08	23.69	5.78
Average	3.85	4.07	5.39	5.82	4.56

Fiscal Year 2016–17

Explanatory Information

Service Level and Delivery

The City of Asheville provides recreation services through the separate Parks and Recreation Department. The city has formal agreements and partnerships with athletic associations, non-profits, universities, individuals, and for-profit organizations for the provision of recreational services.

The city has forty-seven separate parks and sites. These parks cover 869 land acres; about three-fourths of them are currently developed. The city has nearly six miles of trails.

In addition to the core parks and recreational facilities, Asheville has two large outdoor performance event sites and runs an eighteen-hole municipal golf course. The operation of these other facilities is not included in the Core Parks and Recreation comparisons reported here. These facilities are not included here in dollars or staff as part of core parks and recreation facilities and activities.

Conditions Affecting Service, Performance, and Costs

Parks and Recreation is a new service area for the benchmarking project beginning with the FY 2012–13 reporting year.

Municipal Profile

Population (OSBM 2016)	91,929
Land Area (Square Miles)	45.52
Persons per Square Mile	2,019
Topography	Hilly, mountains
Climate	Moderate; ice and snow

Service Profile

Parks and Recreation Staff	
Administrative Position FTEs	18.0
Maintenance Staff FTEs	40.4
Program and Facility FTEs	62.2
Other Staff FTEs	12.2
TOTAL	132.7
Number of Parks and Sites	47
Total Land Acreage in Parks	869.0
Miles of Trails in Parks	5.5
Recreational Facilities	
Indoor and Outdoor Pools	3
Recreation Centers	13
Outdoor Basketball Courts	15
Outdoor Tennis Courts	26
Playgrounds	24
Diamond Fields	19
Rectangular Fields	5
Other Athletic Fields	3
Picnic Shelters	11
Parks and Recreation Revenues	
User Fees	$1,795,270
Grants	$180,698
Sponsorships	$7,075
Donations	$125,549

Full Cost Profile

Cost Breakdown by Percentage	
Personal Services	51.7%
Operating Costs	36.8%
Capital Costs	11.5%
TOTAL	100.0%
Cost Breakdown in Dollars	
Personal Services	$5,914,877
Operating Costs	$4,210,677
Capital Costs	$1,313,264
TOTAL	$11,438,818

Asheville

Core Parks and Recreation

Key: Asheville ▒ Benchmarking Average — Fiscal Years 2013 through 2017

Resource Measures

Core Parks and Recreation Services per Capita

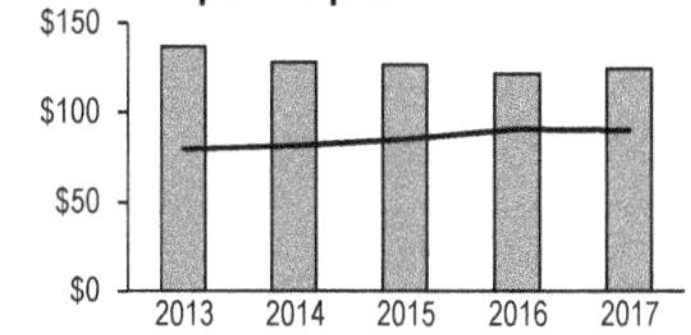

	2013	2014	2015	2016	2017
Asheville	$137	$128	$127	$122	$124
Average	$80	$82	$85	$91	$91

Core Parks and Recreation Staff per 10,000 Population

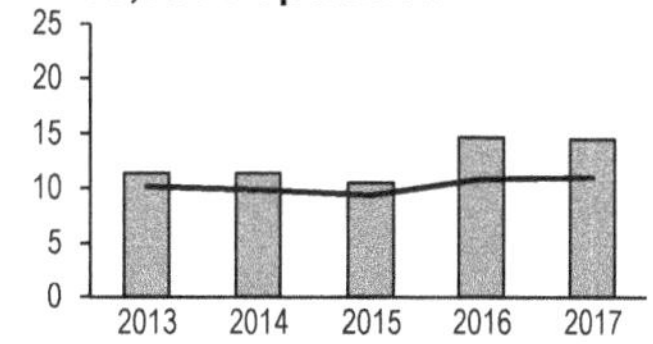

	2013	2014	2015	2016	2017
Asheville	11.3	11.3	10.5	14.6	14.4
Average	10.1	9.8	9.3	10.8	10.9

Facilities Measures

Land Acres of Parks per 10,000 Population

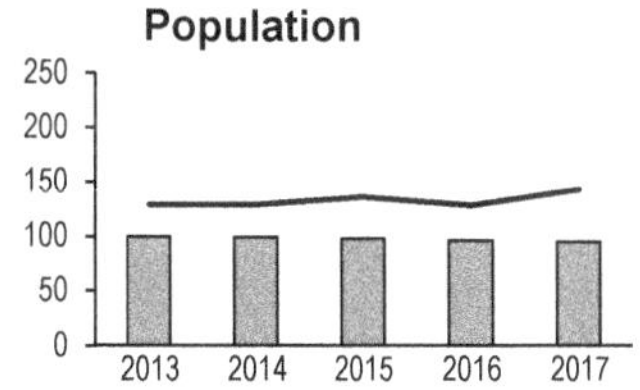

	2013	2014	2015	2016	2017
Asheville	99.47	98.74	97.36	95.58	94.52
Average	129.38	129.25	136.59	128.88	143.58

Recreation Centers per 10,000 Population

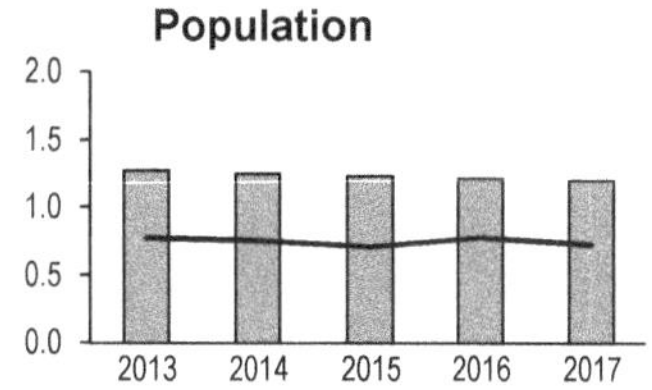

	2013	2014	2015	2016	2017
Asheville	1.28	1.25	1.23	1.21	1.20
Average	0.77	0.75	0.71	0.77	0.72

Swimming Pools per 10,000 Population

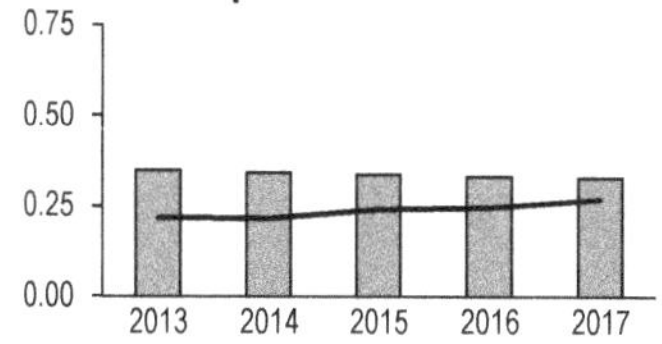

	2013	2014	2015	2016	2017
Asheville	0.35	0.34	0.34	0.33	0.33
Average	0.22	0.21	0.24	0.24	0.27

Athletic Fields per 10,000 Population

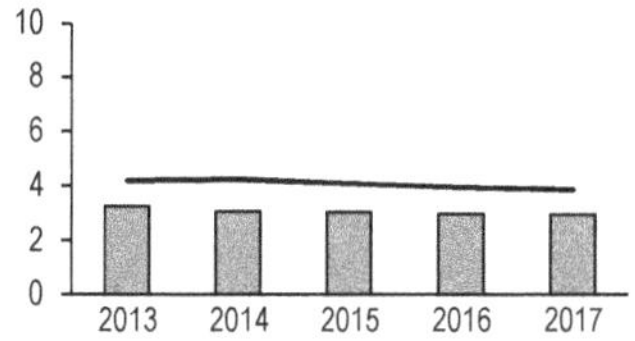

	2013	2014	2015	2016	2017
Asheville	3.25	3.07	3.03	2.97	2.94
Average	4.18	4.23	4.08	3.94	3.85

Playgrounds per 10,000 Population

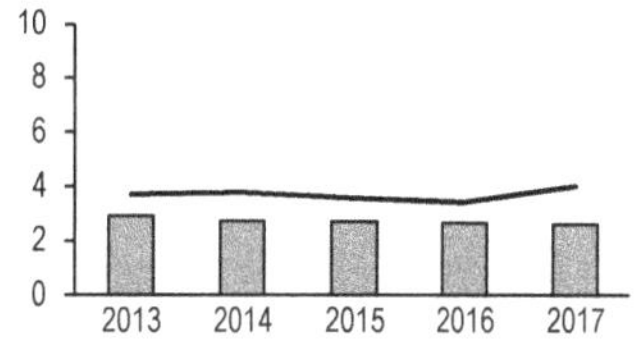

	2013	2014	2015	2016	2017
Asheville	2.90	2.73	2.69	2.64	2.61
Average	3.70	3.76	3.54	3.41	4.01

Miles of Land Trails per 10,000 Population

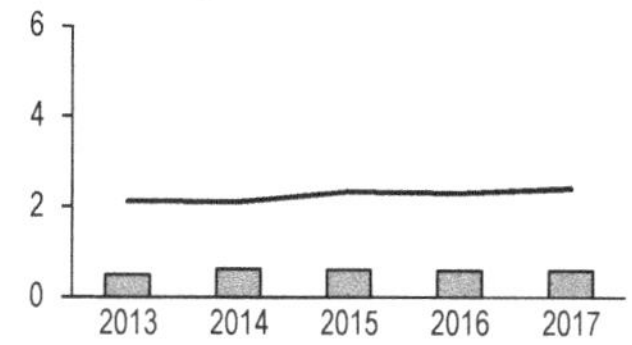

	2013	2014	2015	2016	2017
Asheville	0.50	0.62	0.61	0.60	0.59
Average	2.11	2.10	2.32	2.29	2.41

Efficiency Measures

Total Core Parks and Recreation Costs per Acre

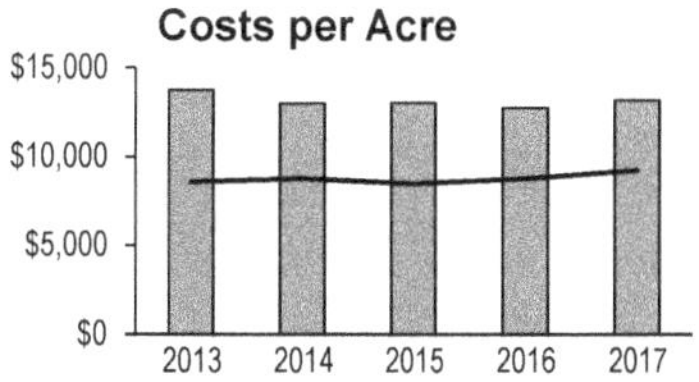

	2013	2014	2015	2016	2017
Asheville	$13,748	$12,977	$13,013	$12,720	$13,164
Average	$8,582	$8,783	$8,478	$8,783	$9,233

Acres of Park Maintained per Maintenance FTE

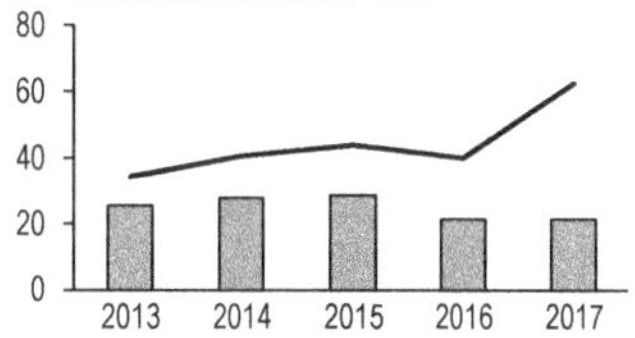

	2013	2014	2015	2016	2017
Asheville	25.4	27.8	28.7	21.5	21.5
Average	34.3	40.5	43.9	39.9	62.5

Volunteer Hours in FTEs as a Percent of Paid Staff FTEs

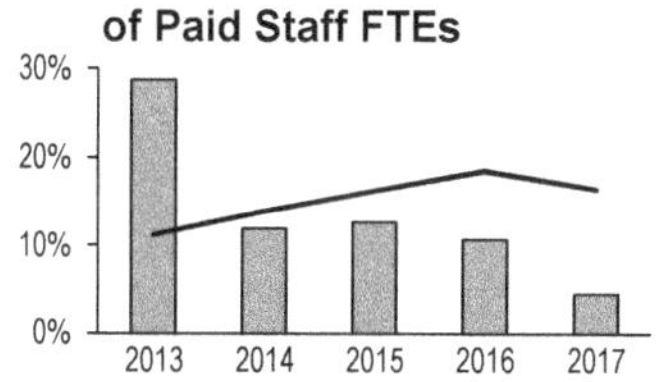

	2013	2014	2015	2016	2017
Asheville	28.7%	11.8%	12.6%	10.7%	4.5%
Average	11.2%	13.9%	16.2%	18.4%	16.4%

Effectiveness Measures

Revenue Gained as a Percent of Total Core Costs

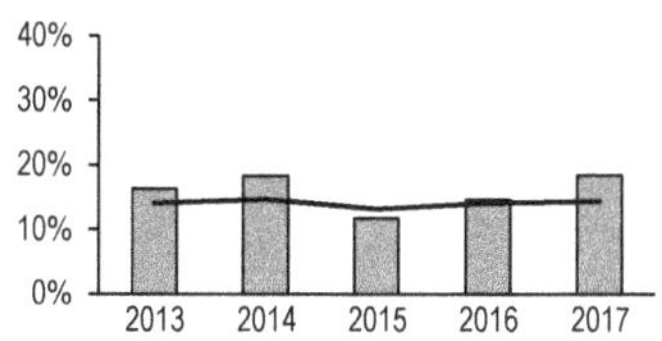

	2013	2014	2015	2016	2017
Asheville	16.3%	18.3%	11.7%	14.6%	18.4%
Average	14.1%	14.7%	13.2%	14.1%	14.4%

Acts of Vandalism at Parks Facilities per 10,000 Population

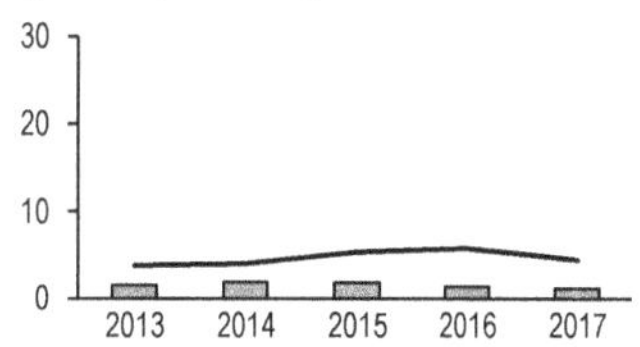

	2013	2014	2015	2016	2017
Asheville	1.62	1.93	1.90	1.43	1.20
Average	3.85	4.07	5.39	5.82	4.56

Fiscal Year 2016–17

Explanatory Information

Service Level and Delivery

The Town of Chapel Hill provides recreation services through the separate Parks and Recreation Department. The town has agreements with Orange County for use of the senior center and county resident participation in other programs. The town also has agreements with the Town of Carrboro, the Street Scene Teen Center, Holmes Childcare Center, and Chapel Hill-Carrboro City Schools.

The town has thirty-one separate parks and sites. These parks cover 1,114 land acres much, of which is currently undeveloped. The town has about twenty-four miles of trails.

Conditions Affecting Service, Performance, and Costs

The Town of Chapel Hill began participation in the benchmarking project in July 2015, with FY 2014–15 being the first reporting year.

Parks and Recreation is a new service area for the benchmarking project beginning with the FY 2012–13 reporting year.

Municipal Profile

Population (OSBM 2016)	59,852
Land Area (Square Miles)	21.21
Persons per Square Mile	2,822
Topography	Flat; gently rolling
Climate	Temperate; little ice and snow

Service Profile

Parks and Recreation Staff	
Administrative Position FTEs	6.0
Maintenance Staff FTEs	13.5
Program and Facility FTEs	57.3
Other Staff FTEs	0.0
TOTAL	76.8
Number of Parks and Sites	31
Total Land Acreage in Parks	1,114.0
Miles of Trails in Parks	23.6
Recreational Facilities	
Indoor and Outdoor Pools	3
Recreation Centers	2
Outdoor Basketball Courts	7
Outdoor Tennis Courts	18
Playgrounds	11
Diamond Fields	7
Rectangular Fields	9
Other Athletic Fields	0
Picnic Shelters	8
Parks and Recreation Revenues	
User Fees	$1,067,971
Grants	$0
Sponsorships	$50,725
Donations	$37,593

Full Cost Profile

Cost Breakdown by Percentage	
Personal Services	56.0%
Operating Costs	34.3%
Capital Costs	9.7%
TOTAL	100.0%
Cost Breakdown in Dollars	
Personal Services	$3,744,358
Operating Costs	$2,293,312
Capital Costs	$646,061
TOTAL	$6,683,731

Key: Chapel Hill ▒ Benchmarking Average — Fiscal Years 2013 through 2017

Resource Measures

Core Parks and Recreation Services per Capita

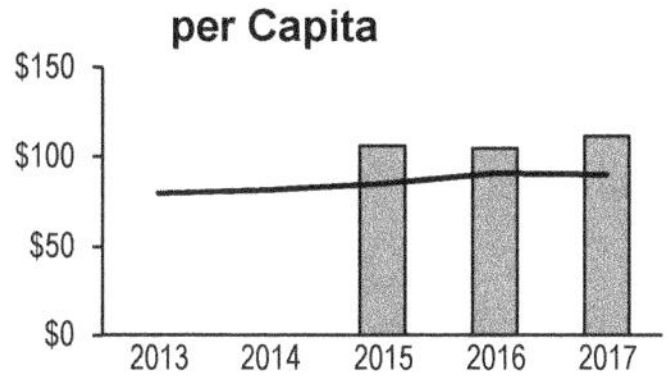

	2013	2014	2015	2016	2017
Chapel Hill			$106	$105	$112
Average	$80	$82	$85	$91	$91

Core Parks and Recreation Staff per 10,000 Population

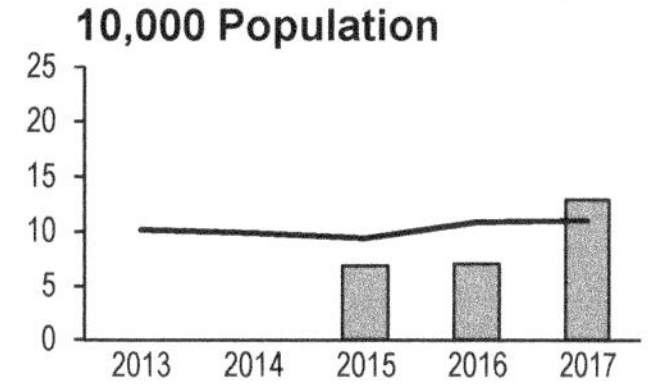

	2013	2014	2015	2016	2017
Chapel Hill			6.8	7.0	12.8
Average	10.1	9.8	9.3	10.8	10.9

Facilities Measures

Land Acres of Parks per 10,000 Population

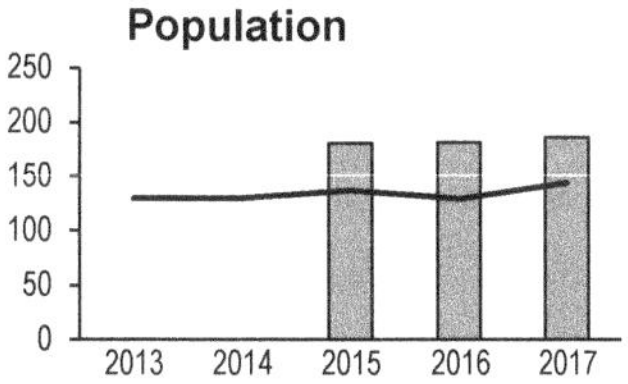

	2013	2014	2015	2016	2017
Chapel Hill			180.73	181.53	186.13
Average	129.38	129.25	136.59	128.88	143.58

Recreation Centers per 10,000 Population

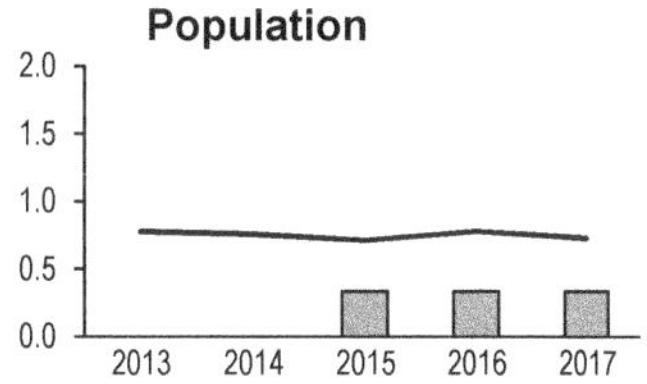

	2013	2014	2015	2016	2017
Chapel Hill			0.33	0.34	0.33
Average	0.77	0.75	0.71	0.77	0.72

Swimming Pools per 10,000 Population

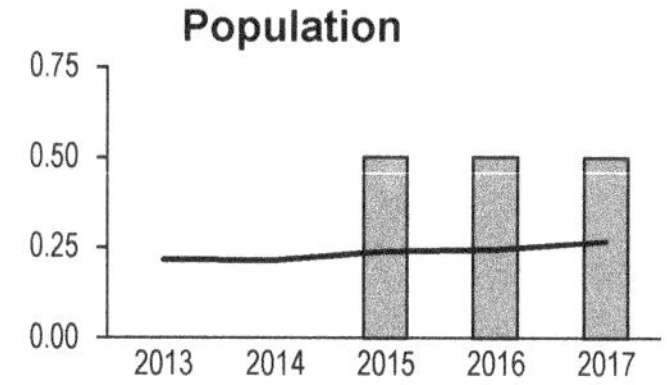

	2013	2014	2015	2016	2017
Chapel Hill			0.50	0.50	0.50
Average	0.22	0.21	0.24	0.24	0.27

Athletic Fields per 10,000 Population

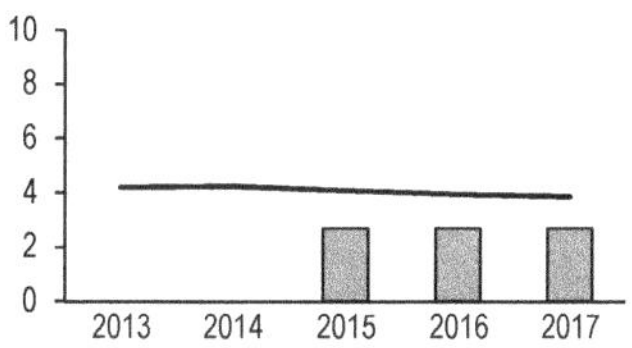

	2013	2014	2015	2016	2017
Chapel Hill			2.68	2.68	2.67
Average	4.18	4.23	4.08	3.94	3.85

Playgrounds per 10,000 Population

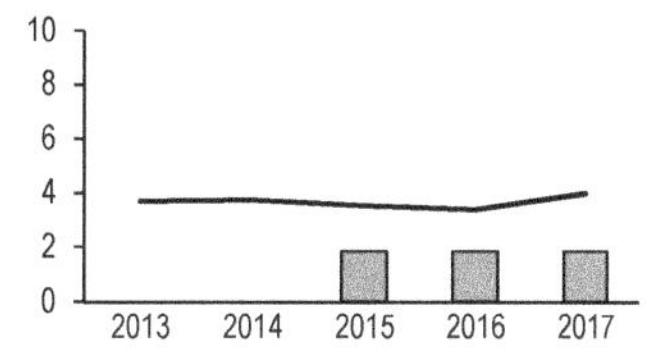

	2013	2014	2015	2016	2017
Chapel Hill			1.84	1.85	1.84
Average	3.70	3.76	3.54	3.41	4.01

Miles of Land Trails per 10,000 Population

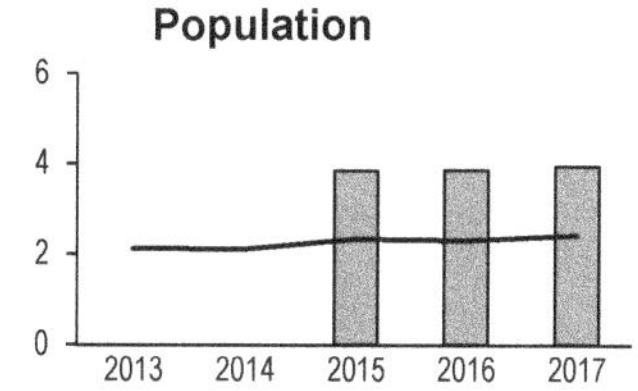

	2013	2014	2015	2016	2017
Chapel Hill			3.84	3.85	3.94
Average	2.11	2.10	2.32	2.29	2.41

Efficiency Measures

Total Core Parks and Recreation Costs per Acre

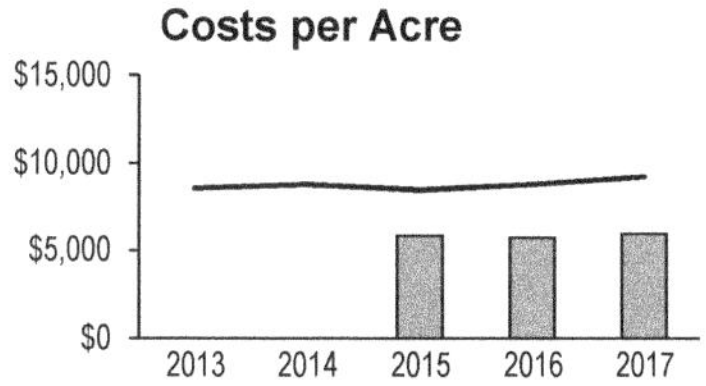

	2013	2014	2015	2016	2017
Chapel Hill			$5,875	$5,780	$6,000
Average	$8,582	$8,783	$8,478	$8,783	$9,233

Acres of Park Maintained per Maintenance FTE

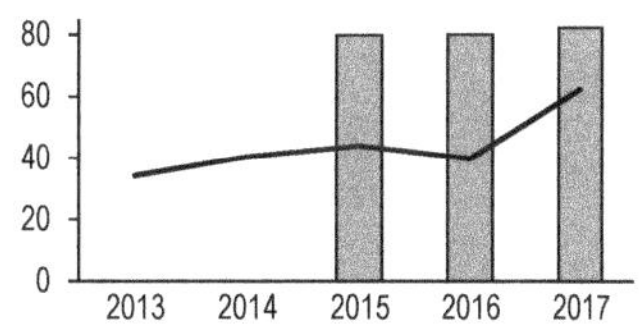

	2013	2014	2015	2016	2017
Chapel Hill			80.0	80.1	82.5
Average	34.3	40.5	43.9	39.9	62.5

Volunteer Hours in FTEs as a Percent of Paid Staff FTEs

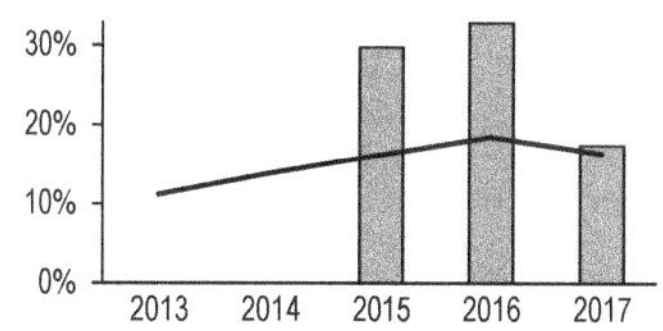

	2013	2014	2015	2016	2017
Chapel Hill			29.8%	32.8%	17.4%
Average	11.2%	13.9%	16.2%	18.4%	16.4%

Effectiveness Measures

Revenue Gained as a Percent of Total Core Costs

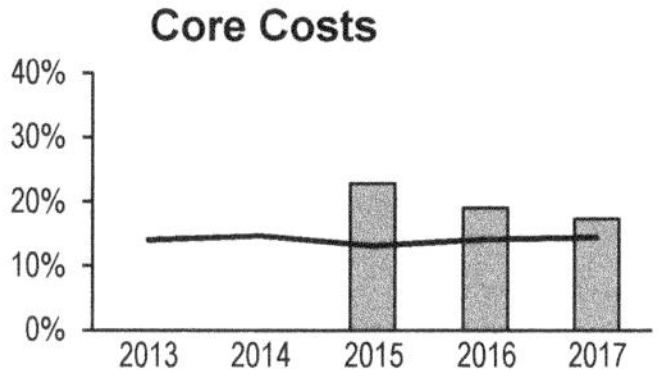

	2013	2014	2015	2016	2017
Chapel Hill			22.8%	19.1%	17.3%
Average	14.1%	14.7%	13.2%	14.1%	14.4%

Acts of Vandalism at Parks Facilities per 10,000 Population

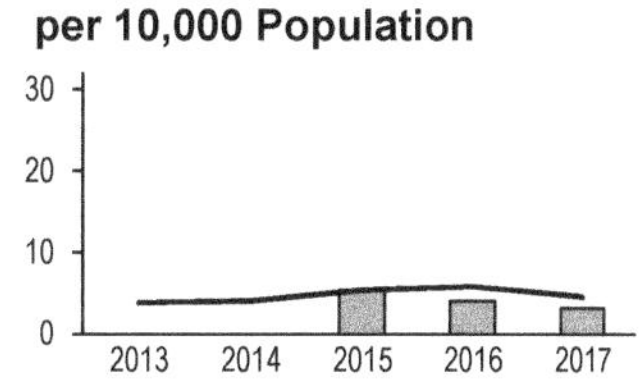

	2013	2014	2015	2016	2017
Chapel Hill			5.35	4.03	3.17
Average	3.85	4.07	5.39	5.82	4.56

Fiscal Year 2016–17

Explanatory Information

Service Level and Delivery

The City of Concord provides recreation services through the separate Parks and Recreation Department. The city provides an array of facilities and activities for recreation.

The city has nine separate parks and sites. These parks cover 226 land acres. The city has about eleven miles of recreational trails, most of them paved.

In addition to the core parks and recreational facilities, Concord has one large outdoor performance event site and one boat ramp. The operation of these other facilities is not included in the Core Parks and Recreation comparisons reported here. These facilities are not included here in dollars or staff as part of core parks and recreation facilities and activities.

Conditions Affecting Service, Performance, and Costs

Parks and Recreation is a new service area for the benchmarking project beginning with the FY 2012–13 reporting year.

Municipal Profile

Population (OSBM 2016)	88,815
Land Area (Square Miles)	62.61
Persons per Square Mile	1,419
Topography	Flat; gently rolling
Climate	Temperate; little ice and snow

Service Profile

Parks and Recreation Staff	
Administrative Position FTEs	5.0
Maintenance Staff FTEs	0.0
Program and Facility FTEs	17.5
Other Staff FTEs	10.9
TOTAL	33.4
Number of Parks and Sites	9
Total Land Acreage in Parks	226.0
Miles of Trails in Parks	10.7
Recreational Facilities	
Indoor and Outdoor Pools	1
Recreation Centers	3
Outdoor Basketball Courts	9
Outdoor Tennis Courts	14
Playgrounds	14
Diamond Fields	12
Rectangular Fields	7
Other Athletic Fields	3
Picnic Shelters	14
Parks and Recreation Revenues	
User Fees	$322,637
Grants	$18,000
Sponsorships	$8,575
Donations	$0

Full Cost Profile

Cost Breakdown by Percentage	
Personal Services	27.1%
Operating Costs	68.0%
Capital Costs	4.8%
TOTAL	100.0%
Cost Breakdown in Dollars	
Personal Services	$1,414,459
Operating Costs	$3,543,436
Capital Costs	$252,655
TOTAL	$5,210,550

Key: Concord ▒ Benchmarking Average — Fiscal Years 2013 through 2017

Resource Measures

Core Parks and Recreation Services per Capita

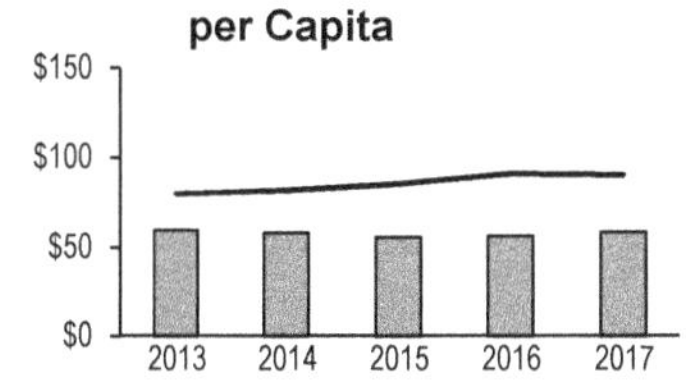

	2013	2014	2015	2016	2017
Concord	$60	$58	$56	$56	$59
Average	$80	$82	$85	$91	$91

Core Parks and Recreation Staff per 10,000 Population

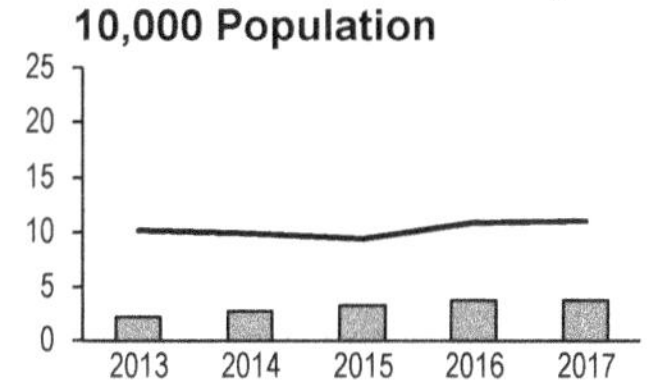

	2013	2014	2015	2016	2017
Concord	2.1	2.8	3.3	3.8	3.8
Average	10.1	9.8	9.3	10.8	10.9

Facilities Measures

Land Acres of Parks per 10,000 Population

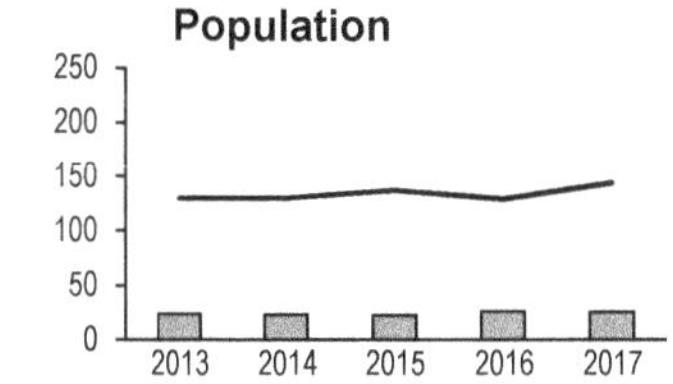

	2013	2014	2015	2016	2017
Concord	23.31	22.80	22.23	25.94	25.45
Average	129.38	129.25	136.59	128.88	143.58

Recreation Centers per 10,000 Population

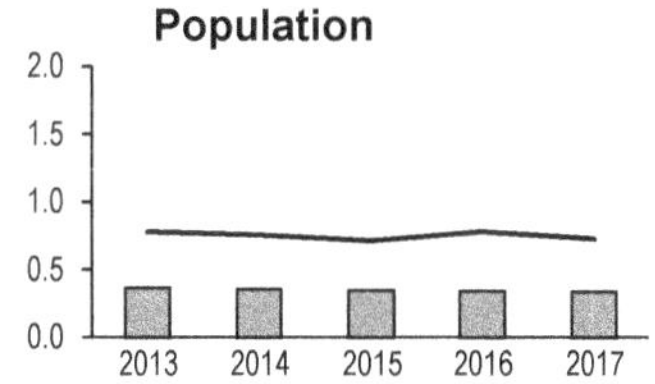

	2013	2014	2015	2016	2017
Concord	0.37	0.36	0.35	0.34	0.34
Average	0.77	0.75	0.71	0.77	0.72

Swimming Pools per 10,000 Population

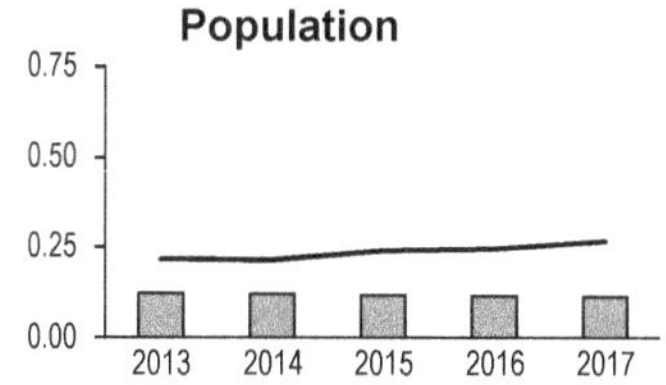

	2013	2014	2015	2016	2017
Concord	0.12	0.12	0.12	0.11	0.11
Average	0.22	0.21	0.24	0.24	0.27

Athletic Fields per 10,000 Population

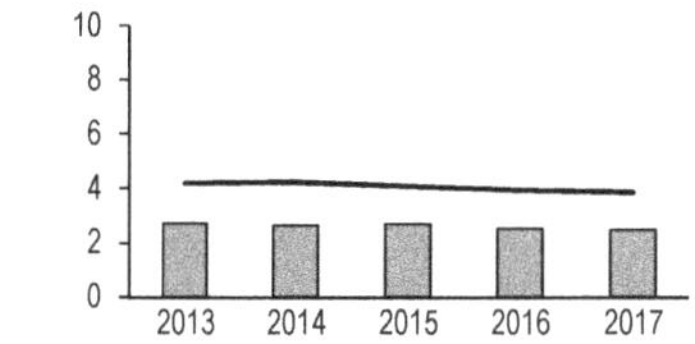

	2013	2014	2015	2016	2017
Concord	2.70	2.64	2.69	2.52	2.48
Average	4.18	4.23	4.08	3.94	3.85

Playgrounds per 10,000 Population

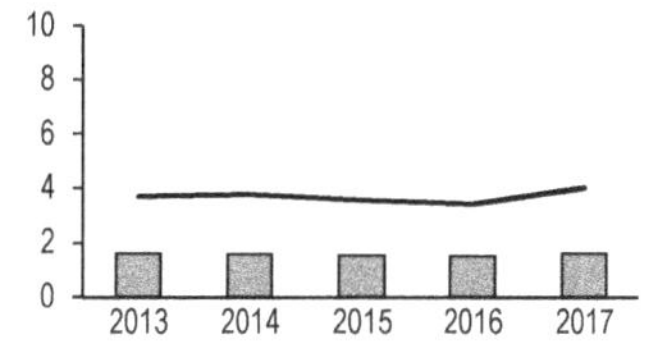

	2013	2014	2015	2016	2017
Concord	1.60	1.56	1.52	1.49	1.58
Average	3.70	3.76	3.54	3.41	4.01

Miles of Land Trails per 10,000 Population

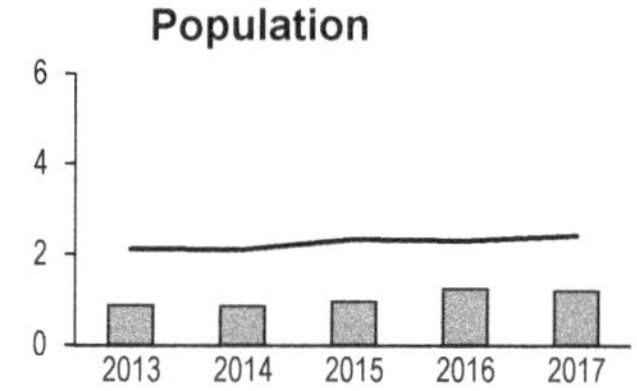

	2013	2014	2015	2016	2017
Concord	0.87	0.85	0.95	1.24	1.20
Average	2.11	2.10	2.32	2.29	2.41

Efficiency Measures

Total Core Parks and Recreation Costs per Acre

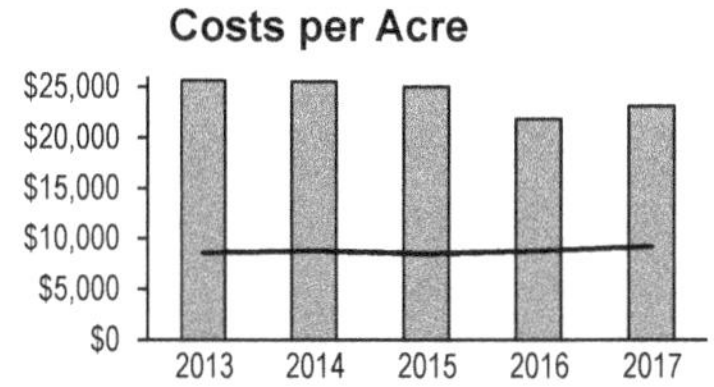

	2013	2014	2015	2016	2017
Concord	$25,633	$25,464	$24,980	$21,782	$23,056
Average	$8,582	$8,783	$8,478	$8,783	$9,233

Acres of Park Maintained per Maintenance FTE

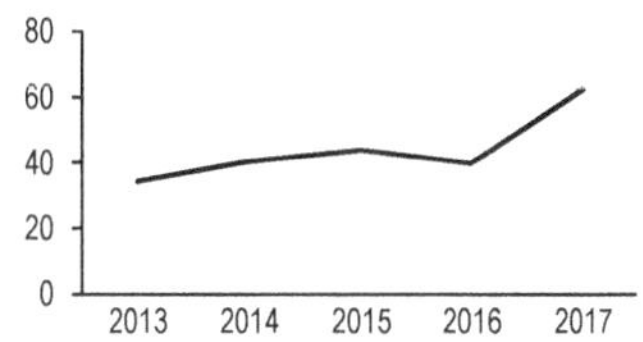

	2013	2014	2015	2016	2017
Concord					0.0
Average	34.3	40.5	43.9	39.9	62.5

Volunteer Hours in FTEs as a Percent of Paid Staff FTEs

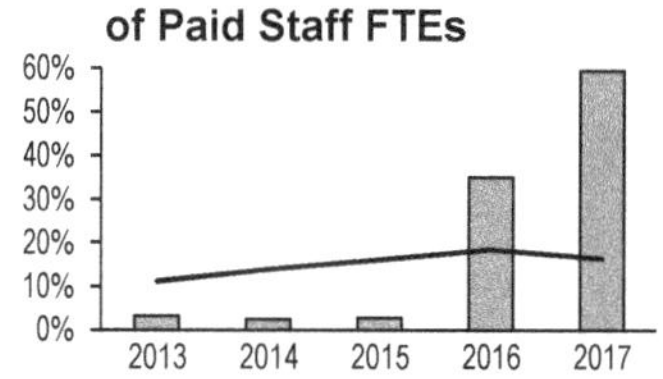

	2013	2014	2015	2016	2017
Concord	3.2%	2.4%	2.8%	35.0%	59.5%
Average	11.2%	13.9%	16.2%	18.4%	16.4%

Effectiveness Measures

Revenue Gained as a Percent of Total Core Costs

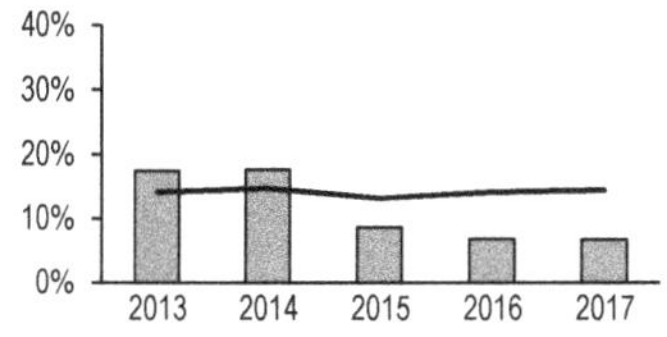

	2013	2014	2015	2016	2017
Concord	17.4%	17.6%	8.7%	6.8%	6.7%
Average	14.1%	14.7%	13.2%	14.1%	14.4%

Acts of Vandalism at Parks Facilities per 10,000 Population

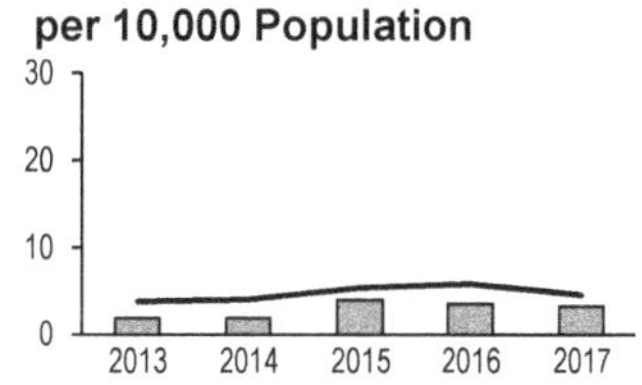

	2013	2014	2015	2016	2017
Concord	1.96	1.92	3.98	3.56	3.27
Average	3.85	4.07	5.39	5.82	4.56

Fiscal Year 2016–17

Explanatory Information

Service Level and Delivery
The City of Goldsboro provides recreation services through the separate Parks and Recreation Deparment. The department aims to serve the community through programs in youth athletics, adult athletics, seniors, and special populations both adult and youth. The city has a cooperative agreement with the public school system. The city has also formalized an agreement with the U.S. Air Force Base Seymour Johnson for the use of certain base facilities. County residents from outside the city are also users of the Goldsboro city system facilities and programmed activities.

The city has eleven separate parks covering almost 169 acres. There are five miles of trails, two outdoor pools, greenways, and a number of school indoor and outdoor facilities.

In addition to the core parks and recreational facilities, Goldsboro has a historic property and a farmers' market. The city also runs a municipal golf course. The operation of this course is not included here in dollars or staff as part of core parks and recreation facilities and activities.

Conditions Affecting Service, Performance, and Costs
Parks and Recreation is a new service area for the benchmarking project beginning with the FY 2012–13 reporting year.

The city of Goldsboro joined the Benchmarking Project in July 2017, with the first year of data showing for FY 2016–17.

Municipal Profile

Population (OSBM 2016)	34,793
Land Area (Square Miles)	29.35
Persons per Square Mile	1,186
Topography	Flat
Climate	Temperate; little ice and snow

Service Profile

Parks and Recreation Staff	
Administrative Position FTEs	6.0
Maintenance Staff FTEs	19.0
Program and Facility FTEs	17.0
Other Staff FTEs	4.4
TOTAL	46.4
Number of Parks and Sites	11
Total Land Acreage in Parks	168.8
Miles of Trails in Parks	5.1
Recreational Facilities	
Indoor and Outdoor Pools	2
Recreation Centers	3
Outdoor Basketball Courts	8
Outdoor Tennis Courts	18
Playgrounds	37
Diamond Fields	4
Rectangular Fields	5
Other Athletic Fields	6
Picnic Shelters	14
Parks and Recreation Revenues	
User Fees	$115,980
Grants	$405,883
Sponsorships	$33,100
Donations	$3,480

Full Cost Profile

Cost Breakdown by Percentage	
Personal Services	65.7%
Operating Costs	29.4%
Capital Costs	4.9%
TOTAL	100.0%
Cost Breakdown in Dollars	
Personal Services	$2,169,109
Operating Costs	$970,059
Capital Costs	$163,289
TOTAL	$3,302,457

Key: Goldsboro ▒ Benchmarking Average — Fiscal Years 2013 through 2017

Resource Measures

Core Parks and Recreation Services per Capita

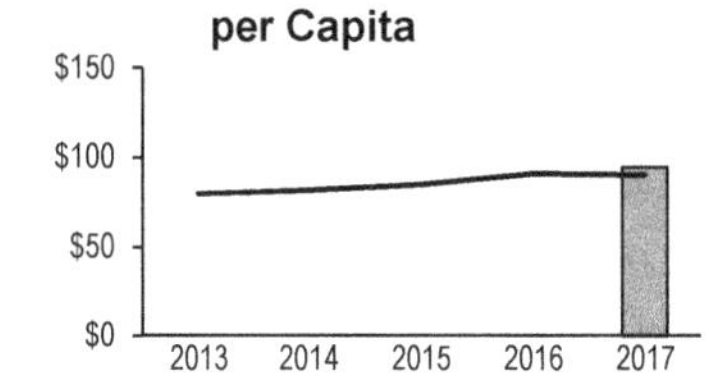

	2013	2014	2015	2016	2017
Goldsboro					$95
Average	$80	$82	$85	$91	$91

Core Parks and Recreation Staff per 10,000 Population

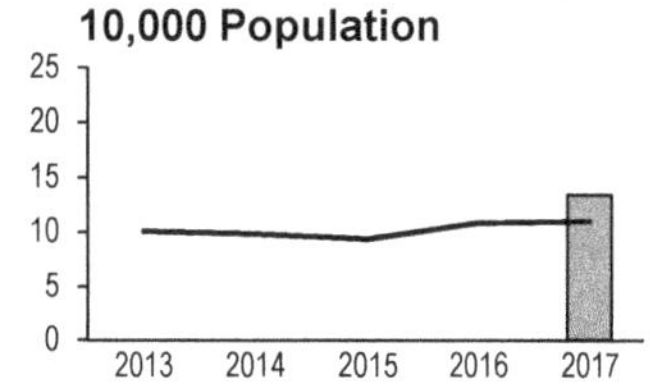

	2013	2014	2015	2016	2017
Goldsboro					13.3
Average	10.1	9.8	9.3	10.8	10.9

Facilities Measures

Land Acres of Parks per 10,000 Population

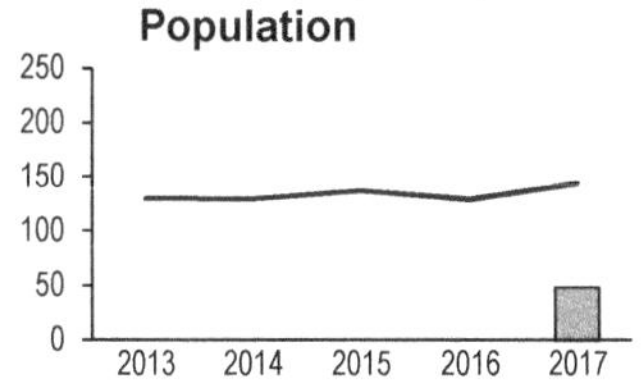

	2013	2014	2015	2016	2017
Goldsboro					48.51
Average	129.38	129.25	136.59	128.88	143.58

Recreation Centers per 10,000 Population

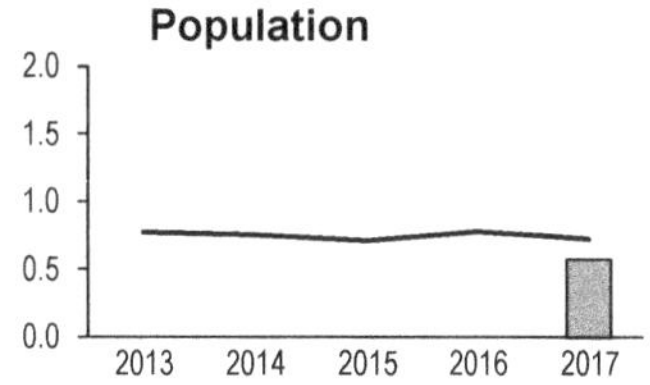

	2013	2014	2015	2016	2017
Goldsboro					0.57
Average	0.77	0.75	0.71	0.77	0.72

Swimming Pools per 10,000 Population

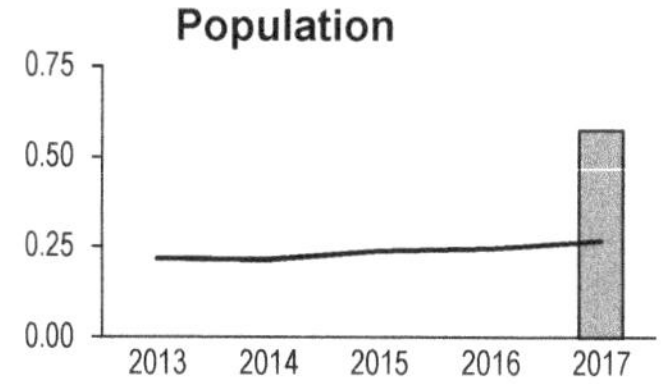

	2013	2014	2015	2016	2017
Goldsboro					0.57
Average	0.22	0.21	0.24	0.24	0.27

Athletic Fields per 10,000 Population

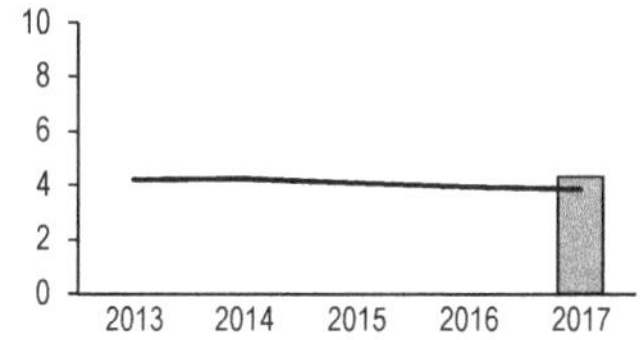

	2013	2014	2015	2016	2017
Goldsboro					4.31
Average	4.18	4.23	4.08	3.94	3.85

Playgrounds per 10,000 Population

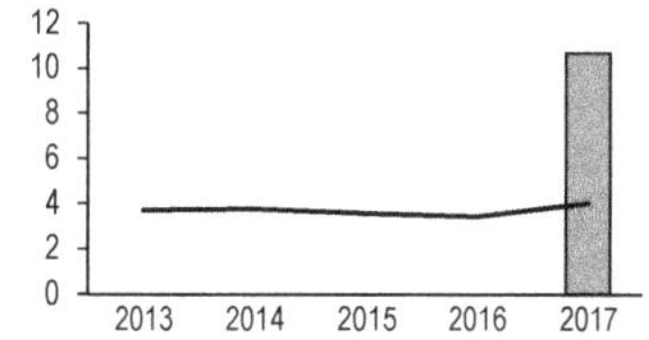

	2013	2014	2015	2016	2017
Goldsboro					10.63
Average	3.70	3.76	3.54	3.41	4.01

Miles of Land Trails per 10,000 Population

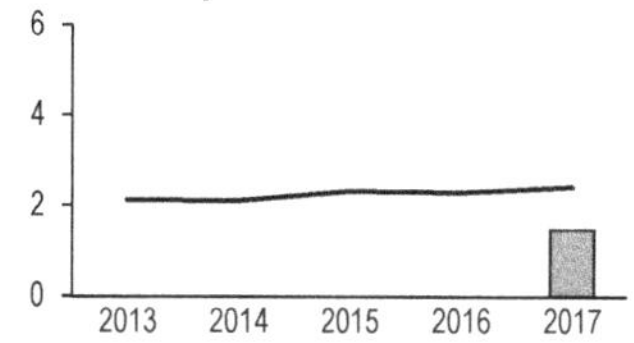

	2013	2014	2015	2016	2017
Goldsboro					1.47
Average	2.11	2.10	2.32	2.29	2.41

Efficiency Measures

Total Core Parks and Recreation Costs per Acre

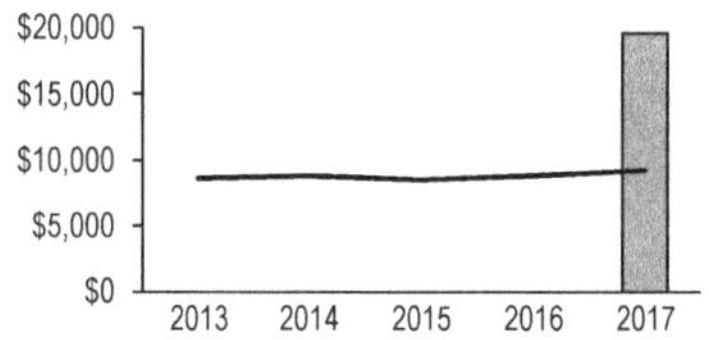

	2013	2014	2015	2016	2017
Goldsboro					$19,567
Average	$8,582	$8,783	$8,478	$8,783	$9,233

Acres of Park Maintained per Maintenance FTE

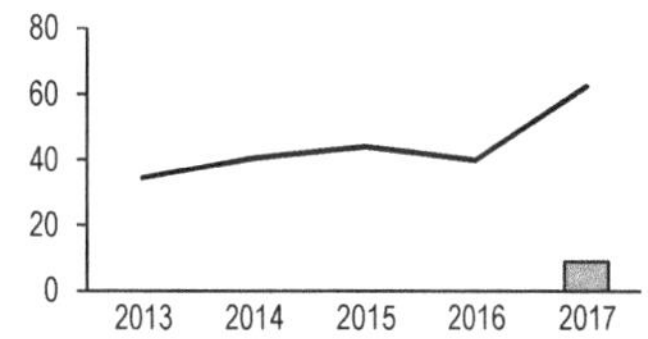

	2013	2014	2015	2016	2017
Goldsboro					8.9
Average	34.3	40.5	43.9	39.9	62.5

Volunteer Hours in FTEs as a Percent of Paid Staff FTEs

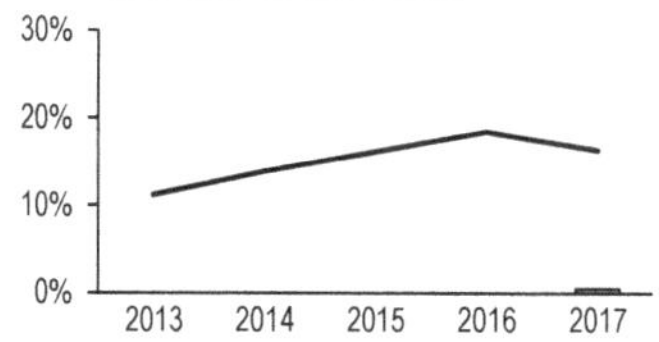

	2013	2014	2015	2016	2017
Goldsboro					0.5%
Average	11.2%	13.9%	16.2%	18.4%	16.4%

Effectiveness Measures

Revenue Gained as a Percent of Total Core Costs

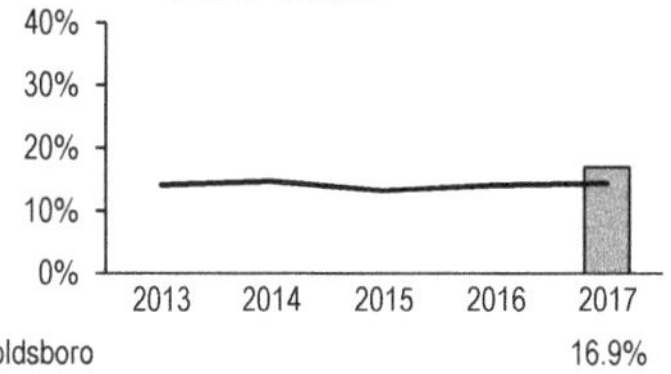

	2013	2014	2015	2016	2017
Goldsboro					16.9%
Average	14.1%	14.7%	13.2%	14.1%	14.4%

Acts of Vandalism at Parks Facilities per 10,000 Population

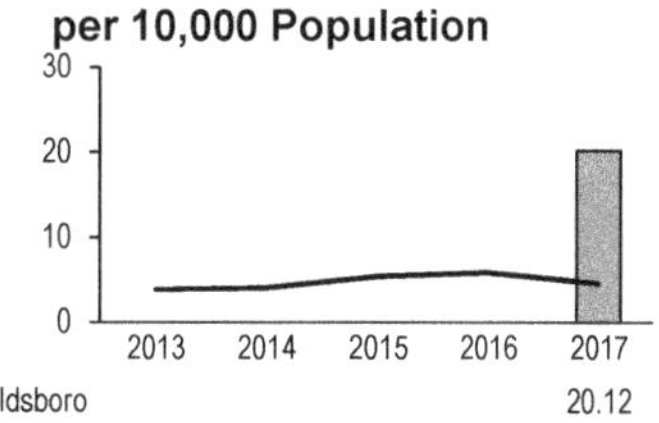

	2013	2014	2015	2016	2017
Goldsboro					20.12
Average	3.85	4.07	5.39	5.82	4.56

Fiscal Year 2016–17

Explanatory Information

Service Level and Delivery

The City of Greensboro provides recreation services through the separate Parks and Recreation Department. The city has several cooperative agreements with the local schools and some non-profits for the provision of services or use of facilities. The city provides a full array of recreational facilities and activities.

The city has 342 separate parks and sites. These parks cover 10,907 land acres; most of them are developed. In addition, 2,641 acres in water space is part of the parks system. The city has eighty-eight miles of trails.

In addition to the core parks and recreational facilities, Greensboro has a large outdoor performance event site, a historic property, a famers' market, a boat ramp and marina, and operates a nine-hole municipal golf course. The operation of these other facilities is not included in the Core Parks and Recreation comparisons reported here. These facilities are not included here in dollars or staff as part of core parks and recreation facilities and activities.

Conditions Affecting Service, Performance, and Costs

Parks and Recreation is a new service area for the benchmarking project beginning with the FY 2012–13 reporting year.

Greensboro did not report data for Core Parks and Recreation services for FY 2015–16.

Municipal Profile

Population (OSBM 2016)	284,343
Land Area (Square Miles)	128.72
Persons per Square Mile	2,209
Topography	Flat
Climate	Temperate; little ice and snow

Service Profile

Parks and Recreation Staff	
Administrative Position FTEs	16.5
Maintenance Staff FTEs	78.5
Program and Facility FTEs	66.0
Other Staff FTEs	0.0
TOTAL	161.0
Number of Parks and Sites	342
Total Land Acreage in Parks	10,907.0
Miles of Trails in Parks	88.2
Recreational Facilities	
Indoor and Outdoor Pools	5
Recreation Centers	12
Outdoor Basketball Courts	45
Outdoor Tennis Courts	82
Playgrounds	108
Diamond Fields	40
Rectangular Fields	39
Other Athletic Fields	0
Picnic Shelters	39
Parks and Recreation Revenues	
User Fees	$1,655,168
Grants	$48,843
Sponsorships	$2,070
Donations	$62,552

Full Cost Profile

Cost Breakdown by Percentage	
Personal Services	58.8%
Operating Costs	41.2%
Capital Costs	0.0%
TOTAL	100.0%
Cost Breakdown in Dollars	
Personal Services	$9,578,153
Operating Costs	$6,704,186
Capital Costs	$0
TOTAL	$16,282,339

Key: Greensboro ▒ Benchmarking Average — Fiscal Years 2013 through 2017

Resource Measures

Core Parks and Recreation Services per Capita

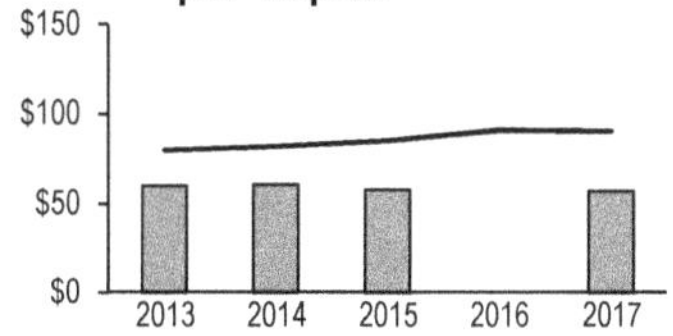

	2013	2014	2015	2016	2017
Greensboro	$60	$61	$58		$57
Average	$80	$82	$85	$91	$91

Core Parks and Recreation Staff per 10,000 Population

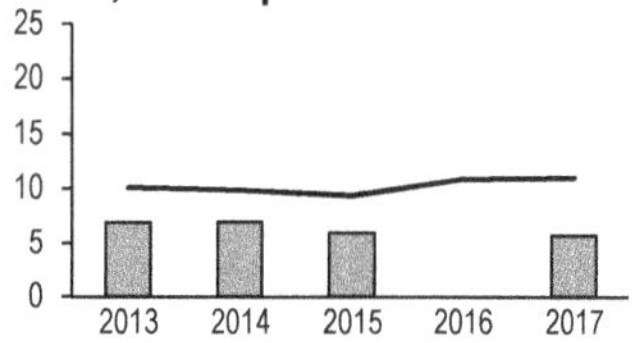

	2013	2014	2015	2016	2017
Greensboro	6.8	6.9	5.9		5.7
Average	10.1	9.8	9.3	10.8	10.9

Facilities Measures

Land Acres of Parks per 10,000 Population

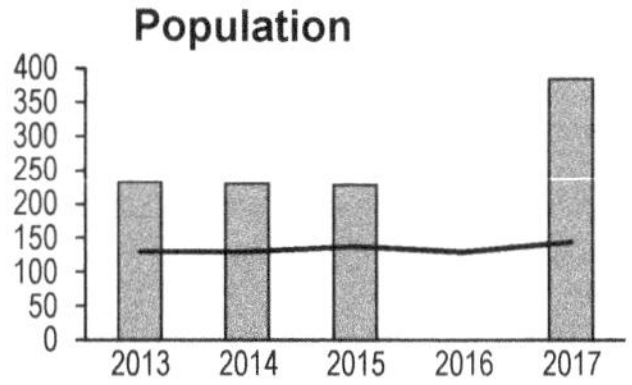

	2013	2014	2015	2016	2017
Greensboro	231.56	228.96	227.21		383.59
Average	129.38	129.25	136.59	128.88	143.58

Recreation Centers per 10,000 Population

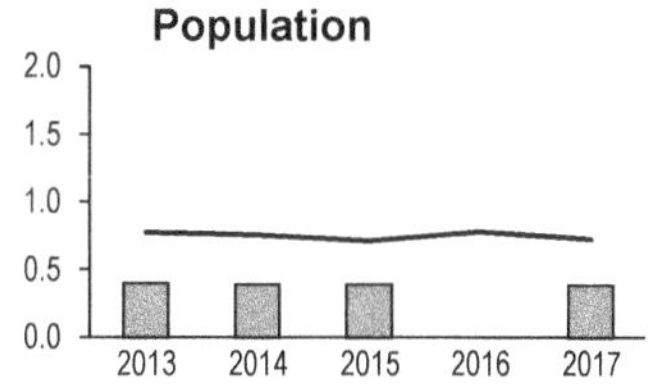

	2013	2014	2015	2016	2017
Greensboro	0.40	0.39	0.39		0.39
Average	0.77	0.75	0.71	0.77	0.72

Swimming Pools per 10,000 Population

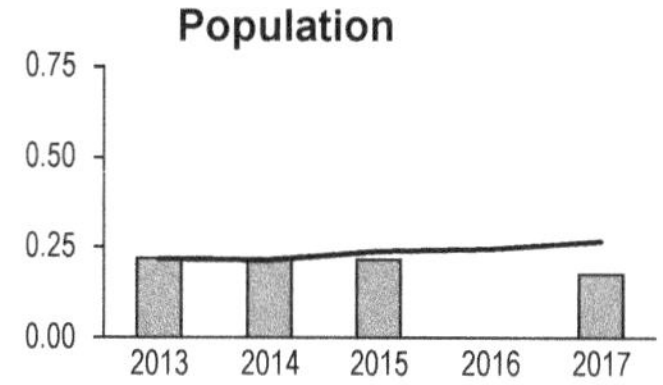

	2013	2014	2015	2016	2017
Greensboro	0.22	0.22	0.21		0.18
Average	0.22	0.21	0.24	0.24	0.27

Athletic Fields per 10,000 Population

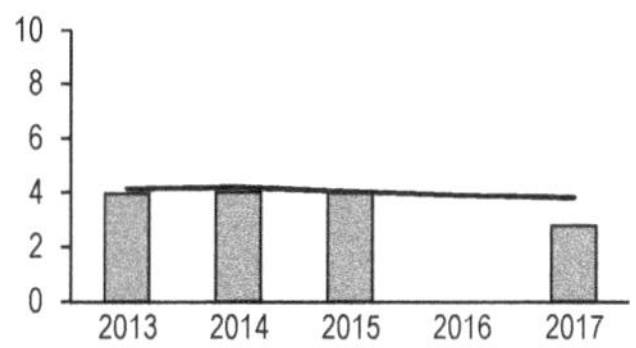

	2013	2014	2015	2016	2017
Greensboro	3.96	4.02	3.99		2.78
Average	4.18	4.23	4.08	3.94	3.85

Playgrounds per 10,000 Population

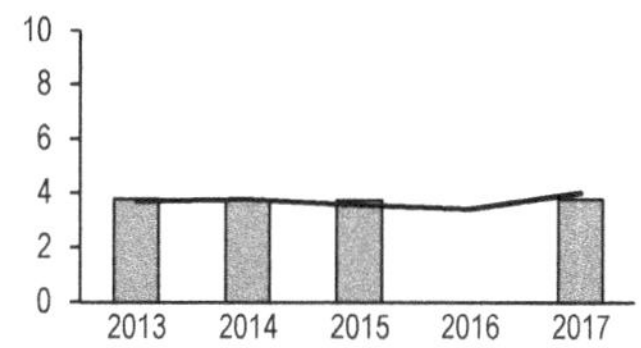

	2013	2014	2015	2016	2017
Greensboro	3.78	3.73	3.74		3.80
Average	3.70	3.76	3.54	3.41	4.01

Miles of Land Trails per 10,000 Population

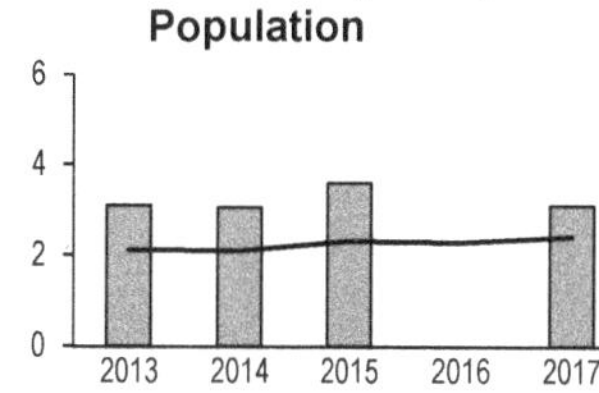

	2013	2014	2015	2016	2017
Greensboro	3.09	3.05	3.60		3.10
Average	2.11	2.10	2.32	2.29	2.41

Efficiency Measures

Total Core Parks and Recreation Costs per Acre

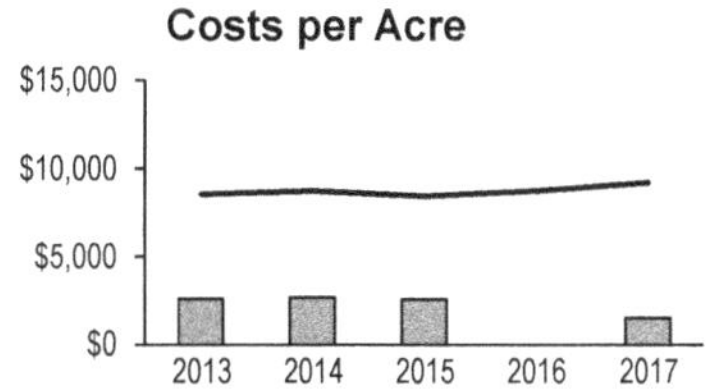

	2013	2014	2015	2016	2017
Greensboro	$2,591	$2,647	$2,553		$1,493
Average	$8,582	$8,783	$8,478	$8,783	$9,233

Acres of Park Maintained per Maintenance FTE

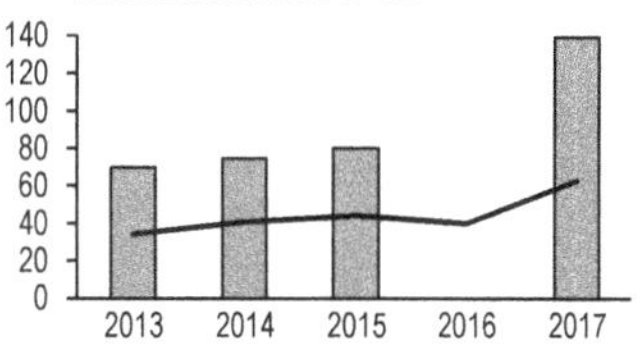

	2013	2014	2015	2016	2017
Greensboro	70.0	74.8	80.3		138.9
Average	34.3	40.5	43.9	39.9	62.5

Volunteer Hours in FTEs as a Percent of Paid Staff FTEs

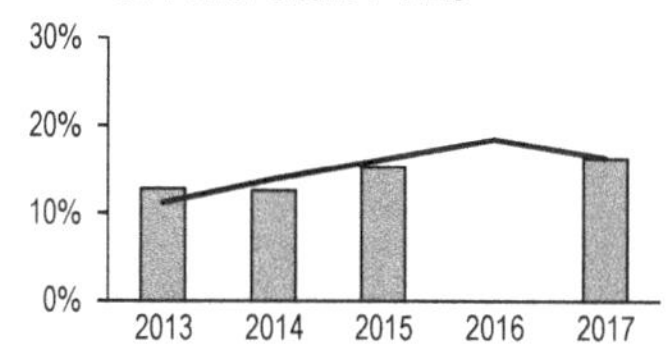

	2013	2014	2015	2016	2017
Greensboro	12.8%	12.5%	15.2%		16.3%
Average	11.2%	13.9%	16.2%	18.4%	16.4%

Effectiveness Measures

Revenue Gained as a Percent of Total Core Costs

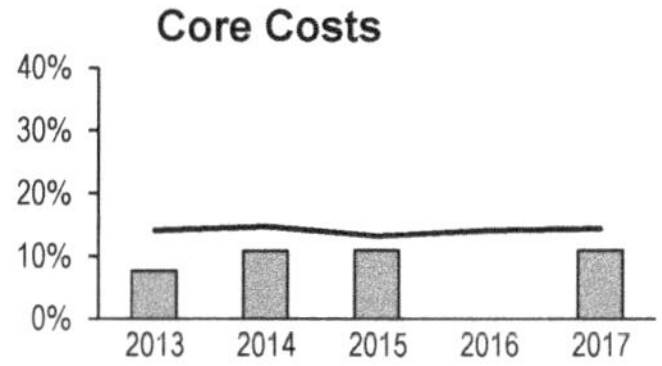

	2013	2014	2015	2016	2017
Greensboro	7.6%	10.8%	10.9%		10.9%
Average	14.1%	14.7%	13.2%	14.1%	14.4%

Acts of Vandalism at Parks Facilities per 10,000 Population

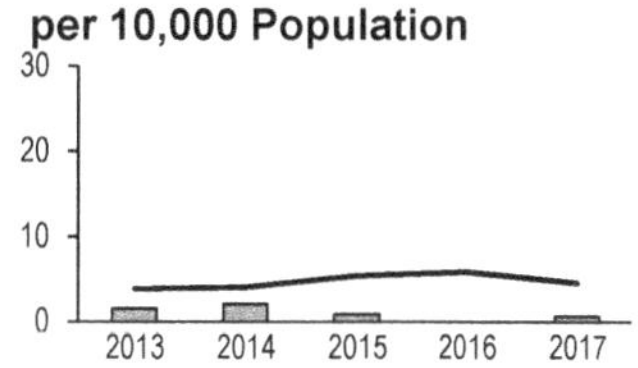

	2013	2014	2015	2016	2017
Greensboro	1.53	2.05	0.85		0.67
Average	3.85	4.07	5.39	5.82	4.56

Fiscal Year 2016–17

Explanatory Information

Service Level and Delivery

The City of Greenville provides recreation services through the separate Recreation and Parks Department. The city has a number of ad hoc or handshake agreements with other organizations but is moving to more formal agreements. Partner groups include Pitt County, local sports organizations, and concert entertainment groups.

The city has twenty-six separate parks and sites. These parks cover 1,461 acres; about two-thirds of them are developed. The city has nearly eight miles of trails.

In addition to the core parks and recreational facilities, Greenville has a large outdoor performance event site, a historic property, a boat ramp, a museum, and an eighteen-hole golf course. The operation of these other facilities is not included in the Core Parks and Recreation comparisons reported here. These facilities are not included here in dollars or staff as part of core parks and recreation facilities and activities.

Conditions Affecting Service, Performance, and Costs

Parks and Recreation is a new service area for the benchmarking project beginning with the FY 2012–13 reporting year.

Municipal Profile

Population (OSBM 2016)	87,989
Land Area (Square Miles)	35.41
Persons per Square Mile	2,485
Topography	Flat
Climate	Temperate; little ice and snow

Service Profile

Parks and Recreation Staff	
Administrative Position FTEs	7.0
Maintenance Staff FTEs	38.3
Program and Facility FTEs	82.5
Other Staff FTEs	1.5
TOTAL	129.3
Number of Parks and Sites	26
Total Land Acreage in Parks	1,460.9
Miles of Trails in Parks	7.8
Recreational Facilities	
Indoor and Outdoor Pools	2
Recreation Centers	8
Outdoor Basketball Courts	1
Outdoor Tennis Courts	20
Playgrounds	17
Diamond Fields	16
Rectangular Fields	5
Other Athletic Fields	3
Picnic Shelters	23
Parks and Recreation Revenues	
User Fees	$1,100,000
Grants	$300,050
Sponsorships	$5,200
Donations	$7,500

Full Cost Profile

Cost Breakdown by Percentage	
Personal Services	57.4%
Operating Costs	38.4%
Capital Costs	4.2%
TOTAL	100.0%
Cost Breakdown in Dollars	
Personal Services	$5,061,525
Operating Costs	$3,381,722
Capital Costs	$371,189
TOTAL	$8,814,436

Key: Greenville ▒ Benchmarking Average — Fiscal Years 2013 through 2017

Resource Measures

Core Parks and Recreation Services per Capita

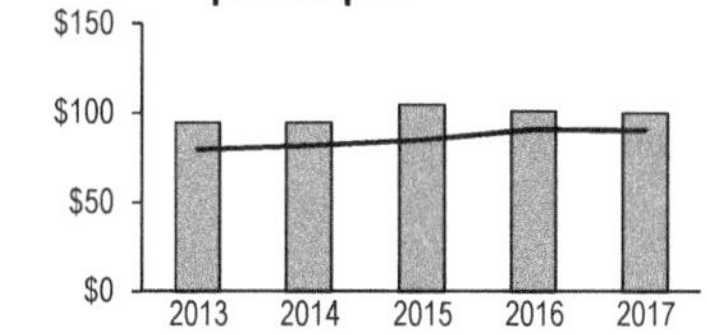

	2013	2014	2015	2016	2017
Greenville	$95	$95	$105	$101	$100
Average	$80	$82	$85	$91	$91

Core Parks and Recreation Staff per 10,000 Population

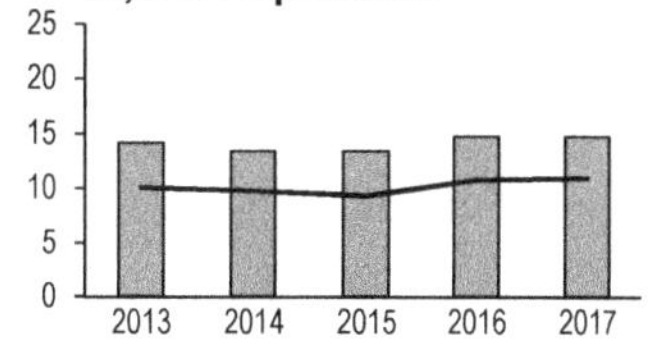

	2013	2014	2015	2016	2017
Greenville	14.1	13.4	13.3	14.7	14.7
Average	10.1	9.8	9.3	10.8	10.9

Facilities Measures

Land Acres of Parks per 10,000 Population

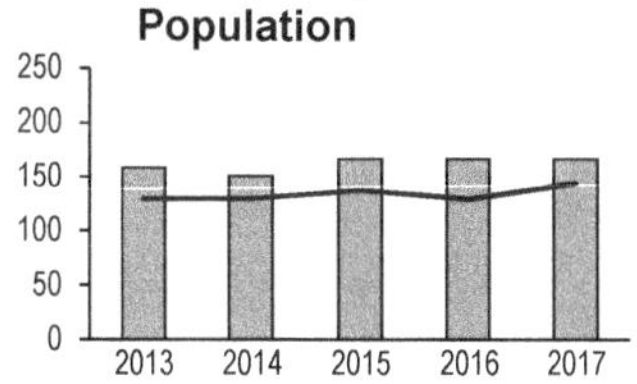

	2013	2014	2015	2016	2017
Greenville	157.99	150.11	166.29	166.08	166.03
Average	129.38	129.25	136.59	128.88	143.58

Recreation Centers per 10,000 Population

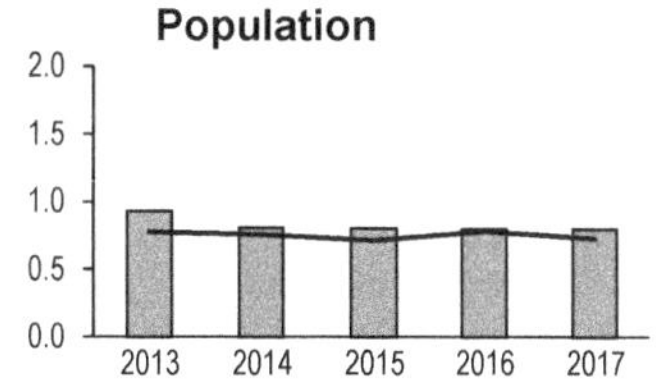

	2013	2014	2015	2016	2017
Greenville	0.93	0.80	0.80	0.80	0.80
Average	0.77	0.75	0.71	0.77	0.72

Swimming Pools per 10,000 Population

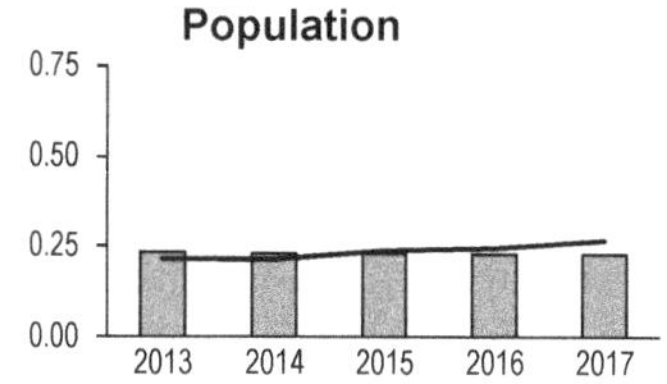

	2013	2014	2015	2016	2017
Greenville	0.23	0.23	0.23	0.23	0.23
Average	0.22	0.21	0.24	0.24	0.27

Athletic Fields per 10,000 Population

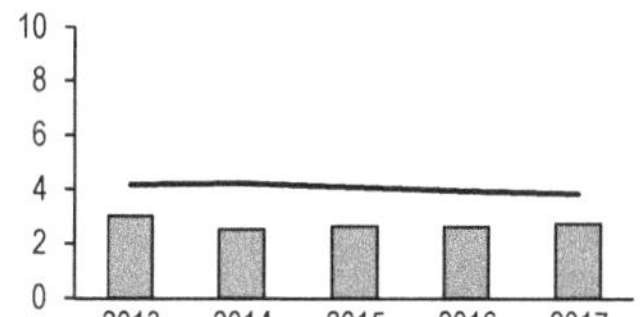

	2013	2014	2015	2016	2017
Greenville	3.02	2.52	2.63	2.61	2.73
Average	4.18	4.23	4.08	3.94	3.85

Playgrounds per 10,000 Population

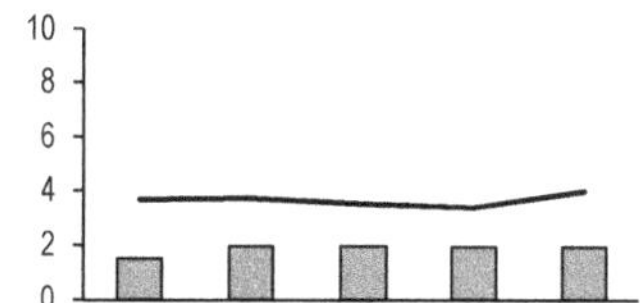

	2013	2014	2015	2016	2017
Greenville	1.51	1.95	1.94	1.93	1.93
Average	3.70	3.76	3.54	3.41	4.01

Miles of Land Trails per 10,000 Population

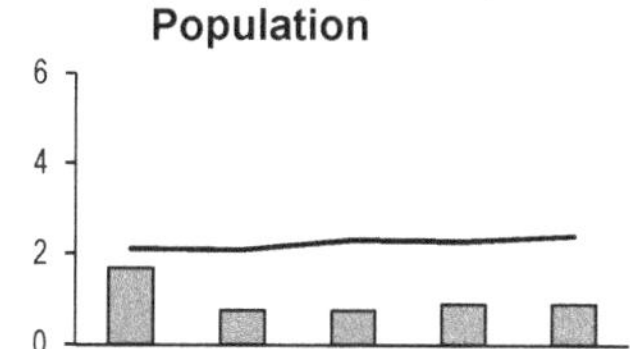

	2013	2014	2015	2016	2017
Greenville	1.68	0.75	0.74	0.88	0.88
Average	2.11	2.10	2.32	2.29	2.41

Efficiency Measures

Total Core Parks and Recreation Costs per Acre

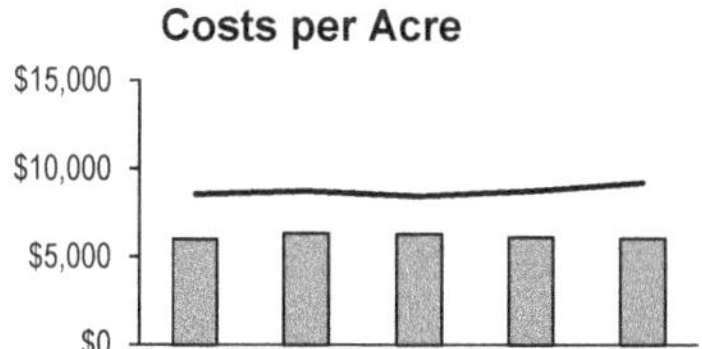

	2013	2014	2015	2016	2017
Greenville	$6,013	$6,320	$6,307	$6,106	$6,034
Average	$8,582	$8,783	$8,478	$8,783	$9,233

Acres of Park Maintained per Maintenance FTE

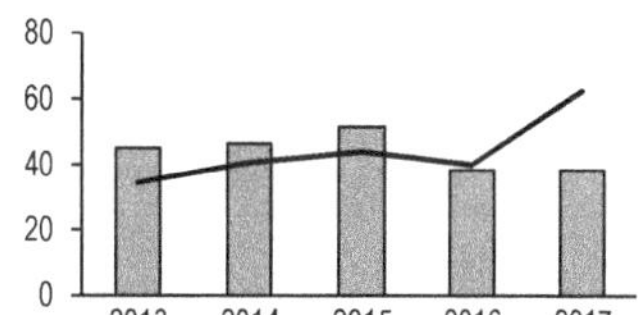

	2013	2014	2015	2016	2017
Greenville	45.0	46.4	51.5	38.2	38.2
Average	34.3	40.5	43.9	39.9	62.5

Volunteer Hours in FTEs as a Percent of Paid Staff FTEs

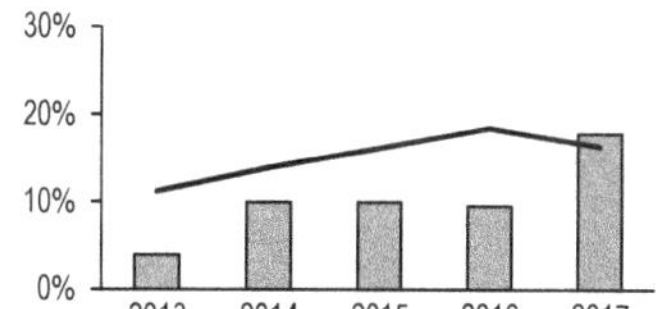

	2013	2014	2015	2016	2017
Greenville	3.9%	9.9%	9.9%	9.5%	17.9%
Average	11.2%	13.9%	16.2%	18.4%	16.4%

Effectiveness Measures

Revenue Gained as a Percent of Total Core Costs

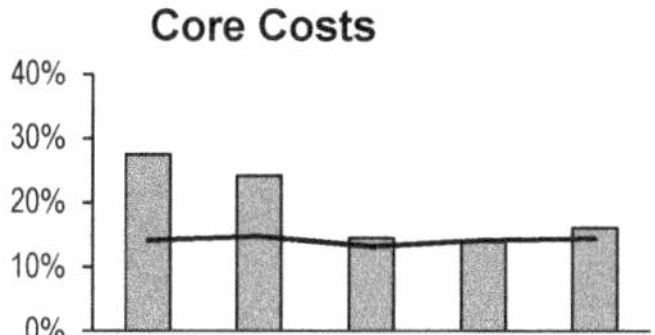

	2013	2014	2015	2016	2017
Greenville	27.4%	24.1%	14.4%	13.9%	16.0%
Average	14.1%	14.7%	13.2%	14.1%	14.4%

Acts of Vandalism at Parks Facilities per 10,000 Population

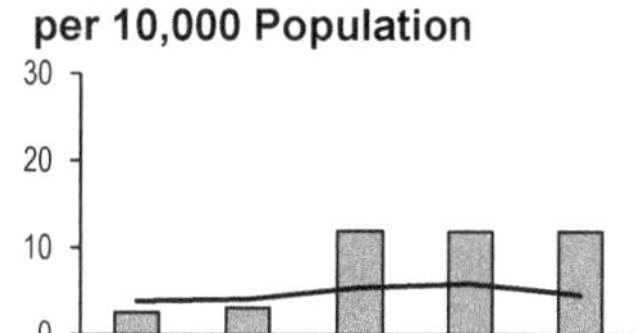

	2013	2014	2015	2016	2017
Greenville	2.55	3.09	11.89	11.82	11.82
Average	3.85	4.07	5.39	5.82	4.56

Fiscal Year 2016–17

Explanatory Information

Service Level and Delivery

The City of Hickory Parks and Recreation Department is a separate department under the city organization. The city has partnerships with other organizations to provide recreational services, including a priority use agreement with local schools for use of facilities over other non-school users and a priority use agreement with Catawba Valley Youth Soccer for use of city soccer fields.

The city has twenty-six separate parks and sites. This includes 515 acres of park acreage; 429 of these acres are developed. The city has twelve miles of trails; about five miles are paved.

In addition to the core parks and recreational facilities, Hickory has one historic property, one professional sports facility, one boat ramp, one museum, two community gardens, and a tower ropes course. The operation of these other facilities is not included in the Core Parks and Recreation comparisons reported here. These facilities are not included here in dollars or staff as part of core parks and recreation facilities and activities.

Conditions Affecting Service, Performance, and Costs

Parks and Recreation is a new service area for the benchmarking project beginning with the FY 2012–13 reporting year.

Municipal Profile

Population (OSBM 2016)	40,453
Land Area (Square Miles)	29.90
Persons per Square Mile	1,353
Topography	Gently rolling
Climate	Temperate; some ice and snow

Service Profile

Parks and Recreation Staff	
Administrative Position FTEs	4.0
Maintenance Staff FTEs	27.5
Program and Facility FTEs	27.5
Other Staff FTEs	0.0
TOTAL	59.0
Number of Parks and Sites	26
Total Land Acreage in Parks	515.0
Miles of Trails in Parks	12.0
Recreational Facilities	
Indoor and Outdoor Pools	0
Recreation Centers	8
Outdoor Basketball Courts	17
Outdoor Tennis Courts	16
Playgrounds	40
Diamond Fields	13
Rectangular Fields	12
Other Athletic Fields	0
Picnic Shelters	18
Parks and Recreation Revenues	
User Fees	$182,074
Grants	$0
Sponsorships	$37,629
Donations	$148,459

Full Cost Profile

Cost Breakdown by Percentage	
Personal Services	47.9%
Operating Costs	36.4%
Capital Costs	15.6%
TOTAL	100.0%
Cost Breakdown in Dollars	
Personal Services	$2,267,799
Operating Costs	$1,723,039
Capital Costs	$738,725
TOTAL	$4,729,563

Key: Hickory ■ Benchmarking Average — Fiscal Years 2013 through 2017

Resource Measures

Core Parks and Recreation Services per Capita

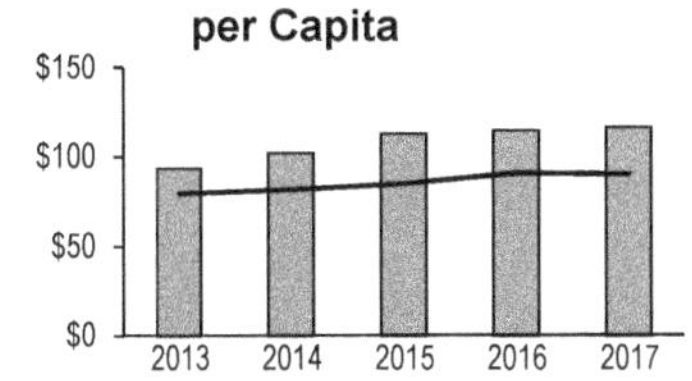

	2013	2014	2015	2016	2017
Hickory	$94	$103	$113	$115	$117
Average	$80	$82	$85	$91	$91

Core Parks and Recreation Staff per 10,000 Population

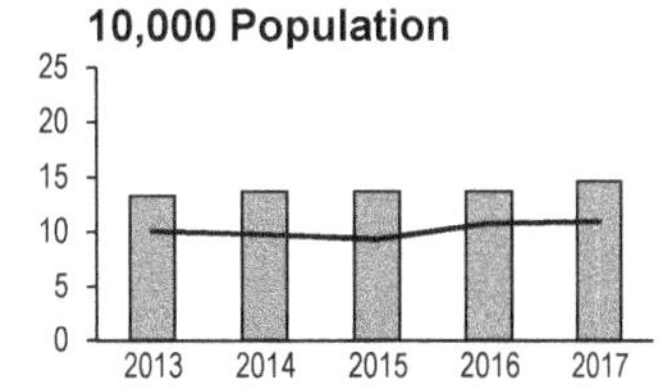

	2013	2014	2015	2016	2017
Hickory	13.2	13.7	13.6	13.6	14.6
Average	10.1	9.8	9.3	10.8	10.9

Facilities Measures

Land Acres of Parks per 10,000 Population

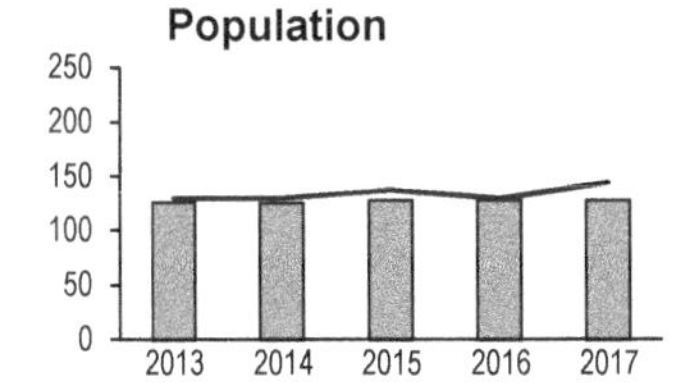

	2013	2014	2015	2016	2017
Hickory	125.88	125.30	127.44	127.38	127.31
Average	129.38	129.25	136.59	128.88	143.58

Recreation Centers per 10,000 Population

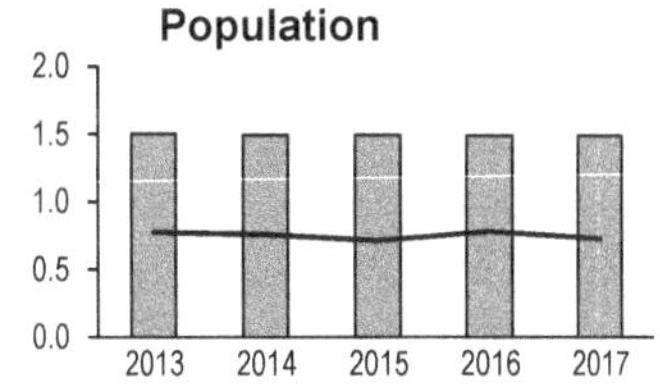

	2013	2014	2015	2016	2017
Hickory	1.50	1.49	1.49	1.49	1.48
Average	0.77	0.75	0.71	0.77	0.72

Swimming Pools per 10,000 Population

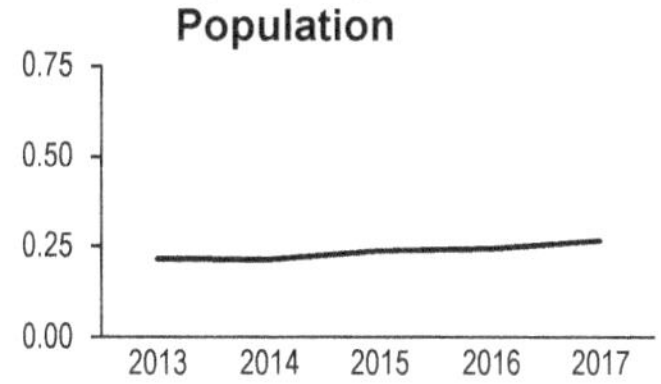

	2013	2014	2015	2016	2017
Hickory	0.00	0.00	0.00	0.00	0.00
Average	0.22	0.21	0.24	0.24	0.27

Athletic Fields per 10,000 Population

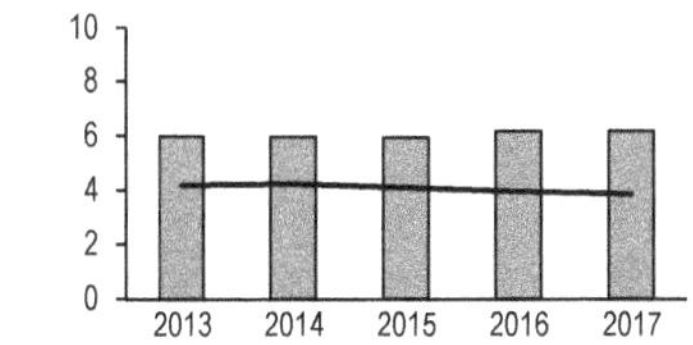

	2013	2014	2015	2016	2017
Hickory	5.99	5.97	5.95	6.20	6.18
Average	4.18	4.23	4.08	3.94	3.85

Playgrounds per 10,000 Population

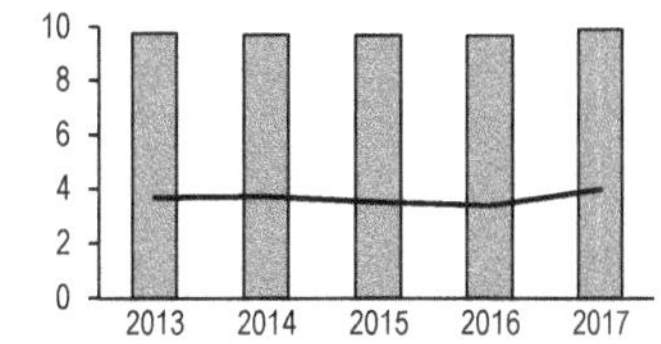

	2013	2014	2015	2016	2017
Hickory	9.74	9.70	9.67	9.67	9.89
Average	3.70	3.76	3.54	3.41	4.01

Miles of Land Trails per 10,000 Population

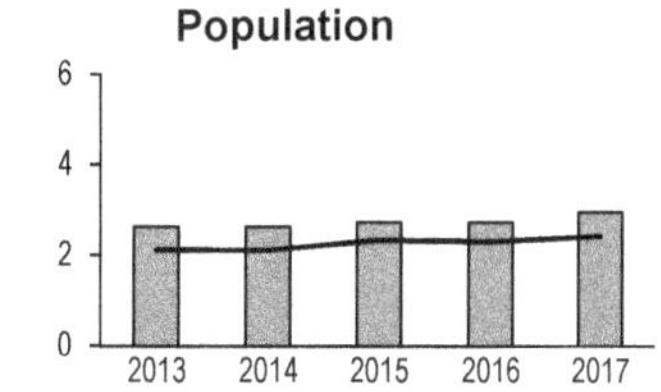

	2013	2014	2015	2016	2017
Hickory	2.64	2.63	2.73	2.73	2.96
Average	2.11	2.10	2.32	2.29	2.41

Efficiency Measures

Total Core Parks and Recreation Costs per Acre

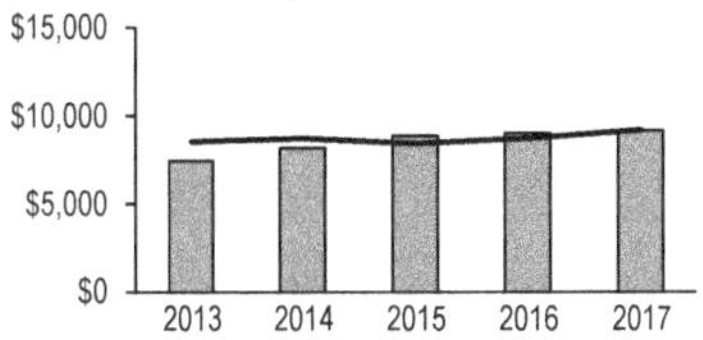

	2013	2014	2015	2016	2017
Hickory	$7,463	$8,188	$8,875	$9,020	$9,184
Average	$8,582	$8,783	$8,478	$8,783	$9,233

Acres of Park Maintained per Maintenance FTE

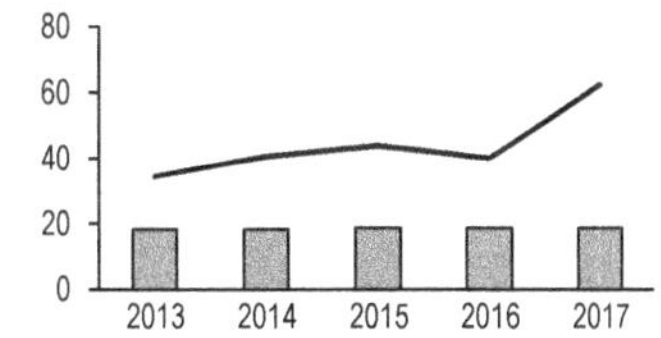

	2013	2014	2015	2016	2017
Hickory	18.3	18.3	18.7	18.7	18.7
Average	34.3	40.5	43.9	39.9	62.5

Volunteer Hours in FTEs as a Percent of Paid Staff FTEs

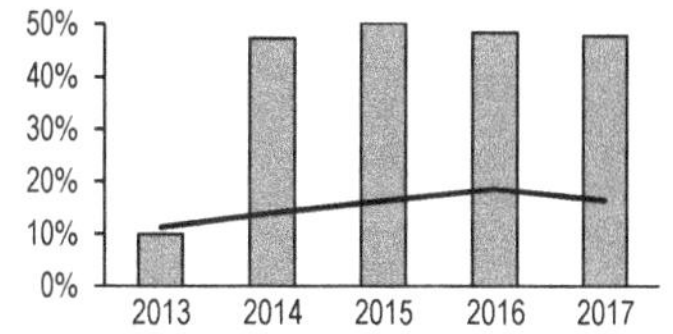

	2013	2014	2015	2016	2017
Hickory	9.8%	47.2%	50.1%	48.3%	47.7%
Average	11.2%	13.9%	16.2%	18.4%	16.4%

Effectiveness Measures

Revenue Gained as a Percent of Total Core Costs

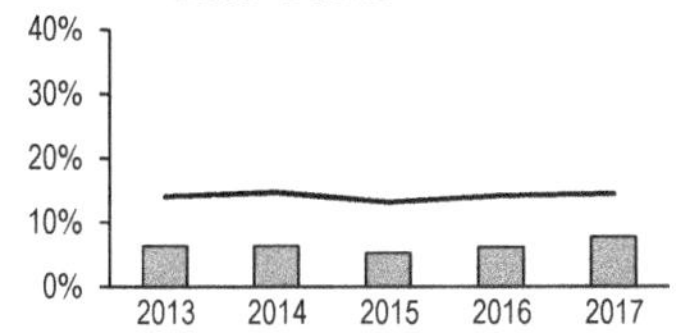

	2013	2014	2015	2016	2017
Hickory	6.4%	6.4%	5.3%	6.2%	7.8%
Average	14.1%	14.7%	13.2%	14.1%	14.4%

Acts of Vandalism at Parks Facilities per 10,000 Population

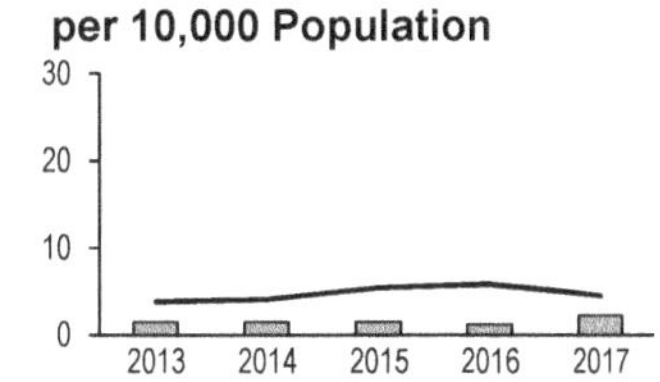

	2013	2014	2015	2016	2017
Hickory	1.50	1.49	1.49	1.24	2.22
Average	3.85	4.07	5.39	5.82	4.56

High Point

Core Parks and Recreation

Fiscal Year 2016–17

Explanatory Information

Service Level and Delivery

The City of High Point's Parks and Recreation Department is a separate department within the city. The city has a full array of recreational facilities and programs available.

The city has forty-six separate parks with 2,058 acres; most of this acreage is developed. Additionally, 1,569 acres of water space are part of the parks system. The city has 23.5 miles of trails; just over half of them are paved. All of these are multi-purpose trails, but equestrian riding is not permitted.

In addition to traditional core recreational facilities, High Point has two public boat ramps as part of the department's operations. These facilities are not included here in dollars or staff as part of core parks and recreation facilities and activities.

Conditions Affecting Service, Performance, and Costs

Parks and Recreation is a new service area for the benchmarking project beginning with the FY 2012–13 reporting year.

Municipal Profile

Population (OSBM 2016)	110,244
Land Area (Square Miles)	55.14
Persons per Square Mile	1,999
Topography	Flat; gently rolling
Climate	Temperate; little ice and snow

Service Profile

Parks and Recreation Staff	
Administrative Position FTEs	12.8
Maintenance Staff FTEs	58.1
Program and Facility FTEs	62.2
Other Staff FTEs	5.0
TOTAL	138.1
Number of Parks and Sites	46
Total Land Acreage in Parks	2,058
Miles of Trails in Parks	23.5
Recreational Facilities	
Indoor and Outdoor Pools	3
Recreation Centers	7
Outdoor Basketball Courts	14
Outdoor Tennis Courts	27
Playgrounds	35
Diamond Fields	23
Rectangular Fields	28
Other Athletic Fields	3
Picnic Shelters	37
Parks and Recreation Revenues	
User Fees	$1,570,935
Grants	$16,524
Sponsorships	$17,300
Donations	$24,513

Full Cost Profile

Cost Breakdown by Percentage	
Personal Services	54.2%
Operating Costs	37.3%
Capital Costs	8.5%
TOTAL	100.0%
Cost Breakdown in Dollars	
Personal Services	$4,997,734
Operating Costs	$3,443,214
Capital Costs	$783,050
TOTAL	$9,223,998

Key: High Point ▒ Benchmarking Average — Fiscal Years 2013 through 2017

Resource Measures

Core Parks and Recreation Services per Capita

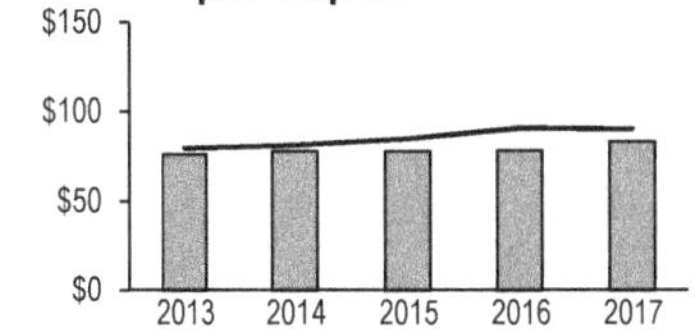

	2013	2014	2015	2016	2017
High Point	$76	$78	$78	$78	$84
Average	$80	$82	$85	$91	$91

Core Parks and Recreation Staff per 10,000 Population

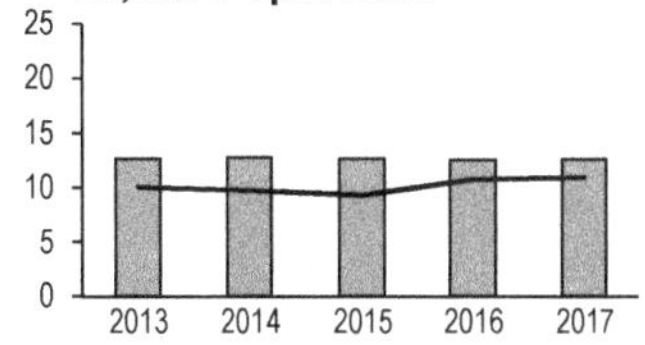

	2013	2014	2015	2016	2017
High Point	12.6	12.7	12.6	12.5	12.5
Average	10.1	9.8	9.3	10.8	10.9

Facilities Measures

Land Acres of Parks per 10,000 Population

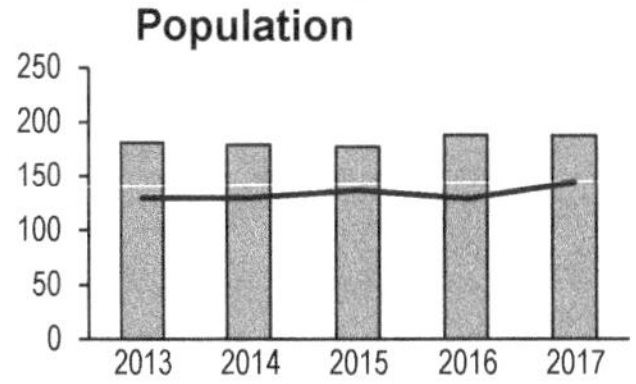

	2013	2014	2015	2016	2017
High Point	180.35	178.54	177.05	187.52	186.68
Average	129.38	129.25	136.59	128.88	143.58

Recreation Centers per 10,000 Population

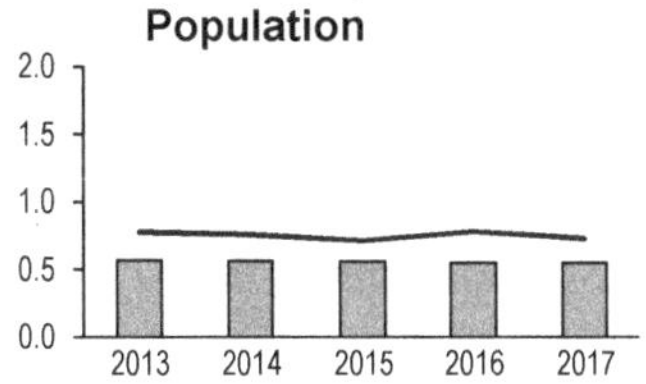

	2013	2014	2015	2016	2017
High Point	0.56	0.56	0.55	0.55	0.54
Average	0.77	0.75	0.71	0.77	0.72

Swimming Pools per 10,000 Population

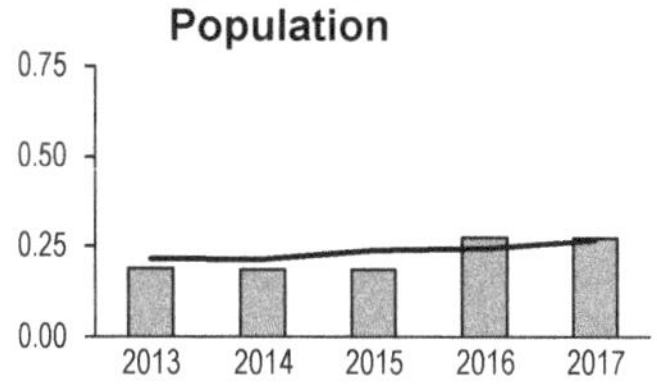

	2013	2014	2015	2016	2017
High Point	0.19	0.19	0.18	0.27	0.27
Average	0.22	0.21	0.24	0.24	0.27

Athletic Fields per 10,000 Population

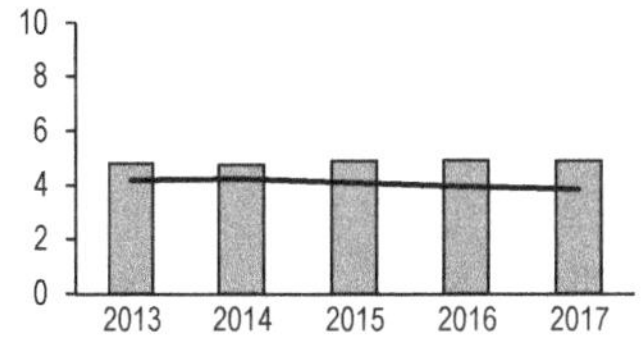

	2013	2014	2015	2016	2017
High Point	4.79	4.74	4.88	4.92	4.90
Average	4.18	4.23	4.08	3.94	3.85

Playgrounds per 10,000 Population

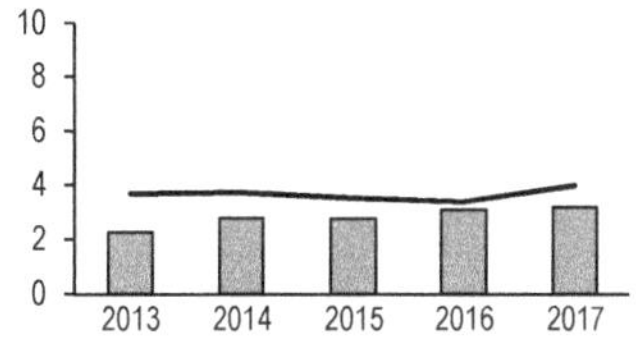

	2013	2014	2015	2016	2017
High Point	2.26	2.79	2.76	3.10	3.17
Average	3.70	3.76	3.54	3.41	4.01

Miles of Land Trails per 10,000 Population

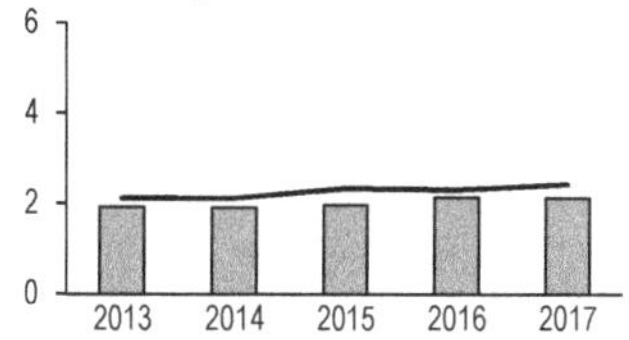

	2013	2014	2015	2016	2017
High Point	1.93	1.90	1.97	2.14	2.13
Average	2.11	2.10	2.32	2.29	2.41

Efficiency Measures

Total Core Parks and Recreation Costs per Acre

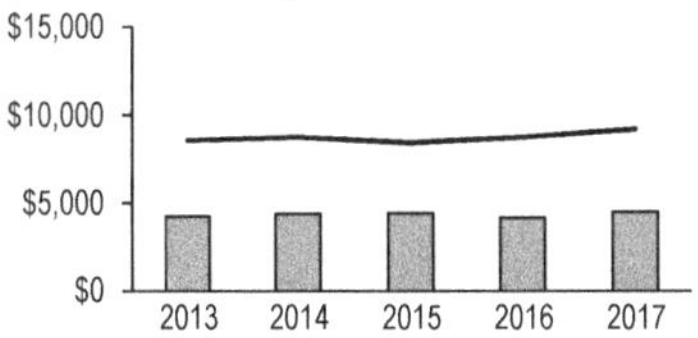

	2013	2014	2015	2016	2017
High Point	$4,235	$4,375	$4,414	$4,179	$4,482
Average	$8,582	$8,783	$8,478	$8,783	$9,233

Acres of Park Maintained per Maintenance FTE

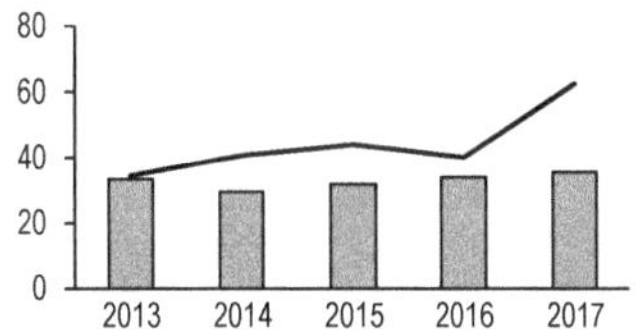

	2013	2014	2015	2016	2017
High Point	33.4	29.5	31.8	34.0	35.4
Average	34.3	40.5	43.9	39.9	62.5

Volunteer Hours in FTEs as a Percent of Paid Staff FTEs

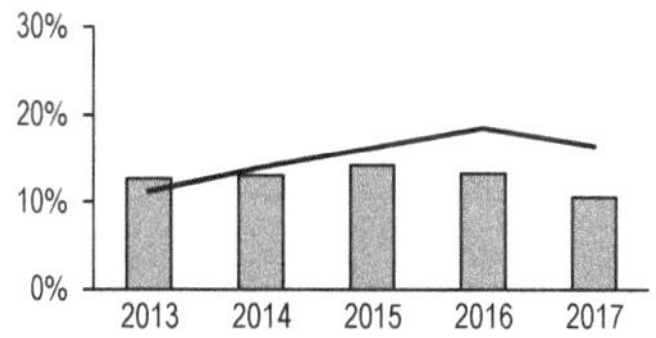

	2013	2014	2015	2016	2017
High Point	12.7%	13.0%	14.2%	13.2%	10.6%
Average	11.2%	13.9%	16.2%	18.4%	16.4%

Effectiveness Measures

Revenue Gained as a Percent of Total Core Costs

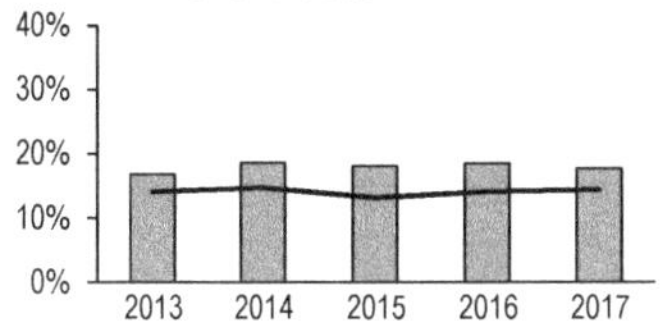

	2013	2014	2015	2016	2017
High Point	16.8%	18.6%	18.1%	18.5%	17.7%
Average	14.1%	14.7%	13.2%	14.1%	14.4%

Acts of Vandalism at Parks Facilities per 10,000 Population

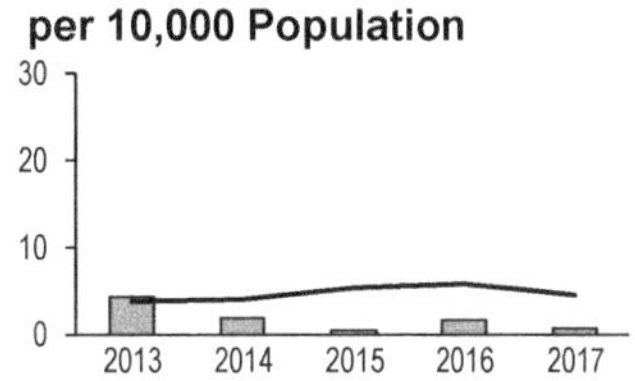

	2013	2014	2015	2016	2017
High Point	4.32	1.95	0.55	1.73	0.73
Average	3.85	4.07	5.39	5.82	4.56

Fiscal Year 2016–17

Explanatory Information

Service Level and Delivery
The City of Raleigh Parks, Recreation, and Cultural Resources Department is a stand-alone unit within the city. The department includes of six divisions: Business Process Management; Design and Development; Parks; Recreation; Resources; and Strategic Planning, Communication, and Analytics.

The department has a public/private partnership with the Dix Park Conservancy to provide funding for master planning and programming at Dorothea Dix Park. The city also has joint use agreements and memorandums of understanding with other entities, including Wake County, Wake County Public School System, NC State University, and local non-profit organizations.

Raleigh has a full array of recreational facilities available. The city has 175 parks and sites covering over six thousands acres and 146.3 miles of trails in parks.

In addition to traditional recreational facilities, Raleigh has a large outdoor performance event site, historic properties, a performing arts center, boats ramps, and city museums. These facilities are not included here in dollars or staff as part of core parks and recreation facilities and activities.

Conditions Affecting Service, Performance, and Costs
Raleigh rejoined the Benchmarking Project in July 2016 with the first year of data showing for FY 2015–16.

Parks and Recreation is a new service area for the benchmarking project beginning with the FY 2012–13 reporting year.

Municipal Profile

Population (OSBM 2016)	448,706
Land Area (Square Miles)	145.57
Persons per Square Mile	3,083
Topography	Flat; gently rolling
Climate	Temperate; little ice and snow

Service Profile

Parks and Recreation Staff	
Administrative Position FTEs	11.5
Maintenance Staff FTEs	172.7
Program and Facility FTEs	533.0
Other Staff FTEs	0.0
TOTAL	717.2
Number of Parks and Sites	175
Total Land Acreage in Parks	6,164.3
Miles of Trails in Parks	146.3
Recreational Facilities	
Indoor and Outdoor Pools	9
Recreation Centers	41
Outdoor Basketball Courts	54
Outdoor Tennis Courts	112
Playgrounds	96
Diamond Fields	62
Rectangular Fields	3
Other Athletic Fields	48
Picnic Shelters	88
Parks and Recreation Revenues	
User Fees	$10,472,779
Grants	$421,662
Sponsorships	$0
Donations	$224,674

Full Cost Profile

Cost Breakdown by Percentage	
Personal Services	58.1%
Operating Costs	35.0%
Capital Costs	6.9%
TOTAL	100.0%
Cost Breakdown in Dollars	
Personal Services	$31,542,199
Operating Costs	$18,989,446
Capital Costs	$3,752,558
TOTAL	$54,284,203

Key: Raleigh ▒ Benchmarking Average — Fiscal Years 2013 through 2017

Resource Measures

Core Parks and Recreation Services per Capita

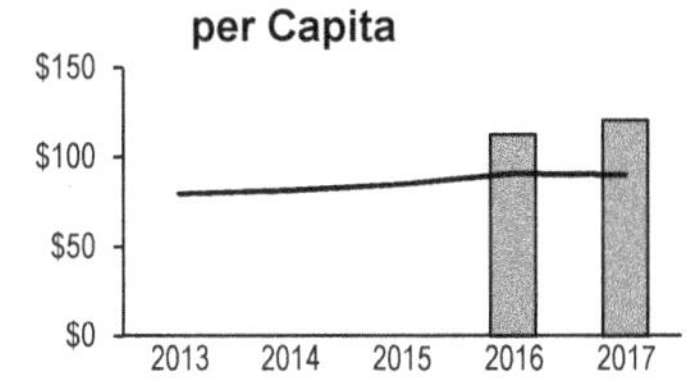

	2013	2014	2015	2016	2017
Raleigh				$113	$121
Average	$80	$82	$85	$91	$91

Core Parks and Recreation Staff per 10,000 Population

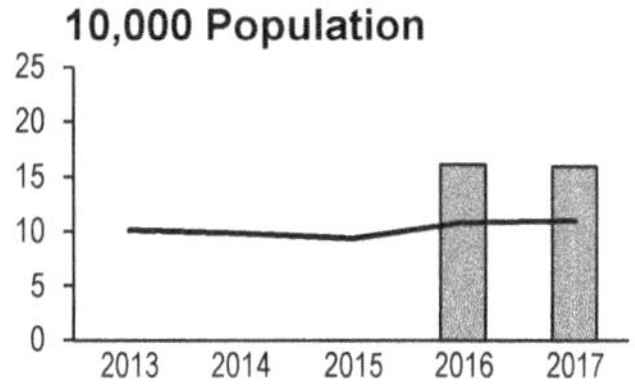

	2013	2014	2015	2016	2017
Raleigh				16.2	16.0
Average	10.1	9.8	9.3	10.8	10.9

Facilities Measures

Land Acres of Parks per 10,000 Population

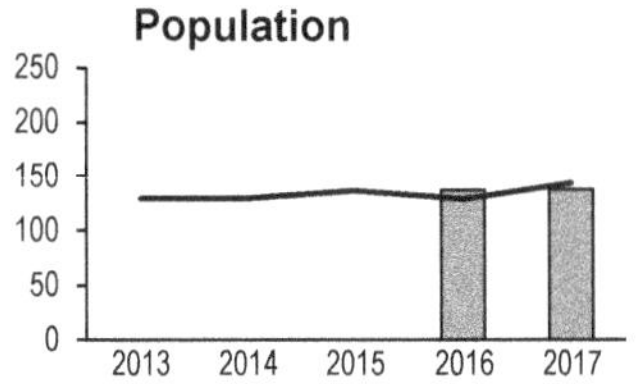

	2013	2014	2015	2016	2017
Raleigh				137.03	137.38
Average	129.38	129.25	136.59	128.88	143.58

Recreation Centers per 10,000 Population

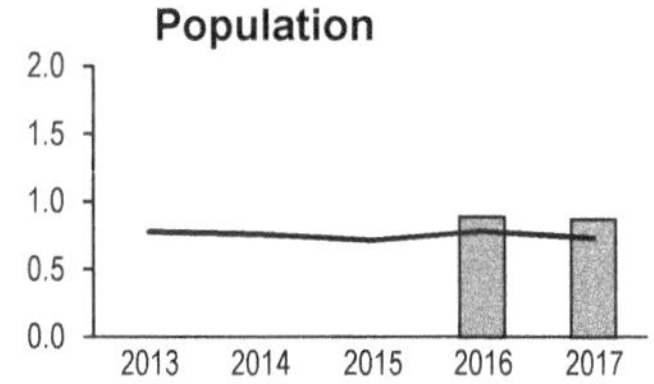

	2013	2014	2015	2016	2017
Raleigh				0.88	0.87
Average	0.77	0.75	0.71	0.77	0.72

Swimming Pools per 10,000 Population

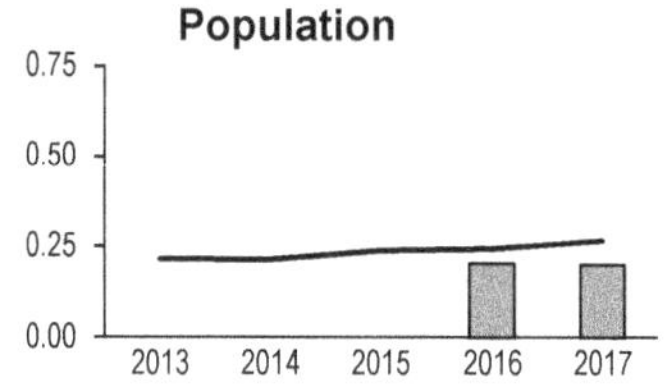

	2013	2014	2015	2016	2017
Raleigh				0.20	0.20
Average	0.22	0.21	0.24	0.24	0.27

Athletic Fields per 10,000 Population

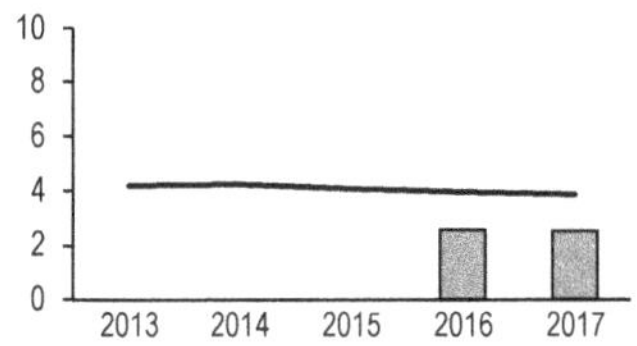

	2013	2014	2015	2016	2017
Raleigh				2.56	2.52
Average	4.18	4.23	4.08	3.94	3.85

Playgrounds per 10,000 Population

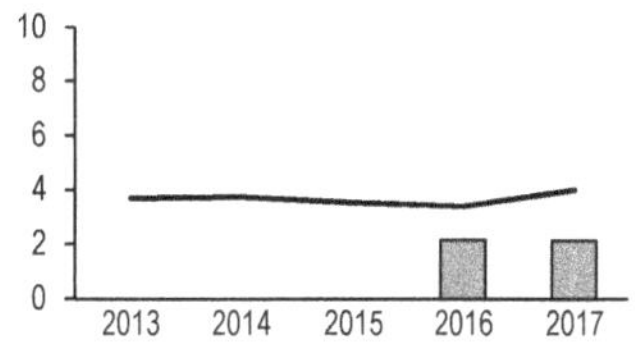

	2013	2014	2015	2016	2017
Raleigh				2.18	2.14
Average	3.70	3.76	3.54	3.41	4.01

Miles of Land Trails per 10,000 Population

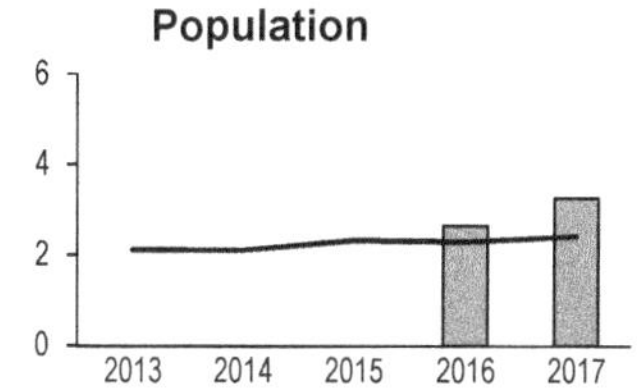

	2013	2014	2015	2016	2017
Raleigh				2.65	3.26
Average	2.11	2.10	2.32	2.29	2.41

Efficiency Measures

Total Core Parks and Recreation Costs per Acre

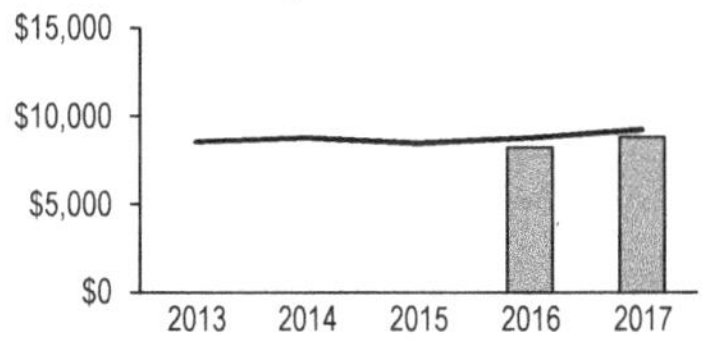

	2013	2014	2015	2016	2017
Raleigh				$8,240	$8,806
Average	$8,582	$8,783	$8,478	$8,783	$9,233

Acres of Park Maintained per Maintenance FTE

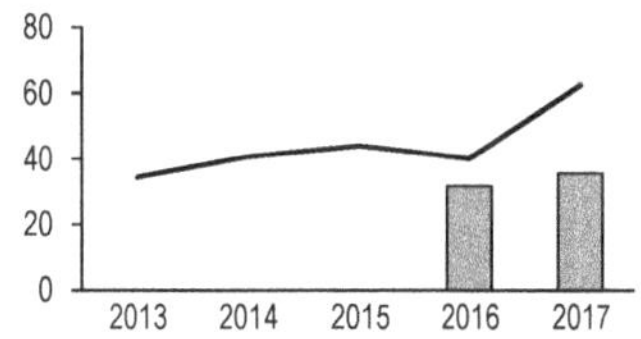

	2013	2014	2015	2016	2017
Raleigh				31.8	35.7
Average	34.3	40.5	43.9	39.9	62.5

Volunteer Hours in FTEs as a Percent of Paid Staff FTEs

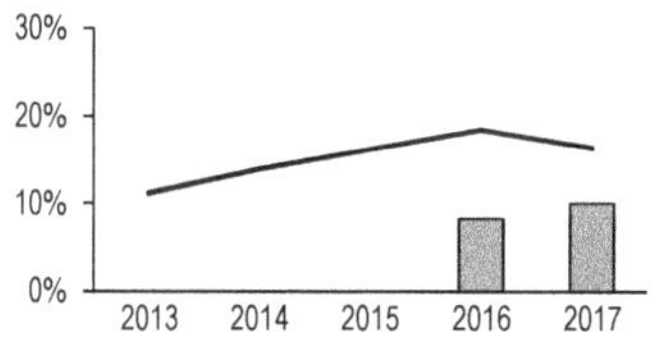

	2013	2014	2015	2016	2017
Raleigh				8.3%	10.0%
Average	11.2%	13.9%	16.2%	18.4%	16.4%

Effectiveness Measures

Revenue Gained as a Percent of Total Core Costs

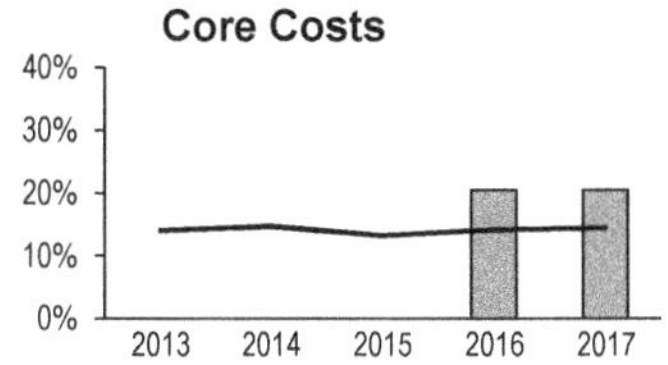

	2013	2014	2015	2016	2017
Raleigh				20.5%	20.5%
Average	14.1%	14.7%	13.2%	14.1%	14.4%

Acts of Vandalism at Parks Facilities per 10,000 Population

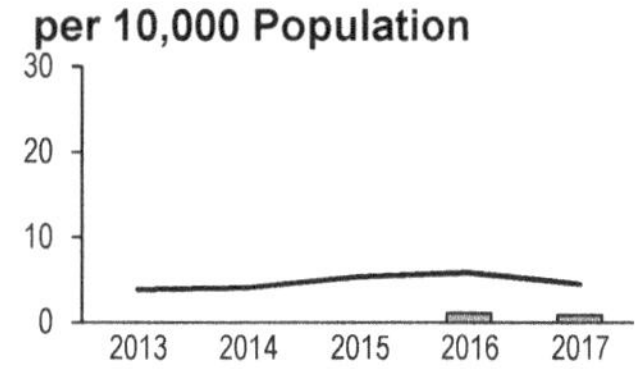

	2013	2014	2015	2016	2017
Raleigh				1.09	0.85
Average	3.85	4.07	5.39	5.82	4.56

Fiscal Year 2016–17

Explanatory Information

Service Level and Delivery
The City of Salisbury provides parks and recreation services through a separate department. This department includes other functions, such as services related to landscaping, rights-of-way and trees. These other functions are not counted in the employees or dollars shown here. The city has an agreement with Rowan County for providing certain services for special populations. The city also provides funding for senior recreation services at the Rufty Homes Senior Center.

Salisbury has a full array of recreational facilities available. The city has 518 acres of parks; more than half are developed. The city has 16.9 miles of trails.

In addition to traditional recreational facilities, Salisbury has a large outdoor performance event site and six historic sites. These facilities are not included here in dollars or staff as part of core parks and recreation facilities and activities.

Conditions Affecting Service, Performance, and Costs
Parks and Recreation is a new service area for the benchmarking project beginning with the FY 2012–13 reporting year.

Many of Salisbury's neighborhood recreational facilities are forty years or older and somewhat dated. There is a YMCA in the city for paying members. The city programs primarily serve those who cannot afford the YMCA programs.

Municipal Profile

Population (OSBM 2016)	34,459
Land Area (Square Miles)	22.28
Persons per Square Mile	1,547
Topography	Flat; gently rolling
Climate	Temperate; little ice and snow

Service Profile

Parks and Recreation Staff	
Administrative Position FTEs	2.0
Maintenance Staff FTEs	2.0
Program and Facility FTEs	9.0
Other Staff FTEs	0.0
TOTAL	13.0
Number of Parks and Sites	28
Total Land Acreage in Parks	518.0
Miles of Trails in Parks	16.9
Recreational Facilities	
Indoor and Outdoor Pools	1
Recreation Centers	4
Outdoor Basketball Courts	12
Outdoor Tennis Courts	10
Playgrounds	18
Diamond Fields	8
Rectangular Fields	4
Other Athletic Fields	0
Picnic Shelters	14
Parks and Recreation Revenues	
User Fees	$2,500
Grants	$2,500
Sponsorships	$5,000
Donations	$19,167

Full Cost Profile

Cost Breakdown by Percentage	
Personal Services	55.1%
Operating Costs	41.1%
Capital Costs	3.8%
TOTAL	100.0%
Cost Breakdown in Dollars	
Personal Services	$1,049,839
Operating Costs	$783,983
Capital Costs	$72,109
TOTAL	$1,905,931

Key: Salisbury ▒ Benchmarking Average — Fiscal Years 2013 through 2017

Resource Measures

Core Parks and Recreation Services per Capita

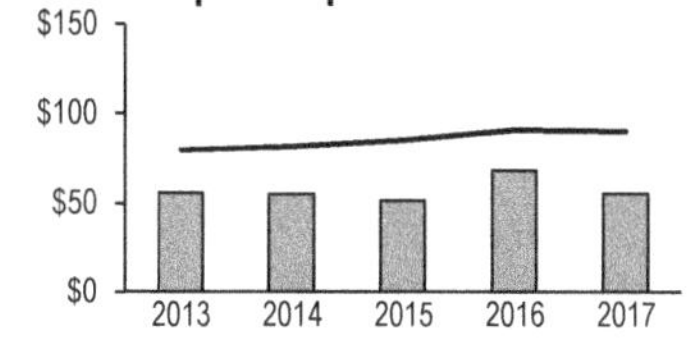

	2013	2014	2015	2016	2017
Salisbury	$56	$55	$51	$68	$55
Average	$80	$82	$85	$91	$91

Core Parks and Recreation Staff per 10,000 Population

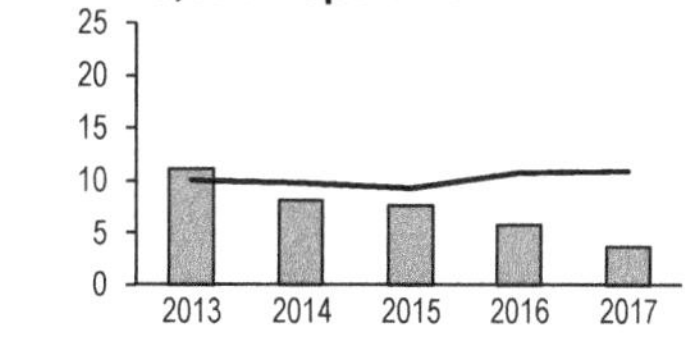

	2013	2014	2015	2016	2017
Salisbury	11.1	8.2	7.7	5.8	3.8
Average	10.1	9.8	9.3	10.8	10.9

Facilities Measures

Land Acres of Parks per 10,000 Population

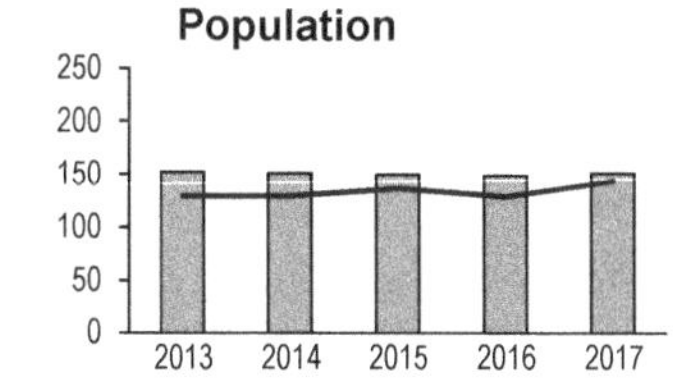

	2013	2014	2015	2016	2017
Salisbury	151.90	150.63	149.61	148.17	150.32
Average	129.38	129.25	136.59	128.88	143.58

Recreation Centers per 10,000 Population

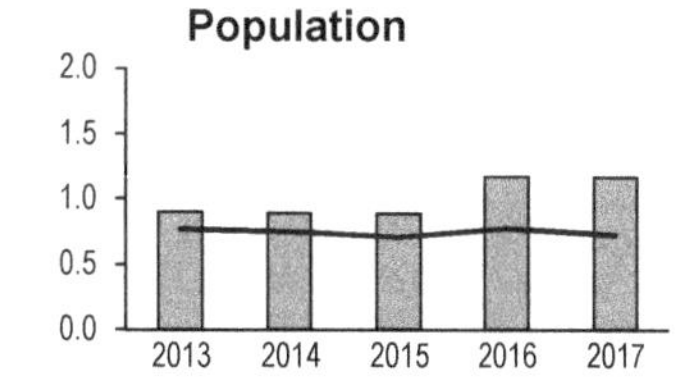

	2013	2014	2015	2016	2017
Salisbury	0.90	0.89	0.88	1.17	1.16
Average	0.77	0.75	0.71	0.77	0.72

Swimming Pools per 10,000 Population

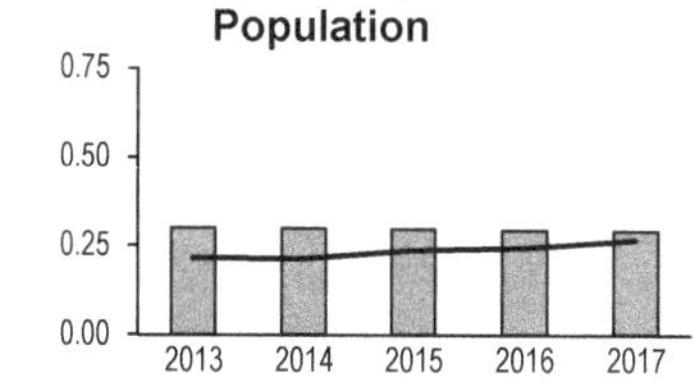

	2013	2014	2015	2016	2017
Salisbury	0.30	0.30	0.29	0.29	0.29
Average	0.22	0.21	0.24	0.24	0.27

Athletic Fields per 10,000 Population

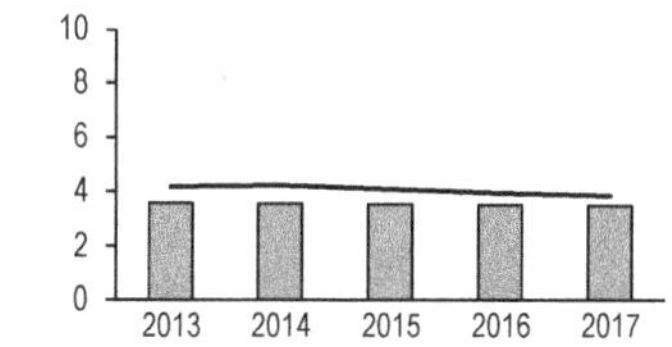

	2013	2014	2015	2016	2017
Salisbury	3.59	3.56	3.53	3.50	3.48
Average	4.18	4.23	4.08	3.94	3.85

Playgrounds per 10,000 Population

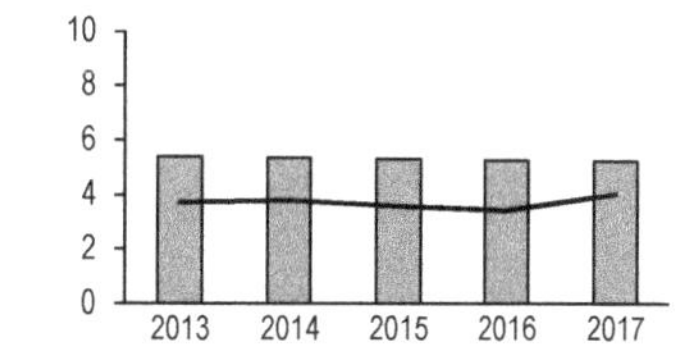

	2013	2014	2015	2016	2017
Salisbury	5.38	5.34	5.30	5.25	5.22
Average	3.70	3.76	3.54	3.41	4.01

Miles of Land Trails per 10,000 Population

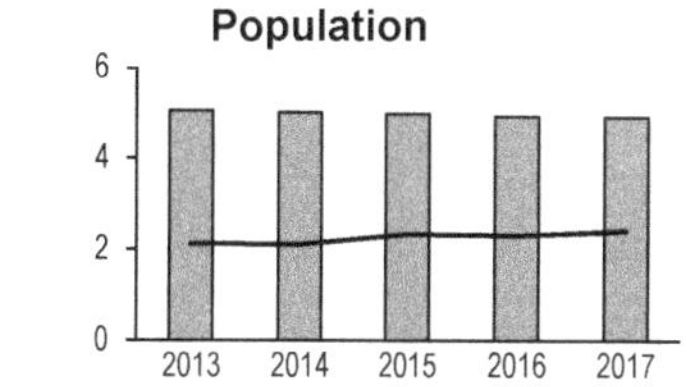

	2013	2014	2015	2016	2017
Salisbury	5.05	5.01	4.98	4.93	4.90
Average	2.11	2.10	2.32	2.29	2.41

Efficiency Measures

Total Core Parks and Recreation Costs per Acre

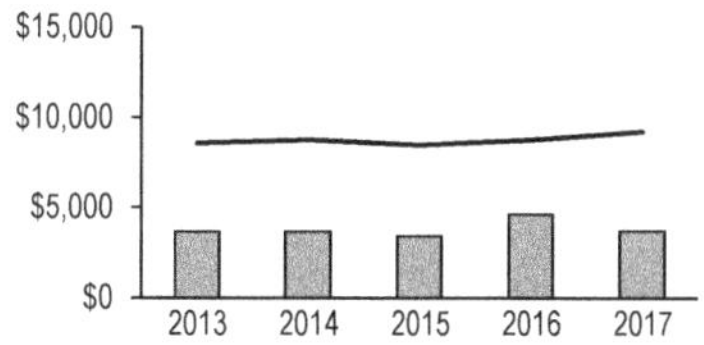

	2013	2014	2015	2016	2017
Salisbury	$3,662	$3,646	$3,418	$4,609	$3,679
Average	$8,582	$8,783	$8,478	$8,783	$9,233

Acres of Park Maintained per Maintenance FTE

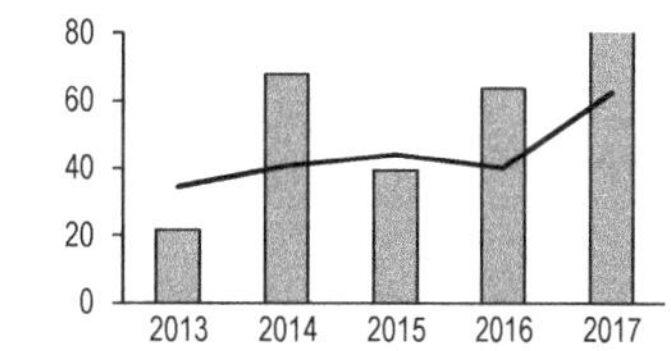

	2013	2014	2015	2016	2017
Salisbury	21.6	67.7	39.1	63.5	259.0
Average	34.3	40.5	43.9	39.9	62.5

Volunteer Hours in FTEs as a Percent of Paid Staff FTEs

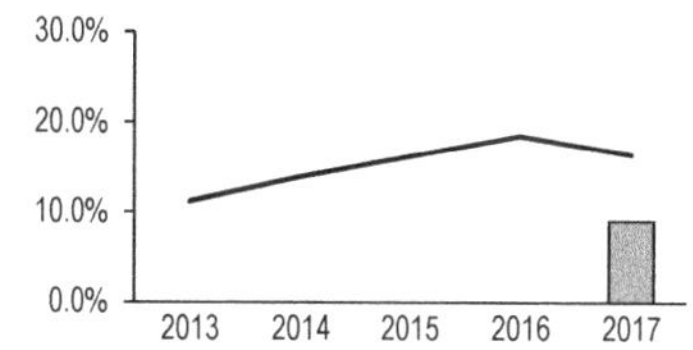

	2013	2014	2015	2016	2017
Salisbury					9.0%
Average	11.2%	13.9%	16.2%	18.4%	16.4%

Effectiveness Measures

Revenue Gained as a Percent of Total Core Costs

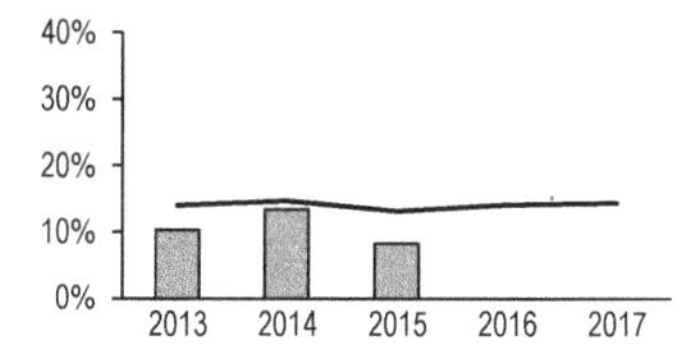

	2013	2014	2015	2016	2017
Salisbury	10.3%	13.4%	8.2%		
Average	14.1%	14.7%	13.2%	14.1%	14.4%

Acts of Vandalism at Parks Facilities per 10,000 Population

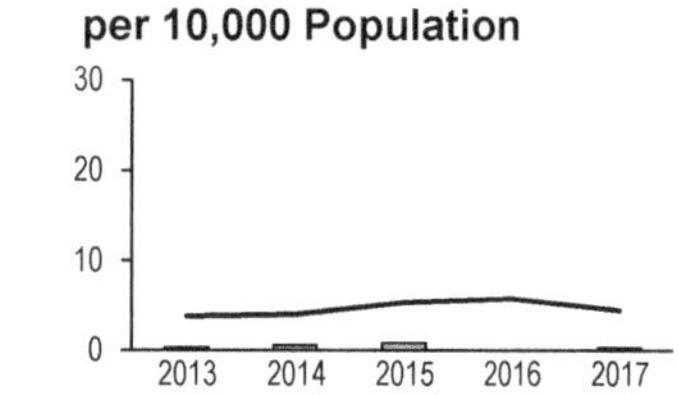

	2013	2014	2015	2016	2017
Salisbury	0.30	0.59	0.88		0.29
Average	3.85	4.07	5.39	5.82	4.56

Wilson

Core Parks and Recreation

Fiscal Year 2016–17

Explanatory Information

Service Level and Delivery

The City of Wilson Parks and Recreation Department is a separate department under the city organization. The city has partnerships with other organizations to provide recreational services, including the Wilson County Schools, the Wilson Youth Soccer Association, Wilson City Little League, Special Olympics, Youth Soccer Association, the Senior Games of North Carolina, and the Wilson Arts Council.

The city has twenty-eight separate parks and sites. This includes 400 acres, most currently undeveloped. The city has fourteen miles of trails.

In addition to the core parks and recreational facilities, Wilson has three boat ramps and one museum. The city also runs a municipal eighteen-hole golf course. The operation of these other facilities is not included in the Core Parks and Recreation comparisons reported here. These facilities are not included here in dollars or staff as part of core parks and recreation facilities and activities.

Conditions Affecting Service, Performance, and Costs

Parks and Recreation is a new service area for the benchmarking project beginning with the FY 2012–13 reporting year.

Municipal Profile

Population (OSBM 2016)	49,406
Land Area (Square Miles)	30.60
Persons per Square Mile	1,615
Topography	Flat
Climate	Temperate; little ice and snow

Service Profile

Parks and Recreation Staff	
Administrative Position FTEs	4.0
Maintenance Staff FTEs	13.0
Program and Facility FTEs	47.0
Other Staff FTEs	4.0
TOTAL	68.0
Number of Parks and Sites	28
Total Land Acreage in Parks	400.0
Miles of Trails in Parks	14.5
Recreational Facilities	
Indoor and Outdoor Pools	2
Recreation Centers	4
Outdoor Basketball Courts	7
Outdoor Tennis Courts	16
Playgrounds	25
Diamond Fields	11
Rectangular Fields	14
Other Athletic Fields	1
Picnic Shelters	17
Parks and Recreation Revenues	
User Fees	$500,000
Grants	$50,000
Sponsorships	$22,000
Donations	$0

Full Cost Profile

Cost Breakdown by Percentage	
Personal Services	55.4%
Operating Costs	36.5%
Capital Costs	8.2%
TOTAL	100.0%
Cost Breakdown in Dollars	
Personal Services	$3,056,848
Operating Costs	$2,013,491
Capital Costs	$450,658
TOTAL	$5,520,997

Wilson

Core Parks and Recreation

Key: Wilson ▒ Benchmarking Average — Fiscal Years 2013 through 2017

Resource Measures

Core Parks and Recreation Services per Capita

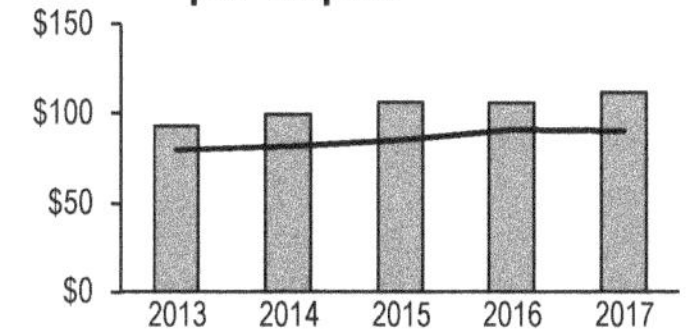

	2013	2014	2015	2016	2017
Wilson	$93	$99	$106	$106	$112
Average	$80	$82	$85	$91	$91

Core Parks and Recreation Staff per 10,000 Population

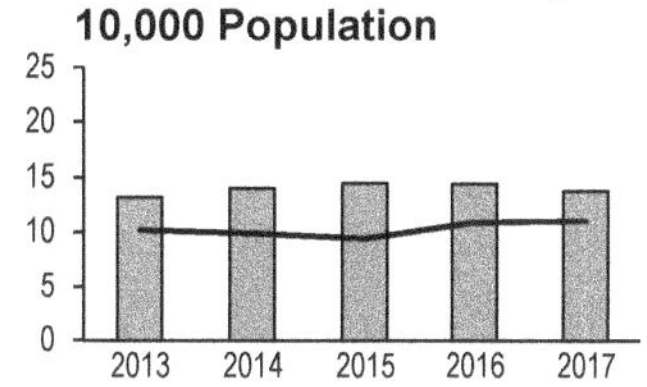

	2013	2014	2015	2016	2017
Wilson	13.1	14.0	14.4	14.4	13.8
Average	10.1	9.8	9.3	10.8	10.9

Facilities Measures

Land Acres of Parks per 10,000 Population

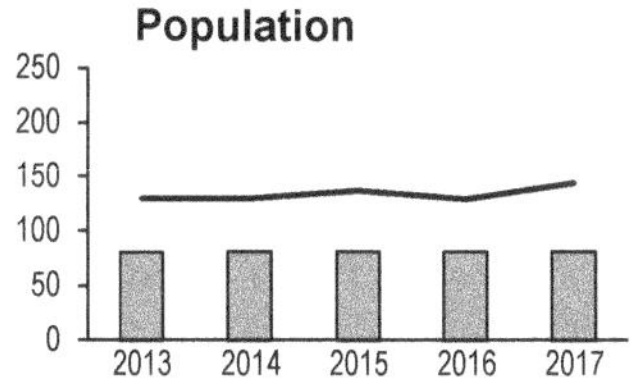

	2013	2014	2015	2016	2017
Wilson	80.91	81.47	81.26	81.04	80.96
Average	129.38	129.25	136.59	128.88	143.58

Recreation Centers per 10,000 Population

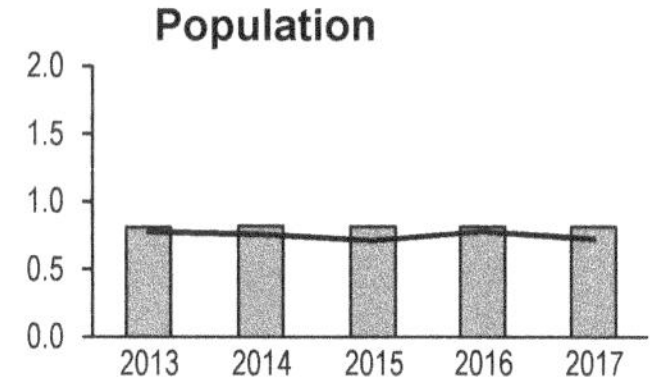

	2013	2014	2015	2016	2017
Wilson	0.81	0.81	0.81	0.81	0.81
Average	0.77	0.75	0.71	0.77	0.72

Swimming Pools per 10,000 Population

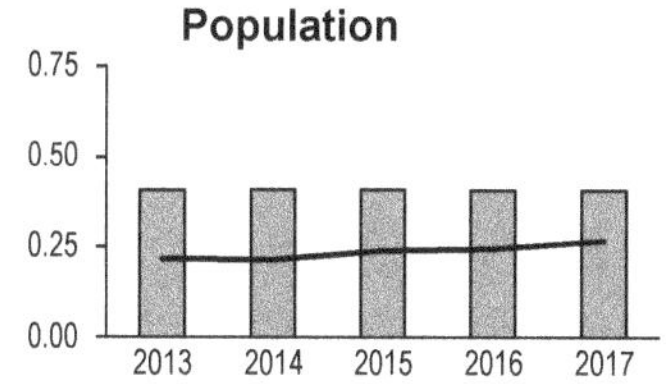

	2013	2014	2015	2016	2017
Wilson	0.40	0.41	0.41	0.41	0.40
Average	0.22	0.21	0.24	0.24	0.27

Athletic Fields per 10,000 Population

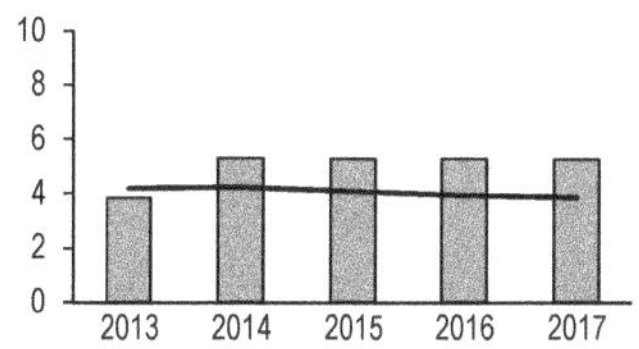

	2013	2014	2015	2016	2017
Wilson	3.84	5.30	5.28	5.27	5.26
Average	4.18	4.23	4.08	3.94	3.85

Playgrounds per 10,000 Population

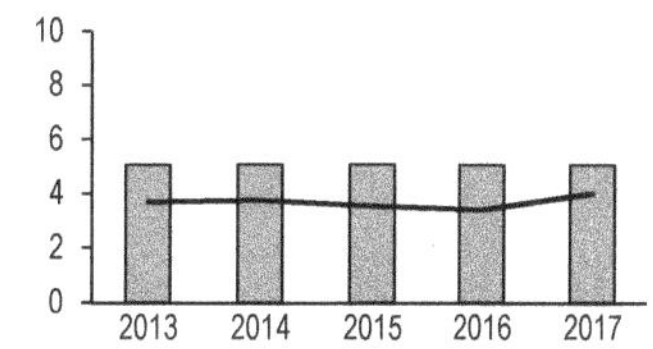

	2013	2014	2015	2016	2017
Wilson	5.06	5.09	5.08	5.06	5.06
Average	3.70	3.76	3.54	3.41	4.01

Miles of Land Trails per 10,000 Population

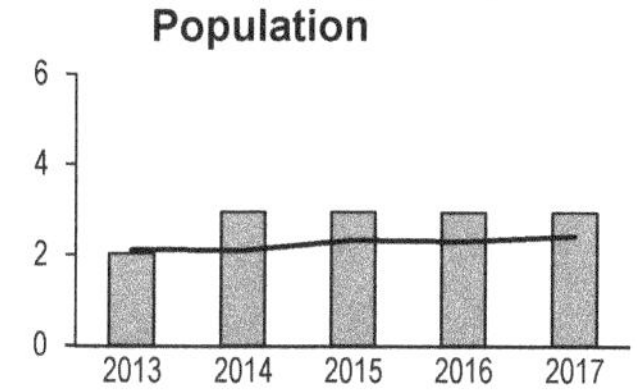

	2013	2014	2015	2016	2017
Wilson	2.02	2.95	2.95	2.94	2.93
Average	2.11	2.10	2.32	2.29	2.41

Efficiency Measures

Total Core Parks and Recreation Costs per Acre

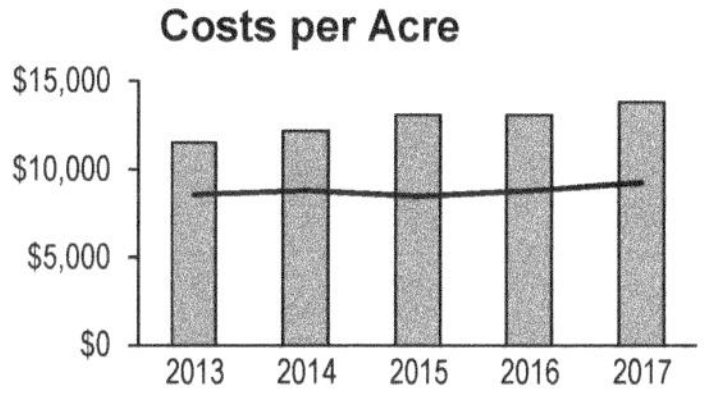

	2013	2014	2015	2016	2017
Wilson	$11,508	$12,184	$13,062	$13,079	$13,802
Average	$8,582	$8,783	$8,478	$8,783	$9,233

Acres of Park Maintained per Maintenance FTE

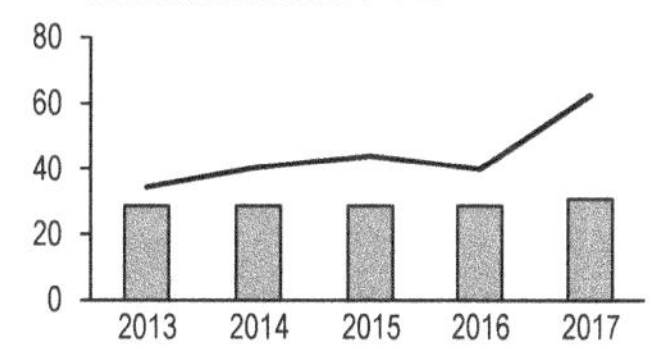

	2013	2014	2015	2016	2017
Wilson	28.6	28.6	28.6	28.6	30.8
Average	34.3	40.5	43.9	39.9	62.5

Volunteer Hours in FTEs as a Percent of Paid Staff FTEs

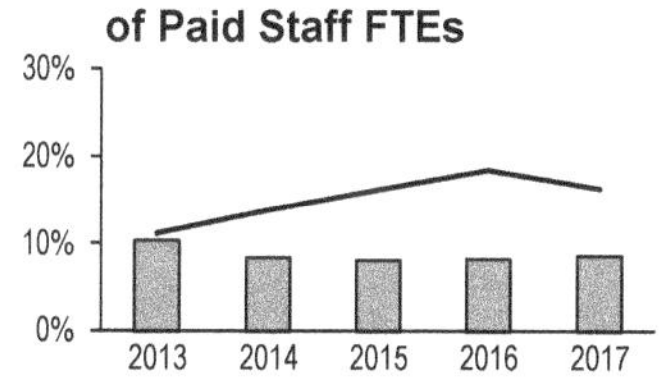

	2013	2014	2015	2016	2017
Wilson	10.4%	8.4%	8.1%	8.3%	8.6%
Average	11.2%	13.9%	16.2%	18.4%	16.4%

Effectiveness Measures

Revenue Gained as a Percent of Total Core Costs

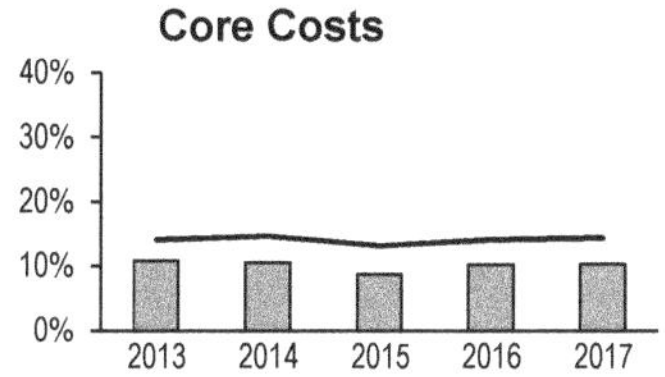

	2013	2014	2015	2016	2017
Wilson	10.8%	10.5%	8.7%	10.2%	10.4%
Average	14.1%	14.7%	13.2%	14.1%	14.4%

Acts of Vandalism at Parks Facilities per 10,000 Population

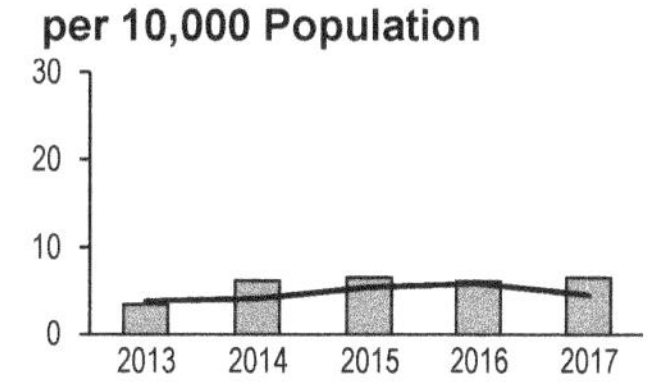

	2013	2014	2015	2016	2017
Wilson	3.44	6.11	6.50	6.08	6.48
Average	3.85	4.07	5.39	5.82	4.56

Fiscal Year 2016–17

Explanatory Information

Service Level and Delivery

The City of Winston-Salem Recreation and Parks Department is a separate department under the city organization. The department is overseen by the advisory Parks and Recreation Commission, which has eleven members appointed by the mayor and approved by the city council. The city has formal cooperative arrangements with Foryth County and various public-private partnerships with other organizations to provide recreational services.

The city has seventy-nine separate parks and sites. This includes 3,852 acres of parkland, most of which is developed The city has twenty-three miles of trails, about two-thirds of which are paved.

In addition to the core parks and recreational facilities, Winston-Salem has two large outdoor performance event sites, a historic property, one boat ramp, and one museum. The city also runs two municipal eighteen-hole golf courses. The operation of these other facilities is not included in the Core Parks and Recreation comparisons reported here. These facilities are not included here in dollars or staff as part of core parks and recreation facilities and activities.

Conditions Affecting Service, Performance, and Costs

Parks and Recreation is a new service area for the benchmarking project beginning with the FY 2012–13 reporting year.

Many Forsyth County residents make use of the city's parks and recreational facilities. Most of the city's facilities were built in the 1960s to 1980s and are aging. Several support services are in other departments to improve efficiency and reduce costs including property maintenance and vegetation management.

Municipal Profile

Population (OSBM 2016)	240,603
Land Area (Square Miles)	132.55
Persons per Square Mile	1,815
Topography	Gently rolling
Climate	Temperate; some ice and snow

Service Profile

Parks and Recreation Staff	
Administrative Position FTEs	24.9
Maintenance Staff FTEs	72.8
Program and Facility FTEs	100.6
Other Staff FTEs	2.0
TOTAL	200.2
Number of Parks and Sites	79
Total Land Acreage in Parks	3,852.0
Miles of Trails in Parks	23.3
Recreational Facilities	
Indoor and Outdoor Pools	9
Recreation Centers	17
Outdoor Basketball Courts	23
Outdoor Tennis Courts	107
Playgrounds	45
Diamond Fields	47
Rectangular Fields	50
Other Athletic Fields	0
Picnic Shelters	51
Parks and Recreation Revenues	
User Fees	$837,461
Grants	$704
Sponsorships	$0
Donations	$61,629

Full Cost Profile

Cost Breakdown by Percentage	
Personal Services	54.1%
Operating Costs	34.6%
Capital Costs	11.4%
TOTAL	100.0%
Cost Breakdown in Dollars	
Personal Services	$6,465,192
Operating Costs	$4,134,536
Capital Costs	$1,358,639
TOTAL	$11,958,368

Key: Winston-Salem ▒ Benchmarking Average — Fiscal Years 2013 through 2017

Resource Measures

Core Parks and Recreation Services per Capita

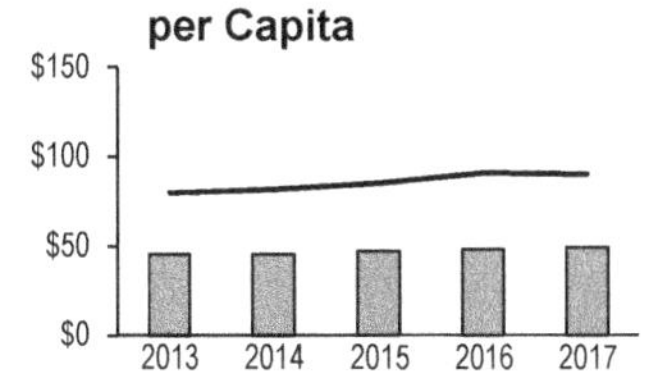

	2013	2014	2015	2016	2017
Winston-Salem	$46	$46	$47	$49	$50
Average	$80	$82	$85	$91	$91

Core Parks and Recreation Staff per 10,000 Population

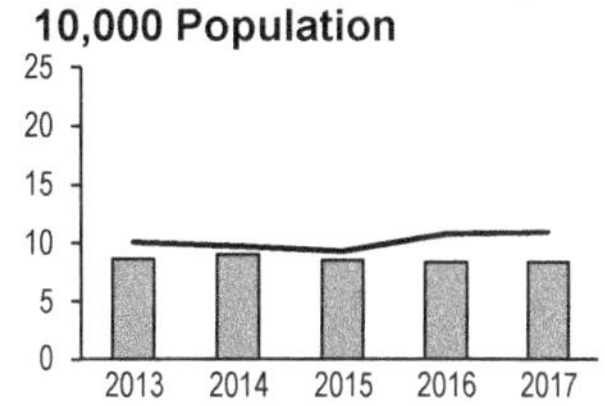

	2013	2014	2015	2016	2017
Winston-Salem	8.6	9.0	8.5	8.4	8.3
Average	10.1	9.8	9.3	10.8	10.9

Facilities Measures

Land Acres of Parks per 10,000 Population

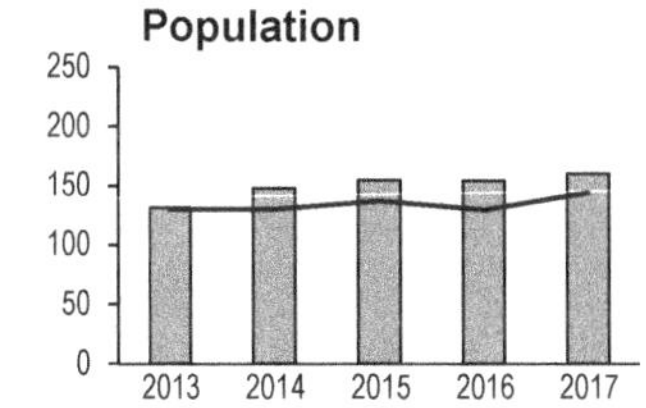

	2013	2014	2015	2016	2017
Winston-Salem	131.07	147.71	154.81	154.37	160.10
Average	129.38	129.25	136.59	128.88	143.58

Recreation Centers per 10,000 Population

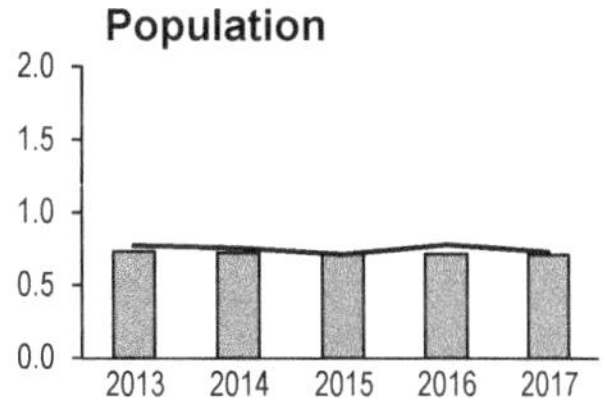

	2013	2014	2015	2016	2017
Winston-Salem	0.73	0.72	0.71	0.71	0.71
Average	0.77	0.75	0.71	0.77	0.72

Swimming Pools per 10,000 Population

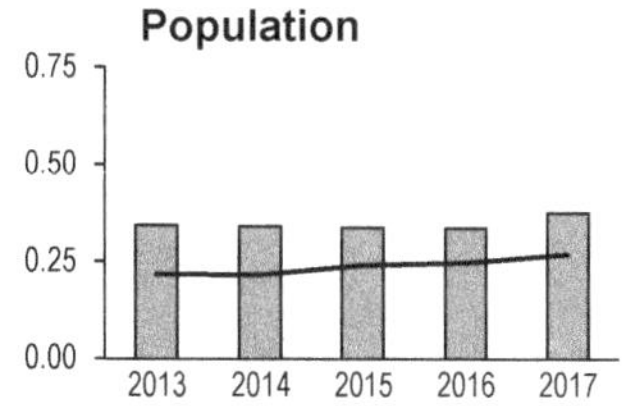

	2013	2014	2015	2016	2017
Winston-Salem	0.34	0.34	0.34	0.33	0.37
Average	0.22	0.21	0.24	0.24	0.27

Athletic Fields per 10,000 Population

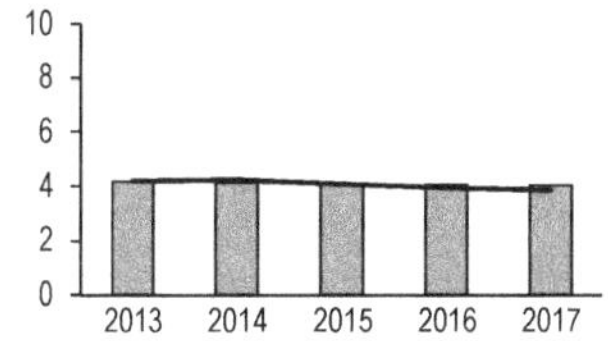

	2013	2014	2015	2016	2017
Winston-Salem	4.16	4.12	4.08	4.06	4.03
Average	4.18	4.23	4.08	3.94	3.85

Playgrounds per 10,000 Population

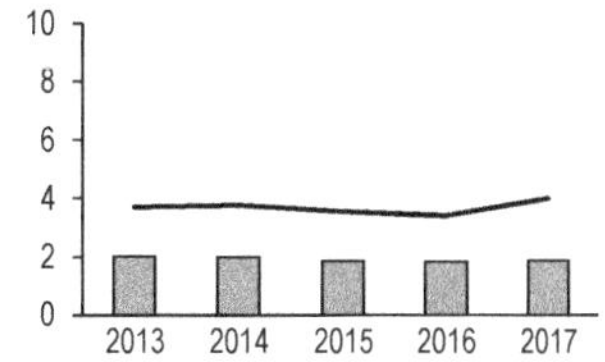

	2013	2014	2015	2016	2017
Winston-Salem	2.02	2.00	1.85	1.84	1.87
Average	3.70	3.76	3.54	3.41	4.01

Miles of Land Trails per 10,000 Population

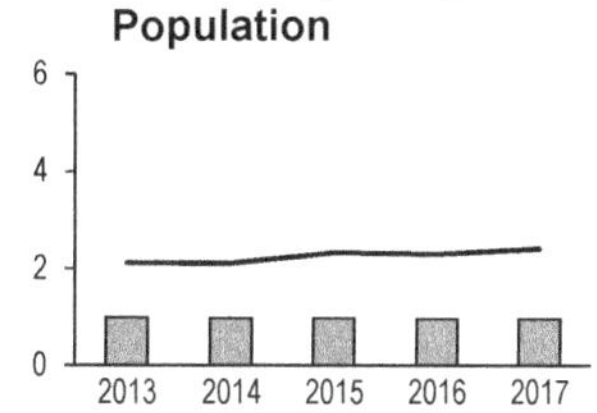

	2013	2014	2015	2016	2017
Winston-Salem	1.00	0.99	0.98	0.97	0.97
Average	2.11	2.10	2.32	2.29	2.41

Efficiency Measures

Total Core Parks and Recreation Costs per Acre

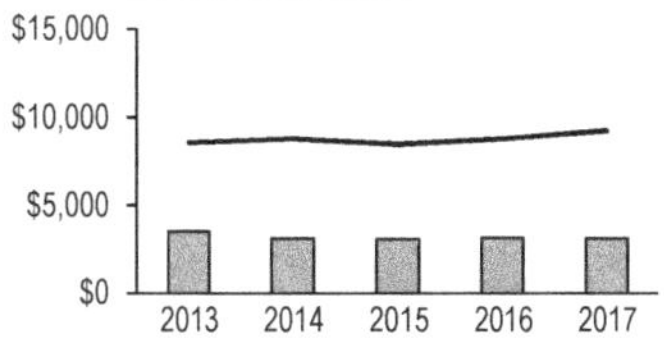

	2013	2014	2015	2016	2017
Winston-Salem	$3,478	$3,094	$3,060	$3,147	$3,104
Average	$8,582	$8,783	$8,478	$8,783	$9,233

Acres of Park Maintained per Maintenance FTE

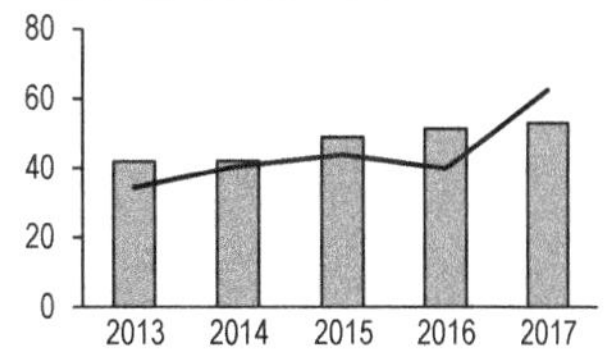

	2013	2014	2015	2016	2017
Winston-Salem	42.0	42.0	48.9	51.2	52.9
Average	34.3	40.5	43.9	39.9	62.5

Volunteer Hours in FTEs as a Percent of Paid Staff FTEs

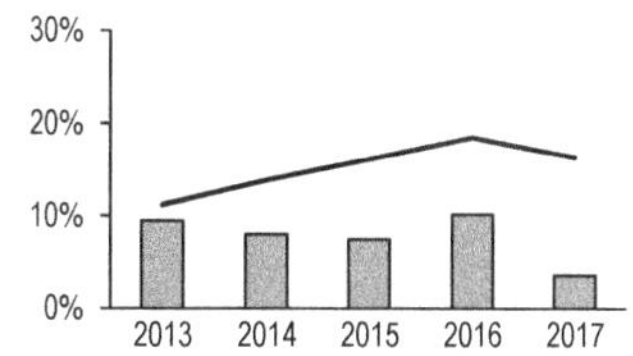

	2013	2014	2015	2016	2017
Winston-Salem	9.4%	7.9%	7.4%	10.1%	3.5%
Average	11.2%	13.9%	16.2%	18.4%	16.4%

Effectiveness Measures

Revenue Gained as a Percent of Total Core Costs

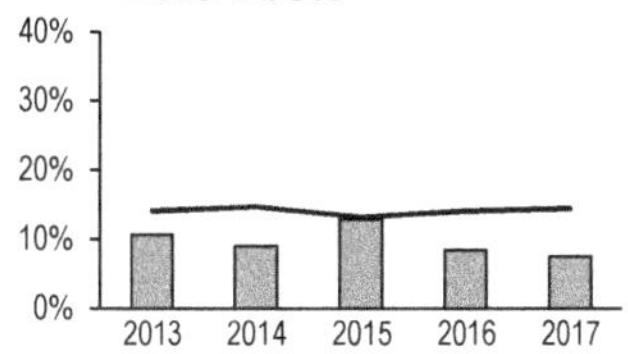

	2013	2014	2015	2016	2017
Winston-Salem	10.6%	9.0%	12.9%	8.4%	7.5%
Average	14.1%	14.7%	13.2%	14.1%	14.4%

Acts of Vandalism at Parks Facilities per 10,000 Population

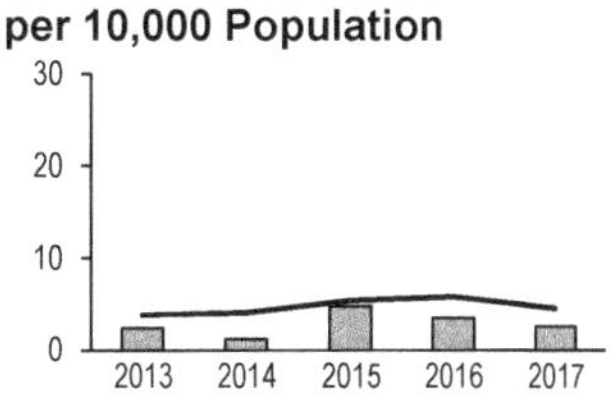

	2013	2014	2015	2016	2017
Winston-Salem	2.44	1.23	4.79	3.56	2.66
Average	3.85	4.07	5.39	5.82	4.56

SCHOOL OF GOVERNMENT
North Carolina Benchmarking Project

CPSIA information can be obtained
at www.ICGtesting.com
Printed in the USA
BVHW01s0933120718
521469BV00011B/72/P

9 781560 119258